Her Brilliant Career

Her Brilliant Career
The Life of
Stella Miles Franklin

Jill Roe

The Belknap Press
of Harvard University Press
Cambridge, Massachusetts
London, England
2009

Library of Congress Cataloging-in-Publication Data

Roe, Jill.
Her brilliant career : the life of Stella Miles Franklin / Jill Roe.
p.   cm.
Includes bibliographical references and index.
ISBN 978-0-674-03609-3 (alk. paper)
1. Franklin, Miles, 1879–1954.   2. Novelists, Australian—20th century—Biography.
3. Feminists—Australia—Biography.   I. Title

PR9619.3.F68Z86 2009
823'.912—dc22
[B]
2009008286

To the memory of my grandmothers,
Elizabeth Norman Heath and Anna Elizabeth Roe,
Australian girls of the period

CONTENTS

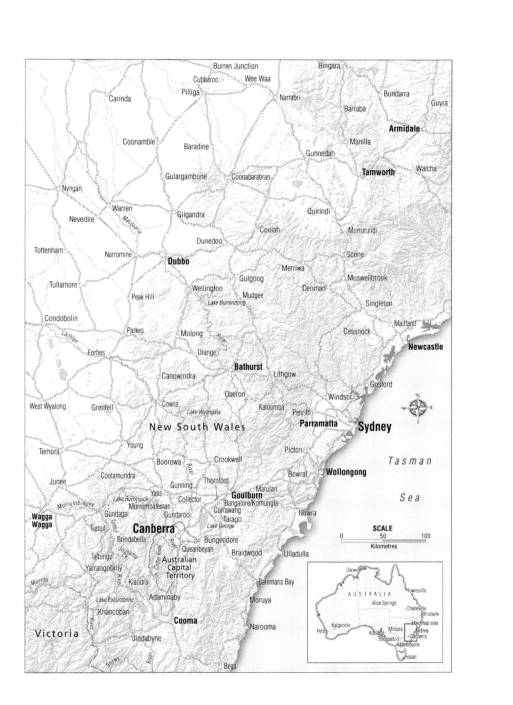

Burren Junction
Cubbaroo
Wee Waa
Bingara
Pilliga
Narrabri
Bundarra
Guyra
Carinda
Barraba
Armidale
Manilla
Coonamble
Baradine
Gunnedah
Walcha
Gulargambone
Coonabarabran
Tamworth
Nyngan
Quirindi
Murrurundi
Warren
Gilgandra
Coolah
Nevertire
Macquarie
Scone
Tottenham
Narromine
Dunedoo
Dubbo
Merriwa
Muswellbrook
Tullamore
Peak Hill
Wellington
Gulgong
Denman
Mudgee
Lake Burrendong
Singleton
Condobolin
Lachlan
Parkes
Molong
Cessnock
Maitland
Forbes
Orange
River
Newcastle
Bathurst
Lithgow
Canowindra
Gosford
Oberon
Windsor
West Wyalong
Grenfell
Cowra
Lake Wyangala
Katoomba
Penrith
New South Wales
Parramatta
Sydney
Young
Temora
Picton
Boorowa
Crookwell
Junee
Cootamundra
Thornford
Bowral
Wollongong
Yass
Gunning
Marulan
Murrumbidgee
Lake Burrinjuck
Collector
Goulburn
Wagga
Wagga
Gundagai
Murrumbateman
Bangalore/Komungla
Nowra
Tumut
Gundaroo
Currawang
Tarago
Lake George
Canberra
Brindabella
Bungendore
Talbingo
Jounama
Queanbeyan
Braidwood
Ulladulla
Yarrangobilly
Australian
Capital
Territory
Kiandra
Batemans Bay
Lake Eucumbene
Adaminaby
Moruya
Khancoban
Cooma
Narooma
Victoria
Jindabyne
Snowy
River
Bega

Tasman
Sea

SCALE
0   50   100
Kilometres

AUSTRALIA
Darwin
Townsville
Alice Springs
Charleville
Brisbane
Kalgoorlie
Main map area
Perth
Mildura
Sydney
Adelaide
Shepparton
Canberra
Melbourne
Hobart

PROLOGUE

On Sunday 1 June 1879, a young woman set off from Brindabella Station in the high country of southern New South Wales to ride to Talbingo, some 50 kilometres south-west as the crow flies. Susannah Margaret Eleanor Franklin, née Lampe, wife of John Maurice Franklin, co-occupant of Brindabella Station, was over four months pregnant and she was going to her mother's place before winter set in to give birth to her first child.

For reasons unknown, possibly to do with the weather, Susannah took the less direct northern route to Talbingo, following a bridle track westward over the Fiery Range through Argamalong to Lacmalac, east of the township of Tumut, turning south thereabouts for Talbingo, where, at the junction of Jounama Creek and the Tumut River, her redoubtable mother, Sarah Lampe, oversaw a considerable estate. On her journey, Susannah passed through some of the most mountainous terrain in Australia, so rugged it had only ever been lightly touched upon by the indigenous Ngunawal and Ngarigo peoples. It is not recorded whether she was accompanied.

In the manner of the day, Susannah rode side-saddle, attired in a fashionably tight riding habit, and it is said that her sure-footed horse, 'Lord Byron' — the same horse that had borne her from Talbingo to the fastness of Brindabella as a bride less than a year before — was up to the girth in snow for miles.

On Wednesday 4 June she arrived at Talbingo and four months later, on 14 October 1879, she gave birth to a daughter. Seven weeks after that, on 6 December 1879, at All Saints' Church of England, Tumut, the baby was baptised Stella Maria Sarah Miles Franklin.

This impressive name captured much of the child's diverse Australian inheritance dating back to 1788. Stella's mother, Susannah, was the great-granddaughter of English convicts Edward Miles (a First Fleeter) and his wife, Susannah, who arrived in Sydney in 1803. Their native-born daughter Martha, who married an emancipist, William Bridle, was Susannah Franklin's grandmother, and her mother was their first-born daughter, Sarah, who married Oltmann Lampe. Oltman was the younger son of a small landholder near Bremen, Germany, who emigrated in the 1840s and in 1866 took over Talbingo Station.

In marriage, Susannah became the wife of John Franklin, a younger son of Irish immigrants of the 1830s, Joseph Franklin and his wife, Mary (known as Maria). A native-born bushman, John Franklin had a touch of poetry in his make-up. Perhaps the name Stella, meaning star, was his idea.

Mother and daughter left Talbingo for Brindabella the following January, when the last of the snowdrifts had melted, according to Miles Franklin's memoir *Childhood at Brindabella*. They travelled 'over the daisied plains, by the sparkling rivulets', probably eastward over Talbingo Mountain, turning north near Yarrangobilly up the gullies to Brindabella. This time Susannah was definitely accompanied, by one of her brothers, William Augustus Lampe, who bore the sometimes noisy infant — always called Stella by her family — before him on a purple pillow strapped to the saddle.

Nothing now survives of old Talbingo. The Lampe homestead site was submerged in 1968 under Jounama Pondage, part of the Snowy Mountains Hydro-Electric Scheme, which today waters much of inland Australia. A fingerpost pointing mid-pond indicates the spot. But a new Talbingo has been established uphill, and in 1979 residents built a memorial to mark the centenary of the birth of Susannah and John Franklin's daughter. Much of the terrain traversed by Susannah a century before is now part of Kosciuszko National Park, an area of great natural beauty that lies between the Australian Capital Territory and the Victorian border and encompasses well over half a million hectares.

Although in recent years the desert may have supplanted the mountains in Australian iconography, the high country still has the power to sustain and uplift the human spirit. For Susannah and John Franklin's daughter it became a special place. 'No other spot has ever replaced the hold on my affections or imagination of my birthplace,' she states in the opening lines of *Childhood at Brindabella*. Any account of the life of the spirited individual known to history as Miles Franklin must start in this beautiful place, and end there too. What lies between is a remarkable story, especially for an Australian girl of the period.

PART I

AUSTRALIA

1879–April 1906

1

CHILDHOOD AT BRINDABELLA:
1879–1889

'… I was not the least suprised when your book came before the public and I often told my frends of a wonderful child I met in the bush with a grate force of character and would some day be heard of.'[1]

The childhoods of writers vary greatly, but they often contain books and solitude. Brindabella, Stella Franklin's first real home, was an even more out of the way place than Talbingo, her birthplace, which is pleasantly situated upstream from Tumut on the Tumut River, along today's Snowy Mountains Highway. By contrast, Brindabella is tucked away in an isolated valley in the Great Dividing Range at the northernmost end of the Australian Alps, through which runs the still-sparkling Goodradigbee River on its way north to join the Murrumbidgee. In today's terms, Brindabella is about halfway cross-country between Canberra in the Australian Capital Territory and the New South Wales town of Tumut, which dates from the 1820s. However, this remote setting at the edge of Empire was far from solitary, as the mature Miles Franklin recalled in the posthumously published *Childhood at Brindabella* and portrayed in her most enjoyable pastoral novel, the prize-winning *All That Swagger*.[2]

The name Brindabella is said to go back to Aboriginal times and mean 'two kangaroo rats'. According to *All That Swagger*, the valley was a stopover for Aboriginal people making their way south annually to feast on bogong moths, and preliminary feasting occurred there. Some sources refer to a less benign environment than the one Miles Franklin evokes, describing fierce clashes with the first squatters, of whom her paternal grandfather, Joseph Franklin, was one; others tell of inter-tribal conflict. Whatever the truth, it was a special place. Miles Franklin was fortunate in her childhood, and she knew it. When the family left the mountains for more cramped circumstances of the Goulburn Plains in April 1889, it was like an 'exit from Eden'.[3]

It seems somewhat astonishing that shortly after mother and newborn daughter arrived at Brindabella, the family set off for a brief visit to the great city of Sydney, some 240 miles (386 kilometres) to the north. As recorded by Susannah Franklin, 'We all went to Sydney International Exhibition February 1880', probably by train from Queanbeyan, over the range to the east of Brindabella. They returned to Brindabella in mid-March. This adventure could not have impinged significantly on Stella Miles Franklin, but it is a sign of connectedness with the wider world, and an earnest of things to come.[4]

Susannah Franklin also recorded that about that time, aged five months, Stella cut her first teeth. The infant already had the makings of what her mother would later describe as an exceptionally healthy child: by eight months Susannah's first-born had six teeth and was sitting up strongly; within twelve months she could stand alone; she walked at fourteen months and talked at twenty months; and all her teeth were through after two and a half years.[5]

According to *Childhood at Brindabella*, Miles Franklin's earliest recollection was of a red nightgown and a candle flame flickering in the wind as she was being carried by her father along the verandah to bed. She was ten months old and just weaned. It was cold and she cried. Although her parents disagreed — Susannah said Stella was too young to remember, while her father asserted that he too could remember things from his first year — it confirmed for Miles Franklin that she had always had 'a clearcut sense of place and direction'.[6]

Another early recollection suggests a distinctive personality in the making. This concerns an incident said to have occurred when Stella was about one year old. Seated in a high chair between her parents at the midday dinner table one Sunday, the child decided she wanted meat like the adults, not her egg, and she could not be persuaded otherwise. When, at Susannah's request, her cousin Joe tried to feed her, she threw the egg-laden spoon at him. For this naughtiness she received an instant switching about the wrist. Susannah did not believe in beatings, but the child, she thought, should be taught self-control. 'I stiffened my spine, yelled and thrust myself into space, regardless of consequences, the normal act of spirited infants,' Miles recalled. This reaction disconcerted her mother, and the gentle Joe was told to take the child away to the sheds.[7]

Bush-bred Susannah Franklin had high expectations of her first-born. Herself an eldest daughter, Susannah had been 'stiffly governessed' at the original Lampe homestead, 'Wambrook', west of Cooma, and was thoroughly grounded in the domestic arts and feminine accomplishments. From the age of fifteen when Susannah's family moved to Talbingo until her marriage to John Franklin thirteen years later, she was the mainstay of her mother's household. The difficulty that arose for Susannah with the onset of motherhood was that whereas she was a well-regulated and rather humourless person, her daughter Stella was, in her own words, possessed of 'an uninhibited ego', and a lively sense of humour.[8]

The relationship between Stella Franklin and her father seems to have been less challenging. In their early years daughters often idolise their fathers, and it is not until puberty that the relationship becomes problematic. So it was for Stella and John Franklin. Very little contemporary evidence survives, but there are many later literary references. The portrait of Richard Melvyn, the unsuccessful selector-cum-horsedealer with a weakness for the drink in *My Brilliant Career*, is the best-known instance.

That fierce portrayal in what Miles Franklin always insisted was an adolescent work was regretted by some at the time and has been contested by relatives since. Miles' younger sister Linda felt she had been 'pretty hot on … poor father', and her aunt Helena Lampe felt sorry for him being used as material 'for a not very creditable character'. It seems clear the young writer was not only mortified at the too-close identification of her characters by some locals, but also at pains to correct the impression that Melvyn resembled her father. Responding to a letter from an admirer of *My Brilliant Career* in 1902, Miles described him as an indulgent father, of the 'Man from Snowy River' type; and in the late glow of *Childhood at Brindabella* she recalled him as 'irresistible', 'proud of his capable young wife and full of good humour'.[9]

In *All That Swagger*, written shortly after John Franklin's death in 1931, the tall, willowy men of the Delacy family, especially the sensitive Harry whose only son saves the family fortunes, seem close to John Franklin. And in the opening chapter of *My Brilliant Career*, where the onset of disillusion is directly portrayed, 'that reprehensible individual' Sybylla

Melvyn is forever riding about the run with her father. More importantly, perhaps, for the development of his daughter as a writer, John Franklin was of a philosophic and poetic cast of mind, even though his education, at the Reverend Cartwright's church-school, Collector, had been limited. Miles believed that this was due to his having been left alone for long periods in the bush when young: 'He retained his sense of wonder'. He also developed advanced political views and was capable of a well-argued letter to the press.[10]

Nothing now remains of the slab house with its roof of mountain ash shingles built by John Franklin for his wife and family at Brindabella except a pile of blackened stones — possibly the remains of a chimney — on a rise in the valley about a mile south of the main homestead, where John's older brother, Thomas, resided with his growing family. A charming watercolour of the house by Brindabella tutor Charles Blyth survives, and Miles gives an affectionate account of the house in *Childhood at Brindabella*, especially the garden of roses and sweet william, lilies and honeysuckle, with a lilac tree, poplars and a picket fence, on ground laboriously prepared by her father, and still partly identifiable sixty years later. In due course she would be given her own patch and a tulip bulb to plant.[11]

Bush houses such as the Franklins' were pleasing to the eye and soothing to the spirit, but required continuous domestic labour to maintain standards. Susannah Franklin was determined about that. She had occasional help, and her home in the wilderness soon boasted those quintessential markers of colonial respectability: a piano brought up by bullock dray, which she played in the evenings with more precision than feeling, according to her daughter; a Singer sewing machine on which, with the aid of the latest paper patterns, she made the family clothing; and an enormous perambulator, apparently never used. Miles could not recall ever sitting in it, only that when it was sold nine years later it was in pristine condition.[12]

Miles Franklin claimed that she could say nearly every word in the dictionary at two. If the titles in her library at her death are any guide, it seems that, except for poetry, the books in that early household were mostly of the useful kind: dictionaries, settlers' handbooks, guides to modern etiquette and reference books such as gazetteers make up most of the very early titles, along with the seed catalogue from which tiny Stella chose her tulip bulb. Susannah Franklin also possessed a first edition of Mrs Beeton's famous cookbook, with its delectable illustrations and array of advice on household management, as well as a number of Bibles, including Cassell's *Illustrated Family Bible*, inscribed by her uncle William Bridle, 'To my niece Susannah on her wedding day with a sincere prayer for her happiness'. Once the young Stella could read well enough, she and her mother would speak aloud the prescribed Sunday chapter of the Bible, verse and verse about, and she was supposed to read a chapter of both the New and Old Testaments daily.[13]

The household was also witness to the avid reading of newspapers, for example by her grandfather Joseph Franklin (Stella never saw him write, although it is sometimes said he could) and by her Aunt Annie Franklin, who would sometimes pause in her busy round at Brindabella to 'clear up the North-West Frontier'. Amid such high-mindedness, it is a relief to find that the nursery rhymes of 'Mother Goose', *Aesop's Fables* and some children's stories were allowed — though not many, as Susannah dismissed fairies as 'unwholesome imaginings' and guarded her children against the harrowing tales of her own mid-Victorian childhood. It was Susannah who gave Stella one of her few juvenile books, a *Picture Alphabet of Birds*, when she was about three years old.[14]

Outside the house lay the wonders of Brindabella Station, a vast, wild domain of mostly leased land. Its exact extent is now difficult to determine, due to the ever increasing complexities of colonial land legislation and the uses the Franklins and others made of it through purchase, grazing licenses and scrub leases over time. But the figure of 16,000 acres (6500 hectares) is mentioned in the 1860s, and there were still some 3000 hectares attached in 1979. It probably reached its greatest extent in the early twentieth century. When it was sold in 1928 the run covered almost 29,000 acres (11,700 hectares), though very little of it was freehold.[15]

As a younger son, John Maurice Franklin's part in this story of gain and loss is small but significant. In what became a standard practice for squatters seeking to retain large holdings in the new age of 'free selection before survey', inaugurated in New South Wales by the Robertson Land Act of 1861, in the early 1860s Joseph Franklin, Miles' grandfather, purchased a homestead block and a grazing licence on the Brindabella run, while his sons selected blocks to secure the water frontage to the Goodradigbee River. Thus John Franklin, Miles' father, though scarcely into his twenties, was one of the first free selectors in the area, and from the outset a junior partner in the Franklin family operation at Brindabella. It was a relationship which lasted for almost twenty years, until significant changes to land legislation occurred and the family partnership disintegrated — due to what John

Franklin would later refer to as serious disputes, the precise nature of which are undocumented.[16]

Up to that time, Brindabella Station was home to all the Franklins except, formally speaking, Stella's grandfather Joseph and his wife, Maria. Maria — the model for 'my brave Johanna' in *All That Swagger* — had long since refused to live in the isolated valley and had retreated over the range to settle at 'Oakvale' on the Murrumbidgee, west of Murrumbateman in the Yass district, near where she and Joseph had started out as immigrant farm servants in 1839. However, it seems clear Joseph spent most of his time up at Brindabella, where he became a law unto himself and a delight to his granddaughter. It was not until the family partnership was dissolved in 1889 that he finally retired to 'Oakvale'.

It was Stella's Uncle George who first moved away from the property. In 1884 George, the oldest of the brothers — and said to have been the most astute — married and moved out to 'Oakvale'. About the same time, John Franklin also made a move in that direction, selecting three small blocks of 180 acres (70 hectares) altogether in area in the adjacent parish of Bedulluck, near Gundaroo, north of today's Canberra. He was at one stage listed as a resident in Gundaroo but it appears he never actually lived there, and the selections were probably intended as holding paddocks for stock.[17]

In 1884, John Franklin was in his mid-thirties and his wife, Susannah, turned thirty-four. Their prospects at Brindabella still seemed good. If the place that had seemed so secure was in reality far from it by then, no hint reached their increasingly precocious eldest child, who revelled in her surroundings: 'The open air furnished with miles of flowers, streams, orchards and mighty trees was my nursery-playground and there was a variety of living toys.'[18]

At this early phase of white settlement in the high country, the native fauna was as abundant as the flora, and young Stella's earliest acquaintance was with the platypus, the wombat, the echidna and the goanna, and the sounds she mostly heard came from a great and colourful array of birds — kookaburras, curlews, magpies — and from the weather. In a letter to a fellow writer during World War II she recalled that she was 'reared on thunderstorms in the mountain country'.[19]

Another letter conjures up fields of little white flowers with a delectable fragrance. Later, in *All That Swagger*, Miles Franklin sought to recapture a still mostly pristine environment as experienced by her forebears:

> Harry and Mike roamed the far recesses of their region, where
> only a shadow people, who neither despoiled nor left any
> monuments, intervened between creation and the young men's
> reign in an emptiness awe-inspiring and splendid. Thousands of
> magpies showered mellow notes like jewels into the aromatic
> silences; butcher birds practised their rich phrases; the crashing
> mockery of jackasses echoed near and far; a feathered host threw
> their small harmonies into the interstices of a spring orchestra,
> with the alien rhythm of hoof-beats as its drums. Crystal water
> rilled hill and plain; flowers were everywhere — a carpet of blue
> and gold underfoot, an arras of lower scrub, a canopy overhead
> exuding honeyed incense which tempered the winds swept pure
> and free from eternity to eternity.[20]

Whether or not she succeeded in capturing the essence of her earliest
environs — and perhaps only the poets Douglas Stewart and, more
jovially, David Campbell have — she was surely right to conclude that
they provided her with a considerable store of cultural capital: 'To grow
up in intimate association with nature ... is an irreplaceable form of
wealth and culture.'[21]

The personal autonomy and self-assurance bred of such circumstances
are significant too. Miles Franklin was brought up to appreciate the natural
world, not to fear it, nor the people in it: 'I was without fear of horses, cattle,
dogs or men,' was how she would put it. Once, with an uncle's whip in
hand, she successfully urged a bullock team forward, 'a stupendous
moment', recalled as a first exercise in power. The ease she felt was no doubt
mostly due to early familiarity and to her parents' attitudes, but also to the
fact that even as a very small child she was already something of a prodigy
and accustomed to being the centre of attention. Moreover, there was no
shortage of people to watch out for her. Many more 'hands' were needed in
the country in those days, and there were men everywhere. In 1885, there
were still as many as fifty-eight people living on Brindabella, and the two
remaining Franklin brothers, Thomas and John, ran considerable stock on
and beyond the 1500 acres they actually owned: some forty-five horses, 650
cattle, and an estimated 31,750 sheep. The portrayal of the young Clare
Margaret, 'the pride of the station', in *All That Swagger*, conforms closely to
Miles' own recollection of that gone-forever pastoral age, when women
were scarce and young women were placed on pedestals:

> Little Clare Margaret … held court with station hands,
> squatters, drovers, remittance men and relatives in her kingdom
> of eucalypts … At three, and four, and five, there were males
> slaving for recognition, and opportunities for mischief were
> illimitable.[22]

An undated verse, possibly written by a station hand, with compliments of
the season to 'Miss Stella Franklin', recalls early experiences simply and
nostalgically:

> Bring back the happy days
> when roaming free and wild
> I played around my mountain home
> a merry Mountain Child.[23]

By the time she was capable of enjoying such personal freedom, the merry
mountain child had several siblings, all born at Talbingo, as she had been;
and she always journeyed there with her mother on these occasions. The
first trip was for six months in 1881, for the birth of Ida Lampe Franklin
(known as Linda) on 12 September, shortly before Stella's second birthday;
the second between August and December 1883 for the birth of Mervyn
Gladstone Franklin on 3 October 1883 (Miles' favourite brother, who
caught typhoid fever and died in 1900); the third in early 1885 for the birth
of Una Vernon Franklin (who died at Brindabella that same year, aged six
months, and was buried there in a bush grave). The last of these birthing
trips occurred in 1886, when her longest-lived brother, Norman Rankin
Franklin, was born at Talbingo on 26 September 1886. Subsequent Franklin
children — there were to be two, Hume Talmage ('Tal') and Laurel — were
born at home.[24]

From a child's point of view the contrast between Brindabella and
Talbingo must have been quite marked. At Brindabella life consisted of an
array of Irish uncles and aunts and their families, and a motley of station
hands, with men preponderant, whereas the Lampe connection at
Talbingo was English and German, and under Grandma Lampe women
set the tone. Although neither family was Catholic and it is said in *Ten
Creeks Run* that religious difference did not affect things in such distant
parts in the early days, the social distance between the English and the
Irish was of considerable significance. It made little if any difference that

the Irish-originated Franklins were free settlers and the Anglo-German Lampes derived from convicts on the Bridle side, this latter fact being well hidden. To the Lampes, the Irish were low socially, and intellectually 'half way to lunacy'. Grandfather Lampe, who had migrated to New South Wales in 1841, on the other hand had been 'of the Herrenvolk': the Lampe line could even boast a coat of arms. In any event, Talbingo was bigger and better established, and a much more comfortable environment.[25]

There a stable matriarchal order prevailed. Sarah Lampe had been widowed since 1875, when Oltmann Lampe's years of increasing help-lessness following a bush injury ended, and thereafter she ran the property with great and much admired acumen. Her own family was not so long completed — Alice Helena, the last of her nine children, had been born in 1868 — so the tiny Stella was surrounded by young aunts and uncles who found her frank curiosity amusing and treated her as a pet. Her strongly evangelical and greatly revered grandmother was not deceived, however, especially when Stella refused to participate in standard religious observances (which Sarah Lampe conducted herself in the absence of clergy): this was a 'froward' child.[26]

'Froward' is an old word, but a good one. According to the *Macquarie Dictionary* it dates back to medieval times, and the meanings given are 'perverse; wilfully contrary; refractory; not easily managed'. When her baby sister Una died on 11 September 1885, according to Miles she saw her mother cry for the first time. She realised then that it was a solemn occasion, and though told not to, followed the men to the burial site.[27]

Soon after, as recorded by Susannah Franklin, there was another trip to Sydney: 'John, Stella and I went to Sydney ... stayed away about a fortnight.' Most memorably, they went to the zoo, then at Moore Park, where the child delighted in the elephant and became interested in animals from other lands. Later, when she heard the story of St George slaying the dragon, she declared protectively, 'I will be a dragon myself,' which amused her father.[28]

It was on this occasion, shortly before Stella Franklin's sixth birthday, that a photographic portrait of her was taken at the studio of W. Norton of George Street, Sydney. She is portrayed in a customary decorative setting and dressed as a typical late-Victorian child, upright in a close-fitting suit with pleats and buttons and a ruffle at the neck, shod in high boots and holding a basket of flowers in her left hand. Possibly due to the strain of standing perfectly still for quite a time, as was necessary in early photography, the expression on her plump face is unsmiling and she looks somewhat bemused, not at all like a merry mountain maid or even a froward child.[29]

Even before the trip to Sydney, Stella had begun to learn her letters. On return, Susannah set to work in earnest to prepare her oldest daughter for school. Stella was told to fetch her slate and practise: 'You will be all behind like the cow's tail if you can't write.' She was required to learn her figures too. In Miles Franklin's Printed Books Collection, held at the Mitchell Library with the Franklin Papers, the earliest schoolbook is a first book of arithmetic inscribed in her own hand 'Stella Franklin, Brindabella, June 8th, 1886'.[30]

There has never been a public school at Brindabella, and at least until the end of the nineteenth century education was a matter of private tuition. About this time, probably late 1885, Thomas and Annie Franklin employed Charles Auchinvole Blyth as resident tutor for their then four children, and Stella was expected to join her cousins at the homestead under Mr Blyth as soon as possible. As things turned out, that was in 1887. This may seem rather late, since she was by then seven years old; but a good part of the previous year had been spent at Talbingo for the birth of her brother Norman. As recorded by her mother, 'Stella went to school to Mr Blyth 1 January 1887, got her second front teeth the same year.'[31]

For Stella, the beginning of formal schooling was momentous. It was not just a matter of contact with other children, for she now had three siblings, as she noted in her *Floral Birthday Book*, an enchanting gift from Aunt Metta Lampe in 1886, and the second surviving book of her own. School became her entrée to another wider world. Talbingo would remain a touchstone, but as she put it in *Childhood at Brindabella*, where, perhaps playfully, she used fictionalised place names: 'Bobilla proper and the schoolroom swept Ajinby away from me ... I loved lessons.' In the schoolroom at Brindabella she felt she was, if not out in the world, 'at least on the ledge before the nest'; and at this moment, we begin to hear Miles Franklin speaking for herself.[32]

Stella Franklin's first known literary effort, a verse entitled 'Man's a Fool', is dated 5 November 1887 (with an attribution 'written by S. M. F. at age of 8 years' added in a more mature hand). The twelve lines are pure doggerel of a markedly rural kind, but for the record, they read:

As a rule
Man's a fool.
When weather's hot
He wants it cool;
When it's cool
He wants it hot;
Always wanting
what it's not;
Never liking
What he's got.
As a rule
Man's a fool.[33]

She could also write a creditable letter by this time. The first of three letters written to 'My dear Auntie', Sarah Metta Lampe, at Talbingo in 1887 — and the first of thousands of letters she would send and receive in her lifetime — was written on 6 June 1887, the second on 8 October and the third on 5 December.[34]

These three letters are all quite short, and much as might be expected from a conscientious seven-year-old, but they are also, as noted approvingly by tutor Charles Blyth, 'nicely written and spelled'. They convey a child's-eye view of the world: of the weather, from mid-year snowstorms to boggy roads afterwards, dried out by December; animals ('How is your pet lamb getting on … and how is the magpie?'); the changing seasons, with long green grass up in spring and the summer flowers coming on; and the latest on her siblings (baby Norman is crawling; sister Linda has had another haircut, which suits her better). In the third and last letter of 1887 to Aunt Metta she reports that her mother was making pretty pink dresses for Christmas, and she wishes she could see Grandma Lampe to thank her for the material. Regrettably, since Miles thought she was 'the loveliest of relatives' and always valued her insights, Aunt Metta's apparently pithy replies have not survived.[35]

The first letter in an extended correspondence between Stella Franklin and her tutor, Mr Blyth, dates from 10 December 1887. In contrast with her letters to Aunt Metta, the letters remaining from this correspondence are all from Charles Blyth; none of Stella's replies has survived. However, her side of the correspondence may be inferred from Blyth's courtly and sometimes quite lengthy missives, which provide direct insight into her schooldays.

It seems there was a certain 'congeniality' — very much a Miles Franklin word — from the beginning between Blyth and the bright, curious girl. As she wrote to Aunt Metta, once she started at his little school she never missed a day, even when it snowed.[36]

Several images relating to this turning point in Stella Miles' life survive: a pen portrait from *Childhood at Brindabella* of her setting off for school, and some contemporaneous watercolours of Brindabella homestead by Charles Blyth. To these may be added the biographical sketch which appears below of Charles Blyth, a somewhat shadowy figure.[37]

The pen portrait is of seven-year-old Stella walking to school. Although in those days children were taken by their elders on horseback from early infancy, it was not until she was four years old that Stella first rode a horse without a lead, and even aged seven she was not allowed to ride the mile or so between the two Franklin houses alone. So, as she tells it in *Childhood at Brindabella*, she had to exercise her legs, her bobbing bonnet watched from home until it disappeared over a rise, soon after which she could be seen by Mr Auchinvole (as Blyth is named in the memoir), awaiting her at Brindabella homestead. His description of 'a very small girl, mostly sun-bonnet, moving at a pace scarcely perceptible' is a reminder that for all her precocity Stella Miles Franklin was a small child, and that although her height when fully grown, as recorded on her passport in 1923, was '5 ft. 2½ in.' (about 159 cm), other evidence suggests it may have been an inch or so less, and the passport is not a wholly reliable document.[38]

The contemporary watercolours painted by Charles Blyth of Stella's destination, Brindabella homestead, which had been built by her uncle Thomas Franklin in the 1870s, are held in the pictorial collection of the National Library of Australia. The earliest of these was probably done in the mid-1880s, about the time Stella joined her cousins in the schoolroom. The watercolours are appealing period pieces, and quite stylised, especially the bonneted and pinafored little girls in the foreground of two of them, but they give a good impression of the site itself (the same site as Brindabella Station homestead occupies today), and an accurate southward perspective of the establishment on the banks of the river, with its increasing number of outbuildings, trees and domestic animals (horses and cows), and its mountain backdrop.[39]

Blyth was the first to see that his latest pupil was more than 'a pet and a prodigy', and he did much in the short time he tutored her to advance her knowledge of the world and its literary culture. For this, Miles Franklin was always thankful: 'Mr A. gave me a grounding in composition and love of literature, advanced for my age.'[40]

In Miles Franklin's writings, Blyth is presented as the gentlest of men but spoiled by drink and despatched to the colonies for this weakness. One of several possible portrayals appears in *Back to Bool Bool*, where an old tutor disgraces himself at the centenary celebrations (in the 1920s) by drinking too much. Another portrayal in *Childhood at Brindabella*, which also conveys a sense of the flow of life at the station in the 1880s, has an Indian hawker and a Chinese retainer caught up in the story of 'Mr A.' being tempted by an old sea captain, and all of them sitting on the verandah drinking rum until cleared off by Aunt Annie Franklin. 'Behaving like a grog shanty!' she snorted at the drinkers and called her husband, the imposing Thomas Franklin, master of Brindabella, who is said to have looked and behaved like a Spanish hidalgo in his prime. 'The gentlemen disappeared.'[41]

Auntie Annie was a formidable woman much admired in real life by her niece for her competence and vitality: 'Aunt was an exceptional woman … She ran an establishment without conveniences and only "brumby" help that was as full as a beehive and included seven children, for whom she made all the clothes for both sexes.'[42]

Many of the men of uncertain social status who came to Australia during the nineteenth century fell into irretrievable obscurity. This may well have been the case with Charles Blyth had he not taken the job at Brindabella in the mid-1880s, when he was already almost sixty. Born on 11 October 1825 at Glassford in County Lanark, Scotland, he was the eldest child of Charles Berry Blyth, a merchant from Birmingham, and Robina Hannah Blyth, née Auchinvole, a Scotswoman.[43]

Blyth was said to have had a university education in Edinburgh, where he claimed to have been trained for teaching. There is no record of his enrolment at or graduation from the University of Edinburgh, but he may have taken some classes, or failed to complete them, because towards the end of his life he regretted not having taken his education seriously enough. His first employment was in journalism in Birmingham, but by 1860 he was in Tumut, New South Wales, tutoring the children of his eldest sister, Mrs Margaret Vyner, and soon afterwards he was appointed teacher at a new national school in the picturesque gold town of Adelong, nearby.[44]

In 1863, Blyth resigned from Adelong school due to 'a sudden and severe illness', and by his own account was 'up country' for many years. Little is known of his whereabouts or circumstances during this time. What is certain is that Brindabella was his final post, lasting until the onset of ill health in 1899 compelled him to seek medical treatment in Sydney. He died at the Coast Hospital in Sydney on 1 April 1902 in his 77th year, and was buried there.[45]

Blyth's death certificate lists him as a journalist, but in New South Wales, he was better known as an excellent teacher, as evidenced in the following commendation of his work at Adelong National School in the early 1860s:

> He evidently possesses two qualities essential to an instructor of youth, patience and a power of adapting his explanation of a subject to the comprehension of his scholars. He strives, it appears to us successfully, to render the school lessons interesting as well as instructive, and to secure the attention of his pupils by kindness, not harshness or menace.[46]

Much later, Miles Franklin referred to him simply as 'a famous tutor'.[47]

Charles Blyth came to Brindabella powerfully recommended. His sister, Mrs Vyner, was undoubtedly one source of recommendation. She was principal of the first girls' high school in Goulburn from 1883 to 1886 and on familiar terms with George Reid, Free Trade Premier of New South Wales in the 1890s (and later Prime Minister of Australia), who is said to have been a pupil of hers. Another recommendation may have come from Fred Vernon, Susannah Franklin's brother-in-law and long-time editor of the *Tumut Times,* for which Blyth occasionally wrote leading articles in the 1890s. Even so, Blyth's gentlemanly manner — as Miles Franklin recalled, he was a credit to the British public school system, though he couldn't boil an egg — would alone have stood him in good stead in the colonies. Had it not been for the drink problem, he would have been enjoying golf with Scottish lairds, she believed, instead of eking out a lonely existence in remote New South Wales.[48]

Charles Blyth's approach to teaching and learning was early made clear to Stella. In his first known letter to her, written on 10 December 1887 at the end of her first year under his tutelage, having said he liked to keep in touch with his pupils during the holiday period, he listed eleven poems he expected his charges to learn by rote over the break. They included 'Mary's Lamb', 'The Naughty Boy', 'The Voice of Spring' and 'We Must Not Be Idle'. He also gave an intimation of his method of maintaining discipline in the schoolroom. This amounted to a combination of praise and the 'peck' — described in *Childhood at Brindabella* as an unpleasant fillip on the cranium which hurt the boys more than the girls, who were only pecked on the pigtail. Blyth wrote that Stella had been 'a very good little girl at learning' and made great progress; and that he would be lenient with his charges when they came back. But if after the first weeks they had not done as asked there would be pecks. Like a good Victorian, Blyth insisted on the importance of perseverance. Things might come more easily to the cleverest people, but everyone has to try, he told Stella in his second letter of 1887; learning is lifelong, and people don't value things they learn easily.[49]

At Brindabella, the classroom was situated on the verandah behind the post office, and the pupils sat each side of a table under a window with Mr Blyth. Teaching in the country, where more exciting activities than reading and writing lie just outside the schoolroom door, could be a dispiriting calling, even for highly conscientious teachers such as Charles Blyth, who prepared lessons in advance despite his small number of pupils and always acknowledged their individual differences. 'My pupils, though few, take a good deal of teaching', he once wrote, noting subsequently that:

> Home education has some advantages, and is the only mode available up here; but it lacks other advantages that the public school system possesses, such, for example, as the impetus to energy and effort that competition between pupils gives, and the very necessary self-confidence and composure that having to read, recite and answer questions before an audience helps to bestow.[50]

The drawbacks did not apply to Stella, deemed in retrospect his brightest pupil. She particularly enjoyed Friday afternoon poetry classes, when they read Scottish border ballads (though the boys had to be bribed with adventure serials such as 'Sinbad the Sailor').

In Stella, Charles Blyth had found the conventional reward of teachers: the responsive student. His appreciation is evident from the third oldest of the books belonging to her to survive in her library: W. Meynell Whittemore's *Sunshine for 1888: For the Home, the School and the World*, a typical Victorian miscellany of useful knowledge and moderately entertaining material. It includes a nice piece of exotica for British readers, an eleven-part serial entitled 'Queensland Sketches' by one Millicent Shooter. On the front page of this substantial volume is written: 'Presented to Stella Franklin, for marked progress in all branches of education taught by her friend and teacher, Charles A. Blyth.' Unfortunately the year of presentation has been torn from the inscription, but '1 April' remains and it seems most likely that it was 1889, when Stella was nine years old and her time at Charles Blyth's little school was coming to an end.[51]

Looking back on the years she spent with him between 1887 and early 1889, Blyth would summarise Stella's abilities in the following way:

> I always felt you would progress educationally for you have not only the ability but the desire to do so, and the energy to persevere with your studies; besides a love of reading, which I consider essential to success in that way. I regret to say I have not found the latter a distinct trait in the majority of my pupils hereaway.[52]

That was written in 1895. By then, Charles Blyth had realised that his star pupil would not become a teacher like himself, as he had first thought she might, recognising that she aspired to be a writer. In the beginning, however, what mattered most was that he took her seriously; and the epistolary relationship that developed between the old tutor and the young girl is remarkable for its intellectual focus. Charles Blyth would not have put it this way, nor would his pupil, even in later life, but his letters strongly suggest that in Stella Miles Franklin he recognised the elements of that distinctive figure of old Australia, the bush intellectual — like her great-uncle George Bridle, who early showed a preference for scientific pursuits over farming and is now best known as a photographer, and the self-educated writer Joseph Furphy.[53]

As to what Stella actually learned in Charles Blyth's 'shabby little school room', little contemporary evidence survives, and no schoolbooks, though she may have used the previously mentioned first book of arithmetic, which predates the school years. But, since memory and mastery of content were the thing in those days, no doubt she learned a great deal. Certainly the approach to learning was very different then; a quick glance at the arithmetic book suffices to make that point. It would not be necessary for children today to undertake such elaborate computations, and what a more advanced book of arithmetic would have required of them is difficult to imagine; poetry on Fridays seems a well-deserved reward for such heavy fare. Still, the rigours of the Brindabella classroom would have been greatly mitigated by personalised tuition. Aged eight or nine, Stella felt she could read anything, later claiming to have read some of Shakespeare and Dickens before she was ten. She was delighted when her mother gave her Dr Wood's *Illustrated Natural History*, recalled as 'a nice fat book containing most of the known animals and their pictures'. What a treasure; and she was allowed to read it on Sundays![54]

By her own account Stella learned other important lessons in Charles Blyth's schoolroom, about interaction with peers and her place in the wider world. Thus, she soon realised that her cousin Annie May was more worldly-wise than she was, and that small boys often enjoy teasing girls. When she complained about her cousin Don's ways, her mother's advice was to rise above the teasing, as girls have done from time immemorial. The suggestion that she might not be able to go to school at all if she continued to cause trouble for her aunt and uncle with such complaints — they were a 'more striking edition of my parents' — introduced a new perspective and marked the dawning of a critical self-awareness. 'This,' she recalls, 'was the first hint I ever had that I might be a trouble to anyone, or be excluded from their company as unwelcome. It was sobering.'[55]

An area of some later importance to Stella in which Mr Blyth was unable to instruct his charges was music. Boys did not learn music in his day, he reflected ruefully. But girls were expected to, and musical skills were highly prized in the bush. Moreover, music was one of the few fields in which Australian girls might respectably aspire to a career. Unfortunately for Stella, neither of her parents was particularly musical. Susannah Franklin may have been competent on the piano, but she never sang, and John Franklin had 'a poor ear'. He recited poetry quite well, and entertained his first-born with ditties, but all in the same chant. And they were too distant at Brindabella to attend church, where they might have enjoyed organ music and congregational singing on a regular basis. Only at Grandma's was the Anglican *Hymns Ancient and Modern* regularly in use.[56]

Yet Stella Franklin was not to be bereft of an essential accomplishment. A broken-down prospector called Hopkins, said to have once been a distinguished musician, sometimes played Susannah's piano, and from time to time a piano teacher was employed at Brindabella Station. By 1889, aged nine, Stella had learned the rudiments of the keyboard: 'I am keeping up my practice,' she wrote to Aunt Metta in February 1889, adding that she was beginning to play a few little tunes. Mostly these seem to have been popular ditties and dances, such as the songs of Demmy Blake mentioned in *All That Swagger*, and the polka — the kind of thing that so appalled the ladies of 'Caddagat' in *My Brilliant Career*.[57]

Another hidden bonus of schooling at Brindabella — certainly to Susannah Franklin — must surely have been that her determination for her children to speak 'properly' found strong reinforcement in Charles Blyth, an educated immigrant of middle-class background. Not only did Susannah eschew baby talk, but she also insisted on correct usage and pronunciation. Intonation mattered too. It is only since the 1960s that it has been acceptable for respectable folk, especially women, to speak with an Australian accent. Miles later told the Angus & Robertson editor Beatrice Davis that, when she was in London after World War I, people would not accept she was Australian 'because I had not the distinctive accent'. A woman who knew her in Sydney in the 1940s said she spoke with 'no particular accent', which suggests that she was taught to speak in what was known in the nineteenth century as a 'pure English', that is, without provincialisms. As for the sound of her voice, there is no recorded evidence, but later Stella would aspire to be a singer; and, by all accounts, in maturity she possessed a deep, resonant, well-modulated voice.[58]

The Franklin family left Brindabella for good on Tuesday 30 April 1889. There is no hint of this prospect in Stella's only known letter of that year, a spritely effort written on 2 February, again to Aunt Metta, all about calves and chickens and flowers and 'the blight' that was afflicting family members. She mentions that her father had been away to vote and inquires about Grandma Lampe's trip to Melbourne to see the 1888 Exhibition, mentioning also that Mr Blyth had been to say goodbye (because he wished to consult a doctor, not because of the family's looming departure from Brindabella). Perhaps she was unaware of the tension between the Franklin brothers that seems to have developed earlier, or perhaps the move, still some three months away, had yet to impinge — although that seems unlikely since, according to Annie May's daughters Ruby and Leslie, Grandma Lampe had long been urging it on the grounds that Brindabella was too isolated if the children became ill and for the sake of their education. Since the reasons for the move are otherwise undocumented, we can only speculate on Stella's state of mind at this time of upheaval. It may be that she was excited, as children often are under such circumstances. As for the actual departure, only Mr Blyth mentions it, and then apologetically and in retrospect, fearing his health had made him seem cross during her final week at Brindabella.[59]

The family were barely settled into their new home near Goulburn in time for the birth of Hume Talmage Franklin on 3 July 1889. Grandma

Lampe arrived for the event with Linda, who had been staying at Talbingo. Afterwards, in response to impassioned pleas, Stella was allowed to return to Talbingo with her grandmother. There is a vivid account of the trip by train and buggy in *Childhood at Brindabella*, and the child's delight at her return gives the memoir its dramatic tension. Although at first the place seemed smaller than when she had last been there, it was late winter when she arrived and it soon came to life again with the arrival of spring.[60]

On 14 October 1889, at Talbingo, Stella turned ten. She was now 'a *big girl*', who did her own hair and would soon wear gloves. Problems began to arise. Some would be easily remedied, her weakness at sewing, for example (though the Bridle sisters thought a surviving sampler of 1890 was probably her only bit of fancywork). Others proved more difficult. With a new baby in a new district, things were doubtless stressful for Susannah at the time, so Stella had been allowed the trip back to Talbingo as long as she kept up her lessons. This she did, more or less dutifully, working alone on the verandah. But before long there was no one able to guide her more advanced studies, nor even her music practice. And as the girl rebelled against restraints — was it really the will of God that she should stay inside? — so Grandma Lampe found aspects of her behaviour cause for concern, reproaching her from time to time for 'running about like a gypsy', and for being 'idle like a boy'.[61]

Grandma Lampe warned her granddaughter that her 'froward heart' would bring her trouble, and urged her to pray to God to cure it. But prayer had failed to mend Stella's doll's broken hand — a tall order, since the doll had china feet and hands — and she was already dissatisfied with God, especially for allowing his only son to suffer the agony of crucifixion, an attitude well beyond her grandmother's range (though her mother sympathised, having suffered similar distress and doubt herself when young). In retrospect, Miles Franklin saw her youthful attitude as a sign of an inquiring mind. It is also evidence of a mind already exposed to influences such as the fiercer versions of evangelicalism circulating at the time, and the secularist reaction.[62]

Stella's last days at Talbingo brought a memorable aesthetic experience, the sight of a splendid black snake sunning itself by a creek in the hills:

> A big black snake lay full-length at his ease beside the water in the thin fringe of maidenhair ferns that were sprouting after

winter retreat. The creature's forked tongue flickered rapidly in and out, his new skin gleamed blue-black with peacock tints, a little of his underside was showing like blended scarlet and pomegranate. I stood a fascinated moment … The experience was not startling, merely surprising.[63]

Given the fear with which most settlers regarded snakes, and the skill and expedition with which they killed them, the child's response is indeed surprising. Even more so is the fact that the image of the snake in that spot stayed with her for thirty years:

As I have sat in some great congress in one of the major cities, or in a famous concert hall, or eaten green almonds on a terrace in Turin in the early morning, or worked amid the din of the Krupp guns on an Eastern battle front, or watched the albatrosses in stormy weather off Cape Agulhas, or have been falling asleep in an attic in Bloomsbury, that snake has still been stretched in the ferns beside the creek, motionless except for the darting tongue.[64]

As observed in Marjorie Barnard's early biography of Miles Franklin, this memory of an ineffable moment brings us to the threshold of the unknown in human experience. Barnard interpreted it as Miles Franklin's first artistic experience and wondered how many more like it occurred in her childhood. Around such insights may be discerned a vague penumbra, suggestive of usually overlooked religious beliefs, or more accurately an aspiration to them, as in Miles' wonderfully cryptic remark that it takes a greater mind to find God than to lose him. The bush had transcendental powers for her as a child, as for her father and grandfather before her, and she often uses religious language to describe its impact. Of that final immersion in Talbingo in late 1889, she wrote, 'Heaven could be no more magical and mystical than unspoiled Australia.'[65]

Stella was allowed to stay at Talbingo for the opening of the Tumut Bridge in late November, but after Christmas she was to return home. The death of an injured chicken she had been nursing on the way back to Goulburn seemed somehow a significant calamity. But, she recounted, due to the excitement of receiving her first pair of gloves for the trip at the same time, memory of it passed quickly into a submerged sense of bereavement, later lamented as the loss of innocence.[66]

This trope is to be found in many Australian memoirs and autobiographies. Indeed *Childhood at Brindabella* is a classic of the genre, as well as an essential biographical source for Miles Franklin's earliest years. That acknowledged, it is the case that foundation myths have their limits in personal (as well as national) histories, and a more conflicted and challenging psychological perspective is the other one offered by Miles herself: that an idyllic childhood at Brindabella left her ill prepared for life beyond its confines. In some understandings, conflict and creativity go together. Certainly life 'near Goulburn' would be very different.[67]

2

NEAR GOULBURN:
1890-1898

'Remember me to Goulburn, drowsing lazily in its
dreamy graceful hollow in the blue distance.'[1]

When Stella Miles Franklin first saw the site of her new home in the
district of Bangalore to the south of Goulburn, she was disappointed
by its low contours and scrubby aspect. But the new environment and the
novel experience of state schooling soon absorbed her. Although the
coming years would often be grim for the Franklin family, and grimmer still
for their fictional counterparts in *My Brilliant Career*, the place had its own
appeal, and it was near Goulburn, a sizable colonial city of almost 11,000
people.[2]

For John Franklin the new locale represented a bid for freedom. After
serious disputes with his brother Thomas, he had, by his own account,
'visited different places to find a suitable place to take my wife and family';
and on 11 April 1889, at the Goulburn Land Office, he selected on
conditional purchase a block of 160 acres in the parish of Tarago, County
Argyle, midway between Goulburn and the smaller southern settlement
at Collector on the northern edge of Lake George, where he had been
educated. He later added a further 434 acres by taking out leases on two
adjacent blocks, confirmed in the Goulburn Land Court in January 1890
and duly certified five years later. With one John Mather he also purchased
a further parcel of mainly freehold land from a neighbour, W. J. Neely,
his share being recorded by Susannah as 320 acres, making 914 acres (370

hectares) in all, near enough to the 1000 acres mentioned in *My Brilliant Career*. His aim was not to become a farmer, as some contemporary documents have it, but a trader in livestock at Goulburn, an occupation for which the years spent on the horse and cattle runs in the mountains further south seemed to equip him, without loss of status.[3]

That plan would prove unrealistic, as Susannah Franklin soon appreciated. Perhaps she was ambivalent from the beginning. Something of this is expressed in the name she chose for the new site, with its tussocks and lagoons so unlike the fast-running rivers up the country: she called the place 'Stillwater'. Nonetheless, with the act of naming she laid claim to that touch of class that she always felt her family rightly possessed, even though her husband was now really only a poor selector. As at Brindabella, she would maintain social and domestic standards. According to her daughter's writings, a young domestic servant came with her from Brindabella. (There was a farm servant too, but he stole from the Franklins and was committed to Goulburn jail in March 1890.)[4]

Of the six-roomed house John Franklin built on the hillside of the newly purchased block, only archaeological evidence survives. A cairn halfway up the hill, erected in 1971 by the then owners, the Frazer family, to mark the spot where 'Miles Franklin lived and wrote her first book', as the plaque added by the local historical society puts it, commands a view through brittle gums towards a series of lagoons, but the Franklin house itself was situated some metres further up on a slight plateau, now a grass and rubble clearing. Recently relocated lines of foundation and their corner posts, and the probable outline of the separate kitchen, appear to correlate well with extant photographs. These show a typical late nineteenth-century Australian bush house built of weatherboard with a corrugated iron roof and a long low front verandah. A couple of semi-domesticated shrubs still survive nearby, and further uphill again, in a crevice created by run-off, is what may have been a domestic water catchment.[5]

Altogether the new house cost £400, a considerable sum at that time. The expenditure represented John Franklin's commitment to the new life and the wellbeing of his wife. 'Dear old Father always wanted to give Mother of the best,' his eldest daughter wrote fondly, recalling especially a fine kitchen, which had 'smooth slab walls and a vast hearth with a colonial oven at one side, then an advance on the camp ovens of the neighbours'. It even had a proper ceiling, unlike most kitchens of the day; and the house itself, with its back and front doors and storerooms, was boarded with soft white pine throughout, including the front verandah ends, 'a great extravagance everyone thought' and 'as dainty as a band box', Miles added, noting that her family always lived 'housily and socially above our income'.[6]

Miles Franklin's recollection of the house at 'Stillwater' dates from 1945, sparked by a press notice of the death of Madame Weigel, a Polish-born paper-pattern maker who established a superior fashion journal in Australia in 1880. Susannah Franklin subscribed to *Madame Weigel's Journal of Fashion* and her children were dressed in clothes made in accordance with Madame's patterns. The journal also provided fashion plates for Stella's scrapbook, which survives, and published romantic serials. Most relevant and poignant, however, is that, along with the *Bulletin,* the paper was used to line the slab walls of the new house, in particular the pantry, the lavatory and the kitchen. Some of those same slabs with their wisps of blue and pink paper survive to the present day, having been re-used soon after the Franklins left the district in the building of a still-operational shearing shed on the then adjacent landholding.[7]

As wisps of colour from an 1890s fashion journal still clinging to the walls of a turn-of-the-century shearing shed are an eloquent reminder of Miles Franklin's distant girlhood, so the vista from the long-gone house she lived in at 'Stillwater' during the 1890s gives pause. Eastward from the 'Stillwater' lagoons, running along the row of hills that hides Bangalore Creek from view, lies the line of the main watershed of the Great Dividing Range. The uplands to which Stella Franklin had been brought could not rival the high country she had left for natural beauty, and the land worked by small settlers on the scrubby hills and ridges of the interfluves was typically poor. Yet the location is of symbolic significance. To the east of the watershed, the rivers run quickly through grandly varied terrain to the Pacific seaboard; to the west they move slowly towards the Murray–Darling basin, and on through dry and thirsty inlands to the Southern Ocean.[8]

The lands once selected by John Franklin have long since been subsumed within larger properties, and the 'Stillwater' site is now inaccessible, except by permission of the owners. However, a good general idea of Stella's girlhood environs can be obtained from approximately midway along the Thornford road, which links the Federal Highway with what is now a back road from Goulburn to Currawang. From there, looking due south towards Telegraph Hill, the main features present themselves: spare and undulating uplands, reedy valleys with seasonal lagoons, and overhead the high, bright skies of a typical continental climate zone.[9]

The address given by John Maurice Franklin for land records in Goulburn in 1890, and as his place of residence on the electoral rolls of democratic New South Wales, was Bangalore. Originally a farm site, Bangalore is now known as Komungla, and the earlier name survives only on topographical maps which pinpoint Bangalore Creek and the Bangalore trig station. Always a sleepy locale, the tiny nineteenth-century community may have been the subject of Stella's earliest journalistic writings. The sharp comments in some unattributed pieces in the *Goulburn Evening Penny Post* in the early 1890s sound like hers — and it was from Bangalore that she despatched the manuscript of *My Brilliant Career*.[10]

My Brilliant Career itself describes Bangalore's location. In the novel, the heroine's father, Richard Melvyn, believes 'Possum Gully' will be ideal for stock trading: 'only seventeen miles from a city like Goulburn, with splendid roads, mail thrice weekly and a railway platform only eight miles away, why man, my fortune is made!' Assuming that 'Possum Gully' was a thinly disguised 'Stillwater', he was out by some miles — Goulburn was more like 21 miles away by road from 'Stillwater' — but right about the railway platform. According to old timetables, Bangalore was half an hour from Goulburn by train on the Sydney–Goulburn–Cooma line, opened in 1875. Today there are still a few buildings at Bangalore/Komungla, and a small overgrown cemetery nearby contains the grave of the namesake of the heroine of *My Brilliant Career*, native-born Penelope Sybilla Macauley, a dairy farmer's wife who died of pneumonia on 15 July 1899, aged forty-seven. John Franklin was a witness at the burial.[11]

The Franklins had arrived at 'Stillwater' on 7 May 1889. From then on, we may imagine them traversing the bridle tracks east to the rail to despatch and receive goods and otherwise link up with the wider world, or travelling to the siding on the more roundabout dirt road running through the locality of Thornford, a mile or so north of 'Stillwater'. Another route to the wider world lay to the west, over the windy high plain to the Goulburn–Collector road, then through Yarra, the nearest postal town. Probably the road to Goulburn was best from Bangalore, but the way through Yarra was more direct and better for riding.[12]

'Stillwater' was one of twelve households in Thornford. As has been pointed out by the copious chronicler of Goulburn history Ransome T. Wyatt, in the late nineteenth century the area was more densely populated than either before or since, due to free selection; and while the Franklin holdings were less than 2 miles across at their widest extent, mostly the distance was much less, as contemporary land maps show. 'I felt cramped on our new run,' says Sybylla Melvyn.[13]

Having so many neighbours close by was a new experience and a mixed blessing for young Stella, though probably less so than for her mother. Flinch as she might at the neighbourly calls and the friendly small talk of matrons from surrounding small farms whom she could not help looking down upon, even Susannah sometimes found it handy when stores ran out; and the proximity of numerous large families enhanced the natural exuberance of the Franklin children. At 'Stillwater', Miles Franklin concedes, the water was soft and the air fresh; there were places to play (and to hide) among the shrubs and she-oaks on the hillsides, where wallabies and 'native bears' (koalas) and lordly goannas were frequently to be seen; and in summer the children frolicked in the waterholes (boys and girls separately), where tortoises abounded, and sleepy lizards sunned themselves on every fence post.[14]

Three of the Franklin children were now of school age, and there was an elementary school to the west of 'Stillwater', at Kirkdale, in the district of Yarra, where from March 1889 Miss Mary Ann Gillespie (known as 'Mae') was teacher-in-charge. If Stella Franklin or any of her siblings ever attended Kirkdale School, however, it was only for a short while, and the experience could not have been pleasant. Kirkdale School had been conducted for some years in the Anglican church of St Michael's and All Angels, the picturesque ruins of which may still be seen from the Federal Highway some kilometres south of Goulburn, but fewer than twenty children attended in the late 1880s, as it was too far from most of the selections. Lacking a chimney, the tiny stone building could not be heated in the freezing winters. Not surprisingly, parents petitioned the Department of Public Instruction for the school's removal to a more convenient location, in the Wesleyan church at Thornford. In mid-1889, soon after the Franklins arrived in the district, the Department acceded to their wishes.[15]

Although no records of attendance remain, it was undoubtedly at the school in the Wesleyan church at Thornford, with its increased number of pupils (thirty) and Miss Gillespie still in charge, that Stella enrolled on her return from Talbingo in 1890. Within months the school was once more moved, again on the petition of the parents (one of whom was J. M. Franklin) because of flooding and the inconvenience of having to shift the furniture several times weekly, presumably to accommodate the frequent Wesleyan meetings in those days. With commendable alacrity, a purpose-built weatherboard on higher ground south of Thornford was opened in August 1890, Miss Gillespie continuing as teacher-in-charge.[16]

No roads went by the new school. But there was a stock route and the school was far more convenient, especially for the Franklin children, who now had a considerably shorter daily trek, less than a mile, up the valley from 'Stillwater'. Miss Gillespie, who boarded with local families during the week and spent her weekends in Goulburn, sometimes drove to school in her horse-and-buggy. There was plenty of room for horses on the hillside site, the location of which is still identifiable from the Thornford road, thanks to the stock route and tree plantings of a century or so ago.[17]

At Thornford Public School Stella Franklin obtained an elementary education, which was at that time compulsory in New South Wales to age fourteen, when grade 7 was normally reached, but might be extended to grade 9, by which time pupils would be aged fifteen or sixteen. Exactly how long she spent at the school is now uncertain, but it seems she left in 1894.[18]

Throughout those years at Thornford Public School, her teacher was always Miss Gillespie. Possibly untrained and never more than a Class C teacher — that is, the lowest of teacher classifications — Miss Gillespie was close to her pupils in origin. The sources indicate she was born in 1856, the eldest daughter of an Irish immigrant, James Gillespie, a freeholder of Grabben Gullen, a hamlet north of Goulburn, and his wife, Frances, and that she began teaching in 1884. During her time at Thornford from 1890 to 1913 (when the school closed due to declining enrolments) she was esteemed by both parents and pupils, as recounted in press reports of school events, and she became a personal friend of both Miles Franklin and her mother. Although the records show that she continually failed further examinations, for example in dictation and history in 1891, Mae Gillespie had skills beyond those looked for by the system and the censorious male inspectorate which policed the new state schools.[19]

Other Australian girls of the early 1890s in more advanced urban contexts were just then reaping the benefits of expanding educational opportunity, most notably at the Presbyterian Ladies' College in Melbourne, of which Miles Franklin's mentors and peers suffragist Vida Goldstein and writer Ethel 'Henry Handel' Richardson were star products. But the one-teacher schools and their mainly female teachers should not be underestimated. As anticipated by Charles Blyth, Stella Franklin responded well to competition, attracting favourable attention from the inspectors, winning numerous school prizes for proficiency in her subjects and earning commendations for her work at the Goulburn Show.[20]

She learned about something else too: the democratic outlook. Her mother may have had misgivings about state schooling (as did Sybylla Melvyn's mother in *My Brilliant Career*), and her new classmates were the children from the surrounding blocks — the Patons, the Macauleys, the Somervilles and the Neelys — but John Franklin supported the new system, and with an ever expanding family, there were no other options for educating his children.[21]

A group photograph of Thornford Public School students, taken according to a handwritten attribution in 1892, but on the basis of enrolment figures, possibly earlier, captures some of the realities. Miss Gillespie, ungainly at one end of the back row, head to the side and slightly lowered, looks hopefully towards the camera. One of the girls is almost as tall as she is. Her pupils, thirty-six in all, are arranged in four rows and dressed in their best, the girls with their hair tied back in ribbons and the boys with hats in their hands. Some boys even wear ties. All wear shoes. But the rows are ragged and the little ones at the front sit on the ground amid the stones and tussocks. Squinting into the sun, they are a typically scruffy lot.[22]

Standing in the middle of the back row in a high-necked white dress is Stella Miles Franklin. Shorter than average, clear skinned and round faced, and already displaying a likeness to her Grandmother Lampe with her hair pulled well back off her forehead, she appears well fed and unfazed. By this time she was approaching twelve and was a senior, though she doesn't look it. Indeed, she looks child-like, and but for the attribution, and perhaps the bold expression, it would be hard to say if it was her. Linda stands two along, and Mervyn Franklin may be somewhere there too.[23]

The photo hardly leaves an encouraging impression of the little school. Nor is this counteracted by its fictional counterpart in *My Brilliant Career*, Tiger Swamp School, with its sometimes inebriated teacher 'Old Harris' (obviously a refraction from poor Mr Blyth, a faithful and encouraging correspondent during the Thornford years). It may be that Miles Franklin was embarrassed by her plebeian schooling. A journalist interviewing her in 1903 was at pains to emphasise that she was not uneducated: 'The idea that Miss Franklin is uneducated is erroneous. She has not been to school [but has had] sound private tuition.'[24]

In fact, Thornford School was a positive experience for Stella Franklin. Enrolments increased to over fifty children in the mid-1890s and the school environment soon improved. A school garden was established — Stella had a flowerbed from the beginning — and over 100 trees were planted, so that soon the school perimeter was ringed with shade. When the school fence collapsed, Miss Gillespie and the boys built another (to keep out the rabbits). They also built a bush shed, and Miss Gillespie procured an apiary 'for the benefit of scholars'. Best of all, Miss Gillespie held a school picnic every year, during which the prizes were awarded by local dignitaries, and hundreds of people from all over the district came. Trees were planted annually on Arbor Day.[25]

Responding to a letter from his ex-pupil on 4 October 1890, Charles Blyth was pleased to think that she now had a chance to show 'what a smart little girl you are'. He urged her to make the most of her chances, and hoped that, having impressed the school inspector, she would continue to acquire and retain knowledge. This she did. She became one of the stars at Thornford Public. For an essay on 'Perseverance' in 1891 she was awarded a special prize (Uncle John's *Wonders of the World*, donor Mr Thomas Rose, MP). In 1892 she won a copy of the *Poetical Works* of Oliver Wendell Holmes for an essay 'On Education', her first prose writing to survive (a rather stilted effort in fair copy, still tucked inside her prize), and also received a copy of *Dombey and Son* by Charles Dickens (one of her early favourites) as half-share of the clean boots prize. In 1894 she topped the school in the general proficiency examination and won the teacher's prize for the best-kept exercise book. She also won prizes for geography, writing (girls) and dictation. The dictation prize was *Routledge's School Reciter for Boys and Girls*, containing speeches from Shakespeare, extracts from Milton's *Paradise Lost*, and various nineteenth-century classics such as Dickens' 'The Death of Little Nell'.[26]

Blyth, who apparently had been jealous of the state schools with their superior resources, soon changed his mind. He was eager to know about the facilities, and keen to hear about the books his ex-pupil was reading; and it seems Stella kept him well informed about her activities and progress. On 27 July 1894, apologising as usual for a delayed reply, he envisaged Stella back at her schoolwork: 'I suppose you have now resumed school and are composing essays, analysing sentences, solving intricate fractional problems and otherwise exercising and developing your intellectual faculties.'[27]

This gives some idea of the curriculum at the upper levels of the state school system in the 1890s. Beyond the standard fare of the three Rs lay a progression of spelling, dictation, grammar and composition, ever more complex arithmetical computations, the appreciation of poetry and prose, and heavy books on history and geography, the latter two subjects mostly learned by rote — which is possibly what put Stella Franklin off history until much later in life. In one of few references to her experience of school history, she deplored the 'dull droning' about Joan of Arc she had endured from a 'brief history of England'.[28]

To this diet Miss Gillespie added a leavening of moral instruction, backed up by the threat of caning. A vignette survives in a letter to Miles Franklin from a schoolmate, Edie — probably Edie Paton, as she signs herself 'Edie (formerly Patent Door Springs)' — Reading in the papers about the now celebrated authoress brought back the memory: 'I can't help smiling for it sets me back thinking of the old school days, when we were scampering over the poor old stony ground at Thornford, and Miss Gillespie standing at the doorway with a moustache of tea on her lips, & rinsing her teacup and then a yell of You girls! You girls! March straight here, & get your hair combed, before I cane the fingers off you. I suppose,' Edie continues, 'Miss Gillespie thinks the good seed of the moral lessons and lectures she used to favour us with fell on barren soil, in my case I can assure her it is not so.'[29]

Presumably the cane was not needed on either of them. Charles Blyth, who relied on 'pecks' to keep his charges in order, concluded that Miss Gillespie must be a good, efficient teacher, asserting that the Franklin children had been fortunate in attending such a well-organised little public school. (By contrast, the best verdict Mae Gillespie ever won from the inspectors was 'very fair to fair', in 1892, but mostly they deemed her work merely 'tolerable'.) In later life Miles Franklin would extol both her teachers as 'rare and precious' and 'wonderful beings that could tell me the things I wanted to know'.[30]

Even so, Miles Franklin's schooling had a great many gaps. She was well grounded in botany — there is a copy of colonial botanist Baron von Mueller's school text in her library and her work is full of botanical references — but her knowledge of science and physiology is another matter. Like many Australian girls in times past, the heroines of her early novels were unafraid of men but terrified by sex, and often feared that a kiss was enough to cause pregnancy. This ignorance may surprise the modern reader, now unfamiliar with rural codes of respectability, and considering the then superabundance of males in rural Australia, where, as Miles Franklin once tartly observed, 'every girl who had four limbs and reasonable features lived in a state of siege from the age of fourteen until she capitulated'. No doubt strange practices sometimes occurred in the paddocks, and there probably was some indecent exposure by station hands, but socially speaking, competition for female favours rendered the males more circumspect, and being in 'a state of siege' strengthened the cult of respectability for females. Silence on such topics was the norm. Nor was extracurricular study likely to have made much difference. In 1895, Stella Franklin won a prize (six shillings) in a temperance physiology examination sponsored by the Woman's Christian Temperance Union, which she had sat one Saturday the previous November at Thornford, but it was probably more about temperance than physiology.[31]

Other sources of worldly information were scarcely more revealing, but far more thrilling. The most striking feature of Miles Franklin's intellectual development during her girlhood (adolescence was not then an established concept) is her voracious appetite for the latest novels. How she responded to Charles Blyth's request that she send 'particulars of the books you read' is unknown, but his replies, discussing the works of Scott, Dickens, Thackeray and other nineteenth-century favourites, are indicative, and doubtless helped shape her taste, which under the additional influence of Miss Gillespie soon ran ahead of his to include the most controversial novels of the 1890s — Du Maurier's *Trilby* and George Moore's even more daring *Esther Waters*.[32]

Miss Gillespie was then boarding with the Franklins, and it was she who brought *Trilby* into the house. 'It was not considered reading for a young girl, but it could not have escaped me,' Miles Franklin recalled. In fact, she doted on the story of young British artists in 1890s Paris and the wicked Svengali who captures their model, Trilby, and by hypnotic means makes her a famous singer: 'what intensity, what poignancy of enjoyment, what glamour!' Fifty years on, she still felt it retained its 'infinite seduction'.[33]

Miss Gillespie also brought *Esther Waters* to 'Stillwater'. The harrowing tale of the lifelong struggle by London-born domestic servant Esther Waters to support her illegitimate son similarly thrilled the young reader in far-off New South Wales. Many years later she recalled the fuss made about the book, noting that she had taken the precaution of reading it under the bed in the spare room, and adding that it never cast a slur upon her mind. Rather, its style excited her. Today *Esther Waters* reads as a moral tale exalting purity, condemning gambling, and making motherhood its own reward. To young Stella it was 'like a poem'.[34]

Many years later, Miles Franklin recorded that the novels she read between the ages of thirteen and twenty remained her favourites. The list included not only the already acknowledged nineteenth-century classics *Les Misérables* by Victor Hugo, Leo Tolstoy's *War and Peace* and Thomas Hardy's *Far from the Madding Crowd*, but also *The Story of an African Farm* by Olive Schreiner, a more recent and controversial work in which the bleak farm on the South African veldt undercuts the heroic image of the imperial frontier, and the rebellious heroine, Lyndall, dies in childbirth. If, as she would also recall, Thackeray's *Vanity Fair* lasted best of all, at the time of first reading, *The Story of an African Farm* and *Trilby* were the most exciting: they were 'the two most exalting novels read in my girlhood'. (Miles in fact didn't read *The Story of an African Farm* until 1901, when she was already past twenty.) In both novels, death and sexuality went together. These were the new themes of 1890s novels, but the effect was uplifting rather than informative. By contrast, the idealistic moralism of *The Lost Manuscript* by Gustav Freytag, a Germanic gloss on town-and-gown relations, which she won in the Amykos short story competition in 1896 (run by the Swedish consul in New South Wales and sponsored by a Swedish mouthwash firm), was probably too dull and unreadable to convey any useful information about male–female relationships.[35]

Whatever the schoolgirl may have gleaned from the reading of romantic novels, she was unprepared for the advances of the local boys. Some never openly declared themselves: an undated 1890s Christmas card simply says 'from a boy you do not know whose heart beats true to you'. Others were unable to refrain. By the age of fourteen, Stella had already had a suitor who claimed to have loved her for two years but was now leaving with the cattle, since his presence was so obviously distasteful to her. Perhaps he was the prototype for the elderly suitor lampooned in the sketch 'Gossip by the Way'. The jaunty response to unwanted suitors in *My Brilliant Career*, that they should send their love to her father, who would put it in a bottle for the Science Museum in Goulburn (he once donated a centipede in spirits to the museum), seems in retrospect to prefigure Miles Franklin's final stance, that romantic love was illogical and human sexual energy was far in excess of all needs for propagating the species. But that was much later. Looking back, she described herself during her second decade as 'bewildered and tormented and rebellious'.[36]

Organised religion was no help. In May 1894, Stella Franklin was confirmed at All Saints' Church of England, Collector. A skilfully composed and suitably serious photographic portrait was taken by Stinson of Goulburn to mark the rite of passage. The ceremony was conducted by the bishop at the village of Collector, not in St Saviour's Cathedral, Goulburn. Evidence of the impact of the event on its subject is non-existent. Like so many New South Welshmen, the Franklins were respectable if largely nominal Anglicans (though the niceties of denominationalism may be misleading, since there was a Wesleyan chapel at Thornford, where Miles later recalled having seen missionary slides of the South Seas; and a scene in *My Brilliant Career* describes Sybylla walking to a weatherboard 'house of prayer' with Harold Beecham one hot Sunday afternoon, which sounds like the chapel). As for Sunday school, it had proved disagreeable during an early stay at Tumut with relatives. Although one source has Stella attending St Saviour's aged thirteen and fourteen, she was already by then impious, baffling her mother. As an early essay, 'A Dialogue: An Infidel and a Religionist', shows, and *My Brilliant Career* stridently affirms, she was soon to become a full-blooded rationalist like her father, the efforts by conscientious local clergy to help her cope with doubt notwithstanding. A dreamy quality pervades the confirmation portrait, however, and a pensive air. Perhaps Stella Franklin was already anxious about her appearance. She may not have been fully grown by then, but the pose — she is resting her elbows on a ledge — indicates a short torso and some puppy fat about the face, with the snub nose for which she became famous very much in evidence, and wispy hair, crimped and tied back for the occasion.[37]

Of necessity, housework took up most of Stella's time outside school hours. When the whole Franklin family but her succumbed to measles in early 1894, she had to do everything, including baking the bread. The situation was compounded by the cult of domesticity, informal but powerful. By all accounts she was capable at cooking, cleaning and the rest from an early age, but the literary record emphasises little time and no priority for her own interests. In *Cockatoos*, a later novel, Miles wrote, 'Ceaseless activity was the ideal of the homes of the Ridges ... the foremost consideration was that Ignez [the heroine] should help with the work'. This may have been set in a slightly later period, but was surely the plain truth for the schoolgirl Stella.[38]

For all that, farm girls often gained enjoyment from games played in the course of outdoor work, and the natural world always has its own entertainments to offer. Yet little is made of these opportunities in the early writing, maybe because as the eldest child Stella often had to look after her siblings, which left limited time for recreation. The exception was galloping across the hills. Evidently horse-riding was the most exhilarating thing in Stella Franklin's life. And here she excelled, having a good seat and hands, and a certain dash. Some of Sybylla Melvyn's most rebellious scenes are to do with riding or driving horses, and in *Cockatoos* Ignez Milford is a wonderful rider who boldly prefers to ride astride rather than use the more decorous side-saddle. Stella would go even further and ride bareback. However, photographs show her sitting side-saddle, on neighbour and sometime suitor James John Ranger Baxter's racing stallion 'Lord Clive', in accordance with prevailing notions of decorum. For some of her peers, J. J. Baxter's brother Andrew, for example, and Tina Coles of Yarra, the most memorable thing about the young Miles Franklin was her horsemanship.[39]

'My sphere of life is not congenial to me,' says Sybylla Melvyn in *My Brilliant Career*. Increasingly her story is of adolescent angst, so it comes as a surprise to learn that as a girl Stella enjoyed a game of draughts. Sybylla, by contrast, lives in a dream world with writers, artists and musicians. Not only does she borrow every book in the neighbourhood, but music becomes a passion: 'I longed for the arts,' she says. In *Cockatoos*, which is set at the end of the nineteenth century, Ignez Milford is sent to stay with her relatives at Oswald's Ridges to enable her to take music lessons in Goulburn, but she is always in trouble for practising the piano when she could be helping with the housework, and she studies musical theory in the interstices of her busy life.[40]

Piano lessons begun at Brindabella continued at Thornford, and in June 1894 Stella Franklin gained an impressive 95 per cent for theory in the Trinity College (London) examinations conducted in Goulburn Town Hall, though she attained only a bare pass from the Sydney College of Music in early 1896. It may be significant that whereas in 1894 Miles sat as a pupil of Percy Hollis, a professional music teacher in Goulburn, in 1896 she was entered by Miss Gillespie. (In *Cockatoos*, a similarly humiliating result for Ignez is explained by the alteration of her mark by a rival teacher.) In later life, Miles would recall that her great ambition when young was to become a singer, and the stage had had its appeal too.[41]

There was plenty to stimulate those dreams in 1890s Goulburn. The organ music at the cathedrals was inspiring, and the Liedertafel's concerts were of a good standard under Percy Hollis. Moreover, Goulburn was a convenient stopover on the main Sydney–Melbourne rail route for entertainers of all stripes, and in the later 1890s the young folk from Thornford would have seen some of them, as did those portrayed in *Cockatoos.* However — and this would be elaborated in the suffrage novel *Some Everyday Folk and Dawn* — in real life acting was beyond the pale for respectable girls. Even a musical career was an impossible dream, as lamented in *Cockatoos* and elsewhere.[42]

Some time after Stella left school, she wrote to Mr Blyth of her regret at receding girlhood and anxiety about looming womanhood. He was a feminist and he did his best to reassure her. In another letter at this time he kindly added that he had never thought her plain. Nothing direct survives to illuminate her feelings about the transition, which in physical terms had in all likelihood already occurred, as the average age of puberty for females in the colonies was then fourteen. Certainly a new stage had begun: in 1895, Stella would turn sixteen, and by that age, young women were ripe for courting.[43]

As Miles Franklin rightly claimed in the Preface to *Cockatoos,* her early writings enable us to hear the authentic voice of 'the really young'. Some tolerance of adolescent angst, as well as the historical context, is necessary to fully appreciate their value. They capture well the liminal character of this stage of a girl's life, with its heady mix of dreaming and recalcitrance, and also show a marked sensitivity to class differences, which were still significant in the area. Sybylla Melvyn protests that she would not be able to compete against Goulburn girls in pupil-teacher exams, as they all had good teachers and time to study, and she complains that she has been born out of her sphere. Ignez Milford suffers the ignominy of hauling Larry Healey out of the 'Mantrap' pub in Goulburn under the eye of the publican's dainty daughters, and persists in longing for a career in London.[44]

Yet, as Stella really knew, the very concept of a career was outside the frame for most girls of the period, especially ordinary country girls: brilliant careers were the preserve of men. What really lay ahead was marriage. As a recent study of the construction of girlhood in English fiction suggests, a young girl's consciousness of growing up was differently shaped from that of boys, not by fear of failure or mortality but by the prospect of marriage. The lesson from literature was that the successful girl would internalise and transcend the contradictions involved in learning 'womanly conduct' — between girlish freedom and marital constraints — and fit into a place 'already prepared for her'. The contradictions were even more marked for Australian girls, reared in greater freedom, and then caught in the contracting economy and demographics of the 1890s.[45]

It has been remarked of many outstanding late-Victorian women, for example Fabian socialist Beatrice Webb, that it is a pity they did not undertake further education. Since Stella Franklin did so well at school, she should surely have gone on to higher studies, as Charles Blyth hoped she would. Instead she became a farm hand. No more compelling expression of her situation is to be found than the heavily ironic 'Bush Idyll' in Chapter 5 of *My Brilliant Career*, where Sybylla wearily lifts bogged cows from the soaks in the boiling sun: 'This was life — my life — my career, my brilliant career!' she cries.[46]

How had it come to this? It was not that secondary schooling for girls was unavailable in the colony, or in Goulburn for that matter. Although the state high school for girls established there in the 1880s had failed, there were private providers, for example Our Lady of Mercy College and St Werberg's College for Girls.[47]

The answer is to be found in an austere entry dated 'Feb. 95' in Susannah Franklin's notebook: 'got separator'. This means John Franklin had become a dairyman. His dream of livestock trading was over. What is more, financial records show that he had to borrow to purchase the separator. But it promised cream for sale, probably to the recently established Thornford Butter Factory, and a small regular income of about fifteen shillings a week — and, since cows must be brought in, fed and milked twice daily for most of the year, it meant an unremitting regimen for his family, made worse by the extended drought of the mid-1890s. Under the circumstances there was not the slightest chance of further education for the eldest of his six children, even if it had been contemplated.[48]

A year later John Franklin went into voluntary bankruptcy. It emerged that his land purchases had involved a mortgage obligation to the Bishop of Goulburn and a larger mortgage to the Bishop of the Riverina taken out in 1893, such property dealings being a standard way in which colonial bishops generated funds. In 1896, the Bishop of Goulburn's solicitor called up arrears on the former mortgage, and as John Franklin could not pay, sent the bailiff in. On 25 March 1896 a notice appeared on the gate leading to 'Stillwater' announcing that all the farm and household equipment (including the separator) would be sold by public auction on site the following week. The final date of sequestration was 19 August 1896, and it was not until 24 August 1897 that John Franklin obtained a certificate of release.[49]

Many small selectors failed in the terrible slump of the 1890s, but the humiliation for Susannah would have been intense. Her family rallied, providing neighbours with the means to purchase and return household goods, and John's brother George took over the lease and paid the rent on the land. So despite everything the family stayed put and had a roof over its head, with a few cows, hens and a garden, but it was the end of John Franklin as a landholder.[50]

Aged forty-eight, John Maurice Franklin became a day labourer. In the first of two surviving letters to his eldest daughter, written to her while she was visiting Talbingo from 'Stillwater' at the end of that terrible year, he was working by the week on fencing at 'Longfield', the Baxter property next door. It is a long and revealing letter, weak on spelling and punctuation and somewhat distraught, but without self-pity: his garden is doing well, with tomatoes in bloom and potatoes on the way, and his god is still reason. He hopes that his daughter will be able to think for herself too:

> I know I have a law full right to think simply because no one else knows what my thoughts are thank god for that otherwise I may have to consult some of my reverend seniors & those educated in the school where nature is only a fool I suppose that you will be glad to hear that I thank god for some thing, well I do but not the god of gold selfishness envy hatred malice pride pomp & worldly show & hundreds of other names, but the one I thank is the god of reason science art love & beauty … now as you maybe endowed with the power to think for yourself, you can think out what sort of a god I thank.[51]

The following year he was hunting for gold reefs at Brindabella.[52]

Any parental authority John Franklin may have retained over his daughter was now gone. 'Near Goulburn' had not been good for him. Whether or not he had become a drinker remains a sensitive point, but on balance it seems he indulged to a certain extent, and his daughters certainly thought he should be kept out of pubs. But too much can be made of his weaknesses, in that the authority of fathers over daughters was wavering everywhere by this time, and his influence can too easily be overlooked. It was from her father that Miles Franklin imbibed political, as well as religious and poetical, values. The contempt for 'spouters' (politicians) noted by Blyth in her letters and the view expressed in *My Brilliant Career* that 'there should be a law' to prevent poverty came directly from her father's radical political circles in Goulburn and the pages of the *Penny Post*. The *Post* was an ardent supporter of Henry George, the American advocate of a single tax on land as the solution to the then highly conspicuous problem of poverty and wealth. As well, in 1894 John Franklin hosted election meetings at Bangalore for his local member of parliament, E. W. O'Sullivan, who advocated protection of local industries, state investment in public works, and votes for women.[53]

Just as the father–daughter bond was becoming strained under trying circumstances, so the mother–daughter relationship intensified with Stella now at home all the time. From Susannah Franklin's point of view, the completion of her eldest's schooling was a godsend. With five younger children and a herd of cows to milk by hand, the work was endless. From her daughter's point of view, however, the timing was most unfortunate. The literary evidence is of cross-purposes and seething tensions, of an intensity previously noted only between fathers and sons on small holdings.

Susannah Franklin was not unsupportive of her clever daughter, but inevitably the demands of home and husband were draining. Aged forty-six in 1896, she may have been thankful that her child-bearing years were over. Yet her rebellious daughter made fresh demands. At a time when anger, sanctioned by feminism, was no longer a totally taboo emotion for girls, though still deplored in etiquette books as unladylike, there seems to have been plenty of it in the Franklin household. *My Brilliant Career* reproduces and elaborates on some of the conflicts, and others are depicted in *Cockatoos*, where the capable but unhappy Dot Saunders cannot stand young Ignez's constant thumping on the piano, and an irretrievable clash occurs between Dot and the younger Freda, who aspires to be a writer. Like Stella Franklin, neither Ignez or Freda showed any sign of settling down in the traditional way; and like her, both Sybylla and Ignez rejected entirely eligible suitors. However, in fiction at least, the misery was shared by the young women, and it was not all misery. Furthermore, it is probably true that Susannah Franklin has been misunderstood to some extent on the basis of literary evidence, as there is nothing to suggest that she sought to push her daughter into marriage. In *My Brilliant Career* the mother openly regrets her own marriage.[54]

Apparently an effort was made to get Stella Franklin into teaching at this critical time. In June 1896 glowing testimonials as to her suitability were written by the Reverend Williams and E. W. O'Sullivan, and a notification allowing her to sit for a competitive examination for pupil-teachers in Goulburn in July, despite being over the age limit of sixteen, survives in her papers. No record survives of the outcome, but subsequent events suggest she did sit the exam and passed.[55]

Stuck at 'Stillwater' her education was not leading anywhere, and no Svengali appeared to liberate her musical talents. But she could write. Miss Gillespie had noticed it: 'She's very good at compositions,' she told her teacher friend Eliza Kellett, with whom she shared weekends in Goulburn. 'I've been encouraging her to write stories. I think she has quite a talent for it.' Just as the young Olive Schreiner was drafting stories in the remote Eastern Cape Colony in the 1870s with only local libraries and a few town friends to rely on, so twenty years later on another edge of the Empire, with the help of Miss Gillespie and the cultural resources of 1890s Goulburn, Stella Miles Franklin tentatively embarked on a literary career.[56]

Various dates have been given to mark its beginning, not least by Miles Franklin herself. Sometimes, like Sybylla, she said she began writing aged thirteen; that is, in 1892–93. Elsewhere she claimed she was writing about 'lords and ladies' even earlier, aged twelve, and that she won a prize for an essay on punctuality at that age. As she had a good memory, this may well be true. The essay on punctuality does not survive in her papers, but she certainly won prizes for school essays around then. However, sustained literary work appears to date from 1895–96, when she was sixteen. *My Brilliant Career* was not begun until 20 September 1898, when she was eighteen, though many people, including her young relative Ruby Bridle, thought it was started earlier, probably because by the time they knew her Miles had been understating her age for years.[57]

Given that in many ways she was turning out to be an archetypal Australian girl of the period (who was thought to be bolder and freer than her British counterpart), it seems only right that like many other early women writers, Catherine Helen Spence and Mary Gilmore, for example, Miles Franklin made her debut in the newspaper press. Her report on the Thornford School picnic in the *Penny Post* on 26 March 1896 was a good start, even if, when ex-journalist Charles Blyth caught up with it, he had kindly advice to offer on the overuse of linking words such as 'after', for example. (Miles used it six times in the article.)[58]

Nothing further seems to have appeared until 1901, though over time her output of topical writings would be quite substantial. Indeed, from 1896 until at least the 1920s, a career in journalism was always a possibility, at least as a supplement to an always meagre income; and Miles' experience in the genre is highly relevant to her approach to literature. But the scope for a woman to succeed in journalism was limited, and it was to literature that she aspired.[59]

The discipline of reportage is not evident in three early manuscripts: 'A Pair of New Chums', dated 5 May 1896; 'For Sale to the Highest Bidder', dated 8 June 1896; and 'Within a Footstep of the Goal; An Australian Story', dated August 1896. The latter two are signed with the ornate and unrevealing but truthful 'S. M. S. Miles Franklin', the first recorded use of the name Miles. None attained publication, and the full text survives for only one, an unsigned manuscript of 'A Pair of New Chums', an 'Australian tale' written for the Amykos short story competition in mid-1896. This was the story which won the book prize mentioned earlier. It was, she later recalled, her first attempt at a short story, and one can see why the judges thought well of it. It takes two young men up the country for Christmas at Jinningningama Station in the year of the great Shearers' Strike, and the priggish one receives his comeuppance on a camping trip arranged for that purpose. It is a conventional tale, but suitable as exotica, and has the bonus of mentioning Bin Bin Station — Bin Bin East and Bin Bin West are referred to in *My Brilliant Career* and the placename later served to locate Miles Franklin's most successful pseudonym, 'Brent of Bin Bin'. It also contains descriptive passages that read like an early version of *All That Swagger*. The address given on the back of the manuscript is 'Miss Gillespie, Public School, Thornford, near Goulburn'.[60]

'For Sale to the Highest Bidder' is a total contrast. Set in the West End of London, it deals with the forced marriage of eighteen-year-old Desdemona Gawler to a wealthy bachelor aged seventy-three. The manuscript is annotated at page 77 'incomplete' in the author's hand, as if, perhaps, she was worn out by the time the heroine says no at the altar. More of a foretaste of later work is the also incomplete manuscript 'Within a Footstep of the Goal', dated August 1896 (that fatal month for the Franklin family when John Franklin was declared bankrupt). Here something more like experience is in evidence, in that it tells how an old-fashioned bush girl with a gift for love and service wins over the Sydney sophisticates with whom she has come to stay.

A quickening correspondence between Stella Franklin and Charles Blyth in 1896 suggests that these unsatisfactory items may not have been the only ones.

Although Blyth's expressed interests by now extended to spiritualism and theosophy, he did his best to deal with current books, commenting in early January, for instance, on the latest novels by Marie Corelli, then at the peak of her popularity ('trashy'), and to encourage Miles, assuring her that there was no intellectual conversation to be had at Brindabella either. Replying in April to a query about one May Hall, reportedly lauded as 'a literary genius' and published in the *Yass Tribune*, he wrote that she had probably copied her stories from some girlish publication and that he felt sorry for her, 'a poor girl … in a bush hut'. In a subsequent letter, written in September, referring to a reply from Stella on 5 June, Blyth notes something more substantial: her confession that the query about May Hall had been prompted by her own aspirations in that line, 'having secretly written a tale or a novel', and sent it to Angus & Robertson, Sydney's leading publisher, to no avail.[61]

Blyth had suspected as much, and was most sympathetic, 'really sorry that after your brain labour, purchase secretly of stationery and burning of midnight oil, your work did not pass from manuscript into type'. But, he went on, she should persevere; many writers suffered such setbacks. One day she would take her place in Australian literature, he assured her.[62]

From this, it seems clear that Miles Franklin had written her first novel well before June 1896. For a long time all that was known of this work was *Penny Post* editor Thomas J. Hebblewhite's recollection of a manuscript Miss Gillespie once brought him to read, and the letter he wrote to its author after he had done so. As he recalled:

> I do not know how many years ago it is since Miss Gillespie, then in charge of the little public school at Thornford, came one Saturday morning into the office with a parcel of manuscript. She said one of her girl pupils had written it, and would I please look it over. It was a story of the London West End, conventional in character and treatment, but well put together for a bush girl in her early teens. I wrote to the young aspirant and pointed out kindly how she could not possibly of her own self know anything of high life in London, and encouraged her to write the things she knew best, the life she understood, and the scenes and people that were familiar to her.[63]

In the letter of 8 September 1896, beginning 'Dear Miss Franklin', Hebblewhite advised the young writer to study the classics and pay attention to style, urging her to leave the unfamiliar world of lords and ladies behind and concentrate on 'the soul and meaning of things which are at hand'. As examples of close observation, he recommended the New England sketches of American writer Miss Wilkins and 'the marvellous rural pictures' of Richard Jefferies, a British naturalist who died in 1887. 'For those who can voice fittingly the life that lies about us there is always an appreciative audience,' he sagely observed.[64]

What, then, was this manuscript? Hebblewhite does not say, and Miles Franklin never did. However, a likely answer is not far to seek. Tucked away in the Franklin Papers, near the end of an otherwise chronological sequence of mostly unpublished manuscripts, is the fair copy in Stella Miles Franklin's youthful hand of a substantial novel about 'lords and ladies'. The novel is entitled 'Lord Dunleve's Ward', by 'S. M. S. F.', and Miss Gillespie's name is inscribed on the title page, with her Thornford address.[65]

Written in lined notebooks bound into two volumes, 'Lord Dunleve's Ward' is a major piece of juvenilia, well over 100,000 words in length. Lynn Milne, in a first study of the text, concludes that it almost certainly is the manuscript in question, and she suggests that although it is not all set in London's West End, Hebblewhite's advice with regard to style and construction fits it 'like Cinderella's glass slipper'. Hebblewhite thought 'the writing [gave] evidence of literary ability, though naturally untrained and inclined to run into the diffusive'.[66]

This is fair comment. The plot is difficult to summarise briefly. First the mother of the anti-heroine, Sybil, then her father, and then her nominated guardian, Lord Dunleve, die, and Lord Dunleve's eighteen-year-old son takes over. He comes to feel more than a brother to Sybil. Grown up, she has three suitors: the earnest young Dunleve; her grandfather's stepson Cyril, a soulmate; and an aristocratic trickster called Dunraven. After she is persuaded by the self-sacrificing Cyril to marry Dunleve, Dunraven succeeds in undermining Dunleve with insinuations of infidelity. The unworldly Sybil then fakes her own death, adopts a false name, and travels the Continent for eleven years doing good works, returning to England with a bad heart to die. Which she does, without ever discovering what really happened.

For all its schoolgirl melodrama, lengthy diatribes on topics such as religion, money and motherhood, and many exotic episodes as the heroine travels Europe, not to mention the flowery style, points of real interest and import do emerge. Not least is the fact that the heroine is called Sybil, which became a favourite name with Miles Franklin, conjuring up — perhaps paradoxically — the prophetesses of classical legend, who were believed to accurately foretell the future. She is an isolated child and clever — 'having no congenial company made her a curious child' — but purblind. Due to her emotionally deprived background, she simply cannot work things out when it comes to love and marriage and men. For Sybil, the young writer observes, 'marriage meant a congenial companion, a confidant, love, life, sympathy, being understood, a home'.[67]

Whether or not Stella Franklin paused to reflect that Hebblewhite's own paper carried serials about lords and ladies, or wondered how to obtain copies of the recommended books, his response to her work was a step on from anything previously available. Miss Gillespie had her limits and knew them, and Charles Blyth, though supportive, generally gave technical advice. Here was a guide that might yield much, and there seems no reason to disbelieve its efficacy. Miles never wrote about lords and ladies again until the 1920s, when she drafted the first volume of the 'Brent of Bin Bin' saga, *Prelude to Waking*, set in London's Mayfair; the writings of her youth were determinedly local, especially the sketches. If anything, in the urgency of youth she took Hebblewhite's advice too much to heart.[68]

From later writings one might think that being 'near Goulburn' was a negative experience for Stella Franklin: her musical education had been thwarted by poor results; she could not compete with Goulburn girls in examinations; the place was full of pubs; and the clergy were mostly hypocrites. But Hebblewhite's response to her first novel casts her situation in a more realistic light. The reality was that she benefited from the proximity. Goulburn has always prided itself on being Australia's first inland city. Laid out in the 1820s, it is one of the oldest cities in Australia, and as was the case in many colonial cities, the 1880s had been a boom time. That much is evident in the built environment even now. St Saviour's Anglican Cathedral was finished in 1884; Sts Peter and Paul's Catholic Cathedral in 1890; the Post Office dates from 1881; the Court House (one of the grandest in New South Wales) from 1887; and the Town Hall, also imposing, from 1889. Less obvious is a cultural infrastructure dating from that time. In addition to the Academy of Music, which was housed in the Odd-fellows' Hall, 1890s Goulburn boasted a Mechanics' Institute Library and a Technological Museum, and in 1890 there were as many as four newspapers, not to mention numerous clubs and associations. Altogether, it was sufficient to sustain a thriving provincial culture, and Hebblewhite was one of its ornaments. An outstanding journalist, he is also remembered for his large personal library. Perhaps Stella Franklin followed up on his recommended reading there.[69]

While it is reasonable to conclude that the extant copy of 'Lord Dunleve's Ward' was both the manuscript she sent to Angus & Robertson and the one seen by Hebblewhite, a century later we cannot of course be absolutely sure. Unfortunately, the relevant publishing records do not begin until October 1896, and although she kept the manuscript of 'Lord Dunleve's Ward', Miles seems to have never mentioned its existence in her diaries and letters, at least by name. Here, then, is the first intimation of that secretiveness that would irritate her contemporaries and critics in later life. For a writer who drew so closely on her own experience, the lengths she would go to do seem extraordinary. Yet even then she lamented being 'driven inward' for lack of peers, and her secretive behaviour seems to have been essentially self-protective, positional and strategic rather than pathological, as has often been implied. After all, there is nothing to be gained in this world by advertising one's failures.

As we know, the young Stella Franklin also tried her hand at poetry, but it was not her métier. Certainly the unsigned verses preserved in the Franklin Papers are unimpressive. Four of six handwritten lines entitled 'Visions of the Past' read:

> The sun is sinking in the West
> All crowned with crimson glory
> The sky is blood-red colour dressed
> Like battlefield when gory.[70]

A line added later, 'I am going for a gallop', seems positively refreshing.

The fact that Miles Franklin kept such slivers is more interesting. Their preservation points to the priority given to poetry over fiction in the nineteenth century, and its prestige in the Australian colonies in the 1890s as a vehicle of nationalist values. John Franklin's only claim to book culture was his love of poetry, and his children followed his taste. Stella's favourite brother, Mervyn, was a vigorous reciter, and there are references to the colonial poets Henry Kendall and Adam Lindsay Gordon scattered through the early manuscripts. When a new nationalist school emerged in Australia in the 1890s — A. B. ('Banjo') Paterson's *The Man from Snowy River and Other Verses* appeared in 1895, and *While the Billy Boils* and *In the Days*

When the World was Wide by Henry Lawson in 1896 — it attracted Stella Franklin's enthusiasm, and the greater power of poetry would become for her a lifelong belief, reasserted in the 1940s. She also liked Ambrose Pratt's 'The Woman Speaks', first published in the *Bulletin*. Forty years later she could still recall its 'glint of glamour', and the hostility it aroused in men.[71]

Whatever her literary prospects, Stella Franklin had already been overtaken by events. In the spring of 1896, she was returned to Talbingo. Uncle Gus Lampe met her at Cootamundra, and they picked up an aunt at Gundagai en route. Bowling along the rich flats of Gundagai in Uncle Gus' buggy, they sang popular ditties such as 'Kate Kearney Who Lived on the Banks of Killarney' and 'I Wandered Today to a Hill, Maggie'.[72]

Just enough evidence survives — a birthday letter from her brother Tal, another from Blyth, her father's only letter — to confirm that for the rest of the year she was at Talbingo. What she did during those months is unknown, except for her memory of a day at Yarrangobilly picking wild raspberries, but it was probably there, when the household gathered around the piano in the evenings, that she first realised she had a good natural singing voice. In *My Brilliant Career*, Sybylla Melvyn is elated when Grandma Bossier's adopted son, Everard Grey, says all she needs is training. John Franklin had some good advice for his excitable daughter: 'do not argue with [your grandmother] wether you think she is right or wrong as she is as good as nature ever made & you only grieve her & do not alter her convictions.' During this time, it has been claimed by Lois Adam, a granddaughter of Susannah's cousin Emma Kinred of Tumut, that Stella fell in love with an (unnamed) young man, who became the basis of Harold Beecham, Sybylla's rejected suitor in *My Brilliant Career*. Other sources indicate that he was a young cousin of Susannah Franklin, Herbert (Bertie) Wilkinson, of nearby 'Yallowin', and that he and his older brother Phillip probably served as models for Harold Beecham.[73]

What happened next we do not know, but Susannah Franklin's record of family events states that Stella went to Tumut for a visit over Christmas 1896, from 17 December to 7 January 1897, and it goes on in its wonderfully plain way: 'Left Stella on Yass [railway] platform Thurs night 11 o'clock pm.' Just so does *My Brilliant Career* deposit Sybylla Melvyn at the Yarnung platform in the middle of the night, for collection by Mr M'Swat. The next we know of Stella Franklin, from an envelope containing a missive from Charles Blyth dated 4 February 1897, is that she has a new address: 'c/– Mr George Franklin, Oak Vale, Jeir PO, via Yass'.[74]

On 8 January 1897 Stella was dropped into a career as a governess. Why this occurred is not recorded. If *My Brilliant Career* is to be believed, Stella had no say in the matter. However, she was undoubtedly under pressure to find employment and, like Sybylla, she was probably to be paid £20 a year. Sybylla finds the dirt and squalor of her new surroundings horrifying and teaching her small charges more or less impossible. By August, she is prostrate with the effort and returns home, the kindly M'Swat cancelling the family debt. This outcome differs from the film version of *My Brilliant Career*, which makes the M'Swats' misinterpretation of her relationship with their oldest son, Peter, the pivot. Moreover, the story common to both novel and film differs in subtle ways from the available evidence of Stella Franklin's experiences.

So far as can be ascertained, Stella spent the first half of 1897 as governess to the children of her Uncle George and Aunt Margaret Franklin, who were by then quite substantial landholders in the parish of Jeir, between Murrumbateman and the Murrumbidgee River. All that is left now of Jeir is a creek crossing the Yass–Canberra road, but 'Oakvale' is still marked on topographical maps, and although it was less isolated than 'Stillwater', the work was intolerable to Stella Franklin. 'My poor child,' began Charles Blyth, as he attempted to pass on his own experience of teaching bush children and to reassure her that no experience was wasted, so long as she hung onto her literary aspirations. 'Keep a diary,' he suggested, and sent her *Jane Eyre* to read, which she enjoyed. Since her mother and several siblings came to stay in April, her living conditions could not have been as bad as those portrayed for Sybylla in *My Brilliant Career* and its film adaptation.[75]

Perhaps Stella was just too young to impress her unruly young cousins. By mid-year she was back at Thornford. Evidently she had already sat a pupil-teacher exam: when Miss Gillespie took sick in mid-July, she requested that Stella be allowed to take over for a week, stating that she had passed an examination towards teacher qualification and had some teaching experience. The request was approved by an inspector, who noted that the school would not be closed, as Miss Gillespie had asked Miss Franklin, an ex-pupil and teacher, to take over her duties.[76]

Stella was still at Thornford in September, when she was among the singers at a coffee supper at the Wesleyan church (she sang 'True Till Death'). Soon afterwards came another unwelcome family imperative, this time despatch to the family of her father's older sister Frances, married since 1874 to one Horace Hayes and living on a smaller holding adjacent to 'Oakvale'. It must have been a service position, in that the youngest of four known Hayes children was already eighteen years old in 1897, and Aunt Hayes was in poor health. When she heard the news, Linda Franklin, then living semi-permanently at Talbingo in delicate health, wrote on 20 September 1897, 'In for the Hayes are you, I pity you,' and a month later, 'Sorry to hear Aunt F Hayes is so bad.'[77]

Linda also referred to the fact that Stella had hydatids disease, or tapeworm, a common and potentially fatal rural infection until well into the twentieth century, usually caused by eating poorly cooked meat. It could be cured, Linda said reassuringly (presumably then by emetics, now by drugs). Precisely when Stella returned home from the Hayes establishment is not known, but doubtless it was because of the debilitating infection. By October she also had 'a bad shoulder'.[78]

Whereas *My Brilliant Career* refers to only one site of unpleasant toil for its heroine, in real life there were two, and the M'Swat subplot probably drew on both of Stella's work experiences — governessing and charring. While it is understandable that Uncle George Franklin (or, as family lore has it, his wife, Margaret) was angered by the representation in the book, it seems Miles was at least partly justified in her denial that his family were the M'Swats. 'I wonder did [the M'Swats] recognise themselves?' mused Aunt Lena much later — which suggests that they had not, and that the life portrayed owes more perhaps to the Hayes household (though it is unlikely that the family protested, since Aunt Hayes died on 29 August 1901, shortly after copies of *My Brilliant Career* arrived in Australia). Of course, in such small interrelated communities the risks of following Hebblewhite's literary advice were high, and whatever her models, Miles Franklin would pay a considerable psychological price for the use she made of her time at 'Oakvale'.[79]

'You are really a very useless girl for your age,' Ma says crossly to Sybylla early in *My Brilliant Career*: she is too young to be a servant or a cook, lacks the experience to be a housemaid, is not keen enough on sewing for dressmaking, 'and there is no chance of being accepted as a hospital nurse'. By this presumably was meant that in those days girls had to pay for the privilege of nursing. Nonetheless the evidence is that in late 1897 Miles did try to get into nursing. E. W. O'Sullivan promised to do his best for her at Sydney Hospital, but warned that it would be difficult to get in, which proved to be the case.[80]

Apart from the death of her grandfather Joseph Franklin at 'Oakvale' in May 1898 and the excitement of contact with her older German cousin 'Uncle' Theodor Lampe, only three things are really known about Miles Franklin's eighteenth year. The first is that in April she and her mother took a trip to Sydney for Susannah to see a doctor. During that trip, lasting about a fortnight, they attended a concert in Sydney Town Hall. The program survives in Stella's scrapbook. The second is that she visited Brindabella for the first time since the family's departure in 1889. This time she found her cousin Don, her childhood tormentor, a charming caballero with whom she could easily hold her own. The third is that on 20 September 1898 she began to write another novel. Six months later, on 25 March 1899, it was done, and on 30 March 1899, accompanied by one of Miles Franklin's most famous and oft-reproduced letters, headed 'Bangalore, Goulburn, NSW', the manuscript went off to Angus & Robertson in Sydney:

> Dear Sirs
> Herewith a yarn which I have written entitled 'My Brilliant(?) Career'. I would take it very kindly if you would read it & state whether or not it is fit for publication.
>
> Nothing great has been attempted. Merely a few pictures of Australian life with a little of that mythical commodity love, thrown in for the benefit of young readers (always keeping in mind should there be readers of any age).
>
> There will be no mistakes in geography, scenery or climate as I write from fact not fancy. The heroine, who tells the story, is a study from life and illustrates the misery of being born out of one's sphere.
>
> Awaiting reply
> Faithfully Yrs
> S. M. S. Miles Franklin[81]

Purportedly written from 'Possum Gully, near Goulburn, NSW' by its heroine, Sybylla Penelope Melvyn, *My Brilliant Career* is addressed to 'My dear fellow Australians'. It tells the story of the down-in-the-world selector's daughter who prefers a career to marriage. To curb her rebellious spirit she is sent up country to stay at her maternal grandmother's property, 'Caddagat'. There she experiences a more cultured and sophisticated way of life, and meets a suitable marriage partner, the handsome, though taciturn, squatter Harold Beecham. But she cannot bring herself to marry him, though he makes every effort to allay her doubts and even endures a long secret engagement. Meanwhile, she is obliged to take up governessing with the M'Swat family at Barney's Gap to help pay off family debt, a sobering experience. The story ends where it began, with Sybylla back at drought-stricken 'Possum Gully'.

The film of *My Brilliant Career* ends with Sybylla Melvyn leaning on a gate, staring into the distance, having posted her manuscript to publisher William Blackwood in Edinburgh, Scotland. It is not how the book ends, nor was 1899 the end of Stella Franklin's life 'near Goulburn'; but scriptwriter Eleanor Witcombe knew her trade and her author too, and the film's finale tacitly acknowledges the book's ultimate publication and success. In the book things are not so clear. Sybylla asks herself, 'Why do I write?' and she worries that she will not get a hearing because she is 'only an unnecessary, little, bush commoner, only a — woman'. But, she reminds herself, she is also a proud Australian, so, with the great sun 'sinking in the west, grinning and winking knowingly', she concludes: 'With much love and good wishes to all — Good night! Good-bye. AMEN.'[82]

3

FROM 'POSSUM GULLY' TO PENRITH: 1899–1902

'… you have made the Australian girl appear from
behind her gum-trees.'[1]

My Brilliant Career was the first and most famous of Miles Franklin's
published books and plays. Now regarded as an Australian classic, its
path to publication in 1901 has been closely scrutinised — but the original
manuscript has been lost. The nearest whiff of it comes in a relative's claim
that her mother saw the original manuscript in a pile of exercise books in
Miles' bedroom on a visit to 'Stillwater' in January 1901. Not even the
publisher's proofs survive, or if they do, they have not been seen for over a
century.[2]

A surprising amount of evidence exists on the prehistory of the
manuscript. Most likely Miss Gillespie and her teacher friend Miss Eliza
Kellett from nearby Run-o'-Waters School were the first to see it. Miss
Gillespie's support for her pupil's writings was unwavering, and Miss Kellett,
who attended Thornford School picnics and met the young Stella there,
became interested too. 'One day Stella showed Eliza the book she had
written, *My Brilliant Career*, and asked her would she please correct the
grammar, [which] she did with pleasure.' Miss Gillespie was weak on
grammar (as was young Stella Franklin). Later, Eliza was given a copy of *My
Brilliant Career*, and fifty years on, Miles visited her in retirement on
Sydney's North Shore.[3]

Next to see the manuscript was T. J. Hebblewhite, the Goulburn news-paperman whose advice on her previous effort was so apposite. Hebblewhite is vague about dates, merely stating that Miss Gillespie brought a revised manuscript along to his office on Auburn Street one Saturday morning, but his recollection of first seeing the manuscript is vivid:

> I heard nothing further for some time, and then, again on a Saturday morning, there came Miss Gillespie with another bulky collection of manuscript, foolscap size, written in a firm but unformed hand and headed 'My Brilliant Career'.
>
> I sat down to its perusal that evening, and had not covered half a score of pages before I knew that here was a true Australian atmosphere and a descriptive capacity marvellous in a country girl still a long way from being out of her teens. I had often seen where a reviewer of a new book wrote how ... he found it impossible to stop before reaching the end, and reckoned that this was only an exaggerated way of saying that the book would meet the requirements of an idle and casual hour. But in this case it was the literal truth: I read until I had come to *finis* in the early hours of Sunday morning. I invited the writer to come into the city, telling her how highly I thought of her new attempt.[4]

Hebblewhite goes on to describe his meeting with the writer:

> In due course she came, a shy, plump girl, the picture of rosy health, with a thick braid of hair nearly a yard long hanging down her back. I went over the manuscript with her, pointing out minor literary defects due to lack of training and experience, but had only praise for a realistic fidelity that was everywhere in evidence.

When copies of the book arrived Miles sent Hebblewhite one of them, and much later, when that was lost, another, inscribed 'Mr T. J. Hebblewhite in affect. remembrance from his pupil Miles Franklin'. Evidently it was one of the highlights of his life that 'the bush girl ... sent the first fruits of her pen' to him, and he remained convinced that, as a transcript of the Australian bush, *My Brilliant Career* was the most minutely faithful of all he had seen.[5]

Miles Franklin probably called on Hebblewhite in August 1899, when she was approaching her twentieth birthday. A handwritten calendar in the

Franklin Papers states that she finished writing *My Brilliant Career* on 25 March 1899 and undertook the revision from 18 September through to November 1899. Given that she had submitted the first version of her 'yarn' to Angus & Robertson on 30 March 1899 — whose reader famously rejected it within the week, 'a serious mistake' publisher George Robertson later acknowledged, but he was away at the time — and that in tandem with domestic duties it would hardly be possible to have completed more than technical revisions in two months, the first substantive revision must have occurred in the months between April and September. The first revision was, by Miles' own account, on the basis of advice proferred by Alex Montgomery on behalf of the *Bulletin*'s editor J. F. Archibald, to whom she sent the manuscript immediately after the rejection by Angus & Robertson, a sensible move in days when the *Bulletin* encouraged all sorts of bush writers. It was this second version of the text that Hebblewhite read with such enthusiasm. On 30 July 1899, he wrote to her that he had read her manuscript and it was 'a distinct and big advance' on her previous effort. After going over it with her, he offered to send the revised manuscript to literary friends in Sydney. (He also wrote to the British publisher Chapman, referring to Olive Schreiner, possibly the first occasion Miles Franklin heard of the famous South African writer.)[6]

Hebblewhite's are the first extended comments on the original manuscript of *My Brilliant Career*. His reactions echo down the years. 'Is Sybylla's story partly autobiographical?' he asked tentatively. With sympathy for 'the heart-breaking torment of it all', he ventured to suggest that '[Sybylla's] unfulfilled aspirations and her baffled ambitions were too earnestly, and in places too bitterly, chronicled to be wholly fictitious and baseless romance'.[7]

He also noted a pessimistic tendency. From a reading of her earlier work, it seems it was there from the beginning, though whether as a matter of temperament or of genre it would be hard to say. Hebblewhite took the broader view: if her temperament did run to pessimism, that was only typical of a native Australian literature. A significant piece of advice is included: to try her hand at sketches and short stories on bush life at some later time.[8]

Hebblewhite returned the manuscript via Miss Gillespie on 16 September 1899, again stressing the importance of style and practice in writing. Two days later, on 18 September, Miles began her final revision. Two months on, it was done. The next day, signing simply as 'Miles

Franklin', she wrote to the well-known writer Henry Lawson, asking him to read her book. It may be that Hebblewhite's sympathetic remark about pessimism encouraged her in this bold step, as well as Lawson's current success with his bush sketches *While the Billy Boils* (though she admitted she had not had an opportunity to read his prose; it was his poetry that had helped her). With the self-assurance of youth, she went straight to the point, stating that she was merely asking him to 'run through' her yarn; if he could advise her on editors and publishers, it would help her 'out of a deep hole'.[9]

It seems she made a similar approach to the critic A. G. Stephens, who ran a literary agency as well as editing the *Bulletin*'s 'Red Page'. However, Stephens advised 'Mr St. M. S. Miles Franklin' that he charged a fee for the revision of manuscripts — which presumably meant it was out of the question. By contrast, the approach to Lawson paid off. Indeed, it was the making of Miles Franklin.[10]

Something in her letter appealed to him. He called for the manuscript, and as soon as he read it one Wednesday, probably in early January, he recognised 'a big thing'. Responding to 'Miles Franklin' that same day, he asked if he could keep the story until his publisher George Robertson returned from England. At that stage he couldn't tell if it was the work of a man or a woman.[11]

He soon found out. In January 1900, Stella Franklin was enrolled as a probationer at Sydney Hospital. There had been talk of her becoming a nurse for some time, and an application was lodged mid-1898, shortly before she began writing *My Brilliant Career*, but the idea seemed to have fallen into abeyance. According to the six-part serial Miles wrote subsequently, 'A Ministering Angel: Being the Real Experiences of an Australian Bush Girl', published in *New Idea* in 1905 (which is recounted in the first person and is the only surviving evidence) she unexpectedly received an offer of an interview for a month's position as a trial nurse probationer, unpaid if not continuing afterwards, which she accepted. She was enrolled on condition that her teeth were attended to, and subsequently she had two fillings and two extractions.[12]

Once settled in at the hospital in Sydney's Macquarie Street, it was a simple matter for Miles and Lawson to meet on her day off. As she recalled that first meeting, Lawson called on her 'to find out what sort of an animal I was — whether a mate or mere miss', and arranged for her to visit him and his wife, Bertha, at the Lawsons' picturesque cottage in North Sydney the next day. Miles was thrilled to find that 'the perfect big brother of our dreams' fulfilled all her expectations:

> He was beautifully dressed. His linen was irreproachable. He was tall and slim, with exceptional physical beauty. The beauty of his eyes is also part of his legend. His manner — it had that sensitive warmth, that winning gentleness, that understanding — well, Lawson was as Lawson wrote. You had not to work up to friendliness with him: he was spontaneously a mate.[13]

Lawson's reaction is not recorded but by then he had decided to go to London to further his literary career, and when from there he wrote a preface for *My Brilliant Career*, he recalled: 'I saw her before leaving Sydney. She is just a little bush girl ... She has lived her book and I feel proud of it ...'[14]

Meanwhile, E. W. O'Sullivan was pleased that his representations on Miles' behalf had at last succeeded, and she was invited to visit his family, then living at Craigend Street, Kings Cross.[15]

Nursing did not suit her any more than governessing. Since she was physically quite small, she may have found the work too hard. In 'A Ministering Angel', 'the Australian Bush Girl' felt she would have made a good nurse, but she was highly critical of working conditions at the hospital and said more than once that it was just a version of domestic service. Others had their doubts, too, thinking her 'too clever' for the job. More to the point, she was not really interested in it. A sister at Sydney Hospital at the time remembered her as 'an unusual applicant', who arrived from the country dressed in a strange tartan outfit and told the matron she had an urge to write and thought a nurse's training would give her something to write about.[17]

For all that, the serial tells humorously of her experiences as a nurse probationer, and Miles' only recollection of her time at the hospital is a positive one. In 1951 she recalled the nurses' quarters in 'a new, tall, high building ... where I slept and wrote letters in a sitting room to tell how wonderful life was'. In the serial, though the nurses are only allowed two or three hours off-duty daily, during the one instance of leave that is mentioned, the probationer goes to church and is walked back afterwards by an unnamed young man.[18]

Miles Franklin was not to be a nurse probationer for long. On 22 January she resigned, 'for private reasons'. Relatives were disgusted that she did not 'take to something useful'. However, she may have been worried about things at home. Not only was her mother's health a continuing concern to her daughters — possibly due to menopausal symptoms — but her brother Mervyn, who had only recently escaped the confines of 'Stillwater', was seriously ill at Talbingo. On 15 February, Susannah Franklin got him to a doctor in Tumut, but Mervyn Franklin, 'boundary rider', died of typhoid fever at a relative's place on 21 February 1900, aged sixteen. He was Miles' favourite brother, 'so fair-haired and cheerful, you liked comic songs and derided my youthful nostalgia for the moaning ballads,' she wrote years later when recalling the agony of that time.[16]

In retrospect, it seems clear her main reason for leaving nursing was Lawson's good opinion of her book, which, in a covering letter when resubmitting the manuscript to George Robertson on her behalf in April 1900, he described as 'the Australian *African Farm*', 'immeasurably ahead of *Jane Eyre*'. Hebblewhite had advised that she should consider sending material about Australian bush life to English magazines, and Lawson also suggested that she try short sketches.[19]

Miles apparently stayed on in Sydney for a month or so after leaving nursing, using the postal address c/– Mrs Gell, 235 Victoria Street, Darlinghurst. Mrs Gell was the older sister of Edmund G. Barton, a law clerk from Picton, not Edmund Barton, the first prime minister of Australia, as previously believed, and Barton escorted her to the station and bought her a copy of the *Bulletin* before she boarded the train for Goulburn. The train was noisy and crowded, and it would be a sad homecoming, but she had had a stimulating time in Sydney and she now saw a way forward in her quest for a career and money of her own. She was not so naive as to suppose literature would provide her with a livelihood, but writing sketches seemed promising.[20]

She certainly needed to do something remunerative to avoid being trapped at 'Stillwater'. Aged twenty-one, with a passion for the arts and a desire to travel, marriage was not on her agenda, and she had now rejected nursing as well as teaching. The most that country girls like her could hope to earn was pocket money from the sale of eggs or cream, which in her case would surely have gone straight into the family coffers.

Typically, Miles left clues in her writings and fragments of memoir as to what she had in mind. Like many other Australian girls of her day, she thought to become a singer, with writing as a back-up: 'In those days with the dream idol of [the fictional] Trilby and the living person in Melba, glorious Melba,' runs a tantalising fragment, possibly from a draft of the novel *Cockatoos*, which is set in this period.[21]

The idea had been growing on her for some time. When Amy Castles, a young singer of about her age who was hailed as the next Melba, sang in Goulburn in mid-1899, Miles did not attend the concert, but she obtained a photo of the young diva. 'Oh what a treasure. I doted and gloated on her. I have it y[e]t,' she recalled. In *Cockatoos*, the heroine Ignez Milford hears 'Monica Shaw' in concert in Goulburn and is 'there and then deracinated':

> The contralto tones struck chords of unfathomable emotion in her. She was instantly aware that what was 'the matter' with her own voice was its unusual quality, and that that was its glory. She had been teased as a bullfrog, and infinitely worse, accused of mannish tones. The volume of her unwieldy organ sometimes frightened her that she might be a freak, and abnormalities were horrifying to her. Now she sat rapt, released into a larger self.[22]

Later — in January 1900 — Ignez takes a holiday in Sydney, the secret purpose of which is to seek an assessment of her voice. The best advice available to her is that she must learn to sing the scale evenly and that an experienced teacher would be required. Back at 'Oswald's Ridges', she hastens to expend the considerable sum of three guineas to enrol with a newly arrived singing teacher, an elderly Englishman named Archibald Jupp, organist at St Saviour's, who unfortunately turns out to be a third-rate choirmaster and the ruination of her voice.[23]

Like the fictional Ignez, Miles was in Sydney in January 1900. What she did between leaving her position at the hospital and returning to 'Stillwater' is unknown. Several reasons for her departure have been suggested already, but literary evidence points to another. In 'A Ministering Angel', the probationer nurse leaves her hospital work because she receives information that makes it advantageous for her to do so. What might that information have been?[24]

No answer is given. But it is possible Miles heard news of singing lessons in Goulburn, as mentioned in the fictional *Cockatoos* and in fact advertised in the *Penny Post* by the newly arrived organist and choirmaster of St Saviour's Cathedral, T. C. Webb, announcing that he was ready to receive pupils in singing and voice production.[25]

Years later Miles would recall with horror that she took lessons from 'old Webb' when she returned from Sydney. Elsewhere she recalled riding into

Goulburn and sitting in Belmore Park reading mail beforehand. However, the tuition is unlikely to have lasted long, since Webb was replaced at the cathedral after little more than a year, and Miles' dream was perforce on hold.[26]

Of particular interest now is how she saw the relationship between singing lessons and writing at that time. This is explained in a (disappointed — and erratically punctuated) recollection of Amy Castles in Sydney in 1902:

> I reme[m]ber her as today Amy and her dress and her singing and my description to someone. It was lacking in 'expression' force soul just ladylike and quiet as a trained spaniel I though[t] in my ignorance of music no doubt. I though[t] then that I might be on the wing for glory — my voice had gone I had ruined it in ignorance and the ignorance of that horrid old Webb (see Cockatoos) but I still thought that the pedestrian writing wd supply me with money to go abroad and get it 'cured'.[27]

Once home, she set to work. Six sketches in the vernacular on 'Bush Life', written in 1900, all but one signed 'S. M. S. Miles Franklin', survive either in manuscript or in print. All are set locally and sometimes linked by narrator Jim Blackshaw, with occasional references to 'Sybylla Melvyn' and her cousin Dick (who otherwise made his bow in 'On the Outside Track', an early version of the published *Cockatoos* and her next major piece of writing). The short story 'Jilted', likewise by 'S. M. S. Miles Franklin', dates from February 1900. Two other sketches, subsequently published as 'Of Life', may date from 1900 as well, and there are several more known by name only; for example, 'Match-breaking' and 'One Bushman's Wooing'.[28]

Two of the early sketches are dated February 1900; that is, immediately after Miles returned from Sydney. 'The Tin-potting of Jim Jones' is a memorable colonial rendering of the traditional European practice of *charivari*, conducted in part vengefully due to Jim Jones' shamefully speedy remarriage after years of meanness to his first wife; while the over-packed but still interesting 'Half an Idyll. Half a Yarn' concerns the stickybeak habits of the local mailman and other eccentricities. The next month, March 1900, Miles completed two more sketches: one on a clandestine meeting one summer's night between a girl and her impatient lover, who curses her bitterly when she admits she doesn't give 'a straw' for him, then kisses her fiercely and leaves her in a fearful state, entitled 'Of Love'. In 'Gossip by the Way', two roadside yarners enjoy the pathetic tale of the ageing Ned Lynch, who came 'a beautiful cropper' when he took Jenny Dane to a dance at Kaligawa (the place name is a variant on 'Caligda', the Aboriginal name for Collector), having bought her a dress for the occasion, only to be unceremoniously dumped on arrival.[29]

More stories were written later in the year. 'How Dead Man's Gap was Named', written in May and signed simply 'Miles Franklin', is especially poignant, telling of the accidental death of handsome bush worker Bob Wallace on his way with an engagement ring in his pocket to the twenty-first birthday ball for Honore Gillespie, who never recovered from the loss. Then, on Boxing Day 1900, Miles finished 'Ben Barrett's Break Up'. An only too plausible tale told in the first person, it recounts an end-of-year concert given by a Goulburn music teacher at Kaligawa, and the unappreciative reception accorded an accompanying violinist. This does nothing to lift the spirits of the narrator, who does not stay for the dancing after supper, sneaking away instead for a soothing ride home alone.[30]

When she named her sketches to Jessie Paterson, the list included the short story 'Jilted'. Here dairyman selector Bob Fuller suffers a crushing blow when jilted; and, having contemplated milking twenty cows by himself, marries Bella on the rebound, under the illusion that one woman would be as good as another, with the result that Bella is doomed to a loveless life of hard labour and he takes to the drink. The story ends parenthetically, 'By the way, who or what is to blame that none of us toe the line?', surely an oblique comment on Miles' own sense of self at this time, just as the fiercer comments on rebellious young women and male inadequacy in the sketches seem as telling as the local colour.[31]

Also among the collection are two or possibly three sketches written in 1901 and 1902. The two dated June 1901 toy with wider concerns: the turn-of-the century themes of rural depopulation and the social consequences of the apparent demise of religion. In the reflective piece 'An Old House Post', a post is all that is left of a once overflowing family home up country as succeeding generations leave for the city; and the would-be essay 'Of Humanism' — in which Miles has clearly bitten off more than she could chew — struggles to come to terms with a latter-day 'City of Dreadful Night', probably Sydney because it is said to have a fine harbour. However, in what appears to be a draft for a late inclusion, 'One Bushman's Wooing', dated April 1902, local colour is again at the forefront.[32]

Although the early sketches rarely discussed issues of fundamental importance, they were in tune with the literary times both in terms of content and genre, and Miles Franklin thought them valid. As well, they did provide her with a little income, and — perhaps equally importantly — emotional release. To a suggestion that her sketches should be more 'Addisonian' — that is, laid-back in the eighteenth-century clubman manner — she responded stoutly that she had earned her bread by manual labour since age fourteen, and that lacking skill in 'flirting, foot-balling, smoking, gossiping and such recreations patronized by the other youth in the small sphere in which I [lead?] a cramped existence', she wrote for relaxation. Her unpretentious word pictures were after all harmless, she had no grand ambitions, and she preferred to stick to her own phraseology and mannerisms. Yet on one occasion at least, the sketches reveal a transcendence through landscape: in 'Of Life', a vista from the sweeping north-west plains south 'peak on peak and tier on tier' as far as the time-worn Bogong Mountains is uplifting. 'Not a breath is stirring, not a sound to jar the ear. All is purity, hush! holiness.'[33]

Few of these early sketches and essays were published at the time, and only three have been thought worth reprinting since: 'An Old House Post', 'Of Life' and 'A Common Case'. Although still readable, they vary in interest and significance, and their value is not so much literary as biographical: unlike most of Miles' work at this time, they have not been tampered with since, by her or anyone else, and so offer access to her state of mind during what has always been one of the most uncertain periods in a woman's life — the period between youth and maturity when marriage is a fundamental issue. The girl in 'Of Love' is baffled by her suitor's sudden passion, and amid spirited observations of rural life in various sketches the reader will notice a melancholy strand.[34]

Meanwhile, in mid-April, just before he left for London, Lawson had written to Miles at Bangalore that George Robertson was back in Sydney but had not had time to read her manuscript and his firm was umming and ah-ing over it. 'Shall I leave the story with them or take it with me to England?' he asked. Miles hastened to forward the necessary powers of attorney to Lawson, who asked Robertson to post the manuscript to him in London, which Robertson duly did. Angus & Robertson may have been the flagship of literary nationalism, but the closest the firm came to 1890s feminism was publishing Louise Mack's *Teens* in 1897 and *Girls Together* in 1898.[35]

Five months later, on 6 September 1900, Lawson reported that Edinburgh publisher Blackwood was interested in Miles' manuscript, and that he had put the matter in the hands of his literary agent, J. B. Pinker, who counted Joseph Conrad, H. G. Wells, and Henry James among his clients. Lawson enclosed Pinker's memorandum of agreement for signature (a fair copy of which survives in Miles' publishing records): 'He'll get more money than we can, and look after your interests.' Once more she had cause for gratitude to Lawson — especially since his own circumstances were increasingly clouded by Bertha's ill health.[36]

Pinker's representations soon bore fruit. On 30 January 1901 he wrote to Miles, advising that Blackwood had accepted her manuscript for publication, provided certain passages that the publisher thought would prejudice readers were removed or toned down. This would be done in consultation with Mr Lawson. Miles took this in her stride, approving the rate of royalty proposed by Blackwood (the print run is not mentioned), requesting the return of her manuscript when the publisher had done with it, and firmly expressing her concerns. These were that the question mark after 'Brilliant' in the title be retained, that the word 'Miss' on no account be used, as she did not wish to be known as a young girl but rather 'a bald-headed seer of the sterner sex', and that any 'toning down' would be very much against her principles. In language steeped in the nineteenth-century radical tradition she declared that her story had been written in the teeth of people's prejudices and did not look at life 'through the spectacles of orthodox cant-ists'; but if there were really unpublishable passages, of course they would have to go. What might they be, she wondered.[37]

By the end of February the novel had been typeset and pages sent to Pinker, with passages marked for revision by Lawson, who had undertaken to see the work through the press. Apologising for the time it took, Lawson wrote to Blackwood in early April that he and his friend Dubbo-born Arthur Maquarie had been through the story together 'and made it as perfect as possible'. Although there were numerous corrections, 'I can assure you every one is necessary,' he noted. He still felt it was a brilliant piece of work, and that it would be a hit, especially in Australia. Blackwood was pleased with their efforts, and wrote back advising that the proofs had been returned to the printer and that, as requested, the revised version would be returned 'very shortly'.[38]

A few days later, Pinker wrote to tell Miles that her book was in press and informing her of an agreement between Blackwood, Lawson and himself that certain pages had to be omitted; but he assured her nothing 'essential to [her] effect' had been lost. Lawson later recalled that Blackwood had given him more latitude than Robertson would have, which presumably meant that whereas as a businessman Robertson preferred 'a happy sentimentality' in fiction, what troubled Blackwood, a man of sound Tory stock who ran a successful empire-wide publishing company, was anti-imperial attitudes. Arthur Maquarie, who apparently had done most of the editing, recalled Miles as 'the little firebrand'.[39]

Back in 'the land of wattle & gum', a new and more cheerful dimension to Miles Franklin's young life is evident. To all appearances she was a lively young woman among her schoolfriends, now grown up too. Whereas the culture of Goulburn might have seemed more attractive to Miles earlier, the social life of young people to the south of Thornford, at Currawang and Collector, now featured strongly. It was not just a matter of dreariness at home with occasional days in Goulburn to relieve the monotony, especially on a Sunday when wonderful music could be heard at the cathedrals. In the southern settlements, 'the houses were full of young people' and there were 'beats we all followed', she recalled after a visit to the area in 1936. Just because she had written a book, been to Sydney, made contact with one of Australia's most famous writers, and was now negotiating with people in faraway London did not alter the fact that she was still John Franklin's daughter, learning to play tennis at Stella O'Brien's at Currawang and winning the approval of young men like the nearby grazier's son Charlie Graham for her 'good strokes' and dashing horsemanship. Charlie would write to Miles on 1 September 1901 that he had always felt he had a true friend in her 'and more than that', and wishing she had a better opinion of him.[40]

The handsome photograph of Miles sitting side-saddle on J. J. Baxter's horse looks as if it dates from around this time, while something like the Baxters' 1902 hare drive (ninety killed on the day) found a place in 'On the Outside Track'. Also around this time, Miles helped arrange for the presentation of a gold bracelet to Miss Gillespie at the annual Thornford School picnic in March, and read an address testifying to the esteem and affection in which the teacher was held. (Miss Gillespie taught at the school until its closure in 1913, when she was transferred to the Sydney.) By then Miles' book was in press.[41]

Miles Franklin was quite unprepared for the shock of seeing her work in print. In *Cockatoos*, the arrival of a parcel for Ignez containing six books, all the same, is a turning point. The book is '*Nita. The Story of a Real Girl* by Bryan Milford'. An entirely credible description of shock ensues. 'Horrors! It was her own book!' Dumbfounded, Ignez realises there is no way of hiding the enormity. There follows an account of how she copes with various reactions to her writing. Fact and fiction may have become entwined, perhaps irretrievably, as to how in real life Miles Franklin coped with responses to her first book, but so far as Ignez is concerned the royalties help her to leave home. Nonetheless, the trauma remains. When Arthur Masters later sees a photo of Ignez, 'her face was now a mask'.[42]

My Brilliant Career appeared in London on 8 July 1901, and the customary six author's copies were forwarded to Miles by Pinker the next day. Evidently the news had reached rural Australia by late August, when a relative, Edgar Vernon, wrote to Miles wanting a copy (and hoping she didn't recall meeting him in Sydney, as he feared he would otherwise appear as 'a comical character': he'd heard 'the tribe is fairly sprinkled'). The copy Miles Franklin gave her mother, with the rather self-conscious inscription 'To Mrs J. M. Franklin with best love and respectful compts. From the scribbler,' is dated 3 September 1901. She also sent copies to Linda at Talbingo, to Hebblewhite, to the *Bulletin*'s editor J. F. Archibald and, at his request, to 'Red Page' editor A. G. Stephens. Ten days later copies were available from Foxall's in Goulburn, price 3s 6d cloth, 2s 6d paper.[43]

It must have been a relief that her immediate family approved. No word of reproach has ever been noted from Miles' parents, and when Linda received her copy at Talbingo she was delighted and reported 'there was great excitement in the camp'. 'I am so proud to be the sister of an authoress,' she wrote, recounting also that Grandma Lampe had found it all very amusing and took a businesslike approach to those who wanted to borrow the book — '"Let 'em buy it," she says.' As well, she wonders if 'The Lordly Phillip', presumably Phillip Wilkinson, brother of the young man Miles is thought to have fallen in love with at Talbingo in 1896, would recognise himself 'partly in it'. Maggie Bridle, Susannah Franklin's cousin, wrote with congratulations, asking where she could obtain a copy. And then came Aunt Metta's warm response to the book, in time for her niece's twenty-second birthday, that Miles Franklin was the first of her tribe to attempt such a thing, and approving that she had dropped a few of her given names. (Nonetheless, Miles Franklin's birthday present from Susannah Franklin that year, *The Poetical Works of Sir Walter Scott*, is inscribed 'To dear Stella, with Mother's love'.)[44]

How much more would the Talbingo–Tumut connection have praised the prodigious Miles Franklin had they known what had already been said at the heart of the Empire. When precisely the first batch of London reviews arrived at Bangalore is unknown, maybe by late March 1902, after Henry Lawson wrote he was posting a packet — the mail from London to Goulburn usually taking about forty days. However, even before Miles received author's copies her name was made on the wider stage, with ten or more favourable reviews appearing in the British metropolitan and regional press in July–August 1901.[45]

The British reviewers recognised the youthful promise of the book, praising its vitality and innocent audacity, while identifying some problems. Four days after J. B. Pinker despatched the six author's copies to Miles, a first brief notice in the London *Academy* saw it as a story of 'sheep-farming in the solitudes', and in acclaiming the author as the 'Marie Bashkirtseff of the Bush', introduced an impressive topical reference to a rebellious young Russian diarist, then well known. Next was the *Manchester Guardian,* whose reviewer deemed it 'a vivid and entrancing autobiography', written in a style 'as yet uncultivated and unrestrained', but not thereby diminished. And it was the *Glasgow Herald* that first linked Miles Franklin with the Brontës — 'This girl writes as the author of *Jane Eyre* wrote — out of heart, with a hatred of shams.' The Glaswegian reviewer was taken aback, however, by the amount of slang, evidently used unawares. The most critical response came from the *Spectator* (interestingly, published by Blackwood): this was a girl's book, often slipshod and excessively egotistical, but written with passion and power. It concludes: 'Her style wants chastening and she should renounce once for all the pose of a defiant woman who attracts all men and sends all men away.' The London *Times* followed with a pointed comment: 'When the young lady leaves realism for romance we doubt her.' Like some readers to come, the reviewer was incredulous that a girl in Sybylla's circumstances could turn her back on wealth and happiness.[46]

Around Thornford the reaction was mixed. One admirer from Currawang took great pleasure in the novel, and expected the characters would recognise themselves; the writer couldn't place the hapless English jackeroo, Hawden, but claimed to have no trouble with Harold Beecham. Charlie Graham, an early admirer of Miles, confessed he was jealous of the book. Miles' portrayal of local reaction in 'On the Outside Track' is probably faithful enough: that at first it was thought shocking and uppity to have done such a thing, then that anyone could have done it and done it better, finally settling down to pride and claims of friendship when external opinion was known, to the point that Linda became tired of hearing about her. 'Are you still getting as much praise as ever?' she asked in March 1902.[47]

The main hostile response came from 'Dear Uncle' — George Franklin — who wrote that it was all malicious lies, and criticised her parents. To this Miles replied in a dignified tone that it was simply a story of Australian life and she did not mean any of the characters as real; that he and his wife had been good to her; and that others thought she had portrayed families 'down here'. As for her parents, they had known nothing of her book. His letter made her angry and upset, but she remained his affectionate niece. Later, some younger men expressed reservations: Herbert Wilkinson, the cousin from 'Yallowin' Miles is thought to have fallen for, felt he had been treated unfairly but tried to rise above it, and Edward Bridle, another of her mother's cousins, told Linda he didn't like the book. Otherwise, it seems negative reactions were mostly expressed verbally.[48]

Amid the flood of words that followed the publication of *My Brilliant Career* one set of responses was strangely muted, and the apparent silence has become more puzzling as time goes by. What did Goulburn make of Miles Franklin and her book? A week after she presented copies to family members, the *Penny Post*, previously edited by Miles' mentor Hebblewhite, and since 1900 by Henry Pinn, reproduced a paragraph from Sydney's *Daily Telegraph*, introduced by the observation that 'a young lady resident at Bangalore has written a novel'. The paragraph highlighted Henry Lawson's preface (which, as has often been pointed out, said straight out that the story had been written 'by a girl', despite her wishes and her leaving her own preface unsigned). The remainder of the notice offered a grudging response to the book itself. Fidelity to local colour was conceded and an amateurish construction could be set aside, but apart from realism in presenting 'the hard facts of Australian life', the interest 'is not strong'. Most revealing is the benign gloss placed upon the portrayal of Sybylla Melvyn's parents, 'the manly, big-hearted, squatter father who is driven down by adverse circumstances, and down until he is a miserable "cockatoo" and hotel loafer; of the refined mother worn by hopeless work into unreasoning ill-temper'.[49]

Eight months later, a more substantial review appeared in the *Penny Post*. The review, by 'Heather', was for the most part patronising and negative. While commending a young girl's realism about the bush, 'Heather' found 'a cynical view of life', and asked rhetorically if it was good taste to depict one's parents in such an unpleasant light. The likelihood of a man in possession of 200,000 acres giving it up for dairy farming is derided. So is the inconsistency of Sybylla's preaching against the subjection of women while rejecting Harold Beecham as too weak, which might also lead overseas damsels to imagine that rich bachelors hung off bushes in New South Wales. Likewise, the bishop responsible for the repossession of the Melvyn household goods is defended as only a nominal figure. The most distasteful aspect for 'Heather', however, was the book's depiction of local class relations, especially a lamentable ignorance of the ways of people of culture and refinement, and the absurd prediction about 'the iron hand of class distinctions', whereas in reality people with brains could rise easily in Australia. Perhaps, it is opined, Miss Franklin, who does have brains, will yet find herself 'an honoured guest at Government House'.[50]

What an insight this belated and mean-spirited review is. Reading it now is to be reminded of the strength of the old squatter culture in the Goulburn area. The reviewer's stance highlights not only the book's radical reaction against the squattocracy but also the radicalism that kept the book alive through the Cold War, when only literary women and the Left remembered its existence. No doubt it was the same radicalism that had to be toned down for the novel-reading public of the Empire, who were happy for 'New Woman' novels to be published, but not if touching too closely on religion, sex or politics, that trio of subjects unmentionable in respectable society in New South Wales, as elsewhere, until the 1960s. As foreshadowed by 'Lord Dunleve's Ward', some of Miles' manipulations of radical thought were doubtless too crude to stand unchallenged, but the class-based view from Goulburn goes a long way towards explaining the puzzling silence from the city's press and notables upon the publication of *My Brilliant Career*, hitherto thought to originate in the writer's harsh depiction of the landscape and references to the locals as 'peasants' and 'cockatoos'.[51]

On 15 October 1901, George McAlister of Goulburn, possibly a relative in the Bridle connection, wrote to Miles Franklin that local papers had failed to respond to her book in a fair and encouraging way. McAlister was right about the local papers. The same could be said about the Sydney press. Three weeks after the *Daily Telegraph*'s grudging paragraph, another appeared in the *Sydney Morning Herald*. No doubt Miles could have done without it. While asserting that *My Brilliant Career* was a creditable novel by a young Australian girl, it found the heroine, though moral, 'distinctly unpleasant'; 'not a person whose acquaintance in the flesh it would be desirable to make'. This was not a correct representation of the Australian girl, asserted the *Herald*. 'It would be a matter for regret if she — "Sybylla Melvyn" is her name — could possibly be taken as a type of Australian bush girl. Bold, forward, and selfish, Sybylla is the sort of girl that is happily rare in Australia.'[52]

How wrong contemporaries can be. Miles Franklin's generation had good reason to be uneasy about marriage, and it was that 1890s generation that created the modern image of the Australian girl, a big step from previous crude imitations of English ladies. Between 1890 and 1910, hardly a year went by without a book or two written by and about this new Australian girl; for example, Catherine Martin's *An Australian Girl* and *A Little Bush Maid* by Mary Grant Bruce.[53]

It seems the *Bulletin* was the only other Sydney publication to notice *My Brilliant Career* when it came out. On 28 September A. G. Stephens filled the *Bulletin*'s 'Red Page' with a resoundingly positive review of lasting value, highlighting the authentic voice of an Australian girl in 'a book full of sunlight', and pronouncing that this was 'the very first Australian novel to be published'. When she read it, Miles recalled in a letter in 1902 that felt she could hug the *Bulletin*: 'Tho' it did not rear me I always call myself a near relative and am glad it did not deny me as one of its youngsters.' But, she protested, '*My Brilliant Career* is not the story of my *own* life.'[54]

Henry Hyde Champion's Melbourne monthly, the *Book Lover*, also noticed *My Brilliant Career* in September. Soon after, Champion's friend F. W. (Fred) Maudsley was in touch with Miles on Champion's behalf, promising a full review in the November issue. In the review, Champion reiterated Stephens' view that this was 'the most thoroughly Australian novel' yet to appear. Like the *Age* later that month, Champion assumed the book to be autobiographical — 'she tells us so in an introduction' — and the first Australian comparison with the journals of Marie Bashkirtseff appeared in print. When others failed to echo his views, Champion did not resile, commenting that the *Age* had been patronising (the *Age* reviewer acknowledged painful themes but thought the writer had been warped by hardship), and drawing attention to what was the most important British review, in the London *Sun*, where it was Book of the Week, while the M'Swat section was compared with the work of the great French realist writer Emile Zola. The London *Sun* reviewer, Henry Murray, concluded: 'Franklin has written a really good book. She will write a better one before long or I am no prophet. She may even some day write a great book.'[55]

In the December *Book Lover* a photograph of the author appeared on the front page, and there was a positive comment by the renowned children's author Ethel M. Turner inside ('the most convincing "local colour" that has been arrived at in any Australian book'). However, while the book probably did reach 'a fairly large public' through the Book Lover's Library, run by Champion's wife, Elsie Belle Champion (the sister of Vida Goldstein), such enthusiasm did not necessarily translate into sales. Miles had already complained to Pinker that copies were slow to reach Australia, and did not arrive in any quantity until early 1902, according to the Champions. In August, Elsie Belle reported that '*My Brilliant Career* is still selling well for us', and that copies were to be seen in other city bookshops, but it was probably the case that Melbourne paid more attention when Miles herself turned up in 1904.[56]

As time went by, responses became increasingly variegated, as they usually do. A difference of opinion between town and country emerged, exemplified by the opposing views of the *Stock and Station Journal* and the *Worker*, the former responsive to the plight of suffering country people and the latter thoroughly hostile at what it saw as rural self-indulgence. (Miles Franklin marked this as the only dissident review, which suggests she had repressed the *Penny Post* review and never saw the Adelaide *Critic*, where 'Iris' objected to a naive 'howl of discontent' and the 'adulation of Lawson'.)[57]

In due course new approaches also surfaced. In 'Fiction in the Australian Bush', a review article published in the Paris-based *Weekly Critical Review* on 17 September 1903, the eminent British sexologist Havelock Ellis noted that *My Brilliant Career* was 'a vivid and sincere book', of psychological interest but painfully crude, too crude to impress as literature. Six weeks later, a résumé of Ellis' comments appeared on the *Bulletin*'s 'Red Page', the bailiwick of A. G. Stephens, who was alert to the new sexology. A few months earlier he had written to Miles about Sybylla's satisfaction at the bruises inflicted on her person by Hal ('Hal, we are quits'): 'Do you mean that you or another woman likes to be hurt and bruised by the man she loves?' This was a very interesting question, scientifically, he added, a point elaborated subsequently by Ellis in his *Studies in the Psychology of Sex*, in which he cites the bruises scene as evidence of a positive relationship between love and pain experienced by women during courtship.[58]

To this inquiry Miles made no reply. If *My Brilliant Career* carried the Australian novel into new territory, now recognisable as the psychology of desire, she had not intended it, and it is not until after World War I that she mentions Ellis' work, in a 1918 book review. In 1920 she told her friend Alice Henry how she had saved a copy of his *Man and Woman* from disposal and sent it home for her library as a classic, albeit an outdated one: 'Fancy we went through a phase of reading him,' she wrote. Nonetheless, it is evident that the new perspective was embarrassing and irritating. 'I always did resist Havelock Ellis's findings,' she recalled decades later.[59]

Though Miles was dismissive of Ellis, A. G. Stephens was not quite right to conclude that here was 'an innocent heart'. In later life Miles many times referred to a consuming interest in sex when young. But as Stephen Garton has argued, she wrote *My Brilliant Career* within an older literary paradigm — the master–slave paradigm popularised by Harriet Beecher Stowe's *Uncle Tom's Cabin* — and although the satiric Adelaide weekly *Quiz* dismissed the idea out of hand, and it is not known if Miles read the great work, it seems reasonable to suggest that the scene where Sybylla strikes Hal with a riding whip when he tries to kiss her provides a formal link with anti-slavery literature. Even so, there is a down-to-earth aspect to it too. The whip was near to hand, and whips were something Miles had grown up with. In *Childhood at Brindabella* she recalls that handling a whip as a small child had given her great satisfaction; and as a young woman she was the proud owner of two, gifts from admiring stockmen. When her book arrived with a whip-cracking girl rider on the hardcover, she was delighted. In a recently located letter to William Blackwood dated 3 March 1902 she wrote: 'I feel impelled to express my pleasure in the binding of my story ... The stockwhip especially takes the fancy.'[60]

The two oddest contemporary responses to *My Brilliant Career* came from New York, where a reviewer, having received a photograph of the author stating she was native-born, supposed this meant black, and from a Sydney schoolboy, who was already the publisher of his own little magazine. The New York reviewer noted that she was pale, and said colour should not matter anyway. The schoolboy, Sydney Ure Smith, later a renowned publisher and artist, reserved judgement: was Miss Franklin a real writer or only a cheap Kodak, he wondered. As for women's assessments, it seems only two more appeared in print: by Evelyn Dickinson in the Federation journal *United Australia*, where it was noted that the author was obviously from New South Wales and her use of 'good unmitigated Australian slang' is applauded; and the other by veteran Anglo-Australian writer Ada Cross (Cambridge), who contributed a brief and equivocal paragraph to the Melbourne *Argus* much later, in 1905. Miles would later reciprocate by deeming Ada Cambridge one of the last of the ladies in the literary paddock.[61]

The extent of 'toning down' gradually became clearer too. A. G. Stephens regretted that Blackwood had 'cut out the plums'. Clearly it wasn't really the style that proved objectionable — Lawson and Maquarie had done their best to improve upon that — it was the overall world view. *My Brilliant Career* is an angry book, and well-brought-up young women were still not supposed to express anger. It is also a wonderfully rebellious book, and it came down on the side of the poor and the oppressed. At that time the 'wretched of the earth' were not understood to be Aboriginal Australians but the failing 'cocky farmers' who had been granted land rights from the squatters in the 1860s only to be defeated by depression and drought in the 1890s; Miles Franklin was firmly on their side. Sybylla Melvyn declines to marry into the squattocracy; she ridicules Empire types like Frank Hawden, and she puts her faith in land taxes, not God. In declining to marry, itself a radical position at that time, she defied respectability and right thinking. Although 'only a girl', she concludes that she is proud to be 'a daughter of the mighty bush', close to the people and part of the new nation. A publisher might well decide that book buyers were entitled to some protection from such rabid views. That is to say, while psychology and gender have since become the main issues in discussion of *My Brilliant Career*, for contemporaries they were autobiography and class.[62]

So what did the readers think? The fan mail is an exceptional cache of some sixty letters, mostly written between September 1901 and December 1902, with one as late as 1904. The letters came from all over Australia, but mostly New South Wales, with a couple from England and New Zealand. Some were simply addressed to 'Sybylla Melvyn, Possum Gully, near Goulburn'. And while some writers ventured criticism, especially of the author's pessimism, suggesting remedies such as Catholicism and theosophy, all were moved by her achievement and felt impelled to communicate. Writing in March 1902, M. J. Purcell of Transfield Park, Melbourne, thought *My Brilliant Career* second only to *Robbery Under Arms* for Australian life, and approved its ending; too many books, he thought, were spoiled by happy endings.[63]

About half of the surviving letters are from women, many of them under thirty and mostly single, and all eager to commend Miles Franklin and her book for its fidelity to Australia and their own lives. Pearl Wilson of Jenolan Caves thought it 'the very best Australian tale I have ever read'. Mary Dunster, a dairy farmer's daughter of Singleton, New South Wales, wrote that she had had the same experiences, though not so bad, as her father was more successful. Stella Simpson of St Kilda, Melbourne, had the same rebellious attitudes: 'I am an Australian girl like yourself & I have had the same longings & I think exactly the same things as you do, and how I have revolted against being a girl.' Even Ethel Lloyd from 'Westralia', a belated reader who wished that some men of Harold's calibre could be sent her way, admitted she had been a prickly person herself.[64]

Amongst the readers' responses, a significant gender difference becomes clear. Whereas most of the men were well-known literary figures or family associates, the women readers, with a few exceptions such as leading Sydney feminist Rose Scott, Elsie Belle Champion and Ethel Turner, were unknowns, and remain so. Among younger women, Agnes Brewster, later founding principal of Hornsby Girls' High School, and the thirteen-year-old Molly David, daughter of Professor Edgeworth David of Sydney University and his wife, Cara, wrote to Miles. However, the letters mostly came from women in lower class positions on the land or in unspecified city jobs; and they instantly recognised themselves in *My Brilliant Career*.[65]

This was more or less as A. G. Stephens expected:

> All over this country, brooding on squatters' verandahs or mooning in selectors' huts, there are scattered here and there hundreds of lively, dreamy Australian girls whose queer, uncomprehended ambitions are the despair of the household. They yearn, they aspire for what they know not; but it is essentially yearning for fuller, stronger life — the cry of their absorbed, imprisoned sunlight for action, action, action! 'Miles Franklin' is one of these 'incomprehensible' ugly ducklings who has luckily escaped from the creek and is delightedly taking her swan-swim on the river of literature.[66]

Miles Franklin was astonished at this outpouring. She sometimes complained that every unhappy girl in Australia wrote to her after *My Brilliant Career* came out. They confessed their miseries, asked for a biography of Miles or a photo, invited her to visit them. Some wanted her help with their own writing. Others wanted to help her. Narrandera squatter's daughter Struan Robertson couldn't, as she had nothing of her own, not even a dress allowance. A few, notably Edith Twynam of 'Riversdale', North Goulburn, one of the daughters of retired New South Wales Surveyor-General Edward Twynam, both asked for and offered help.

Nothing came of Miss Twynam's suggestion that they might collaborate, and her own literary efforts have not so far been traced. For the most part, however, in an era of rampant masculinism, the overlooked Australian girl appreciated the attention: 'you have made the Australian girl appear from behind her gum-trees'. Women writers of the next generation, Katharine Susannah Prichard, for example, certainly took heart, and well into the twentieth century there were still dreamy girls on squatters' verandahs — most notably the poet Judith Wright, stuck on the family property in New England.[67]

Some have wondered at Stephens' claim that *My Brilliant Career* was the very first Australian novel to be published. The view is, however, accurate, provided you accept his definition of 'Australian', which was far from post-colonial. Miles Franklin herself later gave a good account of that perspective in her history of the novel in Australia, *Laughter, Not for a Cage*, where she noted that verse and the sketch had characterised the optimistic literary nationalism of the 1890s, and two very different first novels, the 'adolescently vehement' *My Brilliant Career* and Joseph Furphy's mature work, *Such Is Life*, continued the tradition into the twentieth century. Thus, she wrote, *My Brilliant Career* was hailed for its 'Australianism' and attracted wide attention. It was undoubtedly the literary event of 1901, the only significant Australian novel in the year of Federation; and by now it is more or less recognised that in Australia at the turn of the twentieth century, feminism and nationalism went together as radical forces.[68]

Many people asked Miles Franklin how she could possibly have written *My Brilliant Career* while working as a farm hand at 'Stillwater'. In *Cockatoos,* the young heroine Ignez and her friends gather on a she-oak ridge in the back paddock to read their writings at their Saturday afternoon 'School for Literature'. They swear secrecy and the locals suspect hanky-panky, but all they are up to is reciting Australian ballads and discussing their ideas.[69]

Ignez plans a novel on Nita, a girl with a smudge on her face, no beauty and a bad temper. Later we read that after telling stories to put her young sister to sleep at night, Ignez would creep out and write until the small hours, with pen and paper hard to come by. That is probably how it was for Miles too. The small hours have traditionally been women's only time for writing in Australia. And if Susannah Franklin knew, perhaps she was pleased to have such an aspiring daughter, so long as the work got done during the day. Susannah was not, after all, an uncultivated woman. At some stage she, too, read and marked passages in *The Story of an African Farm,* and in her literary notebook Miles Franklin recorded that her mother preferred Shakespeare and Milton to Byron, the favourite of John Franklin and herself.[70]

My Brilliant Career made Miles Franklin's name, but not her fortune. Envious locals thought she must now be rich, to which Linda snorted that she should be. By August, Miles was waiting impatiently for her first royalty cheque, and by year's end she seemed ready to give up on writing as insufficiently remunerative. Her records indicate that the book sold 1399 copies in 1901, 1012 of them in the cheaper colonial edition, which received lesser royalties, and a similar number in 1902 (1134). By December 1903 fewer than 500 additional copies (449) had been sold; and although the novel went into its sixth impression in 1904, as late as 1938 Blackwood still had a few copies in stock. And when the first royalty cheque arrived in 1902 it was not very encouraging, amounting to £16 5s 6d, about what Miles might have earned as an unskilled hand in the clothing trade for the year. By December 1904 the author had received a total of £27 8s 10d in royalties for her work, a meagre amount even for a young working woman of the time.[71]

Of course money is not everything. Miles never made much, either from her books or from paid employment, at least until the interwar years; and single women were able to make do on very little in those days. Miles was mostly sustained by a feminist network, beginning with her mother; and for all her dissatisfaction with the limited monetary return on writing, a problem faced by many Australian writers then and now, she was encouraged by the critical reception of her book. Apparently the family supported her renewed efforts. They certainly knew about a next book, and both Linda and Charlie Graham, who had by now focused his affections on Linda, worried that she was working too hard on it. Linda at Talbingo urged her to come to the Tumut Show on 26–27 January 1902: 'Let your book go for a while & have a change, it will do you good,' she wrote.[72]

The record is imperfect, but the work referred to is surely 'On the Outside Track', and probably a further attempt was made to publish the sketches. Although these early writings are still readable enough, they vary in interest and significance, and it is hardly surprising that nothing came of Miles' tentative approach to her London literary agent, J. B. Pinker, in late 1901, presumably regarding publication. Miles was anxious about her contracts, and whether she could also publish her work in Australia. The original contract with Blackwood for *My Brilliant Career* has not been preserved, but the agreement with Pinker included in Miles' publishing papers specifies twelve months' notice of termination. Miles believed she was bound to offer her new manuscripts to Pinker, but as she put it to George Robertson, 'The unbusiness like engineering of the first book has been unsatisfactory and unremunerative to me and I should like my next venture put on our own market with a local firm.'[73]

Later in life Miles wondered if she could have developed 'into a professional, unashamed writer' if she had had an understanding literary friend when young. She was largely reliant on Lawson for advice but he was still in London. Then, on 16 February 1902, one of the admiring readers mentioned earlier, Edith Twynam, wrote to say she was sorry to hear Miles had had unsatisfactory reports of her book, and that she would be pleased to help in any way she could, adding that 'Mr Patterson' was a friend of her sister Mrs Wesche in Sydney. The upshot was that Phoebe Wesche spoke to 'Banjo' Paterson, a solicitor as well as a poet, and on 25 March, in reply to a note from Miles, Paterson said he would be happy to advise her on contractual matters, free of charge. A week later he wrote again, urging her to come to Sydney soon, otherwise she might miss him. The exchange marks the onset of an emotional relationship, which in a subterranean way dominated 1902.[74]

Another important letter from Sydney arrived at 'Stillwater' soon after. Rose Scott, suffragist and doyenne of the Sydney liberal establishment, had just read *My Brilliant Career,* and was keen to meet the author. Would Miles Franklin be visiting? Were there books she would like sent? Could they be friends? The great Rose, who had campaigned for women's suffrage in Goulburn in 1901, was really taken with the young writer: 'Let me, my dear fellow Australian, my dear fellow woman, serve you in any way I can.' Soon she was recommending poems by 'Mrs Stetson' (Charlotte Perkins Gilman) and the works of transcendentalist Ralph Emerson, both leading American intellectuals of the mid- and late-Victorian period. So began a life-enhancing relationship, which expanded Miles Franklin's horizons and brought her nearer to the world. Amid the excitement, no one seems to have noticed the death of Charles Auchinvole Blyth at the Coast Hospital on 1 April 1902.[75]

By the second week of April, Miles was in Sydney. Details of the trip are nonexistent but her mother probably paid for it, and from the fragments of evidence pertaining to her accommodation it seems she stayed at a boarding house in Cleveland Street run by a friend of Aunt Mary Neall's, maybe for a week, possibly longer. 'It is very necessary for me to be in Sydney,' she wrote on arrival.[76]

On Monday 7 April Paterson wrote in his flowing hand from the Australian Club inviting her to lunch the following Wednesday, 'and you can tell me what you have done re agreements'; he would be waiting at the door and she would easily recognise him, 'a sad-looking person with a very hard face'. Given the stereotypes of the Victorian era, it may seem strange that a young woman would be free to travel about unchaperoned and to lunch alone with a male person, but girls were somewhat freer in the colonies, and in a small society there were usually plenty of people such as landladies, relatives and family friends happy to look out for girls from the country. The Australian Club was ultra-respectable too, so that Miles was unlikely to have had qualms about meeting Paterson there during the day. What eventuated is undocumented, but it sounds as if the UK contracts were tighter than he had supposed in prior correspondence, where he thought if she had entered in agreements when under twenty-one, she was probably 'free as air'. Nonetheless he was encouraging about the sketches, and set about getting them published locally, merely advising she should satisfy herself as to her position with Blackwood and Pinker.[77]

To be helped by yet another famous writer, who was handsome and as yet unmarried, must have been tremendously exciting. A few days later, most likely at the *Bulletin* office, she met A. G. Stephens, who gave her a copy of his book, *Oblation*, signed also by artist Norman Lindsay, and a book of poems by Will Ogilvie entitled *Fair Girls and Gray Horses*. Of these men only Stephens was to prove a lasting friend. Norman Lindsay, especially, was too inclined to see Miles simply as an attractive bush girl, though to be fair, when *My Brilliant Career* appeared they had all welcomed a woman's voice in the great project of shaping a national literary culture.[78]

At Stephens' suggestion, Miles also called on Ethel Curlewis (Turner), hoping for encouragement in her 'hard struggle', but Ethel was out at the time and slow to respond. Though she had praised *My Brilliant Career* in the *Book Lover* and had sympathised with the struggle, as a happily married young wife and mother, Ethel Curlewis probably did not believe that 'men are so cruel'. Perhaps it was at this time too that Miles first attended one of Rose Scott's famous Friday soirées. As she remembered the occasion many years later, librarian Margaret Windeyer was co-opted to collect her from Mrs Wesche's at Double Bay. Other delightful events included a picnic on the harbour with E. W. O'Sullivan and his family, who were always hospitable to Miles and supportive, and the boxer Larry Foley, deemed an ideal man. She also met Rose Scott's cousin, the library benefactor David Scott Mitchell, and heard Amy Castles sing in the Town Hall.[79]

Assuming that *Cockatoos* indeed conveys the gist of Miles' dream of a singing career, once more she had an ulterior motive for her travels. In the novel, her second trip to Sydney enables Ignez to consult a throat specialist, Dr Bramson on Macquarie Street, only to be told that the recovery of her voice would be impossible at her age, and she must rest it completely for a year. All Dr Bramson can do is treat her for severe laryngitis. Since music has become Ignez's passion, and a singing career her main hope of escape from 'Oswald's Ridges', she plans to concentrate on her writing to earn enough money to get away to Paris or some musical centre for proper voice training. This strategy is not very successful, though it does get her away in the end. For Miles the dream had not quite died, but she was no longer so impressed by Amy Castles.

By the end of April 1902, Miles was back at 'Stillwater' feeling poorly and scribbling feverishly. The important outcome of her trip lay not with the publishers — nothing came of Paterson's approach to George Robertson, despite Paterson's good opinion of some of the bush sketches ('among the best things I have read'), and Alfred Rowlandson of the New South Wales Book Stall Company did not take 'Dead Man's Gap', which Paterson thought 'splendid' — but in personal relations. She and Paterson were delighted with one another. She wished she had a recording of his voice, and he wished she were back in his flat to read his words and sing and play the piano to him, inviting her to visit again. They both had other motives, professional and literary, but a strong mutual attraction is obvious in the correspondence even now.[80]

Miles was again working hard on 'On the Outside Track' but she was also agitated. In the draft of a letter, located among several such, now filed at the end of her Lawson correspondence and difficult to decipher, she asks, 'Dear Sir [Paterson], Have you been doing anything desperate lately?' and goes on in playful mode:

> I nearly married since my return. Was so sick of myself & everything about ink that I nearly gave in at last. The man who thinks I am the one woman to whom all servants shall refer as 'Missus' … doesn't know one tune [word illegible] from another

… has no appreciation of blank verse poetry and I think would wither me in a fortnight, and as I feel a gamer flip now, have determined to hang out a bit longer.[81]

A short story, 'One of Our Old Maids', dating from this time, may contain clues about her state of mind. In the story, Lottie Goslett of Tullengah homestead, aged twenty-five, is restless after her first trip to Sydney. Tullengah may have had its interest for 'humanitarians', with 'tramps, hawkers, agents, drovers, callers, squatters and miscellaneous individuals by the score', but it has lost its charm for Lottie, who determines to accept 'none but a city man'. The days drag on, and the story ends with her sending to Gundagai for a hair tonic.[82]

As it does for the fictional Lottie, the great world lay beyond Miles Franklin's reach. On 31 May 1902, Paterson left on an imperialistic assignment in the New Hebrides (now Vanuatu). Apparently he had suggested Miles might like to come too. He was probably just flirting with her but Miles found the prospect exciting. With no idea of what was really going on in the islands, she replied she would have loved to go, fantasising about dressing up as his valet and wondering whether he would be a good boss; but it was impossible. The surviving evidence says more about their literary than their emotional relationship. Paterson wanted her to collaborate with him on a sporting yarn that needed human interest, or, as expressed by George Robertson whose idea it was, some 'blood and tears'. She, on the other hand, wanted Paterson to improve her poems, by adding 'a little more grammar and rhythm'. Later they might do a dictionary together, she added playfully.[83]

It seems Miles was greatly disconcerted by Paterson's plan for collaboration. Linda reported the view at Talbingo that he would probably take over and claim all the credit. Fred Maudsley of the *Book Lover* in Melbourne was even firmer: 'you simply *must not* entertain the idea'. So she declined. Paterson was too cynical, she recalled many years later. At the bottom of his letter accepting her decision, Miles Franklin wrote 'Finale'. But it was not to be. One of them — possibly Miles — suggested they might collaborate on a play. Paterson was very taken with the idea: 'I feel certain we can do well at the drama you can do the thrill & tears & I can do the villainy & the fighting,' he wrote. What she made of the four-page sketch of an Arthurian drama he later sent is unknown; but when he suggested another visit to Sydney to discuss the subject, and she saw the chance to obtain further advice about her voice as well, she responded immediately, arriving three days later by train from Goulburn on the morning of 21 August, to stay this time with Rose Scott. She had recently finished 'On the Outside Track', which she felt was superior to *My Brilliant Career* — as conceptually it possibly was — and had been angling for local publication.[84]

Miles knew that Paterson was off on another Pacific trip on 26 August, to Fiji. He had again invited her, adding that his sister could come too; but the ship's manager had objected to 'lugging two women around', so neither of them could go, to Miles' considerable disappointment. (Charlie Graham, Miles' rural neighbour and erstwhile admirer, thought it served her right; she always rushed into things.) In any event, Paterson was held up at Coonamble. What actually passed between them, and exactly when, or even if, they got together before he left for Fiji, is undocumented. Whatever it was, their fling was over.[85]

Who dropped whom? Quite possibly it was Miles Franklin, with the question of control, so important to Sybylla in *My Brilliant Career*, the decisive factor. Paterson's sister Jessie, who had done her best to help the collaboration along, regretted it hadn't come off, believing that the two could have rectified each other's deficiencies, but there would always be trouble 'if one is subordinate'. And did it come to a marriage proposal, as is often assumed? The evidence is inconclusive. Miles' fiction depicts a sexually naive young woman who in *Cockatoos* fears a kiss will lead to pregnancy. In *My Career Goes Bung* a country girl traumatised by witnessing the suicide of a prostitute is revulsed by keen male advances; but letters written at the time suggest that — at least in Miles' mind — Paterson made advances. Her sister Linda, for example, wrote, 'I always thought you *might* have him.' Paterson's feelings, on the other hand, are almost impossible to pin down. Sometimes he seemed puzzled by her and in general was less deeply involved. Plainly Miles did not know how to deal with him: he was 'the most sophisticated man that ever attempted to woo me sexually,' she later reflected. Charlie Graham, now engaged to Linda and surprised to be remembered when Miles was among her 'society friends', declined to help Miles ascertain (presumably from local sources, since Paterson grew up near Yass), what sort of man he really was, 'if he be a cad or a man', but said it was correct to have refused him. And when Miles confided in the Lawsons, back from London and living at Manly, their marriage in a fragile state, Bertha replied that she guessed the problem had been Paterson, and that she was thankful Miles had rejected him: 'He did not want your love but your brains.' In December, Miles repaid the £5 Paterson had lent her for her fare to Sydney; by which time he was engaged to be married to Alice Walker, a grazier's daughter at Tenterfield.[86]

Apart from Paterson, Miles Franklin had a fine time in Sydney and stayed several weeks. Young Molly David, one of Miles' admiring correspondents upon the publication of *My Brilliant Career*, was incredulous that anyone could like city life, but Miles Franklin now had entrée to the best circles, and in later life would recall 'fairy days' trotting around with Miss Scott. They went to Parliament House, where Miles sat on the front bench of the Legislative Council with eminent member Sir Normand MacLaurin, and to see Miss McDonald, first principal of Women's College at the University of Sydney. At Miss Scott's soirées she met leading writers, such as E. J. Brady and Roderic Quinn, and the Minister of Justice, B. R. Wise. She also encountered significant women such as feminist Dr Mary Booth and Florence Earle Hooper, teacher and writer; maybe also Margaret Hodge and Harriet Newcomb, doughty Empire feminists who established Shirley, a progressive girls' school just up the road from Miss Scott's at Woollahra. People were 'charmed with this gifted young lady', and Scott wrote a six-stanza poem to her 'Dear little girl'. The poem, and some of the great names, are to be seen in Miles' 'writing album', an Edwardian autograph book given to her by Rose Scott (and known as 'the waratah book' in the 1940s).[87]

Back home she focused on 'On the Outside Track', the novel begun in late 1901, some time after copies of *My Brilliant Career* arrived. Its title may have been a tribute to Lawson, whose poem 'The Outside Track' appeared in 1896 — 'For my heart's away on the Outside Track/On the track of the steerage push' (meaning the cheapest fare on a ship) — and to his 1900 short story collection entitled *On the Track*. Oddly enough, *On the Track* begins with a vignette of a 'bad girl', who had 'the most glorious voice of all' and was as spirited as Miles Franklin's heroines of the period.[85]

The narratives of *My Brilliant Career* and 'On the Outside Track' overlap. *My Brilliant Career* is an 1890s story, and it ends on a definite date — 25 March 1899 — after Sybylla has finally rejected Harold Beecham, recognising that he could give her 'everything but control'. Back at 'Possum Gully', Sybylla's future is unclear, but she remains defiant, and true to the populist and radical values of the day. The book ends on a revolutionary note, with the possibility of class distinctions worse than in Russia overtaking the struggling selectors of Australia. 'On the Outside Track' (which later develops into the published *Cockatoos*) begins in the mid-1890s, when Ignez Milford is sent from the mountains to live with and help out relatives at 'Oswald's Ridges', so she can study music in Goulburn. But the action is mostly turn-of-the-century and spans the Boer War and its aftermath in a manuscript Miles sent to her agent, Pinker, in September 1902. (In *Cockatoos* the story runs on well into the twentieth century and follows later events in Miles Franklin's life quite closely.)[89]

When first advising Pinker of her new work, Miles hoped her 'yarn' would be an embodiment of 'the atmosphere, morals and ethics' of the people it painted, and that it was not anywhere too bold, being, she asserted, less outspoken than 'the unsurpassable *Story of an African Farm*'. (She had at last read this powerful semi-autobiographical novel of religious and sexual revolt on the South African veldt — a *cause célèbre* of the 1880s — thanks to an ardent admirer, Morton McDonald of Uriarra, who had acquired a copy in the mistaken belief it was an agricultural text.)[90]

When many years later she entered an extended form of 'On the Outside Track' in a literary competition, Miles summarised the plot as follows:

> A novel of the life among the selector-farmer-dairymen of the Southern Tableland, near Goulburn at the turn of the century. The milieu is presented in detail through two families as a core with the neighbours, friends and relatives who associate with them. The elders struggle along in droughts and wet seasons before motor vehicles and advanced agricultural machinery were in use. One theme deals with the rising discontent of youths with the land and their hankering after the city and its easier jobs, and the ambition of every talented person to take his wares to London. The Boer War comes and passes with its lure of adventure for young men, some of whom do not return. The young people flirt and win or lose in love. Ignez and Sylvia are two of the principals. Ignez is ambitious for a career. Sylvia, the beauty, desires love.[91]

The story is dreadfully detailed, bound to try the patience of a modern reader, but it is the real sequel to *My Brilliant Career*, and an important source on what happened to Miles after her first publication. The original manuscript does not survive, but according to Miles' instruction to Pinker in 1902, it was arranged in two parts, 'Bush' and 'City'. As everywhere in her early writings, the stultifying effects of life on poor land are manifest. The young are divided about leaving; but they know they must go. Mid-story, at the Boxing Day races at 'Armstrong's Folly' overlooking Lake George, Ignez, 'panting for escape', rides off with cousin Dick, a budding poet, to a high knob and silently takes in the great southern vistas which Miles Franklin would so often struggle to describe: 'Inner response to outside influences was drawing them both out and away; but they were impregnated as with life itself with this soil and air, they were under its spell … They could not stay but it was grief to go.'[92]

Authentic settings are one thing in a novel. Historicity is another, here especially the impact of the Boer War, which inflamed the young men of Miles' circle and offered them a version of escape, but proved not such a jaunt after all (as may be appreciated from the Boer War Memorial in Belmore Park, Goulburn, one of the most impressive in Australia). Ignez Milford in *Cockatoos* is against the war, a highly unpopular position. But like a tiny minority of Australian women and men, her creator knew about South Africa from reading Olive Schreiner and the *Bulletin*, and in all probability from listening to Paterson, who had been at the war as a newspaper correspondent and was now a critic of its conduct. Ignez notes that women don't have the vote in South Africa, thereby connecting the oppressions of gender and war. For her the war is like romance, a distraction from her dream of a career as a famous singer. But, predictably, neither romance nor the singing career eventuates. Ignez loses her voice; the devoted model dairyman, Arthur Masters of Barralong, is abandoned; and ultimately she gets away to London, with 'two undeclared packages' in her luggage, 'a dead Cupid and a ruined singing voice'.[93]

The expression is clumsy, the inferences oblique, but links can be made with what was happening to Miles herself in the first two years of the twentieth century. Like Ignez, she was still hopeful of a singing career until 1902, the point at which the original tale ended; and she did then have plans to leave Australia, possibly as a travelling companion of Florette Murray-Prior, a niece of expatriate writer Rosa Praed, who had offered to help her with her singing when she was in Sydney. She also had a problem with romance. The list of her would-be suitors was lengthening — there had been maybe half a dozen by the time she was twenty-five — and some, such as J. J. Baxter and Morton McDonald's brother Alex, had been persistent. In the novel, the turning point for Ignez comes when the lovely Sylvia becomes engaged to Malcolm Timson, a scion of the squattocracy. Ignez realises she is stranded in 'a world of dreams' and must now act. In real life, Paterson had proved unsuitable and Miles' younger sister Linda was engaged to Charlie Graham, who had until recently pursued Miles. As she had not yet given up on marriage, to have a younger sister engaged first was embarrassing.[94]

Pinker received the manuscript of 'On the Outside Track' in late November 1902. In the covering letter Miles stressed that there should be 'no "toning", as I have taken great pains to express the war fever as it <u>actually was</u> [Miles' underlining]' — a plausible selling point six months after the execution of 'Breaker' Morant in Pretoria — and that her own 'peculiar view of things' was grounded in colonial experience. No doubt it was, but it told against her when it came to publication, and the note she wrote directly to Blackwood requesting an advance in the event of acceptance so that she could get away somewhere 'until the fuss about it dies down' was surely premature. Blackwood promptly rejected the manuscript and when Pinker tried the newer English publishing house Duckworth, the reader — English man of letters and supporter of Henry Lawson, Edward Garnett — reported that although there had been a 'dark brilliancy' to *My Brilliant Career*, 'On The Outside Track' was 'impossible':

> As it stands the MS is a very curious illustration of the fact that good matter, or good literary material, is one thing — & that good style is quite another thing. The style of 'The Outside Track' is very very bad … We feel, we know that with a little more sense & more modesty, [the authoress] could have made a good novel … But … she takes no pains with her expression; she is only desperately anxious to throw her thoughts & feelings at the reader's head.[95]

The letter Garnett drafted for Pinker was hardly more complimentary, and in one respect fiercer: 'the authoress uses language, on almost every page, which is crude, grotesque, & often very inflated'. The conclusion was inevitable: '"The Outside Track" requires nothing more or less than rewriting.'

Miles was not one to languish while waiting to hear from far-off publishers. On 27 October she had begun 'The End of My Career'. It was written in just four weeks, and submitted in part to George Robertson even before that. It was to be taken, she told him, as a satirical skit on things 'in jinril' (an instance of Miles Franklin's frequent use of now quaint-sounding colloquialisms) and as a 'takeoff sequel' to *My Brilliant Career*. She thought it would be a hoot to have two books come out at once, one ('On the Outside Track') by Miles Franklin and this one by Sybylla Melvyn. Neither did. Indeed, neither was heard of again until the 1940s, by which time both were much changed, by Miles Franklin herself.

It is often thought that *My Career Goes Bung* was written at this time. However, it seems clear that while 'The End of My Career' did form the basis of *My Career Goes Bung*, the book which appeared under that title in 1946 had been so drastically revised as to be in effect a different document. As recounted in the Preface to *My Career Goes Bung*, Miles thought the original manuscript had been accidentally destroyed after she left Chicago, but when she returned to Australia she found her mother had preserved a copy. Like several other early manuscripts, it has not survived to date. However, there is a typescript dating from the 1930s which contains a three-part contents list of twenty-nine chapters, along with a publisher's note, a preface by 'Peter M'Swat', and an introduction by 'Sybylla'. There are also some typed chapters; and it is still called 'The End of My Career', with an added subtitle, 'A Study in Self Analysis (Not Necessarily a Sequel to *My Brilliant Career*)'. A third version, handwritten and apparently the earlier of the two versions to survive, is in two parts: the first, amounting to over 100 pages and headed 'Chapters 15–23', deals almost entirely with Sybylla in Sydney and the outcome; the second has material on her prior experiences.[96]

There is a strong family resemblance between these documents, but the material does not correlate, and to understand the first part of the earliest manuscript the reader must refer to letters and the later Contents page. After revising the original text in 1936, Miles told Alice Henry she had 'yards of it', meaning sex, though 'the sex row as conceived by me still exists', and there were the problems of 'the eternal feminine', later given as the title of the first section. Among aspects maintained throughout the versions are the positive picture of Ma and Pa, and Sybylla's return to the drought-stricken land after seeing the superficialities of Sydney. Many of the main characters also remain recognisable throughout, though names are changed: the host in Sydney being originally Mrs De Gilhooley, for example. Perhaps the most enticing aspect is the subtitle of the 1930s revision, referring to self-analysis, which is a strong theme running through the text, though the concept is more lightly treated in the final published version.[97]

The unpublished texts that survive suggest Robertson remained unresponsive to feminism. It may be that all the editing of *My Brilliant Career* by more experienced hands had been the making of it. However, the most skilled editor would have had a hard time making something of this material, as what remains is very thin and altogether immature. *My Career Goes Bung* is much stronger and more amusing, in a radical period way. Most surprising is that at the end of the 1930s rewrite of 'The End of My Career', Sybylla marries Harold Beecham and goes to live at 'Five Bob Downs'; and there is a postscript pretending that the preceding is the work of an old man. Here are shades of *My Brilliant Career*, and Miles' later pseudonym, 'Brent of Bin Bin', supposedly a male landholder of mature years, and with all the criticisms of the ending of *My Brilliant Career* taken to heart. Charlie Graham, who seemed still fond of Miles despite his engagement to Linda, and who wished she did not regard him as an antique, would doubtless have approved.

Running through 'The End of My Career'/*My Career Goes Bung* is the protagonist's wounded sense of self, as an impostor in society and especially the literary world, and her regret and embarrassment at having tossed off a novel. Thus the attentions of the more superficial members of Sydney society earn the country girl's contempt, likewise press interviewers. Robertson recognised most of them immediately, adding, 'You've made me jolly glad I didn't meet you!' By contrast there are very favourable portraits of 'Aijee Refusem' (A. G. Stephens); the encouraging 'Violin Dodson' ('Banjo' Paterson) and his sister, Miss Dodson; and of 'Miss Maynall' (Rose Scott), whose soirées proved enjoyable. 'With Mr Dodson's championing somewhat of a literary career might have been possible; under Miss Maynall's wing a society career would have been a fairy tale.' But Sybylla was already on her way home to good old Harold, and apparently all too feminine. 'In the end lack of concentration in spite of unusual talent invariably plucks its disciple bare, while concentration rewards its servant with a coat of many colours.'[98]

In *My Career Goes Bung*, Ma is forever harping on Sybylla's lack of experience. Miles was certainly learning from hers. Thanking Robertson for his 'kind letter' (as it probably was), she wrote, 'Alack and Alas! My gift or curse of impersonation seems to be fatally real — last venture had on an average three people to every character hunting me for my scalp. I didn't mean the characters for real in this last affair but if they struck you so emphatically as such I owe you a deep debt of gratitude.' In fact, she felt dismayed and embarrassed. Years later she recorded that she read the letter only once and then tore it up, and that she hid the returned manuscript 'in rushes in the flat beyond the pigsty'. By then she understood why, as Robertson put it, publication was not feasible, adding with a touch of bitterness, but also some justice, that it was acceptable to mock 'country nonentities ... but not the better class'. His comment that it 'was too audacious to print and might cause a disturbance' made her wonder if it was not in fact dangerous for her to write.[99]

Back at 'Possum Gully', the drought had worsened. The locals gloomily reflected that they would soon be driven off the land and have to take government jobs. In fact, Christmas 1902 was the Franklin family's last at 'Stillwater'. In a matter of months they were packed and off to Penrith, leaving 'Possum Gully' for good.

4

WITH PENRITH AS A BASE:
1903–APRIL 1906

'Miss Franklin ... has got into the habit of writing books.'[1]

In all probability the Franklins were driven off the land by the great drought that settled over much of Australia from the mid-1890s to 1903. John Franklin's tenure at Thornford had always been precarious, and the drought had affected southern New South Wales severely, with 1902 the worst year of all for men like him. He had survived the crisis of 1896 with the help of his brother George, and it rained at Bangalore in the spring of 1902, but presumably it was insufficient to restore his fortunes. A report from nearby Currawang six months later stated that even the fittest would not survive unless weather conditions changed.[2]

The decision to move to Penrith had been taken by mid-January 1903, as may be inferred from details in an undated letter from Linda Franklin to her sister Stella, written from Talbingo where Linda remained for her health. From the letter it is clear that this is the first Linda had heard of the relocation. She thought moving would be 'a great bother', and did her best to contain her anxiety: 'I do hope you will be able to get some sort of place.' Apparently the idea was that John Franklin would run a butcher's shop at Penrith, which Linda thought mad, and bad for their father too. 'Poor you would have all your time taken up pulling him out of Pubs,' she sympathised with her sister.[3]

The fact that the Franklins were moving soon became well known. On 5 February the *Penny Post* noted the donation of an old man saltbush to the

Botanic Gardens 'by Miss Miles Franklin, who is leaving the district', and a few weeks later the *Post* reported that the annual school picnic had been brought forward in order to farewell the family. However, as is often the case, when the time came for them to leave it was a rushed affair, with a clearing-out sale advertised at 'short notice' on 14 March.[4]

A few days later they were gone.

John Franklin, Stella, Norman and Tal set off by buggy, sulky and spring dray on the eighteenth, leaving Susannah and the youngest child, eleven-year-old Laurel, to follow by train. It was good fun, according to a postcard Stella wrote to Linda from a camp between Marulan and Moss Vale, with good grass and lots of fish: 'wish you were here'. Four days later, on Sunday 22 March, they arrived at their new home, 'Chesterfield', about 2 miles north of Penrith, in the Lambridge area off the Castlereagh road. Susannah and Laurel arrived the next day.[5]

'Chesterfield' is a grand name, and the small brick house with a return verandah looks attractive enough in photos — the house was demolished in the 1980s, with only a peppertree left to mark the spot — but some floors were made of dirt, the location close to the river meant a plague of mosquitoes, and there were spiders everywhere. It took the family two days to clear the place out. Grandma Lampe said to send samples of the mosquitoes so she could advise how best to deal with them. Had they taken fowls, she asked? Did they have fruit? Vegetables? (If not, these would not have been hard to obtain from the surrounding market gardens.) Grandma was shocked to learn subsequently that John Maurice Franklin had sold 'what did not belong to him' at 'Stillwater' and brought little of use to the family.[6]

Penrith is an old town by Australian standards. Its site was known by 1789, and European settlement dates to the 1820s or even earlier. With the coming of the rail in the 1860s, it became an important town on the line over the Blue Mountains to the west, with agriculture and horticulture the main local industries. By the beginning of the twentieth century, with a population of some 4000, it was also a well-established pleasure resort, due to the fine-flowing Nepean (Upper Hawkesbury) River and its fertile valley.[7]

Stella Franklin's schoolfriend Edie Paton, stuck back at Burrowa, felt sure Penrith must be much nicer than Bangalore. No doubt it was in some respects. It was certainly closer to Sydney. However, its fictional counterpart, 'Noonoon', in Miles Franklin's second published novel, *Some Everyday Folk and Dawn*, is portrayed as yet another country town, and grubbier than most:

The journey through the town unearthed the fact that it resembled many of its compeers. The oven-hot iron roofs were coated with red dust; a few lackadaisical larrikins upheld occasional corner posts; dogs conducted municipal meetings here and there; the ugliness of the horses tied to the street posts, where they baked in the sun while their riders guzzled in the prolific 'pubs', bespoke a farming rather than a grazing district; and the streets had the distinction of being the most deplorably dirty and untended I have seen.[8]

Apart from the river itself, the only grandeur was the spectacle of freight trains rattling over the noisy iron-covered bridge that then spanned it. In time Miles Franklin would be more appreciative of 'this land of melons and other fruits and vegetables'.[9]

How exactly John Maurice Franklin proposed to support his family at Penrith is not clear, or even why he chose Penrith. Certainly it was not to take up butchering, as his daughters had feared. He appears on the 1903 electoral roll as a farmer (along with his wife and eldest daughter, both listed as engaged in 'domestic duties'), and an advertisement in the *Nepean Times* for a clearing-out sale at 'Chesterfield Farm' prior to his arrival indicates the land was leased. From Penrith council records and other sources, the owner was Henry Bellingham of Narellan, whom John Franklin may have known through the horse trade, and the land leased from him amounted to 47 acres (19 hectares), a little less than the landholding described in 'The Case of Tom Staples', a feature article published by Miles Franklin in 1905 that draws on her father's experience.[10]

Such a small holding could hardly have sufficed, especially for a man for whom farming was never the main endeavour, much less horticulture (although he was always a keen gardener). Later, in association with Labor League activist Dan Clyne, he took up auctioneering, but the business did not last long, a mere six months from April to September 1906. A stray envelope gives some of the details: 'Franklin & Clyne, Auctioneers, General Commission Agents, Land and Estate Agents, Penrith'. Advertising material preserved among Miles Franklin's literary manuscripts further indicates that they operated at Cobborn Budgeree Sale Yards on High Street, West Penrith, and the accompanying doggerel has it that:

Franklyn's [sic] the Boy with the Hammer,
D. Clyne is the coon with the PEN
Of Cattle, and dear little piggies
The Rooster and loud cackling hen.[11]

Miles recalled Clyne, a railway worker born at Bathurst who became Speaker of the New South Wales Parliament in the 1940s, as having lived with them for a year, 'while he and my father tried a business'; and Clyne, who became a staunch friend of the family and of Miles Franklin, in turn recalled her father as 'a Keen Political Student'.[12]

It was in the political sphere that John Maurice Franklin did best at Penrith, though his success was short-lived. In February 1904, less than a year after arriving in the district, he was elected unopposed to represent Castlereagh ward on the Penrith Municipal Council. As Alderman Franklin, he performed his duties with due diligence until poor health in 1905 and business failure in 1906 overwhelmed him, though it was not until September 1907 that he was obliged to resign. During those years in Penrith he was also a supporter of the Women's Political and Educational League, formed by Rose Scott to encourage newly enfranchised women to back the 'non-party' cause.[13]

For Miles, who turned twenty-four in 1903, Penrith served as a base in the unending quest for a vocation. Having failed so far to produce a successor to *My Brilliant Career*, she now embarked on something completely different: participant investigation of domestic service. This was an enterprising move, in line with contemporary concern about 'the servant question', and had encouraging literary exemplars: Israel Zangwill's 1893 novel *Merely Mary Ann* became a play in 1903, and the year before American journalist Elizabeth Banks was said to have made a 'considerable profit' from her book on 'Maryanning', as domestic service was generally known by the later nineteenth century. No doubt Miles thought she could do something similar. She certainly canvassed a play idea with Rose Scott's nephew Nene Wallace once she had acquired some experience, and something may have come of it (see Chapter 5). Still, it is hardly to be wondered at that it took 'lengthy agitation' for Miles Franklin to convince her parents that her 'long cherished scheme' was safe. Perhaps it was the support of good-hearted Mrs O'Sullivan, who provided a start-up reference, that reassured them. That she would also be earning a living, albeit meagre, must have had some bearing, given the ongoing slide in family fortunes. In the opening paragraph of the account of her experiences, entitled 'When I was Mary-Anne. A Slavey', she remarks, 'I was yet so hopelessly domesticated that I possessed no bread-winning equipment save this.'[14]

So began Miles Franklin's personal turn-of-the-century social experiment. Disguised as 'Sarah Frankling' and later 'Mary-Anne Smith', she spent a year in service in Sydney and Melbourne, trying as many jobs as possible in order to experience at first-hand the grievances of servants. It was time, she thought, for domestic work to be properly valued, and with material gathered incognito she aimed to cast light on the problem of relations between mistress and servant: 'No-one could understand the depth of the silent feud between mistress and maid without, in their own person, testing the matter.'[15]

Her first job was as a general servant in Sydney's eastern suburbs for Mrs Finlayson, an engineer's wife, at 34 Brae Street, Waverley (the house survives), where, to the horror of Rose Scott, she worked as 'Sarah Frankling' for three months with scarcely half a day off. When she left in June, Mrs Finlayson gave her a good reference: 'honest, obliging, clean and quick'. Her next documented positions were across the harbour, perhaps at the suggestion of Mrs O'Sullivan, the MP's wife, then living nearby, from June 1903 at 'Elsiemere', a boarding house at 55 Campbell Street (later renamed Kirribilli Avenue), North Sydney, run by Mrs Vance, wife of a manufacturer's representative; and from about October with Mrs O'Connor, wife of R. E. O'Connor, KC, at 'Keston', 11 Carabella Street, Kirribilli, where her health almost gave out. Her mother wrote urging her to come home — 'no necessity to work hard for the information you want' — but Miles was still there in late November 1903.[16]

It seems she even took another position in Sydney in 1903. 'When I was Mary-Anne', written from diary notes, sketches four employers: 'Mrs Tomlinson', a clerk's wife in a seaside suburb; 'Mrs Michelstein', a Jewish merchant's wife at Darling Point (the only harsh one); 'Mrs Bordinhous' at 'Maria's Dingle', a 'first class boarding house' on the harbour; and 'Mrs Kingconsil' of 'Geebung Point', also on the harbour, the wife of a leading politician. In the real-life counterparts of these establishments, Miles worked as a general servant, a kitchen maid, a parlour maid and a housemaid, earning between ten and twelve shillings per week. It was evidently a struggle to gain a footing in an overcrowded job market, and the first six months were very hard, even with breaks at Penrith. She was at

Penrith in early October, when her youngest sister, Laurel, died from pneumonia. Laurel was 'bright and clear to the end', and the sad occasion was no respite for Miles. After six months in service 'Mary-Anne' would conclude that the boarding house was the hardest work, but the most fun, and that relations between mistresses and servants left much to be desired.[17]

After Christmas, Miles went by boat to Melbourne, interim capital of the new Commonwealth of Australia, where she worked for three months. How did she like 'Marvellous Melbourne', asked Rose Scott. Very well, it seems. It was Mary-Anne's 'Enchanted City'; and when Miles' time in Melbourne was almost up, she told the *Bulletin* she had had an uproarious time. Her alter ego, 'Mary-Anne', sailed steerage on the *Carbuncle*, and after spending the first night at a superior servants' employment registry, obtained a job as a kitchen maid at 'Nabob Hall' at twelve shillings per week. After nine weeks at 'Nabob Hall' (a thinly disguised Toorak), with its endless dinners and entertainments, Mary-Anne moved on to the most agreeable of all her positions, as nursery maid to a doctor's wife in East Richmond (later identified as the establishment of Dr Charles Sutton). She had an amusing time helping with the patients as well. 'Mary-Anne' took two more jobs, one with a shop family called the 'Everybodies', and another up the country, with 'Mrs Topset'.[18]

Miles Franklin's self-imposed time as a slavey in Melbourne was up on 7 April 1904, the beginning of the Easter break. Presumably by then she felt she had enough material and that it was safe to 'come out' among friends. Although there had been a few rather lukewarm notices of *My Brilliant Career* in Melbourne — the socialist weekly *Tocsin*, for example, saw wonderful promise but a lamentable lack of art, suggesting the writer did not yet know the difference between journalism and literature — Miles made some life-enhancing associations in Melbourne that Easter, thanks to the *Book Lover* and its circle.[19]

Henry Hyde Champion and his wife, Elsie Belle Champion, had been among the first to notice *My Brilliant Career*, and it seems Miles had made contact with them soon after her arrival in Melbourne on New Year's Day 1904. In February 1904 Henry Champion wrote to Rose Scott that 'your Stella is having great fun in a variety of ways', adding that she was now quite fat and laughed at everything. She would soon learn more sense, he opined, and make her way in the world. He found her wonderfully amusing, and had invited others to meet her. The Prime Minister of Australia, Alfred Deakin, regretted that he was unable to accept Champion's invitation. Bernard Hall, director of the National Gallery of Victoria, took her on a tour of an artist's studio to gauge the effect of the paintings 'on one who had seen none', as she much later recalled. Miles was amazed by her reception: 'The most exclusive people want to meet me, tho' I have nothing but Mary-Anne clothes,' she wrote to Mrs O'Sullivan.[20]

The Champion–Goldstein circle gave Miles Franklin a new kind of encouragement. The women of the group furthered her intellectual development, showering her with books when she left their city. Elsie Belle gave her a copy of Michael Fairless' *The Roadmender*, while her younger sister Aileen Goldstein's gift was Macaulay's *Essays*. They also tried to enhance her self-esteem by introducing her to the currently fashionable teachings of Mary Baker Eddy, founder of the Christian Science Church. Aileen especially, but also her mother, Isabella, and eldest sister, Vida, the famous suffragist, were all three recent converts to the faith.[21]

On 13 April, having been thoroughly lionised by the literary and artistic circles around the Champions and the Goldsteins, Miles was driven in a flower-decorated carriage to the docks, where she received from an unnamed admirer a spray of roses and a card urging 'little Miles' to remain innocent and unbroken through life. According to press reports, her passage back to Sydney on the SS *Peregrine* was courtesy of the management.[22]

In an interview — apparently with art critic William Moore — on the eve of her departure from Melbourne she spoke positively about her experiences and did her best to avoid talking about *My Brilliant Career*, now three years behind her: 'I like the life,' she said, '… if only you could raise the status of servants.' But she would be leaving that problem to others. 'At present I am too ambitious to be content with the life of a servant.' That sounded assured, but when a fellow passenger on the boat coming down had guessed she must be twenty-nine, she had tossed her head and said that was what seasickness did for you; she was only twenty-one (which would have been true had she been born in 1883, as she was soon to claim in *Johns's Notable Australians*, first published in 1906). Although women have often lowered their ages, that Miles should start doing so while still in her twenties is unusual, an indication of the value she attached to her image as an Australian bush girl, and suggestive of a need to obscure the fact that she was already past the average age at marriage (then 21.9 years in New South Wales).[23]

Rolf Boldrewood, an older writer who met Miles Franklin at the Champions' apartment that April, found her 'a pleasant, unaffected damsel'. At the time, Miles was cock-a-hoop at the success of her efforts, writing back to Mrs O'Sullivan in Sydney that she had finished her career as a

'Mary-Anne' and had been able to carry it through successfully, with never a whisper of her true identity and no reproaches from mistresses, all of whom asked her to stay on. This seems to have been true enough. A report in the *Bulletin* a week before Miles left Melbourne that one 'missus' had been alerted within a week of the miscreant's arrival possibly referred to her time in Sydney, and in any event came too late to blow her cover. There is even a story of a fellow servant bursting into tears on learning her associate's true identity, lamenting that 'Miss Franklin' would nevermore be the friend of 'the likes of me'.[24]

Nor was that all Miles Franklin took away from Melbourne. In late December 1903 a most unusual book had appeared. Published by the *Bulletin, Such is Life* by 'Tom Collins' (Joseph Furphy) was destined to become an Australian classic. Soon after its publication, in February 1904, in all ignorance of her whereabouts, Furphy had written to Miles at Bangalore to introduce himself and to point out the striking coincidences of thought, expression and description he perceived to exist between his book and *My Brilliant Career*, which he liked very much:

> Let me congratulate you on your book. ... It is marked by a departure from the beaten track ... Within my own small circle of observation it is widely read and much discussed, finding as good a reception as you could possibly desire. I like the concluding pages better than any Australian writing I have met with.[25]

In response, Miles sent him her photo as requested, and a meeting was arranged in Melbourne over the following Easter. Joseph Furphy's high opinion of her book endeared him to her, but she was hardly prepared for this 'bush Hamlet', a self-educated up-country foundry worker already sixty years of age, a man who was at once controlling and eager for intimacy. Furphy's biographer John Barnes traces an uneasy relationship between the older man and the young woman after their meeting at the National Gallery of Victoria, where to Furphy's dismay Miles was monopolised by his young women friends who made it their business to be there too. Even so, he found her immensely satisfying, despite her nose, famously snub. He described her afterwards to a friend as:

> ... pure Aboriginal ... Yet when you have listened for two minutes to the torrent of commonsense, pathos and humour,

clothed in mingled poetry and slang, and delivered in a deep, sweet contralto, you wouldn't … have a feature of her face altered. She is right enough as she is. Spontaneous![26]

Teacher and Furphy acolyte Kate Baker, who was at the gallery that day, had a comparable reaction: 'I had conceived you as another Jane Eyre … but you are just yourself.' As for Miles, Furphy at first reminded her of one of her favourite uncles, and she moved into her 'Merrily, Miles' mode, full of laughter and fun, which further pleased him. What she would find increasingly difficult were his high expectations of her, when she knew that she had already twice failed to produce the looked-for second book, and his firmly expressed objection to suggestions she might leave the country as there was so much literary work to do in Australia (though he later softened his view, fearing that she might 'wear out [her] pinions against the bars of the cage').[27]

Miles Franklin and Joseph Furphy met again the following day, but only for an hour. That would be their last meeting. In early 1905 Furphy and his family moved to Western Australia, where he died in 1912, by which time Miles was in America. After 1907 it seems Miles and Furphy did not even correspond (though she sent him a copy of *Some Everyday Folk and Dawn* in 1909).

Penrith must have been quite a contrast after that last week among the book lovers of Melbourne. But back home by May, Miles' first priority was to write up the 'Mary-Anne diary'. Rose Scott, miffed that she had not been told of the Melbourne jaunt, read the news of her return in the *Bulletin*: 'Everyone knows you are home writing the book', she wrote on 3 May 1904.[28]

The fair copy of the Mary-Anne manuscript surviving in the Franklin Papers gives the answer; though when, where and exactly how long the writing took is unclear. Miles told Mrs O'Sullivan that she was going away into oblivion, to 'do justice to all concerned', and *Woman's Sphere* reported that she thought it would take a couple of months. It is possible that she went to stay with feminist Cara David, mother of young Molly, who had so enjoyed *My Brilliant Career*. Mrs David had read an earlier manuscript, possibly 'On the Outside Track' or maybe 'The End of My Career', which she had thought unpublishable. However, Cara had approved of the domestic service project, congratulating Miles on her persistence, and was keen to help, offering her a quiet place to write at the Davids' weekender at Woodford in the lower Blue Mountains, just a few stations up the line from Penrith (and Linda did ask her sister about the food there — Mrs David was a well-known vegetarian). Alternatively, Miles simply lay low at 'Chesterfield'. An annotation on a stray exercise book cover indicates that wherever she was, once she got going she worked quickly, with the sketches of 'Geebung Villas' and 'Nabob Hall' finished by 26 May 1904. The task was well and truly completed by April 1905, when Miles mentioned having finished her 'servant book' to the editor of the *Sydney Morning Herald*, T. W. Heney. What happened to the completed manuscript is unknown, except for a passing commiseration from Sir Francis Suttor, president of the Legislative Council and a new patron in Sydney, that Mary-Anne 'did not take on' with the publishers. In 1903, Rose Scott had dreamed that between them they would 'do something for the working girls', and Scott had already done a lot by promoting reform legislation, but Miles' manuscript still awaits its publisher.[29]

The 'Mary-Anne' sketches fill two volumes, a unique account of life in service by an Australian-born woman. For various reasons, such as length and the sensitivity of the approach (Grandma Lampe characteristically thought it deceitful), it could hardly have been published at the time; and while its findings may seem tame today — 'I think it's nearly time that the big part we working girls play in life was better recognised' — such historicity does not diminish the interest and value of the 'Mary Anne' manuscript. Quite the reverse: close examination shows that it is characteristically quirky but comprehensive in its understanding of one of the great questions of the day, and well-written too. From a biographical point of view its very existence is significant, because of its evident commitment to the problems of working women.[30]

The non-publication of 'Mary-Anne' made three manuscripts in three years held over. What should Miles do? Grandma Lampe thought she should marry. This had been the constant concern of her letters over the preceding year. Of course she would not advise marriage with a man her granddaughter didn't like. But why, she wondered, did Miles lead so many of them on? (Which she evidently did, though perhaps unwittingly. Miss Gillespie too wondered how many poor heartbroken fellows Miles had left behind in Melbourne.) By February 1904, Grandma was becoming impatient: 'Have you found anyone you like better than yourself?' she asked sharply. In her next missive, she said flatly that Stella should come home and settle down before it was too late: 'When you get old there will be no chance, you could write all the same.'[31]

The pressure to marry was terrific. Young women today can have no idea of it, nor of the fate of the unmarried daughter in the old Australia.

Grandma Lampe, accustomed to having her say in the extensive intermarriages up country, was quite willing to help, offering a couple of likely names only some of which can now be identified. For example, Grandma's 'Mr Mac' was probably Alex McDonald, one of the McDonald brothers of Uriarra, who wrote in 1902 that he was fond of Stella's company 'simply because you are different from all other girls … All other of my friends would no doubt be good wives & mothers, you to my idea is above all this. Now I had better say no more.' Similarly, Grandma's favoured candidate, 'Baxter', most likely 'Jay Jay', the previously mentioned owner of 'Lord Clive', made no progress; nor did a younger brother, Sam. Charlie Graham was already engaged to Linda. Occasional extant letters from men in the Goulburn district, such as Harold Hammond of Yarra, who said he had a library of 500 books and felt he was losing a real chum when the Franklins left for Penrith, suggest no shortage of suitors, and the poem 'Buried Feelings', given to Miles by bushman W. G. Hoole in November 1905, confirms her popularity. Grandma Lampe warned Stella these men might start to treat her as she treated them: she should change her attitude 'while [she had] a chance'.[32]

In truth Miles had not totally given up on marriage. The evidence, literary and other, indicates that, in the absence of the ideal man, she was trying to reconcile herself to reality through eugenics, another fashionable prescription of the early twentieth century, in which good genes were the basic consideration. Miles Franklin's ideal man remains a shadowy figure, perhaps best indicated by the (still unsatisfactory) Harold Beecham of *My Brilliant Career*. In Arthur, the model dairyman in 'On the Outside Track', a tolerable husband had also been envisaged, though not, after the collapse of a secret provisional engagement, for the heroine — or for that matter for the writer, for whom the device of secret engagement was becoming almost a trademark.

Miles' approach becomes clearer in *Some Everyday Folk and Dawn*, her next major literary foray. Here she analyses 'the marriage market', which in fact as well as fiction was in increasingly bad shape due to the misfortunes of depression and drought in the 1890s. One of the characters opines, 'It's like a year the pumpkins is scarce, you can sell a little thing you'd hardly throw to the pigs another.' In this context a girl might as well go for brawn. 'Some men have brains and muscle, but this combination is as rare as beauty and high intellect in women … apart from the combination the wholesome athlete is generally the more loveable.' And the reality was that no matter how hard Grandma Lampe pressed, the depression of the 1890s, which made such a sharp dent in Australia's hitherto upward demographic history, significantly diminished the scope for marital choice for Miles Franklin's generation of Australian girls. But did she really care? In *Some Everyday Folk and Dawn* romance is never serious. To Joseph Furphy Miles wrote with insight that even if she were to go abroad and marry some nonentity and thus be forced to endure a death-in-life existence, as he predicted, she would still persist with the life of the mind.[33]

Miles tackled the marriage problem by writing about it. Suddenly the necessary inspiration came to her at Penrith. Linda pinpoints the moment for posterity: 'I wish,' she wrote from Talbingo on 23 July 1904, 'we could get worked up about our election like you all at Penrith.' They had three candidates at Talbingo, none of them any good, she complained. Thirteen days later, on 5 August, she wrote again, about her forthcoming wedding to Charlie Graham, to be celebrated at Penrith on 23 November, with the added injunction: 'Great day tomorrow. Don't go up to town and forget to vote.'[34] Excited by the coincidence of the vote and Linda's wedding, and always quick off the mark, Miles began the political romance eventually published as *Some Everyday Folk and Dawn*.[34]

The 'great day' referred to by Linda was the New South Wales election of 6 August 1904, the first election in which women were eligible to vote at state level. The women of New South Wales, along with all other Australian women of European origin, and even a few Aboriginal women in South Australia, had been enfranchised by the Commonwealth Constitution in 1902, and had voted in Federal elections for the first time in 1903, but enfranchisement at state level was a spread-out affair, with South Australia first to give women the vote in 1894 and Victoria last in 1908. New South Wales came in between, in 1903. To fully appreciate the coming of the 'great day', it needs also to be remembered that the states were still immeasurably more important to most people than the fledgling Commonwealth. Furthermore, tension over 'votes for women' continued at grassroots level, and not only for the voters: many electorates doubled in size with the inclusion of women, an uncertain prospect for politicians, although voting then was optional, not compulsory. In this situation, last-ditch opponents hoped the new woman citizen would be too frightened to venture forth on polling day or would mess up her ballot if she did. Statistics for New South Wales (as elsewhere) show nothing of the kind: the self-respecting and highly literate women of the state participated in at least equal numbers with men in the election of 1904, and nothing special happened to the informal vote. These women were leading the world, and they knew it.[35]

Some Everyday Folk and Dawn is set in a country town called Noonoon — the word is a palindrome, we are informed — across the river from Kangaroo (obviously Penrith and Emu Plains) during the 1904 state election. The title refers to the novel's two main subjects: the people of Noonoon, and Dawn, an Australian girl of the period. It is 'affectionately' dedicated 'to the English <u>men</u> who believe in votes for <u>women</u> … because the women herein characterised were never forced to be "SUFFRAGETTES", their countrymen having granted them their rights as SUFFRAGISTS in the year of our Lord 1902', and there is a quaint accompanying glossary which translates Australian slang and colloquialisms into American and English equivalents; for example, 'blokes' to 'guys'. These were mere marketing devices, however, inserted by the author in 1909 when the book was finally published in England, as the militancy of the British suffragettes was mounting. By then interest had abated in 'votes for women' in politically advanced Australia, where, as Miles rightly observed, there had never been a need for suffragettes.[36]

The book presents several major obstacles to the reader. The first is the unnamed narrator, portrayed as a prematurely grey-haired woman in her thirties who comes to Noonoon for her health. Previously an actress, now burned out, her only dynamic is in saving others from the 'savage disappointments' which have blighted her life. While she eventually succeeds as a self-appointed matchmaker for the beautiful and spirited Dawn, who has been prevented from taking up a career on the stage by her grandmother (a redoubtable figure of familiar type in the Franklin armoury) and is in full-scale rebellion against marriage Noonoon-style, the pivotal narrator remains a dispiriting figure, broken down and on the verge of self-pity. Even a whiff of crypto-lesbianism in the bedroom she shares with Dawn at Mrs Clay's boarding house amounts to nothing more interesting than a soothing cuddle at moments of stress.

A second, more complex problem lies with the 'everyday folk'. On the one hand, they are the saving of the book, but on the other, even Miles acknowledged that not everyone cares for 'life in the actuality', and she worried that her characters might be 'not swell enough'. Thus, it is the women of Noonoon who make the case against marriage as it was then, not the rebellious Dawn, and the same who deal forcibly with opposition to votes for women. Witness Mrs Bray slaying Uncle Jake's biblical objections:

'Cowards always drag in the Bible to back theirselves up … there's always one thing as strikes me in the Bible, an' that is w'en God was going to send His Son down in human form, He considered a woman fit to be His mother, but there wasn't a man livin' fit to be His father.' Likewise, Grandma Clay understands the limitations of the vote: 'It ain't what things actually are, it's all they stand for,' she says, clutching her elector's right. And Mrs Bray advises Dawn to 'get some property or something in your name so [your husband] can't make a dishcloth of you altogether'. They have plenty to say too about 'the female Gethsemane' (birthing), the mindless masculinism which dismisses midwifery as 'rabbit ketchin', and the then compelling question of the decline in the birthrate.[37]

Following the real-life urgings of Rose Scott and her Penrith supporters, including Susannah and John Franklin, to rise above party and vote for the best man (literally, as women were not eligible to stand as candidates in New South Wales until 1918), the new women voters in the novel decide to support the Opposition's Mr Walker, a temperance man from Sydney. According to Dawn, Walker is 'nice and thin and speaks beautifully without shouting and roaring — not like the old beer swipers who buy their votes with drink'. Even so, as Rose Scott may have feared when she predicted 'rocks ahead', the incumbent who goes on buying drinks at Jimmeny's Pub wins. Yet all agree that 'Mrs Gas Ranter' is the best speaker. And so it goes, for three months and more, from June to September 1904, through the entire local campaign, to its still-cheerful aftermath, when, as really happened, the narrowly defeated temperance man is carried through the streets and given a silver plate for his efforts. At Noonoon, it is observed at one point, the fighting was more 'hand-to-hand' than at national level; but the outcome is accepted, and 100 years on, the motley cast will be recognisable to anyone who has ever known or lived in an Australian country town, including (once dressed in modern clothes) the appalling Mr Pornsh and his victim, the feeble Miss Flipp, figures straight from the radical 1890s *Bulletin*.[38]

Miles Franklin had produced a topical political novel which research shows to be remarkably accurate in matters both large and small. The flow of election meetings in Noonoon, for example, is convincingly relayed in the vernacular: 'Don't smooge old cockroach, let the other blokes blaze away as we [the taxpayers] are paying dear for this spouting,' shouts one good-humoured male heckler.[39]

In opting for realism, the narrator was on strong ground, as in her apologia for what modern film-makers sometimes call *cinéma vérité*:

I liked life in the actuality, where there was no counterfeit or make-believe to offend the sense of just proportions. Not that I do not love books and pictures, but they have to be so very, very good before they can in any way appease one, while the meanest life is absorbingly interesting, invested as it must ever be with the dignity of reality.[40]

Australian 'actuality', however, was not much of an export commodity, as Miles was to discover. This was explained to her by (Baron) Hallam Tennyson, a former governor-general of Australia and son of the English poet laureate, who had enjoyed *My Brilliant Career* and was an author himself, although unsuccessful at the time he tried to interest English publishers in another manuscript, probably 'On the Outside Track': 'What interests English people is the *bush-life* of Australia.' As well, what is taken to be 'actuality' by contemporaries may not seem the most significant thing to later readers, as in the case of *My Brilliant Career*, where contemporary reviewers most frequently commended the M'Swat scenes, now seen as condescending. Thus, if the multifaceted problem of 'actuality' is added to the obstacles of a lifeless narrator, the address to English readers, and the novel's interest in grass-roots politics, the recipe for a reception of equal parts disdain and neglect seems more or less complete. Perhaps what might be called respectable or sentimental realism was going out of fashion. The approach first recommended by T. J. Hebblewhite back in Goulburn days still had enough purchase to see the book into print, but not to win it esteem.[41]

On 22 June 1905, Miles Franklin wrote to publisher George Robertson asking if he would look at the manuscript of *Some Everyday Folk and Dawn*, which she was just completing. 'It has often been suggested to me,' she went on, 'to put the life of a small country town in a story as part of Australian life not depicted to any extent, and as an opportunity of studying one together with women's first appearance at the ballot has lately come my way, I have seized it.' It was not an adventure story, like some favourite American yarns, but it had quite as much plot as *Winslow Plain*, and the characters were all alive, she averred.[42]

Robertson would have appreciated the reference to *Winslow Plain*, by the New England writer Sarah P. McLean Greene, as he had published an Australian edition in 1903 and sent Miles a copy. In her letter of thanks, dated 4 January 1904, presumably from Melbourne, she said it gave her 'great pleasure' and that 'it deserved all the kudos'. If it was an inspiration, all that can be said today is that she greatly exceeded her model. Compared with *Winslow Plain*, a dour, pious and self-punishing New England novel of now forbidding length, *Some Everyday Folk and Dawn* is an up-to-date work of marvellous vitality.[43]

Alas! The Angus & Robertson reader could only get through six chapters, finding them tedious and dull, accurate in the vernacular no doubt, but 'very small beer'. Reviewers were kinder when the book finally appeared in 1909, published, apparently without difficulty, by Blackwood; but by then it had dated. The *Sydney Morning Herald* welcomed a book with 'strength and insight and a sense of humour', rightly regarding it as more factual than novelistic; but the *Bulletin* merely commented that Grandma Clay was the best thing in it, and that the story itself was uninteresting.[44]

A little of Sybylla survives in Dawn, and although *Some Everyday Folk and Dawn* lacks the force of *My Brilliant Career*, it is recognisably the work of Miles Franklin. In the long run she proved more percipient than most of her readers. Returning to Penrith in mid-1904 she recognised a vital moment in the history of democracy, which she interwove with a sharp look at marriage from the female point of view. That is to say, despite the stodgy romance, her commentary on the times still holds good.

Rose Scott had been exhausted from campaigning in the elections. In September 1904, she wrote inviting Miles to stay with her at 'Lynton', as Vida Goldstein was there on a visit from Melbourne. It was the first of several invitations to Sydney in the coming months, and in this instance it appears Miles declined. She would always extol Vida, who helped her and sympathised with her troubles — 'I have the same problem to work out — a financial problem, & I, too, *seem* the plaything of circumstances,' Vida replied to a note from her young friend on 16 October — but it is unlikely that the younger woman found sustenance in the Christian Science literature she forwarded. In truth Vida was not such a warm personality, and it probably told in Sydney, where she felt her lectures were 'a ghastly failure'. She had been advised by Susannah Franklin's political associate Miss Hamilton (possibly the model for Ada Grosvenor in *Some Everyday Folk and Dawn*) to 'keep off the grass' at Penrith. Vida suggested instead that she might see Miles on the railway platform if she went to stay with Mrs David in the Blue Mountains.[45]

From this brief communication, it seems that by late 1904 Miles Franklin was unhappy. As a single woman just turned twenty-five with no visible means of support, she was unlikely to relish her role as principal bridesmaid at Linda's forthcoming wedding at Penrith. In the wedding photo she looks pensive (though that may simply be *à la mode*). However, she managed to write a 'splendid description' of the ceremony to her brother Norman, who was working up country and unable to attend.[46]

During her extended stay at Penrith in the later months of 1904, occasional trips to Sydney kept her 'in the swim'. Sir Francis Suttor, recalled by Miles Franklin as 'one of the most charming, lovable and best-looking men in Australia', sometimes took her to lunch at Parliament House. In a note arranging one such meeting, he urged her to leave Penrith: 'You must not live at home and let your brain rot.' On another occasion, Rose Scott introduced her 'spirit child' to Sydney Jephcott, a self-educated poet from the Monaro, like Sir Francis now in his later years and, rather like Joseph Furphy had been, greatly excited by the prospect of meeting Miles. (He later moderated his hopes for her, recalling the 'long disappointment' which followed Olive Schreiner's debut.) At that same soirée at Miss Scott's in December 1904, Miles encountered more of the liberal intelligentsia of Edwardian Sydney, including the patrician politician Bernhard Ringrose Wise, whom she thought a cold fish but who proved handy for her later as agent-general for New South Wales in London. Wise's testimonial at that later time stating that she was an author and journalist and a lady of good social standing came straight out of these years when Penrith was her base.[47]

Elders like Sydney Jephcott could not credit that she feared she was 'such a burnt out case' by mid-1905, and her confession, if such there was — probably more like a cry for help — did not staunch his hope of collaboration on a novel. Perhaps it was just a kindly gesture. The reality was that the contradictions of Miles' life increased year by year. It was nothing but the truth when she referred to her stationary career in a letter to A. G. Stephens in March 1905. A note from Hallam Tennyson dated 24 February 1905 with the main message torn away appears to be yet another dismissal of her work (and the end of any hope she might have had of help from him); and the non-publication of the domestic service manuscript has already been noted. Paterson mentioned seeing an article by Miles on 'Servitude' in *Life* in 1905, but this has not so far been traced. At the same time, aspiring bush authors sent Miles their work, and she was still receiving fan mail about *My Brilliant Career*, which, along with the two stories published that year, 'Gossip by the Way' and 'A Ministering Angel' — both dating back to 1900, but who was to know? — must have been enough for the *Bulletin* to list her as a leading Australian writer in 1905 along with

Lawson, Paterson, Will Ogilvie, Mary Hannay Foott, Mary Gilmore and others. The Broken Hill *Barrier Truth*, edited by Robert Ross, greeted the Sydney Hospital serial 'A Ministering Angel', run in *New Idea* from July to December 1905, as the work of 'Miss Miles Franklin, author of that magnificent Australian book *My Brilliant Career*', and in a subsequent mention in the column 'The Moving Finger' went so far as to say that Olive Schreiner's *Story of an African Farm* was somewhat similar, though by no means equal to it. Such a lavish and well-meant but belated encomium gives some idea of the perpetual state of embarrassment in which Miles Franklin must have lived at this time. About then she had to face Angus & Robertson's rejection of *Some Everyday Folk and Dawn*.[48]

In retrospect, in London during the Great War, just before she left for the Balkans in 1917, Miles recognised that Rose Scott had been her anchor during these years. 'I just want you to know in passing how you have always lived in the middle of my heart as the most beautiful and lovely in every way, as you came to me when I was so wayward and dissatisfied ...' But even the devoted Rose seems to have become a little distant in 1905, as it became clearer that her 'spirit child' was slipping away from her. When, on 4 March 1905, Sir Francis Suttor blotted his copybook by inviting the younger woman to a dinner-cum-theatre party without including Rose Scott, though protocol meant he should have, since Miles was staying with Rose, Rose's uncharacteristically angry reaction spoiled Miles' enjoyment of what was in other respects a memorable occasion, which included meeting folklorist Catherine Langloh Parker, author of *Australian Legendary Tales*. (One wonders what Rose Scott would have thought had she known that Sir Francis was also offering to help her protégé 'walk the boards'.) And when Rose, then in her mid-fifties, realised that Miles was set on going to America, she cried out: 'I know nothing of your plans ... why this long journey? why, why, why?'[49]

Rose Scott's letter, written on 13 March 1905 or thereabouts, also contains some unexpected advice about marriage and consanguinity, to the effect that there was no problem about marrying a cousin's child. Consanguinity is not the only unexpected feature of the letter. The other is that it was written in reply to one from Miles at Peak Hill, a small settlement in the Central Lands Division of New South Wales some 250 miles (400 kilometres) north-west of Sydney on the other side of the Great Dividing Range. In north-south terms midway between Parkes and Dubbo on today's Newell Highway, Peak Hill was a significant place in the life of Miles Franklin. Among other things, it was where she went for solace when her mother died in 1938. Mention of Peak Hill in March 1905 serves as a timely alert to the possibility that something new, maybe decisive, was in the making for Miles Franklin west of the Great Divide.[50]

The originating letter to Rose Scott from Peak Hill does not survive. But there is no great puzzle about Miles being there. No doubt she went to stay with William Augustus Lampe, her Uncle Gus, he who had borne her on a purple pillow over the range from Talbingo to Brindabella as an infant, and who would in later life become a favourite relative. In 1885 Lampe had visited his uncle, Thomas Bridle, brother of Grandma Lampe and previously of Tumut, at 'Wilga Vale', north of Peak Hill towards Narromine. Some time after William's marriage to Martha Wilkinson of 'Yallowin' near Talbingo in 1894, he purchased a property some 5 kilometres north of Peak Hill, where he became a successful sheep breeder. He and Martha called the property 'Brohucting' (changed during the Great War to 'Buddong', after the Buddong Falls on the Tumut River), and there they reared five children, the oldest of whom, Thelma, later Perryman, cared for Miles Franklin in Sydney in her last days.[51]

Nor is the timing of Miles' visit to Peak Hill in the summer of 1905 particularly problematic. Her brother Norman was working at 'Brohucting' in late 1905, and her German cousin Theodor Lampe Jnr, who was visiting Australia in 1905–06, may have been there too (though it was probably later in the year).[52]

There is an unpublished short story by Miles entitled 'The Divided Cup', dated 13 April 1905, which begins, 'It was Jan. 18th, the day of the Wilgandrah races.' The story traces a competition between two horses and their owners which ends in a dead heat, and seems to have a suppressed or stalemated romance as a subplot. The handwritten text is not now entirely legible, but the story is set on the plains 'several miles from anywhere', the first of several stories to be set there, with 'Wilgandrah' homestead (probably a play on 'Wilga Vale') in one direction and evidence of closer settlement in the other, and a vista of blue ranges in the far distance, 'the beauty of their contours [softened by] the summer haze'. Miles Franklin seldom failed to respond to the stimulus of a new place.[53]

So what was afoot for Rose Scott to embark on the subject of consanguinity? Was marriage on the agenda for Miles Franklin at last? An answer may be pieced together from various fragments surviving from 1905 which suggest that the origins of the only romantic relationship of her early years for which Miles saw fit to keep the evidence lie here. The relationship was with the sixth child and longest surviving son of Thomas and Mary

Ann Bridle, Susannah Franklin's young cousin Edwin Ernest Bridle, farmer, of 'Wilga Vale'. However, from other writings, to be discussed in more detail shortly, it seems clear that the actual romance blossomed later, in the spring of 1905, when Miles was back again at Peak Hill recording aspects of life on the plains for the *Sydney Morning Herald*. Amid a vivid catalogue of flora in 'The Woods of the West', memories of horses up to their hocks in green wheat emerge and enchanting journeys through starlit pines and plains, with ducks and cranes rising from the gilgai (sun-created cracks in the ground which act as dams and harbour wild fowl). For his part, in a letter written on 10 August 1906, Edwin would recall 'the heavenly time I was having with you last spring-time', and in another of 9 September 1906, 'all the little jaunts we had together this month last year'. There were pleasant excursions in Sydney after the shearing too.[54]

After Miles left Peak Hill in mid-October, Edwin Bridle wrote apologising for not having written earlier; he had been like 'a sick porcupine' since she left and found it hard to write to 'My Guiding Star', 'My First and Only Love'. He was planning to visit her at Penrith in about a week; and the Sydney excursions may have occurred then.[55]

Altogether Miles kept thirteen letters, plus a few loose pages, from Edwin Bridle, written between 27 October 1905 and 20 March 1907, all but two after her departure for America in April 1906. They make poignant reading today. At first Edwin was flabbergasted to have found a 'perfect woman' and overjoyed when he 'found she cared for him'. That she had called him 'silly' and 'mad' when he first told her he loved her only made him love her more, he said. Later, possibly during the pleasant excursions, she apparently made certain promises, only to retract them almost immediately; but he could not believe it, and doggedly sought to hold her to them. The letters reveal that he was prepared to make every sacrifice, including conjugal relations, and that he made ever more drastic promises, seeking to pin her down. But as he struggled with increasing loneliness awaiting mail from America, it becomes obvious that however the relationship began, it soon became one-sided. If the only reassurance Miles Franklin sought from Edwin Bridle at the outset was that he had led 'a clean and virtuous life', his prospects were surely poor from the start. He said she should have rejected him then, but it was too late now: 'I will wait on *patiently* until your mind is calmer,' he wrote on 24 November 1905.[56]

Perhaps he overwhelmed her with his passion. Maybe she led him on and then got cold feet. We do not know. Her letters do not survive. The question must be, why did she keep only *his* letters? Was it to placate Grandma Lampe, who wrote to her in America the following September asking if the rumour around Tumut that she was going to marry Edwin Bridle was true? Did she regret her apparently fickle behaviour? Or did she hope a later generation would understand her better? There is something oppressive about Edwin's letters, and while he was by no means thoughtless or insensitive, it is evident he was not her intellectual equal. His candid and possibly despairing confession in his last surviving letter, dated 20 March 1907, that he could not give her a lovely congenial home but felt they would get along very well if she loved him as he loved her, could hardly have helped her to make up her mind in his favour.[57]

Of one thing we may be sure: any explanations for her behaviour would not be simple or straightforward. There may be a clue to Miles' feelings in the protracted affair of Ignez with the model farmer Arthur in 'On the Outside Track' (*Cockatoos*), which ends eventually with his marriage to a less turbulent girl. There are echoes of Linda's recent marriage to Charlie Graham. Linda had confided to her sister something of the horrors of her first week of marriage and her wish that Stella would never have to endure such a thing — 'I really wished I would die'. It is not surprising that Miles Franklin's romance with Edwin Bridle was short-lived. Still, she had made one of those bargains which abound in her early fiction; and so began the evasions and the ever lengthening silences from America. It is tempting to conclude he deserved better and leave it there; but it is also possible that it was a case of spring fever, that Miles Franklin had set her heart on wider spheres and once more felt trapped. In geographical terms, Peak Hill put her back on the wrong side of the Great Divide, or kept her, as she used to feel at Thornford, 'on the outside track'. Maybe she took heart from the old Indian woman at the Peak Hill Show in October who predicted that she would have a long life and attain success.[58]

Prior happenings back at Penrith add a useful perspective. Earlier in the year, Miles Franklin had been trying to get some of her old supporters to read what she had written to date of *Some Everyday Folk and Dawn*. She asked J. F. Archibald to do so in secret, and to give her an opinion 'from a publisher's point of view'. She also asked A. G. Stephens for an opinion. This was after sending the first half of the manuscript to T. B. Symons at Angus & Robertson earlier in the month with an assurance that she had toned down the politics, and hearing nothing. Stephens tried to wriggle out of it by suggesting she contact the editor of the *Sydney Morning Herald* and offer to write articles on such subjects as women's work. He thought this might be an opening in journalism and 'would enable a country girl to come & live in Sydney if she wanted'. It might be worth three or four pounds a week, he suggested. That was the male basic wage at the time, and as much as the best-paid women journalists might hope to earn. Miles wrote to *Herald* editor Thomas Heney immediately, suggesting articles about the farming district where she lived, on the effects of drought, or on women working at grape, tomato and other fruit packing, even on the killing of caterpillars.[59]

Heney must have been agreeable, for Miles began writing for the *Herald* right away. Her articles appeared in the Saturday edition under the pseudonym 'Vernacular' (pseudonymous bylines being customary in newspapers until the mid-twentieth century). She also wrote a few features for the rival *Daily Telegraph* as 'Old Bachelor' between April and June 1905, mostly for the Wednesday edition. Counting an article for the *Herald*'s Wednesday 'Page for Women' on 'Women and Humour', a perceptive piece on gender difference in humour which appeared on 10 January 1906 over her own initials 'S. M. F.', Miles wrote thirty-one feature articles for the Sydney press between 19 April 1905 and 13 January 1906. For these she may well have earned two guineas apiece.[60]

The first thing that strikes the reader of these writings is that they are all substantial pieces, usually at least a column and a half and mostly more. Altogether they amount to something like 50,000 words. More striking still is how accomplished they are. In producing them Miles Franklin drew on the full range of her experience, and deployed a surprising amount of technical knowledge. The articles can be classified into five subject groups: four according to place and a fifth encompassing general topics such as the very first (and entirely sensible) article on infant welfare called 'Baby-Culture and Socialism' and the final lyrical article entitled 'A Summer Day', plus articles on gardens (one of these in Melbourne) and topics such as women's irrational dress (a favourite theme), always from a farm woman's point of view. The articles shaped by place move in roughly chronological order through 1905, beginning with Penrith topics, then on to the Southern Highlands and the Monaro and the mountains, north to the western plains, and back to Penrith. Once the pseudonym is identified it is obvious from the content that they are all by Miles Franklin; and although quite impersonal, they contain or confirm a good deal of biographical material.[60]

Miles had plenty to write about Penrith, starting with 'The Case of Tom Staples' (mentioned at the beginning of this chapter) and concluding with a feature on the Nepean, admittedly not quite the Rhine, but 'one of the pleasantest holiday haunts'. These local stories have considerable charm and on occasion mild bite. 'Concerning Cabbages and Some Other Matters', for example, turns out to include a case for increased immigration to enhance market size. The articles offer a more likely picture of life as lived by the Franklins on their few acres at Penrith than any other source. The one on 'Remunerative Recreation', describing a girl's success with grape-growing, is so vivid it may well be the writer's own experience, while 'The Lads from the Land', who threaten to leave because of poor wages and cramped circumstances, sound just like Miles' brothers. Norman had already left Penrith and Tal was trying to go to sea by this time, though he only got as far as the Sydney industrial suburb of St Peters.[61]

When the Southern Highlands articles by 'Vernacular' are perused, they turn out to contain partly familiar material too. We have already met 'The Peripatetic Music Master' and his end-of-year concert at Kaligawa, and heard a little of the dairy farms at Thornford. (Dairying, specifically as an occupation for women, was taken up by 'Old Bachelor' too, in an appropriately astringent piece in the *Daily Telegraph*.)[62]

'Across Lake George. A Moonlight Gallop' is one of the finest of the articles. It describes the view south from Macarthy's Hill beyond Currawang, 'one of the most perfect inland views to be found', a case of 'Nature's masterpiece in blue', and the amazing but not unprecedented circumstance of the completely dried-up lake bed. This article mingles personal experience, geography, geology and history with ease: too young to recall previous occurrences of the lake's recession and having only enjoyed Boxing Day race picnics there, 'Vernacular' found 'a ghastly, ghostly contrast to the sunlit holiday field', a scene lifeless without the usual birds:

> Where were the great flocks of pelicans that used to retreat like droves of sheep, and the goodly company of graceful swans and lively water hens that fairly blackened the dancing wavelets, also skimmed by dainty gulls? They were fled ... The bed of the lake faced us like a pall.[63]

Further south, in August 1905, 'Vernacular' attended the Kiandra snow races and participated in a cattle muster in the mountains, both described in such a way that the reader wishes they had been there. It was at this time too that

'Vernacular' worried about 'The Passing of the Possum'. We now think of them as amiable pests, but 'Vernacular' emphasised the economic aspect:

> Not merely to those sentimentally and scientifically concerned regarding the disappearance of native flora and fauna, but from a practical, commercial standpoint, it is alarming to observe how rapidly these little animals — among the best of fur-producers — are diminishing in numbers.[64]

The article contains an excellent account of how in more abundant days most houses had a tanning pit and everyone had two or three nice warm possum rugs. There was too much wanton killing now, and readers were reminded that possums made excellent pets if properly treated, 'desirable little Australians'. The 'gentle koala' was likewise seldom to be seen.

In September, 'Vernacular' was out on the western plains. Five topics are featured between 16 September and 4 November: spring, tramps, jackeroos, the trees out west, and a crop-flattening hailstorm. 'Vernacular' had little to add to such well-worn topics as jackeroos and tramps. By contrast, 'The Woods of the West' is fresh and informative. The article begins by contrasting the flora of the mountains with that of the plains, and the subject is developed in such a way that the reader can appreciate the great variety of shrubs and trees on the flat land beyond the Great Divide, learning, too, that wilgas are thought to be the most graceful of western trees:

> They have a small white flower and thick foliage of the weeping willow design, and of a bright green ... Of uniform size and shape, they afford a beautiful shade, and clipped as they are by the sheep ... they beautify any locality where they are to be found, and by many are considered ... the belles of the western woods.[65]

A final tantalising biographical dimension is present in 'Christmas Greetings'. This late article would be of interest in any case, due to its view that 'a lighter, gayer age' had begun, and that outdoor recreations on Christmas Day indicated an Australianisation of the religious holiday. Of more immediate interest, however, is a list of postcards said to have been received by the 'average stay-at-home individual'. Could it be that at Christmas 1905 Miles

Franklin received greetings from a Japanese midshipman, as well as from well-wishers at Niagara Falls, Bremen, Florence, the island of Dobu off New Guinea, New Zealand, London's West End and from 'a one-time bush woman who is to spend her revels in one of the lesser European courts', as well as cards from all over the Commonwealth and little local country towns? Bremen is explained by the Lampe connection; Arthur Maquarie lived in Florence; and the bush woman might have been Barbara Baynton, though most of the senders cannot be identified. If so, the article is further evidence that Miles Franklin's generation had many international links.[66]

What a boost publishing those articles must have been to Miles, even though they appeared pseudonymously. Mostly they are still very readable a century later, a nicely crafted compendium of contemporary topics, and they serve to strengthen the hypothesis that Miles Franklin was really cut out to be a journalist, a possibility sustained during her American years. It seems people other than A. G. Stephens began to think so. For instance, Paterson, now editor of the *Evening News,* offered to publish any sketches of life in country towns she cared to send, and others said they would have published her work but were unable to pay contributors. The articles also go some way to explaining how she could afford a fare to America, and, since Heney of the *Sydney Morning Herald* was happy to receive other pieces from her (though wary about how much he would be able to publish), how she imagined she could live there, apart from the old standby, domestic service.[67]

Still, as the newspaper editor Robert Ross wrote from Broken Hill, 'to be a gifted Australian in the literary field is to be born to struggle'. Actually, Miles was remarkably productive during these years at Penrith, writing the equivalent of a book a year, and she had found her métier as a social commentator. The problem was that none of the books had been published, and after three strenuous years she remained 'an outsider' who badly needed a peer group (and a helpful editor), rather than elderly patrons who, like Rose Scott in her last surviving letter to Miles, still thought of her as a little girl. More than that, she was way ahead of her time. While there may be many more women as social commentators in Australia now, they seldom achieve comparable authority with men. How much truer this was a century ago.[68]

As far back as 1904 the Champion–Goldstein circle in Melbourne had strongly encouraged Miles to try her literary fortunes in America, an idea which had been building in her mind since a reader of *My Brilliant Career* in 1901 suggested she try the American magazine market. Vida, who in 1902 had attended an international suffrage conference in Washington as Australasian representative and made an impression, was particularly encouraging and supportive. [69]

In mid-1903 Miles had asked George Robertson about literary agents in America, and by early 1904 all sorts of ideas about escape were swirling around her head. 'Are you really going to New Zealand?' asked Sir Francis Suttor, and 'Why *Canada*?' wondered Cara David. By mid-1904, it seems clear she was intent on going to America. In May Aileen Goldstein urged her new friend to get her priorities right — 'You seem to think if you had a couple of thousand pounds all would be well' — and suggested that if she did go there she would meet Christian Scientists who had been through similar trying experiences. 'I have read of many splendid financial demonstrations' (a Christian Science term, meaning demonstrations of the truth of Christian Science), she added. Two months later Linda assumed it was all happening: 'When are you going to America?' she asked.[70]

Miles Franklin set sail from Sydney for San Francisco on RMS *Ventura* on Monday 9 April 1906, alone and unchaperoned. It was a bold thing to do, but not as bold as it might seem. Sydney was after all a long-established Pacific port. And although it was still unusual for young women to travel unchaperoned, her mother approved: 'Did I tell you about going to the USA?' Miles asked friend and fellow writer Henrietta Drake-Brockman in 1950. 'As soon as I began to agitate Mother understood. She said she had always longed to do likewise, but had married.' She also had Vida Goldstein's assurance of a feminist network when she got there, and the possibility of sending articles back to the *Herald*.[71]

She was twenty-six years old and she was right to go.

PART II

AMERICA
May 1906–October 1915

5

AMONG THE 'MURKANS': MAY 1906–FEBRUARY 1911

'I guess this is the place for me.'[1]

Miles Franklin was one of 162 passengers aboard the RMS *Ventura* when it steamed out through Sydney Heads for San Francisco on the afternoon of 9 April 1906. Advertised as a 'magnificent new twin screw ship', the 6200-ton *Ventura* would call at Auckland, Pago Pago and Honolulu. The ad offered travellers an enjoyable experience among interesting up-to-date people, with great scenery and cheap through-fares to England. Fares to San Francisco ranged from £16–£40, and the voyage normally took twenty-one days.[2]

Like Vida Goldstein, who four years earlier had travelled (also alone) to the United States on a sister ship, the *Sierra*, to represent Australasia at the inaugural International Woman Suffrage Conference in Washington, Miles had trouble with the ship's vibrations at first, but according to a postcard to Linda from Auckland, she soon settled down. By then she had met 'a nice girl', Edith Jones ('Jonesie'), an Adventist nurse from Sydney. Edwin Bridle received a letter from Auckland, and it seems there were more cards and letters posted en route; but apart from that early postcard to Linda, the only item to survive is a snapshot of a group of young men and women sitting on the ship's deck, with Miles hanging onto her hat and looking distinctly queasy. In later correspondence with Jonesie, Miles portrayed herself as 'a rotten sailor'. She also mentioned several young men on the *Ventura*. Allan Levick, sometimes said to have been a resident of Tumut, was one. Another was a journalist (and later a Queensland politician) named Ryan, who rang when *All That Swagger* appeared in 1936 and insisted he had proposed to her on board, though she could not recall it. More memorable was Oscar Unmack, a New York insurance agent who sent Miles the snapshot and remained in touch until 1912.[3]

For Miles, Honolulu was a beautiful locale — 'a place of sunshine and flowers', as Vida Goldstein described it — but the *Ventura* arrived there to appalling news. As Miles reported in an article published in the *Sydney Morning Herald* on 23 June 1906, when the ship drew in, locals shouted news of the San Francisco earthquake six days earlier (18 April 1906), in which at least 1000 people were said to have been killed and the great city wrecked. The news cast gloom 'on the scented day'; many were distraught, and extra coal was taken on to hasten the *Ventura* through the six days it would take to reach its destination.[4]

Miles' first glimpse of mainland America on the morning of 1 May 1906 could not have been more dramatic. In the aftermath of the earthquake had come a great fire, and at first light the once beautiful west-coast city was obscured by mist and smoke. With daylight, the extent of the devastation became apparent: the city 'looked like a series of great rubbish tips cut out in squares where the streets had been, and from it all arose the odour of a great burning'.[5]

The immediate dilemma for arriving passengers that morning in May 1906 was how to find their friends. Miles' contact was Miss Carrie Whelan, a friend of the New York suffragist Carrie Chapman Catt, and through her, of Vida Goldstein. In later life Miles thought of Carrie Whelan as 'my first American friend', and in affectionate letters to Carrie written from 1929 to 1937 she showed she never forgot her, nor her sister Ella. With reason. Ella chartered a tug to get Miles off the *Ventura*. It was Miles' first encounter with confident American women and the national 'can do' attitude. 'Your sister opened up a whole new world,' she wrote to Carrie twenty years later.[6]

The address Miles had for Carrie Whelan was in central San Francisco: 307 Kohl Buildings, on the north-east corner of California and Montgomery streets, a site of great devastation. The Whelans had relocated to 1217 6th Avenue, East Oakland, where Miles advised folks back home to send her letters; and they not only took her in but Jonesie as well. Thirty years later 'Jonesie', who returned to Australia in 1911, still remembered their kindness to two lonely girls.[7]

What Miles did immediately after her arrival in America is still somewhat vague. What is clear is that at first she teamed up with Jonesie, who was an ardent adherent of the predominantly American Seventh-Day Adventist Church and had a ready-made support system. Apparently the two young women spent some time working in an Adventist relief camp in San Francisco, though this remains unsubstantiated. A recollection by Miles simply states that she and Jonesie were together in the San Francisco earthquake debris, and then Jonesie took her to 'a great sanatorium' south of Los Angeles.[8]

Within weeks the two young women had set off for the Seventh-Day Adventist health resort at Loma Linda, a salubrious spot in the foothills near Redlands in southern California. What Miles did at Loma Linda we don't know. Maybe she again worked — in August Edwin commended her for good work 'with those missionary people' — but quite possibly she was there to rest and recuperate. If so, the sojourn at Loma Linda was the first of many indications of the toll taken by stress on Miles, whose cheerful persona disguised many anxieties. One setback at this time was a reply from radical American writer Jack London declining, on principle rather than anything personal, to help her place her writings.[9]

Whatever Miles was doing at Loma Linda, it was a refreshing experience. In August, back in San Francisco, she sent Linda a booklet promoting the health resort, dated by her 26 May 1906, which states that among other benefits the sanatorium was an Eden of repose for the nervous woman seeking rest from the burdens of society, and that rates were kept as low as possible ($15 per week is the lowest rate listed). Her accompanying postcard reported she was 'much better'. Nearly fifty years later, in March 1954, some six months before she died, Miles delighted to recall 'the sweet peas and opulence of Redlands, California, and Los Angeles when Hollywood was a big name on a rough hillside'.[10]

None of Miles' letters home in 1906 has survived, though she certainly wrote to friends and family. Linda reported the consternation of her mother-in-law at news of the earthquake, and later that at Talbingo everyone gathered for readings: 'They would all muster like church to hear yr letters with their mouths open.' And as already indicated, Edwin Bridle received numerous letters. Of the fourteen letters Miles received from home at this time which survive, ten are from Edwin.[11]

The penny postcards and strip photos she sent back to Australia have survived, however, mostly in an album created at her request: 'Keep the photographs and postcards I send you please. We will make a collection some day,' she instructed her mother on an undated card from New York. Now volume 111 of the Franklin Papers, the resultant album with its decorative strip of waterlilies is inscribed in Susannah's distinctive hand: 'This book is for Stella'.[12]

A few postcards are also preserved in a Lampe family album in the National Library of Australia. Altogether well over 100 of the cards sent by and to Miles Franklin survive for her nine American years. One of the first was to her brother Tal at Emu Plains near Penrith, postmarked San Francisco, 11 July 1906. It features a drawing of the devil ('Why in the Devil don't you write?'), and complains that Miles had received nothing from home last mail, but adds that she is well and happy. Presumably she was back from Loma Linda by then. A strip photo of her in a Mexican hat on a one-cent mail card (the previously mentioned card sent to Linda from San Francisco on 20 August 1906) is another early item. Here Miles responds with relief to the news from Linda that she now had a nephew, Edward John Mervyn Graham, born on 16 July 1906 at 'Montrose', the Graham family home, after a difficult pregnancy.[13]

Miles was not planning to stay away for very long. Detail is lacking, maybe deliberately so, but her main aim undoubtedly was to get more of her work published — as we have seen, plenty had accumulated — and even allowing for evasions and prevarications in letters to Edwin Bridle, it is obvious from his replies that she meant to return quite soon. Sometimes it seems she hoped to be back in Australia by year's end; and until his very last extant letter of 20 March 1907, Edwin Bridle was hoping she would soon fulfil her mission and return to become his bride.

Return was contingent on literary success. Her first objective was New York: the address she gave to *Ventura* shipmate Oscar Unmack was Carrie Chapman Catt's, and by September Edwin (rightly) thought she was on her way there. If she didn't make it in New York, there was always London (perhaps via the *Ventura*'s offer of 'cheap through fares to England'). Sometimes Germany was mentioned, but that was early on, and somehow it never eventuated. The imperative was to get more of her work out wherever she could find a suitable publisher. Only in that way could she escape the tyranny of the second-book syndrome, which all writers must suffer.[14]

Miles Franklin's aim was to establish herself as an Australian writer what-ever it took, and despite many disavowals, for example to H. H. Champion in 1913, that she had abandoned literature, she never gave up — diversions, distractions and disappointments notwithstanding. The idea that Miles escaped from Australia is valid only in the most superficial sense, if at all. It was quite normal at this time, and for long afterwards, for creative Australians to seek recognition abroad. Only a few years earlier her first sponsor, Henry Lawson, had sought to establish himself as a professional writer in London, though this did not work out. Compared with Lawson, who was accompanied by his wife and young family, arguably Miles was the bolder figure, though she had the benefit of a vigorous international feminist network, which saw Australasian women as advanced, due to the early success of woman suffrage in the Antipodes. It was probably because of, not despite, her Australian aspirations that Miles Franklin went to America — more fun, more radical than England — in 1906.[15]

Miles left San Francisco for the east coast some time in late August. The railroad route took her first to Salt Lake City, where she worked briefly at the Kenyon Hotel. She thought it 'a lovely city', and the Kenyon was 'then the best hotel'. By 1 September she was working at the Hotel Colorado, Glenwood Springs. Back in Tumut, Grandma Lampe was horrified to hear that her granddaughter was working in hotels, but in a group photo of Hotel Colorado staff taken in lush grounds it all looks highly respectable. Thirteen women in high-necked, long-sleeved white shirts and full-length black skirts — except for Miles, sitting demurely centre front in a light skirt — surround the lone male staff member.[16]

Miles had a great time in Colorado; in fact, the trip to the east left her with some of her most exuberant memories, as recaptured in the previously cited letter recalling the opulence of Redlands.

> Then [came] the beauty of Salt Lake City and its Wasatch mountains, then the Rockies with Hanging Lake, to reach which I astonished the guides by hanging on to my horse's tail and making him tow me up as we used to do beyond Canberra. It was a new trick to them. I had been lent a lovely roan pony belonging to some rich lady at the rich hotel. So they thought I sat special and handed me a rifle and insisted that I shoot something. We were riding up the pass where the Shoshone rapids come down, and in them was a little log about the length of two fence posts. I just pulled the trigger and by chance the bullet hit it. I suppose I had previously fired a gun as many

as half a dozen times, and at a fixed target. I loathed the repercussion or percussion of the beastly instruments. All my denials were no good after that. I got an offer to go in a circus and the strong man of a vaudeville act proposed to me. Such a nuisance! But how gorgeous were Mt Sopris and the Roaring Fork.[17]

It sometimes seems more men proposed to Miles than to Elizabeth I of England. Linda told her she was a naughty girl to leave so many broken hearts behind her. But it was too bad for the latest would-bes, as for those who had gone before: at this stage it was the American people, not the male component in particular, who excited her. Recalling also the Santa Fe crossing of the Rockies, Miles wrote: 'Heaven can offer nothing more satisfying and exciting, and the people! All ranks, from the rich and cultured down to the workers, everywhere I went, I used to say I had only to present myself and the Americans did all the rest, and adopted me and kept me in cotton wool.'[18]

The catch was, she thought in retrospect, that she lacked the acquisitive impulse. 'If only I had had the qualities to acquire and be on the make what a success I could have been.' Maybe she was already in love with America. Aged seventy-four, she could still say, 'I love the beautiful land & its people forever, and in eternity if there is identity there ...'[19]

Jack London had commented that Miles set herself 'a big adventure' playing 'Mary Ann' in the United States. According to 'Concerning Helps', which appeared in the *Sydney Morning Herald* on 13 April 1907, she spent her first nine months in America studying the servant question. The article was written in response to a report of a meeting of ladies in Sydney Town Hall on 3 December 1906 calling for more domestic servants through increased immigration. Miles argued that the answer did not lie in immigration (unlike 'Vernacular' on farm produce in 1905) or even in better pay, but in progressive labour legislation and enhanced status, as demonstrated by her American experience: 'Through the west of the United States the dearth of domestics is so great that wages are high and the liberty allowed them beyond what Australian girls dream of.' But immigration did not make a difference, since all it had done was push American girls westward: 'In California, Colorado and Utah I came in contact with scores of American domestics and was surprised that not any of them were natives of the state in which they were earning their living.'

She further reported that having got as far east as Chicago, she had made a study of employment agencies and found that the first criterion of mistresses was that their servants could speak English. Her experience provided her with material for what seems to be her first American publication, 'No Dignity in Domestic Service', by 'Mary Anne', published on 14 April 1907 in the *Chicago Sunday Tribune*. Perhaps an even more substantial manuscript ensued, as tantalisingly suggested by an American school exercise book cover filed among her unpublished plays with a pencilled heading 'The Misdemeanours of Mary-Anne', and by a passing reference in the Sydney *Worker* in 1913 to her as author of 'Merely Mary Ann'.[20]

Miles had reached Chicago some time in October 1906, during unseasonal snow. In early December, in reply to 'a beautiful letter', Edwin Bridle said they could do with some Chicago snow out Wilga way and apologised for not sending emu feathers, adding that he was sending her a half sovereign for Christmas. Susannah Franklin's Christmas greetings, sent in October to Oakland 'from the Sunny South', wished her wandering daughter 'the gayest of gay times', though winter in grimy, icy Chicago was unlikely to provide that. Vida Goldstein had disliked Chicago, remarking that for miles before reaching the city the air was thick with coal smoke from myriad factories, which, when combined with the 'overwhelming breeziness' of Chicagoans, made the then second city of America, with its almost two million inhabitants, 'much more than the average person can stand'. Others, however, found it a wonder, as in Theodore Dreiser's novel *Sister Carrie*.[21]

It is not immediately obvious why Chicago should have been more than a stopping point, much less how Miles came to stay there for the next nine years. Although it already occupied a significant place in the American imagination, Chicago was not then thought of as a literary magnet. Quite the reverse. By the late nineteenth century it had replaced industrial Britain's Manchester in urban iconography as the most shocking city in the world, due to its phenomenal growth, its industrial pollution and its robber barons, who exploited a largely immigrant work force remorselessly. As most famously portrayed by Upton Sinclair in his 1906 novel, *The Jungle*, behind the gracious lakefront boulevards and the astonishing skyscrapers lay 'a jungle' of meat and other noxious industries. Its climate was unattractive to say the least, not only in the winter, when the place was 'dreary with blackened, bedraggled snow and all the ugliness of this season in a soot-ridden city', as Miles would later describe it, but much of the time. Situated on the south-western edge of Lake Michigan, Chicago was not called 'the windy city' for nothing.[22]

An adequate explanation for Miles' stay in Chicago goes well beyond the fact that it was the next major city on the rail route east. When they learned that Carrie Chapman Catt, Miles' contact in New York, had gone to Europe for a long stay, Miles' Californian friends contacted Jane Addams at Hull-House, on Halstead Street, Chicago. Hull-House, a 'social settlement' house founded in 1889 by Addams and Ellen Gates Starr in the heart of the Stockyard district as a means of bridging the chasms of class in Chicago, was by then one of the most influential sites of social reform in America. 'Social settlement' was a late-Victorian movement whereby better-off people settled in poor areas to improve urban living conditions and promote social cohesion through educational and like facilities. At Hull-House, Miles immediately encountered the progressive side of the city. Chicago would become Miles Franklin's university.[23]

She found lodgings with Miss Stout, a dressmaker, at 268 South Wood Street in the inner west, then nearby with Miss Staller, at 1505 Edgecomb Road. Later in life, Miles forgot about these brief stays, recalling only that when she first went to Chicago, she and Alice Henry lived at 71 Park Avenue, the inner north-west residence of Josephine E. Young, a graduate of the Chicago Women's Hospital Medical College, with links to urban reform. It was to remain Miles' address until late 1907.[24]

Alice Henry, a distinguished-looking Melbourne journalist in her late forties, who had been using a modest inheritance to visit England and America lecturing on the British suffragettes and social legislation in Australia as she went, arrived in Chicago a month or so before Miles. She had been invited there by Jane Addams and the Progressivist Lloyd family to lecture in the cause of municipal reform, and was staying at Hull-House. Apparently Miles and Alice had not met before, as Alice did not recognise the name 'Miss Franklin' to begin with; but on realising it was 'merely Miles', as Miles reported in a letter to the Melbourne *Book Lover*, it was all jolly comradeship, and 'she annexed me at once'. Since Miss Henry had 'a wide circle of very delightful friends' and was much in demand as a speaker, to be taken under her wing was quite an experience: 'there was a tremendous crowd of vital mid-westerners in those days', Miles found. And they in turn took to Miles, whose 'initiative' and 'easy adaptability' (Alice Henry's words) would make her 'a valuable addition' to reform circles.[25]

Not immediately, however. Except for a report in A. G. Stephens' *Bookfellow* dated 21 March 1907, indicating that Miles was still intent on trying her luck in New York, and a letter to Rose Scott noted in the *Sydney Morning Herald*'s 'Page for Women' on 29 May 1907, where it was reported that she was going to 'batch' with Miss Henry at Park Avenue (and could now walk about in the cold without discomfort), there is a gap in the record of almost a year between Miles' arrival in Chicago and finding a niche.

It has been suggested that she worked in a department store, which may be so, though she never wrote directly about shop work, for all that it is roundly condemned as exploitative in her American novels. The literary and other evidence suggests that if she did, it was not at the counter but as a clerk. In *The Net of Circumstance*, the only novel from her Chicago years published (pseudonymously) in her lifetime, Constance Roberts, the 'New Woman' heroine, newly arrived in Chicago from the rural mid-west in hope of a different, more cultured life, first takes a course in book-keeping and stenography. She then obtains a job in 'a well-ordered business house' and subsequently works for a while for a relief aid society. All of which proves exhausting and unfulfilling, especially because to save money Constance must live in a 'Mary-Anne' hostel for working girls, including shop girls. This seems more like it: 'Stella Franklin' is recorded in American labor history as one of the new breed of working women coming to positions of leadership in the union movement after 1907, in her case representing department-store clerks. Her friendship with Emma Pischel, daughter of a German-American lumber merchant and a clerk at City Hall at the time, dates from 1907 and may also have had some bearing on her choice of occupation.[26]

If the story of Constance Roberts is any guide, it was during these early years that Miles Franklin learned the office skills that would enable her to earn a living in coming decades. Too little evidence survives to say when she took up typing, but her first known play, signed and dated August 1908, is in typescript; and her shorthand, which she does not mention until 1916 and which remained impenetrable until the 1980s, may date from this time as well. Even so, it was social inquiry, not clerical work, that attracted her. In this she was doubtless encouraged by Alice Henry, who had been speedily recruited to serve as office secretary to the Chicago branch of the Women's Trade Union League (WTUL), and not long after that became editor of the league's section in the Chicago Federation of Labor's monthly *Union Labor Advocate*. In a letter to the *Book Lover* published in September 1907 Miles said she was in perfect health and getting to the bottom of social evils by studying 'the terrifying work dens of Chicago', eliciting an editorial comment that she had given no sign yet of return. It was thought she would see the east coast, and perhaps visit England, before she did.[27]

Suddenly, from Australia, came tragic news. On 30 August 1907 Susannah Franklin wrote from Penrith to her dearest Stella that Linda had died of pneumonia on 24 August, nine days after reaching her new home at Dalveen, near Warwick in southern Queensland. Having 'suffered so' since her baby was born, Linda had often wished to die and be free of pain, and had died quietly 'in a strange land'. Both John and Susannah Franklin had been with her. Now they were back at Penrith for a clearing-out sale.[28]

Miles was devastated. She could not have known from Linda's letters how bad she was. In them Linda had worried more about the hard time her sister was having than herself. Now Miles had lost her only surviving sister and her best friend. Furthermore, business problems had forced her parents to sell up at Penrith, and they were now homeless. Susannah was obliged to return to Tumut, while John Franklin became a day labourer again, in Queensland and elsewhere.[29]

In the following weeks, alone in Chicago, Miles had something like a nervous breakdown, from which she was still suffering several months later. Back home her elders worried about her. Evidently the concern was justified, and Miles was unwell. Many years later, she recalled being visited by Alice Henry in Passavant Hospital (now Northwestern Memorial Hospital) 'when the news of my last sister's death came'.[30]

How long she was in hospital is undocumented, but it was Alice Henry who came to the rescue. In a postcard to her mother from Winnetka, Illinois, dated 14 November 1907, the young invalid reported that she would not be fit to work for months, and that she was getting 'jolly sick of it'. The postcard identifies 'Wayside' on the shore of Lake Michigan, 30 kilometres north of Chicago, as the home of the Lloyd family, where the previous Saturday Miss Henry had taken her to recuperate. In her biography of Henry Demarest Lloyd, who established 'Wayside' as a family home and as a place of both repose and stimulus for like-minded people, his sister Caro described it as 'part of a social settlement':

> Under its roof was usually found someone wounded in body or soul, some outsider with no claim of friendship or kinship ... Now it was some lonely self-supporting woman, now an over-

worked mother ... now some young man away from home for the first time ... 'A bit of nineteenth-century heaven,' a friend described it.³¹

Miles probably knew the Lloyd family already. She certainly knew one son, Harvard-educated lawyer and Chicago estate agent William (Bill) Bross Lloyd, as she and Alice Henry had sat either side of him at a St Valentine's Day dinner earlier in the year. She may also have met his younger brother Demarest, also Harvard-educated, an employee of the American Automobile Company, Boston, from 1907 to 1911, at 'Wayside'. Both were personable young men, and as beneficiaries of the estate of their maternal grandfather William Bross, part-owner of the *Chicago Tribune*, extraordinarily rich. Later she recalled she was grateful that Bill was kind 'when I was desolate after the death of my sister'. In due course, in a review of Caro Lloyd's book for the Women's Trade Union League journal *Life and Labor*, she would pay tribute to the breadth and warmth of the hospitality at Winnetka.³²

Miles Franklin was homesick as well as heartsick. An unpublished story, 'The Old House on the Corner', subtitled 'Among the "Murkans"', with its bumptious young Australian hero, Jack Sutherland, opens with Fourth of July celebrations similar to those reported in the *Book Lover* in September 1907, and the new Commonwealth of Australia flag flying alongside the Stars and Stripes at his grandparents' abode in Chicago. The plot, not fully developed, revolves around Jack's plans to return to his homeland. He admires American cosmopolitanism and its comfortable houses with running water, even in bedrooms, but with 'the raw lake wind' and another cold Christmas approaching, he yearns for home, even fantasising about shifting Chicago to somewhere between Bourke and the Riverina: 'things would hum'.³³

'The Old House on the Corner', probably written in 1910, was never finished — it peters out into a series of drafts, and the romantic interest is undeveloped. As well as those early reactions to American life, it hints at Miles' speedy adjustment; for example, her appreciation of the liberating effects of American speech. Whereas in Australia it mattered socially if you mispronounced words and she had often felt inhibited because there was no one to advise her, in America such things didn't matter. An unrelated literary fragment recalls her delight: 'I remember one evening early after I arrived there, at the home of Chicago's most brilliant university professors, [what] a great bag of words I got.'³⁴

As Miles gradually regained her equilibrium, Alice Henry led her into the women's trade union movement. Shortly before she went to Winnetka that November, Margaret Dreier Robins, recently elected president of the National Women's Trade Union League of America (NWTUL), had written inviting Miles to become her personal secretary when she was well enough to undertake the duties (which she was assured would not be very onerous at first). The charismatic Mrs Robins, who was a wealthy woman in her own right, offered a small salary of $12 a week. As president of the Chicago branch of the league as well as national president, she needed help, regardless of the league's capacity to pay; and as Alice Henry once remarked, Mrs Robins had the knack of picking people whose prior experience would be useful. She probably heard from Alice Henry of the writing skills that Miles would bring to the job, and knew of her empathy with working women, as evinced by the domestic service article in the Chicago *Sunday Tribune*. Miles in turn was keen to begin. Instead of setting off for Christmas in California, as Jonesie had hoped, she was back at Park Avenue, feeling fine and looking forward to 'a more fruitful year'.[35]

Miles began work on 1 January 1908. The news appeared in the *Sydney Morning Herald* on 29 January 1908:

> The latest news from Chicago tells us that Miss Miles Franklin is engaged as secretary to a woman of great wealth, whose sociological and philanthropic work gives the young Australian writer an opportunity of seeing a side of American life which is not usually seen by a stranger.

So it was that Miles Franklin stayed on in Chicago. She was twenty-eight and had a more or less regular job at last. 'I guess this is the place for me,' says Jack Sutherland in 'The Old House on the Corner', which is quite possibly just how Miles felt.

A few handwritten letters to Margaret Robins, along with the pages of the *Union Labor Advocate*, tell us a little about Miles' new job. There were regular office meetings on Wednesday mornings, and during the week she undertook research as well as clerical tasks for Mrs Robins. Even before she began, she was 'looking out for [court] cases', and in April she was researching *Adair v. the US*, an important case which invalidated 'yellow-dog' or anti-union contracts. According to the activity lists published in the Federation of Labor journal, the *Union Labor Advocate*, she also attended meetings of the knee pants makers' union and the Political Equality League during the year.[36]

Sometimes she feared she had overestimated her strength. But the work was part-time, and from postcards we know she was not missing out on the pleasures of Chicago. Relaxation was to be had from walks along the lakeside; there was skating at Union Park; and some Sundays she went 'automobiling'. On one notable occasion, Dr Allan Johnston of Passavant Hospital took her to the vaudeville to see the whip-cracking Fred Lindsay, an Australian-born adventurer. (She criticised his act, and he offered her a job.) Miles never forgot Dr Johnston, not surprisingly if, as she more than once recalled, he was sacked for proposing to her when she was a patient at the hospital.[37]

She also had time to write. The play previously mentioned as preserved in typescript, and a short story, also unpublished, are both dated 1908. The four-act play, a Chicago-influenced sociological drama entitled 'The Survivors', gives an inkling of her thinking on the relationship between art and life at this time, and is characteristically spirited. It tackles a big theme: the relationship between rich and poor in the modern city; and the romance between wealthy actress Avis Gaylord and the embittered working-class intellectual Dick Dallas is a touch on the times. Recently praised as 'highly actable' and an example of a now forgotten genre, the suffrage play, it was the first of five plays the always stagestruck Miles would write in America. (She wrote some thirty plays and film scripts overall, most of them never published.) The short story, 'Uncle Robert's Wedding Present', revolves around the marriage question and the benefits of a spirited approach to it — more familiar territory.[38]

Both writings are signed 'Miles Franklin, Shawondasee', a placename in Connecticut. As evidenced by postcards home, in the summer of 1908 Miles went east from Chicago for the first time. She stayed with the writer and suffragist Jessie Childs and her husband on Riverside Drive, 'the most fashionable part of New York', and took a trip to Stonington, Connecticut, with Margaret Robins' younger sister, Mary E. Dreier, president of the New York WTUL. There had been an earlier break too, in the Illinois lake country. Summer breaks would become a regular feature of Miles' life in America.[39]

On 1 January 1909 Miles Franklin made the first of the brief daily entries in her pocket diaries that run in a virtually unbroken series to 1 January 1954. Early entries confirm that in her own time she continued to write, though she told no one. They show too that she was often unwell, from the cold and possibly from nervous exhaustion, perhaps partly as a result of being alone and far from home. In consequence some weeks she seems to have spent almost half her time in her room at the Harvard Hotel on Washington Street, West Side. When she moved there from Park Street is undocumented, though she sent a postcard from there in November 1908; nor do we know why she left this comfortable-looking abode for less satisfactory accommodation on 12 East Indiana Street after she returned from an extended break in Wisconsin later in the year. Apparently Mrs Robins had a hand in the first move: in an undated letter to Alice Henry she admitted she was glad she had intervened to move Miles from Park Street to another part of the city once she had recovered from the harsh winter, as she feared anxiety about Miles was affecting Alice's health too. A more mundane consideration surely was the saving on rent over the summer breaks away from Chicago. Rules also varied in the residentials. When Miles moved into Indiana House after her summer break in 1909, she was able to hire a piano and resumed lessons.[40]

No matter how demanding the work — and by 1909 Miles was *de facto* secretary of the league — the reality was that single women like her, 'women adrift' as they were often called, had a lot of time in which to pursue their own interests. Despite bleak moments, which reliance on daily diary entries may easily overemphasise, Miles was forever gregarious. Some weeks she was out most nights. For example, in January 1909 she was singing in the league chorus, attending a 'reading class', and going to a stenographers' dinner on a weekly basis. Even when she was not out, she seldom ate alone. Dutch-born mathematician and musician Arnold Dresden and his wife, Louise, the league's shipping clerk, who became Miles' lifelong friends, must have lived nearby, as they often dined with her at the Harvard; likewise she often ate at the Robinses' apartment in nearby West Ohio Street, or with Alice Henry, with whom she also attended concerts and events at the Art Institute. She even attended church occasionally, to hear the famous Episcopalian Bishop Samuel Fallows of Chicago, and at a Christian Science church.[41]

A highlight was the Chicago league's Anniversary Ball on 22 February 1909. Miles and three of her colleagues — Agnes Nestor of the glove workers' union, fellow office worker and member of the stenographers' union Olive Sullivan, and Mary McEnerney, founder of the bindery women's union — were among those chosen to sing that night. Dressed in Norwegian peasant costumes, the ensemble sang the 'Spinning-Wheel

Chorus' from *The Flying Dutchman*: 'a great success', she recorded. Another notable outing was a league delegation to the state capital, Springfield, in late April, led by Mrs Robins, to further the league's legislative program. Agnes Nestor and Elizabeth Maloney of the Chicago waitresses' union addressed the Illinois Senate on working conditions, to great effect; and Miles, who helped with lobbying at Springfield, went to see Abraham Lincoln's house. She also had a taste of industrial action closer to home when, a month earlier, led by temporary union president Magdalen Dalloz, stenographers at various union offices in Chicago walked out after their demand for a half holiday was rejected by their bosses (though it is unlikely she was personally affected, as she was privately employed by Mrs Robins, who took charge of the protest).[42]

In mid-1909, from June to September, Miles took a lengthy and beneficial break in adjacent Wisconsin, during which time she attended a summer school at the University of Wisconsin, Madison. While at the summer school, she stayed at Kappa Kappa Gamma House and studied French and the poetry of Tennyson, made new friends and, as usual, enjoyed the attentions of several young men. Her Chicago friends missed her, but she was refreshed by walks 'on the hill' and canoeing on the lakes, musical evenings, even attending a circus. It was all great fun, she told the *Book Lover*. When she returned to work in September, Mrs Robins was pleased to note how well she looked: 'All the lieutenants are returning from their vacations and Stella Franklin has brought back red cheeks.'[43]

Miles Franklin delighted in Mrs Robins as her 'good fairy'. By late 1909, with the larger picture in mind, she described her employer to Australian readers as follows:

> In a country where brilliant women abound at every turn, Mrs Robins is easily one of the ablest and most remarkable of living Americans. The prominence which is her due is forced upon her daily in increasing degree … In the prime of the early thirties, she has beauty, birth, wealth, superb physical strength, a brilliant intellect, a vivid and delightful personality, and a few years since formed a romantic and ideal marriage with Raymond Robins, who brought his Brooklyn heiress to live the life of the people in a fourth-floor tenement flat in the most congested of Chicago's broad acres of slums. With the executive ability of a Prime Minister, intensely practical, and at the same time imbued with

lofty ideals and infectious enthusiasm, anything she undertakes is sure of success.[44]

That justifiable assessment was written on the occasion of the second biennial convention of the NWTUL, held in Chicago from 27 September to 1 October 1909, when Miles, who was listed as office secretary and representative of the stenographers and typists' union, served as convention secretary. The league, founded in Boston in 1903 on a British model by William Walling and Mary Kenny Sullivan, had been organised on a national basis at the first convention in Norfolk, Virginia, in 1907, following smaller interstate conferences earlier in the year that addressed the question of how women's trade unionism could be strengthened, and resolved that the league should pursue the twin aims of full citizenship for women and closer association with the American Federation of Labor (AFL). In Chicago in 1909 there were seventy-one delegates from sixteen cities in attendance. A feature, duly reported, was that of those seventy-one women, fifty-nine were working women, the rest social settlement women and 'allies'; that is, non working-class women who supported the league's aims or delegates from women's clubs. A handsome NWTUL medallion, designed by Chicago sculptor Julia Bracken Wendt in 1908, depicts a mother with child before a factory clasping the hand of Justice over three slogans — the eight-hour day, a living wage, and 'To Guard the Home' — and in her left hand Justice carries a shield inscribed 'Victory'. The alliance of working and non-working women under Mrs Robins was to make the league a success in coming years, and is one of its most significant historical features, in that the alliance made working women's unionism both respectable and effective, at least until World War I.[45]

A second significant factor in the league's success was its relationship with the AFL. Although the early years were difficult, devoted to trying to build up the organisation on meagre resources and gradually discovering what its role as a national body was to be, Mrs Robins and her trade union associates early understood that the league's relationship with the AFL, which consisted mainly of skilled male workers led by the redoubtable (and initially sceptical) Samuel Gompers, was essential if the league's work were to be situated in the mainstream of American industrial relations. With the league's national headquarters in Chicago, an important labour city, the association gradually strengthened. Starting from little more than a desk shared with the Chicago league at the Chicago Federation of Labor's building at 275 La Salle Street in 1908, when Alice Henry began to edit the *Union Labor Advocate* women's section, the national body progressed to shared rooms in the CFL's new premises on the even more central Dearborn Street, and ultimately a space of its own there.[46]

As assistant to Margaret Robins, Miles did not even have a desk to begin with. However, it probably did not matter much. A lot of her work was done at the Robinses' apartment, which it seems was not far from the Harvard Hotel where she also took work, mainly typing. From the apartment it was only a few blocks south to the league desk on La Salle Street, if she was needed there. Moreover, like Mrs Robins, she got along with the CFL men very well. Against her memories of tiptoeing around male sensibilities — 'we *were* as quiet as mice and as chaste and correct as dedicated nuns' — was 'the fervour and self-sacrifice' of those days, when increasing worker militancy coincided with heightened suffrage energies in America, as in Britain, and the league's participation in strikes assuaged male doubts about the capacities of women workers and their 'allies'. As the league historian Gladys Boone noted, the years 1909 to 1913 put the league on the map.[47]

The NWTUL September 1909 convention was Miles' first, and marked the onset of increasingly arduous duties. With the first great uprising of clothing workers in New York in late 1909, followed by a strike that lasted from 22 November 1909 to 15 February 1910, the league won its industrial spurs by supporting the strikers in various essential ways, and its role became increasingly clear. Although Miles was not directly involved — her time would come the following year — the combination of the convention and the New York strike made for more clerical work in Chicago, and year's end found her very tired.

In late 1909 the personal column of the *Sydney Morning Herald*, which carried gossipy items contributed by readers, noted that she was thinking seriously about returning to Australia. 'I am now well enough to be growing outrageously homesick, so intend to work very hard so I can make tracks for the Great South within a year or so,' she wrote from the summer school in Madison on 21 August. 'I have just finished correcting the proofs of a yarn that is to appear in book form in the near future, and mean to take up my rusty pen again.'[48]

Buoyed by the imminent publication of *Some Everyday Folk and Dawn* by Blackwood, and by references to it in the press at home (supplied by whom is unclear), and by the publication of a short story — the previously mentioned 'Jilted' — in the *Australasian* of 14 August 1909, Miles was now admitting to renewed literary aspirations, but she made no mention of new work, of which it turns out there was a good deal. Not all the output that survives in manuscript in the Franklin Papers is dated, but it seems clear that when she told the *Sydney Morning Herald* in August 1909 that she was considering returning to the literary life in Australia, she had already that year written three short stories (possibly more) and another novel ('When Cupid Tarried', later turned into a play). The irony for her would be that the Australian reception of *Some Everyday Folk and Dawn* was lukewarm, and worse in England, as noted by the *Book Lover*, which loyally rose to her defence; and the short story 'Jilted' dated back to 1900.[49]

The *Australasian* said the story was interesting, and it kept Miles' name before the public. What seems more significant now is her resuscitation of the tale at this time. Possibly it has a bearing on the otherwise impenetrable silence that descended on her relationship with Edwin Bridle back in 1907. On 27 May 1908, at Waverley, Sydney, Edwin Bridle married Australia Wentworth Lea Little, known as 'Trallie'. Miles apparently made no comment on this or later events in his life, such as the five children borne by Trallie or the family's move to Queensland in 1928. Yet it is likely she knew of the marriage, and she was aware of Edwin's death in 1953. Moreover, she developed a distinctive angle on jilting in her second Chicago novel, *On Dearborn Street*, begun in 1913 and published posthumously (1981). Here a woman, Sybyl, is the jilted one, as she defiantly says to her would-be suitor:

> One man nearly as good as you was once engaged to me, yet I'm free! Thank God! They say any fool can get married but it takes a devilish clever woman to remain an old maid, so that is the distinction I covet. When a man becomes too vigorously engaged to me, I change my geographical location and then he jilts me. I just love to be jilted. It relieves me of all responsibility and leaves the other fellow a friend for life.

Sybyl then produces a wedding ring: 'He had the ring all ready and then I moved, so he jilted me. He was so sorry for me that he sent me the ring as a souvenir.'[50]

If this vignette has any basis in Miles Franklin's experience — and according to her early biographer Marjorie Barnard, she was wearing a wedding ring when she returned to Australia in late 1932, though no one knew why — it suggests that with Edwin Bridle her bluff had been called. It is also the case that she would become increasingly preoccupied with positive roles for older unmarried women in her writing from 1909.[51]

The new writing included a campus tale dated June 1909, set in Wisconsin, in which a brilliant young graduate solves 'The Mystery of Her Parentage' (viz. the mother died in childbirth and she was fostered out by her distraught father). Another more amusing effort was the futuristic novel 'When Cupid Tarried', set at Illiwah Point, Sydney, and of uncertain provenance but recast as a play ('The Love Machine') late that year. 'Old Fawcett's Delusion', a ghostly story set somewhere like Uncle Gus' property at Peak Hill, was probably written about this time too, and there is a fleeting reference to a story about one Phillip Bohrer in Miles' diary. Although none of these writings reached publication, those extant are not without interest today (especially the novel/play, sent to Blackwood in 1910 and later to Lothian), not just as a measure of Miles' literary pulse, but in themselves. Harrie, the eccentric younger sister in 'When Cupid Tarried'/'The Love Machine', believes that hope for her sisters' unfulfilled romances lies in a scientific advance, the 'love machine', invented by an isolated professor living nearby: with it she would fix things, including her own emotional needs. This she manages to do, due to her 'experimental mind': 'A free untrammelled spirit [would be] neither narrowed nor embittered by the subjection of her sex, but possessed of a soaring, experimental mind of high intelligence and quick perceptions ...' It is surely of some significance that Miles was reading H. G. Wells' *Ann Veronica*, depicting a young woman's struggle for autonomy and independence, at this time.[52]

On 14 October 1909 Stella Miles Franklin turned thirty. There is no mention of her birthday in her diary (nor would she ever mention her birthday, at least not until very late in life, and then only because her Aunt Lena insisted on marking it). Sometimes she worried that the strain of her dual life would prove too much, and that her strength would fail, which is hardly surprising. Most of her work involved traipsing around the crowded and noisy streets of central Chicago, from her residential to Mrs Robins' flat, to the league 'office' at La Salle Street, to meetings. Her hours were variable, with a good deal of evening activity, as was inevitable in a semi-philanthropic organisation whose executive consisted mostly of working women. 'You can imagine me walking these pavements,' she wrote on a postcard of the thirteen-floor Monadknock Building on West Jackson Boulevard, off Michigan Avenue. But stylised images of impressively tall buildings scarcely convey the reality of life within 'the Loop' (a term describing the route of the elevated railway, or 'El', encircling the central business district, built in the 1890s and still operating). The rush and crush were phenomenal. In 1902 Vida Goldstein had feared she would be knocked over in the streets: 'the Chicagoans tear along like perfect tornadoes,' she later said.[53]

Chicago's dramatic changes of season made Miles feel homesick. Living alone in a strange city was hard, she was not well off, and there were few opportunities for supplementing her income. Presumably she was paid for contributions to the *Sydney Morning Herald* — financial records of any kind are lacking for Miles until 1911 — but it is unlikely that she received anything for her contributions to the *Union Labor Advocate* during the year, and the news about *Some Everyday Folk and Dawn* was disheartening ('a disappointing start'); and in a long letter published in the December issue of the *Book Lover*, she feared she might be overwhelmed by homesickness.[54]

Even so, there is no evidence of actual want in her diary, nor of numbing isolation. At year's end Miles Franklin weighed a healthy-for-height 116.5 pounds (53 kilos), and some interesting compatriots helped keep her buoyant. Sydney portrait painter Portia Geach passed through Chicago in April; July brought the wealthy Melbourne suffragists and Christian Scientists Annie (Nancy) Lister Watson, who had encouraged Alice Henry's desire to travel, and her husband, the retired squatter Philip Sidney ('P. S.') Watson. The Newsham family, also from Australia, living in Chicago from 1906 to 1912, were always hospitable. Besides, the circle of friendship encouraged by the league was large and strong enough to sustain Miles on a daily basis. Arnold and Louise Dresden and the Posts — Alice Thacher Post, chair of the NWTUL Board in 1908, and her husband, the Free Trade intellectual Louis — were among many supportive friends and associates. Christmas Day 1910 was spent at East Indiana House with Alice Henry, the librarian Editha Phelps, a special chum (Miles shared Editha's sense of humour when she said that though not needed in library work, the male organ was a great advantage there), and Leonora Pease, a teacher and part-time student at the University of Chicago. Miles' diary entry for New Year's Eve was forward-looking: 'Thus endeth the old year's record ... Hoping the coming one will be more eventful, less futile, and very lucrative.'[55]

Such sentiments suggest that Miles' primary concern remained her writing. In 1910 she joined the British Society of Authors, and it was in early 1910 that Blackwood withdrew *My Brilliant Career* from sale, in accordance with her instructions. There had been six editions since 1901, and there were 168 copies in stock in December 1909. But it was still selling, with £16 12s in royalties paid to Miles in March 1910. Although Miles' letter of instruction does not survive, it seems clear she wanted to move on. She needed to distance herself from *My Brilliant Career*, particularly in the British market, where *Some Everyday Folk and Dawn*'s suffrage theme was topical, and if the book sold, she would do well out of British royalties as compared with the lower rate she would receive back in Australia. However, she was willing for remaining copies of *My Brilliant Career* to be sold back in Australia, provided no more were printed, adding brightly that she had on hand 'a most inimitable sequel' (evidently 'The End of My Career'), which she suggested Blackwood might like to publish for sale in Australia: 'it contains a story and sketches of Australian people hit off very naturally but withal safely disguised'.[56]

These two occurrences of 1910 point to Miles' strengthening sense of herself as a professional writer and her more business-like approach to writing. Nonetheless, the quickening pace of events in Chicago, and her own capacities, took her deeper into the work of the league. Meanwhile, readers of the *Sydney Morning Herald*'s 'Page for Women' learned how well the wild colonial girl was doing in America:

> Miss Miles Franklin has done more than write a book since she left our shores for America. For the last two years she has been acting as secretary of the National Women's Trades-union League … and was also secretary of the recently-held convention. She and Miss Henry, another Australian, were both delegates … and received a special vote of thanks for their excellent work.[57]

By contrast, Miles' own account of the Chicago convention in the *Union Labor Advocate* was signed 'Mere Onlooker'.

In the wake of the convention came a clear legislative and organisational program. There were eleven points to the legislative program for the protection of wage-earning women, most of whom were young, unskilled and inexperienced, the first two being the enshrinement of the eight-hour day and the elimination of night work, and the last the procurement of a legal minimum wage in the sweated trades. The organisational program addressed other needs, for example, for a district organiser. All that meant more administrative work for Miles. Then came the New York garment workers' strike, and the need to clarify the function of the national league during strikes. Whereas the NWTUL had developed in a somewhat haphazard way, it was now recognised that its affairs should be put on a sound business basis, rather than relying on the philanthropic impulse. Thus it was decided at an executive meeting in St Louis in May 1910 that Stella Franklin would be employed as league secretary fulltime and paid $25 weekly from the league's treasury rather than Mrs Robins' private purse, more than twice what she had been receiving.[58]

One of the most appealing photographs of Miles Franklin dates from around this time. In it, she is relaxing in a deckchair on the rooftop at 12 East Indiana Street, her hat in her lap, with the city in the background. She seems settled, and indeed her life was now considerably more predictable. It was shaped by the seasons, with much culture consumption in winter months, a long break away from the city in summer, and renewed league activity on her return. Thus her outings in January included park concerts on Sundays, opera matinées, a sculpture exhibition at Hull-House, and hearing the fiery freethinker Emma Goldman speak; there were piano and singing lessons during the year, and among the many evening meetings Miles continued to attend were those of the stenographers' union, where she was elected to the executive.[59]

In August came the summer holiday, in 1910 spent with Editha Phelps at a bungalow camp at Harbor Springs, near Petoskey on the north-eastern shore of Lake Michigan, a restful period, with walks on the shore and canoeing, and since Miles immediately hired a typewriter, presumably there was time to write. The highlight of her holiday came in mid-August, when she visited Hiawatha country, a 'red-letter' day: 'Indians lovely', she enthused in her diary. In one of several postcards to her mother, from We-que-ton-sing, she said it reminded her of Brindabella. Another, of the imposing Chief High Horse, signals the importance of the American experience in her later approach to indigenous Australians.[60]

Perhaps Miles Franklin worked on 'The Old House on the Corner' at this time, or started a modern tale of experimental marriage and its consequences, 'Not All a Coward', dated October 1910, and bearing some slight resemblance to a later play, 'Virtue', also unpublished, the only two identifiable new fictions of the year. More likely, she prepared 'When Cupid Tarried' for publication. It was certainly despatched to Blackwood on her return to Chicago. Her only actual publications for the year were résumés from league publications: 'Cheap Blouses' in the *Sydney Morning*

Herald and 'The Price of Cheapness' in the Sydney *Worker* (with Miles urging all women in the former to refuse to wear garments produced by sweated labour, and in the latter to vote for more labour men in parliament).[61]

Miles was just back from Harbor Springs, with barely time to send 'When Cupid Tarried' off to Blackwood when, on 22 September, a small group of girls working for the clothing manufacturer Hart, Schaffner and Marx struck against a wage cut, followed by another group on 29 September. So began the Chicago garment workers' strike of 1910–11.[62]

Within three weeks of the first small strikes, over 40,000 garment workers were out, directly affecting some 100,000 families in Chicago, and by late November, the entire city. The workers' grievances were many, from wage cuts to heavy fines for damaged work. There was no minimum wage as in England and Australia, or, at the outset, any recognition of collective bargaining rights. Not surprisingly, some women workers would soon seek league support.[63]

The new militancy among the unskilled and mainly immigrant workers in the sweatshops of Chicago did not find the league unprepared, though it was a few weeks before it was called in, and Miles continued to work on other projects. An article called 'Cotillion', possibly for the *Union Labor Advocate,* went to the printer on 27 October, for example, and on 5 October she accompanied Mrs Robins on a speaking engagement at Oshkosh, Wisconsin. Later that month she helped to entertain visiting British unionists Margaret Bondfield and Marion Ward. There was even time for a concert at Orchestra Hall. But the pace of work was tiring, and the league was about to move into overdrive.[64]

Even before the national council of the United Garment Workers of America called a general strike, some women workers had asked the Chicago WTUL for help; and it was not long afterwards that the union accepted a formal offer of assistance from the national league. The league itself formed a strike committee at a meeting at Hull-House at the end of October, with Mrs Robins chairman-treasurer and subcommittees set up on picketing, grievances, organisation, publicity and so on. Miles Franklin became chair of the publicity committee.

She had plenty to work with. The grievances committee under Katharine Coman immediately collected strikers' stories, and the citizens' committee, also formed at the Hull-House meeting, produced its own report, based on worker testimony from the worst of the sweatshops. Miles joined picket lines, organised by Emma Steghagen of the boot and shoe makers' union, where she saw police brutality at first-hand, attended rallies, including one at Pilsen Park where Mrs Robins spoke, and, on 14 November, 'went out investigating conditions on the N. W. side'. Her diary for the crowded days of November records the early preparation of a statement from the league for general distribution, and the establishment of effective contacts with churchmen (a Church Cooperation Committee was formed on 18 November of which she was a member). She also attended court as a witness for picketing workers over several days (but was not called). All in all, her efforts were rewarded in that by the end of the month the public had been aroused, calls for arbitration were heard, and, though this was not her responsibility, considerable sums were being raised by the league to support the strikers, who were by then, with winter setting in, in great need but standing firm.[65]

The league was especially important in sustaining their resolution. On Friday 11 November Miles' diary records, 'Terrible jam of people at 275 La Salle [headquarters of the Chicago Federation of Labor] coming for money.' Most of them were unorganised workers without strike funds, and the local council of the United Garment Workers was already in the red. There was nothing in the kitty for the 10,000-odd workers who waited patiently through the day. In consequence, CFL leader John Fitzpatrick organised commissary stores to dispense strike benefits in kind, obtained at cost from wholesalers and paid for by the national garment workers' union, and run by league workers for up to 50,000 claimants daily when the strike was at its peak. What a task it was to obtain the food and meet other urgent needs, such as for rent assistance and coal, and deal with the voucher system established by the experienced Fitzpatrick; but evidently it worked, as there was virtually no violence at CFL headquarters (or in any other aspect of the strike). However, since the strikers at first shrank from what seemed like charity, it was necessary to prepare a bulletin explaining the situation. No doubt that too was the responsibility of 'S. M. Franklin', as she usually signed herself in America. Later she and Alice Henry would claim of the scheme adopted for the provision of groceries on a fixed rations scale at commissary stations: 'As far as we know such a plan has never before been adapted to the needs of women nor carried out by organized labor for the benefit of a large unorganized group.' The contribution of the 'allies' was also significant. In March 1911, after what Mrs Robins defiantly called 'the hunger bargain' was struck by early February, it was estimated that the league had raised about two-thirds of the strike funds, some $40,000 of the nearly $65,000 raised by the league and the CFL combined.[66]

By December 1910, it had seemed that the strike might succeed. Reconciliation between the largest of the employers, Hart, Schaffner and Marx, and its work force had begun, and would soon be successful. Although the more obdurate employer associations remained opposed to any recognition of workers' rights, the strikers were not about to capitulate, as demonstrated by a great parade through the streets of Chicago by some 30,000 strikers to cheer a phalanx of speakers in West Side Ball Park. As recounted by Miles and Alice Henry, they 'evinced their faith in the common brotherhood of labor'.[67]

That ringing phrase concludes the first of three articles on the strike written by the two Australians at the time, entitled 'Chicago at the Front: A Condensed History of the Garment Workers' Strike'. Miles was working on it at Dearborn Street on 5 December, and Mrs Robins called by to approve it soon after, on 7 December. Nine days later, on Friday 16 December, Miles' diary entry records that she went to 'make up on [the] magazine'. This seems to be her first reference to the league's latest initiative, *Life and Labor*, a monthly publication of thirty-two pages geared to the needs of working women, which first appeared in January 1911, selling at 10 cents a copy and featuring the still very readable 'Chicago at the Front'. (The second and third articles on the strike appeared in subsequent issues.) The last days of 1910 saw Miles running between Dearborn and La Salle streets, from strike committee meetings to 'getting out magazine', as the diary entry for 29 December has it, and she was too busy on New Year's Eve for resolutions.[68]

The league executive appointed Alice Henry editor-in-chief and Stella Miles Franklin assistant editor of the new publication. As will be seen, Miles became a substantial contributor too. For all her cautiously revived hopes for her singing voice and her numerous literary endeavours since leaving Australia in 1906, a career in journalism had long been more likely; and now, in addition to her other responsibilities, it would come close to reality. Amazing to relate, news of her new role appeared in the *Nepean Times*, Penrith, on 18 February 1911, where it was noted that the first issue of *Life and Labor* contained a condensed history of the garment workers' strike as it stood at the time of going to press.

6

THE NET OF CIRCUMSTANCE:
MARCH 1911–OCTOBER 1915

'I love my work very much …'[1]

The Chicago garment workers' strike was brought to an abrupt halt on 3 February 1911 by the leader of the national garment workers' union, Thomas Rickert, an old-style craft unionist more concerned about securing agreements with employers than the problems of unskilled workers, who in consequence gained little from their heroic struggle. The sudden ending of the strike left many loose ends to be tied up by the strike committees, and it was not until March that the Women's Trade Union League and its officers could feel their duties done. Inevitably there was much suffering in the aftermath — as Mrs Robins said, 'the hunger bargain' had been struck — and small prospect of returning to old ways back at the office, with a monthly magazine to get out as well.[2]

These later American years were perhaps the most astonishing of Miles Franklin's life. She held down a demanding job in one of the most rackety cities in the world while in her own time writing compulsively, producing some three novels and at least two plays over the next four years. And although there was no phrase for it then, her biological clock was relentlessly ticking over. Now into her thirties, and in her prime, it was time to take romance seriously. At the same time the social politics of which the Women's Trade Union League was part took an exciting new turn with the foundation of the Progressive Party in Chicago in 1912, and first-wave feminism faced new issues. Could she encompass it all?

An answer of sorts is to be found in the net of circumstance, which was also the title of her third published novel, begun in 1911 and published in London in 1915 under the extraordinary pseudonym 'Mr & Mrs Ogniblat L'Artsau' (a play on 'Austral Talbingo'), a work that remained virtually unknown until the 1980s, mainly because Miles never divulged the pseudonym. In those years in Chicago before the Great War, Miles Franklin sought to reinvent herself as a modern writer, and so great was the stimulus of time and place, she very nearly succeeded. In political terms, what happened was not so much a reinvention of self as a natural development, since the optimistic Progressivist reform ethos that she enthusiastically espoused flowed readily from the radical politics of New South Wales in which she had been reared. Writing to T. J. Hebblewhite in Goulburn in late 1911, the way Miles put it was that her character was broadening and mellowing, or at least having some of its excessive provincialities and intensities rubbed away 'in the maelstrom of Chicago life'. The imprint would be lifelong.[3]

Back in Australia the Sydney *Worker* welcomed news of 'a new American magazine edited by Alice Henry and Miles Franklin', and the Melbourne *Book Lover* was pleased to note that the first issue of *Life and Labor* carried a poem by local intellectual Bernard O'Dowd: 'This is another step in advance as showing that even among the couple of million fighters for freedom in Chicago, an Australian poet is quoted by an Australian editor of a labour journal.' But for assistant editor S. M. Franklin it was far more complicated than that, of course. With its endless westward-extending grid pattern, Chicago could seem like a web to confuse and trap the individual. On the other hand, it threw up some of the most powerful works of contemporary American literature, not only Theodore Dreiser's *Sister Carrie* and Upton Sinclair's *The Jungle* but also *The Song of the Lark* by Willa Cather. A similar upsurge of creativity occurred in architecture and town planning, poetry and the theatre. Dull would she be of soul to remain unaffected, and whatever else Miles Franklin may have been, dull she was not.[4]

For the moment, however, she was exhausted, or close to it. No sooner had the strike fund been dispersed and a second issue of *Life and Labor* produced, with 'Holding the Fort' the second of the editors' three substantial (unsigned) articles on the strike, than suffrage was back on the agenda. Thus on the morning of 7 March 1911, along with several hundred others, Miles boarded a 'suffrage special' for hearings at the state capital, Springfield, as one of a delegation led by Mrs Robins to represent working women. Two days after they got back, she was called in to help the Chicago league when the switchboard operators went on strike. Thereafter, Miles often went early to the NWTUL office on Dearborn Street and worked there all day, and sometimes also at the Chicago league's office on La Salle Street. There was a statement by Mrs Robins to edit and papers to prepare for monthly executive meetings, along with material for the next biennial convention to be held in Boston in June, which included the draft of an amended constitution.

As well that March, with Alice Henry she wrote the final article on the garment workers' strike for *Life and Labor*, and prepared another account for the *Englishwoman*, published as 'Why 50,000 Refused to Sew' in June 1911. (An edited version also appeared in the Melbourne *Age*.) Mrs Robins, enjoying a break with her husband, Raymond, and two of her sisters, Mary and Dorothea Dreier, at Chinsegut Hill, the Robinses' summer home outside Brookesville in southern Florida, was pleased with the edited statement and wished her 'Dearest little Stella-girl, Most Imperial and Efficient NU Secretary' could be there too.[5]

So much responsibility soon weighed upon Miles. She entered a string of concerns about her health in her pocket diary: her shoulder, her throat, her teeth, her eyes all gave trouble, and she undertook various unspecified treatments in early 1911. An almost devastating blow came when it was decreed that she needed glasses: 'My life has been a series of forcing against the grain & I feel I have no more forcing material left for this last straw,' she wrote on Saturday 29 April, adding irritably that she couldn't see to read or write all day due to the drops administered for her eye examination, and got a blinding headache in the evening. 'Went to bed in despair.'

For all the gloom of her diary and the insomnia which would become such a debilitating feature of her life, her workaday routine, with its ebb and flow of lunch companions and weekly meetings, and the rich cultural round, continued in the now familiar way. For example, one Sunday in March she heard the great African-American leader W. E. Du Bois at the Ethical Society, and she attended several matinées at the Majestic Theatre in April. And in addition to treatments with Hugo Oldenborg, a masseur, she continued to take music lessons.[6]

According to the literary notebooks Miles kept along with her pocket diaries in the 1930s and 1940s, which include reminiscences as well as topical comments, she still harboured hopes for her voice: 'What I want is an income that would free me to study music & to try some method that might mend my voice, & free me to write as a second interest.' She also managed to keep up with the latest novels, reading hot off the press H. G. Wells' *The New Machiavelli*, a New Woman novel with a eugenic slant, his next after *Ann Veronica*, with its then frank treatment of sexual relations, which she had read in 1909. What she thought of either is not recorded but she was no advocate of free love: just another term for promiscuity and thoughtless exploitation of women by men, such as her friend Margery Currey's husband, the journalist Floyd Dell, and others of Chicago's South Side Bohemia, she wrote scathingly in her literary notebook years later. And she had a very different idea from Wells of what the New Woman would be like, preferring to envisage her as more highly evolved, 'nervous and refined' (the word 'nervous' then connoting 'highly strung' or 'sensitive'). Moreover, it seems she was right about Floyd Dell, whose career benefited from Margery Currey's superior social status and skills. Born in Evanston, Illinois, Margery was a Vassar graduate who worked first as a teacher and then as a journalist in Chicago. Due to Floyd's behaviour the marriage lasted only four years, from 1909 to 1913. It was Margery's wit and intellectual vitality that delighted Miles, who seems to have met her before 1912, and ensured a lifelong friendship.[7]

Although she was again becoming terribly tired through the spring of 1911, Miles still had the energy to attend to her own work. On 15 April 1911 she sent three short stories off to a literary agent in New York, and copies to another in London. The three stories were 'Mrs Mulvaney's Moccasins', 'Not All a Coward', and 'The Mystery of Her Parentage', the only new one being 'Mrs Mulvaney's Moccasins', which does not survive in its original American form. It was to be hoped, she wrote to the New York agent Mr D. Murphy, that he would have better luck with these than with her stuff to date (the word 'stuff' replacing 'yarn' in her vocabulary in the United States).[8]

Since the stories were quite slight, more like sketches, their lack of success now seems unsurprising; and if the blushing end of the British version of 'Mrs Mulvaney's Moccasins' is indicative — after crossed wires over a Christmas present meant for housekeeper Mrs Mulvaney, romance develops between the stenographer who sent it and the great author who employs both women and accidentally appropriates the moccasins — no progress had been made on the creative front. Yet all three stories concern women perplexed by modern life, and it seems somehow significant that after a long day typing them up at the office one Saturday, Miles wrote in her diary 'tired but content'. The day after she sent them off, a Sunday, she resumed work on 'The End of My Career'.[9]

Working in the office on the weekend was not unusual for Miles. Long and irregular hours were the norm in partly philanthropic, partly reformist work. By the end of April Miles was feeling 'pretty ill', and her eyes became so troublesome she had to try the 'damned glasses' (a rare instance of swearing). Now she seemed set to become not only patron saint of the snub-nosed but, as used to be feared before the coming of plastic frames in the 1950s, of the socially handicapped. The first photographs of Miles Franklin in glasses date from much later in life, when she was back in Australia, so perhaps the despised glasses were primarily reading glasses. On the other hand, most of the photographic portraits from Chicago days are quite formal (and sometimes almost voluptuously posed), and she did at first wear the glasses outdoors, where they caused her to fall over. In any event she was traumatised.

Miles' uncertain health worried her friends. In the summer approaching, her now close friend the librarian and league ally Editha Phelps invited Miles to go with her on her customary summer vacation to England; and when approached, Mrs Robins, back from Florida, responded generously to the proposal. It was, she wrote to Miles on 17 May, 'a great and beautiful opportunity', and two months' leave was granted, one paid, the second unpaid, as apparently proposed by Editha. Once the Boston convention was over in June, they would be on their way.[10]

Soon Miles was packing for Boston and London. It was a bit awkward, as she had to move out of Indiana House, and in the remaining week in Chicago she and Chicago WTUL ally Zelie Emerson stayed at Ellen Gates Starr's flat at Hull-House, sleeping on the floor. Then, on 6 June, with convention preparations completed and her secretary's report done, she packed her grip and, along with twenty-eight other delegates from Chicago, took the afternoon train to Boston.[11]

In those days inter-urban trains were a treat, provided you travelled in a Pullman car and could avoid the spitting which so appalled many women visitors to America; and this was Miles' first trip to historic Boston. That summer, however, North America was experiencing a heatwave, so that the mid-westerners arrived in Boston on the evening of 7 June feeling distinctly grubby, and although Miles was met by Mrs Robins, who took her by taxi to her billet, for some reason the accommodation proved unsatisfactory.[12]

The convention opened in Barnard Hall on Monday 12 June with seventy-nine delegates. The tone was upbeat. Affiliations had increased since 1909, and more young working women attended. A bill limiting hours of work to ten hours a day had just been passed in Illinois. And in her presidential address, Mrs Robins issued a special call to the women of America to unite with the league and their working sisters to set new standards of social justice: 'The world-old struggle between human slavery and human freedom is being fought out in this age on the battle fields of industry.' Since the situation of women workers she outlined was only too true — 'long hours, small pay, despotic rules and foremen … and the haunting fear of losing one's job' — there was much that a strategic alliance of workers and allies might still hope to achieve. Mrs Robins urged a minimum wage law, necessarily state by state, and always the vote for women (achieved nationally in the United States in 1920).[13]

What Secretary Franklin thought of these recommendations, some of which applied to her own situation, is a matter for speculation. She might be excused a degree of *déjà vu*, in that they mostly already operated in Australia. She was proud of 'advanced Australia' and felt she could contribute to a program predicated on class co-operation. Certainly at this stage she and Alice Henry were valued as officers of the league because they were Australians, and under the new constitutional arrangements for direct election to the NWTUL executive, 'Miss S. M. Franklin, Chicago' was elected national secretary at the convention.[14]

With reports in and agreement reached to convene again in St Louis in 1913, the convention closed on Saturday 17 June. Secretary Franklin was 'thoroughly exhausted'. With Alice Henry, she stayed on (in new accommodation) to catch up on sleep before more league meetings in New York. 'I was very played out after the Convention … I had to sleep for about four days,' she wrote to Isabella Goldstein in Melbourne; but she recovered enough to take in some of the sights of old Boston before leaving for New York.[15]

New York was not a new city to her. Her first visit had been in the summer of 1908, when she resided with Jessie Childs and visited Mary Dreier in the country. This time she stayed with league supporter Violet Pike (later Penty), and the Pike family looked after her between meetings and calls on various colleagues, including Mary Dreier. On one occasion they took her to hear the Russian Symphony Orchestra at Madison Square Gardens. 'New York is a wonderful city,' Miles wrote on a postcard to

Grandma Lampe, dated 26 June 1911, and on another, of Trinity Church, to Aunt Lena next day, she noted that the church drew 'part of its revenue from brothel rentals'. The excitement of her impending departure for London was palpable: 'Miss Phelps is taking me to London for a few weeks to see if it will set me on my feet ... [she] is a dear. She is going to take care of me & arrange things so that I will have nothing to do but enjoy myself,' she wrote to Susannah Franklin. They would be leaving from Quebec on 30 June and be back in Chicago by 1 September.[16]

Miles left New York on 28 June 1911. She travelled north by train to Montreal, where she met Editha and sent her mother another postcard, then she and Editha continued together to Quebec, arriving on the 30th to catch the *Empress of Ireland* later that day. They disembarked at Liverpool nine days later, having passed through ice floes in the Atlantic, and by the shores of 'poor old Ireland' and the beautiful but bleak coast of Scotland, glimpsing also the Isle of Man (where, as Miles Franklin had noted in *Some Everyday Folk and Dawn*, women had had the vote since 1881) as they came in from what was an uneventful trip. Miles early decided the other passengers were dull.[17]

As it happened, the weather was warm in England too. Miles was delighted by the trip south to London via Stratford-on-Avon, where she saw Shakespeare's house and sent a postcard to Susannah Franklin. Like so many New World visitors steeped in the old culture, Miles' response was heartfelt: 'England is beautiful beyond words.' Then it was on to Oxford and London, arriving at Miss Brennan's boarding house at 22 Upper Woburn Place on 10 July.[18]

What a contrast with the previous year's break at Harbor Springs. Here at the heart of the British Empire, Miles, who, like all Australians until 1949, was a British subject, felt quite at home. Even the food agreed with her. Her eyes must still have been bothering her, as Lord Tennyson, now living in Sussex, sent her a recommendation for an oculist. But she saw all the sights, starting with the National Portrait Gallery, and was kept busy visiting friends and associates. Almost first thing she went to a Women's Social and Political Union (WSPU) meeting and heard the Pankhursts speak (having first heard Emmeline Pankhurst in Chicago eighteen months earlier); later, with Editha, at the home of Raymond Robins' sister, the suffrage actress and writer Elizabeth Robins, in Henfield, Sussex, she met Christabel Pankhurst socially, finding it an enjoyable experience. Vida Goldstein was in London too, and she had already made quite an impact; so were young Molly David and Agnes Murphy, formerly social editor of Melbourne *Punch* and now biographer of Melba. As secretary of the National Women's Trade Union League of America, Miles also made contact with prominent British labour women Mrs Philip Snowden, Mary Macarthur and Margaret Bondfield, and with Miss Moore of the People's Suffrage Federation (some of whom were previously visitors to Chicago).[19]

This was Miles Franklin's first encounter with the liberal intelligentsia of London. Among the interesting people she met in 1911 was Florence Dryhurst, translator of the Russian anarchist Kropotkin and a friend of Editha, who in turn introduced her to the well-known radical journalist Henry Woodd Nevinson. She also met the McMillan sisters, Margaret and Rachel, already famed for their child welfare work, and the redoubtable Charlotte Despard, leader of the Women's Freedom League (WFL), a breakaway group from the Pankhursts' authoritarian WSPU. Radical, reputable and progressivist, the largely middle-class WFL was a natural affiliation for Miles and she joined the organisation in 1913.[20]

Editha Phelps, considerably older than Miles (and once mistaken as her chaperone), was, as Miles recalled, 'of the H[enr]y Jamesian school, which still looked to England and Paris for culture', and judging by her contributions to *Life and Labor*, something of a Francophile. Perhaps Editha was the more ardent personality, a strong supporter of the suffragettes and of subject peoples — though she did not care to be touched by them, as Miles reported when they were both warmly welcomed by Maoris at an assembly of 'lesser Colonial breeds' to mark George V's coronation (a traditional event, unlike the Universal Races Congress, for which Miles attended a related meeting in July). According to Miles 'practical equality came to me naturally'. It was Editha's wit that Miles most enjoyed; also, she was very well read. Certainly Editha went down well in London, especially 'at her sparkling unusualest'. It seems that despite the age difference, Miles Franklin had found a fine friend in Editha, what the Irish called an *aquil*.[21]

In early August the two women took a trip to Paris, travelling via Dieppe and Rouen. Miles' diary indicates that she saw the main sights, and postcards were sent to Australia, including one of L'Opéra (where she and Editha saw *Coppelia* and *Rigoletto*). But she didn't enjoy herself greatly. There is a vignette of her and Editha sitting in a typical street café (which Editha liked to do), being pestered by Afghan carpet-sellers. Helen Marot, a league colleague from New York who was also in Paris at the time, later commented that it was a pity Miles had not stayed long enough to appreciate all the city's charms — to which Miles replied that her French was not good enough (alas for the lessons in 1909), and the food had upset her finicky stomach, so she hied herself back 'to the heart of my British Empire'. 'You could not believe what a rest and joy it was to me,' she added, going on to say that the trip had assuaged her homesickness and restored her strength.[22]

Back in London until the end of the month, Miles resumed sociabilities. The 'subject people's exhibition' (as Miles dubbed the coronation event) made her hanker for some 'fun and flirting' — and glamour. One summer's day Mr Michael Valtico, a Greek barrister in London for the coronation, took her to Greenwich by boat. But, she recalled, he was 'druv out' by one Ruiz from Lisbon, also very handsome. There was also Georgie Maquay, son of Florence Dryhurst's sister, 'about whom hang many tales of this London trip, as well as generally in Chicago' (but none are told), and later deemed 'insufferable'.[23]

Altogether more substantial than these flirtatious interludes was an interview for the Women's Freedom League weekly, the *Vote*, which appeared in the September 1911 issue. There had already been a hint in postcards home that the poverty of London was hard to take. The day she returned from Paris, Miles noted a great dockers' strike and later she went down to a strike of women factory workers at Bermondsey. In the *Vote* interview she made so bold as to say that she was glad that the workers of England still had enough stuffing in them to strike. It was in fact the summer of the Triple Alliance, when the coincidence of syndicalist industrial action, suffragette militancy, and the Ulster rebellion against Home Rule for Ireland heightened fears of revolution.[24]

In the interview Miles expressed her commitment to the 'splendid work' in Chicago, and explained that although the vote was her passion, in America it made more sense to address the industrial question first. Never one to miss a trick, however, she referred obliquely to *Some Everyday Folk and Dawn* to underline her suffrage credentials: 'You will judge how I have been "on the active list" if you will do me the honour of reading my book on a political campaign in Australia.' At that moment, as one of the world's few enfranchised women, and as a significant figure in the rising women's trade union movement in America, she occupied the high ground. She was abreast of the most advanced feminist thought too. Editha encouraged her to read Olive Schreiner's *Woman and Labour*, the bible of Edwardian feminism, and for Miles as powerful in its impact as *The Story of an African*

Farm. The new work, she opined, was 'as relieving as rain on the dust after drought'. From London, she sent her mother a copy, along with another book important to her, *Women and Economics* by Charlotte Perkins Gilman, with instructions to read the latter carefully if she had not already done so, and Aunt Lena too.[25]

Then, on 29 August, Miles and Editha left London for Liverpool, where they set sail on the *Empress of Britain* for America later that day. It was not a good trip. They were both seasick most of the way, and glad to be recovering by landfall. From Quebec they caught through trains to Chicago, arriving on 7 September 1911.

Secretary Franklin went straight to the office. It was good to catch up with friends but within days she noted 'no rest or peace at the office'. With post-convention tasks (editing the convention proceedings would occupy her on and off for several months, and the finished product would later be noted by the *Sydney Morning Herald*), fresh administrative demands (for example, Helen Marot, secretary of the New York WTUL, wanted up-to-date league statistics), and getting *Life and Labor* out every few months, there was much to be done; and until the end of September she was again camped in the 'beastly flat' at Hull-House. But she felt much stronger for her summer break and was enjoying Chicago's culture with Editha, including its political culture. Perhaps it was at a single-tax conference she attended with Editha and Alice Henry later in the year that Miles Franklin first encountered the architect-planner Walter Burley Griffin and his brilliant wife, Marion Mahony Griffin, who were to win the international competition to design a new Federal capital of Australia on the Yass-Canberra Plains in 1912.[26]

On 29 September 1911 Miles moved into a new residential hotel north of the Loop at 200 East Superior Street, a main east-west thoroughfare running between Lake Shore Drive and North Michigan Avenue, within easy walking distance of the office on Dearborn Street. 'I pay three dollars a week ... for a big back room [on the fourth floor]', she wrote of it in 1915. 'It is in a house among working people ... a very humble place, but I can squark on my piano without getting on anyone's nerves.' Since her salary, paid by the league from 1910, was and remained $25 per week, $3 a week for accommodation suggests exceptional frugality. However, she had then to pay for meals, cheap as they seem to have been, and outlays for full board of $7 a week in 1911 make it appear more realistic.

These figures come from a notebook in which Miles recorded her weekly personal expenditure from 1911 to 1917. The first week, ending 7 October

1911, records a total expenditure of $19.59, covering the usual things —
board, laundry, fares, a hair net, a theatre ticket, union dues and so on.
More often, however, the amount would be around $12, and one week she
managed on less than $7. The big expenditures, on clothes and health and
travel, would sometimes cause the amount to soar, but on the whole,
like most working women, Miles kept her costs down. Occasional
entertainments aside, piano hire and a post-office box seem to be the extent
of personal indulgence.[27]

What did she do with the rest of her pay? The short answer seems to
be that she saved it. The entries in her Illinois Trust and Savings Bank
passbook, which begin in March 1911 at $100, by January 1915 had reached
$661.26, and when she left for London later in the year she still had $500 in
the account. She also did what migrant workers often do: she sent money
home. According to the notebook, between June 1912 and March 1915 she
sent her mother £190.

Miles Franklin and money is a vital subject. Money was never far from
her mind; and it is obvious from even a cursory glance at early records that
although she never had much, she paid careful attention to it, and that she
was a good saver from the moment it was possible. The frugal habits so
characteristic of her first become apparent at this time.

In October 1911 Miles took two train trips with Mrs Robins on league
business: an overnight trip to Springfield (17–18 October), to promote a
state legislative committee, as determined at the convention; and to attend
a conference in the industrial city of Pittsburgh, Pennsylvania (24–27
October), where the league sought to assist striking mineworkers and their
families. '"It takes some hustling", as the Murkans would say, to be an
executive officer of an organization representing about 40,000 people, and
this is such a vast country,' she wrote to Isabella Goldstein, somewhat in
trepidation of the impending trips. Her report to the national executive on
conditions among the mine workers and their families around Pittsburgh is
one of the most effective pieces of writing about her league work extant: on
the first day of her visit she met with miners in their homes and saw 'the
terrible living conditions, the utter lack of sanitation as represented by
choked drains, and the general desolation of the mining camps'. There were
many meetings over the four days thereafter.[28]

From diary entries it seems Miles did most of the dogsbody work on *Life
and Labor,* preparing dummy issues and endlessly negotiating with Saul
Brothers, the printers, several blocks away on 'Printers' Row' in Federal

Street. Bringing out a journal was very different from what it is today, involving much physical running around, with Miles more than ever on the streets of Chicago. She was often tired out by her day. At first, very little of her own signed work appeared in the magazine, but a vivid piece of reportage, 'More About Pearl Buttons', appeared in December 1911. The button workers of Muscatine, a small factory town on the Mississippi, had originally been locked out, and after the employer failed to honour an agreement, went on strike over union rights and unfair working conditions. At the time of Miles' writing, morale was high, and the article begins with a handsome girl striker from Iowa dancing at the Union Halloween Ball in Chicago in November; however, the dispute dragged on to a stalemate in 1912.[29]

An article on 'The English Labor Uprising' in the October 1911 issue of *Life and Labor* attracted critical comment from Mrs Robins. She complained to her sister Mary that Alice Henry had published it despite other (unspecified) options, remarking, rather obscurely, 'Stella Franklin spent two days in England ... to get the best articles ... and sent them over.' It appears that the article in question, which was unattributed, failed to mention that a spectacular woman suffrage parade in London in June 1911 was part of a coronation procession, hence problematic for the women's movement in republican America. But she was reassured with Miles back: 'Now that Stella is back, and back with a great deal of strength and a great deal of spirit, I am sure there will be fewer mistakes and she has good judgement.' Meanwhile, assistant editor Franklin was not much upset at being drawn into the contretemps, replying jauntily that there were many opinions on the monarchy in America and that they had thick enough skin to cope: 'It is a good thing we were pretty well seasoned before we started upon the innocent diversion of running a magazine or we should never have survived the strain, should we?'[30]

Life and Labor was more than a 'diversion'. It might have been a whole career, as seemed likely for a brief time in 1915 when Miles succeeded Alice Henry as editor. In Chicago, Miles learned to write 'on the stone' — that is, dictating copy directly to the typesetter: a method too speedy for later Australian colleagues like Dymphna Cusack, and probably for her own good. From 1912 she contributed feature articles to the magazine under her own name (plus occasional articles to the Australian press) at an increasing rate. She also contributed an irregular book review page, 'When We Have Time to Read', which first appeared in June 1911 with a gentle reminder of league policy that working women would not be able to keep up with modern thought without an eight-hour day and the living wage. Under this rubric 'S. M. Franklin' would later review topical titles such as *The Promised Land* by Mary Antin, said to be one of the first great works of Jewish-American literature, and Elizabeth Robins' most recent suffrage story, *Way Stations*.[31]

Alongside the first 'When We Have Time to Read' column, Alice Henry, as editor, extolled Chapter 14 of Lester Ward's *Pure Sociology*, a book that would have a significant impact on Miles at this time. She ranked it 'among the very few works which have revolutionised thought and helped humanity along a fresh line of progress'. All but forgotten today, except in the history of American sociology, where his creative environmentalism has been seen as foreshadowing the criteria of evolutionary biology, Lester Frank Ward was to become *Life and Labor*'s favourite thinker: his 'gynaecentric' theory made the female sex primary and the male secondary in the organic scheme, and the age-long masculine supremacy but a passing phase. The times, Alice Henry wrote, gave every hope of a restoration of 'a better balanced world': 'The present tremendous uprising among women, so long kept down, and the parallel uprising among the working folks also so long kept down and suppressed, are linked together and seen to be both different expressions of a sound and normal impulse under which the world promises to progress as never before.'[32]

The entry on Ward in *American National Biography* states that in *Pure Sociology* Ward built a kind of scientific theory in support of women's freedoms and rights, arguing that in nature, femaleness was basic and maleness accidental or variational. Thus today's woman was at least equal to man and, with more opportunity, might well surpass him in talent and genius. 'In my young days we used to set great store on Lester Ward's *Pure Sociology* the Fourteenth Chap.,' Miles advised a young playwright in Brisbane in 1948, and a copy of the 1911 edition of *Pure Sociology* is to be found in her library.[33]

When Ward died in 1913, *Life and Labor* saluted 'the greatest American sociologist', and noted among his most important followers another profound influence on Miles, Charlotte Perkins Gilman. The journal's view of Ward was one that Gilman was happy to uphold in word and deed. In her autobiography, *The Living of Charlotte Perkins Gilman*, she extolled Ward as 'quite the greatest man I have ever known', and woman's struggle to circumvent the constraints of male-dominated society was among the most common themes in the *Forerunner*, a monthly magazine she wrote and published single-handedly from 1909 to 1916 to promote her ideas, including those on literature. In 'Masculine Literature', Chapter 5 of *The Man-Made World: Or Our Androcentric Culture*, Gilman elaborated on an 'over-masculine' influence on literature, seen in the dominant modes of story-as-adventure and the love story (dismissed as little more than tales of premarital struggle). 'Today,' she wrote, 'the art of fiction is being re-born. Life is discovered to be longer, wider, deeper, richer, than these monotonous players of one tune would have us believe.'[34]

Gilman was certainly one of the leading intellectuals of the women's movement in the United States. She had been famous as an author since *The Yellow Wallpaper*, the classic portrayal of a woman's nervous collapse caused by a repressive marriage, which appeared in 1892, and *Women and Economics: A Study of the Economic Relations Between Men and Women as a Factor in Social Relations,* first published in 1898, made her name as a theorist by identifying the sex relationship as an economic relationship as well. Interestingly, she did not call herself a feminist, rejecting gender definitions of the world as too narrow for the liberal evolutionary processes she believed were, or could be, under way, preferring the term 'humanist'.[35]

Both Ward and, especially, Charlotte Gilman were crucial to Miles Franklin's way of thinking by 1911 and to her efforts to reinvent herself thereafter. *Life and Labor* published snippets of Gilman from time to time, and advertised her *Forerunner* magazine (Miles' friend Margery Currey was Gilman's agent). And according to Miles, who heard her speak several times in Chicago in 1912, Mrs Gilman was 'incomparably the greatest American woman alive ... a vivific force who promulgates new thought'. In October 1912, the great one autographed the first of two bound volumes of the *Forerunner* which Miles had earlier purchased; and when Mrs Gilman returned to Chicago in December, Miles acted as her 'page' and dined with her at the plush new La Salle Hotel — on which occasion Miles also souvenired a wash rag from Mrs Gilman's bathroom to send home to Rose Scott, who had first introduced her to Gilman's writings. 'I told her ... you were the first to put *In This Our World* into my hands when my young heart was breaking with the immorality of a man-worshipping society,' Miles wrote to Rose.[36]

The case for Gilman's influence on Miles rests on three points: that Miles thought enough of the early issues of the *Forerunner* to purchase a set (the volumes were purchased in August 1912 and January 1913); that in those early issues Gilman nominated fresh fields of fiction germane to Miles' plight as a writer; and that recent research into the intellectual underpinnings of Edwardian feminism casts what Miles did write in a fresh light.[37]

The first point requires no further comment. The second takes us back to 'Masculine Literature' and Gilman's view that 'the humanising of woman' had opened up fresh fields for fiction. Five such fields were identified by Gilman. First is the young woman who is obliged to give up her 'career' — meaning her humanness, says Gilman — for marriage, and who objects. Second is the middle-aged woman who finds her discontent is due to 'social starvation', that it is not love but more business in life that she needs. Third is the interrelation of women with women, not previously envisaged except in convents and harems. Fourth comes the lifelong interaction between mother and child. Fifth, and here it is best to quote directly, is 'the new attitude of the full-grown woman, who faces the demands of love with the high standards of conscious motherhood'. The list is merely indicative, she concludes, with many other broad and brilliantly promising fields possible. (Had the concept of life cycle been invented then she would surely have used it.) The third point is that there is a marked congruence between Miles Franklin's writings over the coming decade and the content of New Woman fiction as sketched by Gilman.[38]

These writings of Miles consist of five 'Chicago novels', only two of which ever attained publication: the 'lost' novel, *The Net of Circumstance*, which dates from late 1911 and was published in 1915, and *On Dearborn Street*, from 'Notes for Sybil: A Magdalen's Dream', begun in 1913 and published posthumously in 1981. Still in manuscript are 'Red Cross Nurse and Armoured Chauffeur', subtitled 'Confessions of a Frustrated Grandmother' (now known simply as 'Red Cross Nurse'), dating from 1914; 'Love Letters of a Superfluous Woman' (c.1919); and 'Sam Price from Chicago' (1921). There are also a number of unpublished (and almost certainly unperformed) plays, mostly only vaguely dated: 'Mag-Marjorie', a dramatisation of a novel by Gilman, and 'Aunt Sophie Smashes a Triangle' (both c.1913); 'Virtue: A Comedy in Four Acts' (c.1916 or later, by Mr & Mrs O. L'Artsau); 'Somewhere in London' (c.1916); 'The English Jackeroo' (1916); and 'By Far Kaimacktcthalan' (c.1918). Finally, there is a handful of short stories, such as the undated 'Teaching Him' (about a wife's need for economic independence); 'When Bobby Got Religion' (1914); and 'A Business Emergency' (1915). These writings are almost all set in a city, either Chicago or London; they mostly revolve around 'the full grown woman'; and they variously address the question Carolyn Heilbrun identified in *Writing a*

Woman's Life as the great stopper of women's biography, the question that Miles herself was asked at the time by free-love advocates such as Floyd Dell and his then complicit wife, Margery Currey: 'What do you want?'[39]

This body of work constitutes Miles Franklin's middle period, and provides a glimpse of its vitality. Except for *On Dearborn Street*, however, none of it is accessible except via the Franklin Papers in the State Library of New South Wales, or in the case of *The Net of Circumstance*, the British Library, London, where a copy was deposited by the publisher, as required by British copyright law, and where it was first rediscovered. Thus the writings of Miles' middle period remained hidden away for some sixty years, and very little of it has been published or subjected to critical scrutiny since.[40]

Overall, the writings show not just that Miles' creative drive did not dry up away from Australia, but that in America she sought to enter new terrain as a writer. Whereas it may seem the Chicago novels all start from much the same place as *My Brilliant Career*, this is not quite right, as literary history would also suggest. Modern research on the previously overlooked New Woman fiction phase in English literature, which lasted from 1880 to 1914, has unearthed a number of early twentieth-century feminist writers who were bringing new psychological, though not necessarily progressive, insights to bear on the paradoxes of 'love and freedom' (Olive Schreiner's formulation). As mentioned earlier, Miles was scathing about the fevered sexual experiments of bohemian associates in Chicago, whose blandishments she firmly resisted; indeed, as a social purity feminist of the dominant turn-of-the-century school, she found their proposals revolting. But what did this mean creatively speaking? In seeking to reinvent herself, her problem was to find a way between the sexual preoccupations in the writings of her contemporaries and her own fastidiousness as an older-style feminist. As Ann Heilmann, a leading scholar in the field of the New Woman genre, has noted:

> New Woman fiction constitutes a boundary marker between nineteenth and twentieth-century variants of the female *Künstlerroman* ... This transition was by no means an easy one. Indeed ... many writers concentrated on the factors which conspired to turn the gifted woman into an *artist manqué*.'[41]

It is a surprise to find that *The Net of Circumstance* appeared under the imprint of Mills & Boon, as it seems much closer to New Woman fiction than the purple heart-throb tales for which the publishing house is now famous. However, in the early years of the twentieth century, Mills & Boon was a relatively new publishing house with a range of titles and the work of other Australian writers appeared under its imprint too; for instance, Dorothea Mackellar and Ruth Bedford's *Outlaw's Luck*. In essence, *The Net of Circumstance* is a richly woven document of contemporary Chicago life as experienced by Constance Roberts, a youngish working woman from the rural hinterland whose hopes for a new life in the city have been stalemated by low pay and the daily grind. At the outset of the tale, all Constance has is her pride: 'There was nothing creative or expansive of her left.' Worse, she was now feeling old and defeated as she sensed that the 'struggle during the spring-time of life robs her of life's fulfilment for all time'.[42]

The Net of Circumstance provides a more or less happy end to the tale of Constance Roberts, but her sufferings are great, due to overwork, poor food and noise at the Mary-Anne residential she is obliged to inhabit, and the bouts of illness which drive the plot. Worse still are the philanthropic interventions of 'steatopigious' persons (Miles' wilder words usually relate to something arcane, in this case 'steatopygia', meaning excessive fatness of the buttocks), and a confusion of suitors.[43]

Most problematic for Constance is the male feminist. She would probably have preferred the 'unadulterated maleness' of the rich and wholesome young Tony Hastings to the earnest playwright Osborne Lewis, to whom she eventually commits herself, but this was not to be, due to Tony's wicked mother and the onset of war in Europe. What Constance most objects to about Osborne Lewis is his unintentionally exploitative attitude to her as a source for better women characters in his plays. Perhaps he grasps the dimension of the problem but his articulation makes him sound as if he is trying to come to grips with Charlotte Perkins Gilman:

> The realization, still rare in this age, that woman is the more complex vessel, to the requirements of whose happiness and honour social and industrial conditions have need to be adjusted with so much greater delicacy and ethical precision than is necessary in the case of the more elemental male, had led him to study with keen sympathy the underlying trend of the feministic movement filling song and story.[44]

At first Constance is unimpressed and evasive: Osborne Lewis has 'no conception of the heart of a free woman'. Still, he does learn, and he does give Constance the credit by declaring her the co-author of his next play; but that is the *artist manqué* solution predicted by Heilmann's analysis of New Woman fiction, and he is, after all, rather feeble. Perhaps Constance is making the best of things. At least she rejects the pure motherhood option represented by an appalling widower of considerable wealth, Uncle Robert Van Dorn, who in the Chicago way fully expects her to capitulate to the dollar in time. As a sideline, there is the alienist Dr Duff Devereux, 'an antlered lord' and positive version of the patronising Dr Weir Mitchell in *The Yellow Wallpaper*, who understands the whole of the problem (and facilitates some kind of emotional transference of Constance's yearnings for love from himself to Osborne). Women like Constance, the author comments, were ahead of their time, 'the too early flowers of the spring of progress.'[45]

Maybe that was how Miles saw herself. However, one must always remember that hers was a double life, especially in Chicago, where she was forever busy with union affairs and no one seems to have paid any attention to her literary endeavours. As well there were many new and exciting aspects to her daily life. These included contacts with Australia and Australians. 'Australia Is So Far Away' is the title of one of the unpublished sketches; but Australia had always found a place in *Life and Labor* due to its ongoing 'labour experiments', and there were always Australians in Chicago and Australian passers-through. Furthermore, throughout 1912 there was a sense that American women were again 'on the march', and to add to the excitement, that year Miles seems to have found a new patron at Sydney's *Daily Telegraph*, probably Florence Baverstock, once a *Bulletin* columnist, and editor of the *Telegraph*'s 'Woman's Page', from 1907 to 1914. The '*Tele*' published three features by Miles (to be noted shortly) in 1912. Baverstock then moved to the *Sydney Morning Herald*'s women's section, which, and it hardly seems coincidental, resumed publication of Franklin features in 1916.[46]

On New Year's Eve 1911, which she spent with fellow expatriates the Newshams, Miles felt 'cold in the joints'. It turned out that she had measles, not a simple thing in adults, and was out of action for over a month, the latter part of which she spent at Resthaven Sanitarium some 60 miles up country at Elgin, Illinois; she returned to Chicago by train on 4 February. A costly sojourn at $15 per week, the benefit was that she was able to finish a first draft of *The Net of Circumstance* and it gave her the locale for the dénouement of the play 'Aunt Sophie Smashes a Triangle', set in 'Chicago now' and probably written in 1913. Also, as she later told New York league worker Leonora O'Reilly, 'you get a lovely rest and everyone sympathizes'.[47]

Leonora O'Reilly was one of the most impressive figures in the early years of the American women's labour movement. Originally a garment worker, later a domestic science instructor and always an ardent socialist, she was a source of inspiration and a tower of strength to all who knew her, especially, it seems, the allies. In 1911, it had been hoped she would become the league's first paid organiser; and it was to her that Mrs Robins turned when, due to her illness, Miles was unable to go to Kansas City and Pittsburgh in January (Mrs Robins regarded Miles as 'especially helpful in bringing about cooperation' at this time). The correspondence between Secretary Franklin and O'Reilly when Miles resumed work in February gives a rare glimpse of Miles at work in the office. Their letters survive as a unique sequence among the vast number of missives, mostly now lost, that undoubtedly passed between Miles and the many women with whom she was working in Chicago. Miles and Leonora grew closer as time went by.[48]

In February 1912, the main concerns of the league were that typically American hazard, judicial setbacks, and a strike of textile workers faced with wage cuts at Lawrence, Massachusetts. In mid-February, Secretary Franklin and President Robins again took the train to Springfield to defend the ten-hour law of 1911. Two months later, on 15 April, the day of the sinking of the *Titanic*, they were off again, to a special executive board meeting in New York to address problems arising from Boston league's participation in the Lawrence strike, which had been led by an organiser of the militant Industrial Workers of the World and not authorised by the American Federation of Labor. The main outcome of the two-day meeting was a successful request for funding by the men's unions to employ a fulltime organiser, on the grounds that 'the organization of the unskilled is imperative and [its cost] must in part be borne by the organizations of the skilled'. The league then appointed the secretary-treasurer of the glove-workers' union, Agnes Nestor, as national organiser. Nestor was a winning figure who rose to national prominence after World War I and whom Miles was proud to call a friend.[49]

The list of lifelong friendships Miles cemented during these prewar years is a long one. Mostly they were with league associates, though a few were with allies, some, but not many, of whom were grande dames and, being very rich, were regarded by Miles with a mixture of awe and hostility. Her close friends Arnold and Louise Dresden, and Margery Currey Dell, a Vassar girl, she informed Rose Scott, were more plainly middle-class allies, while the Lloyds of Winnetka belonged in a class of their own. Of the league's leadership, first in Miles' estimation came Margaret Dreier Robins, her mainstay, and her sister Mary Dreier. Of fellow league workers, Alice Henry, her mentor and educator in journalism, later sometimes addressed as 'Pa', remained pre-eminent. Of members, mostly working women, in addition to 'my beloved Editha [Phelps]', Miles' close friends included Emma Pischel, Agnes Nestor, Leonora Pease, Mary Anderson and Elisabeth Christman, all of whom she saw on a more or less daily basis. Leonora O'Reilly died in 1927, too soon to be counted as a truly long-term friend, and was in any case a New Yorker, as was the diminutive Jewish clothing worker Rose Schneiderman, the New York league's fulltime organiser from 1910, when Miles seems first to have encountered her.[50]

Many others well known to Miles Franklin in literary and social reform circles, though not personal friends, were simply part of the texture of her busy life, which straddled the classes and proved intellectually congenial. Such figures as Carl Sandburg and Theodore Dreiser were part of 'our crowd', she would sometimes say breezily back in Australia, adding that she did not like Dreiser personally, as may be imagined from the amoral passivity of *Sister Carrie*. 'Life goes with a rush and a swing over here I can assure you and the Americans are simply adorable. They have none of the Britishers' tendency to grumble and grizzle,' she enthused in a letter to E. W. O'Sullivan's daughter Eva written on return from a trip to New York, where she had again stayed with Jessie Childs on Riverside Drive, 'in a vast apartment building that nearly reached the sky'.[51]

In the higher latitudes of the northern hemisphere the onset of summer usually lifts people's spirits. To Miles the year 1912 brought a great sadness, as well as much excitement. The sadness dated from 11 June 1912, when Sarah Lampe died at Tumut aged eighty-one. When this news reached her eldest granddaughter, and how she coped, is unknown, but it would certainly have been a great blow. By 1914 she was beginning to feel that her grandmother was the only person who had never let her down ('the supreme love of my life' is how the heroine of 'Red Cross Nurse' puts it, which now seems rather extreme). 'Oh how I wish I could go home, if I had a little strength perhaps I would,' she wrote to Rose Scott six months later. Joseph Furphy also died in 1912, though she seems not to have known of it.[52]

That summer the suffragists of Miles' circle were galvanised by successful suffrage referenda in several states and increased suffragette militancy in England: 'Yes, [it's] "our" suffrage campaign!', begins a report by Editha Phelps in June's *Life and Labor* of a local pre-primary campaign conducted by the league in which the question of woman suffrage was put to the (all male) voters of an inner-city ward. (Two-thirds of the respondents, a significant number of them European immigrants, were against votes for women, an outcome Miles Franklin recalled when a mass immigration program was proposed for Australia.) About this time came the news that Walter Burley Griffin had won the Australian capital city design competition, to the pride and delight of Miles Franklin and Alice Henry, who went to Walter's office to congratulate him and subsequently wrote to the Sydney *Daily Telegraph* to inform their fellow Australians of their good fortune in obtaining the services of one who practised the new art of urban design: 'The new art has sprung to life at the bidding of the new civic conscience. This conscience prompts the community to plan for higher social standards, a larger, loftier civic and national life,' they wrote, adding how pleasing it was that Australia would be leading the world once more.[53]

In addition to the other extraordinary events of that year, in June the Republican convention was held in Chicago. At the convention a great upset occurred when the incumbent president, Theodore Roosevelt, was dumped as presidential candidate in favour of Robert Taft, and the 'Grand Old Party' split. A mere six weeks later, a newly constituted Progressive Party met at the Chicago Coliseum on South Wabash Street to declare Roosevelt its candidate ('Give me Teddy or give me death'). The hastily cobbled together but long-gestating platform comprehended everything the league had been calling for, including equal suffrage, and there were even two women delegates, who were given a historic suffrage escort through the streets to the opening of the new party's convention. The escort was headed by the distinguished sociologist Sophonisba Breckenridge and thirty female students from the University of Chicago, and included a contingent representing working women, among whom the *Chicago Daily Tribune* listed 'Stella Franklin'. At the opening, Roosevelt announced to cheering delegates that he felt as fit as a bull moose, hence the subtitle of Miles Franklin's account published in the *Daily Telegraph* on 28 September, 'Mr Roosevelt and the New Party: Some Sidelights of the Bull Moose Convention'.[54]

Miles had a thrilling time in the press gallery: the suffrage escort down Michigan Avenue on Monday 5 August had opened 'a great and glorious day'. The following day was 'another great day', and the third and final day simply 'glorious'. So exciting was it that she had to take a sleeping draught to calm down at night. 'Never enjoyed myself so for years.' And others found it equally exhilarating. Mary Dreier was delighted by the new party's 'splendid suffrage plank' and by a social and industrial plank 'which surpasses our wildest dreams'. A letter from Miles Franklin to Rose Scott gives a personal reaction:

> These have been stirring times for our circle as Mr & Mrs Robins are in the thick of the fight of the new Progressive Party to elect Mr Roosevelt ... His humanitarian plank has attracted a great many reformers. Of course I am against his military ideals and certain characteristics, but it is a great thing that he has come out for the suffrage. One gets bored to death with all the old, old discussion still going on about this simple thing. I feel as if I had lived before the flood having come from a universal suffrage country ... I had a seat in the press section. I was next to the London *Times* representative ... within four seats of the speakers and had a fine view of Teddy, teeth and all.[55]

The main reason for her letter, however, was to inform Rose Scott of the embarrassment occasioned by Sir George Reid, the Australian High Commissioner in London and former Australian Prime Minister, who visited Chicago in early September. Reid had declined to be received by suffragists in Chicago seeking to know about the achievements of women in advanced Australia, due, he said, to feeling against the suffragettes in England (and according to hearsay, his wife backed him up by asserting that the best women in Australia did not vote anyway). The protest letter written by Alice Henry and Miles Franklin to Australia's Labor Prime Minister, Andrew Fisher, duly appeared in the Sydney *Daily Telegraph*:

> Dear Sir,
> Sir George Reid, High Commissioner for Australia, at present on a visit to the United States, has refused to accept the courtesy of a reception to be tendered to Lady Reid by the suffragists on the ground that it would not be politic (see clippings enclosed). It seems to be a strange position for an Australian official to take, that when in a foreign country, he cannot stand for the principle of equal suffrage embodied in the laws and Constitution of Australia ... As Australians we should like to know what is the explanation of the High Commissioner's attitude, which tends to

discredit Australia among the women of this country, for the question inevitably arises, is Sir George Reid High Commissioner for Australia or for Great Britain. [56]

There were other reasons for feeling good towards year's end. In mid-September Alice Henry had returned from a long break; Charlotte Perkins Gilman would soon be back in Chicago; Miles had finished typing *The Net of Circumstance*; and she had one Guido Mariotti in tow. Not for much longer, however. Poor Guido, who gave Italian lessons to Editha Phelps and many times walked Miles home after an evening meal in one or other lakeside diner, was dismissed by Miles in mid-November as 'a most vacuous specimen of humanity'. Soon afterwards, letters started to come from playboy Demarest Lloyd, the younger son of the Lloyds of Winnetka, where Miles had convalesced in 1907. He was still living mainly in Boston but by 1912 was a journalist and enthusiast for Christian Science. Emma Pischel's older brother Fred, who worked in his father's lumber and estate business in north-west Chicago, had also become an admirer. Somehow Miles never lacked for admirers. It was partly because of her relatively diminutive size, which kept her looking young: she weighed a mere 104 pounds (47 kilograms) at this time, and had to buy clothes from children's departments. No wonder 'Demy' Lloyd called her 'little rascal'. And often she seemed fragile (in particular, her teeth were giving her trouble again).[57]

In December, following the disappointment of Roosevelt's election loss (to Democrat Woodrow Wilson), Margaret Robins wrote approvingly of Miles' work as national league secretary: 'Don't you think it fine,' she wrote to a colleague, Mary Spaulding Lee, 'the amount of work that that girl has pushed through this summer. Not only has she attended to all the National correspondence, but she has edited four numbers of *Life and Labor* while Miss Henry was away, and this year will see her one of the editors of the paper'. Mary Dreier, who visited Chicago at this time, thought the office workers 'a stunning lot of women ... so full of enthusiasm and happiness'.[58]

The December 1912 issue of *Life and Labor* carried an announcement that after two years the production team felt confident the magazine had found its footing, and outlined plans for the coming year: 'When space permits the assistant editor S. M. Franklin will review books that are analogous to our story, from the sociological point of view, and will continue to adjure all in the struggle for industrial justice to keep up their spirits, to preserve and enlarge their sense of humour, and to beware of making contributions too long or too dismal.'[59]

Several clouds may be discerned on Miles' horizon, however. The announcement also encouraged new subscriptions: 'the problems which of necessity face a young and non-commercial magazine have to be overcome'. And the industrial scene gave pause for thought. Mrs Robins was aware that 1913 would see the league enter its second decade and that it could not be led 'from the outside' forever. And what did Miles mean when she wrote glumly in her diary on New Year's Eve, 'Went to P.O. no results'? Had *The Net of Circumstance* been offered to an American publisher? It was certainly not sent to England until early 1914.[60]

According to Miles' eugenical romance *On Dearborn Street*, set in Chicago during 1914–15 but begun on 1 January 1913 and including some references to the New Year, a 'desolate swamp of weeks' follows the festive season:

> … when January has been beaten back into the arctic, and weak-minded February tries to capitulate with the calendar by coming out in the sheep's wool of spring … when there is nothing like fall or Christmas to work up to, when spring and summer vacations are still a long way distant, a dreary stretch to those chained by circumstances to one spot …[61]

During the harsh winter months, colds and the exhaustion born of traipsing around icy streets were, and still are, the norm in such places. Miles' diary for 1913 shows that she suffered her fair share of inconvenience from the weather in the streets and variable steam heating indoors, and that she paid numerous visits to doctors practising in the Loop, especially in the harshest months, from January through to April. Entries suggest that she suffered period pain, being regularly 'unwell', 'very weak', 'not fit for anything'. In early March, she was 'feeling utterly defeated and worn out', and a month later, 'ill and ghastly depressed'. Most puzzling is the diary entry for 14 April: after consulting Dr Young, owner of the house at Park Avenue where Miles lived in her early days in Chicago, she wrote: 'got the familiar old death sentence', leaving her depressed and unable to sleep. Of the doctors she consulted in 1913, three who have been identified were general practitioners: Dr Young, who became a lifelong friend; Dr Bertha Van Hoosen, staff physician to the league; and the 'blessed' Dr Favill, prescriber of veranol for insomnia, whose splendid consulting rooms in the People's Gas Building occasioned mention in a postcard home. Dr Schenkelberger (possibly the prototype of alienist Dr Duff Devereux who appears in both the Chicago novels) was surely the most costly — in the final months of 1912 Miles paid him $60 for 'treatments'. However, her diary also contains instances of resolve to fight feelings of depression, and there are a number of entries saying she felt wonderfully well, with many 'lovely warm days' recorded in the spring and summer months. Nor did she fail to fulfil her obligations. Indeed, she appears to have been busier than ever.[62]

The call for the fourth biennial convention of the league, to be held in St Louis in June, was drafted on 2 January 1913. Miles had been with the NWTUL for five years, and was still enjoying working in the Loop. In her writing there is a sense of her feeling for Dearborn Street, as Cavarley, the male narrator of her novel of that name, finds it:

> I stood awhile on Dearborn Street as I came out of the old Concord Building. I looked south where, unlike its fellows, this street is broken by an obstruction, and is marked by the spire of Polk Street Station. I looked north, where it runs under the elevated [railway] and falls into the Canal when the bridge is open. It was very ugly, and dirty, and blatant, lacking in any character excepting of course the earmarks of driving Business.[63]

But, he concedes, the details depend on whether one is elated or depressed. Sybyl Penelo, his passion, and a fair copy of Miles Franklin, revelled in it:

> Each morning when I wake to find the far quietude replaced by the roar of the traffic, I arise with fresh joy and relief. The thunder of the Loop is sweetest music to me. It tells me the day is to be full of motion and people, that I am going to work among others, that there will be common confidences, jokes and arguments. I love every minute of it.[64]

In the naming of Sybyl Penelo, Miles also summoned up her first heroine, the redoubtable Sybylla Penelope Melvyn of *My Brilliant Career* fame. The implication, for those who caught the echo, was that where Sybylla Penelope Melvyn could not go, Sybyl Penelo might. Miles was still in prophetic mode.

By now there was a firm shape to Miles' working day, even though she had no fixed hours and never had to record her arrival or departure from the office. Almost every day she would lunch with fellow office workers, or callers, at nearby cafeterias, in 1913 most frequently the Hearth. (In *On Dearborn Street*, when Cavarley joins Sybyl at her favourite cafeteria, the Fireside, having never entered such a lowly establishment before, he overloads and then drops his tray.) In the evenings she dined at nearby tearooms, often the Lincoln Parkway Tea Room. (At no time prior to 1914 did she mention cut lunches or cooking for herself; it may not have been feasible in residentials until gas rings were installed.) On special occasions, for example when Mrs Robins called at the office, they took tea at Marshall Field's, the great department store a block or so away, and Miles was sometimes taken to dine at classier establishments such as Blackstones and the La Salle by visitors and suitors. Most nights — and this seems surprising given Chicago's rough reputation, but it was a mark of the modern woman — she would walk home from the diners to her room on East Superior Street, sometimes accompanied by fellow residents, occasionally escorted by male friends.[65]

Less surprising is how ill-defined her week was. Throughout 1913 Miles took French lessons on Saturdays. Otherwise she worked at the office most days, usually on league work, sometimes typing up her own writings. She had a typewriter in her room at the residential too, so she could work at either place. One of the appeals of her job, in addition to its sociable nature, must surely have been the relative freedom she enjoyed to arrange her time to suit the work in hand. She usually worked long hours, but she still had a good deal of latitude day by day. Only on Sundays, when she often spent a good part of the day in bed, did she stay totally clear of the office, though even then there were frequently meetings somewhere.

Nonetheless there is a discernible rhythm to her month, largely dictated by the production schedule for *Life and Labor*. As previously remarked, most of the dogsbody work involved in getting the magazine out on time fell to Miles. And with Miss Henry — Miles usually referred to her colleagues in accordance with the formal modes of address normal in her day — away for several months mid-year, 1913 was a bumper year for contributions from 'S. M. Franklin' (after 1905 the most ever in her journalistic career: seventeen items in all). In addition, Mrs Robins took off for Europe after the St Louis convention, to the initial dismay of Secretary-Treasurer Franklin (as she became post-convention). Writing to 'My Dearest

Mrs Robins' on 17 June 1913, she said it felt as if her 'rock of refuge' had gone when the train pulled out, but that she must learn to get by alone, and she thanked her 'for all you are to me'. No doubt the yellow roses from Mrs Robins awaiting her in the evening helped.[66]

One thing was certain: the work would increase over the year; and with both Alice Henry and Margaret Robins away, more responsibilities fell upon the secretary-treasurer. Yet allowing for the need to put a good face on things in letters home, Miles clearly relished the situation. As she put it in a letter to Aunt Annie Franklin at Brindabella, 'I have done the whole business for months' and 'I have given my opinion on settling strikes and sent organizers and investigators hither and yon,' she added. Apparently the arrangement was that in return for shouldering so much responsibility she was to get five months' leave on full pay in 1914 to visit Australia. Not mentioned in the letter but clear from Miles' diary are the respites, especially in August, when she often spent time at Winnetka with the Lloyd family, and thrilled to the modern recreation of 'automobiling'.[67]

The letter to Aunt Annie includes a sketch of her workplace, which in its wide-eyed simplicity offers convincing evidence that for all her more intimate anxieties, Miles enjoyed her position:

> We have an office suite of four rooms in one of the big skyscrapers and one of them is my private office. I have an assistant to help me. I have my own telephone switch and all sorts of conveniences … We have a mail chute just outside our door in which we drop our letters and when we want a telegraph messenger to take things we touch a button in the wall. The building has a barber's shop and a restaurant and all sorts of things. There are some thousands of people quartered here. It is a great sight when the big buildings light up at night.[68]

'Quite a change from the life of an Australian bush girl,' she remarked. Not only could she boast a big office, but an important job and many friends, some to become significant in American history, such as leading Chicago Progressives Mr and Mrs Harold Ickes, the former Secretary for the Interior in Roosevelt's New Deal administration, and Louis and Alice Thacher Post — Louis serving as Assistant Secretary for Labor under Woodrow Wilson from 1913. Others were more obscure but of personal significance, like the Dresdens (who had moved to Madison, Wisconsin), English couple A. K. (Ken) and

'Mab' Maynard, the Pischels, and 'my sweet Ethel Mason' (later Nielsen) at the office, another special chum of Miles' own age, the granddaughter of Edward Mason, mayor of Chicago during the Great Fire of 1871, and by all accounts a most pleasing person, well dressed, serene and cultivated. Miles noted encounters with the Burley Griffins at both the Maynards' and the Pischels' in January 1913; and the Maynards would be a vital link when she moved to England. Ken Maynard was business manager at the Chicago School of Civics and Philanthopy on South Michigan Avenue, and his wife, Mab, was a graduate of Newnham College, Cambridge, a Quaker and an ally. Both were part of a great British Liberal connection, the Unwin-Byles family (a branch of which migrated to Sydney in 1912 and produced New South Wales' first woman solicitor, the remarkable Marie Byles).[69]

After seven years in America, Miles Franklin could honestly say that she loved Americans and wished that relations between Australia and America were closer (a process already under way informally, though Australia would not appoint its own representative in Washington until 1937). In the despatches of information about her work — she scored at least ten Australian press mentions in 1913, including four in the *Worker*, where Mary Gilmore ran the 'Women's Page', and she exchanged trade union journals with the prominent Sydney labour leaders Annie and Belle Golding — and in the letters she wrote introducing Raymond Robins and Walter Burley Griffin to Australians in 1913, she was a forerunner. (Raymond Robins was in Australia in March and April 1913 on a world crusade to bring men back to Christianity, during which time he met Miles' mother, 'a dear old lady'.)[70]

It used to be said of 'exodists' (Miles' word in *Cockatoos* for talented people leaving Australia) that if they stayed away longer than three years they were unlikely to return. Clearly after seven years the capacity of America's second city to stimulate and delight was far from exhausted. The net of circumstance was so richly woven, with new threads all the time. Thus the very first evening of 1913 found her at the latest site of cultural innovation, the Little Theatre, located at first in the Fine Arts building, then on the city's South Side. A month later she saw a performance of Euripides' *The Trojan Women*, produced by theatre founder Maurice Browne, which she reviewed enthusiastically in the next issue of *Life and Labor*: 'What a mighty tragedy wrought in the lives of women this is.' The review concludes with a request for the young director to find an adequate labour play and give a Women's Trade Union Night.[71]

The Little Theatre, which presented experimental and poetic plays, became one of her enthusiasms. It only held ninety-nine people — a darling place, she wrote to Rose Scott — with a tearoom attached where she sometimes went on Sunday evening and met 'the geebungs in art and literature'. It was, she said, 'quite a jolly highbrow affair' (though she elsewhere abhorred its bohemian aspects, especially its sexual culture), and it made a lasting impression.[72]

This new enthusiasm fed into romantic interests. William Bross Lloyd often took Miles to opera matinées in 1913 and to dine in the great hotels. No correspondence remains to clarify the relationship, but it seems clear that Bill Lloyd was entranced by Miles, once saying she was the most complex mortal he had ever known, and that he wanted to marry her or at least have an affair. The trouble was he was already married, with a wife, Lola, in Winnetka whom Miles knew well, and several children. Worse (in Miles' eyes), it seems Bill Lloyd resorted to prostitutes. As she put it in her literary notebook in the 1940s, 'when he wanted me to marry him, I said scornfully I cd not undertake the heavy burden competing with all the "sporting" women in town' ('sporting' being a North American usage denoting a prostitute or loose woman). To this Bill Lloyd replied that he had exempted himself from such services since pursuing her; but when he could not recall any of the women's names, it disgusted her all the more. (Miles probably took this stand later, as the relationship continued until 1914. The Lloyd marriage lasted a year or two longer, by which time he was 'poor Bill Lloyd'.)[73]

Miles never said she regretted not marrying Bill Lloyd. With his younger brother Demarest, who came to the fore a little earlier, the story would be different, as she confessed to Ethel (Mason) Nielsen in 1951. Born in 1883, Demarest was a few years younger than Miles and by all accounts a fine specimen of manhood. When he died in 1937, Miles wrote, 'I knew him intimately', meaning not sexually, but closely, or very well. She kept his letters too (as she did those of Edwin Bridle and later some from Fred Pischel), bizarre and one-sided as they mostly are. All but two of the surviving thirty-six letters were written during 1913 and 1914, and among them are a few responses from Miles (though these seem to have been composed as much to obscure as to illuminate what was really going on).[74]

On paper, at least, the story began on 19 December 1912, when Demarest Lloyd wrote to 'Miss Franklin', thanking her for a copy of her review of his aunt's life of his father. By this time he was a political commentator on the

Boston Journal, while maintaining a presence in Chicago, where his interests were substantial. How much more Miles knew about him is hard to say, since neither she nor any of her associates mentioned certain pertinent facts until 1951, and they were not reported at the time in the *Chicago Daily Tribune* (of which he and his brother were major shareholders). However, on 5 November 1912 the *New York Times* reported that Demarest Lloyd had recently instigated divorce proceedings in Boston against Mayme ('May') Fisher Lloyd on the grounds of adultery. He had married May in 1905, when he was aged twenty-two. There were no children, and due to certain incidents in a hotel in New Hampshire, apparently involving Fisher rather than Lloyd, as was usually the case, the divorce was uncontested. A decree nisi was granted on 13 January 1913 and was to become absolute six months later. It was on that same day that Demarest Lloyd next wrote to Miles Franklin, thanking her for a bright and cheery note.[75]

Through 1913 the relationship between Demarest Lloyd and Miles Franklin developed in a haphazard manner, due in part to his lavish lifestyle — according to the *New York Times*, he was worth $9 million at this time — but also to her characteristically unpredictable demeanour. At first it was just a matter of his calling in at the league office when in town and her sending him playful notes. Perhaps it was sponsorship of a theatre somewhere unspecified that Miles wanted of him: Demarest Lloyd undoubtedly could have afforded it, but in the only documentation of this extraordinary idea, a long and otherwise largely content-free letter from Boston on 27 March 1913, he dismissed it as too expensive. In that letter he addressed her as 'You dear fascinating little rascal', and signed himself 'Sinbad the Sailor'.[76]

As his life revolved around sailing and automobiles, his letters came from up and down the east coast — from Boston, New York, and Miami — and in August 1913 he was in France, where she wrote to him. At that stage he was still not taking her too seriously, rejecting playful reprimands 'for various imaginary offences and shortcomings'. Perhaps responding to her teasing that she felt an affinity with famed English playwright George Bernard Shaw, he wondered if he should go to England and find out what this 'affinity' business was all about. More seriously, he sent Miles some Christian Science literature. But he failed to respond to invitations to attend a welcome-home dinner for Mrs Robins in September, and although he was tempted by her invitation to the union Halloween Ball the following month, he did not make that either.[77]

What he did perceive was that his 'dear fascinating little rascal' was 'in some kind of trouble'. This he attributed to associating with 'materialistic' people, labour and socialist people; or perhaps it was her work that made her nervous? His prescription that she see a Christian Science practitioner 'where you can open up' seems hardly that of a suitor. The problem, he concluded, possibly correctly, was his beloved brother, whom Demy (as he now signed himself) also mistrusted. Demy urged Miles to keep 'our little secrets' from Bill Lloyd, and to conclude the relationship with him.[78]

These lightly flirtatious letters may seem tiresome to the present-day reader, stripped of any charm by the demise of what historian Manning Clark once called 'the chocolate box culture' of courtship, and even distasteful, with Demy's occasional references to 'spanking'; and on the mysterious concept of theatrical sponsorship little more can be inferred from them. But it is clear that Miles did want something of him. Was it romance? Probably. Doubtless his attentions were flattering, even intriguing. And marriage? Maybe. He fitted the eugenical bill well, and as 'Bobby Hoyne' he served as a literary model for the possibility in *On Dearborn Street*. But she avoided him when he came to Chicago for a family Christmas that year, and Demy Lloyd was often mystified by Miles. Certainly, she found his Christian Science hard to take, as the draft short story 'When Bobby Got Religion', dated 1914 and incorporated into *On Dearborn Street*, would make abundantly clear: 'the only religion that can be made to comfort the rich'.[79]

Meanwhile, Miles was reading the latest works of Raymond Robins' sister Elizabeth Robins, whom she had visited in England in 1911. Reviewing Robins' 'white slave' novel *My Little Sister*, for *Life and Labor* in March 1913, she asserted that 'Art and its henchman culture have fallen on … democratic days', and that in the newer culture emerging, the novel would become a greater educational force than the sermon. In her June review of a second Robins publication, *Way Stations*, which documented the militant suffrage movement in England since the Pankhursts' formation of the WSPU in 1905, she deemed it 'an inspired and authentic piece of history' and defended militancy, predicting that 'the women's war' would crack 'the crust of ages'. Thanks to Lucy Bland's study of the English feminist campaign on sexual morality from the 1880s to 1914, *Banishing the Beast*, subtitled *Sexuality and the Early Feminists*, it is now clear not only that Miles Franklin was a product of social purity feminism — Rose Scott being the outstanding Antipodean representative — but also that she believed the ongoing struggle against the double standard of morality had placed men on the back foot at last. The apocalyptic moment came in 1913, when the suffragette militancy in England reached a new pitch of intensity and the publication of Christabel Pankhurst's pamphlet on venereal disease, *The Great Scourge*, popularised the medical estimate that up to 80 per cent of men were infected by gonorrhea or syphilis, translating to the slogan 'Votes for Women and Chastity for Men'. But gaining the intellectual initiative was not simple, and some positions were soon to be outdated by the new sexology and psychology.[80]

A hint of the impending clash may be heard by juxtaposing a brief but supportive 1913 review by S. M. Franklin of a now forgotten reform novel, *V V's Eyes*, about the awakening of a young woman to the sufferings of her working sisters and her own parasitism, and a passing reference in Miles' pocket diary to the *Freewoman*, a short-lived sexual anarchist journal from England which stressed women's independent sexuality. Miles Franklin was stuck somewhere between the old and the new: an impassioned upholder of social purity and chastity but increasingly conscious that, aged thirty-four, her experience of sex was, to say the least, limited. Whereas both virginity and chastity had their place in Catholic teaching, the mostly Protestant-reared first-wave feminists had no such justification to fall back on when new approaches challenged their faith in self-restraint. Lack of sexual experience presumably was worse than not being able to dance, at a time when Americans were doing the turkey trot, or not being able to drive. Miles got Bill Lloyd to teach her to dance, and Fred Pischel would soon offer to teach her to drive; but she thought it best to hold to the old truths about sex. Self-restraint, however, may not have been enough, if the alarmingly brutal account of the abduction and attempted rape of the young working woman narrator by a wealthy suitor in 'Red Cross Nurse' is based on her own experience, as seems to be the case. During a lengthy break in Boston in 1914, Demy Lloyd took Miles driving and dancing and apparently tried to assault her after one dangerous trip to Providence, Rhode Island. The relevant diary entry reads: 'He was desperate & brutal in an unprecedented degree when drunk. Escaped death or tragedy by v. small margin.' She began 'Red Cross Nurse' three days later.[81]

Her state of mind is apparent from some harsh lines written to Rose Scott on 19 June 1913:

> I am very discouraged by what you tell me of the man-serving propensities of the Australian women and I know it's true, as Miss Henry and I discover it in the newspapers' tone. It is terrible

all together that women are such fools. I have come to the conclusion they are not worth worrying about. They are happier serving men ... than some of the rest of us are in our hot demand for freedom and a system of society which will nurture self-respect.[82]

'Do you suppose', she went on in a more reflective manner, 'we are really ahead of our time, are we deluded fools or are we merely conceited?'

In November 1913 Emmeline Pankhurst came to Chicago. There had been quite a fuss about it, as the United States government had at first tried to keep her out of the country, to the huge indignation of the citizenry. Her lecture tour and the fundraising that was the main purpose of this, her third visit to the United States, were subsequently a great success. Miles, who claimed to have joined the WSPU as a gesture of solidarity back in 1911 when a prior tour by Sylvia Pankhurst had to be cancelled due to public hostility to militancy, went to all the Chicago events and wrote a pointed article for *Life and Labor*: 'The government that sends a woman of such high qualities and unswerving purity of purpose before us as a felon ... while the white slaver flourishes untrammeled in Piccadilly, is in need of profound condolences.'[83]

At the league convention in St Louis mid-year, where she appeared in the local press as a union leader, Miles presented a forward-looking secretary's report, and was 'as busy as an ant'. The league's organisational and legislative agenda was a lengthening one, and as Gladys Boone first pointed out, in many respects well ahead of its time, but hard to implement too, due to the problems inherent in organising unskilled and mostly young working women, and having to push labour legislation through state by state.[84]

In addition, there was the challenge of establishing a training school for women trade unionists. There had been a strong general emphasis on education at the convention, and Mrs Robins was clear that the time had come for trade unionists to take over from the 'allies'. Having become secretary-treasurer (after the convention), Miles had to help find the not inconsiderable sums of money needed for the pioneering effort, which began in a small way in 1914 and lasted until 1926, when the challenge was passed to the newly established Labor colleges. She also contributed supportive features in *Life and Labor*, on Elizabeth Maloney of the Chicago waitresses' union, and on Agnes Nestor, who succeeded Margaret Robins as president of the Chicago WTUL in 1913.[85]

After such a year, it is something of a shock to come upon Miles' last diary entry for 1913:

> Looking back over the year I cannot recall one thing of usefulness or worth that I have accomplished for others nor one of pleasure or satisfaction for myself. The futility of my existence, my weakness in effort, my failure in accomplishment, fills me with a creeping melancholy that grows more impenetrable. I will fight against it once more by hard work & if in two yrs the results are no better than in the past I shall die of my own volition.

Of all Miles' black moments this was surely the blackest, yet she determined to struggle on, at least for the time being. Fortunately, the new year began well. The Chicago league celebrated its tenth anniversary in January 1914; the organisers' training school, which included public-speaking classes, was under way by March with three enrolments (the faculty greatly exceeding these in number); and cordial relations were obtained with the American Federation of Labor, which was reserving its judgement on such a costly and long-term project as a training school.[86]

When the league's public-speaking classes began, Miles played the back-room girl, insisting that the very thought of public speaking made her feel ill: 'I knew I had it in me to be either an actress or a *diseuse*, but not even fabulous bribes could have tempted me to overcome that wild sick agonising fright each time I faced an audience.' She began by observing the classes, and when pressed to participate starred in them, and, by her own account at least, delighting more earnest colleagues with a speech on coloured wigs for men. And when sometimes she was required to convey league greetings at union gatherings, she enjoyed the experience. At a miners' convention in Indianapolis in January 1914, despite poor acoustics she could be heard all over the hall, and it was like being back with 'the shearers and drifters at home', she wrote to Susannah Franklin. Later she spoke to a large assembly of women high-school teachers in Chicago; and although her colleagues doubted her suitability for the occasion, possibly because she was from the office rather than the shop floor, the teachers were impressed, especially by her 'beautiful English'.[87]

On the face of it, things were proceeding as normal. The usual round of work and play resumed in the new year. Money was needed for larger office premises as well as the new school, and Miles wrote twice about funding to

Dorothea Dreier (sometimes it seems the league was entirely funded by the Dreier sisters). There were judicial decisions, trade agreements and the rather complex waitresses' hearing to be attended to — where human rights were at stake — and articles for *Life and Labor* to be written. Singing lessons, now with Mrs Fieldcamp at Kimball Hall, resumed. Miles' teeth became a problem again, and Bill Lloyd became ever more attentive, which, like Cavarley in *On Dearborn Street*, he could easily do, with the Lloyd offices recently relocated downstairs at 127 Dearborn Street. Demarest Lloyd also turned up in January, and there were the usual stimulating visitors to Chicago, notably Helen Keller ('Wouldn't have missed it for anything'), the Christian Scientist Nancy Lister Watson and her husband, P. S., again, and mid-year, the distinguished Australian arbitration court judge Henry Bournes Higgins (who felt he was in a 'new America', so evident was the industrial progress since his last visit).[88]

Perhaps the Watsons' influence, as well as the hurtful behaviour of that 'conceited and inexplicable boor' Demarest Lloyd, led Miles to a Christian Science reading room in late February. She resolved to pursue Demarest for copy — the furious manuscript 'When Bobby Got Religion' is dated 20 February 1914 — and dreamed out loud of returning to Australia: 'I am getting very snappy and disagreeable and there is a movement on foot to send me back to Australia for several months,' she wrote to Dorothea Dreier. 'How I wish you could come too,' she continued, forgetting for the moment her own propensity to seasickness: 'We would lie on the decks in the lovely tropic sun … and watch the flying fishes play and the porpoises also.' The plan must have been for the southern hemisphere spring in September, as she suggested that Dorothea could paint some of Australia's unique wildflowers.[89]

The year 1914 also brought progress on the suffrage front in America. Though things got fiercer in England (evidence of progress, Miles suggested), partial enfranchisement was obtained in the state of Illinois by mid-year, thanks to support from the twelfth biennial meeting of women's clubs in Chicago in June, which she attended and wrote up for *Life and Labor*. 'The city is infested with club women,' she wrote in private to Raymond Robins. They were trying to handle things working women had been grappling with for a quarter of a century; but with Jane Addams and Carrie Chapman Catt among the speakers, the convention was testimony to the tremendous force of the American feminist movement, and further evidence of progress.[90]

There is a fine studio portrait of Alice Henry and Miles Franklin taken about this time, showing both to be clear-eyed, coiffured, confident, modern women. The younger Miles is posed behind Alice, and there is a hint of mirth in the set of her mouth, with the merest trace of a wrinkle at the corners of her large and luminous eyes (the colour of which would become a matter of dispute after her death, but apparently it varied; they were officially grey, though here they look brown). In reality, however, both women were feeling badly overworked, and were in trouble with Mrs Robins over the printers' bills for *Life and Labor*, already a worry in 1913. Mrs Robins was still the financial mainstay of the league, and as she explained to the league's business manager, Jim Mullenbach, the whole burden of financing the magazine, and the legal liability, fell on her: '… although I have begged and pleaded and spoken sternly regarding the necessity of financial support and working for it, I have not been able to make Miss Henry see the necessity for it, or at any rate act upon it.'[91]

And while she would have been willing to support the journal at $1000 a year for ten years, she was not willing to bear the entire burden of publication, especially since in her view the magazine did not even reach union leaders. She was already thinking of paring it down to a bulletin, which she felt would more closely meet the needs of working girls. Alice Henry resisted, but things had changed a little in 1913, with Henry and Miles announced joint-editors mid-year. Then when a printers' bill for $700 came in February 1914, sparks began to fly.[92]

A sadly familiar story of workers defending a good product in the face of financial stringency and plans to downsize began to unfold. Mrs Robins wanted Alice Henry to stand down and finish her long-promised history of women and trade unions, and Miles to take over (an idea to which Miles was not averse). But Alice Henry was appalled, and raised the latent issue of overwork, as Miles had a few days before. One person could not do all that work. The fault lay with the NWTUL's overambitious plans, and what was proposed meant the exploitation of the most efficient workers. It was wrong, Henry further asserted, that 'we who carry so much of [the league's] administration should be leading lives utterly at variance with what we are standing for'. A reading of Miles' diary supports Henry's claim that they were working night after night, due to an increased amount of work and many distractions during the day, with unexpected crises and a constant flow of visitors to be dealt with.[93]

As we know from the modern-day politics of downsizing, such complaints don't wash with financial managers following new agendas. Mrs Robins was highly critical in reply. Alice Henry should economise on her activities and deploy her great gift of teaching others, 'a quality absolutely lacking in Miss Franklin', she added gratuitously. As for Miss Franklin, she could be relieved of her secretarial duties and, in the meantime, she should take a long-delayed holiday: 'it is not only lacking in commonsense [not to] but her refusal to take care of herself is unfair to other workers as well'.[94]

Matters remained there for the time being. Alice Henry was not standing down and Miles was not going anywhere. On 13 April she received an offer from Mills & Boon for *The Net of Circumstance*, which she had been asked to send in January, and immediately accepted it. The following evening she cut fifty-six pages from the text in three hours then slept well. A month later, on 16 May, she returned the revised manuscript 'to West', and two days later mailed a second copy to the New York publisher Doubleday, Page and Co. Presumably West was an agent, and what happened to the second copy that went to New York is presently unknown, but a contract duly arrived from Mills & Boon on 19 June. All she had to do now was await the proofs. Her New Woman novel was coming out![95]

A mystified Demy Lloyd, yachting off Newport, would wonder about references to 'a change' and 'a decision'. As might we. No more than Mrs Robins can we know all of Miles Franklin's life exactly. Perhaps because she was often too tired at the end of the day for reflection, perhaps due to 'the web of indirection', her inner life at this point becomes as unclear as the intentions of Sybyl Penelo were to the hapless Cavarley in *On Dearborn Street*. 'Wish I had a little income so I cd get off the wheel for a little while,' Miles wrote on 30 May. Her perspective differed from that of Mrs Robins, but money was beginning to matter to Miles too.[96]

The arrival in April of Margaret Hodge, a friend of Rose Scott, Dorothy Pethick from London, and young Kathleen Ussher from Sydney to study at the Art Institute added spice to the daily round; and in May, Edith Ellis, the English socialist and wife of Henry Havelock Ellis, turned up at Hull-House, and Miles was invited to dine with her there to help combat Edith's anti-Americanism. Later that year Miles heard Edith lecture on 'The Love of Tomorrow'. It is unlikely that Miles approved of her message, since Edith Ellis was proudly avant-garde and 'a vigorous defender of the abnormal'; but Miles did appear to be making progress with romance. Decorous crosses in the diaries in May indicate that relations with Bill Lloyd had become amorous, though it seems he was about to be superseded by Fred Pischel, whose long-promised driving lessons began in June. 'Automobiling' and the long evenings were good for romance. The rows of kisses increased, and for a time Fred was 'very dear'. Miles was encouraged to return to her Cupid story.[97]

But by mid-June her teeth were troubling her again. An abscess developed, and so began a painful and protracted round of treatment, including the insertion of what sounds like primitive caps in August ('At dentist from 8.45 to 10.45. Cut off two front teeth on left side and put in two temporary'), as well as fillings (requiring numerous visits in the days when injections and high-speed water-drills were unknown), at a total cost of $190, almost two months' salary, and as recorded in her pocket diary, paid off by December.[98]

She was mid-treatment when Britain declared war on Germany on 4 August 1914. Despite fears and warnings, especially of 'the menace of great armaments' (the title of an article which Miles and Alice Henry began for *Life and Labor* immediately after the British declaration of war), the war came as a terrible shock to radicals and progressives everywhere. A firm believer in the gospel of progress, Miles was horrified by 'this vile war'. Until then, the forces of evolution had seemed unstoppable, and the women's trade union movement had been riding the wave of the future. Now came confusion, division and recrimination, unfortunately for Miles Franklin at every level of her life.[99]

At the office, 'No-one thought of anything but the war,' and Miles became depressed by 'the staggering calamity'; 'life seemed hardly worth living', she recalled. In retrospect, she would say simply that as an alien in then neutral (until 1917) America, she regretted that she had been unable to put her affairs in order beforehand, meaning perhaps that she wished her book was out and she was free to move on if she chose or it became necessary. To make things more difficult, in her immediate circle loyalties were divided, as was the case with Margaret Dreier Robins, of German extraction, and her husband, Raymond, who supported the British Empire, and Miles had many other German-American friends, such as the Pischels.[100]

On 4 August, Miles finished retyping 'When Cupid Tarried' and later in the month prepared the typescript to send to H. H. Champion in Melbourne, presumably hoping for his help in placing it, maybe in his *Book Lover* magazine (nothing appeared there, however). On 13 September she finished the proofs of *The Net of Circumstance*, only to hear the next day that publication had been postponed due to the war. Ever resilient, she rang Fred Pischel and had 'a long session' with him (eight crosses). Since the Chicago broom-makers, young immigrant girls on starvation wages, had struck, she was involved immediately in supporting their cause, writing an article on their plight for *Life and Labor* as well. She also joined a picket line in support of striking embroidery workers, and on the lighter side, took her first dancing lesson at the new North West Trade Union headquarters on Milwaukee Avenue.[101]

In need of a vacation (as Mrs Robins had urged), on Saturday 3 October Miles took the train to Boston: 'I am leaving Mrs Robins in the office,' she wrote to Leonora O'Reilly in New York. 'To have her [there] is something like hitching a Baldwin engine to a baby's go-cart, but I leave with a free mind.' She had plans for a good long break. After Boston she would go to Philadelphia for a league executive meeting, to be held in association with the 34th annual Federation of Labor convention, beginning on 9 November, and would be away until the 16th.[102]

Arriving in Boston the following evening, she was met by a league member, Octavia (probably Pinchot), with whom she stayed for a few days until she found lodgings. More precisely, her old friend Aileen Goldstein found her a room, at 113 Gainsboro Street, where Aileen was staying herself.

One reason for Miles' going to Boston, apart from league connections dating back to 1911, was the number of Australian followers of Mary Baker Eddy assembled there in October for the annual Christian Science convention. Thus, in addition to Aileen Goldstein, who was intending to train as a Christian Science practitioner, Miles enjoyed the company of the Watsons, Edith Malyon, Agnes Locke, Anne Worthington, and the artist Geraldine Rede, and attended services with 'the girls'.[103]

This was as near as Miles came to organised religion at this time. Her life coincided with the rise of Christian Science, which attracted many thinking women. In Chicago she had recently attended a Presbyterian service with Alice Henry, but it only confirmed her distaste for traditional teachings: 'Same old stuff I heard in the Bush, nothing to satisfy intelligence or common sense.' Which suggests that Miles was open to the new prescription, notwithstanding 'some rare gems' she had noted in Demy's literature, and her previously expressed views on its appeal to the rich. Hope of relief from ailments as yet untouched by medical science, especially women's health problems, made Christian Science attractive, and Baker Eddy's core teaching, that spiritual self-discipline is the key to salvation, that it is 'all in the mind', struck a chord with the idealists and intellectuals of her generation. While Miles never became a member of the church, and it is hard to imagine her enjoying such a highly regulated form of worship, a relative, Leslie Bridle, recalled Miles reading Christian Science literature in later life.[104]

Demarest Lloyd may also have influenced her being in Boston. A queer and now incomplete correspondence between the two at this time suggests that Miles had something more than romance in mind, and it would be characteristic of her to have kept the clues but not the key to her intentions. Writing to her as 'Dear Friend Bull' from Boston, probably early in September, Demy said he was thinking of starting a newspaper, and if so would offer her a job. A telegram dated 18 September stated he was 'confident all your requirements can be met'. For her part, 'The Bull' declared herself willing to stay in her present position for the time being but referred to the possibility of something 'more congenial to my temperament'. Demy returned from New York when he heard she was definitely coming to Boston, and even after his unwanted advances on the alarming drive to Providence during the previous Boston stay she seemed unwilling to close things off completely: 'Did we quite finish the game of chess?' she asked of him.[105]

If this interpretation of Miles' mind games with Demy Lloyd is correct, the vacation soon proved a dead end. On the surface, the diminished contact between Miles and Demy during the latter part of this stay in Boston is adequately explained by his brutal behaviour, for which she largely forgave him (though the preserved correspondence ends soon after). And she did get new copy ('Red Cross Nurse' was ready to be sent off by the end of the year). Yet her days in Boston seem to have been increasingly perfunctory, and despite lovely weather, she was often depressed. On one occasion she wrote fretfully in her diary that life was 'a hoax'. Not that she looked forward to Chicago again. Indeed, she was 'shuddering at the thought of being compelled to go back'. Perhaps the best things to come out of the foray were *The White Feather*, a sketch of her by Geraldine Rede, now owned by the National Library of Australia (the feather was a gift from Mrs Robins), and a photographic portrait with Aileen Goldstein preserved in the Franklin Papers, where, compared with an austere Aileen, Miles looks quite cheerful.[106]

Miles left Boston by boat on the evening of 7 November, arriving in New York the next morning in time to catch the 9 o'clock train for Philadelphia, where she was pleased to find herself in an agreeable billet at 1822 Pine Street. After lunch she went straight to the first of several lengthy board meetings held over the next few days. The idea of meeting in Philadelphia was to learn from the AFL and remind it of the league's importance, so the league women participated in convention activities. Miles rode in the opening parade on the

Monday, when she was delighted to see colleagues from Chicago again, and she enjoyed all the convention outings during the week, as well as attending to such matters as the AFL's attitude to a minimum wage. Her enjoyment is evident in her report for the December issue of *Life and Labor*, 'The A.F. of L. Convention: Some Snapshots of the Historic Assemblage', where it is noted that only eight of 359 accredited delegates were women. But then Miles always enjoyed being with manly men.[107]

What a contrast awaited her back in Chicago. 'Poor old 200 E. Superior St how dirty and dreary after 1822 Pine St, Philadelphia.' It was 'joyous' all the same to see Miss Henry and Ethel Mason at the office, and she dined with Editha Phelps at the Hearth. As Editha (and Emma Pischel) had been caught in Europe when war broke out, there was a lot to catch up on. Whatever the real purpose of her trip to Boston, she had been strengthened by her time away and by Philadelphia, and was in a sense relieved to be back on the job. Apart from anything else she had run out of money, not having been paid for six weeks. Although feeling 'supertoploftical', meaning a bit overwhelmed, she was hopeful that things would 'come all right'. In a letter to league vice-president Melinda Scott of the hat trimmers' union, written her first day back, she urged Melinda to remain with the league, despite hard times:

> If nothing more comes of going to Philadelphia, I think it was worth it to have become better acquainted with you, which I have never had a chance to do before, and I want to say this here and now: we all have to meet hard situations and I guess you have had more of the brunt of them than many of … us. We all realise this, and please never think of dropping out.[108]

She went on:

> I have felt like pulling out more than once but since I have been talking to you and see how hard your row is to hoe I feel that I want to stay and help you tooth and nail until you can get someone better to put in my place. I guess the fighting never was better than it is now.

Though provisional, there was still commitment and some bounce in Miles Franklin. Its positive expression would be in the cause of peace. Its negative was not of her doing, and concerned the fate of *Life and Labor*.

Grandma Lampe with daughters Sarah Metta and Helena Lampe, possibly at Talbingo, in the late 1880s.

(MITCHELL LIBRARY, STATE LIBRARY OF NEW SOUTH WALES, PX *D250/2, NO. 157)

The homestead at Brindabella Station, where Stella Miles Franklin began her schooling; from an oil painting by her tutor, Charles A. Blyth, c. 1898.

(NATIONAL LIBRARY OF AUSTRALIA, PICTORIAL COLLECTION, R 8957)

An 1895 photograph of
Miles Franklin's mother,
Susannah Franklin.

(Mitchell Library, State
Library of New South
Wales, PX *D250/2, no. 90)

Miles' father, John Maurice
Franklin, in the 1890s.

('Hillview' Wilkinson Family
Album, courtesy Tom and
Colin Wilkinson)

Stella Miles Franklin in 1885.

Miles' teacher and family friend, Mary Anne Elizabeth ('Mae') Gillespie, 1895.

Thornford school and its pupils, with Miss Gillespie, c. 1893; Stella Franklin is fifth from left, back row, and her sister Linda is tenth from left, middle row.

(MITCHELL LIBRARY, STATE LIBRARY OF NEW SOUTH WALES, PX *D250/1, NO. 2)

The Franklin family on the front verandah of 'Stillwater', c. 1893, with Pat O'Rourke (far right, possibly a neighbour) and a dog. Stella Franklin is seated behind the dog, far left.

(MITCHELL LIBRARY, STATE LIBRARY OF NEW SOUTH WALES, PX *D250/1, NO. 3)

Stella Miles Franklin at the time of her confirmation; portrait by Stinson of Goulburn, 1894.

(MITCHELL LIBRARY, STATE LIBRARY OF NEW SOUTH WALES, PX *D250/1, NO. 7)

The cover of the first edition of *My Brilliant Career* (1901).

(MITCHELL LIBRARY, STATE LIBRARY OF NEW SOUTH WALES, MILES FRANKLIN PRINTED BOOK COLLECTION, NO. 156)

A portrait of the young author:
Miles Franklin, with riding crop,
by Henry Dorner of Goulburn, 1902.

Henry Lawson in his early thirties, c. 1890,
ten years before Miles met him.

Leading Sydney feminist Rose Scott,
who befriended Miles in 1902.

Miles spent a year working incognito as a domestic servant. Here she is as 'Mary-Anne' in Melbourne in 1904.

Joseph Furphy in 1899. Furphy published *Such is Life* in 1903. Miles Franklin's own photograph of Furphy, which he gave her in 1904, is inscribed 'This is a very precious possession'.

Miles with suffragist and friend Vida Goldstein, Melbourne, 1904.

Linda Franklin's wedding at Penrith, November 1904, with the groom, Charles Graham, seated, sister Stella (as bridesmaid) seated on Linda's right, and Aunt Helena Lampe on her far left.

(Mitchell Library, State Library of New South Wales, PX *D250/1, no. 32)

Mr and Mrs Charles Graham, 1905.

(Mitchell Library, State Library of New South Wales, PX *D250/2, no. 95)

This picture of Andrew Barton Paterson was taken after his return from the Boer War. Miles described Paterson as 'the most sophisticated man who had so far attempted to woo me sexually'.

(*SYDNEY MAIL*, 22 SEPTEMBER 1900)

Edwin Bridle, one of Miles' many suitors, 1905.

(MITCHELL LIBRARY, STATE LIBRARY OF NEW SOUTH WALES, PX *D250/3, NO. 170)

A. G. Stephens, editor of the *Bulletin*'s 'Red Page' from 1894 to 1906.

(MITCHELL LIBRARY, STATE LIBRARY OF NEW SOUTH WALES, P1/S, STEPHENS)

Alone and unchaperoned, Miles Franklin left Sydney, bound for San Francisco, aboard the *Ventura*, in 1906. Miles is second from left.

THE CHICAGO 'RECORD-HERALD.' SATURD

SINGERS PICKED FOR WOMAN'S TRADE UNION LEAGUE EVENT.

AGNES NESTOR.
STELLA FRANKLIN   MARY McENERNEY   OLIVE SULLIVAN

Stella Franklin (as Miles was mostly known in America) with three other members of the Chicago league's chorus. The chorus sang 'The Spinning Wheel' from *The Flying Dutchman* at the league's annual ball, in February 1909.

Mrs. Raymond Robins and "Cabinet" in Strike Conference; Armed Patrolmen on Guard in Vicinity of a "Storm Center."

[From photographs taken for THE TRIBUNE.]

Miles Franklin was responsible for publicity during the Chicago garment workers' strike of 1910. She is seated second from right in this picture.

(*Chicago Daily Tribune*, Friday 4 November 1910, p. 4)

A place in the sun: Miles relaxing in a deckchair on a Chicago rooftop, 1910.

(National Library of Australia, Bridle Collection, MS 681, Box 1/3)

LIFE AND LABOR

September, 1911

On we march then, we, the workers, and the rumor that ye hear
Is the blended sound of triumph and deliverance drawing near

PRICE 10 CENTS   100 PER YEAR

Cover of the September 1911 issue of the NWTUL journal *Life and Labor*, with the league's logo and photo of a street march (the first banner reads 'We have an eight hour day').

Margaret Dreier Robins, president of the NWTUL, 1907–1913, in campaign mode.

(MITCHELL LIBRARY, STATE LIBRARY OF NEW SOUTH WALES PX *D250/3, NO. 103)

Miles Franklin with her friend and colleague Melbourne-born journalist and labour reformer Alice Henry, in Chicago, 1914.

(STATE LIBRARY OF VICTORIA, J. K. MOIR COLLECTION, BOX 32/6 (c))

Right: An undated photograph of
Demarest Lloyd, playboy millionaire,
whom Miles might have married in
America.

(REPRODUCED FROM MILES FRANKLIN IN
AMERICA: HER UNKNOWN (BRILLIANT)
CAREER, BY VERNA COLEMAN)

Left: Demarest Lloyd's older brother,
William Bross ('Bill') Lloyd, man about
town and political radical, who also
flirted with Miles Franklin in Chicago.
This picture was taken in 1920.

(CHICAGO DAILY NEWS NEGATIVE COLLECTION,
CHICAGO HISTORICAL SOCIETY DN-0072195).

Dreamy Miles, with hair
ornament, 1914.

(MITCHELL LIBRARY, STATE LIBRARY
OF NEW SOUTH WALES, PX *D250/1,
NO. 14)

A friend from Miles Franklin's Chicago days, Ethel Mason Nielsen,
with husband Niels Christian Nielsen, probably in the 1920s.

The NWTUL biennial conference, New York, June 1915. Secretary-Treasurer Franklin is at
the centre of the front row.

Margaret Hodge (left) and Harriet Newcomb (right),
English educators and suffragists (undated).
(MITCHELL LIBRARY, STATE LIBRARY OF NEW SOUTH WALES, ML MSS 1745/1, BOX 3)

Lady Sarah Byles,
a leading figure
in London liberal
circles and important
influence on Miles
during her London
years. This portrait is
dated 1907.

(MITCHELL LIBRARY,
STATE LIBRARY OF NEW
SOUTH WALES, PX
*D250/3, NO. 14)

Prior to the war in Europe the peace movement had been a sedate affair. Mrs Robins had been encouraging people to think about outlawing war or how to translate the military ethos into a citizen ethos. But such a lengthy perspective was increasingly inappropriate, and a new and urgent movement was taking shape in late 1914, in which Miles was a participant. On 24 November she dined at Hull-House with the Hungarian-born peace campaigner Rosika Schwimmer: 'We spent a terrific evening on the war.' Soon there were peace rallies to attend, with Bill Lloyd an organiser, and just before Christmas she attended a rally in Chicago at which all the luminaries spoke — Jane Addams, President of Indiana University David Starr Jordan, and the poet Harriet Monroe amongst them.[109]

As for the situation at *Life and Labor*, it was difficult, to say the least. On her return from Boston, Miles had found Alice Henry in distress, with another, bigger, printers' bill due. She did what she could by putting out an appeal for support, but was overruled by Mrs Robins now on vacation in Florida. Staff meetings were called and it was decided to establish a sustentation fund, as Miles had in effect suggested in the first place. Clearly *Life and Labor* was in crisis. Moreover, Miles had not been paid for two months. As Christmas approached, she was obliged to stay in for lack of cash.[110]

As the cold set in, she concentrated in the evenings on typing up the Boston story, which was ready to go to an agent early in the new year. Of men she seems to have had very nearly enough by this time. Tender references to Fred Pischel were a thing of the past. She continued to see him occasionally and stayed close to the family, German-Americans as heartsick as she was about the war; but Fred, 'a blundering donkey', increasingly irritated her. The Lloyd connection, too, became strained. All Miles now had in common with Bill Lloyd was the campaign for peace. As for Demy, he continued to bluster and bully her until dismissed from the record as a 'silly ass'.[111]

Perhaps she drove them all to distraction with that aura of indirection documented in *On Dearborn Street*, but none of them were really so very impressive in their own right, though all were modern men. All three were involved in the real estate business: the wealthy Lloyd brothers in a desultory fashion; Fred Pischel in more practical ways. Of the three, Bill Lloyd was the most politically appealing, but married, a philanderer, and trying to divorce his impressive wife, Lola, a leading pacifist. Fred Pischel was probably the nicest, but it is not apparent that he had the same stuffing as his sister Emma, by now an inspector at City Hall, and a long-standing ally of the league. As for Demarest Lloyd, he was divorced, an uncommon and socially suspect status at the time, with an ex-wife said to be running about the country as well, and, as Miles was to conclude, 'spoiled by wealth'. There was one last bizarre exchange in 1920, between Mr O. L'Artsau, c/– Mills and Boon, and Demarest Lloyd, president of the 'Loyal Coalition' in Boston, regarding the Irish question, by which time Demy Lloyd was a pompous British Empire loyalist (and from 1922 to 1930, diplomatic correspondent for the *Christian Science Monitor* in London, where he famously travelled to assignments in a chauffeur-driven Rolls Royce). As mentioned previously, she did note his death in 1937, shortly after his second wife divorced him for cruelty. Ultimately Miles gave them all up: 'I could have had money with a man attached several times but death was preferable to "living in sin" to one of my codes and sensitiveness.'[112]

By contrast, conflict at work drew the employees — for that is what they really were — closer together. Leonora Pease, a teacher whose poems *Four and Twenty Dollies* survives in Miles Franklin's library, inscribed 'To Stella Franklin who first loved my rhymes', was one supportive ally at this troubled time. A veneer of normality was maintained by them all. Thus, just before Christmas Editha Phelps and Miles enjoyed George Bernard Shaw's *The Philanderer* at the Little Theatre — not surprisingly, Shaw, with his advanced views and iconoclastic wit, became a great favourite with Miles. She caught a whiff of home when Nell Malone, a Queensland nurse who later became a close friend, and Nell's companion, Eve Midgely, arrived in September and stayed for several months; Sydney gossip was always welcome, as when Ada Holman, journalist and wife of the then Labor Premier of New South Wales, W. A. Holman, turned up in 1915.[113]

Just as Miles never referred to her birthday in her diary, so Christmas Day abroad was usually something to be endured. Alice Henry hosted a dinner in her room for a few friends, including Miles, on Christmas Eve, but Miles spent the next day in her room typing: 'Quite alone. Never said a word to any one or saw a soul all day.' On Boxing Day it was back to the office, lunch with Bill Lloyd, and more typing in her room. Her isolation over Christmas seems emblematic of the larger reality: that she was beginning to feel like a displaced person. Denying all chauvinism, she told Leonora Pease that 'Life grew difficult, I was at last rendered unhappy being an alien, in my beloved America, where it had not mattered previously.' By way of a 1915 New Year's resolution, all that Miles was prepared to say was that 'I hope I can make it a busy and therefore satisfactory division of my hitherto unsatisfactory life'.[114]

At the same time, after seven years without a home since selling up at Penrith, her parents were settled in a cottage at 26 Grey Street, Carlton, a southern suburb of Sydney, where they remained for the rest of their lives (which meant that Miles would have a proper home to return to one day). In the interim, John Franklin had taken labouring jobs up country and Susannah had lived at Tumut and Talbingo until her mother's property was sold in 1911. She then lived with relatives in western Sydney until, after her mother's death in 1912, her share of the estate enabled her to purchase the modest weatherboard house at Carlton, at a cost of £510. Possibly Miles helped with the purchase, as she sent her mother £105 in early 1914, and an annotated house plan sent to her by Susannah states, 'I am quite satisfied, hope you are.' Susannah also purchased two shops at Willoughby on Sydney's North Shore for rent at this time.[115]

In 1915 Jane Addams (then reviled as a pacifist but joint winner of the Nobel Peace Prize in 1931) once more became a vital figure in Miles Franklin's life. Just as the declaration of war tested the claims of international socialism and found them wanting, so feminism faced a great challenge. An American response came when Addams and Carrie Chapman Catt called a meeting of representative women in Washington early in the new year. Rightly, Miles felt the league should be there, but as Mrs Robins was out of contact in Florida, Miles asked Leonora O'Reilly 'to represent working women and keep the economic causes of war to the front'.[116]

Leonora couldn't go. But she rose to the call in April when a 'peace ship' sailed from New York for Rotterdam, Holland, carrying a delegation of American women to the International Congress of Women to be held at The Hague from 28 to 30 April, in hope of paving the way for a comprehensive peace. Much ridicule was directed at this initiative, but as 'S. M. Franklin' noted in 'Peace Ahoy! Crusaders of 1915', published in *Life and Labor*'s April edition, there were still women in America who'd had mud thrown on them when they began professional nursing, and 'every upward human effort in the germ stage has seemed about as imposing as a grain of mustard'. As in the labour movement, it was soon enough learned that only some women were against war; but a gender difference is still evident today in measures of support for peace, and an enduring organisation, the Women's International League for Peace and Freedom, dates back to the assembly in The Hague in 1915, at which Leonora delivered a resounding message on behalf of working women. Meanwhile, a Woman's Peace Party had been established in America, led by Jane Addams, and a 'Stop the War' group headed by Rosika Schwimmer, composed mainly of women, was campaigning for an American peace initiative.[117]

Miles Franklin never changed her view that war was a prime example of male lunacy. Likewise, she had no time for the now rabidly patriotic Christabel Pankhurst, lecturing in Chicago in December 1914 on the war. But by May 1915 she was becoming restive after too many meetings: 'Why should there be any meaning?' she asked Rose Scott just after the sinking of the *Lusitania* on 8 May 1915. She lamented 'these mad days' and mocked the male mind ('a wonderful invention', with now two 'unsinkable' ships gone down), announcing that she had taken refuge in sophistries, since 'all philosophies fail in the teeth of such a debacle'. With a touch of the old bravado, she added, 'Let us not die of sorrowful sympathy, but eat, drink and be as merry as we can, help as much as we can and for the remainder, not become deranged.' Miles was tired of listening to speeches. However, July found her organising a rally to welcome Jane Addams back from The Hague where Addams had been chosen as Congress president, and in October she attended another rally addressed by Schwimmer and the leading Dutch activist Dr Aletta Jacobs.[118]

An underlying anxiety, about which there is almost no evidence, was the fate of *The Net of Circumstance*. If she knew that it was in production, she does not say. The only known English notice appeared in the *Times Literary Supplement* on 13 May 1915 with a brief résumé: 'Mr & Mrs Ogniblat L'Artsau are very much concerned on the subject of the economical independence of woman, her destiny, and her emancipation. Their story (American) is a careful and very very serious study of a highly-strung young female who insists on enduring great privations rather than marry before she has found her soul-mate.' Miles noted in the privacy of her diary that six copies arrived from Mills & Boon on 28 May 1915, and two survive in her Printed Books Collection. One went to the *Book Lover*, which listed it under 'Fiction' in August, the only known reference in the Australian press, and a fleeting one at that, since no review appeared on its pages subsequently. What happened to the other copies is an interesting but now unanswerable question; perhaps Miles gave them to American friends.[119]

The immediate issue was, of course, *Life and Labor*. 'It looks to me as if *Life and Labor* must go under — I see no way out unless I accept full responsibility, and this I refuse to do,' Mrs Robins wrote to Mary Dreier from Florida on 17 January 1915 when faced with another substantial bill. A dispassionate observer might think that the overall deficit was not irredeemable, but Mrs Robins had been troubled for a long time, and was determined that business management be brought under the control of the executive board. When she returned to Chicago in February, a ghastly round of meetings ensued, the upshot being an agreement that publication was to be suspended while the sustentation fund was raised. There was also a proposal from the journalist Zona Gale, conveyed by Jane Addams, that in the interim subscribers would receive copies of the respected Charity Organization Society journal the *Survey*, with a WTUL insert; but this did not find favour with the *Survey*'s editor, Paul Kellog. In March it was proposed by a league ways and means committee member, Edith Wyatt, that Miles be relieved of her duties as associate editor of *Life and Labor*, as her dual role as national secretary-treasurer and associate editor was too burdensome. Alice Henry foreshadowed her own resignation, on the grounds that she wished to undertake less harassing and fatiguing work, adding, her non-concurrence with the plan to deprive her of Miss Franklin's assistance when she later learned it was actually going to happen. (It could be that Miles had a hand in all this, but the diary entry for the day the two women met Mrs Robins to resolve the issue of Miles' dual role reads, 'I was the one decapitated this time.')[120]

These matters rested until the June biennial meeting. Some money was raised for the magazine, enabling the February number to appear, and further issues were produced in the following months. However, these were smaller (and the printers' bill less), and the staff was reduced to three: Alice Henry; Mary Galvin, a stenographer; and Ethel Mason, the book-keeper; and moved to a cheaper office. The plan was that Alice Henry would continue as editor until June, when she would formally resign and become the league's national lecturer, a position vacant since the death of Frances Squire Potter in 1914. Henry would then be replaced by Stella Franklin. (When Mary Gilmore heard of this, she suggested Alice Henry should be invited to lecture in Australia on the need for organisation among women workers.)

'The steam roller has gotten busy,' Margaret Robins told her sister. She worried, though, about replacing Alice Henry with Miles Franklin: 'Miss Franklin has some excellent qualities both as a writer and an editor but … she has neither Miss Henry's knowledge of the labor movement nor her fine vision.' According to Alice Henry's biographer, Diane Kirkby, there had been a contest between two different conceptions of what the magazine should be. Whereas Alice Henry and Miles envisaged an expressive and elevating magazine, Mrs Robins believed the primary purpose of the publication should be propagandist. Perhaps they were unrealistic, and since Mrs Robins held the purse strings, in the end she won. The loss was significant. Though the name was retained, vitality gradually drained out of what became in effect a bulletin, appealing to neither the middle-class allies nor to working women.[121]

Miles felt only relief that it was over. Little did she know what else Mrs Robins had in mind for her. Not until May did she learn that Mrs Robins planned to replace her as national secretary with league stalwart Emma Steghagen of the boot and shoe makers', a far less volatile personality. Mrs Robins was tired of the complaints about overwork and misery in the *Life and Labor* office emanating from Miles and Alice Henry, reared as they were on protective labour legislation in Australia; and she got what she wanted. 'Sister Emma' was duly elected at the fifth biennial convention in New York in June.[122]

There are only two Australian press references to Miles in 1915, both convention-related: in the *Worker* (where Mary Gilmore kept an eye on her compatriots) and the *Sydney Stock and Station Journal*, run by R. McMillan. These indicate that Miles made sure that back home they did not fully appreciate her demotion. In Chicago, however, things were tricky. After an enjoyable post-convention break in New York with league friends (Miles sent four postcards to her mother), including an overnight stay with Leonora O'Reilly and her mother in Brooklyn, the new regime had to be faced. In administrative terms, Miles was now merely a member of the executive board. She handed the books over to Emma Steghagen and on 12 July began as editor of *Life and Labor*. Stenographer Mary Galvin was dismissed in early August, ensuring that the new *Life and Labor* would cost less. As Ethel Mason had already left, this meant, as Miles wrote to Leonora O'Reilly, she was 'the sole survivor'.[123]

Relations with Mrs Robins were now poisonous, and Miles was determined to leave. She would have liked to edit a real working woman's magazine, but Mrs Robins had made that impossible. A plan advanced by Miles envisaged the use of voluntary labour to bring out the magazine, though the board prevailed upon her not to resign formally just yet. She told Leonora O'Reilly she was thinking of coming to New York.[124]

When she did leave, it was as much as Mrs Robins could do to call by *Life and Labor*'s new drab little office at 166 West Washington Street to say goodbye. After such a long and rewarding association, that seems very sad. But the cultural gap had widened, and the socially hybrid league's moment was passing. Miles was not only stoical but determined to get away, though unsure about how and where to go. At one stage, Ethel Mason proposed they set up a chicken farm, where Editha Phelps could stay over summer. Miles told Leonora O'Reilly that she might give it out that she was returning to Australia. But she was not serious. In a letter to Eva O'Sullivan in Sydney on 23 September advising she would not have a permanent address until after the new year, she said that the war had spoiled her plans to visit Australia, and now she was 'a seething mass of indecision', awaiting some unspecified information, unsure whether to go to London or California. Acknowledging the lure of London, she added that she would not want to arrive just as the Germans were taking over, as both defeatist and pro-German friends alike kept telling her would happen.[125]

There is no clear record of her decision to go to London. She seems to have confided in no one, not even her diary. However, on 18 September she invited a few 'faithful friends' to a farewell afternoon tea party at the Narcissus Room on the top floor at Marshall Field's department store. In her invitation to Bill Lloyd's wife, Lola, she reassured Lola that the peace movement or some good angel had sufficiently relieved her 'mysogyny (but applied to all the race)' for the tea party, deemed a great success on the day. Not all the names of the fifteen friends assembled are now recognisable, but Editha Phelps, Margery Currey, Emma Pischel and her mother, Agnes Nestor, Ethel Mason and Mary Galvin were there, and Leonora Pease came late. 'Perhaps it was the general war poison which has affected me this last year to the extent of feeling that I had never met one single human being, not excepting my mother, who would not exploit me to the last inch for what of usefulness or entertainment was in me and then throw me on the scrap without a qualm,' she explained in her diary. Her anger at Mrs Robins was especially long-lasting, as expressed in a letter to Alice Henry from London in 1918: 'I am afraid I am not sympathetic with her yet … If she hadn't a penny, had no health as well as suffered since she was 15 every tooth torture known, no beauty, and no-one to lean on for profit or pleasure, then I might be able to use the word sympathy … [but] perhaps not even then.' In retrospect Miles' memory was of exploitation: 'I was always sweated to obliteration by those reformers.'[126]

When young in Australia, Miles Franklin had lacked a peer group. This she acquired in abundance in America. Her circle in Chicago was large, and many of those closest to her became lifelong friends. Eventually she even forgave Margaret Dreier Robins. However, by the time she came to reflect on the significance of her Chicago years, many of those women had died. There is no doubt that although few were literary, these were vital and sustaining associations, both emotionally and intellectually, of the kind taken for granted among gifted men. 'It's lovely riches to have a friend,' she wrote to Margery Currey on her return to Sydney in 1933, and more extensively in 1950:

> I was going over my days in the USA and totting up what I had got out of it. The things through affection are the only ones that ever meant anything to me. I hadn't the gifts for acquisitiveness. Affection plus intelligence is the most delightful mixture of friendship and friendship the warmest most permanent thing in this existence, and I thought further that Editha, you and Ethel were my most beloved girl friends. Editha was unique, Ethel was so lovely and soft — not an inharmonious or suffering note in her and you my dear well, we had such a congeniality in impishness, audacity of thought and in every way you are a delight to remember.[127]

Miles kept working at the office until mid-October, where she wrote what turned out to be her last signed article for *Life and Labor* and prepared the next issue. To all intents and purposes, she was simply taking leave, and it was conceivable, though unlikely, that after a break she would return. She had submitted a letter 'providing for my extermination' from *Life and Labor* in early October, but its timing displeased Mrs Robins and was ignored, so that her name appeared on the publication until the end of the year, at which time she sent a letter of resignation from London and it was 'accepted with regret' by the board. It was not until 1917 that she formally resigned from the executive board.[128]

Meanwhile, the farewell round in Chicago continued, with lunches (two with Mrs Maynard, a significant transatlantic link) and dinners — with Bill Lloyd at the Automobile Club and at Hull-House with Jane Addams, who, as Miles recalled many years later, when asked if there was anything Miles could do for her in London, said she would like to know if it was true that soldiers had stimulants before going over the top, a claim that had brought abuse upon Addams when she returned from The Hague. Friends took her to the theatre and the vaudeville, and to a gramophone concert. Fred Pischel hung about, no doubt miserably, but by now superfluous. Travel documents, needed in wartime, were being pursued, along with testimonials from prominent labour leaders.[129]

What then was the 'information' she was awaiting, mentioned in a letter to Eva O'Sullivan on 24 September? Could it be that she was hoping to hear from a publisher? In August she had set to work in earnest on *On Dearborn Street*, and diary entries suggest she finished a first version before leaving Chicago. This is confirmed by a letter to the Chicago bookseller and publisher McClurg & Co, dated 24 October 1915, the day she arrived in New York from Chicago. It reads in part, 'With regard to the manuscript entitled "On Dearborn Street", which I asked you to be so good as to read, will you do me a favour …' Posing as G. Marrriott of Chicago, she apologised for not having time to call for mail before leaving and asked that the manuscript be mailed to Marriott, c/– literary agent A. P. Watt in London. Mysteriously she also asked that 'the book' be mailed to another literary agent, Horace Paget, in New York. Perhaps she was trying to interest American publishers in the forthcoming *Net of Circumstance*.[130]

On Dearborn Street was perhaps Miles' boldest throw. Unusually in works by Australian women writers before the 1980s, the narrator is male, and the tale is told from his point of view. Practically all the elements of the New Woman novel are there for the finding in *On Dearborn Street*, along with outspoken commentary on the double standard of morality and the war. In essence it is a sustained attempt to answer the old question: 'What do women want?'[131]

The setting is Chicago, and the wooing of Sybyl Penelo, stenographer, stretches over some two years, from 1913 to early 1915. Cavarley, the narrator, is an older and rather ordinary man, an architect now in real estate (shades of Bill Lloyd), of uncertain origin but having been reared by Aunt Pattie, and proprietor of the Caboodle, a male-only residential in inner-city Chicago. While visiting a lady oculist, he encounters the appealing ingénue Sybyl, a girl with greeny-grey-blue-brown eyes and an impertinent twist to her chin, and is encouraged by Sybyl's employer, the mild Miss Maguire (perhaps based on Ethel Mason), to entertain her, as she 'had no home life and no one to take care of her'.[132]

Sybyl, too, is of hazy origin, maybe Canadian, and although fond of men, having been reared among them, proves elusive, despite Cavarley's best efforts to understand the mind of a modern woman. Cavarley is in love at last. How disconcerting, then, that when his young friend, playboy Bobby Hoyne — handsome, rich and an adherent of Christian Science — meets Sybyl, an outrageous flirtation begins, ending only with Bobby's accidental death. Cavarley had been appalled and bewildered by Bobby's success: 'What she could see in him besides his teeth and hair and his ready money almost shook my faith in women's selective instinct' (a sentiment straight from Lester Ward's *Pure Sociology*). And even though his own near-disastrous attempt at aviation heroics upsets her, she resists marrying him: she is not going to marry anyone.[133]

The war is pivotal. Bobby had planned to join up with Tony Hastings (a prior manifestation in *The Net of Circumstance*) in Paris, in an ambulance service — Miles' wartime male heroes always do this — funded by Chicago wealth, and Sybyl was to go too. Cavarley reflects bitterly that now he will have nothing, that brute force is all that mattered:

> There had been a few of us — congenital idiots apparently — who had thought the world growing saner and more democratic, really moving towards more far-reaching justice, hygiene and comfort. These dreams were now proven to be of the pipe ... We now awoke to reality — such a reality! The realisation that the dominating ideal of the world was still brute force ...[134]

The ambulance support plan is nullified by Bobby's death and Sybyl stays in Chicago. The second half of the novel consists of Cavarley's quest to win her, 'a wild bird on the bough'.[135] After all, he is as complex as she is; and she is surely worth the effort. Making slow progress, he realises there must be a screw loose somewhere: 'Perhaps women do not care to be worshipped or appreciated or understood — they want — God knows what they want! The screw that was loose with me was that the one woman of them all did not want me.'[136]

War is not, after all, the final consideration. But, the attentive reader will not be surprised to learn, it takes Aunt Pattie to get things straight. Rather than give the plot away, suffice it to say that the underlying problem pertains to sexual purity. Sybyl insists they must live at the Caboodle, not in the suburbs, and the final resolution lies ahead. Cavarley accepts this: 'I had never been a follower of the popular schools of manhood', and it would be a matter of 'gambler's luck'. Sybyl herself was 'weary of working for unpopular causes' and all three — Cavarley, Sybyl and Aunt Pattie — sail away. The novel ends some time in 1915.[137]

This résumé has been made from the published version of *On Dearborn Street*, which in turn reproduces the typescript preserved in the Franklin Papers, probably dating from 1920. Nonetheless, for all the probable subsequent revisions, this is unmistakably Miles' verdict on her Chicago experiences, and an informative if inconclusive representation of the net of circumstance as it fell apart. The personal cost of singledom remained high, but where was the resting point if not in marriage? Thus, for all its boldness and topicality, the novel's timing and irresolute ending were unfortunate, and it is not surprising that it remained in limbo for so long.[138]

Perhaps Miles suspected as much. She certainly wasn't admitting to anything on the literary front when she wrote to Kate Baker in Melbourne on 23 September 1915. Baker, standard-bearer of Joseph Furphy, had written inquiring about publishing Furphy's work in America. Miles replied that there would be no possibility, as Americans were not interested in Australian books and the war made things more difficult, as she knew, having had a publication held up herself. But then she went on to say, 'I have written nothing since I came over — nothing to speak of — it is impossible to write and live as full a life as I have been doing.'[139] It was true about the full life, but it would have been more accurate to say that she had not succeeded in getting any of her work published. But she still hoped. And planned. Between *The Net of Circumstance* and *On Dearborn Street*, under the now familiar pseudonym Mr & Mrs Ogniblat L'Artsau, she had apparently written 'A Business Emergency', an unpublished play in which Mrs Mabel Dodge Reber, who regards marriage as business, deals with her wandering husband and his paramour in fine style. Mr & Mrs O. L'Artsau also scripted another play at this time, likewise unpublished, an allegedly comic four-acter entitled 'Virtue', set in New York and Chicago. In this play Maisie Pierce, a working girl, escapes from being a kept woman, and resolutely refuses to be trapped by the double standard. She is saved to marry the right man by the intervention of Antoinette Toby, an older woman who sounds rather like Antoinette Donnelly, the then beauty editor at the *Chicago Tribune*. Antoinette Toby lives in an elegant apartment on Chicago's North Side, where Miles had lived for most of her time in the city.[140]

On Friday 22 October 1915, having done all the usual things one does before leaving on a holiday — been to the bank, said goodbye at the office (and the Hearth), and visited a colleague in hospital — Miles went to hear the Russian, later Bolshevik, diplomat Alexandra Kollontai speak at the Commonwealth Club, and at 10.30 p.m. caught the train for New York.

'Emma and Editha saw me off with violets.' Even the weather was pleasant. In New York, she took a room for the coming week, and saw numerous colleagues and friends. Fittingly, on her last night in America she dined with Alice Henry at the Liberal Club; and at noon the next day, 30 October 1915, New York league officer Alice Bean, and Leonora O'Reilly and her mother, saw Miles off on the *St Paul*.[141]

So ended Miles Franklin's life 'on Dearborn Street'. Although she was left with mixed feelings about Mrs Robins, she must have felt a pang about leaving: 'I do hope I can come back again, & be a useful or entertaining member of the modern sisterhood,' she wrote to Leonora O'Reilly as the ship neared England. And she never lost her admiration for the strong women of America.[142]

If Miles Franklin did not quite succeed in reinventing herself as a writer during her American years, she'd certainly had a good try.

PART III

ENGLAND & AUSTRALIA

November 1915–December 1932

7

PACK UP YOUR TROUBLES — LONDON AND THE BALKANS: NOVEMBER 1915–SEPTEMBER 1918

'The desire to find out can lead one far afield.'[1]

In November 1915, there were over a million British and imperial troops facing the German army on the Western Front, and until evacuation the following month, another 90,000 at Gallipoli on the South-Eastern Front, while a small Allied force for the relief of Serbia had landed in Salonika in northern Greece in October 1915. That same month saw British casualties top the half-million mark, and a political crisis over inept military leadership was brewing in London, soon to be followed by turmoil over conscription and the supply of munitions.[2]

The realities of war in Europe emphasised the remoteness of American politics at this time, and formed the backdrop to the 'European turn' in the life of Miles Franklin, who arrived in London on 7 November 1915. She was now thirty-six and, as Alice Henry later observed, she needed to be there. Her frame of mind was not so far removed from that of the soldiers who made 'Pack up your troubles in your old kitbag/And smile, smile, smile' the most popular refrain of 1915.[3]

After an uneventful Atlantic crossing, as in 1911 she made straight for Miss Brennan's boarding house at 22 Upper Woburn Place, off Euston Road, where Nell Malone met her and took her to see Kathleen Ussher and her mother. Soon afterwards Miles found a room of her own, first at 91 Holland Road, Kensington, and then with the Usshers at 1 Milton Chambers,

128 Cheyne Walk, Chelsea, on the Thames Embankment just beyond Battersea Bridge, where she delighted in her 'dugout'.[4]

Aileen Goldstein and artist Geraldine Rede were also in London in late 1915 on an extended visit to see relatives and friends, presumably after the annual Christian Science convention in Boston the previous year. Thus on her fourth day in England Miles lunched with Aileen at the Women's Freedom League (WFL) headquarters at 144 High Holborn. Afterwards they attended a recruiting rally in Trafalgar Square, where those men eligible and willing to serve were supposed to 'attest' to it, an approach superseded by conscription in January 1916, so that soon Miles would be attending anti-conscription rallies. Within the week she had also visited munitions workers at Fulham, and on 18 November met blinded soldiers. Nonetheless, London seemed surprisingly calm, and she was feeling better all the time, lunching with old friends, enjoying the shops — Selfridge's on Oxford Street, founded by an ex-employee of Marshall Field's in Chicago, was the latest thing and her favourite — and attending various matinées.[5]

All of Miles' networks were in evidence, and most of the people she saw were either Australians who had visited her in Chicago or people she had met before in London or in America, such as Violet Pike (about to become Mrs Arthur Penty). Surrounded by familiar faces, Miles found it easy to relax. Within ten days she was helping Mrs Ussher at the depot distributing babies' kits. These were prepared by members of the Babies' Kit Society for the Allies' Babies, founded by Dr Mary Booth in Sydney in November 1914 to provide needy soldiers' wives with useful items such as babies' bonnets and cot covers. The London depot was in an old chapel in Carton Street, off Baker Street in the West End.

After contacting Margaret McMillan, whom she had first met in 1911, Miles decided to help the McMillan sisters at their 'baby camp' at Deptford, near Greenwich on the Thames, one of the famous child-welfare projects of the day. There, at 232 Church Street, the McMillan sisters and their helpers ('pink-cheeked English maidens', according to Miles) ran a school-cum-clinic for kindergarteners and provided long-day care for the babies of women munitions workers. Miss McMillan advised that she needed someone to help with the toddlers in the mornings and that she could put Miles up, though not very comfortably. It was years since Miles had had anything to do with babies, but as the oldest daughter in a family of seven, she had plenty of experience. Part-time war work minding toddlers and a saving on accommodation would have suited her. She chose not to stay fulltime at the camp, however, preferring to keep her room at Holland Road for weekends and respite.[6]

She began at Greenwich on 23 November. The 'baby camp' was partly outdoors, and Miles caught a cold more or less immediately; but she persisted with the camp until February 1916, when she caught German measles (for which vaccines were not then available). A young nurse, May Meggitt, and her sister, Phyllis, a trainee teacher, who were also working at the camp and became lifelong friends, took Miles home to Newport, Wales, to recover, which she found a pleasant experience. At Newport she was able to visit a dentist. She also attended a meeting of the local trades council, where as ex-secretary and treasurer of the National Women's Trade Union League of America she addressed 'a few words of hearty greeting', courtesy of May and Phyllis' mother, a suffragist and ardent trade unionist.[7]

Another new friend was Annie Beatrice Champion, sister of H. H. Champion of the *Book Lover*, a British nanny resident in central London, whom Miles met through Aileen Goldstein. Aileen and her friend Geraldine Rede left for Melbourne on the SS *Medina* on Christmas Eve; but by then Miles had renewed contact with those redoubtable Englishwomen who had founded Shirley School near Rose Scott's home in Sydney, the Misses Margaret Hodge and Harriet Newcomb. Hodge and Newcomb now lived at Temple Fortune Court, a model apartment building in Hampstead Garden Suburb near Golders Green tube station. They became important to Miles during her London years, especially Miss Hodge, an ardent feminist, socialist and devotee of Empire, who seemed to be in danger of losing her mind over the war. As well, 'Mr and Mrs P.', possibly Louis Post and his wife, Alice, whom Miles recalled as having been 'like a family to me' in Chicago, arrived from New York in December. There was no need to face a bleak Christmas: 'Went to Mrs Ussher's for dinner. Nell came for supper. I stopped all night.' Nor was there the usual New Year resolution: the diary entry for 31 December 1915 reads simply 'Down at baby camp till late because short of help. Came home & pottered, washed head & went to bed about ten.'[8]

Two days earlier, on 29 December 1915, Miles wrote to the NWTUL executive board formally resigning as editor of *Life and Labor*. However, she remained on the board and as an ordinary member of the Chicago league, so it is not clear what she intended to do now that the three weeks' vacation leave on full pay she had been granted had expired. It was not clear to her either. In May she said as much to Alice Henry, but supposed she would have to return. 'You will have to wait until I get back to hear the news,' she wrote to Agnes Nestor on 21 October 1916.[9]

No doubt the motto of the WFL, 'Dare to be Free', had a special resonance for her now she was on her own. On 13 December 1915 she had hired a typewriter. Soon she was writing full tilt, and as usual she kept the typescripts. A year later, by December 1916, she had written some eighteen features for the press (eight published), two short stories (neither published), two or three plays (likewise unpublished), and between April and December 1916, a longer narrative in diary form which is of some significance, as are the unpublished feature articles (to be referred to shortly), and one of the plays, 'The English Jackeroo' (see Chapter 8). The longer narrative, 'How the Londoner Takes his War By a Dissenting Diarist' and addressed to 'Dear E', possibly Editha Phelps, consists of some forty-three sketches drawn from Miles' daily experience during her first year in London (as may be checked against her diary), amounting to about 20,000 words. Retitled 'Diary of a Dawdler' and sent to Watt, the literary agent, in December 1916, it seems to have fallen into limbo; but a favourable reader's report survives.[10]

'How the Londoner Takes his War' is exceptionally valuable as a guide to the direction of her thinking throughout 1916. It even casts light on Miles' income. It was amazing, wrote 'the Dawdler', how much enjoyment could be had in London for a pound or 30 shillings a week. That was what she got for an article in the *Sydney Morning Herald*, maybe a bit more if longer than one column; and as her account book shows, it was what she actually expended in a week initially. Things looked grim in April — 'starvation full steam ahead' — but there were many Australian women of small means resident in early twentieth-century London doing a lot on a little. Hence Miles, with writing now her priority, managed to spin out her American pay, plus at least £6 from her journalism by mid-year. Since its opening in June, she had been working on a voluntary basis a day or two a week at the Minerva, a vegetarian café established by Mrs Maud Fisher at 144 High Holborn, which gave its profits to the WFL; but in November she decided she could no longer afford this and would have to look for paid employment. In consequence, the Minerva took her on, presumably with pay and meals, for four days a week as cook/waitress.[11]

The publisher's reader who provided the favourable report described 'How a Londoner Takes his War' as wide-ranging, broad-minded and humorous. Offered as 'modest notes on common life in these days', on the basis of desultory participation 'in the activities of a number of friends and acquaintances … throughout half-a-dozen circles in varying social grades', the narrator — the Dawdler — begins by expressing relief and pleasure at being in London and states her desire to make a fresh start 'ethically'. After the 'stupendous din and glare' of an American city, she finds London restful, and realising that strident views are counterproductive, hopes for a new sense of proportion about the war. By 1916's end the Dawdler understands that London's 'astounding normality' reflects not just good humour but self-assurance and 'the sole desire to chastise the Germans'. The conclusion to be drawn seems inescapable. The time for peace is not yet, and most of the talk of awakening is claptrap: much as the British need to understand that their right over the earth is challenged, the British Empire will survive the inferno of war.

Although Miles had not become a supporter of the war, the Home Front appealed strongly to her as a subject, and she was being drawn ever closer to the war effort. Something more profound than war fever was at work, nonetheless. As Miles/the narrator made her way around the imperial capital — to lectures and meetings, to churches, to concerts and the theatre, to observe or help with war work, to rallies and conferences, and to tribunals to hear the claims of conscientious objectors, noting as she did such events as the Easter Rising in Dublin, the death by drowning of Lord Kitchener and zeppelin raids overhead — she encountered the soldiers themselves. Many were Australians, on their way from Gallipoli to the Western Front, heroes of the hour. On 26 January she was at 'an Australian corroboree' at Caxton Hall. On 25 April — 'a day to dim the eyes and fill the throat, a day to go in silence' — she saw them marching to Westminster Abbey. A few called on her, and she visited her cousin Claude Kinred in hospital in Birmingham.[12]

It was not just a resurgent sense of Australian identity that moved her, though there was that, as she felt much nearer Australia than she had in America. She was proud of the Australian soldiers and their unabashed ways; and until it was lost in the Balkans, she always wore an Australian flag brooch. But more than that, it was the same deep-seated humanism that characterised so many responses to the wanton waste of the Great War: 'It is impossible to live in any of the belligerent countries without feeling a deep affection for the soldiers … just gentle, ordinary people', full of gaiety and bravado, Miles felt, despite being assembled for the slaughter, just like the cattle in the Chicago stockyards.[13]

On reflection, Miles found the soldiers' gaiety the hardest thing to bear. And she felt strongly the constraints of gender: 'A woman can only look from the windows.' More ebulliently, she hoed into the Tories, who said they were protecting women. Protection! An offending party was told to read the American Commission's report on Serbia and he would see what wars did for women (a reference to the Austrian army's slaughter of 9000 Serbian civilians earlier in the year). Far from protecting women, war exposed them. But then, at the end of the text, she wonders if she would draw similar conclusions if writing from within the German Empire.[14]

The roles available to women in World War I were extremely limited. Even a non-combatant role was not easily come by. Writing to Leonora O'Reilly in New York on 14 May 1916, Miles said she would like to go to France but it cost $25 for three months to work in the soup kitchens there. She said much the same to Agnes Nestor in October.[15]

Her best chance lay with the Scottish Women's Hospitals (SWH) for Foreign Service, an all-women organisation established by Dr Elsie Inglis in 1914 under the auspices of the National Union of Women's Suffrage Societies (NUWSS) 'for both country and Suffrage'. It was funded by private donations and local groups, and run on a voluntary basis by women doctors until 1917, when Dr Inglis died, and others stepped in. The British War Office repeatedly declined its services, but it found plenty to do on the Continent, where it served mainly alongside French armies. Thus it tends to be overlooked, but it was a unique organisation, and a successful one too, with some fourteen hospitals sent to the field during the war. Harriet Newcomb was co-opted to the SWH London committee in November 1916, and was an obvious contact for Miles Franklin.[16]

The evidence suggests that the WFL's stance on the suffrage issue also played a significant part in shaping Miles Franklin's desire to get closer to the war. As a democratic but still militant breakaway from the Pankhursts' Women's Social and Political Union (WSPU), the WFL sought to occupy the middle ground in the long struggle for votes for women in Britain (which did not end until adult women under twenty-eight were enfranchised in 1928). It consisted, it has been said, of 'serious feminists'; and although the smallest of the three main suffrage groups, it was articulate, innovative and arguably more visionary in approach than either the WSPU or the older NUWSS. It was also the only suffrage society to survive the war, lasting to 1961. When in 1914 it suspended militancy, it still kept the suffrage flag flying — as the WSPU famously did not — and undertook various forms of war work for women and children.[17]

At the same time, it kept an eye on the wider world. Margaret Hodge, from 1915 the WFL's hardworking literature secretary and wont to proclaim 'I have had the vote in Australia', was valued for her international experience. Very likely she was involved with the league's publishing arm, the Minerva Publishing Company, located at WFL headquarters on High Holborn, along with the Minerva café. Certainly her sympathies lay with causes such as that promoted in the company's 1916 publication *The Retreat from Serbia: Through Montenegro and Albania,* a brief but vivid memoir by Olive M. Aldridge, a suffragist who served with the 3rd Serbian Relief Unit in the second half of 1915 and participated in the Serbian army's terrible winter trek to the Adriatic to escape advancing Austrian forces. Mrs Aldridge signed off on her book in August 1916 with the hope that Britain would do everything within its power to help the Serbs: 'In the final adjustments of this terrible war may my country do all within its power to secure justice for the liberty loving people of this eastern land.'[18]

Miles already knew Mrs Aldridge. She first called on her at 41 Russell Square, Bloomsbury, in April 1916, two months after Mrs Aldridge had addressed the WFL on 'Our Retreat from Serbia' at Caxton Hall. Later in the year, together they attended meetings about Serbia with Miss Hodge. Mrs Aldridge was also an organiser for the SWH, and she departed again for the Balkans in December 1916 (as did Nina Boyle, director of the WFL's political department), remaining there until October 1917. So Miles was well aware of the Balkan situation, though still thinking in terms of France regarding her own war contribution.[19]

In London houses lacked heating and hot water, and derogatory remarks about women were often to be heard on the buses. But by November 1916, according to 'How the Londoner Takes his War', 'I have had a glorious time wherein to regain poise and regenerated vision wherewith to hold fast to that which I believe is the truth.' That truth involved a certain purposefulness of mind, bravery even, to attain an active and realistic ethical position when confronted by the war. 'We have gone through Verdun and lived hourly on the news from the Somme and the Balkans ... Nearly every day there is a political crisis'. If the fiercely anti-war short story 'The Kookaburras Laugh Good Night', set at Wilga, is any guide, the first step was to acknowledge that progress is not inevitable and that wars are systemic, which unpalatable truth Miles realised sooner than many prewar pacifists. There was much jingoistic hysteria to contend with day by day, and also masochism, as criticised by George Bernard Shaw in a lecture on war economies to the Clapham WFL on Empire Day 1916, enthusiastically reported by 'S. M. F.' for the WFL's *Vote,* and to the *Book Lover* in Melbourne ('Mr Shaw denounced, as a tenet of the worshippers of Baal, the ancient instinct which feels the way to placate fortune is to injure ourselves', excessive economies being both dangerous and inefficient, in his view). Thus, despite second thoughts about conscription as maybe more democratic, she remained emphatic that it was wrong. She and Charlotte Despard, sister of the distinguished soldier Sir John French, and grande dame of the WFL and the Nine Elms social settlement at Battersea, danced with delight when in late 1916 the news came through that Australians had voted against conscription. (The soldiers Miles spoke to said it was because politicians were — splendid phrase — such 'unmerciful twisters'.) And after all, she observed, war was 'the one thing in all creation for which men do not blame women'.[20]

Meanwhile, she resumed French lessons and began brushing up her shorthand. With a new friend, expatriate Australian Mrs Maud Walsöe, a niece of P. S. Watson and like him a Christian Scientist, she learned to swim at St George's Baths between visits to such places as Holland House and the London Zoo. She and Nell Malone went to the theatre weekly, seeing in September 1916, for example, *Peg o' My Heart, Daddy-Long-Legs* and the Chicago-born Edward Sheldon's hit *Romance* (unlike the other two plays now quite forgotten, but Miles thought this teary tale of a young minister's passion for an opera singer the best thing since *Trilby* and saw it several times subsequently), and also the remarkable documentary film *The Battle of the Somme.* On weekends she often went to Hyde Park to hear the speakers: on one occasion a jingoistic ex-suffragette, and on another, two patriotic bishops on their soapboxes, more effective than any recruiting sergeant, she thought, and more appalling. (In 'How the Londoner Takes his War', a recollection of the Archbishop of Canterbury blessing flags and opposing wage rises for munitions workers provoked a ferocious comment: 'Go to any church and count the monuments to slaughter and to those who have distinguished themselves in massacring and being massacred and if you [believe] in Christ, come decorously away and marvel how the church can consider itself His bride.') She also took occasional trips: in addition to Newport with the Meggitts, there was a day trip to Birmingham in January.

In late July she spent a fortnight 'doddering' about in Canterbury with Miss Hodge, after the second British Dominions Woman Suffrage Union conference at Westminster, for which she had worked on publicity beforehand and which she later reported on for the Charity Organization Society's journal the *Survey* in Chicago.[21]

Miles' literary notebook contains some delectable recollections of encounters with the great at this time, mostly at public meetings. On one occasion her idol Olive Schreiner, who was in London during the war, caused a scene when her presence was noticed in the hall and she had to be removed. Miss Hodge, a terror for freedom, though Miles admits 'a bit dotty', also created some memorable, not to say amusing, situations. Thus when supporting a charming Zulu nationalist, Mr Gunnmede, she first took him to the Minerva — 'Mrs Despard's group baulked at none striving for freedom' — and then to the Lyceum Club, where his skin colour displeased some American members, to which Miss Hodge replied that Mr Gunnmede's countrymen had shed their blood in war to save those assembled, and that if such men were good enough to die for us, it was damned impertinence to consider ourselves too good to eat with one of them. Proceedings against her were 'squabashed', that is, crushed.[22]

In London Miles Franklin continued to enjoy the simple things of life. She delighted in the swans and ducks on the Thames, and travelling about 'on top o' bus' (they were open then, and had women conductors, in knee-length skirts). She relished London's changing seasons, which even at their worst were much milder than in Chicago: 'I had forgotten that life could be much less worse under different climatic conditions,' she later wrote to her mother on a postcard of Temple Fortune Court. Although her diary often records depression and anxiety, there is also evidence of exuberance, as in a cheerful informal photograph of her with Australian soldiers dated 6 October 1916, and she had put on 16 pounds (7 kilos) since leaving Chicago: 'I never felt better in my life,' she told Agnes Nestor. In the last quarter of 1916 she finished the 'Jackeroo' play in a matter of days and reworked 'How the Londoner Takes his War' (sent to the agent A. P. Watt on 18 December).[23]

By mid-1916 Miles had acquired a new friend and mentor in Lady Sarah Anne Byles, an aunt by marriage of the Maynards of Chicago days. 'Did I tell you,' Miles wrote to Alice Henry on 26 September 1916, 'that Lady Byles is one of the loveliest people I have met over here … She is a beauty as well as most sympathetic and broad-minded.' Soon after they met, Lady Byles and her husband, Sir William Byles, MP, took Miles to tea at the Palace of Westminster, and Miles soon turned the outing into a sketch, 'Tea on the Terrace', written for (but apparently not published by) the *Sydney Morning Herald*.[24]

A degree of mystery hangs over Miles' literary goals during this time in London. Probably she was most concerned about her American novels. On 25 November 1915, A. P. Watt had advised 'G. Marriott' that Mills & Boon had returned *On Dearborn Street*, saying it needed revision and that many of its Americanisms would not be understood in the United Kingdom. Six months later, on 4 May 1916, Watt further advised that the publisher Duckworth had also declined it. The style was 'very attractive' but it was too 'native'. Duckworth did suggest, however, that if an American publisher could be found, the firm would consider an edition from unbound pages. Meanwhile, *The Net of Circumstance* had proved a deep disappointment, with no known reviews and few, if any, sales (a royalty statement dated June 1918 recording 1167 copies in stock is marked 'NO SALES'), and it is possible Miles was angling for an American edition. According to a diary entry, by October she felt up to answering a letter to 'Marriott'. To whom it went or what it said we do not know, but she was by then pottering at *On Dearborn Street*.[25]

One Wednesday afternoon in May 1916, Miles and Nell Malone visited a fortune-teller on the Strand, leading to another unpublished London sketch, this one entitled 'Fortune by Mascott on the Strand'. In the sketch, a fortune-teller predicts a bright future for the narrator, a female client aged about thirty. This woman has a great deal of personal magnetism, and should succeed as a writer; she will marry someone she has already met who has been married before, and will soon take a short trip over the seas to a place she has been before. Success as a writer was what Miles wanted to hear; but the other predictions seem somewhat surprising. Of course, it *is* only a sketch. But she still thought she might be returning to Chicago, and she had recently heard via Editha Phelps that Bill Lloyd was now divorced. On 7 January 1917 she wrote to him, but the letter has not survived and its content is unknown. In any event, he remarried quite soon, and there would be another child (John Lloyd, born 1919). From what Miles had previously written to Alice Henry, it is probable that she had come to regard the wayward Bill Lloyd with affection, like a labrador dog: big, warm, around all the time, but a bit hopeless. Maybe it was really the rejected younger brother Demy, who remarried in 1916, who was being conjured up in the sketch.

Maybe it was both. Still, she had not quite done with romance, though she had certainly finished with poor, cowed Fred Pischel, who wrote on 28 February 1916 that she was 'so many, many times' in his thoughts. That was his last letter, and as far as is known he never married.[26]

In Chicago, Miles once said that what she wanted was a career as a singer, with writing as a second string. By now, she had given up on singing, except to delight in the great British contralto Clara Butt, 'that modern goddess towering like the Himalayas above every other singer enchanting us today', but she went on writing. On 27 April 1916 she applied for a reader's ticket to the reading room of the British Museum in Bloomsbury (where the British Library was then located). The application reads in part: 'I should like the privilege of the reading room for an indefinite period for use when writing magazine articles on current affairs, stories and plays, but would need to use it only for references not procurable in the libraries nearer my place of residence.'[27]

The application, signed 'Stella Miles Franklin', cites a letter of introduction from B. R. Wise, Agent-General for New South Wales, describing her as 'a well-known author and journalist' and 'a lady of good social standing', and it refers to another introduction from Miss Edith Quinlan, to be submitted separately. Quinlan, a New South Wales-born journalist residing in London, was equally supportive, stating that Miles was 'an Australian lady interested in journalism on a visit to Britain'. A reader's ticket was ready for collection on 29 April and Miles picked it up on 5 June.[28]

Initially, Miles was hoping to survive in London as a freelance journalist. With nine articles known to have been published in the twelve months following her application for a reader's ticket, six of them paid at the *Sydney Morning Herald*'s standard rates, she was surely keen, as evidenced by those vivid London sketches (unpublished, however, to this day). The quality of the articles published in Sydney was exceptional (though perhaps a little florid for modern tastes), especially three articles on babies' kits which appeared under her own name in the *Herald* in 1916, discussing the work of the McMillans at Deptford, suffragette Sylvia Pankhurst's creche-cum-clinic at Bow in the East End (Sylvia was a socialist, unlike her famous mother Emmeline and older sister Christabel), and Charlotte Despard at the Nine Elms settlement. The kit items sent from Australia were said to be much appreciated.[29]

On 6 May 1916 Miles Franklin attended a conference on the problems of women war workers and spoke briefly. Her attitude to women's war work comes out strongly in another *Herald* article of 1916, on an exhibition of women's work at Knightsbridge (where she helped out on a WFL stall). There was far too much fancy work and practically nothing from the basic industries, and she was disappointed by the lack of 'the potato-digging and wheat-growing elements of life' — the solitary example of the rural industries being a humble hen. (Hens were always a favourite with Miles.) In a flurry of mixed metaphors, she urged *Herald* readers that if Australia were to run such an exhibition, women should be more practical: 'I hope the women roll up their sleeves and get down to brass tacks, and that the baby-rearers and baby-kit makers, and fruit-raisers and bootmakers, and jam-and-pickle makers and cooks and bottle washers will be there in force.' The real workers of London may have been too busy to enter the exhibition, she concluded robustly. Slighter but equally characteristic is her account of 'A Journalist's Summer Outing', describing a trip to Richmond on 2 September 1916 with the much depleted British International Association of Journalists. It was all very pleasant and interesting, but there were occasional aircraft overhead, and her dominant feeling was 'a dizzying sense of unreality'. The concluding sentences read:

> Can there be a combat near at hand, where similar peaceful scenes have been reduced to charnel houses and vast junk heaps? There is an echo of it in Richmond across the river, where the blue-painted glass roof of a munitions factory shows through the trees, where 1700 Belgian workers turn out shells, estimated at about a million per week.[30]

Unfortunately for Miles Franklin there was limited scope for expatriate women journalists in the Australian press during World War I, and it seems her attempt to short-circuit the red tape involved in sending articles to the United States in early 1917 failed, despite her being granted a dispensation freeing her work from postal censorship. Inevitably the Home Front was of less interest to readers than the progress of the military; and with the Russian Revolution and America's entry into the war in 1917, it became harder to write interesting or useful copy from London. Moreover, British political trends became more difficult to pick. Thus the 'Welsh wizard', David Lloyd George, was vital as Minister for Munitions from 1915 to 1916, and in retrospect it is clear that when he ousted H. H. Asquith as Prime

Minister in December 1916 he inaugurated the demise of the British Liberal Party, but Miles rarely mentions him. Likewise, London in late 1916 looked much the same as it did in 1911 (except for the men in uniform and women bus-conductors).[31]

One significant thing Miles did do in late 1916 was to arrange for an English edition of Sydney de Loghe's *The Straits Impregnable*, an autobiographical account of the Gallipoli campaign, first published by H. H. Champion in Melbourne earlier that year. In the first edition Champion had described it as fiction, thus evading the censor. Emboldened by its success, in the second edition he acknowledged it was autobiographical, and the book was banned in Australia, so Champion sent it to his sister Annie to promote in London, and she passed it on to Miles. Miles privately thought the book lacked drama and political point, but that it would help the British to understand what the Anzacs had been through. To Elsie Belle Champion she wrote that it was 'lively and amusing, with poetic descriptions of the landscape of Gallipoli'. Interestingly, she missed the authentic laconic tone of this rare contemporaneous example of Australian World War I writing, now seen to be of both literary and historical value.[32]

The possibility of returning to Chicago began to exercise Miles' mind. But she was not ready to leave London: 'I had hoped to be sailing for home by now but I can't manage it yet,' she wrote to Agnes Nestor in late October. Why that should be so is never explained, though it was probably due to a lack of funds and the progress she seemed to be making with her writing. Maybe she should resign from the league executive. This she finally did in a letter to Emma Steghagen dated 31 December 1916. It would not be possible to return to America in time for the next convention, she advised (which means she now intended to stay in London until at least mid-1917).[33]

In coming months she continued to potter over manuscripts: in addition to occasional items for suffrage journals, there was 'Virtue', a play by 'Mr & Mrs O. L'Artsau, authors of *The Net of Circumstance*', a New Woman comedy set in London and Chicago, which went to the redoubtable Lilian Baylis at the Old Vic in January (and later to agent Watt); and having turned 'How the Londoner Takes his War' into a play, in March it too went to Watt; then in May, she was finishing a revision of *On Dearborn Street*. Nonetheless, 'helping to save the Empire by cooking for it one day a week, and waiting on it another, at the Minerva', made the prospect of 'active service' increasingly attractive. Some of the energy of the suffrage movement was being translated into humanitarian war work. Here was something Miles could do.[34]

According to a draft application retained in her papers, on 12 March 1917 Miles Franklin applied to the SWH administration in Edinburgh to serve, preferably in France, indicating that she was available right away, and giving her age as thirty-something. (The second digit has been erased, possibly because the age limit for orderlies was forty, and she was coming close to it.) Under 'Father's Occupation and Nationality', the draft states that he was Australian-born, 'now retired, was a large landholder', which was true enough and seemed to smooth her passage as a colonial in London.[35]

Miles nominated as her three referees Miss Margaret McMillan; Miss Harriet Newcomb, in her capacity as honorary secretary of the British Dominions Woman Suffrage Union ('she knew me in Australia and is also conversant with my work both in the USA and Chicago'); and Mrs Cobden-Sanderson, daughter of Richard Cobden of anti-Corn Law/Free Trade fame, wife of the radical London printer John Sanderson, and a founding member of the WFL. They were required to testify that she was 'first class', thorough, competent and healthy, and a woman of high principles.[36]

A carbon copy of a covering note appears on the back of the draft application. Typed the same day, in it Miles explains how well qualified she was to serve as an assistant cook, due to her background in Australia and her work at the Minerva. Two months later, the *Bulletin* reported that Miles Franklin's latest ambition was 'to join the woman's army in France'. However, there were no vacancies for cooks in France. Would Corsica suit, asked administrator Beatrice Russell in late May. Or Greece, an SWH area of activity since 1915, when a unit had accompanied the French Expeditionary Force to Salonika? Miles replied she was willing to go to either place, but preferred Greece, even though the position there was for an orderly rather than a cook. The question of pay arose also, or at least expenses. Then, quite suddenly — probably because Scottish cook Ishobel Ross left at this time — there was a vacancy in Macedonia for an assistant cook. Would Miles go? She would be serving in the 'America' unit under Dr Agnes Bennett, and she would need to be robust. The unit was attached to the Serbian army, and she would be leaving in less than three weeks. Miles responded that she would be delighted, especially to serve under Dr Bennett, a fellow Australian whom she had met in Sydney when young: although not strong 'in a muscular sense', she declared herself wiry and 'free from hysterical tendencies'. Presumably Russell's advice that assistant cooks were paid at the rate of £25 per annum was a consideration.[37]

Salaried employees such as cooks were normally required to sign on for twelve months. However, Miles' contract, preserved in SWH records in Glasgow and signed and dated 27 June 1917, the day her employment by the SWH formally began, is an agreement to serve as an unsalaried cook for not less than six months. A related agreement regarding travel arrangements with the British Red Cross and the Order of St John, preserved in the Franklin Papers and signed and dated 28 June 1917, specifies that after she had served six months the arrangement could be terminated by four weeks' notice in writing. It seems that the call came suddenly and Miles negotiated a shorter term in return for expenses-only service, due to (unspecified) literary expectations, which she evidently still held despite an extremely critical reader's report forwarded by the Paget Literary Agency, New York, on the '"advanced" feministic views' and poor workmanship in her American novels *The Net of Circumstance* and *On Dearborn Street*. Miles' initial reaction to the sudden call-up was telling: 'This call was a nuisance, and from a worldly point of view, disastrous to me.' As it turned out, she spent the latter part of her time in Macedonia as a superior kind of orderly; and despite some agitation at the time, orderlies were never paid.[38]

By 1917 the SWH was an impressive organisation, proof positive of women's capacities to serve in, without promoting, national crises. From small beginnings at Calais in 1914, it was now fielding some twelve units in Europe, two of them in Greece. Considerable sums of money were being raised to support the work, a fair proportion in Australia, where the SWH was well known. When an SWH fundraiser, Mrs Abbott, arrived in Sydney in November 1917, the *Herald* said the organisation did heroic work, and noted that Mrs Abbott hoped to raise £20,000 from the people of New South Wales. In its own way the organisation was a demonstration of imperial values, or more precisely Empire feminism. It was said, no doubt correctly, that women from all over the British Empire served in its ranks.[39]

Despite her early irritation, the appointment suited Miles well. The Balkan Front was a known cause; Macedonia was exotic; and she would be joining the SWH's America unit, so called because it was supported by funds raised in America. Miles would have liked the efficiency of American administration as well as American backing but, she reported to American friends, 'no such luck'. The bonus would be working with a number of fellow Australians, since Dr Bennett and 'Franky Doodle', as Miles became known, were not the only Australian women to serve in the unit. Others included Dr Bennett's successor as chief medical officer, Dr Mary De Garis, and the fearless dressing-station sister, Agnes Dorothy Kerr. Unbeknownst to Miles at that stage, from July 1917 there would also be numerous Australian nurses working in British army hospitals near Salonika (modern-day Thessaloniki), including Matron Prichard, who would become an associate in Sydney in the 1940s.[40]

On 13 June Miles passed a medical. Soon after, she underwent the requisite inoculations; on 18 June her kitbag and haversack arrived; and on 27 June she had a farewell lunch with an admiring compatriot, Ada Holman, whom she had met in Chicago in 1914. (Reporting to Rose Scott, Ada said, 'She is the kind of girl who always takes up the roughest work, and does it thoroughly too'.) That same day Miles signed the unsalaried employees agreement to serve in the America unit at Ostrovo in north-west Macedonia, with uniforms provided and all costs and expenses (but not medical liability) covered. Then on 30 June, shorter-skirted, high-booted, and adorned with the tartan accoutrement of the SWH, she moved to the Wilton Hotel near Victoria Station with her luggage, ready for departure.[41]

At the hotel she joined two other 'refills': Ostrovo-bound orderly Jean Lindsay from Glasgow, and Sister Margaret Scott Russell, sent to join the Salonika unit, which Kathleen Ussher would also join as an orderly in a matter of weeks, serving until April 1918. In March 1918, Nell Malone too would join the Salonika unit. (Nell was remembered by her superiors in the Balkans as an Irish-Australian who looked after the mule teams and was accustomed to wide open spaces. No wonder Miles was fond of her.)[42]

After a short delay over passports, during which period of barely suppressed excitement Miles wrote letters, on Monday 2 July 1917, the new recruits caught the train to Southampton, and the following day set off for Paris and beyond. Miles was somewhat disappointed to be going overland, but apparently insouciant: 'I hear there are plenty [of] horses in Macedonia, so I shall be in my element,' she wrote in a last-minute letter from London to her dearest Rose Scott.[43]

The Melbourne *Book Lover* reported that Miles had taken charge of a hospital in Macedonia, an embarrassing but not untypical home-town inflation. It was true, however, that Miles was now 'On Active Service', as she advised Alice Henry.[44]

The seven months between leaving England on 3 July 1917 and her return after the contracted six months' service on 14 February 1918 represent an exhilarating and influential chapter in Miles' life, as recorded in her diary and elaborated in her writing, most notably in another vivid set of sketches, 'Ne Mari Nishta (It matters nothing): Six Months with the Serbs' by Miles Franklin, 'Outlander'. She was warm, she enjoyed camp life and she collected a lot of copy. Indeed, 'I never expected to be so happy again,' she wrote shortly after her return from Macedonia. Miles also saw at first-hand the clash of old empires and small nations which characterised the later stages of the Great War.[45]

Much of what she wrote during or about her time in Macedonia has either been lost, or remains in manuscript. SWH personnel were required to sign an undertaking not to write for the press while on service, and only three press articles detailing her experiences ever appeared: the touching 'Active Service Socks', published in the *Sydney Morning Herald* on 20 February 1918, which describes dispensing gift items originally intended for Australian soldiers at Gallipoli; 'Fred's Letter', about a Serbian soldier's pleasure at a schoolboy's letter found in warm clothing sent from New Zealand, published in the *Auckland Star* on 3 July 1918; and a vivid account, 'Where the Ambulance Has Rested: On the Way to Monastir', by 'Outlander', published in the *Daily Herald,* London, on 6 May 1919. However, a surprising amount of other material from her Balkan days has survived, all written during or immediately after her six-month sojourn in Macedonia; for example, the sequence of twelve sketches that make up 'Ne Mari Nishta'; a further four discrete and fragmentary sketches; at least two contributions to a camp magazine (yet to be traced); and the play 'By Far Kajmachtchalan: A Play of Now in Four Acts' (alternative title 'By Far Kaimacktchalan: A Play of the Balkan Front Today'); plus a related fragment, 'Zabranjeno' (Forbidden Valley). Because of its documentary character, it is a significant source of information and insight into what might otherwise remain a largely inaccessible experience.[46]

Thanks to Susannah Franklin, some postcards survive. Miles sent at least half a dozen to her mother en route to Salonika (or Salonique, as she usually spelled it, French being the lingua franca in the Balkans), from Le Havre, Paris, Turin, Rome, and Taranto on the southern tip of Italy. Arriving at Taranto on 8 July 1917, the SWH trio got a taste of what lay ahead. There had been no cakes in Paris, and no butter in Rome; now it was all mosquitoes and flies, with noise and men everywhere. The three were the only women among 3000 men on the troopship which took them via Corfu and Milos, to arrive at Salonika after almost a fortnight's travel on 15 July.[47]

Miles' initial impressions of Greece were scarcely enthusiastic: from Milos Harbour, the view was of 'treeless lands under the glaring sun and funny little white villages looking like cemeteries on the ribbed hillsides'. Contemporary visual records confirm this first impression of treeless lands. But she soon came to terms with the spare scenery, and within a week she was enjoying it all: 'The landscape grew hourly more beautiful to me'.[48]

Likewise, Miles came to enjoy prowling around Salonika, now Greece's second city but until 1912 a garrison town of the Ottoman Empire. By 1917, the city and its region were what she would later describe as 'a great international stew', where Christians, Muslims and Jews lived side by side, and regional flows from Serbia, Bulgaria and Albania added to the confusion. Salonika had always been the focus of Austrian hopes for a port in the Aegean, and it was to this still-neutral port that Allied forces had come (too late) to defend the beleaguered Serbs, who had the misfortune of being in the way. Salonika was also the focus of political turbulence in a war-divided Greece. It was not yet a Greek town, more Turkish and Jewish. But Miles Franklin was hardly there long enough to notice more than the famous White Tower. Falling into a hole in the main street, Venizelos Street, could hardly have cheered her, even if it happened to others too. It was a colourful town. The medieval city was still intact, though only just: the Great Fire of 18 August 1917 destroyed much of it.[49]

Since it was past 2 p.m. when she disembarked, Miles thought she would be sleeping in Salonika overnight. But Dr Bennett arrived to collect her in the early evening. She gathered up her things and they set off almost immediately in the hospital 'Tin Lizzie' for Ostrovo, about 160 kilometres west along the ancient Via Egnata, then known as the Monastir road and now a busy European freeway. It was, Miles recalled, 'the roughest journey I ever underwent' (which was fair comment, considering others described the roads beyond Salonika as 'fit only for bullock transportation'); but with the SWH's (male) mechanic-chauffeur, known only as Fitzpatrick, at the wheel and the passengers acting as 'shovers' when they reached the hills, they arrived at their destination some five or six hours later, at 1.45 a.m., without incident.[50]

Next morning Miles was up and on the job by 8 o'clock. Like many country people, she took no pleasure in roughing it. The tent cookhouse proved to be 'a beastly little gunyah … placed in the open'. Moreover, July was scorchingly hot, and there were no trees to shade the orderlies' tents. Nevertheless, she soon learned to cope with the food and adapted readily enough to camp routine, rising at 6 a.m. and working a long day until 7 p.m., with a rest period in the afternoon.[51]

Looking about her in the light of day, she found the country traversed the previous night had changed from the alluvial Plain of Salonika to a landscape of woods and hills, 'pretty as a picture'. The 200-bed tent hospital nestling in a grove to the north of Lake Ostrovo was located about 5 kilometres from the tiny village of Ostrovo, just before the road ascended to Gornichevo on the way to Monastir, and surrounded by a rim of mountains topped by the majestic Mount Kaimacktchalan. Dr Isabel Hutton, chief medical officer at Ostrovo in 1918, wondered had ever a camp more Arcadian surroundings: 'It lay quite by itself on a green sward in the hollow of the hills which rose on every side; close by was a clump of elm-trees … and beyond the white tents of the hospital lay Lake Ostrovo.' Although placenames have changed, with Ostrovo now known as Arnissa, Lake Ostrovo as Lake Vegoritis, Mount Kaimacktchalan as Mount Voras (or Kaimaktsalan), and even borders have shifted, with Monastir now Bitola in the Republic of Macedonia, the hospital's remote rural site is still much the same, and today's visitor can readily appreciate Dr Hutton's response.[52]

Within a month, Miles reported she was feeling fine, though her luggage had yet to arrive. In the only known extant letter, submitting expenses to Edinburgh, 'Stella M. Franklin' went on in cheerful vein:

> We had a very happy journey out and in our expenditure kept both economy and the good name of our distinguished regiment in mind. Sad to say our luggage has not yet turned up but we are still hoping. We are taken care of here & enjoying our work immensely. The heat of course is rather ennervating in the kitchen but we get good rest time & I am very well.[53]

To the *British Australasian*, a news weekly published in London from the 1880s to the 1960s for expatriates and others with interests in Australasia, she said she was hot and destitute, with only one set of underwear and in need of a decent pair of shoes. It was a great day when she came upon a good pair of boots.[54]

The work itself was no problem to Susannah Franklin's daughter. Miles' competence was soon recognised, first by Dr Bennett, who wrote back to Edinburgh within weeks for permission to make her head cook at £35 per annum, which might encourage her to stay longer — a move not appreciated by the existing incumbent. Miles withdrew: 'I just let 'em muddle along & take no notice as I've had a year's training in London of English ways. Will think my own thoughts & write a book if the plot comes into my head.'[55]

This was not to be. Noticing that Miles did as much work as two, Matron Nye made her matron's orderly, in charge of the stores: 'I looked after the linen and all the clothing and bedding supplies and gave out the dressings.' She also did mending, and on Sundays distributed tobacco. 'I had not been so housewifely for years,' she reflected. Literary inspiration was slow to come.[56]

There is a box brownie photo of a broadly smiling Miles with a group of Serbian orderlies and drivers under one of the elm trees, with the lake in the background. From this and other sources it is obvious that her new position suited the gregarious side of her nature. More like an aide-de-camp than a hospital orderly, she 'cavorted all over the camp on errands for the matron' in a manner reminiscent of early days with Mrs Robins in Chicago; and with ample afternoon rest time, she often went swimming with colleagues. The strong sense of sisterhood noted at the camp by others (for example, Dr Hutton) was agreeable to Miles. Although she did not occupy an important position, she seemed to know most people, and about a quarter of the 300 or more people apparently associated with the hospital are named in her pocket diary. She was always trekking about the countryside with other *sestres* (as patients called the nurses) on her days off. There were evening entertainments with the officers too, mostly Serbian, but also French and Italian, and occasionally Englishmen. Except that she never did get to ride their horses, it all sounds rather like her young days near Goulburn.[57]

The hospital was attached to the Royal Serbian Army, and Miles' experience was specific to unique and mostly forgotten circumstances. The Serbian army, described by military historians as 'a genuinely national army', had been forced west in a bitter winter retreat through Albania to the Greek island of Corfu after a third Austrian assault in 1915. When the survivors revived sufficiently to fight back through Salonika, pressing northward in mid-1916, some gains were made, especially when, after an enormous struggle with many losses, the Serbs re-took Mount Kaimacktchalan, straddling the Greek–Serbian border some 16 kilometres due north of the recently established tent hospital at Ostrovo. However, when the front moved north over the mountains onto the plateau lands of southern Serbia to pass through Monastir, it became stalemated (rather like the Western Front) for the next two years, which meant that by the time Miles got there in mid-1917, Ostrovo was well back from the front line, the hospital's work was less dramatic, and many men had been away from home for several years.[58]

Miles and the rest of the women in the SWH — indeed the entire Allied force, it seems — sympathised with their plight. One of Miles' jobs was to cheer patients up with games in the evenings, which she found easy, despite language barriers, commenting sharply on one occasion, 'How very simple the male of the species is. With him running the planet, little wonder it is being run off its axis.' More benignly, she reflected that Ostrovo was really a royal holiday after the fret of reform in Chicago; and the *sestres* never thought of themselves as anything but lucky to be there, albeit dropped into something like 'the Balkan trance', with history passing them by.[59]

The image of the Serbs during World War I is very different from that of the twenty-first century. They were, Miles wrote, a strange remnant — simple mountain men, chivalric and chaste, almost aristocratic, and impeccable in their behaviour to the *Englesky sestres*, very few of whom managed to master more than a few words of the Serbs' difficult Slavonic language. (Miles' somewhat tattered textbook, *Key to Servian Conversation Grammar*, survives in her book collection.) 'Oh! *Sestra*,' the Serbs would say at mispronunciations. No matter, it was all great fun, with moments of enchantment too — as perhaps captured by a handwritten poem dated 14 September 1917 and retained in Miles' papers. A translation from the Serbian reads:

> Who took the necklace from your throat;
> Who spilled around pearls and beads?
> Last night I went to the garden
> To collect some lilac.
> A branch of lilac [has] hit me
> And that has broken my necklace
> And spilled diamonds and pearls all around.
> And why are your eyes so dark
> Like you didn't have any sleep?
> Somewhere a nightingale sang his song [in] the tree;
> I was listening to it until the early dawn.
> That is why my eyes are dark.[60]

In Miles' writings, some of the characters were actual people, such as a much-loved driver, Bogoljub, in 'Zabranjeno', a sketch subsequently worked into the play 'By Far Kajmachtchalan'. The Serbs might have fitted Miles' idea of real men — Dr De Garis observed that on average they had better physiques even than Australian men — but she seems not to have fallen for any of them. And camp discipline mostly held. The indiscretions of a Miss Dick who drank and flirted were greatly frowned upon.[61]

On days off, the nurses would sometimes visit outlying villages. There they observed local women. The best Miles could find to say about their lives was that it explained how easy it was to exploit the migrants in Chicago: 'Not one hot-water tap of progress since the days of the bible,' she snorted. The men were worse; so exploitative. When the hospital opened a small ward for civilians, some women came or were brought by their wary husbands. The amusing little sketch 'Mrs Mackadoughnut's Hen' shows that at least one was grateful. The women could also be critical of the *sestres*, with their machine-made uniforms. But contact was limited, which is not surprising, since the villages they visited might be Greek, Turkish, Romanian or Bulgarian.[62]

From the campsite at Ostrovo, the mountains to the north were clearly visible, especially the snow-tipped Mount Kaimacktchalan, which at over 2400 metres (7800 feet) could be seen from distances even a day's travel from the tent hospital. As previously noted, the mountain was a site of great significance to the Serbs, who built an obelisk at the top commemorating the great losses experienced during its recovery in 1916, sometimes to be seen glinting in the sun. It became emblematic to Miles of all that was splendid in this ancient and very beautiful place. She first went there on a day off in August, pausing to eat wild strawberries halfway up. In 'Ne Mari Nishta', the changing moods of the mountain 'K' are almost a touchstone: 'K wrapped himself in clouds for days at a stretch', 'K glorious tipped in the rising sun', and so on. She felt fortunate to possess some sketches by fellow orderly Mabel C. Pollard from Cornwall, said to be a well-known portrait artist. Pollard also helped Miles transcribe entrancing folk tunes, 'so strange, so sad, so gay'. The *sestres* took similar pleasure in the changing light of Lake Ostrovo, especially under the brilliant Macedonian moon.[63]

Gradually Miles began to get a grip on the ancient cultures still co-existing in the area. The most frequently visited site was the old Turkish town of Vodena (now called Edessa), 'a queer old city' of around 14,000 people some 19 kilometres to the east by rail, primitive but colourful, and famed for its waterfalls. In Vodena the *sestres* enjoyed the hospitality of Serb and Allied officers, and Miles was able to see a dentist. It is fascinating how much there is about teeth in 'Ne Mari Nishta'. Dental health among the hospital staff was appalling. Whereas both Miles and other observers noted that the Serbs had wonderful teeth (indeed, it was the first thing she noticed about them upon arriving in Salonika), apparently there was only one sister who could boast a full quota of natural teeth. Miles found the locals were astonished at her gold patches and supporting bridges, and treated her as if she were a walking mint, even trying to feel inside her mouth, while she in turn could tell who among the villagers had been to America by the state of their dental work. The Serbs also wondered why so many of the *Englesky* had 'machines' in their mouths; that is, false teeth. All in all, teeth provided good copy for Miles in Ostrovo: there is also a sketch entitled 'The Dentist in Macedonia', based on her visits to the Serb dentist in Vodena.[64]

Despite her pleasure in the region, Miles Franklin left no official imprint on it, unlike some others, such as the English 'military maid' Flora Sandes and the Sydney-born Olive Kelso King, the legendary driver who had her own car and, like Sandes, served with the Serbs. Sandes and King both became famous in Serbia. The much-decorated Queensland-born humanitarian and writer Joice Nankivell Loch is another later instance of someone having a regional impact. Even Nell Malone, who went on to work in an orphanage in war-ravaged Monastir (rather, said Miles, than face London buses again), left a trace or two in SWH literature. Not Miles. Except for a few fragile files in the records of the SWH in Glasgow, and the unpublished manuscripts in her own papers, there is barely a trace of her presence. Was it a case of 'Ne Mari Nishta': 'It Matters Nothing'?[65]

According to her pocket diary, Miles was unwell for most of her time in Macedonia. Despite its beauty the Ostrovo site was an unhealthy spot. Early on Miles had noted that all the disagreeable features of Australian bush life were in evidence: flies, fleas, mosquitoes, wasps and snakes. She suffered greatly from accidentally swallowing a wasp — Dr De Garis noted that wasps were a great trial, making eating hazardous — and the treatment, consisting of quinine injections in the buttocks, made things worse. When it grew colder she got chilblains, and on one wintry occasion she lost her voice for a time. However, all the armies in Macedonia suffered from fevers and other ills and at Ostrovo the staff sick tent was always full.[66]

The greatest scourge was malaria, that debilitating and recurring affliction characterised by attacks of chills, fever and sweating, for which the main treatment, then recently discovered, was quinine; with the onset of war there had been a resurgence of the disease. Carried by the *anopheles* mosquito, it did not often kill people, but it laid them out in droves. It was estimated that in October 1917 as many as 20 per cent of the British force on the Eastern Front was hospitalised at the one time with malaria, and it is notable that both the Ostrovo chief medical officers in Miles' time there, Doctors Bennett and De Garis, had to leave after contracting the disease. Miles was not lucky enough to escape it; and although it is unclear when she was infected, she certainly suffered back in London. Acknowledging advice in early January 1918 that Miles would be leaving Macedonia after six months' service — a decision that may have been due to malaria, though it seems more likely that it was simply because her time was up and she was ready to leave — SWH's Beatrice Russell replied that it was delightful that Miles had enjoyed her time in Ostrovo, and that they would be glad to have her again.[67]

Miles Franklin retained fond memories of her time in Macedonia, and her links with old comrades, such as Sister Kerr, who ended her days working in a hospital at fever-ridden Burketown on the Gulf of Carpentaria in remote north Queensland. In an undated fragment to an unknown colleague from those months, she wrote: 'Those days of glorious warmth under the old beech trees at Ostrovo camp hospital now have the charm of remembered youth' (which age-wise was gilding the lily somewhat). She also had pleasant memories of occasional trips to Salonika, as for 'a banquet of allies — the people on the same side of the dog-fight', where she sat next to a nondescript male who turned out to be the editor of the *Balkan News*, and on 7 January 1918, an Australian dinner in the White Tower.[68]

In 'Ne Mari Nishta', completed in London in April 1918, which she modestly sought to place in an unresponsive world as 'the comments of a camp cook', she attributed her enjoyment to a natural affinity with the Serbs. The text contains scattered but telling references to Australia. Thus, the landscape intensified her longing for the Bogong Mountains; one bright winter's day reminded her of Australia; and her work caused her to think of her mother and of home. She also noted the surprising fact that a force of eighty Serbs from Australia arrived in Salonika. There are similarly telling links made in 'Active Service Socks', which begins with Miles in October 1917 wearing a pair made by Mary Mission of Lang Lang, Victoria, then refers to Mount Kaimacktchalan as the Kosciuszko of the region.[69]

Nor was that all. She felt at home with people as well as place. This meant with the Serbs rather than the Greeks, due to a melange of political, cultural and institutional tensions which kept the Greeks and the Serbs apart. The Serbs may have been a primitive people, but: 'It is why I have been so at home among them, for, reared in the far solitude of great forests, I too am primitive and unlettered, and the doubtful highway of sophistication has never disclosed anything to me but soul impoverishment and spiritual distress.' Too much may be read into such sentiments, but they sound remarkably like those one might expect from John Maurice Franklin's daughter, with her limited bush education. Furthermore, she asserted, the world's young men would have been sacrificed in vain if little lands like Belgium and Serbia — and Australia, it might have been added — were not to be given the right to mind their own business and evolve in their own way, 'free of dictation', as she put it.[70]

Here may be detected the glimmering of that new ethical position she had sought when leaving America. From old empires, new nations might arise. The war itself could provide the leavening, as she observed after attending a concert in Vodena given by refugee schoolchildren. And as if to show she had not lost her sense of humour and proportion when traversing these heady prospects, she remarked wittily on the social hazards of the alien education the children would receive: 'Fine though this is, it has possibilities which may be fraught with pain and disappointment to those concerned … Relatives can get along much more comfortably with different religions than with a different manner of drinking soup.'[71]

Miles left Ostrovo on 3 February 1918, after an unusually warm January, during which her main problem had been lack of sleep. Two days later, she sailed from Salonika for Toulon on the *Lafayette*, arriving in London on 14 February. She seems not to have enjoyed the trip much, although decades later she recalled baking on deck in her cotton uniform and the smell of wattle along the south coast of France; and she managed to finish her play based on the 'Zabrenjeno' fragment, a rather arch drawing-room style comedy set in the camp. It involved deliberately mixed identities, including that of the Ostrovo chauffeur Bogoljub, who turns out to be of aristocratic lineage, thus removing the obstacle to marriage to the Lady Guinevere, who had in the first instance persuaded her female driver to change places with her so that she could experience the full benefit of service. It was a silly tale, though not entirely unreal — a figure rather like the Lady Guinevere's mother did descend upon the camp hospital in January 1918 — and soon Miles would be reading it to Miss Hodge and others in London. As usual, she sent postcards to her mother en route from Marseilles and Paris, and her return was duly reported by the *British Australasian*.[72]

The colleague to whom Miles recalled her time in Macedonia as having the charm of remembered youth must have been having difficulty settling back to regular 'civilian' life, as the text goes on to say that Miles hadn't been troubled, but she had been weakened by malaria and the need to earn a living. She had nowhere fixed to stay and London was experiencing air raids. For the first month or so, when somehow she managed to concentrate on her writing, she shuttled back and forth between Miss Hodge's at Golders Green and 22 Harley Road, South Hampstead, where Miss A. A. Smith (Nan), the long-serving editor of the WFL's journal, the *Vote*, lived when not pursuing good causes elsewhere. After some prompting, in April Miles returned her badges and tartan to Glasgow, her travel expenses having been settled previously.[73]

The Macedonian sketches went off to agent Watt at the end of April. But no one was interested (H. W. Massingham of the *Nation* would prove unable to use 'the interesting book you were so kind to send to me', due to space considerations, and he lost unique photos of the dead on Mount Kaimacktchalan as well). The collection of anecdotes on London and the war signed 'Stella Miles Franklin, 15 June, Harley Road', was probably the one sent to America in 1917, now a bit stale. She was, in fact, adrift and unwell, having experienced since mid-March some half-dozen malarial attacks. Worse, she feared her money was running out. For a time she helped Miss Newcomb prepare for another Dominions suffrage conference in June and she managed a book review for the *Vote*, but by the end of May she was back at the Minerva. She even thought of joining the Women's Royal Air Force.[74]

Some good things alleviated the gloom. Agnes Nestor turned up as part of an official goodwill mission from America to England and France in April, and they had a fine time together. Miles even had a new admirer, Fred Post, a young American working in the office of the Scientific Attaché at the American Embassy, possibly a relative of the Chicago Posts, and enjoyed a last Indian summer of romance, marked by five crosses in her diary. Some Serbs turned up too. Recounting her experiences with Agnes to colleagues back in Chicago, she gave a spirited description of her men friends:

> There is a beautiful boy from California attached to the American Embassy now ... and he is always at my ear wanting to know this that and the other just like Agnes used to be when I was natl sec. I am training him up in the way he should go and

am very much pleased to note he finds no one's analysis of things satisfies him like mine — but such eagerness, such liveliness — after the placid British who never want to know anything … I introduce him to one young beauty but no, he is back there again the next time we meet as full of a desire to know as ever. I had him on one arm of my chair the other night and George of Serbia on the other and a beautiful young Serb lieutenant nearby, and as I was deaf in one ear and couldn't hear out of the other thru' big doses of quinine taken for malaria, I was in parlous condition. But he fell in love with the Serbs, so I was content. The unspoiled Serbs are the nicest men I have ever met.[75]

Even with warmer weather Miles did not feel well, despite two short breaks from London, one with Maud Walsöe in Hampshire in July and another longer stay near Hitchin, Hertfordshire, in August, where she met up with Matron Nye and other colleagues back from the Balkans.[76]

In early August Sir James Cantlie diagnosed her as suffering from influenza as well as malaria. Still, she managed to get on with her work. Though her diary entries record a pitiful state of weakness and depression, she was able to re-type *On Dearborn Street*, and in late August she started a new narrative sequence, 'Sam Price from Chicago', and wrote several book reviews for the *Vote*, along with other unspecified articles, maybe including the fragment 'Sammies in London', based on the sight of 3000 newly arrived American troops in Piccadilly in May, causing her to emit 'a timid yodel'. What a contrast, she added, to the demoralised Serbs she had seen marching in the Balkans, recalling 'that fainting step which has left behind the mounds beside the way from Kaimacktchalan and Monastir to Salonique'.[77]

Within days of returning from Hitchin to that 'cold and comfortless house' on Harley Road, where she struggled to put down depression by burying herself in letters and came again to feel that there was no joy in life, 'only dull stagnation of body and soul', she booked into Merchant Taylors' Convalescent Home for Ladies at Bognor, on the coast of Sussex.

Unlike her sojourn at Redlands, California, in 1906, this was not a good move. According to the *Rules and Regulations for the Guidance of Patients* preserved in the Franklin Papers, the home had been established for the benefit of ladies in need of rest and open air, due to overwork or illness. Miles fitted the bill, but found the home odious. She hated its pervasive snobbery and smell of pauperism. At least the weather remained fine, and daily walks on the seashore and inland with one or two reasonably agreeable souls proved refreshing. On one of several postcards to her mother she marked a spot by one of the groynes where she sat regularly in the hope of catching the sun, but 'Ah for Manly Beach or Waverley or Bondi or Coogee!' On another, of the adjacent resort of St Leonard's, she wrote that it would have been nicer to be there in the summer and with a companion.[78]

She stuck it out from 2 to 21 September, mainly by writing and studying shorthand. Towards the end, on 16 September, her diary reveals she finished a novel, though what this was is unstated. Returning by train to London on the morning of 21 September, a Saturday, she spent the evening with Miss Hodge at Temple Fortune Court, and on the Sunday took tea with Olive Aldridge (the chronicler of the retreat of the Serbian army, and an SWH agent in Britain) in her top-floor flat at 41 Russell Square. Suddenly her life took another of its dramatic turns. Immediately after the reference to tea with Mrs Aldridge comes the laconic line, 'Took on a job with Mr Aldridge.'

Henry R. Aldridge was the founding secretary of the National Housing and Town Planning Council (NHTPC), a semi-philanthropic reform body and pressure group dealing mainly with local authorities. Town planning was a new and increasingly respectable cause, and by 1918 housing was a big issue, one in which the WFL was keen to see the woman's outlook represented. The very next day, Monday 23 September 1918, she began work at the council's office at 41 Russell Square, Bloomsbury, just around the corner from the British Museum.[79]

8

AT THE HEART OF
THE EMPIRE:
OCTOBER 1918–OCTOBER 1923

'I'm a daughter of the Empiah come to help save it,
and they have to put up with me.'[1]

The British Empire and its allies won the Great War, but with over
eight million dead and approaching three times that number of
wounded worldwide, few felt good about it. Miles Franklin observed the
street celebrations in London on Armistice Day from her recently obtained
perch at 41 Russell Square, Bloomsbury, headquarters of the NHTPC since
1913; but she could not accept Fred Post's invitation to join in, as she had to
get council secretary Henry Aldridge off to a conference.[2]

She often complained — with reason — about muddle at the office. The
same could be said of the postwar world, and of her own life. Seen from
London, the world was more than a muddle; it was tense and divided. On
the one hand, the triumphant British Prime Minister, the ex-Liberal David
Lloyd George, had promised 'homes fit for heroes', and legislation in 1919
encouraged public investment in housing, as the NHTPC had urged since
before the war. However, Lloyd George also promised to make Germany pay
for the war. Reaction rather than reform soon became the order of the day in
post-World War I Britain. To this reaction Lloyd George was himself soon to
fall victim, as a reinvigorated conservatism swept away his war-winning
coalition, while the British Labour Party, which would first win government
in 1924, gained in strength, leaving the old Liberals in the middle.

It was the Liberal intelligentsia with whom Miles Franklin was associated in London in the 1920s, and the radicals among it remained radical and in important respects creative; but the rise of Labour had to be faced, and class conflict was a renewed and formidable reality of the immediate postwar years, which saw many great strikes. Likewise, the Empire was in an uproar. In Ireland, the rise of Sinn Fein ('Ourselves Alone') spelled the end of the Liberals' thirty-year commitment to Home Rule, and beyond, in India, another nationalist leader, Mohandas Gandhi, was making his mark with the doctrine of non-violent resistance to imperial power.[3]

In such a volatile world, housing was evidently not of crucial significance. William Ashworth's authoritative history of town planning in Britain acknowledges the NHTPC as one of the most influential propagandist groups of the Edwardian period, notable for its clarity of aims, the quality of its membership, its conferences and international contacts, and its influence through reports and other forms of pressure on local authorities. This assessment, and a reception at Buckingham Palace in 1919, suggest that by Miles' time the political point had been won, and that the council was now respectable, almost establishment. The membership lists of the day look altogether worthy, as do the council's aims. The names of famed Liberal reformers, like George Cadbury, Seebohm Rowntree and the influential town planner Professor Patrick Abercrombie, appear on the council's general committee, and there are a number of individual architects, town planners and the like listed in the early 1920s, yet by then most council members represented relevant interest groups. In particular, local government, employer and employee associations connected with the building trades, trade unions and women's organisations were represented at the council, the latter from 1918 when the vote was extended to women over thirty as well as to working-class men.

Similarly, the council's aims seem proper and appropriate but less than uplifting. Its constitution — a draft with corrections in Miles' hand survives in the council's records — lists them as being to stimulate local authorities to fulfil their obligations with respect to the improvement of housing; to campaign for the abolition of poor housing nationwide; to promote better housing policy at all levels of government; and to foster a strong public opinion in support of these objects. Such a program and constituency suggest a cause effectively bureaucratised. On the other hand, under the reforming leadership of Neville Chamberlain, these would be great days for housing and the state in Britain.[4]

Miles worked hard at the council. The worthiness of it all was too much at times, as revealed in her observations on the plainness of certain distinguished persons encountered at council gatherings, but she was not one to bite the hand that fed her. At £144 per annum, her salary was much the same as that earned by female clerical assistants and typists in the civil service in 1924, and above the rate paid them at that time by the benevolent Liberal employer Cadbury (£127 per annum in 1924). It should be added that given the niceties of class in British society at this time, these rates were well above the prevailing pay rates of skilled female manual workers, very few of whom received over £100 per annum, and of domestic servants, who, although classified as semi-skilled, in an era of rising shortage could by 1924 command up to £115 a year, more than trained nurses (£106 per annum).[5]

As a reasonably well-paid clerical worker in London Miles Franklin had once more caught the wave, and had found a niche in the lower professional classes. But housing never claimed her as women's trade unionism had. As she wrote to Eva O'Sullivan in August 1919: 'I am in the housing work. It is a thing any one can believe in without controversy, and the English houses are terrific … It is impossible to depict the discomfort of the English home.'[6]

Her duties in some respects resembled those of her Chicago days, when she ran around town on errands and back and forth to the printers. But Mr Aldridge was no Mrs Robins when it came to work practices: it was maddening to type memos up to twenty times, and the amount of work that she and the other office women put into his magnum opus, *The National Housing Manual*, over four years can hardly have been rewarding, adequate acknowledgements notwithstanding.[7]

Miles understood from personal experience the great need for reform and planning in British cities. She was still living with the suffrage journalist Nan Smith at 22 Harley Road, a three-storeyed semi-detached brick house located just beyond Primrose Hill in what is now one of inner London's most attractive and expensive areas. Number 22 Harley Road also served as the London base of the extended Smith family, especially Nan's worldly brothers, Thomas Brook Smith, a tourist agent in Yorkshire, and Horatio Nelson Smith, a pharmaceuticals manufacturer in Lancashire and Birmingham. Hence there was much coming and going, sometimes to the detriment of Miles' own work. Nonetheless she stayed on after Miss Smith's sudden death in May 1919, possibly at a reduced rent, as she seems to have helped out with cooking and chores on occasion (though there was a housekeeper, apparently Ethel Bull at first, and from 1923 Miss Peak). More importantly, from diary entries it is evident that she could not rely on having a room of her own. When there was an influx of Smiths and their associates, she had to share her first-floor room with the housekeeper, which meant no privacy, or go up two floors to the housekeeper's room, which she regarded as degrading. Such was her unusual status in the household, however, that she also went to the theatre with family members, and for walks and drives on Sunday. The family was genuinely regretful when she moved to the WFL's Minerva Club in Brunswick Square in 1924. Moreover, the Smiths remained her friends; and until reminded by World War II — 'how we struggled along with rationing and other things during the last war and after,' she wrote to Ethel Bull on 29 September 1942 — she seems to have forgotten how often she had been cold, and sometimes hungry, at Harley Road. There was surely an economic motive to explain why she stayed put for so long in such unstable accommodation.[8]

Harley Road was within walking distance of Lady Byles' home at 8 Chalcot Gardens, a small planned development off Haverstock Hill on the old Eton College estate. It would be difficult to overestimate the importance of Lady Byles as a reference point for, and influence on, Miles Franklin in her London years. Miles had first met her in 1916, most likely through Ken and Mab Maynard, who were resident in Chicago from the 1890s to 1919, but maybe through the Sydney branch of the family, of which the solicitor and conservationist Marie Byles was a prominent member. Lady Byles became her 'refuge and sheer delight', as near as she found to a replacement for Alice Henry and Editha Phelps, as Miles wrote to Alice Henry in February 1919.[9]

Sarah Anne Byles, née Unwin, was advanced in years when Miles met her, but still handsome and strong. Her husband, Sir William Byles, originally a northern newspaper proprietor and 'Lib-Lab' member of parliament for the wool manufacturing city of Bradford since 1890, had died in 1917, by which time she was an esteemed elder of the Liberal world, where she belonged in her own right as the daughter of the Colchester Unwins, a literary and public-spirited family, and as president of the Women's National Liberal Association (later Federation) from 1906 to 1921. (The suffrage issue had caused a division among Liberal women between 'progressives' and 'moderates', with the Association supporting a moderate 'waiting policy' for fear of losing Home Rule for Ireland. Reunion was achieved through federation in 1919, during the final years of Lady Byles' presidency.) Like many, the Fabian socialist Beatrice Webb thought Lady Byles a stronger personality than her husband, and noted that she was sympathetic to labour.[10]

When she died in 1931, one of several admiring obituaries referred to Lady Byles' 'long and enviable life, crowded with public service in many directions, and enlivened by the affectionate companionship of distinguished and clever people', noting also the number of young people she counted among her close friends in later years. Miles, though not exactly young still, was one of them: 'a dear sunbeam', Lady Byles once called her. It is easy to see why Lady Byles appealed so strongly to Miles. The same obituary is particularly apposite:

> She had the platform manner of a cabinet minister — easy, eloquent, authoritative — and in the days of her prime she moved audiences to enthusiasm by the strength and unmistakable sincerity of her convictions. She was a great believer. Having made up her mind she harboured no doubt. She was sure, and she helped other people to be sure.[11]

At Chalcot Gardens in the 1920s, Miles enjoyed Lady Byles' easy hospitality, and encountered many significant people, for example J. A. Hobson, alternative economist and critic of imperialism. She was at once soothed and stimulated, and over time, strongly influenced by the thinking of Lady Byles and her circle. As evidenced by her association with the Meggitt and Smith families and her work with the McMillan sisters at Deptford and the SWH in Macedonia during the war, and even earlier through its transatlantic manifestations, Miles' entrée to English political culture had been through the progressive but largely provincial Liberal network, encompassing (broadly speaking) suffrage and social reform, of which Lady Byles was such an ornament. Her employment at the NHTPC, probably at the suggestion of Olive Aldridge, was an extension of that network. Through Lady Byles she came closer to the heartbeat of Empire.[12]

As British historian Pat Thane has shown in a study of women, liberalism and citizenship in Britain after 1918, although the British Liberal Party never regained the ground lost by Lloyd George's perfidy in abandoning the party to lead a nationalist coalition in 1916, liberalism itself provided a practical framework and set of concepts for the new woman citizen. The Women's National Liberal Federation (WNLF) strongly supported internationalism, seeking to combat slavery and advance women's rights and world peace through the League of Nations. At the same time, while critical of coercion in Ireland and India, the WNLF was committed to a liberal imperialism. Recognising that the Empire was changing — and that it should — the federation reiterated the underlying liberal principle of freedom within the Empire and the promotion of mutual trust and affection, accepting also that 'backward people' must be governed 'in their own interest with protection and development and without exploitation'. 'Liberal policy is based on the principle that self-government should be granted as a right to advanced and responsible peoples,' one prominent Liberal woman stated in 1928. This benign and hopeful view of the imperial mission probably sounds patronising today, but it was a position held by many, perhaps the majority, of progressive persons throughout the British Empire up to and even beyond World War II. While the extent to which Miles Franklin agreed with it emerged only gradually, by the 1920s she had absorbed the main elements of the liberal imperialist position as represented by Lady Byles and her circle.[13]

There may even have been direct links between the world of Lady Byles and Australia. From J. S. Mill onwards, feminism had been part of liberal philosophy; and it is possible to discern through Miles' response to Lady Byles something of the common ground between the incipiently liberal nationalist feminism she had known in Australia and the stronger imperial version she now encountered in London. With its emphasis on mutual aid between women of the Empire, Miles' fourth and final babies' kit article, 'The Home-Going of the Babies' Kits', on the distribution of leftover babies' kits among British war brides emigrating with infants to Australia after the war, written on 10 August 1919 and published in Sydney two months later, is one indication.[14]

Like most writers Miles usually had two jobs, one paid, the other unpaid. This was as true in postwar London as it had been in Chicago, though she had hoped that leaving Chicago for London would enable her to concentrate on her writing, and that she would at last establish herself as a writer. Unfortunately *The Net of Circumstance* had failed to attract attention; nor had she managed to break through in journalism. Thus, although she was again accumulating manuscripts (which she seems to have stored in a trunk), a month into her job with the NHTPC she was already finding it 'a hard struggle to type and earn a living as well'.[15]

Reconstructing Miles Franklin's years in London after World War I is not easy, though she must have meant it to be, given the records she retained.

On the one hand, the diaries are almost overwhelming in their dailiness, and mostly depressing in their references to bother at work and discomfort at Harley Road. 'I hope this is the purgatory of the Catholic faith and something better will come later,' she wrote to Alice Henry on 6 February 1919. On the other hand, few items of what was clearly a well-maintained correspondence have survived: except for the earliest years, this is the thinnest of all periods for extant letters, with an average of about twenty-five items surviving from each year, many of them postcards sent during summer breaks. Had Alice Henry not kept the letters she received, there would be a mere smattering to 1921. In marked contrast to this dearth of letters are the literary manuscripts. These increased exponentially during Miles' almost nine years in London after World War I.[16]

Here perhaps is the measure of Miles' own pulse at the heart of Empire, or at least what she intended us to think of as her core concerns. Altogether, counting published items, items in manuscript, and items referred to in the diaries (whether or not extant), her output in various genres during these London years adds up to some forty writings. This is an approximation only, since the number includes titles referred to in the diaries but not otherwise known, extant undated manuscripts evidently from this period, and some double-dipping, as materials were recycled in hope of catching the new fashions; for example, as plays or film scenarios.

There are at least seven novels or novellas and linked sequences of sketches; as many as fifteen plays; three film scenarios; and some sixteen topical pieces, consisting of single sketches, short stories, anecdotes and other fragments. Sadly for her, of all this work only a handful of topical articles and one novel achieved publication during the London years, and since then only three of the novels have appeared and two of the topical pieces have been reprinted.

Amazingly, Miles never complained about the rejections, at least in print, though she did keep careful records of where her manuscripts were sent, and probably talked about her work to close friends. She just resubmitted, and kept writing. Nor did she ever mention her age, which was becoming a significant consideration: the 'now or never' factor. On 14 October 1919, Stella Maria Sarah Miles Franklin turned forty. As usual, there is no reference to a birthday in her diary. The entry reads simply 'went home and went to bed early … no hope of privacy or comfort'. At least on her thirty-ninth birthday the previous year, she had dined at the Lyceum Club as a guest of Mrs Bage (probably the mother of Queensland feminist Freda

Bage), though it caused her to weep with boredom, and she escaped early. In 1920, when she turned forty-one, the entry on her birthday reads 'feeling life a great burden', and in 1921 comes the entirely perfunctory 'office routine'. If the passage of time was corroding her still-youthful self-image, she was not about to concede it, as is clear from her application for a passport in September 1923 where she understated her age once more, giving it as thirty-eight instead of forty-three, going on forty-four.[17]

Reactions to anniversaries such as fortieth birthdays are culturally conditioned, and it is probably too early to think in terms of an impending life crisis; but with average life expectancy for Australian women then at fifty-five, Miles was well past the halfway mark, unwilling as she was to acknowledge it. And at forty, in the modern world, a life transition of some kind is under way for many women. But there are some classic statements among Miles' diary entries: for example, 'Wish I had means for rest & beauty & to educate myself', a sentiment not so very different from the view of one of the then popular English writer Rose Macaulay's women characters that, 'The thing [is] to defy life; to fly in the face of nature … wrest something for oneself by which to live at last.'[18] A literary fragment cast in narrative form, undated but redolent of the 1920s, possibly casts some light on Miles' attitude at this time:

> 'One must do something. Oh God,' she exclaimed, 'I must do something with the kind of mind with which I have been endowed even as those who have been endowed otherwise who play bridge or mah jong all day, who shake dice all day, who flit about from one big hotel to another, I have a right to the exercise of my faculties even as they are. And I would like to make this life an experiment … It would occupy us and there is just a gorgeous glimmering … that … man … might be able to do wonderful things.'[19]

Irritability, anxiety, depression, frustration and fatigue had been her constant companions in Chicago and even Sydney before that; in the early 1920s they seemed to appear more frequently. And while there were good reasons for recording them in her diary — it is, after all, better to 'let go' — it may also be that a person differently placed in the life cycle would not have reacted so strongly to the incessant demands of Mr Aldridge. Nor might sleeplessness and what Miles called the 'blackfella' fires heating

English homes, which left people cooked on one side and freezing on the other, have afflicted her so badly.

At forty, Miles was evidently set to defer middle age; and she seems to have drawn the line between the private and the public more determinedly than ever. She may have felt miserable a lot of the time but she was not feeble-minded, nor was she neurotic. Rather, as Jungian analysis has it, it is the process of accommodation that matters; and, as will be seen, there were already signs that she was coming to terms with middle age at war's end, though the process would be a protracted one.

Often it is the photographer who best captures character at a given moment. There are two studio portraits of Miles Franklin at the heart of the Empire, one taken quite soon after the end of World War I, probably in 1920, since it was taken in Newport, Wales, when Miles again visited the Meggitts. The other is her passport photo, taken in London in mid-1923. In the first photo we see Susannah Franklin's 'dearest girlie' (as she wrote when learning of her daughter's impending trip home) in her maturity: softer, calm and serious, with just a hint about the eyes of the imp. The second portrait is perhaps more percipient, portraying as it does a personality open to experience — smiling, but with some sadness about the eyes.[20]

In some ways, as in the deferral of middle age, Miles Franklin was ahead of her time. In others — her writing most clearly — she was, or tried to be, in step. War and its aftermath proved a stimulus, suggesting new characters and themes, as for Arnold Bennett in his prize-winning *Riceyman Steps,* a Gothic tale of central London, with its happy ending for general servant Elsie and her troubled 'Tommy', Joe. Of the new novels of women and middle age, neither Radclyffe Hall's *The Unlit Lamp,* perhaps the most appalling, nor May Sinclair's masterpiece *Mary Olivier: A Life* are in Miles' book collection, but she was thinking about much the same things, and in due course she would certainly pay attention to Virginia Woolf. However, she did not really belong in the mainstream of English cultural life among the domesticated middle classes between the wars, since apart from being an 'outlander' (ever a favourite pseudonym), she had already lost her youthful idealism when she left America. Even so, 'the death of romance' in the aftermath of war affected everyone, and when she again addressed the problem of men (the problem which, as Stephen Garton has argued, sits at the core of *My Brilliant Career*), her characters confronted contemporary problems.[21]

The last sentence in Miles' diary entry for Sunday 16 September 1918 reads simply, 'Grey day. Finished novel.' The unidentified novel was undoubtedly 'Sam Price from Chicago', 'by the authors of *The Net of Circumstance*', which she had finished typing in early November and straightaway sent off to the literary agent A. P. Watt. The immediate outcome is unknown, but maybe it was not too discouraging, as she began revising the manuscript in January 1919, an extended process that took until August that year, when she again sent it to Watt. The extant typescript is quite long, some 80,000 words, and considering the extended and irregular hours she put in at Russell Square, and that she was also revising and resubmitting *On Dearborn Street* at the same time, she worked quite fast.[22]

The fact that 'Sam Price from Chicago' failed to find a publisher despite Watt's best efforts — by 1922 it had been rejected by no fewer than eleven publishers — does not diminish its biographical interest. Set in London during the last year of the war, 'Sam Price from Chicago' is about a romance between Sam, a newly arrived and idealistic young American, and Dorothy Latimer, brought up in Gippsland, Australia, with several years spent in America and recently back from service with a field hospital in Belgium, and those who aid and abet their ultimately successful courtship. The supporting cast is mostly quite recognisable, being modelled on Miles' associates in London and Chicago (Kathleen Ussher's mother, for one, is the template for Mrs English), or culled from the hectic social world around her, with two Anzacs thrown in for good measure.[23]

Obviously Fred Post gave Miles the idea for the story and served as the prototype for Sam, and much of Miles went into the construction of Dorothy (even though she is described as tall and aged only twenty-five). The interesting thing is that after their relationship — 'brimming over congenially' — has been temporarily undermined by Gerry Evans, a more determined Chicagoan, Sam takes up with the shallow society figure Mrs Cornelia Newberry, one of the 'war-winners'. Having dealt with the manipulative Evans, who has in effect kidnapped her in hope of a 'honeymoon', Dorothy, it seems, will just have to bear life alone: 'She was of a virginal, fastidious mold. She would love once and never again, but she was no morbid melancholic. She was vigorous and healthy. She would have to face it ... The loneliness terrified her but it was better than a companionship that would gall.'[24] It is Sam and Sam alone that she wants. In Sam, Dorothy has found a really acceptable man, a man reared by women to a positive view of the world:

Men had interested her, disturbed her, distressed her, disgusted her, but never had one made her heart sing and her soul respond like this unpretentious, unambitious young man from Chicago with his beneficent theories, woman-nurtured.[25]

The tale does run on, but in due course, with the aid of two sensible American matrons, the pair are eventually reconciled. Both have been too fastidious. But then Sam's conscience drives him to enlist. Happily, Dorothy overcomes his fears of marriage under the circumstances, and although he returns blinded, she is able to save him from postwar despair. And thanks to the generosity of another attractive male character, Malcolm Ross, a wounded British soldier to whom she became secretly engaged post-Evans but who died a timely death of Spanish flu soon after, she now has quite a considerable income. The novel ends on a highly emotional note. Dorothy Latimer feels that she has been saved. The gods had been cruel, but whereas so many lost their all, Sam is safe. She is 'a treasure-seeker rewarded'; and in an extraordinary flourish of Australiana, 'a shred of mateship had been left her'.

This is a far stronger ending than that devised for the final version of the prewar tale *On Dearborn Street*, where the narrator Cavarley and the mercurial Sybyl Penelo sail away, with Cavarley's aunt as chaperone and guarantor of a still-to-be-assured happy outcome. The same American elders in 'Sam Price from Chicago' carry Dorothy Latimer through to marriage. Though war mars her man, she is happy and fulfilled.

Compared with Miles Franklin's next attempt to essay the pain of women after the Great War, 'The Love Letters of a Superfluous Woman', 'Sam Price from Chicago' is an optimistic work. As the (no longer cited) first half of the title 'There, Where Have You Gone?' sought to emphasise, 'The Love Letters' are a cry of grief and rebellion, barely mitigated. Written in the spring of 1920 in the then popular form of a series of letters (compare, for example, Jean Webster's light-hearted *Daddy-Long-Legs*, an American college girl's romance in letters) to Dan, killed in France, the twenty-two letters are dedicated, somewhat cryptically, 'To those who understand — how many? And those who may agree — if any.' In the first letter, 'Come back to me!', the letter writer, having no faith in spiritualism, tries to comprehend the silence. In the last, 'Au revoir', she turns her back on the senses. But even there all is not lost. Having traversed diverse aspects of opinion and behaviour in postwar London, most of it deemed hypocritical and deplorable, if not downright disgusting, as in the case of ageing superfluous women with sagging breasts and ill-fitting false teeth, the stricken 'superfluous woman' resolves to leave the city: 'I shall get away from this old city so that the memory of you shall not stab anew at each street corner, at each park entrance, and every house of entertainment.' More surprising still, she thinks to go far away around the Cape of Good Hope to Australia 'to see the dear sunny Anzacs', and back to America via Cape Horn.[26]

The letters are not easy to read today. Though totally accessible, they seem high-pitched, and it is hardly to be wondered that no publisher took them up. There is workmanship, but 'insufficient detachment', as a publisher's reader remarked of *On Dearborn Street*. But then there wasn't meant to be. And there is a boldness in the way psycho-social realities are addressed; for example, the superfluous women are not the youthful prewar women too far ahead of their time to find happiness, as in the first title to deal with the subject, Emma Brooke's *A Superfluous Woman*, published in 1894, and as in Miles' own writings in Chicago. Rather they are women well past the first flush of youth, doomed to loneliness and a hideous old age. Miles herself could not have been surprised at the lack of interest. Her observations contained 'too much real feeling' for her to attach her name, she explained in letters to publishers. Instead, the typescript, about 22,000 words in length, was submitted pseudonymously, as by 'Mrs O.'.[27]

In the years to 1921, according to her diaries, Miles wrote a third novel, 'Estelle'. It probably became 'Mrs Dysart Disappears' by 'Brent of Bin Bin', which survives in a typescript dated 1931. The heroine of this post-war mystery novel, 'with a double solution but no material explanation', according to the cover note, is Estelle Dacre, a beautiful singer with a pure contralto voice. Three novels in three years is quite a lot for someone in full-time employment; and in 1920 Miles was also working on 'the bus' story, 'Hold Tight!', begun during the war, which did the rounds in England or the United States in 1921, to no avail.[28]

The output of minor pieces — anecdotes, sketches, short stories and comment — during these troubled years is equally noteworthy, though some are mere fragments, or even more fugitive, their existence known only from diary references. Their subjects ranged widely, and she was quick to try her hand at new genres with two film scenarios drafted in 1920, 'A Beauty Contest, or Venus Here and Now' and the evidently recyclable 'Mrs Dysart Disappears', said to be a synopsis of a novel adapted from one of a series of six novels and plays. The fact that such items are known to exist is not meant to suggest recoverable literary merit or significance, merely that Miles Franklin always had to be writing something, and she found a lot to write about after the war. Moreover, she was always on the lookout for new opportunities to earn money from her writing. In 1920 she read a book on making moving pictures, though given her rather arrogant comments on the film scenarios she submitted it is not to be wondered that her efforts sank without a trace. For instance, to the scenario to 'Mrs Dysart Disappears', submitted first to Astra Films in 1920, she appended the comment: 'The authors [sic] cannot understand how film actors can construct their parts with artistic satisfaction from the mere bones of a synopsis, so, should this MS. meet with approval, the authors will be pleased to lend a copy of the complete work if desired.' The scenario was for return to 'John Maurice'.[29]

The most substantial of the topical writings at this time is a series entitled 'Irish Sketches', again by 'Outlander', ten written during and immediately after a three-week break in Ireland with Miss Hodge in August 1919, and two later, in 1920. The thought of visiting Ireland had filled Miles with glee, notwithstanding the tense political situation, with the Sinn Feiners refusing to take their seats in the House of Commons after the general election of December 1918, which resulted in a coalition government led by Lloyd George. 'I am going to Ireland and am going to see all the Sinn Feiners I can, and I wish I could see the other side too. They seem to be unable to agree among themselves,' she added blandly, or perhaps in Shavian mode.[30]

The two women left England on 15 August, returning to London on the morning of 2 September. Civil war had not yet broken out, and unlike another interested Australian visitor to Dublin in 1919, Joice Nankivell Loch, who very nearly fell foul of the authorities, Miles had a trouble-free time, and met 'the other side' as well, thanks to Miss Hodge's political connections.[31]

Although they got away to a bad start on the overcrowded Irish Mail and she fell sick at the end of her stay, due to what sounds like a recurrence of malaria, Miles enjoyed the trip mightily, complain though she did in postcards to her father of antiquated accommodation and 'damp rheumaticky green' (a common enough Australian response to lushness in the Old World). Not that she slept well in Dublin. Miss Hodge was a snorer.[32]

They spent most of the time in Dublin, with two trips beyond, by train for two days in the old market town of Ennis, to the west in County Clare, and a day trip by charabanc (a long, light vehicle with transverse seats facing forward) to the picturesque Glendalough lake district in County Wicklow to the south, where it rained and reminded Miles of the discomforts of the bush, 'of which I had too much in my young days'. The very first thing they did when settled in their Dublin accommodation at 55 Upper Leeson Street was attend a matinee at the renowned Abbey Theatre. The next day, a Sunday, they did the rounds of cathedrals and museums, and, having met some Sinn Feiners with the Australian-born Sinn Fein MP for South Dublin, George Gavan Duffy, visited Sinn Fein's headquarters, finishing up at Queen's Theatre in the evening. Among other significant Irishmen met subsequently were Desmond Fitzgerald, Cruise O'Brien, Arthur Griffiths and, at Liberty Hall, the prominent and to many frightening labour leader Jim Larkin. Miles also met some agreeable Unionists who assured her that Sinn Fein was all talk. One old gentleman who said that the Irish were only 'dear, dear children', who would not be able to manage for an instant without the English, reminded Miles of the anti-suffrage fogeys. 'Is the paleolithic reactionary always to be with us?' she asked rhetorically.[33]

At the Dublin horse show, she thought the jumping superior to anything she had seen in Australia; and when she saw George Bernard Shaw's mercilessly iconoclastic play *John Bull's Other Island*, also at the Abbey Theatre, she enjoyed herself 'uproariously'. It was a rare privilege to see Shaw presented in his native city by native-born players, and it made her more than ever confident of the social value of theatre: 'when the drama becomes an integral part of the life and recreation of the people ... we shall be a deal further on the road of that culture which promotes mental health,' she later wrote.[34]

Other aspects of the Irish cultural revival appealed less, however. In her 'The Abbey Theatre' sketch she expressed reservations about the Irish preoccupation with oppression, necessary and inevitable as the subject was, and about reviving Gaelic as a national language: the Irish, she thought, had a right to their language, but 'I should hate to face the world with nothing but Gaelic on my lips.'[35]

It was the 'disease of poverty' that really raised her ire. Much later, in a commentary on Sean O'Casey's autobiographical *Drums Under the Windows*, written at the onset of the Cold War, Miles recalled her horror, especially in Dublin:

> The poverty is shocking, and no rage and rebellion against those responsible for upholding such a state of affairs cd be unjustified

or excessive. Dublin poverty is renowned for its depths. It filled my head with lice on the only day I made contact with it in a R.C. church congregation.[36]

That was in St Patrick's Cathedral in 1919, after which experience she wrote, more diplomatically: 'Oh that St Patrick had abolished the fleas from Ireland instead of the snakes.' Not for the first time, a fiercely anti-church paragraph came to her:

> I said upon my first visit to the architectural treasures of the old world, I repeat it now and always, that if a few of these roomy edifices could be converted into comfortably warm and convenient, free, hot water depots with bath room and rest room attachments for the suffering and disinherited peoples that exist within their shadow, they would be more acceptable to God, more in accordance with my vision of Christianity.[37]

Politics, as always, interested John Maurice Franklin's eldest daughter. It had been clear to her from the outset that this was the main point in Ireland in 1919, and she had her own take on the situation: 'The interest of Ireland today is neither its scenery nor its ancient relics, but the form of its immediate political demands, which make it the militant suffragette of the nations.' The analogy may be unexpected; but it was not wrong to suggest that these latest militants were distinguished by that same spiritual exaltation and passion for martyrdom which characterised the prewar women rebels in Britain, the additional factor being, in Miles' opinion, the extent of support worldwide: 'The Irish secessionists have a larger and more powerful army of sympathisers and supporters in the world at large than ever the women could have hoped for.'[38] Miles took the analogy a step further in 'The Three Mutineers', where she saw a close parallel with the British suffrage struggle. Just as the militant suffragettes had made the liberal suffragists respectable, so the republican Sinn Feiners made Home Rulers look mild, and their Unionist opponents were just like the 'antis', with their heads in the sand, but with their own particular bogey: anti-popery. Her conclusion is drawn with conviction: 'Today in watching the Irish fervour and imagination squandered on a ceaseless struggle to secure a simple elemental right like national freedom ... the heart is wrung with despair.'[39]

These sketches should have found a publisher. They nearly did. Miles' American friends tried to place them straightaway, and at least one editor found them extremely interesting, judging the material well-handled and the point of view excellent. But space was a problem for him, and apparently nothing eventuated elsewhere. The literary fruits would be a long time coming.[40]

Most years thereafter Miles managed to take recuperative breaks away from London and its winters, when the streets were hazardous and, until the passing of the Clean Air Act in 1956, thick fogs frequently engulfed the city. Although not always very enjoyable, the breaks were at least in pleasant places: Newport in 1920; St Leonard's, Sussex, in 1921; Scarborough (with the Smiths) in 1922; and Stratford-on-Avon (with Miss Hodge) in 1923. In 1924 she went to Cambridge; in 1925 to Exeter; and in 1926 to Scotland and Ireland with Aunt Lena, who visited England in 1926–27. In addition, the NHTPC held its national conferences at salubrious sites, usually spa towns: Harrogate in 1919; Leamington Spa in 1920; and on three occasions in Miles' time in Buxton. However, if her dumpy-looking presence in a press photograph of 'Housing and Town Planning Experts in Conference' in Cardiff in May 1920 is any guide, they were not much fun, while international conferences, no matter how successful, invariably meant more work.[41]

Numerous American friends passing through London after the war also provided respite. Agnes Nestor had been the first of her old associates from Chicago to arrive, in April 1918. In a letter to Mrs Robins, Agnes wrote, 'Last Sunday I spent with Stella Franklin. She is looking so well and could hardly wait to see me.'[42] Later that year, by chance, Miles ran into Ethel Mason in the street and they had a happy reunion. Over the next few years there would be many other visitors, mostly en route to postwar labour and peace conferences in Europe: Mary Dreier, Mary McDowell, Rose Schneiderman, Mary Anderson, an unnamed settlement house director, and Jane Addams, who was accompanied by the pioneering American occupational health researcher Dr Alice Hamilton. In May 1921 Editha Phelps arrived to stay at Miss Brennan's boarding house at Upper Woburn Place, as in 1911, which was fine until Miles contracted shingles and Editha, by then aged sixty-six, proved 'worse than useless'. And Margaret Dreier Robins passed through twice in characteristic style: first in 1921, and again in 1923 with Raymond Robins, whose great cause now was to outlaw war. [43]

The meetings with Mrs Robins represent a kind of endnote to Miles' association with women's trade unionism in America. After the war Mrs

Robins had conceived of an International Federation of Working Women, over which she would preside, and in 1921 she was on her way to its first congress, held in Geneva. In 1923, she was en route to Vienna for the second congress. The federation did not come to much, due to irreconcilable differences between American and European approaches and perhaps Margaret Robins' philosophical differences with the Australian-born chief woman officer of the British Labour Party, Dr Marion Phillips, not to mention Mrs Robins' own grand ways. By this time, however, Miles enjoyed a peaceable relationship with Mrs Robins, having been deployed to send food parcels to her relatives in Germany in 1920 and been helpful in arranging meetings with British women labour leaders, notably Dr Phillips (whom Miles also detested), and in other ways in 1921. In 1923, Miles was again among those who welcomed the Robinses on their arrival in London (the others being Raymond's sister Elizabeth and the Maynards) and provided a public support system during their stay at Almond's Hotel in Bond Street (where the plumbing left much to be desired and Mrs Robins felt like joining what she called 'Stella Franklin's religion of HOT WATER and a BATH'). Miles had lunch there with Mrs Robins one day. But she had ceased to engage with her politics, as Mrs Robins reported to her sister Dorothea Dreier in 1921: 'Stella is just the same as ever and tells me she has passed entirely through the stage of wishing to reform the world and so she can be amused at others who do or don't.'[44]

Alice Henry was thankful that Mrs Robins had seen Miles and that she had found her much the same, 'in spite of her present woes and troubles', a reference to her health problems, perhaps, or overwork at the office, evidenced by her hostile attitude to hypocritical social reformers. Writing to Alice Henry after a big international housing congress in London in 1920, Miles expressed herself freely: 'I hope they will burn as they deserve in hell fire for what they have done to me. They are the most godless sweaters and blatant megalomaniac egotists.'[45]

There was also a steady flow of compatriots to entertain and be entertained by, lower as her profile at home seems to have been immediately after World War I. Only three articles by Miles Franklin appeared in the Sydney press between 1918 and 1923, and there were fewer references to her, though Dr Mary Booth mentioned her 1905 articles as 'Vernacular' to a Select Committee of the New South Wales Legislative Council on the condition of agriculture in November 1920. Nonetheless she remained in touch with literary developments, thanks to George Robertson, who sent her some new titles for Christmas in 1920, and to the Australian bookshop on the Strand, where she obtained a copy of May Gibbs' delectable children's book *Snugglepot and Cuddlepie,* now an Australian classic.[46]

If the demands of birds of passage were a drain — being well brought up, Miles would always make an effort to see them — they also served to keep her in touch with her homeland. Some, like her cousin Claude Kinred, who had returned to England to work in munitions, and Stanley McKay, a Tumut-born theatre man and ex-soldier who encouraged her to write a play entitled 'Down Under' (of which no more is presently known), were gone by 1920. Others were around for longer, notably her old and still-admired mentor Vida Goldstein, who went to a peace conference in Geneva in 1919 and stayed on in London until 1922, sometimes with Miss Hodge. And whereas the Walsöes left England in September 1920, they were soon replaced by P. S. and Nancy Lister Watson, who arrived in London in June 1922 and stayed for over a year, during which time Miles heard many stories of the old Australia from P. S., who, with his brothers, had taken over the huge grazing property 'Gregory Downs' in north Queensland's Gulf Country in the 1890s.[47]

At the same time came a clutch of New South Welshwomen of much the same vintage as Miles: Marguerite Dale, née Hume, from Yass, the first Australian woman delegate (alternate) to the League of Nations in 1922; Persia Campbell, MA, from Sydney University, whose successes in London included impressing philosopher Bertrand Russell, which provoked Miles to the tart private observation that it was to be hoped that his interest was not allowed to be anything but academic, also in 1922; Lute Drummond, opera coach and friend of Stanley McKay and a leading Australian follower of Rudolf Steiner, met by chance at Stratford-on-Avon in 1923; and Marjorie Chave Collisson, Sydney University-educated lecturer and feminist, a friend of Rose Scott's niece Mollye Scott Shaw, who arrived from the United States in 1922.[48]

News from home was all very well, but it was to trends in politics and culture at the heart of the Empire that Miles responded most keenly. In a letter to Alice Henry and other American friends written on 18 October 1920, she reported with some astonishment that the new Liberal proposals for economic transformation through partnerships in industry read rather like the Russian program, a reference to that 'big revolution which is still struggling to get its head above international tzarism'; also that worker militancy had put a stop to further warmongering and was making the West

End clubmen more respectful of the trade unions: 'Hats off to the British Workman ... he is certainly trying to keep alight those lamps of freedom which England has indisputably lighted of old.' The danger was, as radical journalist H. N. Brailsford had impressed upon her consciousness in 1918 (and was soon to be evidenced by the deportation of radicals from the United States and the foundation of Interpol in 1923), that there would be an international solidarity of 'the potentates' rather than the people.[49]

Included in this densely packed letter are two vignettes of upper-class contempt for Ireland and for working people, which evidently annoyed Miles Franklin. In 1920, the Lord Mayor of Cork fasted unto death in Brixton Prison protesting against the partition of Ireland (which became a reality in December 1921); and there was a big miners' strike in 1920–21, which saw the miners federation struggling on alone after the collapse of the militant prewar triple alliance of mining, railway and transport unions, until the government agreed to subsidise the troubled coal industry. Here Miles really laid into what she called 'fatuous knowingness'. One old gentleman, said to be off to the Dominions to fill some educational position, thought Ireland 'a nothing', and considered that the outcome would depend entirely on the next US presidential election. Another know-all, a company promoter met at a dinner, maybe with Thomas Brook Smith, asserted that the miners' strike was simply fomented by men who did that sort of thing for a living, and wished that they could be deported. In the only act of sabotage open to her after her objections failed to make any impact, Miles took a second helping of fowl, a luxury to which her London wage did not run.[50]

If Miles often found British complacency irritating and was for the most part unimpressed by postwar reconstruction rhetoric, she was also on the lookout for positive aspects of the polity. Even the unfortunate and unhealthy denizens of the Dublin slums were not really tamed, she thought; and the workers might yet deal with the British junkers. Nor, despite assertions to the contrary, had she abandoned the hopes that war seemed to destroy for so many of her generation and the following one. With Miss Hodge now a Labour councillor for Hendon and Lady Byles still an informed voice in Liberalism, that would have been impossible, even had it been her inclination. She was just looking for a new ethical base; and as with so many colonials before and after her, the harshness of British class structure heightened her awareness that something must be done. In that respect it is interesting to find her attending meetings of the Emerson Club in London in early 1923. Not that she was impressed by one Horace Thoroughgood's 'dull trivial irrelevant remarks'. Such experiences would stand her in good stead once back in culturally timorous Australia, but the energy and transcendence once inspired in so many intellectuals by the great American Transcendentalist Ralph Waldo Emerson would have to come from somewhere else.[51]

Her letters at this time also contain numerous sharp comments on international affairs. The world seemed to have learned nothing from the war, she wrote to Agnes Nestor in June 1919: 'They still believe in running things with a big stick'. A few months later, having heard at a lecture at the National Liberal Club, 'crammed with the flower of mental mediocrity', that the effect of a British-led intervention in Russia had been to install the Soviets more strongly, she commented that the peasants would never have put up with the Soviets otherwise, but obviously preferred them to foreign devils. Surely, she added, the Empire was large enough to contain British energies, haywire as it had gone in places. In another letter to Alice Henry written in May 1922 she commented, quite accurately, on the problems of the lascars, the ill-paid Indian seamen who crewed British ships in the age of steam, observing that an incident in which Australians had refused to give a mail contract to a steamer crewed by lascars was probably an expression of the White Australia Policy, 'which in its turn is rooted in fear of the coloured man lowering Australian working man standards'.[52]

With so much to say about class and Empire, there was little room in Miles' letters for commentary on feminism. Her comparative silence on a once consuming subject requires some explanation. It is not far to seek. Although the suffrage struggle was not over, with women in their twenties still unable to vote in Britain, it had become a low-key issue. The main challenge, as Alice Henry saw, lay with the newly enfranchised woman citizen: 'Once you can make voting women into feminists you have a genuine, solid backing, such as women have never had before.' This was something on which Miles had had her say twenty years before at far-off Penrith. Moreover, she had believed from the beginning that war was no good for women, as proved to be the case of advanced Australia, where the war and its aftermath proved a setback for the woman citizen. Nevertheless, she was able to turn out a formal tribute to Mrs Robins for a greeting organised by Alice Henry in 1922, in which she stressed that women would need vision and courage to face the challenge of the postwar world, and that the less encumbered women of the New World now had a chance to organise 'so that we may build anew and better on the partial wreck of civilisation that lies around us'. A better indication of her personal position is probably the sentence marked in the Preface of her copy of *War, Peace and the Future: A Consideration of Nationalism and Internationalism, and of the Relation of Women to War* by the influential maternal feminist Ellen Key, given to her by the American Left-wing poet John Varney in 1919: 'Even after the women and the working-men have attained political power and responsibility, centuries will probably elapse before humanity, by conscious effort, can overcome the madness of a world at war through the organization of that world.' It was not that feminism ceased to matter, but that it had been overtaken by events.[53]

Feminism had not ceased to be part of Miles' world either. She would continue to eat at the Minerva café from time to time, and like everyone else she went to hear Lady Astor, Britain's first woman member of parliament; the Misses Newcomb and Hodge's British Dominions Woman Suffrage Union would soon be transformed into the British Commonwealth League (founded in 1926 and of strategic significance to Australian feminists in the interwar years); and she was aware of such developments as the Six Point Group, founded in 1921, with its program of legislative demands. Somehow, though, the great days were over, and the dreaded British dowdiness that Miles had remarked upon back in 1911 after meeting Christabel Pankhurst, 'hair flying [and] untidy like all the suffragettes', seemed the more evident, as Freud and the flappers impinged on the survivors of prewar feminism. Where was she to turn? When Miles hosted a dinner for Mrs Robins at the International Club on her first visit to London, Mrs Robins noted privately that while she had enjoyed the occasion, the guests were all middle-aged or older ladies, with only a meagre number of men. The Women's Freedom League was no longer what it used to be. Impressive as leader Charlotte Despard always was, she was now well into her seventies. As for the league's journal, the *Vote*, Miles assured Alice Henry it was no longer worth reading, as it had been taken over after Nan Smith's death by 'a doddering nincompoop': 'Some man married her late in life which so elated her that she thinks all the feminist ramping is a deplorable sex antagonism — men are better than women etc.'[54]

Meantime antiquated views about women resurfaced. When the famous writer Arnold Bennett asserted that the lack of women writers of the first rank showed that women were intellectually inferior to men, Miles responded vigorously, though if her response was published it has not so far been traced. By this time too, as she noted warily, an assault on old-style feminist values was under way throughout the English-speaking world. Thus, in January 1922, the year in which the first English translations of Freud became available, she attended a lecture on psychoanalysis and sceptical references to psychoanalysis began to appear in her writing. On learning that her old friend and former landlady in Chicago Dr Young was going in for it, she wrote to Alice Henry, 'Psycho-analysis is like everything else, for those to come, but it is very crude so far — another form of egotism kindly called self expression — but I suppose human beings must puddle through dark to the light.' Old-style feminism, which valued chastity for its own sake, was being undermined by other forces as well as the new sexology. The weakening of the class structure, for example, took with it the protective idea of 'the lady' (and 'the gentleman'), though its observance lasted Miles' lifetime.[55]

Fred Post, whose presence she had been enjoying for over a year, left for Chicago in July 1919, a real desolation. One of his last English letters to his 'dearest twin' ends 'Goodnight with XXXX'. In Washington working in the consular service office by November, he wrote urging her to pack her trunk and join her loving friends in America; but she stayed put. Her response does not survive, only a passing remark to Alice Henry that he was 'a forgetful dreamer', so it is hard to know how she really felt. However, there is something deferential in his letters, as to an older woman, and she obviously thought he was too young for her. (He was thirty-one, but he looks younger in his passport photo.) It seems she did write to him in Washington, but it was a case of 'Amiably yours' in his last communication, dated 4 May 1920. Between March and August 1919, Miles also saw a good deal of the American poet John Varney living nearby at 157 High Holborn — possibly another late romantic figure, to whom she was eventually obliged to speak 'too plainly'.[56]

At least there was an abundance of culture. Chicago had been a great stimulus, in effect her university. London would be equally significant, although its influence is harder to pin down, being the product of a milieu and a mood rather than of social movements. Miles had always read a lot and gone to the theatre whenever she could. It seems she read more and went more often to the theatre in the early 1920s than ever. She was seeking to find new themes and approaches, even new media, to fit her writing to the postwar world, which was no longer distracted by romantic possibilities. The record of her reading and entertainments in the early 1920s is interesting in its own right but also provides clues as to 'the way home', over which she was puzzling.

During 1921 some eighteen titles, mostly novels, are mentioned in her pocket diary, including such classics as *Under the Greenwood Tree* by Thomas Hardy; *Wuthering Heights* by Emily Brontë; *Of Human Bondage* by W. Somerset Maugham; George Meredith's *The Egoist*; and Herman Melville's *Moby Dick* (the only American title); also 'a little Thackeray'. Contemporary titles are fewer and mostly unmemorable, except for Katherine Mansfield's collection of short stories, *Bliss*, and although it is not referred to, Miles was at least aware of D. H. Lawrence's *Women in Love*, thanks to John Varney, who thought it 'too physiological'. As well, Miss Hodge would read aloud to her on visits to Temple Fortune Court (she was usually there on public holidays): in 1921 it was from *David Copperfield* and *Great Expectations*.[57]

Thackeray was a constant in Miles' reading at this time. In 1919, she read *The Newcomes*. Subtitled *Memoirs of a Most Respectable Family*, this panoramic novel was regarded by contemporaries as his masterpiece, the richest of his fictions. In 1919 she also read the earlier *History of Henry Esmond, Esq.*, a somewhat problematic historical novel first published in 1852, which is set in the age of Queen Anne; and in 1920, if an incomplete reference can be relied upon, *Pendennis* (full title *The History of Pendennis: His Fortunes and Misfortunes. His Friends and Greatest Enemy*). Then she re-read what is now Thackeray's best-known novel, *Vanity Fair*, subtitled *A Novel Without a Hero*. All these titles are to be found in her library, and although commentary by Miles is lacking, in retrospect it seems obvious that the worldly, sceptical and at core melancholy mid-Victorian and his characters would appeal to her, especially perhaps the women characters. After all, *Vanity Fair*'s Becky Sharp and Sybylla Melvyn are both bright, bold and flirtatious and, as pinpointed by Ina Ferris, the more complex Ethel Newcome suffered significant inner conflict: 'Ethel's conflict between accepting and rebelling against worldly values defines her and gives her character its depth.'[58]

Not much of Miles' reading at this time seems to have been non-fiction. Yet she took note of, for example, *The Economic Consequences of the Peace* by John Maynard Keynes, and, on Lady Byles' recommendation, *Disenchantment* by C. E. Montague. Like the string of references to Thackeray, this title now stands out as a lasting influence on Miles' thinking. Montague, a brilliant and versatile journalist, put his finger on a key psychological characteristic of the postwar world. In his time he had been a Home Ruler, pro-Boer and a supporter of women's rights, and in 1914 he enlisted as a private in the British army, later being recruited to intelligence. His book, a study in postwar disillusion, consists of a series of powerful and beautifully written essays which enable the reader to understand how during the war 'the common man' lost faith in his betters — politicians, generals, the clergy, journalists and so on — and ends with a 'fair warning', given the rise of fascism in Italy and Germany, of renewed militarism (obliquely expressed as 'piping in Thessaly'), characterising ex-soldiers as 'the most determined peace party that ever existed in Britain'. 'Let them,' wrote Montague in conclusion, 'clap the only darbies they have — the Covenant of the League of Nations — on to the wrists of all future poets, romancers, and sages. We must beware in good time those boys [who will respond to new war cries], and fiery elderly men, piping in Thessaly.' Miles re-read it in 1924, and still cherished the thought of it in 1950, when, recalling that she had lent her own copy to fellow writer 'G. B. Lancaster' (Edith Lyttleton), who never returned it, she sought Elsie Belle Champion's help to replace it.[59]

This résumé indicates that the writings Miles was most interested in were the grand narratives of the nineteenth century and the latest versions of the New Woman novel, with scant attention paid to now familiar experimentalists. However, it is as well to recall that in the early 1920s some of the most important literary modernists such as Dorothy Richardson and James Joyce were either little known or had major works yet to come, and enthusiasm for the historical novel and its downmarket cousin, the imperial romance, was just beginning.[60]

As with books, so with theatre. For the years 1921 to 1922 there are at least thirty-five diary entries indicating that Miles attended a play, a concert or, occasionally, a film. As was normal in the pre-radio era, people went out in the evenings for entertainment. Miles' taste was quite catholic, stretching from Shakespeare to drawing-room comedy, from classical concerts to *opéra bouffe*, from the Russian ballet to song-and-dance and vaudeville. She went to performances in most if not all of the great London venues during these years: Wyndhams, St Martin's, the Old Vic, the Albert Hall, to name just a few of central London's forty-two theatres. There she saw many of the great performers of the day, such as legendary actor Mrs Patrick Campbell (deemed powerful but repulsive) and the great Russian dancer Karsavina. She was especially keen on Sybil Thorndike, and in 1922 was delighted to see again leading American dancers Ruth St Denis and Ted Shawn. (She claimed not to have noticed his near nudity, as it 'gives a sense of self-respect to see at least one human being that looks well uncovered'). In 1923, just in time — as this was to be the actor's last London season — she saw the great Italian Eleanora Duse in Ibsen's *Ghosts*; also Karel Capek's *R.U.R.*, in which the machines take over.[61]

A number of the plays were by novelists who were successful in both genres, a combination now rare. On 26 April 1922 Miles went to see John Galsworthy's new comedy, *Windows*, at the Court Theatre, which she liked, and on 6 October of the same year, at the Regent, Arnold Bennett's not very successful comedy *Body and Soul*. Writing plays could be lucrative for novelists, due to the practice of optioning, whereby theatre managers paid considerable sums for the exclusive rights to new plays, whether or not they ever put them on. Bennett received £200 for an option on another of his 1922 plays, *The Love Match*, though it was never performed.[62]

No wonder, then, that Miles Franklin turned to writing plays with enthusiasm in the early 1920s (especially given that one after another her postwar writing in other genres had failed to find a publisher). She was always keen on the theatre, but seems to have had a rush of blood to the head in the early 1920s (though she apparently passed up an opportunity to work at the Old Vic for the legendary Lilian Baylis, who was looking for a secretary in 1919, probably because the job was less well paid than the NHTPC position and less flexible). From diary references and extant manuscripts, it appears she tried her hand at up to fifteen plays in London between 1918 and 1927, from Stanley McKay's encouragement of 'Down Under' in 1918 and her efforts to interest the leading provincial producer Annie Horniman in 'Virtue' in 1919 through to 'Bouquets. By a Practising Nonentity' in 1926. Eight were written between 1921 and 1923. Quite a few are known only as diary references, and three of the 1921 titles were said to be 'playlets' (though at least one was finished: 'Geese and Ganders', which she sent to Sybil Thorndike). Miles' propensity for recycling is again evident, with some three titles redrafted from prose, two recognisably so — 'Hold Tight!' and 'Phoebe Lambent and Love' (both in 1922), and a third, 'Three Women', dating from 1925. No doubt she hoped they would do better that way. Under the circumstances, keeping track of pseudonyms is almost impossible, but as with 'Virtue', 'Mr and Mrs O.' still did occasional service and there were some new ones, the not so mysterious 'J. Verney' (probably a variant on Varney), and 'Punica Granatum' for a version of 'Three Women'.[63]

Of these mostly fugitive efforts, only a few scripts survive. These Miles presumably thought the most important to keep for posterity. In chronological order they are: 'The English Jackeroo', her first effort at writing a play in London, begun in 1916 and finished in 1922; 'Quite!', begun that year under the name 'Pasquinade' (how typical of Miles to hit on this archaic word, meaning a lampoon, squib, libel or other piece of satire) and sent to C. E. Montague, to unknown effect, ultimately to be redrafted as a revue in the 1940s; and the recycled 'Phoebe Lambent and Love', which she ultimately planned to take home to Australia.

The plot of 'The English Jackeroo' involves a great leap in time, from Somerville Station in the Australian high country in the 1890s in Act 1 to 1920s London in the second and final act. In Act 1, Smith, the 'English jackeroo', who has been sent to Australia to get over his musical ambitions, survives the customary ribbing and finds a soul mate in the squatter's rebellious daughter, Dulcie, whose singing voice impresses him, but not her parents. She wants to run away. He promises to help when he returns to London, but she never hears from him again. (This act has a lively scene about collecting wild honey, a subject on Miles' mind after receiving some from Australia and writing about it for the *Sydney Morning Herald.*) Act 2 has 'Madame Ingera', a prima donna fresh from triumphs in America, arrive in London to help out in an opera. As it turns out, the opera is by Smith, now a great composer; and when Madame Ingera sings for him on a trial basis, beginning with a coo-ee song, her true identity as Dulcie emerges. It is too late for romance — she is now married to Froggart, once a jealous swain at Jingerah and now one of the 'geebungs' of the wool boom — though Smith had written 'a thousand times'. Probably Froggart intercepted the letters. Since both have now fulfilled their ambitions, sleeping dogs are left to lie.[64]

When the play was finished, in September 1922, Miles asked a well-known actress, Phyllis Neilson-Terry, if she would read the script, because she had a good singing voice — Miles had heard Neilson-Terry play Trilby in New York — emphasising that the play's provenance must be kept 'a strict secret'. As 'J. Verney' of 41 Russell Square, Miles would later suggest to a magazine editor that s/he might like to read it and make an offer for the serial rights, as this was a subject taken from real life and would be of interest to women.[65]

Miles Franklin's enthusiasm for writing plays was in accord with, and in good part a product of, the times. In J. C. Trewin's valuable account, *The*

Theatre Since 1900, the theatre of 'the feverish twenties' is characterised as full of contradiction and paradox, but also of zeal and energy: 'The theatre of the 1920s seemed always to be working at full and anxious stretch.' Comedy continued to be a core component, and amid the alternatives, the work of elders was frequently produced: George Bernard Shaw's 1920s plays included *Back to Methuselah* and *St Joan*; Arnold Bennett was 'prolific and efficient'; and Galsworthy wrote as many as twelve plays over the decade. It should perhaps be added that some major British dramatists of the 1920s left plays which have never been acted, for example Sir Arthur Wing Pinero. Meanwhile, among the new contributors, two playwrights from Ireland, Sean O'Casey and St John Ervine, were to be of lasting significance to Miles Franklin. Miles heard St John Ervine lecture on the future of the theatre in late 1922, though she had probably encountered him earlier, as suggested by the first of almost forty letters between them over the next thirty years, during which time he became drama critic of the London *Observer* and Miles' man in London theatre.[66]

Miles' effort to adapt to post-World War I literary modes and pre-occupations was more strenuous than successful. She was not well equipped to deal with Mayfair or the flapper in the novel, and her London plays are too arch for modern tastes, even allowing for the popularity of drawing-room plots and a still class-based humour. Nonetheless, she learned a lot about the upper reaches of class society from H. H. Champion's sister Annie, whose work as a nanny gave her entrée to aristocratic circles. And she never gave up trying to innovate and earn money, no matter how discouraging the circumstances — so long as they were also stimulating.

'I wish I could get home to a bit of sunshine,' she wrote to Eva O'Sullivan on 5 August 1919. She often seemed homesick, in spring especially, and unsettled, writing to American friends that she was thinking of returning to Chicago. In May 1920 she wrote to Mrs Robins that she wished she was back in the United States, but could not make up her mind what to do: 'I know I don't want to be marooned in the old world for life, but when I'll bestir myself ... I don't know. I'll get up with a snort one of these days I expect, and take ship.'[67]

The evidence does not disclose when exactly she decided to 'take ship'. Judging by the first surviving letter from Susannah Franklin for this period, it seems Miles must have booked her passage to Australia some time in July 1923. Writing from Sydney on 14 August 1923, to her 'dear little girl',

Susannah advised that Aunt Sarah Lampe had set up a coded address for cables — 'Wambrook', Sydney; 'Wambrook' being the name of Susannah's birthplace in the Monaro and now of her home in Carlton — and that she was looking forward with keen anticipation to 'good news': 'The time will soon fly by, when we shall see your dear long lost face once more, & I do pray you will have a pleasant and beneficial trip — won't we chatter.'[68]

Miles' diary entries beginning 31 August spell out the procedures for departure, the laborious business of obtaining that irritating document then newly required for peacetime travel, a passport, along with a visa for the United States, and the farewells. On a draft passport application dated 1 September 1923 and endorsed by Lady Byles, JP, Miles gave her occupation as literature secretary and the purpose of her journey to Australia via the United States as being to visit her family. And here at last are those elusive physical details about 'little Miles' by her own report (not that that was always accurate, as has been noted already with respect to her age and perhaps also to her height, later given as an inch less): height 5 feet 2½ inches (158 centimetres), hair brown, eyes grey. The passport itself was issued two days later on 3 September, valid for three years; and on 4 October Miles went to the US Consulate in London for a visa.[69]

The diary entries also present a saga of dental work over the six months preceding departure. X-rays disclosed that Miles' mouth was 'a horrible sink of iniquity', probably due to bridges and crowns imperfectly installed in Chicago. Several operations were necessary, and, rebel against it as she might, the fact was that she would have to have the dreaded false teeth. The smiling passport photograph referred to earlier was taken the day before the dental work began: 'As I would never have teeth like that again, I took the opportunity to show them for the last time,' she later recalled. Fortunately, dental science had advanced sufficiently for her to be fitted with a quite convincing false set, as subsequent photographs indicate; and although her gums were still not properly healed when she left, she seems to have borne it with surprising equanimity.[70]

There was no suggestion that she would not be returning to her job. On 26 October 1923, the executive of the NHTPC granted her six months' leave without pay, and arrangements were made to cover her duties for the duration. Mrs F. G. Hamilton of the Women's Housing Council, the only woman on the executive, reported that the co-treasurer, Major C. P. Lovelock, MBE, feared someone might persuade her to stay away. In a farewell note, Mrs Hamilton wrote: 'If you had been a man we would all have been singing about what a good fellow — for that is what you have been all along and through most difficult times, but we all feel it, only men are either shy or afraid of setting women up by too much recognition of their virtues.'[71]

Miles' workload certainly had increased. In 1921, she was required to take over the day-to-day office organisation, and from 1923, responsibility for banking cheques — leaving Mr A. freer to swan around Europe, as was increasingly his wont. At least she would miss out on the frenzy of getting his *National Housing Manual* out in December 1923.[72]

In retrospect, a homeward drift may be observed in Miles' literary interests by the early 1920s. Thus in 1921 she wrote to George Robertson that she wished there could be a good Australian play (doubtless thinking she had written one); in 1922 she enjoyed the film of C. J. Dennis' classic *The Sentimental Bloke* at Camden Town; and in early 1923 she was looking up old Australian papers in the British Museum. She also kept in touch with the expatriate literary community in London, sometimes calling on 'those sweet *British Australasian* folk', where she first met, for example, fellow Australian writers Alice Grant Rosman and G. B. Lancaster.[73]

Her play 'Quite!' offers an insight into her thinking by 1923. 'Quite!' was written in 1922, and later rewritten 'By an author who at the age of seventeen inadvertently wrote a best seller and who at the age of seventy — more or less — is again lured into the realistic fields of fiction', which explains why it has hitherto been dated about 1949. In 'Quite!', the key figure is Callie, an Australian office girl in London, 'perversely pre-psycho-analytical and anti-complexical'. Callie evades an unimpressive English doctor's marital intentions (he is said to stutter, which may have been meant as a class marker rather than a reference to disability), not wanting to enter into unfair competition in the marriage market with English girls. She also struggles with regret over a lost younger suitor, her mixed feelings about London ('I love even the things I hate') and with the fear that if she left she would never get back, not to mention weariness at being always muffled up in woollens. She suffers most of all from postwar dislocation: 'I'm homesick for something like a spiritual derrick to lift my soul out of the morass in which the war has left us,' says Callie. But, 'When in a sentimental fix, leave the country. That's my motto. I have ever found it efficacious and so, though my heart will break for London, I'm going home.' She decides to book. Apparently the doctor does too. He has the last word: 'Quite! S-s-s-s-so-have I.'[74]

The question remains: how could Miles afford to go? 'Ah if I cd afford the move when the heart-breaking spring comes again,' Miles had written in one of her notebooks on 10 February 1923. According to a contemporary advertisement for the Union shipping line on which she travelled across the Pacific, a second-class Sydney-to-London (via the United States) fare cost £89, presumably one-way; and if so, the whole trip must have cost at least £130. (She returned to London by the shorter Suez route, via Melbourne, for which the minimum single fare was at that time £37, with an extra sum of £2 13s for the Sydney–Melbourne rail fare.) Reasonably paid as she was, and frugal, that amounted to almost a year's salary, and it seems unlikely that she could have saved such a substantial sum in inflation-ridden London, with her postwar writing bringing in only a few pounds. The author of 'Quite!' was fearful of the cost of Callie's trip. Although technology had lessened distance, apart from 'a few rioting profiteers' most people simply could not afford to travel, especially if they hoped to return: 'this moving from one country to another with but little hope of return, aches like death,' says Callie.[75]

Maybe Miles still had savings from her Chicago years. Alternatively, perhaps Susannah Franklin helped her out. Unfortunately only a few postcards from what was a regular correspondence between mother and daughter during the immediate postwar period have survived, and no financial records; but Susannah Franklin was astute with her money, and sometimes sent some to her daughter in London.[76]

On Sunday 28 October 1923, accompanied by Mrs Aldridge, Miles Franklin caught a bus to Liverpool Street and a train to the docks to board the *Minnewaska* for Sydney, via America. According to Olive Aldridge, she looked like the legendary Mohican maiden Minnewaska herself as she sailed away, feathers flying, 'from our ugly old docks to your far off home'.[77]

9

TO BE A PILGRIM:
NOVEMBER 1923–JUNE 1927

'The pluck that has carried you on so far is not going
back on you now …'[1]

Miles was returning home for the first time in almost eighteen years. Her diary entries tell us that, like most people, she was exhausted on embarkation and that for the next six days she and many of the other passengers were horribly seasick. She was able to read a little at first, Shaw's play *Back to Methuselah*, for example, and later to write a few letters, but after a week at sea her gums were too sore to eat, and it was not until the last day of the voyage that she felt well again. 'Lord how I loathe sea travel,' she exclaimed.[2]

After the Atlantic crossing, and a night spent anchored in view of the lights of New York, Miles found herself disembarking on the morning of Tuesday 6 November in what seemed like a London fog. She was met by the Childs, with whom she had stayed on her first visit to the city in 1908. Later that day, in yet another instance of her remarkable gift for retaining friends, she met the Gilmans and John Varney and his wife. In all, she spent four days in New York, catching up with old friends and WTUL colleagues, including Rose Schneiderman, who invited her to lunch at the league's office at 247 Lexington Avenue; Mary Dreier, who gave her a copy of Freud's *General Introduction to Psychoanalysis*; and Mary Anderson, now an important figure in national politics as founding director of the United States Women's Bureau. A particular pleasure was an overnight stay with 'my darling Ethel'

(Mason) at the progressive Edgewood School at Greenwich in nearby Connecticut, where she was taken by Mrs Gilman and met Count Tolstoy, possibly Alexei Tolstoy, a leading Soviet writer; and she was able to see Leonora O'Reilly and her mother one evening.[3]

Then, on Friday, after lunch at the Women's Club, it was off by train to Chicago. The overnight trip was unpleasant, due to overcrowding with immigrants and no diner; but after eight years' absence it was 'a great joy' to be met by Editha Phelps and Dr Young when she arrived at Union Station. For the next five days, staying at Dr Young's flat on Harper Avenue, she enjoyed revisiting old haunts and catching up with more friends from league days, though it was a shock to find Alice Henry looking frail. As in New York, she took an overnight trip out of town, this time to Madison in Wisconsin to see the Dresdens, who were among her earliest associates in Chicago; and interestingly, back in Chicago, she called on Doctors Schenkelberger and Van Hoosen, who had treated her so often in times past. She saw Bill Lloyd, too, though no comment survives to illuminate the encounter. One evening she attended a play at Hull-House, and on another evening Mrs Robins gave a little dinner for her at 1437 West Ohio Street.[4]

The next day, Friday 16 November, five old associates — Editha Phelps, Alice Henry, Agnes Nestor, Dr Young and fellow office worker Olive Sullivan — saw her off on the train for Los Angeles, where she arrived mid-afternoon on Sunday 18 November, to be met by Kathleen Ussher and her mother, now living in Hollywood. There was much yarning. After an overnight stay with the Usshers, she set off on another pilgrimage of congeniality, to visit the Pischel family, who had also moved to the west coast and were living in San Diego. There she saw Emma and Fred — now aged fifty-five and, Miles was surprised to find, white-haired like his mother. Back in Hollywood the next afternoon, she spent a pleasant couple of days with the Usshers, until the evening of 21 November, when they put her on the train for San Francisco, her place of departure.[5]

Another troupe of friends awaited her in San Francisco, where she lunched with Carrie Whelan and supped with the Newshams. Afterwards Isabel Newsham saw her onto a ferry for an overnight stay with Edith Malyon (an Australian Christian Scientist she had met in Boston in 1914) at Mill Valley, prior to embarkation the following day, Friday 23 November. It seems appropriate that Carrie Whelan, who had met Miles on arrival in the United States in the aftermath of the great earthquake of 1906, was the one to see her off on the last leg of her journey.

It took the *Tahiti* twenty-five days to cross the Pacific, a few days longer than her sister ship the *Ventura* had in 1906, due mainly to the International Date Line. They sailed via Papeete, Raratonga and Wellington, to reach Sydney on 18 December 1923. This time the traveller was not seasick, and the sense that it was getting warmer all the time had a calming effect on her. She tried writing a bit — drafting an outline for a story to be called 'Clare and Margaret' — but mostly she just relaxed on deck, enjoying the tropical fish, joining in with shipboard entertainments. She did not even complain about her fellow passengers. Indeed one, John Kinsman, she found 'most congenial'. At Raratonga she received several letters, including one from Susannah Franklin dated 11 November, evidently in response to news of the rough Atlantic crossing. After Wellington, where she spent an agreeable two days and visited a Maori museum, the remaining passengers started packing up. It was, she much later recalled, 'the happiest journey I ever made'.[6]

On the morning of 18 December, Miles rose early. The Sydney fog lifted onto a 'warm happy day', the temperature reaching 94 degrees Fahrenheit (34°C). The family, her old teacher Miss Gillespie, and Eva O'Sullivan were there to meet her at Number 5 Wharf, Darling Harbour. So was the press. She told the Sydney *Sun* that she wanted to see the bush again and asked to be excused, as her parents were waiting and she was trembling all over with excitement. After she cleared customs, they went back to 26 Grey Street, Carlton, the family's modest home in the still rather raw southern suburbs of Sydney.[7]

So Miles Franklin was home at last, just in time for Christmas. She settled in easily (though one of her first outings was into town to see her mother's dentist), and a quiet Christmas was spent, with Miss Gillespie, now retired to the adjacent suburb of Hurstville, joining the family on a coolish day. The family now consisted of John and Susannah Franklin, Miles, her brother Tal and his new wife, Eva, but not her other surviving sibling, Norman, apparently up the country. In the days leading up to New Year, she lazed about, went for swims at nearby Sans Souci, and ventured into the city again to see Rose Scott, also Dr Mary Booth. Evidently it was not a triumphal tour, as she might sometimes have dreamed of, but rather a revisiting of family and old friends, and in the new year, of favourite places. Towards the end of her homecoming, Miles characterised her stay for the benefit of Mrs Robins: 'I've just rushed about all over the country seeing old friends. I have made the pilgrimage definitely for this & have very firmly ruled out meetings and entertainments.'[8]

This clarifies Miles' intentions: she had come on a 'pilgrimage'. Her itinerary over the next three months bears this out.

With her father, she first visited old haunts near Goulburn, where she spent four days, from 9 to 13 January. They went by train, through Goulburn to Komungla (as Bangalore became known), and then by car to Currawang, possibly to stay with the Grahams. On the second day, the Baxters drove her around Mayfield and Longfield, and to 'Stillwater', where, she recorded, 'I went up and looked at [the] kurrajong tree and had mulberries off tree (struck by lightning). Noted grass along wire fence like mat. Old places changed by killing timber … I went over to look at old school ground & found old tree blown out, got some wattle gum.'[9]

Two strenuous days at old Yarra and in Goulburn followed. She stayed with the John McDonalds at 'Landsdowne' — John McDonald was the younger brother of Alex and Morton McDonald, her one-time suitors. Goulburn was deemed to have improved considerably. There were some 'lovely receptions', and much running around in the town, where she saw Thomas Hebblewhite's daughter Mary ('Timpy') among others, and visited the cathedral to sit in the pew she had occupied as a child (according to the *Penny Post*), before catching the late train to Cooma, some 160 kilometres to the south as the crow flies. Arriving at Cooma early the next morning, on Monday 14 January — now travelling alone — Miles went by coach to Talbingo and Tumut for a wonderful ten days with Lampe relatives, ending on 23 January, when she caught the overnight train back to Sydney (a sleepless night).[10]

After a few days back at Carlton for the Australia Day weekend, on 27 January she was off again, on the Northwestern Mail for Cubbaroo, a siding beyond Narrabri on the Sydney–Walgett line, to visit her brother Norman, travelling with Norman's wife, Irene, and their two-year-old son, Jack. This was another enjoyable but low-key time up country. Over ten days, she did little except go riding and take dips in the artesian bore, on one occasion losing her teeth. Fortunately, Norman retrieved them.

A week later she again caught the train, this time travelling south with her mother to Melbourne, still the virtual capital of Australia. Over the next fortnight, staying with the Lister Watsons at 'Iona', Studley Park Road, Kew, with Nancy as obliging chauffeur, Miles, mostly with her mother, was able to see a good deal of the Goldstein–Champion household, and to catch up with Maud Walsöe and her son, Olaf, at South Yarra, and with Agnes Murphy, who agreed to read 'Phoebe Lambent and Love'. One Sunday Nancy drove them out to see Walter and Marion Griffin at Heidelberg; 'Mrs Griffin enlarged her theories,' Miles noted laconically in her diary. (By this time Marion Mahony Griffin was interested in Rudolf Steiner's teaching of anthroposophy, soon to be reflected in the Griffins' experiment in community building at Castlecrag, Sydney.) The next Sunday, Nancy drove Miles and Susannah to Ferntree Gully in the Dandenongs. (In 1953, Miles Franklin would recall that she had wanted to take her mother on such a trip, and could not have done so but for Nancy's generosity.) The *Melbourne Herald* noted her departure, on 27 February; on the train back to Sydney she read C. E. W. Bean's classic account of life in the outback, *On the Wool Track*, possibly a significant experience, though she made no comment in her diary.[11]

That was her last big jaunt, though there were several small ones to come: before she went to Melbourne, she and John Maurice Franklin ('dear old Dad') had gone to Windsor on the Hawkesbury River, to see the grave of her maternal forebear and namesake, the First Fleet convict Edward Miles; and after she returned from Melbourne Miles and her father took a day trip to Wollongong to see her cousin Annie May Bridle and Annie's husband, Henry. (Kept home from school to meet her famous relative, their daughter Ruby was unimpressed, recalling that Miles was 'very short and had flat feet', with 'a real old Bridle nose', though her eyes were 'startling', and she had 'a lovely mouth'.) Later, Miles went with her mother and Miss Gillespie to Rooty Hill to see the Lawsons from Goulburn days, and their daughter Ruth Horwitz with her baby. Mr Wilkes, her sister-in-law Eva's father, took her for a last drive, to South Head. And there was one more special excursion. On the first Sunday of March, a lovely day, clear and warm, Tal and Eva hosted a family picnic in the Royal National Park, south of Sydney.[12]

Otherwise, Miles spent her last two weeks in Sydney saying goodbye to friends. Virtually every day she went to town for that purpose. The day she went to purchase her train ticket to Melbourne, from where her ship would leave, she called on Maud Walsöe's mother, Mrs Black, Bertha Lawson and Portia Geach in the morning, and then went to lunch with Marguerite Dale at the Women's Club, where she also said farewell to Dr Mary Booth and her sister Bay. Sometimes she just dropped in on her friends at work, as she did librarian Margaret Windeyer. Likewise, having earlier met A. G. Stephens and his journalist daughter, Connie, and also the theatrical entrepreneur Stanley McKay (last encountered in London in 1918), one day she called at Angus & Robertson's bookshop in Castlereagh Street and at last met George Robertson, 'who gave me a lot of books'. Others she visited several times, especially Rose Scott, now aged seventy-seven, frail and in hospital in the Eastern Suburbs; and although fatigued with so much rushing about, she and Susannah still had to see the Griffins' experiment at Castlecrag.[13]

On Friday 14 March, Susannah Franklin, the aunts, Eva Franklin and Miss Gillespie saw Miles off on the train for Melbourne, from where she was to embark five days later, on 19 March. (Her father did not come to the station because of a recent facial operation for what were probably skin cancers.) In Melbourne she stayed again with the Lister Watsons, and even went to the Christian Science church with P. S. on the Sunday, though by then Miles was so tired she could hardly stand up. The weather in Melbourne was perfect, and Miles was able to see Agnes Murphy again about her play 'and other literary possibilities'. But 'The last day comes at last'; 'There is no compromise with Time,' she wrote. And so, on the appointed day, having farewelled Walter Burley Griffin and Elsie Belle Champion at the Book Lover's Library, Miles was taken by Vida and Nancy to Williamstown and held ribbons as the ship pulled out. In Adelaide Miles delighted in an overnight stay with Lucy Spence Morice, Catherine Helen Spence's niece, and purchased a deckchair to sleep out in, having decided that the *Moreton Bay* was 'a floating slum' below deck. When the ship left Fremantle eight days later, Vida Goldstein sent her a wonderful telegram: 'Come back soon. You belong to Australia.'[14]

Just out of Fremantle, with unthinking sexism, a 'young flunkey' ordered her to move her chair to the upper deck because the main deck was for men at night, 'as if he were speaking to cattle'. She wrote in her diary, 'Thank God I'm *leaving* Australia.' But other sources tell a different story. The day before leaving Sydney she had written to Mrs Robins of a wonderful reunion with her parents, and that having found them strong and active and comfortable in a small way, she felt content about them, adding that she would now be 'freed for the adventures & experiments that entice me'. But she did not look forward to the cold grey world that awaited her, as she had confessed to Rose Scott when leaving Sydney. Awaiting departure from Fremantle, she wrote in her diary, 'Never felt so dreary and unhappy in my life at the thought of the old folks left behind.'[15]

She had reason to feel miserable. There had been sad and stoic farewell letters from her mother awaiting her in Melbourne and again in Adelaide and there were sadder still to come. 'I begin to feel you are gone now & miss you so much, I would always like to keep you near me, but knowing your work calls you to other lands, I must not be selfish', wrote Susannah shortly after Miles' departure from Sydney, adding, 'if at any time I can help you moneytarily let me know, *don't be in want*'. Then it was 'Goodbye darling, goodbye until we meet again,' sent to Adelaide. Susannah's next letter, in reply to one from a miserable Miles at Fremantle, is even more poignant: she wonders if Miles was not sadly disappointed with the whole thing and regrets that she seemed averse to any show of affection, even though Susannah had done all she could to make her 'somewhat happy'.[16]

The truth is that Miles Franklin had a divided response to this first homecoming. To place, she responded wholeheartedly. Though she found a harbour trip 'not a bit interesting or beautiful', she enjoyed Sydney and its environs; and she had a pleasant time in Melbourne. But her response to people seems more muted, perhaps because so much of her time was spent with relatives, of whom there were many. Indeed, Aunts Lena and Metta Lampe were living at Grey Street with her parents.[17]

Her time 'up the country' had elicited a stronger response than Melbourne or Sydney. It was over twenty years since the Franklins had left Thornford. As the train had approached Goulburn a great wind had come up, and it blew for most of Miles' time in the district, even paradoxically blowing out a bushfire. Fellow passengers said nothing happened in Goulburn these days except the rail. Miles was appalled: 'High winds, & I hated the old horrible places and their aboriginal lack of progress.' However, her comments on what seemed at first a static scene became more benign as she saw more and found so many old schoolmates unchanged.[18]

Ten days in the high country lifted her onto a new emotional plane. From the moment she looked out of the train window onto a lovely morning and beautiful bush en route to Cooma, to boarding another train back from Tumut with a sprig of kurrajong given to her by the mayor in her hand, the trip was an unmitigated delight; and the old bush hospitality of the John Theodore Lampes at Talbingo charmed her. At Adaminaby, where she was obliged to await further transport and there were fleas in her hotel bed, she found the country looking lovely, delighting to see 'fairy trees & black thorn & gum blossoms wafting honeyed perfume' along with the old brittle gums and sallies, and to hear 'kookaburras laugh goodnight uproariously & frogs croaking once again'.[19]

The high country was at its best that January. Once there, Miles Franklin experienced a kind of re-enchantment. Coming across the plains towards Talbingo that Tuesday in January 1924 was for her akin to that moment of awe and excitement the poet Keats captured in his great sonnet 'On First

Looking into Chapman's Homer'. A long diary entry for that day of return through Kiandra reads in part: 'Oh the loveliness of the snow gums in bloom for miles like giant fairies in an unspoiled paradise, & everywhere bubbling streams and the sunlight dazzling, sparkling, swooning in the distance in beauty, and burning me even through a stout blouse and heavy sweater.' This was the longed-for transcendent experience, part intellectual, part emotional. As she would afterwards put it to George Robertson, she felt herself to be in 'my own, my unbelievable country, as I have been dreaming it'. In an undated notebook entry she wrote:

> I found out that I was indelibly, dyed in the wool ineradicably Australian — and also that it was no small or unhappy thing to be — and that no matter how cosmopolitan I might also be through decades [word illegible] work & residence in other lands, my cosmopolitanism supplemented (only supplemented) but not in the least replaced my Australian nativeness.[20]

On her last day at Talbingo, and after one last swim in the waterhole, she tried again for the words: 'Oh! Those lovely little streams like laughing crystal fountains over the beautiful rock and bordered by fairy ferns and the warm fragrant sun-rayed bush all around with sage (old man) blooming.' But with that heightened environmental consciousness which was partly ingrained, partly newly awakened in the 1920s by people like her friends the Griffins, but mostly just obvious to the naked eye, Miles noted as well that some of the hills nearby had been denuded of timber. Still she 'heard the kookaburras laugh in the feathery peaks opposite until long after dark'. Back in Sydney, she would tell Rose Scott that unspoiled Australia was 'an unbelievable treasure trove' — neither preserved nor developed, only defaced.[21]

Her trip up country to see Norman was like a grace note. Passing through the Hawkesbury, Miles thought the gorgeous shrubs and spotted gums were 'like a sunburned lady powdered [with] some freckled'. Next morning she was out in 'the land of mirages', where she was quick to note the same distinctive vegetation of wilgas, swamp wattles and belah as she had first seen at 'Wilga Vale' back in 1905. To the discerning eye there is beauty also in flatness, and it is still possible to catch sight of kangaroos and adult emus 'capering across the plains' as she did. At Cubbaroo she developed a passion for the spotted goanna, a beautiful creature to her eye though not to many Australians then.[22]

It was from Cubbaroo that she wrote to Rose Scott about the appeal for a memorial to Henry Lawson, who had died destitute in September 1922, and was the subject of an editorial in the *Herald* the day she arrived back in Australia. She never forgot him — his beauty as a young man, his sensitive and gentle manner, his goodness to her when she was trying to find a publisher for *My Brilliant Career* — and she contributed her mite to the appeal. But she was not happy about statues to dead poets. 'Poor old Lawson,' she wrote, 'he had great gifts and in a less inefficient community, might not have drunk himself into years of imbecility and a premature grave.' In reply to Rose Scott, she explained that a scholarship for young writers would be her preference, and that by her reference to an inefficient community she had meant psychological inefficiency. There had to be something wrong with a society where so many felt impelled to take strong drink. And when Rose Scott objected to Miles' enthusiasm for goannas, because they ate eggs, she retorted that it illustrated their 'efficiency as dieticians'. Miles was seldom at a loss for an answer and she was buoyed up by sunshine.[23]

The previously quoted letter to Mrs Robins casts a clear light on her disappointment with Australian society. Australia had become a backwater:

> [I]t seems to me that Australia, which took a wonderful lurch ahead in all progressive laws and woman's advancement about 20 years ago has stagnated ever since. At present it is more unintelligently conservative & conventional than England, & I am sad to see the kangaroo and his fellow marsupials & all the glories of our forests disappearing.

The wonder is that scarcely a whiff of those thoughts reached her diary.

It was a long trip back. Sailing via Ceylon (as Sri Lanka was then known) through Suez to the Mediterranean and around the Iberian peninsula to England took some forty-five days. The books George Robertson gave her, such as the latest editions of Lawson's works, helped while away the time, with Paterson's *The Man from Snowy River* a special delight. Although in her letter of thanks she said the ship was too crowded for her to write, she did draft a sketch, 'Twin Screw Chowder Bay', and tinkered with the novel 'Maybe!', referred to in her diary as the 'Clare and Margaret story'. Important also, but not until she got back to London, was Mary Fullerton's *Bark House Days*, published in Melbourne in 1921, a gift sent after her departure from Melbourne by Alice Henry's brother, Alfred. Miles was sorry to see the last of the sun in the Mediterranean; but when the winds blew up in the Bay of Biscay she was not sick, recording that it was the steadiest passage she had ever known. And somehow it seems appropriate that the last day's sailing came on 25 April, and Anzac Day ceremonies were observed on deck. Typically, Miles was more impressed that the 'Last Post' was sounded in the evening rather than at the morning service, which was deemed platitudinous.[24]

The sun shone briefly as the *Moreton Bay* docked at Southampton on the morning of 26 April 1924, but by the time Miles Franklin had arranged transportation for her trunks, 'down came the rain & dank cold'; and although Olive Aldridge and Miles' colleague Emmy Lawson were at the station to meet her in London, they missed each other, so she went straight to the office in Russell Square. Realising what had happened, she went back to look for them, and having found her friends, spent the rest of the day with them. Miss Lawson had obtained an attic room for her at the Minerva Club in nearby Brunswick Square, and in the afternoon the three went to see Monckton's *The Conquering Hero*. All of which Miles appreciated. With customary resilience, she concluded the day's long diary entry with the signs of spring: 'Tender green on early trees. Hyacinths & tulips set out in the Square.'

The let-down was as speedy as it was inevitable. Delightful as it was to be returned from the cultural crudities of Carlton, and to lunch again with Lady Byles, the weather did not improve, and within days the attic room at the Minerva proved 'miserable, cold, frowsy', also noisy, with inner-city horse traffic clomping by at all hours. Henry Aldridge was worse than ever, rushing in from a Continental trip for a mid-morning meeting on Miles' first day back at the office. Within weeks she was worrying about him manipulating the accounts, and angry at having to work on his next 'so-called book', *Guide to the Administration of the Housing Acts, 1923, 1924*, a task that not surprisingly drove the office staff to distraction by year's end when it was published, historic as the legislation itself was.[25]

Furthermore, it seems that living close by had its costs: it emerges that not only Aldridge and his wife, Olive, but also his parents (certainly his mother), lived in a flat above the office at Russell Square. This meant that 'Mr A.' (as Miles almost always referred to him) could keep irregular hours, and took it for granted that his trio of women staff, Miles, Miss Hodgson and Miss Lawson, would do likewise; it was nothing for Miles to be kept on until 11 p.m. She was also asked to stay after hours as companion and cook for one or other of the Mrs Aldridges, which she often did because she liked them, and perhaps because her attic was so cold. Though her job as 'literature secretary' at the council was similar to that which she had held in Chicago, the diminutive and indeed distinctly weedy-looking 'Mr A.' was exploitative in ways that no woman could have been. Why she put up with it now seems a puzzle, but he was an unworldly figure, apparently oblivious to all but the cause that had brought him to London from the provinces in the first place; and a billet in Bloomsbury suited Miles in other ways.

As well, she was back at the heart of the Empire in time to experience the first Labour government in British history. One of her most audacious of London experiences dates from soon after her return from Australia. Seated on the platform immediately behind Labour Prime Minister Ramsay MacDonald at a labour women's demonstration at the Albert Hall in May 1924, she dealt with his legendary verbosity by tweaking his coat-tails. He was astonished, but it worked, and off he went to the House of Commons, where he was urgently needed. His government, a minority government reliant on the support of radical Liberals, fell five months after this incident, and by then Miles was well and truly fed up with politicians.[26]

A week after returning to London she resumed work on the Clare and Margaret novel, roughed out months before on the *Tahiti* en route to Sydney. This unpublished novel, which she pottered away at on weekends until August and then set aside for several months to write plays, then completed in 1925, survives in typescript as 'Maybe!', subtitled 'A Novel Concerning Two Women's Reactions to Current Philosophies'. It deals with the gender crisis that, coinciding as it did with the onset of middle age, so affected Miles in the early 1920s. The work is ascribed to 'Mr and Mrs O., Joint Authors of *The Net of Circumstance*'; that is, Mr and Mrs Ogniblat L'Artsau, with the additional information that 'Mr O.' was the author of *On Dearborn Street* and 'Mrs O.' of 'Love Letters of a Superfluous Woman'.[27]

The genesis of 'Maybe!' would seem to be quite mundane. The idea of a novel featuring Clare and Margaret relates to a publisher's competition in 1922 for a book of 'self-revelation' by a woman. The competition resulted in two stories being declared co-winners (one was by Miles' compatriot and soon-to-be close associate Mary Eliza Fullerton), and a conjoint anonymous publication in 1923 as *Two Women: Clare: Margaret*. (According to Miles, Fullerton won the prize for 'writing intimately of a woman who had no lustful urges' and the publishers found another, presumably more 'lustful', story by a woman whose name is not mentioned, to balance it.) No doubt Miles thought she could do something with the idea too.[28]

Bearing in mind the focal figures and plots of the three preceding novels by the redoubtable 'Mr and Mrs O.', it is easy enough to see how she could have arrived at that conclusion. 'Clare' is simply the unnamed writer of 'The Love Letters of a Superfluous Woman' a few years on, the proud frontier girl who lost her only love during the war, and here decides to return to Chicago. Likewise, 'Margaret' is a renamed Sybyl Penelo of *On Dearborn Street*, eight years into marriage with architect Roswell Cavarley and now needing to be saved from inanition by Tony Hastings, the would-be lover of Constance Roberts, despatched to Paris by his ruthless and disapproving mother at the onset of World War I in *The Net of Circumstance.*[29]

Equally recognisable is the intended clash of philosophies, and behind that a clash of aspirations. Whereas Clare decides to stay in Chicago to try a new approach to women's emancipation — 'the movement for women's emancipation had gone wrong [and she] wanted to help in righting it' — the sensitive Margaret is still drifting after the war, clear only that art must not be sacrificed to reform ('no reform for me'). Thus, the clash of ideologies would be between art and social reform, and the problem one of fresh ideas. America, it is asserted in a faint and disillusioned echo of things past, doesn't have them; indeed never did have them.[30]

While Clare's story is straightforward, that of Margaret, a married woman, is not. Since the stories are told more or less sequentially, with the former more a matter of social commentary and the latter spun too finely around awareness of the new theory of psychoanalysis, the likelihood is that Miles had bitten off more than she could chew. Margaret's story is much the more modern and complex, with its inbuilt ideological conflicts. By contrast, the interest of Clare's story is by now limited largely to its obvious biographical content.

Clare's story elaborates on Miles Franklin's journey across America in 1923. The author is surprisingly frank. Clare finds her New York friends still foolishly cast down by the war, and *in extremis* about the extent of immigration. On the train trip to Chicago, however, Clare experiences the migrant problem, and she finds much to perturb her in Chicago too. There her elders are still fine people; but her now married peers seem mostly preoccupied with beauty parlours and chiropractics, with the young suffering from 'nerves'. She concludes that Americans are like 'over-indulged children … in their sumptuous nursery'. And good heavens, the shops are not so impressive now that she has seen London's Oxford Street. As for the dirt and the noise of Chicago, how did she ever stand it, she wonders.

Nonetheless, having travelled to the west coast for family reasons and there decided against college or a career in business, Clare comes back to Chicago to settle and start on her project, which seems to be the provision of clubs and suitable housing for working women (as the *Bulletin* had reported Miles would be doing after her time in Australia). A reaction of longer-term interest and significance is to the mutual antipathy Clare encounters between the Americans and the English, which certainly existed and her new found aspiration is 'to interpret the old world to the new and vice versa'.[31]

Clare, who likes to think of herself as a 'one-love' woman, has no problem with sex, or men even. Once settled back into Chicago, she fades in and out of the text, serving mainly to meet the requirement of a dialogue between conflicting philosophies. But Margaret *does* have a problem both with sex and with men. After eight years of a marriage entered into on her terms and evidently chaste, she is vaguely aware of personal dissatisfaction. Since she now feels uninterested in sex, and indeed dislikes being touched, but is also aware that this may mean there is something psychologically amiss, she faces 'the quagmire of sex'. Yes, she may have 'a complex', and she worries that she is 'abnormal', but concludes she is free to be abnormal; indeed, that it is quite abnormal to want to think, and that she could endure the loneliness that would follow if her husband, Roswell, were freed from her, as she feels he will have to be. No, Margaret decides, her problem is not sex, but lack of culture: she has no one to guide her intelligence, and her early gifts of music and writing have atrophied. If only she could sing again. Clearly, whatever happened to the young Miles Franklin's voice in Goulburn caused a deep trauma. There it is again in 'Maybe!': the wonderful contralto voice, with its lost middle register and 'emotional trill'.

At this point in the narrative, enter Tony Hastings, now a successful musical impresario home from Paris, the perfectly pure and self-controlled man, apparently made so by Christian Science. Amazingly, he finds time for lessons, and restores Margaret's voice; but in the end she finds him a hollow man, held together by illusions, not so much refuting Freud as she first supposed but in retreat from the world. His Christian Science is no help to her either. Meanwhile, her husband has been tempted just a little by a nubile niece. The old Adam is too easily aroused, Margaret decides. But the focus is femininity, not masculinity.

By 1924 Miles had read at least two core books on psychoanalysis. Travelling across America in November 1923, she dipped into what is generally regarded as Freud's most appealing and accessible work, *A General*

Introduction to Psychoanalysis, given to her by Mary Dreier. She also had to hand an autographed copy of Charlotte Perkins Gilman's 'latest contribution', the gift of Jessie Childs, possibly *His Religion and Hers*. (In prewar *Forerunner* articles, Gilman had opposed the ideas of both Freud and the influential Swedish maternalist Ellen Key, insisting that the emancipation of women must be by collective, not individualistic, means.) As Miles put it in June 1924, 'I have already digested (or rather have chewed up and swallowed) [Freud], and Mrs Gilman's latest on him.'[32]

'Maybe!' suggests she had not swallowed much. The amazing thing, she thought, was that a work so dull and badly written as Freud's should be taken up to such an extent. Presumably Clare speaks from Miles' experience when she observes that it was hard to concentrate on such stuff: 'From time to time she dipped into Freud but he was so pathological.' It is like wading into a clogged-up sewer, Clare complains; and the idea that the suppression of sexuality is harmful she finds irritating, like hearing 'several unsubstantiated rumours about the unconscious' at a Women's Club meeting in Chicago: a sharp phrasing which shows Miles Franklin to have been at odds with the majority of 1920s feminists, now deemed by some scholars to have suffered from a lack of healthy scepticism.[33]

As Miles admitted, she did not read the lectures in their entirety, and since the words do not appear in the manuscript, she seems to have missed the 'Oedipus complex' and the 'libido'. (Freud had yet to develop that *bête noire* of late twentieth-century feminism, penis envy.) Nonetheless she got the point, supported by modern historical scholarship, that the new sexology confounded the prewar feminist challenge to the double standard of morality, by urging women to behave more like men, instead of vice versa; and she saw intuitively what had happened to women: 'the grey-wolf androcentric cunning of the flesh had once more engulfed them'. British historian Susan Kingsley Kent has called the result 'a conceptual bind'.[34]

To this, Miles added her own twist, on the way fear of feminism had operated: 'The high priests of the fleshly instinct, seeing ahead of them a pale sea of continence where the red fleshpots had glowed in a drab world, had become deeply alarmed. Than to lose male license, better it were ... to make it convenable for women to share it.' Even more uncompromisingly (euphemisms such as 'the daughter of joy' notwithstanding), she wrote: 'They saw some of us were going to martyrise the daughter of joy, we were going to insist upon logic for her which could not result in anything but her abolition, so they consciously or subconsciously tolerated whoreishness for both sexes.' On this basis she roundly condemned feminist complacency and naivety: 'the inner feminist crowd that had found a grand zest in crusading up till the outbreak of the war, [had] since then largely enjoyed themselves in celebrations of feminist victories which had become automatic from lack of fresh inspiration and … postponed by the great phallic renaissance.'[35]

It is hard to resist the temptation to interpret the now middle-aged Miles Franklin's reaction to the new sexology as a reassertion of outdated values. But the effort is worth making. Alongside older values must also be placed the felt need for newer ones, which would take account, as Freudianism to date had not, of a specifically female sexuality and quest for identity that did not coerce married women by also demonising single, lesbian and chaste behaviours, as the new sexology did. The problem was to find a middle way, such as Charlotte Perkins Gilman had sought in the redemptive power of struggle and work, and by her abandonment of the word 'feminism' for 'humanism' after the Great War. If there was no simple going back, then there was also good reason to fear the forward march of male demands and the deregulation of sex, as research into the effects of venereal disease on women's reproductive health and the incidence of botched abortion in the interwar years amply demonstrates.[36]

Margaret's (and Miles') problem now comes into clearer focus. Margaret says she simply cannot come at sex under present circumstances. She asserts, no doubt correctly, that she is not the only one to have 'a sex complex'. And she explains how hers dates from youthful discovery of venereal disease and prostitution. Now she is just too fastidious, and all she wants is her own identity back. To this project men are almost irrelevant, but not quite.

Miles Franklin never had a problem with femininity. Her exemplars were, after all, Rose Scott and Vida Goldstein, both handsome and stylish women; and Miles shared what Australian feminist Susan Magarey has in a neat double entendre called the 'passions of first wave feminists'. Living in London on a modest but adequate income enabled her to at last enjoy both fun and freedom. The stumbling block was always, for her, marriage. So, as usual, having tested all the men in the Clare and Margaret story, she has her protagonist, Margaret, wish it could be more like friendship. Thus masculinity remained an unresolved and largely unaddressed problem for Miles, though some women writers were turning to it: for example, the well-regarded May Sinclair, author of *Life and Death of Harriett Frean* and *Arnold Waterlow*, which Miles read before resuming work on 'Clare and Margaret' in late November. Arguably, Miles was ahead of her time in thinking about friendship between the sexes, which was always a dream of gifted girls and may have come to pass less than a century later among the young, but was nowhere in sight in the 1920s.[37]

Margaret's husband, Roswell, however, believes in 'deathless love' and is prepared to carry on. Finally, in a truly surprising throwback, there comes a rather tormented rewriting of the Edwin Bridle affair of 1905–07, here portrayed as having generated a vast one-sided correspondence from an unnamed suitor, explained as maternal entrapment of a troubled girl and unmanageable male persistence, culminating in betrayal and her release from this unsuitable 'man of the plains'. A still-cynical Margaret plans to destroy the letters, but is placated by Roswell's understanding that the Bridle-like character's sudden decision to marry someone else is that of 'a real man', in that it frees her, explaining also that in marriage the pair have found refuge in each other.[38]

From now on, for Miles, life and art must go together. It would be a matter of 'technique', a concept also central to an unpublished play of 1926, 'Bouquets'. But, as will be seen, 'technique' would not be so easily acquired, resting as it did on an independent income. As early as June, a mere matter of months since returning from Australia, Miles' diary entries become black again: 'feel no pleasure in anything,' she wrote. Ada Holman, who turned up again in 1924, had the bright idea that the two of them should collaborate on a play about the Aztecs, but even after reading the standard works and attempting a little Spanish, there was the seemingly insurmountable problem of creating a love interest, and nothing came of it, except that Miles had a chance to use her British Museum reader's ticket. Despite summer and a pleasant break in Cambridge in early August 1924 with Miss Hodge, housing work seemed ever more uncongenial; and a proposed collaboration on a play with fellow expatriate novelist G. B. Lancaster came to even less than the Mexican effort with Ada Holman.[39]

'I can't go on indefinitely without fruition,' reads the diary entry for 8 August, after the Cambridge trip. But, Miles added with her usual optimism, 'it must come soon, and effulgently'. Despite the disappointment with 'G. B. L.', she suddenly thought of a play of her own: 'feel I have a good one coming'. That was on 11 August. A week later she had written the first act of the play tentatively titled 'The Ten Mile', soon renamed 'Old Blakely of the Ten Mile' and later known as 'Old Trask of the Ten Mile'. By 9 September the script was completed; a typescript was finished a week later. Early the following year Miles once more retitled the play, calling it 'Old Blastus', and also toyed with the phrase 'of Bin Bin', a play on the name of a run on the east bank of the Goodradigbee River held by George and John Maurice Franklin as Bimben East Pastoral Holdings in 1889, and first used by her in the Amykos story competition in 1896.[40]

The play 'Old Blastus', one of the few known to have had a reading, though not until the 1940s, is set in the southern tablelands of New South Wales at the turn of the twentieth century. Old Blakely/Trask/Blastus is a rural tyrant saved by grace and a bushfire, and by romance in the next generation. There are several surviving versions, but an original typescript does not survive, and it was years — and not a few genre transitions later, including a screen scenario in maybe 1925 — before the idea finished up as a cameo novel, the first published in her own name since *Some Everyday Folk and Dawn* in 1909 and still one of her best: *Old Blastus of Bandicoot*, whimsically subtitled *Opuscule on a Pioneer Tufted with Ragged Rhymes*.[41]

During this burst of creativity, Alice Henry arrived in London in August to attend conferences in England and Europe. At sixty-six, she had recently been retired by the league (though voted a generous allowance, she was relieved to learn in December). Miles, cast in a quasi-daughter role, found her very demanding, and altogether too close at 9 Brunswick Square, but dutifully took her about, and to many plays.[42]

Perhaps for respite, on 18 September Miles caught a train from Euston to Liverpool, then a boat to Port Erin on the Isle of Man in the Irish Sea. There she was met by the Smiths' Harley Road housekeeper, Miss Peak, who took her to a boarding house at 31 Royal Avenue West, Onchan, north of the main town of Douglas, where she once more faced the horrors of British housekeeping, finding it stupid, wasteful and uncomfortable to a degree: 'England will have to revolutionise her domestic arrangements at once,' she noted irritably in her diary. A picture postcard duly went home to Carlton, of a dour Victorian resort development overlooking the sea. On the positive side, she visited Ballamanaugh Farm at Sulby, birthplace of her uncle Fred Kinred, and wrote to him that it was a very pretty place with a lovely stream which reminded her of Jounama Creek.[43]

After a week, the possibilities offered for diversion by the Isle of Man and Miss Peak's company had been exhausted. They had travelled around the island by charabanc, been on a train trip, and visited the shops in Douglas several times. In keeping with the island's reputation for mild but changeable weather, it was wild and windy on the day they left for Liverpool, where Miles took a room near the railway and spent a week alone looking around the great maritime city, prior to returning to London on 1 October. Most of the time she wandered around the cathedral precinct and its adjacent slum — the Anglican cathedral was a grand Neo-Gothic edifice, begun in 1904 and, though still under construction, consecrated in 1924; 'a Temple of Mars' to Miles nonetheless. She spent her evenings at the theatre, where she saw the famous actress Mrs Patrick Campbell twice, to varied effect.[44]

Back in London, she attended a matinée of Part I of G. B. Shaw's *Back to Methuselah*, starring Edith Evans, which, in the words of A. M. Gibbs, 'presents a vision of humanity that has evolved to a state where sex and other fleshly pleasures have been superseded by contemplation as the principal enjoyment of humans'. At work, she found an ever worsening situation with Mr A., and wondered if his irresponsible behaviour was merely egotism, 'or is he living a dissolute life abroad'. Most trying was the task which occupied the staff at Russell Square seemingly until Christmas, described to her mother as sending out circulars about slums, apparently flyers for Mr A.'s 'abominable book'.[45]

On her forty-fifth birthday, unremarked upon as usual, Miles sent her play to G. B. Lancaster, and the next day to Madge Titheradge, an Australian-born actress prominent on the London stage in the 1920s, resolving as she did so to cut 5000 to 6000 words from the dialogue at a later date. Otherwise there was nothing of import related in her diary: the weather was mild, the fog rendered the sky over London a beautiful rose colour, and she minded the premises for the Aldridges in the evening.[46]

The arrival a fortnight later of her German cousin Theo Lampe, last seen at Talbingo in 1906, gave her a boost. Since attractive men were now few in her life, she made the most of his brief presence, with outings and several shows. It was too wet for them to join the crowds gathered in the streets of London on 29 October 1924 to hear the results of the general election (the Tory victory was virtually a foregone conclusion, due to the withdrawal of Liberal support for the Labour government, and the notorious Zinoviev letter, which smeared Labour as pro-communist). Miles thought Theo looked very nice and well dressed when he left from Liverpool Street Station on 31 October; she may even have planned to visit him, since she later set herself to learn German. But she never went there, a fact that rather undermines the idea that she took special pleasure in her more socially elevated Lampe connections.

A year had now passed since she had left for the Great South Land. One weekend she despatched forty-eight Christmas cards to Australia. 'I wish I could be with you again this Christmas,' reads the card to her father. Instead she spent the day with her elders in London: after lunch with Alice Henry, she called on Miss Hodge, then in the evening dined with Agnes Murphy and her friend Miss Moore. Two days later she saw Noël Coward's controversial drama of postwar decadence, *The Vortex*, starring the author. Its exposé of drugs and adultery, and whiff of homosexuality, since deemed more significant, made her wonder if any Englishmen were such cads or any of the women so disgustingly disreputable. Her own thoughts ran along simpler lines. Purchasing a new pair of boots, the first since leaving for Australia, gave her an idea for a play but no more was heard of this.[47]

Despite her urge to write, her only publication in the coming year was an article in the Sydney *Daily Telegraph*, 'A Coué Lecture', which she attended with Miss Hodge on 12 December 1924. Emile Coué was a French self-help lecturer popular in the jazz age; Miles thought she knew why. He was reassuring in a world of upheaval where so many behavioural landmarks had been blown away. In the article, sent to Sydney a few days after the lecture, she wrote that he did not ask too much of people. It was all a matter of 'method', he taught with self-deprecating Gallic charm: 'He only commands one to whisper to one's unconscious self, "Every day in every way I am getting better and better."' Miles liked his modesty, and was inclined to think his approach preferable to 'the jungles and quagmires of psychology'.[48]

With Miss Henry safely Australia-bound by year's end, Miles got back to work, reading, writing and attending the occasional film and play in her spare time. One night she walked to the Old Vic to see if the lead actress in a performance of *She Stoops to Conquer* would suit for 'my girl in the Ten Mile'. (She wouldn't — 'not enough zip'.) On another, she saw *Pearls and Savages*, a film about an Australian in the Pacific which reminded her of lantern slides seen in her youth at Thornford and Penrith.[49]

Then came terrible news. On 9 February 1925 her youngest brother, Hume Talmage Franklin (Tal), died in Sydney aged thirty-six, a victim of Bright's disease, a kidney disorder now treatable with antibiotics. He had been hospitalised some six weeks earlier, and according to her pocket diary Miles had already received 'two heart-breaking letters' from her mother, who had now lost all but two of her seven children, Miles and Norman being the only survivors. Although the letter from Susannah to her daughter at this sad time, written the day after Tal's death, urged Miles not to fret, it is apparent that they were both distraught. Lady Byles and others helped her through the grief, but she was very low. She must have read through her diaries, for she was relieved that she had not entered anything distressing in her diary about 'my little Tal' during her visit, and hoped that 'his frail body and sensitive generous soul' were somehow now comfortable and at peace, taking some comfort in the thought that he had had a happy marriage. Later in the year, her diary reveals, she destroyed her mother's other letters about Tal's death. The grief was almost overwhelming: 'I seem to have too much leisure & shudder at my own society which I so craved.' It seems her father was unwell by now too. Anxiety about her family became one of the factors turning Miles Franklin's mind back towards Australia in the mid-1920s.[50]

Two significant events occurred in June 1925 to lift Miles' spirits. The first was on Wednesday 10 June, when Mary E. Fullerton called on her at Russell Square. They had met before, in 1924, but Miles had been too busy then with an international women's housing conference to talk for long, and possibly even earlier. (Miles certainly knew of her long before, as a correspondent of Alice Henry in Chicago.) But closer association dates from this time, when Fullerton, with her English-born friend from the days of suffrage struggle in prewar Melbourne, the now widowed Mabel Singleton, and Singleton's young son, Denis, moved from Letchworth in Hertfordshire to west London. In 1922, aged fifty-three, Fullerton had left Melbourne in a bid for love and freedom to join Mabel, with whom she lived for the rest of her life, and to devote herself to her writing, free of inhibiting family pressures. She was over a decade older than Miles; and although they were travelling in opposite directions geographically speaking, their literary aspirations were similar. From the moment she read Fullerton's delightful memoir of her Gippsland childhood, *Bark House Days*, it was clear to Miles that they were kindred souls, as she explained in her first known letter to Fullerton, written shortly after her return from Australia in apology for not having had time to talk during the housing conference:

> My *dear*, it brought the tug to my throat so often, and there has to be rare artistry as well as sympathy of treatment to affect me like that.
>
> Every word of that sweet little book with its sweet little brown cover and its sweet little bark house drawing — why it's like gum blossom honey! I wonder can it — *can it* — no, it cannot surely, for all its charm, mean so much to outsiders as it does to those of us whose mother tongue it is in every syllable.

Your cranberries I think are my groundberries, and the potatoes, how I should like again to see them unearthed! I have lately been to the old places where once these homes were seats of hospitality and flirtation and industry. Ah, the charm of it and the wistfulness! You have caught it all with your exquisite, delicate strokes ... I want to talk to you.[51]

The 1925 meeting marks the beginning of a vital conversation which continued until Fullerton's death in 1946. It was another step along 'the way home' for Miles.

Miles' diary entry for Sunday 28 June signals the second significant event: starting a story 'as novel in parentheses', which soon took on a life of its own — 'not the story I intended'. Although referred to thereafter in the pocket diary as 'the Natalia story', it was submitted to publishers at the end of the year as 'Not the Tale Begun', and ultimately published by Angus & Robertson as *Prelude to Waking: A Novel in the First Person and Parentheses* by 'Brent of Bin Bin' in 1950, under the auspices of senior editor Beatrice Davis. The original manuscript has not survived, but the Author's Note attached to the published version gives the date of completion as December 1925 and the author's address is given as Brunswick Square, London (the address of the Minerva Club). Though of its time and place, and a manifesto of kinds, the contemporaneous rejections of the manuscript are unsurprising (and Davis' decision to publish is generally regarded as one of her least impressive).[52]

This 'novel in parentheses', with its male narrator and mercurial heroine, Merlin Giltinane, was a mouthpiece for Miles' thinking at the heart of the Empire as her time there drew to an end. Even in this most arch and apparently unreal writing, some immediate links with reality are evident, one being that on 28 April 1925, as Miles' diary reveals, she entertained several European visitors at the office, including a former consul in Moscow named Giltinane, 'an Irishman with glittering eyes'. However, the important point is simply that she had begun work on what would be her most important literary endeavour since *My Brilliant Career*.

In mid-1925, with Mr A. onto another book and 'bolting' to Paris at alarmingly short intervals, and her gums playing up again, she had summer conferences to attend, a Dominions women's conference (an important one for Australian feminists but merely a duty for Miles) and a Labour Party summer school at Hatfield on unemployment, which she found uninformative and lugubrious. At the time Miles was reading the recently published *Life of Olive Schreiner*, the story of that earlier paradoxical daughter of Empire who had died in Cape Town in 1920 aged sixty-five, written by Schreiner's husband, Samuel Cronwright-Schreiner. Miles found it 'very sad, and [a] very great warning. For in addition to terrible asthma, she evidently was not trained to work, or would have accomplished something.' As she would later tell Mary Fullerton, she read Schreiner's letters too (also published by Cronwright-Schreiner in 1924) and took note:

> ... concerning Olive Schreiner. I carefully read her life and also letters by her husband ... Yes she was a great and rare soul but lost to the world for want of a little Christian Science. She lacked self-discipline. You'll see it in those books ... If she had written only half a page a day — the amount of work in her letters, she would have had the thing done. It was a terrible warning to me and I therefore set out at once to do these books. [Evidently Miles had softened her views on the value of Christian Science.][53]

The thought of Olive Schreiner's sad decline drove her on. A first draft of 'Not the Tale Begun' was finished on 19 September 1925, by which time she had also revised 'Old Blastus of Bin Bin', and was reading both works to various friends. That summer brought others back. Emma Pischel was in London in late July; and in the second half of August Miles spent a fortnight or so in Devon, at Broad Clyst, just outside Exeter, with Leonora Pease, the teacher from Chicago days whose poetry she had encouraged. When she returned to London, who should be at the Minerva but Nell Malone, on three weeks' holiday from the south of France. Ada Holman was in London too; and Rose Scott's niece Mollye Scott Shaw, soon to marry the economist (and son of Sydney theosophists) Jules Menken.[54]

Back from the break in Devon, Miles found the situation at Russell Square worse than before. The endless demands of the Aldridges had exhausted her. Privately she now regarded them as 'selfish vampires' and shameless exploiters of defenceless persons (by which she probably meant her fellow office workers Miss Lawson and Miss Hodgson as much as herself). There had been an awkward inquiry about Mr A.'s personal accounts from the bank in June, after which the office staff had agreed it was best to leave him 'to cut his own throat'. Miles, who was the most experienced of the office staff, knew her work was valued by the executive of the council, but it was all very difficult. After a particularly bad day on Mr A.'s circulars, she concluded he had softening of the brain.[55]

Mr Aldridge resigned as secretary of the National Housing and Town Planning Council on 12 November 1925, after an office meeting called on 5 November to regularise the council's accounts, and in the face of an interim audit of the council's books instituted by a meeting of the general council on 11 November. The general council declined to grant his application for two months' leave, citing 'grave irregularities' and 'private difficulties'. Piecing together evidence from Miles' diary and letters written to her by the council's president, Frank Elgood, and Mrs Hamilton, a council member, she had felt obliged to act at least a month before: on 14 October 1925 she had spent a most unusual birthday, dining, at his invitation, with president Elgood at Fleming's on Oxford Street to discuss what to do about Mr A. 'We were both shocked at his depths of moral obliquity,' Miles recorded. Writing the following week to Mrs Hamilton, she urged the council to intervene, not by moralising but policing his behaviour. He must be made to realise that he could not live on the Riviera at the rate of between £5000 and £10,000 a year when his income was between £500 and £1000, she urged. The letter was written in association with Miss Hodgson, and though they were still trying to save him, the office workers had had enough. It seems that in addition to cavorting on the Continent, Mr A. had taken advantage of his wife's absence on a lecture tour of North America, trailing women through the office: as Miles would later tell Eva O'Sullivan back in Sydney, it was all very surprising from an 'eccentric unfleshly professor sort of old chap', who never said a bad nor a harsh word, did not drink or even smoke, but there it was, 'gambling & women & embezzling — the whole gamut'.[56]

Concern about the council's deficit dated back to 1921. (Some of the council's impeccably drawn-up financial statements belatedly tabled for executive perusal are in Miles' hand.) Now, despite the office women's best efforts to bring him to his senses, and Mrs Hamilton's hope that the rebuke and constraints of the first meeting might suffice, there was no way out for Mr A. Having allegedly spent all night burning papers at Russell Square after the 11 November meeting, he did what he had done so often before: he bolted, leaving behind a pathetic letter of resignation. For quite some time it was unclear where he had gone, apart from abroad. (Miles had earlier sent Mr Elgood a Paris address.) When Olive Aldridge rushed back from Canada, she could not believe what she found. An undated letter from Nell Malone in the south of France, probably written early in 1926, reported that the Aldridges were there, regretting that Mrs Aldridge no longer had the staying power of her 'dugout days' in Serbia. They returned to the obscurity of south London when the dust had settled at Russell Square. Later Miles would grieve for 'little Mrs A.', who died in London in 1950. Appropriately Mr A. died in Paris, in 1953.[57]

With Mr A.'s resignation and departure, the council's executive was determined to restore order. A special meeting at Russell Square on 20 November 1925 appointed Miles Franklin interim secretary. Donations were sought, an advertisement drawn up for a new appointment; and with Miles' help, the press kept at bay. It had been, Miles wrote to Marian Dornton Brown, an associate of Olive Aldridge, one of the most terrible experiences of her life. Her own health had suffered. She told Eva O'Sullivan with just a touch of pride that 'off my own bat I averted one of those big postwar, headline scandals, but at what a cost to myself few can realise'.[58]

Mrs Hamilton knew the cost, because Miles told her. She was shocked to hear of the mounting impoverishment of both Miles and Miss Hodgson, caused, Miles asserted, by the executive's failure to rein in Mr A.'s profligacy with council funds, which fortunately, she added, were derived from private donations rather than public monies. Miss Hodgson, a loyal servant of the council, had resorted to bread and dripping to spin out her meagre wage, while Miles' situation deteriorated markedly, partly due to inflation, but mainly due to overwork and Mr. A.'s incompetence. A glimpse of how she managed comes in a letter: aunts and uncles sent her a £10 note now and then to protect her against 'dreadful cold and fogs'. Then just before Christmas, on doctor's orders, Miles Franklin, secretary *pro tem*, took several days' leave. By this time she was worried about the effects of the crisis on her heart. Events at Russell Square in 1925 gave her palpitations.[59]

From her letters to Mrs Hamilton, it is clear that Miles felt her time was up at Russell Square. She would stay to clean up, making sure that her colleagues were looked after and that satisfactory arrangements were made for the rehousing and care of Mr Aldridge's mother, and for re-letting the top-floor flat; but new hands were needed at the tiller. Unlike her disappointment with the way things turned out after the financial crisis in the league at Chicago, she had no wish to stay on: 'The lure of England is dulled.' Unfortunately her hope of fresh leadership at the council was soon disappointed — she found the new secretary appointed in March 1926, John G. Martin, previously of the Alliance for the Suppression of Liquor

Traffic, good at raising money though lacking in flair — but she stayed for another year, with ever diminishing enthusiasm.[60]

Under such tumultuous circumstances, coping with an invitation to represent the Women's League of New South Wales at the International Woman Suffrage Alliance in Paris in 1926 seems to have been beyond her. (Her response to the invitation, if any, does not survive.) There had scarcely been time to reflect on the death of Rose Scott back in April, or to recover from the sad news of the death of Aunt Metta Lampe, so dear to her from Talbingo days, in August. Come Christmas Day, it was enough to rest in her room at the Minerva and join club residents for a communal meal. On Boxing Day she set off for a few days' rest with Mrs Hamilton and her sister at Rottingdean, near Brighton, returning by slow train on 28 December to resume work at the office. Apart from comforting the still-distraught Olive Aldridge, Miles ended the year quietly and made a final diary note: 'The opening year *must* be better.'[61]

Somehow she had persisted with her writing, and now went all out on 'Not the Tale Begun', with one or other of its early subtitles: 'Prologue/ Divertissement' (as later recounted to the American publicist C. Hartley Grattan); or maybe 'A Novel in Parentheses, and Slightly in the Mayfair Manner, though with a Difference and Divergences', a spectacularly obscure formation used in the only original typescript to survive, from details attached to a 1931 version. The published subtitle, 'A Novel in the First Person and Parentheses', was definitely an improvement, as was the name given the central character, ultimately Merlin, but initially Natalia and later Mervynda. By April 1926, the 'Novel in Parentheses' had been rejected by three publishers: on 28 January by Jonathan Cape (who were told by Miles' alter ego, the addressee 'H. F. Malone' — that is, Helen Frances Malone, 'Nell' — that the manuscript 'bristles with overseas view points', and that the author wished to remain anonymous); then on 8 February by Cassell; and thirdly on 22 March by Chatto & Windus.[62]

The response is unsurprising. Few readers today could credit this tale within a tale — or story 'in parentheses' (there are nineteen) — and full of words such as 'caracole', 'a-whoop', 'robustious' and 'burstatious', or be able to stomach the idle lives of characters called Merlin Giltinane, Hugh de Courtenay la ffollette and Lady Pamela Clutterbuck-Leeper, who live in Mayfair and enjoy weekend house parties at Great Snippington. According to an Author's Note attached to the 1931 version, some of the characters were at least partly based on real life; but it seems extraordinary to have

Merlin say her father, Daddy Giltinane, is based on 'my own father', a pioneer, and an Oxford don, and that 'a brother sat for the younger Giltinane', Guy. Obviously this is a period piece; but it did not attract interest then, and it would be a determined reader now who persisted past the first parenthesis, where Nigel the narrator, a thirtyish male writer, meets the enchanting Merlin in her genteel little slum flat in Mayfair and takes up the challenge to write 'a smart novel in the Mayfair mannah' around their *liaison de covenance*, brushing aside her warning that it would end up as self-revelation, especially as there could be no sex interest, sex being 'a phase of adolescence' which she has passed through.

Yet Miles Franklin was not the only Australian expatriate writer to attempt a Mayfair novel at this time, as evidenced by Martin Boyd's pseudonymous *Brangane: A Memoir*, published in 1926. And on closer perusal, *Prelude to Waking* turns out to be as much a résumé as a prelude: a résumé of Miles Franklin's years at the heart of the Empire, starting with Merlin's war service in the Balkans and passing through the Mia Mia restaurant experience to end with the narrator's belated recognition that although Merlin has been his true love all along, due to immutable circumstance it is too late, and they all must learn that renunciation is sometimes the only way to preserve ideals. Parenthesis XIX in the published version concludes in capital letters:

PRESERVATION OF THINGS
MOST PRECIOUS TO THE HUMAN SOUL
SOMETIMES LIES IN RENUNCIATION

There is no mention of unemployment or other social questions in this thwarted romance. What is being explored instead is Merlin's journey through the best that England has to offer in terms of progressive culture and prospective husbands, culminating in a chaste marriage with a noble man thirty-five years older than herself as the only viable (and admittedly very comfortable) option. Also under the microscope was Miles' new cause: imperial renewal, as heralded in verse preliminary to the text, beginning, 'Mother England, lead us still!'[63]

A strategic figure in the parentheses is Lady Courtley, directly modelled on Lady Byles. It is she who supports Merlin's marriage to an old beau of her own, and she who encourages Merlin to write her very successful pamphlet 'Wake up, Mother England': 'It is for you brave young people from the new worlds to retrieve us from reaction and unreality,' says Lady Courtley.[64]

Merlin has in mind waking up to the wonders of Australia; her creator, Miles, had at last found something refreshing, something transcending the personal, in the Liberal version of Empire renewal (and the Empire immigration so desperately sought by Australian governments in the 1920s). Merlin herself does not leave England for her native land, but her beloved Daddy and brother Guy return to Coolibah on the western plains of New South Wales, where Nigel, the narrator, has previously spent a wonderful interlude, the place being 'my latest, most commanding love', he writes. Meanwhile, the death of Guy on the homeward passage is a major trauma for Merlin in the (thankfully) quickening narrative. It is early agreed by Merlin and the narrator that while England is wonderful in its way, and cosmopolitanism is the ideal, the day of a true internationalism is a long way off in terms of socio-political arrangements, and that it is impossible for an individual of any strength of character to be denaturalised. Considerable space is devoted to descriptive writing extolling the Australian landscape.[65]

Obviously the tale is not about the lower orders, though those featured do behave splendidly, especially Mrs Brindle, the widowed London charwoman who decides to go to Australia with Daddy and Guy De Giltinane, and adapts unexpectedly: declaring herself to have been a housekeeper in the old country, she marries Daddy, to the approval of all but Merlin. The set piece of the story is a weekend house party at Snippington Manor with the advanced Liberal set, where the narrator (who has already attracted police attention for a talk on the great Bolshevik experiment after returning from Russia) wonders if this elite 'can save the city'. From Friday evening to Tuesday morning the guests reconstruct the Empire and examine attendant 'isms', seeking sources of renewal amid postwar drift and profiteering under Lloyd George: 'The most popular idea for reorganisation and renovation of England was through an aristocracy of intellect and idealism to supersede the moribund oligarchy of privilege and primogeniture. Education was the cry, to pave the way for a bloodless revolution.'[66]

Literary fragments indicate that Miles herself entertained that idea (as did many members of the European intelligentsia in those troubled times, when the relationship between culture and democracy seemed unpromising) but with reservations. 'I believe,' she jotted down, 'that inside a nation or a race even, there is no such thing as aristocrat and plebeian under our present way of mating [though] eugenics might change it,' adding that 'brain is the only kind of royalty'. Even so, she mused, such a regime would be hard to maintain; and what about beauty? Nor could age and death be avoided. And fierce as some of these jottings are about the 'masses', or the 'mob' (both elitist words of the interwar years), as dupes of public schoolboys or easy prey for dictators, how could such 'nonentities' put on side when they faced the same fate as a dog? Increasingly, in both literature and life Miles Franklin was pained by her own lack of a systematic education, and her heroines often entertain regrets at missed educational opportunities, so the new prescriptions were not entirely reassuring to her. In her own case, it was the freedom to be eccentric she found most welcome in England, and it is the idea that originality could still seep up through the cracks in the social mould that lies behind the bizarre dedication to *Prelude to Waking*: 'To England's Genius Cracks, Appraisingly Dedicated'.[67]

It is important to note that, just as many of the preoccupations of the 1920s intelligentsia are echoed in Miles' writings, so she sought to exploit then fashionable genres. In *Prelude to Waking* she was on her way to historical fiction, one of the rising genres. However, towards the end of the book one or two of Miles' prior unpublished writings of the postwar years are recycled, notably the play 'The English Jackeroo', depicted as a great operatic success, and there is a passing reference to the unpublished play 'Bouquets'. There are also some comic touches, though the intent throughout is too fervent for many laughs, the best being the narrator's other current literary effort, a Mayfair thriller temporarily titled 'The Lady with Natural Back Teeth'.[68]

By the end of January 1926, Miles confided to her diary that she was feeling like a dish rag, looking after the office and the older women there, for whom she cooked meals and otherwise soothed. She was sustained by hope of 'Old Blastus', her play of 1924–25, and in coming months made numerous attempts to get it staged. People said it was a good, even excellent play (Agnes Murphy said it was magnificent); but she had no success with publishers, and the London theatre world proved unresponsive. As 'H. F. Malone', she first tried to get it published with 'Not the Tale Begun' and then sent it to the London *Daily Telegraph* and to Blackwood, with a note that both works were by the same author 'who wishes to remain anonymous' — presumably she had yet to devise a suitable pseudonym. Thereafter, as 'J. Verney', and then

'Sarah Miles', she approached numerous London theatre managers and actors, such as Margaret Bannerman at the Globe Theatre on Shaftesbury Avenue, and on 12 December 1926 the Shakespearian actor Robert Loraine, again to no effect. So she was obliged to set aside what on one occasion she sought to promote as 'a play of Empire', and on another as 'shorter than *Hedda Gabler*'.[69]

She turned to other manuscripts. She re-read 'The Other Side of Love', retitled it 'Three Women', then sent it off. 'What am I to do?' she cried to her diary when yet another script came back. What she did was predictable. She wrote another play, a comedy in three acts 'by a practising nonentity', called at first 'Daphne' then 'Bouquets'. Begun in August 1926, it was finished at the offices of Minerva Club resident Hilda Mary Baker at 275 High Holborn just before Christmas, for immediate despatch to the theatre producer Alban Limpus (and was under revision the next month).[70]

Bouquets, in the eponymous play, stand for 'technique' — what we might call today 'life skills', these being possessed by Daphne, an American-trained businesswoman who solves romantic misunderstandings with ease, just as she helps her brother out of financial difficulties caused by over-borrowing. When words fail, flowers serve to smooth things over, and people are able to take a more realistic view of one another despite postwar tensions and artificialities. A topical effort, set somewhere like Harley Road, after the General Strike of May 1926, which brought the country to a standstill and caused many to fear that the revolution had come to Britain at last, 'Bouquets' is hardly a great work, but it is another biographical marker, in that the sensible older woman triumphs. Indignantly denying that she is 'normal', Daphne asserts that art/technique is all: 'I have made an art of business ... of life. I have a technique welded from my amorous life, from my artistic talent (if ever I had any), from other elements.' It was, she went on, 'complex and broad based', and she was interested in applying and reinforcing it.[71]

To challenge her flapper niece Phyllis, she explains: 'A technique will stand by you something like armour — or a mask. You must put it on no matter if your heart is broken or bored to the death. That is the difference between being a trained artist — a professional — and a merely self-indulgent amateur in the game of life. Do you think you can rise to that?'[72]

For Daphne, a character very much of the age and circumstances of Miles Franklin, 'technique' is a way to manage the stresses that beset her in the postwar world. And although her diary never reveals such a thing, the implication is that Miles was preparing to don her armour, or find a mask that would enable her to press on: 'Levity, is the saving grace of life.'[73]

In March 1926, Mr Martin, the new head of the NHTPC, took up his position at Russell Square. It was not too long before Miles decided he lacked stamina. In April, Aunt Lena Lampe and a friend, Barbara Donaldson, arrived from Australia for a lengthy stay; and by July other old friends had again turned up, including Miles' Welsh friend Phyll Meggitt and Amy Somerville, Miles' god-daughter, originally from Penrith. Amid the outings and entertaining, such as she normally enjoyed, Miles was increasingly perturbed by what she took to be heart trouble, not helped by the strengthening conviction that she was wasting her life on dunderheads. Nell Malone urged her to leave the council, but what, she asked herself, was she to do.[74]

A fortnight's holiday in August with Aunt Lena and Barbara Donaldson failed to lift her spirits. They travelled by train to Glasgow on 13 August, and from there to Loch Lomond and a highland gathering at Oban. Aunt Lena was a trial at first with her constant talk. However, things improved when they took a steamer to Ireland for a few days in Belfast, where Miles enjoyed the sights, especially the Giant's Causeway, and were better still during a week in Dublin, where they saw all the cultural sights and Miles had more time to herself. As it happened, Agnes Murphy was there too.[75]

Arriving back in London on 27 September, Miles dashed around seeing all the new season's plays before returning to the office, but felt too stale and dispirited to write anything. She had become an occasional literary adviser to Mary Fullerton, and Mary, in turn, was increasingly supportive of Miles. But Miles had begun seriously contemplating leaving London and was now looking for a way home. In April 1926, shortly before Aunt Lena's arrival, she had written to A. G. Stephens, then travelling in Europe: 'I'm getting so embedded here that I'll never get out and I want to tell you what I've been up to, and get your advice and assistance.' In August she must have told her mother she was thinking of returning. A reassuring reply from Susannah dated 19 September 1926 reads as follows: 'If you intend coming home … how glad I'll be to see you & what a warm welcome waits you'. Susannah Franklin warned that she was not strong financially but would do all she could to help, adding that she supposed Miles would be loath to break up her connection in England, 'but what is the use if it is a continual strain on your health'.[76]

The decisive moment came on Wednesday 24 November 1926. Miles had felt a little better the previous day, but her heart was bad again, and she was depressed, so she went to her doctor. The doctor told her to give up work immediately. She did so. At one o'clock on Thursday 25 November she left the office at Russell Square 'for ever': 'thus ends an ignoble and deteriorating situation'. At its next executive meeting, the council determined that Miles Franklin's job should terminate on 1 December 1926 and voted her an honorarium of £50 in lieu of notice. The minutes conclude the matter with a decision to send Miss Franklin a letter of thanks for her service together with best wishes for her future.[77]

'I have treated myself to a nice little Corona [typewriter],' Miles wrote to Eva O'Sullivan on 15 January 1927. Although still feeling unwell during this coldest of months, she was now free to concentrate on her own work. She had been dealing with the Mervynda tale ('Not the Tale Begun') through Kath Baker's office on Oxford Street (the sources are silent on who precisely Kath Baker was, though maybe she was associated with Hilda Baker on nearby High Holborn); Mary Fullerton was reading 'Old Blastus'; and she finished 'Bouquets', which went off to publishers soon afterwards. On 20 January Aunt Lena left, a further liberation (though her companion, Barbara Donaldson, who had been helpful when Miles fell ill, stayed on). At this time and subsequently, she consulted Dr Una Fielding, a New South Wales-born medical researcher who arrived in London in late 1923 and stayed at the Minerva Club.[78]

In her diary on 3 February 1926 Miles recorded that she rose at eleven and tried to do work on a new manuscript, 'Three Rivers'. The next day, having written a little, she went to the British Museum to look up old Huguenot names and locate old Australian works. And after some ten days in the museum consulting works on early Australian history, including Henry Parkes' letters, works by the Reverend D. Mackenzie (probably David Mackenzie, author of *The Emigrant's Guide* of 1845) and others on bushrangers, she resumed her writing. By the end of the month she was reading bits of her 'old time novel' to friends, like Mollye Menken, who responded enthusiastically. Mary Fullerton was especially encouraging: 'Like Oliver Twist I want more. Your story delights me. I think you have hit it. Found yourself and your theme.' She encouraged Miles to try to place the manuscript, and significantly for the future, she offered to try to place it for her later, if Miles' efforts were unsuccessful. She told Miles that an epic of Australia had not been attempted before. 'Can she be right?' Miles wondered.[79]

The first draft of the 'Three Rivers' story, which became *Up the Country* (a phrase from Henry Lawson), was written at speed. Tucked into the 1927 diary is a typed memorandum, summarising its progress in three points:

> Really got steam up on February 14 and finished on March 20 — five weeks, averaging 3500 words a day.
>
> Began second draft 27 March, typing and licking into better shape, and in spite of much other diversions, finished on May 8 — six weeks.
>
> Began typing third and final draft on Monday August 29, and finished Sunday, September 18, 1927 — really 19 days as I did only a page or two the first Monday and last Sunday.[80]

By the time she began the third draft of the 'Three Rivers' story, Miles Franklin was back in Australia. When she finally decided to leave is unclear, but it was undoubtedly a writing-related decision. By March 1927 London friends such as Mary Fullerton were already expecting her departure.[81]

Before she left London, she had an offer of publication for the 'Three Rivers' story. After two knockbacks — she first sent it to Duckworth and Chatto & Windus — on 25 May, writing as Miss S. Miles, c/– H. M. Baker, she had sent it to Blackwood. Going by a typescript dated May 1927, it was then entitled 'Up the Country', with, according to an accompanying cover sheet, the subtitle 'A Novel of the Australian Squattocracy', though the typescript's title page, which is generally regarded as more reliable, was 'A Tale of Not So Long Ago'. The author was given as 'Blake of Bin Bin', and there is an author's note and a dedication:

> To the Old Hands
> Both Here and There and Everywhere
> Most Affectionately Dedicated by One of Themselves.[82]

In a covering letter 'Miss S. Miles' (or maybe Mills) apologised for sending an unsolicited manuscript, explaining that the author (unnamed), who had already left for Australia, had specially requested that it be sent to Blackwood, and stated that she was leaving the country herself shortly. It was, she continued, still a rough draft, but an experienced reader would be able to judge its potential, and, she affirmed, there would be no problems with context: 'The writer of the story has read widely to be sure of the vocabulary and detail of the time, and is familiar with the environment through being a member of an old squatting family in the area.'[83]

The evolution of Miles' 'Brent of Bin Bin' pseudonym, under which she published six books and kept secret from the reading public until well after her death, can be traced back to these last days in London, when she amused Mollye Menken with readings from 'my old squatter friend and his saga'. But the name when it first appeared in print in late 1928 took English friends by surprise. Writing to thank Miles for a volume by Brent, Lady Byles exclaimed, 'Where on earth did you get *that* christening? I was staggered.'[84]

Blackwood's prompt response to 'Miss S. Miles' came in the form of a letter of acceptance dated 27 May 1927, in which terms were discussed and an understanding sought that the firm would have right of first refusal on the next two or more works. 'Sarah Mills' (as she now clearly signed herself) was, however, cool-headed and, confident of her product, was still negotiating minor details in the Memorandum of Agreement prepared at her request on 14 June at the time of her departure for Australia. Although Miles made a last-minute commitment, recording in her diary on 22 June, the day before she left, 'At 11 p.m. wrote to Blackwood finally', there was a hitch: who precisely should sign the agreement? 'S. Miles' responded to Blackwood's politely worded inquiry of 17 June that 'It would be quite in order for me to sign on behalf of the author but it was my intention to send it to him in Australia and let him go on with the affair himself now.' Would Blackwood prefer her to sign or to await signature from Mr Blake, she asked, naming an author for the first time. Blackwood felt it would be better if the author signed.[85]

With that clarified and time to think it through, Miles was ready to leave London. She departed for Australia on Thursday 23 June 1927, probably from Southampton, since she first caught a train and her initial comments refer to rain and mist in the English Channel. Only the two Maynard women, Mab and her daughter, Frieda, and the mysterious Kath Baker saw her off; Lady Byles, now very frail, sent a farewell note. Miles' diary entry reads: 'Feeling alright.'

10

ENTER BRENT OF BIN BIN:
JULY 1927–DECEMBER 1932

'… one must keep faith — with reality …'[1]

The TS *Barrabool* sailed for Sydney via the Cape of Good Hope. The long way home, fifty-four days in all, gave Miles Franklin plenty of time to revise her 'Three Rivers' story. Typically, the job was done before Cape Town, and after a pleasant day ashore, she was back on deck, writing and chatting with fellow passengers, rough conditions in the 'roaring forties' permitting.[2]

Stopovers in Australian ports made the journey seem even longer. During five days in Adelaide, where she was relieved to get news that all were well at home, Miles called on Lucy Spence Morice, now aged sixty-eight and frail, as she had done when passing through in 1924. When the *Barrabool* arrived in Melbourne for a two-day stopover, the Lister Watsons collected her from Victoria Dock and Nancy took her for 'a heavenly drive to hear bell-birds and kookas and black maggies and see wattles'. As usual, she called on the Champions at Punt Road — to where Joseph Furphy's admirer, Kate Baker, sent a note welcoming her home — and, for the first time, she visited Mary Fullerton's family.[3]

At last, after a fine final day at sea, she was home again, landing in Sydney on Tuesday 16 August. It was warm, and she thought the harbour looked better this time, but when the family finally turned up at the wharf, her father (whose deteriorating health may well have been a factor in her return) 'looked terrible'. This time the press did not notice her arrival, probably because the *Barrabool* was a migrant ship and she was not on the passenger list as released, or maybe simply because she was not particularly newsworthy, having published virtually nothing since her visit in 1923–24. The small welcoming party, which included Aunt Lena and Miss Gillespie, went straight back to Carlton for lunch. Later she met neighbours and relatives. Within days she was feeling stressed, due to the daily chores and the noise in the small bungalow crowded with relatives and a constant flow of visitors. After a week came the first of many desperate diary entries for late 1927 and over the coming decade: 'My God, what a wasted day. Deliver me speedily or my punishment would be greater than I could bear.'[4]

She knew that, unlike Olive Schreiner, she must keep writing and that meant lying low. Within days she found her way to the Mitchell Library, that great repository of Australiana on Macquarie Street, opened in 1910. After a fortnight, on 29 August, she was able to get down to typing 'the old time novel'. That took three weeks. Then came a version of delivery: on Tuesday 18 October, writing for the first time as 'W. B.' [William Blake], c/– Mrs Lister Watson in Melbourne, she advised Blackwood that she was sending under separate cover the final typescript of *Up the Country*. W. B. apologised for not including the agreement, still unsigned due to the 'stultifying' effect of legal documents on his mind. The letter is also unsigned, possibly because Miles had still to devise a suitable signature for William Blake.[5]

The 'Author's Note' included with the rough draft of *Up the Country* sent by Miss S. Miles to Blackwood in May had been signed 'Blake of Bin Bin'. Now, William Blake advised that 'Brent' was to be substituted for 'Blake'. In the only known rationale for the change, Miles (as W. B.) explained, 'I have chosen Brent as nom de plume [because] Blake would be a nuisance in view of the revived interest in the great William' (1927 was the centenary of the death of the artist and poet William Blake). In choosing 'Brent', maybe she was thinking of the small migratory geese known as brent which breed in high northern latitudes and migrate south in autumn, or of the River Brent, a tributary of the Thames running through north-west London near Miss Hodge's apartment, or even of someone she knew at the time, a possibility suggested by the discovery of a man's collar, made in London and marked 'Brent', among her possessions at the time of her death. Perhaps she just liked the sound.[6]

By contrast, no such mystery attaches to the etymology of 'Bin Bin'. It appears on the opening pages of *My Brilliant Career* and was part of the

'Australian turn' in Miles' writing in London — she had used 'of Bin Bin' for her play in 1925 ('Old Blastus of Bin Bin') — and, as previously noted, its relationship to family land-holdings in the Brindabella valley has long been established by literary critics.

The name 'Brent of Bin Bin' may have been serendipitous, but it is possible Miles Franklin also had in mind the old stock brands of New South Wales. Some early letters purportedly from Brent of Bin Bin, for example, to Mary Gilmore, were signed 'the old brand BBB'. It sounds like whimsy, but the brand 'BB' was still in use by stockholders at Currawang and Adaminaby in 1923.[7]

Many women writers of the nineteenth century, most famously George Eliot, adopted a male pseudonym, in the belief that women writers were discriminated against. Miles' attempt when young to pass as a male writer might have worked — it is still sometimes assumed today that Miles Franklin was a man — but for Henry Lawson, who revealed in the Preface to *My Brilliant Career* that it was 'written by a girl'; and then when she tried to capitalise on her famous name it did not seem to work very well (except in journalism, where she mostly used versions of her given names). During the years away she almost always submitted literary work under pseudonyms, over time devising quite an array of them (Mary-Anne, Mr and Mrs Ogniblat L'Artsau and Outlander being the main ones before Brent of Bin Bin), and many were merely to meet the requirements of literary competitions). Probably because of her feminist principles, she usually devised something non-specific, like Outlander, or ambiguous, as with Mr and Mrs O., though Old Bachelor in 1905 was an exception. With Brent of Bin Bin, she seemed to be creating an amiable older country gentleman who would be a convincing author for the historical novels she had in mind, and which she feared would not be credible coming from a woman whose literary reputation was still that of a young girl.[8]

From the outset, Miles Franklin went to extraordinary lengths to protect her Brent pseudonym. She was not only her own literary agent, operating as Miss Mills (or Miles), but also the author, operating as W. B. or William Blake, and she communicated with her publisher via the addresses of trusted friends, not her home address. For an author to conduct her business in such a secretive manner would probably not be tolerated today, though it is possible, since most professional writers have literary agents, and there are valid reasons for pseudonyms, which may be adopted for commercial reasons or to protect an author's privacy, or even, as in the case of Doris Lessing, to test the critics; and anyone can get a post-office box. Very few, however, make it a lifelong enterprise. Even if, as Carolyn Heilbrun has suggested, writing under an assumed name is a way to create a space for the self and secrecy a way of controlling one's destiny, it can be a hard thing to live with. Miles maintained it for the rest of her life. Indeed, she ensured that, in theory at least, Brent outlived her: the link was not definitely established until 1966, twelve years after her death, when her papers became available.[9]

The inaugural letter to Blackwood from William Blake on 18 October 1927 stressed that anonymity was necessary 'to facilitate the progress of my work'. If making any announcement, the publisher must be indefinite 'on whether the author is a be-shingled flapper under twenty or a be-whiskered squatter over fifty'. Clearly, however, Blake/Brent was no flapper. Otherwise, as the firm responded to an inquiry a year or so later on behalf of Lord Novar, a previous Governor-General of Australia, 'we know practically nothing about the author of *Up the Country*'. All they had ever been told was that he was a member of an old squatter family.[10]

From a business point of view, these matters were finalised in a letter dated 24 October 1927, when William Blake returned the agreement to Blackwood, complete with a small crabbed but clear signature written in black ink. Meanwhile, with the help of the poet John Varney in New York, Miles was looking for literary agents in America.[11]

To come home to get on with her work was a gamble for Miles. In August, just prior to arrival, she had been nominated for inclusion in a popularity poll to be conducted by Melbourne's Australian Literature Society, but she had not published anything under her own name for nearly twenty years and attracted few votes. Having returned to live with aged parents, she could easily be trapped as a dependent daughter, or demeaned as an 'old maid'. She needed time to write but the moment she finished typing her old-time story, she became ill and depressed. Her diary — since 1926 kept securely in shorthand — records: 'Cannot live long in this awful atmosphere. Awful old people killing me by inches.'[12]

Some unspecified shock soon after left her sleepless, and after less than six weeks of life at Carlton, she feared she would not be able to go on, that her mother was beyond bearing. Over many years, distance had enabled Miles to maintain an affectionate relationship with her mother, and vice versa. In the same house, they grated on one another. The strain is apparent in early diary entries:

Find mother very wearing. Just as hard on me as she always was
(11 September 1927).

Mother terrible. More intransigent than ever (30 September
1927).

I can't go on with it. Mother is just as terrible as she was of old
(1 October 1927).

Help me as before dear God. Poor old Mother is happier with
strangers so help me to provide her with a companion and to do
my own work well (8 November 1927).

By year's end, it seems clear that the homecoming was provisional (as Mrs
Robins envisaged when she wrote in her slightly off-beam way that she well
understood why Miles' parents wanted her home because 'Dear Stella you
are so full of wit and the joy of living,' adding the hope that she would
return soon as 'we need you'). Miles was already wondering if she would
have to go, writing on 11 November, 'Mother intransigent. God help me to
bear it or let me get away.' (Since there is little enough evidence of religious
belief in Miles' life at this or any other time, her reference to the deity was
most likely an expression of exasperation.) By late November it seems the
situation had further deteriorated: her supplication reads, 'God help me to
endure Mother. Deliver me from this trouble.'[13]

Christian Science, advocated by the Goldsteins since 1904 and still
ardently pressed by P. S. Watson, was probably some help. The ex-squatter
Watson most obviously features as an old-timer influence in Miles' life, but
he also came from a Victorian family interested in alternative spiritualities,
and when Miles met him in Chicago and again in London he was an
accredited Christian Science practitioner. Hence the 'cheer up' letter to Miles
shortly after her arrival in Sydney, which deals first with the average speed of
bullocks and then recommends a passage in Mary Baker Eddy's *Science &
Health*. Christian Science was at its most popular in the 1920s, and with its
message of bodily transcendence and mental discipline it appealed to many
intellectual women. Clearly Miles Franklin's need was very great, and it must
have strengthened her to be told that her mind would carry her through: 'Its
mind not Blood, Bones & Beef that lives. You are the Mind that runs the
Body ... dictate terms to what ever is no good,' Watson urged.[14]

Not only was Miles in great need psychologically, but since American
days, her physical health was always of concern. Her letters at this time are

full of it. Although her heart had apparently ceased to worry her — 'Women don't die of hearts,' she would say — she experienced persistent insomnia and she once more felt pressured. Certainly she was no longer young; on at least one occasion, she wrote of having returned 'an old woman', possibly a reference to the menopause. She turned forty-eight in October 1927, and having survived thus far could expect to live another twenty years or more (and maybe even grow more like her mother, grim thought).

Still, Miles was no wimp. Evidently, as with Bernice Gaylord's homecoming in the 1920s in *Gentlemen at Gyang Gyang*, anxiety about her health was really a cover for stress. After eighteen months at Carlton, she would confide in Alice Henry that she had been 'kicked out of London', due to the precarious state of her heart, with instructions to take a year's break in the sun, but this had proved impossible. Her homecoming had been the worst period of her life, 'purest kind of hell'. However, given space she felt sure she could accomplish something.[15]

Still, there were the daily chores, and more. When on 30 December Susannah Franklin insisted on washing all the curtains and quilts (perhaps as a New Year's gesture), the day was thoroughly disrupted by the steaming copper and mounds of heavy washing being heaved in then out to the clothesline. Soon Miles Franklin would be saying, as she did for the rest of her life, that Australian women were 'wood and water joeys', nothing more. She would often begin a diary entry with 'charring', from which there was no escape in the modestly respectable reaches of the old Australia, where electricity was still on its way and there were no washing machines. As for surrounding amenities, having seen the suburban development along the railway line through Carlton on her first trip home, her expectations could not have been high. In her first Christmas letter to Alice Henry from Sydney she reported that 'Australia is a wilderness of arrested mental development in all its arrangements,' and in the next that she considered life in Carlton the dreariest possible kind of incarceration.[16]

Driven by desperation, she wrote at speed in whatever space there was at 26 Grey Street (it could not have been much, probably only the small bedroom situated midway along the corridor that runs down the centre of the bungalow, on the western side). A fortnight after she finished typing 'the old time novel', she began work on another, which was entitled 'Ten Creeks Run' from the outset and would be Brent of Bin Bin's second novel, published by Blackwood in 1930. The first draft was finished in a little over six weeks, on 25 November 1927. A mere ten days later, on 5 December

1927, she made a start on what is rather loosely described in her diaries as a new story, called 'Cockatoos', based on an old manuscript, 'On the Outside Track' (see Chapter 3).[17]

Thus, in three years, from 1925 to 1927, Miles Franklin had written the first three of the six sequential volumes of the Brent of Bin Bin saga of settler families in south-eastern Australia and embarked on a fourth. It was a pity, William Blake wrote to Blackwood on 6 February 1928, that there was no chance to talk about the series, which spanned the decades from the 1850s to the 1920s, but 'I have planned the whole thing architecturally,' and its interest would build; a further volume, presently in note form, would bring the series up to the present.[18]

The four volumes to 1928 were, in chronological order of writing: 'Not the Tale Begun' (also called by Miles the 'Mervynda story' and the Merlin story and ultimately published in 1950 as *Prelude to Waking*), set in 1920s London; the first substantive volume of the saga, *Up the Country: A Tale of the Early Australian Squattocracy*, covering the period from the 1840s to the 1860s, this having first been thought of as the 'Three Rivers' story (presumably referring to the confluence near Talbingo of Buddong Creek and Jounama Creek with the Tumut River, where the Mazere, Labosseer, Brennan, Poole, M'Eachern, Healey and other clans portrayed first squatted); then *Ten Creeks Run: A Tale of the Horse and Cattle Stations of the Upper Murrumbidgee*, which takes the families into the 1890s and a second generation, with particular emphasis on the young Milly Saunders, who marries the much older Bert Poole, the nearest thing to a hero in the saga; and finally *Cockatoos: A Tale of Youth and Exodists*, set among the small farmers and selectors near Goulburn, running through the Boer War to about 1906. The escape overseas of the central character, Ignez Milford (a thinly disguised Miles Franklin), occurs in this volume.[19]

Hard on the heels of this output would come the first draft of *Gentlemen at Gyang Gyang: A Tale of the Jumbuck Pads on the Summer Runs*, set on the high plains north of Kiandra and featuring the return from London of Bernice Gaylord in the 1920s. In 1928, too, came a first draft of *Back to Bool Bool*, subtitled *A Ramiparous Novel with Several Prominent Characters and a Hantle of Others Disposed as the Atolls of Oceania's Archipelagoes*, which, despite its capacious subtitle, is set in Sydney and around Tumut in the late 1920s and deals with the return of a new generation of 'exodists', who try to make something of their limited cultural heritage.[20]

Miles' diary entry for 21 August 1929, as she was completing the rough draft of *Back to Bool Bool* preparatory to typing it up, reads 'writing is like walking in heavy mud, but must press on to finish'. By year's end it was done. In *Back to Bool Bool*, several descendants of the early clans — Major-General Sir Oswald Mazere-Poole, the diva 'Madame Astra' (Mollye Brennan, said to be based on Dame Nellie Melba) and the poet Richard Labosseer Mazere (Dick Mazere) — return to the 'atoll' (as Australia may still seem from afar) as international celebrities homesick for the bush. Also returning is the journalist Freda Healey, to report on immigration issues, which is Sir Oswald's concern also. Judith Laurillard, a celebrated English actress recovering from 'an affair with an unspoiled youth', adds to the galaxy. While Sir Oswald, the diva and the actress travel in comfort via the Pacific on the RMS *Papeete*, Dick and Freda endure a migrant ship, the TSS *Barryphule* via the Cape; and in due course they all join in centenary celebrations at Bool Bool (Tumut), a great success. William Blake wrote to Blackwood that it was the best volume in 'the Up-country tetralogy': 'Instead of so much geographic and mechanical detail, there is some setting out of what people think.'[21]

At some stage, a further three volumes were envisaged: 'Uncle Joseph Comes Home', possibly about go-ahead George Stanton, who returned from America for the centenary celebrations in *Back to Bool Bool*; 'Coolooluk', which picks up the name of the river flowing through the story and would feature the widowed Emily Mazere (a practical woman modelled on Susannah Franklin), who sets up on the other side of the mountains; and 'Laleen. Ah! Laleen', the name of Dick Mazere's young half-sister and inheritor of the mantle of Ignez Milford, 'the girl who got away' in *Cockatoos*. From the titles, it seems the intention was to situate the families in the modern world, but the volumes were never written. Perhaps they did not need to be. Literary criticism advises that no matter how closely the historical novel sticks to its period, it is always, inevitably, of its time. Only the most superficial reading of the saga could fail to notice its contemporary import, or mistake it for the then popular Empire romance, in essence an escapist genre.[22]

Brent of Bin Bin was a demanding pseudonym, not merely a nice-sounding phrase but a pledge of authenticity, and so much writing was a drain on Miles' intellectual and creative energies. One consequence was that, having immersed herself in Australian history and the bush, she was increasingly avid for contemporary works, like the American realist Sinclair

Lewis' *Main Street* and *Babbitt*, both published in the early 1920s. Yet the historical novel was increasingly popular; and when Katharine Susannah Prichard and M. Barnard Eldershaw (the pen-name of literary collaborators Marjorie Barnard and Flora Eldershaw) were declared joint winners of the *Bulletin*'s inaugural literary prize in 1928, Miles thought Prichard's now classic *Coonardoo* all very well but considered Barnard Eldershaw's *A House is Built*, a historical novel of mercantile Sydney, the real find.[23]

Three years is a long time to keep writing with nothing to show for it (as noted, 'Not The Tale Begun'/*Prelude to Waking* dates from late 1925, and *Up The Country*, the first volume to be published, did not appear until late 1928). 'God help me through this year,' Miles prayed in her diary on 4 January 1928. With the new year, however, came sad news: the sudden death in Melbourne of Nancy Lister Watson. Miles was shattered by the loss of her generous, trusted friend, who had characteristically allowed Miles to use her address as part of William Blake's smokescreen. Miles now turned to her old teacher, Miss Gillespie, nominating her residence, nearby at 45 Hudson Street, Hurstville, as the address of Brent of Bin Bin's agent. It was from there, on 6 February 1928, as William Blake, that she returned the proofs of *Up the Country* to Blackwood, appending a chronological chart showing the sequence of the four volumes already drafted; and it was to Miss Gillespie's address that the publisher replied encouragingly about *Ten Creeks Run*, and then wrote that publication of *Up the Country* would be delayed until the northern autumn, due to the poor state of the book trade.[24]

In accordance with an emerging work pattern of completions, despatches, breaks and fresh starts evident over the next two years, on 8 February 1928, two days after despatching the proofs of *Up the Country* to Blackwood, Miles caught the overnight train for Cooma and beyond, travelling by motor coach to the old gold town of Kiandra the following afternoon. There she was collected by her Uncle Fred Lampe and his wife, Eliza, and taken to Gooandra, on the long plain to the north, over which she had first travelled as a three-month-old infant.[25]

The daily round in the high country was not very restful, nor even companionable — 'Am I never to be with anyone who understands?' she cried mid-stay — but wonderfully exhilarating. 'I love the bush,' she would write to Mary Fullerton. One day she was taken to Canberra. On another she rode with Uncle Fred Lampe towards Tantangara, on the edge of what is now Kosciuszko National Park, with its awe-inspiring southern vistas. There were old sites to visit and a sports day at Rules Point. Inevitably, Miles began another story. As she wrote in a long-overdue letter to Kate Baker praising *Such Is Life*, she had such a lot of stories in her head craving expression — if only she could find peace and quiet.[26]

After Gooandra, Miles spent two months at Talbingo with the Theo Lampes, interspersed with visits to other relatives in Tumut. On 3 March at the Tumut Show she remembered how all those years back poor Linda had been unable to go; and she heard about the town's centenary celebrations in 1924, which were to feature in a fictionalised version in *Back to Bool Bool*. Mostly, though, she simply immersed herself in local life, riding about and playing cards at night. Soon — 'God speed me with my work,' she implored on 8 March — she felt she was writing well.

The story, begun 'near Kiandra', was *Gentlemen at Gyang Gyang*. With this realisation, the reading of the bizarre work is transformed. Not only does the descriptive writing seem less overblown, and its slight and distended plot become more bearable, but the ideological import of the whole saga becomes clearer. It might as well have been in a letter to a friend like Mary Fullerton that Miles (as Brent) described the environment wherein Bernice Gaylord, the painter nursing secret wounds, finds herself temporarily stranded: 'She was in the middle of a treeless piece of country surrounded by hills crowned with timber. Away, away down a valley was a transcendent view of peaks, rising tier upon tier, as blue as the skies above. From half a mile away she could have faintly discerned Kosciuszko.' Bernice relaxes. The creeks, the basaltic rocks, the wildflowers, even the sheep at summer pasture, all delight her. As for the light and the birdsong, words could scarcely convey Bernice's dawning realisation that she is free of the cliques of London and Paris: 'It came to her as distinctively as the blazing quality of the sunlight, while the gyang gyangs, kookaburras, magpies, wagtails and other friends chattered about her, that these men, living so far from the world of exquisites, were gentlemen, entitled to association with other gentlemen at home and abroad … with the refreshment of a new idea'. Though Cedric Spires blackmails both Bernice and 'Black Peter', great-grandson of Boko Poole in *Up the Country*, about secrets in their pasts, art and romance together win through.[27]

Miles Franklin was not only making her peace with Australian men but also laying out an imperial typology along advanced liberal lines of the kind Lady Byles strongly approved. 'Better, far, your half-developed colonials. *They* know love and loyalty,' was Lady Byles' throwaway assessment of sensational dancer Isadora Duncan, whose autobiography Miles had been reading. And so Bernice Gaylord found.[28]

A handwritten draft of the *Gyang Gyang* story dated 16 April 1928 survives in a ledger given to Miles by a woman at the old Talbingo pub. Back in Sydney in May, she typed her story up for the *Bulletin* novel competition. Two typescripts resulted, one engagingly titled 'Snow Daisies: A Tale of the Jumbuck Pads on the Summer Runs' by 'Saddle Flap', and the other 'Piccadillian Pantaloons on the Hoof' by Brent of Bin Bin. Both are said to have been entered. However, a third typescript (undated) entitled 'Gentlemen at Gyang Gyang: A Tale of Piccadilly's Pants A-hoof' by Brent of Bin Bin, or alternatively (the choice was left up to the judges) 'Piccadillian Pantaloons on the Hoof', might have been the one that actually went in (it came 'from an accomplice of BBB'). Also entered in carbon copy was Brent's *Up the Country*, then in press. It is now almost impossible to follow all the goings on, but a notice in the *Bulletin* in July stated that 'Gentlemen at Gyang Gyang' by 'Australian Born' and 'Up the Country' by 'Squatter' were among the entries received for which sealed envelopes enclosing names and addresses of the authors were awaited. (This procedure ensured blind assessments.)[29]

Apart from the competition judges, no one saw *Gentlemen at Gyang Gyang* for almost thirty years. Miles herself did not live to see it in print, and by that time the intellectual milieu that generated it had passed away. But *Gentlemen at Gyang Gyang* is nonetheless the novel of her return to Australia, and should be read as such.

Unlike the two previous mountain tales, *Up the Country* and *Ten Creeks Run*, it has no Preface. In a sense, a preface would have been superfluous. However, it takes some awareness of historical contexts to understand who exactly the author was addressing in those prior introductions, and to appreciate that Brent of Bin Bin's approach, called 'possuming', is what in modern times would be recognised as discursive. More straightforward is the dedication of *Up the Country*: 'To The Old Hands'. The 'Old Hands' were to be found both at home and abroad, not just up the country (as the pioneer legend would have it); they were the cultivated few, those who were mature enough to be cultured 'by contact either with nature or with humanity's stored knowledge'. Arguably, Bernice Gaylord and Peter Poole are Miles Franklin's first attempts to characterise an 'aristocracy of intellect' in the Antipodes.[30]

When she returned to Sydney, Miles was once more beset by sleeplessness and anxiety. It was during this period that a friend of Miss Gillespie, the Adelong-born Will Carter, a near-retirement bush teacher and prolific contributor of 'Australianities' to country newspapers, turned up at Miss Gillespie's 'to spy on me', according to Miles (and later fall in love with her, a futile thing to do). More ominously, it gradually became clear that her mother, now aged seventy-eight, was suffering from encroaching senility, and that with her father's increasing frailty, Miles must reconcile herself to the roles of charwoman and nurse, at least for the time being, keeping away from people due to 'limitations of strength'. Mary Fullerton's letters provided her with 'some refuge and comfort'.[31]

As winter set in, Miles resumed work on *Ten Creeks Run*, now pushed back in the publication schedule due to Blackwood's delay in bringing out *Up the Country* — 'the swine', Miles wrote fiercely to Mary Fullerton. She finished typing *Ten Creeks Run* at the end of July 1928. Was her work any good, she sometimes wondered. Fullerton had no doubts, and Miles reassured her in return after an appalling review of Mary's descriptive work, *The Australian Bush*, in the *Times Literary Supplement*. The important thing was to lie low, and to get some sleep.[32]

By August 1928 Miles had completed a draft of *Back to Bool Bool* and resumed work on 'Mervynda' (*Prelude to Waking*), which she found good and later sent off to Blackwood on the off-chance that they would slip it into their schedule as 'a merry, perhaps satirical interlude'. Blackwood said they looked forward to seeing it, but did nothing when it came. Miles assumed that she should be getting along with 'the second Australian volume', that is, *Ten Creeks Run*. She also remarked, probably correctly, that it was a pity not to have stuck with the 'Three Rivers' title for the first volume, leaving 'Up the Country' for the series as a whole.[33]

No doubt some people wondered what Miles Franklin was up to these days, and would have liked to make something of her return. But with so much work still to do on the saga — and to protect her cover — she eschewed 'tuft-hunters'. The Society of Women Writers invited her to a lunch, but it is unclear whether she went. Likewise, the Fellowship of Australian Writers (FAW), which was to flourish as the main support and advocacy body for Australian writers in coming decades, was starting up in Sydney, but Miles was too absorbed in her own work to pay attention. In general, apart from some outings in the city with friends, such as Eva O'Sullivan and Stella Kidgell (Ada Holman's sister), and visits to the Griffins at Castlecrag, Miles' contact with the wider world was at this time quite limited. Alice Henry, now retired to Santa Barbara, and Mary Fullerton in London were her principal confidantes. To preserve her privacy, with the help of her father's old Penrith associate Dan Clyne, now a state parliamentarian, she obtained a post-office box in the city, and soon after she decided she must find somewhere quiet to write. Probably a generous bequest of £200 from Nancy Lister Watson made it possible.[34]

When on 23 October 1928 Miles set up office in the old Council House at Hurstville, about one and a half kilometres from Grey Street, it felt like bliss, and from then on, insomnia was less of a problem. For one thing, walking is a recognised antidote. For another, she had somewhere to sleep in the daytime as well as to work without interruption. And Miss Gillespie's residence — the business address for Brent of Bin Bin — was conveniently en route.[35]

On 10 November Miles called in to her old teacher's residence to collect a parcel. It contained six copies of *Up the Country*, one of which she straightaway sent to the Prime Minister, Stanley Bruce; another, from Brent of Bin Bin, went to Mary Gilmore. Mary had recently declared the expatriate writer Dorothy Cottrell a genius for her novel *The Singing Gold*. Was *Up the Country* the work of a genius or a geniass, Brent asked provocatively. There is no record of a response. A few days before, as William Blake, Miles wrote to Blackwood urging the firm to fend off inquiries about the identity of Brent of Bin Bin: 'I am most desirous of preserving my "nonentity" for twelve months at least. It will be more interesting than details in these days when the public is bored as to authors' braces and actresses' hair washes etc; besides it will give me quiet, which I must have to live.'[36]

Fortunately, Miles already had her retreat in place when on 14 December 1928 Susannah Franklin installed a wireless at Grey Street. On 23 December, in the quiet of her office at Hurstville, she put the final touches to *Ten Creeks Run*, and on Christmas Eve she despatched a copy of the typescript to the New York publisher Harper.[37]

When Aunt Lena handed her niece the issue of the *Bulletin* for 2 January 1929, she had not noticed anything unusual. Miles saw it immediately. There, on page 5 in a column headed 'An Australian Classic', was an enthusiastic review of *Up the Country* by Brent of Bin Bin. It was not Brent's first review — numerous short and sometimes bemused notices had appeared in the British press late in 1928, and the Sydney journal *Country Life* had been quick to applaud a notable chronicle — but the *Bulletin* was the first to celebrate literary achievement, comparing the method of narration to that of Thomas Hardy's *The Dynasts*. The anonymous reviewer passed quickly from the question of Brent's identity to his 'smiling knowledge of Australian country folk'. 'In this book,' the review continued, 'Australia's countenance beams'; and although Brent was said to have no style as understood in literary cliques, the book was deemed true to life and to contain some of the most tender writing in Australian literature. In the death by drowning of Bert Poole's betrothed, the beautiful young Emily Mazere, in the Mungee Fish Pool, 'the prose sings'. Yet as Lady Byles would remark with some surprise, most reviewers missed the woman's voice in *Up the Country*.[38]

Miles was triumphant, straightaway sending a copy of the review to Blackwood, and to Mary Fullerton. To Blackwood, as W. Blake, she wrote that hiding under a pen-name was after all an advantage for publicity, and urged that the other volumes be published quickly. To Fullerton she expressed relief, on two grounds. Firstly, that she was 'completely under cover for the start ... To be in the limelight now would kill me, I know,' she wrote. 'I feel like some cowering exhausted animal in an inadequate cover which cannot last long.' Mary must stand firm and hide her. Secondly, although she had entered *Up the Country* in the *Bulletin* competition in 1928, no one had noticed it; it had not even made the commended list. She didn't care to have it said that she had no style, and the *Bulletin* had gone down in her esteem, but she wasn't going to argue. It had done her proud: 'When I came out as a girl I found myself famous overnight because of the *Bulletin*, and now, coming back as an old woman, I find them "discerning" me immediately again.'[39]

Mary Fullerton, observing from afar the success of women writers such as Katharine Susannah Prichard, exulted that they would soon be 'top dogs' in Australia. The close literary friendship between the two women which had been developing since 1924 was cemented at this time. The flow of letters from 1927 to Fullerton's death in 1946, approaching 600 preserved in the Franklin Papers (the largest single correspondence), is remarkable not only as a friendship but also as a professional partnership. It reveals two bush intellectuals who were also vulnerable women navigating the quickening, multi-directional tides of an emergent Australian literature. Miles' success encouraged them both. Who was Martin Mills (Martin Boyd) and how good was his Melbourne saga *The Montforts*, they asked each other. And what about the phenomenon of Henry Handel Richardson, who had to date published two acclaimed volumes of her magnum opus *The Fortunes of Richard Mahony*, with a third imminent, of whom very little was known? (Even Nettie Palmer was unaware until 1928 that 'H. H. R.' was a woman.) As for the hazards facing women writers in the 1920s, events like the censorship of Radclyffe Hall's taboo-busting but grimly determinist lesbian novel *The Well of Loneliness* in 1928 were a warning to keep to the higher ground. 'Yours also a pilgrim,' Mary once signed off.[40]

Among the plaudits in the Australian press in the early months of 1929 came an especially significant one by Nettie Palmer in the *Brisbane Courier*. More than verisimilitude, Palmer wrote, Brent of Bin Bin had achieved 'something like communicable delight in fine memories'. Here, she said, was a novel that met the call for books about pioneering that were not just struggles with drought, but a record of 'some of the dignified, complex lives of the prouder kind of pioneer'. She was particularly impressed by the characterisation of Bert Poole: 'If Brent of Bin Bin had done nothing more than render the personality of Bert Poole and make him credible, this book would have been worth writing.' But, she went on, a man is incomplete without his environment, and what Brent had successfully essayed was a kind of ecology. Nor did Palmer miss the book's contemporary thrust, pointing out that to see the characters as old-fashioned was to look through the wrong end of the telescope: they might wear crinolines, 'but their hearts and speech are young, contemporary', and some of the young women sounded like 'flappers'. There was no equivocation in Palmer's generous response to the adventures and the huge, growing homesteads of the principal families. Finally she pointed out that the town of Bool Bool was an old settlement, a historical perspective sometimes overlooked.[41]

No wonder Miles Franklin came to see Nettie Palmer as her preferred candidate for a founding chair in Australian literature. Her review showed 'the deepest understanding'. She was especially happy with the phrase 'communicable delight', and in due course as Brent of Bin Bin, c/– Blackwood, Edinburgh, she responded to 'Dear, delightful Nettie Palmer, (Mrs)'. In the first of a handful of early letters from Brent of Bin Bin to Nettie written between 1929 and 1932, Miles further outlined Brent's approach to writing. The letter explained that the book attempted to convey the atmosphere and unique qualities of the Australian landscape, 'which are spiritual breath to me', and that the author had found a way to detail the subtleties of Australian life based on old pioneer yarning techniques. Brent also promised to send Nettie's elder daughter, Aileen, a copy of the next volume (as she instructed Blackwood to do in 1930, when it appeared), Aileen having apparently made a genealogical chart after reading *Up the Country*. Brent added for Aileen's information that he had made such charts too, along with an index of people, horses, pubs etc.

Nettie's review was 'balmfully free from any interest in the person of the writer', Brent noted.[42]

There had already been a good deal of speculation about Brent of Bin Bin. The address given in the Author's Note to *Up the Country* was 'Brent of Bin Bin, S[eat]. 9, Reading Room, British Museum', which suggested an expatriate. In mid-March, attending a meeting of the 'Literary Fellowship' (probably the FAW) with Eva O'Sullivan, Miles heard the matter discussed, and letters came to her from friends conveying the gossip in London: from Mary Fullerton, for example, that Kathleen Ussher had guessed Brent was Miles Franklin. In April 1929 the *Bulletin* reported that Brent of Bin Bin had written to the Victorian writer Bernard Cronin congratulating him on a serial in the *Bulletin* about dairy farming in Gippsland, adding that Brent had so far succeeded in preserving his anonymity despite numerous efforts to get behind it.[43]

Undoubtedly many people knew the truth — family, friends in London — but out of loyalty or simple kindness no one gave her secret away. Ruby Bridle, daughter of Miles' cousin Annie May Bridle, née Franklin, said that when the Brent books came out she and her family knew who wrote them but were never game to say: 'they were full of stories we'd been brought up on'. Winnie Stephensen, the long-suffering wife of nationalist publisher P. R. 'Inky' Stephensen, who had been cared for in Melbourne by Nancy Lister Watson when young and first met Miles in America, had only to read a few pages to encounter an anecdote she had heard P. S. Watson tell Miles many times in London. And it could well have been Kate Baker who arranged for an excerpt from *Up the Country* by Brent of Bin Bin to appear in the Victorian Education Department's *School Paper* in September 1929. Even so, it seems clear that only a few London friends — Mollye Menken, Lady Byles and Mary Fullerton — could have been absolutely certain that Miles was Brent.[44]

After a while interest abated, and it seems Miles relaxed, even enjoying the challenge of outwitting those who sought to smoke her out. In June 1929 as 'The Old Brand BBB' she wrote to *Country Life* to thank it for its welcoming review ('like a celebration in the home paddock'), and as Brent, again to Bernard Cronin, who decided Brent was 'a lady' (leading the *Bulletin* to refer to 'Mr or Mrs Brent'). Meanwhile, it was reported in the Sydney press that Miss Miles Franklin was living quietly in Sydney. With that, the inquisitive had to be content.[45]

There were anxious moments nonetheless. In all innocence, Mrs Robins almost exposed the secret of Brent's identity by cabling congratulations to

Miles on her great book (which Miles had sent to her). 'Please keep absolutely secret or all ruined financially,' Miles cabled back. A letter followed, explaining that if the public suspected she had anything to do with it, it would finish her. Hopefully no one at the post office had noticed the cable's contents. 'No one in Australia has been confided in.' Nor would they be. Miles was vigilant. When she heard there was a rumour going around Melbourne that she wrote the Brent of Bin Bin books, she telegraphed Elsie Belle Champion to correct the impression. Charles Peters, the manager of Robertson & Mullens bookshop, who had made the connection in his weekly book program on radio 3LO, subsequently retracted his remarks, as he explained to Miles in an apologetic letter.[46]

'The strength and repose at my command for this undertaking are precarious,' Brent wrote to Nettie Palmer on 22 July 1929. Nonetheless, Miles kept a straight course. By the end of the month she had finished a rough typescript of *Back to Bool Bool*, despatched a final version of *Ten Creeks Run* to Blackwood, and sent a typescript of *Gentlemen at Gyang Gyang* to the literary agent A. P. Watt in London. Unfortunately sales of *Up the Country* were not yet to Blackwood's satisfaction, especially in the home (that is, British) market, where after eight months a mere 307 copies had been sold, as compared with 918 on the colonial market. But it was hoped sales would improve, and in due course a modest annual royalty payment of £22 19s made its tortuous way to Miles via Mary Fullerton. While Brent regretted that the publisher was not making a profit, he felt sure *Back to Bool Bool* was superior to the previous volumes.[47]

In a letter to Mrs Robins, Miles reflected fiercely on her loneliness:

> Australia is the unique place to study the common man ... A special condition creates him. There is first a small community ... Then there is our isolation ... [but with] imperialism to dictate what we shall think and sterilise originality of mind, and every one of any note ... drawn off to London ...[t]he result is the highest community of common people in the world. Also they are the richest per capita, I am sure.[48]

Despite, or maybe because of, her isolation, Miles Franklin took a close interest in international affairs and literary trends, devouring the magazines forwarded by far-off friends and emphasising the need for modernity in Australian literature, lamenting also the worn-out character of women's politics in Sydney in one of numerous letters to Alice Henry in California. She was disgusted by Adela Pankhurst Walsh's rantings (Adela had emigrated to Australia in 1914 and moved far from her radical roots), though her response to Virginia Woolf's *Orlando*, which appeared in 1928, was merely that she found it 'stimulating'.[49]

News of the death of H. H. Champion's sister Annie Beatrice Champion in late 1929 saddened Miles, who recalled that 'A. B. C.' had done much for her in London by introducing her to the aristocracy and educating her about London ways, and it strengthened her desire to escape from Australia again. But with so much literary work in train, this was not yet possible. The proofs of *Ten Creeks Run* came and went in December. Soon after, she drafted a retrospective rationale for the series as a whole, declaring that it recorded a phase of human life close to nature, now passing in Australia and elsewhere vanished entirely, and drew on the experience of old hands: 'What an enrapturing literary adventure to limn that life while it still quivers in the air.' To keep her spirits up, just before Christmas, as Brent of Bin Bin, she wrote an optimistic article entitled 'Our Literary Turkey Nests', suggesting that Australian writers were like the brush turkey, a native of eastern Australia, whose eggs are incubated in large mounds and whose chicks are able to fend for themselves if and when they hatch.[50]

Being Brent could be fun. However, it seems probable that the years away in larger, more complex societies left Miles Franklin unprepared for the contradictions now apparent in her position. Although Brent's books had good reviews, literary life in Sydney was limited, even claustrophobic. It was hard to maintain the fiction of Brent, though without it she felt all would be lost. If exposed prior to completion of the saga, she would lose momentum and face, and — by now it was an article of faith — sales. The underlying problem was that although Miles badly needed to succeed as a writer, the task she had set herself, and the terms on which she felt strong enough to carry it through, meant it could only be in the long run. For now, she must hold her breath, and manage her fear of premature exposure. At stake, it now seems obvious, was the creative process itself, as she experienced it. It was the point she was driving at when, as William Blake, she wrote to Blackwood shortly after copies of *Up the Country* arrived, stressing the need for anonymity: 'I could not survive personal publicity at the moment.'[51]

Meanwhile, there was the irony of her role as the dutiful daughter to be endured. The situation with her parents got worse and worse. Susannah was maddening, and John Franklin was obviously deteriorating. Maybe she could leave them for a while after Christmas. In the meantime she fiddled about with articles for the *Sydney Morning Herald* and the old silent film scenario 'Old Man of Bandicoot', adding dialogue for a competition. But it wouldn't work: 'too tired, too stupid, too old', she wrote in her diary on 21 March 1930. To further dampen her spirits, the first American knockback for *Back to Bool Bool* had arrived.[52]

Unbeknownst to Miles, a potentially serious situation arose when Agnes Murphy more or less blew her cover with Blackwood at this time. Once again it was her own doing. Apparently Miles had written Murphy an anonymous letter from Sydney with no return address, promising to send a copy of *Up The Country*, adding a giveaway reference to meeting her once in Ireland. Murphy subsequently speculated in a letter to Blackwood that Brent might be Miles. Nothing came of this possibly deliberate indiscretion except that William Blake was not so convincing as the real author of the Brent books thereafter, and Blackwood could treat Brent of Bin Bin with some detachment. Murphy, who died the following year, was not bothered by the situation either, and subsequently wrote enthusiastically about both Brent books, as did Kathleen Ussher, who was still sniffing about in London ('simply splendid').[53]

Tension could only intensify when *Ten Creeks Run* appeared in late April. This time the dedication read:

> To
> My Father and Mother
> With due recognition of their
> valiant share in the life depicted.

And this time Brent gave his address as 'New South Wales'. Once more there was speculation about his identity, with the *Launceston Courier* and then the *Advertiser* in Adelaide declaring categorically that Brent was Miss Miles Franklin — to which the *West Australian* replied that she had officially denied it. Meanwhile, Mary Fullerton had reacted instantly with vehement congratulations. Subsequently she did much to advance Miles' cause, including, in a comment on the London literary scene entitled 'A Note on Australian Writers: Some Women and an Unknown' in Melbourne's *Table Talk*, highlighting Brent's work ('magnificent stuff') and speculating that Brent was a woman (although 'Brent and his publishers lie low'). Australian women writers, she reported, were doing well in London; Australian writing was being treated with respect by critics for the first time; and the rising popularity of long novels was 'good for Australia'.[54]

Between April and August 1930 numerous notices and reviews appeared, first in Britain and then in Australia, beginning with the London *Daily Telegraph* on 1 April: 'one of those rare narratives that recapture the very essence, sap, savour and force of the old days they set out to describe'. Brent had passed the 'second book' test with flying colours. A few reviewers thought the canvas too crowded, and the *Times Literary Supplement* concluded its warmly welcoming review with a comment on 'the hideous place-names'. In general, however, it was thought that *Ten Creeks Run* was probably a better novel than its predecessor, and reviewers found much to commend. Some noticed that the horses were as heroic, if not more so, than the people. Nettie Palmer, who showed great perspicacity when dealing with Brent, said that the horses were 'fit to be celebrated by Pindar'. And she recognised the splendour of the funeral of the matriarch Emily Mazere with which the book concludes. Others picked out the romantic interest, with Milly Saunders happily marrying the much older Bert Poole and the unfortunate Aileen Healey unable to resist family pressure to marry Jack Stanton, also a much older man, despite her passion for flash Ronald Dice. Nettie Palmer concluded simply that *Ten Creeks Run* was 'a landmark in Australian literature'. Nettie also recognised that in the sudden flowering of the Australian novel of which the Brent books were part there was hardly a glance at Aboriginal life except by Katharine Susannah Prichard (though there are some references in the saga; for instance, Milly is sickened by Red Jimmy's tales of 'shootin' the blacks' in Queensland).[55]

The imperial dimension was noticed by very few friends or reviewers. This is not surprising, since of the first three volumes in the Brent saga, *Ten Creeks Run* is the one in which the families are most firmly settled on the land, and is of particular interest in its portrayal of a whole community under circumstances where the laws of primogeniture no longer obtained, as they did in England. (In the Author's Note, dated November 1927, the setting is described as 'a patternless, trackless region'.) A reviewer in Glasgow was grateful for a tale from the Dominions rather than yet another American Western, and the *London Daily News and Westminster Gazette* observed the underlying reality that the novel represented 'a strange and compelling chapter in the history of imperial development'. Writing to Nettie Palmer after a review in the *Tasmanian Illustrated Mail*, Brent provided an explanation:

I had read one book after another acclaimed in current literary circles, full of detail, detail — sordid detail of sordid lives — and mostly sex detail, detail with which I am chock a block. Said I, I'll sit me down and give detail, detail, detail with which I'm chock a block. Detail entrancing to me, which though trivial, nevertheless in the mass, embroiders a record of the lives of people in an unworked part of the globe, units of a master race in our day, units of a great Empire, a life as you have expressed it, otherwise hidden past all knowing ...[56]

The publication of *Ten Creeks Run* prompted Miles' most significant reflection on John Galsworthy, whose work has often been thought to have inspired the Brent books. Aunt Lena had given her a copy of the Heinemann edition of *The Forsyte Saga* when it appeared in 1922, and there are five other Galsworthy titles from the 1920s in her library; Miles admired his work immensely. 'G[alsworthy] wears wonderfully well,' she wrote to Alice Henry in November 1928. 'His writing is beautifully easy reading and full of delicate observation.' The extent to which her work was shaped by his approach is less easy to estimate, however. 'Of course I don't try to set myself against Galsworthy or HHR [Henry Handel Richardson] ... both of those have done a different thing,' she wrote to Mary Fullerton on 20 May 1930, by which she meant that she had worked not through one person or one family, but 'on whole cloth'. Moreover, extol Galsworthy's gifts as she did, she could not help but compare his achievements to her own. If she was less successful, 'partly it wd be because I lacked the God-given power, and more because circumstances erode what I had, lack of those conditions so well-known to be Mr Galsworthy's'. (Miles was referring to an impression of privilege, confirmed when she read H. V. Marrot's 1935 biography of the great man.)[57]

When copies of *Ten Creeks Run* arrived, Miles could not at first muster the strength to open the packet; and when she did, she was displeased by the jacket's graphic, of an 1890s girl a-horse. (Although she thought it better than the Aboriginal warrior on the jacket of *Up the Country,* the horse had been given a cropped tail, an affectation found on imported horses only.) At least the delay in opening the package enabled her to reply truthfully to reporters seeking to flush out Brent that she had not seen the book. Inevitably the renewed interest in Brent upset her.[58]

As a diversion, she had been trying to turn 'Old Blastus' into a novel to appear under her own name. It was a job done quickly. One Sunday she managed 6000 words. In June 1930, before finalising the text, she took a trip to Queanbeyan, where she spent a week with her cousin Ivy Maxwell and Ivy's ranger husband, Jack, checking contexts and consulting Ivy's mother, 84-year-old Aunt Annie Franklin (to whom the novel would be dedicated when it appeared in 1931, along with her daughter Annie May and granddaughters Ruby and Leslie, and Miss Gillespie, 'who encouraged my earliest attempts'). One day when Miles and Ivy walked to the top of Jerrabomberra Creek, her thoughts turned to Greece: the headwaters of the creek being the only place she had seen with vistas to compare was Edessa (that is, Vodena), she told the *Queanbeyan Age*. When *Old Blastus* was finished a fortnight or so later in Sydney, she sent it to newspapers in Sydney and Melbourne for possible (and lucrative) serial publication; and then in hope of a quick local publication, 'as my father is very old', to Angus & Robertson, but to no avail. By then, however, the Melbourne publisher Thomas Lothian, with whom she had been in contact since January, had offered to seek a London publisher and 'to take the Australian market ourselves', anticipating 'a very good sale' (and possibly the rights to *My Brilliant Career*).[59]

In the ongoing struggle to sustain Brent — the extent of which only Mary Fullerton knew — Miles presented a cheerful face, enjoying friendships old and new in the city, where the entertainments of 1930 included 'talkies' at the gorgeous new State Theatre in Market Street and concerts by 'Madame Austral', and sharing the excitement over aviatrix Amy Johnson's successful solo flight from England to Australia. She took pleasure too in her young nephew, Norman's son, Jack, when he visited Sydney. (After his mother, Irene, died in 1925, Jack went to live with Irene's sister Xenia Harkin at Ardglen near Murrurundi, where he attended primary school, and his father continued to work up the country.) And she did her best to keep calm in the face of her mother's relentless criticism, playing cards with all and sundry on Saturday evenings, when her widowed sister-in-law, Tal's wife, Eva, usually visited and cheered them all up. The worst problem was a neighbour's blaring radio which kept her awake.[60]

The long nights did mean that she could read voraciously — 'To keep me in decent reading is like trying to keep an elephant in hay' — and with a sharp eye, especially for current Australian literature. Henry Handel Richardson was a continuing (and to some extent mutual) preoccupation. Considering Richardson's narrow focus upon one man, and her lack of humour, Miles puzzled about the secret of her success. Norman Lindsay's *Redheap*, banned when it first appeared in 1930, she welcomed as the work of 'our first mental housekeeper'. In the Mitchell Library, she noted the communist writer Jean Devanny's first novel, *The Butcher Shop*, published in 1926, and caught up on Louis Stone's Sydney classic *Jonah*, which dates from 1911.

By July she was writing, 'I must get away. Feel I shall die of mental starvation.' Apparently her parents were now strongly anti-Labor. In New South Wales in 1930, unemployment was high and the populist Premier Jack Lang led an anti-deflationary Labor government from October 1930 until his dismissal in May 1932, amid constant turmoil. Like Lady Byles, Miles probably believed that 'Inherently, truly we are all Labour — we cannot be anything else.' But she and Lady Byles both felt its limitations. Miles had delighted in George Bernard Shaw's *The Intelligent Woman's Guide to Socialism, Capitalism, Sovietism and Fascism* — though fearing isolation might have relegated her to the ranks of 'Victorian and prewar drivellers' — and she understood that Labor could only go so far before capital reasserted itself. No doubt her association with guild socialists and other under-consumptionist critics, such as Arthur Penty and Lady Byles' friend J. A. Hobson in London, and the strong Catholic orientation of New South Wales Labor in the 1920s, made her antipathetic, but she supported Labor in 1930, and again in 1939, when the lawyer Clive Evatt became the Labor member for Hurstville.[61]

When the old Council House at Hurstville was demolished mid-year, Miles had to look for a new office, which was found nearby at 336 Forest Road. By October, buoyed by news of a third impression of *Up the Country* and the stronger sales of *Ten Creeks Run* (1650 copies sold in the first three months, though again mostly on the colonial market), and with over £37 in royalties for the period at last on its way, via Mary Fullerton, she had more or less decided on one more trip before she was too old. 'I may be leaving Australia soon,' William Blake advised Blackwood on 14 October 1930. Soon Miles was searching pawnshops for a fur coat. Mary Fullerton's sister Em, who seems to have run a dress-making shop in Melbourne, said she would get one for her, and sent £50 as well.[62]

Miles was prepared to go steerage, but she still did not have enough for the fare. Ultimately the key was none other than Mrs Robins, now retired to Chinsegut Hill, Brookesville, in north-central Florida, where the Robinses lived in seigneurial style and Raymond Robins continued his campaign to outlaw war while Mrs Robins undertook cultural work, running a bookshop in the town. In what might be read as a skilful begging letter, Miles outlined the situation to Mrs Robins. Her brother, Norman, was likely to be laid off for three months after Christmas due to 'financial stringency' — she probably meant in the pastoral industry, where he had been employed in the 1920s — and could watch over his son and their parents, which she said would keep him from brooding on his financial situation, so she could get away for a time, but she needed another $50. Mrs Robins cabled her the money. Miracles sometimes happen, Miles cried on receipt. That was on 8 November. Soon after, she began assembling the requisite travel documents; and later in November Norman obtained a part-time job as a supervisor at the Metropolitan Milk Board. With a final version of *Old Blastus* sent to Lothian earlier that month for placement with a British publisher, *Back to Bool Bool* off to Blackwood just before Christmas, and her parents planning a holiday in the new year, the way was clear for her to go.[63]

Lothian was told she wanted to keep her trip as quiet as possible, which was perhaps wise, since she had published nothing under her own name during her homecoming, not even any journalism. As in 1906, she said she would be seeking publishers in New York. Although prior attempts to interest American publishers in Brent's books had been unsuccessful, the reviews of *Ten Creeks Run* had been good, and on re-reading the Merlin story (*Prelude to Waking*) and that other unpublished manuscript *Cockatoos*, she thought they might appeal. For good measure, she packed *Back to Bool Bool* and *Gentlemen at Gyang Gyang* as well. (Shortly before departure in the new year, as S. Mills she sent *Gentlemen at Gyang Gyang* to Blackwood too, though only to give them first option.) She also hoped to find an American publisher for Mary Fullerton's work. Through 1930 she had tried without success to persuade George Robertson to reissue *Bark House Days*, and she loved Mary's poems, believing the grave quatrains were as good as those of Emily Dickinson.[64]

On 21 January 1931, the eve of her departure for San Francisco on RMS *Monowai*, Miles wrote a reassuring letter to her mother (on holiday in the country), that she had done the washing and cleaning and paid the bills, swept the side path, and made some plum sauce, even left some books and her best dictionary for reading. Thanking Susannah for money, Miles urged her to take a rest: 'I'll be back before you remember I have gone.'[65]

According to the date stamp in Miles Franklin's passport, the RMS *Monowai* arrived in San Francisco on 13 February 1931. As in 1906 and 1923, she spent time with Carrie Whelan at Grand Avenue, Oakland, and also with Edith Malyon, before boarding the train for New York via Chicago, where there were more reunions, including with Agnes Nestor and Dr Young, and a health check (the result was reassuring).

This time Miles delighted in the trains, 'thundering up like polled angry bulls', and the Pullman attendants pleased her too: they were so attentive. The luxury of America struck her once more. There were clean sheets every night on the train, and the terminals were like vast cathedrals. 'No wonder Australia doesn't seem real to the rest of the world,' she wrote to Leslie Bridle. Even so, 'everything has gone smash'; people were to be seen wearing any old thing.[66]

Arriving in New York on 24 February, she was met by Rose Schneiderman and again stayed with old friends, giving her address variously as c/– Mrs E. M. Childs, 55 East 10th Street (Jessie Childs), and Mrs Swartz, 102 East 22nd Street, NYC (possibly Maud Swartz, national league president in the 1920s). Among other old friends seen during her two-month stay were Mary Dreier, Margery Currey and Magdalen Dalloz, as well as John Varney and his friend Mary Barnicle. One weekend she had a 'wonderful reunion' with the much-loved Ethel Nielsen, previously Mason, now an up-country farmer's wife in Goschen, Connecticut.

Apart from the strain of pursuing publishers, there was much to enjoy in New York that autumn: the music of Prokofiev and Stravinsky, Pirandello plays, the art of Nicholas Roerich, a Dorothea Dreier exhibition, and the 'talkies'. A highlight was seeing the Adelaide-born actress Judith Anderson in performance. Miles was very proud of her, as 'our own Australian. She has it advertised on programmes that she is from Australia, God bless her, as it is no credit to be an Australian these days.' As ever, America stimulated her cultural antennae. Commenting on Alice Henry's concern about the conventional character of Australian art, Miles sagaciously identified the double burden of the creative classes in Australia at that time: a still-atrophying isolation and the superimposition of English values — making it difficult to depict 'a new milieu which is not exciting'.[67]

Of immediate import was a cable from the Melbourne *Herald* offering to serialise *Back to Bool Bool,* then in press. She was interested, provided the price was right, but soon became exasperated at the *Herald*'s apparent desire to capitalise on the Brent of Bin Bin mystery. Under her resumed identity as Brent's agent, S. Mills, Miles haggled over the rates due to 'native brains', and asked such a high price to begin with (£500 for the Australian rights) that ultimately it came to nothing; but the offer encouraged her with her main objective, the publication of Brent titles and Mary Fullerton's poems.[68]

'Many times en route I have lost my courage,' Miles had written to Mary on her arrival in America. Mary encouraged her to 'dig in'. But strenuous efforts to interest publishers over the next two months were unavailing. One youthful editor at Doubleday asserted that Brent's work was too highbrow for American readers (a problematic reaction which nonetheless served to obscure the possibility that the Americans were waiting on British responses to unpublished material such as *Gentlemen at Gyang Gyang*). Although 'near despair' in April, Miles started Brent on a new novel, 'Mrs Dysart Disappears', begun as a film scenario in 1920. As well she found articles by the young American publicist Hartley Grattan, whose pamphlet *Australian Literature* had appeared in 1929, approving her personal touchstone, Furphy's *Such Is Life*: 'bless the boy', she added in a letter to Alice Henry of 29 April.[69]

Next day she sailed for London. Before leaving Sydney in January she had obtained a letter of introduction from Premier Lang, stating that she would be proceeding to visit Great Britain and Europe. However, it seems she did not finally make up her mind to go there until her New York options were exhausted. On arrival in New York in February she had advised Blackwood that the forwarding address for Miss S. Mills, who had resumed responsibility for Brent's affairs, would be c/– Mary Fullerton; but Mary seems not to have known she was definitely coming until mid-March, and it was not until late April that the booking was made. 'Think I'll take a run over to London on the 27th, but do not broadcast to Australia please,' she wrote to Alice Henry.[70]

Arriving at Southampton on 8 May, she caught the boat-train to London, to be met by Mary Fullerton and taken back to the Fullerton–Singleton abode, an apartment at 181C High Street, Kensington, where she was invited to stay, and remained until September 1932. She was just in time to visit Lady Byles in hospital. Now very frail, Lady Byles died two months later on 19 July 1931, aged eighty-eight.[71]

Miles was not impressed to learn that Blackwood might postpone publication of *Back to Bool Bool* due to a depressed economy and, as S. Mills, responded that she had before her another new novel, 'a work of genius, outstripping any other novel circulating in its time and place'. (Probably it was 'Helen of the Headland' by Mary Fullerton.) However, the possibility of a German translation of *Ten Creeks Run* cheered her. And though Mary's refusal to polish her work or improve her typing skills irritated Miles, she had faith in her friend and was determined to help her.

According to her diary, by 13 July she had two manuscripts typed ready for Mills & Boon: Fullerton's 'Rufus Sterne' and Brent's 'Mrs Dysart Disappears'. Soon after, she experienced several all-too-prompt rejections from other London publishers.[72]

Of necessity, Miles was very focused in mid-1931, although she did find time to see numerous friends and associates. Aunt Lena was in Europe on a second overseas trip (but was in hospital in London when Miles arrived); Rolf Wahmann, a young German cousin, briefly visited; and she spent time over summer with the Meggitt sisters, Miss Hodge (whom she found very trying, due to Miss Hodge's obsession with losing her hair) and Miss Newcomb (now living separately). She also saw the Dresdens from America, and enjoyed an occasional jaunt about London 'on top o' bus' with Mary Fullerton (as vividly recounted in a letter to her mother dated 18 August). With the summer over, she was more or less fully occupied in August and September with work. The proofs of *Old Blastus* had arrived early in August from Cecil Palmer — 'to my horror', since she had only recently been advised by Lothian of this minor London publisher's readiness to publish and had yet to finalise the contract. No sooner had she finished with those pages than Blackwood sent the 'Bool Bool' proofs. Worse, she was running out of money, and the exchange rate was so poor it was doubtful whether she would receive more from home. Still, she managed to do a little writing on a tale about which nothing further is known, 'Tadpole', and other stories, and some reading. Interestingly, it was the novels of Thomas Hardy that appealed at this time, and a few nineteenth-century Australian novels, such as Ada Cambridge's *The Three Miss Kings*, Louis Becke's *By Reef and Palm*, and *Blood Tracks of the Bush* by Simpson Newland.[73]

Most exciting was a book exhibition at Australia House on the Strand. On learning that the English humorist A. P. Herbert was to open it, Miles wrote to him as Brent of Bin Bin, noting that no Australian writers appeared on the invitation. She was anxious to see if Brent's work was included, but was nonplussed to find *My Brilliant Career* in the middle of Henry Handel Richardson's showcase. On a later visit, however, she discovered both *Up the Country* and *Ten Creeks Run* prominently displayed. It was at the exhibition that she met the Victorian-born Henry Handel Richardson for the first time. Richardson's success with the Richard Mahony trilogy, completed in 1929 with the publication of *Ultima Thule*, had taken Miles' circle by surprise. Miles' Printed Books Collection contains the 1929 edition of *Ultima Thule*; and in May 1930, Brent told Nettie Palmer that he had carefully read all the volumes and rejoiced in Richardson's success, but was otherwise noncommittal.[74]

What did Miles really think of this formidable competitor's achievement? In essence, she thought Richardson's tragic tale of gold-rush Victoria was 'unAustralian', the unleavened product of a European imagination, appealing mostly to European readers. (It strongly appealed to American readers too.) The child of an older and more secure colonial culture in New South Wales, Miles had a point, though unable to articulate it, or the literary perspectives on which it relied. Her old mentor A. G. Stephens agreed, asserting that Richard Mahony was 'a morbid microscopic study'.[75]

Miles and Richardson were not temperamentally attuned. When on 26 February 1932 Kathleen Ussher took Miles to tea at Richardson's residence, 90 Regent's Park Road, Chalk Farm, the visit was not a success: Miles envied Richardson's creature comforts, and Richardson, willing but typically remote, perceived her guest as rather odd. (Miles liked the other guest, New Zealand novelist Jane Mander, whose *The Story of a New Zealand River* is thought to have inspired the film *The Piano*, much better.) Between the two Australian writers lay the chasm of Edwardian feminism and colonial nationalism. Although Miles could characterise Richardson's novels well enough, she could not really sympathise with them. Ultimately she thought Richardson was going in the wrong direction by highlighting Old World pessimism. Clearly, the literary purposes of the two writers differed markedly: whereas Richardson's Mahony was the wandering Everyman, Miles' characters are meant to be the settled children of Empire, distinctively Australian.[76]

Meeting Richardson was by no means the only notable event of October. Another was the British general election, which saw erstwhile Labour Prime Minister Ramsay MacDonald successfully head a coalition of conservatives and liberals to stabilise the recently devalued British pound in a time of financial crisis. 'Listened to election returns and heard the stampede back to the reactionaries,' reads Miles' disgusted diary entry of 27 October. The dream of a Liberal resurgence in Britain was thus over, and in Miles' sharp comment we may foresee an intensification of nationalist reaction to imperial constraints which became a hallmark of cultural life in Australia in the 1930s.

The very next day, 28 October 1931, in the *Publishers' Circular*, Blackwood announced *Back to Bool Bool* by 'the anonymous but already famous Australian author' Brent of Bin Bin, price 7s 6d net. Miles had been expecting it. Writing as Brent of Bin Bin from Blackwood's address to Nettie Palmer some time in October, she noted that 'it shd have been out today', adding that Brent had two more volumes ready if wanted. Brent was not always so circumspect. Early in September he informed P. R. Stephensen that his contribution to the coming field of fiction would be out soon, and later that month boldly sent a leaflet to Sir Otto Niemeyer, the Bank of England's adviser to the Australian government, hoping that *Back to Bool Bool* would help in a study 'of the cross-currents at work in our Empire'.[77]

Melbourne readers could be excused for thinking the book was already out. Mary Fullerton's puff for *Table Talk* appeared on 8 October, and a few days later in *All About Books* it was said, probably on the advice of Kathleen Ussher, to be arriving in Australia shortly. That was well ahead of time. There was welcoming doggerel in London in *Punch* in mid-November, but the published volume did not make it to Australia until December — Norman Franklin gave his mother a copy for Christmas — and it was too late to do well.[78]

Miles was annoyed at the poor timing. The reviews were slow over the holiday period, and when they did come they were rather mixed. Whereas British reviewers favoured the book's contemporary Australian outlook, Australian reviewers enjoyed the gusto with which people and place were portrayed. Some worried about a supposed absence of literary values. Expatriate characters' comments on some migrants as 'riff-raff' and worse caused one reviewer to remind Brent that his forebears had been immigrants too.

At 351 pages, *Back to Bool Bool* was the longest of Brent's novels, and arguably the most readable, due to its topical edge. It was strong on environmental degradation and suburbia, while Madame Astra, the diva, dreamed that 'art could become the fashion among the squattocracy'. Although its defence of the White Australia Policy has not stood the test of time, that was a widely approved position then. As for sex, Brent made an effort at modernity. The pivotal figure Freda Healey 'had always meant to satisfy [her] curiosity before [it was] too late ... [but when the major-general sought to seduce her] She did not want to surrender. *She did not know how!*' Instead she took refuge in 'the old bush chastity' and self-restraint, as approved by the *Bulletin*.[79]

On balance, the reception of *Back to Bool Bool* was positive. But somehow it lacked the bravura of its predecessors, and as the third and now final volume of a trilogy — it was stated in the Author's Note that one volume (unnamed) had been omitted for the sake of topicality, and this one is marked 'The End' — it did not quite succeed as a culminating creative achievement. Lower sales figures bear this out: it sold less than half the number of copies of *Ten Creeks Run*, and as late as 1937 sales had barely topped 1000 copies. Richardson, who had responded sympathetically to the earlier volumes, after reading a critical review in the *Times Literary Supplement* ('the whole atmosphere is falsified with affectations'), wondered if Brent was 'going dotty'. A. G. Stephens decided he was suffering from nervous fatigue.[80]

A thoughtful review appearing in the Adelaide journal *Desiderata* on 2 February 1932 pointed out that Australian readers have not always risen to the challenge of cultural criticism. Yet compared with the contemporary Canadian family saga writer Mazo de la Roche, for example, Brent was a radical voice. Indeed, as suggested by Drusilla Modjeska's approach in *Exiles at Home*, *Back to Bool Bool*'s discursive, multi-voiced exposition of the limitations of progress and development in 1920s Australia makes it the most interesting of all Brent's now neglected writings. It was easier for contemporaries such as Ussher and Stephens to appreciate Brent's grasp than it is now. Ussher, recycling an article on Brent's earlier volumes for the *Launceston Courier* in mid-1931, put it this way:

> Academic critics might dismiss them as an ingenious record of day-to-day events, but the more discerning will perceive here the born narrator, the gossiper, the eavesdropper, the teller of tales. Brent does not possess his subject. It possesses him. When he writes of the 'squatters' and the small selectors of the cattle regions of the Upper Murrumbidgee, the ruggedness of his theme takes control of his style, making it jerky and uneven, like the late work of Rodin …[81]

For Stephens, although *Back to Bool Bool* was unsatisfactory, the overall plan was spectacular, and the keynote of Australia well sustained: 'The author loves and praises his land and his people.' This understanding of the book held till the 1950s, as in Arthur Ashworth's overview in the Sydney literary journal *Southerly* in 1951 — after which time reviewers found it hard to say a good word about such a period piece.[82]

In any modern consideration of the trilogy, its imperial framework is inescapable. Drawing *Back to Bool Bool* to the attention of the Canadian-born British press baron Lord Beaverbrook, Brent suggested that literature was a potent force for bringing the Empire together; and further, that his great chronicle was a response to an earlier call from Beaverbrook's *Express* for writers to leave the pavements and lickspittles of London and go to the farthest ends of the Empire to write about real people. Ever hopeful, Brent added that the forthcoming 'Piccadilly's Pantaloons on the Hoof' (that is, *Gentlemen at Gyang Gyang*) was consonant with Beaverbrook's interest in wool, and would make a nice serial.[83]

Brent wrote as well to the editor of the London Labour newspaper the *Daily Herald* (from 1964 the *Sun*) in March 1932, urging him to read *Back to Bool Bool* for a balanced treatment of the sufferings of British migrants under closer settlement schemes and the negative reactions to imperial migration in Australia at the time:

> I have tried to be fair and fearless. It is my contribution to the solidarity of the British peoples which I have so much at heart.
>
> It would be a tragedy if the British family cannot enjoy that splendid (though capricious) land, where so much arduous pioneering had been done. It would be inexcusable if owing to family disagreements, outsiders should now take the plant so arduously wrought and reap the harvest of endeavour — people of lower standards of life and poorer ideals of political liberty than old Britain sends out.[84]

In Australia, speculation as to the real identity of Brent of Bin Bin was revived. The author again signed off from New South Wales, and the book was dedicated, boldly but obscurely:

> To M.F., but for whose loyalty and support this
> effort could not have thriven.
> To rare MSS., who nourished its inception.
> To D.C., who can keep a secret.
> To Others, to be mentioned later, or excused as
> they stay or betray the course.[85]

The initials, it is usually thought, refer to Mary Fullerton, Mollye Scott Shaw (Menken), and Dan Clyne.

A. G. Stephens thought the saga must be the work of a team of writers. And whereas Mary Gilmore thought it must be a man, others now detected a woman's voice. Miles remained the chief suspect. (When Mary Gilmore found out, she remarked that Miles had always been something of a practical joker.) 'Everyone loves a mystery,' observed 'Yorick' in the Perth *Daily News* on 10 September 1932, but asserted that when *Old Blastus* appeared there could be little doubt that Brent and Miles were one and the same — adding that all the books made jolly fine reading.[86]

The modulated response to *Back to Bool Bool* strengthened Miles' conviction that she had written an important book. This goes some way towards explaining what otherwise must be seen as her shameless plugging of Brent of Bin Bin and his achievements in the years to come. But for all the bravado, she was soon compelled to accept that she was not going to make money out of serious writing. The financial crisis in Australia, and in particular the closure of the Government Savings Bank of New South Wales in April 1931, meant small depositors like Susannah Franklin for a time had no liquidity, and whatever money Miles herself may have had in Australia was diminished in value by an unfavourable exchange rate; the devaluation of the British pound in August 1931 made it worse. New Australian tariffs on books published overseas further dented her prospects. In the second and barely legible of the two surviving letters to his daughter, written on 29 April 1931, John Maurice Franklin railed against 'the money power'. Like many others, Miles was attracted to social credit: 'The whole world is sitting like a lot of scared rabbits while there is a surplus of everything, even money. Only thing missing is logic,' Brent wrote to Mrs E. H. Stephens in faraway Basutoland (now Lesotho), adding that idealists were the only people with practical ideas.[87]

As usual, Miles Franklin's birthday — her 52nd — on 14 October 1931 passed without notice, except by her mother, who hoped she would have a happy day free from worry and taxes. A fortnight later, Susannah wrote that John Maurice Franklin was in hospital, having failed to pick up after a bout of winter bronchitis, but there was no cause for concern, it was only old age.[88]

She was too sanguine. Although John Franklin came home from hospital, he died soon after, aged eighty-three. While it was not entirely unexpected, the news distressed Miles. She felt 'as if the light had gone out'. In untitled verse written 'when Father died', she wondered if ''tis we who died'. His equanimity and unquestioning support over the years had meant much to her, and she learned her first political lessons from him. In later years she came to think of him as 'a spiritual genius' — which would seem to refer to his affinity with the land — and in a sense he had become a lodestar in her literary endeavours. She had tried to help during his last illness in September by arranging to forward money to be paid to her upon the publication of *Old Blastus of Bandicoot*, but it was never sent. In any event it was too late. Now he was gone. Friends, and associates such as Marjorie Chave Collisson, the Sydney University-educated lecturer and feminist, rallied round. Collisson took her to hear Gandhi, then in London (impressive but distasteful when speaking of the hungry multitudes in India who obviously did not practise any form of sexual self-restraint) and the famed Red Dean of London, W. R. Inge (far too academic and Oxbridge for Miles' liking).[89]

On 11 November, as S. Mills, Miles wrote to Blackwood, 'I may have to leave England any day now.' However, her cousin Annie May wrote after the funeral that Susannah had held up well, and had a woman companion until Christmas; neighbours also wrote reassuringly. Susannah herself wrote that if Miles was able to conduct her business better in England and was happy, there was no need for her to come home. It was not until her sister-in-law Eva wrote later that month that Miles learned Susannah had suffered a minor heart attack at home on 20 November, but by then Aunt Lena was on her way home.[90]

Miles threw herself into her work. It was pleasing to hear Blackwood had a reprint of *Up the Country* under way; and as S. Mills she busied herself on Mary Fullerton's behalf when Blackwood agreed to publish *Rufus Sterne*, on which Miles had worked hard earlier in the year. 'Please extend this writer the same splendid and impenetrable mantle of silence as has enveloped Brent of Bin Bin,' S. Mills wrote to Blackwood as she negotiated a pseudonym satisfactory to Mary. It was something, too, when on 12 November Cecil Palmer sent author's copies of *Old Blastus of Bandicoot*, the first novel to appear under Miles' own name since *Some Everyday Folk and Dawn* in 1909. When Eva Franklin told Miles' father about this just before he died, he asked if it was selling. But Miles herself always regarded it as a minor work, a useful diversion from Brent's greater task.[91]

Warmly welcomed when this *Opuscule of a Pioneer Tufted with Ragged Rhymes* appeared in Australia in 1932, under the imprint of William Lothian, as arranged with Cecil Palmer, the circumstances subsequent to publication were lamentable. Palmer was yet another casualty of the Depression, and most of the pages Miles repatriated at her own expense for yet another edition with Inky Stephensen were lost in a warehouse fire. Miles earned nothing. Palmer never paid the £20 that she was to receive on publication and had instructed him to send to her mother, presumably to help with her father's medical expenses. Surviving correspondence with Palmer and Lothian shows the incredible complexity of authorship as a small business. Miles Franklin conducted her affairs with competence, even flair, but the times were against her in 1931, just as they had been in 1914.[92]

Typically, she pressed on. She was still trying to find a publisher for 'Mrs Dysart Disappears' and for Fullerton's poems, and she managed to complete the mysterious 'Tadpole' story. Then in December she finished writing a genre novel, an English country house detective story — or parody thereof — called *Bring the Monkey*, which she described as 'a light novel' and no doubt hoped would sell.

There really was a monkey, a rhesus monkey called Peter, owned by Victorian-born Jean Hamilton, a vivacious redhead who had once worked in Elsie Belle Champion's Melbourne bookshop and subsequently became assistant to the Melbourne University anthropologist Professor Baldwin Spencer. Jean Hamilton had accompanied Spencer on his last, fatal field trip to Tierra del Fuego and supervised the burial of his remains at Punta Arenas in southern Argentina, after which she went on to London, where she worked for a time for Mabel Singleton and became a good friend of Miles Franklin. Miles was as captivated by the monkey as she was by its spirited owner, and seized upon the novelty for a 'potboiler'. Even allowing for fashion — Dorothy L. Sayers set the style — it was slight, but it was witty enough and it kept her busy. Come Christmas, a happy event at 181C, Peter the monkey was the star of the show. Miles' reward for helping Jean Hamilton prepare a lecture on Spencer's last days for delivery at Oxford in January would be the occasional sole care of the volatile creature.[93]

Miles was not yet ready to leave London, but it was a struggle to stay. On 2 January she had heard that her dear Uncle Theo Lampe had died soon after her father, and six weeks later, on 20 February, came 'the dreadful news' that her sister-in-law Eva had succumbed to cancer. 'I feel so desolated by the bereavements in my family since I left, but one must go on,' she wrote to Eva O'Sullivan in May 1932. 'I am aching to be home, and shall leave as soon as I put through things here. It is not easy in these days of financial stringency.' Fortunately, just before Christmas Miss Hodge had generously sent her £15, and Alice Henry lent her $50. But liquidity was always a problem. When she visited Ethel (Henry Handel) Richardson in February, she had 2s 6d to her name, and by April no money at all. The occasional pound note slipped into letters by her mother must have been a relief from reliance on the generosity of friends.[94]

Miles certainly was not earning anything from her writing. The *Gyang Gyang* manuscript went off to Blackwood in January, but nothing came of it, and Palmer's business was in receivership. A new manuscript, the 'Betty Belfrage novel', written full pelt in March and April 1932, which became 'Virgins out of Date' and survives in several typescripts, did no better. It seems to have gone to the publisher Gollancz and the literary agent Francis Jones, and then into an oblivion of failed offerings to await recycling as a play in the 1940s. Nor did Miles' stories and topical pieces fare well. Of several would-be press articles written in London in 1932, only one made it to print, and then belatedly. On 28 May, Miles and Mary attended a Lewis Carroll centenary exhibition at Bumpus' bookshop on Oxford Street, and by chance took tea with Alice Liddell, the original 'Alice in Wonderland', now a gracious old lady of eighty. The resulting article appeared in the Melbourne magazine *All About Books* shortly after Miles' return to Australia. A draft article on British manufactures (by 'Saddle Flap') and two London anecdotes (by 'Corroboree') from about this time survive in typescript, along with some Pacific sketches.[95]

Yet in one respect at least Miles was wonderfully well off. Having taken up residence at 181C with Mabel Singleton and Mary Fullerton, and with Jean Hamilton working for Mabel at the office below (Mabel ran a domestic help agency), she was with kindred spirits: 'We were a great quartette,' she recalled. In her study of their lives together, biographer Sylvia Martin has described the four women as 'passionate friends'. With Mary, she shared the literary life. With Mabel, it was the public pleasures of theatre and politics. With Jean Hamilton, it was the fun of things. 'I am glad you are so happy in your surroundings,' was how the practical but not imperceptive Susannah Franklin saw it.[96]

Even without money, Miles was able to enjoy many outings early in 1932: an Elizabeth Arden cosmetic show at Harrods; the Chelsea Flower Show; the waxworks (to see the image of airwoman Amelia Earhart); the annual rhododendron display at Kew Gardens; Highgate Cemetery; the Tower of London; and more. As well, tickets to shows materialised with surprising frequency, probably from Mabel Singleton's clients. Among other memorable experiences during those later London days, in November 1931 she heard the young Yehudi Menuhin play, and in May 1932 saw *Private Lives* by Noël Coward.[97]

There were also clubs and lectures to attend, as when Miles joined Marjorie Chave Collisson's Query Club, and dined at the Minerva. She even saw Mrs A.

one day, and with some reluctance attended a conference of the British Commonwealth League in April 1932, where she observed that the same few who had been struggling for the good of humanity when she was with them were still active, but looking older and without young ones coming on as far as she could see. She was not impressed by two Australian delegates, Melbourne's Dr Osborne and Sydney preacher Mrs Jamieson Williams, and in the evening was dragged along to a party held by the prominent Sydney feminist Ruby Rich, where she was saddened to find Dora Montefiore, a giant of the suffrage struggle in her youth, sitting alone and blind.[98]

In a series of lectures on Russian literature, then very topical, delivered by Prince Mirsky at the University of London early in the new year, Mirsky observed that people with something new to say often arrive at that position unconsciously, and alone. Miles heard him and was particularly taken with his description of the outcome — 'saturated prose'. In preceding years, to Blackwood and also in eloquent prefaces, Brent of Bin Bin had provided various justifications of his approach, extolling the yarn. Miles could not resist a letter to Mirsky in the character of Brent:

> Saturated prose. I went to Australia determined to present Australia from the inside — not from the outside as is done generally because by force of circumstances most Australian literati become a species of emigrés. I used the material at hand, and the idiom at hand. It was like building and furnishing a house without importing anything. I had no dictionary nor even an associate to consult acquainted with the meaning of a split infinitive. I deliberately eschewed references that might indicate how much I know of the classics, or Rudolf Steiner, or Einstein, or Job, or Jacob. The result is surely saturated prose.[99]

Of course this is a gloss on the creative process, as the research entered in Miles Franklin's literary notebooks clearly indicates. Not only did she love dictionaries, but also, as Brent told Nettie Palmer, he had noted phrases from some thirty-five writings of the times. Moreover, no one can be dissociated from intellectual influences. But Miles' gloss is sincere too, heartfelt even, as is the more evident from the second paragraph:

> I wrote to satisfy an overwhelming craving. I was nauseated with London pavement or drawing-room stories, hashed and re-hashed

about the theme of sex. My craving for primal forests, the divine loveliness of running water, of the view with no limits but eternity overcame me, the results you may read if so inclined.[100]

There is no record of Mirsky answering Brent's *apologia pro vita sua*, but it hardly matters. Mirsky's lecture had lifted Miles to a new level of perception.

It may seem that Miles' year of determined effort in London had been largely unrewarding. Thus Susannah wrote on 10 April 1932 that she was sorry Miles had failed to realise on her writings after working so hard, and not to wear herself out further if it was no good. But Miles hung in. After all, Australian books were like wild turkeys' eggs, left to hatch if they would; and even if she could not 'realise' on her writings, she had had not one but two novels come out in late 1931, with a third in limbo due to the collapse of Cecil Palmer.[101]

Evidently there was something more at stake than the fourth novel with which she had been associated in 1931, Fullerton's *Rufus Sterne*. This appeared in March 1932 under the pseudonym 'Robert Gray' with a dedication to Brent of Bin Bin, and Miles assiduously promoted it in correspondence. But *Rufus Sterne* provides a clue to what she meant. She arranged for Nettie Palmer to be sent a review copy and wrote to her as Brent of Bin Bin foreshadowing the novel as the work of a 'protégé' (Nettie's review noted it did not deal with life in Brent's large copious way but could develop, and that Brent would be an excellent guide). Further, on receipt of the publisher's circular for *Rufus Sterne* in February, as S. Mills, she grandly, if somewhat elliptically, outlined for the benefit of Blackwood Brent's role in the production of this poetic novel: 'Brent of Bin Bin has borne the expense of typing and editing this Australian school he has started, and his judgement was responsible for discovery [of Robert Gray].'[102]

So it emerges that by 1932, Miles Franklin hoped and believed that as Brent of Bin Bin she had founded an Australian literary school or tradition. This may take the reader by surprise; but Miles' confidence was up, and the reviews of Brent's book had been reassuring. Maybe the imperial curtain had lifted at last. As S. Mills, she was now urging Blackwood to reissue Joseph Furphy's *Such Is Life*, something his Melbourne standard-bearer Kate Baker had been urging her to arrange for almost two decades. To Baker, Brent wrote that he would be only too happy to write a preface (though this letter is undated and might refer to a later initiative).[103]

Miles' hopes and beliefs were not without basis. She had not missed the signs that Australian literature was rising, and in March 1932, writing under her own name, sought to respond to an exchange between Nettie Palmer and Hartley Grattan in the Brisbane *Saturday Night Telegraph* the previous year. Her contribution began boldly with a query as to why so many pseudonymous authors, including Brent of Bin Bin, were said to be her. The main point she wished to make was that Australian writers should turn isolation into an asset: just as Australia's innovations in social legislation had been an advantage when Miles first went abroad, with outlets in the daily press and greater financial support something similar could happen with literature. Unfortunately the *Telegraph* felt the subject was stale. Later, as Brent of Bin Bin, she offered a further comment, 'Blazing the Trail for Australian Literature', to *Blackwood's Magazine*, but without success. Here she argued that while Australian writers should not be confined to their own milieu, it was the bush that mattered artistically to Australian writing and for 'social health'.[104]

Meanwhile, her work was being promoted in the German-speaking world. In February 1932, the Austrian writer Helene Scheu-Riesz, the wife of a Viennese professor whom Miles had known in London, sent a copy of an article she had written for the Austrian *Neue Freie Presse* and a German syndicate entitled 'A Young Continent Seeks its Literature'. Madame Scheu-Riesz's article discussed four family histories from Australia — M. Barnard Eldershaw's *A House is Built* and the three Brent books — making reference to Thomas Mann's *Buddenbrooks* and praising Brent of Bin Bin for having written 'the great *Forsyte Saga* of his undiscovered literary country'.[105]

Miles was delighted. She had kept in touch with Helene Scheu-Riesz and had sent her a copy of *Back to Bool Bool* a month earlier in hope of a translation ('I deserve to be Brent's agent'). The prospects for translation were not bright, but she immediately sought to capitalise on the article, which Madame Scheu-Riesz reported in June had appeared in the syndicated paper but not so far in the *Neue Freie Presse*. Mab Maynard translated the article for her, and she contacted another acquaintance from Russell Square days, Dr A. W. Roeder, now a literature teacher near Marburg, who showed interest in the task of translating *Back to Bool Bool*. To Madame Scheu-Riesz, Miles wrote seeking off-prints and further links, enunciating also her aim and vision for Australian literature: 'we should strike out for ourselves, adapting classical forms to our new need and thus contribute something fresh to European fiction'. Soon after, she sent copies of Scheu-Riesz's article to Eva O'Sullivan with the suggestion that the Misses Barnard and Eldershaw might be interested, also to the *Bulletin,* and to Katharine Susannah Prichard in Perth, with whom a long and rich correspondence had begun in 1930 (though most of their surviving letters date from a decade later).[106]

On 18 March 1932 Miles Franklin wrote her first letter to Hartley Grattan in New York about his *Telegraph* exchange with Nettie Palmer, enclosing her response and a copy of *Old Blastus of Bandicoot* with the somewhat outrageous comment that she would have called it 'Old Barry of Bin Bin' but that Bin Bin had been used ahead of her. In a rare reference to Aboriginal culture at this time, she added that the name had several Aboriginal variants, such as *ban ban, ben ben, boon boon* and so on. In the correspondence that quickly evolved between the very able but rather prickly young man and his would-be mentor, Miles conceded that American readers had supported some Australian writers, but what she was talking about was a coming field of fiction, asserting that 'verisimilitude' would ultimately create a market (as it now has, through film especially). Unfazed by Grattan's view that *My Brilliant Career* was neurotic and *Old Blastus of Bandicoot* sentimental, she made arrangements to meet him in New York on her way home. He too would be part of 'the great literary adventure' now under way.[107]

Suddenly, the pieces seemed to fall into place. Just as one option closed — on 9 August she learned that the Melbourne *Herald* had declined to take her *Monkey* book as a serial (as the expatriate journalist Guy Innes had urged it to do) — another opened. Happily, as noted in her pocket diary, Miles had already signed an agreement with Inky Stephensen on 30 July for its publication by the publishing house he was planning to launch on return to Sydney in a few months' time (the contract does not survive, but presumably publication would be under Miles' own name). Oddly enough, it seems that although she had known Inky's wife, Winnie, in America and during her previous time in London through the Watsons, and in the guise of Brent had contacted Stephensen when *Back to Bool Bool* was imminent, she did not actually meet him until invited to tea by Kathleen Ussher on 3 July 1932, along with Ethel Richardson.[108]

For Miles Franklin it was an auspicious occasion. Jean Hamilton had them all to dinner soon afterwards (the meal cooked by 'a Jamaican black', Miles noted) and they talked about the publishing project. Miles was very excited. With Stephensen's recent experience as a quality publisher at

Mandrake Press in London, and with the backing of Norman Lindsay and the *Bulletin* in Sydney, a tremendous vista opened up. Did Inky mean it when he said she could be something in the new firm, she wondered. She saw him as an Australian publisher for Brent but Inky knew Miles only as the author of *My Brilliant Career*, which he would have loved to get his hands on. Miles liked this 'wild man of letters', and his plans for Australian literature were a timely complement to her own. Moreover, his letters to Brent were wonderfully encouraging, and 'the old brand BBB' loved his *Bushwhacker* stories.[109]

She reported these remarkable developments to Helene Scheu-Riesz in Vienna:

> I am still here, having postponed departure for a few weeks to discuss the new publishing venture in Australia. It looks very promising indeed. The managing Director is in London, himself the author of a little volume of short stories that are the real Australian thing. He has a first list of publications made out and in it — the only new novel so far [—] is one of mine that I mentioned you last letter. I meant it for a light thriller but Mr Stephensen … said it kept him up till 3 a.m. and is much, much more, that it contains sophisticated satire and humour to unusual degree. I am pleased about this and shall be in this venture.[110]

Compared with the exchanges between Brent of Bin Bin and Stephensen around this time, this was a restrained account. Stephensen assured Brent that every one of his books was a portent of the future and that the Australian nation would live forever in his characters, urging him to throw his lot in with the new publishing house: 'I implore you to consider the possibilities of your works reaching the post-war Australians quickly through publication by the lively Australian Publishing Firm we are establishing.' In return, Brent enthused: 'I have an accumulating pile of letters and articles on the need for a self-respecting Australian literature, which have been refused by the *Sydney Morning Herald* and similar journals … prophetic in view of what you want to do.'[111]

Miles as Brent went on to suggest negotiations with Blackwood, in order for Stephensen to gain access to Brent's published work — a proposal she soon regretted, fearing Blackwood might inadvertently blow her cover, but thankfully it came to nothing — and then listed 'stuff on hand', including the three still-unpublished volumes in the saga, 'Merlin of the Empiah' (*Prelude to Waking*), *Cockatoos* and *Gentlemen at Gyang Gyang*, three short stories, probably the *Tahiti* sketches; 'Three Little Tales of Shipboard Behaviour'; and several articles on Australian literary subjects, including *Such Is Life*, the Sydney novel *Jonah*, and Australian fiction in general. That is to say, she offered Stephensen almost all of Brent of Bin Bin's unpublished work over the previous five years, and even hinted at the secret of his identity (which Stephensen subsequently claimed to know, though he was always tactful to Miles). Miles also advised Kate Baker that Stephensen hoped to reissue *Such Is Life*.[112]

The Stephensens left for Sydney on the *Otranto* on 3 September 1932. Miles sailed for New York on the *Olympic* six days later, having spent her last days in London at Jean Hamilton's studio in Charlotte Street due to overcrowding at 181C, with Peter the monkey for company. (She sent her mother a cheap picture of them both 'for publicity', Susannah's expressed distaste for monkeys notwithstanding.) It rained heavily as she left, and she felt depressed at leaving Peter behind and the thought of nauseating sea travel.[113]

Once more Miles made the return trip to Australia via America. As usual there was no progress with publishers in New York, where she stayed with Margery Currey from 14 September until 10 October, again meeting old friends such as John Varney (who gave her a copy of his narrative poems *First Wounds*, published in 1926). Happily she also met the Grattans, and was alerted by Hartley to the importance of D. H. Lawrence's Australian novel, *Kangaroo*, first published in 1923. Miles also met Antoinette Donnelly (whose first name she had sometimes used in her Chicago writings) at a party. She later visited Donnelly, a famous beauty columnist, at Larchmont, and attended a Chicago newspaper women's luncheon with her. Whether Miles Franklin also met Margaret Robins is unclear, but she certainly did not get to the Robinses' home in Florida as once envisaged, due to the sudden disappearance of Raymond Robins (he was found three months later in North Carolina, possibly kidnapped by bootleggers or maybe suffering from amnesia).[114]

In retrospect, Miles felt she'd had a great time in the United States, but Margery Currey later deplored the non-response of New York publishers to her 'beautiful Australian epic' when forwarding a parcel of clothes (two dresses, for which Miles was grateful). On 10 October Currey saw her off from Grand Central Station. Her journey to Chicago involved a detour, and a poignant one, to Tecumseh, Michigan, where she spent two days with Editha Phelps. As with Lady Byles, Miles was just in time to see her old friend. Phelps was by then very ill. She died three months later, aged seventy-seven. Miles knew she would never see her again, but when the news came to her in Sydney that Editha had gone, it was hard to bear.[115]

In Chicago she was met and dined by Dr Young. Miles crammed a lot into the two-day stopover, including a league meeting at South Ashland Boulevard on arrival, and a visit with Agnes Nestor to the World's Fair site on South Side the next day, 14 October, her birthday. She also met up with old league associates like Frances Bird and Mary McDowell. It was 'a little bit of heaven' to see old chums, she said; but there were few enough left in the 'Windy City', and by now nothing in particular to hold her there longer.[116]

Late on Saturday, 15 October, she was away on the Santa Fe train to Los Angeles, arriving three days later, to be met by Kathleen Ussher's older sister, Lorna, a musician, and her husband Bruno, a music critic, also named Ussher. Quite a few of the old crowd had moved west, and during her eight days in California she met Emma Pischel and her mother, and Alice Henry, at Santa Barbara. Alice Henry noticed quite a change in Miles, and for the better: 'We had such a beautiful time with Stella Franklin,' she wrote to Margaret Robins subsequently. 'How she has matured and softened, and yet lost none of her brilliance. Her prospects too seem much better than they have been for a long time.'[117]

In San Francisco, Miles again stayed with Carrie Whelan, and then with Edith Malyon at Mill Valley. As in Chicago, she had a happy but brief time with her friends, before boarding the *Monowai* on Wednesday 26 September for the long trip to Sydney via Tahiti and New Zealand, a voyage of twenty-three days in all.

After an uneventful trip during which Miles was able to try out a new typewriter purchased in San Francisco on accumulated correspondence — over thirty items done before Tahiti — the *Monowai* docked at Darling Harbour in the early afternoon of Friday 18 November 1932. There were warships in the harbour, and disembarking was fraught. She evaded reporters by hiding in First Class, and when caught in Customs, refused to be interviewed: 'Rotters will never publish anything I write. How am I to live?' she wrote irritably. (The press did not catch up with her for several months, until *Bring the Monkey* was due to appear.) Nor was she cheered by the welcoming party on the dock at Darling Harbour: her mother, Aunt Lena and two local women, who had yet another death to report, this time of 'little Mary', possibly a neighbour's child. The diary entry continues 'Ghastly home coming'. Miss Gillespie was unwell too.[118]

Still, that very day a warmly welcoming article appeared in the Hurstville *Propeller*, doubtless the work of Miss Gillespie's friend Will Carter. It concluded with a paean of praise for *Old Blastus of Bandicoot*, released in Australia by Lothian in August — 'the local colour has the very glint of the gum-tips'; 'the reader feels he is out in the bush seated upon an old bleached stringy-bark log, which has long since shed its bark' — deeming it a fulfilment of the promise of *My Brilliant Career* all those years ago, and a timely marker of Miles Franklin's return to Australia.[119]

The current issue of *All About Books* carried a more substantial notice: 'A hearty, good-natured book, full of character and good writing, but not handled firmly enough,' was critic Furnley Maurice's friendly verdict. With unusual insight, Maurice noted that Mabel Barry, the disgraced elder daughter of Old Blastus, who bears an illegitimate child and becomes the family drudge, was the most impressive character. Nettie Palmer, who had responded in a balanced way to Miles' challenge regarding Australian authors' proclivity for pseudonyms in 1932, was also welcoming of 'a sprightly comedy'.[120]

With the excitement of a new novel by Miles Franklin, no one paid attention to Brent of Bin Bin. That suited Miles. She had no intention of revealing the truth 'until he finishes his series' — which basically meant until the publication of 'Merlin of the Empiah'/'Not The Tale Begun' (*Prelude to Waking*), *Cockatoos* and *Gentlemen at Gyang Gyang*. With little new work in the pipeline and few remunerative prospects, she was more than ever determined to protect her intellectual capital. Besides, she was still sure the mystery was good for sales.

The return of Miles Franklin with a new book to her name was a significant event. George Mackaness, a person of considerable pomposity, was quick off the mark with an invitation to address the Sydney Fellowship of Australian Writers (FAW) in late November, presumably at the welcome party arranged for P. R. Stephensen to report on his new publishing house. Miles politely declined, pleading exhaustion but offering her support for the cause. Maybe she anticipated a fresh round of questions about Brent of Bin Bin. She also had her own agenda: as she put it to Helene Scheu-Riesz during that letter-writing frenzy on the *Monowai*, 'I had a great time in the USA among literary critics and writers and journalists and [come] home inspired with the faith that Australia may be the coming fashion in fiction.' There was no time for retrospectives. Her *Monkey* book was revised and delivered to Stephensen on 13 December.[121]

Retrospectives were inevitable all the same, and useful, even to a forward-looking Miles Franklin. With advance notice of the Australian release of *Old Blastus of Bandicoot*, Nettie Palmer had published an impressive article on Australian writers in the *Illustrated Tasmanian Mail* entitled 'The "Olive Schreiner" of Australian Literature'. It began with the suggestion that South Africa was fortunate to have Schreiner's *The Story of an African Farm* (1883) as a fictional frontispiece: the novel was written with all Olive Schreiner's young powers and without a hint of colonialism. By contrast, Palmer wrote, it took a long time for Australian novelists to break through colonial attitudes, with Miles Franklin's *My Brilliant Career* (1901) one of the first and most emphatic moves. Franklin, Palmer noted, resembled Schreiner at least in that her book was written 'in girlhood and with passion', adding that although the novel appeared over thirty years earlier and had long been out of print, it had never been forgotten. 'She has always been a symbol,' Nettie said elsewhere. Recounting this to Hartley Grattan, Miles declared: 'I am tired of this symbol business and want now to assert myself as a natural fact.'[122]

PART IV

AUSTRALIA
January 1933–September 1954

11

'As a Natural Fact':
1933–1938

'My struggle was to express something of the life into which I was born.'[1]

With a population of 1.2 million in 1933, Sydney had overtaken Melbourne as Australia's largest city, and also boasted that first great symbol of Australian modernity, the Harbour Bridge, opened in March 1932. But the money was still in Melbourne and a Federal capital was only slowly being established on the limestone plains of Canberra, so that the harbour city had yet to attain the national pre-eminence it always secretly believed to be its rightful position. Although the populist Lang Labor government had been dismissed in mid-1932, recovery from the economic slump was not in sight, and the cultural scene in Sydney was paradoxical. For Miles Franklin, no longer young, to assert herself 'as a natural fact' in such circumstances would take some doing.[2]

First Miles had to make Sydney her own, just as she had previously done with Chicago and London. Although she already knew the city quite well, it was not until her return from London in the 1930s that she really lived in it. There had been the occasional trip from Goulburn as a girl, and she had been back and forth from Penrith many times when young. She had also glimpsed (with some distaste) its postwar modernisation on that first trip home in the 1920s; and after three and a half years of semi-seclusion in suburban Carlton, from 1927 to 1930, she had some tracks marked out already, mostly leading in 'to town'. Now, except for occasional trips up country, Sydney became her home.

Some of Miles Franklin's friends regretted that she was obliged to reside in the unprepossessing suburb of Carlton, and from time to time urged her to move. But if Miles was discontented with Carlton, she never said so. At least, as she put it to Hartley Grattan, 'I have plenty of food, a good roof and bed.' It was a functional location. The shops were adequate; Railway Parade boasted a picture theatre, the Carlton De Luxe; the postman brought the world to her as readily there as anywhere else in Sydney; and provided she could rustle up the fare, it was no more than half an hour by train from the city centre, via Central Station. Being unfashionably located even had its advantages. It protected her from the busybodies of the press, quarantined the flow of country relatives, and somewhat obscured her current status reduced to that of spinster-daughter-cum-housekeeper. (The telephone installed in 1934 would help with the last point, too, though not always effectively, as when Miles answered a call from fellow writer Marjorie Barnard in a pretend maid voice, to Barnard's understandable irritation.)[3]

Miles had not come home to do housework, though she had little choice about that, occasional home help notwithstanding. She had returned as an Australian writer, intending to make her presence felt. Thus on New Year's Day 1933, a Sunday, she set off to spend a couple of days with Norman and Rose Lindsay in the semi-bushland of Springwood in the lower Blue Mountains. The Stephensens were there too, and the recently incorporated publishing company was much discussed.[4]

Miles enjoyed these wild men of art and letters, so full of intellectual energy and, in Inky Stephensen's case, a roaring sort of charm. She didn't care for Lindsay's voluptuary art, but she greatly admired his novels, and she was delighted by his offer to do sketches for *Bring the Monkey*, deemed by him '"a delightful thing", [which] … made him laugh outright in many places'. And she had high hopes for their new national publishing house with its inspired name, the Endeavour Press (after Captain Cook's ship on his voyage of discovery). Correctly predicting that Norman and Inky would fall out when it came to coping with diverse manuscripts, she offered her services: 'You and Inky will grow weary of that publishing house without me. Yessir — remember you have been warned.' Her own problems, she said stoutly, had nothing to do with being female; they were entirely financial, due to lack of time to write.[5]

Thanks to Lindsay's influence, the Endeavour Press was set up as an adjunct of the *Bulletin*. This partnership was not quite what Miles and Inky had envisaged in London, and though seemingly an advantage, it would be a problem all too soon. But with Inky already ensconced in the *Bulletin* building at 252 George Street, and Lindsay's delectable *Saturdee* in hand, Miles felt the Press was away to a good start. Stephensen's list included not only her *Monkey* book, but also a new edition of Louis Stone's *Jonah* and, at Miles' urging, an Australian edition of the Tasmanian saga *Pageant* by G. B. Lancaster, published in London in 1933.[6]

Unfortunately Inky would overreach himself, and tiresome legal battles lay ahead. As early as March 1933 Miles pulled out, claiming that the *Bulletin* was 'a petrified affair'. However, publication of *Pageant*, she wrote to 'G. B. L.' (as Miles addressed her), was 'a great thing towards setting up real Australian publishing and getting authors free from a subordinate tacked-on position in London'.[7]

When *Bring the Monkey* appeared in May 1933, with its dedication to Jean Hamilton and Peter the monkey 'in memory of variegated and heartwarming experiences *London* 1932', it was a *succès d'estime*, but it sold poorly: 584 sales were reported by mid-1933, yielding a modest £8 11s in royalties. Reviewers were keen to welcome Miles Franklin home and to acknowledge the new publishing house; and while some expressed disappointment, most made an effort to understand the tone and setting of the thriller. The monkey's tricks were amusing, and the country house setting showed she had moved in sophisticated circles during the years away. But it was caviar to the general. Freda Barrymore, writing in the *Townsville Daily Bulletin* of 27 June 1933, thoroughly enjoyed the novel as a skit on modernity. It revealed a writer who had learned to say serious things in an amusing way, but she admitted it might be a bit 'highbrow'. Nettie Palmer, ever inclusive, underlined the point, stating that the detective story framework enclosed fragments of social satire and some illuminating social opinions; for example, that Australian tea parties were 'full of mis-placed deference to a title and free from any mental stimulation'. Was this so, Nettie wondered mildly. (Miles would later respond with some grim experiences of her own for Stephensen's short-lived magazine, *Australian Mercury*.)[8]

The explanation for limited sales was that although Miles had merely hoped to cash in on the craze for detective stories, with Jean Hamilton's monkey a nice novelty, she could not help going beyond the confines of the genre. The tale was edgy and up-to-the-minute, dealing with topics such as film-making and long aeroplane flights, and with shots at many of Miles' favourite English targets, such as effete males, cold houses and film plots, 'gathered together without the interference of an author'. But not too many

Australian readers would have got past characters with such names as Zarl Osterley (based on Jean Hamilton), the dazzling film star Ydonea Zaltuffrie, or the second son of Tattingwood Hall, the Hon. Cedd Ingwald Swithwulf Spillbeans, much less tolerate ex-RAF flier Jimmy Wengham, said to have crashed his sacred war machine during a commercial stunt.

In February 1933, before the release of *Bring the Monkey*, Miles had set her mind to arranging another visit by Hartley Grattan. (Grattan had accompanied his first wife, an actress, on a tour of Australia in 1927.) When they had met in New York the previous September, the opinionated young New York writer with a keen interest in both public affairs and Australia, and the older Australian writer who had experienced the Chicago culture in her young days had proved highly congenial. Miles had earlier contested his view of *My Brilliant Career* as 'an outburst of uncontrolled, neurotic energy', but, as she told Kate Baker, he had a proper idea of *Such Is Life*: 'I know Mr Grattan's estimate [of Furphy's book] and consider it his charter to speak on Australian literature.' Now, partly at her urging, partly due to hard times, Grattan was keen to return to Australia to write a big book along the lines of James Bryce's landmark study of *The American Commonwealth*, an exciting prospect.[9]

Miles raised the idea in early February with an exploratory letter to the FAW president George Mackaness, and soon after, Nettie Palmer began inquiries in Melbourne. Over the coming months, they approached everyone they could think of who might support and, more importantly, fund the visit. But, partly in the face of what Miles deemed 'the opulence' of Grattan's requirements, after a time the pair wilted. Whereas Grattan had supposed he would need £900 for the year (a vast sum to Miles' mind), and in that large American way imagined that lectures and a foundation could fund it all, Australians were not accustomed to paying for public lectures, or for that matter attending lectures on America, as proposed by Grattan; and there were no foundations. Moreover, although Melbourne seemed the more promising site at first, Nettie found that Grattan's radical opinions alarmed influential figures like Herbert Brookes, previously Australian Trade Commissioner to the United States. Miles made some progress in Sydney at the Workers' Educational Association (WEA) level but not at the university or the teachers' college, where Mackaness seemed preoccupied with Grattan's qualifications, nor with the press, where she found an unnamed leading newspaper editor 'embalmed in caution and fear of the present [economic] crisis'.[10]

By mid-1933 the two women were obliged to put the project on hold. 'We'll hatch little Grattan out presently,' Miles wrote to Nettie; but there things remained until 1935, when Grattan successfully applied for a Carnegie grant to visit in 1936 — as P. R. Stephensen always said he would have to. Meanwhile, Grattan widened his range of reference in a position with Harry Hopkins' Federal Emergency Relief Administration, and Miles did her best to maintain his interest with book news and hopeful suggestions: 'Australia is all ripe for a wonderful harvesting ... Someone from outside may be the leader. Why shd not an American publisher open a branch in Sydney and put you in charge? He wd have a chance of picking the best of the books fit to publish abroad, and Australia is a coming fictional fashion, make no mistake.'[11]

In response to Grattan's complaint that his Australian visit was slow to get off the ground, she added reassuringly: 'I know how you feel about the Australian venture being so stuffy to start, but I am glad you feel so. It shows I am not such a lone pelican ... presently you will come. It is my hope and desire that you shall. No outsider knows Australia (and few in) as you do ...'

That Australia was a coming field in fiction was a favourite theme of Miles' homecoming, along with her fervent and frequently expressed belief that the time had come to write the Australian story 'from within'.

She had already embarked on her own version. Late in January 1933 she left Sydney for a few weeks, travelling south through the Shoalhaven and on to her heartland. It was at Tallong, near Marulan, just north of Goulburn, where she stayed with relatives Edward and Maggie Bridle (the former a retired drover), that, according to her pocket diary, she noted the name for a new work, 'All That Swagger'. 'It came to me in a flash as just what I wanted while I was listening to an old drover telling me of his exploits. I could see the hardship and difficulties met with fortitude and resource, both gallant and pathetic, as the past came alive before me,' she later recalled. Based on the life of her paternal grandfather, Joseph Franklin, and the fate of Brindabella, after *My Brilliant Career*, *All that Swagger* is now Miles' best-known book. To Arthur Greening at Lothian she wrote excitedly, 'I have a big book in my head,' dealing with 'three generations of Australians.'[12]

Given that these days Miles was urging other writers to face the challenge of the present, it may seem surprising that she herself turned again to the past. One commentator has dismissed *All That Swagger* as a set of warmed-over family stories, a notably superficial view of the historical novel and its place in the making of Australian and other cultures at this time. In fact, Miles had not previously written about the Franklin side of her family.

Furthermore, the story came from deep within her, and was shaped as much by perceptions of the present as of the past. Nowhere is it stated, but it seems obvious now that the trigger for writing was her father's death, and that she seized upon the Franklin experience over time as the perfect vehicle for what she wanted to say about contemporary Australia, with its still-uncertain culture and fragile environment.

All That Swagger was the book she had to write. Her perspectives had been in place since the late 1920s. At that time she had written to Blackwood of a unique era, now passing, but still alive in the fifth and sixth generations of native-born white Australians: 'The first 130 years of British colonization in Australia involved a close touch with Nature which society may not experience again on such a primordial scale this side of Armageddon.' Moreover, most of her thinking about 'the Australian novel' had already been done in London. Now she began writing about her Australia 'from within', and it came quickly, with a rough draft finished in August and a first typescript by October 1933.[13]

Meantime, Brent had lapsed into silence. So far as Blackwood knew, William Blake was struggling with *Cockatoos*, and Mary Fullerton was told to say he was probably in the United States if they tried to sound her out. If 'Miss Mills' was after an advance mid-year when she advised Blackwood that Mr Blake was held up by lack of funds, she got the brush-off. Friends like the Stephensens and Grattan tactfully avoided the subject and others lost interest or simply suppressed it, as Nettie Palmer came to, remarking with some irritation that it was tiresome of Miles not to admit that a writer was known by his style (and, she might have added, his typewriter, since the letters Miles Franklin was now writing to her in her own name evidently came from the same machine as that used for the letters she had earlier written to Nettie as Brent). Miles, however, had by no means finished with Brent of Bin Bin. She'd merely set him aside, dealing with the occasional proddings with evasive élan. Mostly she just said Brent should be left to make his own announcements.[14]

There was a good attendance when on 10 June 1933 'the distinguished author Miles Franklin just back from abroad' addressed the Propeller Young Writers' League at the Strand Theatre at Hurstville on 'Literature and the Australian Outlook'. The league had been established by Miles' admirer Will Carter and the local newspaper in 1931 to encourage talent among the under-twenties. Miles spoke encouragingly to the young hopefuls, and urged them to be brave in the face of rejection; writing was a serious vocation, calling for dedication and sustained mental effort. The door was ajar to 'the [present] opportunity of creating our own literary background, and ... the most unique and magical material from which to fabricate it'. Miles confessed her fear of returning to something less than she had imagined after nearly twenty years in Britain, America and 'the Continent', but said she found herself enraptured. The challenge was not to imitate English writing but 'to prove ourselves worthy of its great traditions by adding to them and by enriching them'.[15]

She had already been among the distinguished writers invited to an evening party given by the FAW on 24 May 1933 — though a report of the event in *All About Books* which referred to her as 'our novelist just returned from eight years' sojourn in America' implied some people had only a vague idea who she was. In fact, as befitted her trade union experience, she had now joined the FAW, which met regularly at the School of Arts, Pitt Street, though it seems meetings were not very stimulating in the early 1930s. (Jean Devanny, a feisty communist writer from New Zealand, refused to join because it was too conservative.)[16]

This conservatism may be gauged from Miles' experience in late 1933 of a debate on the topical question of 'The Feminisation of Literature'. Putting the women's case on 20 September, she said that although women were doing better since the war, they were still underdogs when it came to editorial chairs, top journalistic jobs, and of course income. The fact that women were now writing more freely meant that the old distinction between men's and women's novels had gone: men had discovered that women were not puppets. Characteristically, she asserted that what was important was 'spiritual independence', sincerity and self-respect. A month later, the men spoke: 'terrible — pre-suffragette', she wrote in her diary. Elaborating to Grattan a week later, she excused Frank Dalby Davison, 'a nice man and he had a thought'; otherwise the speakers were 'trivial, offensive and weak', their arguments on the level of 'a whistling woman and a crowing hen'; that is, in the words of the proverb, 'neither fit for God nor men'. 'Think of me among that stuff and no one but myself to feel the mental disgrace of it,' she wrote.[17]

It was not until political conflict arose the following year over censorship, and the visit of the banned Czech communist writer Egon Kisch, in Australia to support the Movement Against War and Fascism, that things improved. Miles was to the fore when younger members called on the FAW to take a stand on Australia's severe censorship laws in April 1934, and when in November Stephensen and others ousted the FAW president George Mackaness, due to Mackaness' objection to Kisch's attendance at a literary luncheon at the Wentworth Hotel for the visiting English poet laureate John Masefield, she supported them. (Mackaness was replaced as president *pro tem* by the journalist Tom Inglis Moore and then by the dynamic Flora Eldershaw.) Because Miles was still in touch with Madame Scheu-Riesz in Vienna and knew about what was going on in Germany from her friend Lute Drummond, the opera coach, the doziness of Sydney in the face of world crisis was hard to take.[18]

Returning had not been easy. As she would express it to Kate Baker: 'You speak of loneliness. Everyone must be lonely after a certain point: the lack is of congenials up to that certain point, which cd be avoided were one in a position to make the necessary contacts.' Contacts, however, take time, and for a while at least the friendships Miles maintained by mail, as with Mary Fullerton and more recently with Hartley Grattan, were more sustaining than organisations of writers.[19]

The letters between Miles Franklin and Hartley Grattan in 1933 add a critical edge to Miles' experience of return. Grattan did not hesitate to challenge her thinking, and this she valued, though she sometimes had difficulty in responding to his firmly expressed views, for example, on the now infamous White Australia Policy. In his writings Grattan recognised that it was 'a racial and economic policy of enormous emotional content making it possible to use white labour in the tropics', but this did not significantly diminish his distaste for it, as he explained privately to Miles: 'I don't, as you guessed, sympathize much with the policy, think it mistaken economically and socially. Also I don't find the U.S. as horrifying racially as Australians seem to ... in Australia I am always a bit upset by the predominance of wizened up British types!'[20]

Miles felt much the same about 'wizened up British types', and she understood his American perspective. But how was she to respond? The White Australia Policy was supported by both sides of politics as, in the words of historian W. K. Hancock in his 1930 classic *Australia*, 'the indispensable condition of every other policy'. Moreover, as Hancock also remarked, it was unreasonable to maintain that the policy was based on loftier grounds than those observed by Grattan.[21]

Protesting that 'you can't bring in a backward (if we must not say inferior) breed of semi-slaves without having the problems so profuse in history', the best Miles could say was that things could change. The currently collapsing world economy needed reorganisation, and a mingling of Asiatic and European types might well make a splendid race eventually. In the meantime, hard-won working conditions should not be undermined by indiscriminate immigration: 'What are we to do after striving for conditions above starvation level?' she asked. Even southern Mediterranean immigration worried Miles in that regard (as it did many people in the interwar years).[22]

Startled, Grattan responded that it was difficult to disentangle racial prejudice and economic fears, something most Australians were far from ready to do at the time. The exclusionary provisions created by the Immigration Restriction Act of 1901 remained firmly in place, and the White Australia Policy would not be seriously challenged until the late 1950s. That is to say, despite a perceptible widening of diplomatic engagement with the region, there would be no new approaches until after Miles' death. Moreover, serious criticisms of the policy which may have impressed her were yet to come. Although she countered Grattan that she thought no one racially inferior, too often it sounded as if she did, and increasingly so as world events prompted more strident and careless expressions of her views on immigration. At least Grattan made her think about the issues, as she had not done since Chicago days.[23]

Grattan also encouraged her work. This may not seem so remarkable, but enough has been written of the unthinking sexism in Australian culture in the interwar years, and the way women writers coped with it, to mark him out as unusual. His enjoyment of her quicksilver personality is evident from the beginning, and he sympathised with her circumstances as a writer: 'I hope your remarks about domesticity do not mean that you are neglecting your proper work. It is only by production that the battle can be won,' he would write robustly.[24]

The puzzle now seems not so much how Miles Franklin managed to maintain a writerly life in such a context — as Drusilla Modjeska first showed in *Exiles at Home* (1981), most women writers in Australia at this time ran houses in the suburbs and cared for variously constituted families, and Miles has left a record in her pocket diaries of how she did it day by day, down to mowing the grass — but rather, where she got the money to purchase typing paper and pay for postage on her correspondence, and how she found room to store it all in her mother's crowded cottage. She could no longer afford an office, and her ever expanding archive contained numerous unpublished manuscripts (among which she reportedly found 'the sequel to *My Brilliant Career*' in mid-1933).[25]

Just how crowded it was at 26 Grey Street is clear from a significant happening of late 1933. On 11 September the 76-year-old Alice Henry arrived in Sydney from Los Angeles on the *Monterey*. She was en route to Melbourne, returning to Australia for good, like Miles really, and likewise out of sheer financial necessity, but much later in life. Miles and Aunt Lena collected her from the dock and took her to Carlton, where she stayed for a month. With Susannah and Susannah's friend from Penrith days Louie Somerville, Aunt Lena and Miles already there, there were now five in a cottage with three small bedrooms and a glassed-in verandah at the back. As well, Miles' brother Norman and his son, her nephew Jack, were often there on weekends. Numerous callers included dear dead Linda's husband, Charles Graham, who had remarried in 1909 and remained in Queensland, but Miles apparently gave him short shrift, possibly due to a family dispute now hard to fathom, related to Linda's son, Ted, or simply because the cottage was already crowded. John Franklin's old associate Dan Clyne also called in on Sundays. No wonder Miles railed against endless hospitality in *All That Swagger*. Marjorie Barnard benignly described the situation as 'a homestead in the suburbs', but Nettie Palmer came to think Miles overdid the hospitality, at least after her mother's death.[26]

Fortunately for Miles, most of the household went out much of the time, and Alice Henry was no trouble. Miles took her old friend to the FAW where she contributed a characteristically calm but challenging perspective to the feminisation debate ('We are still climbing a hill, and a hill with many steep slopes'), and one long weekend Alice went to stay with the Griffins at Castlecrag. Yet one senses Miles' relief at her departure for Melbourne on 11 October: 'Mother and I put Miss Henry on board *Mariposa* and then went to lawyer and optician and newsreel. Lunch at David Jones [department store] and home at 3.45. *Tosca* on radio at night.'[27]

Nonetheless, the Franklins were ever country gentlefolk, and Miles was 'a lady'. The Sydney historian Ken Cable could recall as a boy visiting relatives next door at Carlton but he never knew that 'Miss Franklin' was the writer Miles Franklin. The house might have been bursting at the seams, but appearances were kept up and a gleaming-floored respectability ruled.[28]

Miles recorded no response to Alice Henry's return to Australia. Their partnership had been so productive in Chicago, although Miles' years in London had put that a long way back. But they never lost touch, and Alice continued to support Miles' literary work. Miles was, she said about this time, 'a most unusual and gifted person'. Maybe Miles had enough to worry about with her increasingly demented mother, or she was reassured by the thought that Alice was returning to the care of her much-loved brother, Alfred, and his wife, Jean, in Melbourne. Alternatively, Alice Henry was divided about returning and, arriving so soon after Miles, aroused difficult feelings.[29]

Miles was also keen to get on with her work. Soon after Alice's departure she finished typing a first version of *All That Swagger*. She had already found a niche as a book reviewer, though no one would have known it, due to a flurry of pseudonyms, such as the jokey 'M. Seednuts' and 'Vernacular', the latter first used in 1905. If proof were needed that many novels fall by the wayside, Miles' reviews of twenty-odd mostly forgotten titles over the short life of the New South Wales Bookstall's 'magazine for the booklover', *Book News*, with which Inky Stephensen was probably associated, and the longer-lasting *All About Books*, will serve. Angela Thirkell's novel *Ankle Deep*, deemed to have been compiled in accordance with the *kennel amours* recipe, clearly irritated her — and only one of the titles, *Desert Saga*, by William Hatfield, is likely to be of interest now. The life of a freelance reviewer is a precarious one, however. In 1934 only one item appeared, 'The Prospects for Australian Literature', in *Stephensen's Circular*, reprinted in the *Catholic Women's Review*. Typically, Stephensen never paid the three guinea fee promised, leaving Miles without money even for fares.[30]

Somehow Miles was able to keep a straight course. Self-protective to a degree people still find incomprehensible, she pressed on. December saw her take another trip to Marulan, and make a start on the road to the publication of *All That Swagger*, sending a typescript to Jean Hamilton as her unofficial agent in London. Surprisingly, the ever supportive Mary Fullerton was left out of this new venture, seemingly because Miles mistrusted Mabel Singleton's capacity to keep a secret. (She probably feared that if word of the impending novel somehow reached Blackwood, the remaining Brent manuscripts would be jeopardised.) Sometimes she would write to all three ('My dearest ducks, Virginia [that is, Mabel], Jean, Mary', begins one such letter). But by now, secrecy about her work was almost second nature, and with Jean Hamilton a willing accomplice, it was not hard to maintain another little mystery in London.[31]

After a trip to Queanbeyan at the start of 1934, where she stayed with relatives and visited Yass cemetery, Miles was back at the typewriter. 'I fear my fate will be the beetle with its ball of dung in *Story of an African Farm*,' she wrote gloomily to Hamilton in February, and to Fullerton that she was exhausted. She really needed help with her ever more demanding mother. Numerous gaps in her diary in February, and throughout the year, are testimony to the strain.[32]

Two new novels sustained her spirits: an American blockbuster *Anthony Adverse* by Hervey Allen and a manuscript by Xavier Herbert called 'Capricornia', which Inky gave her to read in March. Here were writings of the kind Miles delighted in — big, bold and realistic. Allen's mammoth historical novel set in the Napoleonic era confirmed her assumptions: 'There is no escape from the frame of reality.' 'Capricornia', she told Mary Fullerton, was 'very lively reporting — and frank about the half-caste situation in North Australia, and shows how the poor blacks are treated and makes them loveable. It shd be very controversial and sell immensely.'[33]

Inky certainly needed some good fortune. Although Miles deplored the commercial decisions he was obliged to make to keep his publishing company afloat, and expended emotional energy on his weak and isolated wife, Winifred, she still admired his vision and style. She also hoped he would publish *All That Swagger*, which she asked Alice Henry and also Ada Holman to read in late March.

Then suddenly she was off to Queensland as a travelling companion for Uncle Gus Lampe's younger daughter, Metta. 'I have always wanted to see Bourke and beyond,' she exulted, and Uncle Gus was paying. Miles left Sydney by train on 5 April to join Metta at Narromine the next day. Two days later, having travelled via Nyngan, Bourke and up the Warrego River to Cunnamulla, they arrived at Charleville, where they spent 'a delightful week' at the recently built Hotel Charleville. There Miles met the local newspaper editor, before she and Metta pressed on to Taylor's Plains, arriving on 17 April after a journey of some 780 miles (1260 kilometres). At Taylor's Plains, a pastoral holding north-east of Mungallala on the Brisbane line, they were, according to the Brisbane *Courier-Mail*, the guests of Mrs Roland Statham, a schoolfriend of Metta's sister, Thelma. Unfortunately neither letters nor diary entries cast much light on Miles' time in central Queensland, except for references to mustering at Taylor's Plains and the unlikely and impractical gift of an echidna. There is only an unrevealing sliver of literary evidence: an incomplete, unpublished sketch, 'La Ville de Ma Tante' by 'Young Bill' and a few lively pages in Miles' co-authored sesquicentenary satire, *Pioneers on Parade*.[34]

Taking the alternative route home via Brisbane, she had a day to prowl about the subtropical city, lunching with Yass-born Firmin McKinnon, editor of the *Courier-Mail*, and his wife, Emmie, another journalist, who failed to smoke her out as Brent. A woman journalist from Brisbane's *Telegraph* also tried unavailingly to get a line on Brent, but to Miles' subsequent relief wrote the interview up in a bland manner. It was Miles' only experience of Brisbane, and although it rained, she enjoyed herself visiting the Art Gallery and eating custard apples.[35]

After a pleasurable five weeks away, she returned to Sydney by crowded overnight train from Brisbane on Friday 11 May. To Jean Hamilton she wrote, 'I love the far out places. Out there one sees what an incredible feat Australia is' — a phrase which reappears at the end of *All That Swagger* and in Miles' World War II journalism.[36]

Among the letters awaiting her return was a positive response to the *All That Swagger* manuscript from Alice Henry. Miles' relieved reply to 'Dearest Pops' reflects on her interest in the passage of generations, and comments on the secrecy surrounding the new novel: 'I have not divulged my attempts because I expect no quarter … [people] always expect the writer to have written something else. If you knew what I have suffered from that!'[37]

To Mary Fullerton, Miles reported that authors were now paying Stephensen to publish their work, and the books were mostly tripe. An exception was Eleanor Dark's startling eugenical novel *Prelude to Christopher*, which Miles liked as much as the manuscript of 'Capricornia' and reviewed for the *Australian Mercury* as a brilliant modern novel (though written without her own experience of 'alienists' and reformers). But she was still unable to make progress with Mary Fullerton's poems. When she took some of her 'pets' in to 'old Forsythe' at Dymocks bookstore in the city, he patronised her, and later treated her as if she was some disreputable acquaintance, saying dismissively there was no money in poems. It was a pity, she wrote, that the passes were so tightly held.[38]

Brent's identity continued to attract speculation. Some thought he might be the Queensland-born William Baylebridge, a dilettante poet living in Sydney, and, being rich, the great hope of Inky Stephensen. 'Well I have met Brent of Bin Bin,' Miles wrote gleefully to Jean, Mary and Mabel on 8 June, having encountered Baylebridge with Inky in a city café the previous day. He seemed like an antipodean Horatio Bottomley, at least at first, all wind and roaring, and Miles had fun with him. It pleased her to report that Brent could still keep even experienced male writers guessing, and gullible. After much talk, Baylebridge confessed that she was not as he had expected, because of the 'pungent virility' of her writing. 'Huh!' said Miles, recognising an implied transgression of the male terrain. 'Had I been young he would have fobbed me off with a "virile" platitude about my glorious eyes and my long lashes, but as I was middle aged he cd not forgive me for anything.'[39]

Miles was in fact fifty-five, and Baylebridge fifty-two. Obviously she had more presence than she realised. Interestingly she got to like Baylebridge, a tall, reclusive man who never married, as she saw he was serious about his work — she had a nineteenth-century romantic's view that poetry was the ultimate art. His exalted ideas doubtless influenced Stephensen, who was at that time publishing an important essay on the recently deceased Sydney symbolist poet Christopher Brennan by Randolph Hughes, a Right-wing expatriate scholar lecturing at the University of London. (How interesting it would be to know what Miles and Inky said as they sat by that wonderful new cultural landmark, the Archibald Fountain, one evening later in the year discussing Hughes' essay, diametrically opposed to their values but impressive on its own terms.) Some strange currents were flowing at this time, and Miles did not always cope well with new directions; for example, she hardly knew what to make of Gertrude Stein, and was shocked to hear from Mary Fullerton that Walt Whitman had been homosexual.[40]

Less than six weeks after her return from Queensland, Miles Franklin set off for Melbourne, where she had literary business. Between 20 June and 13 July she stayed first with Maud Walsöe at 276 Domain Road, South Yarra, then with the Goldsteins at 462 Punt Road, and finally with Mary Fullerton's sisters at Hawthorn. Her first day was spent in town with Miss Henry but, she later told Mary Fullerton, either Miss Henry had deteriorated with age or she had completely outgrown her. Attempts to meet Nettie Palmer and her husband, Vance, a leading Australian writer and cultural commentator, then living in the Dandenongs, failed. She read 'a bush sketch' to the Fullertons (actually a slab from *All That Swagger*, but she did not want to risk news of that getting back to London), and called on booksellers. Maybe she tried to promote Brent in Melbourne, but a concurrent approach as Miss Mills through Jean Hamilton to the *Australian Journal* on Swanston Street regarding serial rights to Brent's stories met with refusal.[41]

Back in Sydney, Miles tried to write a play entitled 'Clive's Wife' (later entitled 'Claud's Wife'). She went to the Mitchell Library and read Leonard

Mann's *Flesh in Armour* and later Catherine Helen Spence's *The Author's Daughter*; and she made the most of the available entertainments: concerts in the Town Hall, movies and newsreels at the State Theatrette, the Art Gallery. However, home and family duties took much of her time. When Maggie and Edward Bridle came up from Marulan for Edward's health towards the end of the year, she looked after them as well.

Miles often went to the newsreels, which, in those days before television news, kept her up to date, along with letters and journals sent by friends. She was missing London, and aware of her intellectual isolation. The letters to Fullerton and others are full of it, raging at the effects of distance on her fellow Australians. That correspondence, mostly with Mary but also with Mabel Singleton and Jean Hamilton, and occasionally all three of them, kept her going through the drear patches. Sometimes her letters to Mary Fullerton ran to four closely typed pages, mostly on literary topics; and Mary, who wrote in hand, was similarly lavish.

Inky Stephensen continued to worry Miles. Whether or not he really intended to publish *All That Swagger*, he had no qualms publishing the Queensland-born journalist Brian Penton's *The Landtakers* in 1934, a black Queensland version of Australian foundation myths and a competitor in the historical novel field. In 1935 Stephensen would become involved in a complex and tedious court case over Penton's critical review of a lesser Stephensen publication, *Mezzomorto* by Vivian Crockett, which Crockett successfully charged was defamatory, winning £1000 in damages from the *Bulletin*. Miles seriously disliked Penton, as she disliked all the 'boho' types on 'the heights of Darlinghurst' (she called them the Parnassians), and she thought his book brutal; but it is unlikely she approved the publication of Crockett's book either, in which an Australian squatter undergoes an experiment with a Viennese specialist out of a desire for romance which his own country cannot satisfy. Of greater concern to Miles, though, was the suspicion that Stephensen was already on the rocks financially. By the end of 1934, she had accepted that he was 'a dead-end'.[42]

In 1934 Miles Franklin voted Social Credit in the federal election, along with other progressives and radicals in New South Wales. It was, she said, her protest against antediluvians, 'the whole tribe of Noah's Ark'. Some of her old American colleagues were now in Roosevelt's New Deal administration, but she had nothing hopeful to report to them, writing that she could detect no leader emerging in Australia 'to make a new pattern in the prevailing stagnation and confusion'; and she lamented that a ghastly conservatism had taken hold, especially in Victoria, then celebrating its centenary with the aid of the Duke of Gloucester. Royalty was more important than God in the British Dominions, she wrote tartly: 'One could blaspheme God without much notice being taken, but a word of criticism of a royal prince wd put one in an unpleasant light.'[43]

In November she was at the Domain to hear Egon Kisch when the Reverend Albert Rivett, a doughty campaigner for peace, suffered a heart attack and died. Though declaring herself anti-war as well as anti-snob and anti-imperialist, spiritually she felt overcome. Commiserating with Jean Hamilton on the loss of her father, she wrote, 'I shall never cease to miss my father. He was wonderful. Life gave him nothing, but he was never spiritually defeated, as I am.' Arthur Greening at Lothian had already reported in December 1933 that *Old Blastus of Bandicoot* had been a great disappointment to the publisher — Nettie Palmer told Miles that readers were repelled by him. Moreover, she was no further ahead with *All That Swagger*, due probably to Inky. She entered the manuscript in the Melbourne Centenary Prize competition, but without success; and when over tea at the Hotel Australia at year's end she offered a copy of the typescript to the visiting British publisher Jonathan Cape, he was noncommittal, suggesting only that she might send any revised version to London.[44]

As usual, letters sustained her spirits. At least 150 items of personal correspondence survive for 1935, as it happens the year in which regular airmail services between the Australian state capitals and London began (though cost probably precluded frequent use). This number is not perhaps exceptional at a time when everyone wrote and received letters, and not many for Miles (there are approaching 400 items preserved for 1936). What is exceptional is that she kept so many of those she received, along with carbon copies of her replies, which she filed according to the name of the writer. Clearly Miles Franklin's office skills carried over to her personal life, which was also a professional life and a small business conducted from home.[45]

Her letters went far and wide. In 1935 she corresponded with some forty-five people, in most Australian capitals, London, the United States and India, as well as family in rural New South Wales, such as Aunt Annie at Queanbeyan and Uncle Gus at Peak Hill, and her nephew Jack, who completed schooling as a boarder at Blue Mountains Grammar School, then located at Springwood. Some were old friends and longstanding correspondents, such as the Goldstein sisters in Melbourne, or enduring associates like the increasingly needy Alice

Henry, or emotional mainstays of the period like Mary Fullerton (to whom Miles wrote, probably in early 1935, 'I so live for your letters'). Others were fellow writers, usually locals and one-off correspondents, or of particular moment, such as Walter Burley Griffin, gone from Castlecrag to work in Lucknow, India, and the Melbourne journalist Guy Innes, a friend of Jean Hamilton, whom they both thought an appalling snob but possibly useful.[46]

Other letters mark the beginning of heartening new associations, as with the Anglican Bishop of Goulburn, Bishop Burgmann, a big bush-bred cleric Miles first heard preaching at the liberal Anglican church of St James', adjacent to Hyde Park in central Sydney in mid-1935: 'I had heard that you were truly Australian,' her first letter to the bishop notes. 'How I wish that when young and seeking there could have been someone like you to whom I could have gone instead of the Canon who was then in charge of the [Goulburn] Cathedral and my spiritual obstruction.' Through the post Miles also learned of inevitable losses, as when she heard from America of the death of the esteemed Chicago progressive Anna Ickes, and the last days of Jane Addams from the Robinses.[47]

Each year would produce its own epistolatory kaleidoscope, with new lights compensating for recently darkened spots, while the absolute size of the archive grew. In the end there would be at least 10,000 items, mostly accumulated after Miles' return to Australia, from 1000 or more correspondents.[48]

Miles was increasingly concerned about the past as well as the future of Australian literature, and her own place in it. Late in 1934 she had contributed an appreciation of Tom Collins (Furphy's pen-name) to a celebration of Joseph Furphy's ninety-first birthday at Yarra Glen in Victoria, organised by Kate Baker, and in 1935, again prompted by Baker (and also Nettie Palmer), she tried to promote something similar in Sydney for A. G. Stephens, whose death in 1933 had passed unnoticed by the Bulletin's 'Red Page'. Likewise, early in 1936 she would attend a ceremony at Wentworth Falls in the Blue Mountains to mark the spot where Charles Darwin had paused on his only inland trip in Australia a century before, and later that year she would begin speaking up for the nineteenth-century South Australian writer Catherine Helen Spence.[49]

Partly it was her age that made her more historically minded. It was also the peculiar cultural situation in which she found herself. In the interwar years, the forces of modernism made more headway in Sydney's 'sea coast of Bohemia' than elsewhere in Australia. Yet with all roads from the depressed hinterlands leading to Sydney, there were plenty of keen (though less well documented) advocates of an Australian bush culture too. The result was 'a conflict of opposites', with ideological and class tensions tending to cancel one another out and little space left for the idea of a national literary culture. Moreover, the whole scene was blighted by heavy censorship and ongoing expatriatism. (Miles thought with some justice that she and Stephensen were exceptional just because they had come home.) There was a post-colonial intelligentsia in Sydney, but support was limited outside journalism; and with only one small and poorly funded state university, it soon became clear that allies in the project to secure a new field for fiction were few. Miles believed that the future of Australian literature was unlimited, and that a distinctive technique, the 'yarn', was being established, but that the lines were simplistically drawn between those committed to the 'gum tree' school and those who felt themselves above and beyond it. As she rightly observed, unlike the English oak, the alphabet of the eucalypt was hardly known.[50]

Nonetheless, although it was not a red-letter year for Miles, 1935 saw her profile rise. In an article on Australian women writers published during Authors' Week in April she was said to be one of the pioneers still doing good work, and she remained to the fore in the campaign against censorship, asserting at a meeting called by the newly formed Left-wing Writers' League that same month that 'if the world were made safe for fools, it wd soon be fit for nothing else'. While the FAW-sponsored Authors' Week irritated her, especially when she was patronised by 'would-be society women' and found that books published overseas, as with Brent, were not on display, she pitched in with a talk on 'Novels of the Bush', delivered at the Blaxland Galleries and broadcast over 2BL. Even Brent seemed to have become part of the scene, as when P. R. Stephensen turned up at the Authors' Ball as Brent of Bin Bin, with Winnie as one of Brent's characters, Mrs Mazere. (Unfortunately Miles was not there to appreciate the joke.)[51]

In May 1935 Miles was awarded a King's Silver Jubilee medal, which she graciously accepted with words commending the New South Wales Governor's support for Australian writing and stressing the importance of a vigorous and distinctive national literature. The award took her by surprise, and the family was unimpressed, except for her cousin Metta at Peak Hill, who sent congratulations to the only member of 'the tribe' to be honoured. Miles still didn't think much of the local literary societies, but she was probably nominated by one of them, and they sought her out, for instance to address the Junior Literary Society and as a judge of plays at the Savoy Theatre in mid-1935. Such occasions enabled her to promote her ideas. Well aware that 'we are roughly divided between those who are satisfied with the gum tree school … and those who are bored to the eyes with it', in her talks she drew attention to largely forgotten writers such as the recently deceased expatriate Rosa Praed, and in public statements emphasised the material circumstances of authors and the 'hegira of talent' as underlying issues. Later in the year, after the FAW came under the leadership of Flora Eldershaw, she prepared a blast on the parlous situation of Australian writers, 'Amateurs but Proletarians: Peculiar Predicament of Australian Literati', which appeared in the *Writers' Annual 1936* (and for which she received the very reasonable fee of three guineas).[52]

Miles' talk for Authors' Week 1935, 'Novels of the Bush', is her first known radio broadcast, subsequently donated to the *Australian Mercury* and in 2004 deemed one of 'the speeches that made Australia'. She was an occasional broadcaster thereafter, giving maybe one or two talks a year, mostly over national networks, until 1951. Jean Hamilton had already been on the BBC, and other women writers in Australia (for example, Katharine Susannah Prichard) had made their debut earlier. Despite anxiety about how she would sound — an anxiety common among women broadcasters until the 1960s — Miles was keen to avail herself of this new and lucrative medium. The new possibilities included radio plays and talks, on which she sought advice about rates from Nettie Palmer. Complaining to Mary Fullerton that she had not entered an ABC play competition, only to find there was nothing special about the winning plays and that the ABC was taking out options as well as awarding prizes, she returned to play-writing with zest.[53]

Her radio talks were not unlike her earlier print journalism. A talk on 'Jane Addams as I Knew Her' went to air on 17 June, and she gave four twenty-minute talks on Wednesday mornings in September and October: 'The Fun of Being a Foreigner'; 'Postscript on Humour'; 'Wit and the Jurist' (on meeting Mr Justice Higgins in Chicago); and 'Why Australian Novels?'. But she was not always paid. At other times she would be paid quite handsomely; for instance, she received three guineas for a schools broadcast on 'My Life and My Books' in 1938.[54]

Baylebridge said her voice carried well. But according to her mother, her timing was bad: 'your voice sounded awful'. However, this seems to be an instance of the strained mother–daughter relations that Miles increasingly complained of in her pocket diary. Except for Susannah's strictures, all sources agree that she had a strong, rich voice and that she spoke well. At a time when Australian women were encouraged to speak in light tones and women's voices were regarded as lacking in authority, hers proved acceptable for radio, where the male voice and Received Pronunciation predominated until the 1970s.[55]

All That Swagger was still in typescript at the end of 1935. The news from London in November had been that although four publishers had rejected the manuscript, Harraps was interested, but it would have to be cut by one-third, and made more of a story. Miles was tempted, wondering if they would give her an advance: 'This book is a big piece of work and I could not afford to mutilate it on mere chance,' she wrote to Jean Hamilton. In fact, she had already retyped the whole thing, cut 100 pages and done what she called 'sand-papering'. Then she decided not to publish a cut version. As she explained to Jean:

> The story does not parallel *Landtakers*, which is a sadistic modernistic rendering of convictism from a clever journalist. I have merely represented the Australia which is in my bones. The continent of Australia has not yet undergone any over-virilising filibustering. Australia opposes nothing in the blood-and-thunder convention to invasion. She has resisted by attrition ... The tale as I envision it has to be painted stroke by stroke — many many many small strokes — as is. It will be falsified if jazzed-up ...[56]

She urged a similar approach — perhaps it could be described as pointillist — on Australian film-makers like Charles Chauvel, who had attracted her critical attention at this time.[57]

Still in search of publishers, she wrote to John Varney in New York before departing 'to look over my territory', as she seemed to do most summers, advising that on her return she would revise and retype the manuscript and make an additional carbon copy for his friend Miss Barnicle, in hope she might recommend it to a publisher there. It was a faint hope.[58]

The biggest disappointment was Stephensen, who, she lamented to Nettie Palmer, had had thousands of dollars but had failed to establish his publishing house or even a literary magazine and was now in liquidation. Still, she said, the Crockett case had taught the *Bulletin* a lesson; and Inky had published some important texts. Although the *Australian Mercury* lasted only one issue, and more of her work went under with it, it was the impetus for Inky's resounding blast at 'the Garrison', *The Foundations of Culture in Australia*, provoked in good part by an infamous article written early in 1935 by the Melbourne English professor G. H. Cowling, who denied the existence of an Australian literature — to which 'weak piffle' Miles responded immediately in the *Age*. Stephensen's forceful and skilled polemic, now a classic if not a cliché, appeared early in 1936.[59]

The international situation was increasingly worrying too. The beginnings of German re-armament were evident in 1935; there were further Japanese incursions into north Asia; and in October, the Italians invaded Abyssinia. Writing to the Robinses at Christmas time, Miles recounted her pleasure at Mrs Griffin's outdoor theatre at Castlecrag, where she had seen a splendid performance of *Iphigenia in Tauris* mid-year — the amphitheatre was one of the features of Sydney in the 1930s, when commercial theatre was depressed — but added that mention of such things seemed trivial 'while the great problems are flouted.'[60]

To this point, Miles Franklin, despite a rich correspondence and her active membership of various writerly organisations, not to mention her continuing literary effort, was not truly part of the mainstream of cultural politics. She lacked real authority, a situation she found puzzling. Why was it, she asked Mary Fullerton after reading a few chapters of M. Barnard Eldershaw's *Plaque with Laurel* in April 1936, which she deemed 'precious stuff quite away from the real life of Australia', that it was acclaimed 'and I am ignored and rejected'?

In answering this question it must be remembered that her known literary output was limited, and since her homecoming somewhat eccentric, and that at first she had been aligned with Stephensen, whose standing diminished by the year. Moreover, although she had a number of women friends in Sydney (and could always call on Eva O'Sullivan to accompany her to events such as the opening of the annual Royal Arts Society exhibition in 1936), most were not writers. The women writers she had met earlier included Marjorie Barnard, who was impressed but too timid for an affinity to develop, and Mary Gilmore, who was older and too established, while the young Christina Stead, whose first fierce novel, *Seven Poor Men of Sydney*, had won Miles' approval, had long since left for London. Perhaps

Miles had been looking in the wrong direction anyway, to the men of the radical nationalist school instead of among the younger women. There in the mid-1930s she found some apparently unlikely 'congenials', such as that wild communist activist Jean Devanny, the brilliant but reserved Eleanor Dark at Katoomba in the Blue Mountains, and the young schoolteacher Dymphna Cusack, a radical literary daughter for Miles to cherish. Early in 1936 Miles also encountered Kylie Tennant, whose first novel *Tiburon* had won the inaugural S. H. Prior Memorial Prize in 1935 and was welcomed by Miles as a work in the Brent tradition of cultural realism.[61]

One small sign of a change in her perceptions at this time was an increasing acknowledgement of Aboriginal Australia. Jean Hamilton had drawn her attention to Herbert Basedow's sympathetic *Knights of the Boomerang*, and Miles told the American advocate of indigenous cultures Alice Thacher Post that Australia was coming around to her wise 'way of thinking'. It was not something she could write knowledgeably about herself, but for all the feminist and nationalist reasons then coming into circulation, she was a strong supporter of Xavier Herbert's 'Capricornia', still in limbo due to Stephensen's business collapse.[62]

Early in 1936 Miles set *All That Swagger* aside and took up the re-discovered manuscript of 'The End of My Career', which she enthusiastically edited and revised. On re-reading, she found it ran 'pretty patly' and thought it 'good fun'. Written as a skit on *My Brilliant Career*, it now struck her as something that could stand on its own: 'Do you know any editor who would think it a scoop?' she asked Elsie Belle Champion. How much of the original 1902 text survived the editing is unknown, but Miles later told Alice Henry she had cut yards of it, along with material used elsewhere, writing modestly, 'It is only a small, slight tour de force of a young ignorant girl.' The new version, dated 7 May 1936, she called 'My Career Goes Bung'.[63]

On 15 February 1936, at the invitation of Edward and Maggie Bridle, Miles once more took the train south 'to look over my field'. She spent ten days with them at Tallong, then Maggie took her into Goulburn, whence she visited old friends over the next ten days, first the McDonalds at 'Landsdowne', then the Baxters at 'Longfield', and finally the Twynams at 'Riversdale', returning for a last night at Tallong on 9 March. While at 'Longfield', she and Dolly Baxter rode over to 'Stillwater', where very little evidence of the Franklin occupancy remained. They visited Currawang and Collector, and on Sunday attended the old Kirkdale church. Back in Goulburn, Miles managed to take tea with Bishop Burgmann. One evening she attended a political meeting, which she privately judged a deplorable example of 'bumble politics' at the local level.[64]

Back in Carlton there were notes from Alice Henry on 'Sybylla' (*My Career Goes Bung*), and Miles was determined to finish *All That Swagger*. Her working conditions, she said, approximated those of a telephone girl in a busy office, and the constant flow of visitors almost drove her mad, but she managed to complete both tasks in her crowded bedroom, 'as a matter of character'. A pettiness from her mother prompted the comparison that 'Dad was a frustrated mystic ... mother a pagan and potential tyrant'. However, things improved when Miss Hall was employed to help with the housework (though Miles still did the garden, the laundry, the fires and the wood, and home maintenance). And she now had a discernible plan of action.[65]

In May, she began plotting to enter her work in the Prior Prize competition. To this end, she arranged to submit a 'short-ish novel' by 'Miss Melvyn' via Freda Barrymore in Townsville. Freda complied (while protesting against Miles' penchant for secrecy). It was probably the manuscript of *My Career Goes Bung* which went in, from the list of entries and pen-names published in the *Bulletin*, as 'From Possum Gully' by 'Cross Stitch'. *All That Swagger*, blandly retitled 'Advance Australia', she entered herself. It went in a week later, submitted with the pen-name 'Captain Bligh', c/– Mr M. A. E. Gillespie.[66]

According to a diary entry for 24 June, she also sent several parcels of work to the United States and London. The package to the United States contained a letter, the manuscripts of *All That Swagger*, *My Career Goes Bung*, and Fullerton's poems, and an unspecified magazine, while a similar assemblage containing the *My Career Goes Bung* manuscript went to Guy Innes in London. She also sent *All That Swagger* to the publisher Jonathon Cape.[67]

Three weeks later, on 15 July, Miles was astounded to learn that 'Advance Australia'/*All That Swagger* had won the Prior Prize. There were over 230 entries in 1936, and according to the terms of the award, if suitable the winning manuscript would be published as a serial in the *Bulletin* on terms to be negotiated with the author, as well as receiving a cash prize.[68]

Announcing the award the following week, the *Bulletin* confirmed that *All That Swagger*, 'this magnificent story' by Miles Franklin, would appear shortly as a serial and would later be published simultaneously in book form in Australia, England and America. Apparently the judges, T. D. Mutch,

Cecil Mann and Stewart Howard, had first thought the manuscript was the work of M. Barnard Eldershaw or Vance Palmer, and the announcement noted that Miles was widely believed to be the author of the Brent books — which showed, she muttered, that most people had no idea who Brent was. Overcoming her panic at having won the prize with a book which stated 'all my views', she set to work, first to advise publishers and agents overseas, then to negotiate with the *Bulletin*.[69]

The prize was worth £100, the serial rights £50, and she would receive £100 against royalties on the book. As well, she would retain overseas rights. Miles feared that people would cut the serial from the *Bulletin* to make their own 'books', damaging sales of the conventionally published version, but with all else to her satisfaction, she began to excise some 40,000 words from the text to fit the available space in the magazine so the first of eight instalments could appear on 16 September. Clearly Miles was a champion cutter.[70]

The congratulations flowed in. 'Now you can swagger', telegraphed Inky and Winnie Stephensen. How exhilarating 'to read such wonderful things about our cousin', wrote the Vallances from Murrumbateman, near Canberra. Mary Fullerton in London was quite blown away: 'The splendid news lifted me right into the air'.[71]

The saga was, according to one of the judges, T. D. Mutch, Miles 'at the zenith of her power', her youthful promise magnificently fulfilled. Further, 'In not one page is there to be seen any evidence of overseas influence. Only an Australian could have written it, and there has been nothing written like it except the Brent of Bin Bin novels'.[72]

Cecil Mann, another of the judges, said the saga of Danny Delacy and his wife, 'my brave Johanna', made him feel better about Australia as a place, a point underlined shortly after by a *Bulletin* contributor, Denton Prout. Responding to an article in the magazine by Miles entitled 'Our Crowded Canvases', which suggested that Australian authors faced difficulties writing about a sparsely occupied continent, Prout asserted that it was simply that they couldn't accept the Australian scene as natural. Thus, from the outset some readers saw *All That Swagger* as a mighty swipe at what was to be defined in 1950 as the 'cultural cringe'. The Rawdon Vale family of Gloucester, New South Wales, wrote to the *Goulburn Evening Penny Post* — quick off the mark to announce a local 'girl's' success these days — that the history of the Delacy family was just like their own. Elsie Barton of Wahroonga thought the work so good it warranted the Nobel Prize (something not achieved by an Australian writer until 1973, when Patrick White received the honour).[73]

Mann also drew attention to the title, noting that swagger was 'not a word that everyone likes'. In one of the first notices of the book version, the Sydney *Truth* began by referring to 'an intentionally ugly name'. When she first heard the title, Henry Handel Richardson thought it bespoke some kind of defect in the writer, and later said it was 'odious': 'Old Blastus was bad enough.' Others, such as Lucy Spence Morice in Adelaide, were intrigued but bemused. Even Alice Henry, reporting the 'joyful news about Stella Franklin' to their American friend Mary Anderson, by then head of the United States Women's Bureau, was uncertain about it — but also perspicacious: 'The title rather puzzles me, but it seems to be part of its popularity.' The *Truth* overstated it when, as illustration that the author knew her background, it referred to 'the supreme masculine insolence of the day for women "of the lowly grade"', but was right when it said that whatever it was, 'it had to go'. For her part, Miles early made the oblique point that women and children had carried pioneering slowly forward to success. To Lucy Morice, she explained that 'swagger' simply meant 'the bravado of the bravura days — 'a little dash, a little extra virility which carried them through hardship and loneliness' — which is nearer today's more positive connotations than those of the 1930s, when, for many readers, the word conjured up insolence and overbearing behaviour, or as in Australian folklore, a swagman.[74]

The *Bulletin* serial ended on 4 November with a four-page Conclusion (previous instalments were ten pages). Reader responses had been positive; and at least one reader thought the last chapter was the best of all. Here Danny Delacy's grandson, the returning airman Brian, flies south in his 'Nullah-Mundoley' (the original Delacy breed of horse) over the road that had taken old Danny and Johanna weeks to traverse, to reclaim the vision of Australia which had sustained his forebears. Landing near the Gap, in sight of Canberra, Brian is uplifted by the view and by the thought of his unborn child. The Delacys may have lost the land, but it is in his bones, and he envisions a new race of men, a people unafraid to dream and worthy to occupy it. 'Australia, the incredible feat!' he chants; and as the plane soars to the stratosphere, he sees a glimmer of the Delacys moving on 'the palimpsest of Time'. In this upbeat ending, Miles Franklin declares Australia, not the Delacy generations, as the real heroine of her book.[75]

One significant reader of the serial was Mary Gilmore, whose life was threaded through the Australian socialist tradition in a way Miles' life was not, or not yet. For reasons not now easy to understand, Miles could not abide Gilmore, perhaps because she came from her own patch in south-eastern New South Wales, or because Gilmore's celebrations of the Australian spirit were unencumbered by ambiguity or critical intent. But Mary, the older, more established writer (then in her seventies), was by contrast always generous to Miles, and never more so than in her response to *All That Swagger*.

> I have not read anything so wise & fine as your *All that Swagger*. I would like to tell you how often it has wrung — not brought but wrung — the tears from my eyes … you don't know how I have felt about your work for Australia … Proud of you, proud for the country that brought you forth, yours very humbly by comparison.[76]

Miles may have suffered from simple professional jealousy. Perhaps Mary's sacred-cow status was trying, and the possibility that imperial honours might be forthcoming had a gender dimension. Although quite normal for men, such rewards were rare for women, and seen as invidious by many. The idea that Mary might become a Dame of the British Empire (DBE), as she did in 1937, riled Miles on principle. Writing to Henry Handel Richardson in September 1936 in the belief that the FAW's behaviour over the Kisch affair in November 1934 had put the kybosh on a DBE for Mary, she snorted, 'A Dame eh? But then no great women writers are dames so perhaps it wd not have disgraced us so irretrievably after all.'[77]

Such Milesian swirls stimulated people, but perplexed them too. Urbane Ambrose Pratt, a Melbourne journalist, met Miles in Sydney in May 1936 and formed the view that she was obsessed, due to being too much alone with her own thoughts and the woman's side of things: 'When writing to me you have been writing to an abstraction'. Certainly, as Miles told Guy Innes at this time, isolation was the origin of her literary notebooks: 'As I have no one to talk to, I have taken to writing in exercise books.'[78]

All That Swagger the book was still to come. Even after the first round of cuts, made immediately after she heard of her win, it was a big book, some 200,000 words on Miles' own estimate, filling 500 pages in the first edition. With Mutch's help, from July through September she worked over the proofs, and when advance copies finally became available on 14 November she expressed herself happy with the *Bulletin*'s production values. A fortnight later, on 24 November, the book appeared.

Stephensen was one of the first to congratulate her. His telegram the next day reads: 'Delighted speechless magnificent swagger feat of bunyip virtuosity.' A fortnight later, on 4 December, Miles apparently netted £30 in two hours at what, it has been suggested, was the first book signing in Australia, at Hordern's department store. (Among those who turned up was one Mrs West from Kirkdale, near Goulburn, who had kept all the press clippings after Miles went to America; whether the man who sent the music for the old song in *All That Swagger*, 'I Am Denny Blake from County Clare', also turned up as Miles suggested is not known.) She hankered for a full window display by a bookseller, but to no avail. Nonetheless, 'it was wonderful how the book sold'. So was its reception, despite few press notices until just before Christmas. It pleased Miles to think that Edward Bridle, who had contributed, she said, so much to the story, especially spiritually, liked the book. On 18 December, she wrote exultingly to Mary Fullerton: 'You should see the pile of letters I have from many parts of Australia, all rejoicing like frogs in the rain after the drought in my book because it is real Australian, Australia under the skin, Australia from the inside.' She was grateful for Hilary Lofting's review in the *Bulletin* on 23 December, which saw in Danny Delacy the embodiment of the Australian 'fair go', and placed him in 'the august company' of Soames Forsyte and David Copperfield. One positive reader reaction was to the language of *All That Swagger*, where words either very creative or startlingly archaic often appeared; for example, the Irish archaism 'streel', meaning a 'waster'.[79]

Overseas rights, so confidently anticipated in July, were another matter. There were no offers from America, and although Harraps was still interested, it was not happy about separate British-only rights. In vain Miles argued that recent titles such as *Pageant* and *The Landtakers* had done well in the United Kingdom after being published first in Australia. However, that window, briefly wrenched open by Stephensen, had closed. The British publishers' Traditional Market Agreement, which divided the English-speaking world in two, to be shared by British and American publishers, with Australia part of Britain's spoils, was firmly adhered to, and Miles' stance merely irritated everyone. By May 1937 the literary agent Innes Rose reported that the manuscript had been refused by all the top British publishers and he could do no more. So it was that Miles Franklin's most successful book, which went through numerous editions during her lifetime and was until the 1970s her second-best-known work, was never published outside Australia, not even in New Zealand.[80]

With scarcely any reviews appearing in the first weeks, Miles was becoming anxious about missing the Christmas market. Of some thirty known reviews, most came in the two months after Christmas. When they did, almost all were favourable, commending the integrity and vitality of the text: as the Melbourne *Age* reviewer put it, 'the story rings true'. And although sales could not be compared with those of the prolific travel writer Ion Idriess or of F. J. Thwaites, a popular romance writer, 1664 copies had been sold by the end of the year and approaching 3000 by the end of February 1937. Miles Franklin was never so well off as in 1937, as the royalties rolled in, and each new edition sold well.[81]

It was from Adelaide, arguably then the least Australian of the state capitals, that the first of the few negative responses came. The *Adelaide Advertiser* said the novel was a disappointment, far too long and heavy to hold. 'Mr' Franklin employed too much padding. Indeed, *All That Swagger*'s length became the most frequently expressed criticism. Some reviewers noticed that it was hard to sustain the emotional intensity of the narrative over four generations, but none suggested that it was really two books (as later), contenting themselves with the observation that Danny and Johanna were the most successful characterisations.[82]

A great deal was said in the reviews about the pioneer past and its hardships. For instance, Will Carter, writing under the heading 'Australianities' for provincial presses such as the Albury *Banner*, listed the characters' travails, describing them as 'faithfully laid out as a feast, of ... real Australian fiction'. The *Sydney Morning Herald*'s review on Christmas Eve 1936 offered a more literary assessment, juxtaposing Brian Penton's Cabell family of *The Landtakers* with Franklin's Delacys. The *Herald* deemed Franklin to have achieved a wholesome balance and congratulated her for breadth, depth, and conceptual coherence, with the young pilot Brian pioneering a new age of air as Danny had pioneered the age of the horse. It concluded:

> There is something heroic in the passionate note of hope on which the book ends. By all mundane standards, the house that had been built on land taken from Murrumbidgee natives had disintegrated and fallen from the hands that made it. The Delacys will not go down in the fictional annals of Australian squattocracy as enduring landtakers.[83]

That must have pleased Miles, who was genuinely puzzled by the ferocity of *The Inheritors*, Penton's successor to *The Landtakers*, remarking on one occasion that she had never known such brutality in convictism as seemed to have prevailed in Brisbane, nor such nightmares of free settlement.[84]

A long review by Freda Barrymore in the *North Queensland Register* is perhaps more interesting. Barrymore had privately promised to give *All That Swagger* a boost. But she did more than that; she touched on most of the aspects Miles herself would have deemed important in a book that was 'essentially Australian in spirit'. Publicity agents were always on the lookout for the great Australian novel, but those who looked for big things from Miles Franklin when young would find much to satisfy them in this book — like an old Norse saga, Barrymore said. Its settings, especially the bush scenery in the early parts, were 'the highest peak of her achievement'. Unusually, Barrymore noticed memorable treatments of Aborigines, asserting, though it may surprise modern readers, that Miles Franklin 'stands with those who understand and sympathise with the original owners of this land'. She noted Danny's 'humanitarian quality' and the characters Maeve, a young Aboriginal girl who becomes Johanna's companion in the wilds, and the disabled boy Doogoolook, whom Danny rescues from a fire and who becomes his devoted retainer. Chinese people too are sympathetically drawn, as in the character of Cantonese-born gold miner Wong Foo.[85]

Barrymore also referred to Miles' new and original sociological ideas, especially her view that the horse kept Australia free of a flunkey class and ensured the transformation of the peasantry: 'No man can remain a peasant and go a-horse'. She might have gone on to say, as did Bishop Burgmann in the *Southern Churchman*, that *All That Swagger* spans the era from the horse to the machine and that the era of the horse had now closed; but she put her finger on the fact that *All That Swagger* is the great novel of the horse era of Australian history, already then passed — as had been apparent to Miles on her visit to Goulburn earlier in the year. Writing to Nell Malone afterwards, she said the horse had gone, 'except as luxury for the rich or a last resource of the poor'.[86]

Two other notices may be mentioned, more for what they say about contemporary expectations and values than as book reviews. Essaying 'The Miles Franklin Country' in March 1937, the Melbourne journalist John McKellar suggested that if the two criteria for the long-looked-for great Australian novel were a work embodying distinctively Australian characteristics and exhibiting features of national development, *All That Swagger* probably fitted the bill. A belated notice in the *Australian Women's Weekly*, the Packer press's triumphant captor of the women's magazine market in the 1930s, though similarly laudatory, nowhere mentions the role of women in the saga of progress it commended — a sign, perhaps, of the timidity of the times, and an unexpected perspective on Miles Franklin, the becalmed radical.[87]

Altogether it seems the reviewers did a good job in a timely manner. Not only is *All That Swagger* a big book, but it covers a considerable time span, from 1833 to 1933. It also treats of four generations, which means a large cast. However, Miles (in the guise of Brent) had already mastered the long-run approach; and the book is very readable. Compared with the three previously published Brent books, *All That Swagger* roars along, due to the immense vitality of the main characters, poor Irish immigrants Danny Delacy and his 'brave Johanna', and the writer's emotional investment in Danny's vision of Australia. Also, the novel's line of thought was readily accessible, more so then than now. In a recent reading of the novel, Brenton Doecke compares its nationalist vision with that of historian W. K. Hancock's classic *Australia*. According to Doecke, *All That Swagger* may be read, not just as a simple celebration of the passing pioneer tradition, nor of its great eccentrics like Danny, but as a critical view of the lost pioneer heritage and an assertion of the relevance of its collectivist values to the 1930s. Doecke's contextual interpretation helps us to appreciate the esteem the novel enjoyed.[88]

There are nonetheless two interesting absences in *All That Swagger*. The first is the impact of World War I on Australia and the consequent creation of the Anzac tradition. The Delacys were not war-minded, Miles wrote in the one short chapter devoted to the war, in which she upheld the anti-war, anti-conscription line: the great thing about the soldiers, Miles maintained, was that they fought as free men and maintained that right 'in the midst of world hysteria' by rejecting conscription. Gallipoli she knew to have been 'a stupid blunder', and having observed Dr Booth's annual women's remembrance ceremony at the departure gates at Woolloomooloo on Sydney Harbour in the 1920s, she was aware of the tragic loss. In an undated reflection in a notebook begun in 1935 she wrote: 'Anzac cannot be glorified except speciously, and to glorify it ... would be to betray again the men who were so basely betrayed by the false glamour of military glory. To contribute to the retribution due the men sacrificed on Gallipoli, youth must be made to see the facts.' With this, Miles expressed her distaste for the increasingly intense observation of Anzac Day, and suggested something of the distaste of rural Australia for the war, and especially for conscription. Like many Australians outside the major cities, the Delacys were more preoccupied with primary production than the conduct of the war.[89]

The second absence in *All That Swagger* is religion. In gliding over the subject, the novel is optimistic, but — it might now be thought — somewhat superficial, just as Mutch's assertion that the book was purely Australian is. The Delacy family is Irish, and sectarianism was present in colonial New South Wales. However, the Delacy family is founded on a 'mixed marriage' between 'Prodestan' Danny and Catholic Johanna, in which religion is deliberately avoided. This accorded with Miles' experience (and probably says something about her class position as well, in that New South Wales sectarianism was more a phenomenon of the lower class).

As for the simplistic 'purely Australian', Freda Barrymore was nearer the mark when she said that 'all that [Miles Franklin] learned abroad has gone into the making of this new novel'. A historical assessment would find many refracted aspects of the wider world, such as town planning and the new environmentalism, evident in the book.

Success with *All That Swagger* immediately encouraged Miles' hopes for her other projects. Nothing more was heard of *My Career Goes Bung*, but a month after the prize was announced, on 20 August 1936, she got out the manuscript of *Cockatoos*. It would need work to put 'blood and tears' into it, she decided. A fortnight later, on 4 September, William Blake wrote to Blackwood announcing that Brent now had time to work on 'the missing volume', that is, *Cockatoos*. Mary Fullerton was delighted to hear this, and the manuscript reached Blackwood a year or so later, but was rejected 'for commercial reasons'; in particular, poor sales of *Back to Bool Bool* on the home market and limited returns on the colonial edition.[90]

Winning the Prior Prize enhanced Miles' standing and increased her authority in the literary community. At an FAW party given in celebration, according to Marjorie Barnard, Miles gave 'a wise and witty address', and soon after, with the journalist Bartlett Adamson, she served as a judge at the annual play night of the Sydney Literary Society, of which she had been made a patron (as she was of the Propeller League) earlier in the year. And she was in some demand as a speaker, agreeing in August to address the Women's Club on 'Australia's Greatest Woman'. That turned out to be Alice Henry's heroine and now Miles' literary touchstone, Catherine Helen Spence, and

Miles spoke for an hour. 'They seemed to find it stimulating,' she remarked afterwards. Elsewhere she asserted that Spence should be on a stamp. (In 2001 Spence appeared on the $5 note commemorating the centenary of Australian Federation.)[91]

Given her increasing interest in historical biography, it was serendipitous that one of Miles Franklin's more recent Sydney friends was Ida Leeson, Mitchell Librarian from 1932 to 1946, a friend of the Griffins and a rare soul, according to Miles. Miles loved working in the Mitchell, and no one knew its research collections better than Leeson. When invited to a meeting with Marjorie Barnard, Flora Eldershaw and Dora Wilcox, another Sydney writer, to prepare a women's memorial volume for the forthcoming sesquicentenary of New South Wales in 1938, she agreed to write a chapter about Rose Scott. A changing focus was inevitable given her stage of life and cultural mission; and as with most things she undertook, her reflections are worthwhile. To Ambrose Pratt, an occasional biographer himself, she remarked upon the peculiar difficulties facing the biographer in Australia:

> That field is still to be pioneered in indigenous literature and is more difficult even than the novel, for which some sort of a track has been blazed. The Australian biographer or autobiographer cannot be so uninhibited as those of Europe and America where there is more jungle to hide in. We are members of a small community which imposes small community decencies upon us.[92]

At the same time she was encouraging Kate Baker to write a biography of Joseph Furphy; and on hearing the unnerving news that *Such Is Life* was to be abridged for publication in London by Cape, she expressed a wish that they lived nearer each other so they could work on a biography together. It was an intriguing suggestion, which would soon enough bear fruit.[93]

Ambrose Pratt had dared to suggest that Miles Franklin was obsessed, and then that she was inhibited, despite what he called her 'glinting' mind. She countered that, with two old friends recently having died, P. S. Watson in Melbourne, and Alex McDonald of Goulburn, she had reason to feel low, and that she had need of money, not a mind doctor. (Other losses around this time included Charlotte Perkins Gilman, whose autobiography Miles was reading in 1936, and the British novelist Winifred Holtby, now best known for a remarkable friendship with fellow writer Vera Brittain.) She might also have mentioned her mother's markedly failing strength, which by year's end led Miles to call on their relative Ivy Vernon as a companion (Ivy was paid fifteen shillings weekly), and the endless hospitality still dispensed in the crowded cottage (there had been seventy visitors over the past two months, she estimated on one occasion). At least Miss Henry, pausing in Sydney for a month or more in October after a trip to north Queensland, stayed at the YWCA, Carlton being too far from the city for her by then.[94]

Pratt had the temerity to ask Miles what it was she was afraid of, really. He probably thought sex. Many have thought that, even in recent times. On this vexatious topic, Miles confessed to Alice Henry that nothing could now be further from her mind or interest even if it had once been a consuming subject, and that she had to be careful to remind herself that sex mattered enormously to the young. Evidently she had passed through her disgust with postwar mores in the metropolis and her own grief at the end of romance, and was now on her preferred path to immortality. Maybe all the evidence so carefully preserved — the letters, the diaries, the rejected manuscripts — in some way served as protection, or a projection of a self uneasily situated in a sexist society. A modern critic might suggest that much, and that the ecstatic approach to the landscape so prominent in *All That Swagger* was itself an erotic displacement; but this would need to be seen against Miles' naturalist approach to landscape writing. Maybe, it would be truer to say that Miles was an extrovert, but this too was problematic for the older woman in Australia then. Perhaps like most writers she feared to fail.[95]

No such complexity obscured Miles Franklin's outlook on international affairs by 1936. If the 1930s were the devil's decade, he was riding high in 1936, with the Nazi occupation of the Rhineland, Mussolini's success in Abyssinia, the military rebellion against the new Nationalist government in Spain and the onset of the Spanish Civil War, the curtain raiser, as many feared, to a second world war. Miles knew, and frequently said, that Europe was a mess, and continued to support the Movement Against War and Fascism that had brought Kisch to Australia in 1934. Likewise, she understood the totalitarian threat. When the New South Wales government acceded to the German Consul-General's demand to stop performances of Clifford Odets' anti-Nazi play *Till the Day I Die*, and the New Theatre League exploited a loophole in the legislation to put on a 'private' performance with his *Waiting for Lefty* as a double bill at the Savoy Theatre, Miles went along and delighted in a fine performance, asserting to

Henry Handel Richardson that if literary societies did not protest about censorship they were 'stuffed fowl concerns'. She soon worked out her position on Spain too, supporting the Nationalist government. When Vance Palmer passed through Sydney in December on his way home from Europe, having observed the Spanish situation first-hand, Miles attended a big meeting he addressed at Transport House. Although she thought him rather dull, she felt he made a valuable contribution by stressing the Nationalists were not anti-religious; and he was grateful for her presence.[96]

Probably very few Australian women at that time were as well informed about foreign affairs as Miles Franklin, and not many Australians, male or female, as clear-headed. However, writing at year's end to the Sydney poet-librarian Kathleen Monypenny, living in London, that Stephensen with retired businessman W. J. Miles had started a new political movement, the Australia First movement, Miles thought it was 'very much needed'. But the theory it was based on was backward looking, and Stephensen's ultra-nationalism soon headed in a fascist direction. His idea was that Australia should stay out of European imbroglios and put 'Australia first', assuming that the next war would simply be a renewal of the last. In July Miles had subscribed to the Australia First journal the *Publicist*, funded by W. J. Miles. What she most feared at this time was conscription.[97]

Amid so much international activity, Miles did not forget Hartley Grattan. He had been busy with his New Deal work — he was employed as research editor with the Federal Emergency Relief Administration in 1934–35 — but not out of touch with Australia, thanks in good part to Miles, who was still confident that he was what Australia needed: 'Sometimes a fresh mind is the miracle necessary to focus things,' she had written encouragingly on 25 June 1935.[98]

On 16 September 1936 Grattan cabled that he had been successful with his Carnegie grant application to study contemporary Australia and would be leaving New York for Sydney on 4 November, travelling via London, where he would seek to penetrate 'the British curtain' that surrounded Australia by meeting significant Left-wing intellectuals such as Harold Laski and Beatrice and Sidney Webb. Miles was astounded to learn that he would have £10 a week for the duration of his two-year fellowship for 'your gorgeous work' — 'you millionaire!!!' — and ironical about his going via London, 'where you will meet all the émigrés'. But she told William Baylebridge that Grattan would be a wonderful help and stimulant, and she began to prepare the ground, with letters and press releases, and advice to Grattan about where to stay, reassuring him that although recently divorced, he need have no fear of a gutter press in Sydney. But she was baffled by his recent anti-war book, the encyclopaedic *Preface to Chaos*, however much she admired it. En route Grattan sent her a cable from Adelaide congratulating her on *All That Swagger*: 'Danny Delacy triumphant creation. Yarn with you first.'[99]

When the *Narkunda* berthed in Sydney on Christmas Eve, Miles was there on the dock to meet him, heading a motley literary delegation, along with P. R. Stephensen. Having prepared to show him the real Australia, she was disappointed when he was whisked off by journalists — the Parnassians — and did not hear from him for a week. But cultural and intellectual affinity, and Miles' worldly-wise approach to the much younger man — he was thirty-four — prevailed in what proved to be a mutually supportive relationship.[100]

Grattan would often need support, both emotional and intellectual. He was on his own, homesick at first and not easily able to meet people his own age, especially women — a situation Miles met with one of her most memorable *bons mots*, that the Australian scene was unnecessarily cluttered with men. Nor did Australians at first accord Grattan the status due to a Carnegie Fellow. The dapper, soft-spoken New York intellectual and writer was being put right all the time by Australian loudmouths and pomposities. He was prickly, said Miles, and outspoken (which she enjoyed). Inevitably he found much to criticise: the poor quality of information available in the press about America and the absence of American studies in the universities, for example; and, once he had surveyed the scene by study and extensive travel, the limitations of Australian foreign and economic policies. Criticism caused upset, as when he dismissed the idea that hope for Australia lay with the inland and deplored the effects of agricultural protection. After travelling in Queensland he said the standard of comfort in Australia was low compared with America. On the other hand, he genuinely liked and cared about Australia, and his lectures and broadcasts went over well. He also established an important niche for himself in Australian cultural history by his recognition of Australian writers. Supporting him so staunchly over the next two years was probably one of the best things Miles Franklin ever did for her fellow writers.[101]

He helped her too. Besides encouraging her work, he supported her literary projects, such as a reissue of *Jonah* and the shaping of a response to the Cape abridgment of *Such Is Life*, which appeared in 1937. More importantly, in due course he helped Miles to think clearly about political trends. Grattan's views were a world away from those of Stephensen. Having previously done his best for Inky's literary enterprises in New York, he soon rejected Stephensen's larrikin chauvinism, arguing against isolationist policies as unrealistic and deploring racism: Stephensen's lurch to the Right was, he said, 'deeply offensive'. Although he could not free Miles from the contradictions of Australia First, he saved her from a deeper descent into the Stephensen mire. When he left, with 'an incredible mass of material', on 5 September 1938, Miles Franklin was one of the last he talked to before departure, 'as you were one of the first', he noted gratefully.[102]

On one issue, though, she needed no help: the abdication of Edward VIII. On 3 December 1936 the British press broke its silence on King Edward VIII's intention to marry the American divorcée Wallis Simpson. The news shook the Empire. 'Hands off our King', one placard protested. But Miles was not in doubt. If, as she wrote to Edward Bridle the next day, there was anything in it, the king should control himself: 'It may be all froth, but if it is not, I think an old man of his age [he was born in 1894] might have held his emotions in the crisis in European affairs.' Later she told Mollye Menken that Australian workmen had a point when they said they had to give up their lives for the king and he could not give up a blooming tart to save his people. Most men had to give up their tarts, they added.[103]

Odd as it may seem, the contradictions that Miles Franklin had been compelled by circumstance to live with since returning to Australia increased throughout 1936. The success of *All That Swagger* restored her name and recast her reputation as an Australian writer among the reading public; it encouraged her in her work, especially in the hope that Brent might yet finish his series, as she replied to friends who suggested that now might be the time to come clean; and it strengthened promising literary associations, such as with Frank Clune and Jean Devanny. She was even mentioned in parliament as 'one of our most brilliant writers'. But her family brought her to despair. 'Petty nonentities all they can do is criticize each other and I am a special mark. I wonder how I came to be one of such relatives. Nothing in common — no discernible spiritual or mental likeness with anyone but my father and grandfather Franklin and Grandma Lampe and Aunt Sara[h],' she wrote in her pocket diary on 28 September. Nor did the next generation show any sign of comprehension. Her schoolboy nephew Jack said she would make someone a splendid wife: 'You could keep house so well and write books in your spare time.'[104]

Christmas Day 1936 merely emphasised the paradoxical situation. There were eight for dinner that day, with both her mother and Miss Gillespie to be put to bed after. Susannah's condition was such that it was only a matter of time, and Miss Gillespie, now aged eighty herself, reported another death in Goulburn. 'Altogether a depressing Christmas,' sighed Miles. How nice then to go into town a few days later to meet Horatio Nelson Smith of inner London days at the Hotel Australia, and to collect some reviews and a cheque from the *Bulletin* office.

On New Year's Day 1937, despite feeling exhausted from lack of sleep and a matinée where the pandemonium of a storm on film coinciding with heavy thunder outside further tired her, Miles tapped out letters to far friends, among them the distinguished New Dealer Harold Ickes in Washington, Margery Currey in New York, and Agnes Nestor and Dr Young in Chicago. She had plenty of news: the arrival of Hartley Grattan, the departure of the Griffins for India, an imminent visit by Emma Pischel and other members of her family, and her success with *All That Swagger*. And, as she told Dr Young, there was 'always the telephone and door bell and a continual stream of people who thought that writing was a way of shirking my womanly duty', with her mother 'always restless and disintegrating'. She went on: 'My mother had a collapse about two months ago, but is slowly pulling around. She is so restless, and would traipse out, and wd explain to her old mates that I was very selfish and would like to keep her in. They all urged her to go out and enjoy herself. Result that her heart gave way at last.'[105]

Under such circumstances, to see Emma Pischel, her old friend and colleague from Chicago, again was 'like a little bit of heaven'. The Pischels, who were on a Pacific cruise, stayed at the Hotel Metropole in the city, and Miles had a delightful few days with them. She took Emma to meet the equal-pay advocate Muriel Heagney, to lunch at Carlton with her mother, and one evening to the Russian Ballet. Afterwards she sent her a copy of *Back to Bool Bool*, 'the best picture' of contemporary Australia, even if it hadn't sold very well. Emma had given her a copy of the recently published *Gone with the Wind*, which Miles deemed magnificent, also instructive: 'My material provides no such massed human drama', with no comparable carnage in Australia, and although 'we murdered the blacks of course … they have not provided poets of it as the American South has done'. In what became standard imagery, she went on: 'This is a strange lone silent land …

the peopling of Australia reminds me of a skeleton crew that is left to run a place at night ...'[106]

At a Writers' League dinner at Pakies, the renowned bohemian restaurant on Elizabeth Street, on 9 January 1937, also attended by Vance Palmer, Katharine Susannah Prichard and Hartley Grattan, Miles sat at the table of a new friend, the tax consultant and travel writer Frank Clune, and seconded a motion protesting against the extent of censorship in Australia. In private, she judged the dinner boring and unimportant. Her mind was now on another vital issue of the 1930s, the peopling of Australia. This was to be the subject of an Australian Institute of Public Affairs Summer School, convened in the Albert Hall, Canberra, at the end of January. 'I have definite ideas of which *All That Swagger* is the protagonist,' she wrote grandly, meaning her emphasis there on natural increase rather than immigration. At her first ever Australian conference she was pleased to find everyone opposed the 'verminous filling up' of Australia — except the captains of industry. Afterwards she wrote to Alice Henry, 'I too have had a spree.'[107]

Then came the news of the death of Walter Burley Griffin in India: 'Desolation.' She wrote a tribute to Griffin for the *Bulletin* and applied herself to her work. Soon after sending a play of postwar identity muddle, *No Family* (previously Act 1 of 'Claud's Wife') to Angus & Robertson for inclusion in *Best Australian One-Act Plays* (1937) — the only one of her plays to achieve publication during her lifetime — she began revising the manuscript of *Cockatoos*, and in April turned to corrections for a third edition of *All That Swagger* (they were not incorporated). In addition to supporting Grattan, she served as assessor for Dr Mary Booth's Anzac Festival literary competition, and persisted with Fullerton's poems, beginning with an address to the Sydney Literary Society. A public reading of the poems organised at the Propeller League on 2 March 1937 won support from the literary commentator Camden Morrisby, who was persuaded perhaps by the argument Miles put earlier to the young writers of Hurstville that 'there was a resemblance to Emily Dickinson, but ... while Emily Dickinson was specialised by the inimitable phrase, my poet was set apart by the meaty kernels of thought'.[108]

The long-awaited abridgment of *Such Is Life*, purportedly by Vance Palmer (actually by Nettie and their daughter Aileen, though this was not known until much later), appeared in May. From her earlier encounter with the English publisher Jonathan Cape, Miles had feared the worst, and here it was — to her mind not so much an abridgment as a humourless mutilation of the noble text, apparently to attract English readers. Immediately she embarked on an insistent campaign to counteract its impact, with articles of her own and increased pressure on Joseph Furphy's 'gallant standard bearer', Kate Baker, recipient of an Order of the British Empire (OBE) earlier in the year: 'Oh, Katy Baker! When we thought a (not the) fort was gained, to find that it was merely a betrayal and we must to arms once more.' Whereas previously she had supported Baker's efforts to republish Furphy's works, now Miles once more urged Baker to write something, and renewed her offer to help with a biography.[109]

Amid the instabilities of magazine publishing in the interwar years, a new one sprang up in Canberra in 1937, the *Australian National Review* (*ANR*), which, although it lasted no longer than many others (till 1939), proved hospitable to Miles' concerns. It was in June in the *ANR* that she began to publicise Mary Fullerton's poetry by announcing the 'Discovery of a Poet', whom she declined to name. Many assumed it was another of her tricks and really her own work, rather than, as stated, a protection against the application of irrelevant criteria such as the recent flurry over Emily Dickinson's virginity, or lack thereof. Later she was able to publish a short review of the lamentable abridgment of *Such Is Life* in the *ANR*, following 'Such Is Colonialism', her first response in the *Bulletin*. By then Stephensen had swung into action in the *Publicist*, though not yet Grattan, who was, however, supportive in private.[110]

About this time Miles avoided what she considered a major embarrassment. On 24 April 1937, she received a telegram from the office of the Governor-General, and on inquiry found she was summoned to attend upon the Official and Military Secretary at Government House in Sydney two days later. There she learned that in his coronation year His Majesty King George VI wished to confer upon her the Order of the British Empire. Miles was mortified, recalling how this award was despised during the Great War (and mocked long afterwards as 'Other Buggers' Efforts') — but also because she was being offered such a lowly honour when that 'slipshod' poet Mary Gilmore had recently been made a dame. Then and there Miles declined the honour, and — as may be inferred from a lengthy account of the incident in her literary notebook — was rather disappointed when the official insisted the whole thing must remain confidential.[111]

Frank Clune provided a welcome diversion. A recent arrival on the literary scene with the rollicking autobiography *Try Anything Once*, Clune subsequently published over sixty books in a variety of popular genres, mostly travel and historical volumes. It was doubtless the sweep of *All That Swagger* which drew him to Miles Franklin in 1936. He was not everyone's cup of tea, but Miles told Freda Barrymore he was a dear, and despite an age difference of almost twenty years, their writerly agendas were not that different. 'We don't want stories of snoopy sex written by anaemic lounge lizards and pub crawlers. Action is the password of these pages, this is reading for men with red blood in their veins,' Clune once asserted. Miles certainly agreed on the first point, and if she did not write for red-blooded men, she undoubtedly preferred 'real men' like Stephensen and Clune. When in mid-1937 Clune determined she should accompany him and his wife, Thelma, on a research trip around the inner west of New South Wales, and then, soon after, on another to Central Australia, she was delighted. (The current home help, Mrs Wilkinson, was able to look after her mother, with Miles' cousin Ruby Brydon for backup.)[112]

The first trip, over nine days from 18 to 26 May, took them in Clune's Pontiac through Goulburn to Canberra and Yass, on to the inland towns of Cowra, Temora and Grenfell, and back to Sydney via Katoomba. Highlights along the way included being photographed at the Henry Lawson Memorial obelisk at Grenfell and lunch with the French-born squatter and fellow writer Paul Wenz on his property at Nanima.[113]

The second trip lasted five weeks, from 8 June to 9 July. To Carrie Whelan in California — her last letter before Carrie's death later in the year — Miles wrote when she got back to Sydney:

> I have had a wonderful change. I was hardly strong enough, or rather was too fatigued when I went away for the hard travelling but the relief from the care of my mother and being confined in such an enervating circle was wonderful. I went with two friends, a Mr and Mrs Clune, by car to Adelaide. We wandered all around inland Murrumbidgee towns (which is called my country as Wessex in England was called 'Hardy's), and then followed the Murray to the sea. From Adelaide we flew to the centre of Australia and then went to the geographic centre ... Look at the map. In all, 3000 miles by car and 2000 by plane. It was a lovely 10 passenger Lockheed Electra and we saw the red heart of Australia and the bed of Lake Eyre and the MacDonnell Ranges — colours ravishing like your Grand Canyon, Colorado stretches, only of course flat.[114]

They returned via the south-east of Australia and the Great Ocean Road, through Geelong (where Miles called on Dr De Garis of Ostrovo days), Ballarat and Melbourne. There Miles saw her old friends the Goldstein–Champion sisters and poor Alice Henry, whose only brother had been recently lost overboard on a trip to Japan, but missed Maud Walsöe, who died the following year.[115]

Miles and Frank Clune usually advised the local press in advance of their coming. Clune told the Adelaide *Advertiser* he was collecting material for two books: a travel book dealing with the Murrumbidgee and a historical romance in collaboration with Miss Miles Franklin, said to be 'a young New South Wales authoress'. (How this must have amused Miles, then going on fifty-eight.) In Melbourne, he told the press he was on the trail of two explorers, Sturt and Stuart, with Miss Franklin helping him, which is probably more like it. Speaking on her own behalf, Miles said she was collecting material for a book on the lower Murrumbidgee, which, given its role in *All That Swagger*, is plausible, though nothing seems to have come of it.[116]

A fine series of photos of their travels survives in the Franklin Papers, mostly featuring Miles as a prop. This, she told the Adelaide *Advertiser*, was the only drawback to the whole trip: 'Due to Mr Clune's insatiable interest in every bushranger's tomb and monument within miles of the track, I had to be photographed beside each one. I look like a corpse of the bushranger come to life and felt that at least to give beauty to his photographs Mr Clune should have asked a film star to accompany him.' In fact, she usually has a big smile, as when standing by an abandoned water cart in the Riverina. There she is in photo after photo with her lisle stockings, lace-up shoes and a trilby, in the same suit every time, possibly because she hadn't any other.[117]

Miles' literary notebook of the time makes exceptionally good reading — often amusing, sometimes uplifting — as a spontaneous response to vast stretches of Australia, more than she had seen before, and the ultimate expression of that alluring western perspective so long ago glimpsed from 'Stillwater' on the cusp of the Great Dividing Range. Of New South Wales country hotels she wrote, 'living in these places is like a bombardment, the noise is so terrific, the country fellows are going to drink till midnight, and the workers are up before six, banging around in the yard'. On one occasion they got bogged in the saltbush of the Old Man Plain near Moulamein and had to spend the night in the car. Apparently Frank Clune, who in

Try Anything Once tells us he was fleetingly part of an opera company, sang Thelma and Miles to sleep. At Leeton, Miles had the pleasure of meeting *Bulletin* contributor 'Jim Grahame' (James Gordon), a friend of Henry Lawson.[118]

In Mildura they went to the Grand Hotel, 'that looks like its name and most unpub-like. Palms and gardens and a glorious view of the Murray.' Next day they went out to Wentworth, at the junction of the Lachlan and the Murrumbidgee rivers, where, according to Miles, the explorer Charles Sturt 'met the blacks like a man and a gentleman'. To her, this unprepossessing spit was a haunted place, 'one of the most wonderful spots in Australia'. Later they called at the Mildura Workingman's Club, famous for a bar as long as two cricket pitches. Miles wrote it was a guzzler's paradise.

Three things stand out in Miles' diaries thereafter. The first is a visit to the great artist of the Australian gum tree, Hans Heysen, at Hahndorf in the Adelaide Hills. After 'a charming lunch' in surrounds which showed Heysen to be 'a man [of] means & taste', the visitors were escorted around his studio, where Miles greatly admired a painting of a red gum, 'magnificent [and] as heavy as marble', the work of a great craftsman. The gum tree would become Miles' shorthand for Australian content, a conceptualisation only recently rescued from cliché by Murray Bail's *Eucalyptus*. Second is the trip to the interior (her first by aeroplane): 'I loved it. I was at home here as some pilgrim reaching the goal.' It was also an adventure, and an exposure to new facets of Australian life, such as she delighted to see Xavier Herbert encompass in *Capricornia* and was always urging other writers to attempt. At Oodnadatta she met Afghans and visited an Aboriginal camp; somewhere near Alice Springs, at the famed bushman Bob Buck's camp, she sat on a camel; and when they reached Central Mount Stuart, she let out a lusty cooee. Back in Adelaide, Miles and Clune told the press that the 'dead heart' was a misnomer; and on 29 June they earned a handy six guineas for an interview on the ABC. The third important event occurred when, in Adelaide, Miles went to the state archives and read Catherine Helen Spence's unpublished novel 'Handfasted'. With the assistance of Spence's niece Lucy Spence Morice, she brought precious manuscript material back to Sydney, gladly received by her friend Ida Leeson, the Mitchell Librarian. Spence became another of Miles' causes — 'Australia's greatest woman', she declared — and she gave a talk on Spence's writings to Grattan's WEA class later in the year.[119]

The immediate task to be faced once back in Sydney, however, was the sketch of Rose Scott (now regarded as an important early study) for the forthcoming sesquicentenary gift book, a task requiring interviews as well as library researches. There was also further revision of the *Cockatoos* manuscript to be done.[120]

After 'a glimpse of heaven' with the Clunes, Miles was back to what she called her 24-hour-a-day job, as charwoman, laundress and housekeeper. To Mary Fullerton she reflected that it was ten years since she had read to them from 'the Australian series' in London, but now she felt herself going dead spiritually and mentally, with nothing but 'a few non-successes' to show, nominating *Bring the Monkey* as the best. (Presumably she meant that she had not managed to bring Brent up to date.) At the same time she asked Fullerton to look for a copy of that prewar favourite, Lester Ward's *Pure Sociology*, which she and Alice Henry had admired back in the Chicago days. Rather like Germaine Greer, whose books have followed her passage through the life cycle, the older Miles, following an earlier intellectual trajectory, now asserted the need for an objective moral standard based on good order and decency, and sexual restraint.[121]

What one would like to do and what one can do are often two different things, especially with encroaching age. Despairing diary entries in the second half of 1937 are evidence of Miles' mounting frustration. After one particularly futile day in December taken up with family, she wrote, 'It is maddening when I have so few days left.' She had no new writing under way. Political trends in Europe were perturbing. Her German cousin was a Junker and a Nazi. Mussolini-admiring Italians were emigrating to Australia, and Tories everywhere were in the ascendancy. As for Australia's own rising conservative, Robert Gordon Menzies, it sounded as if he was getting too big for his boots, letting it be known in London that he could run the British Commonwealth with one hand (so Miles told the Sydney bank manager S. B. Hooper, an associate of Stephensen and a new acquaintance).[122]

Friends continued to warn her against Stephensen's lurch to the Right, not only the Left-leaning Grattan, whose lectures on fascism and the prospects for neutrality in the event of war, as well as other political advice, she found helpful, but also Mary Fullerton, who deplored the coarseness of the *Publicist*, and Lucy Spence Morice, who, like Fullerton, felt that Inky's Australianism was 'too vehement'. But Miles could not yet see this, nor the signs of anti-Semitism, which she claimed to have missed until pointed out by Grattan. After hearing a visiting Canadian-Scot on the need to forget England, and go back as far as Aboriginal Australians to 'find our separate selves', Miles wrote to Fullerton that she agreed, not because she did not love England — she did — but because it was time to do 'something of our own', the political dimension to this position being that it was 'dreadful' that the New World should be dragged into European wars and suffer their tribalism. In her view, as part of the desired new moral standard, small nations off the beaten track should stand out for peace.[123]

Meanwhile, her causes continued to absorb a good deal of time and energy. In September she had further fun with the lamentable Professor Cowling ('Yowling'), who asserted that there were no Australian books suitable for schoolchildren, suggesting instead the feeble English *Troy Town*. Some progress was made too with Fullerton's poetry. A further edition of Dickinson's poetry appeared in 1937. With new research on the emotional lives of these two reticent women, much more could be said now about the parallels between Dickinson and Fullerton. Even then Miles was well aware of the background issues of sexual status, but for the time being she simply persisted with a longstanding commitment. Thus, she sought out Mary Gilmore. Dame Mary was impressed and was persuaded to write something for the *Australian National Review*. (Apparently Dame Mary suspected the poems were by Miles but, she said, 'I ask no questions'.) As for the Furphy abridgment, while Miles was away with the Clunes, Inky Stephensen had taken a hand, with a ferocious assault on Vance Palmer in the *Publicist*. But then Stephensen had long said Australian literature must be 'de-Palmerized', whereas Miles was much milder, and a firm advocate of Nettie, even if she thought the Palmers lacked humour.[124]

Was it not a good thing to get *Such Is Life* back in print, albeit abridged? Having studied the matter, cultural historian David Walker concludes that the fracas amounted to a battle between the 'primitives' and the 'professionals' for cultural leadership. Since both Stephensen and Franklin were thorough professionals, this concedes too much to the Palmers, and diminishes 'unprofessional' Sydney too, but it helps cast the now worn Melbourne-versus-Sydney culture theme in a different light. At the time, Grattan saw the spat as an example of the constant struggle between 'the virus of respectable mediocrity and the virile recklessness of sound unblinkered vision', and assured Miles that the rules of the drawing room did not apply: 'more power to your pen,' he wrote from Queensland. Though himself a graduate, he was, like Mary Fullerton, against 'Universityism'.[125]

Miles really had become an elder, and as is often the way of elders, far from disinterested. She had a view of what was important in Australian literary history, and was prepared to defend it. The preoccupation did nothing for her bank balance, further diminished by helping Mary Fullerton's sister Em, who came to Sydney after her business failed in Melbourne; and it was irrelevant at Grey Street. Susannah Franklin had another fall before Christmas, and Miss Gillespie was visibly failing: to see them together was 'a ghastly spectacle'. This year there were only five for Christmas dinner: Miles, her mother, her brother Norman, her nephew Jack and Mrs Wilkinson, the home help. On Boxing Day, Miles escaped to Castlecrag to see young Sylvia Brose's play *Mirabooka* at the open-air theatre, 'a so-called aboriginal play', she decided (rightly, since it was framed by an idealistic anthroposophy, with little bearing on the harsh realities of Aboriginal life, as exposed by parliamentary hearings on the policy of protectionism, which, like other feminists and nationalists, Miles had attended in November).[126]

Was it on the edge of the Government House fishpond at a morning tea party given by the Governor of New South Wales, Lord Wakehurst, and his wife, Lady Margaret, on 1 February 1938, or was it two days later on the manicured lawns of Admiralty House at an afternoon garden party hosted by the Governor-General of Australia, Lord Gowrie, and his wife, Lady Zara, that Miles Franklin and Dymphna Cusack first thought of writing a satire on the sesquicentenary of New South Wales? The first event was a reception to mark the opening of a Women's International Conference associated with the sesquicentenary, the second to farewell the delegates — none of whom, Miles noted, represented working women. Both she and Dymphna, disgusted by the servility on display, determined not to curtsey when their turn came. From Miles' diaries, it seems clear the project was first mooted on the lawns of Admiralty House. But Dymphna always thought it was at the edge of the fishpond at Government House that the aptly named collaboration *Pioneers on Parade* had its genesis, and hers is the better story, the substance of which rings true. As Dymphna recalled in 1977, the two writers were sitting muttering over their soggy sandwiches and lukewarm lemonade — suitable for a women's event, part of a token conference — when Miles had an inspiration. She poured the lemonade into the pond and said, 'Why don't we write a book about it?'[127]

The only other sesquicentennial event to which Miles was invited — probably by its white supporters, the Australia Firsters — was the then obscure, now historic, Aboriginal Day of Mourning at the Australian Hall in

Elizabeth Street, Sydney, though she did not attend. In any case it was for Aboriginal people only. She did attend the opening of an exhibition at the Mitchell Library, for which, she said ironically, 'Ida Leeson did [all the] work in the way of androcentric society.'[128]

Miles had no time for the celebrations. The 'shivoo' (party) made her 'so wild … that I wrote it all up in a diary … and Mr Miles' *Publicist* immediately wanted it for his paper, but I did not feel like such a fierce bout as it would involve,' she reported to Mary Fullerton. Nonetheless, she still felt 'it should be fictionalized in a satirical novel'. What annoyed her were the 'female excellencies' assembled from all over the country opening things with not a poor old pioneer in sight. (A similar situation pertained at the Sydney Opera House during Australia's 1988 Bicentenary, when *Pioneers on Parade* was reprinted and historians gave the title phrase another run.) Miles' objection was strong enough to carry the collaboration with Dymphna Cusack through, though she had had no success with earlier collaborations, and Dymphna, a teacher at Sydney Girls High School, was already overburdened and far from well.[129]

Most of the writing was done in the months immediately after the sesquicentenary and, it seems clear, Miles was the major contributor. Dymphna wrote chapters of sharp Sydney material at the beginning, while the subsequent undoing of sesquicentenary 'celebrities' at 'Pine Grove' (Grandma Brankston's property at Marulan), the acid asides about the state of international affairs, and the romantic convict- and pioneer-endorsing twist to the plot are all Miles, as must surely be the flight to Charleville to achieve a resolution, which comes with the unexpected arrival there by air of the shameless Lady Lucinda Cravenburn. Arriving back in Sydney, Lady Lucinda facilitates the marriage of her long-neglected daughter, the over-indulged and otherwise useless Lady Lucy, to the besotted 'Little Willie' Brankston, and by playing the maternal card overrides Grandma Brankston's previously immovable objection, an obstinate reverse pride in the pioneer family's hitherto unknown convict origins which precluded association with past persecutors. Along the way, the youth of Sydney get a lesson in proper values, and everyone rejects imperial honours. In *Pioneers on Parade*, headed 'For Australians Only', self-respecting values triumph over 'the silly Sesqui', and some very funny scenes are concocted. Not that all readers thought so: the reviews which followed publication by Angus & Robertson in July 1939 were mixed, and the eminent Shavian St John Ervine warned Miles not to waste her talent in future.[130]

Miles grumbled a bit in private about doing all the work, but the lively Dymphna was stimulating. They shared the editing task — there are four versions preserved in the Franklin Papers — and Miles loved Dymphna's 'fine polemical ideas'. Whoever thought up the Society for Purer Australian History and the Women's Circle of the League of Early Free Settlers (the 'Early Frees' for short) added something to the rather limited stock of hilarity in Australian history; and Miles and Dymphna had fun with the title, which at one stage was the Gilbertian 'The Iron Pot and the Silver Churn' (and apparently entered as such for the Prior Prize in 1938). When in late May Dymphna acknowledged Miles' greater input, Miles was mollified, and later did the proofing and business arrangements without a murmur. Indeed, to far-off friends she sometimes hazarded a reference to *Pioneers on Parade* as 'my Sesqui novel', which was claiming too much. Had she done so at home it might have disturbed the foundations of a developing friendship, of some literary significance.[131]

Dymphna and Miles had met as early as 1935. Between 1938 and Miles' death in 1954, they exchanged well over 200 letters. In 1935, Miles recorded her enjoyment of Cusack's play *Red Sky at Night*, and Cusack recalled Miles delivering her Eleanor Dark review at the FAW. Cusack also recalled that, unlike herself, Miles was a good committee woman, evident in her work in the first half of 1938 on the FAW executive for a scheme for subsidising both the writing of 'worthwhile books' and a Chair in Australian Literature. (When it was said there were no suitable men to fill the Chair, Miles responded that there were two women, naming Nettie Palmer and Flora Eldershaw, clearly a revolutionary suggestion. 'Australia is positively Troglodytic on the woman question,' she sighed to Nettie.)[132]

Having encouraged Alice Henry to write her autobiography and addressed the young women at Dr Booth's Domestic Science College at Kirribilli on pioneer women during the sesquicentenary, in May Miles reviewed Xavier Herbert's Sesquicentennial Prize-winning novel *Capricornia*, which she had already approved in manuscript. Apart from anything else, she thought it a wonderful handbook for 'practising feminists' (this referred to sexual relations on the frontier, a subject of great concern to Australian feminists in the 1930s), and 'definitely of the school led by Brent'. Meanwhile, because Brent was in abeyance, thanks to Blackwood's objectionable commercialism in rejecting the revised manuscript of *Cockatoos* (which meant it could not be entered in the sesquicentennial competition, as that required a certificate of impending publication), she made further efforts with her 1932 play 'Virgins

Out of Date' (which survives in a 1944 version as 'Virgins and Martyrs Out of Date'). And she found nourishment — a favourite Miles word — in public lectures. Early in 1938 she delighted especially in addresses by Eldershaw and Grattan on Australian literature. An earlier series by the librarian H. M. Green had earned judicious praise for openness, as compared with Prince Mirsky, whom she had heard in London in 1932: 'What was lacking in fury or intellectual strain was compensated for by freedom.' More such lectures were needed to cover the geographic diversity of the field and ultimately to assess how Australian material stood in relation to world literature, she thought.[133]

In February Miles had been startled to hear of the death of a girlhood friend, Tossie O'Sullivan. Now in June the losses came thick and fast, and while they were to be expected, no easier to bear for that. Wonderful Aunt Annie Franklin — she who could clean up the North-West Frontier while running Brindabella homestead — died at Queanbeyan on 5 June. A week later on 12 June Miss Gillespie, to whom the first edition of *Old Blastus of Bandicoot* had been dedicated, followed her. Miles did not tell her mother. Then three days later, in the early hours of 15 June, Susannah Franklin's time came.[134]

'You will be alone in this barn,' Susannah had said in her harsh way shortly before her death. Even Aunt Lena had moved to a residential on the North Shore a few years before. But with Jack and Norman coming and going, and with so much support from family and friends, was that the main point? What was? Miles had spent the years of her homecoming, in some ways her best years, caring for her mother, and now she was gone. The loss was very real, and it is not difficult even now to empathise with the grief, guilt and anxiety which threatened to overwhelm her. Alice Henry and Mary Fullerton both wrote wise letters, and as Mary said, 'You have nothing to reproach yourself with,' which was true. Even so it took several months for Miles to regain her equilibrium. To Hartley Grattan's mother she wrote, apropos of his impending return to America, that she understood Mrs Grattan's impatience to see him again, and of her own desolation after her mother's death:

> I, who have been round the world so often, more than understand. At every port my mother always had a letter waiting for me, whether it was the Pacific or the other route ... But there will never again be anyone thus to care about my homecomings or going. Mother passed away last month and if I stop to

remember the desolation, I am all to pieces. For eleven years I have never had Mother off my heart day and night and with her going everything seems to have ended for me too. I feel that I am old — prefer to get the ugly chore of death over now rather than later. I must just sheer away from the emptiness & be passive.[135]

This bleak letter was written from her Uncle Gus Lampe's property at Peak Hill. The cook there had hurt her hand so Miles went up to help out. She stayed for a month, from 12 July until 9 August, and when her aunt and cousin Metta both fell ill, she took on the washing and cleaning as well as the cooking. It filled the time, she wrote to Nettie Palmer, but 'depression supervenes and I'm so far down I don't want to come back to life'.[136]

But she did. Back in Sydney, perspective gradually returned. 'To say I grieve is unanalytical,' she wrote to Kate Baker in October. 'It is merely that the preoccupation and strain was so great for years that I was not strong enough to weather Mother's dissolution ... However, it doesn't matter.'[137]

That bespeaks acceptance. Yet Miles Franklin had felt for a time that her own life was over. 'Don't let your grief and exhaustion turn into an inferiority complex,' Alice Henry warned. The contrast between Miles' cheerful public persona and the depressed tone of much of her private writings raises the possibility of a depressive illness. However, the explanation may lie simply in the lack of real intimacy in her life.[138]

Some things lie too deep for documentation. Maybe it was implicit in Susannah Franklin's last barb about being left alone that, despite Mary Fullerton's reassurance, Miles did feel she had something to reproach herself with. It would be surprising if her mother had not in some way goaded her for remaining unmarried. Susannah quite possibly implied that for all the fuss that had been made of Miles, she was a failure as a daughter, especially an eldest daughter, and what is more, the only daughter to survive. Susannah had certainly made it clear that she was not overly impressed by Miles' literary output.

Among the many emotions Miles struggled with after her mother's death was a feeling of 'financial helplessness'. Susannah had long managed the family finances, and although Miles was careful and persistent about her writing income, she knew she lacked her mother's skill with money. Susannah had long been a termagant (Dymphna Cusack's word), and her death could be seen as a relief, but Miles could not allow herself those comforting clichés. Susannah Franklin's death left her, an ageing woman, alone and insecure in a harsh and moralistic world. She wrote to Alice Henry in October that except for her nephew Jack coming home at nights — he had left school and was employed by the Permanent Trustee Company in the city and living at Carlton with his aunt — she would be tempted to shut the door and lie down to starve to death.[139]

'In Australia,' Miles once said, 'you have to be a self-starter.' After Susannah Franklin's death, she did not feel up to creative work, but on her return from Peak Hill she finished typing *Pioneers on Parade* and prepared it for submission to publishers. Towards the end of the year she managed to review the poems of the vintner and ex-Anzac Harley Matthews, an associate of Inky Stephensen, and gave a broadcast or two. Then she had a bright idea. One of the reviews she had written earlier in the year was of *The Life Story of Joseph Furphy*, by Furphy's nephew Edward Pescott. The subject had been on her mind ever since the lamentable Palmer abridgment of *Such Is Life*, and Pescott's brief account merely drew attention to the need for a proper study. Suddenly she knew what to do. 'An idea has just come to me,' she wrote to Kate Baker in late October. Why didn't Baker come to stay for a few months at no cost, and together they could get Baker's Furphy material into shape? The next *Bulletin* Prize would be for biography. Was it not a grand idea? Baker replied that she lived frugally — it transpired that she had only 28 shillings a week to live on — and it would be an adventure for them both. The letters flashed back and forth throughout November, and to avoid attracting attention it was agreed that they would say that Baker was collecting data in Sydney.[140]

By 8 December 1938 the 77-year-old Kate Baker and her boxes were ensconced in the spare room at 26 Grey Street. The boxes contained 'a magnificent lot of things', but as it soon emerged poor Baker was quite deaf, and to Miles' mind a real amateur when it came to literary work. In consequence, things did not turn out as either of them envisaged. But at least Miles had a preoccupation to replace Susannah, and an important new project for when she returned from her annual summer break.[141]

After the 'virtual holocaust' of deaths in the first half of 1938 came lesser losses in the second, with the departure for America of Grattan on 5 September and of the widowed Marion Mahony Griffin in November, her Castlecrag friends weeping at the dock as the ship drew out. Miles saw them both off. Her emotional sustenance was now coming mainly through her remarkable correspondence (Dymphna Cusack, who saw it at this time, said it was neatly filed in boot- and hat-boxes, where Miles could find items in a trice), and she was effectively re-Australianised, as the Furphy project further signified. On a day-to-day basis she could call on new associates and a new generation of relatives, notably Gus Lampe's daughters Thelma and Phillis, and the Bridle sisters, Ruby and Leslie, with whom she was about to go riding in Cotter River country — she practised astride a chair beforehand. Best of all, she was buoyed by the admiration and friendship of younger women writers like Cusack.

The young writers admired Miles Franklin for her tenacity. Yet there was more than tenacity. They admired — or, like Marjorie Barnard, vaguely resented — her unique blend of cosmopolitanism and nationalism, that experience of the world which gave her some ineffable authority at FAW meetings. Miles Franklin's position as an Australian nationalist by the end of the 1930s has sometimes been misunderstood, not unreasonably, given the excesses of the cultural nationalists and Australia Firsters with whom she associated in Sydney. In fact, her outlook was much the same as that of the anthropologist Margaret Mead, who once said that you can't be a good internationalist if you don't love your own country. When challenged by the spluttery Chicagoan Leonora Pease, last seen in Devon in 1925, and who until the Anschluss of March 1938 lived in Vienna, Miles hastened to set straight her views on 'pacificism' and nationalism, explaining that she still repudiated all talk of wars — 'There is always one last war to end war' — and as for nationalism, 'I so love my own land that I know how to be at one with other people's love of their lands … I think I love the Americans best of all peoples that I know. In England I love the things that men have made, the food for the intellect, the art treasures, the social contacts possible, and in Australia it is the continent itself.'[142]

12

MAINTAINING OUR BEST
TRADITIONS: 1939–1945

'Culture will survive war.'[1]

O n the evening of Sunday 3 September 1939, walking along Pitt Street
with Louis Esson after a reading of Leslie Rees' play *Lalor of Eureka* by
the New Theatre League, Miles Franklin saw a late news poster declaring
that Britain and France were at war with Germany. At first she assumed that
it was 'the same old war', but well before the supposedly impregnable British
naval base at Singapore fell to the Japanese on 15 February 1942, she
understood that it was a 'new war'. The 'new war' for Australians, the war in
the Pacific, lasted until the Japanese surrender on 15 August 1945. It was to
be a long war. Reluctantly at first, but with increasing clarity of mind
following the Battle of Britain in the northern summer of 1940 and
dissociation from the Australia First movement thereafter, Miles rose to the
occasion. She was too old to sign up as a cook again, but still resolute
against armchair warriors. This time she found her métier in what she
described as 'maintaining our best traditions'. Indeed, the Furphy project
ensured she was well placed to perceive the relationship between culture
and society at a time of total war.[2]

Like most thoughtful people, Miles had long been anxious about the war
clouds gathering over Europe. She hung on to her pacificist — the
contemporary adjective indicating that she was close to but not an absolute
pacifist — views as long as she could. Letters written in 1939, particularly to
the Fullerton–Singleton household in London, show her to have been on

the one hand deeply mistrustful of the appeasers, and on the other, resolutely anti-war. She thought, rightly, that the British governing classes feared Russia more than Germany: 'The only ally for England is Russia but the British Fascists and their hankerers like Chamberlain and all that privileged crowd would rather risk losing all than giving in to the possibility of such an experiment in democracy.' She was therefore 'more than thankful' for Virginia Woolf's *Three Guineas*, which showed, she averred, that Charlotte Perkins Gilman was right, that war was the madness of men.[3]

When the Australian High Commissioner in London, Stanley Bruce, reported on 24 January 1939 that the Chamberlain–Hitler meeting in 1938 had saved the world from war, Miles was just back from a three-week camping holiday in the upper Cotter region over the New Year with Ivy Maxwell and her husband, Jack, and Ivy's nieces Ruby and Leslie Bridle (the daughters of Ivy's sister Annie May and Henry Ernest Bridle). Jack Maxwell, formerly assistant manager at Thomas Franklin's Brindabella, an outstanding horseman and the first ranger of the upper Cotter, Canberra's water catchment area, was their expert guide. Miles slept well in her tent by the Cotter River, and delighted to find in riding Maxwell's pet mountain horse that although she might be by now a weak and unpractised 'townie', she was still horse-wise. There were expeditions to old haunts such as Ginini Flats and the Blue Waterhole, and to various peaks such as Mount Franklin. New Year's Eve, with local sheep men and food galore, was followed by 'a great day, a picnic a-horse'; and she was unfazed subsequently by 'the hottest day in history', when bushfires raged around Sydney and further south in the Victorian high country. Box Brownie camera images of Miles in jodhpurs beside the great horse, with her young cousins on top of a mountain, and sitting in a stream in her swimming costume, have survived.[4]

She returned to Sydney by train on 15 January, arriving home just before midnight. It took two days to get through her mail, and with Kate Baker in residence as well as her nephew Jack, Miles had three people to cook and clean for most of the time. Baker, now aged seventy-eight, a pensioner, stone deaf and unable to afford an ear trumpet or to lip-read, was in for her own purgatory: 'Collaboration at best is not a happy thing,' Baker confessed to a friend when safely back in Melbourne after five months' absence. Given Baker's dedication to the memory of Joseph Furphy and her assiduous promotion of his reputation since her retirement from teaching in 1912, also the year of Furphy's death, her literal and grammatical approach to the project, and a self-effacing — perhaps somewhat passive — personality, it is hardly surprising that Miles' energetic, even commanding style at first upset and then overwhelmed her. As Furphy's biographer John Barnes has said, a falling-out was probably inevitable.[5]

The collaboration began unequally, but then came a bombshell. Miles' diary entry for the last day of January reads: 'Got A. Stewart's letter with disclosures about KB [Kate Baker], Leonie and Joe. Not to mention them is making a meat pie without the meat but they have to be kept secret.' Annie Stewart was Furphy's younger sister, and Leonie his wife (she died in 1936). The disclosure pertained not only to the unhappy marriage ('a tragedy for them both,' wrote Stewart), but also to an unfortunate incident when the young Kate Baker, suffering from typhoid, wrote an impassioned letter to Furphy. Leonie saw the letter and wrote to Kate Baker's mother alleging impropriety, though the charge was retracted at Furphy's insistence. Baker never knew a thing about this exchange. She told Miles she could not even remember the typhoid. A further disclosure pertained to Baker's incarceration in an asylum after Furphy's death, which she did acknowledge but apparently recalled nothing of. According to John Barnes' biography, no improprieties occurred, and Miles responded to Annie Stewart wisely. In her Preface to their book on Furphy she simply noted: 'The time is not yet ripe for a definitive biography of Joseph Furphy.'[6]

Over the next three months, Miles worked hard on the Furphy project. In retrospect she said, and she was right, that it was a terrific piece of work under the circumstances. Whereas in Chicago, she had abandoned Furphy due to his embarrassing comparisons between her and such heavyweights as Marcus Aurelius, Daniel Defoe and Jonathan Swift, and knew any account of his constricted life would have limited appeal, personally she found the project of compelling interest. Problems of collaboration notwithstanding, she managed in that short time to produce the draft of a biography which, in published form, was to be for fifty years the best available reference on this 'bush Hamlet'. It is still valuable for, among other things, its penetrating portrait of a shy man, and its bold assessment of his magnum opus, *Such Is Life*, now admired more for its modernity than its bushwhackery. Miles saw this in a highly topical comparison with James Joyce's *Ulysses* (then banned in Australia), and drew a wonderful image of *Such Is Life* as the literary equivalent of Ayers Rock (now Uluru) rising from the plains.[7]

Miles' objective, it may be recalled, was the 1939 Prior Prize. On 5 June, a fortnight or so after Baker's departure, she and her friend, the bank manager and Australia First supporter S. B. Hooper, dropped the typescript, entitled 'Who Was Joseph Furphy?' (by 'Glow-worm') into the *Bulletin* office for judging. Hooper had a high opinion of it. 'Hope he is right,' muttered Miles. She probably had in mind her enticements to Kate Baker the previous year, when inviting Kate to Sydney. However, she had seen all the available materials and was not about to give up hope. The prize had not been awarded since 1936 (the year when *All That Swagger* won), and its scope had been widened to include all prose works, not just novels. Moreover, the prize monies from 1937 and 1938 were to be carried over, so that the amount to be won in 1939 would be £300. Otherwise, the rules were unchanged, that any bona fide resident of Australia or anyone born in Australasia or the British South Pacific islands was eligible to enter, and the work must be the entrant's own original work and previously unpublished in any shape or form. The usual rules to ensure blind assessment pertained (that is, the manuscript had to be submitted under a nom de plume with an accompanying sealed envelope giving the author's true name and address). As an FAW stalwart and its vice-president since March, Miles would have been familiar with the rules, and there would not have been cause for concern on that score.[8]

The next she heard of the biographical essay, as it was originally described, was from fellow writer Frank Dalby Davison, the FAW president in 1936–37, and, as *Bulletin* reviewer, a prize assessor, who remarked that someone had sent in 'a damn good book on Furphy'. The judges, however, awarded the prize to journalist-historian M. H. Ellis, for a mammoth biography of Governor Macquarie. Miles tried to reassure Kate that no one could have won against such a project, especially as Ellis was on the *Bulletin* staff. But Ken Prior, editor of the *Bulletin* and a trustee of the award, was not satisfied, and sent Ellis' manuscript to Ida Leeson at the Mitchell Library as an authority on the subject. After a fortnight's examination, Ida declared the work undocumented and full of inaccuracies, 'altogether in an unfinished condition', Miles reported to Mary Fullerton. So the judges were required to meet again and 'Who Was Joseph Furphy?' was elevated from 'highly commended' to first place, with a rider that entry No. 62 (the Ellis manuscript) would have won had it been fully documented and the references checked.[9]

Ellis was remarkably good about this. Miles was immensely relieved. Replying to congratulations from Jean Devanny, both personally and on behalf of the Communist Party of Australia, Miles wrote: 'I am glad for KB's sake … Otherwise she would have thought that my design and handling of the material which she has so devotedly collected, was at fault.' To Kate Baker she wrote simply, 'I am so glad, for your sake,' adding, 'our work has been recognized to some extent,' and, since Prior wanted to publish as soon as possible, they would need to 'spring off our tails like good kangaroos with the finishings-up'. But something went wrong and the essay did not appear in book form until published by Angus & Robertson in 1944. Pretty soon Miles was complaining that Baker thought the manuscript was perfect and did not want any changes. Still, she generously sent Kate £5 from her advance for *Pioneers on Parade*, and much later, anonymously, more money. They shared the Prior Prize of £100 equally (the prize was awarded 'without accumulations' — a mean decision said Stephensen).[10]

Miles was not so sensitive about the next phase of the Furphy project. As early as 27 August 1939 in a letter to Kate she referred to 'my book', and in the original the word 'my' is underlined by hand, evidently Kate's. A few days later, commending Kate for further work on a proposed Furphy memorial at Kyneton, north-west of Melbourne, Miles wrote, 'my biography will have to be my contribution to memorials'. Despite numerous assertions to the contrary, and careful acknowledgement of Kate's input on the title page of the eventual publication, *Joseph Furphy: The Legend of a Man and his Book* 'By Miles Franklin, in association with Kate Baker', Miles was much more than a midwife.[11]

In the letter to Baker of 27 August, Miles told Baker that the struggle to get the biography to its present state had exhausted her and she would need a small grant to finish it. Once again her work for writers stood her in good stead. The first Commonwealth Literary Fellowships were awarded in 1939, largely due to pressure from the FAW, and she was among the beneficiaries. As announced in December, she was granted a six-month fellowship worth £125 'to complete a biography of Joseph Furphy'. The seriousness of her commitment to the project is evident in the volumes of research material and correspondence generated and preserved in the Franklin Papers. Just as Miles' friendship with Grattan had a supervisory quality, her collaboration with Kate Baker served to rescue historic material which might otherwise have been lost or dispersed. The 'Furphy adventure' had been brought, she assured Baker, to triumphant fruition.[12]

They were fortunate to get so much done before the war, Miles reflected. Later, paper shortages and other factors would hold up publication indefinitely. It was also timely. Interest in Furphy's work had been slowly rising since World War I, when the devoted Baker oversaw a reissue of *Such Is Life* and put together an edition of his poems. The legend of Joseph Furphy assumed a whole new significance in World War II, when Furphy, 'part bushman, part dreamer', seemed to many the archetypal common man, iconic, an answer to 'What are we fighting for?'. Miles had not anticipated that when she first thought of the project in 1938, nor perhaps even in 1939 when working on it, but the 1944 book dedication reads 'For Australia', and the volume ends on a rousing note:

> Few things are more potent than song or story in relating peoples to their soil and in crystalling natural aspirations, a function which expands into the announcement of international understanding. For forty years *Such Is Life* has had significance in the developing Australian way of life. Through his shining faith in the future of his country and his courageous brief for the brotherhood of man Furphy remains a force in Australia's contribution to all freedom-demanding people's concept of New Orders.[13]

After the effort of collaboration, Miles collapsed with a bad attack of pleurisy in the second half of June 1939. There was also bad news for Brent from Blackwood that *Gentlemen at Gyang Gyang* could not be published 'at this time'. On a positive note, Miles had also seen *Pioneers on Parade* through the press while working on the Furphy manuscript, having finished with the text of the sesquicentennial satire in early March. Authors' copies arrived on 4 July. Miles immediately sent one to Prime Minister Menzies, with a note, duly acknowledged by him, expressing the hope that Australia would be a site of citizenship, not military vassalage.[14]

Reactions to *Pioneers on Parade* were mixed. However, the *Bulletin* was kind. 'It is not one book but two — an amusing skit on Sydney's social climbers, and a message about the land.' And the literary world was mainly enthusiastic. Majorie Barnard and Flora Eldershaw promptly telegraphed congratulations ('helpless with mirth'), and the West Australian writer Henrietta Drake-Brockman wrote to record her enjoyment — 'wit is such a rare thing in Australia' — and her envy of Miles' productivity, reflecting that she was constrained by family and her husband's official position. She also promised the publisher to review it favourably ('a laugh on every page'), while the irrepressible Frank Clune told Walter Cousins, the director of publishing at Angus & Robertson, that *Pioneers on Parade* was a bonzer book by a pair of dinkum Aussie sheilas who knew their onions — 'and their snobs'. Vance Palmer would have liked something less hilarious and more searching, but Miles didn't mind that. Nor did she mind that it was too much for the conservative Sydney press types known to be after imperial honours; and as for a 'contemptuous' Adelaide review, well, what could you expect? What probably did sting was the opinion of the English critic St John Ervine: 'If you continue to write smarty-smart novels like *Pioneers on Parade*, you will soon cease to be worthy of any person's serious notice.'[15]

It reminded Miles of the reception of *My Brilliant Career*, except that she quite enjoyed the fuss this time. The basic problem was one of timing. When *Pioneers on Parade* appeared, the war clouds were thickening, and imperial values were again in the ascendant. Any suggestion of disloyalty was frowned upon; and book sales stalled.

Miles returned to the task of publishing Mary Fullerton's poems. On the afternoon of 2 September, Miles Franklin had joined the FAW's annual pilgrimage to Henry Lawson's statue near Mrs Macquarie's Chair in Sydney's Outer Domain. On the way back to the city centre, she enjoyed talking to old Billy Miller (also known as Linklater), who had once worked for P. S. Watson and his brothers up north, and then fell in with Tom Inglis Moore, the writer and critic who had stood in as president of the FAW in 1934 and was still with the *Sydney Morning Herald*. Moore had agreed to help edit a volume of Mary's poems and write a preface, to which Miles would add something on the human side, she told Mary, and although he was more interested in *Pioneers on Parade* at the time, Miles was nursing him: 'I think he is my best bet.'[16]

The pair began meeting over afternoon tea at the Hotel Metropole in December to select the most suitable from among some 350 poems Miles had lovingly collected and typed for consideration over the preceding seven years. A harmonious collaboration ensued, testimony to Moore's affable personality. By August 1940, the preface had been finalised and Moore was in the army. Delayed further by the exigencies of war, *Moles Do So Little with their Privacy* by 'E' was published by Angus & Robertson in 1942. (It seems that only Miles knew the identity of 'E', the nearest Mary Eliza Fullerton could bring herself to a signature, and that Miles did not reveal it until after Mary's death in 1946.)[17]

During the year Miles made some interesting new friends, such as the exuberant bushman and Aboriginal rights advocate Michael Sawtell and botanist and curator Richard Baker, who presented her with a waratah-patterned cup and saucer designed by Lulu Shorter for the English china manufacturer Doulton. Miles developed a custom of offering her 'waratah cup' to special guests who, as they became more conscious of the honour, were nervous about dropping it. Meanwhile, her friendships with younger women writers, especially Cusack and Dark, but also Devanny and, more recently, Drake-Brockman, continued to be sustaining. Yet when she read the young Patrick White's *Happy Valley*, set around Kiandra, her own country, she did not think much of it. (On reflection, neither did he.)[18]

As 1939 drew to an end, the 'phoney war' in Europe was far off. In the quiet of Carlton, Miles was busy with the Furphy project Mark II. She was encouraged by Annie Stewart's good opinion of her work, likewise that of Furphy's son, Sam, and his wife, Mattie. Letters from old associates like Mary Dreier in New York cheered her and provided an outlet for her political opinions, which remained hostile to 'the same old war'. But an atypical dreariness came to pervade her letters and diaries in late 1939. She had complained mid-year to Jean Hamilton about feeling trapped, that looking after two self-indulgent males was getting her down (her brother Norman, now permanently employed as an inspector with the New South Wales Milk Board, was working on the south coast, but made Grey Street his weekend base from mid-1939, and Jack, his son, was still in full-time residence). 'I cannot wait on them and do the garden and three meals a day,' reads one diary entry. Christmas Day was worse than usual. As for New Year's Eve, late in the afternoon Norman and Jack suddenly announced they were off to the city, leaving Miles all alone.[19]

A picnic in the Royal National Park south of Sydney on New Year's Day with her next-door neighbours, the Fogdens, was a poignant reminder of the family picnic her late brother Tal had organised when she left Australia in 1924: 'Poor old Mother used to complain so bitterly that all her mates were gone — mine all going fast.' Such pleasant events helped to put petty irritations in perspective. Norman and Jack were both sullen and secretive, but it was not the same as being bombed, she reminded herself when writing, often at night to stave off sleeplessness, to friends in war-affected England.[20]

There are approximately 350 letters preserved to and from Miles Franklin in 1940. While Miles made no bones about her circumstances, mostly her letters are about her work and the world at war. It was only in passing that she reflected more deeply: 'In youth you only need courage but in years you must have fortitude, and that is infinitely more courageous.' Or, as she had once put it to Frank Clune, protesting against his use of the word 'conquest' as applied to Australian history: 'The one great conquest of man — of each and all of us — is conquest of ourselves.'[21]

On 3 January 1940 Miles banked her first CLF cheque, worth almost £5 a week for six months. This, along with her share of the rent from two shops in Willoughby, a northern Sydney suburb, inherited from Susannah, meant she was better off materially than for years. As well, her resentful attitude to 'the same old war' was being challenged, especially by Mary Fullerton. Fullerton had read Hitler's *Mein Kampf,* and as she explained to Miles in a letter dated 15 January 1940, her feelings were quite different from what they had been in 1914–18: whereas the previous war had seemed a sordid territorial or trade shindig, it was clear the world now faced 'a foul philosophy and the time having come, [that] it is now in action'; 'the Hitler crowd' would lead to enslavement. Their 'Chosen People' attitude, especially towards Jews, was worse than contemptible. Thus, although Fullerton felt that democracy needed reshaping, 'the first and immediate [task] must be the overthrow of Nazism'.[22]

Like most Australians, Miles was slow to fully comprehend the situation in Germany, and in holding to an isolationist position, ill-equipped to do so. Indeed, a friendly letter to the Irish politician and poet Desmond Fitzgerald (whom Miles had met in Dublin in 1919), dated 6 February 1940, barely mentions the war. (Miles was more interested in a vaguely recalled literary prize for writers of Irish extraction.) For the time being, Australia First remained a dominant idea among her immediate associates; and she was all for an independent foreign policy, as she averred in a letter to Prime Minister Menzies expressing hostility to outmoded swashbucklers like Winston Churchill and the British Union of Fascists leader, Sir Oswald Mosley.[23]

Meanwhile, there was the preparation of a new edition of *All That Swagger,* to be published mid-year — the first by Angus & Robertson — and the possibility that S. B. Hooper would sponsor the publication by a local printer, Catts, of the Brent books. When this came to nothing, the possibility of publishing them under the auspices of the *Publicist* was raised. Having polished up 'Not the Tale Begun' (*Prelude to Waking*) early in the year, Miles, posing as agent, offered Hooper nine Brent volumes. 'Ye Aboriginal Gods!', responded Hooper, who was normally chivalric and deferential, addressing Miles as 'Little Ladye': 'This fellow "Brent". Can he produce the three unwritten [volumes]?' In May, Hooper wrote to Blackwood about the Australian rights, only to be told that although Brent owned the copyright, Blackwood retained publishing rights. This, along with Miles Franklin's distaste for Catts' 'shark-like' approach, was probably enough to dish the project.[24]

When Angus & Robertson announced an anthology of Australian poetry, to be selected by George Mackaness, formerly president of the FAW, Miles thought there could hardly be a worse editor, but she hastened to suggest poems by 'E' for inclusion, seeking power of attorney from Fullerton, now frail and living in Sussex, and providing Mackaness with copies of poems as requested. In October he wrote that he had selected twelve poems. (However, his *Poets of Australia* (1946) contained only seven, five by 'E' and two published earlier by Fullerton under her own name.) Librarian H. M. Green, who was invited to prepare another anthology later in the year, thought that 'E' was a poet all right, and a thinker too, but lacked originality. Miles told Mary not to worry, his opinions were always second-hand but he was friendly personally and, as proved to be the case, 'we shall get into that precious anthology'. Green included one poem by 'E' in *Australian Poetry* (1943), and four in his *Modern Australian Poetry* in 1946.[25]

R. G. (Guy) Howarth, who in 1939 with the linguist A. G. Mitchell was a founding editor of the Sydney University-based literary journal *Southerly*, was now seeking contributions. In 1940 Miles made two, the first a sprightly review of the journal's first issue, in which she was particularly pleased to find that it was hospitable to poets: poets could still inspire, whereas scientists and philosophers all too often served the war machine. Her second contribution, a reply to the toast to Australian literature at the annual dinner of the journal's sponsor, the Australian English Association (as the Sydney branch of the English Association was then known), at the University of Sydney in November, was more fearful, suggesting that the war might see the end of the beginning of a native literature. On her trip up country in mid-1937 with Frank Clune — she amused herself by referring to him as 'a great man' — she had found Australian literature in short supply, swamped by imported titles pushed by overseas publishers, who were full of preconceptions. There was always some obstacle facing Australian writers. What lay ahead she could not say, but 'in view of what the war may do to us I feel that any toast to any sprouts and vestiges of Australian literature as we have been dreaming of it needs to be in the form of Hail and Farewell.'[26]

Miles enjoyed herself again when the *Bulletin* caricaturist John Frith made a likeness of her. Apparently the *Bulletin* had not previously allowed caricatures of women in its pages (and even this one seems not to have appeared). The novelty encouraged Miles to indulge in a little fantasy. Just as she sometimes spoke of Cusack and Dark as her literary daughters ('my two gals of whom I am so proud') and had told friends that with *Pioneers on Parade* she was pioneering a new field in Australian literature, so consenting to the caricature meant that 'once again I am leading my flock'.[27]

Delicate issues continued to arise with the Furphy project. Kate Baker was upset when Miles queried her ownership of the copyright on *Such Is Life* (correctly, as it turned out, as Furphy had ceded it to the *Bulletin* in 1903). She was even more annoyed by Miles' Commonwealth Literary Fellowship, which she felt showed lack of recognition of her own contributions and caused her to protest to the CLF. Miles busied herself responding to these matters, to the extent, she recalled many years later, of offering to give the fellowship back, but took heart when Furphy's nephew and first biographer, Edward Pescott, was encouraging. When Sam and Mattie Furphy, who had been caravanning in Sydney over the summer, invited her to join them on their return trip south in February, she gladly accepted, not only for the break but as an opportunity to check Furphy sites in central Victoria and to clear up misunderstandings in Melbourne if possible.[28]

It took four days via Canberra and Wangaratta to reach Colbinabbin, some 70 kilometres south of Echuca in northern Victoria, where they camped for ten days (Miles slept in the car), after which she went on alone to Melbourne by coach. Arriving in Melbourne on 20 February, she stayed at the Federal Hotel, and over the next fortnight saw all her old friends, first contacting Baker to set things straight about the fellowship and checking on Alice Henry. She attended several literary events, including a meeting of the Lawson Society in Footscray, where a poisonous situation regarding Kate Baker's role in the biography was manifest, and a PEN club dinner, attended by all the Melbourne writers, including Vance Palmer.[29]

'Melbourne always uplifts me,' Miles said after the visit — and the writers were hospitable. This time she met the bibliophile John Kinmont Moir. She also visited a fragile Louis Esson in hospital. But it was, Miles wrote to Dymphna Cusack afterwards, 'a queer situation', and she was not after all successful in allaying Baker's concerns, which extended to demanding the inclusion in the biography of a section written by herself, and recognition as the inspiration for *Such Is Life*. Since that was untrue and Miles could not reveal all she knew, she could not allay the concerns of Nettie Palmer either. Nettie, like others, had heard only Baker's side of the story: that her contribution had not been properly acknowledged and her rights were being overridden. It is difficult to know what Miles could have done. 'I shall do everything compatible with literary and biographical proportion … and let her [Baker] retain her heroine-ship,' she concluded. It was a profitable research trip nonetheless, as she met several of Furphy's friends, notably Stanley Cathels and Molly Bowie (née Winter). The journalist John McKellar, who had so favourably reviewed *All That Swagger*, took her for a drive to Yarra Glen where the first memorial to Furphy had been installed in 1934 and she was able to give Ambrose Pratt the manuscript to read.[30]

Miles had hoped that Alice Henry would be able to read it too, but ruefully concluded that Alice was past it. The personal memoir which Miles had urged her to write, though with no great expectations, proved to be dead wood. Happily, Alice was able to get into town from her Armadale nursing home, though not for much longer, as she became bedridden after a fall in October. Miles made sure she saw a lot of her. (It was just as well, since it was for the last time — Alice Henry died in 1943.) To Alice's delight, there was even a little party before Miles left, given by Nettie Palmer. Other significant friends who were visited by Miles included Mary Fullerton's sisters, her goddaughter, Penrith-born Amy McCutchan and the Goldstein sisters. (Talking to Miles inspired Vida to write to her afterwards about the need for a crusade to bring about radical social change.) In due course *Woman's World* magazine reported that the 'famous Australian author' Miles Franklin had been in town.[31]

Miles left Melbourne by train on the evening of 5 March. Back home many letters and a lot of male mess awaited her. Mabel Singleton had advised her to do less housework, but she could not leave the garden untidy or neglect her bantam hens, who would soon be laying for the war effort. Over the next two months she was once more flat out on the Furphy manuscript — 'I must keep to my burrow with this biography,' she wrote to Grattan — and by mid-year she was thinking of it as part of her war work. 'I am coming to the end of the biography,' she wrote to Molly Bowie in June. 'God knows if we will be left with a culture and literature but I have no intention of giving in till I'm ninety, so I did the task that was nearest and am finishing my consignment.'[32]

By August it was done. On 21 August 1940 she sent a copy of the completed work ('by Miles Franklin') to the CLF office, along with 'I Sing

My Own Song' by 'E' and a note to the effect that the six-month grant had also enabled her to type up some poems which had been worrying her for years.[33]

'I struggle like a fly in tar, but get no time and have no strength to achieve much,' Miles wrote to Henrietta Drake-Brockman in response to her admiring remarks about her productivity. She felt flat because Angus & Robertson was publishing *All That Swagger*, but had forgotten to send her the proofs beforehand: 'I had so wanted to improve on the *Bulletin* printing,' she noted ruefully.[34]

But now the whole focus of her work was changing. Creative writing was being overtaken by a preoccupation with other projects, largely historical. Not that this is especially odd — an interest in history, and concern about their place in it, comes to many older people — and it did not preclude other literary work, such as topical writings, short stories and plays. The other reality was that even before the war, Miles had become more than the 'natural fact' she had aspired to on her return to Sydney in 1932. She was now a prominent elder. As such she was increasingly called upon to do the things elders must do: to record and reflect, to supervise the young, to support good causes and to speak out on issues of the day.

For example, in early 1940 she attended meetings of a committee established by Inky Stephensen to raise money for a bust of A. G. Stephens, to be located in the Mitchell Library. Something like this had been attempted before, and once again, although the money was raised and a cast prepared by sculptor Frank Lynch, nothing permanent eventuated. Perhaps it was just as well for the reputation of A. G. Stephens that it did not, since Stephensen was increasingly rabid for Australia First and looking for heroes.[35]

A better cause championed by Eleanor Dark, Marjorie Barnard and Flora Eldershaw was free speech. As wartime censorship began to bite, writers had reason to protest, and the reluctance of some FAW members to do so ('the oddments', or, as in the pocket diary, 'nitwits') made Miles cross. When the police raided the New Theatre for playing Rupert Lockwood's *No Conscription* (it was banned after the first performance on 17 May), she signed a protest drafted by Barnard and Eldershaw. It reads in part: 'Even in these difficult and dangerous times … we would deplore any suppression of those civil rights contained in free expression, and most earnestly and respectfully urge our authorities to leave untouched those liberties that are the basis of our life and for whose continuance we are fighting.'[36]

This was what Miles Franklin meant about maintaining 'our best traditions'. Civil censorship had been a thorn in the side of the Australian intelligentsia since the 1880s, and a blight on cultural life in the interwar years, when Australians were unable to read James Joyce's *Ulysses*, Aldous Huxley's *Brave New World*, and many other modern works, most of which Miles had read as a matter of course in London. Military censorship made things worse. On another front, in early 1940, due to her association with Michael Sawtell as well as Stephensen, she also supported the Aboriginal Progressive Association's campaign for an Aboriginal representative on the recently constituted Aborigines Welfare Board in New South Wales.[37]

More difficult were her responses to some other war-related issues, notably Japan and refugees. If it was fortunate for the reputation of A. G. Stephens that Inky Stephensen's memorial project fizzled out, it was unfortunate for Miles Franklin's that she maintained her association with the *Publicist* crowd for so long, out of loyalty perhaps, having learned a lot from Inky and all the while supporting his long-suffering and needy wife, Winnie. Miles had ceased to see Inky as a literary saviour and she had no time for his patron since 1936, W. J. Miles, due to his anti-feminism; but she continued to subscribe to the *Publicist*.

On 14 June 1940, the day France fell and Britain stood alone against the Nazis, on A. G. Stephens Memorial Fund letterhead Stephensen wrote to Miles as follows: 'Great changes are coming, as the entire bluff of "Democratic" Plutocracy is called in Europe by the desperate "Have Nots"! The German victories reveal culpable inefficiency [of] Britain. Australia must stand *alone* — our best friends will be the Japanese.'[38]

Presumably she ignored this outburst. She often regretted that she was too old to serve: 'I wish they would take me to record the history of the Australian women in the campaign,' she wrote wistfully to Molly Bowie. But as late as November 1940 she did not know what to think about Japanese objectives.[39]

Inky Stephensen's just-quoted words express his muddled transition from far Left to far Right; and his anti-Semitism became more pronounced. Miles did not know what to think of this either. Responding to Nettie Palmer's concern about anti-fascist refugees, she was unable to sympathise much, on the grounds that many refugees in the Sydney suburbs seemed to be quite rich, and some were underselling local labour, while her Chicago experience had been that immigrant men, once settled, opposed votes for women. It worried her that Jewish teachings reduced intermingling with gentiles to 'miscegenation'. 'Can you give me an answer to these problems?' she asked Nettie. In that same letter to Nettie Palmer, she said far worse: that she was sick of the paranoid slaughter of all the blue-eyed, fair-haired youth, German or British, and of the Islamic and Mongol hordes 'breeding and breeding'.[40]

In May 1940 she told Alice Thacher Post she was reading H. C. Peterson's *Propaganda for War: The Campaign against American Neutrality 1914–1917*, which she'd had specially imported from the United States, and Hartley Grattan's follow-up, *The Deadly Parallel*, approving in particular Grattan's Chapter 14, 'So You'd Like War' — America having yet to join what seemed still to be a noxious European war. But after the Blitzkrieg began in late May, and the British evacuation of Dunkirk in June, anxiety about English friends softened her attitudes. It might still be the same old war, but 'the letters I get from England amaze me. The writers seem to be less worried about the war than I am myself,' she wrote to the T. B. Smiths. The same day she also wrote to Phyll and May Meggitt: perhaps they could come to Australia with evacuated children — she had a spare room — and she would help the war effort in every way she could. Miles also reported (ominously) that her nephew Jack hankered to join up.[41]

As the Battle of Britain got under way in August, Miles wrote to Margery Furbank of Minerva days, last seen in London in 1930 and now living in New York with Margery Currey, inquiring of old associates such as H. M. Baker and noting with some bemusement that, from radio news, the British seemed to be enjoying themselves coping with the air raids, whereas she was so fearful: 'These are terrific days and as each day draws to a close I wonder how England has weathered the night.' Memories of Macedonia came flooding back, and she wrote to Dr De Garis in Geelong, who would still be able to serve whereas she, Miles, probably could not: 'Remember the time we went to Salonique together and also on that trip up the mountains?' A few days later, Sister Kerr turned up from her hospital at Burketown in Far North Queensland for lunch at the Metropole and 'a talk over our Ostrovo days'.[42]

It was en route to lunch with Sister Kerr that Miles picked up a copy of Havelock Ellis' recently published autobiography, *My Life*, something different to reflect on amid the world crisis. He still intrigued her, even if he was an 'old ass', and the ruination of his poor wife: 'I always did resist [his] findings.' They did not accord with imagination, she said. No doubt his approach to homosexuals as an intermediate or third sex did not accord with Miles' views either.[43]

On 19 August Miles Franklin was in the Mitchell Library consulting G. B. Barton's *Literature in New South Wales* and Desmond Byrne's *Australian Writers*. She was preparing a paper on literature for a conference on culture in wartime to be held in the rooms of the FAW at 38 Clarence Street on 1 September, and sponsored by the Central Cultural Council, which had been formed in 1937 'to facilitate harmony of effort between organizations interested in the cultural development of Australia'. Miles had a fine time at this inspiring event, held at the height of the Battle of Britain. It went from 10 a.m. to 10 p.m. and attracted an overflowing crowd in the evening, concluding with anti-censorship motions. During the day speakers included W. J. Cleary, chairman of the ABC; Doris Fitton, actor and proprietor of the Independent Theatre; Frank Dalby Davison; and Dymphna Cusack. In the evening, the prominent lawyer A. B. Piddington, KC, and Justice Evatt spoke.[44]

Miles had prepared her talk on literature well. 'Literature is the articulate soul of a nation,' she began. 'While our youth is sacrificing life itself to preserve our liberty … it is imperative for those who cannot serve in that way, humbly and industriously to do their share by protecting and enlarging our culture right here and now.'

Miles had five suggestions for the protection and enlargement of an Australian literature: first and foremost she focused on freedom of expression, and then on public libraries, state support for writers and publishers, public broadcasting ('a tremendous opportunity'), and co-operative publishing to encourage young writers. 'Do you think,' she concluded challengingly, 'that a vigorous, hardy, vocal, free people like ourselves has not enough internal fizz to brew a virile literature?'[45]

The conference resolutions were printed after Miles' contribution, the main points being that censorship had gone too far, and that accredited cultural bodies should be consulted in order to maintain the important distinction between military censorship and censorship of opinion.

Controls on the press had been imposed in May. The Communist Party was banned in June. Miles was among the 'liberty-loving citizens of Australia' who protested against the seizure of Left Book Club property in July; and another speech on 'Our Constitutional Rights' was apparently made in support of protest against the banning of the Australian Youth Council in August. These occurrences may have stimulated contact between Miles and Katharine Susannah Prichard in 1940, when Miles encouraged her to apply for a literary fellowship. Prichard, a leading communist writer, responded that she didn't think she would find favour. Standing up for Katharine would become an important aspect of Miles' 'maintaining our best traditions'. 'For the present we try to keep the way open for freedom and constitutional civil rights,' she wrote to Mrs Robins in Florida. Or as she said in a radio talk at that time, 'Knitting is not enough'.[46]

Following the culture in wartime conference, on 10 September Hartley Grattan arrived back in Sydney, this time for a two-month visit to Australia as a fellow of the Institute of Current World Affairs, a New York think tank, to survey Australian opinion and outlook on the war. Miles was delighted. They had kept in touch, and she had always hoped he would return. She sent a welcoming telegram, and the next day they had tea together at the Hotel Australia. With a different brief and support at the highest levels, Grattan got the red-carpet treatment this time, and his determination to visit all the capitals (he didn't make Brisbane) meant Miles saw little of him until shortly before he left on 31 October, when she again took tea with him. She noted with satisfaction that he was 'harmonious' and improved by remarriage ('helpless without a woman to potato him'), and gladly provided him with ten points characterising Australia for the American press, citing the White Australia Policy and such issues as water and soil erosion, and concluding with the need for an alert population. 'I have always enjoyed [Grattan's] intelligence,' she later wrote to Guy Innes' wife Dorothy in London.[47]

Meanwhile, possibly inspired by a new friend, Welsh-born Pixie O'Harris, a successful children's artist-writer, she was working on a children's story about the Sydney Royal Easter Show. On her way to that second tea with Grattan she dropped her manuscript off at Angus & Robertson. (It was eventually published by Shakespeare Head in 1947.) To Noël Coward, in town on a morale-boosting visit in November, she sent a copy of *Pioneers on Parade*.[48]

In December 1940, what with FAW committee meetings, reading a play by Marguerite Dale ('my debut as an actress'), a prize-giving at Dr Booth's domestic science college at Kirribilli ('rivetting on the [nearby Harbour] Bridge made the whole show inaudible'), enduring Xavier Herbert's monomaniacal telephone calls ('I got a cushion to put under my elbows'), and lecturing on Furphy at the FAW, along with the effort she put into sustaining letters to frail elders throughout the year, it is a wonder she got anything of her own done. 'Spent the last day of this year quite alone,' she noted on 31 December.[49]

She would soon be spending even more time on her own. Her brother Norman was never well again after suffering a coronary occlusion in May 1941, though Miles thought he mostly looked healthy enough afterwards. Then, shortly after Australia was placed on a war footing on 17 June 1941, her nephew Jack was called up — he entered the Ingleburn camp two days later to serve as a driver in the Transport Division — and he too became seriously ill, with pleurisy and pneumonia. Miles herself recorded sore throats, dizziness, toothache, the old heart trouble, stomach pains and more (at one point she feared a growth on the brain) as afflictions, while she struggled to cope with her ailing menfolk, and to rise above their indifference. Alone at Carlton in the middle of the year, she noted despairingly, 'Quiet no good to me now as I am too old to write — the spring has run dry — dissipated by frustration, hostility and constant fatigue.'[50]

Some six deaths in 1941, including that of Banjo Paterson in February, caused her to think about death as a way of escaping the gathering blows, but reflecting on the suicide of Virginia Woolf in March, she could not approve. 'I have suffered despair to such an extent that had I the pluck of Virginia Woolf I wd do as she did, but also had I that pluck I would not do as she did because of that pang ... to perhaps a few sensitive souls here and there,' she wrote to Desmond Fitzgerald in Dublin a few months after the event. In her diary on 10 August she wrote: 'If I directed the courage it is taking to go on living to facing the fact of dying, perhaps I cd go in peace.' But 'I wanted first to straighten my papers & Mss.,' she continued. Then, 'Why don't I simply burn them all and be done with the futile struggle?' Fortunately — and typically — she went to an FAW meeting instead, where she chaired a lecture by H. M. Green on Mary Gilmore.[51]

Miles' miseries for the most part reflect a writer's response to the human condition. She thought she was super-sensitive, and hence felt things very deeply. But her ability to express what she felt uninhibitedly gave immense pleasure to her friends, and later to readers of her published letters and diaries, where she also recorded the brighter moments.

Thus she enjoyed a goodwill visit of United States warships in March (the ratings had excellent teeth, and it was oh so lovely to hear the American voice), and she had 'a good bout' with H. M. Green, when he rang about Mary's poems, on 'the feebleness and expatriatism of Sydney University'. She was again assiduous at the FAW, where a drama circle had begun, and in support of the Propeller League, and as ever was conscientious in responding to appeals for help from aspiring writers during the year, such as Eila Barnett from up-country Wellington. When the playwright Betty Roland gave her a manuscript by a boy called Alan Marshall (later famous as the author of *I Can Jump Puddles*) entitled 'How Beautiful Are Thy Feet' to read in January 1941, Miles commented, 'there may be a writer here'. Meantime, she was fielding Prior Prize judge T. D. Mutch's idea that they could collaborate on a biography of Henry Lawson, and when it was proposed to erect a memorial seat to Louisa Lawson in the Domain, 'Miss Stella Miles Franklin' was listed as a patron, but nothing seems to have come of this.[52]

Miles' writing in 1941 remains something of a mystery, except for a draft story, 'Give Battle', and an unpublished novel set in 'Jones Street, Ashville' during the initial period of Nazi aggression, 'Let Go of Grief. By Young Bill et al. A Tale of Talkers Far Far from the Mad Mad War', which she entered in the Prior Prize competition in June. A by-product of the 'phoney war', 'Let Go of Grief' contrasts the attitudes of young and old to a distant war and strives for a realistic response. Although it may have been among those short-listed for the prize — the judges' report refers to a novel based on life in a Sydney suburb as one of those having possibilities — it was very long, with too much bush philosophy and backyard moralising. As the judges observed, great novels could be made from ordinary events, but they had to have depth. In the end no award was made.[53]

In December, Miles was still revising 'Give Battle', also referred to as 'The Pattern', begun on New Year's Day and typed up by May, possibly a 102-page short story she mentioned giving to Hooper later that month. A few items were submitted to competitions and the press, including a play entitled 'Release', entered in a West Australian drama competition in March, and a story sent to the *Daily Mirror* in October, the outcomes of which are unknown. Thanks to the drama editor Leslie Rees, and with the help of Joan Browne, a copywriter who lived nearby in the 1940s, there was a reading of *All That Swagger* on the ABC at Christmas.[54]

Miles now had a new poet to enthuse over: Adelaide-born Ian Mudie. Gregarious and egalitarian, with an intense love of the land and its inhabitants and fiercely critical of the Europeans' treatment of Aborigines and the environment, Ian Mayelston Mudie and his passionately nationalistic poems were just about ideal as far as Miles was concerned. In an early letter, she wrote that his first collection, *Corroboree to the Sun*, intoxicated her, and that he had gone 'farther than any of us in capturing the spirit of Australia', thus foreshadowing the view that Mudie embodied much of the traditional version of Australian identity. He probably embodied Miles' idea of masculinity as well. More than thirty years his senior, she delighted in the tall, wiry South Australian, an occasional bush worker. His poetic career, which dated from 1931, showed promise through the *Publicist* in 1937 and developed further via the Jindyworobak poetry movement (founded in Adelaide by Rex Ingamells in 1938 to promote 'environmental values'), really took off in the 1940s with Miles' support and tutelage. A difference to emerge between them (which did not undermine their lifelong friendship, due to their shared passion for an Australian literature) was that whereas he would be elected to the executive of the Australia-First Movement (AFM), as constituted in Sydney in October 1941, she did not even join it.[55]

Miles usually took in the latest newsreels at the State or Wynyard theatrettes when in town, thus keeping a keen and increasingly perturbed eye on the war. Mechanised war horrified her; and with the bombings of English cities, including historic London, the enthusiasm in *All That Swagger* for the aeroplane as a remedy for distance fell right away. Now there was nowhere safe, she lamented to Mary Fullerton in a comment that presciently conjures up the terrorist attacks of 11 September 2001: 'There will always be some conquest maniac arise and with long range air machines and mighty explosives it is a poor lookout. Think what a mess Hitler's Blitzkrieg would have made on a city piled as high as New York.' She worried that she had not heard from the Dutch-born Dresdens with whom she had shared so much in long-ago Chicago — and what of Rika Stoffel in Deventer in the Netherlands, whom she had known in London in the early 1920s? Often she felt sick at heart, especially as she believed the 'Japs' would pounce as soon as Hitler got to Suez.[56]

But before that horror took hold came the German repudiation of the Nazi–Soviet non-aggression pact and the invasion of the Soviet Union, beginning 30 June 1941. As the panzer divisions rolled over great stretches of Russian Europe, with Kiev and Leningrad under threat by August, opinion in Australia, as elsewhere, rose in support of the Soviets. Though not yet aroused by 'this Russian business', Miles went to a lecture on Russia by the trade unionist Lloyd Ross on 14 August, with Guido Baracchi, a founder of the Australian Communist Party ('a bore'), in the chair. She was now more worried about the defence of Australia. A postscript to the day's diary entry reads, 'Radical Australians are all for worshipping & saving Russia. Status quo-ers are all for worshipping England. Is there anywhere …

any group dedicated to saving & praising — worshipping and developing Australia: or is she a detached orphan?'[57]

The *cri de coeur* was justified by the increasingly unstable nature of Australian party politics. However, as subsequently recounted to Mary Fullerton, on the last weekend of August 1941 a Sydney Congress for Friendship and Aid to the Soviet Union, which she attended as a delegate of the FAW, attracted enthusiastic crowds: 'My friend Dr Burgmann was a convenor. There were over 2000 delegates from nearly 600 organisations. First day was in Town Hall and the second in Leichhardt Stadium.'[58]

On that occasion Miles Franklin did not speak. But on 8 November, some two months later, with Moscow besieged, the New South Wales Aid Russia Committee sponsored a second cultural conference. This time she did speak, as chair of the afternoon session on women and children in Great Britain and the Soviet Union, and then as opening speaker of the evening session. Her speech, entitled 'Literature and Drama', reminded listeners that they were lucky to be meeting in comfort and sanity, not huddled in cellars in fear of their lives or bludgeoned into concentration camps. She sought to clarify the value of culture in a world at war, intimating that postwar culture would have to be on a new basis, of brotherhood and equality, and asserting that cultural advance came from experiments in living such as were being conducted on a grand scale by the Soviet Union, embracing not only workers but women and children. Turning to Soviet culture, she stressed the importance and value of open communications. Her talk ended on an impassioned note: 'I should like to say God help the USSR and help them to save from total destruction their vast social experiment on which the hopes of the world are set, give them unity, faith and strength to repair it and to extend and develop its best features.' There is a final fervent plea: 'May Australia be saved from the final horror of invasion.' From the point of view of literary history, perhaps the most interesting aspect of her speech was her reference to Chekhov's *The Cherry Orchard*, a play based on 'quiet prosaic material' and illustrative of the passing of a system, 'something like that of our old squattocracy'. It was, she said elsewhere, her favourite play.[59]

Running through all Miles Franklin's talks on culture and war is the golden thread of free speech. Hence she avoided a parting of the ways with P. R. Stephensen, even though he now advocated only 'legitimate' speech. Nonetheless, the political distance between them was widening. Whereas Stephensen had been opposed to the FAW since before the war (due to what he believed to be communist influence in its ranks following the amalgamation of the largest grouping in the communist-inspired Writers' League, the short-lived and broader-based anti-fascist Writers' Association, with the FAW in 1938), Miles was more active in it than ever. In 1941, she joined other members of the FAW in the formation of a Civil Defence League and became one of its patrons. Her friends included several communists and communist sympathisers: Eleanor Dark, Katharine Susannah Prichard (in Sydney in October–November as part of a lecture tour of the eastern states for the Australia–Soviet Friendship Society, and looking frail), and Jean Devanny, the self-styled 'Red Menace', now living in Queensland, unwell, and threatening to visit. On no account would Miles compromise these friendships because of political circumstances. At the FAW, she chaired two meetings late in the year for literary critic Camden Morrisby on Brent of Bin Bin (one wit said the real question was who wrote the books by Miles Franklin), and another for Norman Haire, the eminent sexologist (Miles found him creepy). She also endured Michael Sawtell on oratory ('a male disease') one night in December, and gave at least two talks herself during the year: one in April on her experiences in Serbia to the Anzac Fellowship of Australian Women, a patriotic organisation founded by Dr Mary Booth in 1921 to promote the Anzac tradition, the text of which seems not to have survived; another, at the Women's Club on 2 December, was on Australian writers and readers (where she was appalled to hear the suppression of *Capricornia* advocated).[60]

The following evening, with T. D. Mutch, she attended a public meeting under the auspices of Australia-First, addressed by the ex-communist Leslie Cahill, with Stephensen in the chair. It was noisy, and they slipped away when the bawling got too much: 'Reds or pinks or "rightists", all showed their ignorance,' reads the day's diary entry. It goes on in a mode less comprehensible since 1945: 'One Jew was frothing at the mouth.' Clearly, however, no one behaved well: 'One ½ witted old digger was sneering at unsexed old maids.'[61]

That was her first attendance at Australia-First's weekly public meetings at the Australian Hall, 148 Elizabeth Street, held in November and December 1941. At the next meeting on 10 December, when Stephensen spoke against conscription, her verdict was much the same, except that it was limited to 'Noisy meeting, abuse and counter-abuse & little intelligence displayed'. The noise was only to be expected, since between the two meetings Japan had bombed Pearl Harbor; Britain and Australia had (separately) declared war on Japan; and the Japanese had invaded Guam.

Miles realised that this 'altered everything', that the 'same old war' was becoming a 'new war' — 'our war' — but she continued to attend Australia-First meetings, in the face of 'devastating' news. Before the next meeting, on 17 December (which she attended following artist Dattilo Rubbo's party in aid of dependants of the crew of the sunken HMAS *Sydney*, with her Melbourne house guest, journalist John McKellar), had come the Japanese advance to Malaya and the Philippines, and the destruction of two British battleships off the Malayan coast. The good news was the relief of Tobruk and that the Russians had repelled the Nazis; but the 6th and 7th Divisions of the AIF remained in the Middle East, and until the arrival of the first American troops on 22 December, it seemed Australia (and New Zealand) stood alone in the south-west Pacific. Inevitably, the Australia-First meeting was rowdy.

If there was a fourth Australia-First meeting in December, it is not recorded in Miles' pocket diary. S. B. Hooper rang on Christmas Eve, but what passed between them is blacked out in the diary. Still, she was there for the first meeting in January, when she took Dymphna Cusack and the Melbourne-based American-born psychoanalyst Dr Anita Muhl with her. It was again noisy; apparently Dr Muhl was surprised. Dr Muhl's presence suggests that Miles thought of Australia-First meetings as part of the old public-lecture, free-speech culture, and that she still hoped Australia could somehow be kept out of the war. This was not how its opponents saw Australia-First, especially with the pro-Japanese Adela Pankhurst Walsh an organiser and Stephensen all for a separate peace (not the same as a negotiated peace, but too fine a point under the circumstances and in any event premature and entirely opportunistic).[62]

What Miles Franklin feared was war on Australian soil. On Boxing Day 1941, reading Eleanor Dark's historical novel *The Timeless Land*, then enjoying success in America, she commented on Dark's treatment of the Aborigines: 'If Australia escapes desolation and devastation, we must make amends to the remnants of the blacks.' On New Year's Day 1942, when she could hear the thud of training guns at Liverpool, she hoped for the best: 'May it never be more or nearer'. And after a hot day on 13 January, longing to hear rain on the roof, she wrote, with mounting anxiety: 'May we never awake to ... shrapnel.' When the Japanese landed in Borneo, that seemed ever more likely, and Miles' tension was palpable.[63]

Suddenly, sadly, on 24 January 1942, Norman Ranklin Franklin died at the Pacific Private Hospital, Brighton-le-Sands, aged fifty-five, due to heart failure. The doctors were right after all. At some time later, Miles went back to her recording of the early diagnosis to add, in grief and guilt, 'If only I had known he was really so ill.' Now she was the only one left of the seven children of John and Susannah Franklin, and all she had for consolation was young Jack. It was something that the Lampe relatives rallied, and to hear from Alice Henry, now unable to write her own letters, who understood from personal experience the blow rendered by loss of a brother.[64]

Letters to American friends indicate that Miles Franklin had no idea of what was coming to the Australia-Firsters. She was at Adyar Hall on 19 February for what turned out to be Australia-First's last meeting, when what the *Sydney Morning Herald* described as a minor riot occurred, and enraged wharfies, aiming (according to the unionist Tom Nelson) to wind up the pro-Japanese movement, beat P. R. Stephensen up — though they did not stop him speaking at length afterwards.[65]

From the vivid account preserved in the Mudie Papers in Adelaide, it seems clear that Miles was present for the whole meeting, but not, as has been asserted, on the platform or hustled away when the police came. Despite occasional assertions to the contrary, Miles had played no part in the formation of Australia-First. It was an unholy alliance between Adela Pankhurst Walsh and P. R. Stephensen forged in mid-October 1941, Stephensen's hand having been to some extent forced by Walsh. Miles did not attend its rowdy inaugural public meeting in November, or any other meeting that month. Nor did she join Australia-First subsequently, though she attended public meetings and, as is now obvious (as perhaps it was not then), she sailed close to the wind by continuing association with its leaders. Moreover, although she was a long-time subscriber to the *Publicist*, even writing to owner-editor W. J. Miles that the July 1941 issue was 'great' (for what reason is now hard to discern, but it could hardly have been for the bio-politics of W. J. Miles' favourite ideologue, the prolific English travel writer Morley Roberts), yet she never wrote for the journal. As she later told Ian Mudie, 'I did not join the AF movement for the same reason that I did not accept Mr Miles's invitation to write for him, that is because I was at variance with his views,' meaning his rabid misogyny. W. J. Miles had once shouted her down at the Yabber Club, an informal gathering of Stephensen and his associates at the Shalimar Café in the city, and even without W. J. — he died in January 1942 — the AFM platform was anti-woman. 'To me the position to be accorded women in any political movement is always a sure test of that movement's democracy,' she said to Mudie. As noted earlier, she had never had much time for Adela Pankhurst Walsh either.[66]

Because she was a woman Miles Franklin was tangential to the Australia-Firsters; and although their concerns overlapped with hers, hers was an apparently old-fashioned evolutionary nationalism, which had room for Britain and America as well as Australia, whereas they were narrower, modernistic, anti-democratic, and looking for the main chance. Not for the first time, Miles Franklin experienced a clash between feminism and nationalism, this time involving different understandings of nationalism as well.[67]

Australia-First was not really illegal or disloyal, though it looked like it. With the fall of Singapore four days before the meeting and the bombing of Darwin that morning, Stephensen's timing was disastrous. Although he was correct that the fall of Singapore heralded the end of the British Empire in the Far East — Australia's Near North — it did not mean that his fellow Australians were ready for a national liberation movement on authoritarian lines; and but for an intelligence conspiracy in Perth purporting to document Australia-First plans to aid the invading Japanese, his movement might have disappeared. Indeed, it had begun to fizzle out in early March. Yet, acting on a secret intelligence report, New South Wales police rounded up thirteen bemused Australia-First men on the night of 9–10 March and took them to Liverpool internment camp (plus another the next day). Most were released by September, but Stephensen was interned for the duration of the war, though no charges were ever laid.[68]

When Miles heard Stephensen had been arrested, she commented in her pocket diary, 'no wonder', adding, 'I always said I cd not have anything to do with his politics.' She had known 'dangerous days' in America during the previous war, and urged a distressed Ian Mudie to stay calm. Later, as the dust began to settle, she put it in a nutshell for Hartley Grattan: 'We have had a Quisling scare in a small way.'[69]

The people Miles Franklin felt sorry for were poor Hooper, aged seventy-two, and Winnie Stephensen, who had contracted tuberculosis some months earlier, also Harley Matthews, an occasional contributor to the *Publicist*. She did what she could for them. 'Believe me,' she assured Mudie on 21 April, 'I am quietly doing what I can towards maintaining our best traditions, even in war time.' However, her efforts behind the scenes did not extend to Stephensen, who later accused her of not doing enough for him. When she was approached by a Stephensen defence committee in June, she declined to appear on his behalf, on the grounds that he would implicate her in his politics as she believed he had done before. She even lost patience with Winnie for a time.[70]

It was literature, not politics, that mattered most to Miles. Towards the end of 1941, she was contacted by Clem Christesen, founder and editor of the new *Meanjin Papers*, then based in Brisbane, inviting her to contribute. 'When is your deadline?' she replied in mid-1942. However, she was too late for the proposed short piece on 'the importance of Australian writers at the present juncture'. Perhaps it was due to the atypically speedy print publication of a radio talk series organised by the FAW soon after the fall of Singapore, 'Is the Writer Involved in the Political Development of his Country?', to which she had contributed on 27 April. At a time when 'we have our backs to the wall', Miles had shown herself a sharp performer — though Katharine Susannah Prichard was upset when her friend's talk was presented on air by 'a very lah-de-dah young English woman' instead of in 'your own crisp, witty voice'. When FAW secretary George Ashton put it to her that writers could be very dangerous to politics, Miles responded, 'I should hope so!' Writers were, or should be, disturbers of the status quo and the pioneers of politics, their effect like the potato crops planted of old to make virgin soil more friable. (Not surprisingly, this line of thought failed to impress the Sydney University English lecturer Wesley Milgate, who in a review for *Southerly* cited the conversation as the inconsequence of talk leading to 'inconsequence of thought'.)[71]

Later Miles had something for Christesen. On 5 September 1942, she delivered the annual Lawson oration in the Domain, and then over radio station 2FC. Afterwards she grumbled that few of those assembled in the Domain had appreciated what she had to say, which may be so, as it was 'a humble personal tribute'. However, she also voiced her fears that an Australian identity might not survive the war. (The Americans had arrived in Australia, and the Japanese were on the Kokoda Track, making for Port Moresby. As she said elsewhere, when the clearing up finally came, Australia would present a complex problem, which 'breeding' would not settle.) But the Lawson oration reads well, and is of particular interest today for its recollection of the quickening of a nativist culture in the 1890s, and the pleasure it gave the young at seeing their own idiom in print: 'Due to Lawson and his colleagues … were the gums, the bush, the creek: gully and spur and sideling: the paddock, the stockyard, the sliprails. We were on the track, and burning off down in the gully; hobble chains and camp were jingling to a tune.' Lawson was a hero to them, 'glamorous with success', and moreover of 'exceptional physical beauty'. Christesen received the text in November, and it appeared in the Christmas issue of *Meanjin Papers*.[72]

Already an early contributor to Sydney's *Southerly*, in *Meanjin Papers* Miles found her cultural home. She was a valued if sometimes prickly contributor to both journals from time to time thereafter. In 1942, *Southerly* carried her review of Tom Inglis Moore's *Six Australian Poets*, with its Preface by Hartley Grattan; and in November, the editor, Guy Howarth, promised to publish her short story 'Australia Is So Far Away', about a bogus British war bride (though it does not seem to have appeared).[73]

Moore was pleased with her review. Of his six poets — Hugh McCrae, John Shaw Neilson, Bernard O'Dowd, William Baylebridge, Christopher Brennan and R. D. FitzGerald — Miles privately thought McCrae probably should not be there; and of the others, Shaw Neilson, Baylebridge and FitzGerald had special resonance for her in that Neilson and Baylebridge both died in 1942. She had always admired the former, and the latter had become a friend while, as it happened, FitzGerald, the rising star of poetry in Sydney in the 1940s, was editor of Angus & Robertson's *Australian Poetry 1942* and held the pass when it came to including 'E'. Happily, FitzGerald's initial wariness abated with skilful handling by Miles and, *mirabile dictu*, he became supportive. Angus & Robertson paid for 'Unit', the poem by 'E' that FitzGerald selected.[74]

When Alice Henry first heard of Miles Franklin's determination to get Mary Fullerton's poems published back in 1933, she dismissed the project as impossible. Nine years later, Mary Fullerton was a frail 74-year-old living under the flight path of the Luftwaffe and still not prepared to attach her name to her work; but it was published, thanks to Miles' tenacity and the support of Ida Leeson, who helped with proofreading ('She thinks I am "E",' said Miles), and in time for Mary to see the volume. On 5 November 1942 the Angus & Robertson editor Beatrice Davis rang Miles to say that *Moles Do So Little with their Privacy* by 'E', with Miles' Explanatory Note and Tom Inglis Moore's Preface, had been published. A couple of days earlier, in a letter documenting her efforts, Miles had written to Fullerton: 'I grin, I grin,' and then, 'I gloat, I gloat.' Douglas Stewart immediately offered to support a second volume, which Miles had already advised CLF administrator H. S. Temby was possible. The *Bulletin* welcomed 'E' as a fresh voice.[75]

Probably 'E' was the beneficiary of war, when poetry was in demand. Not only would H. M. Green decide to include 'E' in the Angus & Robertson anthology for 1943, as had FitzGerald in 1942, but by 1942 Guy Howarth had also published seven poems by 'E' in *Southerly*, and a new friend, Victor Kennedy of the Jindyworobak cultural movement, had shown enthusiasm for the poet's work. Congratulating Kennedy on his 1942 *Jindyworobak Anthology*, Miles commented: 'We are now beginning to enjoy the fruits of the last thirty years (or more) of revolt against the accepted forms. The modernists are getting their house in order — not so many stumps, rocks, fallen debris, obstructing their crops and our view.'[76]

In due course Beatrice Davis would become one of Miles Franklin's congenials, but when Miles submitted a short story based on an old manuscript, 'Nedda Rich', for inclusion in the annual anthology *Coast to Coast*, with a metaphorical toss of her head, thinking it better than many published the previous year, evidently Beatrice did not. To Miles' irritation, she returned it in October. After attending the annual Australian English Association Dinner, Miles confided to her pocket diary that Beatrice and the other speaker on the night, Elisabeth Lambert, were menaces and obstructionists to Australian development. However, no Sydney writer could afford such pique for long; and when, with 'E' at last published, Miles managed to face the Furphy manuscript again, it was Beatrice Davis who gave it the go-ahead. Miles' pocket diary of 30 December 1942 reads, 'I got out my Furphy biography resolutely.'[77]

Japanese submarines entered Sydney Harbour in May 1942. Miles took the blackouts and the rationing in her stride and was uncomplaining about the trains crowded with soldiers. One day she spoke to a 'Negro' from Chicago, and at home for sustenance she had her chooks. She was at a low ebb creatively, but as usual she persevered. Between March and May 1942 she worked at a revision of 'Let Go of Grief'. The second version, entitled 'Jones Street', has the same time frame, but all the lads in the street have now gone to war, not just Alby as before, and their mothers wait anxiously for news: 'The devil knows where it will end.' Throughout 1942 she also worked at another story, 'The Thorny Rose', sometimes referred to as 'Evadne', which finally achieved publication in 1947. That nothing was ever wasted with Miles is further evidenced by a retyping of 'Old Blastus' for the FAW play-reading circle on 2 August 1942. Miles thought that it went well for a scratch effort, and that it had possibilities.[78]

That was unusually modest for Miles. When she heard paeans of praise for other writers, such as the frail Louis Esson, whom she respected and wrote about perceptively, she would mutter, 'Nothing left to say about

Shakespeare' — a phrase she'd probably heard from Editha Phelps. Deep down, she knew her own oeuvre was substantial. More astonishing was her ongoing effort and high regard for Brent. Having failed with Hooper the previous year, in mid-1942, in her circumlocutory way, she asked Hartley Grattan (whose fortunes were at a low ebb) to see if he could get the Brent series published in the United States, where Blackwood's rights did not hold. Her comparison with the Nobel Prize winner Thomas Mann's *Buddenbrooks*, first suggested to her by her Austrian friend Helene Scheu-Riesz, may be comprehensible, but it seems somewhat disproportionate. Grattan was doubtful, but willing to try.[79]

In mid-1942, she began agitating about the centenary of Joseph Furphy's birth in 1843; in response, the FAW secretary, George Ashton, advised that a subcommittee consisting of Flora Eldershaw, Frank Dalby Davison and herself had been established. In August, Miles was seated with other patrons at the Town Hall supporting the Pageant of Youth, a rally of the young to win the war and the peace; the same month she also attended and spoke at a Labor tea at Mark Foy's department store to celebrate the fortieth anniversary of women's suffrage, written up afterwards in her most uninhibited style, especially the scathing portrait of the guest speaker, Mrs Quirk, a member of the New South Wales Legislative Assembly. In October, when old Billy Miller decided to return to the north, she went to the send-off at the Sawtells. (Apparently Billy got as far as Tibooburra before he raffled the iced plum cake she had made for him with precious bantam eggs.) And she kept up with FAW activities, not only the play-reading circle (which read some good plays that year, notably Betty Roland's *A Touch of Silk* and Dymphna Cusack's *Morning Sacrifice*), but with the Aid Russia Committee, and attended the occasional party (though she never touched a drop of alcohol). As well, she joined a poetry circle established by the Eng. Ass. (as she always called the English Association), where she read some poems 'by the mysterious "E"'; and she fulfilled her responsibilities as patron of the Propeller League with customary diligence, assessing entries for a short-story competition early in the year.[80]

She also kept up her reading: Ernestine Hill's popular novel based on the life of Matthew Flinders, *My Love Must Wait*, she described as 'lush', while non-fiction choices included *Inside Asia* by John Gunther, and Nordhoff and Hall's *Botany Bay*, a second edition of which was then doing well in the United States — Miles thought it was easily dismissed. Her initial response to Eve Langley's picaresque *The Pea Pickers* was quite balanced. Langley, then living in New Zealand, was delighted to hear from the great Miles with her 'telegraph pole' signature (a fair comment on the uprights in her 'M'). From the whirlpool of Washington, Women's Bureau head Mary Anderson found time to send her a copy of Gladys Boone's history of the WTUL, which Miles thought dull and colourless, though valuable for its references to Alice Henry. It reminded her of how much of the primary material cited she had written anonymously long ago, including 'Miss Coman's articles which I wrote about the strike'.[81]

Alice Henry was scarcely well enough to share her response. In lieu of another trip to Melbourne, Miles kept writing to her, as Alice's carer, Isabel Newsham, urged her to do. Time was slipping away from them both. After Jack Franklin achieved his heart's desire and was accepted by the RAAF in October 1942, he told his aunt that in the event of his being killed he wanted to be buried with his parents. She despaired of this cult of death, brought on, she believed, by male belligerence. And she privately despaired for herself too. 'There are none to grieve for me, who has grieved so desperately for each as he or she went.' Her observation that time does not lessen grief, only rounds the memories up and intensifies them, will strike a chord in many.[82]

In public she was still spirited. Though travel was restricted and her jaunts seldom extended beyond outer Sydney, one of her few delights was a long weekend in Newcastle in October 1942 to see Dymphna Cusack, when she met a posse of young writers and intellectuals, in particular Esmonde Higgins, Harry Hooton and Godfrey Bentley. Responding to Bentley's later complaint that she had called him 'child', she offered him a glimpse of her technique on living: 'Keep your decades fluid, don't let them congeal into separate compartments and make a period piece of you. You'll then find out as you grow older that the oppression of age will lighten or at least mellow with progress.' One day, cleaning out her brother Norman's things, she found some old music, and for the first time since 1914 played the piano. Maybe the tide of war was turning. Maybe modernism was over. Maybe next year would be better. It was time to get back to Furphy.[83]

The year 1942 proved to be a turning point in the war, but as we now appreciate, in January 1943, with much of the world in the grip of the Axis powers, peace lay a long way ahead. The reality of a long war was something civilians were learning to live with. With Jack Franklin in training for the RAAF and so many old friends sitting it out in Europe, talk of a New Order, signalled in Australia by the establishment of the Department of Post War Reconstruction in January 1943, did nothing for Miles. No New Order would get her to see those old friends again, she wrote gloomily to Mary Anderson, it would probably be the same old story, 'with the haybags and gangsters enjoying all the loot and the rest of us struggling to pay the taxes and scrimping to keep body and soul together'.[84]

On 14 February 1943, Alice Henry died in Melbourne, aged eighty-five. When Isabel Newsham's telegram reached Miles, it was no surprise, but it left 'a great blank', especially regarding the American years. Miles was a beneficiary of Alice's estate, but it seems she was never able to express how she felt about her. She owed Alice a great deal, both personally and professionally, and practically through her links with Melbourne. Subliminally, at least, the older woman had also been a calming influence on her rebellious spirit. This, along with Alice Henry's own eccentricities, seems to have underlaid Miles' apparent ambivalence about her 'Dearest Pops'. When, later in the year, as Alice Henry's executor, Nettie Palmer asked if Miles would help with a limited-circulation memoir, she could not bring herself to do it, neither for love nor money (maybe also in part because the fate of her Furphy book was still undecided): 'I don't seem to be able to rise to the job emotionally.'[85]

The dangers facing her nephew, now known by his baptismal name, John, were a worry. It became a relief simply to hear his voice on the phone, a pleasure to provide a meal when he arrived at short notice. As with Miles' literary reputation, so with her closest remaining family relationship: war improved it. There is a sharp portrait of the two of them, taken at Falk Studios, Sydney, in February 1943, with John handsome and winning in his uniform, and Miles determinedly bright, smiling, with teeth in good order, wearing rimless glasses, her hair well set (and still without a hint of grey), in a classy top and a pendant.

Her 'natural outlook' was not morbid or defeatist, she assured that great old literary booster and *Bulletin* balladist E. J. Brady. Elsewhere she asserted that at her best she was 'a sane kind of extrovert'. Moreover, it is apparent from her letters that there were many among her extended family and fellow writers who cared about her wellbeing. Jean Devanny from the north (with plenty of troubles of her own) urged her not to worry so much about her nephew, but to 'look after yourself, Miles. There is only one Miles Franklin.'[86]

Devanny's warm urging ended on a significant note: 'Aren't you writing at all?' The literary round itself took up much of Miles' time and energy.

Although she declined the FAW presidency in 1943, she accepted the position of vice-president, and with President Flora Eldershaw now working in Canberra, chaired many meetings on Sunday evening at Clarence Street. She was frequently there again on Tuesday evenings for executive meetings. From the FAW's rather chaotic papers in the Mitchell Library, it is obvious that it was extremely active during the war years, with Miles in the thick of it, wearying though she often found some of the members and the meetings. George Farwell, an executive member who became president in 1944, was at pains to dispel any impression that Miles was some little old lady in a hat. Bart Adamson's son, Don, who as a boy saw her there, recalled her as a strong presence. By her own account, at an FAW meeting in 1943 she floated the idea of a short-story collection, resulting in *From Pillar to Post*, to which she contributed her Nedda Rich story, entitled 'From Merely Looking On' (deemed 'a good story in essence but not handled in a sufficiently up-to-date way' by a reviewer, 'R. G. H.'); she kept up with the play-reading circle, her reward being a reading of 'Old Blastus' mid-year; and a publishing co-operative came into existence in 1944. In addition, Miles was re-appointed as patron of the Propeller League in July. And (with Farwell, whose good looks and urbanity were what Miles liked in men) she once more judged short stories for the Modern Writers' Club, an offshoot of the 1930s Writers' League that workshopped manuscripts (the prize going to 'the least worst').[87]

All this literary business meant endless phone calls at Carlton, but Miles found much of it stimulating, as when American soldiers dropped in on the Sunday FAW meetings; and she enjoyed the contact with aspiring writers in the field, like Frank Ryland. In reply to a letter from Ryland serving 'somewhere in the north' dated 21 April 1943 which covers considerable ground, including her attitude to Aboriginal people ('I always spell them with a capital A') and the writer Theodore Dreiser ('he was in my clique in Chicago'), she urged him to write a novel if he felt like it: 'a first novel is a grand adventure. You are young enough, you are mature enough and you are poised in a marvellous moment of history and of time and your material is gorgeously new and vivid.' The elder's supervisory tone is unmistakable but appreciated ('you really understand our past,' wrote a grateful Ryland).[88]

She also had some projects of her own. *Moles Do So Little with their Privacy* was going well, and after Douglas Stewart said there should be a second volume of the poetry of 'E', Miles fell to with alacrity, though as usual an outcome lay far ahead. Her own writing was harder. She tackled the Furphy biography again in January. It made her feel awful ('a dead albatross'), but by 1 April it was done. Then came the business of getting it published. As intimated earlier, it was not to be published by the *Bulletin* but by Angus & Robertson; and when the paper shortage eased mid-year, Walter Cousins, as director of publishing, seemed agreeable. That meant more 'finishing touches'. However, the typescript was not to pass by Beatrice Davis' editorial eye until December. Miles was duly thankful for Beatrice's 'toe tracks over my saga'.[89]

Although her book was not published in time for the centenary of Furphy's birth (on 26 September 1943), she contributed a broadcast on the ABC in August; Clem Christesen wanted something for *Meanjin*; and another tribute, written at the behest of Katharine Susannah Prichard (then living in Sydney to be nearer to her son, Ric, serving in the north), appeared in September in the *Communist Review*. Miles also sent a statement to a tree-planting ceremony in Melbourne to be read by Nettie Palmer. These occasional pieces seem repetitious now, but at the time they had a stirring effect. The article for the *Communist Review*, entitled 'Joseph Furphy, Democrat and Australian Patriot', concluded: 'Furphy ... kept his shining faith in his fellow men and in the future which Australians could win for themselves and for the world.'[90]

When asked after the war what she had contributed to the war effort, Miles replied, 'Nil.' However, this was not quite the case. She joined a play-reading group established by the FAW to entertain the troops, and she wrote many letters to servicemen like Frank Ryland who were aspiring writers. There are also occasional references in her letters to contributions to 'my soldier affairs', one of which may have been the Australian Comforts Fund, a major voluntary organisation.[91]

It was through topical writings and talks that Miles Franklin contributed most in the later war years. She produced 'Australia, the Incredible Feat', a commissioned piece published in mid-1943 in Mildred Seydell's *Think Tank*, a fortnightly paper based in Atlanta, Georgia, and in October gave a talk over the radio station 2BL entitled 'The Birth Pangs of the Australian Novel'. In 1944 she would give at least five talks, and one, possibly two, broadcasts on Australian writers. In addition to 'The Need for Australian Literature', an address to the Newcastle WEA when she was there for a reading of 'Virgins and Martyrs Out of Date' organised by Godfrey Bentley in April, she made a speech at the annual Lawson pilgrimage to the Domain in September, and was invited to speak in July at the Newtown Teachers College on Australian books and the people who wrote them. She also gave the main address at a Lawson afternoon at Marx House, the headquarters of the Communist Party of Australia at 695 George Street in September, and in November she spoke for an hour on Furphy at the Hunters Hill Forum, a neighbourhood discussion group held at the home of teacher Donald McLean and his wife, Thelma.[92]

Speaking 'over the air' and writing about other people's work certainly kept Miles' name before the public, and broadcasting paid handsomely; but as Jean Devanny said, what about her own writing? A pocket diary entry for 2 May 1943 reads: 'Can't write. Must just turn to chores till I end. Nothing to hope for now'; and to Frank Ryland she confided: 'I have lost heart as the old bushmen used to say of a horse. Bullocks, dear souls, never lost heart.'[93]

Xavier Herbert suggested that she had been 'boned' — from the Aboriginal ritual, to 'point the bone' — and offered to sing the evil spirits out of her. A small measure of literary success would have sufficed to cheer her up. None was forthcoming. Hartley Grattan had been unable to arouse interest in the Brent books in New York, and at a time when theatre and radio plays were in demand, she had nothing to offer except 'Phoebe Lambent and Love', last heard of in 1922 and now retitled 'Three Women and Love'; and 'Virgins and Martyrs Out of Date', subtitled 'A Play of the Lost Generation in the No-Prudes' Revolution in Behaviour which took place between the World Wars', recast from 'Virgins Out of Date', a London novel on the consequences of sexual 'experiment', written in 1931. Both works were from her social satire phase, and were rejected by all to whom they were offered. More recent ventures into national historical drama fared no better: 'Scandal at Glenties', set south of Sydney during the Boer War, in which a young girl is taken advantage of and commits suicide, was unsuccessfully entered in an ABC play competition in 1944, as was 'Comedy at Runnymede', a play set in the Riverina in 1884 which she based on an incident in *Such Is Life*.[94]

The resuscitation of 'Virgins Out of Date' in wartime suggests either courage or desperation. It appears Miles had been reassured by a talk given by the Sydney University anthropologist Camilla Wedgwood: 'She evidently believes in chastity same as I do, but the fashion has been so much otherwise for a generation that one has had to … keep quiet … The funny thing is I am at work on a play with Camilla's thesis but it is very difficult [and] was too advanced even for New York ten years ago.' At that time she had seized on the British anthropologist J. D. Unwin's treatise *Sex and Culture*, which posited a direct relationship between the degree of high culture and the intensity of sexual prohibitions and offered indirect support of Sigmund Freud's views of sublimation and civilisation. A decade on, after attending the reading of 'Virgins and Martyrs Out of Date ' by Godfrey Bentley's group at Newcastle in April 1944, she commented that its reception showed her how far behind 'current sophistication Australians are', which suggests disappointment. When the young Melbourne actor Catherine Duncan read the typescript she remarked, 'it's about the only chance I'll ever have to play [a virgin]'. By this time Miles was also against romance, and had recently destroyed many love letters ('scores', she told Dymphna Cusack, mostly from the Lloyd brothers), to ensure that there would be no data on her own love life left.[95]

There were three things to keep Miles going through the later war years. One was her 'homestead in the suburbs'. She had her weekly round of housework and hospitality, by now second nature and a kind of discipline, tending to the chooks and her astoundingly productive garden, with its yield of potatoes (among other vegetables), plums, guavas and lemons, and flowers too, like the sunflowers planted by her father and still blooming abundantly.

She began to note what she cooked for visitors. The meals were usually quite substantial. On one occasion in 1943, her nephew was given a hot dinner consisting of roast lamb and mint sauce with butter beans, potatoes and cold beetroot, then stewed peaches with raspberry jelly and junket. She cooked a similar meal for Aunt Lena and for the impecunious critic Camden Morrisby, who would have liked more. When she went into town, Miles would often take home-grown produce for friends — eggs and plums and the like — to supplement rationing. She also took gifts of food when seeing them off on trains and ships, as Nettie Palmer had gratefully recorded when the Palmers were farewelled for Europe in 1935.[96]

A second sustainer was that great gift for friendship. It is impossible to measure such things, except perhaps by the extent of her correspondence, or by the range of family and friends recorded in the diaries. All too few of them are mentioned in this book; while only occasional mention can be made of others when in fact Miles saw them quite often, such as the opera coach Lute Drummond (first encountered at Stratford-on-Avon in 1923); Mary Fullerton's sister Em (who seems to have run boarding houses in Sydney from 1937 to 1951); and Eva O'Sullivan (though Eva talked too much about Catholicism these days for Miles' liking). While some old acquaintance passed out of range — Dr Mary Booth accused her of being a communist, to which Miles responded 'poor old thing' — others stayed, like Ada Holman and her sisters, with whom Miles usually spent an evening after Christmas; and new ones appeared on the scene. There would be 'a real spree in congeniality', Miles said, if Godfrey Bentley came to stay. How wonderful if Henrietta Drake-Brockman did too: 'We could hatch things up.'[97]

During these years, Miles got to know and like numerous younger people active on the cultural scene in Sydney and Melbourne. Among them were the poets Muir Holburn and Marjorie Pizer, the 'little theatre' director Neroli Whittle, the playwright Musette Morell and the actor Catherine Duncan. A more fleeting association dating from Miles' visit to Newcastle in 1942 was with the anarchist poet Harry Hooton, who — like historian Russel Ward — was surprised to find her 'young intellectually', and a different kind of feminist, highly evolved; he thought her a 'man-woman', but gender proud. Miles' association with Glen Mills Fox also strengthened. Victorian-born Mills Fox, a journalist active in the FAW and first wife of the communist journalist Len Fox, latched on immediately to (as she later addressed her) 'The One & Only Great & International Miles'.[98]

The third sustainer was Miles' own unflagging spirit. The word 'courage' appeared with increasing frequency as part of her vocabulary in the 1940s. You need courage to grow old. Australian writers would need courage postwar. It was her capacity to keep going that so endeared Miles to many younger writers. With them she made no claims, put on no side, was as one with them in the struggle to get things published, and was a help in withstanding disappointments. As well, she was positive. History was on their side, or rather that of the cultural nationalists. If only Hartley Grattan could get back, she mused, they could bring literature and society together in Australia.[99]

There was also a responsiveness to the world in Miles. She was incurably political. She remained in touch with Harold Ickes (how many other Australians were in personal communication with a member of Roosevelt's cabinet, one wonders); with Mary Anderson, head of the United States Women's Bureau until mid-1944; and with Anderson's friend Elisabeth Christman, still soldiering on with the Women's Trade Union League; and with the Robinses in Florida. A steady flow of news came from Mary Fullerton and Mabel Singleton in England, and she received the occasional communication from others there, such as Kathleen Ussher. At home she kept up her subscription to the Friendship with Russia League (as the NSW Aid Russia Committee became in 1942), and from time to time spoke at meetings. She responded, too, to the resurgence of feminism in 1943, attending various conferences, including the first Women's Charter conference in November, and contributed to the new journal of the United Associations of Women, the *Australian Women's Digest*, edited by Vivienne Newson — as it happened, a Goulburn girl of the next generation. Her first piece was a page on Rose Scott for the second issue, and she joined the editorial board in 1944.[100]

There was no summer holiday for Miles in 1943. Instead she went to Melbourne to see John Franklin get his wings at Point Cook in September ('a sacrificial offering to the gods'). Even Melbourne failed her this time. She was shocked to find that Geraldine Rede, the artist and Christian Scientist who had sketched her in Boston long ago, was dead. And when she went with Vida Goldstein to the grand Christian Science church on St Kilda Road, there was hardly any congregation. Although she did all the usual things and saw all the old friends, she felt like a ghost.

It was a relief to get on the train for Sydney, back to the familiar round. Indeed, so much did Miles still propel herself around her home city, one is reminded of her young days in Chicago. Now, however, she circulated in the cause of literature, not politics. Miles continued to read surprisingly widely, from Aldous Huxley's *Point Counter Point* to Plato's *Dialogues*, but mostly Australian books. She now deplored Eve Langley's *The Pea Pickers* as 'phoney'; but when she learned that Eve was incarcerated in a mental institution in New Zealand, she relented: 'We are frail mortals — all sorts of devils lurk to defeat and devour us'. These days Miles sometimes woke in fright and sadness, after dreaming of her sister Linda and her mother. When Louis Esson died at year's end, his wife, Hilda, seemed almost as anxious to help Miles through her grief as vice versa.[101]

A three-week holiday at Brindabella — 'my native fastness' — in February 1944 refreshed Miles' spirit. She had not stayed there since 1900. The station was no longer in the family, but she found the company of her now frail cousin Les Franklin, who lived on the edge of the old run, relaxing, and it was easy to slip back into the bush life, of which there were many poignant reminders, including the remains of her mother's first home. As if to confirm that for Miles Franklin bushmen were the only real men, there was young Lindsay Franklin, recently released from the army: 'Six feet or over and perfect in face and body — I have never seen a film star more beautiful,' she wrote to Mary Fullerton.[102]

Revitalised by her break, Miles wondered if she should withdraw from the FAW for a year. By early 1944 it had become too politicised for her liking, and its play-reading circle was threatening to focus on European plays. Probably because George Farwell was the incoming president she decided to stay on; but Bart Adamson, twice president of the FAW between 1938 and 1946, had joined the Communist Party in 1943, and emphases were changing. (Frank Ryland later reported that in Melbourne they thought the Sydney FAW was too Red.) The Propeller League seemed dull, and the FAW-perceived threat of a market swamped by light fiction from overseas was dispiriting. When she and Dymphna Cusack toured the bookshops in February looking for Australian novels they found lamentably few on the shelves. (Presumably this little adventure was the genesis of their satiric one-acter set in a bookshop, 'Call Up Your Ghosts!', which won a small prize in 1945, shared with Katharine Susannah Prichard's son, Ric Throssell.)[103]

On 30 October Miles received copies of the Furphy biography 'at last', she recorded in her pocket diary. She immediately sent a copy to Mary Fullerton. However, as is often the case when authors see copies of their work for the first time, the euphoria was short-lived. On closer inspection, she found that the bibliography had been omitted, a ghastly slip — 'It made me feel sick put me in a class where MB [Marjorie Barnard] would have a right to sneer at me as an illiterate,' and likely to upset her informants as well — but soon remedied, as the publisher was persuaded to paste the necessary page into copies of the book. By then Kate Baker had seen the book and discovered some slips, and also read a critical review in the *Bulletin* which complained about evasion and 'scrappiness'. However, Miles managed to reassure her, and Kate had a share of the royalties. In general, apart from the *Bulletin* review and that of the poet A. D. Hope (who gave credit for industry but stressed lack of critical skills), the reviews were positive. The response of the Melbourne *Argus* was glowing — 'the first complete authentic account of Furphy and his work' — despite what it saw as an overemphasis on Kate Baker and some 'inept' literary comparisons. The Palmers, it seems, maintained a patrician silence. Maybe they were just too busy to comment, as Nettie's mother died at this time and Vance was working in the Commonwealth Public Service.[104]

To further lift her spirits, the second edition of Ian Mudie's long poem *The Australian Dream* arrived. Its Margaret Preston cover, featuring a swagman and Aboriginal shield, struck Miles as 'just right'. Dedicated to his son Bill's generation, Mudie's poem was inspired by the American Stephen Vincent Benet's long narrative poem, *John Brown's Body*, to which Miles had introduced him. It envisaged the dawning of an independent Australia:

> Down time and down the future they shall hail
> their destiny along the swagman's trail,
> and with his cross of stars for totem team
> Forward shall drive the Australian dream.
> Then shall the love and strength of this our earth
> and all our national pride have singing birth.[105]

Unannounced visitors and phone messages for neighbours still took up much of her time, but as far as possible Miles tried to focus on her own writing. She continued to have hopes for *My Career Goes Bung*, which she noted had been too advanced for the duds at Harraps back in 1937, and she sent it out to, among others, Katharine Susannah Prichard, who found it interesting but less forceful than *My Brilliant Career*, and also to her FAW colleague the journalist Les Woolacott. Likewise, on 7 September 1944, Miles returned to the first of the unpublished Brent volumes when she opened up 'Merlin' and decided to call it 'Prelude'. The extent to which she revised it thereafter is unknown, but she worked at it on and off throughout October 1944, when she apparently set it aside again.[106]

The immediate thing was a new edition of *Old Blastus of Bandicoot*, selected as one of ten fiction titles in a CLF-funded library of Australian classics, a cheap wartime series published in response to the demand for Australian books and known as the Australian Pocket Library. (The price per copy was to be between 1s 3d and 2s, depending on size.) Publisher George Clune of Allied Authors and Artists was in touch with Miles on 21 April, the day the initiative was announced. Irritable negotiations ensued, possibly over the sale price; but this seems to have been smoothed over, perhaps with the help of Frank Clune, George's brother. The proofs were sent to Miles just before Christmas, and the book appeared soon after. The paper was poor, but she felt it an honour to be included in the series. A. D. Hope said that it was not only odd that it had been chosen but that 'it should ever have been printed at all', and R. G. Howarth wrote that it was 'a failure that might well have been a success', but in 1945 it sold 25,000 copies, and it remains a vivid document of the era when young women's lives could be destroyed by pregnancy outside marriage. This point Miles stoutly defended when the book was privately criticised by Howarth as unrealistic: 'You can be sure that the material in *Blastus* is as sound as something a doctor might assemble on the basis of his case book.' (She was probably referring to 'Miss Gillespie's tragedy', a real-life story about Gillespie's sister Addie and Addie's illegitimate son recorded in her literary notebooks.) Miles also made an ironic comment on Howarth's view: 'Contraceptives must have resulted in an even greater revolution than I had realized.'[107]

Hope and Howarth were both academics. Their views did not impinge on George Clune's proposal in November to republish *Bring the Monkey*, which reached galley stage eighteen months later, but then disappeared, presumably into another publishing black hole. However, Miles also realised that she would have to cope with academic critics, whom she referred to sardonically as the 'dominies' (from the old Scottish word meaning 'schoolmaster'), as well as the publishing industry and the Left faction of the FAW. As Lesley Heath has explained in a study of literary societies in Sydney in the interwar years, such societies strengthened cultural nationalism in the face of public indifference, but at the same time the academic study of literature was taking hold and 'the passing of judgement' became the province of universities, where the imprint of class and wealth was still very strong, and many senior writers found this irritating.[108]

Two instances of academic interference in literary affairs upset Miles Franklin in 1944. In the winter of that year Marjorie Barnard and Flora Eldershaw delivered the annual Commonwealth Literary Fund lectures at the University of Sydney on Australian literature. When on 9 August Barnard lectured on 'Miles Franklin and "Brent of Bin Bin"', Miles, with characteristic insouciance and somewhat to Marjorie's consternation, turned up to listen. Afterwards she declined to eat with Barnard, and when she got home she wrote in her pocket diary that Marjorie Barnard had delivered 'a venomous & cowardly attack on me; every detail of calculated malice to bring ridicule on me before [a] university group'.[109]

Barnard subsequently protested her innocence and asserted that Miles had taken offence when students laughed at quotes read out by way of illustration. This she no doubt believed to be the problem, and she did read out some funny bits (both intentionally funny and otherwise; for example, a reference to 'hirsute ornaments', that is, beards, one of Miles' pet dislikes, and Brent's extolling of Peter Poole as the perfect male type). But it was not how Miles Franklin saw it.[110]

From the text of the lecture, which survives in the Barnard Papers in the Mitchell Library, it is clear enough what the problem really was. The lecture began by outlining the pioneer novel as an established tradition, a genre that offered plenty of action and required no great labour by the author, and noted that it was the main channel of romanticism in Australian literature. The novels of Miles Franklin and Brent of Bin Bin — Barnard had no doubt they were one and the same, which on its own was enough to irritate Miles — were of 'historic and symptomatic interest' in this regard. Most attention was devoted to *Old Blastus of Bandicoot*, 'the perfect type of the whole tradition', located 'somewhere between the beard and the motor car'. When dealing more speedily with the Brent books, Barnard highlighted 'local colour', noting also the writer's many 'distracting opinions' about women and war and the environment. In short, Barnard's lecture placed Miles' writings in historical perspective and adopted a critical approach; and in doing so, exposed a generation gap.[111]

Beyond pain and pique, the incident at Sydney University illustrated changing literary values. Miles had welcomed the first Barnard Eldershaw novel, *A House is Built*, but the collaborators' subsequent work had lesser appeal, being weakened, she thought, by modernism. When earlier in the year she read Marjorie Barnard's collection of short stories, *The Persimmon Tree*, deemed by many to contain Barnard's most stylish writing, she took a dim view of its literary merits. Although she conceded that, like Barnard Eldershaw's earlier novel *The Glasshouse*, *The Persimmon Tree* contained some good things — for instance, the story 'Habit', showing that 'habit is stronger in an old maid than the chance to marry' — it was overall too precious for her taste: 'What is Marjorie on about in her persimmon tree. It seems faintly unwholesome, faintly — well faintly, faint.' 'Why,' Miles wondered, 'should so many women be so neurotic & so dull?' Fortunately for her, Miles Franklin did not live to see the extent to which new literary and critical values which stressed structure and style would take over in the 1950s, to the detriment of the reputations of realist writers in general and her own in particular.[112]

Miles' response to Barnard's lecture exposed something deeper and more personal as well. Like Mary Fullerton, Miles Franklin was still sensitive about her limited bush education. In her young days, women were not deemed to need much in the way of formal education. However, by the 1940s, some younger women, including a few women writers (such as Dymphna Cusack), had degrees. Marjorie Barnard, an outstanding history and English graduate of Sydney University in 1920, personified the new order. And here she was, apparently mocking a less privileged predecessor.

Generational change is never easy, and Miles was not one to take slights lying down (soon after, Katharine Susannah Prichard was set to defend her friend's work at the University Book Club). Tension between writers and critics is inevitable. Perhaps the demarcation lines had yet to be clearly drawn up. As Miles said self-mockingly to Fullerton when she first heard that Douglas Stewart favoured a second volume of the poems of 'E': 'an illiterate non-university unconforming oddity [such] as myself' could still discover and promote a poet. No matter that liberals like Howarth did their best to defend academic training, Barnard's lecture ensured that from then on Miles Franklin's mistrust of 'examination passers' was never far from the surface. (Interestingly, the young South Australian graduate and modernist Max Harris and his 'uni-journal' *Angry Penguins* did not bother her greatly at first, since the young were bound to find their level later and, as she remarked, the young should be rebellious and if they could not manage that they should at least be noisy. Later, though, she thought he deserved to be 'put down' for being so egotistical.)[113]

Then on 17 August 1944 the second disturbing literary incident began when Miles Franklin met Colin Roderick, then a Gympie schoolteacher, on the steps of the Mitchell Library. Roderick had earlier sought permission from Blackwood to reproduce a chapter of Brent's *Up the Country* in his forthcoming anthology, *The Australian Novel*, and the matter was referred to 'the author' via Mary Fullerton. According to Roderick, the outcome was an 'untraceable' permission from William Blake, and an apparently genial meeting in Sydney to discuss his decision to invite Miles Franklin to write a preface. However, when she later received page proofs and saw what he proposed to do, she was enraged on behalf of the authors, whose financial rights had not been considered, despite lengthy ('stupefying') selections. (The selection from *Up the Country* amounted to sixteen printed pages.) It was, said Katharine Susannah Prichard (also included in the anthology), 'barefaced insolence'. Then when Roderick told Miles he was doing it for the good of Australian literature but expected to get a D. Litt. for his efforts, she set about organising a boycott.[114]

Miles Franklin had felt disadvantaged by the unequal relationship between writers and publishers. But this was a case of exploitation for academic purposes. (A later generation of writers faced a similar situation with photocopying and the student 'brick' or reader.) At first, Miles seemed to have some success with her proposed boycott. But in the end she had to give way, as there were no legal constraints, and goodwill — or maybe vanity — among the anthologised authors won out. When she at first declined to write the preface, Roderick replied regretting her decision, but assuring her that all the other writers were satisfied and wished the book complete success, Prichard among them. So she gave in to Roderick, deemed in her diary a 'thick-skinned go-getter', and wrote the requisite page and a half.[115]

That autumn Viennese-born Paul Frolich, a music commentator, theatre aficionado and part-time sculptor, proposed a bust of Miles, in hope of becoming a celebrity himself, she supposed. At the first sitting, he had her looking like 'a kindly sheep'. The second left her speechless: 'Good Lord!' After the third, she asked herself why was she doing it — because 'I am a drifting derelict'. When she saw the final thing at the Society of Artists exhibition at the Education Department art gallery in Loftus Street on 31 August, it made her feel ill. Tom Inglis Moore, who was with her, said comfortingly that current artists compared poorly with Tom Roberts and the old crowd; and Miles decided that unless people looked at the catalogue they would not know it was her. However, neither Frolich's 'atrocity' nor the controversial portraits of Joshua Smith and Brian Penton by William Dobell in that year's Archibald Prize exhibition ('a decayed corpse' and 'a sinister eunuch' were her verdicts) prevented her from later hoping to have her portrait done.[116]

With only the one not very impressive Nedda Rich story published in 1944 and no new novels in sight, Miles despaired of herself as a creative writer: 'Wish I cd drive myself to my own work, but desolation paralyses me, also the long Australian struggle against the tide — one is never established but always at the beginning,' she wrote in her pocket diary on 2 September 1944. Like everyone else, her efforts were framed by the war.

She continued to attend conferences on war and culture; mostly they were about maintaining Australian culture and emphasising its value for the war effort, and the planning of postwar reconstruction, as at the People's Conference on Culture in the War and the Peace, held from 30 June to 2 July 1944 in Federation House, Phillip Street, Sydney, which called for a comprehensive national cultural policy. Conferences in support of the Soviet Union carried a strong cultural message too. Less well discussed in public fora was the state of the book trade, which Martyn Lyons has emphasised was disrupted by the war in several ways, in particular through severe paper rationing, limiting local productivity at a time when restrictions on shipping also diminished the flow of imported books. The *Annals of Australian Literature* shows, for example, that of the fifty-five titles listed as appearing in 1944, only two were paper-greedy novels: Lawrence Glassop's *We Were the Rats* and Christina Stead's *For Love Alone* (but it was published overseas); whereas there are twenty-seven volumes of poetry listed. With two books published during the war years and both her pet poets in print, Miles Franklin was actually doing quite well. Even so, it was hard for an older woman far from the front to be sure what to write about next. She mostly told younger writers to concentrate on data collection and new experiences. A good war novel was unlikely anyway. Australian writers seemed to her to lack 'the disgust ... that informs the best war books from other nations'.[117]

By late 1944 it was clear that the course of the war had changed. With the Normandy landings and the Battle of the Bulge under way in western Europe, and Australian troops mopping up in New Guinea, the Allies were on the offensive at last. As early as mid-year, Miles Franklin had detected a relaxation in suburban Sydney: 'More people on the streets in Carlton these days. Lots of men in civvies & I saw a young woman in [the] middle of the day without babies or errand boys. Commodities creeping back into the shops. Got rolled oats — plenty of eggs, a little bacon, & a flint for [a gas] lighter' reads the pocket diary entry for 22 July 1944.

Miles had her thoughts on the New Order ready. She made one of Katharine Susannah Prichard's friends gasp at what she called her 'simple and cogent formula': that it would abolish brothels for women and breadlines for men. Bishop Burgmann was a beneficiary of zanier thoughts: if she were a world dictator, Miles would ensure a quota of single American women teachers over the age of forty-five to work alongside Nehru et al to soothe India, while a good dose of Soviet comradeship would fix Japan, and she would bring England and China closer together. Australia, she thought, could safely be left in Burgmann's hands, 'provided you did not allow it to be too thickly over-run with human epizoa'. To Mary Fullerton, she wrote equally frankly that she did not want the dead heart of Australia overrun by swarming millions of lesser breeds with their downtrodden women. Clearly she was unaware of how such unguarded statements would seem to posterity, for the copies remained in her correspondence, unlike those love letters and whatever else she destroyed during intermittent episodes of clearing and pruning of her papers.[118]

Her nephew John Franklin turned up to spend New Year's Eve with her, reminding her that the war was not yet over. 'I can't bear much more of the war,' she wrote to Ian Mudie on 19 January 1945. In the circumstances it didn't worry her that some people were finding the Furphy book a bit indigestible ('I attempted nothing more than a sourcebook'), nor had the unfriendly review in the *Bulletin* concerned her. And yes, she confided to Mudie, she had capitulated to Roderick, but maybe she had been too harsh to begin with ('sometimes … the pirate is the most gentlemanly man in his community'), and there were 'hilarious aspects' to his project, such as listing her among the expatriates in volume 2. 'What a lovely lot there is to be done as soon as the lunacy goes into recess for a while,' she mused, which, with the Americans in Belgium and the Red Army in Budapest, was now a real prospect. She also mentioned having had a great time a few days earlier addressing teachers, some 600 of them, on Australian literature at a summer school at the University of Sydney. The historian Dr Currey and others treated her with respect, as she reported to Kate Baker. Apropos of the Furphy book, in February she collected £50 in royalties, a goodly sum even when shared with Kate Baker; and to Roderick, when later granting permissions, she suggested he might one day write her biography.[119]

The surviving Franklin–Mudie correspondence for 1945 amounts to some forty-five items. Mudie, she felt, could 'sing the bone' out of her (unlike Herbert); and when she found that the last poem in his collected *Poems: 1934–1944*, 'Unabated Spring', was dedicated to her ('my own beeyootifulll poem') she was so thrilled she spent a whole day (2 April) in reply. These letters include some lovely things, a memory of rain on the corrugated iron roof, for instance. 'Is the rain *loud* on the iron roof to you? … Knowing it only on the iron roof for so long in my formative years, that was the right way for rain to sound to me … One of the indignities in London was that one had to look out the window to see if it were raining.' Another is of 'ducks on the pond'. 'I recall my father and another old hand talking of them one night, and how they would sometimes be frozen in the ice on winter mornings up there where the wind from Kosciuszko would freeze you, or shave a gooseberry.'[120]

Miles Franklin regarded Mudie as a kind of literary son, just as she felt Dymphna Cusack was her darling daughter. She thought his poetry captured the core of what she had so haltingly expressed, and evidently, as earlier with Hartley Grattan, she spared no effort in supervision and support. Thus she emphasised that the creative process was a matter of liberating what was within, as when (probably with regard to *Up the Country*) 'I carried a single sentence with me for months … when I could get it down it was like a popping cork and about 200,000 words spurted out ... What we people who are overwhelmed by it need is discipline and selection.' Likewise, she laid out the task ahead for 'bigger and more wayward souls':

> You know we are in danger of exploding at the ferment of all the intoxicating things there are to be won from and done for our very own land, that the Aborigines — under sacrifice — gave to us, kept for us unspoiled ... [The land] was so beautifully kept by the blacks, and they were banished and vanished so heartbreakingly that the conscience of the place can only be appeased by retribution to those remaining, and by the whites making themselves worthy of holding the land and spreading from it the news by example of a worthwhile way of life ...[121]

Otherwise, she added somewhat illogically, the place would be overrun from the north.

Mudie didn't really need strengthening on the environment or the Aboriginal cause. Probably it was the undivided attention of another writer that he particularly valued. Most interesting now are the contemporary values expressed in Miles' letters. It seems that while she had fully absorbed Eleanor Dark's *The Timeless Land,* she struggled to get past her belief in white Australia. Yet correspondence at this time suggests that her views were in fact changing. Replying to a letter from Catherine Duncan which included a criticism of the White Australia Policy, Miles entered the usual historical account, but went on to doubt the future of racism: 'If the world becomes a unit and all receive education, tribes will not be able to look down on one another because of complexion. They will intermingle wholesale and become shaded down. In the light of new studies it appears that all brains are much the same.'[122]

Miles' relationship with Dymphna Cusack was somewhat similar, though the outspoken Dymphna was already a celebrity in her own right. In early 1945 Dymphna and her friend and future collaborator Florence James had moved with Florence's two young daughters, Julie and Frances, to 'Pinegrove', Hazelbrook, in the lower Blue Mountains, to concentrate on their writing. Miles Franklin was among their first visitors, staying for five days, from 14–19 February. To the delight of the children, she arrived by train with three bantams in a hatbox. She in turn delighted in them, and in the surrounding bush, identifying twelve birds from the verandah next morning, before finding a possum had pinched her toothbrush. It was her substitute for a summer break that year. Riding in the bush, knee-deep in ferns, was a happy reminder of her childhood, 'the enchanted core of her life,' Dymphna later recalled. On Saturday 17 February, Miles recorded in her pocket diary, 'I continued reading', but if it was Dymphna and Florence's work, she does not say. (It could not have been the classic Sydney war novel *Come in Spinner*, which Cusack and James began later, on 30 July 1945, but it possibly was their children's book *Four Winds and a Family*, published in 1947, or maybe an early draft of *Caddie: The Autobiography of a Barmaid*, a Cusack collaboration with Catherine Elliott, who came weekly to do the washing at 'Pinegrove'.)[123]

In turn, when Dymphna stayed a couple of days at Carlton in early March, Miles gave her *My Career Goes Bung* to read in bed, and next day Dymphna expressed herself enchanted by the first nine chapters. Dymphna would also urge Miles on with her Easter Show story, *Sydney Royal*, which Miles completed in December 1945 despite much lamenting of loss of momentum along the way. And their literary partnership continued beyond that. In mid-1945 at Carlton, with Dymphna in residence for the purpose, they worked on their bookshop play, 'Call Up Your Ghosts!', in which the ghost of Australian literature booms from above shelves bereft of Australian books.[124]

Dymphna later wrote from Hazelbrook: 'My friendship with you … has not only brought me great joy … but … our relationship has been of the greatest value in re-orienting me in my own country. All the corrupting influences of academicism and expatriatism had left their mark on me and meeting you swung me to my own pole again … You have been a touch-stone of essentials for me.' (The academicism and expatriatism she rejected were particular features of the University of Sydney when she was a student, due to an emphasis on early modern literature by English professor Mungo MacCallum, also to the pervasive influence of the philosopher John Anderson.) Elsewhere Dymphna remarked on Miles' unfailing intellectual energy, and it is she who has left the vivid image of Miles at work, marvelling at the clean copy of their play which Miles produced at speed for submission to the Melbourne New Theatre's Tom Collins Drama Competition in late July: 'I don't believe that little chaff-cutter of yrs could possibly have turned that out.' Given Australian writers' fear of a flood of imported literature after the war, 'Call Up Your Ghosts!' was a timely spoof, and there were several readings, in Melbourne and Adelaide as well as in Sydney later in the year.[125]

As the Allied momentum was maintained in early 1945, those who recalled the reactionary aftermath of the Great War of 1914–18 preached 'reconstruction' and 'never again'. Miles doubted the efficacy of political programs, and would not be sidetracked by fashionable nostrums. Stalin's regime was the 'bravest attempt to give women a square deal,' she told Frank Ryland, then based in Singapore; but, as she wrote to the Melbourne poet Frederick Macartney, with thanks for an ode he had written: 'I am all for the Marx Lenin doctrine being given a full chance as a tremendous experiment, but when it is established the poets, dreamers and thinkers will have to struggle out of its clutches, which will be as stifling as Czarism, or capitalism etc. Progress depends on creative minds.'[126]

FAW plans to ensure the survival and development of Australian literature when the war was over took several forms. First was the already established Pocket Library. The series had print runs of 25,000, an astonishing figure today, and Miles would do well out of it herself: by May 1945 *Old Blastus* had earned £95 in royalties. By then she was working to get Catherine Helen Spence's *Clara Morison* included in the series as well. (As time went by Miles became ever more enthusiastic about Spence, then almost totally neglected as a writer, partly it seems because she saw in Spence a prior instance of a writer swamped by social reform, the now routine rationale for her own apparently limited output.)[127]

There was a related Co-operative Book Publishing Program, a project in which Miles also had a personal interest. Unlike Nettie Palmer, Miles Franklin did not think Australian literature securely established, and she believed a nationwide publishing co-operative was the surest hope. A third initiative, the FAW Book Society, a club along American lines with a Book of the Month, was launched at a literary luncheon on 4 June 1945 by a Yale literature professor, Henry Seidel Canby, who was passing through Sydney. Miles gave the vote of thanks. In her response she sounded a warning note, however. American big business was on its way and its impact on the book trade would not be benign so far as authors were concerned; Australian writers would need courage. Perhaps they would have to live off the proceeds of two-up. Meanwhile, would Australian publishers co-operate with the book club? Fortunately Canby approved of what she said, and received from Miles a copy of *Back to Bool Bool*.[128]

As a long-serving member of the FAW executive, she had worked hard on the co-operative publishing program, and then on the Book of the Month plan, which came to fruition in September 1945, when Sidney J. Baker's *The*

Australian Language appeared as the first title. Miles, who served as chair of the judging committee, would have preferred Eleanor Dark's sombre study of frustrated creativity in wartime Sydney, *The Little Company*.[129]

With any mooted publishing venture, Miles invariably thought of Brent. She even had the temerity to send *Back to Bool Bool* to the Pocket Library Advisory Committee; and there were negotiations on his behalf in 1944–45 with the Sydney bookseller and publisher Dymocks, and a vague publishing possibility arose with someone Ian Mudie referred to only as 'Brown'. Miles had been working over the first volume, retitled 'Prelude to Romance', in January, and when she re-read *Gentlemen at Gyang Gyang* a few months later she decided it needed very little revision. Indeed, there was scarcely a time between 1931 and 1948 — when Beatrice Davis finally proposed their publication by Angus & Robertson — that Miles was not scheming to get her outstanding Brent books published.[130]

Reporting to Mary Fullerton on the FAW initiatives, Miles compared the problems of the book trade with those of the theatre: 'I said in the thanks speech that we had seen what big business in the commercial theatre had done to drama in America — ran it into the ground.' Commercial theatre had collapsed in Australia in the 1930s and drama had survived best in the little theatres, along with radio, in the 1940s. 'It is desperate that we have no working theatre here,' Miles wrote to Catherine Duncan, and without that, as she argued later, no matter how many subsidised buildings were erected, there would be no national theatre.[131]

On 22 April 1945 she attended a conference convened by the People's Council for Culture, a 'New Theatre League's shebang' at the league's new location, 167 Castlereagh Street, to consider proposals for a national theatre. The gathering was full of 'importers and expatriates', and a 'host of parasites, pretenders and axe-grinders', whose idea of 'international' was 'to receive humbly and greedily from other national cultures'. But the valiant few who spoke up for a national drama also displayed a limited outlook, and 'a turtle-like lack of a sense of humor' pervaded the whole proceedings. Considering that Miles had attended plays at the Little Theatre in Chicago and the Abbey Theatre in Dublin, as well as the commercial theatre in Chicago and London, her reaction is scarcely surprising. Moreover, as recalled by Mila Kronidov, she still took real pleasure in local theatre. Among plays seen or heard on the wireless at this time Miles commended *I'll Meet You at Botany Bay*, a radio play by Ruth Park (about whom she later wrote harshly); and although she was more critical of Paul Frolich's production of Dulcie Deamer's *Judgement* at the Maccabean Hall in August — 'phoney sawdust' — it was a brave effort, and they had to be praised for staging it.[132]

Miles persevered with her own plays too. 'Sophistication', a drama about divorce set in Sydney in 1939 featuring Nedda Rich, 'the last word in sophistication', was typed and entered in the Montague Grover Memorial Award for a satire under the pen-name 'Sceptic' in May. 'Comedy at Runnymede', revitalised by her reading of the pastoral novelist Henry Kingsley in the Mitchell Library and retitled 'Tom Collins at Runnymede', by 'Narangy', went off to the ABC drama competition in August (having been 'tossed out' the year before). When a scratch cast at the New Theatre read it in October, she consoled herself with the thought that 'Even such experiences show me "Blastus" and this work are pretty well fool proof.' A second entry — her 'Glenties' play — entered in the Tom Collins competition under the pen-name 'Botany Bay', did no better; but with the help of Musette Morell (unfortunately now 'a poor, frail thing'), she sent it to the 2UW Lux competition in November as well, along with 'The Thorny Rose' (which had begun life as a radio play in 1942), and possibly others, since she wrote doggedly in her pocket diary on 4 September that she was reassembling herself regarding the rejected plays and would send them all to the Lux competition.[133]

Neroli Whittle, first encountered by Miles in the FAW play-reading circle and now running a little theatre at Greenwich, tried to help with rehearsals of *No Family* in November. It was an ordeal for Miles, but at least it showed her that 'the play has no superfluous verbiage & cd be perhaps all right with real actors'. However, no one turned up for the next rehearsal on 20 December. And although Catherine Duncan came to Sydney in October, she had given up acting, so there was no hope there. When the FAW read 'Call Up Your Ghosts!' one Sunday evening in November, Miles couldn't face it. She got as far as the door but heard a dull voice and fled. Later, Musette phoned to tell her that the reading was 'an unqualified success'. So she persisted. Just before Christmas, she began fixing 'Release', subtitled 'A Modern Drama in Three Acts'.[134]

Miles had been writing plays on and off since 1908, and she probably hoped to make money from them, at least in the 1920s. But of nearly thirty plays written by 1945, only three had been read or performed, and she never made money from any of them. Evidently the competitions of the 1940s renewed her enthusiasm for playwriting. Perhaps it was her competitive streak: with so many women doing well in the field, why should not she? She had plenty of plots from Australian history, and the prize money was good. At a deeper level, she had always believed the theatre could be a powerful force in people's lives, and she yearned for its influence and immediacy, just as she yearned for a best-selling novel. But her sense of what the public wanted was never very good, and there was an off-putting element of preaching in most of her dramatic writing.[135]

If Miles Franklin did not succeed in making an impact via the theatre in 1945, other opportunities seemed to come her way. In January she prepared a five-minute talk for the United States Office of War Information, and when G. B. Lancaster died in London in March, it was Miles who delivered the tribute on national radio (2BL, on 6 May), for which the script and two versions published in 1946 survive (plus a poignant footnote, appended to G. B. L.'s last letter to Miles: 'I was always going to answer this and now she is dead'). And Miles was there at a United Associations of Women party to farewell Jessie Street when she left for the founding conference of the United Nations in San Francisco in April 1945. Although she believed that a new generation of women should be on the job, she again contributed to the *Australian Women's Digest*, this time a review of a pamphlet by Bishop Burgmann entitled 'The Education of an Australian'. In fact, with nine pieces published during 1945 — another instance being a review of Margaret Trist's suburban novel *Now That We're Laughing* for the FAW's short-lived quarterly *Fellowship* — it was a bumper year for her occasional writing. She spoke at various events throughout the year too: at the previously mentioned teachers' summer school in January and to the Lawson Society in October (having paid tribute to Lawson, she fished *Poets at War* out of her bag and began on Mudie). When interviewed by Freda Barrymore for the *Australasian* in October, Miles returned to the gum tree as a metaphor for getting Australia into literature: she was, Barrymore reported, 'quite exalted' on the subject.[136]

In October 1945 she wrote to Ben Chifley, Australia's new Labor Prime Minister following the death of John Curtin that month, on the need for protection for Australian literature: 'Without a literature of our own we are dumb. In the disturbed world of today, more than ever we need that interpretation of ourselves … which is the special function of imaginative writers.' As a result of such pressures, an inquiry by the Tariff Board was established. Frank Clune was one who appeared at the hearings in Sydney in

November, though very little in fact eventuated. Writers in Australia were still caught somewhere between the overseas publishers and local booksellers. 'Aust. Lit. tried for its life,' Miles reported in disgust to Ian Mudie.[137]

She often felt weak, and worried now about passing symptoms of stress and decay. With her weight down to just under 8 stone (around 50 kilograms) in June, there was perhaps cause for concern about occasional aches, trembling of the knees, chest pains and the like. Home maintenance worried her too: 'the house is a chaos of papers & books, the garden a wilderness of weeds & rubbish'. However, it was poorly fitting dentures in the second half of the year that caused her the most trouble. An underlying psychological problem surely was that her characteristic approach to life — just pick yourself up and get on with it — did not work so well when confronting the ageing process and the inevitability of death. When Margaret Dreier Robins died in Florida in March, a great light went out of Miles' life; and with Susannah Franklin and Alice Henry gone, there was no one to share her grief. 'Only one or two people in all the world meant as much to me as Mrs Robins. With her rich generosity and warm courage she made life a feast and an adventure,' she wrote in respectful longhand to Raymond Robins.[138]

When Aileen Goldstein visited Sydney in October, Miles reflected that she had known her for forty-one years; Aileen was sixty-eight, but then Miles was almost that too. For once she mentioned her birthday in her diary. On 15 October 1945, the day after her sixty-sixth birthday, Aunt Lena took her to see *National Velvet* starring the young Elizabeth Taylor, and then to David Jones for lunch.

On 13 April Miles Franklin saw 'the troops hanging out their washing on the Siegfried Line at last' on a newsreel, adding to the entry in her pocket diary that the cost of fulfilling 'that rooster boast' of 1939 had been very high. Then after peace was declared in Europe on 8 May 1945 came reports from the concentration camps: 'German horrors,' she noted on 30 May. On 8 August, when the news of the American bombing of Hiroshima and Nagasaki came through, she noted, again in her pocket diary, the advent of 'atomic bomb destruction, dismaying in its possibilities'. On 16 August, after the Japanese surrender, she took the train into town to join the peace celebrations in the Domain, her diary comment on this happy occasion being, 'It was the nearest approach to a crowd I ever saw in Sydney.' Even then her nephew John in air transport was still fully occupied in possibly dangerous work.

But she decided the time had come to remove blackout material from her windows and to look for old friends trapped in Europe. After a long silence, she heard from Arnold Dresden, whose family had suffered greatly in Holland, and made contact with Rika Stoffel, whose family had also experienced great losses in Deventer, Holland, now largely destroyed. Ever practical, she invited the Meggitt sisters in Cheshire, which had had its share of aerial bombardment, to join her for a break. She had a house and some £3 a week. As nurse and teacher they could work, and share it. 'We are still young enough to get something out of life,' she wrote optimistically. Of course, they didn't come; Australia was too far away.[139]

It was, she wrote to Mabel Singleton, like pulling out of a whirlpool. 'What is to be the end of us few Australians with our big territory?' she asked of Frank Ryland. When John came home for Christmas smelling of beer she felt ill. Like many women she had reason to fear the after-effects of war. Meanwhile, she sought to reassure Ryland: 'For the present we home birds will try and keep societies and things from dying right out till the boys come home to jump into them and give them a new start.'[140]

13

THE WARATAH CUP:
1946–1950

'We are such tiny sparks …'[1]

'What awaits us I dunno,' Miles wrote in a postwar catch-up letter to expatriate poet-librarian Kathleen Monypenny in London. Australia was 'sinking back into normality', but with the prospect of another bout of profiteering, most people would be left 'poorer and older and sadder'. The war had consumed six years; from 1942 more people had to pay taxes, and two big wars in a lifetime was a lot to bear. But with fewer casualties than World War I and a reforming Labor government in power in Australia until December 1949, hopes ran higher than in 1918, and reaction was slower to take hold.[2]

Miles knew that Mary Fullerton was now quite ill, and fearing that every letter would be her last, kept writing as normally as possible, but could barely suppress her anxiety, even when it was deflected to the abstract idea of death: 'Is there to be no going-on — no continuance, no conscious carrying on of the beauty of character wrought here?' she wrote to Mary and Mabel Singleton on 5 February 1946. For comfort, she re-read Virginia Woolf's *Mrs Dalloway*, and then her favourite girlhood novel, *Trilby*.[3]

On 25 February she wrote again: 'Mary, my precious, my dear, have you gone beyond our voices to something splendidly different, or to blessed sleep and relief from pain?'; and on that same day she received a letter from Mary. But Em Fullerton rang the following day to say Mary had already died, on 23 February.

Miles' letter to Mabel Singleton the next day is one of her best. Urging Mabel to rest now that Mary's 'heroic suffering' had ended, she encouraged Mabel to make a record of a 'glorious and rare friendship' when she felt up to it. The world was too disorganised by the war at present, but leaving aside the threat of the atomic bomb, one day people would be avid to know more about Mary Fullerton. Miles was right — though it was not so much about her work as about her friendship with Mabel in which interest revived in the late twentieth century, due to new research into the lives of lesbian women. Strenuous though her own efforts for Mary's work now seem, she felt she had accomplished practically nothing, that it would take someone better equipped; but she had saved the poems. To Mary Fullerton's sister Lydia Chester she wrote in May that Mary had been 'one of the richest things in my life', that she had found her 'brave and lovely and gifted beyond ordinary people'.[4]

The last big thing Miles Franklin was able to do for her friend was see a second volume of verse by 'E', *The Wonder and the Apple*, through the press. Colin Roderick brought copies to Miles on 13 May, too late for Mary of course, but she had seen the proofs. Two days later, on 15 May, '"E": The Full Story' by Miles Franklin appeared in the *Bulletin*. It makes poignant reading today, as Miles explained what lay behind Fullerton's insistent anonymity: 'She was discouraged and self-doubting because of her lack of education.' To this Miles added that when she pooh-poohed this, Mary pointed out that Miles had escaped from Australia early, whereas she did not leave for England until much later in her lifetime. And from this we may glimpse what Miles Franklin really valued and admired in Mary. Despite constraints and discouragements, she was 'self-mastered'.[5]

What Miles did not realise — though she did say Mary's letters to her contained enough effort for many novels — was that their vast correspondence would itself be a rich legacy. Mary's handwriting got worse as she aged and some of her letters were written in pencil on flimsy paper, but it remains a rare record of a conversation between two highly intelligent, talented and largely self-educated Australian bush women.[6]

Miles was now anxious about her own letters. In January she had written urgently to Mary: 'I am worried because you said you kept my letters and to you I have always written spontaneously straight onto the machine without pre-meditation, discretion or reserve.' She asked Mary to instruct Mabel to return them, unless they were to be burned. Apart from anything else, they contained the full story of Brent, for whom Miles still had hopes. 'Don't be smoked-out,' she wrote to Singleton, who had earlier taken over as Brent's agent and was also Mary's literary executor.[7]

It was not, however, Brent's year. On 11 June 1945, a month or so after the war in Europe ended, Miles had signed a contract with the Georgian House for the publication of *My Career Goes Bung* in 1946. Probably it came about through Ian Mudie and his association with the founding Jindyworobak poet Rex Ingamells, then a traveller for the Melbourne publisher Georgian House. On 26 February 1946, the galleys of *My Career Goes Bung* turned up from Georgian House, and Miles found perusing them 'interesting'. When the novel appeared in August, it was warmly welcomed by her friends. Beatrice Davis called it 'a delicious book'; Henrietta Drake-Brockman thought it 'enchanting', better than *My Brilliant Career*, and Miles assured her that it was written 'at the time' (which may be true though there had been a lot of tinkering subsequently). Dymphna Cusack thanked her stars that she had been born a generation later. Miles was pleased to hear from younger women that it still rang true — as it certainly did for Rose Lindsay, Norman Lindsay's wife and muse, who said she enjoyed being reminded of a period and people she had known well. But was Henrietta Drake-Brockman right to see it as a study in feminine adolescence? Probably not, according to Miles, 'since I think much the same still but with tremendous enlargement'. As for Aileen Goldstein, who objected that the book was too sexy and had funny words, Miles was amused, recalling that when she was young she had been accused of being 'not a woman but a mind'. To Raymond Robins she wrote, somewhat immodestly, that it was the most interesting thing to hit the book world in years, a claim only partially supported by male reviewers, who tended to see it as merely a period piece.[8]

Broadcasts and topical writings in 1946 kept Miles busy and supplemented the income she received from her mother's estate. Radio continued to pay best. For 'What Can Be Done to Assist Australian Literature?' on 25 March, Radio 2FC paid three guineas; and Miles made at least two other paid contributions to radio during the year, speaking on reading Australian books on 2KY, and recording extracts of *All That Swagger* for schools on the ABC. By contrast, her print contributions were almost certainly unpaid. Occasional pieces, such as her tributes to 'dear little G. B. Lancaster' in 1945, belatedly appeared in the ABC monthly *Talk* in April and subsequently in the *Australian Book News and Library Journal*. In October, after a celebration of Katharine Susannah Prichard at Marx House, Miles' salute to 'Australia's Most Distinguished Tragedian' appeared in the

Tribune, the communist weekly; and that same month, in one of two reviews of *The Roaring Nineties,* in the *Australian Women's Digest,* she commended Prichard's portrayal of women on the West Australian gold-fields. There was also a brief but charming appreciation of Louis Esson, who had died in 1943, in *The Southern Cross and Other Plays,* a posthumous edition of his work. Her most substantial general comment, occasioned by the first anniversary of the book club and published in the *Labor Digest,* was 'Not Angels but Australians', which asked 'Is there an Australian way of life?', a highly topical question as things settled down after the war. (Miles urged Australians to rise to the challenge or lose the right to occupy the country.)[9]

The young loved such forthright remarks, and Miles' sharp wit, just as much as her apparently unquenchable spirit, delighted her friends. Pixie O'Harris struggled to put it into words: 'The personality ... the soul, the staunch heart, the mixture of courage and timidity, the mixture of all that you are. We are, each one of us, only you are more so than most people. There is a greatness in you, Miles ... [You are] more personally loved in our circles than most.'[10]

Maybe, but Miles could be cruel. Some of her private comments on the work of her fellow writers were harsh: for instance, her declaration that M. Barnard Eldershaw's *The Glasshouse* — which she attributed solely to 'that bobby-dazzler' Marjorie Barnard — was 'imitative, eviscerated, pretentious', and her response to *The Harp in the South* by Ruth Park, which won the *Sydney Morning Herald's* literary competition in 1946, as 'that infernal *Harp*'. Even Kylie Tennant, previously approved of as a contributor to 'the Brent school', was now deemed to lack pity. Still, as Dymphna Cusack said, who of us is not unkind from time to time; she herself dismissed *The Harp in the South* as a 'mere stencil of all the Hibernian slop from Galway to Brooklyn'.[11]

A good proportion of Miles' correspondence throughout 1946 was with Dymphna Cusack and Florence James as the two younger women struggled to finish *Four Winds and a Family* and then *Come in Spinner,* one of the great World War II novels of Sydney. When Miles read a first slab of *Come in Spinner* she was thrilled by its scope and verve, urging even greater verisimilitude, at the same time advising that the authors needed to yard the galloping horses. She liked succeeding drafts even better (although in retrospect Dymphna felt Miles never really understood the work). 'We are enormously grateful to you,' wrote Dymphna on receipt of Miles' initial response; and by working full tilt, she and Florence managed to meet the 30 October deadline for the *Daily*

Telegraph's new £1000 literary competition, entering the manuscript as 'My Unabated Spring' under the pen-name 'Sydney Wyborne'.[12]

Not surprisingly Miles did not mention that she too had entered the competition, with a story about two women, Elspeth Jane and Evadne — evidently a version of 'The Thorny Rose', the play drafted in 1942 and initially recast for competition purposes as 'In Pursuit of Glamour' by 'M. Alletts' (that is to say, 'Stella M[iles]' reversed). Evidently her hopes were not high. Having suggested a temporary address for 'Sydney Wyborne', she remained supportive of her friends during the drawn-out judging process — her own entry did not make the short list — and when *Come in Spinner* won, she delighted in their success. (The *Telegraph* never announced the winner however, and failed to publish the novel, due, it now appears, to ideological as well as moral objections of increasing force in the Cold War era).[13]

Miles seemed to be at a standstill, creatively speaking. It was probably true, as she wrote to Nettie Palmer, that she had not written anything for six years (presumably she meant a new novel). Meanwhile, apart from a performance of *No Family* at the Independent Theatre, North Sydney, in June and a production of 'Call Up Your Ghosts!' in Adelaide later in the year, her plays failed to attract interest. Nonetheless, she still had things in hand, for instance, her 'Glenties' play, recast as 'The Scandal-monger'; and she kept hoping for success with a serial, even though an approach by 'Miss S. Mills' to the *Sydney Morning Herald* to publish 'Gentlemen at Gyang Gyang' earlier in the year had come to nothing. Until it stalled at the galley stage mid-year, there was also the proposed Clune edition of *Bring the Monkey*, and the prospect of another edition of *All That Swagger* as well as the excerpt from it in Colin Roderick's second anthology, *20 Australian Novelists*. Possibly spurred by the formation of the Children's Book Council in New South Wales in 1945 and news of the inaugural Children's Book of the Year Award in 1946, she was also working on a book for children, *Sydney Royal*, first mentioned in 1940 as 'The Ballad of Sydney Royal', which would be accepted for publication by the Packer press book publishing subsidiary, the Shakespeare Head Press, at the end of the year.[14]

Suddenly, in September 1946, Miles' pocket diary reads: 'Got out my war novel with [a] view to final form'. This was undoubtedly 'War Comes to Jones Street', entered in the Prior Prize in 1941 as 'Let Go of Grief', and revised as 'Jones Street' in 1942. As updated, the story ended in December 1941, with 'the Australian way of life' threatened and Jones Street engaged at last: 'Everyone has settled to the war now, with Russia and the United States with the British again, there is no longer any hesitancy.' Nonetheless it concludes with the mocking laughter of the kookaburra. Miles' résumé of the final version reads:

> This story might be termed a diary of war emotions. It concerns the reactions to the outbreak of war among the people of a small street in the outer suburbs of Sydney. It gives the isolated life in this small back-stream of a big city against the backdrop of the holocaust in the northern hemisphere. The old and the middle-aged discuss politics and fear of recurrence of unemployment. The youngsters act and re-enact love, war and discontent.[15]

The story was so close to home it might as well have been called 'War Comes to Grey Street'; but by 1946 its time had surely passed. However, it has some documentary as well as biographical value; and it serves as a reminder of Miles' earlier war series, 'How the Londoner Takes his War'.

In December 1946 Miles' fellow writer and FAW activist Dora Birtles reported to Miles that William Dobell was interested in painting her portrait. After the frightful Frolich head sculpted during the war, and a 'footling effort' by Alice Cooper Stewart mid-year, entered for but not hung in the Archibald Prize exhibition, this was a challenging prospect. On the one hand, Dobell was the outstanding portrait painter of his day, with three Archibald prizes to his credit by 1945. On the other, Miles did not want to finish up looking like Joshua Smith, whose portrait by Dobell had been seen as a caricature. Miles feared that the effects of all that dubious dental work in Chicago on her jaws and cheeks offered an opportunity for similar treatment.[16]

Miles had already encountered Bill Dobell at events about town, and somewhat to her surprise, had found him 'gentle and quiet'. He had been taken by her new spring hat, reportedly 'as bright as a Persian garden'. So despite feeling 'like a bird with a shiny object luring it to its doom', Miles made her way to his studio in the new year. It emerged that Dobell *was* thinking about painting her for the Archibald. Having heard her concerns, he said he would try, 'and if you don't like it, we can tear it up'. Apparently the issue was unresolved, since nothing more seems to have happened.[17]

Christmas Day was no longer the same. After Norman Franklin died in January 1942, there were no more distressing gatherings at Grey Street. That year Miles, her cousin Ruby Brydon, and Norman's son, John, joined Aunt

Lena Lampe for Christmas dinner at 'Rothesay', Wycombe Road, Neutral Bay, where Lena had boarded since leaving Grey Street. Thereafter, with John away in the air force from 1943, the three women usually went on to afternoon tea at the home of one or other of Uncle Gus Lampe's daughters, Thelma Perryman and Phillis Moulden. In 1945, at the Eastwood home of Phillis and John Moulden, Miles recorded that Thelma and her husband, George, were there too, and 'we had a very pleasant party, with children, nice garden etc'. Jenn Lane, née Moulden, Phillis and John's daughter, has since re-created the scene from a child's point of view: the three maiden aunts, Miles, Ruby and Lena, 'sit straight-backed in a row on the sofa' in old-fashioned clothes. 'They seem to me, at the age of eleven, to be creatures from the distant past.' When in 1946 Miles and Ruby dined at the Hotel Metropole without Lena and then went on to the Perrymans' at Cheltenham, it was a minor variation on a lasting arrangement. Miles' links with the Franklin family were weaker, or perhaps just intermittent, due to distance and dispersal. Les Franklin of Brindabella died in November 1946, and Miles' nephew John was developing a heart-breaking drinking habit.[18]

Needy friends overseas were not forgotten. Food parcels were a popular and much appreciated gesture of solidarity among English-speaking peoples after World War II. In 1946, as well as letters, Miles sent food parcels to Miss Lawson in Lancashire and to Miss Hodgson in Leeds, both of whom she had worked with in Bloomsbury in the 1920s; and she continued sending them to numerous English friends in the coming year. In return, she received a flow of grateful letters, and news of once significant people, such as 'Mr A.' and his successor at the National Housing and Town Planning Council, Mr Martin, and even of poor 'little Mrs A.', last seen in 1932, now living in south London with Mr A., who was having his last fling at social reform by advising Londoners on compensation for wartime housing damage. Thus there was the pleasure of renewed associations, but each with its own poignancy: Emmy Lawson, for example, now retired to Southport on the Lancashire coast and probably lonely, later sent Miles her precious postcard collection. Miles accepted the gift graciously. After all, she too was, in effect, alone.[19]

In Sydney, 1947 began with a severe hailstorm. As Miles worried about her English friends, then enduring a ferocious winter accompanied by strikes and food rationing, they worried about her. But, Miles assured Emmy Lawson, she had escaped the storm, although 'It was like a rain of blue metal on the roof [the hail] as big as golf balls ... in other places it was as big as cricket balls.' Whatever Australians might still be putting up with, it was as nothing compared with the Europeans, she added.[20]

Most of the images of Miles Franklin at this time come from her friends' recollections of life at Grey Street. A homesick Florence James, who left with her daughters, Frances and Julie, for England once *Come in Spinner* had been edited and resubmitted to the *Daily Telegraph* in mid-1947, wrote: 'I just can't bear the thought of not coming back ... I can see you in my mind's eye tapping away at terrific speed on your typewriter in the sunshine, with [the bantams] Ginger's and Greedy's friends and relations conversing at the far end of the garden ... How I'd love to stretch out on the floor in your front room and have you read poetry to me.'[21]

Miles' hospitality was by now legendary, and came to be symbolised by the bestowal of the waratah cup on favoured guests. When Florence James received an invitation to visit and take tea from the cup, she felt honoured: 'I shall really feel I belong to the sisterhood of Australian women writers.' On another occasion, the young poets Muir Holburn and Marjorie Pizer came for 'delicious food' and experienced 'widehearted' encouragement. 'If we continue our work and make some small contribution to Australian literature,' Marjorie wrote later, 'it will be due, in large measure, to encouragement from such persons as yourself.'[22]

Miles even started giving little (non-alcoholic) literary parties. After a gathering at Grey Street on 13 March 1947, a new congenial, Rex Ingamells, wrote in effusive Jindyworobak style: 'Many thanks for the bonzer corroboree and champion tuck-in of the other night.' Others present included Harley Matthews, Roland Robinson and his first wife, Barbara, the poet Gina Ballantyne, Glen Mills Fox, and 'some Cahill', the erstwhile Australia-First organiser Les Cahill. On that occasion it was Ingamells who drank from the waratah cup; he also entered a spontaneous verse entitled 'Lubra' in the waratah book, another symbolic item, given to Miles by Rose Scott in 1902, now back in use, having being in abeyance since 1908. One Saturday evening in May, fellow writers Nancy Cato and her husband, Eldred Norman, Anne Williams and the Jindyworobak poets Roland Robinson and Flexmore Hudson joined Miles and Glen Mills Fox (a house guest) for the evening, and they stayed until nearly 1 a.m. However, Miles thought the discussion dull, maybe because of the predominance of the Adelaide-based Jindyworobaks, people of one big idea, the incorporation of 'environmental' values, including Aboriginal values, in Australian literature. Hudson, who edited several

Jindyworobak anthologies in the 1940s, was given the waratah cup and Nancy Cato signed the waratah book.[23]

Another positive feature of daily life in the late 1940s, which, amid frequently articulated tribulations and loneliness, Miles never mentioned, was that apart from John's occasional stays and her visitors, she had the house to herself, and it was much easier than when Susannah and Norman were alive to get on with her work. In the new year she turned again to her plays, once more revising 'Scandal at Glenties'/'The Scandal-monger'. In October 1947 she sent a three-act version to the New Theatre, without success.[24]

Mid-1947 brought — as Miles said herself — a windfall, when the *Newcastle Morning Herald* published 'The Thorny Rose' as a serial. This was the Evadne and Elspeth Jane story, which dated back to 1942. As promoted by the Newcastle *Herald*, the 'new and previously unpublished story' was written 'with a light touch and not a little humour … [it] concerns a Sydney girl who took a liking to a young airman. The romance has many novel complications.' Told in twenty-one episodes and set during the 'brown out', the story features the young Evadne Jordain, a volunteer pianist at the Kookaburra Club who wants to be closer to the action. Evadne falls for fickle Billy Badminster from Melbourne, and pursues him there. A tangled tale of sexual misdemeanour and cover-up in the previous generation then unfolds, with the more advanced Elspeth Jane turning out to be Evadne's half-sister as well as her rescuer from illusion. A Greek medical student named Archie also assists, and the novel concludes with the raising of Archie's longstanding hope of a more mature Evadne. Her 'mother' and 'aunt' back in Sydney, proud and self-sacrificing women who rose above the male misdemeanours in the past which drive the plot, reflect ruefully on how the world has changed, and get on with their professional lives.[25]

Evadne is scarcely a convincing figure, especially as she and others dash back and forth between Sydney and Melbourne trying to sort things out, and Miles could almost never bring her heroines to the altar. As for the plot, it deploys many familiar tricks: the jiltings (this time by women betrayed), the double standard, the secret arrangements to evade the marriage knot, and the self-respecting single woman of mature years. Of most biographical interest is the way these older women characters think about the effects of war on younger women. Whereas the previous generation had been trapped by the double standard — 'girls were reared in a sweet dream of monogamy and waked up in a nightmare of polygamy,' says Evadne's Aunt Olive — and there was 'no room for experiment', they now wondered if they should have 'grasped the rose regardless of its thorns', recognising that premarital sex no longer turned women into 'damaged goods', and that divorce was more socially acceptable. As for the war itself, it was utterly different from the last one: according to Elspeth Jane, 'life goes at such a pace … we have to catch it as it flies past'. But as Evadne's unhappy experiences reveal, war was destroying the balance of the sexes again, and 'young women … have to scramble for the men', with unhappy consequences. Thus older values still triumph, as does a nativist preference. In 'The Thorny Rose', Miles Franklin is surprisingly antithetical to the 'Yanks'; for example, Elspeth Jane finds her American suitor, Elmer, too conventional when he rejects her offer of a secret arrangement which she says could be easily abandoned after the war if need be. As in an earlier short story still in typescript, 'One Touch of …', the 'Yanks' seem rather crass.[26]

Comparing 'The Thorny Rose' with M. Barnard Eldershaw's *Tomorrow and Tomorrow* and Cusack and James' *Come in Spinner*, both of which were written at much the same time, it is obvious that Miles' war romance was tame: 'nothing in it but that the milk and waterest haven't done, I bet,' she wrote to Florence James. But she thought it better than its predecessor as a serial, Lawson Glassop's 'Lucky Palmer', which she described as mere 'chaff'; and at least one reader, an Oliver Holt, admired her story. Moreover, it was well rewarded: 'Gave me 50 pounds and very pleasant attention.'[27]

Later in the year Miles cleaned up 'War Comes to Jones Street' and sent it off to yet another competition, an experience that led her to write amusingly about men in post offices: experience of petty bullying by postal clerks around the world convinced her they were unsuited to the work. Meanwhile, George Ferguson at Angus & Robertson had advised that decent white paper — a scarcity in the war years — was to hand for a new edition of *All That Swagger*. This was welcome news, since *All That Swagger* was Miles' most popular work. The new edition would be the sixth since it first appeared in 1936, and the third since Angus & Robertson took the title over in 1940. It was always her best earner, with the 1943 edition bringing in £86 in royalties for the financial year 1947–48.[28]

Copies of *Sydney Royal*, over which Miles had laboured in 1946, arrived on 20 February. The proofs had caused her concern, having been returned for checking without the original manuscript, and Nan Knowles' drawings certainly were rather conventional; but at least Shakespeare Head had not let her down, as she had sometimes feared. Subtitled in manuscript 'A

Modern Fairy Tale — Trading in Australia as a Furphy', it was dedicated 'To All My Young Friends Everywhere under Sixteen Years of Age'. Children's literature was a new genre for Miles, which she had been encouraged to try in part by the availability of T. D. Mutch's historical researches on Sydney's Royal Easter Show (duly acknowledged); maybe by Dymphna and Florence's *Four Winds and a Family*; and no doubt by Pixie O'Harris, who began with fairy stories and by the 1940s was writing romantic stories for girls. According to Pixie, children were honest and 'your audience doesn't grow stale, there's always another batch coming along, like scones'. Offered as a gift item, 'a rich entertainment spiced with humour, fantasy and drama', the publisher's idea was that one of Australia's most famous writers combined with one of Australia's most famous institutions was bound to succeed. The published version nominates *Sydney Royal* as a 'divertisement', in hope, as the blurb put it, of appealing to the 'Young in Heart' as well as the young in years.[29]

The story begins 'It was a grand morning, a fairytale morning in the fabulous age of once upon a time.' It was written when the Easter Show was at a peak of popularity, with 1.23 million attending in 1947, and it celebrates a great populist event dating from early colonial times: 'Every Easter, all the families, from the Governor-General's to the general slavey's, flock around in exhausting gregrariousness.' Over one day and into the next, the cast, consisting of sideshow folk and the state governor's household, plus a few passing Americans, get thoroughly and agreeably mixed up, and the unhappiness of the governor's daughter Rosalie Coppem is miraculously relieved when 'Queensland Jack', a rider at the show, turns out to be none other than Bob of Black Swan, who, due to a fit of amnesia, had jilted her back in England. Things turn out well too for a parallel cast of children: Rosalie's young sisters Tootles and Toddles; Hoppie, a crippled working-class boy from Woolloomooloo; and Junior Otis, a previously pampered American boy, who mingle at the sideshows and ultimately help bring the adults together at Government House. All but fortune-teller Gypsy Rose's illegitimate daughter, Queenie, who also loves Queensland Jack, and an old horseman are present at the wedding next day at St James.'[30]

For all that it has a large cast and there are some unusual twists in the plot, *Sydney Royal* is slight and rather patchy; the Melbourne bibliophile John Kinmont Moir felt it was mainly of local interest. Beatrice Davis loyally said it had a fairy tale quality, but sales were disappointing, and Miles was forever sending copies off as gifts, to the Alice Springs Kindergarten in 1947, for instance. She was inclined to blame the publisher, with whom she had many disagreements along the way: 'it never had a chance'. One of only two reviews located, a brief note in the FAW's *Fellowship*, said the book 'breathed youth' and that it would make a fine bit of publicity for intending immigrants. That was Miles' view too; maybe she even wrote the review (though more likely it was the work of Glen Mills Fox). The other notice, in *Book News* (by an unnamed author), said the show was the real protagonist, and that while it was hard to take the book seriously as a story for young people, grown readers would enjoy its vigorous style and pithy phrasings, and the realism of its setting and atmosphere.[31]

Late in life Miles recalled that she first went to the show when she was seventeen, which would mean in 1896 or 1897. In another instance she said it was 1898, which is more likely, since she came to Sydney with her mother that year. She may also have attended while living at Penrith. After she returned to Australia in 1932, she always went with family or friends. In 1947, she visited on the second day, 3 April, with a 'Beatrice', probably Beatrice Bridle, wife of her mother's cousin John Bridle. According to her pocket diary: 'We did Agricultural Hall, flowers, fowls, pigs & dogs and then went to the Coronation Stand & had our lunch & stayed there until 9 p.m., when we tired of the horses jumping ... & came home.' It is this core experience, affectionately recalled in *Sydney Royal*, her last published fiction under her own name, and its ideological underpinning that now make the book interesting. In Australia the local agricultural show has long been a great day out. The Sydney show was special, the oldest in the country, part of the New South Wales experience, as the Melbourne Cup was part of the Victorian one, and a true people's festival, according to Miles. Moreover, just as her little story celebrates the healing effects of Australia and the ordinary folk on mixed-up imperials, so its descriptions of particular classes and their interaction are vivid and, if not exactly attractive, realistic:

> Woops, from Woop Woop, come to make whoopee in the wood-chopping and sheaf-tossing and sheep-dog contests, and to marvel at the ignorance of the townies, who don't know a Hereford from an Ayrshire, a come-back from a merino or a stringy bark from a mulga. The wallops, from Woolloomooloo, look on them with a grin of superiority and the hope of pickings. Sometimes they all can dote and gloat on three or four representatives of the King, for nothing is more official than a

democracy, nor more snobbish. A democracy breeds officials like rabbits, and worships its swells as long as they are pets rather than pests, and can be worn on the tassles of a fez rather than felt as the thongs of the knout. And none can be more democratic than ploots [plutocrats], whose logic in being select is demonstrated by associating with the masses at a distance. How could folks be superior if none were inferior?[32]

During 1947 Miles took only a couple of weekend breaks, in February and June, to Hazelbrook to stay with Dymphna and Florence and the girls. Otherwise, it was a matter of into town as usual, almost always on literary business, mostly to the FAW or Book Society meetings. Les Haylen had succeeded George Farwell as president of the FAW in 1946, and Miles was again elected vice-president, which meant chairing numerous meetings when Les, a Federal parliamentarian, was in Canberra. (Thankfully, Marjorie Barnard now chaired 'that infernal Book Society', as Miles described it to Dymphna Cusack.) With Glen Mills Fox, who served as secretary at this time, Miles also edited *Fellowship* (published 1944–c.1948), a tricky job involving in-house reviewing. She wrote a couple of minor reviews herself, welcoming an unabridged edition of Furphy's *Rigby's Romance* in March and commenting on 'The Landscape in Our Stories' in J. K. Ewers' *Men Against the Earth* and other works in June. But the big books written by members had to be treated with great care, especially the literary event of the year, M. Barnard Eldershaw's *Tomorrow and Tomorrow*. A good deal of the correspondence between Glen Mills Fox and Miles when Glen was in Melbourne recuperating from an operation and wondering what to do about her failing marriage is about finding a generally acceptable reviewer. (Margaret Trist was the answer.)[33]

Miles' view of *Tomorrow and Tomorrow* was that it was a great feat of composition, but lacked the creative spark. She had a point, for as we now know, the novel had been effectively gutted by censorship. But its cerebral structure and futuristic themes were unlikely to have appealed to her anyway. Much more to her liking was a new novel by her friend Henrietta Drake-Brockman, *The Fatal Days*, a wartime romance set in the provincial city of Ballarat, which takes a positive view of the 'Yanks' in Australia. Miles loved the book, and found the characters refreshingly normal, which, compared with Xavier Herbert's *Soldier's Women* (begun at the time though not published until 1961), they certainly were.[34]

Unfortunately for Miles, conflict was beginning to replace consensus at the FAW. Two alarming issues came before it: the prosecutions of writers Robert Close in Melbourne and Howard Fast in Washington. Close was charged with obscene libel for his rough seaman's story with its 'nymphomanic' cargo, *Love Me Sailor*, and despite protests from the literary world, in due course, successfully prosecuted. Late in 1947 Glen Mills Fox advised Miles that Close thought they were not doing enough in Sydney to support him. Miles was also involved when the FAW sent a message to Washington over the jailing of Howard Fast for refusing to testify to the House Committee on Un-American Activities, not so straightforward an action as might be supposed, due to a fit of FAW 'constitutionalism' by Bart Adamson of which Miles disapproved: 'I don't go much on constitutions. No use having the constitution I warned them if we make a schism.' Which was what she feared — or worse disintegration.[35]

In the literary politics of the day, the relationship between Sydney and Melbourne was often tense. By 1947 tensions were also apparent within the Sydney FAW, which regarded itself as the premier Fellowship. The tensions, which Miles sought to moderate, were largely ideological, a reflection of the emerging Cold War and as fierce in Australia as in America.

It would be wrong to cast Miles Franklin as anti-communist here. As early as 1946, there were suggestions that she was a communist, a charge she made merry with, as in her response that the young Red-baiting W. C. (Billy) Wentworth was 'a bright little fellow, apparently with a semi-detached intellect'. Nothing gave her more pleasure than outwitting mindless conservatives whom she derided as a bunch of blimps, with no ideas since the Ark. 'You know I *can* be brilliant if I bestir myself,' she remarked to Katharine Susannah Prichard after one such triumph. And as she implied when writing to Raymond Robins, it rather pleased her to think she had earned the Right's disapproval due to her membership of the Friends with Russia Society and being 'often called to speak for its adherents'. One wholesaler even wanted to ban her books; the prospect filled her with mirth, which seems about the only sane response. Her favourite riposte, that in one slap Joe Stalin had taken women off the midden and put them in parliament, was guaranteed to throw all Right-wing types off-guard.[36]

Miles was probably under the threat of surveillance herself. It was, as everywhere in those paranoid years, a case of 'guilt by association'. There had been communists in the FAW in Sydney since the merger with the Writers'

Association in 1938, and Bart Adamson, who joined the Communist Party in 1943, was conspicuous in its affairs. And as bolder, more intellectual women made their way to the Communist Party, Miles' personal friends were among them. Although she often lamented that communists spent all their energy defending Russia, they too were optimists, with a passion for 'the people' and for ideas, and she had much in common with them. Whenever Miles walked through Darlinghurst to work on *Fellowship* at Glen Mills Fox's flat, 'The Gwydir', at 167 Forbes Street, she was entering a communist household.[37]

Sometimes she met Katharine Susannah Prichard there. Katharine was the best-known communist with whom Miles Franklin associated, and was back and forth from Perth in the 1940s. In mid-1947 she was again in the east, travelling to Sydney via Canberra, where she stayed for a time with her diplomat son, Ric Throssell, and his new wife, Dorothy (his first wife died in Moscow in 1946). She arrived to stay at Carlton on 22 August. John Franklin, in one of his uncontrollable moments after excessive drinking, threatened to denounce his aunt to the authorities for having communists in the house.[38]

But Miles was opposed to communist doctrine. She acknowledged that in theory it marked a step on from liberalism, but it tended to conflict with her basic beliefs in several ways. To start with, the communist focus was international first and national second, whereas Miles believed it should be the other way round. Secondly, it was, or rather its followers made it, a rigid creed, whereas iconoclasm was second nature to her. She sometimes spoke at Marx House — for example, in May 1947 on early Australian novels — but if Marx House was in some respects a people's university, it was not so for her. 'In evening went to Marx House to [a] very dull religious gathering of communism and Russia,' she wrote in her pocket diary on 8 March 1947. That is hardly surprising given that in London in the 1920s she heard first-hand reports of life in the new society and was an avid reader of the international press.

Thirdly, she always stood for complete intellectual freedom. No matter how valuable new teachings were, writers would ultimately have to break free of them. How interesting it would have been as a fly on the wall at Carlton when she and Katharine argued these points. If their letters are any guide, she probably had the better of it.

In these years Miles Franklin was progressive or Left leaning. The Irish Catholic complexion of New South Wales Labor did not appeal to her. Her friends the O'Sullivans were Catholic, and she had contributed to the *Catholic Women's Review* in the 1930s, but Catholic teachings on sexuality were anathema, and she was never keen on organised religion. However, she supported the Labor stalwart Dan Clyne, her father's old mate, at state level; and Carlton was represented by members of the Evatt family, whose Left-liberalism she found highly congenial, at both state and Federal level during the 1940s.[39]

The main thing — and surely what her radical friends found so comforting in her — was not to be intimidated. 'All the world is afraid of USA and Russia now, some think one is the greater menace, others think the other, depending upon their political outlook,' she wrote to Emma Pischel in May 1947, commenting thereafter on the problems of postwar Japan ('a prize for big business and as a bulwark against communism') and India ('a nice mess'). To Emma she also vouchsafed her view that war was the madness of men, a point sustained to her satisfaction by renewed intermarriage between the English and the Germans, and her amusement at her German cousin's pleasure that his nephew was marrying an Englishwoman who had her own coat of arms, so there would be two crests on the wedding invitations. Vida Goldstein, referring to the atomic bomb, was of the same opinion about the world, though she was critical of women for not doing more to prevent the recurrence of crises.[40]

In August 1947, Anne Barnard, daughter of Eileen Barnard, a friend of Dymphna and Florence in the Blue Mountains, wrote on behalf of the Sydney University Labour Club seeking support for the nationalist struggle in the Dutch East Indies. Miles answered that of course she supported the Indonesians' struggle for freedom against European overlords, but felt it unnecessary that the club should throw its weight against a threatened scorched-earth policy, given the end of British India and currents in world opinion, and inexcusable in the face of world famine: 'There has been too much destruction and death.' The letter goes straight on to what Miles deemed urgent local issues:

> I feel deeply about Australia's position in the holocaust. How are we to give power to our ideas or methods whether blimpish, imperial ideal or merely impish? What about our own Aborigines? What about our own men who will not give women equal pay for equal work … What about the imprisonment of women in brothels — regulated in two states? I would like to discuss the whole question with you … but there is no time … all sorts of picayune engagements await me and nag me.[41]

She did discuss some of these questions, however, in a lecture on 'Puritanism,' on 7 March 1947, to the FAW Young Writers' group (which according to Glen Fox's husband, Len, Miles founded) and for which her notes survive. Miles argued that puritanism had once been 'a godly self-discipline', which saw its greatest outcome in the dynamism of America: 'America was the most tremendous up-surging force in the world. Un-standardised, uneven, full of lawlessness and sins as well as Puritanism, it was the coming power … What a cauldron it was. And the greatest spiritual power bringing some kind of co-ordination was Puritanism.' Three centuries on, it had withered to 'Victorianism', a blight that nonetheless had not affected her personally: 'My blight was poverty, lack of opportunity.' Moreover, it was now the scapegoat for the problems of society. On the one hand, the old code no longer held since World War I had seen the dam burst; on the other, the ensuing licence was not the same thing as freedom, and a 'lost generation' followed. The reality was that 'Each generation must fight for freedom', and never more so than now, when everything must be faced anew due to the possibilities of the atomic bomb.[42]

The problem was that the old Puritan inheritance was entirely played out. What to put in its place? Here Miles' thinking reflected her enthusiastic reading of J. D. Unwin's theories in *Sex and Culture* in the late 1930s, which held that the energy saved over time by chastity was a cultural dynamic. 'I think myself we may go back to very rigid self-discipline in one particular … sex.'

How the young writers took such a message is hard to imagine. But these lecture notes show how Miles Franklin was trying to marshal her thoughts on the challenges of the postwar world, facing such major issues as the population explosion in the yet-to-be-defined Third World, and Australia's commitment to a mass immigration program. Ultimately she came back to demography, always a vital and sensitive issue in Australia and just then being established as an academic discipline at the Australian National University, and also to the end of Empire, heralded by the departure of the British from India in August 1947, the biggest political event of the year.

In mid-1947 Miles began re-reading *Cockatoos* (and soon after re-read *Up the Country* and *Ten Creeks Run*). She enjoyed *Cockatoos*, and immediately began to retype it for entry in the *Sydney Morning Herald* literary competition for 1947, along with the updated 'War Comes to Jones Street'.

(The prize for fiction was £2000.) *Cockatoos* was entered as 'The Exodists' by 'Banksia', and the manuscript was to be returned to 'M. Blake'.[43]

It did not win. Later Miles reflected irritably that it was a tragic story but would not be recognised as such because it lacked crime and perversion. Interestingly, *Cockatoos*, published posthumously under the Brent pseudonym, is now attracting attention from historians as a study in rural depopulation.[44]

In August, at Kate Baker's behest, Miles despatched a strong message to a ceremony at Shepparton commemorating the 104th anniversary of Furphy's birth, in which she envisaged pilgrimages to the site in the twenty-first century. Although she was happy to oblige, it was another instance of the energy Miles Franklin expended on public and professional affairs in later years. That she had reached 'the contemplative stage', as she assured Mabel Singleton, seems doubtful. But having had the last tooth removed from her mouth, she was well aware of the remorseless march of time. 'Yes,' she wrote to Emma Pischel, 'growing old is sad because so many of our generation drop out and leave us desolate, and because of the physical inability to do for oneself.' That was a special problem in Australia, where people lacked the British gift of enjoying being looked after, and in any event there was no one to do it: 'Underdogs have been very scarce and always on the rise to become top dogs themselves.'[45]

Regrets surfaced occasionally in her writings, as when the senior aunt in 'The Thorny Rose' reflects that the new morals might make people happier. They were evident too in a vivid correspondence with Nettie Palmer in 1947, mainly about Alice Henry and her eccentricities. Nettie suggested that an outline of Miles' own life would be a welcome addition to the manuscript being prepared by Alice's friends in Melbourne as a record of Alice's life, in association with the eminent American historian Mary Beard. Miles responded that it was flattering to be asked, but there was nothing to say, beyond a blurred scratch or two, and even there she had failed to do anything worth reporting: 'I've had the flattest, respectabilist life, the only remarkable thing about it, and that cd not be made into news, is that it was 100% frustration.' Meantime, since most of her friends in the United States were by this stage out of office, and news of the deaths of working colleagues came in every year from London and America, she felt such an outline would lack readers.[46]

Most probably she now regretted her single state. (Indeed, if Dymphna Cusack is to be believed, it was virginal also.) But how could she have known that she would be the last of her family, with only John, and Linda's son, Edward, in Queensland, to follow her? She had been trapped by the code of respectability — though there was more to it — as she recognised when she said she was not internally frustrated, merely defeated. She would have been irritated if she'd thought posterity would pity her. Although she wrote much about loneliness in her diaries, it should be remembered that diaries serve as a form of emotional release and self-discipline as well as a record; and that in addition to the loss of her immediate family, she endured a seemingly inexorable loss of friends. Except for Raymond Robins, all of her old mentors were gone by 1947. Even Godfrey Bentley, one of her young Newcastle friends, died in September, aged thirty.[47]

Miles always regarded herself as lucky to have a roof over her head, and continued to resist suggestions that she move to a more salubrious suburb. Wherever she was, maintenance would have been an increasing problem. Old friends from the area rallied around to help her at Grey Street. Harley Matthews, whom Miles had supported during the Australia-First fiasco and now regarded as 'a tremendous original', was one such loyal friend, ever ready to do a few jobs. Miles' gift for friendship, in life as in letters, stood her in good stead. 'Tho' we meet rarely, we are true friends, I am proud to say,' wrote opera coach Lute Drummond on 28 September 1947. And Miles no longer complained about too many phone calls.[48]

At least her authorial earnings were higher these days. With £200 earned in addition to the estimated £160 from the Willoughby shop rentals, she was in receipt of over £6 a week pre-tax in 1947, about what a fulltime female worker in New South Wales could expect to earn as a minimum. (It has been estimated that her net income seldom exceeded that after 1945.) Still, she owned her own home and the rent came in regularly from the shops; and sometimes she earned considerably more from her writings: in 1944–45, for example, she made over £400.[49]

Miles' will had been hanging in limbo since the time of Mary Fullerton's death. She still could not quite face it; but she made extensive notes. Preserved in her papers, they serve to clarify her financial position by 1947. They show that she had almost £1250 in savings accounts, £1247 in the Commonwealth Savings Bank and maybe £20 in the Bank of Westminster, London; that is, over £2500 in savings. She also owned £300 of Water Board bonds, £250 of retrievable War Savings and £700 of Treasury Bonds (war loans); that is, another £1250 in investments. In addition, she held two mortgages at Tumut, amounting in all to £650, each earning 5 per cent interest per annum. She also listed 'a few household effects' and her library at

26 Grey Street, plus her published books (but not those by Brent of Bin Bin or Mr & Mrs Ogniblat L'Artsau) and a number of unpublished manuscripts and stories.[50]

After the royal wedding in November 1947, and while Princess Elizabeth was awaiting the birth of her first child, Miles expressed the hope that it would be a girl. In the event it was a son, Prince Charles, born on 14 November 1948. In her sixty-ninth year, reared in the republican tradition, Miles observed the resurgence of enthusiasm for royalty with something like incredulity. Obviously postwar reaction had well and truly set in, and here she was marooned in suburban Australia, where, she wrote on March 1948, her life was now merely a low form of existence, sunk in a stream of interruptions, with little chance of innerness or intellectual cultivation.[51]

More than once in 1948 Miles Franklin said she felt like an exile in Australia. 'I know the pull of London. You see, I had the uprooting to suffer from the USA and then London, and my life is a shattered exile of pieces,' she wrote to Florence James, undergoing an unpleasant divorce in London. Similarly, Miles longed to see surviving friends in the United States, such as the former WTUL stenographer Magdalen Dalloz, heard from in 1948 for the first time since 1931. Scarcely an overseas letter went off without the wish that Miles had the reason or resources to visit the recipient. That applied to Melbourne associates too.[52]

Such sentiments went beyond pent-up affection or a desire to travel. They pointed to general unhappiness, and to intimations of mortality. In ''Twas Ever Thus', celebrating the Jindyworobak's first ten years (and apart from a pointed paragraph contributed to the *Bulletin's* series 'Authors on Censorship', her only published topical writing that year), she was still arguing for an Australian culture. But Cold War Sydney was not a pleasant place for uncommitted intellectuals, and she was unwell in the latter part of the year, possibly due to stress.[53]

By now Miles was really irritated to be dubbed a communist. As she wrote to Emmy Lawson on 6 January 1948, 'I loved the old Liberalism of England' (as distinct presumably from the new 'Liberalism' of Robert Menzies in postwar Australia, meaning in fact bourgeois conservatism). These were dangerous days for the unaligned Left. Late in January 1948, in an address to teachers on the difficulties faced by Australian writers, she spoke of a 'postwar convalescence', referring, perhaps, to Australia as an enfeebled or divided state.[54]

Jean Devanny, who had been expelled from the Communist Party during the war under controversial circumstances but was now back in the fold, arrived from north Queensland in March 1948 for a three-week stay. This did nothing to reassure Miles. Their friendship survived the 'siege', but only just. When the botanically minded Devanny criticised the state of her garden, Miles could barely refrain from pointing out that she was cooking Jean's meals, and her notebooks contain an extended critique of Devanny's views: 'Torquemada would be a soft angel compared with what she would decree for infidels.'[55]

It proved impossible for them to discuss the problems of the divided FAW. While Devanny agreed that the FAW was a mess and so far reduced as to look like a subcommittee of the Communist Party, she said it was because Camden Morrisby had sabotaged it. 'He is ... specially employed by Catholic Action to destroy the FAW because the RCs know that writers are dangerous. The communists know that writers are the most important people in the world and want them to be strong.' The thing to do, said Jean, was to clear out the parasites, pimps, etc. and be more subtle about the Communist Party presence. Miles could not believe this of Camden, feeble as she thought him. She was not interested in helping the Party, only writers. She thought the FAW should be like a trade union: 'I believe that now more than ever Australian writers need a strong non-sectarian organization on trade union lines.' But if no writer of significance was willing to stand for the executive in the upcoming elections, she would withdraw.[56]

This she did, remaining a member but declining to stand for any position. Her pocket diary account of election night in March 1948, and her subsequent report to Katharine Susannah Prichard, suggest that at the time she was as affected by reports of wild parties held by 'Dulcie Deamer's crew' as by communist domination. Katharine Susannah agreed that the wild parties were deplorable: 'I'm sure every reputable writer would object if they knew what was happening.' Miles was also tired of chairing meetings attended by what she privately described as 'a handful of old sleepers' in the front row and 'park intellects and cranks' in the others. Jean Devanny was humiliated to find the Party did not want her to stand. However, Glen Mills Fox (just back from Melbourne) was elected secretary; and with Muir Holburn as president, the overall result was not so bad. (Miles was fond of Muir's wife, Marjorie Pizer.)[57]

There was a strong FAW protest in Sydney in May 1948 after Robert Close was convicted of obscenity in Melbourne, but as far as Miles was concerned

— maybe she overstated it but Pixie O'Harris for one shared her views — most of those left in the FAW were fanatics who spent their time sending cables telling England to get out of Greece and urging the United States to stop disgracing itself over Howard Fast, leaving no time for local issues.

On 14 December 1948, the Fellowship of Australian Writers celebrated its twentieth birthday. Miles went to the party and spoke on members' writings. But after the March election she no longer attended executive meetings and for a few months she did not even go to monthly meetings. It was the third time in her life that she had been forced to back away from a cause: the first was in Chicago in 1915 when Mrs Robins withdrew funding for *Life and Labor*, and the second in London in 1925 when Mr Aldridge's antics at the National Housing and Town Planning Council nearly destroyed it. According to Dymphna Cusack, Miles became increasingly bitter that '"the Reds" made her leave her own Society'. She also declined office in the Book Society mid-year, on the grounds that she would be out of place amid the examination passers and blimps. Her concession was to continue for a second year as FAW representative on a (possibly advisory) UNESCO committee in July. Meantime, she went with Jean Devanny to the Easter Show. Later she decided to end her subscription to the Australian Russian Society, 'as I must send my meagre shillings to the United Relations [sic] Children's Fund.'[58]

Such circumstances made for melancholy, to some extent inevitable at Miles' age; and her anxiety about death increased. To long-silent Jean Hamilton in London she wrote that she had nothing except death to look forward to now, 'and I loathe and fear that'. Miles' best hope, she felt (if it was not just a witticism), was that she had already been punished enough in this life to be let off in the next. The whiff of rebellion in her stance bespeaks both entrapment in, and reaction against, prevailing attitudes of death denial and silent grief. Thus she managed to muster a jokey paradox: 'To be Irish I'm so afraid of death that I'm sure when I wake up some day and find I'm dead it will kill me with fright.'[59]

Seventeen years on, she still marked the anniversary of her father's death, and invariably paused over those of Susannah and Norman too. Some comforter might have helped. But she found none. Leonora Pease, last seen in Devon in 1925, had apparently taken up some form of spiritualism. On learning this, Miles remarked that she had been interested in that sort of thing once, but these days found that only her small needs were met, such as finding a newspaper on the train when she wished to read one, never the big things like contact with her family. Nor was there any respite from the passing of old friends. When Hildegarde Pischel wrote from Salt Lake City in mid-February to say that her Aunt Emma had died, it was a heavy blow, the end of 'a perfect association' over forty-one years. And after visiting Dymphna's friend Kay Keen, who died in May aged thirty-eight, she wrote: 'It was so sad, going there with the angel of death waiting.'[60]

By now Miles was 'haunted by the necessity of tackling my silly will'. She had been sorting her notes since at least 1946 (one source says 1943) and clearing up her papers for even longer. (As may be recalled, the need to do so was a consideration in her thinking about suicide in 1941, and in 1943 she told Dymphna Cusack that she had been through a trunk and destroyed 'scores of letters' relating to her love life.) The final version of the will was signed on 9 July 1948.

It shows she had four main concerns. The first was with various small treasures, to be distributed among family and friends, as named; the second was her nephews, primarily John, who was to receive £100 and her piano, plus an allowance of 10 shillings a week as an annuity (he was already the beneficiary of his father's will), while Edward Graham was to receive £50. Miles' third concern was her papers, willed to the State Library of New South Wales and today one of its treasures; and fourth, the big surprise when revealed by her trustees, was the provision for the Franklin Award, as it was originally named, perhaps inspired by the Pulitzer prizes, but more likely the Prior Prize, awarded for the last time in 1947.[61]

Unlike many writers, Miles gave careful thought to the administration of her literary estate. The bequest of her personal papers to the State Library would ensure that her literary remains (and those papers of Mary Fullerton and Alice Henry which had passed to her) would be in permanent professional custody. Likewise, her financial affairs, including the copyright on her published works, were left in the hands of the Permanent Trustee Company, which was to be responsible for the administration of the Franklin Award.[62]

Maybe Miles' realisation that John Franklin was suffering from war neurosis was a spur to her will-making. Day by day, he remained her greatest worry. Despite his aunt's urging, he could not give up flying, and she lived in constant anxiety that the next crash would involve him, a realistic fear given that over one-third of those killed in World War II were airmen and that terrible accidents were still occurring in Air Transport. When he turned up, at all hours of the day and night, he was usually the worse for drink, and babbling, 'poor nervous boy'. News that he had a month's leave in January 1948 made Miles anxious as to how she would cope. On one occasion he brought what sounds like pornographic pictures home, and threatened to burn the house down. Then, as usual, he left her feeling ill and despairing, the more so for having 'no one to turn to, all dead'. Nonetheless they remained loyal to one another. Each was all the other had left of immediate family, and on the rare occasions John was unaffected by beer, they got along well enough; and Miles was able to look after him properly whenever he returned home unwell, with gastric and other disturbances. For the most part, though, all she could do — apart from his laundry and preparing his meals — was be there, and see him off on the next assignment, which might take him to Perth or Tokyo or some equally far-off place, such as 'that blasted rocket range' (a reference to Woomera, and a rare instance of Miles swearing). The irony of the airman as saviour in *All That Swagger* must have been obvious.[63]

Dymphna Cusack's experience of coping with her own health problems and those of her brother who had been treated for shell shock were invaluable. She was there one weekend in March when John returned home 'practically out of his mind' after a disaster at Amberley air base in Queensland, in which sixteen of his mates had crashed just ahead of him, and were incinerated in front of their wives. Dymphna recalled:

> God help me, I was the only one who could do anything with him. I don't know why. I gave him two full grams of Phenobarb[itone, a sedative] (am I a menace?) and he grabbed the bottle and took two more. With Miles' horror of drugs I daren't tell her what they were and I dragged Jack around — when he wasn't dragging me — and it took him 12 hours to pass out and he slept for 12. I think it saved his sanity, poor kid.[64]

It was probably Dymphna's phenobarb. Not only did Miles distrust drugs (even commonly used ones like aspirin), but like many women of her generation she never drank alcohol. She was probably quite inexperienced in its use — it was not kept at home — and even fearful because of her youthful memories of her father's drinking problem. John's stress-induced drinking was a tragedy for them both. She told Frank Ryland, then serving in the occupying forces in Japan, she was often depressed but had been before and must not give way to it. Perhaps for her own benefit as much for Ryland's she wrote: 'If you let your sympathies derange you, you become merely one more soul lost and destroyed by war.'[65]

Arguably Miles Franklin's anti-war attitudes were a further, if subliminal, barrier between her and her unhappy nephew: 'The warrior is never a hero to me.' The most she could manage (as in the letter to Mary Dreier from which this uncompromising remark comes) was that soldiers were victims of mass hysteria, rooted in fear. Nor should her lifelong habit of self-protection be omitted from the equation. At one point she recalled that her brother Norman had once said his son was his punishment, to which she added fiercely, 'I don't see why he should be mine.' To two Queensland journalists, John Adam and Brian Dobbyn, seeking help for a proposed writers' manual, she responded that technicalities were of no importance and her only interests now were inner consciousness, experience of life and freedom of speech. But reflexivity was never her forte; in literary terms, her sensibility was more like that of Thackeray than George Eliot.[66]

A sense of time running out is evident in her correspondence. To Katharine Susannah Prichard in January, she had mentioned trying to finish a novel set locally, to no avail. She found her manuscript too boring. As earlier to Nettie Palmer, she confessed to Ian Mudie (among others) that she had not written a novel since 1942. Clearly in both instances she was talking about 'War Comes to Jones Street', which she called her 'marooned novel'.[67]

Sometimes the level of frustration seems to have been almost unbearable. After the funeral of Dr George Lawson, a surgeon in 1890s Goulburn, at Rookwood on 2 November — '52 years I believe since I first saw him!' she recalled — her pocket diary entry reads: 'Trivial, segregated, exiled, futile', without even the energy for chores. Katharine Susannah did her best to keep her friend's spirits up, and she was onto something when she remarked that Miles' letters to her were like jewels that sparkled. She suggested a novel in letter form. Nothing came of this promising idea, nor, for the time being, of Nettie Palmer's urging that she should write her memoirs, but Miles did work on her diaries. The late 1940s brought some wonderful reminiscences, and 1948 was a vintage year, with, for example, Miles' recollection of first reading *The Story of an African Farm* and her disappointing encounter in London with its famous author, Olive Schreiner. Her letters contain ever more reminiscences of her time in the United States and London. To be so far from old associates and with no prospect of seeing them again was another form of bereavement, but it brought forth some vivid memories, of inspecting cesspits in London, for instance, when the Housing Council men would not do such work if there was a woman to hand.[68]

In her blacker moments Miles Franklin felt she was finished as a writer, that she was better employed on the daily round, which, with her notions of neighbourliness and hospitality, could have filled her days, and for all the irritations did bring satisfaction. Moreover, she was often thankful for her routines, and for the flow of guests who helped keep melancholy at bay. To Pixie O'Harris, 'The house seemed to be the right setting for her.'[69]

Though Miles may have felt from time to time that there was no point trying to write any more, she often returned to her plays. Early in 1948 she was reworking 'The Scandal-monger'/'Scandal at Glenties' as two plays, and later in the year she embarked on a romantic comedy entitled 'Johanna versus Hennessy', based on an incident in *All That Swagger*. Set in the upper Murrumbidgee in the 1860s, it survives in manuscript, as does another version entitled 'Models for Molly', dated 1948 and known to have been submitted to the Commonwealth Jubilee Competition in 1951 under that old standby pseudonym Mr & Mrs O. Like 'Scandal at Glenties'/'The Scandal-monger', the Johanna/Molly play has a complicated plot revolving around the misguided matchmaking efforts of elders, but at least it was a new idea for a drama. Written quite quickly, it was posted, presumably to another competition, in September. (These historical plays were still doing the rounds in 1953, along with others yet to be written in 1948.) Clearly it was a thin year creatively, and Miles' tenacity seems misplaced. But the prizes were big, and as with Miles' protective attitude to her Brent pseudonym in times past, money — not psychology — was the key.[70]

Whatever else kept her working on plays, Miles Franklin's commitment to and enthusiasm for the theatre are beyond question. As she explained to the critic St John Ervine, she was well acquainted with the theatres of postwar Sydney, in particular the New Theatre and Doris Fitton's Independent Theatre in North Sydney, the other great survivor of the little-theatre movement in Sydney in the 1930s. The Old Vic toured in 1948 too, with Laurence Olivier and Vivien Leigh. Thanks to Katharine Susannah Prichard, 'Call Up Your Ghosts!' was chosen to launch a new workers' theatre in Perth, playing at the Modern Women's Club on 10 August 1948, and there was the prospect of a presentation in Brisbane. But the best thing in 1948 by far, seen at the Independent in October, was Sumner Locke Elliott's soldiers' camp play *Rusty Bugles*, set in northern Australia. Miles knew his aunt, and Alice Henry had been a friend of his long-dead mother,

Sumner Locke. This play, not his first, delighted Miles: 'Well, Sumner my dear you've done it … the Australianness was so authentic, so original and actual, and so gifted … The play shows how life and its tragedies catch all.'[71]

Another young man of the theatre, Laurence Collinson from Brisbane, brought himself to her attention in 1948. Miles had met him before, and had invited him out to Grey Street in 1947, but for reasons now clear — he was a troubled homosexual — she found him unresponsive. This time he asked her to read one of his plays, in which a character, Em, refuses to marry. Miles thought the play remarkable for such a young man — Collinson was in his early twenties — but the treatment needed depth. In reply to his request for further reading on sexual matters, she dredged up her old favourites: Lester Ward's *Pure Sociology*, Chapter 14, and Olive Schreiner's *Woman and Labour*. If he could not find John Stuart Mill's *Subjection of Women* in Brisbane, she would consider lending him her own precious copy, plus her current favourite, Dr Unwin's *Sex and Culture*, 'which deals with sexual indulgence'.[72]

Like many first-wave feminists, Miles was perplexed by the latest thinking on sexuality. When she read Christina Stead's novel *Letty Fox: Her Luck*, she waxed indignant to Margery Currey that there seemed no place left for chastity in America, where phallic worship was apparently now rampant. And when Walter Cousins at Angus & Robertson lent her a copy of Alfred Kinsey's *Sexual Behavior of the Human Male*, all she could say was: 'My, oh my! how tastes differ.' She could not bring herself to read it closely: 'kangarooing' through its pages was quite sufficient. It made her wish there was a worthy successor to Charlotte Perkins Gilman. She decided the emancipation of women had not yet begun. Elsewhere she worried that young women were no longer rebellious, as her generation had been.[73]

So true was Miles Franklin to the feminism of her youth, she could even, in a rare positive reference to Australia's Asian neighbours, wish she was in Japan with Frank Ryland. The position of women in Japan would make a great subject, she suggested. Otherwise she maintained the Malthusianism which carried over into first-wave feminism, that there could be no accommodation with Asia until the men there controlled themselves and the population explosion was constrained. Her intemperate expressions of this view have been referred to earlier, and they did not improve as she grew older. Interestingly they seem to have been more candidly expressed when she was writing to American friends such as Leonora Pease, to whom she reported on 28 May 1948 that she had recently heard on the radio the

British nutritionist Sir John Boyd Orr, Sir William Beveridge (designer of the British welfare state and a visitor to Sydney in May) and the Australian physics professor Marcus Oliphant variously advocating 'birth control, girth control and earth control': 'Very few countries other than America overeat today, we must awake about ruining the earth and as for birth control I think over fecundity reduces people to the most disgusting kind of vermin … they could control themselves.'[74]

By the late 1940s, such assumptions were radically out of step with both national policy ('populate or perish') and international demographic concerns, which focused on the problem of feeding an exploding world population, with birth control the only known answer in the long run. To this prescription the Catholic Church was then, as now, opposed. As it happened, the American Cardinal Spellman and 'some prelate named Sheen' were also in Sydney in May, for a 'great Catholic corroboree', and they made no bones about it: the world's choice was between Moscow and Rome — so Australian women must fill up their cradles. 'Catholic prelates never say one uplifting word, nor give any great message to lead mankind … but they are astute politicians and in democratic countries will prevail by getting a lot of adherents and then telling them how to vote,' Miles wrote to Emmy Lawson on 3 June 1948.[75]

The candid expression of opinion to overseas friends included comment on the American ascendancy: 'Wall Street has the British Lion by the tail.' Her years in Chicago had given her a critical perspective on big business, and along with the rest of the Left, she fully expected Wall Street to foment another war, while America had the advantage of the atomic bomb. Would there be enough like her old associates in Chicago to fend off the danger, she inquired anxiously of Mary Dreier.[76]

Even for an adept like Miles Franklin, it was difficult to cope with Cold War tensions. 'I'd be for Moscow in the dogfight if it could be clear cut and the rest of the world unharmed'; but that she doubted. If it came down to support for the United States or Joe Stalin, she'd be for the United States, as she knew the language, and the Americans knew how to keep their feet warm in winter and the flies out of their food. That was flip, the kind of thing one writes in letters to make old friends smile. In Australia, however, the communists were set to challenge the Labor government on the coalfields, and it seemed to Miles that they would be willing to provoke civil war, even though Katharine Susannah Prichard argued that if there was violence it would be the violence of bourgeois reaction.[77]

The letter to Emmy Lawson cited above shows how fiercely she could express her political views in personal letters. But perhaps this was how distant friends remembered Miles of old. Margery Currey, one of those friends from Chicago days, to whom she sent a copy of *My Career Goes Bung*, recalled 'your own gallant and high-flying self'.[78]

Face to face it was different. While incorrigibly political, Miles Franklin was also a lady of standing in literary Sydney, and usually polite in her dealings with people. At a party given by Dora Birtles at Balmoral the previous year, however, one of the guests had been obliged to quickly change her tune after Miles made it plain that she had overheard the woman's dismissive remarks about her good self. Miles later reproved herself for being so blatant: 'I am [not so] quick on [the] trigger as in my alerter days (I'm inclined to go off into my own thoughts nowadays).'[79]

Mostly she still enjoyed social occasions like the now frail Ada Holman's birthday in March. And on 15 July 1948, at Angus & Robertson's first postwar staff ball at Paddington Town Hall, she was placed at Beatrice Davis' table, in effect in the official party. However, the next day she came down with a chill, then cystitis, and was in bed for a week. When she went to a local doctor with a head cold she was obliged to wait two hours in what she described as workhouse conditions, and had no relief. Then there were problems with a terrific pain up the sciatic nerve, something like she had experienced from wasp bites at Ostrovo.[80]

Worse was to come, with shoulder pains, and in October, shingles. Dymphna Cusack came to Carlton to care for her, and neighbours did their best. But her ailments did not seem to stop Miles' trips to town, or get her to bed earlier. It was a rare night, and a sign of feeling poorly, that she went to bed before midnight. She seems to have been unconcerned about travelling alone late at night on public transport. There were some cars, but they had not taken over the city in Miles' time. It was a treat when gallants like Beatrice Davis' partner, Dick Jeune, drove her home.[81]

In July 1948 Miles wrote to Magdalen Dalloz: 'I am beginning to feel old. I get skinnier and wrinkled and wrinkleder, and my hair is beginning to go grey around the temples. If I live long enough I suppose it will be quite grey.' Then, in November, commiserating with Margery Currey's loss of a kidney, she commented that although women could lose all manner of parts without loss of longevity, she didn't know about kidneys; but according to family wisdom only men died of heart failure. This, she hazarded, was because women's hearts learned to live in so little sustenance.[82]

One mild winter's afternoon in June Miles called in to see Lute Drummond, the opera coach she had first met at Stratford-on-Avon in 1923 and now an oft-visited friend in Sydney's Bond Street. Lute was a month older than Miles, and had suffered a stroke, but otherwise, Miles recorded, was her radiant, transcendent self. Two months later Miles attended a testimonial for Lute at the Theatre Royal; however, it would not be many more months before she attended Lute's memorial service at Christ Church St Laurence on Broadway, Sydney's most important High Anglican church, where, appropriately, the singing was wonderful. (After the ceremony Miles vigorously defended herself and Dymphna against the dramatist Sydney Tomholt's charge that they were communists.)[83]

When Beatrice Davis broke her ankle, Miles loyally trekked across the harbour to Cammeray to visit her several times, on one occasion to cook lunch, shelling peas en route. Beatrice was one of the younger women who became important to her in the 1940s. Except for Katharine Susannah Prichard and Jean Devanny, all were born in the first decade of the twentieth century, a generation after Miles: Beatrice Davis, Dymphna Cusack, Florence James, Henrietta Drake-Brockman, Glen Mills Fox, Pixie O'Harris, Delys Cross (an FAW member). Their support of her was quite touching. She was, of course, a strengthener, and they valued her for that. When *Come in Spinner* was at last published, in London in 1951, it bore a dedication to Miles Franklin. Likewise, Miles did not forget those elders to whom she owed much. One of the last things she did in 1948 was send £5 to J. K. Moir in Melbourne as a New Year's gift for Kate Baker, in 'complete secrecy'.[84]

In late 1947 Angus & Robertson had honoured Miles with a special two-copy edition of *All That Swagger* printed on rag paper. One copy went to the British Museum, the other to the National Library of Australia, which she and George Ferguson, as representative for the firm, signed for despatch on 16 February 1948. In 1948 Angus & Robertson also published a new popular edition, the seventh since 1936. Now Miles welcomed the paperback revolution:

> I find that I'm inclined to shy away from beautifully produced books because so often they are pompous shells and the matter does not live up to them. This feeling has come to me from my childhood when a tattered volume of Aesop was my delight and good works in stuffed-shirt gilt-edged bindings were like those

mausoleums that rich nonentities erect over their dead in a vain attempt to be what they are not. And today such a lot of treasure is to be found in paper-covered flimsies while many of the well-produced books are mere lumber.[85]

That year she had enjoyed Virginia Woolf's *To the Lighthouse*, and she wanted Jean Hamilton to send her a cheap second-hand copy of Woolf's *The Waves* too. She thought Eleanor Dark's latest novel, *Storm of Time*, 'a tremendous thing' (and told her so), and Malcolm Ellis' life of Governor Macquarie pleased her, as did Katharine Susannah Prichard's *Golden Miles*. That she kept up with the market is apparent from her reading of such popular titles as *The Herb of Grace* by Elizabeth Goudge and Neville Cardus' *Autobiography*, which she privately panned. Probably she had not seen what would now be thought of as the book of the year, Patrick White's *The Aunt's Story*. A brief, bleak review appeared in the *Sydney Morning Herald* in mid-1948, but copies of the novel were slow to arrive from England, and it was not until 1950 that a more informative notice appeared in Sydney.[86]

Published in the year of White's homecoming, the novel is about a spinster aunt of landed stock, born in the Southern Highlands of New South Wales, who is troubled by questions of identity. The first and last of the three sections are prefaced by quotations from Olive Schreiner. In an unpublished short story dated 17 February 1949 entitled 'Gentleman Encounters Lady' and featuring Tommy Kingston, a wild man from the hills, Miles drew upon local lore reminiscent of the opening section of White's novel, though there is no record of her ever reading it.[87]

White is said to have been fond of *The Aunt's Story*, and it is easy to see why: the single woman, like the homosexual male, was a marginal figure in prewar Australia. Theodora Goodman, the ageing spinster who seems to have a diminishing grip on reality, is an outsider whose odyssey from the Southern Highlands through harbourside Sydney to extensive travel and the south of France, then homewards, reaches its apotheosis in the American high country, where she meets Holtius, another wild man from the hills — or maybe the same man as she had encountered as a girl in Australia — and attains the longed-for state of selflessness, which some see as madness.

Arguably, at least some aspects of this story — not just the settings and the sequence, but also the themes — have a bearing on the later experiences of Miles Franklin. Over time, literary critics have made some pertinent comments on it; for example, calling the novel a work of great beauty, close to the human heartbeat, a compassionate treatment. Of these, for present purposes, the comments of Adrian Mitchell seem most apposite:

> Within the dissolving order of the normal world, the disappearance of provincial Australia and the collapse of the 'gothic shell of Europe', Theodora undergoes not so much a crisis of identity as an eventual release from the constraining sense of self. Her rational intelligence, initially unconventional but acute, is gradually abandoned as she pursues the desirable state of selflessness, and at the end of her spiritual odyssey she achieves a new personal calm that may also be madness.[88]

This commentary sketches the changing world also experienced by Miles Franklin, and the possibility of personal transcendence. But as emphasised by Mitchell, the price for Theodora is high. Nor does the fictional Theodora ever return to Australia, as Miles did in 1932 (and Patrick White in 1948). Moreover, it seems clear that Miles never actually achieved, maybe never even aspired to achieve, Theodora's transcendence of self. Even less did she seek Theodora's ultimate calm and acceptance of the world. To some extent, that was due to generational shifts in understanding: for example, whereas the essentially early twentieth-century Theodora could treat death as a nothing, late nineteenth-century Miles remained puzzled about what the *Bulletin* used to call 'the silence', and raged against it until too weak to do so. Miles also had the stronger, more gregarious personality, and wider purposes, which despite advancing age she still hoped to fulfil. That is to say, the fictional Theodora was a gnostic, whereas Miles Franklin was rationalist and intellectual. Nonetheless, Patrick White, a younger writer with a fresh approach, captured the ground they shared more extensively than might be imagined. When the young Theodora understands that the decaying family home 'Meroe' was eternity 'and she was the keeper of it', it might be Miles Franklin speaking. In the themes of renunciation and return to Australia, do we not catch a distant echo of 'Merlin of the Empiah'/*Prelude to Waking*?

The year 1949 was a momentous one for Australia, beginning with the enactment of Australian citizenship (though Australians remained British subjects until the 1980s) and ending with the defeat of the Chifley Labor government by a conservative Liberal-Country Party coalition, which remained in power for the rest of Miles Franklin's life (and long after, to

1972). Older Australians, however, may remember it as the year when *Blue Hills*, the long-running ABC serial of rural family life, came on air, and for the mid-year coal strike, when Chifley called the communist bluff by sending the troops to work the mines. For Miles Franklin personally, it was the year of Brent, and of John Franklin's discharge from the RAAF on 21 February 1949 — starkly contrasting experiences.

John Franklin's discharge from RAAF Transport after seven years' service, six as a pilot, brought him no joy nor his aunt. It was preceded by his now familiar communist taunt and unpredictable behaviour, with cross words when it seemed to Miles he was taking her for granted and would not help around the house: 'By tolerating him I have not helped him, he only gets worse & thinks he can use me as he likes. It makes me ill to see him drunk and I *can't* stand [it] & don't know what to do.' He in turn accused her of not doing anything to help him. By year's end he had yet to make the psychological transition to civilian life. No doubt the thought of returning to clerking with the Permanent Trustees was unappealing, and he could not give up drinking.[89]

Miles often did not know his whereabouts. When his long-term girlfriend, June Marshall, announced her engagement to someone else, Miles could only agree with her decision. Hearing just before Christmas that he was ill, she contacted one of his maternal cousins, Claire O'Connor, at Chatswood. Claire's mother, Xenia, who had cared for John Franklin as a child at Ardglen, told Miles that they were taking him in, that they would help him find a job after the holidays, and that he was his handsome, charming self with them. That, wrote Miles in her pocket diary, was like 'an answer to a prayer'. To Claire's youngest sister, Enid, to whom John had been close as a boy at Ardglen, she expressed her relief, writing on 23 December that she had often pleaded with him to visit his cousins, but 'the bright lights of the town were too much for him':

> He needs to be with young people his own age & children & people of congenial pursuits and interests. As he truly says my acquaintances are only a few old writing people. He has nothing in common with them & they cannot be of any use to him. With the love and attention of his own family around him I hope he will recover from the strain of the flying and get a settled job on the ground … He had the luck to come through [the war] so must be meant for some good & useful life.[90]

Regarding Brent of Bin Bin, his fortunes had improved. As noted, Miles had continued to seek publication outlets during the war, but since Hartley Grattan's fruitless approach to American publishers in 1943, she had concentrated on local possibilities. The conditions she imposed were always a stumbling block, however. In 1944 she had become aware that Dymocks Book Arcade was seeking to acquire the Australasian rights from Blackwood; but once Dymocks realised copyright rested with the author, they insisted on face-to-face negotiations with his representative, William Blake. A little later, in May 1945, Colin Roderick had the temerity to write directly to Miles from Gympie High School to inquire about an edition of *Up the Country* for Queensland schools. Needless to say he got a dusty answer and there is no record of him approaching Blackwood for permission. Perhaps he was unable to find a publisher.[91]

Nor had the negotiations with the Melbourne bookseller and publisher Robertson & Mullens, which had begun in late 1945, resulted in publication. Prompted by the Commonwealth Literary Fund, the managing director Charles H. Peters (the same Charles Peters whom Miles had taken to task for linking her with Brent on radio in 1931) had sought permission from Blackwood to reprint *Up the Country* in the Pocket Library. After a hold-up due to Mary Fullerton's failing health, William Blake had responded positively, provided all of Brent's six volumes were to be published. But when Peters then suggested that maybe the time had come to lift Brent's anonymity, a stalemate ensued. On 8 February 1946 Blake advised there was no point in proceeding unless the entire series was involved, and anonymity was maintained. Miles was still keen to do business on that basis, however, and the correspondence between William Blake and Charles Peters flowed back and forth in a predictable manner for months. It was probably the insistence in September that 'Prelude to Romance' (as *Prelude to Waking* was then titled) appear 'without delay' that finally discouraged the firm from bringing out the series, though formally speaking Peters had already accepted 'Prelude' and the project was merely deferred in October 1946 'until conditions improved'. In June 1947, William Blake tried Peters once more, reporting that although Brent had received no new offers, interest was rising: perhaps the firm would like to have 'Prelude to Romance' on its Christmas list? There is no record of a reply.[92]

Angus & Robertson also became interested in the Brent books after World War II. In late 1946 the firm contacted Blackwood with a proposal to purchase the copyright on the three published volumes for £50 a title; and on 6 January 1947 the publishing director, Walter Cousins, wrote to Miles directly, indicating that he would like to speak with her about 'the Bin Bin series'. Since by now most people in the book trade in Sydney believed she was at least Brent's agent, this is not as surprising as it may sound, but Miles kept up the charade. Understandably, the proposal did not appeal to her, and as William Blake she immediately sought clarification from Blackwood regarding her rights. In response, Blackwood assumed that since it did not own the copyrights, the proposal really related to republication of the volumes in Australia, and as it did not wish to reprint the volumes itself, it would not make any claims (which could also be interpreted as a general relinquishment of the firm's rights). But it strongly advised William Blake not to accept the offer. Brent of Bin Bin replied he had no intention of doing so, adding that there would be no further proposals for republication, as 'the author has no wish to be published except in Australia as a record of life here'. From the accompanying warm reflections on Brent's long association with the firm, it seems clear that this represented the end of Miles Franklin's relationship with Blackwood; except for a letter in 1948 from an otherwise unknown Miss Marjorie Hetts of Spilsby inquiring of Blackwood if any further books had been written by Brent, this was the last letter in a file that extended back to May 1927.[93]

Meanwhile, Miles had followed up Cousins' approach by writing as Brent of Bin Bin to Colin Roderick, who now occupied an influential position as director of educational publications at Angus & Robertson. Brent told Roderick that he had received 'a comprehensive offer' from elsewhere (meaning Robertson & Mullens) but it was held up by conditions in the printing trade, and he would like his books to appear sooner, especially 'the preliminary story'. No more than before did this attempt to get 'Prelude to Romance' into print succeed; but in Roderick, Brent had an ally: Angus & Robertson's publishing schedule was full for 1947, but Roderick was sure *Up the Country* would last, and he hoped the firm could bring out the whole series at a later date, 'spaced so as to bring the fullest possible return to the author'.[94]

In private Miles thought Roderick 'so mediocre' that it is doubtful whether she had much faith in his projections. However, on 17 September 1948, when Miles visited Beatrice Davis at Cammeray, as Miles' pocket diary records, Beatrice 'gave me a letter for Brent'. Beginning 'Dear Sir', it reads in part:

> We should be glad to discuss with you the rights to publication
> of your novels *Up the Country*, *Ten Creeks Run* and *Back to Bool
> Bool*, which apparently are not being kept in print. Recognizing

their importance to the Australian literary scene, we feel they should be available to the public; and we should be proud to become Brent of Bin Bin's publisher. It has been suggested that there are also further works, as yet unpublished; and it would naturally interest us to see any such manuscripts.[95]

Despite this much-desired development, Miles hesitated. Beatrice went to Queensland to recuperate for her ankle injury in November, and as so often over the summer months, Miles had several smaller projects to finish. On 3 January 1949 she resumed revision of her 'Johanna versus Hennessy' play, for entry in the Maie Hoban Pilgrim Theatre competition in Melbourne later in the year (she also entered 'Scandal at Glenties'), and in early February she sent 'The Scandal-monger' (under the pen-name 'S. Bruce') to the Western Australia Drama Festival competition. At much the same time, she was acting as go-between for young Ric Throssell's plays, assuring him she had gained some efficiency in keeping secrets. However, neither she nor Throssell had any luck in the competitions, and another reading of 'Call Up Your Ghosts!' at the Players' Club in Sydney in June was discouraging.[96]

There were sketches and short stories to get off as well, and a broadcast to record for the ABC. In January 1949, having heard Jean Batt, a lecturer in French at the University of Tasmania, say on radio that women had not yet made the grade in the arts, she was driven to reply. 'Women Haven't Yet Made The Grade — But Which Grade?' appeared in the *ABC Weekly* a few months later. There she wrote, 'Feminism is an experiment unnaturally based. Feminism merely attempts to free women to an equality with men in men's physical and mental pursuits', as if she had recanted on long-held principles. But the original text has a concluding sentence which makes all the difference: 'As a beginning of woman's emancipation the female ego must first be fully released.'[97]

Other pieces dating from these uncertain months were finished but never published — a pity in the case of the spiky 'Syntax is not Sufficient', by 'One of the Illiterates', a response to 'R. G. H.' (presumably R. G. Howarth), whose 'Writers from the Universities' had appeared in the *Bulletin* in January. Miles listed many unlettered Australian writers, including herself, to make her point: 'Candidates for immortality [should] remember that syntax, like patriotism, is not sufficient to produce a worthy contribution to the archives of literature.' She also polished several short pieces, including 'Gentleman Encounters Lady', the Tommy Kingston story previously mentioned in relation to *The Aunt's Story*; 'The Robinson Story' (about an up-country confidence trick perpetrated by a cross-dresser); and 'The Hat', apparently based on a gift from John Franklin to his aunt, and later entered in a *Herald* competition. Of the writings worked on in this period, however, only a paragraph or two of her earliest memories written for Donald McLean's *Easy English for Young Australians* ever appeared (in 1951).[98]

It was time to take a break. On Thursday 24 February 1949 Miles caught the overnight train to Cooma. There she was obliged to spend the night in an uncomfortable hotel. But a warm day and summer flowers in the town park, and an evening spent at the pictures, enabled her to sleep soundly, ready for a week with her cousin Pearl Cotterill (née Lampe) and her husband, Bruce, at Yarrangobilly, halfway between Cooma and Talbingo. 'I have run away from myself for a week or so,' she wrote to Beatrice Davis.[99]

The next morning Bruce Cotterill collected her by car and they drove to Yarrangobilly via the historic Cooma Church of England where Susannah Franklin had been confirmed, and 'Wambrook', Susannah's birthplace, arriving late in the afternoon in time for a Country Women's Association event. As ever, Miles had a lovely time in the high country, relaxing among busy and undemanding relatives and basking in memories, as of a settler's old home, 'where I stayed last aged four', and in the atmosphere: 'bright white light like eternity'. One afternoon she and Pearl visited the Yarrangobilly Caves, and they took a short walk down a ravine, at the bottom of which Miles saw a dead snake. They picked native raspberries 'as 52 years and 2 months before', and one evening Bruce drove them to see 'the rubbishy pines' now driving out 'the dear old eucalypts'. [100]

A week later the Cotterills drove Miles to Tumut, through Talbingo — 'Sad to see no trace of the old Talbingo', burned down long ago, in 1912 — where she stayed for the weekend in a hotel, visiting the remnants of her tribe. Lily Kinred was in hospital, but Miles attended church with Ethel Bridle. Next morning it was raining, and she packed to leave, walking first over the bridge towards the poplars, but it was too mucky to go far. Then (since she travelled via Wee Jasper) she must have caught a bus, probably to the train at Yass. It rained all the way to Sydney, a rather miserable end to what turned out to be her last trip to the high country. She had been following Brent's trail to Kosciuszko, as she wrote to Beatrice Davis, and although still unsure about the Brent business, due to the amount of work 'which will mostly be thrown on me', she would 'hunt through those books with renewed zest when I return'. Writing to Ian Mudie later, she put it more grandly: 'I was absent visiting a couple of the parishes of my literary diocese of Monaro.'[101]

On her return to Sydney the first matter requiring attention was the closure of a tent theatre mounted the month before at Rushcutters Bay to present the controversial play *Love Me Sailor*, adapted from Robert Close's novel. It represented a big investment by the actors Philip and Sarah Myers, and Miles had been at the opening night in February, enjoying herself and helping as dresser to Mrs Myers. 'We had a good night,' she wrote to J. K. Moir, 'I hope the venture succeeds. There are splendid possibilities in it.' But it was not to be. After the Chief Secretary's Department declined to renew the tent theatre's permit beyond the standard month, and the promoters announced it would have to close as they could not afford to move, she and other theatre people tried to save the day by urging the state government to buy the theatre as a nucleus for a national travelling theatre. Since this was a cause dear to her heart, she may even have been a prime mover. In any event, the government proved unresponsive, and her efforts were unavailing.[102]

On 17 March 1949, Miles lunched at the Queen Victoria Club with Beatrice Davis, '& we fixed up the matter of BBB'. Beatrice was the soul of tact, and Miles overcame her misgivings about the amount of work involved. A few weeks later, on 11 April, having checked the Blackwood agreement, she went to Glen Mills Fox's flat and typed a letter to Beatrice from Brent, with a covering note written under her own name the next day beginning, 'Here goes.' Nonetheless, in her diary she remained anxious — 'I have hesitated & quibbled, and on the brink, wish I hadn't jumped into this' — and vague about Brent: 'If only it could have been completed when Mary Fullerton was alive. However,' she went on quasi-dutifully, 'I must gather up the ends.'[103]

Any suggestion that Beatrice Davis was merely an agent for Angus & Robertson is surely dispelled by her response two days later. It was exciting to hear from Brent via Miles, she wrote, and she was keen to see all the volumes. She hoped it would not be too much work for Miles but she was just as anxious as Miles to see all the volumes out, and bearing the Angus & Robertson imprint. She would have to consult with George Ferguson, but Miles could take it from her that it would all happen as she wished: 'I can tell you now that we will want to undertake all the works and will do our best to get them out in reasonable time.'[104]

On 19 May Beatrice Davis wrote a formal letter on behalf of Angus & Robertson to Miles Franklin as Brent of Bin Bin's representative, stating that the firm would bring out all six Brent novels, and thanking her for a copy of the agreement with Blackwood, a page of which survives on Angus & Robertson's files, with a mark next to the clause stating that the right to publish the work would revert to the author if the publisher declined to reprint. The publisher would respect Brent's wish to remain anonymous, Beatrice told Miles, but was puzzled about his negative attitude to granting United States rights. (Possibly this was due to Miles' earlier failures there with Brent.) The first two volumes, *Prelude to Waking* (as it was now called) and *Up the Country*, were scheduled for publication in 1950.[105]

When in April Beatrice invited Miles to let her know if she could be of any further use, Miles responded with four exclamation marks: 'If you can be of use!!!! The whole thing depends on you, otherwise it cd all go to oblivion, and my indifference go with it.' Angus & Robertson's undertaking to publish all of the Brent books rescued Brent's saga from obscurity. Otherwise the volumes published in London years earlier would have mouldered on the shelves of a few libraries while the rest remained in manuscript — that is, if Miles had not burned them, as she apparently threatened she might, unlikely though it was. Despite cold feet, she did want the books published in Australia, especially those in manuscript. As she said to Ian Mudie, 'I'd like my writing to appear here and now; no one knows what will survive or why; and whether to survive pleases dead writers we don't know ...'[106]

The record now shows that the Brent saga was a live issue within Angus & Robertson from 1946 onwards, and that Beatrice's overture of 1948 amounted to a coming together of the optimism of Walter Cousins (who envisaged the firm as the leading player in Australian publishing after World War II), the unquenchable zeal of Colin Roderick for Australian historical fiction, and Beatrice Davis' determination that Angus & Robertson should remain 'the literary hub of Australia'. The record reveals that it was Beatrice who finally overcame the obstacles to republication; years later she divulged that the agreement finally reached was that all the volumes would be published in the order Miles specified, the unpublished ones sight unseen — a brave undertaking which from Miles' point of view ensured the publication of *Prelude to Waking*. In addition to Beatrice Davis' close personal association with Miles, and her persuasive powers within the firm, there was perhaps also a sentimental factor at work: Angus & Robertson's rejection of *My Brilliant Career* would in effect be remedied. (They had also declined to publish 'On the Outside Track'/*My Career Goes Bung* and several other titles, but those rejections were not so significant.) That four editions of *All That Swagger* had appeared under the firm's imprint since it was first published by Angus & Robertson in 1940, with a fifth to come in 1949, may have been another variable.[107]

By June Miles had still not begun work on the volumes, having been held up by a bad cold through April and May, and an extended visit by the Melbourne journalist John McKellar, as well as the loss of old friends Ada Holman and Lute Drummond. Ada's death was the more wrenching, since their association reached back to Rose Scott's salon. Ada, who lived alone, had suffered a stroke at her flat and lain unconscious for some time before being found. By then it was too late, and she never regained consciousness. Writing to Dr Josephine Young, by then living in a nursing home at Evanston, Illinois, Miles wondered if that would be her fate too, but gathered herself together to make a memorial speech at the FAW on 12 April. News of the death of Agnes Nestor in Chicago late in 1948, and then of Emma Pischel, came soon after. 'Ah me, they all go,' Miles wrote sadly in her pocket diary. Dymphna Cusack's departure in May for England was also a loss.[108]

Mid-winter, Miles was shivering and suffering the ignominy of chilblains, not experienced since London, so that it was not until late July that she was ready to make a start on 'Merlin of the Empiah' (*Prelude to Waking*), a work that seems to have undergone many revisions (last known as 'Prelude to Romance'). But incredibly she could not find the manuscript, 'a great blow': it was 'irreplaceable and years of thought gone', she lamented. Strenuous searches having failed to locate the lost manuscript, she was obliged to turn to the already published volumes, *Up the Country* and *Ten Creeks Run* — and, reluctantly, her income tax. A few days later, however, to her great relief, she found 'Merlin of the Empiah' on a shelf in her bedroom, 'where I had tidily placed it. I can tackle the tax or anything now.'[109]

It took Miles six weeks to review *Up the Country*, *Ten Creeks Run* and the manuscript of 'Merlin of the Empiah'. When she was working, she was wont to say it felt as if she was in solitary confinement. But solitude is essential for literary work, and besides there were often outings: to the FAW (she had resumed attending meetings), and to the Rachel Forster Hospital for women and children at Redfern to sign verses she had written to accompany murals painted by Pixie O'Harris; and there were occasional friendly visitors at Carlton. Henrietta Drake-Brockman came to stay in late July, and Glen Mills Fox was sometimes there over the weekend. For a Moulden family visit earlier in the year, as recalled by Jenn Lane, her young cousin, Miles provided 'a wonderful afternoon tea of bread and butter spread with … fig-jam, topped off by wedges of watermelon', and Jenn's sister Rosemary was allowed to drink from the waratah cup as a reward for winning an exhibition to the University of Sydney. Moreover, although she wrote fewer letters than usual — Cusack and James in London were her main correspondents in 1949 — Miles continued to read widely. Of many titles, she particularly enjoyed Frank Clune's *Wild Colonial Boys*, Nettie Palmer's reminiscence, *Fourteen Years*, and that great South African novel by Alan Paton, *Cry, the Beloved Country*: 'I wish we could present our Abo. tragedy as gently and yet as compellingly,' she wrote in May when returning the book to Walter Cousins.[110]

Pixie O'Harris sometimes feared loneliness might defeat her friend. 'Don't let your lovely spirit be overwhelmed by sadness,' Pixie urged. Probably the hardest things to bear were the rare upsetting calls from her nephew John, and the cold, exacerbated by the national coal strike, which lasted from 27 June to 15 August, affecting electricity supplies. Yet by mid-August Miles had prepared the two previously published Brent volumes for the printers and was ready to see Beatrice about the Merlin/*Prelude* tale.[111]

'The temerarious hour has come,' she announced. She now found the Merlin manuscript tantalising, or, more precisely, puzzling: it was not a thriller, more like a prophecy fulfilled. There is a somewhat desperate edge to her wishful recollection that Robertson & Mullens had accepted the manuscript in 1946, so 'it must be interesting', and to her uncertainty as to genre, which may refer to a passing remark by Beatrice that it was not a novel (as is perfectly correct: see Chapter 9 for the argument that it is a reformist tract of the imperial period). So Beatrice must come to Carlton for a private meeting to discuss the next step. It would not be necessary for her to bring so much as a hairbrush, Miles told her. She could even use the embroidered hand towel Nettie Palmer had sent as a peace offering after getting it wrong in *Fourteen Years* about Miles giving her a pot of pineapple jam, though Miles loathed it, and preferred to use the towel as a bathmat (it was probably made of hessian).[112]

On 25 August, after a typically generous meal, the text of *Prelude to Waking*, as Miles was now calling it, was finally passed to Beatrice Davis, and the book Marjorie Barnard felt should never have been published was on its way to print. Like most authors Miles felt anxious, hopeless even; and when nothing had happened by October, she began pressing for a publication date. Another publisher had shown interest, she claimed, referring perhaps to the stalled negotiations with Robertson & Mullens. Not to worry, came Beatrice's reply; and when the two women met again in December, Miles was reassured to find that the editing had scarcely changed a thing, and to hear that the book would go to the printer in January. After revising proofs in May 1950, Miles finally received printed copies of the book in September. Thus, after a 25-year wait, she had the satisfaction of seeing Brent's first book in print.[113]

At a meeting of the FAW in April 1950, Miles had met the Hungarian-born writer and peace activist David Martin, a new, true congenial of the next generation. His intellectual energy reminded her of Prince Mirsky in London in 1932. 'Listening to him I felt my own mind all still there, tho' so long exiled from any give and take with its equals and superiors. He is analytical resulting in penetration: I am penetrating which results in analysis.' A mutually admiring exchange of books ensued, and Martin's comments pleased Miles greatly. He saw that her greatest strength was her identification with the people she wrote about, but thought that this had limited her too, remarking apropos of Sybylla Melvyn in *My Brilliant Career*, that Miles' personal rebellion had not gone far enough; and from a Magyar perspective that there must be something terribly wrong with Australian manhood if not one in seven could have won Sybylla. When he observed that she had a unique way of spreading self-traces around the characters in *My Career Goes Bung*, even the negative ones, resulting in an 'auto-spread' rather than an autobiography, Miles responded that few women and no men had seen so far into the novel.[114]

Martin had a fine turn in political analysis. Not only did he see Australia clearly, but his experience as a journalist in Europe and India equipped him also to understand the complexities of the atomic age, which increasingly perplexed Miles Franklin. What would it be like in another fifty years, following the debacle of the British Empire, she asked Mollye Menken in London on 19 December 1949: 'Trying to take hold of life these days is like catching at a fireman's hose and being thrown about.' And how could she align herself with the emergent peace movement when it was unclear who was behind it?[115]

On one point, the position of women, she was not in accord with Martin, who was at that time a member of the Communist Party. She accepted that the Soviet Union was trying to emancipate women in the workforce, but what would women really be like if their egos were as liberated as those of men, she wondered. Elsewhere she worried that young women did not seem to want liberation these days. All they wanted was to marry and breed. The death in August of Vida Goldstein seemed like the end of an era.[116]

Miles Franklin still saw no reason to abandon her version of first-wave feminism. During a trip she made to Newcastle for Authors' Week in September 1949, John Metcalfe, the state's head librarian, ruined the launch with an hour-long speech, not on books or publishing or even libraries, but amazingly — and exhaustively — on Mexican bulls (he had recently been on a trip to Mexico). Even Miles, who knew Metcalfe of old, was taken aback, almost running out of exclamation marks in the telling. But on the way back to Sydney in the Angus & Robertson car, recalling Editha Phelps' quip that the genital organs of the male were not needed in library work but commanded more pay, she told her disappointed fellow authors Ion Idriess and E. V. Timms that it served them all right. No doubt she was thinking of her friend Ida Leeson, who in the 1930s had been passed over for the position now occupied by Metcalfe.[117]

While in Newcastle Miles told the local press she was thinking of writing a book on immigration, as it might influence Australians to 'an honest pride' in nationality. The accompanying photo catches her smiling broadly. And for once she thoroughly enjoyed the annual dinner of the 'Eng. Ass.' in November. University types seldom met with her approval, but this time the speaker, the newly appointed Professor of Town and Country Planning at Sydney University, Denis Winston, earned it, as he had read Stephensen's *Foundations of Culture in Australia* and had the temerity to criticise plans for a railway at Sydney's Circular Quay. Then, despite the kerfuffle about his literary anthologies, Colin Roderick dedicated his latest work, *Wanderers in Australia: A Book of Travels*, to Miles, calling her 'a thorough-going Australian'.[118]

On 14 October 1949 Miles turned seventy, although for public consumption she was four years younger, 1883 being the year of birth she maintained (intermittently) in *Who's Who in Australia*. At least some people knew it was her birthday. The local children came in, each with a handkerchief, and Aunt Lena sent her a necklace. By now she thought it was a puzzle still to be standing herself, and instead of dwelling on losses, of which there were ever more, she came to cherish those elders who survived with her — even Mary Gilmore — and later helped to memorialise some who did not, such as the popular poet Roderic Quinn, another of those she had first met at Rose Scott's salon, and who had died in August. Happily, not all her old associates were gone into 'the silence'. Nell Malone was still alive in Paris, having survived civilian internment at Vittel in Vichy France.[119]

When the idea of Miles Franklin delivering Commonwealth Literary Fund lectures at the University of Western Australia was first raised is unclear. There had been talk of her visiting Perth for several years, as there had been of her going to Queensland to stay with Jean Devanny. She had also been invited to Hobart to deliver CLF lectures before but had declined, fearing the winter winds of Australia's southernmost state capital. Apparently some time in 1949, when she was in the eastern states, Henrietta Drake-Brockman sounded Miles out on behalf of Professor Allan Edwards of the university's English Department; and having ascertained that she was not averse to the idea, Edwards wrote with an informal invitation on 16 January 1950.[120]

For once Miles would be adequately paid. Under the CLF scheme, inaugurated in 1940 at the instigation of the FAW (but now a thing of the past), universities were granted a small subsidy to sponsor a series of public lectures on Australian literature by a practitioner of their choosing, with the money to go to the lecturer as a fee and to cover travel costs. In this case, for an 'Eastern Stater' of eminence, the subsidy would be £150.[121]

Although it was not until April that Miles heard from the vice-chancellor of the university, Dr George Currie, that she had been appointed as Special Lecturer in Australian Literature for 1950, by then all the arrangements had been made with Edwards, and she had already done a good deal of work. In fact she began on 18 January, immediately on hearing from Edwards for the first time: 'I should enjoy making a survey of Australian writing,' she responded. A few weeks later, on 4 February, having been assured that Perth winters were milder than the Riviera's, she told Edwards she found the project irresistible, and had dived into her subject, 'Australian Writing from the First Fleet to the Atom Bomb'.[122]

Once committed, Miles took the work very seriously. Henrietta declared that she should just talk in her own stimulating way and especially about the old traditions, now slipping away — 'I do not *oppose* [that] but the nucleus of the old should be retained, & who better to magnify that on … young minds than yourself,' she urged — emphasising that it would be good for students who thought the study of Australian literature dull. To this Miles responded that she had had to put up with dull lecturers herself: 'We are as we are, and can't help it if we are bores, in fact bores are the basis of society and the most successful individuals in it.' She planned to chronicle Australian writing from the First Fleet to the present with the Australian novel as heroine.[123]

If the outline sent to Edwards in June for publicity purposes is a reliable guide to what she actually said, the lectures were good value. She began reading old novels, mostly in the Mitchell Library, and sorting through what at first felt like 'a tangled skein', writing and typing the lectures one by one until she had eight prepared, ready in good time for her departure for Perth on 26 June. Edwards had asked for ten lectures, but she did not feel up to so many, nor to additional lectures for the Adult Education Board, as he had suggested.[124]

There was no summer holiday that year. Once more, Miles had something to finish (if one can say she ever finished with an unpublished manuscript) or at any rate to tidy for yet another competition, possibly her Furphy play. 'Johanna versus Hennessy' had been commended in Maie Hoban's 1949 competition, despite 'unpleasant aspects', and by St John Ervine, who had praised the characterisation and dialogue, so it was worth another try. She sent copies to the Sydney actors James Pratt and Kevin Brennan in the new year for comment (a move that proved unproductive), also to Perth, where Henrietta Drake-Brockman would later read it and comment positively.[125]

There were seasonal letters to answer, too. Deplore as she did the commercialisation of Christmas, at least she heard from old friends once a year. Especially cherished were letters from Mabel Singleton, a loyal correspondent, who was working in the north of England as a housekeeper, although Miles complained she had taken up that newfangled writing implement, the biro. Even so, Mabel could give her news of the remaining Fullerton sisters. Old associates in America also wrote. Elisabeth Christman, still secretary-treasurer of the now virtually defunct WTUL, replied to Miles' Christmas letter in February, advising that the biography they had been preparing of Margaret Robins would be out in April. Better still, Margery Currey sent a timely box of clothes, which Miles had altered and wore as soon as the weather permitted. Recalling the clothes Margery gave her in 1932, she wrote: 'judging by how long the others lasted me I am now set till the end of my days and can give more attention to world affairs and the chore of dying, which comes terrifyingly nearer and nearer.' When her only known Canadian friend, Dr Burnham of Balkan days, sent her a portrait of the king, she replied that he had very generously sent her the same picture in 1948, but she had been able to sell it for £4, and would buy a new handbag for Perth. Apparently he sent her an inhaler too, which she hoped would relieve the hoarseness afflicting her from the beginning of the year. Sydney to Perth was like Quebec to Vancouver, she explained to him, 'but at least I'll have a change'. Emmy Lawson in Lancashire was asked to slip an aerogram into a roll of newspaper 'to mislead the heads of a literary competition that is coming off some months hence'. Miles' plan was to write in it and send it back for Emmy to post.[126]

From time to time she spent whole days replying to old friends. But as she told Margery Currey, 'friendship [is] the warmest most permanent thing in this existence'. New friends gave just as much pleasure, particularly the Martins: 'Your letter is a tonic,' she wrote to David Martin and his wife, Richenda, in her first letter of the year, and in the South Australian outback writer Myrtle Rose White she had a new and loyal — if somewhat earnest — friend. Myrtle Rose was thrilled to meet Miles and so nervous she nearly dropped the waratah cup when invited to Carlton. Her strength was probably her spiritualistic belief that there is no death. Though she had once taken an interest in spiritualism, Miles had not found it helpful — but Myrtle Rose was kind.[127]

Her health again gave cause for concern. Accompanying her throat infection was a persistent cough of varying degrees of severity, at times sounding like whooping cough. She jokingly reassured Henrietta it was probably because her doctor advised she lacked thyroid, 'so if he doesn't turn me into a baboon I may improve'. She was not as strong as her mother had been at seventy-five or even eighty, she said. The evidence suggests she got worse with the approach of winter, but the lectures gave her a purpose and a focus.[128]

John Franklin's summer sojourn with his maternal relatives, which had seemed so promising, ended in the same old way. By mid-January they had had enough. In their view shock treatment was the only answer. Miles was able to arrange a birthday lunch for John at David Jones with Aunt Lena. She still longed to rescue him, despite the abusive phone calls and late-night visits which began again, and the signs of deterioration which had led his maternal Aunt Xenia Edwards to contact Alcoholics Anonymous in February.[129]

The crisis came at midnight on 15 March 1950. Miles' pocket diary records:

> Jno. came in maudlin and incapable with drink with much
> [word illegible] to foist himself upon me. I went for Mr
> Andresen [a neighbour] and summoned Dr Whittemore. The Dr
> gave him a needle. A. brought in J's gear & put him to bed, he
> was too incapable to be undressed. He bucked and snored all
> night. I lay awake feeling all ill & trembling so I cdn't sleep or
> stand — What am I to do?

The next day was no better. Mr Andresen came in early to urge Miles to go
to a chamber magistrate and have her nephew committed to a reception
centre for assessment, under the New South Wales Lunacy Amendment Act
of 1881. This she could not bring herself to do. She managed to get John to
eat a saveloy and drink some coffee, and then he said he was off to find
lodgings. When she said no one would have him in his present state and
begged him to let her help, he left. When she telephoned Alcoholics
Anonymous (AA), she found they could only help if John would admit he
had a problem. That, he never did.

The next night at 2 a.m. he rang to say he was wandering the streets of
Kingsford and had no money. When he arrived home at dawn he was 'a
terrible wreck'. Miles persuaded him to eat something and put him to bed,
whereupon he locked the door and a few hours later jumped out the
window and went raving up the street. Mr Andresen again helped, and John
quietened down until the evening, when according to the diary record he
became violent. After Mr Andresen had to struggle with him because he had
a razor, Miles called the police. They came but did nothing, except that it
did quieten him down, and he agreed to see an AA representative.

By this time Miles had had three sleepless nights and unfortunately the
AA man did not get there in time to see John the next day. The doctor had
come with an ambulance and, with a policeman present, a reluctant John
Franklin was removed to the Darlinghurst Reception Centre. The stigma of
incarceration at that time cannot be overstated. Miles had tried to avoid it by
saying John had war neurosis, though it was actually the DTs. She told
Dymphna Cusack, 'I really thought I would die of anguish and desolation.'[130]

Neighbours, then friends and relatives, helped her through the ordeal.
The next day Glen Mills Fox contacted the government agency responsible
for the repatriation of servicemen, 'the Repat', and Persia White, apparently
a close friend of John's, arrived to help. The choice was between treatment
at a repatriation facility, Broughton Hall, for war neurosis, and the mental

asylum at Callan Park. When it was decided that John drank because of his mental state and thus would be admitted to Callan Park, it was 'a cruel blow'; but perhaps, Miles mused, it would help him. On 28 March he appeared before a magistrate for committal and the next day she went to see him at Callan Park, as she had at the Darlinghurst Reception Centre.[131]

John Franklin blamed Miles for the electroconvulsive therapy with which he was treated for schizophrenia at Callan Park. After the third application, probably administered without muscle relaxants, he told visitors it was she who had put him there — which in a way was true, but beside the point. On 10 May, nearly two months after his violent behaviour at Grey Street, Miles learned that despite earlier expectations of release he was not yet well enough, and there would be more shock treatment. A week later the doctors advised that John was not insane but not sane either.[132]

Miles was now worried about going to Perth. She and Persia White visited John regularly with laundry and provisions, and Miles was still his prime carer with respect to his non-medical needs and affairs. The doctors' advice was for Miles to go, that they'd keep him at the hospital, where he would be helped to act as an adult, with jobs around the place. As for John, he claimed he was only occasionally a drinker and his problem was money. (This, Miles thought, could not be the case: even if he had run through his deferred service pay, he had savings and accumulating income from his father's estate.) A week later he was planning to go crocodile hunting on release.

The final straw came on a Sunday visit in late May, when, far from showing any appreciation of the clean clothes and cigarettes Miles had brought him, John Franklin told his aunt he hated her, that he never wanted to see her again, and that she had never done a thing to help him. 'I endured it when he was drunk,' she wrote, 'but he is stone sober now and deadly.' It seemed to her he had 'no character'. Miles blamed the air force, since like Jane Addams before her, she believed stimulants had been provided to give young men false courage. Even so, Glen Mills Fox was persisting with the Repatriation Department, so maybe there was a way forward.

The hospital was full of broken men and it was terrible for Miles to see the stress placed on wives and mothers. Possibly at John's insistence, but more likely out of self-protection, she began to organise his papers so that Glen could act as his contact when he was released (a prerequisite for which was usually satisfactory participation in jobs around the hospital). Newly released from Callan Park, John called on Glen Mills Fox on 23 June, shortly before Miles left for Perth. The news made Miles feel queer, especially as she heard he had been drinking, just as she had predicted. But he did not harass her, and she was able to concentrate on her packing for Perth.[133]

While John was in Callan Park, she had been researching and writing her lectures, and in May checking the proofs of *Prelude to Waking*. Such demanding tasks gave her a purpose and occupied her mind. But her health did not improve.

She did go to the Easter Show, with her neighbour, Mrs Fogden. She scarcely went anywhere else, however, and she wrote fewer letters than usual during those months. It was not until June that her life looked more normal. That month she was at Malcolm Ellis' 'christening' of the Greenway flats at Kirribilli and the birthday party of her local member of parliament, Clive Evatt, an above-average affair on the enjoyment scale. 'I can still enjoy my congenials,' she wrote to Ian Mudie, and these days, as she would tell the Perth English lecturer David Bradley, she didn't care what age they were — the wider the range the better. Meantime, with the introduction of the Communist Party Dissolution Bill in Canberra in April and the onset of the Korean War in June, and Australian troops committed soon after, the world was again an increasingly unstable and alarming place. Never far below the surface, Miles told Katharine Susannah Prichard, she felt 'a tatter of dissatisfaction, at having done nothing but squander my natural talents and I'm not yet quite reconciled to dying — though I have to face it any day now.'[134]

Prime Minister Menzies' bill to ban the Communist Party enraged Miles. In February she had mourned the demise of the Liberal Party at the British general election as the end of the old tolerance and freedoms in the face of big business. Not long after, she affirmed to David Martin the truth learned by progressive liberals in the early twentieth century, that 'of course labor's cause is the only fundamental cause'. She cheered 'good old Chif' — the Labor Opposition leader, Ben Chifley — in May for defending freedom of expression. She did not belong to any political party, she told Henrietta Drake-Brockman in June, but felt that the anti-communist bill was 'sheer Hitlerism', warning that they could be had up for associating with Katharine if it passed. At the state elections in June, Miles mocked the conservatives: when she went to vote, two men with leaflets approached her in the customary way but she waved them aside, saying, 'Gentlemen, don't waste paper on me, I'm bent on preserving my habeas corpus,' whereupon two women standing by with notebooks said, 'One for Evatt!' Altogether, she deemed it a deplorable situation, with the communist scare causing

Catholic Labor to support the bill. People seemed unaware of the danger of ceding freedom of association and expression to a conservative government. No doubt it would take the restriction of beer, tobacco or cheap women to arouse them, she wrote irritably to Katharine Susannah Prichard in a letter beginning on a splendidly defiant note: 'Mr Menzies would be one of the chief reasons I'd like to stay with you.'[135]

Katharine Susannah Prichard had been urging writers to protest at the turn of events for months. Miles defended Katharine's political rights and Katharine upheld Miles as an Australian writer 'of tonnage'. The strength and character of their friendship were evident when the West Australian writer J. K. Ewers decided, with support of the local branch of the FAW, to nominate Katharine for a Nobel Prize, and Rex Ingamells (who was also consulted by Ewers) then added the names of Eleanor Dark and Miles Franklin. What eventually went forward is unclear, but when Ingamells told Miles what he had done, she did not excite herself or try to push herself forward. Rather, she immediately offered Katharine her support — 'it seems a sure thing' — and told her that no other candidate had been mentioned in Sydney. A win by Katharine would be worth a whole battalion in the current situation, and justifiable on the basis of the tragic cross-cultural love story *Coonardoo* alone, she later asserted. There was, perhaps, a sting in the tail of the account she gave to Margery Currey: that although she had been nominated, nothing would come of it because everyone approved of the Prichard nomination 'also she is an ardent communist and all her fellow religionists are pledged to her'.[136]

Miles did not stay with Katharine in Perth, however. Apart from the fact that accommodation had already been arranged at the new Highway Hotel at Claremont, near the university, Greenmount, the suburb where Katharine lived, was a long way out, nestling at the edge of the Darling Ranges, and moreover Katharine had suffered a coronary occlusion on 21 June. Miles had a fall in the street about the same time. Katharine had another heart attack while Miles was in Perth; and Miles herself had to take a fortnight's rest from her schedule due to the recurrence of her throat trouble. It was a great disappointment to them both that their contact was perforce limited to two visits.[137]

On the morning of Monday 26 June, friends drove her to town to catch the bus to the airport, where she took the morning flight to Adelaide, en route to Perth. On arrival at Parafield (the old airport site), she was met by none other than 'Jonesie', now Mrs H. P. (Edith) McKenzie of Mile End, with whom she had sailed to America in 1906, along with her husband. Contact had been resumed in 1937 after 'Jonesie' saw an article about Miles in the *Women's Weekly*, and later wrote with news of the women they had stayed with on disembarkation and at Loma Linda. During the 48-hour stopover Miles recalled what a poor sailor she had been, and how much stronger 'Jonesie' was: 'You could have lifted me up with one arm.'[138]

Happily, the stopover was a success: restful, with a good meal and a glorious sleep on the first night. The next day they drove to the beachside suburb of Glenelg and saw there the Pioneer Memorial. That evening they went to a Bible talk, really an exposition on communism as an apostasy from Romanism, according to Miles' diary entry. (Jonesie had been an Adventist in 1906 and the McKenzies were ardent Adventists still.) The next morning, after Miles enjoyed the luxury of breakfast in bed, the McKenzies took her to the railway station on North Terrace and she caught the Transcontinental to Kalgoorlie.

Miles Franklin always enjoyed a long train trip, and this one across the great saltbush plain was 'lovely, lovely'; there were even singsongs on the train at night. At Cook on the South Australian side of the Nullarbor, Charlie Nalty, an admirer of her work, took her to see his school. When she returned to Sydney Miles sent the school a copy of *Sydney Royal*.[139]

All too soon, on the morning of 30 June, Miles was in Kalgoorlie, Prichard country, where friends of Katharine collected her for the day and showed her around the goldfields, including Boulder. Then came the last leg of her westward journey, overnight to Perth, by state rail. The food was not good and she had too little sleep, but the adrenalin rush came the next morning when the train pulled in to Perth railway station at 7.20, and a welcoming party was waiting from the English Department at the University of Western Australia, led by Professor Edwards and including lecturers David Bradley and Jean Tweedie. They took Miles to breakfast at Henrietta Drake-Brockman's home on Perth's Esplanade, and afterwards to the Highway Hotel. Miles' room was next to a noisy bathroom, and she was not impressed by the journalist who came to interview her at lunchtime ('some ass named Waddy'). But the *Australian Women's Weekly* did better, describing her as a professional writer of merry disposition, who lived alone and enjoyed cooking and gardening. Among the new faces at a small reception hosted by the vice-chancellor and his wife later that day were fellow writers J. K. Ewers and Dorothy Sanders. There was a dinner at a pub afterwards.[140]

The following day, Sunday 2 July, Henrietta and her mother, the pioneer feminist Dr Roberta Jull, took Miles to see a frail-looking Katharine Susannah at Greenmount in the afternoon, and in the evening she dined with the Drake-Brockmans and others. Unfortunately, an open door at the dinner brought on a chill, and the sore throat was back, so she was unwell even before the lectures began.[141]

The lectures were scheduled for delivery twice weekly on Monday and Wednesday evenings in the arts lecture theatre at the university, and Miles managed the first four before her voice gave out. The rest were postponed, on doctor's orders. After the ordeal of the fourth lecture, Joseph Furphy's only daughter, Sylvia Pallot, removed Miles from the noisy hotel and nursed her at her home in nearby Nedlands. Miles recovered enough to resume on 24 July, 'with my congregation halved'. In all, as anticipated she gave eight lectures, the last on 2 August, when, according to an article by Henrietta Drake-Brockman commissioned at the time, she concluded by simply folding her hands, and saying with a diffident smile, 'That is all.'[142]

The faithful enjoyed what she had to say, with many questions and much talk after the later lectures. Notes made at the time indicate that the lectures began with the earliest attempts by Europeans at the novel in Australia and 'our first novels of tonnage', moved towards contemporary novels by younger writers, and concluded with a challenging question: 'What next?' Along the way she covered *Robbery under Arms* by Rolf Boldrewood and Catherine Helen Spence's *Clara Morison*; the 1890s; the new century from Furphy's *Such Is Life* to Anzac writing; a period of hibernation (in which Henry Handel Richardson was placed); and Aborigines as a theme in novels. The *West Australian* said the lectures were some of the most brilliant delivered at the university, remarking also on the lecturer's challenging and witty approach, while the two students who interviewed her afterwards — the future historian Geoffrey Bolton was one, Lila Hanson the other — declared that the university had been well served by an 'interesting and stimulating series of lectures'.[143]

Miles Franklin could hardly complain about lack of attention during those last weeks in Perth. She could not thank the Pallot family enough: 'You retrieved me from disaster and defeat.' Sylvia's husband, Victor, became her chauffeur, and took her to see Furphy's grave. One night they all went to an Australian film night at Shell House, where Miles was given a picture of Furphy to take home and met D. H. Lawrence's collaborator, Mollie Skinner, and the broadcaster Irene Greenwood. Miles evidently took to

Irene, who afterwards annotated her own copy of *All That Swagger*, 'Your book and mine, Miles Franklin, August 1950'.[144]

Miles earned a little from broadcasts too. There had been an interview with Henrietta soon after her arrival for the ABC 'Women's Session', for which she was paid two guineas; and on 25 July she was heard on the 'WA Parade' program, the four-minute interview earning her another guinea, the same amount received for appearing a second time on the 'Women's Session' on the day of her departure. What or whether she was paid for an interview with Irene Greenwood as 'Woman of the Week', which played on commercial radio after she left is not known, but since Irene was a fierce feminist, perhaps she was. There would also be an article on Australian theatre for the *West Australian*, which earned her 33s 9d when it appeared in September.[145]

There were invitations to clubs and lunches. After the sixth lecture, the University Wives Club gave Miles a supper, where she met the aspiring writer Alexandra Hasluck, and the Women's Service Guild invited her to a conference, less to her taste. No feminist would pass through Perth without a visit to the Karrakatta Club; and at the Modern Women's Club, as arranged by Katharine Susannah Prichard, she was treated to written speeches commending her lectures. The Fremantle Rowing Club got in touch too. Most striking, she spent an hour in informal discussion with each of the five tutorial classes in English II at the university, and two hours with Professor Edwards' honours seminar. (Edwards felt she was better with small groups, telling Colin Roderick many years later that she was 'nervous and coquettish' in front of larger ones.) For Miles, her health problems diminished whatever satisfaction she may have felt from being able to promote her view of Australian literature to a younger generation. She was simply relieved that she had managed to get through it all.[146]

So much teaching brought that troublesome throat back, and Miles found herself voiceless again. However, she seems to have been in good spirits in the snaps of her wearing a suit which were taken in Henrietta's garden on the afternoon of 7 August. In the evening, after a tea party at their house, the Pallots drove her to Guildford airport for her flight to Adelaide, a thoroughly enjoyable experience due to a chivalric young man who 'looked after me like an angel'. She was not so lucky the next day. After a dawn touchdown and transfer of planes at Parafield, a military type seized her specially allocated seat and prevented her from gaining all but fleeting glimpses of the Southern Alps and Canberra, where they made a brief stopover, arriving back in Sydney at noon. It is a measure of how much air travel has improved over the last half century that the trip took fourteen hours, about three times as long as nowadays (though there *was* the detour). At least it was dry in Sydney, though the place seemed very dirty after Perth.[147]

Plaudits from friends followed. Katharine Susannah Prichard heard the plane pass over the Darling Ranges and wrote a caring letter the next day to underline her regret at missing the lectures and to report the positive responses of her friends at the Modern Women's Club. Furthermore, she announced she was going to write to Beatrice Davis about getting the lectures published: they had been such a success, better than the likes of Colin Roderick could do (Roderick had recently published *An Introduction to Australian Fiction,* a variant on Miles' theme) and under the circumstances 'a triumph of spirit'.[148]

Beatrice soon wrote that Henrietta had told her how splendid Miles had been, and that it would have been good to hear her make the academic ones sit up and take notice, though she made no mention of publication. Beatrice's mind was on Brent: but for a bad printing slip *Prelude to Waking* would have been out, but it would be a few weeks longer. Meanwhile, Beatrice was trying to organise some publicity. Miles replied that she was still too poorly to see anyone, or even answer the telephone, but she had fulfilled her contract 'as a matter of character'. She, too, was thinking ahead to Brent's reappearance, having been gently badgered in Perth on that score, due to Glen Mills Fox's efforts in alerting booksellers. Miles said that she had heard Brent was about to break out again before she left Sydney. She later remarked that Glen was a natural publicist, 'like a kelpie pup who will work chickens and ducks or children if no sheep are handy'.[149]

Without an immediate prospect of publication for the lectures, Miles did not begin reworking them into what she came to call 'my essay' for quite some time, as there was a Jubilee play competition to prepare for (though she did have a typescript entitled 'Notes on Australian Fiction' ready for entry in the non-fiction section of the Jubilee competition in 1951). Much remained to be done; and she was unable to complete the work to her satisfaction until April 1953.[150]

The road to publication proved long. Professor Edwards' plan to publish the lectures in the local *Arts Quarterly* with CLF funding soon fell through, and English publishers were not interested. Thus, although Angus & Robertson was not Miles Franklin's first choice of publisher, ultimately Beatrice Davis agreed to take them on. *Laughter, Not for a Cage,* with its lengthy and quirky but quite accurate subtitle *Notes on Australian Writing, with Biographical Emphasis on the Struggles, Function, and Achievements of the Novel in Three Half-centuries*, was published in eleven chapters by Angus & Robertson in 1956.

The title is appealing, but obscure, and very Milesian. Its meaning does not become apparent until the last page of the book, indeed the last sentence: 'Truly there are no nightingales to enchant the night, but the mellow carillon of the magpies enlarges the spacious sunlit days and the mocking laughter of the kookaburras is not for a cage.' Maybe it helps to know that there was a kookaburra on the original dustcover, and to recall that Miles Franklin often expressed the view that there was not enough humour in Australian writing.[151]

According to the opening chapter, *Laughter, Not for a Cage* was written 'without regard for academic pretensions or the shifting and doubtful vogues of standardized reviewing'. Furthermore, 'No anatomical fragmentation or exhaustive analysis' would be attempted. There would be a purposeful re-reading of selected stories. A few lines later, readers are told what to expect: 'Writings are valued on the basis of containing something of the essence of a new literary continent.'[152]

Despite the disclaimers, *Laughter, Not for a Cage* is an ambitious work. Though the acknowledgement modestly refers to 'these notes' and 'talks', it goes on to explain that the 'notes' have been expanded from ten talks, eight of which were delivered to members of the public and students of the English Department at the University of Western Australia under the auspices of the Commonwealth Literary Fund; and that it would have been 'impractical and pretentious' to append a bibliography, so references to authors consulted are included in the text. However, specific mention is made of Morris Miller's pioneering bibliography, *Australian Literature*, and the Catholic historian Eris O'Brien's *Foundations of Australia*. For the remainder, it continues, 'these notes rest upon personal knowledge and years of reading — desultory or intensive — everywhere, including the John Crerar Library in Chicago, the Metropolitan in New York, the British Museum, the Kensington Public Library, the New South Wales Parliamentary Library, and happy days in the Mitchell Library, Sydney'. The book itself amounted to 238 pages including references and an index, and was by any standard a substantial work of literary criticism.

It opens at 'the fiftieth anniversary of our Federated Commonwealth', in 1951, by asking: 'what of Australian literature — if any?' over three half-centuries of British settlement. Its theme, stated soon after, is 'the pioneering of Australia for literary occupation'. Thereafter, chapters move along at a steady pace, tracing the fortunes of the novel in Australia from Henry Savery's efforts in Hobart in the early 1830s to 'the reappearance of the novel in force' in the 1930s. Having argued that by then the quantity and quality of novels in Australia were comparable to the mid nineteenth-century peak, *Laughter, Not for a Cage* addresses 'Aborigines as a theme', and the work of younger writers, concluding in the final chapter with the question: 'Where does the Australian novel stand today?'[153]

Miles Franklin was often at her best in topical writings. In this instance, however, it becomes increasingly obvious that novelists are not the only ones for whom 'the present is the most difficult'. Black velvet — that is, the sexual abuse of Aboriginal women — had become highly topical with the publication of *Coonardoo* and *Capricornia*, and Miles' choices in this area still seem reasonable. However, the coverage of 'younger writers' is noticeably selective. Kylie Tennant's work certainly deserved to be highlighted, and it was both diplomatic and consistent with Miles Franklin's experience to conclude with an instructive novel of Americans and the Australian home front in World War II by Henrietta Drake-Brockman, *The Fatal Days*. But in her survey of some 115 novels, there is no systematic account of M. Barnard Eldershaw, whose *Tomorrow and Tomorrow and Tomorrow* had appeared under the truncated title *Tomorrow and Tomorrow* in censored form in 1947, and Patrick White's *The Aunt's Story* is not mentioned. The literary historian Elizabeth Webby once observed if Miles did not like the sound of something she simply left it out. She did, however, make a tongue-in-cheek comment on White's *Happy Valley*: a 'Lawrentian-Joycean novel which gained praise as showing that the Australian novels were at last outgrowing squatters and gum-trees to become adult and modern'.[154]

Laughter, Not for a Cage argues that in the process of imaginatively possessing the land — 'an unsung land does not exist' — the novel ultimately outstripped other forms of writing. But as a form, it remained 'British Colonial', with 'the conquest of environment its most prominent characteristic', the argument continues. Yet the texture of Australian life was changing with the mass immigration program; Australia's place in the world had already changed, from British colony to American satellite; and science was transforming everything:

> The bush settlers wrung a wealth of fresh folklore from existence, and just as a distinctive way of life became mature for literary harvesting, it is being swept away in the gulf which has opened between yesterday and tomorrow, marked by the loosing of an atom bomb on Hiroshima … What next?[155]

Not that Miles knew the answers. Indeed, her realist approach probably precluded fresh insight. Her focus was the consolidation of a nativist tradition since *My Brilliant Career* and *Such Is Life*, hampered as it had been by censorship and the difficulties of publishing Australian material. In Miles' view, the mid twentieth-century novel, like Australia, was entering a new era without having attained a regional maturity. 'Native literature has remained chronically incipient' is her final verdict.[156]

It was not necessarily a gloomy verdict, though Katharine Susannah Prichard understandably thought so. While the kookaburra had not triumphed over the nightingale and Australian writers still lacked 'tradition', it was not fatal. Anzac was a tradition of sorts, and writers should beware of the false gods which had brought on the 'de-civilization' of Europe since 1914. Here Brent came into his own, according to Miles, as a writer who accepted Australian life 'on its own terms'; and Furphy, favourably compared with Henry James as in her 1944 study, remained the great autochthonous voice (i.e. home-grown).[157]

As for the work of Miles Franklin, *My Brilliant Career* is considered briefly alongside *Such Is Life*, and deemed inexperienced and impatient compared with Furphy's mature and methodical treatise, but also 'free of inherited nostalgia'. Citing A. G. Stephens, 'when estimating the realism of more mature works' (an oblique reference to Stephens' enthusiastic review of *Back to Bool Bool* in 1932), she describes *My Brilliant Career* as inadvertently demonstrating the suitability of Australia for novel-writing, despite the young writer's expressed view to the contrary. *All That Swagger* is not mentioned, nor are any of her other works.[158]

Miles Franklin's friends waited patiently for the work to appear. When it did, it was after her death, and the warm welcome it received is both sad and a little ironic. The first and in some respects the most illuminating review appeared in the *Bulletin*, on 16 May 1956. There, the (anonymous) reviewer noted capricious aspects and a certain amount of 'conscientious plodding', also an 'alarming' feminine bias, but concluded that the book rose triumphantly over its limitations 'because of the vital personality pervading it'. In a fine phrasing, *Laughter, Not for a Cage* was deemed 'wayward, original and — it is hardly too much to add — grand'. *Overland*'s review appeared soon after, in the Spring issue of 1956. There Marjorie Pizer was more positive. *Laughter, Not for a Cage* was 'undoubtedly the most stimulating and exciting volume of criticism of Australian literature, novels in particular, ever to appear' in 'a comparatively dull field', a welcome nugget which did not hesitate to attack windy Anzac rhetoric and intrusive psychologism; certainly quirky, and in places a bit pedestrian, but overall radical and refreshing. Leonie Kramer, writing in the *Sydney Morning Herald* on 21 July 1956, noted Miles' aggressive anti-academic attitudes and literary chauvinism, but allowed that the history was good; and found it 'refreshing to discover a critic who does not regard *The Fortunes of Richard Mahony* as an Australian counterpart of *The Brothers Karamazov*'. In the December issue of *Meanjin*, Tom Inglis Moore offered a carefully modulated response, beginning with the irony that Miles seemed to have joined the critics at last, and pointing out some 'breath-taking' effects, most striking (and noted by all the reviewers) the dismissive treatment of *The Fortunes of Richard Mahony*. But the generous Moore struck a positive note overall too, finding 'something more' in the volume: 'the personal viewpoint of an original personality', and 'a lively vibrant critique, irreverent, provocative and stimulating'. Moore's comment that 'as one reads one can hear her speaking and see her eyes twinkle once again' is just right.

Miles did not live to see *Laughter*, nor to read these reviews. In 1950, after her return from Perth, the publication claiming attention was Brent's *Prelude to Waking*. Miles received a copy on 30 August. Her dearest friends did their best to respond positively, but Henrietta Drake-Brockman had scarcely been able to hide her impatience over the Brent business even before, and Katharine Susannah Prichard obviously thought the book's dismissive attitude to sex unhealthy, while praising it as 'a strange, beautiful piece of work'. The Sydney press was unimpressed, to say the least. To the *Sydney Morning Herald* reviewer it was 'a shallow tale of unreal people'. 'Miss Bronte' in the *Daily Telegraph*, whom Miles thought spiteful, said it was a piece of juvenilia better left unpublished. Not worth worrying about, was the verdict in the *Sun*. Ian Mair was even more cutting in the Melbourne *Argus*: 'To write about sophisticated persons of any rank in society, one must be more sophisticated than they are.'[159]

Such responses made Miles feel black, in that she felt they showed that despite her efforts over fifty years she had not become part of the literature of her country, as she put it to David Martin, who would soon write the most positive review in *Meanjin* in July 1951. Noting the novel's arch mannerisms, and a 'bee in her bonnet' about 'Asian fecundity', he nonetheless commended *Prelude to Waking* as brave, witty and true to the period in which it was set. He was the only reviewer to recognise the political point of the title, that it was time for a realignment of Australian loyalties.[160]

In his review, Martin dealt with the disappointing reception of *Prelude to Waking* and Miles' complaint about lack of recognition in a forthright manner. The underlying problem, he said, was Brent of Bin Bin. People were tired of the 'mummery', but if the whole of Brent's very substantial literary record — 'a dozen big books' — could be taken into account, it would be seen that 'she is Australia's most formidable literary figure'. In a postscript he referred directly to 'all of Brent-Franklin books'.

By this time, it was widely assumed that Miles and Brent were one and the same. However, secure in the knowledge that three of the four people to whom she had ever actually admitted it (that is, Lady Byles, Mrs Robins and Mary Fullerton) were now dead, and that the fourth, Rose Scott's niece Mollye Menken, was still in London, Miles was not about to respond to the challenge of disclosure. *Prelude to Waking* was merely a curtain-raiser to the projected publication by Angus & Robertson of the five substantive volumes of Brent's saga, and her intention was to come clean when they were all out. Jean Hamilton was more or less right, after reading *Prelude to Waking*, when she said that Miles was too clever for the real world.[161]

When asked if she would contribute to the United Associations of Women's plans to include the experience of women in the Commonwealth of Australia Jubilee celebrations in 1951, Miles was slow to answer. Her response is of considerable interest now, though it was probably disheartening for the recipients. She felt there was little to celebrate:

> I think women have slipped back since those days [1901]. This is
> inevitable following the states of war which have existed much of
> the time since. Women cannot hope to be in a dignified position
> as mothers of the race while the slaughter of males destroys the
> balance of the sexes and Asiatic women continue to swarm.[162]

The onset of the Korean War and Australian participation in it was fulfilling the Australian nightmare, and she expressed it out loud. She was reminded of the conscientious objectors of World War I, the real heroes, though doubted that such a response would be relevant any more. It seemed that the world she knew was slipping away: 'We dyed-in-the-gum-and-wattle British Australians are passing like the bandicoots and lyrebirds,' she wrote to Ric Throssell, then serving in Rio de Janeiro.[163]

One would never know from the pleasure expressed by Beatrice Davis in September 1950 at her amazing vitality, wit and intelligence that most of the time Miles was feeling unwell. Nonetheless she could still astonish her young cousins on Christmas Day by doing her Charlotte Perkins Gilman act: putting her big toe in her mouth to demonstrate that she had a flat stomach and no need of corsets.[164]

14

'SHALL I PULL THROUGH?':
1951–1954

'Hold on to your essential self.'[1]

The first of January 1951 marked the beginning of a new year, and also the fiftieth anniversary of the Commonwealth of Australia. Ahead lay the consumer society and the worst of the Cold War. The prospect of affluence left Miles Franklin unimpressed, but the return to power of the conservative governments led by Winston Churchill and Robert Gordon Menzies in the United Kingdom and Australia, and the elevation of Eisenhower in the United States, kept her feisty. The Jubilee year meant there were literary prizes to be won, and into her seventies, she still had much to do. 'Struggled again on the writing — shall I pull through?' she wondered in her pocket diary on 22 September 1951.

Though she still liked a new hat, and went into town to meet people, to read at the Mitchell Library and to see newsreels, with the increasing pressure to finish her books — given her diminishing energy — life for Miles rested even more on the neighbourhood, for the most part an undemanding place. Harry Andresen, the Ukrainian immigrant at number 28 who had been so helpful with John Franklin, added a dimension to life along Grey Street, but otherwise Miles' immediate neighbours were much the same as in 1932: on her side of the street there were the Fogdens at number 22, the now widowed Mrs Coates at number 24, and further up, the Bennetts; opposite, the Jervises remained at number 23 and Mrs Morgan at number 25, with a vacant block at number 27.[2]

These names and more from along Grey Street feature prominently in Miles' diaries in later years. Many neighbours still did not have telephones, and Miles was forever running messages or being interrupted as they came to use her 'machine' — but these days she complained less about that than about not getting calls herself.

Few, if any, of the neighbours shared Miles' concerns: of some 260 electors recorded as residents of Grey Street in 1950, the men were mostly in skilled working-class or lower middle-class occupations, with a sprinkling of clergy, teachers and manual labourers, while as many as 80 per cent of the women were engaged in 'h.d.' (home duties), including 'Stella Franklin', who was one of four women (and one man, a seaman) to be entered as sole elector in a residence. However, the rural society from which 'Miss Franklin' sprang had always been a social microcosm of New South Wales. Except when noisy at night, her neighbours were companionable and helpful, as good neighbours are, though probably more so in the 1950s, when exchanges of food and other surpluses were common, even in the city.

When a neighbour passed her a hot meal, Miles would return the dish washed, with flowers or other garden produce, such as peaches or plums, or that sun-loving green vegetable the choko; if Mrs Andresen, the wife of Harry, a 'stereo-typer' in a printery, threw stale bread over the fence for the five remaining bantams (bread which Miles sometimes rescued for her own lunch), there might be an egg or two in return. The children of William Goggins, a motor mechanic, and his wife, Mildred, a tailoress, came and went as it suited; and Miles often went to the Carlton picture house with the most nearly congenial, Mrs Fogden, a joiner's wife, or her widowed daughter Mary (called May by her family and friends).[3]

According to a local historian, R. W. Rathbone, by the 1950s the suburb of Carlton had settled into 'useful old age'. In 1951 there were some thirty shops on Carlton Parade, and Miles continued to do her own shopping, though the fifteen-minute walk to the grocer, the butcher (but maybe not the baker, as there was one nearby at 19 Grey Street at that time), the post office and the bank often wore her out. So did gardening, on which she still expended a good deal of energy. The alacrity with which she lopped branches from fruit and other trees around the house, for exercise and due to the ongoing unreliability of electricity supplies after the 1949 coal strike, is quite startling.[4]

But she no longer dashed about as in Chicago and London or even wartime Sydney; and she went less often to meetings in the city at night due to feeling the cold. However, that was no loss after what she still saw as the communists' destruction of the FAW. Nonetheless, she still got about a good deal, mostly by public transport, even at night, though more of her friends now had cars. She was not sleeping any better, perhaps because of taking rests during the day, but it was not from want of trying: after a lifetime of retiring late, at midnight or even after, Miles would often go to bed at ten when home alone.[5]

It was the larger tasks of home maintenance that really tested her, and led to rising anxiety about what she called 'my humpy'. When better-off friends urged her to shift to a classier area she was dismissive: those in 'the snubbubs' needed people like her to look down on, she retorted. Perhaps she did not think she could afford to move — she was always complaining about inflation, which was bad at this time, especially for people like her on fixed incomes — even supposing that at her stage of life she could have borne the inconvenience and loss of time involved. She had sentimental attachments: to the double sunflowers first planted by her father, the wisteria along the west side of the house grown by her mother from a cutting from Talbingo (and still there in the 1990s), and the peach tree given to her by Miss Gillespie; maybe even the hollyhocks grown from seeds gathered by Aunt Lena at Windsor Castle in 1926. At least the house was hers. (Aunt Lena Lampe, who lived in various residentials on the lower North Shore after leaving Grey Street in the early 1930s, seems never to have had a home of her own.)[6]

Fortunately Miles was able to call on outside help. Literary friends living in southern Sydney mowed the lawn and did odd jobs, generally keeping an eye on her, especially Joe Salter, 'a kind and generous creature' of humble origins who had belonged to the Modern Writers' Club in the 1940s. With his wife, Lorna, Joe lived at Como, further down the Illawarra train line. Happily, the Crosses, Arthur and Delys, were within reach at Caringbah. Other friends included the journalist Frank Ryland, and Allan Dalziel ('Dal'), aide to Dr Evatt, a frequent caller but usually feeling exhausted. In return, Miles offered support and encouragement and many scratch meals.[7]

Miles' gregariousness stood her in good stead. If she did not go about quite so much, people still came to her. Often they, too, were lonely or in some way needy, like Dalziel, and Glen Mills Fox, in the throes of divorce, and always they were fed well. Frequently they would arrive with contributions to the table — a couple of extra chops, a fish, or an onion or two. Occasionally they came unannounced, as when the Jindyworobak poets Roland Robinson and Rex Ingamells turned up at 26 Grey Street one wet evening in August 1951 with the young writer Nancy Keesing in tow. Confessing in her memoirs to being 'scared stiff', as Miles always '*sounded* so redoubtable, despite her usually gentle appearance and demeanour' at literary gatherings, the young Nancy was soon at ease. The men had to stand on the verandah while Miles helped Nancy dry her hair: 'You must *never* be a doormat,' she said. Later, in 'her small, warm, living room', with decorative soil samples collected by Miles from different parts of Australia glowing in jars on the mantelpiece, she served supper. Nancy took tea from the waratah cup, which — like many other guests — she feared to drop, and signed the waratah book. She did not care for the writings of either Miles or Brent, but she found Miles Franklin 'an irresistible woman': 'I almost loved her. Her conversation was fun.' Soon after, Ingamells gave Miles a copy of his *The Great South Land*, a vast opus in blank verse on the discovery of Australia 'in the spiritual and the geographic sense'. Miles welcomed the gift, but ultimately found it a bit overpowering ('a great Ayers Rock').[8]

In *All That Swagger* Miles Franklin had lamented the unstinting hospitality that frittered away the Delacy legacy at Burrabinga. Yet she maintained the old ways herself. She always made careful preparations for guests, and was never at a loss coping with unexpected visitors. The back garden remained productive, thanks to its sunny northerly aspect, and Susannah's values held when it came to housework. Miles seems to have spent a lot of time 'redding' (a favourite archaism for cleaning), perhaps necessarily, given the heavy Victorian furniture she inherited: all must be spick and span, with meals provided in several courses plus supper served off a traymobile in the evenings.[9]

Miles Franklin owned a radiator and an electric jug, but if the frequency of her trips to the butcher is any guide, she did not have a refrigerator, only a weekly ice delivery. Nor does she seem to have had a washing machine, a floor polisher or a vacuum cleaner. 'Did a line of washing' was shorthand in her diary for a morning's work over the tubs and copper; polishing lino floors was hard on the knees. References to the occasional 'plunge bath', and more frequently to a 'sponge bath', suggest the bathroom facilities may have been limited — although it is recorded that Beatrice Davis once took a shower during an overnight stay. A classic Australian Early Kooka gas stove was standing on the back porch in the 1990s and probably dated back to Miles' day, so there may have been a gas heater too. The lavatory was outside but connected to the sewer. Much of the household equipment we take for granted today was only just becoming the norm in Australia, where there was a profligate dependence on women's unpaid labour. Miles' frequently reiterated line that in Australia women were 'wood and water joeys, nothing more' applied to her as much as anyone.[10]

A random excerpt from Miles Franklin's pocket diary gives a feel for her daily life. On 30 January 1951, a Tuesday, she wrote:

> Warm day, but showers. When I finished bagging & gathering the figs & other chores, went to butcher. I thought to straighten 1st draft of first act of the war play. Mrs Bennett in to telephone. Then as I was so feeble I lay down & was nearly asleep when Mrs Fogden came & I had to listen to her for half an hour & she left me with an important message to come at 3 pm. So I started to mow the front esp. under the trees. The children & Mildred came upon me wanting lollies & flowers, & by that time it was 6.15 & I was exhausted. May Fogden came for a couple of hours in the evening. I made another pan of fig jam.[11]

The telephone was an important assurance of connectedness beyond Carlton, though not, as today, internationally or even nationally. In those days a long-distance, or 'trunk', call was costly and probably presaged bad news. Local calls enabled Miles Franklin to keep in touch with family and friends, and to conduct her literary business in Sydney in these later years without too much rushing about.

Wider links depended on the letterbox and the newspapers. One of her paperboys, the previously mentioned historian of Carlton, Ron Rathbone, recalls that she took numerous papers and magazines, including the *Australian Women's Weekly* and both evening papers (and that it was hard to collect the money, as 'Miss Franklin' could never find her purse). She herself records a postman's polite incredulity at the extent of her Christmas mail. Letter-writing continued with verve at the customary rate: 'Your letters have been wonderful. So full of life and vitality. They enchant me and I feel I'm living it thru' you,' Dymphna Cusack wrote from London on 14 January 1951.[12]

That panic about death in her sixties seemed to have faded somewhat, though she feared to lose Aunt Lena, who said she hoped to die before another winter (but happily for Miles did not, surviving as a link with Talbingo for the Lampe tribe until 1964). Increasingly though, Miles would say she would do things 'if I live'. Inevitably, memories flooded in as she pressed on with her work. How much she valued her German cousins is apparent from letters to Theo Lampe at this time, and how much fun there had been with them when young: 'I used to tease young men, did I not?' she asked him. When the singer Amy Castles died in November 1951, she felt the urge to contact Eva O'Sullivan as one of the few remaining who would recall the magic of fifty years ago. That same month, writing to Ethel Mason Nielsen, Miles confessed for the first time that she would have married Demarest Lloyd, except that 'He had a fully fledged divorced wife running about the country and I was too proud and too rigidly grounded in monogamy to enter a harem, even if he was running them tandem.' Such was the legacy of respectability.[13]

It was difficult for Miles to obtain information about her nephew John. Although he had been released from Callan Park in June 1950, it seems he was recommitted soon after, as Miles was anxious about another release in November 1950, and he was back for a third time in the new year. (Apparently inebriates could only be held for six months, with the possibility of recommital and day release for chronic cases.) Thanks to Dymphna Cusack's experience with her brother, Miles had sought help from Dr William Farquhar Fraser, previously a medical officer at the Darlinghurst Reception Centre and now in charge of the microbiology unit in the Public Health Department. His inquiries confirmed that John Franklin was 'somewhat psychopathic — plainly a war-broken case': 'they call it schizophrenia', Miles reported to Dymphna. She still blamed the war and the drink. Passing the asylum one day in February 1951 en route to a meeting made her feel ill, 'But what can I do?'[14]

John's occasional phone call when on day release shattered her by its coldness: he still blamed her for his plight, predicting that she too would finish up in an asylum. Vulnerability to such calls was one factor in her uncharacteristic unwillingness to sign petitions intended for publication in the press. She was distressed when one of John's maternal cousins, Brenda Fitzpatrick, pressed her about his debts, though Brenda had thrown him out as hopeless the year before. As a matter of policy, Miles Franklin never disclosed her nephew's whereabouts, directing all inquiries to his trustees, the executors of his father's estate.[15]

Support came from an unexpected quarter. Miles first met Wagga Wagga-born artist and cousin of Mary Gilmore Marie McNiven through Myrtle Rose White in 1950. Like Myrtle, Marie was a spiritualist and she thought she could help John by taking Miles to a medium. Apparently this was supposed to disclose alcoholism in John's family. The medium also told Marie to paint Miles' portrait; Van Dyck 'came through' urging her to it, Marie asserted. Nothing more was said of this at the time. The main thing was that Marie was kind and Miles was grateful for Marie's ongoing efforts to help John. Likewise, she paid no attention when 'an artist of sorts' associated with the Packer Press, Herbert Kemble, offered to paint her later in the year: 'No gout for the Packer gang,' she wrote dismissively after meeting him at a dull dinner.[16]

If Miles Franklin had no luck with painters, a snapshot could arouse her ire too, as when Henrietta Drake-Brockman published the 'Miles-in-her-suit' photo taken in Henrietta's backyard in Perth in the popular monthly *Walkabout* in March 1951. She seems to be laughing but Miles thought it made her look like a scarecrow up against a wall. The accompanying text, affectionately written by Henrietta, includes a closely observed description of the older Miles Franklin:

> Physically she is petite; with quick, bright, hazel-grey eyes that miss little from behind rimless glasses; with an almost solemn expression breaking readily into a wide smile, that not only turns up the corner of her lips but also turns down the corners of her eyes so that she smiles with all her face. She has a repertoire of smiles. Often impish, sometimes mocking, I have yet seen a sweet, almost diffident smile.

Her hair, which had been her youthful glory and remained long until Charlotte Perkins Gilman persuaded her to have it cut in Chicago, was still brown, with just a few grey threads. It was now too wispy for a 'perm', she told Arnold Dresden, and anyway she couldn't afford it. As for hair dye, it was out of the question: 'old women with a lot of discoloured hair thinking it is still a glory are like an old sofa with the stuffing bulging'. Still, she was glad not to be bald. And she tried to dress respectably. The suit she was wearing in the Perth photo was made for her in the 1940s at the (to Miles) exorbitant cost of £15.[17]

Drake-Brockman's article conveys well how Miles Franklin struck many people — as one of Australia's most provocative talkers, a gregarious person with a gift for friendship:

> Her wit is herself. Spontaneous, springing from a mind stored with knowledge of three continents, crystallized by contact with

the famed of many countries, flavoured with the spice of wide reading, it is nevertheless a wit still drawing on the essence of Australia.

According to Drake-Brockman, Miles Franklin had 'that rare appeal peculiar to women who keep alive both youthful zest and a fresh outlook un-harassed by the complications of matrimony'. Not too many men would credit that, but plenty of intellectually starved women with limited life experiences surely did. Admittedly, her little mysteries were a perpetual irritant, but Miles had a heart as wide 'as her country's "back paddocks"', Henrietta declared.

On 12 February 1951 Miles Franklin wrote to Bruce Graham, the Liberal member for St George, her Federal electorate, to deplore the 'haphazard' application of immigration policy. The new arrivals were causing discomfort to old Australians, she wrote, 'invaded by wads of nationals that are a menace to the Australian way of life'. Graham's assurance that the aim of the program was to ensure that Australia remained a British country 'for the next twenty years', and his enclosure of copies of speeches made by the Minister for Immigration, Harold Holt, probably did nothing to diminish her concern.[18]

Two weeks later, on 26 February, a Citizens' Protest Committee on German Migration, chaired by a Methodist minister, W. J. Hobbin, called a meeting in Sydney Town Hall to protest against 'large scale admittance of Germans', meaning ex-Nazis, under the postwar immigration program. Miles' name was listed on the committee, along with those of Dr Evatt and a professor of law, Julius Stone, though the meeting was so crowded Miles was unable to get in on the night. It seems she was drawn into Hobbin's circle by some of his associates who wanted an Australian slant on their concerns, as she had attended several meetings earlier in February and later gave a talk on early Australian writing ('very few there').[19]

Italian immigration bothered her just as much, if not more. The Italians were Catholic, and it seemed to Miles — and she was not alone — that some conservatives were hell-bent on a Catholic Australia. She reacted adversely to the plan for a Catholic university in Sydney, floated between 1949 and 1951. On 3 June, along with Dalziel and one Fitzpatrick, possibly the controversial Bankstown businessman Raymond Fitzpatrick, she attended an 'anti R.C. University meeting ... [Anglican Archbishop] Mowll in the chair'. Strongly opposed by Protestant and liberal opinion (and also by the Catholic Archbishop Mannix in Melbourne), nothing came of the university idea, as she explained to Arnold Dresden — though it would surely come again.[20]

Opposition to a Catholic university probably seems simply sectarian nowadays, but in 1951 the politics of religion were tense. Miles' youth had been spent in notoriously sectarian Goulburn, still a strong Catholic town. By 1951 she was both anti-Catholic and anti-communist, and anti-American big business as well. She put it lightly for the benefit of Jean Hamilton: the Pope had pulled a great scare about the Reds and the silly Protestants had all rushed into the pen with the RCs. With the Cold War, she could hardly stand the sound of American voices 'bleating about democracy' over the radio; and she was clear that communism could not be stopped by bullets.[21]

In mid-1951, the former prime minister Ben Chifley died. Like other Australians, Miles mourned his passing. She had listened with approval to his speeches on behalf of the Labor Party during the Federal election campaign in April (and shaken her head at her neighbour Mrs Bennett's support for the Menzies-led Tories, 'now trading as "Liberals"'). When the country was riven by a second attempt to ban the Communist Party, she stood firm. You must vote 'No' in the referendum on wider Commonwealth powers to combat communism because it was so hard to undo oppressive legislation, she told Pixie O'Harris, who was still smarting from FAW politics. But Miles steadfastly avoided any appearance of political alignment, even declining an invitation to stay with the Evatts in Canberra in November: 'I wish to remain free.'[22]

There were some sharp exchanges with Katharine Susannah Prichard, a constant correspondent in these fearful times. Though they were as one on civil liberties and the referendum, Miles did not yield to her friend when it came to the Communist Party line on the writer's role in society, believing that the writer must always be free to dissent. In similar vein she urged Katharine not to kill herself with peace work, much as it was needed in 'a war-demented world'. Miles was particularly irritated by communist domination of the peace movement and the scant space left for the cause in Sydney: 'You daren't even say you would like to see peace today or they put you down as a communist', but 'without two great disciplines it doesn't matter whether we vote for … Uncle Joe, Churchill or Buddha or the Star and Crescent, unless the human race can regulate its verminous fecundity and abstain from war it is doomed, if not today then tomorrow'.[23]

Problematic as these sentiments seem today — and Miles could put them roughly, claiming, for example, that race suicide would ensue 'unless the occident abandons war and the orient abandons rabbit-swarming' — they were common coin in Britain and Australia after World War II, when the Asian demographic revolution was in full swing and the contraceptive pill had yet to be invented. A Malthusian pall hung over all, even inland Australia. This is how she put it to Katharine Susannah Prichard:

> Only a third of the inhabitants of the globe [are] fully fed at present. No matter how scientific they are about agriculture and distribution, if the human race keeps on increasing at present Asiatic rate the whole globe won't keep them forever. Also, why shd the whole globe be spoiled by agriculture to keep creatures that are no joy or delight compared with virgin forests and our dear, dry inland, not even if they were your pet communists or my libertarians.[24]

The Australian Security Intelligence Organization (ASIO) had Miles on file from 1949, when it was founded, for no better reason than that she had been seen to attend a premiere at the New Theatre that year and might therefore be a member of the Eureka Youth League — what a loss to hilarity that she did not know about that — and because her name appeared on the address lists of individuals and groups such as her FAW colleague Alexander Bookluck, the pro-communist New Housewives Association, and the Democratic Rights Council, set up in Victoria to oppose the Communist Party Dissolution Bill in 1950. She was also a person of interest as a member of the FAW, on which substantial files were compiled at this time. And though Frank Hardy was acquitted of a criminal libel charge in mid-1951 in connection with his novel *Power Without Glory*, Miles' fear had been that FAW protests were too feeble, and it was obvious that writers would be subject to ongoing political harassment by the state.[25]

When, about this time, Miles heard that well-meaning colleagues had sought to obtain a Commonwealth Literary Fund pension for her, she responded with four exclamation marks. On Friday 2 March 1951 she went to see the fund administrator, H. S. Temby, about the proposal: 'I was much hurt & depressed.' She refused it, 'though gratefully'. Temby's file note reads: 'Miss Franklin explained her position to me & said she did not desire to accept a pension until forced to do so by economic necessity.' Perhaps the offer made Miles feel she was finished as a writer. There was her pugnacious streak too: 'Beware the government stroke,' she would say.[26]

'There is no chink or gleam of anything hopeful for me,' she reflected on 9 January. 'I struggle like a fly in tar.' As ever, the imperative was her writing. There was a broadcast on Rose Scott in January, the 'Johanna versus Hennessy' play was still on the go, and she had begun an anti-war play, 'The Dead Must Not Return', after Christmas.[27]

Miles invested a good deal of emotional energy in 'The Dead Must Not Return'. The play is set in the shabby living room of the Fisher family's bungalow in 'Ashville', an imaginary inner Sydney working-class suburb, at the onset of the Korean War. Apart from sundry items of furniture, the main prop is a mantelpiece adorned with two photographs, one of a World War I subaltern wearing a distinguished service medal and the other of a World War II private. An instruction at the head of the script reads: 'To be acted quietly without ranting. Action is inner, and not to be confused with mere motor activity or restlessness.'

The play is constructed in two acts. Act I opens in late 1950 with Myrtle Fisher, a World War II widow, and her daughter, June, returning from the posthumous investiture of Myrtle's husband, Ernie, with a Victoria Cross. Myrtle's aunt by marriage, Miss Flora Fisher, an elderly housewife, recalling her brother Harry, thought to have died at Gallipoli, comments that the dead must not return: 'They could not stand it and neither could we.'

But in this play, the dead do return. Harry, who somehow survived 'from Anzac to Okinawa', arrives first, followed by Ernie, 'last heard of in the islands', now 'a piteous human scarecrow', a madman clutching an old rifle and hiding behind the sofa. The men have made their way home, like animals. Myrtle is appalled. Her opportunistic flame, Ivor Cadman, determines to get rid of the nuisance. But young June is more caring, especially as it dawns on her that Ernie is her father; and when the police arrive, they say that they cannot arrest the men as they are in their own home.

In Act II, the family is beginning to comprehend the situation. Maybe some hospital treatment is available, and Ernie need not be rejected. Then Ernie disappears. He is found yelling in the street and brandishing his rifle. Once more the police decline to act, and only June can calm him down. Harry, who is guilt-ridden by an incident in World War I and tempted by alcohol, remembers how Ernie was brought to them after his father died, 'a soft sort of little fellow', and is determined to look after him. The play closes with Cadman ('Shiny Bum') ousted, and Harry pinning the Victoria Cross on the bewildered Ernie. June clutches Ernie affectionately, and Flora gathers Myrtle to her.[28]

The imprint of Miles' painful struggle with John Franklin is obvious. More complex is the analysis of gender and war that takes up a good deal of the second act. As Harry and Flora argue, Flora concludes that the male is both saint and fiend, doomed to fight, and that woman is the more unified sex. But when Harry asserts that 'It's woman's final destiny to abolish war,' Flora responds that women have been bamboozled, 'fooled and frustrated by men'. And whereas the men think the current war is inevitable, Myrtle says the army ought to give war a break, and Flora asks, 'Why can't Australia stay neutral for a change?' But both women are powerless; all they can do is face the consequences. Ultimately Flora declares the problem of men and war is beyond rational analysis: 'I'm old now and have learned that forgiveness is not for me to give or to withhold from men, nor even from myself. I still can't understand why man, the only beast endowed with reason, should be the only one to degrade his mate.'

David Martin, who later advocated armed neutrality for Australia, thought it a brave play, and its main idea still has some purchase. Nonetheless, like so many Franklin plays, it was never performed, and remains unpublished. Miles tossed her head. 'I've written a play against war — indirectly — no sectarian bias or political partisanship. Just the facts of men returning blasted and wasted.' And because he seemed to be saying something similar, Miles approved of the prize-winning novel by T. A. G. Hungerford, *The Ridge and the River* — 'real good stuff' about soldiering, she wrote to Florence James mid-year.[29]

Again, it was the (admittedly faint) prospect of a prize that kept Miles at her typewriter. She entered her anti-war play in the annual *Herald* literary competition in May but had no luck (no one won the first prize of £2000). A few weeks later, she submitted both the Johanna play, under the title 'Models for Molly', and 'The Dead Must Not Return' to the Commonwealth Jubilee Stage Play Competition (first prize £500), the first play forwarded in her own name, the second as 'O. Niblat', but again with no success. Her scripts came back the day after the *Bulletin* announced Kylie Tennant the winner for a play on Federation's founding father Alfred Deakin. In August, she entered the same two plays in a West Australia Theatre Council competition, won by James Crawford's *The Governor's Stables*. Then in September she began to polish 'Furphy Today', which had been read for her by various people during the year, including Professor Keith Macartney in Melbourne and Fred Robinson's English class at the University of Queensland.[30]

With 'Furphy Today', which had begun life as 'Comedy at Runnymede' in 1943, most likely Miles was tending the Furphy flame in the year of the national Jubilee. Hearing St John Ervine broadcast on Thomas Hardy one night, she wrote admiringly in her pocket diary of his beautiful speaking voice and diction, and his love for his friends. 'Oh to have a friend like that when I am dead,' she wrote, adding, 'I do my best for Jos. Furphy and Rose Scott.' Happily, with regard to Furphy she would have a helper in John Barnes, a student who wrote to her in 1951 and later became Furphy's next biographer.[31]

Even in her later years, Miles Franklin seems always to have been peering hopefully through the footlights, watching plays and trying to write them. 'The Australian theatre is a burning interest to me,' she wrote to a new acquaintance, Eleanor Witcombe, in April 1951. When young Eleanor, who later wrote the script for the screen version of *My Brilliant Career*, invited Miles to a matinee of the Children's National Theatre at St James' Hall in April, she took 'a child friend' and thoroughly enjoyed herself; and she was much interested in a play by the newspaper proprietor Warwick Fairfax entitled *A Victorian Marriage* later in the year. Although she thought it flawed, she was sufficiently stimulated by reminders of her mother's generation to write him an encouraging note afterwards. Likewise, she kept in touch with Ric Throssell in case he needed help in submitting plays to competitions, and she was thrilled by news of the success of Sumner Locke Elliott on Broadway in October with a show called *Buy Me Blue Ribbons*. (It didn't last long though, Sumner responded from New York.)[32]

Miles saw *Lysistrata*, the great Greek anti-war comedy, whose sentiments she agreed with entirely, at the New Theatre in 1951, and there are many comments on the latest broadcasts and shows in her diaries and letters. She dismissed T. S. Eliot's *The Cocktail Party* as warmed-up Noël Coward with a dash of stale psychoanalysis and a bit of blasphemy (though she had been admiring of his earlier *Murder in the Cathedral*, performed in the Sydney Town Hall in 1948 with Camilla Wedgwood leading the chorus), and privately deemed Musette Morell's *Webs of our Weaving* odious due to a 'male point of view'.[33]

Eleanor Witcombe and others, such as the forthright Melbourne writer Jean Campbell, were among those to whom, with customary tenacity, Miles turned in the early 1950s seeking outlets for her theatrical work. She was disturbed, however, by the reported prevalence of homosexuality among actors, including Sumner Locke Elliott. It was a subject she found shocking and depressing, and mostly beyond her range, though there had been rumours of goings-on at a long-ago camp at Thornford, she recalled, and she had heard about Dobell and Walt Whitman.[34]

Among the literary prizes offered for the Commonwealth Jubilee was one for a non-fiction prose work, worth £1000. In March 1951, soon after the prizes were announced, Miles began to revise 'my essay' (her Perth lectures). This involved much more work in the Mitchell Library, where, according to the *Bulletin*, she seemed to live these days. One day in May she found Tom Inglis Moore there writing an essay for the non-fiction prize, covering much the same ground. He seemed keen to see her work, but there was no way she would allow that. Moore's work would be so orthodox it would be bound to win, she muttered into her diary, and she was not going to supply ideas as usual, 'only to be overlooked and denigrated by my [word illegible] and inferiors'. Even though the writing felt like 'walking up a hill of sand', by the end of September it was done.[35]

According to a surviving brochure, she sent it to the Jubilee competition as 'Bunyip' on 26 September 1951 under the title 'Notes on Australian Writing'. When the awards were announced in February 1952, no first prize was awarded, but Tom Inglis Moore's manuscript, 'The Australian Mirror — Social Patterns in Australian Literature', shared second place with the Perth writer J. K. Ewers. There was no mention of Miles' entry in the press, just the usual return of her manuscript.[36]

Writing in October to David Martin, now living in Melbourne 'among the blest', but not as she had feared forgetful of her, amid enthusiasm and encouragement for his writing Miles made no mention of 'my essay', lamenting instead her own limited output in a vivid horsy image: 'I am completely winded. None of my horses are out of the stable, let alone running. They have long ago eaten their heads off. I have had only two foals in the last decade.' (Presumably that meant *Sydney Royal* and *My Career Goes Bung*.) And whereas she was generous about the success of colleagues in other sections of the competition, notably Vance Palmer's double win in the radio serial and short story awards, and the Northern Territory writer Tom Ronan's *Vision Splendid*, which won second prize for fiction, there was an understandable silence about the non-fiction prize. It seems unlikely that she would have got anywhere anyway, with the vociferously 'anti-gum tree school' A. D. Hope as one of the judges. However, Miles did beat Moore to publication, albeit posthumously: Angus & Robertson published her *Laughter, Not for a Cage* in 1956, and Moore's *Social Patterns in Australian Literature* not until 1971. (Moore joined the teaching staff of the ANU after World War II and was unable to complete his work until he retired in 1966.)[37]

Miles Franklin knew that more work was needed on her essay; and it would absorb most of her energy over the next two years. Living alone made work easier, but 'it takes will power to suffer it without depression'. She knew just as well, however, that creative work is its own reward. As she said to the younger West Australian writer Dorothy Sanders, 'Writing depends on an inner core of stillness.'[38]

Miles also advised Sanders not to worry about having been described as a 'frustrate', asserting that it was an out-of-date concept, now replaced by the equally dubious 'schizophrenic'. She seems to have been unaware that 'frustrate' by then meant sexually unfulfilled, but Miles had long since dismissed psychoanalytic ideas. According to her, the reality was that 'every single one of us is schizophrenic and everyone is frustrated'. She did concede that to be 'schizophrenic' might be useful to a writer, while maintaining the traditional meaning of 'frustrate': 'We must cling to the firm inner core of ourselves, then outside circumstances will not frustrate us.'[39]

For Miles Franklin the inner core was no fragile thing, and we may safely infer it lay somewhere beyond both the private and the public personae she so successfully articulated over time, to a fair degree with an eye to posterity. Artful remarks, such as to Florence James after reading Katherine Mansfield's journals, that she would hate to be exposed like that after death, merely suggest a smokescreen, and the ongoing game.[40]

It is also true, and kinder, to recall that most of her peers were dead and gone, and with them irreplaceable understandings. In 1951 Em Fullerton returned to Melbourne, and although Miles had limited contact with her by then, it meant losing her last local link with Mary Fullerton. Similarly May 1951 marks her last known contact with Nell Malone, unwell and housekeeping near Fontainebleau in France. On the other hand, there were always new friends and associates and fresh ideas to keep her going. 'The joy of creative activity and congenial and stimulating association with one's fellows is the nearest to happiness one can get,' she once told Dymphna Cusack.[41]

Miles Franklin's personal and political values at this time were eloquently expressed in letters to David Martin. Her uninhibited engagement with his views was one of the brightest things in her later life. 'I enjoy his mind,' she said and in return she taught him her Australia. Expressing relief when the referendum on banning the Communist Party failed, she cited the popular attitude to politicians and proposals for constitutional change: "'They got enough power already. Let 'em get on with it.'" A substantial exchange on Katharine Susannah Prichard's great work *Coonardoo* led her to defend emotion over artifice in writing: 'Now I enjoy Aldous Huxley's *Point Counter Point* immensely, and it is all artifice, but I turn to *Cry the Beloved Country* with envy ... I wish I could write like that, or like Nevil Shute.'[42]

In early 1951, at his request, she reviewed Martin's novel *The Stones of Bombay* for the Sydney Jewish magazine *Unity*.

> Mr Martin is at present in Australia. His published work reveals a man who thinks ... internationally. His quality and linguistic equipment could make him welcome in the ranks of resident writers who are urgently concerned with expressing their country in song and story, a transplanted citizen as valuable as a scientist or mechanician in the development of the new multinational Australia.[43]

A richly woven tale of the plight of refugees from Karachi in overcrowded exploitative Bombay post-Partition (1947), it was exactly the kind of fiction she liked, in terms of both action and background, the latter 'as absorbing as personal news from behind a closed frontier'. She commended its approach to 'the tumultuous and disorganized present', free from propagandist intent. Seldom one to miss a chance herself, she noted that the book contained a warning to any in Australia who would exploit immigration regardless of social and environmental costs.

For this review she earned three guineas. Better still, her name was plastered across the page, with an accompanying statement that she was one of the greatest prose writers Australia had produced, a writer in the democratic tradition, and a militant progressive. In return, when Clem Christesen at *Meanjin* wanted a reviewer for *Prelude to Waking*, Miles recommended David Martin, and he did her proud ('Shavian, captures the spirit of the period'). Apart from the ever polite Vance Palmer, and the *Bulletin*, which acknowledged the book's 'moral purpose', Martin's was the only favourable review.[44]

With the long-awaited publication in London and Melbourne of *Come in Spinner* in January 1951, Clem Christesen asked Miles for a review. She was happy to oblige, though the novel was dedicated to her and she felt she had not been given enough space. When for the first time she read it straight through, she declared it brilliant. It was not necessarily a straightforward assignment, however. The *Daily Telegraph*'s response to the book, headlined 'For Your Literary Dustbin', cried out for rebuttal. But this she did not attempt, on the grounds that the '*Tele*' was beneath contempt. Her review confined itself to outlining the plot; and it may have seemed like fence-sitting. Perhaps it was. One of Miles' neighbours thought *Come in Spinner* pornographic; another local found it surprising that two women could know so much about the seedy side of wartime Sydney. Moreover, it hardly mattered what reviewers thought. *Come in Spinner* was hot stuff, more popular than literary, and as a respectable local elder Miles might well have felt there was no need to say more.[45]

Although she had seemed to agree with Miles' dismissive attitude to the *Telegraph*, when the review appeared Dymphna let it pass without comment — which suggests either irritation or disappointment. Another variable may be relevant. Miles was devoted to Dymphna as a kind of literary daughter and she very much missed her and Florence James when they went to London. Nonetheless, her constant advice was to 'dig in' over there until successful, a refraction of her own less happy experience as an expatriate, along with the realities of publishing; and a rich correspondence lasting until Miles' death ensued, the largest extant cache of letters for any of her congenials in this period. Yet for all the flow of words and affection Dymphna was not being entirely candid, in that she kept Miles in the dark about her longstanding relationship with a communist journalist, Norman Freehill, a married man unable to obtain a divorce. Freehill had joined Dymphna in London in 1949 and was now her permanent partner. Her deception is hard to fathom, except for the climate of the times, and fear of ASIO. Even Miles' gas man thought marriage would be obsolete in fifty years' time, or so she told Emmy Lawson.[46]

Miles could no longer complain that none of her books was in print. Apart from the copies of *Sydney Royal* she held, and *My Career Goes Bung*, in November she learned of an impending reissue by the British publishing firm George Allen & Unwin of *All That Swagger*, the eighth edition. And the entire Brent series was appearing. Angus & Robertson reprinted *Prelude to Waking* in early 1951, the first print run of 1204 copies having sold out by December 1950, a pleasing situation, suggesting that readers were curious about the previously unpublished work, regardless of the reviews. By the end of 1951, Miles had earned almost £87 in royalties from it, and another £55 in royalties came with *Up the Country*, republished mid-year.[47]

When the author's copies of *Up the Country* arrived on 2 June, Miles could not at first face Beatrice Davis because the cover made her feel sick: it showed a grotesque collection of characters 'from Snake Gully and I can't make any of them fit the book.' ('Snake Gully' was the home of Steele Rudd's Dad and Dave in the then popular radio serial.) The 'romantic Zulu', as Mary Fullerton had dubbed the image of an Aborigine that appeared on the cover of the first edition of *Up the Country* in 1927, seemed grand by comparison.[48]

Beatrice was apologetic and promised the firm would do better for the next volume, *Ten Creeks Run*, which was almost ready for printing (Beatrice had received the typescript from Miles on 29 June). Beatrice also reassured Miles that all six Brent volumes would appear as fast as she could manage, and in that respect she was as good as her word, even if it was not quite fast enough for Miles to see them all.[49]

When earlier in the year Dymphna Cusack had asked why Miles didn't come out as Brent ('You don't have to answer that'), Miles claimed that once people knew the truth about a pseudonymous work they lost interest. This now seems doubtful, especially a generation after Brent's debut. But she wasn't risking it. That queer mix of ebullience and lack of confidence was by now a fixed character trait. So a new round of reviews and speculation had to be endured, while her 'essay', which she described as an 'autobiography' of the novel in Australia, kept her busy. The new edition of *Up the Country* was well received. The *Bulletin* said it was unmistakably authentic, and written with the breath of life — though not a work of art.[50]

In Sydney, people were used to Miles' secretive behaviour and valued her nonetheless. She was a speaker at the annual 'Eng. Ass.' dinner in November, where the recently arrived Fulbright scholar Bruce Sutherland, a literature professor from Pennsylvania State University, was the main speaker. In December she was invited to attend the ceremony at Waverley cemetery for the unveiling of a memorial on the poet Rod Quinn's grave. She was even admitted to the international writers' organisation PEN in 1951, despite past smears as a communist sympathiser. Irene Greenwood's Christmas greeting from Perth in 1951 conveys something of the affection she now commanded: 'To dear, brilliant, clever and courageous Miles'.[51]

On 20 February 1952 Miles flew to Melbourne and stayed there until 8 March, when she left for Sydney on the Riverina Express. The trip had been mooted for several months, and although it was true that it made a nice break and Miles wanted to see old friends, there was another purpose. This time she stayed with the twice-divorced *bon vivant* bibliophile John Kinmont Moir, who resided at the back of a disused pawnbroker's shop capable of housing his vast Australiana collection, at 474 Bridge Road in the inner suburb of Richmond. Miles wanted Moir to read the early chapters of her 'essay'. The trouble was that 'J. K.', as she usually called him — an accountant with the department store Bon Marché by day — was a great one for conviviality. So lively was it at Bridge Road, with literary and other visitors night after night, she mostly felt utterly worn out before he was free to discuss her work. When Nettie Palmer made her go to the doctor, it cost three guineas to hear what she already knew: that she was not as strong as she used to be and should take things easier.[52]

Certainly she was not as strong as Kate Baker, still tripping around town aged ninety on nothing more than a cup of tea in the morning, but she was much better than the surviving Goldstein sisters, who now seemed really old. At eighty, Elsie Belle Champion still went to work at Mullen's Bookshop, part-time however; and Aileen Goldstein obviously suffered from arthritis, though not admitting it. The Fullerton sisters, getting on one another's nerves in the suburbs, reminded her once more of the tribulations of her friend Mary.[53]

'Miles Franklin Visits Us' ran the headline of a welcoming article by an *Argus* journalist, Freda Irving; it was Miles' first trip to Melbourne for almost a decade. Irving found her a challenge: 'You need cerebrations at the rate of an express train to keep up with her darting, inquisitive brain, her quick wit, and her ready tongue.' As usual, Miles was unwilling to talk about herself, asserting that she never wrote anything now, and it was the future of writing that interested her. She mentioned Kylie Tennant, Katharine Susannah Prichard and Henrietta Drake-Brockman from among the established writers, and from the world of poetry, the Lyre-Bird Writers, a publishing co-operative recently established by some young Sydney poets. We must, she said, 'put ourselves in' to the world's literature. In the accompanying photograph, she smiles widely (a horrible close-up, she noted privately). The text states that, having avoided the camera on arrival, 'Her happy nature got the better of her.'[54]

As in the past she did the rounds. One day she had lunch with Mollie Bowie, 'Furphy's delight' back in 1904; on another she had afternoon tea with Rex Ingamells and some of his friends in the Botanical Gardens, where she heard the popular Aboriginal singer Harold Blair. The Jindyworobak journalist John McKellar took her to the theatre one evening (as well he might, given his lengthy stays at Grey Street in recent years). He also took her for a drive to Belgrave, his place in the Dandenongs, after which they called on the now relocated David and Richenda Martin. At a PEN Club dinner one evening, Miles met, among others, the best-selling novelist Nevil Shute, whose success she admired and envied. On another occasion, Moir took her to the Australian Literature Society to hear a paper in memory of the recently deceased Jindyworobak poet Victor Kennedy, with whom she had corresponded in 1942 regarding the poems of 'E'. Victor Kennedy's poems were read 'splendidly' by Bernard O'Dowd, one of her few surviving elders. Freda Barrymore, the reviewer and journalist, now widowed and returned from Townsville, was there too and Miles was prevailed upon to make a short speech.[55]

The list of people calling at Bridge Road when Miles Franklin was there reads like a literary who's who of 1950s Melbourne: among them the Palmers, Frederick Macartney, Flora Eldershaw and the forthright Jean Campbell; but not, because of some slip-up with the mail, Clem Christesen, editor of *Meanjin,* nor the critic Arthur Phillips, author in 1950 of the famous phrase 'the cultural cringe', who had once chided Miles (to her amusement) for 'wooziness' in a broadcast. One story has it that when Bruce Muirden, the youthful editor of a new journal, *Austrovert,* turned up, she exclaimed, 'Ah! Someone my own age at last.'[56]

Moir was an excellent cook as well as a generous host, and despite a foot injury, he cooked some agreeable meals for Miles and one of the honorary lady associates of his all-male literary Bread and Cheese Club, Everill Venman. He must have found some time to look at her essay too, as he praised the quality of research, and in coming months made many helpful factual comments on the text.[57]

Everill Venman took Miles to the train at Spencer Street on 8 March. Despite having felt poorly for much of the time, and having failed to meet some important literary associates, her stay in Melbourne had been 'a glorious change'. Perhaps she knew in her bones that this would be her last visit to the great city of the south, where she had first found a peer group almost fifty years before, the home town of some of the most significant people of her maturity: Alice Henry, who welcomed her in Chicago in 1906; Mary Fullerton, who called on her at Russell Square after her return from Australia in 1924; and the Christian Scientists Nancy Lister Watson and her husband, P. S., and his sister, Maud Walsöe, all long gone.[58]

The tent hospital at Ostrovo in north-west Macedonia, where Miles served
as an orderly during the later stages of World War I.

(L. Emslie Hutton, *With a Woman's Unit in Serbia, Salonika and Sebastopol*,
1928, Rare Books Collection, Macquarie University Library)

'Sestra' Franklin with soldiers,
Macedonia, 1917. Miles' handwritten
list at right gives the names of five of
her Macedonian colleagues.

(Mitchell Library, State Library of
New South Wales, Px *D250/1, nos.
68(a) and (b))

Reading from left to right—
Kaplar (Corporal) Milevoje Stekić
Shover (Chauffeur) Milan Stević
" " Bogoljub Djordjević
Sestra Franklin
Podnarednik (Sgt.) Milesov Stojanović
Narednik (Sgt. mjr.) Milan Masalović

Miles received this postcard from Australian nurse Alice Prichard, who served at Salonika. The image is by *Punch* illustrator George Armour, who was also in Salonika in 1917. (MITCHELL LIBRARY, STATE LIBRARY OF NEW SOUTH WALES, MSS 3659/1)

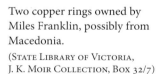

Two copper rings owned by Miles Franklin, possibly from Macedonia. (STATE LIBRARY OF VICTORIA, J. K. MOIR COLLECTION, BOX 32/7)

A 1922 photograph of Nell Malone, an Australian friend in London and the Balkans. Miles kept in touch with her, though Nell spent the rest of her life in Europe. (COURTESY HELEN MALONE, BRISBANE)

Indian summer of romance in London: Fred Post, 1918.

(National Archives, Washington DC, State Department records, Passport Applications Book 1750, no. 2500-2749)

Miles Franklin pictured with Mr Aldridge (second from left) at a housing and town planning conference in Wales in 1920.

(*South Wales News*, Friday 23 July 1920, Mitchell Library, State Library of New South Wales, ML MSS 364/122, press cutting)

Miles Franklin's passport, issued London, September 1923; photo by Florence Carey, Southampton Row.

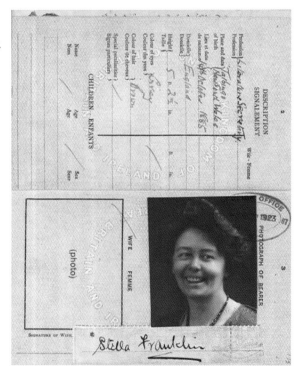

Right: Mary Eliza Fullerton (the poet 'E').

Left: Jean Hamilton with Peter the monkey, c. 1932.

Mabel Singleton with son Denis at the seaside, 1933.

Miles Franklin first met Hartley Grattan in New York in September 1932, the year of this photographic portrait.

Dust cover of the first
edition of *Up the Country*
(1928).

P. R. Stephensen and his wife Winifred (front row, far right) as Brent of Bin Bin and Mrs
Mazere (a character in *Up the Country*) at the Artists' Ball, Sydney, 1935.

Miles Franklin with a Furphy water cart in the Riverina, 1937.

(MITCHELL LIBRARY, STATE LIBRARY OF NEW SOUTH WALES, PX *D250/1, NO. 116)

Miles and her airman nephew, John Franklin, Sydney, February 1943.

(MITCHELL LIBRARY, STATE LIBRARY OF NEW SOUTH WALES, PX *D250/1, NO. 99)

As a girl Stella Miles Franklin loved to go riding. Here she is on her last known horse ride, at Brindabella, January 1939. She practised on a chair beforehand.
(Mitchell Library, PX *D250/1, no. 93)

Miles delivered an oration at the Lawson statue in the Domain in September 1942. In this photograph, another prominent member of the Fellowship of Australian Writers, Bartlett Adamson, stands to her right. The photograph accompanied an article by Dulcie Deamer in the Sunday *Truth*, 6 September 1942.

The waratah cup and saucer, gift of Richard Baker, 1941.

The Frolich head, 1943. When Miles saw this, she consoled herself that no one would recognise her.

Miles Franklin and friends, statue and mural, Hurstville, 2008. The installation, which is located on the corner of Dora and McMahon streets, was unveiled on 19 June 2003. Miles' association with Hurstville included supporting younger local writers.

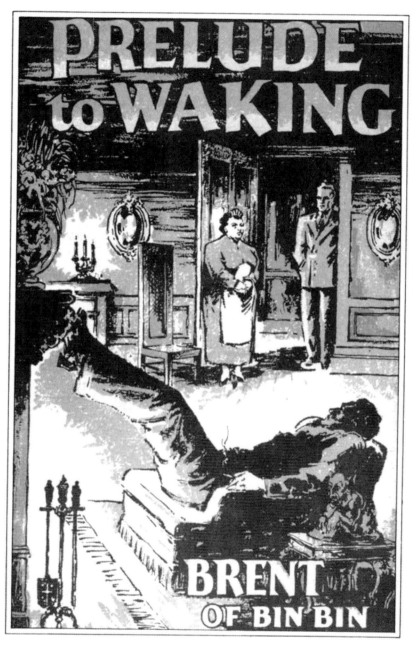

What is the stern man in the doorway supposed to represent? Brent of Bin Bin's first novel, *Prelude to Waking*, drafted in 1925, was published in 1950. It meant a lot to Miles, but the cover suggests the designer had as much difficulty in fathoming its message as most readers. (HARPERCOLLINS ARCHIVE)

26 Grey Street, Carlton, Sydney, the Franklin family home from 1914, where Miles Franklin lived from late 1932 to 1954. (MITCHELL LIBRARY, STATE LIBRARY OF NEW SOUTH WALES, PX *D250/4, NO. 12)

Katharine Susannah Prichard, sketch by Enid Dickson c. 1945.

(MITCHELL LIBRARY, STATE LIBRARY OF NEW SOUTH WALES, P1/P, PRICHARD)

John Kinmont Moir, Melbourne bibliophile and bon vivant.

(HARPERCOLLINS ARCHIVE)

Left: This photograph is inscribed 'To Miles, with love, Dymphna Cusack, 1947'.

(MITCHELL LIBRARY, STATE LIBRARY OF NEW SOUTH WALES, PX *D250/3, NO. 21(a))

Right: Beatrice Davis at her home, 'Folly Point', Sydney, 1953.

(NATIONAL LIBRARY OF AUSTRALIA, BRIDLE COLLECTION)

David Martin, sketch by Noel Counihan. Hungarian-born Martin was Miles' candidate for an immigrant voice in Australian literature post-1945.

(COURTESY MICK COUNIHAN, COUNIHAN ARTWORKS)

Henrietta Drake-Brockman, Perth, 1950, friend, fellow writer and strong supporter of Miles Franklin in the West.

(NATIONAL LIBRARY OF AUSTRALIA)

Children's artist and Miles' devoted friend in later years Pixie O'Harris in her sunroom at Vaucluse.

(COURTESY PIXIE O'HARRIS ESTATE)

Adelaide poet and ardent nationalist Ian Mudie, 1944. Miles delighted in his poems.

Miles with P. R. Stephensen at Bethanga, in north-eastern Victoria, 1952.

Miles Franklin in her sitting room at Grey Street, Carlton, 1952.

A cutting from the Melbourne *Argus*, 27 February 1952, under the headline 'Miles Franklin Visits Us'.

AUSTRALIAN WRITER Miles Franklin avoided the camera when it first appeared soon after her arrival yesterday—but her happy nature got the better of her

Jounama Creek, Talbingo, where Miles Franklin's ashes were spread, in accordance with her wishes.

(COURTESY MARJORIE PIZER, PHOTOGRAPH BY MUIR HOLBURN. MITCHELL LIBRARY, STATE LIBRARY OF NEW SOUTH WALES, ML MSS 2354 ADD ON 921, K 22082)

The week before Miles left Melbourne, P. R. Stephensen had written inviting her to stop over at his post-incarceration abode at Lower Bethanga, an old mining town east of Albury, where he now made a living ghost-writing for Frank Clune. The visit proved a delight. P. R. was still a very angry man, with even more reactionary political views, but he greeted her warmly. The long-suffering Winifred was as brave as ever, and a wonderful homemaker. At Bethanga Miles was thrilled to meet the widowed Tina Mitchell, one of the Coles from Run-o'-Waters near Goulburn, who remembered Miles as a girl riding a black show mare called 'Muriel' and the racing stallion 'Lord Clive', and had on her walls a photograph of another horse, once owned by Charlie Graham, which Miles had ridden when young.[59]

A quaint photograph taken outdoors at the time of the visit of big, be-suited Stephensen standing with his right arm around tiny Miles Franklin — in a spotted dress with a light-coloured belt, Mary Jane shoes and a net-brimmed hat, holding long white gloves — is as good an expression of rapprochement as any. Though they are looking into the light and she has her eyes closed, they are both smiling for the camera. For once, Miles approved of the snap, while correcting Stephensen's later reference to an 'avuncular caress' to 'nephewian', on age grounds. To Moir she wrote: 'P R and Winnie were wonderful to me — not a bit changed from the early days of our meeting in London.'[60]

After Albury the train passed through her old stamping grounds, which Moir had known also as a young man, so she wrote especially for him:

> I felt like a ghost yesterday as I came through Breadalbane and Yarra, where the old de Lisle homestead still looks cosy, and past Joppa Junction picking out the Towers and good old Lansdowne on the Hill and the tower of Bartlett's brewery where old Bartlett's boy played me Bach fugues; and I noted Riversdale, and I ran out in the [Goulburn] Station yard where I came in the middle of the night in my youth. What a cramped place the Station seems today, and I used to feel it the base of all travel-beginning and romance long ago.[61]

It was 'too crowded with the ghosts of my girlhood', and reminders of more recent endeavours. As the train pressed northwards from Goulburn past Marulan, Miles glimpsed the homesteads she had written about in *Pioneers on Parade*, and the great rocks nearby, forever associated in her mind with her old acquaintance the Sydney University geologist Professor Edgeworth David. By nine that evening she was back in Carlton, and very aware of loneliness after the crowded days in Melbourne.

Miles now occupied herself largely with her 'essay'. An article on Fergus Hume's classic thriller of 1880s Melbourne, *The Mystery of a Hansom Cab*, published by the *Bulletin* in December, was a by-product of her research. There were also the demands of Angus & Robertson's Brent publication program to meet, with *Ten Creeks Run* set to appear mid-year. Thankfully this volume appeared with an unobjectionable cover, a line drawing of two horsemen against a mountain backdrop.[62]

In August 1952 the ever loving Pixie O'Harris exhorted Miles to write about her childhood. Although at first loath to do so, feeling it was 'too happy' for the taste of most readers, the proposal suited Miles' mood following the publication of her first memory of Queanbeyan in Donald McLean's *Easy English for Young Australians* in 1951, and her recent traverse of the country by train; and visitors such as Morton McDonald from Uriarra days stimulated her memory. Pixie was so delighted with what her friend first wrote, she demanded more. 'Pixie's demand', completed in January 1953, became the autobiographical memoir originally entitled 'My First Ten Years', which Miles always meant to dedicate to Pixie, and was published posthumously by Angus & Robertson as *Childhood at Brindabella: My First Ten Years* in 1963.[63]

Probably Miles Franklin's best-loved book, *Childhood at Brindabella* is certainly her most accessible. She said she wanted to see how much she could recall 'clear-cut, before my memory is too moth-eaten'. Like many autobiographers, she began with her first recollection, of her red nightgown and a lighted candle on the verandah at Brindabella (which, as if by force of habit, she thinly disguised as 'Bobilla'), when she was ten months old. She ends with the decisive departure from 'Ajinby'/Talbingo, aged ten, in a chapter entitled 'Exit from Eden'. In between, in more or less chronological order, comes a series of stories, among them of her being bald and staying up late in infancy, of driving bullocks at Brindabella as a little girl, and of being too small and naive as a child to defend herself at a Sunday school picnic at 'Gool Gool'/Tumut. There are also recollections of some unusual bush characters, among them Great-uncle George Bridle, a photographer; the gentle 'Uncle Hil' (William Hilder); and his wife, Aunt Aggie (née Franklin). Miles' parents, and especially Grandma Lampe — 'Grandma was

God' — are the crucial characters, apart from herself — a 'prodigy and a pet' among indulgent elders but often at a loss with other more worldly children. Written simply in the first person, her story of childhood in an enchanted world unfolds beguilingly and ends, inevitably, with the loss of innocence and ease.[64]

Our understanding of Miles Franklin's early years would be immeasurably poorer without *Childhood at Brindabella*. It also illuminates her later years. Joy Hooton has suggested that the sequence of memories is more psychological than chronological, and that Miles' personal myth was 'simple, dramatic and tragic'. It is, after all, a short step from the wonder of Grandma's garden to the 'exit from Eden', with all its profound consequences; and familiar as these Edenic symbols are in autobiographies of childhood, they seem especially appropriate in this case. Nonetheless, the reader will find many perspectives drawn from later life, suggestive of something more. For example, Miles recalls as many as eighteen varieties of plum in Grandma's orchard at 'Ajinby', but also that the only other place she has encountered one of them, the delectable gizzard plum, was in a shop on London's Tottenham Court Road; she also remarks in passing that none of the fruit in the orchard was afflicted by the diseases evident in King George V's peaches at the Chelsea Flower Show. And here is her reflection of sitting alone in the hills just before leaving 'Ajinby' the second time:

> This view had nothing to outmatch dawn in the tropics ... or the skyline of New York, challenging God and Nature ... nor the satisfaction of the spires of Oxford, the Cambridge Backs, of the dear familiar outlines of London filtered through racial consciousness ... via our language and literature and direct parentage; nor the haunting mystery of the Giant's Causeway and Glendalough; nor Paris, irresistibly enticing, nor that petrified austere majesty of the Alps, of Rome, of Mt Olympus. Yes, they are all a part of human consciousness; but this obscure view had something that watered existence with the more intimate ecstasy of possession.[65]

Miles Franklin was then in her seventy-second year. Not surprisingly, 'memory work' made her more than ever self-aware. Although she modestly refers to 'these jottings', the interaction between the past and present in *Childhood at Brindabella* develops into something more profound. As already noted in Chapter 1, Miles concluded that the 'self', shaped by her enchanted world was ill prepared for life beyond its confines. Likewise, as has been noted earlier in this chapter, at this time she stressed the importance of holding on to 'the inner core of self', and as she interrogates and reflects upon the images retrieved, she seeks to define that 'self'. Contrary to what is sometimes suggested, she more or less succeeds. Simply put, through those selected memories she defines her 'self' in such a way as to contain, even celebrate, inner contradictions, and to soothe her feelings of inadequacy. Though few have written so well about it, many children from remote or deprived circumstances have come to similar understandings of their strengths and weaknesses in later life. She concludes:

> Goodbye, young thing, perhaps as much a mirage as a reality. Go back into the box of imagination and memory where you belong with those rare people who have retired to that baffling country — the past, lost forever except in these frail inconsequential stories.
> Farewell happy childhood!

On 11 February 1953, Pixie O'Harris sent the memoir, now called 'I Remember', to Frank Eyre at Oxford University Press in Melbourne. Later, at Miles' request, she arranged a meeting between them. Eyre, an Englishman who had arrived in Australia in 1949, responded positively to the text, but they disagreed over the possible illustrations. Eyre felt line drawings would be better than family photographs, but Miles was adamant, and that was the end of it, at least in her lifetime. Apparently she did not see a contradiction between the warm, nostalgic tone of her text and the severely realistic — one hostile reviewer said 'Calvinistic' — photographs she wanted to accompany it, nor the inconsistency of including photographs of people whom she had been at pains not to name precisely. For Eyre the memoir spoke to a romantic fascination with Australia's past, but Miles was strongly committed to the verisimilitude of her account and saw the photos as integral to it.[66]

Meanwhile, Marie McNiven, Mary Gilmore's cousin, was painting Miles' portrait. After 'the [Alice] Cooper [Stewart] atrocity', Miles was ready to swear off portraits forever, but Marie had persevered. When she finished the portrait is unknown, and since Miles seems not to have commented on it, she may never have seen it. If she did she could hardly have been pleased.

No doubt Marie meant well, but the portrait, which is in oils and is now held by the National Library of Australia, makes her look like a frumpish Elizabeth II. Of greater significance are the preliminary photographic studies made by Marie's son Glen on 19 January 1952, of Miles in her living room at Carlton, holding sunflowers. One has her standing in front of bookshelves next to a table scattered with more books, holding the sunflowers upwards. In another, she is seated in a wicker chair in a corner by the mantelpiece, hands folded in her lap, with a glass-fronted bookcase behind her and the sunflowers in a vase on a mat. Miles was nervous, but composed, and the effect of these late, unsmiling images is at once touching and telling, suggesting both physical frailty and strength of mind.[67]

There is another unsmiling snapshot taken outside the Mitchell Library on 22 May 1952 by the visiting Fulbright scholar Bruce Sutherland, just before he left for home with his family. (Miles saw them off on the *Stratheden* on 6 June.) This is the only known image in colour. Surprisingly she approved of Sutherland's photo, at least the colour, despite feeling the scarf she wore made her look strangulated. And the photo is of interest in another respect. Not only do looks matter, especially to young people — and Miles took time to come to terms with hers, if in fact she ever did — but the varying visual representations of an individual over time are themselves essays in character. Thus, if one compares the studio portrait of Miles Franklin taken in Sydney in 1885, when she was aged six, and this penultimate photograph, also taken in Sydney, in 1952, when Miles was approaching her seventy-third birthday, there is that same direct, unsmiling expression. Miles Franklin might not have thought of herself as a success, but certainly from an early age she looked the world in the eye. The last known image is a tiny black-and-white snap of a frail figure crouched on the front steps at Grey Street, dated 1954, in the Cross Papers.[68]

Back from Melbourne, one of the first things Miles did was to send John Kinmont Moir money to purchase a radiator for Kate Baker, who had mentioned in passing that she was cold in the mornings. Moir thought this quixotic, but obliged. Miles in turn thought Moir's work habits quite mad, and for fear of losing this new-found literary brother, another dedicated male cultural nationalist and an expert on Australiana, urged him to slow down. The letters between them now flowed thick and fast. Of the nearly 200 letters they exchanged between 1940 and 1954, over sixty were written in 1952, mostly on literary points, but also on literary politics, tense at the time.

An accountant by profession, Moir was up in arms about supposed Red dominance of the Commonwealth Literary Fund and its awards, not to mention its wasteful ways. Miles did her best to improve his mind, explaining that the purpose of the CLF awards was to advance Australian literature: 'It could flourish from an accountancy point of view and yet become a blimp bridle. The wild obnoxious fellows generally deliver the goods.' It was no good calling for a changeover of board members every two years, given the limited expertise available. 'If they could blackball every writer that was what *they* would class as subversive or sacrilegious you would soon have nothing to collect but Hansard.'[69]

Clem Christesen regretted having missed Miles in Melbourne. In May he invited her to write a satiric piece for *Meanjin* on the Jubilee literary awards. Miles declined on the ground that she was not the person to write it. Someone with a degree would be needed. Clem was puzzled. Miles seemed to him an ideal person to write about 'the Jubilee Sweep', as she called it. But unbeknownst to him, she was implicated. From what she told him, she had contributed nothing more than a radio script to the celebrations (the previously mentioned Rose Scott broadcast, read by an actress, to her indignation). However, the administrators of the awards could have been aware from the application forms that she had been an entrant. Christesen, who genuinely cherished her and thought she should have been made a Dame in the year of the Jubilee, could hardly be told that. He was an ally and in a bad way himself, having felt compelled to resign from the publishing firm Heinemann Australia, where he had been tarred with the Red brush and the prominent Catholic intellectual Paul Maguire was taking up all the space.[70]

These days Miles worried more than ever about her health. It seemed, she recorded on 16 April, that she was deteriorating rapidly. She was often tired during the day and too much typing or heavy shopping or steep stairs caused her limbs to seize up. A cardiogram in February had revealed no apparent irregularity, so presumably it was not arteriosclerosis that caused her to fall a couple of times in the house: 'must be nervous,' she concluded glumly, refusing to take pills for dizziness. She ceased taking her temperature daily, as she had been doing since the beginning of the year — but then bought a new thermometer in May; and colds came in the winter to alarm her. Somehow, she wrote to Ian Mudie, she never felt quite well after Perth, but it was no good 'hypochondriacking' about it.[71]

Jean Devanny urged her to come to sunny Queensland, but somehow she never got there. Perhaps she was wise to conserve her strength for another visit from Jean, which would eventuate in early 1953, and John Kinmont Moir's friend Everill Venman was already threatening to land on her. Since sleeplessness still plagued her, especially when she thought of her nephew John, the prospect of guests made her feel weak. By now Miles Franklin believed she had 'a bent heart', caused by a longstanding curvature of the spine 'which puts the heart in a bent position,' she explained to Les Woolacott.[72]

Friends kept watch, the Crosses in Caringbah especially. Arthur fixed the roof and taps, and Delys did some of the ironing. One day Miles came home to find a box of food on the verandah, thanks to Arthur, *chef de cuisine* (baking) at Sydney Technical College. Another day the lawns had been mowed. Joe Salter helped too, despite personal tragedy when his wife, Lorna, suffered a stillbirth (Miles noted grimly that her analysis of marriage had yet to be proved wrong). Allan Dalziel was usually too tired to do more than talk, but he kept her up to date with political events (even if his views on women seemed pre-1914).

The value of her neighbours' support can hardly be overestimated. Sometimes she went to shows in the city with them, to the Borovansky Ballet at the Empire Theatre with Mrs Bennett in April, for instance, and to hear Elena Nikolaidi sing at the Town Hall with May Smales, Mrs Fogden's daughter, in mid-June. When her neighbour Harry Andresen died suddenly, she recalled that he had stood by her when Norman died, and again when John was raving in the street. And when the Fogdens moved up-market to Castle Street, Blakehurst, in September, she wept.[73]

Family was still there too. Miles' cousin Ruby Brydon, who had been so helpful during Susannah Franklin's last days, sometimes helped again at Grey Street. Uncle Gus, now ninety, always set off a flurry when he arrived from Peak Hill to stay with her Lampe cousins. And Aunt Lena, though frail, was safe at her nursing home at Hunters Hill and in regular contact, as were the Bridle sisters and the Brindabella Franklins, though intermittently. Further away, at Tumut, relatives contributed material to the memoirs that became *Childhood at Brindabella*.[74]

'If I don't get what they call my second wind, I'm a goner,' Miles Franklin had written to Henrietta Drake-Brockman on 3 January 1952. She now needed it for her 'essay'. Sometimes the research was fun, as when John Kinmont Moir drew her attention to *The Pearlers*, a West Australian novel published in 1933 and allegedly burned on the beach at Broome by offended locals. It would be 'germane to my thesis', but when she asked

Henrietta Drake-Brockman about the incident, Henrietta replied evasively that maybe one copy had been burned, due to high spirits. (This led Miles to think Henrietta might have participated.) In the main, however, it was a struggle to finish, with the drudgery of checking references in the library and retyping text at home. At times Miles feared she had the wrong kind of mind for the job, and she dreaded making herself 'a fine target', as she confided to Ian Mudie. This was despite, or perhaps because of, her apparently modest aim: 'I attempt only to shew the struggle the novel here had to be itself and emerge and survive as a new Australian, as if it were a person, and choose only those books that illustrate that bias and promise, but one must know all around a subject to be trustworthy.'[75]

Despite the good opinion of those who had read chapters along the way (Moir, P. R. Stephensen, Delys Cross) and warm responses from J. K. Ewers ('grand, stimulating stuff') and Henrietta Drake-Brockman's husband, Geoff, when she sent the whole draft manuscript to them in July, it seemed there was always more to do. Katharine Susannah Prichard added her comments in August, mostly positive, as in 'pages and pages of brilliant writing', but had some critical observations too — to which Miles responded robustly. She was more anxious about being rendered superfluous by 'academic practitioners' than the comments of congenials. October 1952 found her still labouring 'like a wounded soldier' on her essay; by November it was 'the accursed essay', with still more to be done.[76]

Miles may no longer have been working as a fiction writer, as Marjorie Barnard believed had long been the case, but she was still writing a great deal, and well. Now it was criticism, history, memoir and the daily outpouring of diaries and letters. The recollection from her girlhood of lovely Dolly Wilson from her literary notebook, first published in 2004, is a vivid piece of writing; and despite sometimes feeling 'as dull as a doughnut', writing her memoir of childhood came easily. Arguably it is the best written of all her books. Moreover, *All That Swagger* was back in print, thanks to the recent British edition by George Allen & Unwin, and the Brent books were rolling off the presses in an orderly fashion.[77]

It was quite a feat to squeeze up to 150 words into the small space allocated for a day in her pocket diary. Miles didn't write that much every day, but it seemed that the diary entries got longer as she wrote less elsewhere. She was still tossing off letters, many of them quite long, with a personal to-and-from correspondence in the order of 400 items in 1952. Some are trivial or business letters, but her epistolary network, though shrinking, was still functioning well. She heard again from Madame Scheu-Riesz, recently returned to Vienna from New York, where she had fled the Anschluss in 1938. Mabel Singleton, now working in Surrey, kept in touch and in vigorous exchange. Miles told Florence James that 'no peace movement which has any connection with the communists can do anything except cause more friction'. In one of those earthy analogies that sprang to her mind so readily, she said the situation was like the old cartoon of two litigants, one pulling at the head of the cow, the other at the tail, and the lawyer milking the beast comfortably between, except that this time it was the 'R.C.s' milking the enmity of both sides. Nor did she lose the thread when 'a momentous letter' from Dymphna Cusack informed her of the existence of Norman Freehill, though she was undoubtedly hurt. Soon enough, as Dymphna probably feared, she also heard, from Glen Mills Fox, that Freehill's wife and son were living in poor circumstances in Sydney (but Miles wisely kept her own counsel on a complex situation).[78]

On 23 April 1952 when Lucy Cassidy, a founding member of the FAW, was honoured at the Nellie Stewart Club, Lucy herself invited Miles. The ceremony was presided over by Colin Roderick and attended by other stalwarts in the cause of Australian culture in Sydney: the Catholic archbishop and historian Eris O'Brien, the writer Dora Wilcox, the parliamentarian Dan Clyne and a lawyer, James Meagher (who made a speech, as did Miles). There were usually plenty of people to talk to at the Mitchell Library; for instance, on 27 June she saw the poet R. D. FitzGerald there, the historians George Mackaness and Malcolm Ellis, and Nancy Keesing too. And when Furphy's grandson, Victor Pallot, and his wife, Ivy, turned up on her doorstep to stay for five days in August, they took her on drives around Sydney, to Palm Beach, Katoomba, and as far as Goulburn, and it was 'back to desolation in the disorder of work' when they left.[79]

Though her excursions were not expensive, Miles was still worried about money. For income tax purposes, she claimed to have earned £165 in the financial year 1951–52 from her writings, a figure that more or less accords with royalties received from Angus & Robertson for the two Brent books in print plus occasional fees, but not rental income from the shops. The lot of a landlord was precarious, she wrote to J. K. Moir, with rising repair costs and, in her case, rentals pegged at prewar prices, so that she sometimes got nothing for six months. To be financially secure these days, she told Dymphna Cusack, you needed to write a radio serial for the ABC. But when Cusack later sent her a cheque for £5, stiff-necked Miles would not cash it, replying (with thanks): 'If money doesn't go phut altogether I shall have enough to bury me and eat for a year or two longer.' According to the Bridle sisters she was always lamenting a lack of money. But a lifetime of economic uncertainty had led to habitual anxiety about her finances.[80]

Perhaps her insecurity was social as well as financial. Had family fortunes not collapsed in times past, she might have occupied a more elevated social position. There had been some admired wealthy spinsters in Sydney, most notably the philanthropist Dame Eadith Walker, who had inherited a fortune from her merchant father. Miles' father, on the other hand, left her nothing. Indeed, he did not even leave a will. It was her mother's estate on which she relied. Her royalties were a top-up, and in some years small.[81]

Now reports of deaths came often, each reminding her of her own mortality. In February she heard that her most distinguished American correspondent, the New Dealer Harold Ickes, had died. And hearing of E. J. Brady's death, she reflected that only a few of her literary elders were left: Kate Baker, Bernard O'Dowd, Mollie Skinner, Mary Gilmore, Will Lawson, Bertha Lawson, Professor Murdoch. Hugh McCrae and Norman Lindsay also survived, but were more like Miles' peers.[82]

The gentle, rational Arnold Dresden wrote to her, 'There is no reason I can accept for a fear of death. There is nothing to be concerned about in the prospect of a sojourn in this world coming to an end.' Her fears were unseemly, still church-bound. Dresden, who was suffering from cancer of the tongue and would die in April 1954, was seemingly more distressed by his old friend's anxiety than his own situation.[83]

Arnold Dresden's diagnosis of a church-bound attitude misunderstood Miles' real position. The Franklins were scarcely more than nominal Anglicans, and as she said herself, she lacked 'a believing mind', attending church at most once a year in later life. She probably rejected Christian teachings quite early. An undated sketch in manuscript entitled 'Sequel' portrays a rebellious girl at 'the little church among the eucalyptus trees' who had to conform outwardly, but inwardly reflected on 'ghastly [anti-woman] teachings'.[84]

At least her fictional clergyman was sympathetic: he loved an honest doubter better than a lukewarm believer. Mostly Miles Franklin regarded the clergy as obstructions to religious understanding, if not simply hypocritical, which is hardly surprising when one recalls the Bishop of Goulburn's apparent role in bankrupting her father. The congenial Bishop Burgmann, an intellectual as well as a bushman, was an exception proving the rule, and latterly Archbishop Eris O'Brien. The best that could be said about the churches was the music. She had tried Christian Science, and paid some attention to spiritualism after World War I, but both had failed to satisfy.[85]

Miles seems never to have had a Christian belief in the life hereafter, nor even in 'the Beyond', or in any non-Christian teachings regarding the afterlife, such as reincarnation, though she sometimes regretted it was so. In maturity she had difficulty with the very idea of a soul, as in a fragment to an unidentified American friend, possibly Mrs Robins: 'I've come to the conclusion that our soul is not always with us. It can be chased away by lunacy ... or in abeyance due to fatigue.' Vida Goldstein said flatly that Miles Franklin had no spiritual convictions.[86]

Yet in a way Arnold Dresden was right. For instance, there is a surprising amount of incidental comment on religion in *My Brilliant Career*, though it is mostly hostile in the free-thinking 1890s manner. And in *Childhood at Brindabella* Miles reflects that 'it takes a greater mind to find God than to lose him'. Later, she almost invariably adopted an agnostic position. She did not entirely reject religion, nor did she accept it; and without it or some other understanding, she remained at a loss to comprehend the end of life. In that sense, something of the old church teachings lurked in her mind, as is often the case with non-believers in a Christian culture.[87]

Miles never said as much, but she may have been afraid of dying alone. With no children, siblings or even nieces and nephews near to hand, and some of her most reliable neighbours already gone, that was quite possible. She told Dymphna Cusack on 29 July that she had not heard from her nephew John in two years. The Queensland connection to Linda's family was long broken, possibly as early as Charlie Graham's second marriage, and although his son, Edward, had lived with his grandparents at Carlton for a time after World War I, spent his honeymoon there in 1932, and was acknowledged in Miles' will, it seems she never met him.[88]

Miles Franklin frequently expressed irritation at posthumous honours for writers. With the years slipping remorselessly by and the sense that she was failing physically, she yearned for recognition. But Brent of Bin Bin, not Miles Franklin, was now getting praise, most recently from Archbishop O'Brien, and the *Bulletin* when *Ten Creeks Run* appeared. In reflective mode, she wrote to David Martin that these days she preferred general ideas simply put: 'If only I could get rid of my complexities, my far-flung deviousness, which sweeps me away in cross-currents when one life is sufficient only to get out one idea one aim.'[89]

An enduring reputation — literary immortality — was even more uncertain. The fictional clergyman who appreciated honest doubt in the sketch 'Sequel' predicts the rebellious heroine will become a great thinker. Such an accolade, had it really been bestowed on the young Stella Franklin, would have been burdensome, just as the accolades piled upon the youthful author of *My Brilliant Career* were double-edged: on the one hand confirming an identity, on the other creating impossibly high expectations.

She no longer tried to hide her anxieties. It is striking just how much time even quite casual associates spent reassuring her that she was a good writer: Joe Salter for one, Les Woolacott for another. Woolacott, by that time a newspaper editor and part-time drama lecturer at Dubbo, recalled meeting Miles in King Street in the city in 1952 after a Book Society dinner in a very downcast mood 'because you were a failure, because you couldn't write, and a lot of other rot', and was pleased to hear that she had not stopped writing as she had threatened. (As might be guessed, she was wanting him to read one of her plays as well as put on some of Dymphna's.) In reply, Miles said that much of her literary struggle had been futile and that she had received very little help as a writer: 'I have never had any help except from Henry Lawson when I was a kid. I have done endless ghosting and revisions and readings and advising for love but never had a literary friend.'[90]

There was some truth in what she said. No one had any idea of the extent of her unpublished writings. She had done a lot of other unsung work; and for all her commitment, the FAW had not developed as she had hoped. On the other hand, such retrospections were hard on everyone, including herself, and on all those who had tried to help her, starting with her mother and those Sydney women in the early twentieth century like Rose Scott and Cara David, and especially on Alice Henry, a faithful critic to the end, and Mary Fullerton, who played a vital role during the interwar years, not to mention the friendship of Dymphna Cusack since. Katharine Susannah Prichard, who regretted that she had been unable to do more to boost her friend's confidence, would have been mortified. Younger people such as Eleanor Witcombe and the Australian novelist Dal Stivens in London did their best to be supportive. Stivens wrote an article for the magazine *John O' London's Weekly* in October, as 'a small tribute from one of the many people Miles has helped by her writing ... and her being what she is'.[91]

What she had really needed was professional help, but in her youth it was not available in Sydney except to the young men nourished by George

Robertson, or under unusual circumstances, as in London in 1901, when several people had had a hand in the final editing of *My Brilliant Career*. Unfortunately, as Beatrice Davis would ruefully assert, Miles never could see the importance of style. Alternatively, she could not reconcile herself to being unable to write a bestseller, and envied those who could. In the end she was her own best diagnostician: 'I totally lack self-confidence, but do not give way to self-pity.'[92]

That was the way of the old Australia, where to feel sorry for oneself was a secular sin. In Perth in 1950, Miles had told the *Australian Women's Weekly* she lived alone at Carlton, cooking and gardening and writing. That may have been a bland formulation, but it indicated her determination not to give way to doubt and melancholy. Gardening became her strength and solace. As she recalled in an early chapter of *Childhood at Brindabella*, it was in her blood: 'I was born into a tribe of inveterate gardeners.' The details of her mother's first garden came back to her, as did Grandfather Franklin's eccentricities as a vegetable grower, and her father's passion for gardening in his last years at Carlton. Of her earliest childhood triumph, the raising of an enormous red tulip, she wrote, 'To see the first leaves of plants or seedlings break from the earth is an entrancement that never stales', and as spring came once more in 1952, she noted with satisfaction that her Madagascar beans were coming up nicely, and that she had planted more sunflower seeds.

Ric Throssell had recently returned from his diplomatic posting in Rio de Janeiro. One night he and Miles went to the Independent Theatre to see Warwick Fairfax's latest play: a dreary thing, she wrote to Ric's mother, Katharine Susannah, which made her glad she had two legs so she could cross them one by one. Another evening, she went to the local cinema to see *A Streetcar Named Desire* starring Vivien Leigh, who was very good, she thought, but all that naked lust and brutality was loathsome. Hearing Kylie Tennant's prize-winning Jubilee play read at the FAW one night did nothing for her, nor did a Fellowship party for a young Australian literature lecturer from Adelaide, Brian Elliott; but she religiously attended the year's CLF lectures at the University of Sydney, worthily delivered by Vance Palmer, but 'lifeless'.[93]

It was increasingly difficult to follow where some of her fellow writers were going. Rex Ingamells was always a great puzzle, with his massive works. Though sympathetic, she did not know how to respond when his poem *The Great South Land* won two prizes; now his prose work *Of Us Now Living* was imminent. Modern Australia as it appeared in novels — *The*

Harp in the South, *Come in Spinner* and *The Sundowners* — was 'all *after* American models', she said. The writers might be 'right artistically', but Australia was becoming 'a poor ersatz USA'. And she was discomfited by the way facts were presented. Jon Cleary referred to 'dark-eyed sheep' in *The Sundowners*: 'The merinos are Nordics,' she snorted. A later reference by Erle Wilson to swimming wombats almost floored her (the hairy-nosed wombat, still to be seen in abundance along the river banks at Brindabella, being a burrower). But Gwen Meredith's radio serial *Blue Hills*, which had premiered in 1949, was a great success — 'I do everything I can to be near a radio at 1 p.m. every day' — and she found she could not get served at the grocer's until the other women had discussed the latest episode. Did Nettie Palmer know the writer, she wondered. After a few months, however, she had gained a better perspective, or at least distanced herself: 'Not enough in it for me,' she wrote to a West Australian correspondent, mentioning in passing her pleasure in jam-making, a skill she shared with Dame Mary Gilmore.[94]

The crisis of World War II focused attention on Australian culture and the urge for consolidation remained strong afterwards. The cultural output of the 1950s, from essayist A. A. Phillips' critique of 'the cultural cringe' to Russel Ward's *Australian Legend*, shows how strong it really was. In this respect, Miles' own preoccupation with literary and other forms of Australian history was as much a product of the times as of her stage in life. But in literary politics, fierce contestations and obscurantism continued, and writers on the Left found themselves under siege. When Billy Wentworth went too far in his Red-baiting by referring in the *Sydney Morning Herald* to Katharine Susannah Prichard as 'alias Mrs Thorsell' (a mis-spelling of her married name), thereby implying she lied about her marital status, Katharine sued him for £10,000 through her solicitor, fellow communist Christian Jollie Smith. Miles responded in a forthright manner:

> Dal says that Ric should confront Wentworth on the steps of Parliament in Canberra and punch his jaw … I wish Ric would wait till he sees W coming up the steps and then walk down and soundly smack his face. It makes such a nice sound as I know, through having smacked the faces of tormentors in my day and it doesn't hurt but is much more humiliating than a crack on the jaw. If I had as magnificent an excuse as Ric's I'd enjoy going smack on W's cheek.[95]

Wentworth's unremitting attentions to the CLF — in October 1952 Kylie Tennant gave her award back in protest when he said she would use it for communist purposes — and news of Dymphna Cusack's struggles with European publishers were grist to the mill. Miles was delighted with Dymphna's successes, which seemed to compensate for her own failures and limitations in years gone by: 'I rejoice in your courage ... Every word you tell me is a repetition of what I underwent, but I had no confidence in myself and was defeated.' In similar vein, she encouraged Dymphna to ignore those who said she should come home. Rather, she should make the most of happy days, because 'you can never approximate them back here. I know, I've been through it.' All the gossip was relayed to Dymphna, and to a lesser but still substantial extent, to Florence James, now living in north London, near where Miles had once visited her friends the Maynards.[96]

An invitation in October from her local member of parliament, Clive Evatt, to open the Louisa Lawson flats at Bondi was resisted, and an evening at History House on Macquarie Street proved lamentably dull; but Miles went to Sydney University for the annual Eng. Ass. dinner in November, along with Beatrice Davis, back from Europe. The Douglas Stewarts were also there, and the latest Fulbright scholar, Mentor Williams, like his predecessor Bruce Sutherland an enthusiast for Australian literature and a wonderful source of gossip about the English Department at the university. Miles was not a speaker. That honour went to Florence Earle Hooper, a retired headmistress whom Miles had first met at Rose Scott's many years ago.[97]

To some of the younger generation of writers Miles was now an oddity, almost a museum piece. At an FAW meeting in January 1952, the rising young writer Ray Mathew saw her as 'an amusing figure, a kind of combination of Mrs Pankhurst and Mary Poppins'; but she surprised him by greeting him with enthusiasm for making mud-pies of Australia, a reference to his poem 'Australian-Made', the second stanza of which begins: 'This is my land, I made/Mud-pies of it ...' Later in the year, with other Lyre-Bird folk, Mathew enjoyed a supper at Carlton: 'Miles Franklin's house looks ordinary enough from outside on a dark night but when the door opened and the dear head poked around the corner it was most extraordinary.' The house was neat and tidy (except the bookcases); the conversation was anything but, with Miles telling tales of theatre in New York and expressing her literary likes and dislikes freely, while the waratah cup and waratah book did the rounds.[98]

The 'amusing figure' had become the 'dear head'. When they first met, Mathew had already read *My Career Goes Bung*, but it was not until the end of the year that he read *My Brilliant Career*, and he wrote immediately saying how much it had delighted him — it was so honest and true to Australia. He too had been teaching down among the M'Swats. 'I think *M. B. C.* is your saddest book that I know and your happiest; *Career Goes Bung* funniest and most educationalest; *All that Swagger* your bravest.' Keep writing, he urged her, and bring out those plays. Miles was pleased to hear from him, and in reply expressed the hope that after fifty years he would not find, as she had, a total inadequacy of talents — but then it was a different age, with a different memory, and he was 'a different kind of bird'. 'Write to me when you feel like it and come and see me if you want to,' she concluded.[99]

Then aged just twenty-three, Mathew was a talented and under-appreciated poet and playwright who left Australia for good in 1961, dying in New York in 2002. According to Myfanwy Horne, a friend from student days, he was 'Australian-made' to the last. In 1963 he published a significant monograph on Miles Franklin in the series Australian Writers and their Work. Although short and limited to then published sources, it was the first literary assessment of the whole of Brent's *oeuvre* — Angus & Robertson published the last volumes in 1956 — and it also took Miles Franklin seriously as a woman.[100]

Mathew began by acknowledging that Miles Franklin's literary reputation was fragile and might not last without her vivid personality to reinforce it. In his opinion, nothing from a literary point of view happened in her life after the traumas associated with the reception of *My Brilliant Career* in 1901. Thereafter, he proposed, came despair and incomprehension at a changing world, until the Brent persona set her free and enabled her to write honestly again. Mathew argued that although *Cockatoos* was the only one of the Brent books likely to survive in its own right — 'irrefutable in its own backyard' — the series was her masterpiece, likely to live on in the 'archives of imagination'. A strong but provisional conclusion could then be drawn, as follows: 'On that possibility, on the probability that *My Career Goes Bung* will live as a minor classic and on the certainty that *My Brilliant Career* is a classic (important in our literature, good in any), the case for Miles Franklin ... could confidently rest.'[101]

Mathew's generous conclusion was largely adopted by literary history, but his approach to the Brent series has been less easily accepted. Discussing the published volumes in chronological order, Mathew defended Miles' method of 'possuming' and 'yarning', and pointed to an underlying acceptance of life, albeit variably maintained, coming full circle as it were. Even *Prelude to Waking* is given its psychological due as an awakening, a re-enchantment of the world.

That would have endeared the study to its subject. Mathew's treatment of Miles Franklin as a woman is refreshing, but more problematic. Dealing headlong with Miles' reticence about sex, he postulated an underlying 'sexual confusion' or uncertainty in the plot of *Prelude to Waking*. 'This sexual confusion,' he argued, 'may either irritate or amuse the reader, but it does force the author into extraordinary studies of women desiring but incapable of consummation which are subtle and unique in Australian writing.' Mathew elaborates by analysing women characters in subsequent volumes, such as Milly and Bernice Gaylord, and in this way addresses a difficult and sensitive subject in an appropriately literary manner.[102]

That her reputation might come to rest not on her life or her work but on her approach to sexuality, a subject rarely mentioned directly in her books, would probably have appalled her. Miles' attitude to Freudianism has been outlined earlier, likewise her attempts at a literary defence of chastity and virginity; and her views on the sexualisation of literature and society and the need for self-restraint in an over-populating world have been quoted too.

Mathew was no crass Freudian, and he was right about a confused situation. But it was not as he thought. Mathew recognised a conflicted personality and pinpointed a basic issue, but he thought the problem was 'puritanism', about which she had spoken to the FAW Young Writers' group in 1947. In its mildest dictionary definition, puritanism means strictness in matters of personal conduct, and, at its fiercest, excessive strictness. After psychological approaches came into vogue, the word took on something of a dismissive connotation as well, as in the adjective 'puritanical'. By the mid-twentieth century, puritanism usually meant the unwholesome repression of the sexual self.[103]

That was not how Miles Franklin saw things. No more than Ray Mathew could she assemble the whole picture, supposing she had cared to; but she did leave some clues. Although recent scholarship has concentrated on Miles' many close friendships with women, she came to think she was more at ease in the company of men. At the end of a long discussion of her anti-war play, 'The Dead Must Not Return', with David Martin, dated 3 February 1952, she remarked: 'Somehow I am more intimate with men. Men were plentiful, women a rarity in my youngest years and perhaps being a woman I was not so curious about them, thought I knew them.'[104]

This may come as a surprise. Looking back, however, the names of many men friends spring to mind, not so much from her flirtatious youth, when there were plenty of suitors but records are thin, but rather in maturity: men such as Arnold Dresden, first known in Chicago; P. S. Watson, who gave her Christian Science 'treatments' in Boston; P. R. Stephensen in London with his plans for a literary homecoming; that other wild man of the 1930s, Frank Clune; Ian Mudie, who made the 1940s sing for her; David Martin, her pet hope in more recent years for an immigrant voice in Australian literature; J. K. Moir, Melbourne bookman extraordinaire; the kindly Joe Salter; and Uncle Gus Lampe, who outlived his first niece by five years. Such friendships probably protected her from the worst of the denigration experienced by single women of a certain age in Australia in the first half of the twentieth century, and in one sense she was ahead of her times. In another, she had been trapped by them.

The fact that Miles Franklin remained single did not make her as unusual then as it would later. The proportion of older unmarried people in the population is now negligible (although marriage patterns have changed and marital status is differently regarded). We now have a poor understanding of a world in which a significant proportion of the population never married. According to census figures for 1921, almost 20 per cent of adults aged forty-five to forty-nine had never married; that is to say, one in five of older people. Many of them probably also had no sexual experience.[105]

Theoretically, Miles should not have become one of them. In rural New South Wales there were three males for every two females of marriageable age in 1891, and nearly as many twenty years later. (The ratio was 158:100 in 1891, as compared with 139:100 in 1911.) Considering that fewer than 5 per cent of country women reached their forties unmarried in 1891, and that Miles Franklin reached the median age of marriage in New South Wales (then about twenty-three for women) in 1902, she would seem to have been set to marry easily.[106]

Statistics for slightly different dates tell another story, however. The years between 1893 and 1903 saw a sharp downturn in marriage rates, and the proportion of women reaching thirty while still unmarried in the 1890s rose from 29.4 to 40.3 per cent, a figure that remained stable for another decade or so. The difficulty was that prolonged economic depression and then severe drought created unfavourable circumstances for men to marry.

Basically, those women who were unable to find partners in the 1890s never regained their place in the marriage market.[107]

There was even more to it socio-sexually. Some young women decided not to marry, or not then. Instead, they left for the city; and many stayed there. Again, statistics tell the story, or some of it: by the 1890s the proportion of older unmarried women in Sydney was double that in country areas. As Graeme Davison has shown, following up Miles' own analysis in *Cockatoos*, this was the generation of 'the exodists', female as well as male, when young people left the land in search of economic opportunity. Otherwise, for women marriage was the main option. Indeed, as Miles had so often complained, it was little short of compulsory in the country. Yet marriage in the old Australia was no protection against impoverishment and could mean excessive childbearing, as Susannah Franklin's experience showed, while sex outside marriage was scarcely thinkable in that there was no reliable contraception, while the dangers of venereal disease, not to mention ostracism for being 'fast', were significant. To make matters harder still for country girls, should they 'fall', abortion was illegal, largely unavailable and extremely dangerous, yet the alternatives of unmarried motherhood or adoption were unnerving too. The lesbian option was simply unimaginable, as evidenced by the controversy surrounding 'inversion' in *The Well of Loneliness* and its banning in 1928, and Miles' attitude to any suggestion of it was dismissive, for instance, in the life of Emily Dickinson. In short, the options facing young women in the 1890s were few and harsh. Hence, what might be called 'Miles' choice', except that others must have made it too: to avoid the whole thing.[108]

Hera Cook's important recent study of the subject in England, *The Long Sexual Revolution*, illuminates 'Miles' choice'. Cook argues convincingly that it was not contraceptives, as is usually thought, but the codes of self-restraint and sexual abstinence created by English women for their own protection in the mid to late nineteenth century that brought fertility under control, and that those woman-enforced codes persisted until the 1940s, by which time it was easier to separate sexual pleasure and family planning (and to recognise dysfunctional consequences over time, such as a surprisingly high rate of unconsummated marriages). Things were probably freer, but not necessarily better, in Australia; except during the 1890s Australian women still had more children than English women and they experienced a higher rate of maternal mortality. But probably just as many preferred the culture of restraint and abstinence pioneered by their English sisters.[109]

The implications for understanding the life history of Miles Franklin are clear enough. The period of restraint and abstinence spanned her life almost exactly, and the sexual confusion Ray Mathew refers to, relating to the separation of sex and reproduction, occurred only towards the end of it. This historical perspective has yet to make its way into the common stock of knowledge, and will undoubtedly be carefully reviewed as it does. That doesn't matter greatly for an understanding of Miles' late dilemmas: for her, in the long run, it became a no-win situation. As the historical circumstances that shaped her life choices slowly disappeared — Cook argues the sexual revolution in England was not over until the mid-1970s, when the fertility control now taken for granted was finally secured — so the codes in which Miles was reared and by which she lived came to seem unintelligible, except in the moralistic terms implied by 'puritanism'. That is, as a young woman she made rational choices, based on socio-sexual realities, then she was trapped, not just in personal terms, but worse, in terms of her literary reputation.

It is in this context Miles' friendships with men should be evaluated. These too are taken for granted today. But they were unusual until very recently, and required some skill and sensitivity to maintain, even as an older woman. They were the best she could do in a world where male sexuality and power were still overwhelming. The man she came closest to marrying, Demarest Lloyd, was divorced not once but twice, the second time in 1937, the year of his death, for cruelty, possibly of the kind portrayed in Miles' shocking story of entrapment and attempted rape, 'Red Cross Nurse', written in 1914. In her code, divorce implied serious doubt as to a man's moral and physical suitability as a husband, far from the simple personal incompatibility accepted today.[110]

Mathew's was also a young man's understanding. By her sixties, Miles had lost her once urgent interest in sex. As she said to Jean Devanny in 1954, now that sex had come to stay, it was time to give it a rest. By then she had read Kinsey's *Sexual Behavior in the Human Male* and found elements of the behaviourist approach 'utterly revolting'. In late 1952 she was far more interested in a new round of war novels, especially Hungerford's *The Ridge and the River*, and coping once more with Christmas.[111]

It was time to get Christmas cakes off to Mabel Singleton, Miss Hodgson and her cousin Theo in Germany. Despite a bad summer cold, Miles struggled through the usual December round, with the neighbours passing her hot food, the customary Christmas lunch with Aunt Lena and cousin

Ruby, and afternoon tea with her Lampe cousins. An effort to locate John Franklin beforehand came to nothing; and preparing a lavish lunch at Carlton on 30 December in honour of Lena's eighty-fifth birthday wore her out. Her last pocket diary entry for the year reads: 'Never heard a sound at midnight as 1952 disappeared.'[112]

In the new year another parcel of clothes arrived from Margery Currey in New York. With Margery, Miles was always capable of a light-hearted response to the world, noting that its current 'disturbed ant-bed state' was baffling, except that the United States now ran things, which, she quipped, left women's fashion for France and the British with a coronation coming up. Mostly she was more sombre. Musing on the 'unforgivable' Korean War, then in its third year, Miles told Mabel Singleton that men had made a terrible mess of the world with their belligerence and lust. It was the fourth major war in her lifetime. Huge bombs were being tested in Nevada and in the Australian desert regardless of the presence of Aboriginal people, and the peace movement, in Miles' view, was negated by male and communist dominance.[113]

There were some signs, however, that she was coming to a greater equanimity. Now into her seventies, she more frequently had recourse to her wry, conditional stance which began to appear in her letters in the late 1940s: 'If I live'. Others were rebuked for fatalism. Jean Campbell was told not to give in until she was 'laid out with a wet fish', and when Katharine Susannah Prichard came to stay she rather depressed Miles, not only with her rigid views but also for asserting that her work was done and she wished to die: 'Of course we have to die, but I believe in resisting it to the last breath,' Miles wrote in her pocket diary. David Martin, who did not meet her until 1949, put it this way: 'Miles was a complex person, of great courage, but courage may take all kinds of forms.'[114]

'Hold on to your essential self, swing to your inner pole of integrity in what you have to tell the world,' Miles wrote to Tom Ronan on 13 February 1953. Many people have found Miles Franklin's 'essential self' elusive. P. R. Stephensen said she was as paradoxical as a platypus. But she believed in her essential self, and perhaps it can be glimpsed in these final, driven years, when she struggled to distil her most basic experiences, of childhood and novel writing, and felt an urge to complete other old manuscripts, 'as a matter of character'. She didn't expect to last anywhere near as well as her parents, who both lived into their eighties; but she had no crystal ball, and in these now poignant years, she carried on as usual, extracting what pleasure and amusement she could, all the while struggling to finish her work: 'My book is coming along if I live and can keep plugging,' she wrote to J. K. Moir in October 1953.[115]

By then that book — 'my essay' — had suffered some setbacks. Pixie O'Harris had sent several chapters along with the memoir to Frank Eyre at Oxford University Press in February 1953, and a week or so later Miles began what she hoped would be a final assault on the text. Encouraged by Eyre's positive response, on 20 April she sent the entire typescript, with a covering note advising that it was obviously an illiterate toot from the bush on a bullock horn, 'but my earnest testimony'. Later she asserted it would be 'a salutary toot'.[116]

But to suggest she wanted to dispose of the essay soon, so as to get along with a major work on rabbits, long projected, was probably a mistake, even if it was just a joke. Eyre's reply was very long, and Miles asked Pixie to open it. Unfortunately Oxford would not be able to publish the essay as it stood. It had meat, Eyre wrote, but too few bones, too many verbal pyrotechnics and too little of concentrated effort for it to stand as a coherent critical work. Miles never did take criticism well, but she soon put as good a face on this 'onslaught' as possible, merely asking for the manuscript's return: 'I did not close any doors.' She began to revise, advising Eyre in October that she would resubmit it.[117]

Meanwhile, the good opinion of friends and associates kept her going. Rex Ingamells in Melbourne, to whom she first suggested the title 'Laughter, Not for a Cage', was enlisted to help in mid-1953. Ingamells approached C. E. S. Hall, a Prahran bookseller who had a publishing sideline, called Hallcraft; and in early September Miles received a positive response from him. Hall thought these 'Notes on Australian Writing' a very worthy manuscript, and offered to proceed straight to galleys; but there was no contract. That wasn't good enough for Miles, for whom the essay was, as she said, 'a very serious matter', and there would be too many changes needed if they went straight to galleys and she still had things to check. Her response on 12 September was again to ask for the manuscript to be returned.[118]

Two days later she wrote to Florence James and Dymphna Cusack for advice, and in hope of placement with Constable. (Florence was now a talent scout for the London publisher.) This took both of them by surprise, especially Cusack in the south of France, who vaguely recalled hearing about an article, but never a book. ('Her passion for secrecy is a real disease,' she wrote to James.) Of course they both responded positively. James replied that she would be delighted to read the work, and Cusack that she was tremendously impressed by her friend's 'sheer dogged tenacity', and they would both do all they could to help when she was ready to send it.[119]

Miles was often fatigued these days, and her health was now variable. Sleep continually evaded her. Sometimes she took a sleeping draught, even a sip of brandy. The winter of 1953 brought severe coughs and unidentifiable pains around the heart, so that she longed for summer. Writing is not a particularly healthy lifestyle at the best of times, much less in the creaky years: 'constant work at our age is not only terrifically wearying but so deadening. One cries out for relief,' she wrote to Mabel Singleton on 29 October.[120]

Friends urged her to visit them in exotic places instead of crouching in Carlton. Tom Ronan would have loved her to come up to Katherine; Jean Devanny was forever urging her to leave 'that cold and melancholy house' for Townsville; and Myrtle Rose White wrote from her son's property 'Lalla Rookh', near Port Hedland in Western Australia, inviting her there and later to her home in Adelaide. Twenty years before, any one of these invitations would have been an adventure, but now that she was aged seventy-four, in unreliable health, and with those 'plaguey mss.' hanging over her, such intrepidity was unthinkable.[121]

At Carlton she kept up the ordained level of hospitality. When an unnamed woman on an overnight stay announced she always left 2 shillings on the windowsill to pay for her ablutions, Miles rebuked her for her crassness: Miles' hospitality was freely given. No such irritations arose when Jean Devanny and Katharine Susannah Prichard came to stay. It was a treat, although Katharine sometimes depressed her, and Jean could be a trial, especially later when advising her about her autobiography would take up a great deal of Miles' time. She and Jean went once more to the Easter Show, a thoroughly enjoyable excursion, during which Jean attacked the Angus & Robertson stallholder for stocking only Ion Idriess and E. V. Timms among Australian writers. When Dymphna's barmaid, 'Caddie', later came to Carlton for lunch, she turned out to be a conventional soul and rather too demanding, but Miles was kind and helpful, and they met on several occasions thereafter, with Miles gently fending off approaches for further literary help.[122]

Nice as staying guests could be, they consumed precious time and limited energies. John McKellar arrived yet again in September, and as Miles said to Henrietta Drake-Brockman, 'What is one to do?' Apart from Katharine Susannah Prichard ('it would break my heart to miss *her*'), her favourite visitors seemed to be the regular callers. Allan Dalziel often brought with him the radical bookseller Colonel Alex Sheppard (who served in Greece during World War II and afterwards with the United Nations in Salonika) for insider political gossip, of which there was plenty, what with a new governor-general, Sir William Slim ('an old war cock', Miles said), General Eisenhower's regrettable rise in America, and the tinsel of the coronation in London. She probably went with Dalziel and Sheppard, when on 29 July she attended a debate on the atomic bomb at nearby Kogarah and Dr Evatt conveyed greetings to her from Hartley Grattan.[123]

Without the support of the Crosses, Miles could hardly have managed so well or so long alone. Delys Cross worried about her, and with cause: Miles was an 'aggravating sprite', and as Delys said, it was not realistic to be so independent. On 24 September 1953 a neighbour, Mrs Coates at number 24, died unexpectedly, 'a terrible blow': 'As I expect to be dead here alone I said it wd depend on the neighbour who first found me to let my cousin know, and I wanted her [Mrs Coates] to promise that if it were she that no one must be allowed in to see me, and she promised. Also she had the telephone and said always if I cd crawl to it I had only to hail her and she wd be in.'[124]

Despite such anxieties, Miles was determined to stay put, and there was nothing others could do but help. Fortunately, the Crosses regularly delivered small feasts, which saved shopping and on bills as well. 'My share [of the week's leftovers],' she told Mabel Singleton on 29 October 1953, 'is six eggs, a bream fish, some fowl fried in batter, 2 loaves of smoking hot bread, a cinnamon loaf, a tumbler of lemon butter, a big apple Dutch tart, short-bread biscuits, and you should see the dozen jam puff tarts and tomorrow they are coming with a chook and salad. Sometimes it is soups and stews as well as bread and Madeira cake and jam rolls.'[125]

She was fortunate too in the support of a nurse living on the North Shore, Florence Neely Knox, whose name was cited on the parents' petition for a school in Thornford in 1890. Florrie had been a constant at Carlton for many years, and contact with others from Thornford days was sustaining. Berta Donald of Goulburn, who now ran a business college at Hornsby, sent Miles photos of old Collector, and reported that she kept in touch with Lizzie Gunter, that is, Miss Gillespie's friend, Miss Kellett, of Run-o'-Waters school, who was still alive and 'particularly precious to me', responded Miles.[126]

One day a great box of lilacs arrived at Grey Street, sent by Rene Laws, a friend of Dymphna Cusack in Goulburn, who had invited Miles to address the local historical society (but Miles would not). The lilac is Goulburn's flower, and the gesture stimulated some vivid memories: of causing a sensation dashing down Auburn Street on her charger; of how she had donated an old man saltbush to Belmore Park, where she sat to read her mail before singing lessons; and most notably, of the music in Goulburn's two cathedrals and Miss de Lauret, who donated the superb organ in the Catholic cathedral and was to young Miles the epitome of cultured womanhood.[127]

Other youthful associations were noted in diaries and letters throughout the year. When her god-daughter Amy Somerville (then McCutchan) and her mother, Annie, nearly ninety, took Miles on a drive to Penrith in January 1953, they lunched on the banks of the Hawkesbury and visited all the old spots, including the church where Linda had been married. Miles wondered if Charlie Graham was still alive, which suggests that she never saw him again after his visit to Carlton in 1936. But when she heard that her impassioned suitor of 1905–07, Edwin Bridle, had died, also in Queensland, the relevant diary note (of 18 June 1953) gives no inkling of her feelings.[128]

In October 1953 Miles was taken aback to learn that Phoebe Wesche (previously Twynam), with whom she had stayed when she first visited Sydney, had died three years earlier. Likewise, although Miles had thought her frail when last in Melbourne, it was a shock to hear that Elsie Belle Champion, a friend for nearly fifty years, was dead. The Goldstein family had always treated Miles as one of them, and now only Aileen was left. The death of Louis Esson's widow, Dr Hilda Bull, in a road accident in mid-1953 occasioned the important reflection to Katharine Susannah, a schoolfriend of Hilda, that Miles had not been blessed with such a friend until her mature years.[129]

Kate Baker's death in October 1953, aged ninety-two, caused Miles to reflect that apart from herself and Norman Lindsay, there were now only a few people in Perth left who had known Joseph Furphy. When in August 1953 John Kinmont Moir asked her to identify signatures in Catherine Helen Spence's birthday book, a rare and precious item that had somehow come his way, she was pleased to find she recognised many of them: from her American years there were the Lloyds and Charlotte Perkins Gilman, and some British names as well, such as the founding settlement worker Dame Henrietta Barnett, whom Miles had met at Hull-House. There, too, was the librarian Margaret Windeyer, recalled as having taken Miles to meet

Rose Scott for the first time, and Ada Kidgell, the maiden signature of Ada Holman, wife of the New South Wales Premier who had helped Miles in London.[130]

From time to time she would 'give up a day to letters' to distant congenials. Many nearer home benefited also; for example, Matron Prichard from Macedonian days, now retired. Likewise, 'a busy day on the phone' was confirmation of connectedness with the local literary scene. Although she now kept a low profile in the FAW, Miles accepted a coronation medal in June 1953 and she was pleased to make a little speech at Dame Mary Gilmore's eighty-eighth birthday in August. Age brings its rapprochements, apparently (though not with younger rivals, as per a diary entry noting having seen Marjorie Barnard in the Mitchell Library looking old and fat).[131]

It takes a certain kind of courage to stay the course with a project like the 'essay' at Miles' time of life. Sometimes she called it 'fortitude'. Occasionally she had recourse to 'character'. However, if any one quality comes through strongly at this time, it is surely perseverance, the moral value Charles Blyth stressed in the schoolroom at Brindabella long ago. Today it would probably be called self-discipline. 'To finish the ms. is *all* at present,' Miles wrote to Rex Ingamells on 9 September 1953.[132]

Favourable reviews of *Ten Creeks Run* had appeared at the beginning of the year, with 'D. S.' (Douglas Stewart) in the *Bulletin* concluding, despite reservations, that it was a beautiful but muddled classic. 'D. E.' (John Edward Webb) of the *Sydney Morning Herald* was more or less in agreement: '*Ten Creeks Run* … has plenty of faults, but it improves as it progresses, till, at the end, the reader is left with sharp memories of real and virile people, spirited horses, and some of the loveliest scenery in Australia.' Soon after, Miles had 'a field day' re-reading the manuscript of *Cockatoos*, and Beatrice Davis approved it for publication conditional on some reworking.[133]

With *Back to Bool Bool* and *Gentlemen at Gyang Gyang* still in the print queue, she could not yet admit to being Brent. Once there had been economic grounds for a separate identity. Now Miles hoped for proper recognition for Brent and vindication of her own early promise. Scarcely anyone now doubted her authorship. In his review of *Ten Creeks Run*, 'D. S.' simply said that in the absence of a denial from Miss Franklin, it was a reasonable assumption that she and Brent were one. But she needed all six volumes in print, and she still believed, maybe correctly, that the mystery ensured publishers' attention and kept up sales. Certainly Angus &

Robertson scrupulously adhered to her wishes, as had Blackwood before and maintained sales as well, with author royalties from the three Brent books on sale amounting to almost £42 in 1953, mainly from the latest volume, *Ten Creeks Run* (almost £27). *Prelude to Waking* was still selling fifty-five copies in 1953, resulting in three guineas, and *Up the Country* rather more (186 copies earned her over £11). It was a bonus when Angus & Robertson forwarded £32 in royalties to Miss Miles Franklin from George Allen & Unwin (UK) for the English edition of *All That Swagger* and she earned five guineas for its serialisation on rural radio.[134]

Still she had no success with her plays. A number of people, including the theatre producer John Casson, had read 'The Dead Must Not Return' and 'Models for Molly' in 1953, to no avail. Everyone did their best to think of ways forward, Henrietta Drake-Brockman even suggesting abridgment as radio plays, but they remain in manuscript to this day. Miles herself attributed her lack of success to 'a plague of Shakespeare' — this was the new Elizabethan era, with all the old hams and shysters back, she wrote to Dymphna Cusack. Yet her enthusiasm for theatre remained, extending as far as attending a talk on religious drama because it showed signs of taking a nationalist turn. Early in the new year at the New Theatre she saw and enjoyed the folk musical *Reedy River*.[135]

She could usually (though not always) get a letter published in the *Sydney Morning Herald*, however. On 11 July 1953, in a review headed 'The Great Australian Novel', Sidney J. Baker had the temerity to dismiss both Miles Franklin and Brent of Bin Bin with 'Lord help us'. To this Miles retorted via the *Herald*'s letters page:

> Australian novels are so poor that Mr Sidney J. Baker calls on the Lord's help in contemplating them … The depressing factor in Mr Baker's opinion is not that it is probably true, but that, being in the same provincial category as the novels, it [Baker's opinion] is of no consequence beyond Sydney or Melbourne, certainly not as far afield as Brisbane or Adelaide.[136]

She was still in demand as a speaker. One enthusiast felt she should always give the vote of thanks at the annual English Association dinner, though she had been satirising the event since 1940; but Dorothea Mackellar's friend Ruth Bedford, John Douglas Pringle (the newly arrived editor of the *Herald*), Douglas Stewart and Justice Charles McLelland did the honours in 1953. That night Miles sat between the poet Kenneth Slessor, whom she found rather stodgy, and Angus & Robertson's George Ferguson. Not that it mattered, as such outings helped keep her buoyant. She was, after all, Sydney's literary lady of tonnage, as R. G. Howarth recalled of another gathering held about this time where both Miles and Nettie Palmer were present, which made a 'historic spectacle of two reigning queens of literature'.[137]

A month or so earlier, on 13 October, at the instigation of her young relative Jennifer Moulden (now Lane), Miles had addressed some 300 students and staff of Balmain Teachers College on Australian literature. They all had a great time, 'even me' she recorded, her theme being that bushmen, not professors, wrote the classic Australian ballads. As Jenn Lane recalls, she established excellent rapport with the students, speaking slowly and with assurance in her deep melodious voice, and letting slip the occasional sly smile, just as Henrietta Drake-Brockman had observed in Perth in 1950.[138]

Miles also spoke at an end-of-year party at Dr Booth's domestic science college in early December, though there were only six graduates to celebrate and Dr Booth was just able to walk with two sticks. As so often now, the memories came flooding back: the boarding house in Kirribilli where she had worked as a domestic servant in 1903 was near. 'It made me unbelievably sad — there at "Elsiemere" & just around the corner at "Keston". I was unbelievably high-spirited 50 years ago,' she reflected. As a further sign of longevity, she started to find herself in other people's memoirs, an early instance being Rose Lindsay's mention in the *Bulletin* of Miles' visit to Springwood in 1932.[139]

Still she had to finalise her 'essay'. She had told Frank Eyre in October that she would revise and resubmit it; she also began preparing the text to send to Constable in London. By the end of the year she was satisfied with the text — it had taken seven revisions, she told Jean Devanny by way of encouraging her to do likewise with her autobiography — and on 16 December she sent it to London, evidently by airmail, as she wrote to Florence James advising her that it would be with her any day. The covering letter included a plea for sympathy, which may or may not have been tactful: 'You must remember that I've been chained up here for 20 years without any exchange with my congenials except in short flashes ... You can read it as letters from home.'[140]

For Christmas 1953, Arthur Cross made Miles the most amazing cake, four pounds in weight and decorated with Aboriginal motifs, among them a crocodile, a snake and a boomerang, with her name on it. There was little joy for her otherwise. Hearing from Ruby Brydon that John Franklin had spent the past five months at Brindabella, on 18 December she rang Dr Fraser, who advised that he had been discharged six months earlier. Miles also learned that his cousin Enid knew where he now was. Maybe it was Kurrajong, since he had sent Ruby Brydon a card from there. A sad letter she wrote to him just before Christmas survives in draft: 'I wish you well as always.' It was now over three years since he was 'immured' and 'cast me off', as she expressed it to Dr Fraser; and apart from upsetting phone calls 'from my unfortunate nephew and someone else stuttering for Jack', mentioned in a letter to Moir the following March, the draft Christmas letter appears to be Miles' last effort to communicate with him.[141]

Meanwhile, the 'essay' had reached London. Florence James initially expressed delight with it, but she soon recognised that there would be difficulties. In mid-February she told Cusack that Constable would not be publishing: 'It's highly controversial in spots, very individual of course, stimulating, outspokenly antiwar and Constable found it "bitter".' It should be published in Australia, though, she affirmed. Dymphna did not read the manuscript until April 1954, due to postal difficulties — she was in France — but she and Florence wrote separately before then to Miles, advising there was no possibility of publication by Constable, James adding that *Laughter, Not for a Cage* was the most valuable thing she had ever read on Australian writers and writing, and Cusack assuring Miles that she was looking forward immensely to reading it when she got to London. When she did, she sent a 'gorgeous telegram': 'CONGRATULATIONS LAUGHTER TRIUMPHANT'. Considering she is hardly mentioned in the text, it was a generous reaction. Miles asserted, probably quite truthfully, that she did not care if it was not published in England.[142]

But it was not accepted by the Australian branch of Oxford University Press either. On 1 February 1954 Miles wrote to Frank Eyre saying that she had retyped 'my toot with the Australian novel' and asking if he wished to see it again. He agreed but to no effect. It probably did not help that Miles pressed him for a verdict within the month. On 19 March he wrote that the revision was insufficient. Later, when Miles said she would have liked further editorial input, he said he would co-ordinate the critical comments received from readers and send them. This may refer to factual notes in the hand of J. K. Moir preserved in her publishing papers. No further record of contact with Eyre survives.[143]

When asked about her work, Miles would now vaguely intimate that she had a couple of things held up in press. In fact, both her new books (her memoir and her 'essay') were in limbo. As for Cusack's valid criticism, contained in a letter following the telegram, that she should not try to cover the history of the novel to 1950 but stop at 1939, Miles responded that it would be up to Dymphna to carry on into the next period — which in a way it was. Overall she found Dymphna's response that the book was enormously important, and a crowning achievement, a release.[144]

In 1954 Australia was experiencing 'queen fever'. On 2 February the young Elizabeth II arrived in Sydney for a two-month tour of Australia, departing Fremantle on 1 April. Miles was one of the few to take a dim view of the royal tour, which she regarded as a backward step for Australia — though she did watch the royal yacht *Gothic* enter Sydney Harbour from the balcony of a friend of Pixie's at Watsons Bay, 'a beautiful sight' according to Pixie. Thanks to a local tradesman who told her about the route she also caught a glimpse of 'the living icon' when the royal entourage passed through the southern suburbs. The rest she saw at the newsreels, being too weak to stand in the hot streets with a million other Sydneysiders.[145]

The royal visit reminded Miles of Inky Stephensen and how he had pointed out two decades earlier that, technically speaking, when the Statute of Westminster was passed by the United Kingdom parliament in 1931, the English monarch became the monarch of Australia. Evidently it was now a reality: 'Twenty years behind the times and six months ahead of the crowd' is the way to triumph in the modern world, she observed tartly. The immediate politics amused her even more: 'Looked at from the angle of power politics, I chuckle to note that as an icon Elizabeth out-glittered all others. The RCs gave in and whooped too, as they astutely recognised here a bulwark against communism or any other advanced ism.' The tour was a phenomenal success, with men bowing low and women enjoying the spectacle, especially the clothes. Miles commented to Dymphna Cusack, it was quite something to see a '*young female exalted*'. Ethel Bridle reported, however, that the Queen looked tired and strained by the time she got to Wagga Wagga.[146]

Amid the excitement, John Kinmont Moir's friend Everill Venman arrived at Grey Street, not for a night as arranged, but, as it turned out, five weeks. Venman, a pharmacist, who apparently had been working on a mission on Thursday Island, was both demented and penniless. It took all Miles' forbearance and diplomatic skills to cope with her. She didn't mind so much the big clothing bills Everill ran up in the stores under her address, reasoning the stores could afford it while she could not, or even having to lend her small sums of money (although she was now complaining that inflation had reduced her income to below the old-age pension). It was the mad disruption and the negotiations with the local bishop to get the church to pay Everill's fare back to Brisbane that really wearied her.[147]

It was a relief to see Everill onto the train on 21 March, and to hear later that she had obtained a job at Brisbane Hospital. Everill, when recovered, had the grace to say that Miles had been 'a saint in the real sense of the word' to put up with her. For her part, Miles acknowledged that Everill, a graduate of Brisbane Girls Grammar School, was 'a dignified and well-bred creature in spite of her vagaries'.[148]

Miles was not well when she visited the Archibald Prize exhibition with Pixie O'Harris and Myrtle Rose White in the second week of February, and she had to forgo the Easter Show for the first time since her return to Sydney in late 1932. Soon she was not strong enough to do her own shopping. Her condition puzzled her; on 8 March, she told J. K. Moir that all the bounce and boasting had gone (though Everill was still with her, a sufficient reason, perhaps, for feeling low). Maybe it was a virus, or even anaemia? 'I simply can't make myself go,' she wrote to Winifred Stephensen on 1 May, and the same day to Moir she said she seemed to have a chill, citing the family adage that women don't die of hearts and admonishing Moir to take care of himself.[149]

She also told Moir she had many things she wanted to finish: in particular she had still to ensure the publication of her 'essay' after the rejections by Constable and Oxford in Melbourne. Having had second thoughts about C. E. S. Hall's offer, she asked Rex Ingamells' help again. 'I am no candidate for posthumous recognition,' she urged. It would be 'a salutary blast now in the face of the re-garrisoning of the Australian mentality by Elizabeth's visit and all the mass hysteria [and] hullabaloo, and in every governorship a supernumerary army general'. He responded that Hall was still interested. However, it was decided she should try Perth first, as a university press had just been launched there. So she contacted Henrietta Drake-Brockman, and through her Professor Edwards. But that proved a dead end: the funds had already been committed for the year, and in any event, publication was reserved for 'sacred works by members of the Uni. staff'. She also approached Beatrice Davis to see if Angus & Robertson would be interested, but Beatrice seems to have expressed reservations. 'I guess it will be Mr Hall,' Miles concluded.[150]

She continued to worry about Everill, and kept up her mentoring of needy writers. When David Martin suffered a nasty review of his poems *From Life* by A. D. Hope ('Anno Domino Hopeless') in the *Sydney Morning Herald*, Miles recalled for his benefit a reassurance given to the English novelist Rebecca West when young that the only reason writers need reviewers is for advertising lines. Beatrice Davis was persuaded to take a look at Jean Devanny's memoir as well.[151]

She also commented freely on Federal politics, currently in an uproar. On 13 April, with a general election scheduled for 29 May, a Russian embassy official (and Soviet spy), Vladimir Petrov, defected to Australia, and his wife soon after, under dramatic circumstances. Like most people Miles was taken aback, but was not without a timely response: 'It would seem that the Lord is on the side of Mr Menzies, first the bonanza of the Queen's visitation, now the spy melodrama,' she wrote to Mary Alice Evatt. Sure enough, Mr Menzies defeated Dr Evatt in the election, and Australian politics were cast in a conservative mould lasting to 1972. Whether Miles voted informal as she was thinking of doing is unknown, but she made her feelings known about the election campaign, saying it was a sorry exposé of Australia's satellite position and of tenth-rate politicians. What was needed against the satellite comforters were some good old roosters like Sir Henry Parkes, she declared. In lighter vein, to Eris O'Brien, a friend of Brent and since late 1953 Catholic archbishop of Canberra and Goulburn, she remarked that she had sometimes been called the literary bishop of the Monaro but would be happy if he granted it to her as a parish.[152]

There was no evading the 'bungy heart' though. According to a note Miles wrote to the Howarths, she was already 'out of action' on 26 May and could not say if she would improve or not. The following week, in the last of the several thousand personal letters preserved (mostly as carbon copies) in her files, addressed to 'My dearest Magdalen' (Dalloz) and completed on 4 June, she confessed she had reached her allotted span, but was unsure if it was the end or if she should struggle to go on. One letter was all she could manage to type in a day, she admitted. Nonetheless, having previously asked Magdalen about a copy of Kinsey's *Sexual Behavior of the Human Female*, she now wanted Harper's *American College Dictionary* (Magdalen sent it, and in good time).[153]

'This cold is dreadful — my heart literally won't go,' Miles wrote to Delys Cross on 9 June. On Sunday 20 June, Miles' cousin Joan Lampe in Wagga

Wagga wrote, in response to a letter from her the previous week that does not survive: 'I am sorry to hear you are not feeling well.'[154]

That same day, or possibly the next, Miles suffered a heart attack. When Aunt Lena made a routine phone call to Carlton on 22 June, she was shocked to hear that Miles was ill in bed with a doctor in attendance. Writing the next day, Lena expressed the hope that her niece was not in too much pain, and that the doctor was treating the case properly, adding brightly, 'Cheer up dear: they can do so much for the heart now.'[155]

Delys Cross was the only person in a position to give an on-the-spot account of the situation (and even she was not there when the attack occurred). In a letter to Katharine Susannah Prichard dated 'Sunday' (almost certainly 27 June), she reported that 'Early last week she [Miles] had a severe heart attack, preceded by a tummy upset and vomiting. She was alone, eventually managed to phone dr.' How much time elapsed before Miles was able to call the doctor is unclear, but according to a later letter from Miles to Dymphna Cusack, 'the doctor came after 48 hours and relieved me with morphine'.[156]

Delys had been concerned when her calls to Carlton went unanswered, but she kept trying, and in due course got through to the doctor, who was visiting Miles on a daily basis, and that evening to Glen Mills Fox. The next morning she went to Grey Street, where, as she told Katharine Susannah Prichard, she found Miles very low, very tired, and able to eat very little. The doctor wanted to send Miles to hospital, but she did not want to go and Delys persuaded him to allow her to nurse Miles at home. At least once that first week Delys nursed her through the night. Florence Knox took over on the weekend, and it was arranged that Glen Mills Fox would come to help at nights subsequently. Others such as the Lampe cousins were also willing to help, but unable to leave their families overnight.[157]

After a week Miles picked up a little. This meant she could worry about her 'essay'. On 28 June she sent an urgent (typed) note to Beatrice Davis, saying that she lacked the strength to do more and wanted it out now, 'ahead of the rush': 'I'm conscious of a faulty offering but it is my testament and I am one of the few remaining with a personal knowledge of some of the period — with a vivid memory of the effects of the development of Aus. writing.' In a shaky hand she added, 'This is all I can do.' A covering letter from Delys explained that it was essential that Miles have mental and physical rest, and that she was drugged to keep her mind still, but that she really needed to see Beatrice and to get the manuscript fixed up: 'if you

could reassure her about publication it would mean so much — life itself.'
Beatrice collected it on 30 June.[158]

The day before, Beatrice had sent 'the smallest note' to say that
corrections to the family tree for *Cockatoos* were being made according to
Miles' instructions, and publication would not be much delayed. A file note
in Beatrice's hand records that Miles was sent an advance copy on 12 July.
Later, Miles wrote a note (undated) in pencil to 'George', probably Ferguson,
thanking him for getting the book out, adding in a trembling hand: 'this is
the first time I have attempted anything and it has winded me.' Whether she
was well enough to read it is not known, but she certainly saw Stewart
Howard's 'shallow' review in the *Sun-Herald* later in July, and possibly also
the *Bulletin*'s sympathetic response in early September.[159]

Delys Cross nursed Miles at Carlton for a fortnight with scarcely a break:
'I never leave her at all,' she wrote to Beatrice Davis. But the drugs upset
Miles' stomach, and her condition worsened. 'Miles has been very ill since
approximately the beginning of July,' Delys later told Henrietta Drake-
Brockman. Rex Ingamells recalled visiting her on 8 July and that Miles told
him 'in a matter-of-fact way' that she was dying but he couldn't believe her.
As soon as she was strong enough to be moved, she was taken by ambulance
to her cousin Thelma Perryman's place at Beecroft.[160]

Seven weeks' total rest were prescribed, and at first no visitors were
allowed, not even the dedicated Delys, who continued to take care of
Grey Street (except for the bantams, fed by neighbours): 'It seemed so
strange without our gay darling Miles, for however down she was we
eventually struck the chord of her laughter.' In a letter to Miles at
Beecroft, dated 20 July, Delys hoped her friend's cough had abated, that
she was taking her medication, and that soon she would be 'sparkling on
all sixes' (meaning, presumably, all six cylinders). Miles was not then well
enough to write her own letters, but she loved to get them, as Delys
would later advise distant friends; and despite being unable to sit up 'or
do anything at all', a few days later she managed to dictate a heartfelt
response: 'I shall never forget what it has meant to me to have you come
to me and help so much.'[161]

The same day, 23 July, Miles dictated another letter, to Vance Palmer, to
say she had his new book *The Legend of the Nineties*, and hoped it would be
a great success, and that she had something coming too: 'there is now no-
one living except you and me who has felt the "nineties" emotionally and
the heady joy of the balladry about our very own country.' She also wanted

to ask him about heart attacks, as she knew he had survived a bad one the year before, and wondered how long he had been kept in bed and how he had felt. Her doctors said she was getting better and she was wonderfully cared for, but she felt like a poisoned pup, due to the drugging needed to calm her heart, she told him. Perhaps he had not been so wild and fierce as she was?[162]

From 1 January 1909 to 1 January 1954, there is some kind of record of what Miles Franklin was doing on virtually every day of her life. But after her letters to Delys Cross and Vance Palmer and until her letter to Dymphna Cusack dated 18 August, there is practically nothing. There was a pocket diary for 1954 — Miles checked it in May regarding correspondence with David Martin — but it does not survive; and even if it had, she would hardly have been able to write in it. On 3 August, Beatrice Davis wrote to C. E. S. Hall in Melbourne at Miles' behest, merely advising that, due to Miles' ill health, *Laughter, Not for a Cage* would now be coming out 'with a local firm'.[163]

It was too soon for visitors. The only exception seems to have been David Martin. He visited 'when I first came', Miles told Delys Cross. Many years later Martin recalled that visit to Beecroft. At the time of her heart attack he was in Townsville on literary business, staying with the Devannys. There he received a letter from Miles, presumably dictated, asking him to visit her on his way back to Melbourne (and telling him to announce himself loudly when he arrived, in case he was not allowed in). Although she seemed to be alert, even still slightly coquettish, as he thought she liked to be with men, he realised she was very frail. It was the last time he would see her, she said.[164]

'Jounama', the Perrymans' house on Murray Road, Beecroft, occupied a large corner block amid what was still largely bushland, and the trees and birds in the garden gradually had a soothing effect on the invalid. In retrospect, Beatrice Davis was inclined to think Miles rested too long in these idyllic surrounds (probably because, at Miles' request, in late August she obtained another opinion of Miles' condition from Dr Douglas Anderson, a Macquarie Street physician, who took a rather benign view of the symptoms reported to him). However, the effort of getting up for even two hours daily in mid-August was almost too much for her. It was a wonder she was still alive, she told Dymphna Cusack on 18 August. Her will power must be on some kind of automatic pilot: 'If only I'd relax I'd be gone.' In the letter to Beatrice Davis seeking a second medical opinion, undated, but probably written a few days later, she said she doubted she would have the strength to pull through if she had to become an invalid: 'I have struggled so long already.'[165]

On 24 August, in another letter to Beatrice Davis, she wrote, 'I feel no hope of return to even weak normality.' A few days later she wrote again, still anxious about her 'essay': perhaps Beatrice should post it back for one more look; perhaps it should be burned if she did not recover. Her last letter to Delys Cross dated 30 August was annotated in pencil, 'Dear Delys, I don't think I'll ever see you again.'[166]

Phillis Moulden told her daughter Jennifer that Miles had lost the will to live. Miles undoubtedly felt bleak, fearing that if she lingered she would have to go to 'a home for dying'. Phillis thought it was because of the Petrov affair, and Miles certainly was aware of the Sydney hearings of the royal commission into espionage appointed following the Petrov defection. In her letter of 30 August to Delys Cross, written three days after Dr Evatt denounced the royal commission as an anti-Labor conspiracy, she referred to it directly: 'I hope Dr Evatt will be able to show up the Petrov racket against him.' Phillis Moulden's observation suggests that she also became aware of what actually happened: that on 8 September Evatt was excluded from the commission and that she recognised it for what in the long run it proved to be, a disaster for him and for the Labor Party.[167]

Being able to read her letters and the newspapers again seems to have revitalised Miles. It helped, too, that she was taken off an appetite-suppressing drug. In a undated letter to Marjorie Pizer marked 'one of the last letters from Miles Franklin', she was still struggling to get through a newspaper, but a new literary magazine which had come her way delighted her: 'I will subscribe to *Overland* if I live.' In a subsequent letter to Marjorie, annotated 'Last letter from Miles' and postmarked 2 September she expressed interest in a Henry Lawson letter which Marjorie had apparently sent, and recalled her embarrassment at the flattering way the great men of her youth had responded to her. The next day she wrote to Pixie O'Harris assuring her that the manuscript of 'I Remember' was safe in her cousin's deed box, though the essay on novels had priority.[168]

These are probably the last letters she ever wrote. They make poignant, even powerful reading today. To Marjorie Pizer, she wrote of a haunting sense of failure: 'I have never gained self-confidence & my writing fills me with a sense of tortured failure. Critics don't see the underside or innerness of what I attempt.' To Pixie O'Harris, she sent a strong message for peace: 'The human race has reached such a crisis in politics & science that to survive we must abandon the *idea* of war'.[169]

It still seemed she would get better. She had told Pixie that Beatrice would come and see her about the 'essay', if she was well enough. Beatrice indeed recalled visiting several times. She found Miles sitting on the verandah in the afternoon, able to talk brightly. Nancy Keesing had checked some references in the 'essay', Beatrice had edited the manuscript, and Miles was trying to work through it. There was talk of publication by Angus & Robertson later in the year.[170]

When Delys Cross was finally allowed to visit Miles on Monday 13 September, she found her propped up in the big four-poster bed that had been her grandmother's, in a room looking out to a garden full of spring flowers. As she reported to Katharine Susannah Prichard, Miles seemed weak but content.[171]

Pixie O'Harris agreed. She had been told by Miles there was no need to visit. But she did, and later wrote an account of it:

> I found her sitting on a wide verandah surrounded by the greenery of a beautiful bush garden. I had never seen her so relaxed. When she tried to walk it was agony to watch and not help her; but I had learned never to offer help — it hurt her independent spirit. When I kissed her goodbye, we both knew it was for the last time. She told me so, and I showed her that I understood. But I would not grieve then; I could only think of her finding peace at last. [172]

Suddenly Miles' condition worsened, and she had to go to hospital for an operation to remove fluid on her lungs. She was taken to Seacombe Private Hospital, Drummoyne, and the operation took place on Thursday 16 September. At first it seemed a success. It is said she recognised relatives the next day and was about to leave, when another heart attack occurred. She collapsed and never regained consciousness.[173]

Miles Franklin died in the early hours of Sunday 19 September 1954. The death certificate states that the cause of death was (a) coronary occlusion, and (b) chronic myocarditis and pleurisy, with effusion, in lay terms, a heart attack, with heart disease and fluid on the lungs. She was seventy-four years and eleven months old. When Florence Knox saw her body the next day, she wished she could tell her how really beautiful she looked in death, with no lines and her skin so clear, as in girlhood.[174]

She was cremated the next day, at the Northern Suburbs Crematorium, after a ceremony at the Eastwood Anglican church conducted by a young minister on furlough from mission work in Kenya, the Reverend Keith Cole. In accordance with Miles' instructions, there was no public announcement of her death until it was all over, and attendance was confined to immediate family and friends. Present were Helena Lampe, Annie May Bridle, Ruby Brydon, Thelma Perryman, Phillis Moulden, Leslie Annie Bridle, Ruby Franklin Bridle, George Perryman, Jack Moulden, Ruth Horwitz and her daughter Lillaine, and Florence Knox.[175]

'Nothing broke the drabness of a cold wet day,' Leslie Bridle recalled, '... except the young minister.' He had not known Miles, but he took the trouble to obtain details of her life and work. 'He spoke of Miles Franklin's burning love of Australia, of the work of the pioneers she knew and loved, of our country, and when [making reference] to Kenya & Asia, and the millions of Asians at our door ... asked, "What are you going to do with Miles Franklin's Australia?" (Poor old Aunt Lena, eighty-seven, and the rest of us not far behind, couldn't do much, however we were very thrilled that he had grasped the keynote of all Stella's work).'[176]

Reverend Cole concluded by reading the passage from *All That Swagger* about 'Australia, the incredible feat':

> All too swiftly the day ascended and declined. The shadows lengthened from the cropped tussocks pimpling the hillsides. Perfume of wattle bathed approaching evening in delight. The bright landscape danced in air translucent and dazzling. The westering sun laying vesper offering on the rim of day, melted sky and mountains into a glory of filtered light and retreated to the core of a continent over which as yet man has no sure dominion. A land of distances, a land dependent upon distances for preservation; a land gorgeously empty and with none of the accumulations of centuries of human occupation; a continent surveyed, fenced, patrolled and policed by the nucleus of a nation analogous to a patriarchal family with unwieldy wealth.
>
> 'Australia, the incredible feat!', he chanted ...[177]

It was a pity that in what seems to have been a rigid interpretation of crematorium rules the official who arranged the funeral removed the wildflowers placed on the coffin by the Bridle sisters, Ruby and Leslie. The bouquet of ti-tree blossom and blue field flowers they had gathered was a lovely touch.

Yet in a way it didn't matter greatly. Miles had made sure her remains would be returned to where they grew. On 2 October, in accordance with her wishes, her ashes were scattered by Pearl Cotterill at Jounama Creek, in sight of the original homestead at Talbingo where she was born.

AFTERLIFE

Self-protective to the end, Miles stipulated in her will that no death notice was to be placed in the Sydney press but of course the word was soon out. The first to acknowledge her passing was Marie Marshall, president of the New South Wales Society of Women Writers, who two days after the cremation wrote a letter to the *Sydney Morning Herald* calling on younger writers to abandon inverted snobberies and fill the void Miles left by taking up the cause of the delineation of Australian character, of which Miles, she said, had an instinctive understanding. Henrietta Drake-Brockman was also quick to mark her friend's passing, writing in the *West Australian* on 25 September that 'to meet Miles Franklin was as invigorating as to ride on a spring morning across the Monaro plains she so dearly loved and immortalised for the rest of Australia'.[1]

Many tributes followed, as friends rallied to honour her life and work, and vivid recollections appeared in the literary journals. Beatrice Davis wrote in *Southerly* of 'a true Australian', while in *Overland* David Martin recalled her as 'the Bernard Shaw of the Australian Bush' and Jean Devanny as a wonderful letter writer and 'the truest of friends'. Florence James, in an obituary for the London *Times*, spoke of 'her hatred of shams, and the love of Australia which shines through all her writing', and 'O. C. R.' stated in the Melbourne *Age* that she had long since earned a lasting place 'in a company whose prose and verse have imparted to this land a living quality'. To 'R. J. B.', writing in *Voice*, she was one of the most original and vital creative writers Australia had produced. Perhaps the most apposite was Vance Palmer when he wrote in the *ABC Weekly* that 'a great deal of light and laughter went out of the world when Miles Franklin died'. 'To know Miles Franklin well was to love her,' added Martin, whose critical reflections are still of value. While the twelve contributors to *Miles Franklin by Some of her Friends*, published by the Bread and Cheese Club in 1955, may have valued her in different ways, their affectionate contributions to the publication bear him out.[2]

But — ah! Nemesis — for the most part the press was only interested in one question: was she really Brent of Bin Bin? It was thought she probably was; but while she was alive Miles had resolutely refused to acknowledge it. Now that she was gone, no one could say for sure. The issue was not finally laid to rest until 1966, when the Mitchell Library released her correspondence with Mary Fullerton. And with that, as Miles had predicted, Brent ceased to be interesting. Reviewers found it difficult to find anything positive to say about the posthumous Brent volumes and the accolades never came. It was too late for most readers to care about the pastoral age.[3]

Miles' will was declared for probate on 14 January 1955, and her last and best-kept secret, the literary prize for which she had been preserving her capital all along, became public knowledge. Most of her estate, valued at £8922, was dedicated to it. According to Colin Roderick, literary critics were astonished. Such personal beneficence was unprecedented. However, the *Sydney Morning Herald* noted she was a prize-winner herself, having twice won the Prior Prize. Once her estate was cleared and her intentions regarding the literary prize were translated into practicable terms, the judges nominated in her will — the Mitchell Librarian, Beatrice Davis, Ian Mudie, Colin Roderick (whose early enthusiasm for Brent presumably overrode all other considerations in Miles' mind), and her accountant, George Williams — were able to begin work. They honoured her by extending the name of the prize from the Franklin to the Miles Franklin Award. First awarded to Patrick White for *Voss*, published in London in 1957, and presented in Sydney in April the following year by Robert Gordon Menzies, Prime Minister of Australia, with Dr Evatt, leader of the Federal Opposition, in attendance, it was initially worth £500. Average weekly earnings for men in New South Wales at that time were around £15; for women £11. In 2008, with support from the Copyright Agency and the Nelson Meers Foundation, it is worth $42,000.[4]

The terms of the award are of considerable biographical significance. In accordance with clause 6 of Miles' will, the prize is awarded to the author of 'the Novel for the year which is of the highest literary merit and which must present Australian Life in any of its phases'; and if, in the opinion of the judges, in any year no novel is deemed worthy of the prize, it may be awarded to the author of 'a play for either stage Radio or Television or such other medium as may develop but not for farce or musical comedy'. There is also a sub-clause to protect standards: if no entry is deemed to be of sufficient merit, no award need be made, a situation that has occurred several times. Unlike the Pulitzer Prize in the United States, and some other comparable awards, there are no national eligibility criteria. These terms encapsulate Miles' two great hopes in later life: that Australian writers would be encouraged in their endeavours, and that Australia would become a significant field in world literature. However, debate about an entry written by a non-Australian and published outside Australia has yet to occur.[5]

At the time of her death, Miles was a well-known writer. Although the only title available under her own name was the English edition of *All That Swagger*, there were other relatively recent titles and four still to come, two by Brent and two by Miles. In addition, Angus & Robertson published a new Australian edition of *All That Swagger* in 1956. On that basis, her reputation seemed set to live on. But would it? The world was changing, and with it critical values, as was apparent when Sidney J. Baker concluded Australians had grown up considerably since *Back to Bool Bool* was written, and from the mixed reception afforded *Childhood at Brindabella*, welcomed by Peter Ward as the work 'of a kind of bush Simone de Beauvoir' and condemned by Thelma Forshaw, for whom Miles Franklin was an arrogant woman: 'Colette wins hands down.'[6]

Meanjin editor Clem Christesen had always been interested in Miles Franklin. His mother had kept a scrapbook of Miles' writings as a girl, and Miles had encouraged her to become a writer. She had encouraged Clem too, and from time to time contributed to *Meanjin*. Recognising that the time was ripe for a re-evaluation, in April 1955 Christesen commissioned Marjorie Barnard to write an article for *Meanjin* on Miles' life and work. Marjorie, who seems never to have realised just how much Miles disliked her, welcomed the opportunity. Her article was the first recognisably modern assessment of Miles' work. The opening sentence reads: 'Miles Franklin was a legend in her own lifetime — which is not always a healthy thing for a writer.' For Barnard, *Old Blastus of Bandicoot* — a title last reissued in the wartime Pocket Library edition of 1945 — was the touchstone, not because it was the best of the novels but because 'it was the palette from which they were painted'. This now seems untenable; but Barnard was of her time too, and her historically informed approach was valuable, if perhaps a little patronising. She concluded it was probably unnecessary to evaluate Miles' work as literature: 'The books are there to be read. They are a record of Miles herself, her warmth, her humour, her idiosyncratic mind. They are an index to a period and tribute to the earth she loved.'[7]

Barnard's approach carried over to her critical biography *Miles Franklin*, the first book-length study, published in 1967 and still valuable as literary analysis, though largely superseded as a source of biographical information, having been written prior to the release of the Franklin Papers. Marjorie, who had not been satisfied with her *Meanjin* article and declined Christesen's invitation to review *Childhood at Brindabella*, fearing she would not be able to treat it fairly, found the larger task uncongenial ('it was folly to undertake it'). Although it was in other respects not comparable with Colin Roderick's iconoclastic work, *Miles Franklin: Her Brilliant Career*, published in 1982, well after the release of the papers though without acknowledgement to them, both works now seem like winding-up statements by the succeeding generation: whereas Barnard sought to elucidate the legend, Roderick tried to demolish it. (No doubt Roderick was shocked to discover from her papers what Miles really thought of him.) Miles, who once remarked that the thought of biography added a new dimension to her fear of death, would have recognised the ironies.[8]

In 1959, for the first of many in-depth radio programs on her life and works to come, John Thompson interviewed various people who had known her about 'the mysterious Miles Franklin', but he concluded, rightly, 'we have not yet heard the last of Stella Maria Sarah Miles Franklin'. One of the interviewees, George Farwell, referred suggestively to her diaries. The sale of seventy plays and novels, published and unpublished, and numerous manuscripts deemed surplus to archival requirements by her trustees and their advisers to the Sydney book dealer Isidoor Berkelouw in 1960 was an indication of how much there might be; but Miles' personal papers were embargoed for ten years following her death. Furthermore, her will specified that certain items marked by Miles were to be burned. This was done before the papers were accessioned, but the amount was said to be small and it has never been suggested that anything of importance was lost.[9]

As Susan Sheridan has shown with respect to *My Brilliant Career*, Miles' reputation reached its lowest ebb from the mid-1950s to the late 1970s, when modernist values dominated literary criticism. Without immediate family to maintain her name, she could have been forgotten. Inevitably, the number of people who knew Miles personally slowly diminished, though *My Brilliant Career* was valued by the Left for its class analysis, and many women writers cherished its message, poet Judith Wright for one. When I first read *My Brilliant Career* as a graduate student in the 1960s it was at the suggestion of radical Australian historian Ian Turner.[10]

'The books are there to be read,' wrote Barnard in the *Meanjin* article, but to be read they must stay in print, something that happens to very few Australian writers. Miles has been one of the few, though variably so. By 1981, when the previously unpublished Chicago novel *On Dearborn Street* appeared, Miles' published works, including non-fiction, serials and plays, amounted to twenty-two titles (see Appendix 1). Of these, seven have been out of print for at least fifty years: three have never been reissued — *The Net of Circumstance* (1916), *Sydney Royal* (1947), and *Laughter, Not for a Cage* (1956); one, *Old Blastus of Bandicoot* (1931, 1945), has not been reissued since Miles' death; and four of the Brent titles last appeared very close to it — *Prelude to Waking* (1950), *Ten Creeks Run* (1952), *Gentlemen at Gyang Gyang* (1956) and *Back to Bool Bool* (1957). On the other hand, for the fifty-plus years since her death, one or more of fifteen titles has at one time or another been in print.[11]

This may be due to extraneous events rather than literary merit. The relevance of the struggle of Sybylla Penelope Melvyn to free herself from what Charlotte Perkins Gilman called 'the disabilities of sex' — that is, the unequal position of women in society — was obvious to many with the revival of interest in feminism in the 1970s, and the Margaret Fink-produced film version of *My Brilliant Career*, which appeared in 1979, highlighted this theme for an international audience.

With the onset of second-wave feminism, Miles became famous again, and there was a rush to read her books. At least a dozen editions of *My Brilliant Career* were published over the following decade, not only in Australia but in England, Canada, the United States and South Africa, and in translation in Japan and (later) France. A Braille edition has also been published. *My Career Goes Bung* was reissued four times in the 1980s, and again in 1990. Even *Some Everyday Folk and Dawn* was rescued from obscurity in 1986 by Virago (which was subsequently taken over, causing a planned reissue of the first Chicago novel, *The Net of Circumstance*, to be abandoned).[12]

Other titles were reissued to coincide with national events. In 1988, the year of Australia's bicentenary, *Pioneers on Parade* made an unexpected comeback, published by Angus & Robertson. Likewise, the centenary of

Federation in 2001 saw not only a centenary edition of *My Brilliant Career* published by HarperCollins, but also the first reissue of *Joseph Furphy: The Legend of the Man and His Book* by Halstead Press.

A snowball effect has been at work in the case of forgotten texts. The University of Queensland Press, which was quick off the mark in 1981 with *On Dearborn Street*, languishing in manuscript since World War I, followed with a new edition of *Bring the Monkey* in 1984. Two plays also re-entered the public domain: the previously unpublished 'Call Up Your Ghosts' in a Penguin anthology of Australian women's writing edited by Dale Spender in 1988; and as recently as 1999, *No Family* was reprinted in *Tremendous Worlds*, an anthology of Australian women's drama from 1890 to the 1960s, edited by Susan Pfisterer and published by Currency Press. Perhaps most surprising was the fleeting reappearance of the 1940s serial 'The Thorny Rose' in the *Newcastle Herald* in 1992, following a passing reference in a play prepared for ABC Radio National by a freelance dramatist, Julia Britton.[13]

If most of these were, in publishing terms, opportunistic, they also suggest areas of ongoing relevance in the writings of Miles Franklin. At least they have kept her name before the reading public. Meanwhile, a handful of titles have gone from strength to strength. In 1910 Miles withdrew *My Brilliant Career* from publication, and in her will required that it remain out of print for ten years after her death, probably to protect sales of the posthumous titles. Since 1965, it has been continuously in print, sometimes in tandem with *My Career Goes Bung*; in 2007 it appeared in Penguin Classics, with an introduction by Sandra M. Gilbert, and an annotated edition was published in Canada. Similarly, *Childhood at Brindabella* has been reissued every decade since it first appeared in 1963, most recently in 2003 by Sydney publisher Richmond. Angus & Robertson also published *All That Swagger* four times across the period.[14]

The obvious failure to carry over was Brent. Brent's world was irrelevant to the feminist version of Miles, and of little interest otherwise. To date only two titles have been reissued since the 1950s, both in the 1980s, and serendipity seems to have been at work there. The best explanation for the re-emergence of Brent's *Up the Country* in 1984, and *Cockatoos* in 1989, is probably that Richard Walsh, managing director and publisher at Angus & Robertson from 1972 to 1986, was co-lessee of a cabin once owned by the *Blue Hills* author, Gwen Meredith, in the Brindabella Valley in the 1970s.[15]

In retrospect, 1981 was an *annus mirabilis* in the afterlife of Miles Franklin, with related literary scholarship dating back to the 1970s appearing in print. Drusilla Modjeska's *Exiles at Home*, a study of Australian women writers from the 1920s to the 1940s, allotted Miles 'A Chapter of Her Own'; and Verna Coleman examined her American years in a sound monograph, *Miles Franklin in America: Her (Unknown) Brilliant Career*. Since then, a boom in biography, including collective biography, has been significant for the maintenance of Miles' name, with more and more of her mentors and congenials restored to the cultural mainstream, often with extensive reference to Miles and her papers.[16]

Though such factors as serendipity, circumstance and changing critical values have contributed, they alone cannot fully account for the surge of interest in the life and work of Miles Franklin in the last quarter of the twentieth century, nor its survival into the twenty-first. There has been an ongoing sense that somehow Miles still matters. As more women have entered the public sphere and taken on a larger role in the cultural industries, not only as readers and writers but also as publishers and curators, Miles has become the all-purpose Australian girl, still brilliant a century on. Moreover, although some may have felt that enough is enough, even more of her writings have entered the public domain since the 1980s boom, to add a new dimension to her *oeuvre*. Editions of previously unpublished correspondence and diaries and the retrieval of topical writings from past print media have not only drawn attention to new sources of information about her life and work but also established her as a significant practitioner in those genres, which in turn are now more widely admired. In addition, important new primary sources have become widely available to the biographer. As noted in Chapter 5, in the early 1980s the late Dorothy A. Hayes succeeded in transcribing Miles' daily diary entries for the years 1926–36 from her obscure shorthand; and much of the new information regarding Brent of Bin Bin presented in Chapter 9 and subsequently has been drawn from Blackwood's Brent of Bin Bin publishing file and the Berkelouw manuscript collection, both acquired by the State Library of New South Wales in the 1990s. As evidenced by a centenary seminar on *My Brillian Career* in Sydney in August 2001, the array of new material has slowly but surely brought her historical authenticity into clearer focus.[17]

The centenary of Federation in 2001 was to prove a second high point in Miles' afterlife. She was among those listed as a 'national achiever', along with Henry Lawson and 'Banjo' Paterson; and *My Brilliant Career* was nominated as one of the books 'that tell us who we are and what Australia is'. In 2001 she was the heroine of a whodunnit devised by staff at the *Sydney Morning Herald*, celebrated in an operatic event in Melbourne called *Miles to Furphy, 2001*, and honoured by a seminar and art exhibition in Goulburn. In 2004 the State Library of New South Wales mounted a multimedia exhibition based on materials from the Franklin Papers. By now she is possibly one of the most memorialised of Australian writers: for example, there is an in-ground plaque at Carlton, placed there by the Fellowship of Australian Writers in 1957; a cairn built by the local community at Talbingo in 1979; and a life-sized statue and colourful wall mural created at Hurstville in southern Sydney in 2003. Another tribute is mooted for Goulburn's historic Belmore Park.[18]

Southern New South Wales especially has taken Miles to its heart. An obelisk was erected at the site of the original 'Stillwater' by the Goulburn Historical Society in 1971, and a plaque was attached the following year; there is a Miles Franklin Memorial Park at Tumut; and three public schools in the region are named after her, one at Tumut and two in suburban Canberra. In Goulburn, a young writers' award has been recently instituted in her name (touchingly, it was initially awarded to a young writer whose family live at 'Stillwater', for a story featuring a jilting). Out west, at Wagga Wagga and beyond, Lampe relatives have continued to cherish Miles' name in the context of impressively researched family history. At Murrurundi to the north, there is a regional art prize established by Peter Norvill, the son of John Franklin's favourite cousin, Enid, in which her example as a prize giver has a minor place (as perhaps does her nephew, for when John Franklin died in 1956, Peter Norvill was a beneficiary of his will).[19]

'If ever a soul should go marching on, it is Miles Franklin's. It must, and it will,' wrote Rex Ingamells in the Bread and Cheese Club tribute organised by J. K. Moir. It has. Some people assume she (or maybe he) is still alive. Yet just as writers' reputations often languish after death until rediscovered by a new generation — aided and abetted by literary scholarship — so it is inevitable that reputations will fluctuate over time. In Miles' case there have always been detractors of her work, and from time to time her personality has rubbed people up the wrong way, as in the case of Thelma Forshaw in the 1960s. In the 1990s there was also controversy over the Miles Franklin Award, most notably the so-called Demidenko affair in 1995, when the winner misrepresented her identity, and another writer, Frank Moorhouse, charged that his work had been wrongly excluded in 1994.[20]

The long view is still in the making. Her most recently reprinted book is *My Brilliant Career*, which remains the only one to be adapted for film, despite the popularity of historical drama in recent decades. Many of the issues with which she engaged in her work have either lost their appeal — *All That Swagger* became dated and has disappeared since 1990, despite its filmic possibilities — or have yet to be taken up in a systematic way by literary critics and others, as in the case of her liberalism and environmentalism, and her attitudes to Empire and race. Meanwhile, many readers find it increasingly difficult to understand why Sybylla Melvyn chose not to marry Harry Beecham but to have a career instead. Perhaps most have found the contrast between her creator's public and private selves puzzling. But in fact it is these mysteries that have elevated both *My Brilliant Career* and Miles Franklin above the ordinary. Had *My Brilliant Career* ended conventionally with a happy marriage, it would have the more quickly become a period piece; and had Miles Franklin not created Brent of Bin Bin and hidden her rather extravagant hopes for the future of Australian literature, she may have remained a minor writer in the histories.

As more is known of Miles' life and work, the basis of the paradoxical quality of her creativity is becoming clearer. With limited resources when young, and only *My Brilliant Career* as a bargaining chip with publishers later, she was always on the defensive, creatively speaking; and there were no emeritus writer awards in her day to assuage her mounting sense of failure towards the end. Friends such as Katharine Susannah Prichard tried to reassure her; but few if any really understood the contradictions that caused her unhappiness, and in later life sometimes led to harsh judgements of younger and apparently more successful colleagues.[21]

David Martin, with the insight of an outsider, probably came nearest when he wrote at the time of Miles' death that her position was a tragic one, though there was an optimistic driving force in her work: 'Her wit, insight and genius alienated her from her own class, at the same time as her outlook in many ways bound her to it. Both in time and place she was caught in a contradiction from which she had never quite the strength to escape.'[22]

Thirty years later, in his autobiography *My Strange Friend*, he reflected on her work:

> In the best of her Miles Franklin novels appear women who, as artists or reformers, fight to break free of their background, but the struggle is broken-backed, affection hems it in. These women

fail because they are too close to their roots, which are sunk in the soil of the bush where the battle cannot be waged and won. It is a collective and national dilemma, twice sad because the afflicted do not know their affliction.[23]

To represent the psychological dynamic in another way, women who wish for independence and employment must break into male citadels, which is never an easy or simple thing to do; and the effort has consequences for the individual who tries. As expressed by the philosopher Michèle Le Doeuff in *The Sex of Knowing*, such a woman is 'caught up in a network of representations of the self, of empowerment and inhibitions, which weigh heavily on thought'. And that weight is surely why Miles Franklin seemed 'as paradoxical as a platypus', as P. R. Stephensen put it, and the reason too for what she once confessed was her 'far-flung deviousness'.[24]

If that rings true, it is also true that the old bush culture with its stress on character and self-reliance and a sense of humour stood her in good stead; and for the most part her background and the networks created by first-wave feminism sufficed to carry her through to something approximating the literary career she always aspired to. Though in personal terms the price was high — after her sister Linda's death, she never knew real intimacy and she was seldom happy or content — the richness of her experiences along the way placed her at the forefront of aspiration and achievement among Australian girls of the day, and her example is still encouraging.

Ultimately, and rightly so, it is through her own words that we can best recapture the bright intelligence and irrepressible spirit of Miles Franklin. Though her private life was troubled, and her inner conflicts remained forever unresolved, she persevered and her optimism still shines, if variably, through her books and topical writings, and in her letters and diaries.

In effect, Miles herself ensured her afterlife, thanks to her two great bequests: the 124 volumes of personal papers and forty-one volumes of literary manuscripts left to the State Library of New South Wales (recently supplemented by the Berkelouw and Blackwood purchases) and the Miles Franklin Literary Award. These bequests ensure her continuing participation in Australian life and culture. The papers are far from exhausted; and the prize now has the standing of an antipodean Booker or Pulitzer. Which bits of her own writing will appeal at any given time is a crystal ball issue, but it seems probable that as the historical significance of her life is more widely appreciated, so will be her work. Hopefully more of it will be published too.

As the Fulbright scholar Bruce Sutherland recognised in his last letter to her — dated 3 September 1954, so she may just have seen it — she was 'a vital spark'. [25]

Of one thing we may be sure. So long as personal freedom and national identity are valued in this world, so long will the life of Miles Franklin command attention and affection. In 1955, her cousin Leslie Bridle recalled her as 'the most colourful personality we had ever met ... for us, she can never die.[26]

APPENDIX 1

Principal Published Writings of Miles Franklin

My Brilliant Career, Blackwood, Edinburgh, 1901

'A Ministering Angel, Being the Real Experiences of an Australian Bush Girl',
     New Idea, July–December 1905

Some Everyday Folk and Dawn, Blackwood, Edinburgh, 1909

The Net of Circumstance (under pseudonym Mr and Mrs Ogniblat L'Artsau),
     Mills & Boon, London, 1915

Up the Country: A Tale of the Early Australian Squattocracy (under pseudonym
     Brent of Bin Bin), Blackwood, Edinburgh, 1928

*Ten Creeks Run: A Tale of the Horse and Cattle Stations of the Upper
     Murrumbidgee* (under pseudonym Brent of Bin Bin), Blackwood,
     Edinburgh, 1930

Old Blastus of Bandicoot: Opuscule on a Pioneer Tufted with Ragged Rhymes,
     Cecil Palmer, London, 1931

*Back to Bool Bool: A Ramiparous Novel with Several Prominent Characters and
     a Hantle of Others Disposed as the Atolls of Oceania's Archipelagoes* (under
     pseudonym Brent of Bin Bin), Blackwood, Edinburgh, 1931

Bring the Monkey: A Light Novel, Endeavour Press, Sydney, 1933

All that Swagger, Bulletin, Sydney, 1936

'No Family', in W. Moore & T. I. Moore (eds), *Best Australian One-Act Plays*,
     Angus & Robertson, Sydney, 1937

Pioneers on Parade (with Dymphna Cusack), Angus & Robertson, Sydney, 1939.

Joseph Furphy: The Legend of a Man and his Book (with Kate Baker), Angus &
     Robertson, Sydney, 1944

*My Career Goes Bung: Purporting to be the Autobiography of Sybylla Penelope
     Melvyn*, Georgian House, Melbourne, 1946

'The Thorny Rose', *Newcastle Morning Herald*, 12 July–28 August 1947

Sydney Royal: Divertissement, Shakespeare Head, Sydney, 1947

Prelude to Waking: A Novel in the First Person and Parentheses (under
    pseudonym Brent of Bin Bin), Angus & Robertson, Sydney, 1950

Cockatoos: A Story of Youth and Exodists (under pseudonym Brent of Bin Bin),
    Angus & Robertson, Sydney, 1954

Gentlemen at Gyang Gyang: A Tale of the Jumbuck Pads on the Summer Runs
    (under pseudonym Brent of Bin Bin), Angus & Robertson, Sydney, 1956

*Laughter, Not for a Cage: Notes on Australian Writing, with Biographical
    Emphasis on the Struggles, Function, and Achievements of the Novel in
    Three Half-centuries*, Angus & Robertson, Sydney, 1956.

Childhood at Brindabella: My First Ten Years, Angus & Robertson, Sydney, 1963

On Dearborn Street, University of Queensland Press, St Lucia, 1981

'Call Up Your Ghosts' (1945) (with Dymphna Cusack), in Dale Spender (ed.),
    The Penguin Anthology of Australian Women's Writing, Penguin,
    Melbourne, 1988

My Congenials: Miles Franklin and Friends in Letters, 1789–1954 (2 vols), Jill Roe
    (ed.), Angus & Robertson/HarperCollinsPublishers in association with
    the State Library of New South Wales, Sydney, 1993

A Gregarious Culture: Topical Writings of Miles Franklin, collected and
    introduced with annotations by Jill Roe and Margaret Bettison, University
    of Queensland Press, St Lucia, 2001

The Diaries of Miles Franklin, Paul Brunton (ed.), Allen & Unwin in association
    with the State Library of New South Wales, Sydney, 2004

APPENDIX 2

FAMILY TREES

Stella Miles Franklin: Franklin Family Tree

NOTE
Within generations, only persons referred to in the text are named.

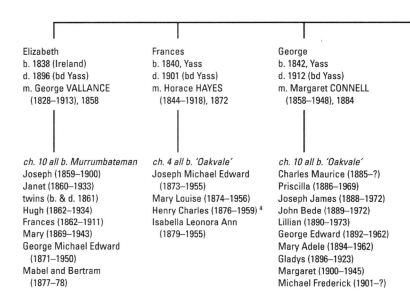

Elizabeth	Frances	George
b. 1838 (Ireland)	b. 1840, Yass	b. 1842, Yass
d. 1896 (bd Yass)	d. 1901 (bd Yass)	d. 1912 (bd Yass)
m. George VALLANCE	m. Horace HAYES	m. Margaret CONNELL
(1828–1913), 1858	(1844–1918), 1872	(1858–1948), 1884

ch. 10 all b. Murrumbateman	*ch. 4 all b. 'Oakvale'*	*ch. 10 all b. 'Oakvale'*
Joseph (1859–1900)	Joseph Michael Edward	Charles Maurice (1885–?)
Janet (1860–1933)	(1873–1955)	Priscilla (1886–1969)
twins (b. & d. 1861)	Mary Louise (1874–1956)	Joseph James (1888–1972)
Hugh (1862–1934)	Henry Charles (1876–1959) [4]	John Bede (1889–1972)
Frances (1862–1911)	Isabella Leonora Ann	Lillian (1890–1973)
Mary (1869–1943)	(1879–1955)	George Edward (1892–1962)
George Michael Edward		Mary Adele (1894–1962)
(1871–1950)		Gladys (1896–1923)
Mabel and Bertram		Margaret (1900–1945)
(1877–78)		Michael Frederick (1901–?)

KEY
b. = born; d. = died; m. = married; bd = buried; arr. = arrived; ch. = children

FOOTNOTES
[1] Bounty immigrants arr. Sydney, 4 April 1839
[2] Roderick, *Miles Franklin*, p. 33
[3] With two siblings, Anne Casey (prev. Franklin, b. c.1812), Robert Franklin (1814–98), d. Goulburn
[4] Sometimes wrongly cited as Charlie Vallance
[5] Laura Bridle was the daughter of W. H. Bridle, oldest child of William and Elizabeth Bridle.

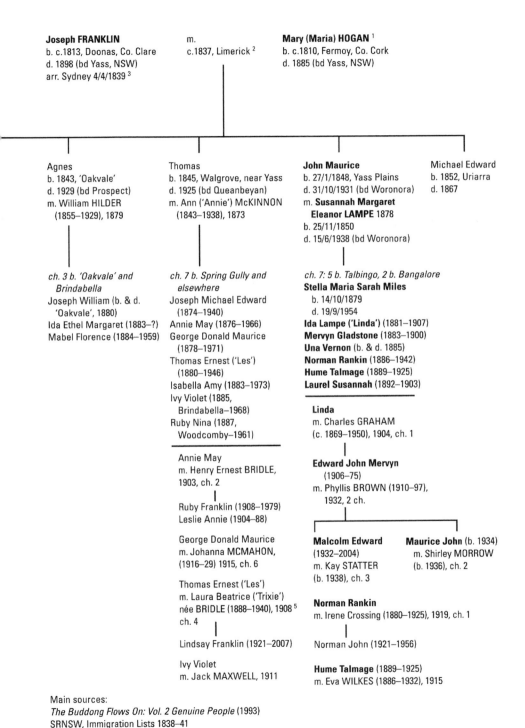

Joseph FRANKLIN
b. c.1813, Doonas, Co. Clare
d. 1898 (bd Yass, NSW)
arr. Sydney 4/4/1839 [3]

m.
c.1837, Limerick [2]

Mary (Maria) HOGAN [1]
b. c.1810, Fermoy, Co. Cork
d. 1885 (bd Yass, NSW)

Agnes
b. 1843, 'Oakvale'
d. 1929 (bd Prospect)
m. William HILDER
(1855–1929), 1879

Thomas
b. 1845, Walgrove, near Yass
d. 1925 (bd Queanbeyan)
m. Ann ('Annie') McKINNON
(1843–1938), 1873

John Maurice
b. 27/1/1848, Yass Plains
d. 31/10/1931 (bd Woronora)
m. **Susannah Margaret
Eleanor LAMPE** 1878
b. 25/11/1850
d. 15/6/1938 (bd Woronora)

Michael Edward
b. 1852, Uriarra
d. 1867

---

*ch. 3 b. 'Oakvale' and
Brindabella*
Joseph William (b. & d.
'Oakvale', 1880)
Ida Ethel Margaret (1883–?)
Mabel Florence (1884–1959)

*ch. 7 b. Spring Gully and
elsewhere*
Joseph Michael Edward
(1874–1940)
Annie May (1876–1966)
George Donald Maurice
(1878–1971)
Thomas Ernest ('Les')
(1880–1946)
Isabella Amy (1883–1973)
Ivy Violet (1885,
Brindabella–1968)
Ruby Nina (1887,
Woodcomby–1961)

ch. 7: 5 b. Talbingo, 2 b. Bangalore
Stella Maria Sarah Miles
b. 14/10/1879
d. 19/9/1954
Ida Lampe ('Linda') (1881–1907)
Mervyn Gladstone (1883–1900)
Una Vernon (b. & d. 1885)
Norman Rankin (1886–1942)
Hume Talmage (1889–1925)
Laurel Susannah (1892–1903)

Annie May
m. Henry Ernest BRIDLE,
1903, ch. 2

Ruby Franklin (1908–1979)
Leslie Annie (1904–88)

George Donald Maurice
m. Johanna MCMAHON,
(1916–29) 1915, ch. 6

Thomas Ernest ('Les')
m. Laura Beatrice ('Trixie')
née BRIDLE (1888–1940), 1908 [5]
ch. 4

Lindsay Franklin (1921–2007)

Ivy Violet
m. Jack MAXWELL, 1911

Linda
m. Charles GRAHAM
(c. 1869–1950), 1904, ch. 1

Edward John Mervyn
(1906–75)
m. Phyllis BROWN (1910–97),
1932, 2 ch.

Malcolm Edward
(1932–2004)
m. Kay STATTER
(b. 1938), ch. 3

Maurice John (b. 1934)
m. Shirley MORROW
(b. 1936), ch. 2

Norman Rankin
m. Irene Crossing (1880–1925), 1919, ch. 1

Norman John (1921–1956)

Hume Talmage (1889–1925)
m. Eva WILKES (1886–1932), 1915

Main sources:
The Buddong Flows On: Vol. 2 Genuine People (1993)
SRNSW, Immigration Lists 1838–41
Biographical Register, ACT (1993)
Birth, Marriage and Death Indexes (NSW)

Stella Miles Franklin: Bridle/Lampe Family Tree

NOTE

Within generations, only persons referred to in the text are named.

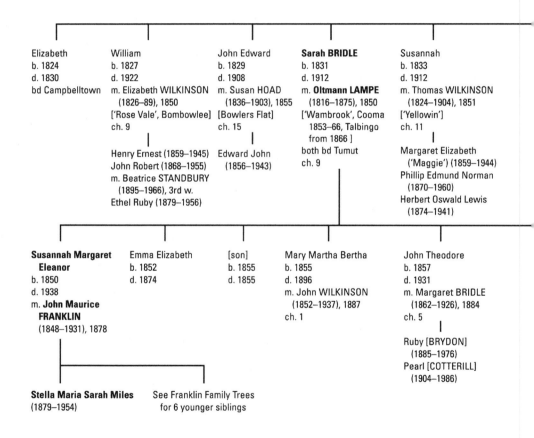

Elizabeth
b. 1824
d. 1830
bd Campbelltown

William
b. 1827
d. 1922
m. Elizabeth WILKINSON
(1826–89), 1850
['Rose Vale', Bombowlee]
ch. 9

Henry Ernest (1859–1945)
John Robert (1868–1955)
m. Beatrice STANDBURY
(1895–1966), 3rd w.
Ethel Ruby (1879–1956)

John Edward
b. 1829
d. 1908
m. Susan HOAD
(1836–1903), 1855
[Bowlers Flat]
ch. 15

Edward John
(1856–1943)

Sarah BRIDLE
b. 1831
d. 1912
m. **Oltmann LAMPE**
(1816–1875), 1850
['Wambrook', Cooma
1853–66, Talbingo
from 1866]
both bd Tumut
ch. 9

Susannah
b. 1833
d. 1912
m. Thomas WILKINSON
(1824–1904), 1851
['Yellowin']
ch. 11

Margaret Elizabeth
('Maggie') (1859–1944)
Phillip Edmund Norman
(1870–1960)
Herbert Oswald Lewis
(1874–1941)

**Susannah Margaret
Eleanor**
b. 1850
d. 1938
m. **John Maurice
FRANKLIN**
(1848–1931), 1878

Emma Elizabeth
b. 1852
d. 1874

[son]
b. 1855
d. 1855

Mary Martha Bertha
b. 1855
d. 1896
m. John WILKINSON
(1852–1937), 1887
ch. 1

John Theodore
b. 1857
d. 1931
m. Margaret BRIDLE
(1862–1926), 1884
ch. 5

Ruby [BRYDON]
(1885–1976)
Pearl [COTTERILL]
(1904–1986)

Stella Maria Sarah Miles
(1879–1954)

See Franklin Family Trees
for 6 younger siblings

KEY

b. = born; d. = died; m. = married; unm. = unmarried; bd = buried; arr. = arrived; ch. = children; w. = wife

FOOTNOTE
[1] First Fleet, 1788

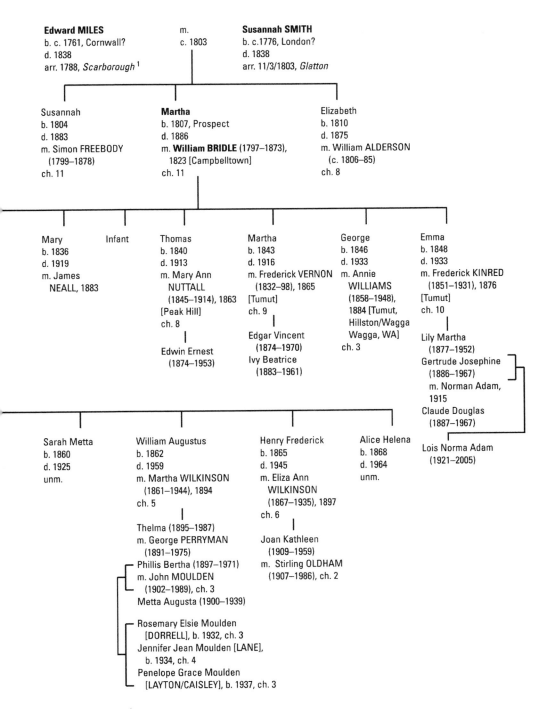

Edward MILES
b. c. 1761, Cornwall?
d. 1838
arr. 1788, *Scarborough* [1]

m.
c. 1803

Susannah SMITH
b. c.1776, London?
d. 1838
arr. 11/3/1803, *Glatton*

Susannah
b. 1804
d. 1883
m. Simon FREEBODY
(1799–1878)
ch. 11

Martha
b. 1807, Prospect
d. 1886
m. **William BRIDLE** (1797–1873),
1823 [Campbelltown]
ch. 11

Elizabeth
b. 1810
d. 1875
m. William ALDERSON
(c. 1806–85)
ch. 8

Mary
b. 1836
d. 1919
m. James
NEALL, 1883

Infant

Thomas
b. 1840
d. 1913
m. Mary Ann
NUTTALL
(1845–1914), 1863
[Peak Hill]
ch. 8

Edwin Ernest
(1874–1953)

Martha
b. 1843
d. 1916
m. Frederick VERNON
(1832–98), 1865
[Tumut]
ch. 9

Edgar Vincent
(1874–1970)
Ivy Beatrice
(1883–1961)

George
b. 1846
d. 1933
m. Annie
WILLIAMS
(1858–1948),
1884 [Tumut,
Hillston/Wagga
Wagga, WA]
ch. 3

Emma
b. 1848
d. 1933
m. Frederick KINRED
(1851–1931), 1876
[Tumut]
ch. 10

Lily Martha
(1877–1952)
Gertrude Josephine
(1886–1967)
m. Norman Adam,
1915
Claude Douglas
(1887–1967)

Lois Norma Adam
(1921–2005)

Sarah Metta
b. 1860
d. 1925
unm.

William Augustus
b. 1862
d. 1959
m. Martha WILKINSON
(1861–1944), 1894
ch. 5

Thelma (1895–1987)
m. George PERRYMAN
(1891–1975)
Phillis Bertha (1897–1971)
m. John MOULDEN
(1902–1989), ch. 3
Metta Augusta (1900–1939)

Rosemary Elsie Moulden
[DORRELL], b. 1932, ch. 3
Jennifer Jean Moulden [LANE],
b. 1934, ch. 4
Penelope Grace Moulden
[LAYTON/CAISLEY], b. 1937, ch. 3

Henry Frederick
b. 1865
d. 1945
m. Eliza Ann
WILKINSON
(1867–1935), 1897
ch. 6

Joan Kathleen
(1909–1959)
m. Stirling OLDHAM
(1907–1986), ch. 2

Alice Helena
b. 1868
d. 1964
unm.

Main sources:
Franklin Papers (Mitchell Library, State Library of New South Wales)
The Buddong Flows On: Vol. 1 The Old Hands (2003); *Vol. 2 Genuine People* (1993)

ENDNOTES

This is the first full biography of Miles Franklin to be based on the Franklin Papers, held in the Mitchell Library, State Library of NSW, Sydney. Numerous related original materials located there and elsewhere in major Australian and overseas libraries have also been utilised. Extensive supporting references are provided for interested readers and to assist future researchers.

The notes are generally grouped by paragraph. Biographical details not included in the text are located in these notes and are indexed. Short titles are used for frequently cited references. Full details are given in the bibliography.

The following abbreviations are used in the notes:

*	in *My Congenials: Miles Franklin and Friends in Letters 1879–1954*, vols 1 and 2
ABC	Australian Broadcasting Commission/Corporation
ADB/ADB S	*Australian Dictionary of Biography/Supplementary Volume* <www.adbonline.anu.edu.au/>
AHS	*[Australian] Historical Studies*
ALS	*Australian Literary Studies*
ANB	*American National Biography* (prev. *Dictionary of American Biography*)
AFWS	Australian Federation of Women's Societies
BA	*British Australasian*
BMD	Births, Marriages and Deaths
CDT	*Chicago Daily Tribune*
CHS	Chicago Historical Society

corres.	correspondence
DD	Dorothea Dreier
d.o.b./d.o.d.	date of birth/date of death
DT	*Daily Telegraph*
ed./eds	editor/s
FAW	Fellowship of Australian Writers
FP	Franklin Papers
GRAGERP	Goulburn and Regional Art Gallery Exhibition Research Project
HA	*History Australia*
HHR	Henry Handel Richardson
JMF	John Maurice Franklin
L&L	*Life and Labor*
KSP	Katharine Susannah Prichard
LN	Literary Notebook
MD	*Macquarie Dictionary*
MDR	Margaret Dreier Robins
ML	Mitchell Library, State Library of NSW, Sydney
ms./mss	manuscript/s
n.d./n.p.	no date/no further details of publication
NAA	National Archives Australia, Canberra
NAW	*Notable American Women*
NLA	National Library of Australia, Canberra
NHTPC	National Housing and Town Planning Council
NYT	*New York Times*
OCAH	*Oxford Companion to Australian History*
OCAL	*Oxford Companion to Australian Literature* (2nd edition, 1994)
ODNB	Oxford Dictionary of National Biography
pb.	paperback
PBC	Miles Franklin's Printed Books Collection
PD	Pocket Diary
Penny Post	*Goulburn Evening Penny Post*
pers. comm.	personal communication
repr.	reprinted/reproduced
RR	Raymond Roberts
RS	Rose Scott
SF	Susannah Eleanor Franklin
SMF	Stella Miles Franklin
SMH	*Sydney Morning Herald*
SRNSW	State Records NSW, Sydney
SWH	Scottish Women's Hospitals for Foreign Service
TLS	*Times Literary Supplement*
ts./tss	typescript/s
VG	Vida Goldstein
WFL	Women's Freedom League
WSPU	Women's Social and Political Union
WTUL	Women's Trade Union League

Chapter 1 — Childhood at Brindabella: 1879–1889

1   J. McIntyre, Bowral, to Stella Miles Franklin, 8/7/1902, FP vol. 8 (spellings as in the original).

2   Margaret Atwood, *Negotiating with the Dead: A Writer on Writing*, Cambridge Univ. Press, Cambridge, New York, 2002, p. 7; Martha Bridle to SF, 31/12/1878, FP vol. 108 ('out of the way place').

3   Paul Mann, 'Brindabella Valley', *Australian Geographic*, 1986, vol. 4, no. 1, p. 106; 'The Story of an Irish Pioneer', *Queanbeyan Observer and Captain's Flat Mining Record*, 2/9/1898, p. 3, and SMF to William Wilkinson, 6/10/1937, FP vol. 50; *Childhood at Brindabella*, p. 151.

4   W. Hanson, *Geographical Encyclopedia of Australia*, Govt Printer, Sydney, 1892, p. 45; SF, Notebook, FP vol. 107 [p. 102]; *Colonial City, Global City. Sydney's International Exhibition 1879*, eds Peter Proudfoot, Roslyn Maguire and Robert Freestone, Crossing Press, Darlinghurst, NSW, 2000. The Exhibition closed Apr. 1880.

5   *Childhood at Brindabella*, p. 65 ('exceptionally healthy child').

6   ibid., pp. 4–5.

7   ibid., ch. 2, p. 8.

8   ibid., pp. 10, 22. Re SF's accomplishments, see NLA MS4771/1 (card album), ML SSV* Art 56 (watercolour, c.1875), and FP vol. 110 (verses); Jane Hunt, 'Unrelaxing Fortitude: Susannah Franklin', *ALS*, 2002; *Childhood at Brindabella*, pp. 65–6. The original 'Wambrook' is located in Somerset (site visit, Margaret Francis, 23/6/2006). Leslie Bridle recalled her aunt Sue (Susannah Franklin) as humourless (pers. comm., 5/12/1982). For Joseph Vallance, see Appendix 2.

9   Linda Franklin to SMF, 16/9/1901, and Helena Lampe to SMF, 6/10/1906, FP vol. 49. Dorothy Mortlock, née Baxter, recalls JMF sobering up at the Baxter house on his way home from Goulburn (cited Jennifer Lamb (comp.) 'Miles Franklin's "My Brilliant (?) Career"! Goulburn and District References', in GRAGERP, in 2001, p. 9). The famous 'Snowy River' poem by Andrew Barton ('Banjo') Paterson, who was also bred on the Yass Plains, was first published 1890; *Childhood at Brindabella*, p. 10.

10   J. M. Franklin, 'The Federal Capital', *Penny Post*, 12/5/1900, p. 5, and 'Using the Cotter River', *Penny Post*, 17/10/1901, p. 4; *Queanbeyan Observer and Captain's Flat Mining Record*, 2/9/1898, p. 3. For Robert Cartwright (1771–1856), Anglican bush parson *extraordinaire*, see *ADB*, vol. 1.

11   *Childhood at Brindabella*, pp. 4, 50–3, 57; SMF to Mary Fullerton, 24/3/1944, FP vol. 18.

12   *Childhood at Brindabella*, pp. 10, 81, 20; 'Taking out the Pram', ML MSS 445/22.

13   Jill Roe, 'Miles Franklin's Library', *Australian Cultural History*, 1992, vol. 11; PBC, nos. 540, Q 23; *Childhood at Brindabella*, p. 109.

14   *Childhood at Brindabella*, pp. 57, 62–4, 72, 93. SMF to Joseph Furphy, 15/11/1904, Baker Papers, also mentions Bacon as 'a childhood friend', presumably Roger Bacon, medieval scholar and educational reformer.

15   Roderick, *Miles Franklin*, p. 39; 'A Trip to Brindabella', a series of jottings by 'Wombat', *Adelong and Tumut Express*, 24/2/1911 [p. 2] (said there to be approaching 200,000 acres) (ML); Jane Brumfield, 'PM Can only Dream of the Catch He Didn't Land', *Weekend Australian*, 15–16/12/1979, p. 3; *Tumut & Adelong Times*, 24/4/1928 [p. 5].

16   Parish Map Preservation Project, Brindabella, Run 58, <www.lands.nsw.gov.au>; 'Wombat', 'A Trip to Brindabella', 14/2/1911.

17   Bedulluck parish (county of Murray) map, 1904 (ML); *Biographical Register of the ACT 1820–1911*, ed. E. Fletcher, Heraldry & Genealogy Society of Canberra, Canberra, 1993, p. 61.

18   *Childhood at Brindabella*, p. 68.

19   SMF to Frank Ryland, 24/4/1943, FP vol. 37.

20   *All That Swagger*, p. 255. SMF to Elsie Belle Champion, 19/9/[1953], FP vol. 8.

21   *Childhood at Brindabella*, pp. 68–9: Douglas Stewart, *Selected Poems*, Angus & Robertson, Sydney, 1973, e.g. 'Brindabella', 'The Snow Gum'; David Campbell, *Selected Poems, 1942–1968*, Angus & Robertson, Sydney, 1973, e.g. 'The High Plains', 'The Miracle of Mullion Hill'.

22   *Childhood at Brindabella*, pp. 59, 31, 11; *NSW: Legislative Assembly, Votes & Proceedings*, 1885, vol. III, Appendix 2; *All That Swagger*, p. 310–11.

23 'The Merry Mountain Child', from Will Kirk, FP vol. 51.
24 SF, Notebook, FP vol. 107 [pp. 46, 49, 25, 81, 83]; see ch. 2 for the birth of Laurel. 'Rankin' was the family name of Maria Franklin; 'Talmage' was the name of a visiting American evangelist, Dr Thomas De Witt Talmage.
25 De Berg interview; *Childhood at Brindabella*, pp. 81–2, 107. A licence on Talbingo Station was obtained in the 1850s; when taken over by Oltmann and Sarah Lampe in 1866, it was 30,000 acres in extent with a grazing capacity of 6,000 sheep, 'Wombat', 'Historical Tumut', *Tumut Advocate*, 11/1/1910 [p. 2]; Colin Roderick, Guard Book 6, Roderick Papers, MS 1578, NLA. 'Herrenvolk': 'master race', (German), (*MD*).
26 *Childhood at Brindabella*, pp. 105, 112, 142.
27 *ibid.*, ch. 10.
28 *ibid.*, pp. 47–8; SF, Notebook, FP vol. 107 [p. 102]; *Childhood at Brindabella*, p. 81.
29 Jill Roe, 'Changing Faces: Miles Franklin and Photography', *AFS*, 2004, vol. 19, no. 43, pp. 43–54. There are two earlier photographs of SMF, as a baby and aged four, the former taken by her great-uncle George Bridle, a photographer among other things (Jill Roe, 'Miles Franklin: Bush Intellectual', p. 3).
30 *Childhood at Brindabella*, pp. 56, 82, and PBC no. 1774.
31 SF, Notebook, FP vol. 107 [p. 45]. Thomas and Annie Franklin had seven children in all (see Appendix 2).
32 *Childhood at Brindabella*, p. 87. The fictionalised place names refer to Brindabella and Talbingo respectively. Sarah Metta Lampe was SF's third sister (see Appendix 2).
33 FP vol. 62.
34 FP vol. 113X.
35 *Childhood at Brindabella*, pp. 151–2.
36 Charles Blyth to SMF, 10/12/1887–28/7/1899, FP vol. 6 (27 letters).
37 The biographical sketch of Charles Blyth is based on research undertaken for this book by Margaret Bettison.
38 *Childhood at Brindabella*, pp. 85; FP vol. 51 (passport); Jill Roe, 'Forcing the Issue, pp. 67–73 (introduction of passports). SMF's passport, p. 2, is reproduced in this book; PD, 1944, Personal Memorandum: 5 feet 1½ inches.
39 Colin Roderick to George —, 30/1/1981, Guard Book 11, Roderick Papers; De Berg interview (paintings preserved by Annie May Bridle, née Franklin).
40 *Childhood at Brindabella*, p. 89.
41 *ibid.*, p. 87.
42 *ibid.*, p. 86; 'brumby': 'wild horse'.
43 *All That Swagger*, p. 312 (remittance men); Index to Old Parish Registers (Scotland), Salt Lake City, c.1990, m/fiche, SLNSW). Blyth siblings known to have migrated to NSW: Margaret (Mrs Margaret A. Vyner, see following paragraph); George (1831–1920), labourer/overseer, Adelong; Sydney (chairman, Armidale Lands Board, 1887).
44 Advice received from Univ. of Edinburgh Archives, 2/7/2002; Charles Blyth to SMF, 8/5/1896, FP vol. 6; *SMH*, 20/2/1852 (shipping lists); form of appointment, Bd of Nat. Ed. (Misc. Corres., p. 257, m/f reel 4018, SRNSW).
45 Blyth's name appeared on the NSW electoral roll at Three Brooks, Beago, 1883–5; Charles Blyth to SMF, 28/7/1899, FP vol. 6; Charles Blyth, *ADB* office file.
46 *Wynyard Times* (Tumut), 10/12/1861, p. 2.
47 *Childhood at Brindabella*, p. 84.
48 Ransome T. Wyatt, *The History of Goulburn, N.S.W.*, Municipality of Goulburn, Goulburn, 1941, p. 375; Mrs Vyner to George Reid, 26/1/1884, Goulburn Girls' High School (SRNSW); FP vol. 113X; *Childhood at Brindabella*, p. 84.
49 *Childhood at Brindabella*, p. 89; Charles Blyth to SMF, 17/12/1887, FP vol. 6.
50 Charles Blyth to SMF, 4/5/1893, FP vol. 6; *Childhood at Brindabella*, p. 88.
51 PBC no. 836 (note: author's name Whittemore, not Whittlemore); SF, Notebook, FP vol. 107 [p. 101].
52 Charles Blyth to SMF, 5/5/1895, FP vol. 6.
53 Roe, 'Miles Franklin: Bush Intellectual', p. 3; see Appendix 2 for George Bridle, and ch. 4 for Joseph Furphy.

54   *Childhood at Brindabella*, pp. 89, 83; SMF to Ian Mudie, 19/1/1945, FP vol. 36; John G. Wood (1827–89) published over 70 books, including *Illustrated Natural History*, Routledge, London, 1861, 1886 (*ODNB*).

55   *Childhood at Brindabella*, p. 91.

56   Charles Blyth to SMF, 6/7/1889, FP vol. 6; *Childhood at Brindabella*, pp. 10, 63, 64, 105. *Hymns Ancient and Modern* was first published in 1861.

57   *Childhood at Brindabella*, p. 11 (the broken-down prospector was probably a nephew of Edward John Hopkins (1818–1901)), organist, (*ODNB*); SMF to W. Stafford, 20/10/1935, FP vol. 28; *Childhood at Brindabella*, pp. 145–6; SMF to W. A. Lampe, 15/1/1953, FP vol. 49 (ditties).

58   Berta Donald to SMF, 11/3/1936, FP vol. 27 ('You had a nice voice as a girl'); SMF to Beatrice Davis, 30/9/1952, FP vol. 38; Mila Kronidov, interview by Stephanie Liau, London, Jun. 2003; Bruce Moore, 'Towards a History of the Australian Accent', in *Talking and Listening in the Age of Modernity*, eds Joy Damousi and Desley Deacon, ANU E-Press, Canberra, 2008, p. 101 (see also ch. 11, n. 55).

59   SMF to Metta Lampe, 2/2/1889, FP vol. 113X; De Berg interview; transcript of 'First Ten Years' by Ruby Bridle in my possession (gift from the Max Kelly estate); Charles Blyth to SMF, 6/7/1889, FP vol. 6.

60   *Childhood at Brindabella*, pp. 99, 100–03.

61   ibid., pp. 106, 99, 136; De Berg interview.

62   ibid., pp. 142, 78, 109; 'Freethought', *OCAH*.

63   *Childhood at Brindabella*, p. 119.

64   ibid., p. 119.

65   Barnard, *Miles Franklin*, p. 16; *Childhood at Brindabella*, pp. 114, 103.

66   *SMH*, 23/11/1889, p. 12 (Tumut bridge opening); *Childhood at Brindabella*, p. 158.

67   *Penguin Book of Australian Autobiography*, eds John and Dorothy Colmer, Ringwood, Vic, 1987. The writing of *Childhood at Brindabella* is discussed in ch. 14.

Chapter 2 — Near Goulburn: 1890–1898

1   Miles Franklin, *My Brilliant Career*, p. 96.

2   NSW *Census*, 1891, Municipalities, Goulburn, p. 22 (population 10,916).

3   'Serious disputes': affidavit in support of certificate of release, NSW Supreme Court (Bankruptcy), 27/7/1897, incl. documents, No. 1124 (ref. 10/23117), and for comment on the breakup, see *All That Swagger*, p. 318; *Penny Post*, 23/1/1890, p. 4, and 2/4/1895, p. 4; SF, Notebook, vol. 107 [p. 97]; *Childhood at Brindabella*, p. 95, and *My Brilliant Career*, p. 8.

4   The Frazer family who owned the property in the mid-20th century also named it 'Stillwater', without knowing that this had been Susannah Franklin's choice (pers. comm., Rose Frazer, Goulburn, 31/3/2002). *Penny Post*, 6/3/1890, p. 4, and *Goulburn Herald*, 6/3/1890. Marcelle Leicht, 'Miles Franklin's Life in the Goulburn District', in GRAGERP, 2001, p. 4.

5   Site visit, 30/3/2002.

6   Literary Notebooks, FP vol. 3, pp. 462–63, repr. *Diaries*, pp. 168–9.

7   Johanna Wilhelmine Weigel (1847–1940), *ADB S*.

8   Great Dividing Range: the generic name for the eastern highlands of Australia, running from Cape York to western Victoria, 150–300 km in width, *Australian Encyclopedia*, Grolier Society of Australia, Sydney, 3rd rev. edn 1979, vol. 3 (*AE*); D. N. Jeans (ed.), *Historical Geography of NSW to 1901*, Reed Education, Sydney, 1972, p. 62.

9   Present-day 'Stillwater' as marked on ordnance survey maps is on a different site, nearer to and visible to the south from the Thornford road. The property, owned by the Baxter family in the 1890s, was then called 'Longfield'. Jacob Baxter purchased the 'Stillwater' blocks in 1906, *Penny Post*, 11/5/1937, p. 4 (Baxter obit.).

10   Land purchases at Bangalore date back to 1833 (NSW Government *Gazette*, 21/8/1833, p. 329) and a farm named 'Bangalore' was established by 1836 (Allan E. J. Edwards, *Earliest Monaro and Burragorang, 1790 to 1840*, Palmerston, ACT, 1998, n.p., pp. 89–90); news from Bangalore, *Penny Post*, e.g. 10/5/94, p. 4. *My Congenials*, vol. 1 has several letters from SMF at Bangalore, 1899–1902.

11   *Alphabetical Index to Country Localities of NSW*: Thornford (13 miles south-west of
     Goulburn); *NSW Government Railways. Timetable & Fares*, Government Printer, Sydney, 1892,
     p. 61; Ray Mooney, pers. comm., Goulburn, 31/3/2002; *My Brilliant Career*, p. 9; Bangalore
     cemetery site visit, 30/3/2002. Re Penelope Sybilla Macauley (1852–99), NSW BMD indexes,
     and *Penny Post*, 20/7/1899, p. 4.

12   *NSW Post Office Directory* 1889–90; *Penny Post* 10/5/1894, p. 4 ('one of the finest roads in the
     colony').

13   *My Brilliant Career*, p. 8; Wyatt, *History of Goulburn*, p. 259. By 1899 there were twelve at
     Thornford in addition to JMF: Jacob Baxter, farmer; Moses Bilton, hawker; Samuel Crouch,
     dealer; Edward McCallister, grazier; Thomas and John Macauley, dairy farmers; William Neely,
     dairy farmer; Walter Oakley, fruit grower; Alex Paton, John Rowe, Henry Taylor and [?]
     Woods, all farmers; *NSW Post Office Commercial Directory*, 1898–99.

14   *My Brilliant Career*, p. 8, but the early chapters of *Cockatoos* are the best source; see also
     Childhood at Brindabella, p. 97.

15   Schools: petition for the establishment of a provisional school at Thornford, 4/3/1889
     (signatories John Macauley, James Smith, Will J. Neely and T. A. Macauley), SRNSW,
     5/17831.3; Index to Teachers' Rolls (m/f, reel 1994) and Mae Gillespie, 'History of Thornford
     Public School', Schools File [1913], NSW Dept of School Education Archives. Wesleyan
     churches: est. Bangalore, 1859 (*SMH*, 26/8/1859, p. 5), Thornford, 1883 (*Weekly Advocate*
     19/1/1884, p. 343). Mary Anne Elizabeth Gillespie (1856–1938), teacher, *SMH*, 13/6/1938, p. 8.

16   Letter dated 28/1/1890, 5/17831.3, and Index to Teachers' Rolls (reel 1994) NSW Dept of
     School Education Archives.

17   Re Miss Gillespie, Dorothy Mortlock, née Baxter, interview 1984, held Goulburn & District
     Historical Society; Marcelle Leicht, 'Miles Franklin's Life in the Goulburn District', in
     GRAGERP, 2001, p. 8.

18   Charles Blyth to SMF, 4/5/1895, FP vol. 6; J. Fletcher and J. Burnswoods, *Government Schools
     in NSW 1848–1963*, NSW Dept of Education, Sydney, 1963, p. 250; Charles Blyth to SMF,
     27/7/1894, FP vol. 6.

19   *Penny Post*, 16/1/1912, p. 4 (obit. James Gillespie); *Penny Post*, 25/2/1892, p. 4 (popular);
     'Grabben Gullen': 'small waters' from the Wiradjuri language (site visit 26/7/2006). Index to
     Teachers' Rolls (n. 15 above) contains a sorry record of unfulfilled aspiration.

20   Vida Goldstein (1869–1949), *ADB* vol. 9, and Ethel Florence Lindesay Richardson
     (1870–1946), *ADB* vol. 11; Charles Blyth to SMF, 4/10/1890, FP vol. 6; *Penny Post*, 26/3/1892,
     p. 3, and *Goulburn Herald*, 25/3/1892, p. 5 (commendations).

21   *My Brilliant Career*, p. 11, and see attachment, 1889 petition, n. 15 above. JMF was a steady
     supporter of the school, e.g. 'Arbor Day at Thornford', *Penny Post*, 19/9/1901, p. 4.

22   ML PX* D250–1, no. 2.

23   Identifications according to Roderick, *Miles Franklin*, p. 63, who had access to family
     knowledge. SMF was like her grandmother Lampe in height, also in appearance (family recall,
     Jenn Lane, pers. comm.).

24   *My Brilliant Career*, p. 12; Zara Baar Aronson, 'Some Impressions of the Authoress of *My
     Brilliant Career*', *Home Queen*, 18/12/1903, p. 2 (*ADB* vol. 7).

25   'History of Thornford School', *passim*; *Penny Post*, 25/2/1892, p. 4 and 27/8/1892, p. 4. Picnics
     were held in Feb., at the beginning of the new school year.

26   Charles Blyth to SMF, 4/10/1890, FP vol. 6; PBC, nos 851, 678, 177B; *Penny Post*: 25/2/1892, p. 4;
     28/2/1893, p. 4; 28/2/1895, p. 4, and 2/3/1895, p. 4; Charles Blyth to SMF, 17/6/1893, FP vol. 6.

27   Charles Blyth to SMF, 27/7/1894, FP vol. 6.

28   Marcelle Leicht, 'Miles Franklin's Life in the Goulburn District', in GRAGERP, 2001, p. 9 (daily
     regimen); SMF to Bruce Sutherland, 18/3/1954, FP vol. 44* re Joan of Arc, first brought alive
     for her by George Bernard Shaw, SMF to Donald McLean, 26/12/1949, ML MSS 3659/1 and
     Jill Roe, *History for the People*, History Council of NSW, Sydney, 1999.

29   Edie P— [Rebecca Edith Paton?] to SMF, 28/5/1903, Plain Farm, Burrowa, FP vol. 9B.

30   Charles Blyth to SMF, 4/5/1895, FP vol. 6; Index to Teachers' Roll, NSW Dept of School
     Education Archives; LN, FP vol. 3, p. 648 and ML MSS 445/36, item 17 (notes on teachers).

31   (Sir) Frederick (Baron) von Mueller, *Introduction to Botanic Teachings at the Schools of
     Victoria, through References to Leading Native Plants*, Ferres, Melbourne, 1877, PBC no. 343,

(and *ADB* vol. 5); *Childhood at Brindabella*, p. 59 ('unafraid'); *Up the Country*, p. 30; *Penny Post*, 6/11/1894, p. 2 and 23/2/1895, p. 2.

32 *Trilby: A Novel*, Bell, London and Bombay, 1894; *Esther Waters: An English Story*, Scott, London, 1894; Charles Blyth to SMF, 24/6/1896, FP vol. 6.

33 LN, FP vol. 3, pp. 464–68.

34 LN, FP vol. 3, p. 464; *A Gregarious Culture*, p. 145.

35 LN, FP vol. 3, pp. 464–68; SMF to David Martin, 26/7/1952, FP vol. 41; Margaret Bettison and Jill Roe, 'Miles Franklin as Reader', in *A History of the Book in Australia*, vol. 2, eds Martyn Lyons and John Arnold, Univ. of Qld Press, St Lucia, Qld, 2001. Olive Schreiner (1855–1920), *The Story of an African Farm*, Hutchinson, London, 1883 (*ODNB*); Kay Daniels, 'Emma Brooke, Fabian, Feminist and Writer', *Women's History Review*, 2003, no. 2; Gustav Freytag (1816–95), *The Lost Manuscript*, Edward Arnold, London, 1887 (first pub. 1865), PBC no. 631. Re the Amykos Educational Competition: *Dawn*, Oct.–Dec. 1894, *Bulletin*, 8/2–7/3/1896, p. 3, and *Young Australia*, 2/4/1896, p. 16, ML MSS 118, all ML; see also SMF to Dear Sirs, 10/12/1936, FP vol. 28.

36 [?] to SMF, n.d., FP vol. 46, p. 109 (a) and (c); W. C. Cooper to SMF, 15/12/1893, FP vol. 6; 'Gossip by the Way', *Book Lover*, Aug. 1905, vol. 7, no. 76, p. 1 (dated 1900); *My Brilliant Career*, pp. 78, 142; 'Goulburn Technological Museum', *Goulburn Herald*, 11/7/1892, n. p., *Childhood at Brindabella*, p. 141.

37 *Penny Post*, 31/5/1894, p. 4 (Bishop conducts confirmations at Collector); confirmation card, 27/5/1894 (signed Rev. J. H. Williams), FP vol. 51; James Herbert Williams, (18??–1913) was the incumbent, Gunning–Collector 1887–1896 (*Crockford's Clerical Directory*, 1911, p. 1615, and *SMH*, 30/9/1913, p. 18). Re SMF's early religious experience: *My Brilliant Career*, pp. 242–3; SMF, PD 22/1/1925; *Childhood at Brindabella*, p. 43; De Berg interview, 1977; J. H. Williams to SMF, 15/12/1903, FP vol. 6, and Rev. Stanley Best to SMF, 30/12/[1901], FP vol. 10; 'A Dialogue…', FP vol. 59/1–3.

38 SF, Notebook, FP vol. 107 [p. 74]; O'Harris, *Was It Yesterday?*, p. 75; *Cockatoos*, p. 35.

39 SMF to J. K. Moir, 14/3/1954, J. K. Moir Colln; Andrew Baxter to Colin Roderick, n.d., Guard Book 10, Roderick Papers, pp. 18–19.

40 Charlie Vallance [Hayes] to SMF, 27/4/1954, FP vol. 50; *My Brilliant Career*, pp. 21, 41; *Cockatoos*, p. 228.

41 FP vol. 111, cards notifying exam time; *Penny Post*, 11/12/1894, p. 2, 16/1/1896, p. 2 and 25/2/1896, p. 4; *Cockatoos*, p. 204.

42 Jill Roe, 'Miles Franklin and 1890s Goulburn', *ALS*, 2002, and Ransome T. Wyatt, *History of Goulburn, N.S.W.*, Municipality of Goulburn, Goulburn, 1945, ch. XIX, Cultural Societies; LN, FP vol. 3, p. 650 and FP vol. 51A, clippings of singers and theatre; *Cockatoos*, pp. 7–8, 101ff.; SMF to Thomas Wood, 31/12/1944, ML MSS3659/1; Wood (1892–1950) was a composer (*ODNB*).

43 Charles Blyth to SMF, 9/8/1895, FP vol. 6; 'Courtship', *Girlhood in America: An Encyclopedia*, ed. Miriam Forman-Brunell, Santa Barbara, Calif., 2001, vol. 1; Janet McCalman, *Sex and Suffering. Women's Health and a Women's Hospital: The Royal Women's Hospital, Melbourne 1856–1966*, Melbourne Univ. Press, Carlton, Vic, 1998, p. 73.

44 Charles Blyth to SMF, 9/8/1895, FP vol. 6; *My Brilliant Career*, p. 31; *Cockatoos*, Preface, p. 183.

45 Lynne Vallone, *Disciplines of Virtue: Girls' Culture in the Eighteenth and Nineteenth Centuries*, Yale Univ. Press, New Haven, c.1995, pp. 2, 5; 'Still Brilliant 100 Years On', *Macquarie University News*, Sept. 2001, p. 6, resume of unpub. paper, Beverley Kingston, 'Miles Franklin: an Australian Girl'.

46 *My Brilliant Career*, p. 26.

47 E. W. Dunlop, 'The Public High Schools of NSW, 1883–1912', *J. Royal Aust. Hist. Soc.*, 1965, vol. 51, no. 1, p. 65; Ransome T. Wyatt, *History of Goulburn, N.S.W.*, Municipality of Goulburn, Goulburn, 1945, p. 362, and *Penny Post*, 1/4/1896, n.p. (advertisement).

48 SF, Notebook, FP vol. 107, back cover. Thornford Proprietary Butter Factory was launched in 1890, probably at Baxter's 'Longfield', Goulburn & District Historical Society *Bulletin*, Jul. 1971, p. 2.

49 FP vol. 50, pp. 129c–130; Papers filed in Bankruptcy, cited n. 3 above; *Goulburn Herald*, 21/8/1896, p. 5; SF, Notebook, FP vol. 107, back cover.

50   JMF, Affidavit, 1897; Tal Franklin to SMF, 10/10/1896, FP vol. 48 (filed 2nd letter), Charles
     Blyth to SMF, 20/3/1897, FP vol. 6.
51   JMF (from 'Stillwater') to SMF, 7/12/1896, FP vol. 48.
52   Charles Blyth to SMF, 20/3/1897, FP vol. 6.
53   'Daughters and Fathers', *Girlhood in America: An Encyclopedia*, ed. Miriam Forman-Brunell,
     Santa Barbara, Calif., 2001, vol. 1; Linda Franklin to SMF [1902], FP vol. 49; Bruce Scates,
     'Miles Franklin's Radicalism', *ALS*, 2002; *Penny Post*, 3/7/1894, p. 3 (advertisement). Edward
     William O'Sullivan (1846–1910) MLA, represented Queanbeyan for nineteen years (*ADB*,
     vol. 11); JMF was enrolled in the Collector division of his electorate; B. E. Mansfield,
     Australian Democrat: The Career of Edward William O'Sullivan 1846–1910, Sydney Univ.
     Press, Sydney, 1965.
54   'Daughters and Mothers', 'Emotions', *Girlhood in America: An Encyclopedia*, ed. Miriam
     Forman-Brunell, Santa Barbara, Calif., 2001, vol. 2, pp. 196, 256; Jane Hunt, 'Unrelaxing
     Fortitude', *ALS*, 2002; *My Brilliant Career*, p. 30.
55   J. H. Williams, 25/6/1896, FP vol. 6, p. 335c, and E. W. O'Sullivan, 26/6/1896, FP vol. 51;
     Marcelle Leicht, 'Miles Franklin's Life in the Goulburn District', in GRAGERP, 2001, p. 24.
56   SMF to Charles Graham, 8/6/1936, FP vol. 49; 'What Now, Eliza? The Chronicles of Lizzie
     (Kellett) Gunter, 1865–1971. Australian Bush Teacher', as told to Jeanne Kellett Cox (unpub.
     ms., courtesy Jeanne Kellett Cox).
57   SMF to Mrs Barnett, 23/9/1941, FP vol. 35, and SMF to Miss Shain, n.d. [c.1940], FP vol. 34;
     De Berg interview, 1977; Elizabeth Webby, Introduction, *My Brilliant Career* centenary
     edition. *Johns's Notable Australians* (George Robertson & Co, Melbourne, 1906) gives SMF's
     birth date as 3/10/1883, maintained in the successor publication *Who's Who in Australia* in
     the 1940s (cf. artist Margaret Preston, who lowered her age by seven years when she
     married at age 45, Janet Hawley, 'Thoroughly Modern Maggie', *SMH, Good Weekend*,
     4/6/2005, p. 27).
58   'Australian girl': see Richard White, *Inventing Australia: Images and Identity 1688–1980*, Allen
     & Unwin, North Sydney, 1981, pp. 77–8. Charles Blyth to SMF, 24/4/1896, 9/5/1896, FP vol. 6,
     and *Penny Post*, 26/3/1896, p. 4, repr. *A Gregarious Culture*.
59   Bettison and Roe, 'Miles Franklin's Topical Writings'; *My Career Goes Bung*, p. 218 mentions
     prose sketches for one of the big dailies, sometimes fetching 25 shillings, but that came later
     (see ch. 4, pp. 110–13).
60   'New Chums', FP vol. 57; 'For Sale…', FP vol. 52; 'Within a Footstep…', FP vol. 53 (and see also
     FP vol. 54 for another version, subtitled 'An Old, Old Story', 1896). Re the Amykos
     competition, see n. 35 above.
61   Charles Blyth to SMF, 27/9/1895, FP vol. 6. Angus & Robertson, established 1886, one of
     Australia's most important book selling and publishing firms, operated from Castlereagh St,
     Sydney, from 1890 until the 1970s, when it moved to N. Ryde, Sydney, and later became an
     imprint of HarperCollinsPublishers, Australia. A search of Yass papers 1895–6 did not disclose
     a writing by May Hall.
62   Charles Blyth to SMF, 27/9/1896, FP vol. 6.
63   'Recollections of a Journalist', *Penny Post*, 3/12/ 1921, p. 2. Thomas (Tom) John Hebblewhite
     (c.1857–1923), a Yorkshireman educated at Manchester Grammar School, first came to Sydney
     in late 1879, and in May 1885 joined the *Penny Post*, which he edited 1885–1900, continuing as
     an associate editor until retirement in 1920 (*Bulletin*, 25/1/1923, p. 44, and Kirkpatrick,
     Country Conscience, p. 215).
64   T. J. Hebblewhite to SMF, 8/9/1896, FP vol. 6.*
65   'Lord Dunleve's Ward', ML MSS 445/15–16 (35 chs).
66   Lynn Milne, 'Lord Dunleve's Ward', unpub. conference paper, Macquarie Univ. 2004, p. 1, copy
     in my possession courtesy the author; T. J. Hebblewhite to SMF 8/9/1896, FP vol. 6.
67   Milne, 'Lord Dunleve's Ward', (see n. 65 above) pp. 5, 14.
68   'Alice Desmond', *Penny Post*, Mar.–May 1894, is an interesting example of a Home Counties
     serial which nonetheless carried a modernising message for girls, see Jill Roe, '*My Brilliant
     Career* and 1890s Goulburn', in *ALS*, 2002, p. 367. *Madame Weigel's Journal of Fashion* also
     carried serials (reading works there by Carmen Sylva, Queen of Roumania, stood SMF in good
     stead in the Balkans in 1917, LN, FP vol. 3, p. 463).

69   Ransome T. Wyatt, *History of Goulburn, N.S.W.*, Municipality of Goulburn, Goulburn, 1945, p. 77; Stephen J. Tazewell, *Grand Goulburn. First Inland City of Australia: A Random History*, Goulburn City Council, Goulburn, 1991; Jill Roe, 'Miles Franklin and 1890s Goulburn', in *ALS*, 2002; Kirkpatrick, *Country Conscience*, p. 424; Mena Calthorpe interview, Giulia Giuffre, *A Writing Life: Interviews with Australian Women Writers*, Allen & Unwin, N. Sydney, 1990, p. 28 (Hebblewhite's library). Works by Mary Eleanor Wilkins, later Freeman (1852–1930) and Richard Jefferies (1848–87) in the Mechanics' Institute library included *A New England Nun and Other Stories* (Wilkins, 1891) and *Life of the Fields* (Jefferies, 1884), Goulburn Mechanics' Institute Library, *Catalogue*, 1898, ML (*ANB, ODNB*).

70   FP vol. 62 n.d. [1896?].

71   JMF's poetry books included Henry Kendall, *Poems* (George Robertson, Melbourne, 1890), a gift from Aunt Mary Neall, née Lampe, 1899, PBC no. 257; 'The Woman Speaks', *The Bulletin Reciter: A Collection of Verses from the* Bulletin *1880–1901*, Bulletin, Sydney, 1901, p. 83: SMF to Ambrose Pratt, 25/6/1936, FP vol. 27 and SMF to George Mackaness, n.d. [1940s], Mackaness Papers, MS 534. Aunt Mary Neall (1836–1919), a woman of some distinction, was Miles' great-aunt (see Appendix 2). Ambrose Pratt (1874–1944), journalist and businessman, was born at Forbes, NSW (*ADB* vol. 11).

72   SMF to Uncle Gus Lampe, 15/1/1953, FP vol. 49; 'Kate Kearney' (possibly a reference to 'Killarney Kate', Melbourne street singer Ellen Cahill (c.1863–1934), *ADB* S.

73   Tal Franklin to SMF, 10/10/1896, FP vol. 48; Charles Blyth to SMF, 21/11/1896, FP vol. 6; JMF to SMF, 7/12/1896, FP vol. 48; Miss (Lois) Adam to Colin Roderick, 10/6/1979, Guard Book 7, Roderick Papers; *My Brilliant Career*, p. 45. Re Herbert (Bertie) and Phillip Wilkinson, see Appendix 2, and Margaret Francis, Stella Vernon, Colin Wilkinson, Barbara Crichton (eds), *The Buddong Flows On*, vol. 1: *The Old Hands*, p. 416 (family photograph), and vol. 2: *Genuine People*, pp. 347ff. (Wilkinson family); Pamela Mathers, pers. comm.

74   SF, Notebook, FP vol. 107 [p. 102]; FP vol. 6.

75   Charles Blyth to SMF, 4/2/1897, 29/3/1897, 18/4/1897, FP vol. 6; 'Currer Bell' [Charlotte Bronte], *Jane Eyre*, Smith, Elder, London, 1847. Re George and Margaret Franklin's family, see Appendix 2.

76   E. W. O'Sullivan to SMF, 10/5/1897, FP vol. 51; M. Gillespie, Application for Leave of Absence, 13/7/1897, 5/17831.3, letter 40555, NSW Dept School Education Archives.

77   *Penny Post*, 16/9/1897, p. 2; Linda Franklin to SMF, 20/9/1897 and 30/10/1897, FP vol. 49.

78   JMF to SMF, n. 51 above, on the prevalence of hydatids, and SF, Notebook, FP vol. 107 [p. 33]; Sarah Lampe to SMF, 29/10/1897, FP vol. 48.

79   SMF to Uncle —[?], 21/10/1901, FP vol. 50, and Aunt Lena Lampe to SMF, 6/10/1906, FP vol. 49.*

80   *My Brilliant Career*, p. 31; E. W. O'Sullivan to SMF, 15/10/1897 and 13/6/1898, FP vol. 6.

81   SF, Notebook, FP vol. 107 [p. 103] and FP vol. 51A, 24; Ruby Bridle, ms. notes on *Childhood at Brindabella*; Theodor Lampe to SMF, 20/1/1953, FP vol. 49; SMF to Angus & Robertson, 30/3/1899, ML MSS 314/31, Angus and Robertson Manuscript Register 1896–1937, ML MSS 269, Box 16, both.*

82   Richard Coleman, 'Surviving as a Career', *SMH* (*Good Weekend*), 23/8/1980, p. 15 (Witcombe interview).

Chapter 3 — From 'Possum Gully' to Penrith: 1899–1902

1   Annie Black to Miles Franklin, Balmain, 17/11/1901, FP vol. 7.

2   Miss [Lois] Adam to Colin Roderick, 10/6/1979, Guard Book 7, Roderick Papers, and Gertrude Kinred (Mrs Adam, 1886–1967), FP vol. 49, p. 283. SMF requested the return of her mss (SMF to J. B. Pinker, 6/1/1901, FP vol. 80), and Henry Lawson promised to return the corrected proofs (Henry Lawson to SMF, 18/3/1902, Goulburn postmark, FP vol. 6).

3   'What Now, Eliza? The Chronicles of Lizzie (Kellett) Gunter, 1865–1971. Australian Bush Teacher' as told to Jeanne Kellett Cox (unpub. ms., courtesy Jeanne Kellett Cox); SMF to E. M. Gunter, 22/11/1947, FP vol. 28.

4   T. J. Hebblewhite, 'Recollections of a Journalist', *Penny Post*, 3/12/1921, p. 2.

5   *ibid.*, p. 2, and T. J. Hebblewhite to SMF, 13/9/1901, FP vol. 6.

6   FP vol. 88, p. 81 (calendar); SMF to Angus & Robertson, 30/3/1899, ML MSS 314/31, Angus & Robertson Manuscript Register 1896–1937, ML MSS 3269, Box 16, both;* SMF to J. F. Archibald, 18/4/1899, FP vol. 80; Alex Montgomery to SMF, 11/2/1902, FP vol. 8; T. J. Hebblewhite to SMF, 30/7/1899, FP vol. 6; LN, FP vol. 3, p. 730. Jules Francois Archibald (1856–1919), *ADB* vol. 3; untitled talk on Australian literature, FP vol. 77, p. 27; SMF to J. F. Archibald, 5/9/1901, FP vol. 7.*

7   T. J. Hebblewhite to SMF, 30/7/1899, FP vol. 6.

8   *ibid.*, 4/9/1899. Re 'Within a Footstep of the Goal' (see ch. 2, n. 60) pronounced 'a fine picture of Australian bush life' but needing revision; also T. J. Hebblewhite to SMF, 16/9/1899, FP vol. 6. 'A Common Case', an early sketch dated Jul. 1898, FP vol. 57, was first published (in part) Kay Daniels and Mary Murnane (eds), *Uphill All The Way: A Documentary History of Women in Australia*, Univ. of Qld Press, St Lucia, Qld, 1980 (repr. 1989 as *Australian Women: A Documentary History*, pp. 118–19).

9   SMF to Henry Lawson, 19/11/1899, FP vol. 6.* Henry Lawson (1867–1922), short story writer and balladist (*ADB* vol. 10).

10   J. F. Archibald to SMF, 18/4/1899, FP vol. 80, and A. G. Stephens to SMF, 3/1/1900, FP vol. 80. Alfred George Stephens (1865–1933), b. Toowoomba, an influential literary critic, edited the *Bulletin*'s 'Red Page' 1894–1906 (*ADB* vol. 12).

11   Henry Lawson to SMF, Wednesday [postmark 18/1/1900], FP vol. 6.

12   Sydney Hospital Nurses' Register, Oct. 1898–Oct. 1907, p. 409, Sydney Hospital and Sydney Eye Hospital Museum Collection, Lucy Osburn Nightingale Museum, Sydney.

13   'Henry Lawson', *Meanjin Papers*, 1942, vol. 1, no. 1, repr. *A Gregarious Culture*.

14   John Barnes, 'Henry Lawson in London', *Quadrant*, Jul. 1979; Henry Lawson, Preface, Apr. 1901, *My Brilliant Career* (1974 edn).

15   E. W. O'Sullivan, 22/1/1900, FP vol. 6.

16   Nurses' Register (see n. 12 above), and Matron Rose Creal Diary (1896–1901), 29/1/1900, p. 44, *ibid.*, re a letter of resignation, which does not survive; SF, Notebook, FP vol. 107 [pp. 85, 25, 103]; SMF, 'Well Mervyn', c.1945, PBC enclosure, ML MSS 3659/1; NSW BMD records, death certificate no. 03599 (transcript) and *Tumut & Adelong Times* 23/2/1900, p. 3. There does not seem to be any basis to the still current legend that Mervyn Franklin died under mysterious circumstances to do with the waterholes at 'Stillwater'.

17   'A Ministering Angel', ch. 2, repr. *A Gregarious Culture*; information from Mrs Orr to Beatrice Davis, Angus & Robertson, ML MSS 3269, vol. 274, p. 515.

18   PD, 29/5/1951.

19   Henry Lawson to George Robertson, n.d. [early Apr. 1900], cited Barker, *Dear Robertson*, p. 28, and Bertha Lawson to SMF, 13/3/1900, FP vol. 6.

20   Edmund G. Barton (1868–1903), law clerk; Linda Franklin to SMF, 9/6/1903, FP vol. 49.

21   Fragment, ML MSS 445/39, p. 473; (Dame) Nellie Melba (1861–1931), *ADB* vol. 10.

22   *Penny Post*, 8/7/1899, p. 4; ML MSS 445/39, pp. 475–7; *Cockatoos*, pp. 103–4. Amy Castles (1880–1951), concert singer (*ADB* vol. 7).

23   *Cockatoos*, p. 151.

24   Theodor Lampe to SMF, 12/12/1898, FP vol. 49 (re JMF's health).

25   *Penny Post*, 23/1/1900, p. 2: fragment, ML MSS 445/39, p. 477 (*verso*).

26   SMF to Rene Laws, 3/10/1953, FP vol. 45; Bertha Lawson to SMF, 13/3/1900, FP vol. 6.

27   Fragment, ML MSS 445/39, p. 477 (*verso*).

28   Henry Lawson to SMF, Wednesday [postmark 18/1/1900], and SMF draft to Henry Lawson, n.d. [Jan./Feb. 1900], FP vol. 6. All sketches, FP vol. 57; 'Of Life' (*Steele Rudd's Magazine*, Mar. 1906, 'by Miles Franklin', repr. *A Gregarious Culture*); SMF to Jessie Paterson 3/6/1902 (list of sketches) and Jessie Paterson to SMF, 2/8/[1902], FP vol. 8 (mentions 'No Man's Land').

29   'Of Love', FP vol. 57; 'Gossip by the Way', *Book Lover*, Aug. 1905, p. 92 ('by Miles Franklin'); Collector/Caligda, NSW Government *Gazette*, 1866, p. 138.

30   'How Dead Man's Gap was Named', *Australian Journal*, 1/9/1904, pp. 505–7 ('by Miles Franklin'); 'Ben Barrett's Break up', FP vol. 57.

31   SMF to Jessie Paterson, 3/6/1902, FP vol. 8; 'Jilted', FP vol. 57, *Australasian*, Melbourne, 14/8/1909, pp. 436–7.

32   Draft, 'Some Letters of a Torn Maid', FP vol. 57; 'An Old House Post', *Australasian*, 26/3/1904, p. 727, repr. *A Gregarious Culture*; 'Of Humanism', FP vol. 59.

33 Undated fragment on style, FP vol. 59/5; 'Of Life', *Steele Rudd's Magazine*, Mar. 1906, repr. *A Gregarious Culture.*

34 Bettison and Roe, 'Miles Franklin's Topical Writings', publications for 1904, 1905, 1906; SMF to J. B. Pinker, 18/11/1901, FP vol. 80* ; 'Emotions', *Girlhood in America: An Encyclopedia,* ed. Miriam Forman-Brunell, Santa Barbara, Calif., 2001, vol. 2, p. 258.

35 Henry Lawson to SMF, 16/4/1900 and her letter of authorisation 19/4/1900, FP vol. 6; untitled talk on Australian literature, FP vol. 77, n.d. [probably 1940s]; Angus & Robertson to SMF, 1/5/1900, FP vol. 80, and Roderick, *Miles Franklin*, p. 78. Caroline Viera Jones, 'Australian Imprint', PhD thesis. Louise Mack (1870–1935), *ADB* vol. 10.

36 Henry Lawson to SMF, 6/9/1900, FP vol. 6 and reply 17/10/1900, ML Doc. 2211, FP vol. 80, p. 17.* William Blackwood (1836–1912) was managing director of the Scottish firm, founded in 1804 in the Tory interest credited with reviving the company's lists in the late nineteenth century (*ODNB*). James Brand Pinker (1863–1922) opened for business in London in 1896 (*ODNB*); John Barnes, 'Henry Lawson and the "Pinker of Agents"', also Lucy Sussex, '"… Riotous Living among the Fleshpots of the West End": Henry Lawson in London and as reported in Australia', ASAL/Webby conference, Univ. of Sydney, Feb. 2006.

37 William Blackwood to J. B. Pinker, 29/1/1900, cited Barnes, 'Henry Lawson in London', *Quadrant*, Jul. 1979, p. 32, and FP vol. 80; J. B. Pinker to SMF, 30/1/1901 and reply 6/2/1901 (possibly a misdating), FP vol. 80.*

38 Henry Lawson to William Blackwood, 8/4/1901, repr. Harry T. Chaplin, *Henry Lawson*, Wentworth Press, Surry Hills, NSW, 1974, p. 69. William Blackwood to Henry Lawson, 12/4/1901, Blackwood Archive, National Library of Scotland, MS 30389 (Private Letter Book, 3/1–15/8/1901). Arthur Frank Maquarie (1874–1955), freelance writer, graduated Univ. of Sydney 1895, went to London (*OCAL*).

39 J. B. Pinker to SMF, 15/4/1901, FP vol. 80; Henry Lawson, 'Culled Contributors', *Bulletin*, 14/2/1903, 'Red Page'; Viera Jones, 'Australian Imprint', PhD thesis, p. 16; Arthur Maquarie to William Blackwood, 15/4/1901, cited John Barnes, 'Henry Lawson in London', *Quadrant*, Jul. 1979; Arthur Maquarie to SMF, 19/12/1901, FP vol. 7; F. D. Tredfy, *The House of Blackwood 1804–1954: The History of a Publishing Firm*, Blackwood, Edinburgh, 1954, p. 154.

40 SMF to Henry Lawson, 17/10/1900, ML Doc 2211;* *My Brilliant Career*, p. 228; SMF to Charles Graham, 8/6/1936, FP vol. 49; Stella O'Brien to SMF, 25/2/[?] and 29/8/1900, FP vols 6, 7; Charles Graham to SMF, 2/9/1901 [postmark], FP vol. 49. Charles Graham (1869–1950) was a son of Edward Graham of 'Montrose', south of Currawang.

41 *Penny Post*, 25/9/1902, p. 3 ('hare drive'); *Penny Post*, 30/3/1901, p. 4 (possibly by SMF).

42 *Cockatoos*, pp. 214, 268.

43 *Times* (London), 8/7/1901, p. 6; J. B. Pinker to SMF, 9/7/1901, FP vol. 80; Edgar Vernon to SMF, 21/8/1901, FP vol. 50; inscription, *My Brilliant Career*, PBC no. 156; Linda Franklin to SMF, 16/9/1901, FP vol. 49 and SMF to J. F. Archibald, 5/9/1901, FP vol. 6, both;* *Goulburn Herald*, 13/9/1901, p. 5. For Edgar Vernon (1874–1970), see Appendix 2.

44 Linda Franklin to SMF, 16/9/1901, FP vol. 49;* Maggie Bridle to SMF, 16/9/1901, FP vol. 47; Metta Lampe to SMF, 7/10/1901, FP vol. 49; PBC, no. 802. Re 'the Lordly Phillip', see ch. 2, n. 73. Maggie Bridle, née Wilkinson, was an older sister of Phillip and Bertie Wilkinson (see Appendix 2).

45 Henry Lawson to SMF, n.d., FP vol. 6. See FP vol. 121A for collected press cuttings of reviews from London and for ts. (edited selection), ML MSS 445/40 (some paginations).

46 *The Journal of Marie Bashkirtseff* [c.1859–84], Virago, London, 1985, English trans. 1890; *Academy*, 13/7/1901; *Manchester Guardian*, 17/7/1901; *Glasgow Herald*, 1/8/1901; *Times* (London), 3/8/1901, p 4.

47 S C—[?] to SMF, 5/10/1901, FP vol. 7; Charles Graham to SMF, 14/10/1901, FP vol. 49; Linda Franklin to SMF, 12/1/1902 and 3/3/1902, FP vol. 49.

48 SMF to Dear Uncle, 21/10/01, FP vol. 50* (see ch. 2 for the likely construction of the M'Swats); Herbert Wilkinson to SMF, 5/2/1902, FP vol. 50; Linda Franklin to SMF, 16/5/1903, FP vol. 49; Edward Bridle, possibly Edward John Bridle (1856–1943), a cousin of SF (see Appendix 2).

49 *DT* (Sydney), 7/9/1901, p. 6; *Penny Post*, 10/9/1901, p. 4 and 14/9/1903, p 3.

50 *Penny Post*, 13/5/1902, p. 4.

51 The *Goulburn Herald* seems not to have noticed either Miles Franklin or her book Sept. 1901–May 1902, except for the ad of 13 Sept. cited n. 43 above.
52 George McAlister to SMF, Montague St, Goulburn, FP vol. 7; *SMH*, 28/9/1901, p 4.
53 Beverley Kingston, *Macquarie University News*, Sept. 2001, résumé. Publication dates in note, 1890, 1905.
54 *Bulletin*, 28/9/1901, 'Red Page'; SMF to A. G. Stephens, 10/10/1902, MA.
55 Fred Maudsley to SMF, 7 and 8 /10/1901, FP vol. 7, and John Barnes, *Socialist Champion: Portrait of the Gentleman Socialist*, Australian Scholarly Publishing, Melbourne, 2006, pp. 252, 262; *Book Lover*, Nov. 1901, pp. 122–3; *Age*, 30/11/1901, p. 4; *Book Lover*, Feb. 1902, p. 162, and *Sun*, 1/9/1902, FP vol. 121 (S. Ross to SMF, 26/1/1906, FP vol. 90, refers to his comparable response in the *Barrier Truth*, 22/9/1905 [p. 1]). Henry Hyde Champion (1859–1929), an erstwhile leading English radical who came to Melbourne in 1894, produced the *Book Lover* 1899–1921 (*ADB* vol. 7, *ODNB*); Elsie Belle Champion (1870–1953), owner/manager of the Book Lover's Library, was also very supportive (Barnes, *Socialist Champion: Portrait of the Gentleman Socialist*, Australian Scholarly Publishing, Melbourne, 2006, p. 300).
56 SMF to J. B. Pinker, 18/11/1901, FP vol. 80;* *Book Lover*, Jan. 1902, pp. 221–2; Elsie Belle Champion to SMF, 6/8/1902, FP vol. 8.
57 *Sydney Stock and Station Journal*, 'Gossip', n.d. (press cutting, FP vol. 121A); *Worker*, 22/11/1902, p. 1, also 21/2/1903, p. 1, and 29/6/1903, p. 1; *Critic*, 22/2/1902, p. 126. Ethel Curlewis (Turner) (1870–1958) author (*ADB* vol. 12).
58 'Fiction in the Australian Bush', repr. *Kanga Creek: Havelock Ellis in Australia*, ed. Geoffrey Dutton, Picador, Sydney, 1989, p. 233; 'Memoranda' (by A. G. Stephens?), *Bulletin*, 29/10/1903, 'Red Page'; A. G. Stephens to SMF, 29/7/1903, FP vol. 7;* *Studies in the Psychology of Sex* by (Henry) Havelock Ellis, Davis & Co, Philadelphia, 1904, pp. 67–8. (Henry) Havelock Ellis (1859–1939), writer and sexologist (*ODNB*).
59 '*In Defence of Women* by H. L. Mencken', *Vote*, 7/12/1918; SMF to Alice Henry, 21/1/1920, FP vol. 114, and PBC no. 610; SMF to Mary Fullerton, 21/11/1940, FP vol. 19; Mathew, *Miles Franklin*, p. 8.
60 Stephen Garton, 'Contesting Enslavement: Marriage, Manhood, and *My Brilliant Career*', in *ALS*, 2002; *Quiz*, 13/5/1904, p. 69, comment apparently by K. Partridge (copy FP vol. 121A); *My Brilliant Career*, p. 140; *Childhood at Brindabella*, p. 31; SMF to Freda Barrymore, 14/9/1936, FP vol. 27, re two whips, one from stockman W. G. Hoole (W. G. Hoole to SMF, 10/7/1947, FP vol. 10), possibly the one bequeathed to Joanie Lampe, photo in my possession courtesy her daughter, the late Susi Baldwin. See also *Bulletin*, 14/2/1903, 'Red Page', for a bizarre contemporary response to the issue of SMF and whips, and SMF to J. K. Moir, 6/9/1952, Moir Colln; SMF to W. Blackwood, Blackwood Archive, Incoming Corres. 1902, National Library of Scotland, MS 30084.
61 *New York Herald* (SMF to J. B. Pinker, 29/5/1902, FP vol. 80), but see also F. C., *Bulletin*, 19/10/1901, p. 13 ('a reversion to the aboriginal type'); *Australian Kat*, 13/01/1903, p. 10; *United Australia*, Jan. 1902, p. 20; *Argus*, 16/3/1905, FP vol. 121A, and *Laughter, Not for a Cage*, p. 89. Evelyn Dickinson, Irish-born doctor and writer, was companion to Louisa McDonald, first principal of Women's College, Univ. of Sydney (Magarey, *Passions of the First-Wave Feminists*, p. 107, and see n. 87 below). Ada Cambridge (1844–1926) *ADB* vol. 3.
62 A. G. Stephens to SMF, 13/9/1901, FP vol. 7; Arthur Maquarie to SMF, 19/12/1901 and following, FP vol. 7; Bruce Scates, '*My Brilliant Career* and Radicalism', *ALS*, 2002; Katie Holmes, 'Spinsters Indispensable: Feminists, Single Women and the Critique of Marriage 1890–1920', *Aust. Hist. Studies*, Apr. 1998, vol. 29, no. 110; W. Blackwood to J. B. Pinker, 29/1/1901, FP vol. 80, and Henry Lawson to SMF [1902], FP vol. 6, also Henry Lawson, 'Culled Contributors', *Bulletin*, 14/2/1903, 'Red Page'.
63 The letters are at FP vols 7–9A.
64 Kathleen Evesson, 'Reactions of Young Female Readers to Miles Franklin's *My Brilliant Career*', unpub. BA (Hons) essay, Macquarie Univ., 2001; Pearl Wilson to SMF, 22/9/1902, Mary Dunster to SMF, 30/4/1902, Stella Simpson to SMF, 12/9/1901, all FP vol. 8; Ethel Lloyd to SMF, 10/11/1904, FP vol. 10.
65 Rose Scott (1846–1925), *ADB* vol. 11; Agnes Brewster (1874–1957), *ADB* vol. 13; Caroline David (1856–1951), *ADB* vol. 13.

66 'A Book Full of Sunlight', *Bulletin*, 28/9/1901, 'Red Page'.

67 Struan Robertson to SMF, 10/4/04, FP vol. 9A; Edith Twynam to SMF, 28/6/1902–24/8/1903, FP vol. 8. Edith Twynam (c.1874–1956), *Penny Post*, 3/5/1956, p. 2; Edward Twynam (1832–1923), Surveyor-General of NSW 1887–90, *SMH*, 3/4/1923, p. 8; KSP to SMF, 1/6/1930, FP vol. 21, and *Judith Wright*, ed. Patricia Clarke, Text Publishing, Melbourne, 1999, pp. 53–4. Katharine Susannah Prichard (1883–1969), writer and political activist (*ADB* vol. 11). Judith Wright (1915– 2000), writer and environmentalist (*OCAL*).

68 *Laughter, Not for a Cage*, pp. 118–19; Graeme Johnston, *Annals of Australian Literature*, Melbourne Univ. Press, Carlton, Vic, 1970 (re 1901), and Nicole Moore and Brigid Rooney, 'The Centenary Celebration/Symposium of Miles Franklin's *My Brilliant Career*', *AHA Bulletin*, Dec. 2001, pp. 78–80.

69 As published in *Cockatoos*, pp. 66–7.

70 Modjeska, *Exiles at Home*, ch. 8; LN, FP vol. 3, p. 728, and PBC no. 743, *John Milton: Poetical Works*, inscribed 'Mrs J. M. Franklin with love and best wishes from her aunt, Mary Neall, Stillwater, 2/4/1899'.

71 SMF to William Blackwood, 31/8/1902, also figures in an entry for *My Brilliant Career* under 'Melvyn' in Blackwood's Publication Ledger (National Library of Scotland MS 30864) which vary slightly, but are difficult to interpret; Linda Franklin to SMF, n.d. [Jan. 1902], FP vol. 49; J. B. Pinker to SMF, 7/4/1904, FP vol. 80; Jill Roe and Margaret Bettison, 'How Did Writers Earn a Living: Miles Franklin', *History of the Book in Australia*, vol. 2, eds Martyn Lyons and John Arnold, Univ. of Qld Press, St Lucia, Qld, 2001.; *Official Year Book*, 1908 (women's wages, 1897); *Laughter, Not for a Cage*, p. 119.

72 Jane Hunt, 'Unrelaxing Fortitude', *ALS*, 2002; Linda Franklin to SMF, 12/1/1902, FP vol. 49.

73 Memorandum of Agreement, FP vol. 80; SMF to J. B. Pinker, 18/11/1901, FP vol. 80; SMF to George Robertson, 29/7/1902, ML MSS 314/31.

74 FP vol. 5/16, p. 16; Edith Twynam to SMF, 16/2/1902, FP vol. 6 *et seq.*; SMF to My Dear Sir [maybe Henry Lawson, but more likely A. G. Stephens], n.d. [1902], FP vol. 6, p. 405 (b), (c); A. B. Paterson to SMF, 25/3/1902, 2/4/1902, FP vol. 7. Phoebe Twynam (1871–1950) married Gordon Wesche (Supt. of P&O Australia in 1912) in 1901 (*ADB* vol. 12). Andrew Barton Paterson (1864–1941), was a poet, journalist and solicitor (*ADB* vol. 11).

75 'Women's Suffrage League', *Penny Post*, 31/10/1901, p. 4; RS to SMF, 31/3/1902 (Scott's postscript acknowledges faults in *My Brilliant Career*) and 22/6/1902, FP vol. 8.

76 SMF to My Dear Sir [maybe Henry Lawson, but more likely A. G. Stephens], n.d. [1902], FP vol. 6, p. 405 (b), (c); undated fragment, FP vol. 6, p. 399 and lettercard addressed by A. G. Stephens, 11/4/1902 [misdated 1901], FP vol. 7.

77 A. B. Paterson to SMF, 7/4/1902, and 12/4/1902, FP vol. 7.

78 A. G. Stephens to SMF, 11/4/1901[2], FP vol. 7; PBC nos Q17 and 357; Norman Lindsay, *Bohemians of the Bulletin*, Angus & Robertson, Sydney, 1965, p. 143, and Norman Lindsay, 'Meeting on the Stairs', *Bulletin*, 18/9/1946, p. 2; Jill Roe, 'What Has Nationalism Offered Australian Women?', in *Australian Women: Contemporary Feminist Thought*, eds Norma Grieve and Ailsa Burns, Oxford Univ. Press, Melbourne, Vic, 1994. Norman Lindsay (1879–1969), artist and a writer (*ADB* vol. 10). Will (W. H.) Ogilvie (1869–1963), poet and journalist (*ADB* vol. 11).

79 *Book Lover*, Dec. 1901, p. 139, and SMF to Ethel Curlewis (Turner), n.d. [1902], ML MSS 667, and Ethel Curlewis to SMF, 17/5/1902, FP vol. 8, both;* SMF to Margaret Windeyer, 19/7/1937, FP vol. 25; SMF to J. K. Moir, 17/6/1953, FP vol. 34; SMF to Tossie O'Sullivan, 28/5/1924, ML Af 64/8, and *Sunday Times* 20/4/1904. Margaret Windeyer (1866–1939), *ADB* vol. 12. Laurence Foley (1849–1917), *ADB* vol. 4.

80 A. B. Paterson to George Robertson, 14/4/1902, cited Barker, *Dear Robertson*, p. 33; A. B. Paterson to SMF, 12/4/, 29/4/1902, and 2/5/1902, FP vol. 7, and draft letter SMF to Dear Sir, n.d., FP vol. 6, p 405 (d); SMF, Oct. 1943, LN, FP vol. 3, pp. 34–5, repr. *Diaries*. p. 146. Alfred Cecil Rowlandson (1865–1922) became the owner of the NSW Book Stall Company in 1897, one of Australia's most successful book publishing and selling ventures (*OCAL*).

81 SMF, undated fragment, FP vol. 6, p. 406.

82 'One of Our Old Maids', undated ms., FP vol. 57.

83 A. B. Paterson to SMF, 31/5/1902, FP vol. 7, and SMF, undated fragment, FP vol. 7, p. 295 (the dictionary idea); FP vol. 62 (four verses, dated 30/6–8/8/1901). See also LN, FP vol. 3, p. 34,

re Paterson's 'yarn', published by Angus & Robertson as *An Outback Marriage* in 1906, and Viera Jones, 'Australian Imprint', PhD thesis, p. 110; Clement Semmler, *Banjo of the Bush: The Life and Times of A.B. Banjo Paterson*, Univ. of Qld Press, St Lucia, Qld, 1974, Sydney, 1977, ch. XI (SMF is not mentioned).

84   SMF to Dear Sir, n.d., FP vol. 6, p 405 (d); Linda Franklin to SMF, 30/6/1902, FP vol. 49; Fred Maudsley to SMF, 8/6/1902, FP vol. 7; Jocelyn Hedley, 'The Unpublished Plays of Miles Franklin', MA thesis, pp. 4–5.

85   A. B. Paterson to SMF, 7/8/1902, 18/8/1902, FP vol. 8; Charles Graham to SMF, 2/9/1902, FP vol. 49 (postmark); Jessie Paterson to SMF, 2/8/[1902], FP vol. 8.

86   *ibid.*, 17/10/[1902, 14/11/1902]; Linda Franklin to SMF, 16/5/1903, FP vol. 49 (and 12/1/1902, engagement); Charles Graham to SMF, 2/9/1902, FP vol. 49 (postmark); Bertha Lawson to SMF, n.d. [from Ladywood, Manly], FP vol. 6, p. 417 (a); Colin Roderick, *Henry Lawson: A Life*, Angus & Robertson, N. Ryde, NSW, 1991, pp. 247ff.; 'The End of My Career', part ms., draft, FP vol. 52.

87   Molly David to SMF, 24/8/1902, FP vol. 8; SMF to RS, 2/7/1917, RS Corres., ML MSS A2282.; LN, FP vol. 3, p. 534; Roderic Quinn to SMF, 4/11/1902, FP vol. 8. Re 'this brilliant and gifted young lady', *A.A.A. All About Australians*, Oct. 1902, vol. 2, no. 18; ML MSS 445/41/2, poem dated 24/8/1904. The waratah book: ML R230c. Henry Normand MacLaurin (1835–1914), *ADB* vol. 10; Louisa McDonald (1858–1949), *ADB* vol. 10; Edwin James Brady (1869–1952), *ADB* vol. 7; Roderic Joseph Quinn (1867–1949), *ADB* vol. 11; Bernhard Ringrose Wise (1858–1916), *ADB* vol. 12; Mary Booth (1869–1956), *ADB* vol. 7; Florence Earle Hooper (1870–1967), headmistress, ML MSS 1553 (*ADB* file); Margaret Hodge (1858–1938) and Harriet Newcomb (1854–1942), *ADB S*.

88   SMF to J. B. Pinker, 31/8/1902, FP vol. 84; *A Camp-Fire Yarn: Henry Lawson. Complete Works 1885–1900*, ed. Leonard Cronin, Lansdowne Press, Sydney, 1984, p. 487, and *On the Track*, Angus & Robertson, Sydney, 1900, repr. *On the Track* and *Over the Sliprails*, Australian Pocket Library, Angus & Robertson, Sydney, 1945 (PBC no. 267).

89   SMF to J. B. Pinker, 27/9/1902, FP vol. 84.

90   SMF to J. B. Pinker, 31/8/1902, FP vol. 84. Morton McDonald (1872–1958), of Uriarra, became a grazier.

91   FP vol. 84, p. 29 (résumé).

92   *Cockatoos*, p. 148. 'Armstrong's Folly': possibly 'Montrose' (see n. 40 above).

93   *Cockatoos*, pp. 124, 145, 161, 241; Shirley Walker, 'The Boer War: Paterson, Abbott, Brennan, Miles Franklin and "Breaker" Morant', *ALS*, vol. 12, no. 2, Oct. 1985, pp. 216–18; Craig Wilcox, *Australia's Boer War: The War in South Africa 1898–1902*, Oxford Univ. Press, S. Melbourne 2002, pp. 21, 59, 315; Sandra McKirdy, 'Lives on the Line: Women of the Empire and the Peace Movement during the Second Anglo–Boer War', BA (Hons) thesis, Macquarie University, 2008.

94   SMF to J. B. Pinker, 31/8/1902, FP vol. 84; Florette Murray-Prior to SMF, 23/8/1902 and 10/1/1903, FP vol. 8; Linda Franklin to SMF, 12 /1/1902, FP vol. 49.

95   J. B. Pinker to SMF, 27/11/1902, FP vol. 84; SMF to Blackwood, 20/11/1902, Blackwood Archive, Incoming Corres. 1902–C, National Library of Scotland MS 30084; 'On The Outside Track', 13/1/1903, and report, Duckworth Papers, Berg Collection, New York Public Library. Edward Garnett (1868–1937), publisher's editor and writer (*ODNB*): 'A Discoverer of Talent', *Times* (London), 22/2/1937, p. 19; see also Garnett's sister-in-law, fellow writer Martha Garnett to SMF [1902] and 8/5/1902, FP vol. 7, that *My Brilliant Career* was 'the cleverest novel of the season' in London.

96   'The End of My Career' [1902], ML MSS 445/2; misc. mss., ML MSS 445/19–20: 'To All Young Australian Writers', *My Career Goes Bung*. SMF to Elsie Belle Champion, 31/1/1936, FP vol. 8. Of a further four bound tss at ML MSS 6035/24, the first, entitled 'My Career Goes Bung' and dated 7/5/1936, is by 'Miles Franklin's understudy', and the remaining three also relate to the published version.

97   SMF to Alice Henry, 11/3/[1936], FP vol. 8; ML MSS 6035/24, 7/5/1936.

98   'The End of My Career', 190[?], ML MSS 445/2; FP vol. 5/16, p. 180; George Robertson to SMF, 30/11/1902, ML MSS 314/31.

99   SMF to George Robertson, 4/12/1902, ML MSS 314/31; FP vol. 5/16, p. 15, c.1949.

Chapter 4 — With Penrith as a Base: 1903–April 1906

1   Melbourne *Herald*, 14/4/1904, p. 4.

2   *Penny Post*, 3/3/1903, p. 4.

3   Linda Franklin to SMF [1902, but from internal evidence after 12/1/1903], FP vol. 49.

4   *Penny Post*, 5/2/1903, p. 2, 19/2/1903, p. 4, 14/3/1903, p. 3.

5   SF Notebook, FP vol. 107 [p. 101]; SMF to Linda Franklin, 19/3/1903, FP vol. 113X; P. M. Woodriff to Miss Bridle, 28/12/1954, Mutch Papers, MSS, Set 426/20. 'Lambridge area': now the Penrith Lakes Scheme area.

6   The dirt floors were treated annually with a mix of fresh cow manure and blood and polished weekly (pers. comm., Mr A. J. Willett, Penrith, 5/5/1985, from his grandfather, a neighbour at Penrith, and *Nepean Times*, 3/6/1905 [p. 4]); Sarah Lampe to SMF, 30/3/1903 and 6/4/1903, FP vol. 49.

7   Frank Walker, 'Penrith and District', *J. Royal Aust. Hist. Soc.*, vol. 12, no. 2, 1909, pp. 43–52.

8   Edi to SMF 28/5/1903, FP vol. 9A; *Some Everyday Folk and Dawn*, pp. 2, 3.

9   *Some Everyday Folk and Dawn*, p. 3.

10 *Nepean Times*, 7/3/1905 [p. 5]; 'The Case of Tom Staples', *SMH*, 22/4/1905, p. 5.

11 NSW Government *Gazette*, 25/4/1906, p. 2506, and *Nepean Times*, 31/3/1906 [p. 5]; *Nepean Times*, 7/4/1906 [Saturday], 29/9/1906 [p. 4]; undated envelope, FP vol. 111; ML MSS 445/41/2/3. The sale yard was at the corner of High and Worth Sts, Penrith (*Nepean Times*, 14/9/1907 [p. 5]).

12 SMF to Alice Henry, n.d., FP vol. 11, p. 23; Heather Radi, Peter Spearritt and Elizabeth Hinton, *Biographical Register of the NSW Parliament, 1901–1970*, ANU Press, Canberra, 1979; Dan Clyne to SMF, 29/10/1930, FP vol. 22. Daniel Clyne (1879–1965) was the state member for King 1927–65.

13 *Nepean Times*, 6/2/1904 [p. 6] and NSW Government *Gazette* 16/2/1904, p. 1395; *Nepean Times* 11/2/1905 [p. 6], 21/9/1907 [p. 4].

14 'Concerning Maryann', FP vol. 59 (extended draft, and *Bulletin*, 31/3/1904, 'Red Page', repr. 'Letter from Melbourne', *A Gregarious Culture*). Israel Zangwill (1864–1926), London-born Jewish writer: play performed Sydney 1905 (*Evening News*, 30/10/1905, p. 8). Elizabeth Banks (1870?–1938) wrote *The Autobiography of a Newspaper Girl* (1902) (*Who Was Who in America 1879–1942* and *Bulletin*, 7/4/1904, p. 14); Nene Wallace (1878–1951), NSW Births, Probate; SMF to Eva [O'Sullivan, c.1924], FP vol. 46; 'When I was Mary-Anne. A Slavey. Sketches 1–4', ML MSS 445/23, p. 1. Note: there are several drafts and variable spellings of Ann/Anne.

15 'Concerning Maryann. First draft', FP vol. 59, p. 17. The standard reference is Kingston, *My Wife, My Daughter and Poor Mary Ann*.

16 'A Domestic Servant', *Australian Woman's Sphere*, 10/7/1903, p. 327 (letter, possibly by SMF); Commonwealth electoral roll and *Sands' Directory*, 1903; Mrs Finlayson, Jun. 1903, FP vol. 51, and S. Vance to SMF, 8/9/1903, FP vol. 9A (references); S. Vance to SMF, 8/9/1903, FP vol. 9A and *Home Queen*, 18/12/1903, p. 3 (FP vol. 121A); SF to SMF, [1903] and 29/10/1903, 19/11/1903, FP vol. 48. Mrs O'Connor, wife of Richard Edward O'Connor (1851–1912), politician and judge, (*ADB* vol. 11).

17 'When I was Mary-Anne. A Slavey: sketches 1–4', ML MSS 445/23. 'Maria's Dingle': see G. V. F. Mann, *Municipality of North Sydney*, Municipal Council, North Sydney 1938, p. 4 ('The Dingle', an old harbourside cottage on Kirribilli Point). Linda Franklin to SMF, 30/9/1903, FP vol. 49. Laurel Franklin died at Penrith on 4/10/1903, SF, Notebook, FP vol. 107 [pp. 85–6].

18 RS to SMF, 3/2/1904, FP vol. 8; 'When I was Mary-Anne. A Slavey: sketches 5–6', ML MSS 445/24; *Bulletin*, 31/3/04, 'Red Page'; Clem Christesen to Marjorie Barnard [1950s], Barnard file, MA.

19 Melbourne *Herald*, 14/4/1904, p. 4; *Life*, 15/4/1904, p. 399, also *New Idea*, 6/5/1904, p. 999; *Tocsin*, 2/6/1904, pp. 18, 19, as edited here; *Australian Woman's Sphere*, 15/4/1904, p. 237 has further comment on the servant question.

20 Aileen Goldstein to SMF, 12/2/1905, FP vol. 10; H. H. Champion to RS, 26/2/[1904], RS Corres.; SMF to Jean Campbell, 21/5/1953, FP vol. 44; SMF to Mrs O'Sullivan, Melbourne, Tuesday [April 1904?], O'Sullivan Family Miscellanea 1901–27, ML MSS 1603;* Alfred Deakin to H. H. Champion, 12/4/1904, FP vol. 121; Lindsay Bernard Hall (1859–1935), *ADB* vol. 9.

21 PBC, nos 618 and 732; Isabella Goldstein to SMF, 28/7/1904, FP vol. 10; Aileeen Goldstein to SMF, 24/5/1904, FP vol. 10;* Jill Roe, '"Testimonies from the Field"', pp. 304–19. Isabella Goldstein (1849–1916) bore five children: Vida Goldstein, Elsie Belle (Champion), Lina (Henderson), Selwyn Goldstein (1873–1917?) and Aileen Goldstein (1877–1960).

22 Farewell telegram to Yarra Basin from Laura Bogue Luffman, 13/4/1904, FP vol. 9A; press cutting (*Book Lover*), ML MSS 3732/2; Cargill and others. Press cuttings, ML MSS 4937/4 ('little Miles').

23 Melbourne *Herald*, 14/4/1904, p. 4; *Johns's Notable Australians*, 1906, and *Who's Who in Australia*, 1947 (d.o.b., 1883).

24 P. De Serville, *Rolf Boldrewood: A Life*, Melbourne Univ. Press, Carlton, Vic, 2000, p. 281. SMF to Mrs O'Sullivan, Melbourne, Tuesday [April 1904?], O'Sullivan Family; *Bulletin*, 7/4/1904, p. 14.

25 Joseph Furphy to SMF, 17/2/1904, FP vol. 9B. Joseph Furphy (1843–1912), *ADB* vol. 8.

26 SMF to Joseph Furphy, 23/4/[1904], Furphy Papers, SLV; Joseph Furphy to SMF, 27/3/1904, FP vol. 9B; Elizabeth Webby, 'The Bush Hamlet', *TLS*, 28/6/2002, p. 27; typed extract, 'Tom Collins' to William Cathels, FP vol. 51A; Barnes, *The Order of Things*, p. 341.

27 Kate Baker to SMF, 17/4/1904, FP vol. 9A;* Joseph Furphy to SMF, 1/8/1904 (postmark), FP vol. 9B. Kate Baker (1861–1953) was a teacher (*ADB* vol. 7). The other young women at the gallery were Molly Winter and 'Lizer Jane' (Miss Drewitt).

28 RS to SMF, 3/5/1904, FP vol. 8; Aileen Goldstein to SMF, 24/5/1904, FP vol. 10.*

29 SMF to Mrs O'Sullivan, Melbourne, Tuesday, O'Sullivan Family Miscellanea 1901–27, ML MSS 1603; *Australian Woman's Sphere*, 14/4/1904, p. 327; Cara David to SMF, 7/11/1903 and 12/4/1904, FP vol. 9A; Linda Franklin to SMF, 23/7/1904, FP vol. 49; ML MSS 445/21; SMF to T. W. Heney, 1/4/1905, FP vol. 55;* Francis Suttor to SMF, 13/2/1905, FP vol. 9A; RS to SMF, 24/8/03, FP vol. 8. Thomas William Heney (1862–1928), first Australian-born editor of the *SMH*, appointed in 1903, was educated at Cooma (*ADB* vol. 9). Sir Francis Suttor (1839–1915), President of NSW Legislative Council 1903–13 (*ADB* vol. 6).

30 Sarah Lampe to SMF, 29/2/1904, FP vol. 49; *Bulletin*, 31/3/04, 'Red Page'; Agnes Stokes, c.1867, *A Girl at Government House. An English Girl's Reminiscences: 'Below Stairs' in Colonial Australia*, ed. Helen Vellacott, Currey O'Neil, Melbourne, 1982 (first published 1932) is the only comparable document.

31 Sarah Lampe to SMF, 27/4/1903, 14/5/1903, 1/2/1904, 29/3/1904, FP vol. 49.

32 Alex McDonald to SMF, 6/3/1902, FP vol. 7; Harold Hammond to SMF, 12/3/1903, FP vol. 9A; Linda Franklin to SMF, 16/5/[1903], FP vol. 49; FP vol. 46, 109A. William George Hoole, b. Bathurst, 1876, FP vol. 121A, see also his 'Appreciation', dedicated to SMF, *Peak Hill Express*, 25/5/1906 (n.p.); Sarah Lampe to SMF, 14/5/1903, FP vol. 49.

33 *Some Everyday Folk and Dawn*, pp. 198, 93; SMF to Joseph Furphy, 15/11/1904, Baker Papers.*

34 Linda Franklin to SMF, 23/7/1904, 5/8/1904, FP vol. 49.

35 Audrey Oldfield, *Woman Suffrage in Australia: A Gift or a Struggle?*, Cambridge Univ. Press, Cambridge UK, 1992; Jill Roe, 'Chivalry and Social Policy in the Antipodes', pp. 395–410.

36 SMF to Blackwood, 2/8/1909, FP vol. 80. The suffragette wing of the British campaign, the Women's Social and Political Union (WSPU), was founded in 1905 but its trademark 'militancy' began later, in 1908.

37 *Some Everyday Folk and Dawn*, pp. 138, 285–6, 244–5.

38 SF to SMF at North Sydney, 19/11/03, FP vol. 48 (organising a meeting for Scott at Penrith); RS to SMF, 8/8/1904, FP vol. 8; SMF to RS, 9/6/1904, RS Corres., and RS to SMF, 11/7/04, FP vol. 8 (Rose to stay with the Franklins for meetings, foresees 'rocks ahead' for women citizens). For selected references to press coverage of the election, see Jill Roe, Introduction, *Some Everyday Folk and Dawn*. On the Franklins, see e.g. *Nepean Times*, 2/7/1904, p. 4 and FP vols 4–7, p. 153.

39 *Some Everyday Folk and Dawn*, p. 184.

40 SMF to George Robertson, 22/6/1905, ML MSS 314/31, 40.

41 Hallam Tennyson to SMF, 31/10/1904, ML MSS 3659/1, PBC enclosure no. 160. Cara David to Hallam Tennyson, corres., FP vol. 9, and Roderick, *Miles Franklin*, p. 90; SMF to A. G. Stephens, 30/3/1905, FP vol. 55.* Hallam Tennyson (1852–1928) was Governor-General of Australia for one year in 1903 (*ADB* vol. 12).

42 SMF to George Robertson, 22/6/1905, ML MSS 314/31.*

43 SMF to George Robertson, 4/1/1904, ML MSS 314/31/399. Sarah Pratt Greene née McLean (1856–1935) wrote numerous novels; *Winslow Plain* was first published by Harper & Brothers, America, Oct. 1902; *History of the Book in Australia*, vol. 2, p. 34.

44 Cited Barker, *Dear Robertson*, p. 40; *SMH*, 30/10/1909, p. 4; *Bulletin*, 11/11/1909, 'Red Page'; ML MSS 314/31, pp. 419–21.

45 Vida Goldstein to SMF, 16/10/1904, FP vol. 10.*

46 Norman Franklin to SMF, 10/12/1904, FP vol. 48; LN, FP vol. 3, pp. 568–9. Linda married Charles Graham at St Stephen's, Penrith, 25/11/1904.

47 Francis Suttor to SMF, 5/11/1904, FP vol. 9A; Sydney Jephcott to SMF, 18/6/1905, FP vol. 10; RS to SMF, 6/12/1904 and 4/1/1905, FP vol. 8; Wise doc., 16/3/1916, FP vol. 51; Sydney Jephcott to SMF, 18/6/1906, FP vol. 10. Sydney Jephcott (1864–1951) was a Monaro poet and farmer (*ADB* vol. 9).

48 Sydney Jephcott to SMF, 18/6/1906, FP vol. 10; SMF to A. G. Stephens, 30/3/1905, FP vol. 55;* Hallam Tennyson to SMF, 24/3/1905, FP vol. 9; Ralph Nattrass to SMF, Mudgee line, 25/6/1905 and 5/7/1905, FP vol. 10; Bettison and Roe, *Miles Franklin's Topical Writings* [1905 listing]; Wilde, *Courage a Grace*, p. 138; *Bulletin*, 12/1/1905, 'Red Page'; *Barrier Truth*, 21/7/1905 and 22/9/1905; ML MSS 314/31, p. 417. Robert Samuel Ross (1873–1931), was father of trade unionist Lloyd Ross (see ch 12 and *ADB* vol. 11).

49 SMF to RS, 2/7/1917, RS Corres.;* Francis Suttor to SMF, 13/2/1905 and 4/3/1905, FP vol. 9A; RS to SMF, 5/4/1905, FP vol. 8; LN, FP vol. 3, p. 581ff.; PBC no. 372 (*Australian Legendary Tales*); RS to SMF, 19/3/1906, FP vol. 8. Catherine (Langloh Parker) Stow (1856–1940), author (*ADB* vol. 12).

50 RS to SMF, FP vol. 8, p. 161, text filed between 13/3/1905 and 19/3/1905.

51 Appendix 2; 'In Peak Hill District', *Peak Hill Express*, 18/8/1905, p. 7; *A History of Peak Hill and District*, Peak Hill Centenary Book Committee, 1988, p. 261.

52 Theodor Lampe (1882–1968) from Uenzen, Germany, was in NSW for about a year, 1905–06, mainly at Talbingo and Penrith, also Peak Hill, SMF to Theodor Lampe, 21/10/1951, FP vol. 49.

53 'The divided cup', ML MSS 445/21.

54 *Peak Hill Express*, 29/9/1905 [p. 10]; Edwin Ernest Bridle (1874–1953), see Appendix 2, and *The Buddong Flows On*, vol. 2, p. 185ff.; Edwin Bridle to SMF, 10/8/1906, 22/8/1906, 9/9/1906, FP vol. 47.

55 Edwin Bridle to SMF, 27/10/1905, FP vol. 47.

56 Edwin Bridle corres., FP vol. 47, *passim*.

57 Sarah Lampe to SMF, 24/9/1906, FP vol. 49.

58 Linda Franklin to SMF, 27/12/1904, FP vol. 49; undated recollection, FP vol. 13.

59 SMF to J. F. Archibald, 25/3/1905, FP vol. 55; SMF to T. B. Symons, 12/3/1905 and 25/3/1905, FP vol. 55; A. G. Stephens to SMF, 31/3/1905, FP vol. 7;* SMF to T. W. Heney, 1/4/1905, FP vol. 55.* Clarke, *Pen Portraits*, pp. 243, 246.

60 Mutch Papers, Index (Franklin), ML m/films, CY572, also Joy Hooton, Franklin entry, *OCAL* (2nd edn, 1994); Wilde, *Courage a Grace*, p. 137. The rate of journalists' earnings cannot be verified, as records do not survive for casual contributions to the *SMH* at this time, but that was what Mary Gilmore was paid for articles on the utopian settlement Cosme a few years earlier.

61 *SMH*, 22/4/1905; 20/5/1905, 24/6/1905; *SMH*, 29/4/1905; *SMH*, 6/5/1905; *SMH*, 27/5/1905. SF Notebook, FP vol. 107 [pp. 100, 42].

62 *SMH*, 10/6/1905, 1/7/1905; *DT*, 24/5/1905.

63 *SMH*, 17/6/1905. See 'Getting to the Bottom of the Lake George Mystery', *SMH*, 30/11–1/12/2004, p. 13 for the latest geological explanation of the lake's fluctuations.

64 *SMH*, 2/9/1905, and previously, 12/8/1905 and 19, 26/8/1905.

65 *SMH*, 14/10/1905.

66 *SMH*, 23/12/1905. Barbara Jane Baynton (1857–1929), NSW-born author of *Bush Studies* (1902), lived in London and Australia, c.1903–14, (*ADB* vol. 11).

67 A. B. Paterson to SMF, 9/8/1905, FP vol. 7; T. W. Heney to SMF, 2/4/1906, FP vol. 55.

68 Robert Ross to SMF, 26/1/1906, FP vol. 90; RS to SMF, 19/3/1906, FP vol. 6.

69 Vida Goldstein to SMF, 26/5/1905, FP vol. 10.

70   SMF to George Robertson, 14/7/1903, FP vol. 90; on similar inquiries overseas, Francis Suttor
      to SMF, 6/2/1904 and 22/1/1904, FP vol. 9A; Cara David to SMF, 12/4/1904, FP vol. 9; Linda
      Franklin to SMF, 23/7/1904, FP vol. 49; Aileen Goldstein to SMF, 24/5/104.* It is ironic that in
      later life SMF would criticise Christian Science as being too commercial: 'Its appeal is in its
      financial hope. If [Mary Baker Eddy's] disciples had gone about healing without being more
      greedy than the medical profession …' Miles Franklin, Notebook, 1935–52, ML MSS 1360,
      p. 59.
71   *SMH*, 9/4/1906, p. 8 and 10/4/1906, p. 8, and *Peak Hill Express*, 20/4/1906, p. 1; SF, Notebook,
      FP vol. 107 [p. 75]; SMF to Henrietta Drake-Brockman, 5/8/1950, FP vol. 33. For Drake-
      Brockman, see ch. 12, n. 15.

Chapter 5: Among the 'Murkans': May 1906–February 1911

1   'Among the "Murkans"', FP vol. 55.
2   *SMH*, 9–10/4/1906, p. 5 and 20/3/1906, p. 1; *DT* (Sydney), 22/1/1902, p. 1. Sophie Corrie
      (1832–1913), NSW orchardist and writer, was one interesting person aboard (*ADB S*).
3   Goldstein, *To America and Back*; SMF to Linda Franklin, 12/4/1906, FP vol. 111;* SMF to Mrs
      H. P. McKenzie, 22/9/1937 and 26/5/1950, FP vol. 10; SMF to Ian Mudie, 5/6/1950, FP vol. 36.
      A. Levick appears on the shipping list but has otherwise proved untraceable; the Qld MP was
      probably Daniel Ryan (1867–1952), MLA for Townsville 1915–20; Oscar Unmack to SMF,
      24/7/1908 and 24/5/1912, FP vol. 111. 'Jonesie': Edith Beatrice McKenzie née Jones
      (1878–1965) came from Wahroonga.
4   Goldstein, *To America and Back*, pp. 2–3.
5   Miles Franklin, 'San Francisco: A Fortnight After', *SMH*, 23/6/1906, p. 11, repr. *A Gregarious
      Culture*, Book Lover, 1/11/1906, p. 131.
6   SMF to Carrie Whelan, 16/1/1929, 2/1/1935, FP vol. 20; SMF to Margaret Dreier Robins,
      8/1/1936, MDR Papers; *Book Lover*, 1/7/1906, p. 77. Carrie Whelan (1862–1937) and her sister
      Ella Greenman née Whelan (1855–1921) were Californian suffrage campaigners.
7   Mrs H. P. McKenzie to SMF, postcard, and 10/9/1937, FP vol. 10.
8   Bruce Sutherland, 'Stella Miles Franklin's American Years', *Meanjin Papers*, 1965, vol. 24, no.
      103, p. 443; SMF to Ian Mudie, 5/6/1950, FP vol. 36.
9   Site visit, 6/8/1982; SMF to Mrs H. P. McKenzie, 22/11/1937 and 5/9/1947, FP vol. 10; Edwin
      Bridle to SMF, 10/8/1906, FP vol. 47; Jack London to SMF, 28/5/1906, FP vol. 10.
10   *Loma Linda Sanitarium*, PBC no. 724; SMF to Linda Graham, 20/8/1906, FP vol. 111 (booklet
      sent 'about a fortnight ago'),* and SMF to Bruce Sutherland, 18/3/1954, FP vol. 44.*
11   Linda Graham to SMF, 28/8/1906 and 6/6/1907, FP vol. 49.
12   Message, postcard of Bona Vista, an apartment building on Riverside Dr., New York, where
      SMF was staying with Mr and Mrs Childs, FP vol. 111. Jessie Childs (1867–1956) was an
      American suffragist.
13   SMF to Tal Franklin and SMF to Linda Graham, FP vol. 111; SF, Notebook, FP vol. 107 [p. 91].
      Re Edward John Mervyn Graham (1907–75), see Appendix 2.
14   Oscar Unmack to SMF, 25/6/1906, postcard, ML PX *D250/1, no. 33(b); Edwin Bridle to SMF,
      9/9/1906, FP vol. 47; *Bulletin*, 28/6/1906, p. 20.
15   Letter, *Book Lover*, Sept. 1913, p. 98; Woollacott, *To Try Her Fortune In London*; Jill Roe,
      'Australian Women in America, From Miles Franklin to Jill Ker Conway', *Approaching
      Australia: Papers from the Harvard Australian Studies Symposium*, eds Harold Bolitho and
      Chris Wallace-Crabbe, Harvard Univ. Press, Cambridge, Mass., 1998, pp. 139–58.
16   [Jonesie?] to SMF, FP vol. 46, p. 91; Sarah Lampe to SMF, 24/9/1906, FP vol. 49;* PX
      *D250/1/33(a).
17   SMF to Bruce Sutherland, 18/3/1954, FP vol. 44.*
18   *ibid.*
19   *ibid.*
20   ML MSS 445/27/7, p. 9; *Worker*, 29/5/1913, p. 17. The article 'No Dignity in Domestic Service'
      is unsigned, but from internal evidence, clearly by SMF.
21   'Ne Mari Nishta', ML MSS 445/4, p. 188 (arrival), and Kirkby, *Alice Henry*, p. 75, also *CDT*,
      22/10/1906, p. 6 (Rocky Mts storm); Edwin Bridle to SMF, 10/12/1906 (postmark), FP vol. 47;

SF to SMF [1906], FP vol. 48; Goldstein, 'To America and Back', p. 5; Carl S. Smith, *Chicago and the American Literary Imagination 1880–1920*, Univ. of Chicago Press, Chicago and London, 1984, p. 111. *Sister Carrie* (Doubleday, Page & Co, New York, 1900) was withheld by the publisher until 1907.

22 Upton Sinclair, *The Jungle*, Doubleday, Page & Co, New York, 1906; Smith, *Chicago and the American Literary Imagination*, p. 165; *The Net of Circumstance*, p. 238.

23 Biographical notes, FP vol. 51, pp. 133–5; SMF, 'Jane Addams of Hull House: Some Personal Recollections of a Great American', *Catholic Women's Review*, Aug. 1935, vol. 6, no. 4, and ML Doc. 812; Spinney, *City of Big Shoulders*, pp. 157–200. Jane Addams (1860–1935) was a settlement founder, social reformer and peace activist (*NAW*); Elshtain, *Jane Addams and the Dream of American Democracy*, is the outstanding intellectual biography.

24 Postcards or early addresses: FP and *Lakeside Directories*, 1906–07 (CHS); 'Jonesie' to SMF, 8/10/1907 and 18/11/1907, FP vol. 10; Josephine Young to SMF, note, Xmas card [1940s], FP vol. 20; SMF to Dr Young, undated postcard, FP vol. 20, p. 255. Josephine E. Young (1866–1950) was a graduate of the Chicago Women's Medical College, 1896 (*Alumnae*, Chicago, 1896, p. 119 and CHS).

25 Alice Henry (1857–1943), journalist, feminist, trade unionist (*ADB* vol. 9); Diane Kirkby, 'Henry, Alice', *Women Building Chicago 1790–1990: A Biographical Dictionary*, Univ. of Indiana Press, Bloomington, 2001; *CDT*, 30/9/1906, p. H2 (Alice Henry, 'The Political Situation in Australia', Political Equality League); *Bulletin*, 11/10/1906, p. 22, also *SMH*, 9/1/1907, p. 5 and 6/2/1907, p. 5; 'Letter from Chicago', *Book Lover*, 1/9/1907, p. 97, repr. *A Gregarious Culture*; Biographical notes, FP vol. 21, pp. 133–5, and 'Stella Miles Franklin', *Memoirs of Alice Henry*, ed. Nettie Palmer, Melbourne, 1944, ts., p. 89.

26 Eleanor Flexner, *Century of Struggle: The Woman's Rights Movement in the United States*, Atheneum, New York, 1974, 2nd edn, pp. 244–5, also MDR to Irene Andrews, Jun. 1909, Sutherland m/film, ML; and see also Susan Porter Benson, *Counter Cultures: Saleswomen, Managers and Customers in American Department Stores 1890–1940*, Univ. of Illinois Press, Urbana, 1986; *The Net of Circumstance*, pp. 8ff., 23, 193. Re Emma Pischel (1870–1948), see SMF to Hildegarde Pischel, 19/2/1948, FP vol. 41.

27 'The Survivors', Aug. 1908, ML MSS 445/25; SMF's version of Clark's shorthand system was first deciphered by the late Margaret A. Hayes, c.1982 (Margaret A. Hayes, 'The Difficulties and Pleasures of Transcribing Miles Franklin's Diaries 1926–36', n.d., ts., ML). Diane Kirkby, 'Class, Gender and the Perils of Philanthropy: The Story of *Life and Labor* and Labor Reform in the Women's Trade Union League', *J. Women's Hist.*, 1992, vol. 4, no. 2, p. 39, and *Women Building Chicago*; 'Miss Franklin Writes from Chicago', *Book Lover*, Sept. 1907, pp. 97–8, repr. *A Gregarious Culture*.

28 SF to SMF, 30/8/1907, FP vol. 48; *Nepean Times*, 7/9/1907, p. 3 (death), p. 5 (sale).

29 Linda Franklin to SMF, 6/6/1907, FP vol. 49; 'homeless': JMF to SF, 17/12/1907, FP vol. 111 (postcard), also SF, Notebook, FP vol. 107 [p. 92], vol. 110 (resignation from Penrith Benevolent Society); electoral roll, Tumut, 1908.

30 C. H. Spence to Alice Henry, 3/8/1907, noted *Ever Yours: C. H. Spence*, ed. Susan Magarey with Barbara Wall, Mary Lyons and Maryan Beams, Wakefield Press, Kent Town, SA, 2005; SMF to Alice Henry, 29/1/1942, FP vol. 11.

31 SMF to SF, 14/11/1907, FP vol. 111;* Caro Lloyd, *Henry Demarest Lloyd 1847–1903: A Biography*, Putnam's Sons, New York, 1912, vol. 1, p. 173 (PBC nos 723, 723A). Wayside Trust pamphlet (CHS). Henry Demarest Lloyd (1847–1903), journalist, social reformer and leading Progressive intellectual ('the first muck-raker'), resigned from the *Chicago Daily Tribune* in 1887 after disagreements with his father-in-law William Bross (1813–90), who in consequence left his estate to Lloyd's sons, but 'shrewd investments' in Chicago real estate enabled Lloyd to devote himself to social and political causes thereafter (*ANB*).

32 SMF to Ethel Mason [Neilsen], 29/11/1951, FP vol. 21; William Bross Lloyd (1875–1946); *Book Lover*, 1/9/1907, p. 1; Demarest Lloyd (1883–1937); Colin Roderick, *Miles Franklin*, p. 128; *L&L*, Sept. 1912, pp. 275–6 (PBC nos, 155, 155A–C).

33 FP vol. 55.

34 ML MSS 445/39, p. 413.

35 MDR to SMF, 29/10/1907, FP vol. 10;* 'Jonesie' to SMF, undated postcard, FP vol. 10, p. 371; SMF to MDR, Wednesday, RR Papers (Additions, Box 1, Folder 13). Brooklyn-born Margaret Dreier Robins (1868–1945), President of the Chicago WTUL 1907–13 and the NWTUL 1907–22, m. Raymond Robins (1874–1954), lawyer, ordained Protestant minister and head of the North-Western University Settlement in Chicago, in 1905, Raymond having settled there in 1901 after goldmining in Alaska which made him moderately wealthy (*Women Building Chicago*).

36 SMF to MDR, Sunday [early 1904] and 10/4/1908, from 71 Park Avenue, RR Papers, also MDR to Mary E. Dreier, 11/1/1908, MDR Papers; *Encyclopedia of American History*, ed. Richard B. Morris 1953; *Union Labor Advocate*, Dec. 1908, p. 53 (CHS).

37 SMF to MDR, Sunday [early 1908] and 10/4/[1908], RR Papers; SMF to SF, 9/3/1908, FP vol. 111, postcard;* Allan Johnston to SMF, 16/1/1908, FP vol. 11, postcard; LN, FP vol. 3, p. 761. 'Fred Lindsay' was the performance name of Australian-born Lt. Col. Holman James (1874–1946), *BA*, 9/1/1908, p. 14, *Argus*, 16/2/1946, p. 3, 3/2/1935, p. 4. Allan (sometimes Allen) Johnston died soon after the incident recalled (LN, FP vol. 3, p 761).

38 ML MSS 445/25 and 21; Pfisterer, *Playing with Ideas*, p. 55; Jocelyn Hedley, 'The Unpublished Plays of Miles Franklin', MA thesis, ch. 2, is a recent sympathetic account. The suffrage theme may have been rekindled by reading *The Convert* (1907) by Margaret Dreier Robin's sister-in-law Elizabeth Robins (SMF to MDR, 31/12/1907, RR Papers). Elizabeth Robins (1862–1952), who as an American-born actress famous for Ibsen roles, moved to England 1888, and became a leading suffragist and suffrage writer.

39 SMF to SF, 20/8/1908, FP vol. 111;* SMF to Miss Lampe, 20/8/1908, Lampe Family Album, NLA; SMF to 24/6/1908, RR Papers. Mary Elisabeth Dreier (1875–1963) was president of the New York WTUL 1906–15 and member of the NWTUL Board until its termination in 1950 (*NYT*, 4/11/1963, p. 35).

40 SMF to SF, 30/11/1908, FP vol. 111; PD Jan.–May 1909, *passim*; MDR to Alice Henry, n.d., FP vol. 116 (at pp. 289–95). To Indiana House, PD, 20/11/09; takes singing lessons with Miss Everett, a student of Mme Marchesi, who taught Melba, PD, 12/8/09; hires piano, PD, 29/11/09.

41 Meyerowitz, *Women Adrift*; MDR to Mary E. Dreier, 12/1/1909, MDR Papers (re Louise Dresden). Arnold Dresden (1882–1954) was survived by wife, Louise, and son, Mark (*NYT*, 13/4/1954, p. 31).

42 Anniversary Ball', *Union Labor Advocate*, Mar. 1909, p. 23, and *Chicago Record-Herald*, 20/2/1909 (CHS, web cat. index); Mary E. Dreier, *Margaret Dreier Robins*, p. 61; 'Unions Shocked by Typist Strike', *CDT*, 25/3/1909, p. 3. Agnes Nestor (1880–1948) was an important Chicago and US labour leader. Magdalen Dalloz (1887–1980) was a stenographer at the Chicago Federation of Labor.

43 PD, 16/6/1909, 14/9/1909; MDR to Irene [Osgood], 2/6/1909, thanks her for finding room 'for Miss Franklin who will appear re the eight hours bill', and 'expects to spend the entire summer in Madison', and to RR, 15/9/1909, in RR Papers in MDR Corres., MDR Papers; *Book Lover*, 6/12/1909, p. 138.

44 'American Working Women', *SMH*, 15/12/1909, p. 5, repr. *A Gregarious Culture*; Stella Franklin to Miss Lampe, 1/9/1908, Lampe Family Album, NLA.

45 *Union Labor Advocate*, Nov. 1909, pp. 18–19; 'Sidelights on the Convention', *Union Labor Advocate*, Nov. 1909, p. 20, by 'Mere Onlooker' [SMF], and Report of the Office Secretary, Nov. 1909, p. 19; ML MSS 445/40/7 (initiated as member of the Office Employees' Association, Chicago Local, PD, 26/3/1909); *Chicago Record-Herald*, 26/3/1909, n.p. (platform and constitution); First Convention report, *Union Labor Advocate*, Dec. 1907, Schneiderman Papers, *Principal Leaders*, microfilm edn (WTUL m/film), reel 2.

46 Boone, *The Women's Trade Union Leagues*, p. 71; Robin Miller Jacoby, *The British and American Women's Trade Union Leagues*; Kirkby, *Alice Henry*, p. 77.

47 Boone, *The Women's Trade Union Leagues*, pp. 71, 113; SMF to Nettie Palmer, 25/2/1947, FP vol. 24, p. 489. Due to the renumbering of Chicago streets in 1910, prior locations are not always certain (see *Christian Science Monitor*, 15/4/1911, p. 2).

48 *SMH*, 6/10/1909, p. 8; see also 22/9/1909, p. 8.

49 *Penny Post*, 21/9/1909, p. 2; *Book Lover*, Nov. 1909, p. 127; FP vol. 57 ('Jilted'); ML MSS 445/40/1; ML MSS 445/40/6 (London *Athenaeum*, 23/10/1909, p. 489, cited *Book Lover*, Dec. 1909, p. 135).

50 *The Buddong Flows On*, vol. 2, pp. 185–7; *On Dearborn Street*, Univ. of Qld Press, St Lucia, Qld, 1981, p. 120 (both quotations).

51 Marjorie Barnard, 'Miles Franklin', *Meanjin Papers*, 1955, vol. 14, no. 4, p. 475.

52 ML MSS 445/18 ('Cupid') and 445/21 (stories); PD, 5/12/1909 and 11/12/1909. *Anne Veronica* was published in 1909.

53 Postcard, Lampe Family Album; Goldstein, *To America and Back*, p. 6; Larry A. Viskochil, *Chicago at the Turn of the Century in Photographs*, Dover Publications, New York, 1984, also Kirby, *Alice Henry*, after p. 118 (traffic jams on Dearborn St).

54 *Union Labor Advocate*: 'Home Problems from a New Standpoint' (book review by 'S. M. F.'), Feb. 1909, p. 33; 'A Certain Rich Man', Oct. 1909 (book review by 'M. F.'), p. 20; and 'Sidelights on the Convention', Oct. 1909, by 'Mere Onlooker' [SMF], p. 20. William Blackwood to SMF, 16/3/1910, FP vol. 80.

55 Portia Geach (1873–1959) *ADB* vol. 8. Annie (known as Nancy in some sources) Lister Watson (c.1869–1928) and Philip Sidney Watson (1858–1936) joined the Christian Science church in 1904, 'P. S.' a practitioner in 1905 (church archives, Boston), Edward Palmer, *Early Days in North Queensland*, Angus & Robertson, London and Sydney, 1983 (1st edn 1903, n.p.), pp. 102–3, 166 (ML). Newshams: after the death of her husband, J. E. B. Newsham (d. Brisbane, 1905), Mrs Newsham, née Roseby, and her four children went to Chicago 1906–12 and remained in America until 1937; Anne Isabel Newsham (1876–1969) was a secretary (Isabel Newsham to Colin Roderick, 5/11/1954, Guard Book 6, Roderick Papers). Louis Freeland Post (1849–1928) wrote *Social Service*, Wessels, New York, 1909 (PBC no. 773 with inscription 6/4/1910) and, with Alice Thacher Post (1855–1947), produced *The Public*, a single tax journal (SMF to Mary Fullerton, n.d., FP vol. 19, p. 343, extract from Alice Henry to SMF re the Posts). Leonora Pease (1875–1958), b. Colorado, died in California. Editha Phelps (1855–1932), b. Michigan, was daughter of an Episcopalian minister (press cutting, FP vol. 12, *Tecumseh Herald*, 29/3/1932; *ADB* files).

56 Blackwood to SMF, 16/3/1910 and SMF to Blackwood, 4 /4/1910, FP vol. 80.*

57 *SMH*, 8/12/1909, p. 5.

58 Margaret Dreier Robins, Welcome and Convention Address, 27/9/1909, and Minutes, National Executive Board, NWTUL, St Louis, 19/5/1910, MDR Papers, Box 13, and WTUL Papers, m/film reel 1.

59 PD, 14/1/1910.

60 Postcards, FP vol. 111; PD, 1/8–5/9/1910.

61 *SMH*, 19/1/1910, p. 5 ('Page for Women'), and *Worker*, 10/2/1910, p. 7 ('Our Women's Page').

62 [SMF and Alice Henry], 'Chicago at the Front', *L&L*, Jan. 1911, p. 5.

63 *ibid*; 'A Sweated Industry', *L&L*, Jan. 1911, p. 13.

64 PD, Oct. 1910.

65 'Chicago at the Front', *L&L*, Jan. 1911, pp. 4–13. Katharine Coman (1857–1915) was an Ohio-born professor of economics at Wellesley College and reformer (*NAW*).

66 Boone, *The Women's Trade Union Leagues*, pp. 94–5; 'Chicago at the Front', *L&L*, Jan. 1911, pp. 4–13, and 'The End of the Struggle', *L&L*, Mar. 1911, p. 89. John Fitzpatrick (1870–1946) was a progressive labour leader in the Chicago Federation of Labor.

67 'Sketches from Life No. 1: The Waiter Speaks', ML MSS 445/22, is set about this time.

68 'Why 50,000 Refused to Sew', *Englishwoman*, vol. 10, 29/6/1911, pp. 297–308, and the *Age* (Melbourne), 24/6/1911, p. 8.

Chapter 6: The Net of Circumstance: March 1911–October 1915

1 SMF to Aunt Annie Franklin, 21/11/1913, ML Doc 2866.*

2 James J. Kenneally, *Women and American Trade Unions*, Eden Press, Montreal, 1981, pp. 71–2; Susan Eastabrook Kennedy, *If All We Did Was Weep at Home: A History of White Working Class Women in America*, Indiana Univ. Press, Bloomington, Indiana, 1981, pp. 129–30.

3 SMF to T. J. Hebblewhite, press cutting, *Penny Post*, ML MSS 3737/2; Bruce Sutherland, 'Stella Miles Franklin's American Years', *Meanjin*, 1965, vol. 24, no. 2, mentions 'the lost novel', identified in Jill Roe, 'The Significant Silence', *Meanjin*, 1980, vol. 39, no. 1; 'Progressivism' (*OCAH*).

4   *Worker*, 2/3/1911, p. 21, and *Book Lover*, Mar. 1911, p. 30; Smith, *Chicago and the American Literary Imagination*, p. 181; 'the Chicago Renaissance', *Atlas of World Literature*, 1996, pp. 154–7.

5   *Englishwoman*, vol. 10, no. 29, 1911, pp. 297–308 (the *Englishwoman*, London, 1909–21, was a monthly published by Grant Richards); *Age*, 24/6/1911, p. 18; 'The End of the Struggle. The Garment Workers' Strike', *L&L*, Mar. 1911, pp. 88–9, and PD, Mar.–Apr. 1911, *passim*; MDR to SMF, 18/4/1911* and 24/4/1911, FP vol. 10. Dorothea Adelheit Dreier (1870–1923) was a well known artist (*NYT*, 16/9/1923, p. 8).

6   She also read Ballinger on 'the singing voice' (title unable to be traced) in the John Crerar Library, a scientific reference library then located on the sixth floor of the Marshall Field building, cnr Wabash and Washington (Viskochil, *Chicago at the Turn of the Century*, Plate 31), now part of Univ. of Chicago Libraries. W. E. B. Du Bois (1868–1963) was a prominent black civil rights leader (*ANB*).

7   PD, Mar.–Apr., *passim* ; LN, FP vol. 3, pp. 615–20; SMF to Florence James, 26/3/1954, FP vol. 30 (the ideal American woman, c.1910) and *Collins English Dictionary*. Margery Currey (1877–1959), teacher then journalist, publicist, Chicago and New York (*NYT*, 17/8/1959, p. 23), was a Vassar graduate (1901), also a Christian Scientist (Vassar College, alumnae records, 1927), and known for her 'airiness and gaiety' (George Thomas Tansell, 'Poet at the Barricades: The Life and Work of Floyd Dell', Dissertation Abstracts 1993, p. 64); Floyd James Dell (1879–1969), prominent in the Chicago literary renaissance, was an editor on *Chicago Evening Post* 1911–13, later a New York writer (*NYT*, 30/7/1969, p. 39).

8   SMF to D. Murphy, 15/4/1911, FP vol. 10 and PD, 15/4/1911; ML MSS 445/22. FP vol. 121A has unidentified page proofs with many corrections by SMF.

9   ML MSS 445/22; PD, 8, 15–16/4/1911.

10 MDR to SMF, 17/5/1911, FP vol. 10. Editha Phelps worked at the John Crerar Library (see n. 6 above).

11 PD, 29/5–6/6/1911.

12 PD, Jun. 1911, *passim*; Goldstein, 'To America & Back', p. 27; 'How Chicago Went to Boston. By a Delegate' (probably SMF), *L&L*, Aug. 1911, pp. 232–4.

13 *L&L*, Aug. 1911 (Convention Report), pp. 228–37 and Sept. 1911 (Presidential Address), pp. 278–80.

14 *L&L*, Aug. 1911 (Convention Report), p. 230; *CDT*, 17/6/1911, p. 8.

15 SMF to Isabella Goldstein, 13/10/1911, VG.*

16 Violet Pike (1885–1978), b. New York, a Vassar graduate and a volunteer picket during the 1910 strikes in New York and Philadelphia (Rheta Childe Dorr, *What 8 Million Women Want*, Small, Maynard and Co, Boston, 1910), m. Arthur J. Penty, English Guild Socialist, in 1916 (see ch. 7, n. 6); FP vol. 111, vol. 113X (*postcards, p. 65); Lampe Family Album, NLA.

17 PD, Jun.–Jul. 1911.

18 FP vol. 111; *London Directory*, 1909, lists 'Miss Lucy Bremian', boarding house, at 22 Upper Woburn Place (site adjacent to Endsleigh Crt, a few steps down from Euston Rd), but the name is probably misspelled.

19 Tennyson to SMF, 11/7/1911, FP vol. 9A; PD, *passim*; SMF to Isabella Goldstein, 13/10/1911, VG Papers;* SMF to Elizabeth Robins, 10/10/1940, FP vol. 13. *Melba* by Agnes Gillian Murphy (c.1875–1931), expatriate journalist and publicist, was published by Chatto & Windus, London, 1909 (see also Clarke, *Pen Portraits*, pp. 214–16).

20 LN, FP vol. 3, p. 560, and *Times* (London), 6/11/1930, p. 17; Personal Account Book, 18/1/1913, FP vol. 110/1. Florence Dryhurst, a member of the WFL, was wife of Albert Robert Dryhurst, Assist. Sec. (ret.) of the British Museum (*Times*, 1/7/1924, p. 14), mother of Sylvia, writer and wife of Robert Lynd (1879–1949) (*ODNB*). For more on radical liberal journalist Henry Woodd Nevinson (1856–1941), social reformers Margaret McMillan (1860–1931) and Rachel McMillan (1859–1917), and the redoubtable Charlotte Despard (1844–1939), see *ODNB*, ch. 7.

21 Editha Phelps, 'The First Suffrage Parade in Paris', *L&L* Sept. 1914, pp. 280–1, and 'French Women at Work', *L&L*, Nov. 1914 (dated Paris, 31 Aug.), pp. 348–51; LN, FP vol. 3, pp. 559ff.; Mandy Treagus, 'Britons of the South Seas: The Maori visit to London, 1911', in *Projections of Britain*, eds Heather Kerr et al., Lythrum Press, Adelaide, 2008; *Times*, 26/4/1911, p. 8, 24/7/1911, p. 4; PDF, 25/8 and 24/7/1911.

22   FP vol. 111 (postcard); LN, FP vol. 3, p. 564; Helen Marot to SMF, 30/9/1911, and SMF to
      Helen Marot, 4/10/1911, NWTUL, Records, m/film reel 1.* Helen Marot (1865–1940), Quaker
      and social investigator, was Secretary, New York WTUL 1906–13 (*ANB*).

23   SMF to Dymphna Cusack, 27/7/1949, FP vol. 30, repr. North (ed.), *Yarn Spinners*; LN, FP vol.
      3, p. 560–1, 567; PD, 13/6/1912. Mrs Emily Maquay (c.1853–1938), Irish-born, was the widow
      of an English electrical engineer; her son George Maquay (c.1875–1964), b. Ireland, an
      electrician, emigrated to Chicago in 1909 (censuses, UK, 1881, 1891, US 1920; *Times*
      (London), 2/9/1886, p. 4 and 5/12/1938, p. 1).

24   'Strike of Women', *L&L*, Oct. 1911, p. 315, and 'Organising Women Workers in America' by A.
      A. S. [A. A. Smith], *Vote*, 16/9/1911, pp. 256–7, repr. *A Gregarious Culture*. George Dangerfield,
      The Strange Death of Liberal England (Constable, London, 1936) is the classic work. Fellow
      Australian Dr Marion Phillips (1881–1932), later first woman organiser of the British Labour
      Party, was an organiser of the Bermondsey strike, but it is not known if Miles met her at that
      time (*ADB* vol. 11).

25   Roe, 'Chivalry and Social Policy'; LN, FP vol. 3, p. 731; SMF to SF, 22/7/[1911], FP vol. 111;
      Olive Schreiner, *Woman and Labour*, 1911, inscribed 'S. M. E. Franklin', PBC no. 799, and C. P.
      Gilman, *Women and Economics: A Study of the Economic Relation between Men and Women as
      a Factor in Social Evolution*, Putnam's Sons, London, 1908, 6th edn, inscribed 'S. M. E. Franklin
      12.12.11' in her hand, PBC no. 647.

26   'American Women and Labour', *SMH*, 5/6/1912, p. 5; Helen Marot to SMF, 30/9/1911, and
      SMF to Helen Marot, 4/10/1911, WTUL Papers;* Second Single Tax Conference, Chicago,
      24–6/11/1912. Census records show Miles and Walter in the same Chicago neighbourhood in
      1910 (Terence H. Hull, 'The Strange History and Problematic Future of the Australian Census',
      unpub. conference address, 2006, courtesy the author), and there was probably a prior link
      between Miles' friends the Pischels and Marion Mahony's family in north-west Chicago.

27   Personal account book, 1911–17, FP vol. 110/1.

28   SMF to Leonora O'Reilly [Aug. 1915], O'Reilly Papers, WTUL Papers, m/film series II; SMF to
      Isabella Goldstein, 13/10/1911, VG Papers and SMF to Exec. Members, 30/10/1911, WTUL
      Papers;* MDR to RR, 24/10/1911, RR Papers, in MDR Corres., MDR Papers.

29   *L&L*, Dec. 1911, pp. 377–9, repr. *A Gregarious Culture*; *L&L*, Oct. 1912, pp. 310–11.

30   MDR to Mary E. Drier, 6/10/1911 and SMF to MDR, 31/12/1911, MDR Papers. Lisa Tickner,
      The Spectacle of Women: Imagery of the Suffrage Campaign 1907–14, Chatto & Windus,
      London, 1987, pp. 122–3.

31   *A Gregarious Culture*, p. xix; Bettison and Roe, *ALS* listing, 2001; *Promised Land* review, *L&L*, Nov.
      1912, pp. 342–4 (repr. *A Gregarious Culture*), *Way Stations* review, *L&L*, Jun. 1913, pp.181–2.

32   Lester F. Ward, *Pure Sociology: A Treatise on the Origin and Spontaneous Development of
      Society*, Macmillan, New York, 1911, p. 188.

33   Laurel N. Tanner, 'Ward, Lester Frank', *ANB* vol. 22; SMF to Laurie Collinson, 23/12/1948, FP
      vol. 41;* PBC no. 857.

34   *L&L*, Jun. 1913, p. 187; Gilman, *Living*, p. 187; Knight, *Charlotte Perkins Gilman*, pp. 59,
      116–24 (quotation, p. 123).

35   This account of Gilman follows Ann J. Lane, *ANB* vol. 9.

36   SMF to RS, 19/6/1913, and SMF to RS, 9/12/1912, RS Corres. *(edited text); and 'Mrs Gilman
      on the Warpath', *DT* (Sydney), 5/2/1913, p. 2.

37   Account Book and PBC no. 644, 644A, 644B.

38   Ann Heilmann, *New Woman Fiction: Women Writing First-wave Feminism*, Macmillan, St
      Martin's, London & New York, 2000, esp. ch. 3.

39   Knight, *Charlotte Perkins Gilman*, p. 123; LN, FP vol. 3, p. 614; Heilbrun, *Writing a
      Woman's Life*, p. 43. Most of the unpublished work is to be found at ML MSS 445, e.g. 'Notes',
      ML MSS 445/22.

40   Roy Duncan, Introduction, *On Dearborn Street*, p. xiii.

41   Heilmann, *New Woman Fiction*, pp. 156–7. '*Künstlerroman*': a novel on the development of an
      artist from childhood.

42   Joseph McAleer, *Passion's Fortune: The story of Mills & Boon*, Oxford Univ. Press, Oxford UK,
      1999. Dorothea Mackellar (1885–1968) wrote the lines 'I love a sunburnt country', *ADB* vol. 9;
      Net of Circumstance, pp. 19, 15.

43 'Mary Anne residential': a fictionalised Eleanor Association residence (Meyerowitz, *Women Adrift*, p. 47).

44 *Net of Circumstance*, p. 29.

45 Elaine R. Hedges, Afterword, *The Yellow Wallpaper*, repr. Virago, London, 1987, c.1973, pp. 46–7 (first published *New England Magazine*, 1892). 'Alienist': one who treats mental diseases, *Shorter Oxford English Dictionary*, see Elaine Showalter, *The Female Malady: Women, Madness and English Culture 1830–1980*, Pantheon Books, New York, 1985, pp. 134–8 re punitive treatments disguised as rest cures; *Net of Circumstance*, p. 212.

46 There are ten references to Australia in *L&L*, vol. 1, including two to Catherine Helen Spence. Florence Baverstock (1861–1937), daughter of Victorian journalist David Blair (*ADB* vol. 3), was much admired by fellow journalist Mary Gilmore (Clarke, *Pen Portraits*, pp. 231–3).

47 PD, 31/12/1911, 1/1/1912–4/2/1912; *Lakeside City Directory*, 1917; ML MSS 445/25/2 (play).

48 *NAW*; O'Reilly Papers, m/film series V (SMF to Leonora O'Reilly, 20/11/1911); MDR to Leonora O'Reilly, 17/1/1912; SMF to Leonora O'Reilly, 19/2/1912; MDR to the Exec. Board, 20/1/1912, NWTUL Records, m/film reel 1; 'Leonora O'Reilly', personal file, MDR Papers, Box 12.

49 PD, 17–18/2/1912 and 15/4/1912; MDR and SMF to Exec. Board, 26/3/1912, NWTUL Records, m/film reel 1; Boone, *Women's Trade Union Leagues*, pp. 101–7 (incl. quotation) and Mary E. Dreier, *Margaret Dreier Robins*, pp. 86–7. See ch. 5, n. 42 for Agnes Nestor.

50 Margery Curry: SMF to RS, 9/12/11912, RS Corres.* Elisabeth Christman (1881–1975) was President of the Chicago glove workers' union 1912–17 and WTUL Secretary-Treasurer 1921–50 (*NAW*). Rose Schneiderman (1882–1972) was fulltime organiser for the New York WTUL from 1910 (*NAW*). For Mary Anderson see ch. 8.

51 SMF to Eva O'Sullivan, 8/5/1912, ML MSS 544.* FP vol. 11 has postcard of the building.

52 Condolence card, Sarah Lampe, FP vol. 51, p. 21 ('For honesty, piety and integrity the deceased had no superiors'); 'Red Cross Nurse', ML MSS 445/3; Jane Hunt, 'Unrelaxing Fortitude'; SMF to RS, 9/12/1912, RS Corres.*

53 'Suffrage Forces Call on Homes', *CDT*, 30/3/1912, p 2; 'Walter Burley Griffin. Winner of the Federal Capital Prize', *DT* (Sydney), 3/8/1912, p 15; Griffin heard the news late May; SMF's first diary reference to the Griffins is 4/6/1912, stating that Emma Pischel's brother Fred took her and Miss Henry to call on the Griffins. On 'civic ambitions', see Daniel T. Rodgers, *Atlantic Crossings: Social Politics in a Progressive Age*, Belknap Press at Harvard Univ. Press, Cambridge, Mass., 1998, ch. 5.

54 'Women to March on the Coliseum', *CDT*, 5/8/1912, p. 5; press cutting, *The World*, 25/8/1912, DD Papers, m/film reel D106; Margery Dell (Currey), 'Chicago Suffragists March', *L&L*, Oct. 1912, pp. 316–17.

55 SMF to RS, 14/9/1912, RS Corres.; PD; Mary E. Dreier to Dear Dodo [1912], DD Papers, m/film reel D106.

56 Alice Henry and SMF to the Prime Minister of Australia, 13/9/1912, RS Corres., and 'American Suffragists Annoyed', *DT* (Sydney), 6/11/1912, p. 15, also *CDT*, 12/9/1912, p. 1 (possibly the cutting referred to); SMF to RS, 9/12/1912, RS Corres.*

57 Frederick Pischel (1868–1920s?), b. Wisconsin, is listed as a clerk in Lakeside Directories, but appears as an architect at the 1900 census. From *CDT* references, he was active on Cook Co realty board 1913–19.

58 MDR to Exec. Board, 20/1/1912, NWTUL Records, reel 1; MDR to Mary Spaulding Lee, 2/12/1912, MDR Papers, Nov.–Dec. 1912 (4); Mary E. Dreier to DD, DD Papers, m/film reel D106.

59 *L&L*, Dec. 1912, p. 356.

60 Boone, *Women's Trade Union Leagues*, p. 109.

61 *On Dearborn Street*, p. 203.

62 *Lakeside City Directory*; Van Hoosen, *Women Building Chicago*; the 'blessed' Dr Favill (PD, 30/10/1913, FP vol. 111, postcard); SMF to Margery Currey, 13/1/1948, FP vol. 22.

63 *On Dearborn Street*, p. 107. 'Canal': what remained of Chicago River.

64 *On Dearborn Street*, p. 29.

65 *ibid.*, p. 25; SMF to J. K. Moir, 17/6/1953, FP vol. 34; Sally Ledger, *The New Woman: Fiction and Feminism in the Fin de Siecle*, Manchester Univ. Press, Manchester, UK, 1997, ch. 6, 'The New Woman and the Modern City'.

66 Contributions to *L&L*, Bettison and Roe, *ALS* listing, 2001; SMF to MDR, 17/6/1913, MDR Papers;* 'Leaders at Union Convention', *St Louis Post-Dispatch*, 3/6/1913, and *St Louis Republican*, 3/6/1913, Jane Addams WTUL Scrapbook, Univ. of Illinois-Chicago Library, Special Collns, folder 6.

67 SMF to Aunt Annie Franklin, 21/11/1913, ML Doc 2866, and SMF to SF, 3/8/1913, FP vol. 111* (both).

68 SMF to Aunt Annie Franklin, 21/11/1913.

69 Harold Ickes (1874–1952); Mr and Mrs A. K. Maynard, *L&L*, Mar. 1914, pp. 90–1 and see ch. 8, n. 9; Marie Byles (1900–79), solicitor and environmentalist (*ADB* vol. 13). Ethel Mary Mason (1880–1967), b. Chicago, m. Niels Christian Nielsen, 1925, d. N. Carolina, pers. comm. Gilbert and Glenn Nelson.

70 Australian press references: *Book Lover*, Mar. 1913, p. 30, May 1913, p. 49 (Raymond Robins' visit to Australia), Jun. 1913, p. 69 and Sept. 1913, p. 98 (sends material on NWTUL Convention), Sept. 1914, p. 106 (SMF said to be a woman of 30), plus separate citations this chapter; *Socialist* (Melbourne), 'A Literary Letter from Myles [sic] Franklin', 12/9/1913, p. 4 (SMF sends *L&L* Jun., Jul. 1913); *Sydney Stock and Station Journal* 5/9/1913, p. 2 (St Louis Conference Proceedings, FP vol. 122/97). *Worker* ('Our Women's Page'): 'Girls and Unions in America', 27/3/1913, p. 15; invitation to send delegates to St Louis Convention, 10/4/1913, p. 15; 'An American Suffragist Leader', 8/5/1913, p. 21; 'Wages and Vice: Are They Related?', 29/5/1913, p. 17 (from *L&L*, Apr. 1913). Letters introducing Walter Burley Griffin: SMF to RS, 19/7/1913 and 23/8/1913, RS Corres.,* and *Book Lover*, Sept. 1913, p. 99. RR to MDR, 7/4/1913, Hotel Metropole, Sydney, RR Papers in MDR Corres. in MDR Papers. ML MSS 445/37/19.

71 'Women and War. Chicago's Little Theater', *L&L*, Mar. 1913, p. 87. Maurice Browne (1881–1955), British-born theatrical producer, and his wife, actor Ellen Van Volkenburg (1882–1979), co-established the Chicago Little Theater, Autumn 1912.

72 SMF to RS, 19/6/1913, RS Corres.; 'The Australian Theatre', *West Australian*, 23/9/1950, p. 21, repr. *A Gregarious Culture*.

73 SMF to Alice Henry, 1/3/1917, FP vol. 114 (after a letter in *Tribune*?);* SMF to Alice Henry, 11/3/[1936], FP vol. 11;* FP vol. 5, item 16 (diary fragments); William Bross Lloyd m. Lola Maverick (1875–1944), WTUL 'ally' and peace activist, in 1902, and they had four children 1904–13; divorced by her in 1916, he remarried in 1918. Opera in Chicago dates from 1910.

74 SMF to C. H. Grattan, 6/9/1938, FP vol. 23;* Demarest Lloyd to SMF, 36 letters 1912–21, FP vol. 12.

75 *NYT*, 5/11/1912, p. 1; Court depositions, Boston, 1912–13 (but the documentation is in archaic language, now difficult to interpret); *National Cyclopedia of American Biography*, vol. XXVIII, 1940; SMF to Ethel Nielsen (Mason), 29/11/1951, FP vol. 21.

76 'Sinbad the Sailor' to SMF, 27/3/1913, FP vol. 12.

77 Demarest Lloyd to SMF, 16/9/1912, n.d. [Oct. 1913], FP vol. 12. George Bernard Shaw (1856–1950), b. Belfast, Fabian socialist and dramatist, was then at the height of his powers (Gibbs, *Bernard Shaw*, ch. 16).

78 Demarest Lloyd to SMF, 22/9/1912, 6/10/1913, 5/12/1913, 8/10/1913, FP vol. 12.

79 SMF to Demarest Lloyd, 26/9/1914, FP vol. 12;* 'When Bobby Got Religion', ML MSS 445/21, and *On Dearborn Street*, ch. 13. Demarest Lloyd's enthusiasm for Christian Science 1913–14 did not extend to church membership (Church records, Boston) and is treated dismissively in the fictions. Charles Manning Hope Clark (1915–91) published a six-volume history of Australia, 1962–87.

80 Bland, *Banishing the Beast*, p. 245 (Pankhurst).

81 'VV's Eyes', *L&L*, Oct. 1913, p. 319; *The Freewoman* was founded and edited by Dora Marsden (1882–1960), *ODNB*; supporters included Floyd Dell and Margery Currey, also Edith Ellis (see n. 97 below). 'Red Cross Nurse', ML MSS 445/3.

82 SMF to RS, 19/6/1913, RS Corres., ML.

83 'Mrs Pankhurst in the United States', *L&L*, Dec. 1913, pp. 364–6, repr. *A Gregarious Culture*; June Purvis, *Emmeline Pankhurst: A Biography*, Routledge, London and New York, 2002, has a fine photographic portrait of EP in Chicago in 1913; SMF expended $3 on tickets to hear Mrs Pankhurst (account book, 1/11/1913); Purvis, pp. 136–41 (1909), 169–76 (1911), 234–7 (1913).

84   'Leaders Who Will Take Part in the National Women's Trade Union League Convention Here', *St Louis Times*, 31/5/1913, and 'She'll Devote her Life to Better her Sex, Trades Head Says', *St Louis Republican*, 3/6/1913, Jane Addams WTUL Scrapbook, Univ. of Illinois-Chicago Library, Special Collns, folio 6; Boone, *Women's Trade Union Leagues*, pp. 110–16.

85   'Fourth Biennial Outlines Organizational Work', *L&L*, Sept. 1913, pp. 273–5; MDR, 'Industrial Education', Presidential Address, 1913, *L&L*, Aug. 1913; 'Elizabeth Maloney and the High Calling of the Waitress', *L&L*, Feb. 1913 (repr. John Hammond Moore (ed.), *Australians in America 1876–1967*, Univ. of Qld Press, St Lucia, Qld, 1977, pp. 123–30); 'Agnes Nestor of the Glove Workers: A Leader in the Women's Movement', *L&L*, Dec. 1913, pp. 370–4 and Mar. 1913, p. 93.

86   'Training School for Women Organizers' and 'Ten Years of Work by the Chicago League', *L&L*, Mar. 1914, pp. 90–1, 93–4; SMF to RR, 11/6/1914, RR Papers in MDR Corres. in MDR Papers.*

87   LN, FP vol. 3 p. 648, (teachers); *diseuse*: French, actress who presents dramatic recitals, usually sung accompanied by music. SMF to SF, 21/1/1914, FP vol. 111; PD, 25/3/1914; LN, FP vol. 3, pp. 641–50, and speech notes, ML MSS 445/36/17.

88   SMF to DD [27/2/1914], DD Papers; 'Elisabeth Martini, Architect', *L&L*, Feb. 1914; *Lakeside City Directory*, 1917; 'Visit of Arbitration Expert', *L&L*, Aug. 1914, pp. 248–9, and John Rickard, *H. B. Higgins: The Rebel as Judge*, Allen & Unwin, North Sydney, 1984, p. 197.

89   PD, 18/2/1914, and ML MSS 445/21; SMF to DD, 14/3/1914, DD Papers.

90   *Prisons and Prisoners*, *L&L*, Jun. 1914, pp. 190–1; 'The Biennial of Women's Clubs', *L&L*, Aug. 1914, pp. 228–31; SMF to RR, 11/6/1914, RR Papers in MDR Corres. in MDR Papers.*

91   MDR to James Mullenbach, 3/4/1913, MDR Papers. SMF and Alice Henry (photo reproduced in this book).

92   *L&L* letterhead, SMF to RS, 23/8/1913, RS Corres.; Diane Kirkby, 'Class, Gender and the Perils of Philanthropy: The Story of *Life and Labor* and Labor Reform in the Women's Trade Union League', *J. Women's Hist.*, Fall 1992.

93   Alice Henry to MDR, 24/3/1914, NWTUL Records, m/film reel 1; SMF to Leonora O'Reilly, 10/6/1914, O'Reilly Papers, m/film series V.

94   MDR to Alice Henry, 18/4/1914, NWTUL Records, m/film reel 1.

95   PD, Apr.–Jun. 1914, *passim*.

96   Demarest Lloyd to SMF, 21/7/1914 (postmark), FP vol. 12; *On Dearborn Street*, p. 97.

97   Dorothy Pethick (1881–1970) was a sister of WSPU's Mrs Pethick Lawrence. Florence Emily Kathleen (Kath) Ussher (1891–1983), b. Qld, second daughter of English-born parents Florence Eleanor Ussher, née Whittle, and Cpt James Ussher, and star student of the Misses Hodge and Newcombs' 'Shirley' school, enrolled briefly in the School of the Art Institute of Chicago in 1914 (transcript copy in my possession). Edith Ellis (1861–1916), socialist and writer, m. Henry Havelock Ellis in 1894, but the marriage failed, due to the unorthodox sexuality of both partners. Martha Vicinus, conference address, Univ. of Adelaide, 28/6/2005, stressed Ellis' avant garde self-image; the short story 'Miss Toby's Party, or How I Queered a Queer's Party' (ML MSS 445/22) mocks 'well-worn lectures on free love'.

98   Maurice Smith, *A Short History of Dentistry*, Wingate, London, 1958, pp. 71–5.

99   'The Menace of Great Armaments', *L&L*, Sept. 1914, pp. 260–3.

100   Jill Roe, 'Forcing the Issue: Miles Franklin and National Identity'; MDR to RR, 23/8/1914, in MDR Corres., MDR Papers.

101   'The New Broom: How It is Sometimes Made', *L&L*, Oct. 1914, pp. 294–6; William Lothian to SMF, 26/5/1930, FP vol. 80 (re return of the Cupid story, held 'for a great many years').

102   SMF to Leonora O'Reilly, 15/9/1914, O'Reilly Papers, m/film series V; MDR to Mary E. Dreier, 2/10/1914, MDR Papers. 'Baldwin engine': Matthias Baldwin was a leading American locomotive designer whose engines were imported by NSW in the early 20th century.

103   Jill Roe, '"Testimonies from the Field"', pp. 304–19. Edith Malyon (c.1876–1942) nurse, Christian Science practitioner, came from Ballarat. Agnes Locke (1869–1950), was a sister of writer Helena Sumner Locke (1881–1917), *ADB* vol. 10. Geraldine Rede (1873–1943) was an artist and friend of Vida Goldstein.

104   Leslie Bridle, pers. comm., 1982.

105 SMF–Demarest Lloyd corres., FP vol. 12: Demarest Lloyd to SMF, 24/9/[1914]; Demarest Lloyd to SMF [Sept. 1914?]; SMF to Demarest Lloyd, 26/9/1914;* SMF to [Demarest Lloyd], postcard, 16/10/1914 [date inserted by SMF], FP vol. 12.

106 PD, 23, 18/10/1914; SMF to Dear D—?, FP vol. 46 (the white feather, reprod. Harry Heseltine, *The Most Glittering Prize*, cover).

107 Postcards to SF, FP vol. 110 and 13/11/1914, FP vol. 111.

108 SMF to Melinda Scott, 16/11/1914, NWTUL Records, m/film reel 1.

109 MDR to Mary E. Dreier, 2/10/1914, MDR Papers; PD, 24/11/1914. Rosika Schwimmer (1877–1948) died stateless, due to her beliefs (*ANB*).

110 SMF to Melinda Scott, 16/11/1914, Alice Henry to MDR, 19/12/1914, appeal 18/12/1914 and staff meeting report, by SMF [?], 31/12/1914, and MDR to Exec. Board, 23/12/1914, NWTUL Records, m/film reel 1; MDR to Mary E. Dreier, 17/1/1915, MDR Papers.

111 PD, 2/4/1915 (Demy Lloyd); PD, 5/12/1914 (Fred).

112 *Lakeside City Directories*; 'Mr O. L'Artsau' to Demarest Lloyd, 27/8/1920 and reply, 11/1/1921, FP vol. 12, and Erwin Canham, *Commitment to Freedom: The Story of the Christian Science Monitor 1908–1958*, Houghton Mifflin, Boston, 1958, p. 159; LN, FP vol. 3, p. 614; SMF to Ethel Nielsen, 29/11/1951, FP vol. 21.

113 PBC no. 769. Helen Frances ('Nell') Malone (1881–1963), b. Stanifer, NSW, near Inverell, a nurse, was last heard of in France in 1953; Ada Augusta Holman, née Kidgell (1869–1949), journalist, m. W. A. Holman in Sydney, 1901; William A. Holman (1871–1934) was Labor, then National, premier of NSW 1913–20 (*ADB* vol. 9).

114 SMF to Leonora Pease, 12/3/1938, FP vol. 13.*

115 SF, Notebook, FP vol. 107, *passim*, vol. 111 (postcards), vols 105, 110 (account books); Roderick, Guard Book 6, p. 15, Roderick Papers; Sarah Lampe (d. 1912), will no. 56750 and estate SR 20/455 (NSW BMD). The cottage was purchased 27/8/1914 and Susannah moved in on 21/9/1914; JMF did not finally retire there until 1917.

116 SMF to Leonora O'Reilly, 5/1/1915, O'Reilly Papers, m/film series V and SMF to Jane Addams, 6/1/1915, Women's International League for Peace and Freedom Papers, Univ. of Illinois-Chicago.*

117 Leonora O'Reilly, 'International Congress of Women at the Hague', *L&L*, Jul. 1915, pp. 127–18; SMF to Leonora O'Reilly, 12/4/1915, O'Reilly Papers; 'Peace Programs', *L&L*, Apr. 1915, p. 47. Jill Roe, 'Peace' in Mary Spongberg *et al.*, *Companion to Women's Historical Writing*, Palgrave Macmillan, Basingstoke, UK, 2005, pp. 401–10. 'Peace Ahoy!', *L&L* Apr. 1915, pp. 66–7, is repr. *A Gregarious Culture.*

118 'Miss Pankhurst in the U.S.', *CDT*, 15/10/1914, p. 7; SMF to RS, 8/5/1915, RS Corres.; G. Bussey and M. Tims, *Women's International League for Peace and Freedom 1915–1965: A Record of Fifty Years' Work*, G. Allen & Unwin, London, 1965.

119 *TLS*, 13/5/1915, p. 163. Roderick, *Miles Franklin*, p. 126, states she mentioned the novel to him in 1947.

120 MDR to Mary E. Dreier, as cited MDR to the Exec. Board, 5/2/1915, MDR Papers, Box 13 (deficit $2996.78, income $9850.19) and MDR to the Exec. Board, 8/1/1915, NWTUL Records, m/film reel 2 (control). Edith Wyatt to MDR, 12/3/1915, MDR to the Exec. Board, 23/3/1915, and Alice Henry to MDR, 6/4/1915, NWTUL Records, m/film reel 2; Kirkby, *Alice Henry*, p. 115. Zona Gale (1874–1938) was a leading journalist and regional writer; Paul Kellog (1879–1958) was editor of the *Survey* from 1912 (both in *ANB*).

121 MDR to the Exec. Board, 23/3/1915, NWTUL Records, m/film reel 2; MDR to Mary E. Dreier, 19/3/1915, MDR Papers; MDR to E. Wyatt, 17/3/1915, NWTUL Records, m/film reel 2; Kirkby, *Alice Henry*, p. 118; Wilde, *Courage a Grace*, p. 191. The *Bulletin* ceased publication in 1920.

122 Kirkby, *Alice Henry*, p. 117; S. M. Franklin, 'The Fifth Biennial Convention', *L&L*, Jul. 1915, pp. 116–22, and 'Prominent Women Leaders in National Union Here for Big Convention', *New York Call*, 7/6/1915 (Jane Addams, WTUL Scrapbook, Univ. of Illinois-Chicago Library, Special Collns folder 9), with SMF and MDR centrally pictured.

123 R. McMillan to SMF, 7/10/1915, FP vol. 13 and 'Miles Franklin', *Sydney Stock and Station Journal*, 10/10/1915, p. 2; [*Australian*] *Worker*, 30/9/1915, p. 9; MDR to the Exec. Board, 10/8/1915, NWTUL Records, m/film reel 2; SMF to Leonora O'Reilly, 9/8/1915, O'Reilly Papers, m/film series V.*

124 SMF to Leonora O'Reilly 9/8/1915 and enclosure, SMF to Emma Steghagen, 9/8/1915, O'Reilly Papers, *both.

125 MDR to Agnes Nestor, 8/1/1936, Nestor Papers, m/film series VII; SMF to Eva O'Sullivan, 23/9/1915, ML MSS 544.*

126 PD, 1915, last page (guest list); SMF to *L&L*, 9/9/1915, FP vol. 13;* SMF to Alice Henry, 27/7/1918, FP vol. 114; LN, FP vol. 3, p. 762.

127 SMF to Margery Currey, 14/3/1950, also 4/1/1933, FP vol. 22.*

128 'Chicago Trade Union Women in Conference', *L&L*, Oct. 1915, pp. 154–6; Emma Steghagen to SMF, 28/1/1916 and 3/4/1917, Exec. Board Minutes, 22–4/1/1916, NWTUL Records, m/film reel 2. Amy Walker Field was listed as acting editor Nov.–Dec. 1915 and subsequently appointed editor; MDR took over in 1916.

129 SMF, 'Jane Addams of Hull-House'; Elshtain, *Jane Addams*, pp. 230–1; John P. White to SMF, 7/10/1915 and Samuel Gompers to SMF, 26/10/1915, FP vol. 51. SMF's AFL membership card is at ML MSS 445/40.

130 MSS 3659/1, 145a (enclosure PBC).

131 *The Detective's Album* (1871) by 'Mary Fortune' (Mary Wilson, c.1833– c.1910, *ADB S*) used a male narrator. Thea Astley is probably the best known modern Australian writer in this regard. 'Miss Toby's Party' is another Cavarley narration, heterosexual in character.

132 *On Dearborn Street*, pp. 19, 22.

133 *ibid.*, p. 83.

134 *ibid.*, p. 115.

135 *ibid.*, p. 110.

136 *ibid.*, p. 108

137 *ibid.*, p. 209

138 Karen Lewis, 'Single Heterosexual Women Through the Life Cycle', in Marsha P. Mirkin (ed.), *Women in Context: Towards a Feminist Reconstruction of Psychotherapy*, Guildford Press, New York, 1990 (cited *Women's Review of Books*, Dec. 2002, p. 17); also LN, FP vol. 3, p. 624, that she felt not sex antagonism but sex disgust at the double standard.

139 SMF to Kate Baker, 23/9/1915, Baker Papers.*

140 Antoinette Donnelly ('Doris Blake', 1887–1964), *NYT*, 16/11/1964, p. 31, was beauty editor of the *Chicago Tribune* later the *NY Daily News*.

141 Alexandra Kollontai (1872–1952) was the first woman in history to hold a senior diplomatic post, as Soviet minister to Norway (1923).

142 SMF to Leonora O'Reilly, 6/11/1915, O'Reilly Papers, m/film series V.*

Chapter 7 — Pack Up Your Troubles: November 1915–September 1918

1 'Ne Mari Nishta (It matters nothing)', ML MSS 445/4, p. 91.

2 'Salonika': historically there have been many variants on the name of the Greek city officially known as Thessaloniki since 1912 (Mazower, *Salonica: City of Ghosts*, pp. 15–16); except in citations with variants, the spelling 'Salonika' is followed hereafter as the main English-language usage at this time.

3 Memoirs of 'Alice Henry', ed. Nettie Palmer, Melbourne, 1944, ts.; FP vol. 51, p 129. '*Pack Up Your Troubles*': words by brothers George Asaf [Powell], music by Felix Powell.

4 Nell Malone now worked at a creche in Argyll Sq and lived at Stevenage Rd (PD, 8/6/1916), which clarifies one of Miles' several London literary addresses, viz. 'c/- H. F. Malone Esq., 42 Stevenage Rd, SW6'. Kathleen Ussher was now settled in London where she became a stenographer with the Australian Naval Office and undertook war work as an orderly at Endell St Hospital, Bloomsbury, and part-time munitions work (SMF to Alice Henry, 4/1/1916 and 7/5/1916, FP vol. 114).

5 Aileen's brother Selwyn Goldstein, an engineer, was then working in the UK; he enlisted in late 1915 and reportedly died on the Western Front (Bomford, '*That Dangerous and Persuasive Woman*', p. 183). Angela Woollacott, *On Her Their Lives Depend*, pp. 27–30, also 'A Journalist's Summer Outing', *SMH*, 1/11/1916, p. 5, repr. *A Gregarious Culture*; Alison Adburgham, *Shopping in Style: London from the Restoration to Edwardian Elegance*, Thames and Hudson, London, 1979, pp. 168–9.

6   Margaret McMillan to SMF, 21/11/1915, FP vol. 13; Miles Franklin, 'The Babies' Kits. Deptford
     and Miss McMillan', *SMH*, 13/5/1916, p. 8, repr. *A Gregarious Culture*; Miles attended the
     wedding of Violet Pike and Arthur Penty (1875–1937), architect and social thinker (*ODNB*),
     on 15/1/1916 (PD), Violet becoming Penty's second wife.

7   Phyll to SMF, undated postcard, 1916, vol. 111; 'Newport Trades Council. No-
     Conscriptionists' Wild Talk', *Monmouthshire Evening Post*, 19/2/1916, press cutting, FP vol.
     122, p. 103, and SMF to Emma Steghagen, n.d. [Feb 1916], NWTUL Records, m/film reel 2.
     May Massingberd Meggitt (1880–1958) and Phyllis Mary Meggitt (1889–1969) were both
     born at Mansfield in the north of England, where their father was a glue manufacturer ('The
     World of Miles Franklin', *Southerly*, 1984–5, Jill Roe) also 'British Labor and the War', *L&L*,
     Mar. 1916, pp. 44–6, unsigned, possibly by SMF).

8   *Bulletin*, 17/2/1916, p. 20 ('Melbourne chatter'). Annie B. Champion to SMF, 23/12/[1916]
     (postmark), FP vol. 13; Hodge and Newcomb lived in Sydney 1897–1908, see ch. 3 and
     Catherine Mackerras, *Divided Heart: The Memoirs of Catherine B. Mackerras*, Little Hills Press,
     Crows Nest, NSW, 1991, for a vivid picture of Miss Hodge in full flight. Annie Beatrice
     Champion (1873–1929), a nanny, lived at 4 Bickenhall Mansions, off Baker St, London, W1
     (*Annie Beatrice Champion: Memories of a Victorian Nursery*, ed. Avis Thornton, Cicerone
     Press, Milnthorpe, UK, 1989).

9   SMF to Alice Henry, 4/1/1916, FP vol. 114; Emma Steghagen to SMF, 28/1/1916, NWTUL
     Records, m/film reel 2; SMF to Alice Henry, 7/5/1916, FP vol. 114; SMF to Agnes Nestor,
     21/10/1916, Nestor Papers, m/film series VII.*

10   WFL motto and banners: see http://ahds.ac./UK/Women's Library; Bettison and Roe, *ALS*
     listing (1916), 2001, and ML MSS 445/21–2 (unpublished sketches, mostly listed n. 12 below);
     'The Kookaburra Laughs Goodnight' and 'Queer Street' (probably a version of 'Miss Toby's
     Party'), ML MSS 445/21–2 (two short stories); 'The English Jackeroo' (set in 'Tucker-time
     Gully on Jingerah Run') and 'Somewhere in London', ML MSS 445/26 and 25 (two plays);
     'How the Londoner Takes his War' (ML MSS 445/21, carbon, ts., pp. 5541–781, plus résumé of
     reader's report).

11   PD, 27/4/1916; Woollacott, *To Try Her Fortune In London: Australian Women, Colonialism, and
     Modernity*, Oxford Univ. Press, Oxford and New York, 2001, ch. 3; FP vol. 105/1, expenses Nov.
     1915–Jun. 1917; SMF to Mrs Laurie, 23/6/1917 and Form V(e), SWH Colln, Personnel file, Tin
     32/F (claim for fifteen shillings to cover two days idleness while she was vaccinated and
     payment of a stand-in at the Minerva). The Minerva: SMF to Alice Henry, 4/1/1917, FP vol.
     14, *Vote*, 22/10/1915, p. 790, WFL Records, 104/37c; *Times* (London), 4/9/1920, p. 1.

12   'Anzac Day', in 'London Sketches', ML MSS 445/21; 'Somewhere in London', FP vol. 445/25.
     SMF to Alice Henry, 1/3/1917, FP vol. 114.* Claude Douglas Kinred (1887–1967) was
     wounded at Gallipoli and repatriated, returned to work in munitions (Australian War
     Memorial Nominal Roll and *The Buddong Flows On*, vol. 2, p. 288).

13   'Hold Tight! Life on a London 'Bus!', ML MSS 445/22; 'How the Londoner Takes his War', ML
     MSS 445/21, pp. 744–5. Unpublished sketches at ML MSS 445/21: 'Easter in London', 'A
     London Flower Show: Holland House', 'The Britisher and his Zoo', 'Hyde Park, London' and
     'Kent, Cradle of Civilization', 'London's Editors', 'Take One Please' (by 'Outlander', a Boer War
     tag meaning the opposite to 'Homelander'), 'Two Years After. London Today'. Unpublished
     sketches at ML MSS 445/22: 'Fortune by Mascott in Strand', 'Tea on the Terrace' and 'Things
     Noted in London'.

14   'How the Londoner Takes his War', ML MSS 445/21, p. 743. 'American Commission': possibly
     the Carnegie *Report of the International Commission to Inquire into the Causes and Conduct of
     the Balkan Wars*, Washington, 1914 (PBC no. 575).

15   SMF to Leonora O'Reilly, 14/5/1916, O'Reilly Papers, m/film series V, and SMF to Agnes
     Nestor, 21/10/1916, Nestor Papers, m/film series VII, both.*

16   'Country and Suffrage': cited Jean H. Quataert, 'Gendered Medical Services in the Mobile Field
     Hospitals (the Balkan Wars and World War I 1912–1918)', conference paper International
     Congress of Historical Sciences, Univ. of NSW, 2005, p. 5, http://www.cish.org; Leneman, *In
     the Service of Life*, p. 220; London Committee 1916–1919, SWH Colln, Tin 1.

17   Linklater, *An Unhusbanded Life*, pp. 248–9; Claire Eustace, 'Meanings of Militancy: The Ideas
     and Practice of Political Resistance in the Women's Freedom League 1907–14', in *The Women's*

Suffrage Movement. New Feminist Perspectives, eds Maroula Joannou & June Purvis, Manchester Univ. Press, Manchester, 1998; Garner, *Stepping Stones in Women's Liberty*, ch. 3; Newsome, *Women's Freedom League 1907–1957*, p. 11 (war work). SMF was billed as 'hostess' at two WFL meetings in late 1916 (*Vote*, 13/10/1916, p. 1207).

18   Re Hodge: *Vote*, 19/11/1915, p. 822, and WFL Annual Conference Reports, 1914–24, 1918 transcript, pp. 17, 20, 172, WFL Records. Olive Mary Aldridge (1866–1950), wife of urban reformer Henry R. Aldridge (see ch. 7, p. 224), was a member of the WSPU in 1913, but eschewed violence, *Times* (London, 7/6/1913, p. 40). Miles sent a copy of Mrs Aldridge's book to Aunt Lena (PBC no. 519).

19   PD Apr.–Oct. 1916 *passim*; Miss Bassnett to Mrs Laurie, 26/1/1918 and related items, and File of Miss Bassnett and Mrs Aldridge, organisers, SWH Colln, Box 26; *Vote*, 11/2/1916, p. 922, and 5/10/1917, p. 383. Constance Antonina ('Nina') Boyle (1865–1943), women's rights activist (*ODNB*).

20   How the Londoner Takes his War', ML MSS 445/21, p. 619, and PD, 1/11/1916; 'George Bernard Shaw on War Economy', *Vote*, 2/6/1916, p. 1058, *Book Lover*, 1/10/1916, p. 161 (ML MSS 445/40/6), and Gibbs, *Bernard Shaw*, p. 349; Howard Weinroth, 'Norman Angell and *The Great Illusion*: An Episode in Pre-1914 Pacifism', *Hist. J.*, 1974, vol. xvii, no. 3; 'The Babies' Kits: Nine Elms Settlement and the work of Mrs Charlotte Despard', *SMH* 17/6/1916, p 7, repr. *A Gregarious Culture*; Newsome, *Women's Freedom League*, p. 18.

21   Maud Walsöe (1872–1939), daughter of George Black and Isabella Emily Black, née Watson, joined the Mother Church, Boston on 3/11/1911 with husband Danish-born Paul Walsöe (d. 1961) when resident at Wilmersdorf, Berlin; their son Olaf Walsöe (b. Hamburg 31/3/1908, d. Wahroonga, NSW, 27/5/1977), was a major in the Australian Army in World War II. Jean Webster (1876–1916) rewrote her best-selling novel *Daddy-Long-Legs* (Century Co, New York, and Hodder and Stoughton, 1912) as a play, which opened in 1914 (*ANB* vol. 22 and *Encyclopedia of American Theatre*, 1980, p. 114). Edward Sheldon (1886–1946), playwright (*ABD*); 'Demand for Somme Battle Films', *Times* (London), 29/8/1916, p. 5, entered UNESCO's Memory of the World Register in 2005; London sketches, ML MSS 445/21, cited n. 12 above; LN, FP vol. 3, p. 479 (bishops); *Times* (London), 7/7/1917, p. 5; 'Women and Imperial Ideals', *The Herald* (later *Daily Herald*), 15/7/1916, p. 16 (possibly by Margaret Hodge), and SMF, 'Conference of the Women of Britain', *Survey*, 19/8/1916, pp. 516–17, repr. *A Gregarious Culture*, also 'London's Editors' and 'Take One Please', ML MSS 445, 21–2; PD, 14/10/1916.

22   LN, FP vol. 3, pp. 731–41.

23   Postcard, 15 May [1918?], FP vol. 110/6; photo with G[unne]r T[homas] C[harles] Adams, 4th Division, Australian Artillery, PX *D250/s, no. 135; PD, 26/3/1916, 26/5/1915; SMF to Agnes Nestor 21/10/1916, Nestor Papers, m/film series VII.*

24   'Tea on the Terrace', ML MSS 445/22, drafted for *SMH* (PD, 12/7/1916 and 8/8/1916); SMF to Alice Henry, 26/9/1916, FP vol. 114.* For more on Sarah Anne Byles (1843–1931), wife of William P. Byles, MP (1839–1917), see ch. 8, notes 9 and 10.

25   The Watt-Marriott letters are at ML MSS 364/84; G. Marriott to H. Paget, 17/1/1917, FP vol. 84 and see ch. 6, p. 191.

26   'Fortune by Mascott in Strand', ML MSS 445/22; PD, 10/5/1916; PD 3/5/1916 (re the Lloyd divorce, *CDT*, 28/3/1916, p. 10 (Lloyd divorce sought), 9/7/1916, p. 7 (Lloyd divorce granted); SMF to Alice Henry, 17/10/1916 and 1/3/1917, FP vol. 114.* Fred Pischel to SMF, 25/2/1916, FP vol. 13 and postcard, Leo [Leonora Pease] to SMF, 13/6/1916, FP vol. 13 (the Pischels 'deeply concerned to know all about you').

27   Application and related documents in my possession, courtesy British Library, and see 'How the Londoner Takes His War' ML MSS 445/21, pp. 567–8. Clara Butt (1872–1936) was made DBE in 1920 (*ODNB*).

28   Edith Quinlan: UK census, 1901, 1916 addresses: 166 Leader Mansions, 166 Shaftesbury Avenue (the original of B. R. Wise's letter is at FP vol. 51; on Wise, see ch. 3, n. 87).

29   All three babies' kit items repr. *A Gregarious Culture*. Harriet Newcomb to Andrew Fisher 12/3/1917, FP vol. 13 (draft) refers to SMF writing frequently for the *BA* but only a few news items about her have been located in period. Two pars by S. M. F., 'Symbolism in War Pictures' and 'Women's War Work', appeared in the *Vote*, 5/5/1916, p. 1023, 19/5/1916, p. 1043.

30   PD, 6/5/1916, also *Vote*, 26/5/1916, p. 1051 (Miss Stella Miles Franklin thanked for help with WFL stall); 'British Women-Workers' Exhibition', *SMH*, 5/7/1916, p. 7, and 'A Journalist's Summer Outing', *SMH*, 1/11/1916, p. 5, both articles repr. *A Gregarious Culture.*

31   Australian High Commissioner's Office and SMF, 16/3/1917, 19/3/1917, 26/3/1917, and SMF to Chief Postal Censor, 16/3/1917, FP vol. 13; David Lloyd George (1863–1945), Liberal/Coalitionist politician (*ODNB*), is referred to in LN, FP vol. 3, p. 460 as 'the execrable Lloyd George'; 'Two Years After. London Today', ML MSS 445/21.

32   'Sydney de Loghe': penname of Frederick Sydney Loch (1889–1954); title reissued as *To Hell and Back: The Banned Account of Gallipoli* with a biographical essay by Susanna de Vries and Jake de Vries (HarperCollins, Sydney, 2007). SMF to Alice Henry, 26/9/1916, FP vol. 114;* SMF to Elsie Belle Champion, 21/10/1916, private colln, cited by De Vries and De Vries, p. xii. Loch's wife was Joice NanKivell Loch (see n. 65).

33   SMF to Agnes Nestor, 21/10/1916, Nestor Papers, m/film series VII, SMF to Emma Steghagen, 31/12/1916, NWTUL Records, m/film reel 2, SMF to Alice Henry, 1/3/1917 FP vol. 114, all.*

34   PD, 22/2/1917, article on the suffrage for the *Woman's Journal*, Boston (not traced), 'A Suffrage Demonstration', *SMH*, 9/5/1917, p. 5 (previously unlisted); *BA*, 1/3/1917, p. 20. Lilian Mary Baylis (1874–1937) managed the Old Vic Theatre from 1898 (*ODNB*).

35   Draft Application, Form IB, 12/3/1917, FP vol. 104, p 37; form 1a (age limit), SWH Records, Box 304.

36   *ibid.*, Form IIB (Referees Request). Julia Sarah Ann (Annie) Cobden (1853–1926) and Thomas James Sanderson (1840–1922) *ODNB*.

37   *Bulletin*, 17/5/1917, p 18; FP vol. 104, pp. 39–49, corres. between SMF and Beatrice Russell, 30/5/1917–9/6/1917, FP vol. 104; Ishobel Ross, *Little Grey Partridge: First World War Diary of Ishobel Ross, who Served with the Scottish Women's Hospital Units in Serbia*, intro. Jess Dixon, Aberdeen Univ. Press, Aberdeen, 1988, p. 38. Agnes Elizabeth Bennett (1872–1960), Sydney-born, obtained her medical degrees in Edinburgh (*ADB* vol. 7).

38   Agreement with Unsalaried Employees, Form IIIb, SWH Colln, Tin 32, Form IIIa, Agreement with Salaried Employees, FP vol. 104, with an annotation by SMF that she was not paid anything is undoubtedly a superseded form, and the annotation, which is undated, probably refers to the changed circumstances. Paget, letter and report on *The Net of Circumstance*, 8/5/1917, FP vol. 84; Gilchrist *Australians and Greeks 2*, p. 144. Colin Roderick to Bruce Sutherland, 8/11/1958, Guard Book 6, states that *The Net of Circumstance* was rejected by several US publishers in 1917 'due to outlandish slang' (Roderick Papers).

39   *The Thistle: Souvenir Book in Aid of Scottish Women's Hospitals for Foreign Service*, John Horn, Glasgow, 1917 (British Library); 'Notes on the Work of SWH for Lecturers and Others': Serbian Units and Summary Account, SWH Records, Box 307; *SMH*, 12/11/1917, p. 6.

40   Bozidar Jezernik, *Wild Europe: The Balkans in the Gaze of Western Travellers*, Bosnian Institute, London, 2004, ch. 9; SWH London units, Statement of Accounts, 1916–19, SWH Records; SMF to [American] Friends, 28/6/1917, Nestor Papers, m/film series VII;* SMF ('Frankie Doodle') to Miss Marx, 2/5/1943, FP vol. 39; *A History of the Scottish Women's Hospitals*, ed. Eva Shaw McLaren, Hodder, London, 1919, p. 243, and Gilchrist, *Australians and Greeks 2*, pp. 111, 131 (ten Australians with SWH 1916–18, c.360 Australian nurses in Salonika). Mary De Garis (1881–1963), *ADB* vol. 8 (p. 271); English-born Agnes Dorothy Kerr (c.1870–1951) joined in Salonika and served Aug. 1916–Mar. 1919, SWH Colln, Personnel files, Box 36 and list of American unit members, large trunk; Alice Marion Prichard, MBE (1877–1964), b. Kyabram, Vic, was matron, St George Hospital, Sydney, 1922–51.

41   Ada Holman to RS, 27/6/1917, RS Corres.

42   PD, Jun. 1917; Kathleen Ussher joined the Salonika unit 7/7/1917 (SWH Colln, Box 38), Nell Malone, SWH Colln, Tin 32 (address, 115 High Holborn) and PD, 15/3/1918; I. Emslie Hutton, *With a Woman's Unit in Serbia, Salonika and Sebastopol*, p. 135.

43   SMF to RS, 2/7/1917, RS Corres.*

44   *Book Lover*, Mar. 1918, p 38; SMF to Alice Henry, FP vol. 1/3/1917, FP vol. 114, p. 3c.

45   SMF to Alice Henry, [26/2/1918], FP vol. 115;* 'Ne Mari Nishta', ML MSS 445/4, plus two ts. copies, ML MSS 6035/7, with different sets of photographs.

46   SMF to Mrs Laurie 13/8/1917, SWH Colln, Personnel files, Tin 32/F; FP vol. 104 (declaration & agreement). The four sketches: 'Zabranjeno (Forbidden Valley)' and 'The Dentist in

Macedonia', ML MSS 445/21; 'On the Way to Macedonia' and 'Mrs Mackadoughnut's Hen', ML MSS 445/22. 'By Far Kajmacktchalan' is at ML MSS 445/25 and the variants are ML MSS 6035/1 and 19. 'Active Service Socks' is repr. *A Gregarious Culture.*

47   FP vol. 111; PD, Jul. 1917.

48   'Ne Mari Nishta', ML MSS 445/4, pp. 23, 38. *The Salonika Front. Painted by William T Wood, RWS. Described by A. J. Mann,* A & C Black, London, 1920, substantiates her impression.

49   'Ne Mari Nishta', ML MSS 445/4, pp. 27, 110; 'Salonika', *McMillan Dictionary of World War I,* 1995; R. Clogg, *A Concise History of Greece,* Cambridge Univ. Press, Cambridge, UK, 1992, p. 93; PD, 15/7/1917; Palmer, *The Gardeners of Salonika,* p. 12. Mazower, *Salonica, City of Ghosts,* is the essential account.

50   PD, 15/7/1917; 'Ne Mari Nishta', pp. 28–31; *Salonika Front, by A. J. Mann,* p. 26; Hutton, *With a Woman's Unit,* p. 61.

51   'Ne Mari Nishta', ML MSS 445/4, pp. 33–5.

52   *ibid;* Hutton, *With a Woman's Unit,* p. 138. Isabel Galloway Emslie Hutton (1887–1960) was a Scottish-born physician who specialised in mental health and social work (*ODNB*). 'Kaimacktchalan' was Miles' usual spelling, e.g. 'Active Service Socks', repr. *A Gregarious Culture.*

53   SMF to Mrs Laurie 13/8/1917, SWH Colln, Personnel files, Tin 32/F.

54   *BA,* 6/9/1917, p. 16.

55   Agnes Bennett to SWH, 2 and 27/8/1917 (extracts), SWH Colln, Personnel files, Tin 3/F; PD, 30/7/1917.

56   PD, 27/8/1917; 'Ne Mari Nishta', ML MSS 445/4, p. 177.

57   Photo, FP vol. 2;* 'Ne Mari Nishta', ML MSS 445/4, p. 177; Gilchrist, *Australians and Greeks 2,* pp. 146–7; Mary C. De Garis, *Clinical Notes and Deductions of a Peripatetic,* p. 165 (the officers); SMF to Jean Devanny, 7/1/1954, FP vol. 32, repr. in Ferrier (ed.), *As Good as a Yarn with You.*

58   'The Serbian Army', *McMillan Dictionary of World War I,* 1995 ('a genuinely national force'); *Salonika Front … by A. J. Mann,* ch. 7.

59   PD, 11/8/1917; 'Ne Mari Nishta', ML MSS 445/4, p. 133.

60   'Ne Mari Nishta', ML MSS 445/4, sketch, 'The Plight of the Serbs' and 'Ne Mari Nishta', p. 36, and *ibid.;* W. H. Petrovitch, *Key to the Servian Conversation Grammar,* Heidelberg, 1914, PBC no. 772; untitled poem, ML MSS 445/41, item 2, translated by Dr Boris Skvorc (punctuation added).

61   De Garis, *Clinical Notes,* p. 162; PD, 8/8/1917 (Miss Dick).

62   'Ne Mari Nishta', ML MSS 445/4, Sketch vi [p.1]; Gilchrist, *Australians and Greeks 2,* p. 149; De Garis, *Clinical Notes,* p. 160.

63   'Ne Mari Nishta', ML MSS 445/4, pp. 37, 113, 173, 179; M. C. Pollard, 'Sketches of Macedonia', ML PX *D253; Serbian songs, words, and music collected in 1917, FP vol. 104; Hutton, *With a Woman's Unit,* p. 141. Mabel Pollard (b. 1885–?), who had prior experience of Serbia with Lady Paget's unit in 1914, served at Ostrovo 15/10/1917–7/7/1918, SWH Colln, Personnel files, Box 36.

64   Roula Palanta, *Edessa: City of Waters,* Municipality of Edessa, Edessa, 1993, p. 35 (population estimate and its mix of Greeks, Serbs and Bulgars); 'Ne Mari Nishta', ML MSS 445/4, pp. 39, 43, 101, 152; PD, 29/11/1917 and 5/12/1917.

65   J. Wheelwright, 'Flora Sandes — Military Maid', *History Today,* Mar. 1989; *One Woman at War: Letters of Olive King 1915–1920,* ed. and intro. Hazel King, Melbourne Univ. Press, Carlton, Vic, 1986, and Hutton, *With a Woman's Unit,* pp. 38, 69, 221; re Malone, SMF, 'Hold Tight! Life on a London 'Bus', ML MSS 445/22, p. 763. Joice NanKivell Loch (1887–1982) was especially honoured by Greece (Susanna de Vries, *Blue Ribbons, Bitter Bread: The Life of Joice NanKivell Loch,* Hale & Iremonger, Sydney, 2000).

66   Gilchrist, *Australians and Greeks 2,* p. 139 (wasps) and SMF to MDR, 7/5/1920, RR Papers in MDR Corrs., MDR Papers (still having trouble sitting);* Hutton, *With a Woman's Unit,* p. 112; *The Salonika Front by A. J. Mann,* p. 107.

67   Dorothy H. Crawford, 'To Clear the Air', *TLS,* 6/10/2006, p. 13; Palmer, *The Gardeners of Salonika,* pp. 142–3; Beatrice Russell to SMF, 7/1/1918, FP vol. 104.

68   'Ne Mari Nishta', ML MSS 445/4, pp. 196–7; FP vol. 46, p. 165; Gilchrist, *Australians and Greeks 2,* p. 109, and LN, FP vol. 3, pp. 543–5; PD, 7/1/1918.

69 'Ne Mari Nishta', ML MSS 445/4, pp. 37, 122, 130, 180.

70 *ibid.*, pp. 196–9.

71 *ibid.*, p. 198; PD, 16/12/1917 (concert).

72 PD, Jan.–Feb. 1918; SMF to Dymphna Cusack, 31/12/1951, FP vol. 30, repr. North, *Yarn Spinners*, p. 306; 'Zabranjeno', ML MSS 6035/19; FP vol. 111; *BA*, 7/3/1918, p. 14, and 30/5/1918, p. 14.

73 PD, Mar.–Apr. 1918; SWH to SMF, 19/3/1918 and 9/4/1918, FP vol. 104, and SWH to SMF, 25/2/1918, SWH Colln, Personnel file, Box 32. Annie Amelia Smith (1863–1919) also contributed to the Indian Press (*Vote*, 6/6/1919, p. 213, copy FP vol. 122).

74 H. W. Massingham to SMF, 17/8/1918, FP vol. 90, and SMF to Elizabeth Robins, 10/10/1940, FP vol. 13; War Office to SMF, 7/5/1918, FP vol. 13, re 'sketches you have written', and collection of anecdotes re London and the war, apparently sent to US newspapers, c.1918, FP vol. 59; 'On Our Library Table: *Mountain Meditations* by L. Lind-Af-Hageby', *Vote*, 28/6/1918, p. 302; SMF to Professional Women's Register, Ministry of Labour, Westminster, 13/7/1918, FP vol. 13. H. W. Massingham (1860–1924), *ODNB*.

75 SMF to Emma Pischel *et al.*, 8/5/1918, FP vol. 114;* PD, 11/7/1918. Frederick Daniel Post (1886–1970), AB Stanford Univ. 1912, b. Illinois, was a clerk resident in Chicago prior to appointment as secretary to the Scientific Attache, US Embassy, London, departing New York 31/1/1918 (US passport application 22/1/1918, State Department Records, Group 59). The letters from 'Fred K—', FP vol. 13, 1918–19, are in his hand, also the postcard from Paris from 'Frederick —', FP vol. 46, pp. 51–3 ('Dear Stella Marie', n.d. [Nov. 1918]); as well, some items 1918–20 hitherto attributed to Frederick Pischel are from Fred Post, but Pischel's corres. in fact ends in 1916. As Fred Post never signed with his surname, he does not appear in the *Guide* to the FP. FP vol. 13 also has postcards from Serbs.

76 Postcard, 13/5/[1918], FP vol. 110/6; PD, May–Aug. 1918. SMF to Sr Kerr [?], FP vol. 164/46, p. 165, n.d.; Matron Nye, b. Poplar 1876, may have gone to Canada subsequently.

77 'Sammies in London', FP vol. 445/21; the four articles in the *Vote* by 'M. F.', Bettison and Roe, *ALS* listing, 2001, included '*Workhouse Characters* by Margaret Wynne Nevinson' (26/7/1918) and *The Coo-ee Contingent* (Aug. 1918). Gladys Hain, *The Coo-ee Contingent: Billjim as Fighter, Good Chum and Lover*, was published in Melbourne in 1917. Sir James Cantlie (1851–1926) was a Harley St surgeon (*Who Was Who, 1916–1928*).

78 *Rules and Regulations for the Guidance of Patients*, FP vol. 13; SMF to [SF], 4 postcards, n.d. [1918], FP vol. 110/4.

79 O. A. [Olive Aldridge?], 'The House of the Future', *Vote*, 18/10/1918, third of three articles on housing; WFL Annual Conference 1918, transcript, p. 84.

Chapter 8 — At the Heart of the Empire: October 1918–March 1923

1 LN, FP vol. 3, pp. 536–7.

2 PD, 11–12/11/1918. The Council remained at 41 Russell Sq. until 1947 and is now known as ROOM, the National Council for Housing and Planning, 41 Botolph Lane, London EC1 (Kelvin MacDonald, 'A Century of Reform', *Axis*, Feb.–Mar. 2000, p. 10 and web data).

3 A. J. P. Taylor, *English History 1914–1945*, Oxford Univ. Press, Oxford, 1965, ch. IV 'Postwar: 1918–22'.

4 Ashworth, *The Genesis of Modern British Town Planning*, pp. 178–9; 'Housing: Past and Present', p. 24, with 'The National Housing and Town Planning Council and its work, 1900–1922', ts., n.d., NHTPC Records (held by the Council, London, copies in my possession). As Minister for Health 1924–29, (Arthur) Neville Chamberlain (1869–1940) was responsible for the building of almost one million houses (*ODNB*).

5 Quarterly balance sheets, NHTPC Records, Minute Books, 1921–26 (SMF's salary, 1921); A. L. Bowley, *Prices and Wages in the United Kingdom 1914–1920*, Clarendon Press, London and New York, 1921, p. 190; G. Routh, *Occupation and Pay in Great Britain 1906–60*, Cambridge Univ. Press, Cambridge, 1965, Tables 1, 33, 37, 42, p. 80; LN, FP vol. 3, 535ff.

6 SMF to Eva O'Sullivan, 5/8/1919, ML MSS 544.*

7 *The National Housing Manual* 1923 (526 pp.); this and two other Aldridge titles are retained in SMF's PBC.

8   The London, Midlands and Scottish Railway Company owned 22 Harley Rd; members of Smith family were listed as occupiers and ratepayers in period (Adelaide Ward rate books, Borough of Hampstead, 1918–28, Local Studies and Archives, Holborn Library, Stephanie Liau, site visit and research, Jul. 2003). For Annie Amelia Smith see ch. 7, n. 73; Thomas Brook Smith (1862–1938), older brother of Horatio Nelson Smith (1874–1960), *ODNB*, and J. Foreman-Peck, *Smith & Nephew in the Health Care Industry*, Elgar, Aldershot, UK, c.1995, ch. 4 (products included Elastoplast and sanitary napkins). SMF to T. B. Smith, 6/7/1940, FP vol. 34, and SMF to H. N. Smith, 13/6/1944, FP vol. 29. Re Primrose Hill, see F. Sheppard, *London 1808–1870: The Infernal Wen*, Oxford Univ. Press, London and New York, 1971, p. 88. SMF to SF, postcard of Harley Rd, n.d., [1919], FP vol. 110/4; SMF to Ethel Bull 28/9/1942, ML MSS 3569/1, p. 531.

9   SMF to Alice Henry, 6/2/1919, FP vol. 114.* Special notes on the Byles/Maynard connection: (1) The Maynard link with the Byles family in England and the US was as close as it is now complex. From Lady Byles' will and other sources, it appears Mary Anna Maynard (Mab) was a younger sister of Sir William Byles, and Ken Maynard was his nephew, son of another sister, Mary Beuzeville Byles. The pair were the same age: Mary Anna Beuzeville Byles Maynard, née Byles (1864–1944), b. Bradford, a graduate of Newnham College, Cambridge, m. Alfred Kenyon Maynard (1864–1924) in America in 1893; they became US citizens, returning to England (Woolwich) in 1919; and in 1923 she became a Quaker (Society of Friends London Yearly Meeting Proceedings, 1945, pp. 171–2, Society Library, Euston Rd, London). (2) Re the Byles family in NSW: Marie Beuzeville Byles (1900–79) was daughter of Cyril Beuzeville Byles and his wife, Ida Margaret, née Unwin; the family arrived in Sydney in 1911 (*ADB* vol. 13).

10   (Lady) Sarah Byles, née Unwin (1843–1931). Re Sir William Byles: J. Reynolds, *The Great Paternalist: Titus Salt and the Growth of Nineteenth-Century Bradford*, M. Temple Smith, London and New York, 1983, p. 323. Lorna Walker, 'Party Political Women: A Comparative Study of Liberal Women and the Primrose League, 1890–1914', in Jane Rendall (ed.), *Equal or Different: Women's Politics 1800–1914*, Basil Blackwood, Oxford, 1987, pp. 187–8; *The Diary of Beatrice Webb. Volume Two 1892–1905*, Norman and Jeanne MacKenzie (eds.), Virago, London, 1986, p. 80.

11   *Yorkshire Observer*, 20/7/1931, courtesy City of Bradford Central Library; press cutting, FP vol. 22, p. 191, M[anchester] G[uardian], 21/7/[1931].

12   J. A. Hobson (1858–1940) wrote the classic critique *Imperialism: A Study* (1902), *ODNB*. Arthur Penty (see ch. 7, n. 6), who later veered to the far right, was another habitué; he gave a copy of his *Old Worlds for Plutes* (1918) to SMF in 1923 (PBC, no. 771).

13   Pat Thane, 'Women, Liberalism and Citizenship, 1918–1930' in E. F. Biagini, *Citizenship and Community: Liberals, Radical and Collective Identities in the British Isles, 1865–1931*, Cambridge Univ. Press, Cambridge, 1996, esp. pp. 88–91 (quotation, Margaret Wintringham, 1928).

14   'The Home-going of the Babies' Kits', *SMH*, 11/10/1919, repr. *A Gregarious Culture*. Sandra Stanley Holton's important work on transatlantic liberal suffragism has yet to lead researchers to an Australian dimension.

15   PD, 4/11/1918.

16   FP vols 14–15 contain the (often scrappy) corres. begun Apr. 1919 and lasting till Nov. 1926, with a few letters to mid-1927 in vols 16, 20; letters to Alice Henry are preserved at FP vol. 114; the postcards are at FP vol. 111 and the Lampe Family Album, NLA.

17   Bage, Anna Frederika (1883–1970), *ADB* vol. 7, refers to her mother, Mary Charlotte, a widow, who took her daughters to England for secondary schooling in the 1890s; see also *Bulletin*, 24/6/1931, p. 33. Draft passport application, FP vol. 51, p. 167.

18   PD, 4/12/1918; Rose Macaulay, *Dangerous Ages*, Collins, London, 1921, p. 51; (Dame) Rose Emilie Macaulay (1881–1958), English writer, became popular in the 1920s when *Dangerous Ages* won the Femina Vie Heureuse Prize (*ODNB*).

19   ML MSS 445/39, p. 399.

20   FP vol. 111 (studio portrait) and FP vol. 51 (passport photo); SMF to the *Book Lover*, from Newport, *Book Lover*, 22/11/1920, p. 137.

21 *Riceyman Steps* (1923); *The Unlit Lamp* (1924); *Mary Olivier: A Life* (1919). On the writings of May Sinclair (1870–1946), see N. Beauman, *A Very Great Profession: The Woman's Novel 1914–39*, Virago, London, 1983, glossary. *Mrs Dalloway* appeared in 1925, *To the Lighthouse* in 1927. Winifred Holtby's *Virginia Woolf* (1932) is at PBC no. 67, also Rose Macaulay, *Personal Pleasures* (1935), PBC no. 731; Garton, 'Contesting Enslavement: Marriage, Manhood, and *My Brilliant Career*', *ALS*, 2002.

22 'Sam Price from Chicago', ML MSS 445/17, carbon ts., n.d.; A. P. Watt to G. Marriott, 24/7/1919, FP vol. 104 (invoice for typing).

23 A. P. Watt to G. Marriott, Esq., 22/2/1922, FP vol. 84.

24 'Sam Price', ML MSS 445/17, p. 154.

25 *ibid.*, p. 155.

26 'Love Letters', ML MSS 445/5, p. 131.

27 Kay Daniels, 'Emma Brooke', *Women's Hist. Review*, 2003; Dear Sir/The Writer, 15/6/1920 and 22/6/1920, FP vol. 84.

28 'Mrs Dysart Disappears', ML MSS 445/10. 'Hold Tight! Life on a London 'Bus' (ML MSS 445/22) was rejected by at least five press outlets by 1921 (ML MSS 6035/3 and FP vol. 84).

29 'A Beauty Contest', ML MSS 445/21; Bettison and Roe, *ALS* listing, 2001; Synopsis, ML MSS 445/28.

30 Articles on Ireland, FP vol. 59, ten plus two items (nine in ML MSS 445/22); SMF to Eva O'Sullivan, 5/8/1919, ML MSS 544;* SMF to Alice Henry, 12/12/[1919], FP vol. 115.*

31 PD 15/8–2/9/1919; *BA*, 2/10/1919, p. 14 (SMF's return from Ireland).

32 SMF to JMF, 16/8/1919 and 28/8/[1919], FP vol. 113X, both.*

33 SMF to Miss Lampe, 28/8/1919, Lampe Family Album, NLA; Irish Sketches, 'Irishmen All!', ML MSS 445/22, p. 1003; SMF to Desmond Fitzgerald, 6/2/1940, FP vol. 33. Gavan Duffy (1882–1951), *Times* (London), 11/6/1951, p. 6. For Desmond Fitzgerald, see ch. 12, n. 23.

34 PD, and Irish Sketches, ML MSS 445/22, 'At the Horse Show' and 'The Abbey Theatre'. 'John Bull's Other Island' was first published in 1904.

35 Irish Sketches, ML MSS 445/22, 'The Abbey Theatre', p. 993.

36 *Drums Under the Windows* (1946), and commentary, LN, FP vol. 3, pp. 749–50.

37 Irish Sketches, ML MSS 445/22, 'In the Shadow of the Church', pp. 969–71.

38 Irish Sketches, ML MSS 445/22, 'In a Proclaimed Area', p, 951. A similar thesis was later advanced in George Dangerfield's *The Strange Death of Liberal England* (1936), which postulated an underlying similarity between the worker, Irish and women's rebellions of the early twentieth century.

39 Irish Sketches, ML MSS 445/22, 'The Three Mutineers', p. 1021.

40 Francis Hackett (*New Republic*) to Rose Schneiderman, 28/10/1919, FP vol. 121.

41 Postcard from Newport to SF, 1/7/1920, FP vol. 108; cutting, *South Wales News*, 23/7/1920, [n. p.], FP vol. 122; SMF to Alice Henry, 14/6/[1920], FP vol. 114 (a 'magnificent congress', with men, and one woman, from 26 countries).

42 Agnes Nestor to MDR, 28/4/1918, MDR Papers and SMF to Agnes Nestor, 20/6/1919, Nestor Papers, m/film series VII.

43 PD, Dec. 1918–Mar. 1919 (Mason), Jan. 1919 and Jul. 1922 (McDowell), Apr.–May 1919 (Anderson and Schneiderman), May–Jun. 1921 (Editha Phelps); SMF to Jane Addams, 6/8/1922.* Mary McDowell (1854–1936) was a social reformer in Chicago (*NAW*). Mary Anderson (1872–1964), Swedish-born union leader, was head of the US Women's Bureau 1920–1944 (*NAW*). Alice Hamilton (1869–1970) (*NAW*), *Exploring The Dangerous Trades*, Little, Brown & Co, Boston, 1943, SMF, PBC no. 665, with inscription, mentions Stella Franklin, 'who had gone back to England' (p. 261).

44 Marion Phillips to MDR, 22/11/1921 (to Savoy Court); MDR to SMF, 14/4/1920, SMF to MDR, 7/5/1920, both,* 11/7/1923, MDR Papers; SMF to Elizabeth Robins, 10/10/1940, FP vol. 13; MDR to DD, 2/11/[1921], DD Papers.

45 Alice Henry to MDR, 22/8/1923, MDR Papers; SMF to Alice Henry, 14/6/[1920], FP vol. 114.

46 The published articles were 'The Home-going of the Babies' Kits. An appreciation and an Appeal', *SMH*, 11/10/1919, p. 7; 'Not Honey — Nectar! Australian Products in England', *SMH*, 20/11/1920, p. 7 (both repr. *A Gregarious Culture*); and 'A Coué Lecture', *DT* (Sydney), 7/2/1925, p. 10; SMF to George Robertson, 16/4/1921, ML MSS 314.* Mary Booth's evidence is

in the *Interim Report*, Acting Govt Printer, Sydney, 1923, pp. 176–7. *Snugglepot and Cuddlepie* was published by Angus & Robertson in 1919. Emile Coué, d. 1926, *Who Was Who 1926–1928*.

47 For Claude Kinred, see ch. 7, n. 12; Henry Stanley McKay (1877–1974), Australian War Memorial Nominal Roll, also *Theatre Magazine*, 1/9/1916, pp. 41–2 (ML); SMF to RS, 28/12/1919, RS Corres., ML (re Vida Goldstein);* Jack Lockyer, pers. comm., 21/10/1992.

48 *ADB* vol. 13: Marguerite Dale (1883–1963), Persia Campbell (1898–1974); *ADB* vol. 14: Lute Drummond (1879–1949); *ADB* vol. 17: Marjorie Collisson (1887–1982). Mary (Mollye) Scott Shaw, later Menken (1891–1976) lived in London for the rest of her life (Deaths index, UK). SMF to Alice Henry, 23/5/1922, FP vol. 114.*

49 SMF to Alice Henry, 18/10/[1920], FP vol. 11;* PD 8/5/1918 (Brailsford). Henry Noel Brailsford (1873–1958) was a journalist and author (*ODNB*).

50 SMF to Alice Henry, 18/10/[1920], FP vol. 11;* 'The Mayor of Cork's Funeral', FP vol. 59, also *Times* (London), 26/10/1920, p. 10c; 'Million Miners Out Today', 18/10/1920, p. 12.

51 PD, 31/1/1923; Ralph Waldo Emerson (1803–82), poet, essayist and lecturer, was the leading Boston transcendentalist.

52 SMF to Agnes Nestor, 20/6/1919, Nestor Papers, m/film series VII;* SMF to Alice Henry, 26/11/[1919] and 23/5/1922, FP vol. 114, both;* also SMF to RS, 28/12/1919, RS Corres.,* ('the Empire seems to have gone mad').

53 Alice Henry to SMF, 9/6/[1920], FP vol. 114.* Roe, 'Chivalry and Social Policy in the Antipodes'; SMF to Mrs Robins, 15/5/1922, 'A garland of greetings to Margaret Dreier Robins', RR Papers, in MDR Corres., MDR Papers, Box 2s. Ellen Key (1849–1926) was a Scandinavian educationalist, lecturer and feminist (*Who Was Who 1916–1928*).

54 SMF to Alice Henry, 10/7/[1920], FP vol. 114;* Jill Roe, 'What Has Nationalism Offered Australian Women?', in A. Burns and N. Grieve, eds, *Australian Women: Contemporary Feminist Thought*, Oxford Univ. Press, Melbourne, 1994; MDR to Dearest Dodo, 2/11/[1921?], DD Papers; SMF to Isabella Goldstein, 13/10/1911, VG Papers.* Dale Spender, *Time and Tide Wait for No Man*, Virago, London, 1984 (Six Point Group). (Lady) Nancy Astor (1879–1964), American-born, was Conservative MP for Plymouth 1919–45.

55 16/10/1920 Submission by Joint Author of *The Net of Circumstance* re Bennett's disappointing remarks, FP vol. 90. 'John Stuart Mill, Arnold Bennett and Time', FP vol. 59; SMF to Alice Henry 23/5/1922, FP vol. 114.* PD, 2/1/1922: SMF consults Dr Burnett Rae, an advocate of cooperation between doctors and the clergy specialising in mental disorders (*Times*, London, 16/11/1960, p. 15); PD, 7/1/1922, hears lectures on 'Psycho-analysis and its Limitations' (Prof. John Adams, *Times*, London, 9/1/1922, p. 5).

56 Fred K [Post] to SMF, 30/7/1919, FP vol. 13, p. 265 and 15/11/1919, FP vol. 13, p. 67a and 4/5/192[0], FP vol. 13, p. 87; SMF to Alice Henry, 26/11/[1919], FP vol. 114;* John Varney to SMF, 30/6/1926, FP vol. 15. John Cushing Varney (1888–1967), poet and communist sympathiser, taught English at Washington Square College, New York Univ., c.1926–53 (*NYT*, 1/10/1967, p. 84), and *Modern American Poetry*, online journal, 'Sol Funaroff: Apollinaire of the Proletariat'.

57 *Under the Greenwood Tree* (1872); *Wuthering Heights* (1847); *Of Human Bondage* (1915); *The Egoist* (1879); *Moby Dick* (1851); *Vanity Fair* (1847–8); *Bliss* (1920); *Women in Love* (1921); John Varney to Dear Stella, 25/9/[1921?], ML MSS 3659/1.

58 *The Newcomes* (1854–55); *History of Henry Esmond, Esq.* (1852); *Pendennis* (1849–50); Ina Ferris, *William Makepeace Thackeray*, Twayne Publishers, New York, 1983, p. 9. This paragraph draws heavily on this excellent study.

59 *The Economic Consequences of the Peace* (1919); *Disenchantment*, MacGibbon & Kee London, 1968, first pub. 1922, p. 163; Charles Edward Montague (1867–1928), *ODNB*; SMF to Mary Fullerton, 10/6/1924, Fullerton Papers* and SMF to Elsie Belle Champion, 29/12/1950, FP vol. 8.* 'G. B. Lancaster', pseud. Edith Joan Lyttleton (1873–1945), b. Tasmania and reared New Zealand, published twelve novels 1904–38 (*Dictionary of New Zealand Biography*).

60 Dorothy Richardson (1873–1957) is now best known for *Pilgrimage*, Duckworth, London, 1919, repr. Virago, 1979. James Joyce (1882–1941) published *Ulysses* in 1922. The first instalment of John Galsworthy's *Forsyte Saga* appeared in 1922, when Aunt Sarah Lampe gave Miles a copy for her birthday (PBC, no. 633); Melman, *Women and the Popular Imagination in the Twenties*, p. 134.

61   Mrs Patrick Campbell (1865–1940), famous and temperamental British actor, the original
      Eliza Doolittle; Tamara Karsavina (1885–1978), Russian-born, helped found Royal Academy
      of Dance, 1920; (Dame) Sybil Thorndike (1882–1976), who played the title role in Shaw's
      'St Joan' (1924), married fellow actor Lewis Casson (1875–1969) in 1908; Ruth St Denis
      (1879–1968), US choreographer, with partner Ted Shawn (1891–1972), a pioneer of modern
      dance; Karel Capek (1890–1938), Czech writer (*R.U.R.*, 1920); Eleanora Duse (1859–1924),
      'one of the world's greatest actors' (all *Cambridge Encyclopedia*, 1992 edn, except Karsavina,
      ODNB).
62   SMF to Alice Henry, 23/5/1922, FP vol. 114;* Margaret Drabble, *Arnold Bennett: A Biography*,
      Weidenfeld and Nicolson, London, 1974, p. 250. John Galsworthy (1867–1933) (*ODNB*) now
      better known as a novelist, wrote over 31 full-length plays.
63   FP vol. 88 and ML MSS 445/27. Annie Horniman [Honimann, FP *Guide*] to Dear Sir,
      21/3/1919, FP vol. 88; *punica granatum*: pomegranate tree. Annie Horniman (1860–1937)
      founded the Manchester repertory (*ODNB*).
64   'The English Jackeroo', ML MSS 445/26 (1922); 'Not Honey — Nectar! Australian products in
      England', *SMH*, 20/11/1920, p. 7, repr. *A Gregarious Culture*.
65   SMF to P. Neilson-Terry, 18/9/1922, FP vol. 88,* and 'J. Verney' [SMF] to The Editor, *Royal
      Magazine*, 22/6/1925, FP vol. 88.* Phyllis Neilson-Terry (1892–1977) was a London actress and
      theatre manager.
66   Trewin, *The Theatre Since 1900*, p. 439; LN, FP vol. 3, pp. 493–7. Sean O'Casey (1880–1964)
      wrote for the Abbey Theatre after World War I and features frequently in Franklin materials
      (*ODNB*); SMF corresponded with St John Ervine (1883–1971), b. Belfast, writer, war casualty,
      and biographer of George Bernard Shaw, mostly in the 1930s and 1940s, FP vol. 14 (*ODNB*);
      Gibbs, *Bernard Shaw*, pp. 362–3.
67   SMF to Eva O'Sullivan, 5/8/1919, ML MSS 544;* SMF to SF, 20/8/1919, FP vol. 108; SMF to
      Agnes Nestor, 20/6/1919, Nestor Papers, m/film series VII;* SMF to MDR, 7/5/1920, MDR
      Papers.*
68   SF to SMF, 14/8/1923, FP vol. 48.*
69   Jill Roe, 'Forcing the Issue: Miles Franklin and National Identity'. SMF's passport (a British
      passport, as for all Australians prior the introduction of Australian citizenship in 1949) is at FP
      vol. 51. PD, 1944, Personal Memorandum: 5 feet 1 1/2 inches.
70   Maurice Smith, *Short History of Dentistry*, Wingate, London, 1958, pp. 74–5; SMF to MDR,
      11/7/1923, MDR Papers; SMF to Mr Greening, 26/1/1932, Lothian Papers.
71   NHTPC Records, Minute Books, 1923–26; F. G. Hamilton to SMF, 26/10/1923, FP vol. 15.
      Mrs Hamilton's home address: 56 South Eaton Place, SW1.
72   NHTPC Minute Book, 7/1/1921, 17/11/1921.
73   SMF to George Robertson, 16/4/1921, ML MSS 314*; Alice (Grant) Trevenen Rosman
      (1882–1961), writer (*ADB* vol. 11).
74   'Quite! A Revue in Type', ML MSS 445/14.
75   Notebook, 10/2/1923, FP vol. 5/10. *SMH*, 19/12/1923, Shipping News; 'Quite! A Revue in
      Type', ML MSS 445/14, p. 176.
76   Apart from a small bank account in Chicago, financial records for SMF are missing for this
      period, but SF's financial records reveal that she lent money to various individuals in the 1920s
      (FP vol. 110).
77   Olive Aldridge to SMF, 26/10/1923, FP vol. 14.* 'Minnewaska' may refer to Ina E. Wood Van
      Norman, *Minnewaska: A Legend of Lake Mohawk, Sequel to Longfellow's Hiawatha and other
      Lyrical Poems*, Donohue & Henneberry, Chicago, 1897.

Chapter 9 — To be a Pilgrim: November 1923–June 1927

1   Nell Malone to Miles Franklin, c.Dec. 1925, FP vol. 15.
2   *Back to Methuselah* (1921); PD, 3/11/1923.
3   Sigmund Freud, *A General Introduction to Psychoanalysis*, Boni & Liverbright, New York, 1922
      (PBC no. 630, with inscription); RS to SMF, 3/11/1923, FP vol. 15. Edgewood School was
      supported by prominent New York women; Count Tolstoy may have been Aleksai Tolstoy
      (1882–1945), Russian author (*Times* (London), 27/2/1945, p. 6).

4   MDR to Mary E. Dreier, 17/11/1923, RR Papers Box 2.

5   *Bulletin*, 22/11/1923, p. 26 (her impending departure).

6   SF to SMF, 11/11/1923, FP vol. 48; SMF to H. G. Kinsman 30/12/1952, FP vol. 44.

7   *Sun*, 18/12/1923, p. 10. Also, *Evening News*, 18/12/1923, p. 10; *SMH*, 19/12/1923, p. 10; *Southern Morning Herald* (Goulburn), 20/12/1923, p. 2.

8   SMF to MDR, 13/3/1924, MDR Papers.

9   PD, 11/1/1924.

10 *Penny Post*, 19/1/1924 [p. 2], 11/1/1924, p. 4 and 17/1/1957, p. 2 ('Timpy' Hebblewhite).

11 SMF to Uncle Gus, 21/10/1953, FP vol. 49. Apparently Susannah stayed for part of the time with her cousin, Mrs Gertrude Adam, née Kinred (Lois Adam in Roderick, Guard Book 7, Roderick Papers). Press interviews recorded in PD, 22/2/1924, were not found in any of the main papers. *On the Wool Track: Pioneering Days in the Wool Industry*, Rivers, London, 1914.

12 De Berg interview; Henry Ernest Bridle was by then a building contractor, at 28 Campbell St, Wollongong. Dr Lawson practised in Goulburn in the 1890s. The children of Ruth Horwitz, née Lawson (1887–1972) were Stanley (b. 1921), who became a publisher, and Lillaine (*SMH*, 20/7/1972, p. 28, and *Who's Who in Australia*, 1998).

13 Mrs Black: Isabella Emily, née Watson (c.1851–1931), of Gippsland, painter of Australian flora and fauna (*Argus*, 12/3/1931, p. 1), was sister of P. S. Watson. Marion Mahony Griffin to SMF, 16/4/1924, FP vol. 15; SMF to George Robertson, 16/4/1924, ML MSS 314.* The Griffins divided their time between Sydney and Melbourne until 1924.

14 Vida Goldstein to SMF, 27/3/1924, FP vol. 10.* Lucy Spence Morice (1859–1953) was kindergarten worker and social reformer (*ADB* vol. 10).

15 SMF to MDR, 13/3/1924, MDR Papers;* SMF to RS, Monday 1924, RS Corres.

16 SF to SMF, 17/3/1924* and 14/4/1924,* FP vol. 48.

17 The Lampe aunts came to live at Carlton in 1916.

18 PD, 10/1/1924 ('aboriginal lack of progress').

19 PD, 14/1/1924.

20 SMF to George Robertson, card, n.d., ML MSS 314;* Miscellaneous Notebooks, FP vol. 5/12, p. 587.

21 PD, 21/1/1924; Marion Mahony Griffin to SMF, 16/4/1924 and 24/12/1929,* FP vol. 15; SMF to RS, 2/2/1924, RS Corres.*

22 PD, Feb. 1922.

23 *SMH*, 18/12/1923, p. 8; 'Henry Lawson', *Meanjin Papers*, 1942, vol. 1, no.1, repr. *A Gregarious Culture*; SMF to RS, 2/2/1924, and Monday [1924], RS Corres. The Lawson statue by George Lambert, near Mrs Macquarie's Chair, was unveiled in 1931.

24 SMF to George Robertson, 16/4/1924, ML MSS 314.* 'The Twin Screw "Chowder Bay" at Sea', ML MSS 445/25 (Act 1) and draft to Nancy W—, FP vol. 46; 'Maybe!' ML MSS 445/7; SMF to Mary Fullerton, 10/6/1924, Fullerton Papers.*

25 Henry R. Aldridge, *Guide to the Administration of the Housing Acts, 1923, 1924*, National Housing and Town Planning Council, London, 1924, PBC, Quarto 20.

26 PD, 13/5/1924, and LN, FP vol. 3, pp. 733–5.

27 'Maybe!', ML MSS 445/7.

28 Martin, *Passionate Friends*, p. 95.

29 'Roswell Cavarley': possibly based on Fred Pischel.

30 'Maybe!', ML MSS 445/7, pp. 84, 93, 103–4, 141a; SMF to J. K. Moir, 18/4/1952, FP vol. 34.

31 'Miles Franklin returns to the States to Handle Town Planning Schemes', *Bulletin*, 22/4/1923, p. 26.

32 C. P. Gilman, *His Religion and Hers: A Study of the Faith of our Fathers and the Work of our Mothers*, Century, New York, 1923, PBC, no. 65, inscribed by Jessie Childs (Buhle, *Feminism and its Discontents*, pp. 39–49 provides context); SMF to Mary Fullerton, 10/6/1924, Fullerton Papers.*

33 'Maybe!', ML MSS 445/7, p. 56; p. 49; Sheila Jeffreys, *The Spinster and Her Enemies: Feminism and Sexuality*, Pandora Press, London and Boston, p. 128 ('healthy scepticism').

34 'Maybe!', ML MSS 445/7, p. 94; Susan Kingsley Kent, 'Gender Reconstruction After the First World War', in Harold L. Smith (ed.), *British Feminism in the Twentieth Century*, Elgar, Aldershot, England, 1990, p. 66.

35   'Maybe!', ML MSS 445/7, p. 143, pp. 119–20.

36   Buhle, *Feminism and its Discontents*, p. 88; Judith A. Allen, *Sex and Secrets: Crimes Involving Australian Women Since 1880*, Oxford Univ. Press Australia, Oxford and Melbourne, 1990, Part III.

37   'Maybe!', ML MSS 445/7, p. 231; Marian Quartly, 'Women Citizens of the New Nation: Reading Some Visual Evidence', *Lilith*, 2002, 11, p. 13, citing *Australian Woman's Sphere* that it was a duty to be attractive; Magarey, *Passions of the First-Wave Feminists*; Heilbrun, *Writing a Woman's Life*, p. 106. May Sinclair (1863–1946), *Life and Death of Harriett Frean*, Collins, London, 1922, and *Arnold Waterlow: A Life*, Hutchinson, London, 1924.

38   'Maybe!', ML MSS 445/7, pp. 228, 220.

39   Ada Holman to SMF, 31/7/1924, ML MSS 3659/1, encl. 775, and BM book request, 29/7/1924, encl. 671; SMF to SF, postcards, 1/8/1924, 5/8/1924, FP vol. 108, and SMF to Miss Lampe, 5/8/1924, Lampe Family Album, NLA. There are two editions of William H. Prescott's classic *History of the Conquest of Peru*, PBC, nos 774A and 772B.

40   W. Hanson, *The Pastoral Possessions of NSW*, Gibb, Shallard & Co, Sydney, 1889, p. 16. There was also a Bimben West holding listed at that time, holders John McDonald, Joseph and William Webb, and John and James Wright.

41   The earliest tss are 'Old Blastus of Bandicoot: Australian Play in Three Acts, by Old Blastus Himself' (ML MSS 445/25, with graphics from the *Sydney Mail*), a shorter version, 'Old Blastus of Bandicoot: Domestic Drama' (also ML MSS 445/25), and 'Old Man of Bandicoot', a dialogue and scenario 'for a talking motion picture' (ML MSS 445/28), all dated c.1925. 'Old Man of Bandicoot' was entered in a scenario competition in Australia in 1930, and 'Old Blastus of Bandicoot: Domestic Drama' (ML MSS 364/61d) is a dramatic version of the 1931 novel, described as 'Introductory to the play form written in 1924', given a reading by the Sydney FAW in 1942. Other undated tss are to be found at ML MSS 6035. As well, there is an undated title page for 'Old Blastus of Bin Bin', showing partial erasure of 'Bin Bin', and a replacement by hand of 'Bandicoot' at FP vol. 88, p 285.

42   Kirkby, *Alice Henry*, pp. 187–90, and PD, Aug.–Dec. 1924, *passim*.

43   PD, 22/9/1924; SMF to JMF, 19/9/1924, FP vol. 113X; SMF to Fred Kinred, 20/9/1924, Francis *et al.*, *The Buddong Flows On*, vol. 1, p. 389.

44   Liverpool cathedral was completed in 1978.

45   SMF to SF, 14/11/1924, FP vol. 108. Gibbs, *Bernard Shaw*, p. 366. Dame Edith Evans (1888–1976), a famous London actress, appeared in plays by Shakespeare, Wilde, and Shaw, and in films.

46   Madge Titheradge (1887–1961) was daughter of George S. Titheradge (1848–1916), a leading actor in Australia in Miles' youth (obits from the *Times* 1961–1970 (1975)), *Companion to Theatre in Australia*, ed. Philip Parsons with Victoria Chance, Currency Press in association with Cambridge Univ. Press, Sydney, c.1995.

47   SMF to JMF, 14/11/1924, FP vol. 113X. Noël Coward (1899–1973), *Plays: One, Hay Fever, The Vortex, Fallen Angels, Easy Virtue*, Methuen, London, 1979. *The Vortex* (1923), Coward's first big success, was launched at Everyman Theatre, Hampstead, 23/11/1924, and moved to the West End 16/12/1924.

48   Emile Coué (1857–1926); *DT* (Sydney), 7/2/1925, p. 2.

49   Alice Henry to SMF, 5/1/1925, FP vol. 114. The film showing at the Polytechnic Cinema Theatre, Regent St, was made by Frank Hurley, *Times* (London), 12/12/1924, p. 12.

50   FP vol. 107, p. 83; SF to SMF, 10/2/1925, FP vol. 48; *SMH*, 10/2/1925, p. 8 (death notice).

51   SMF to Mary Fullerton, 10/6/1924, Fullerton Papers.* (Fullerton's first extant communication with SMF is a postcard from the Lake District, from 'the author of *Bark House Days*', 12/11/1926, FP vol. 16.) The housing conference was held at Caxton Hall, 17–19/7/1924, *Times* (London), 17–19/7/1924, pp. 11 and 9, with Ada Holman in the chair on the final day. Martin, *Passionate Friends*, pp. 99, 110; ADB, vol. 8, Fullerton entry; for Mabel Singleton (1877–1965) and Denis Singleton (1911–2008), Index, *My Congenials*, vol. 2; SMF to J. K. Moir, 15/4/1952, J. K. Moir Colln.

52   Kent, *A Certain Style*, p. 124 ('Beatrice allowed friendship to overrule literary judgement'). Beatrice Davis (1909–92), was the first fulltime general editor at Angus & Robertson, serving in that capacity for 36 years (*OCAL*).

53 Dominion women's conference: Miles was among those suggested as a delegate but not apparently endorsed (Conference Minutes of the Australian Federation of Women's Societies, Adelaide, 1924, AFWS Papers, MS 2818, Box 9, p. 2); ML MSS 445/39, p. 379 (unemployment); PD, 25/7/1925; SMF to Mary Fullerton, 27/3/1928, FP vol. 16. Ruth First and Ann Scott, *Olive Schreiner*, Schocken Books, New York, 1980, Introduction.

54 SMF to Sarah Lampe, 23/8/1925, FP vol. 113X, and SMF to SF, 23/8/1925, FP vol. 108X.*

55 Her work appreciated: F. Elgood to SMF, 12/2/1925, and F. G. Hamilton to SMF, 25/5/1925, vol. 15.

56 NHTPC Records, Minutes, Nov. 1925; SMF to F. G. Hamilton, 20/10/1925, FP vol. 15 and SMF to Eva O'Sullivan, 5/4/1926, ML MSS 544*. LN, FP vol. 3, p. 536 describes Mr A. as a gargoyle, typically English, with horrifying teeth and encroaching baldness.

57 SMF to Frank Elgood, 23/1/1925, FP vol. 15; Nell Malone to SMF, n.d., FP vol. 15. Mr A.'s earlier address in Paris was Cercle Artistique and Litteraire, 7 Rue Volney (H. Reilding to SMF, 12/3/1925, FP vol. 15).

58 NHTPC Records, Minutes; SMF to Marian Dornton Brown, 24/11/1924, FP vol. 15; SMF to Eva O'Sullivan, 5/4/1926, ML MSS 544.*

59 SMF to F. G. Hamilton, [c.21/11/1925] and 15/12/1925, FP vol. 15.

60 John Martin to SMF, 29/1/1926, FP vol. 15; SMF to Helene Scheu-Reisz, 30/9/1952, FP vol. 20.*

61 Women's League of NSW to SMF, 17/12/1925, FP vol. 15; *SMH*, 22/4/1925 (Rose Scott obit., by Maybanke Anderson); SF, Notebook, FP vol. 107, p. 35. Marjorie Chave Collisson was NSW delegate to the Paris conference.

62 FP vol. 23, p. 311 (subtitle given in listing of the Brent chronicle to C. H. Grattan); 'Merlin of the Empiah by Brent of Bin Bin', ML MSS 6035/34/1, gives Miles' forwarding address in New York, 1931; H. F. Malone [SMF] to Cape, 19/1/1926, FP vol. 86 ,* and following items.

63 Brenda Niall, *Martin Boyd: A Biography*, Oxford Univ. Press, Melbourne and New York, 1988, pp. 94–5, 103. Martin Boyd (1893–1972), author (*ADB* vol. 13).

64 Brent of Bin Bin, *Prelude to Waking: A Novel in the First Person and Parentheses*, Angus & Robertson, Sydney, 1950, p. 89.

65 Michael Roe, *Australia, Britain, and Migration, 1915–1940: A Study of Desperate Hopes*, Cambridge Univ. Press, Cambridge, UK, 2002; an undated fragment at ML MSS 445/39/329 goes further, envisaging 'a mighty big scheme' wherein British industrial workers could mingle with native Australians in properly founded towns, and at once keep Australia white and relieve congestion in Britain, a point she hastened to mark as 'private and secret', presumably along with her expectation that this would create a Protestant population (p. 70).

66 *Prelude to Waking*, p. 102.

67 ML MSS 445/39/395.

68 D. L. LeMahieu, *A Culture for Democracy: Mass Communication and the Cultivated Mind in Britain Between the Wars*, Clarendon Press, Oxford, UK, 1988, ch. 2; Alison Light, *Forever England: Literature, Femininity, and Conservatism between the Wars*, Routledge, London and New York, 1991, ch. 4 (women's historical novels and detective stories).

69 Robert Loraine (1876–1935), airman and actor, was a friend of George Bernard Shaw (Gibbs, *Bernard Shaw*).

70 'Bouquets', ML 445/26; Margery Furbank to SMF, 22/4/1939, FP vol. 26, re Baker. 'H. M. Baker' is listed as a tax consultant, *London Telephone Directory*, 1926. Alban Limpus (1878?–1941) produced *Hay Fever* and other successful plays, *Times* (London), 25/3/1941, p 7.

71 'Bouquets', ML 445/26, p. 75 (numbered by hand).

72 *ibid.*, p. 73.

73 *ibid.*, p. 51.

74 Nell Malone to SF, 28/2/1926, FP vol. 15.

75 SMF to SF, 1/9/1926, FP vol. 108, and SMF to JMF, postcard 19/9/1926, FP vol. 113X.

76 SMF to A. G. Stephens, Sunday [18/4/1926], FP vol. 7; and SF to SMF, 19/9/1926, FP vol. 48.

77 NHTPC Records, Minutes, 13/12/1926, and F. G. Hamilton to SMF, 13/12/1926, FP vol. 15.

78 SMF to Eva O'Sullivan, 15/1/1927, ML MSS 544. Una Lucy Fielding (1888–1969), *ADB* vol. 14.

79 Mary Fullerton to SMF, 3/3/1927, from 35 Stratford Rd, W8, FP vol. 16.*

80 'Up the Country': sketch, repr. Graeme Davison *et al.*, *Australians, 1888*, Fairfax, Syme and Weldon, Sydney, 1987, p. 112.

81 Mary Fullerton to SMF, 3/3/1927, FP vol. 16.*

82 'Up the Country', ts., Miles Franklin — Further Papers 1908–c.1950, ML MSS 6035/40, purchased from Sydney antiquarian bookseller Berkelouw, 1994. Re the purchase see Christopher Niesche, 'A Brilliant Collection', *SMH* (*Good Weekend*), 12/11/1994. Berkelouw's catalogue (1962) is at ML MSS 6035/41.

83 Covering letter, preserved in William Blackwood & Sons, Publishing file for Miles Franklin's 'Brent of Bin Bin' novels, 1927–48, ML MSS 6329/1; also FP vol. 85. Special note on Blackwood's 'Brent of Bin Bin' publishing file: This file was purchased by the State Library of NSW from New Century Antiquarian Books, Melbourne in 1997. It contains over 200 letters written between 26/5/1927 and 22/2/1948, almost half of which are new to Franklin studies. A breakdown of contents discloses that 82 of the letters were written by Miles Franklin, the first as noted from the northern hemisphere as 'S. Miles', then as 'S[arah] Mills' (a play on her last two given names, Sarah Miles), and from Australia, as 'William Blake'; 52 are from other correspondents, including Agnes Murphy, still operating as a publicist in 1930; and there are 76 (transcript only) by Blackwood. Estimate from Offer of Sale, Corres. of Miles Franklin and others 1927–48, ts. I am grateful to Paul Brunton for access to this document.

84 Mollye Menken to SMF, 21/5/1928, FP vol. 20; S. A. Byles to SMF, 28/10/[1929] FP vol. 6.*

85 Copy of Memorandum of Agreement, 17/6/1927, signed for Blackwood, but not by Ms Sarah Miles for William Blake, FP vol. 85; Blackwood & Sons to Miss Sarah Miles, 17/6/1927 (transcript) and S. Mills to Blackwood & Sons, 18/6/1927, ML MSS 6329.

Chapter 10 — Enter Brent of Bin Bin: July 1927–December 1932

1 SMF to MDR, 30/10/1930, MDR Papers.*

2 Eric Martin, a Sydney draughtsman, recalled her conversation as delighting fellow passengers (Eric Martin to SMF, 18/9/1927, FP vol. 20). Brent of Bin Bin, *Back to Bool Bool*, Blackwood & Sons, Edinburgh, 1931, pp. 20–1 (a Cape Town stopover).

3 *Age*, 12/8/1927 (Shipping News); A. B. Champion to SMF, 5/10/1927, FP vol. 15; Kate Baker to SMF, 11/8/1927, FP vol. 9A.*

4 *DT* (Sydney), 17/8/1927, p. 10 (the only press reference re arrival); PD, 23/8/1927. Helena Lampe Diary, 16/8/1927, FP vol. 104/112. Re JMF's health: according to SF's records (FP vol. 109X), p. 285, he suffered a nervous collapse in Apr. 1927.

5 W. B. to Blackwood & Sons, 18/10/1927, ML MSS 6329. Some letters in the Blackwood file are preserved in SMF's own Brent file (FP vol. 85).

6 ML MSS 6035/40; Mutch Index, ML m/films, reel CY 572. The collar came from Hine, Parker and Co, a long-established clothing firm in central London.

7 *Large Stock Brands Directory of NSW Brands Registered and Transferred 31 December 1923*, ML; 'The old brand Brent of Bin Bin' to Mary Gilmore, 2/12/1928, FP vol. 119.*

8 SMF to J. B. Pinker, 6/2/1901, FP vol. 80 ('I do not wish it to be known that I am a young girl'); Elaine Showalter, *A Literature of their Own: British Women Novelists from Bronte to Lessing*, Princeton Univ. Press, Princeton N.J., 1977, pp. 57–9; Roe and Bettison, *A Gregarious Culture*, p. xxii, Bettison and Roe, *ALS* listing, 2001.

9 Heilbrun, *Writing a Woman's Life*, pp. 113, 116; W. Blake to Blackwood, 30/11/1928, ML MSS 6329. Nigel Muir, 'Miles Franklin Confesses', *SMH*, 16/7/1966 (*Weekend Magazine*).

10 G. W. Blackwood to Lord Novar, 25/10/1928, ML MSS 6329.

11 W. Blake to Blackwood, 24/10/1927, ML MSS 6329; John Varney to SMF, 17/9/1927, FP vol. 15.

12 *Argus*, 10/8/1927, p. 19, and 22/8/1927, p. 1; PD, 20/9/1927.

13 MDR to SMF, 29/9/1927, FP vol. 10.

14 P. S. Watson to SMF, 22/8/1927, FP vol. 12*; Roe, 'The Coming of Christian Science'; for more on the Watsons, see Philippa Martyr, *Paradise of Quacks: An Alternative History of Medicine in Australia*, Macleay Press, Paddington, NSW, 2002, p. 108.

15 *Gentlemen at Gyang Gyang*, pp. 8–9; SMF to Alice Henry, 23/12/1928, FP vol. 114.*

16 SMF to Eva O'Sullivan, 5/4/1926, ML MSS 544; SMF to Alice Henry, 26/12/1927 and 23/12/1928, FP vol. 114 (all*).

17 A ms. and a ts. of *Ten Creeks Run* dated 1927 are preserved at ML MSS 6035/37–38, also two tss dated 1928. The earliest version of *Cockatoos* is a ts. at ML MSS 6035/30 dated 1927–8, and

a carbon ts. entitled 'Cockatoos, a Story of Youth and Exodists' by Brent of Bin Bin, c.1927, is at ML MSS 445/8.

18 William Blake to Blackwood, 6/2/1928, ML MSS 6329.

19 Other family correlations: Simon Labosseer/Oltmann Lampe, Emily Labosseer/Susannah Franklin, Henry Milford/John Maurice Franklin, Mazere/Bridle, Poole/Wilkinson, Mutch Index, ML m/films, CY 572.

20 'Ramiparous': from 'rami', plural of 'ramus', branch, as of a plant. The 1928 ms. and two tss of *Gentlemen at Gyang Gyang* are at ML MSS 6035/32; the earliest version of *Back to Bool Bool* is a ms. dated (by SMF) 14/7/1927, i.e. it was begun on the *Barrabool*, with ML MSS 6035/27 another early ms. version dated 1927.

21 William Blake to Blackwood, 22/9/1930 and 9/12/1930, ML MSS 6329. A rough ts. of *Back to Bool Bool* dated 1929, plus three undated tss, are at ML MSS 6035/26–8. T. B. Clouston, *Tumut Centenary Celebrations 1824–1924: Official Souvenir*, ML.

22 FP vol. 56, p. 79; Billie Melman, *Women and the Popular Imagination in the Twenties: Flappers and Nymphs*, Macmillan, London, 1988, p. 141, on the Australasian version of 'Empire yarns' as 'romances of the wilds'.

23 *Bulletin*, 22/8/1928, p. 9; SMF to Alice Henry, 23/12/1928, FP vol. 114.* 'M. Barnard Eldershaw': Marjorie Barnard (1897–1989), writer and historian (*ADB* vol. 17); Flora Eldershaw (1897–1956), teacher, writer, and public servant (*ADB* vol. 14).

24 William Blake to Blackwood, 6/2/1928, and Blackwood to W. Blake Esq., 25/4/1928, ML MSS 6329.

25 Fred Lampe was a younger brother of SF (see Appendix 2); 'Gooandra' was a snow lease.

26 SMF to Mary Fullerton, n.d. and 12/6/1928, FP vol. 119;* SMF to Kate Baker, 12/2/1928, Baker Papers.

27 *Gentlemen at Gyang Gyang*, pp. 13, 89; 'gyang gyang': a small dark-grey cockatoo of the timbered slopes and uplands of south-east Australia. The phrase also echoes Gang Gang Mountain, east of Kiandra.

28 S. A. Byles to SMF, 12/9/1928, FP vol. 6. Isadora Duncan (1877–1927), *ANB*.

29 ML MSS 6035/31–3; *Bulletin*, 11/7/1928, p. 51.

30 *Up the Country*, 1928 edn, p. xi; 'possuming': the chaotic movements of the arboreal Australian marsupial, something like a squirrel (*MD*).

31 SMF to Alice Henry, 15/12/1928, FP vol. 11, SMF to Mary Fullerton, 12/6/1928, FP vol. 119. The papers of William Alexander Carter (1867–1956), mainly press clippings of his writings, are at ML MSS 33721 (1).

32 Mary Fullerton to SMF, 27/3/1928, and 31/7/1928, both FP vol. 16, SMF to Mary Fullerton, n.d. and 12/6/1928, both FP vol. 119; supportive letters, Mary Fullerton to SMF, 23/4/1929, vol. 16, and SMF to Mary Fullerton, 3/9/1928, 20/5/1929, both FP vol. 119, also SMF to John McKellar, 6/10/—, FP vol. 28; *TLS*, 26/7/1928, p. 543; Blackwood to W. Blake Esq., 16/8/1929, ML MSS 6329.

33 Exercise books 2–4, ML MSS 6035; W. Blake to Blackwood, 4/10/1928, and Blackwood to W. Blake Esq., 14/11/1928, ML MSS 6329.

34 The Society of Women Writers, founded 1925, is the oldest continuous literary society in Sydney, Florence Baverstock (see ch. 6, n. 46) a founder. Lesley Heath, 'Sydney Literary Societies of the Nineteen Twenties', PhD thesis, p. 101, SWW Minutes, cited n. 134; Fox (ed.), *Dream at a Graveside*, p. 8. Stella Kidgell (1875–1960), a public servant, was Ada Holman's youngest sister (*SMH*, 15/10/1960, death notices).

35 The Old Council House, erected in 1913 on the corner of McMahon St and Forest Rd, was demolished in 1931, *Jubilee History of the Municipality of Hurstville 1887–1937*, Hurstville Municipal Council, Hurstville, NSW, 1937, and advice, Hurstville Library, 14/12/04.

36 *Up the Country* was published in the UK in Oct. 1928 (*English Catalogue of Books*); Brent of Bin Bin to Mary Gilmore, 2/12/1928, FP vol. 119; Dorothy Cottrell (1902–57), writer (*ADB* vol. 8); W. Blake to Blackwood, 30/11/1928, ML MSS 6329.

37 FP vol. 108/10; the most likely ts. is at ML MSS 6035/35.

38 Dated cuttings/transcripts of reviews, FP vol. 121A. *The Dynasts* was published 1903–8. Re the death of Emily Mazere, in the summer of 1881 the young girls Elizabeth and Emma Darlow drowned in a deep hole at Bowler's Creek (Jack Bridle, *My Mountain Country*, Miles Franklin

Memorial Committee, Talbingo, 1979, and see also 'The Ghost Hole. Feet First', ML MSS 445/21). The 1984 edition of *Up the Country* prepared in-house at Angus & Robertson from an early ms. has a different subtitle, 'A Saga of Pioneering Days', and while it renders the work more accessible to modern readers, its historicity is diminished (Laurie Clancy, 'Loss and Recovery', *Australian Book Review*, Apr. 1985, no. 69).

39   W. Blake to Blackwood, 2/1/1929, ML MSS 6329; SMF to Mary Fullerton, 2/1/1929 and reply, 13/2/1929, FP vol. 16; re competition, SMF to Mary Fullerton, 23/8/[192—, annotated SMF, 1929], FP vol. 119.

40   Mary Fullerton to SMF, 27/3/1928 and 30/7/[1929], FP vol. 16, is a good example of the relationship,* also 2/10/1929. 'Henry Handel Richardson': devised by Richardson after her marriage for her first novel, *Maurice Guest* (1908), by replacing her given names, which she disliked, with 'Henry Handel', variously said to have family or musical connotations, to avoid categorisation as 'a woman's novel' (Nettie Palmer, 'Frontier Years', in Smith (ed.), *Nettie Palmer*, pp. 30, 175–6). Marguerite Antonia Radclyffe Hall (1880–1943) was a controversial British writer and radical lesbian (*ODNB*), and see PD, 27/3/1932 re *The Well of Loneliness*: 'damned dull'. Mary Fullerton to SMF 27/3/1928, FP vol. 16.

41   'An Up-Country chronicle. Brent of Bin Bin', *Brisbane Courier*, 2/3/1929, p. 22, also 'Brent of Bin Bin', *Illustrated Tasmanian Mail*, 13/3/1929 [pp. 4–5].

42   Miles' other candidate for a chair was Flora Eldershaw; 'yarn' (coll.): 'a story or tale of adventure, especially a long one, about incredible events' (*MD*). Brent of Bin Bin to Nettie Palmer, 22/7/1929, Palmer Papers, MS 1174;* charts etc, FP vol. 56, p. 79; Notes on characters, ML MSS 445/30; W. Blake to Blackwood, 14/2/1930, ML MSS 6329.

43   Mary Fullerton to SMF, 26/6/1929, FP vol. 16. Bernard Charles Cronin (1884–1968), jackeroo, journalist and prolific writer of light fiction, published *Bracken* in London in 1931 (*ADB* vol. 8); see also 'Miles Franklin reviews Bernard Cronin' [*The Sow's Ear*], FP vol. 60, possibly published *Book News*, Jul. 1933.

44   De Berg interview; 'Cooking for the Wedding', *School Paper*, 2/9/1929, pp. 119–20, Lawson Lit. Soc. Papers, ML MSS 772, Box 28. Percy Reginald Stephensen (1901–65), writer, editor, and publisher, and Winifred Sarah Stephensen, prev. Venus, née Lockyer (1886–c.1967), a British-born dancer (*ADB* vol. 12), also Winifred's son Jack Lockyer, pers. comm., 21/10/1992.

45   *Country Life and Stock and Station Journal*, 9/8/1929, p. 2; *Bulletin*, 4/12/1929, p. 37; *Sydney Sun*, 13/10/1929, p. 19.

46   MDR to SMF, 24/1/1930, SMF to MDR, 30/1/1930, MDR Papers, both;* Charles Peters to SMF, 28/5/1930, FP vol. 90; SMF to Mary Fullerton, 11/7/1930, FP vol. 119.

47   There are several undated tss of *Back to Bool Bool* at ML MSS 6035; 'Ten Creeks Run. A tale of the horse and cattle stations of the Upper Murrumbidgee, Australia', final typed draft, 1928, ML MSS 6035/35; PD, 16/7/1929; Blackwood to W. Blake Esq., 16/8/1929, and W. Blake to Blackwood, 22/9/1930, ML MSS 6329.

48   SMF to MDR, 6/5/1929, MDR Papers.*

49   SMF to Alice Henry, 13/8/[1928], FP vol. 115,* and 22/6/1929, FP vol. 114. Adela Pankhurst Walsh (1885–1960), youngest daughter of Emmeline and Richard Pankhurst, political activist (*ADB* vol. 12), started an Australian branch of the British Guild of Empire in the 1920s, which SF supported (PD, 19/6/1936).

50   *Ten Creeks Run* was published in the UK in Mar. 1930; SMF to Alice Henry, 1/2/1930, FP vol. 114; W. Blake to Blackwood, 20/12/1929, ML MSS 6329; 'Our Literary Turkey Nests' by Brent of Bin Bin, FP vol. 59. Other unpub. sketches by Brent of Bin Bin dated 1929: 'On Vale's Verandah' and 'The King is Cordial', ML MSS 445/21.

51   William Blake to Blackwood, 30/11/1928, ML MSS 6329.

52   *SMH* articles: not located to date; 'Old Man of Bandicoot', ML MSS 445/28 and Commonwealth Film Censor to Mr S. M. Franklin, 1/4/1930, FP vol. 88 (entry unsuccessful).

53   Agnes Murphy to Blackwood, 26/3/1930, ML MSS 6329; Kathleen Ussher to SMF, 8/5/1930, FP vol. 21.

54   Mary Fullerton to SMF, 27/3/1930, FP vol. 16;* *Table Talk*, 15/5/1930, p. 16. Guy Innes, '"Brent of Bin Bin" a Woman. Literary Secret Out', Melbourne *Herald*, 5/5/1930, p. 3, also said Brent was Miles Franklin, based on literary evidence. Guy Edward Innes (1882–1953) was deputy manager, Australian Newspaper Cable Service, London 1926–35.

55 FP vol. 121 (reviews and cuttings); *Ten Creeks Run*, 2nd edn, 1952, pp. 196–7.

56 SMF to Mary Fullerton, 20/5/1930, FP vol. 19 (the literary effect of no primogeniture);* Brent of Bin Bin to Nettie Palmer, Dec. 1930, Palmer Papers (SMF did not write to Nettie in her own name until 1933, see FP vol. 24).

57 SMF to Alice Henry, 11/11/1928, FP vol. 114; SMF to Mary Fullerton, 20/5/1930, FP vol. 119;* LN, p. 214, FP vol. 3; Roderick, *Miles Franklin*, p. 175. H. V. Marrot, *The Life and Letters of John Galsworthy*, Heinemann, London, 1935.

58 Brent of Bin Bin to Nettie Palmer, Oct. 1930, Palmer Papers.

59 *Queanbeyan Age*, 6/8/1930 [p. 2]; George Robertson to SMF, 2/9/1930, and SMF to George Robertson, 14/9/1930, and to Arthur Greening [Lothian], 25/8/1930 and 11/9/1930, all FP vol. 80 (for Greening, see Stuart Sayers, *The Company of Books: A Short History of the Lothian Book Companies 1888–1988*, Hawthorn Press, Melbourne, 1988, pp. 54–5. John Henry (Jack) Maxwell (1885–1954), ranger, stockman, horseman (*ADB S*).

60 SMF to Mary Fullerton, 29/5/[1930], FP vol. 119; family information, Claire O'Connor, pers. comm., Chatswood, 1/8/2003 (Claire O'Connor, b. 1913, third daughter of Irene Franklin's sister Xenia Edwards, previously Harkin, a television actor) and Peter Norvill of Murrurundi, son of Xenia's youngest daughter, Enid. 'Madame Austral', b. Florence Mary Wilson (1892–1968), Australian Wagnerian soprano (*ADB* vol. 7). Amy Johnson (1903–41), British aviatrix flew solo to Australia, arriving Darwin 24/5/1930 (*ODNB*).

61 SMF to Alice Henry, 1/2/1930,* and 23/12/1928, FP vol. 114; Dan Clyne to SMF, 29/10/1930, FP vol. 22;* S. A. Byles to SMF, 16/10/[1930?], FP vol. 6.

62 SMF to Mary Fullerton, 3/8/1930, FP vol. 119; Blackwood to SMF, 14/7/1930, and SMF to Blackwood, 14/10/1930, ML MSS 6329; Em[ily] Fullerton to SMF, 4/11/[1930], FP vol. 20.

63 SMF to MDR, 30/10/1930 and 8/11/1930, MDR Papers, both;* FP vol. 113X (re Norman Franklin): SMF to Arthur Greening, 11[?]/11/1930, Lothian Papers.

64 S. Mills to Blackwood, 2/1/1931, ML MSS 6329; SMF to George Robertson, 15/5/1930, ML MSS 314.*

65 SMF to SF, 21/1/1931, FP vol. 108.*

66 SMF to Leslie Bridle, 2/3/1931, ML MSS 3737/3.

67 SMF to Leslie Bridle, 8/4/1931, ML MSS 3737/3; SMF to Alice Henry, 20/4/1931, FP vol. 114. Judith (from 1960 Dame Judith) Anderson (1898–1992) left Sydney for the US during World War I (*Who's Who in Australia*, 1992).

68 Blackwood to Mary Fullerton, 26/1/1931, S. Miles to Blackwood, 26/3/1931 and cables, [S. Mills] to Melbourne *Herald*, 26/3/1931, 31/3/1931, ML MSS 6329.

69 SMF to Mary Fullerton, 25/2/1931 and Mary Fullerton to SMF, 27/2/1931, SMF to Mary Fullerton, 8/4/[1931], 6/3/1931, FP vol. 16; SMF to Alice Henry, 29/4/[1931], FP vol. 114; '"Mrs Dysart Disappears" by Brent of Bin Bin', ML MSS 445/109, and film scenario c.1920, ML MSS 445/28. Clinton Hartley Grattan (1902–80), journalist, author, historian (*ADB* vol. 14).

70 J. T Lang, travel document, 20/1/1931, FP vol. 51, p. 155; S. Mills to Blackwood, 25/2/1931, ML MSS 6329; SMF to Mary Fullerton, 25/2/1931, and Mary Fullerton to SMF, 17/3/1931, FP vol. 16, SMF to Alice Henry, 20/4/1931, FP vol. 114.

71 Mabel's son Denis had just joined the air force, so there was a spare room at 181C High St.

72 S. Mills to Blackwood, 20/5/1931, ML MSS 6329; Blackwood to SMF, 7/5/1931, FP vol. 85, and S. Mills to Blackwood, 9/5/1931, ML MSS 6329; Curtis Brown to Blackwood, 5/5/1931, FP vol. 86. 'Helen of the Headland' became *Rufus Sterne* (Blackwood, Edinburgh, 1932).

73 Arthur Greening to SMF, 23/6/1931, FP vol. 80 (advising also that three publishers had previously rejected *Old Blastus*). Corres. with Cecil Palmer, May–Aug. 1931, FP vol. 80, S. Mills to Blackwood, Saturday, FP vol. 85. On Cecil Palmer's standing as a publisher, see Society of Authors to SMF, 5/8/1931, FP vol. 80; his most notable previous Australian publication was Norman Lindsay's *Creative Effort* (1924). SMF to —[SF?], 18/8/[1931], FP vol. 108. Stories in ms. dated 1931 include 'Back to Feathers!' and 'Prowling Around', FP vol. 60.

74 *Australian Authors' Week. Catalogue of Books*, 29 Sept.–5/10/1931, N828.9994/26, State Reference Library, State Library of NSW (and list of late titles); Brent of Bin Bin to A. P. Herbert, 26/9/1931, FP vol. 87; S. Mills to Blackwood, 28/7/1931 and 5/10/1931, ML MSS 6329; SMF to Greening, 15/10/1931, FP vol. 80; Brent of Bin Bin to Nettie Palmer,

8–10/5/1931, FP vol. 87. (Sir) Alan Patrick Herbert (1890–1971), a British author, politician and matrimonial law reformer (*ODNB*).

75 'UnAustralian': my emphasis (see *Laughter, Not For A Cage*, pp. 147–9 for SMF's final verdict); A. G. Stephens, 'Brent of Bin Bin. The Wizard of the South', attachment, S. Mills to Blackwood, 16/6/1931, ML MSS 6329, also FP vol. 87.

76 Brent of Bin Bin to Nettie Palmer, 8/5/1931, FP vol. 87. Mary Jane Mander (1877–1949), teacher, journalist, novelist (*Dictionary of New Zealand Biography*).

77 Leaflet with PBC no. 152; Brent of Bin Bin to Nettie Palmer, London, Oct. 1931, Palmer Papers; Brent of Bin Bin to P. R. Stephensen, 8/9/1931, FP vol. 86, and Brent of Bin Bin to Otto Niemeyer, 25/9/1931, FP vol. 87.

78 PBC no. 152C.

79 *Back to Bool Bool*, pp. 108, 266, 270; 'Brent of Bin Bin Again', *Bulletin* 21/5/1930, p. 5.

80 This and subsequent paras are based on cuttings preserved FP vol. 121A, plus local reviews as attrib. by SF, PBC no.152C (*SMH*, 19/12/1931, *Woman's Mirror*, 26/1/1931, *Sunday Sun*, 27/2/1931); Blackwood to Mary Fullerton, 24/11/1937, FP vol. 85; HHR to Mary Kernot, 21/1/1932, *Henry Handel Richardson: The Letters*, ed. Clive Probyn and Bruce Steele, Miegunyah Press, Carlton, Vic, 2000, vol. 2, p. 497, and *TLS*, 14/1/1932, p. 29; A. G. Stephens to Brent of Bin Bin, 11/2/1932, FP vol. 87, and Brent of Bin Bin to A. G. Stephens, May 1932, MA.*

81 Modjeska, *Exiles at Home*, pp. 177–9; Kathleen Ussher, 'The "Inconspicuous" Australian', *Bookman*, Apr. 1931, p. 8, and *Launceston-Courier*, 15/7/1931, [attrib. by SMF], FP vol. 121A. Mazo De La Roche (1885–1961) wrote the 'Whiteoak' series, a family chronicle of three generations set in Ontario (*Hutchinson's New Twentieth Century Encyclopedia*, 1964).

82 Stephens, 'The Wizard of the South', FP vol. 87, p. 225; Arthur Ashworth, 'Brent of Bin Bin', *Southerly*, 1951, vol. 12, no. 4.

83 Brent of Bin Bin to Beaverbrook, 21/11/1931, FP vol. 87.

84 Brent of Bin Bin to *Daily Herald*, 28/3/1932, FP vol. 87.

85 The dedication is included in the 2nd edn of *Back to Bool Bool* (Angus & Robertson, Sydney, 1956).

86 *Bulletin*, 10/4/1929, p. 37, and 4/12/1929, p. 37; Wilde, *Courage a Grace*, p. 283; *Daily News* (Perth), 10/9/1932 (FP vol. 121A).

87 SMF to SF, 12/11/1931, FP vol. 108;* JMF to SMF, 29/4/1931, FP vol. 48; SMF to E. H. Stephens, 3/9/1931, FP vol. 87. Social Credit: a version of political economy popular during the 1930s Depression, based on the teachings of Major C. H. Douglas, that the weakness of capitalism could be remedied by the redistribution of purchasing power.

88 SF to SMF, 11/10/1931, FP vol 48; PD, 28/10/1931.

89 SF, Notebook, FP vol. 107, p. 32; 'Who Are the Dead?', FP vol. 62; SMF to SF, 21/9/1931, FP vol. 48, and Roderick, *Miles Franklin*, p. 191 (column 1); SF to SMF, 12/11/1931, FP vol. 108* (Gandhi, Dean Inge). 'Death of Mr John Franklin', *Queanbeyan Age*, 6/11/1931, p. 1.

90 S. Mills to Blackwood, 11/11/1931, ML MSS 6329; Annie May Bridle to SMF, 4/11/1931, FP vol. 47; SF to SMF, 7/11/1931, FP vol. 48; Eva Franklin to SMF, 23/11/1931, FP vol. 48.

91 Blackwood to S. Mills, 4/11/1931, S. Mills to Blackwood, 2/11/1931 and 17/11/1931, ML MSS 6329; Eva Franklin to SMF, 23/11/1931, FP vol. 48; SMF to Mary Fullerton, 25/2/1931, FP vol. 16 ('that [*OBB*] would mess the trail up a little, wouldn't it').

92 The *Old Blastus* files are at FP vol. 80, and the William Lothian Papers are at SLV, plus materials at FP vol. 92 (Memorandum of Agreement, Aug. 1931); SMF, 'Old Blastus of Bandicoot', FP vol. 80, p. 371, n.d., is a résumé of the affair. The earliest review appears to be *TLS*, 21/1/1932, p. 45 ('uncommon and attractive qualities'); *All About Books*, Aug. 1932 (announcing publication in Australia), and *Bulletin*, 21/9/1932, p. 5 ('more than a fine novel').

93 J. Mulvaney and A. Calaby, *'So Much that is New'. Baldwin Spencer 1860–1929: A Biography*, Melbourne Univ. Press, Carlton, Vic, 1985, pp. 417–18; SMF to SF, 25–26/12/1931, FP vol. 108. Jean Hamilton, 'Notes from my Diary (typed and aided by me M.F., 1931–2)', ML MSS 3659/1, pp. 885–941. Jean Hamilton (1889–1961) was of a pioneering family in Victoria's Western District (Mulvaney and Calaby).

94 SMF to Eva O'Sullivan, 4/5/1932;* PD, 3/3/1932 and after; SMF to MDR, 4/3/1932, MDR Papers; Eva Franklin died at Paddington, NSW, 24/1/1932, aged 46, after three months' illness.

95 'Virgins Out of Date', ML MSS 445/11, and 'Virgins and Martyrs Out of Date', c.1944, ML MSS 445/25; Francis Jones to SMF 29/9/1932, FP vol. 81; *All About Books*, 3/12/1932, p. 199 (plus ts. copies, two by 'Saddle Flap', at FP vol. 60, where items mentioned are listed).

96 Martin, *Passionate Friends*, p. 134; SF to SMF, 21/9/1931, FP vol. 48.

97 SMF to Alice Henry, 21/12/1931, FP vol. 114 (lack of money); PD, Nov. 1931–Jun. 1932, *passim*.

98 SMF to SF, 8/6/[1932], FP vol. 108* (part), and ML MSS 364/5/16. Dr Osborne: probably Ethel Elizabeth Osborne (1899–1955), medical practitioner (*ADB* vol. 11); Mary Jamieson Williams, d. 1947, temperance worker; Ruby Rich (1888–1988), Jewish leader (*ADB* vol. 18, forthcoming); Dora Montefiore (1851–1933), suffragist and socialist (*ADB* vol. 10).

99 PD, 19/1/1932–27/3/1932 (lecture series); Brent of Bin Bin to D. Mirsky, 1/3/1932, FP vol. 87. Prince Dimitri Syvatopolk-Mirsky, better known as D. S. Mirsky (1890–1939), Russian scholar (*ODNB*), published a celebrated *History of Russian Literature* (George Routledge, London) in 1926.

100 Brent of Bin Bin to Nettie Palmer, Sept. 1930, Palmer Papers; Brent of Bin Bin to D. Mirsky, 1/3/1932, FP vol. 87.

101 SF to SMF, 10/4/1932, FP vol. 48; Nettie Palmer, *All About Books*, 1931, vol. 3, no. 7, p. 159 (turkey's eggs); Blackwood to S. Mills, 4/11/1931, ML MSS 6329 (reprinting *Up the Country*).

102 Brent of Bin Bin to Nettie Palmer, 26/1/1932, Palmer Papers; Nettie Palmer, *All About Books*, 1932, vol. 8, no. 4, p. 121; S. Mills to Blackwood, 17/2/1932, ML MSS 6329.

103 Roderick, *Miles Franklin*, p. 146; Brent of Bin Bin to Kate Baker, n.d., Kennedy Papers and Jun. 1932, Baker Papers.

104 Nettie Palmer, 'Australian Letters. Reply to an American Critic. The Advance of the Prose Art', *Saturday Night Telegraph*, 4/7/1931, p. 14, and Grattan's reply, 'Australian Literature. An American Criticism. Mediocrity to be Fought', *Saturday Night Telegraph*, 19/12/1931, p. 13; 'Blazing the Trail for Australian Literature, by Brent of Bin Bin', FP vol. 60; SMF to *Saturday Night Telegraph*, 14/3/1932, and response, 19/4/1932, FP vol. 90; S. Mills to Blackwood, 10/8/1932, and response, 23/8/1932, ML MSS 6329.

105 Helene Scheu-Riesz to SMF, 17/2/1932, FP vol. 20, 'A Young Continent…', FP vol. 121A (orig. text), and ML MSS 445/35, item 14 (transl.). Helene Scheu-Riesz (1880–1970), writer and publisher (*Dictionary of German Biography*, 2005), was active in Social Democratic women's organisations in Vienna; exiled following the Anschluss, she lived in New York until 1951.

106 SMF to Helene Scheu-Riesz, 6/4/1931, 5/1/1932, and Helene Scheu-Riesz to SMF, 13/6/1932, FP vol. 20; A. W. Roeder to SMF, 27/4/1932, FP vol. 32, and SMF to Martin Christensen, Hamburg, 27/12/1932, FP vol. 20; SMF to Eva O'Sullivan, 4/5/1932, ML MSS 544; KSP to SMF, 1/7/1932, FP vol. 21.

107 SMF to C. H. Grattan, 18/3/1932,* and 1/9/1932, FP vol. 23; S. Mills to Blackwood, 17/11/1931, FP vol. 103.

108 Guy Innes to SMF, 9/8/1932, FP vol. 24; Winifred Stephensen, Diary, 3/7/1932, Stephensen Papers, ML MSS 1284.

109 PD, 16/7/1932; Munro, *Wild Man of Letters*, pp. 108–10, and Proposal for an Australian Publishing Company, FP vol. 91/4; P. R. Stephensen, *The Bushwhackers: Sketches of Life in the Australian Outback*, Mandrake Press, London, 1929. Special note: it seems Stephensen may have realised that Miles was Brent at this time (Munro, p. 109).

110 SMF to Helene Scheu-Riesz, 11/8/1932, FP vol. 20.

111 P. R. Stephensen to Brent of Bin Bin, 25/7/1932, and 'The old brand Brent of Bin Bin' to P. R. Stephensen, Aug. 1932, FP vol. 86, both.

112 S. Mills to Blackwood, 18/8/1932, ML MSS 6329 (urging secrecy if Stephensen visited); SMF to Kate Baker, 31/8/1932, Kennedy Papers.

113 *BA*, 8/9/1932, p. 8; SF to SMF, 9/11/1931, FP vol. 48 (monkeys), and SMF to SF, 31/8/1932, FP vol. 108. Guy Innes, 'Author of *My Brilliant Career* Returning to Melbourne', Melbourne *Herald*, 13/10/1932, p. 22.

114 John Varney to SMF, 9/10/1932, in *First Wounds*, Bianco, New York, 1926, PBC no. 352; SMF to A. Dresden, 4/11/1932, FP vol. 24; C. H. Grattan to SMF, 6/12/1932, FP vol. 23; SMF to Antoinette Donnelly, 4/11/1932, FP vol. 24; MDR to SMF, 29/9/1931, FP vol. 10; Elisabeth Christman to SMF, 14/10/1932, FP vol. 24.

115 Margery Currey to SMF, 19/10/1932, FP vol. 22; 'Editha Phelps', *Tecumseh Herald*, 29/12/1931, FP vol. 12; Louise Phelps to SMF, 3/12/1933, FP vol. 3, p. 81.

116 SMF to Agnes & Mary Nestor, 11/11/1932, FP vol. 24.*

117 Alice Henry to MDR, 17/12/1932, MDR Papers; Lorna Mary Ussher (1890–1975) was a violinist.

118 Letters included SMF to Melbourne journalist Spencer Brodney, 2/11/1932, Kennedy Papers, SMF to publisher and fellow writer 'Furnley Maurice' (Frank Wilmot) 4/11/1932, and SMF to Helene Scheu-Riesz, 4/11/1932, FP vol. 24. Arrivals: *SMH*, 18/11/1932, p. 13 (Miles not among the passengers pictured, *SMH*, 19/11/1932, p. 16). 'Back Home. Famous Author in Sydney. Quiet Entry', *SMH*, 28/3/1933, p. 6. (One rejected press item: '"Back to Feathers!" by Miles Franklin', a fashion comment dated Aug. 1931, ML MSS 364/60, and see SMF to Sydney *Sun*, 1/9/1931, FP vol. 90, annotated 'No reply, tho' I thought it was trashy enough'.)

119 'Miles Franklin', 18/11/1932, FP vol. 121A. The *Propeller*, a suburban weekly, founded in 1911, was absorbed by the *St George and Sutherland Shire Leader* in 1969.

120 'An Australian Novel of Note', *All About Books*, 1932, vol. 4, no. 11, p. 175; SMF to Blackwood, 18/8/1932, ML MSS 6329; Nettie Palmer, 'Writing Under a Pen-name: Consistent and Inconsistent Disguises' and 'Old Blastus of Bandicoot', *Illustrated Tasmanian Mail*, 11/8/1932, p. 61, and 24/11/1932, p. 15. For a likely origin of Mabel's story in Miss Gillespie's family, see FP vol. 4, pp. 141–8. Joan H. MacDonald, 'Snow-white and Red-rose in Colonial Novels', *Australian Folklore*, 12, 1997, is a rare modern response to *Old Blastus*.

121 SMF to George Mackaness, 19/11/1932, Mackaness Papers, NLA; *All About Books*, 4, 1/11/1932, p. 181, and *Sun*, 24/11/1932, p. 34. George Mackaness (1882–1968), educationist, author and bibliophile, lecturer-in-charge of English, Sydney Teachers College 1924–46, pres. FAW 1933–4, was awarded an honorary DSc., Univ. of Sydney, 1961 (*ADB* vol. 10).

122 *All About Books*, 1932, no. 4, vol. 6, p. 87; 'The "Olive Schreiner" of Australian Literature', *Illustrated Tasmanian Mail*, 16/6/1932, p. 15; SMF to C. H. Grattan, 21/7/1932, FP vol. 23.*

Chapter 11 — 'As a Natural Fact': 1933–1938

1 Chapter title: SMF to C. H. Grattan, 21/7/1932, FP vol. 23.* Lead quotation: LN, FP vol. 3, p. 594.

2 Spearritt, *Sydney's Century*, p. 8.

3 SMF to C. H. Grattan, 5/5/1933, FP vol. 23; Barnard, *Miles Franklin*, p 3.

4 *Rose Lindsay: A Model Life*, ed. Lin Bloomfield, Odana Editions, Bungendore, 2001, p. 342; Munro, *Wild Man of Letters*, p. 120; Publishing Company, Manager's Report, 25/6/1933, Stephensen Papers, ML MSS 1284 29 (127).

5 SMF to Norman Lindsay, n.d. [Feb. 1933], Harry T. Chaplin Colln, Rare Books Colln., Fisher Library, Univ. of Sydney;* SMF to Margery Currey, 4/1/1933, FP vol. 23;* Publishing Company, Manager's Report, 25/6/1933, Stephensen Papers; John Hetherington, *Norman Lindsay: The Embattled Olympian*, Oxford Univ. Press, Melbourne, 1973, p. 200.

6 SMF to C. H. Grattan, 29/3/1933, FP vol. 23;* Munro, *Wild Man of Letters*, pp. 119, 127. *Saturdee* was published by the Endeavour Press in 1933, and in London in 1936.

7 SMF to G. B. Lancaster, 19/4/1933, FP vol. 20.*

8 'Bring the Monkey', ts. with corrections, Stephensen Papers; Manager's Report, 25/6/1933, Stephensen Papers, ML MSS 1284; reviews, FP vol. 121A, also 'Smart, Banal, Shocking. Miles Franklin's New Novel', *Sunday Observer* (Sydney), 28/5/1933, p. 23; SMF, 'Tea Parties', *Australian Mercury*, Aug. 1935, vol. 1, no. 2, Stephensen Papers (page proofs). *Monkey* was taken over by the *Bulletin* in 1936, FP vol. 81. Freda Barrymore, née Sternberg (1880–1971), b. Deloraine, Tasmania, m. George Barrymore (d. 1944), journalist, in 1929, was a publicist and journalist (*Home*, Jun. 1924, p. 52 has a photograph of Barrymore).

9 Hergenhan, *No Casual Traveller*, ch. 2 (Grattan accompanied his first wife, an actor, on a tour of Australia in 1927); Jill Roe, '"Tremenjus Good for What Ails Us"'. *The American Commonwealth*, Macmillan, New York, 1927–8, 2 vols, was first published in 1888.

10 SMF to George Mackaness, 11/2/1933, courtesy Louise Preston (copy in my possession); Nettie Palmer to SMF, 28/2/1933, FP vol. 24; SMF to Nettie Palmer, 14/6/[1933], FP vol. 24; SMF to C. H. Grattan, 5/5/1933, FP vol. 23; Roe, '"Tremenjus Good for What Ails Us"', p. 83.

11 SMF to C. H. Grattan, 25/10/1933, FP vol. 23;* Hergenhan, *No Casual Traveller*, p. 85.
12 SMF to Randolph Bedford, 21/1/1937, FP vol. 29; SMF to Arthur Greening, 4/2/1933, Lothian Papers; ML MSS 6035/20, 22. Edward and Maggie Bridle were cousins of SF (see Appendix 2).
13 W. Blake to Blackwood, 20/12/1929, ML MSS 6329, attachment.
14 Blackwood to Miss Mills, 21/2/1933, and S. Mills to Blackwood, 26/5/1933, ML MSS 6329; SMF to Mary Fullerton, n.d., incompl. [1933], FP vol. 16.
15 *Propeller*, 6/1/1933, p. 5; *Propeller*, 16/6/1933, FP vol. 121A, repr. *A Gregarious Culture*.
16 *All About Books*, May 1933, p. 79; Fox, *Dream at a Graveside*, pp. 40–3; FAW membership receipt, 7/4/1933, FP vol. 25. Jean Devanny (1894–1962), NZ-born writer, was a member of the Communist Party 1930–49 (*ADB* vol. 8).
17 *All About Books*, 14/10/1933, repr. *A Gregarious Culture*; SMF to C. H. Grattan, 25/10/1933, FP vol. 23. Frank Dalby Davison (1893–1970) was a leading writer (*ADB* vol. 13).
18 Lesley Heath, 'Sydney Literary Societies of the Nineteen Twenties', PhD thesis, pp. 332–3, and Heidi Zogbaum, *Kisch in Australia: The Untold Story*, Scribe, Carlton North, Vic, 2004, pp. 94–5; SMF to Helene Scheu-Riesz, 20/8/1933, FP vol. 23, also Leonora Pease to SMF, 20/9/1933, FP vol. 13, and SMF to A. W. Roeder, 24/7/1933, FP vol. 20; SMF to C. H. Grattan, 25/12/1933, FP vol. 23;* *All About Books*, Feb. 1935, p. 32. Egon Kisch (1885–1948), *ADB* vol. 15. Tom Inglis Moore (1901–78) was a poet and academic who later pioneered the teaching of Australian literature at Canberra University College (*ADB* vol. 15).
19 SMF to Kate Baker, 7/5/1934, Kennedy Papers.
20 C. H. Grattan to SMF, 6/12/1932, FP vol. 23; preceding quotation, C. Hartley Grattan, 'The Australian Political See-Saw', *Current History*, Jan. 1933, p. 435.
21 Hancock, p. 59, cited A. T. Yarwood, *Attitudes to Non-European Immigration*, Cassell Australia, Melbourne, 1968, p. 114.
22 SMF to C. H. Grattan, 29/3/1933 and 21/6/1933, FP vol. 23.
23 C. H. Grattan to SMF, 27/4/[1933], FP vol. 23.* David Walker, *Anxious Nation: Australia and the Rise of Asia*, Univ. of Qld Press, St Lucia, Qld, 1999, p. 232, also ch. 8 (invasion narrative); Alison Broinowski, *The Yellow Lady: Australian Impressions of Asia*, Oxford Univ. Press, Melbourne, 1992, ch. 2.
24 C. H. Grattan to SMF, 13/4/1935, FP vol. 23.
25 Will Carter reported the ms. find in 'Australianities', *Daily Advertiser* (Wagga Wagga), 24/7/1933, FP vol. 121A.
26 Re Ted Graham, *see* Charles Graham to SF, 27/3/1928, FP vol. 49, and SF to Charles Graham, 9/4/1928, FP vol. 113; Barnard, p. 140. Deborah Jordan, *Nettie Palmer: Search for an Aesthetic*, History Dept, Univ. of Melbourne, 1999, p. 229. Annie Louisa Somerville, née Treherne (1863–1958) was a nurse (NSW BMD registers, electoral rolls). Nephew Jack: enrolled for secondary schooling at Blue Mountains Grammar School, from 1932 he spent his holidays at Grey St (SF Notebook, FP vol. 107, p. 30). Lena Lampe left Grey St in Jun. 1934, FP vol. 107, p. 39.
27 *All About Books*, 12/10/1933, p. 170 (Alice Henry at FAW).
28 Ken Cable, pers. comm., 15/5/1987. Kenneth John Cable (1929–2003), historian (*J. Royal Aust. Hist. Soc.*, 2003, vol. 89, no. 12).
29 Kirkby, *Alice Henry*, p. 216 (Alice Henry on SMF).
30 'Unusual Aboriginal Romance. William Hatfield's Novel about the Aruntas', *Book News*, Oct. 1933, p. 16; SMF to MEF, 22/1/1934, FP vol. 16. *Book News* was published in Sydney, Jun.–Oct. 1933, ed. R. J. D. McCallum; *All About Books* was published in Melbourne, 1928–38.
31 Mary Fullerton to SMF 10/8/1936, FP vol. 17 ('unprepared' for news and publication). SMF to Jean Hamilton, 6/12/1933, FP vol. 26.* Jean Hamilton's relations with Mabel Singleton seem to have been problematic by 1933.
32 SMF to Jean Hamilton, 14/2/[1934], FP vol. 26.
33 SMF to Mary Fullerton, 27/3/1934, FP vol. 16. Xavier Herbert (1901–84), *ADB* vol. 17.
34 Metta Lampe: see Appendix 2. Ad for Hotel Charleville, built 1932, with a SMF note, ML MSS 3659/2X, 221, and SMF to Mr McK—[?], FP vol. 46; Eva [Statham] to SMF 5/1/1949, FP vol. 26; *Atlas of [Queensland] Pastoral Holdings*, 2000, map 41, D6, and indexes to Lessees of Crown Lands; *Courier-Mail* (Brisbane) 10/5/1934, p. 20, *Pioneers on Parade*, pp. 248–53.
35 SMF to Dearest Ducks, 14/5/1934, FP vol. 25;* *Telegraph* (Brisbane), 10/5/1934, FP vol. 121A; Thomas Firmin McKinnon (1878–1953), *ADB* vol. 10.

36   SMF to Jean Hamilton, 15/5/1934, FP vol. 26.

37   SMF to Alice Henry, 12/5/1934, FP vol. 114.

38   SMF to Mary Fullerton, 15/6/1934 and 14/9/1934, FP vol. 16, both;* M. F., 'A Remorseless Novel: Review of *Prelude to Christopher* by Eleanor Dark', *Australian Mercury*, Aug. 1935, vol. 1, no. 2 (page proofs), repr. *A Gregarious Culture*. Dymock's Book Arcade, founded 1880, was run by John Malcolm Forsyth [sic] (1878–1963) in the 1930s (AustLit).

39   SMF to Jean Hamilton, Mary Fullerton, Mabel Singleton, 8/6/1934, FP vol. 26;* William Baylebridge (1883–1942), *ADB* vol. 7. Horatio Bottomley (1860–1933) was a British journalist, jingoist, and financial operator post-WWI (*ODNB*).

40   SMF to Mary Fullerton, 14/8/1934, FP vol. 16. Randolph Hughes (1899–1955), lecturer and literary critic (*ADB* vol. 14). *C. J. Brennan: An Essay in Values*, P. R. Stephensen & Co, 1934. Christopher Brennan (1870–1932), poet and scholar (*ADB* vol. 7). The Archibald fountain dates from Mar. 1932.

41   SMF to Mary Fullerton, 13/7/1934, FP vol. 16, SMF to Jean Hamilton, 11/6/1934, 28/9/1934, 28/2/1935, FP vol. 26 (rights). Edward Vivian (Vance) Palmer (1885–1959), *ADB* vol. 11. Gertrude Stein (1874–1946) was an American modernist writer and Walt Whitman (1819–1892) was an American poet (*Cambridge Encyclopedia*).

42   'Through Muddle to Half-death', *Bulletin*, 10/10/1934, pp. 2–5; Miller and Macartney, *Australian Literature*, p. 129; Patrick Buckridge, *The Scandalous Penton: A Biography of Brian Penton*, Univ. of Qld Press, St Lucia, Qld, 1994, pp. 154–60, also *ADB* vol. 15.

43   SMF to Rose Schneiderman, 13/11/1934, FP vol. 15, also SMF to C. A. Whelan, 15/8/1934, FP vol. 20, both.* Clarence Vivian Crockett (1893–1973) AustLit.

44   SMF to Mary Fullerton *et al.*, 19/11/1934, FP vol. 26, and SMF to Jean Hamilton, same date; A. Greening to SMF, 12/12/1933, Lothian Papers, and SMF to Nettie Palmer, Wednesday [mid-1933?], FP vol. 24; 'All That Swagger', ts. with note, 17/12/1935, ML MSS 6035/22; Wright [for Cape] to SMF, 31/12/1934, FP vol. 82. Rivett family entry *ADB* vol. 11.

45   Airmail services to the US began two years later, in 1937.

46   Guy Innes to SMF, 7/3/1935, FP vol. 24. Guy Innes (1879–1953) AustLit.

47   SMF to E. H. Burgmann, 28/3/1935, Burgmann Papers, NLA;* Harold Ickes to SMF, 21/9/1935, FP vol. 12, and SMF to MDR and RR, 16/12/1935, FP vol. 10.* Anna Ickes (1873–1935) was wife of Harold Ickes, US Sec. of Interior, 1933–46 (both *ANB*). Ernest Henry Burgmann (1885–1967), *ADB* vol. 13.

48   Main personal corres. is at FP vols 6–46, with family corres. in the following vols 47–50 and bound in files for each correspondent. Business corres. is bound separately.

49   'The Great Australian novel. Honouring Tom Collins. An appreciation', FP vol. 73; Re A. G. Stephens, part-published *DT* (Sydney), 20/4/1935, p. 5, c. to Kate Baker, 20/4/1935, also a memorial to 'A.G.S', *Australian Mercury*, Jul. 1935, vol. 1, no. 1 (page proofs); Patricia Rolfe, *The Journalistic Javelin*, Wildcat Press, Sydney, 1979. p. 277; SMF to Gus Lampe, 18/1/1935 [1936], FP vol. 49, and *SMH*, 20/1/1936, p. 10; 'Catherine Helen Spence. Australia's Greatest Woman', delivered Women's Club, Sept. 1936 (ML).

50   Kirkpatrick, *The Sea Coast of Bohemia: Literary Life in Sydney's Roaring Twenties*, Univ. of Qld Press, St Lucia, Qld, 1992; Geoffrey Dutton, *The Innovators: The Sydney Alternatives in the Rise of Modern Art, Literature, and Ideas*, Macmillan, South Melbourne, 1986; SMF to C. H. Grattan, 25/6/1935, FP vol. 23; Eileen Chanin *et al.*, *Degenerates and Perverts: The 1939* Herald *Exhibition of French and British Contemporary Art*, Miegunyah Press, Melbourne, 2005, p. 45; Miles Franklin, 'A Book of Lore', *Australian Mercury*, Aug. 1935, vol. 1, no. 2 (review of Gordon Buchanan, *Packhorse and Waterhole: With the First Overlanders to the Kimberleys*, page proofs); SMF, 'The Future of Australian Literature', *Age*, 2/3/1935, p 5.

51   FP vol. 76, item 3 (paras on censorship), and *SMH*, 12/4/1935, p. 6; 'Australian Women Who Write', *SMH*, 4/4/1935, p. 12; 'Novels of the Bush', *Australian Mercury*, Jul. 1935, pp. 51–4, repr. *A Gregarious Culture*; 'Authors' Ball', *SMH*, 15/4/1935, p. 4. The Writers' League, formed by Left-wing writers and FAW dissidents in early 1935 with Katharine Susannah Prichard president and Jean Devanny secretary, was aligned with the Writers' International and thus the Comintern, Julie Wells, 'The Writers' League: A Study in Literary and Working-class Politics', *Meanjin*, 1987, no. 4, and Throssell, *Wild Weeds and Wind Flowers*, p. 255, n. 55.

52   SMF to the Governor of NSW, 27/5/1929, FP vol. 29 (George V's Silver Jubilee fell 6 May 1935 and was celebrated throughout the empire; he died Jan. 1936). Metta Lampe to SMF, n.d, FP vol. 49; SMF, 'Notes for a talk to the Junior Literary Society, Sydney', n.d. [23/4/1935], ML MSS 445/37; Miles Franklin, 'The Future of Australian Literature', FP vol. 59; *Age*, 2/3/1935, p. 5; [W. E. Fitz Henry] to SMF, 17/7/1936, FP vol. 25.

53   Sally Warhaft (ed.), *Well May We Say ... The Speeches that Made Australia*, Black Inc., Melbourne, 2004; Arrow, *Upstaged*, p. 102; SMF to Nettie Palmer, 13/4/1935 [possibly 13/9/1935], FP vol. 24, part ;* SMF to Mary Fullerton, 5/2/1935, FP vol. 17. Broadcasting in Sydney dates from the 1920s, but the ABC did not begin until 1932.

54   Some scripts are at FP vol. 121A; part text school broadcast, FP vol. 76. SMF, 'Jane Addams of Hull House', *Catholic Women's Review*, Aug. 1935.

55   *Australian Woman's Sphere*, 15/4/1904, p. 429, and Joseph Furphy to William Cathels, 11/4/1904, cited Barnes, *The Order of Things*, p. 342 (SMF's voice); Jenn Lane, pers. comm., Sept. 2003, and SMF to Maggie Bridle, 27/11/[1935], FP vol. 47; literary fragment, FP vol. 445/39, p. 475. Sound recordings of distinguished Australians file, Box 38, NLA Archives (corres. only, 1938). Special note: recent research suggests that by the 1930s, after so many years away, Miles' accent may have evolved to something like the now largely superceded imperial status marker 'Cultivated Australian' (see Bruce Moore, in ANU E-Press, *Talking and Listening in the Age of Modernity*, eds J. Damousi and D. Deacon, Canberra, 2008, pp. 101, 107–8), but it may also be that her accent included traces of American as well as English influences.

56   SMF to Jean Hamilton, 6/11/1935, and 3/12/1935, FP vol. 26. See ML MSS 6035/22 for a ms. of *All That Swagger* dated 1935.

57   LN, FP vol. 3, 1935, repr. *Diaries*, pp. 22–4; SMF to Jean Hamilton, 14/1/1935, FP vol. 26. Charles Edward Chauvel (1897–1969) was a pioneer film-maker (*ADB* vol 7).

58   SMF to John Varney, 28/12/1935, FP vol. 15.

59   SMF to Nettie Palmer, 13/4?/1935, FP vol. 24; Patrick Buckridge, *The Scandalous Penton: A Biography of Brian Penton*, Univ. of Qld Press, St Lucia, Qld, 1994, p. 170; SMF to C. H. Grattan, 25/6/1935, FP vol. 23; SMF, 'The Future of Australian Literature', *Age*, 2/3/1935, p. 5, also 'Australians Do Not Exist', *Bulletin*, 29/9/1937, p. 2, repr. *A Gregarious Culture*: 'The Foundations of Culture in Australia: An Essay Towards National Self-respect', was published by W. J. Miles, Roseville, NSW, price two shillings. George Herbert Cowling (1881–1946) was professor of English at the Univ. of Melbourne 1926–43 (*OCAL*).

60   SMF to RR and MDR, 16/12/1935, FP vol. 10.*

61   SMF to Mary Fullerton, 11/4/1936, FP vol. 17; 'A Woman's Letter', *Bulletin*, 5/8/1936, p. 4. Dymphna Cusack (1902–81), b. West Wyalong, NSW, graduated Univ. Sydney and taught until 1944, was a prolific and successful writer in several genres. The Prior Prize was established by the *Bulletin* in honour of Samuel Henry Prior (1869–1933), *Bulletin* editor 1914–33, awarded annually 'for a work of literature' (*ADB* vol. 11). Kylie Tennant (1912–88) was a successful and esteemed writer (*OCAL*).

62   Herbert Basedow (1891–1933), anthropologist (*ADB* vol. 7); SMF to Alice Thacher Post, 23/1/1936, FP vol. 27;* Desley Deacon, *Elsie Clews Parson: Inventing Modern Life*, Chicago Univ. Press, Chicago, 1997, ch. 11. On *Capricornia*, see LN, Jan. 1935, FP vol. 3, repr. *Diaries*, pp. 13–15.

63   *My Career Goes Bung*, ts., 1935–6, ML MSS 6035/24; SMF to Elsie Belle Champion, 31/1/1936, FP vol. 8, and SMF to Alice Henry, 11/3/36, FP vol. 11, both.*

64   SMF to Edward & Maggie Bridle, 4/2/1936, FP vol. 47; *Penny Post*, 28/2/1936, p. 4; SMF to Dolly Baxter, 19/5/1936, FP vol. 27.

65   SMF to Edward Bridle, 7/6/1936, FP vol. 47; PD, 19/3/1936.

66   SMF to Freda Barrymore, 23/5/1936 and 13/6/1936, Freda Barrymore to SMF, 29/5/1936, FP vol. 27; *Bulletin*, 24/6/1936, p. 35.

67   FP vol. 4, pp. 78f., repr. *Diaries*; SMF to Barber & McKeogh, New York, 22/6/1936, FP vol. 90.

68   *Bulletin*, 17/6/1936, 'Red Page', and 24/6/1936, p. 9; *Newspaper News*, 1/8/1936 (FP vol. 121A).

69   *Bulletin*, 22/7/1936, p. 9; *Diaries*, pp. 47– 51 consolidates her reactions; *All That Swagger* corres., FP vol. 82. Thomas Davies Mutch (1885–1958), politician and historian, was editor of the *Bulletin*'s 'Red Page' 1936–7 (*ADB* vol. 10); Cecil Mann (1896–1967), journalist, was a prev. editor of the 'Red Page' (*OCAL*); William Stewart Howard (1903–83), was a Sydney journalist and publicist (*ADB* vol. 17).

70 *Bulletin*, 29/7/1936, p. 2, and 19/8/1936, p. 2; SMF to Freda Barrymore, 18/7/1936, FP vol. 27; the various mss and tss, FP vol. 82 and ML MSS 6035/20–2.

71 Telegram, 22/7/1936, FP vol. 28;* G. and S. Vallance to SMF, 23/7/1936, FP vol. 50; Mary Fullerton to SMF, 10/8/1936, FP vol. 17.

72 *Bulletin*, 29/7/1936, 'Red Page'.

73 *Bulletin*, 26/8/1936, 'Red Page' (Mann); Denton Prout, 'These Australian Writers', 21/10/1936, reply to SMF, 'Our Crowded Canvases', *Bulletin*, 7/10/1936, both repr. *A Gregarious Culture*; *Penny Post*, 14/9/1936, FP vol. 121A; E. V. Barton to SMF, 28/10/1936, FP vol. 28. 'Denton Prout', pseud. Charles Walter Phillips (1910–91), public servant, author of *Henry Lawson: The Grey Dreamer*, Rigby, Adelaide, 1963 and Angus & Robertson, London, 1963 (*OCAL*).

74 *Truth*, 13/12/1936 (FP vol. 121A); HHR, *Letters*, vol. 2, 10/2/1937 and 19/4/1937; Alice Henry to Mary Anderson, 27/8/1936, Mary Anderson Papers; Lucy Spence Morice to SMF, 22/7/1936, and SMF to Lucy Spence Morice, 10/8/1936, FP vol. 22;* *Shorter Oxford English Dictionary* and *Australian National Dictionary*.

75 *Bulletin*, 30/12/1936, p. 9; *All That Swagger*, Sydney, 1936, pp. 494, 500.

76 Mary Gilmore to SMF, 15/10/1936, *Letters of Mary Gilmore*, eds W. H. Wilde and T. Inglis Moore, Melbourne Univ. Press, Carlton, Vic, 1980, pp. 127–8.

77 SMF to HHR, 9/9/1936, FP vol. 25.*

78 Ambrose Pratt to SMF, 29/6/1936, 9/7/1936, FP vol. 27; SMF to Guy Innes, 18/8/1936, FP vol. 24. Ambrose Pratt (1874–1944), b. Forbes, NSW, was a writer and businessman (*ADB* vol. 11).

79 FP vol. 56A (galleys); SMF to Snelling [printer], FP vol. 82; 'Australian Author will Autograph', FP vol. 121A, cuttings, n.d., and *Diaries*, p. 59, n. 55; M. E. West to SMF, 21/7/1936, FP vol. 9 (annotation); 'I am Demmy Blake', 445/41/2, and SMF to W. Stafford, 21/11/1936, FP vol. 20; SMF to Cpt Peters, Melbourne, 1/11/36 and 13/11/1936, FP vol. 82; 'A Mixed Grill', *Bulletin*, 18/11/1936, p. 40; SMF to Mary Fullerton, 18/12/[1936], FP vol. 119; SMF to Hilary Lofting, 29/12/1936, FP vol. 28; SMF to Edward Bridle, 4/12/1936, FP vol. 47. Note: all reviews cited as from the press cuttings (unpaginated) assembled by SMF, FP vol. 121A.

80 SMF to Innes Rose, 15/9/1936, Innes Rose to SMF, 7/10/1937 and 27/5/1937, FP vol. 82.

81 *Age*, 29/12/1936, and 'Australian Books Boom. 1936 Best Sellers', *DT* (Sydney), 3/12/1936, FP vol. 121A. Ion Idriess (1889–1979) had published seven books and Frederick Joseph Thwaites (1908–1979) nine books by 1936 (*ADB* vols 9 and 12, Miller and Macartney, *Australian Literature*).

82 *Advertiser*, 16/1/1937, FP vol. 121A; [H. K. Prior] to SMF, 5/3/1937, FP vol. 82, and royalty statements, *Bulletin* and Angus & Robertson, FP vol. 82.

83 Undated cutting, FP vol. 121A; 'Miles Franklin's Triumph', *SMH*, 24/12/1936, FP vol. 121A.

84 SMF to Vida Goldstein *et al.*, 4/11/1936, FP vol. 10.*

85 *North Queensland Register*, 2/1/1937, FP vol. 121

86 *A Southern Churchman*, 1/2/1937, FP vol. 121A; SMF to Nell Malone, 22/4/1936, FP vol. 15.

87 John McKellar, 'The Miles Franklin Country', *Age*, 6/3/1937, p. 6; 'Lovable Pioneers', *Australian Women's Weekly*, 26/12/1936, FP vol. 121A. John McKellar (1881–1966) was a Scottish-born journalist and writer in Melbourne, associated with the Jindyworobak movement (*OCAL*).

88 Doecke, 'How to Read Pioneer Sagas: Miles Franklin's *All that Swagger*', *Westerly*, Autumn 1998.

89 *All That Swagger*, 1936 edn, ch. XLVI and pp. 446–7; SMF to MDR, 6/5/1929, MDR Papers;* SMF, Notebook, 1935–52, ML MSS 1360, p. 22; see also 'Debunk Anzac', FP vol. 39, p. 487.

90 ML MSS 6035/31 (1927/1937 version of *My Career Goes Bung*); William Blake to Blackwood, 4/9/1936, 'BBB and WB' to Blackwood, 5/10/1937, and Blackwood to Mary Fullerton, 24/11/1937, ML 6329.

91 Marjorie Barnard to Nettie Palmer, 4/8/1936, MA, and Marjorie Barnard to Nettie Palmer, Palmer Papers; Sydney Literary Society, plays program, FP vol. 122, pp. 1–4, and Sydney Literary Society to SMF, 22/10/1936 (thanks); SMF to Guy Innes [4/9/1936], FP vol. 24; SMF's talk on Spence is at FP vol. 64, see also Edith Hubbe, 25/8/1936, FP vol. 64; SMF to Lucy Spence Morice, 13/10/1936, FP vol. 22. George Ernest Bartlett Adamson (1884–1951) was a journalist (*ADB* vol. 13).

92 Marjorie Barnard to SMF, 25/11/1936, FP vol. 32 (committee invitation); SMF to Ambrose Pratt, 2/5/1936, FP vol. 27. Ida Emily Leeson (1885–1964) was Mitchell Librarian 1932–46,

and is first mentioned PD 1935 (Martin, *Ida Leeson*, p. 113, also *ADB* vol. 10). Dora Wilcox (1873–1953), a poet and playwright, was wife of William Moore, art historian (*ADB* vol. 10).

93 SMF to Kate Baker, 25/4/1936 and 9/9/1936, Baker Papers.

94 Ambrose Pratt to SMF, 9/7/1936, SMF to Ambrose Pratt, 21/7/1936, FP vol. 27, Ambrose Pratt to SMF, 6/8/1936, FP vol. 28; SMF to Freda Barrymore, 11/7/1936, FP vol. 27; SMF to M. McDonald, 20/7/1936, FP vol. 28 (deaths); SMF to Ivy Vernon, 11/11/[1936], FP vol. 50; Heilbrun, *Writing a Woman's Life*, ch. 5. For Ivy Beatrice Vernon see Appendix 2.

95 SMF to Alice Henry, 11/3/[1936], FP vol. 11.*

96 Arrow, *Upstaged*, pp. 162–3; SMF to Guy Innes, [1936], FP vol. 24; SMF to HHR, 9/9/1936, FP vol. 25;* SMF to Nettie Palmer, 31/12/[1936], FP vol. 24,* and Vance Palmer to SMF, 24/12/1936, FP vol. 26.

97 SMF to Kathleen Monypenny, 30/12/1936, FP vol. 22; SMF to Mab Maynard and Frieda Maynard, 8/6/1936, FP vol. 27. William John Miles (1871–1942), 'a man with dangerous obsessions and money to spend', was father of Sydney Bohemian Bea Miles (both *ADB* vol. 10). Kathleen Monypenny (1894–1971), Marjorie Barnard, obit., *Australian Author*, 4/2/1972 (unpaginated).

98 The following account of Grattan's second visit to Australia is a résumé from Roe, '"Tremenjus Good"'; FP vol. 23 has additional letters.

99 Hergenhan, *No Casual Traveller*, p. 162 ('British curtain'); SMF to W. Baylebridge, 18/9/1936, FP vol. 27.

100 *SMH*, 24/12/1936, p. 15.

101 SMF to C. H. Grattan, Monday, Grattan Papers. Hergenhan, *No Casual Traveller*, ch. 6, has a comprehensive account of Grattan's presentations.

102 C. H. Grattan to SMF, 8/5/1938 and 17/4/1938, FP vol. 23; C. Hartley Grattan, 'Tom Collins's "Such is Life"', *Australian Quarterly*, Sept. 1937, p. 67ff.; *New York Times Book Review*, 15/8/1937, pp. 8, 20, cited Munro, *Wild Man of Letters*, p. 189 ('deeply offensive'). New editions of *Jonah* and *Such is Life* finally appeared in 1945 and 1948 respectively.

103 SMF to Edward Bridle, 4/12/1936, FP vol. 47, and SMF to Mollye Menken, 12/1/1937, FP vol. 29;* 'The little prince', ML 445/22.

104 Dan Clyne, Hansard, 3/12/1936, p. 996; *Diaries*, p. 21 (20/12/1935).

105 SMF to Dr Young, 1/1/1937, FP vol. 20. The Pischel party consisted of Emma, 'Mrs Pischel, snr' (apparently her sister-in-law Mrs William Pischel, not Emma's mother, Julia, who died in 1936), Mrs William Pischel's daughter-in-law, and Emma's niece by marriage Hildegarde (Mrs Frederick E. Pischel), of Salt Lake City.

106 SMF to Emma Pischel, 22/1/1937, FP vol. 15.* Muriel Heagney (1885–1974) was a trade-unionist and equal pay advocate (*ADB* vol. 9). Margaret Mitchell (1900–49) wrote *Gone With the Wind* (1936) (*ANB*).

107 'Writers Criticise Censorship', *SMH*, 11/1/1937, p. 8; SMF to Alice Henry, 5/2/1937, FP vol. 11.* 'Pakie': Augusta Macdougall (1875–1945), *ADB* vol. 15. Frank Clune (1893–1971) was an accountant and writer (*ADB* vol. 13).

108 SMF, *Bulletin*, 3/3/1937, p. 2 (Griffin died 11/2/1937); *Best Australian One-Act Plays*, eds W. Moore and T. I. Moore, Angus & Robertson, Sydney, 1937, and ML MSS 6035/2, also reviews, *SMH*, 28/8/1937, p. 12, and *Bulletin* 15/9/1937, p. 2; *SMH*, 20/2/1937, p. 10, and SMF to Mary Fullerton, 23/2/1937, FP vol. 17; *Propeller*, 1/4/1937, p. 8. Camden Risby Morrisby (c.1893–1973), clerk and literary commentator, was an occasional broadcaster on radio 2SM (*ADB* file, various Franklin sources).

109 *Such is Life*, Cape, London, 1937; SMF, 'Such is Colonialism', *Bulletin*, 26/5/1937, p. 8, repr. *A Gregarious Culture*; SMF to Kate Baker, 3/5/1937 and 11/5/1937,* Baker Papers. For Vance Palmer's gentlemanly reply, see *Bulletin*, 30/6/1937, p. 8, which reveals that he consulted Edward Garnett (see ch. 3).

110 'Discovery of a Poet', *Australian National Review*, Jun. 1937; 'Such is life … edited by Vance Palmer', *Australian National Review*, Sept. 1937; Munro, *Wild Man of Letters*, p. 175; C. H. Grattan to SMF, 11/7/1937, FP vol. 23,* and C. Hartley Grattan, 'Tom Collins's 'Such is Life"', *Australian Quarterly*, Sept. 1937.

111 *Diaries*, pp. 67–73, has her account.

112 SMF to Freda Barrymore, 21/11/1936, FP vol. 27; Clune, quoted *ADB* vol. 13. *Try Anything Once* was published in 1933.

113 Paul Wenz (1869–1939) grazier (*ADB* vol. 12), wrote *Diary of a New Chum and Other Lost Stories* (1908, repr. Collins/Angus & Robertson, N. Ryde, 1990, preface by Frank Moorhouse).

114 SMF to Carrie Whelan, 22/7/1937, FP vol. 20.*

115 'Writer's Interesting Tour', *Argus*, 7/7/1937, p. 17; Maud Walsöe to SMF, 10/1/1938, FP vol. 29.

116 *Advertiser*, 24/6/1937, Melbourne *Herald*, 6/7/1937, cuttings, FP vol. 121A (no pagination).

117 FP, ML PX *D250/3; 'The Moving Camera Clicks. From Kosciusko to the Sea, by Frank Clune', *Sydney Mail*, 3/8/1938–7/9/1938; *Sunday Advertiser*, 24/6/1937, p. 8.

118 *Diaries*, pp. 73–8 has a substantial excerpt. 'Jim Grahame': James William Gordon (1874–1949), ML MSS 1085 and FP vol. 29, was a contributor of bush verse to the *Bulletin* (*OCAL*).

119 *Diaries*, p. 82; *Sunday Sun and Guardian*, 8/8/1937, cuttings FP vol. 121A; SMF to Guy Innes, 17/8/1937, FP vol. 24 (coo-ee); *Advertiser*, 29/6/1937 ('We interview two world roamers'), and SMF to SF, 30/6/1937, FP vol. 108; SMF to Lucy Spence Morice, 31/8/1937, FP vol. 22,* and Ida Leeson to SMF, 13/10/1938, FP vol. 29. Bob Buck (1881–1960) worked in central and northern Australia from 1905 (*ADB* vol. 7). *Eucalyptus* by Murray Bail was published in 1998.

120 'Catherine Helen Spence', FP vol. 64; SMF, 'Rose Scott. Some Aspects of her Personality and Work', *The Peaceful Army: A Memorial to the Pioneer Women of Australia 1788–1938*, ed. Flora Eldershaw, n.p., Sydney, 1938; Allen, *Rose Scott*, ch. 8. The second revision of *Cockatoos* was typed 17/8/1937–21/9/1937 (Roderick, Guard Book 6, Roderick Papers, pp. 38–9).

121 SMF to Mary Fullerton, 4/8/1937, FP vol. 17; SMF, 'Can an objective moral standard be set up in the present age?', FP vol. 60.

122 SMF to MDR, 14/4/1937, MDR Papers; SMF to S. B. Hooper, 22/10/1937, FP vol. 29; SMF to F. G. Hamilton, 9/9/1937, FP vol. 23. Sydney Benjamin Hooper (c.1869–1959) was a manager, George St branch, Union Bank, and lived at Palm Beach (*Bulletin*, 9/9/1959). Miles' German cousin is unnamed.

123 Roe, '"Tremenjus Good"'; Mary Fullerton to SMF, 14/2/1937, FP vol. 17, and Lucy Spence Morice to SMF, 3/8/1937, FP vol. 22; SMF to Mary Fullerton, 5/8/1937, FP vol. 17; 'Can an objective moral standard be set up in the present age?', FP vol. 60.

124 Munro, *Wild Man of Letters*, p. 175. *Letters of Mary Gilmore*, eds W. H. Wilde and T. Inglis Moore, Melbourne Univ. Press, Carlton, Vic, 1980, pp. 136–9, 185, and 'Poetry: And An Australian Poet', *Australian National Review*, Feb. 1938. When Emily Dickinson (1830–86) (*ANB*), died only seven of c.2000 of her preserved poems were published, and important evidence of her emotional life remained unexamined for over a century, see *Open Me Carefully. Emily Dickinson's Intimate Letters to Susan Huntington Dickinson*, eds Ellen Louise Hart and Martha Nell Smith, Parish Press, Ashfield, Mass., 1998. SMF to Mary Fullerton, n.d. [Sept. 1934?], FP vol. 16, p. 545 ('dePalmerized'). *Troy Town* was published in 1888.

125 David Walker, 'The Palmer Abridgement of *Such is Life*', ALS, 1978, vol. 8, no. 4; C. H. Grattan to SMF, 11/7/1937, FP vol. 23;* Mary Fullerton to SMF, Feb. the end [1938?], FP vol. 17.

126 Mary Fullerton to SMF, 17/5/1937, FP vol. 17; Jill Roe, 'The Magical World of Marion Mahony Griffin: Castlecrag in the Interwar Years', *Minorities: Cultural Diversity in Sydney*, eds Shirley Fitzgerald and Garry Wotherspoon, State Library of NSW Press, in association with the Sydney History Group, Sydney, 1995.

127 *SMH*, 2/2/1938, p. 8, and 4/2/1938, p. 4; Dymphna Cusack, 'My Friendship with Miles Franklin', *Ink*, no. 2, 50th anniversary issue of the Society of Women Writers, Sydney, 1977, p. 111; 'Witty Collaboration by Telephone', *SMH* (Women's Supp.), 3/7/1939, (by Florence James, repr. North, *Yarn Spinners*). (Baron) John Wakehurst (1895–1970), *ADB* vol. 16. (Baron) Alexander Gowrie (1872–1955), *ADB* vol. 9.

128 *Diaries*, p. 97.

129 SMF to Mary Fullerton, 9/3/[1938], FP vol. 115; *Diaries*, pp. 98–9; *Australians. 1938*, eds Bill Gammage and Peter Spearritt, Fairfax, Syme and Weldon, Sydney, 1988, s. 1.

130 Marulan property: possibly 'Glenrock' (Caroline Simpson in *Historic Homesteads of Australia*, Cassell Australia, Stanmore, NSW, 1976; St John Ervine to SMF, 23/8/1939, FP vol. 14, and press clippings repr. North, *Yarn Spinners*, pp. 56–8).

131 Re 'Iron Pots and Silver Churns': 'Silver Churn', from the Maidens' chorus, *Patience*, Gilbert & Sullivan; prize entry, *Bulletin*, 22/6/1938, p. 8 (pen-name 'X Legge').

132 Cusack, 'My friendship'; SMF to Nettie Palmer, 16/5/1938, Palmer Papers. The first chair of Australian Literature was established at the Univ. of Sydney in 1962.

133 SMF, 'Pioneering', 1938, FP vol. 64; Blackwood to SMF, 24/11/1937, FP vol. 85; SMF to Xavier Herbert, 8/3/1938, FP vol. 28,* and review of *Capricornia, Australian National Review*, repr. *A Gregarious Culture*; SMF, 'Lecturers in Literature', *Bulletin*, 5/1/1937, p. 2; SMF to Blackwood 13/3/1938, postscript re 'Capricornia', ML MSS 6329. H. M. Green (1881–1962) published the magisterial *History of Australian Literature* in 1961 (2 vols) (*ADB* vol. 14).

134 *Queanbeyan Age*, 7/6/1938, p. 7, obit. for Aunt Annie; *Propeller*, 16/6/1938, p. 3 death of Miss Gillespie. No obit. for SF has been located to date; probably Miles was too upset to write one.

135 Alice Henry to SMF, 3/7/1938, FP vol. 11, Mary Fullerton to SMF, 30/8/1938, FP vol. 7,* and SMF to Alice Henry, 11/10/1938, FP vol. 11; SMF to Mrs Grattan, 21/7/1938, Grattan Papers, Harry Ransom Colln, Univ. of Texas at Austin.

136 SMF to Nettie Palmer, 21/7/1938, Palmer Papers.*

137 SMF to Kate Baker, 27/10/1938, Baker Papers.*

138 Alice Henry to SMF, 3/7/[1938], FP vol. 11.*

139 SMF to Alice Henry, 11/10/1938.*

140 Harley Matthews review: *Reveille*, Dec. 1938, p. 20. Broadcasts in 1938: 'My Life and My Books', FP vol. 76 (school broadcast 21/3/1938, part text); invited to broadcast on prominent people she has met, Sept. 1938, FP vol. 92; 'Australian literature and its place in social reform', 6/12/1938, FP vol. 77/2. Pescott review, *Australian National Review*, Jul. 1937, p. 78. Re Baker, SMF to Kate Baker, 27/10/1938, Baker Papers,* and 3/11/1938, 22/11/1938, 1/12/1938; Kate Baker to SMF, 1/11/1937, FP vol. 9A. Harley Matthews (1889–1968) served at Gallipoli and became a freelance journalist, later a vigneron (*ADB* vol. 10); Edward Pescott (1872–1954) was a teacher and botanist (AustLit).

141 SMF to Alice Henry, 10/12/1938, FP vol. 115; SMF to Kate Baker, 15/11/1938, Baker Papers.

142 SMF to Leonora Pease, 12/3/1938, FP vol. 13.* Pease spent a year in Paris after Vienna, returning to the US via Holland in 1940, and was last heard from in New York City (Leonora Pease to SMF, 3/7/1940, 15/1/1950, FP vol. 13).

Chapter 12 — Maintaining Our Best Traditions: 1939–1945

1 SMF to Phil and May Meggitt (UK), 6/7/1940, FP vol. 34.*

2 *SMH*, 2/9/1939, p. 9 (amusements); SMF to H. N. Smith, 4/10/1939, FP vol. 29 ('same old war'); SMF to Ian Mudie, 21/4/1942, FP vol. 36.* Louis Esson (1879–1943) was a dramatist (*ADB* vol. 8). West Australian-born Leslie Rees (1905–2000) was drama editor for the ABC from the late 1930s–66 (*OCAL*).

3 SMF to Mabel Singleton *et al*., [7/4/1939], FP vol. 25.* *Three Guineas* was published in 1938.

4 *Chronicle of the Twentieth Century*, 1939; SMF to Mary Fullerton *et al*., 'St Valentine's Day', 1939, FP vol. 17. Stanley Melbourne Bruce (1883–1967), *ADB* vol. 7.

5 Kate Baker to Victor Kennedy, 14/6/1939, quoted Roy Duncan, 'Kate Baker: "Standard-bearer"', *ALS*, May 1980, p. 384; De Berg interview, 1977; Barnes, *Joseph Furphy*, p. x.

6 Annie Stewart's letters and Miles' replies Jan.–Mar. 1939 are at FP vol. 31, also corres. with Furphy's son, Sam, and his wife, Mattie. Re the first incident, see Joseph Furphy to Annie Stewart, 13/5/1888 and 25/7/1888, ML MSS 3659/1, encl. 188.

7 *Joseph Furphy: The Legend of a Man and his Book*, Angus & Robertson, Sydney, 1944, pp. 141 (re SMF), 116 (loneliness), 127 (assessments); Elizabeth Webby, 'The Bush Hamlet', *TLS*, 28/6/2002, p. 27. *Ulysses* was first published in 1920.

8 S. B. Hooper to SMF, 28/5/1938, FP vol. 29; SMF to H. S. Temby, 26/5/1939, Mackaness Papers; SMF to Kate Baker, 14/6/1939, Baker Papers; 'Who Was Joseph Furphy? Biographical Essay. Something of a Man's Life and Legend as Gathered from his Literary Work, his Letters and the Memory of his Friends', ts., [1939] ML MSS 6035/26.

9 *Bulletin*, 23/8/1939, p. 2 (awards and judges, *viz*. F. D. Davison, H. M. Green and Louis Esson), also 30/8/1939, p. 37 ('Melbourne chatter', highlighting Kate Baker); SMF to Kate Baker, Monday night [Jun. 1939], Baker Papers; SMF to Kate Baker, 16/8/1939, FP vol. 9A. SMF to Mary Fullerton, 3/9/1939, repr. *Diaries*, pp. 123–6, is the best account. Malcolm Henry Ellis (1890–1969), *Bulletin* journalist and historian, published *Lachlan Macquarie* in 1947 (*ADB* vol. 14).

10 M. H. Ellis to SMF, 25/8/1939, FP vol. 32; SMF to Jean Devanny, 30/8/1939, FP vol. 32;* SMF to Kate Baker, 16/8/1939, FP vol. 9A; SMF to Mary Fullerton, 20/9/1939, FP vol. 17.

11 SMF to Kate Baker, 27/8/1939 and 30/8/1939, Baker Papers; *Age*, 10/5/1940, p. 8.

12 *Bulletin*, 6/12/1939, p. 4; SMF to Kate Baker, 6/9/1939, Baker Papers.* The other winners were Frank Dalby Davison, Xavier Herbert, Ernestine Hill, Marjorie Clark; Nancy Keesing, *SMH*, 16/8/1981, p. 12 (corrective reply to Colin Roderick, 'Author Would Have Scorned Handouts', *SMH*, 8/5/1981, p. 6).

13 *Joseph Furphy*, p. 183.

14 SMF to R. G. Menzies, 5/7/1939,* and R. G. Menzies to SMF, 10/7/1939, FP vol. 32.* Robert Gordon Menzies (1894–1978), founder of the Liberal Party and Prime Minister of Australia 1950–66, first served as prime minister 26/4/1939–29/8/1941 (*ADB* vol. 15).

15 *Bulletin*, 19/7/1939, p. 2; M. Barnard Eldershaw to SMF, 6/7/1939, FP vol. 32; Henrietta Drake-Brockman to SMF, 20/7/1939, and to W. G. Cousins, 20/8/[1939], ML MSS 3269 (Corres. files), vol. 156, pp. 339–41, and 22/2/[1940], FP vol. 33;* Frank Clune to W. G. Cousins, 22/7/1939, ML MSS 3659/1; SMF to Vance Palmer, 24/7/1939, Palmer Papers; SMF to Alice Henry, 6/8/[1939], FP vol. 115, and SMF to Mary Fullerton, 9/8/1939, FP vol. 119* (re press responses); St John Ervine to SMF, 23/8/1939, FP vol. 14.* Henrietta Drake-Brockman (1901–68) was a West Australian writer whose husband was an engineer and army officer (*ADB* vol. 14). Walter G. Cousins (1886–1949) was director of publishing and chairman of directors, Angus & Robertson 1933–49, Australian Booksellers Association, *Book*, 19[??] (ML).

16 William Miller/Linklater (1867–1959), bushwhacker and writer (*Northern Territory Dictionary of Biography*); SMF to Mary Fullerton, 9/8/1939, FP vol. 119.*

17 Tom Inglis Moore to SMF, 15/7/1940, FP vol. 29;* Miles Franklin, '"E". The Full Story', *Bulletin*, 15/5/1946, 'Red Page'; Martin, *Passionate Friends*, pp. 151–2, 164. 'E': Mary Fullerton's second name was Eliza.

18 SMF to C. H. Grattan, 18/3/1940, FP vol. 23, and PD, 20/11/1940 (the waratah cup); Lulu Shorter, *Heritage*, ed. Joan Kerr, Art and Australia, E. Roseville, NSW, 1995; SMF to Mabel Singleton *et al.*, [7/4/1939], FP vol. 25,* and David Marr, *Patrick White: A Life*, Random House, Milsons Point, NSW, 1991, p. 180. The waratah is the state flower of NSW. Michael Sawtell (1883–1971) was a bushman and Emersonian (*ADB* S); Richard Baker (1854–1941), *ADB* vol. 7; Lulu Shorter (1887–1989), *ADB* vol. 18, forthcoming. Patrick White (1912–1990) was living in England in the 1930s (*OCAL*).

19 Norman Franklin was appointed to a permanent position as a Milk Board supervisor 5/1/1932 (NSW Government *Gazette*).

20 PD, 1/1/1940, and *Diaries*, pp. 127–8.

21 FP vol. 5/9, p. 481 (Miscellaneous notes, 19—); SMF to Frank Clune, Monday night [after 31/10/1936], FP vol. 28.

22 The shops were at 327–29 Penshurst Rd, Willoughby. Mary Fullerton to SMF, 18/1/1940, FP vol, 17. *Mein Kampf* was published in 1925.

23 Paul R. Bartrop, *Australia and the Holocaust 1933–45*, Australian Scholarly Publishing, Melbourne, 1994, p. 199; SMF to R. G. Menzies, 30/1/1940, FP vol. 32; SMF to Mary Fullerton 18/1/1940, FP vol. 17. Desmond Fitzgerald (c.1888–1947), republican and statesman, was elected a Sinn Fein MP in 1918 (*ODNB*).

24 S. B. Hooper to SMF, 19/1/1940, SMF to S. B. Hooper, 22/1/1940, S. B. Hooper to SMF, 7/2/1940 and thereafter, FP vol. 29; S. B. Hooper to Blackwood, 13/5/1940 and Blackwood to S. B. Hooper, 4/6/1940, ML MSS 6329; SMF to S. B. Hooper 14/12/1938 and n.d., Hooper file, ML MSS 330; SMF to Mary Fullerton 1/2/1940, FP vol. 17. Catts: probably J. H. Catts (1877–1951), a unionist and politician who established a successful printing and publishing agency in Sydney, (*ADB* vol. 7).

25 Mackaness–SMF corres., FP vol. 25; SMF to Mary Fullerton, 1/2/1940 and 14/12/1940, FP vol. 17; SMF to Mary Fullerton, 21/11/1940, FP vol. 17* (in part), and H. M. Green to SMF, 13/12/1940, FP vol. 35.

26 R. G. Howarth to SMF, 8/1/1940, FP vol. 33; SMF, [untitled review] and 'Australian Literature', *Southerly*, Nov. 1940, vol. 1, no. 4, pp. 40–2 and Jul. 1941, vol. 2, no. 2, pp. 23–6; *Union Recorder*, May 1941, vol. 21, no 8, p. 69 (SMF's speech); SMF to Mary Fullerton, 21/11/1940, FP vol. 17.* The English Association is affiliated to the parent body in London and was known

as The Australian English Association (founded 1923) until 1944, when it became the English Association (Sydney branch) (*OCAL*). Miles always referred to it as the 'Eng. Ass.'. Robert Guy Howarth (1906–74) became professor of English, Univ. of Cape Town 1955–71 (*ADB* vol. 14).

27 SMF to Mary Fullerton, 1/2/1940, FP vol. 17. John Frith (1906–2000), *SMH*, 12/10/2000 (obit.).

28 SMF to Kate Baker, 9/1/1940, FP vol. 9A; Kate Baker to CLF, 16/12/1940, NAA A 463, 1968/4278; SMF to Temby, 10/1/1940, Mackaness Papers; SMF to Temby, 7/11/1950, NAA A 463, 1968/4278; E. E. Pescott, 2/1/1940, ML MSS 3659/1. Henry Stanley Temby (1890–c.1965) was appointed secretary to the CLF in 1938 (NSW BMD, CLF records).

29 SMF to Temby, 20/2/1940, NAA A463/44.

30 SMF to J. K. Moir, 12/9/1940, J. K. Moir Colln; J. K. Moir to SMF, 20/9/1940, FP vol. 34. SMF to Dymphna Cusack, 12/3/1940, Cusack Papers. John Kinmont Moir (1893–1958) was a bibliophile and literary patron (*ADB* vol. 15). For Cathels and Mollie Bowie, see Barnes, *The Order of Things*, pp. 198–9, 143; for McKellar, see ch. 11, n 87; for Pratt, see ch. 2, n. 71.

31 Vida Goldstein to SMF, n.d., FP vol. 10. Interview by E. E. Pescott, *Woman's World*, Apr. 1940 (cutting FP vol. 122).

32 Mabel Singleton to SMF, 16/2/1940, FP vol. 25; SMF to 'Molly Asthore', 13/6/1940, FP vol. 29; SMF to Mary Fullerton, 30/6/1940, FP vol. 119* (bantams).

33 SMF to C. H. Grattan, 18/3/1940, FP vol. 23; SMF to H. S. Temby, 21/8/1940, FP vol. 90.

34 SMF to Henrietta Drake-Brockman, 29/4/[1940], FP vol. 33.*

35 P. R. Stephensen–SMF corres. 7/2/1940–17/5/1940 on the Stephens' bust is at FP vol. 28, related letters at ML MSS 3659/1; Munro, *Wild Man of Letters*, p. 200.

36 PD, 7/5/1940; the draft protest from FP vol. 46.* Dark–SMF corres. 27/4/1940–15/6/1940 is at FP vol. 26.

37 D. Heath, 'Literary Censorship', *History of the Book in Australia*, vol. 2, eds Martyn Lyons and John Arnold, Univ. of Qld Press, St Lucia, Qld, 2001, p. 72. Sawtell–SMF corres. is at FP vols 32 and 34. *Brave New World* was published in 1932.

38 P. R. Stephensen to SMF, 14/6/1940, ML MSS 3659/1, encl. 450.

39 SMF to 'Molly Asthore', 13/6/1940, FP vol. 29; Alice Thacher Post to SMF, 6/11/1941, FP vol. 27.

40 Nettie Palmer to SMF, 25/5/1940, and SMF to Nettie Palmer, 31/5/1940, both FP vol. 24*.

41 SMF to Alice Thacher Post, 11/5/1940, FP vol. 27; SMF to T. B. Smith, 6/7/1940, FP vol. 34, and SMF to P. & M. Meggitt, 6/7/1940, FP vol. 34,* and SMF to Margery Furbank, 18/8/1940, FP vol. 26; H. C. Peterson was an associate professor of history, Univ. of Oklahoma, *Chicago DT*, 26/11/1939, p. SW4; his book was published in 1939, as was Grattan's follow-up.

42 SMF to Mary de Garis, 6/7/1940, FP vol. 34; A[gnes] D[orothy] Kerr to SMF, 21/10/1940, FP vol. 35 (PD, 12/7/1940).

43 SMF to Alice Henry, 17/7/1940, FP vol. 11;* SMF to Mary Fullerton, 2/9/1940, FP vol. 17; SMF to Mary Fullerton, 21/11/1940, FP vol. 17.* The only Ellis title in SMF's library is *Man and Woman: A Study of Human Secondary Sexual Characters* (1894), saved by Miles from disposal in London in 1920 (SMF to Alice Henry, 21/1/1920, FP vol. 114).

44 *SMH*, 2/9/1940, p. 11 (Brian Fitzpatrick also spoke). The Central Cultural Council was a joint organisation of the FAW and the Writers' Association.

45 'Literature', ML MSS 445/37/14, published in the conference proceedings 'Culture in Wartime', c.1941, repr. *A Gregarious Culture* (text only), also reported J. G. Shain, 'Miles Franklin — Literary Product of Australia', *The Listener In*, Sept. 28–Oct. 1940.

46 SMF to KSP, 6/6/1940, and KSP to SMF, 14/10/1940, FP vol. 23, and Ferrier, *As Good as a Yarn with You*; Helen Thomas to R. G. Menzies, 26/7/1940 and protest (attached), NAA series 1608/1, item A39/2/2 PT; 'Our Constitutional Rights', FP vol. 60, *Freedom*, Bulletin of the Youth Freedom Council, 5/9/1940 (ML), and *SMH*, 13/9/1940, p. 8; SMF to MDR, 17/10/1940, MDR Papers; SMF to Mabel Singleton, 11/10/1940, FP vol. 25; Jean Shain to SMF, 9/10/1940, FP vol. 34; and 'Knitting Is Not Enough', ML MSS 445/37, broadcast 2GZ (Country Broadcasting Services Ltd), 17/11/1940.

47 This account draws on Hergenhan, *No Casual Traveller*, pp. 150ff., PD entries, and personal corres.; Grattan to SMF, 27/9/1940, FP vol. 23, has the points; SMF to Dorothy Innes, 16/11/1940, FP vol. 34.

48　Pixie O'Harris (Mrs Rona Olive Pratt) (1903–91), children's book illustrator and author (*OCAL*), first letter to SMF, 28/7/1941, FP vol. 35; 'Lion Takes Coward's Way', *SMH*, 28/4/2004, p. 17 (Coward's visit). For the publication of the Easter Show story see ch. 13, p. 448.

49　PD, 11/12/1940; Invitation, Presentation of Awards, Memorial College of Household Arts and Science, Kirribilli, 11/12/1940, ML MSS 3659/1.

50　PD, 17/7/1941; N. J. Franklin, Certificate of Discharge, 21/10/1942, FP vol. 113X.

51　PD, 10/8/1941, *Diaries*, pp. 133–4; SMF to Desmond Fitzgerald, 13/7/1941, FP vol. 33.*

52　PD, 20/3/1941; SMF to Eila Barnett, Feb.–Sept. 1941, FP vol. 35; 'Louisa Lawson Memorial', *SMH*, 14/8/1941, p. 5. Betty Roland (1903–96) a Victorian-born journalist and writer, was a communist in the 1930s and wrote many plays. Alan Marshall (1902–84) is best known for *I Can Jump Puddles* (1955); *How Beautiful are thy Feet* was published by Chesterhill Press, Melbourne, in 1949 (*OCAL*).

53　'Let Go of Grief', ML MSS 6035/5; 'Prior Prize Entries', *Bulletin*, 18/6/1941, p. 2, 14/1/1942, p. 2.

54　Joan Browne was a young local writer (in 1942 treasurer of the Propeller League, winning second prize in a short story competition, *Propeller*, 9/4/1942, p. 3); for Leslie Rees, see n. 2 above.

55　Ian Mayelston Mudie (1911–76), *ADB* vol. 15; SMF to Ian Mudie, 20/7/1941, Mudie Papers.* The Franklin–Mudie corres. (FP vol. 39, 1942–54) amounts to almost 500 pages, with later and earlier items in the Mudie Papers. *Corroboree in the Sun* was published in 1930. *OCAL* has a succinct account of Jindyworobak movement. South Australian-born Reginald Charles Ingamells (1913–55) was a poet and editor (*ADB* vol. 14).

56　SMF to Mary Fullerton, 20/4/1941, FP vol. 18; SMF to Arnold & Louise Dresden, 16/3/1941, FP vol. 35.*

57　*SMH*, 9/8/1941, p. 3 (lecture notice). Lloyd Ross (1901–87) *ADB* vol. 18, and Guido Baracchi (1887–1975), *ADB* vol. 13. The lecture was delivered at Federation House in Phillip St, Teachers' Federation HQ.

58　SMF to Mary Fullerton, 22/9/1941, FP vol.18;* *SMH*, 1/9/1941, p. 6 (2300 delegates).

59　'Literature and Drama', *Soviet Culture: A Selection of Talks*, Sydney, 1941, pp. 73–7 (ML), repr. *A Gregarious Culture*; also ML MSS 445/37/19, 'Women and Children'. The day session of the conference was held in the Education Building, the evening session at the New Theatre Club, 36 Pitt St.

60　Australian Civil Rights Defence League, A. H. Garnsey Papers, ML MSS 7101/11/3, and Stuart Macintyre, *The Reds: The Communist Party of Australia from Origins to Illegality*, Allen & Unwin, Sydney, 1998, p. 404; *Bulletin*, 19/11/1941, p. 36; Throssell, *Wild Weeds and Wind Flowers*, p. 108; PD, 4/4/1941, talk on Serbia, PD, 2/12/1941, FP vol. 445/36; Norman Haire (1892–1953) was doctor and sexologist (*ADB* vol. 14). Dr Booth served as president of the Anzac Fellowship until 1956, *ADB* vol. 7.

61　Leslie Kevin Cahill (1902/04–1955), labourer and ex-communist, recruited from Melbourne by P. R. Stephensen, would join the army in Jan. 1942, allegedly to organise nationalist revolt from within (see Bruce Muirden, *Puzzled Patriots: The Story of the Australia First Movement*, Melbourne Univ. Press, Carlton, Vic, 1968, p. 72, and Barbara Winter, *The Australia-First Movement and the Publicist, 1936–1942*, Glass House Books, Qld, 2005, pp. 47, 203). James Jupp, *The Australian People*, Angus & Robertson, N. Ryde, 1988, p. 648, points out that while official attitudes were sympathetic to the plight of Jewish people by 1939, the Australian public both Jewish and non-Jewish was generally cold, aloof and in some cases even hostile. PD, 3/12/1941.

62　PD, 24/12/1941; Dr Anita Muhl (1886–1952) taught at the Univ. of Melbourne 1938–1941 (www.indianahistory.org).

63　For more on *The Timeless Land*, published 1941, see SMF to Grattan family, 10/2/1942, Grattan Colln, and SMF to MDR, 19/2/1942, MDR Papers, both.*

64　*SMH*, 26/1/1942, p. 10 (death notice), Mutch Index, ML m/film C572; Alice Henry to SMF, 2/2/1942, FP vol. 11.

65　*SMH*, 23/2/1942, p. 4; Tom Nelson, *The Hungry Mile*, Waterside Workers' Federation, Sydney, 1957, p. 25; 'The "Adyar Hall" Incident', *Publicist*, Mar. 1942, p. 12, states Stephensen spoke for 90 minutes.

66 SMF to Ian Mudie, 27/2/[1942], Mudie Papers; 'Boos, Blows, Cat-Calls at New Party's Birth,' *Daily Mirror*, 6/11/1941, p. 10; Muirden, *Puzzled Patriots: The Story of the Australia First Movement*, Melbourne Univ. Press, Carlton, Vic, 1968, p. 66; SMF to W. J. Miles, 21/7/1941, ML MSS 330; SMF to Ian Mudie, 23/5/1942, FP vol. 36; Craig Munro, 'Australia First — Women Last: Pro-Fascism and Anti-feminism in the 1930s', *Hecate* 1983, vol. 9, pp. 25–34. The Shalimar Café was located in the basement of the T&G Building, Elizabeth St. Re Morley Roberts (1857–1942) see Miller & Macartney, *Australian Literature*, pp. 404–6 and *ODNB*.

67 Susan Sheridan, 'Louisa Lawson, Miles Franklin and Feminist Writing' *Australian Feminist Studies*, 1988, vols 7–8; I am grateful to Beverley Kingston for discussion of this frequently overlooked distinction.

68 This account is largely based on Muirden, *Puzzled Patriots* (see note 61) and Munro, *Wild Man of Letters*, sixteen men were interned in all, and separately, Pankhurst Walsh.

69 SMF to Ian Mudie, 23/3/1942, FP vol. 36;* SMF to Ian Mudie, 6/4/1942, Mudie Papers; SMF to Ian Mudie, 21/4/1942, FP vol. 36;* SMF to C. H. Grattan, 8/6/1942, FP vol. 23.

70 SMF to Ian Mudie, 23/3/1942 and 21/4/1942, FP vol. 36, both.*

71 SMF to C. B. Christesen, 28/7/1942, MA;* SMF and George Ashton, 'Is the Writer Involved in the Political Development of his Country?', in *Australian Writers Speak*, Angus & Robertson, 1942, repr. *A Gregarious Culture*; KSP to SMF, 9/6/1942, FP vol. 35* (KSP was also a speaker, others included Bert and Dora Birtles, Leslie Rees and the Palmers); *Southerly*, Apr. 1943. Clement Byrne Christesen (1911–2003), whose mother read *My Brilliant Career* as a girl, was founding editor of *Meanjin* 1940–74 (*OCAL*). *Meanjin Papers* (from 1947 *Meanjin*) moved to Melbourne in 1947, and was the flagship of cultural nationalism for two generations. Dora Birtles (1903–94) was a poet and traveller, Bert Birtles was also a poet (*OCAL*). George Ashton was secretary of the FAW in the early 1940s (Fox, *Dream at a Graveside*, p. 186). Wesley Milgate (1916–99), AustLit.

72 SMF to C. B. Christesen, 15/10/1942, MA, and C. B. Christesen to SMF, 9/11/1942, FP vol. 35; 'Henry Lawson', *Meanjin Papers*, 1942, vol. 1, no. 12, repr. *A Gregarious Culture* (the virtually identical ABC script at ABC Archives, Accessioned Talks, Scripts, SP 300, Box 8, was published by Escutcheon Press, Pearl Beach, NSW, 1999, as 'Miles Franklin: A Personal Tribute to Henry Lawson' (*Biblionews*, 1999, vol. 24, no. 4)); Miles received five guineas for the broadcast.

73 'Our Best Poets', *Southerly*, 1942, vol. 3, no. 2; 'Australia is so far away', FP vol. 58.

74 Tom Inglis Moore to SMF, 22/11/1942, FP vol. 29; SMF to John Shaw Neilson, and ML MSS 3659/1; 'Is the Writer Involved…', repr. *A Gregarious Culture*, p. 172 (the three poets); for SMF to R. D. FitzGerald, 1942, see FP vol. 36 (17 ls), and *ADB* vol. 17; A&R to 'E', via SMF, FP vol. 103.

75 Martin, *Ida Leeson*, p. 112, and PD, 8–13/10/1942; SMF to Victor Kennedy, 18/10/1942 and 29/12/1942, Kennedy Papers; W. G. Cousins to SMF, 27/11/1942, FP vol. 103; SMF to Mary Fullerton, 2/11/1942, FP vol. 18; Douglas Stewart to SMF, 6/11/[1942], FP vol. 37, and SMF to H. S. Temby, 2/11/1942, FP vol. 103; *Bulletin*, 3/2/1943, 'Red Page'. The title is from 'Piety' a characteristically terse verse in the volume. NZ-born Douglas Stewart (1913–85) a leading poet, was editor of the *Bulletin*'s 'Red Page' 1940–61, and literary editor with Angus & Robertson 1961–71 (*OCAL*).

76 Index, *Southerly*, vol. 1, 1939–61, p. 67; SMF to Victor Kennedy, 29/12/1942, Kennedy Papers. Victor Kennedy (1895–1952) was a journalist and freelance writer, (*ADB S*).

77 *Union Recorder*, 11/2/1943 (Eng. Ass. Dinner, 19/11/1942); PD, 19/11/1942. Elisabeth Lambert, journalist and poet, was b. England (1915–2003) (*OCAL*).

78 ML MSS 6035/5, 2, p. 299, also ML MSS 445/12; 'Old Blastus of Bandicoot: Domestic Drama', 1942, FP vol. 61 (*Guide* entry); for the publication of 'The Thorny Rose', see ch 13, pp. 447–8. 'Evadne': possibly from Evadne Price (1896–1985) (pseud. Helen Jenna Smith), a prolific writer of popular adult and children's fiction (*ODNB*).

79 SMF to C. H. Grattan 11/8/1942, C. H. Grattan to SMF, postmark 25/9/[1942], SMF to C. H. Grattan, 29/11/1942, FP vol. 23.

80 SMF to FAW, 2/6/1942, and reply 18/6/1942, FP vol. 25; 'Youth Holds Our Future', *Truth*, 16/8/1942, p. 15; untitled speech, ML MSS 445/37, *Bulletin*, 2/9/1942, p. 25, diary entry, repr. *Diaries*, pp. 136–9; W. Linklater to SMF, Sept. 1942, FP vol. 36; *Southerly*, 1944, vol. 5, no. 1, p 57.

81   SMF to KSP [Jun. 1942];* PD, 4/5/1942, and Eve Langley to SMF, 27/5/1942 (p.m.), ML MSS 3659/1; SMF to Alice Henry, 18/6/1942, FP vol. 115,* and SMF to Mary Anderson, 2/8/1942. Eve Langley (1904–74), *ADB* vol. 15.

82   PD, 28/12/1942; FP vol. 4, p. 162, repr. *Diaries*, 28/10/1942, p. 143.

83   SMF to Godfrey Bentley, [Oct. 1942], FP vol. 37. Esmonde Higgins (1897–1960), a WEA tutor, was brother of Nettie Palmer (*ADB* vol. 14); Harry Hooton (1908–61) was a Sydney anarchist poet (*ADB* vol. 14); Godfrey Bentley (1917–47) was a journalist on the *Newcastle Morning Herald.**

84   SMF to Mary Anderson, 24/3/1943, Anderson Papers.*

85   SMF to Isabel Newsham, 19/2/1943, FP vol. 29; Kirkby, *Alice Henry*, p. 223; SMF to Nettie Palmer, 19/10/1943, FP vol. 24.*

86   SMF to E. J. Brady, 10/8/1943, FP vol. 37;* Jean Devanny to SMF, 22/5/1943, repr. Ferrier, *As Good as a Yarn with You*.

87   'R. G. H.' [Howarth], *Southerly*, 1943–4, vol. 6, no. 4, p. 56. George Farwell (1911–76) was president FAW 1944 (*ADB* vol. 14); pers. comm., Don Adamson.

88   SMF to Mary Anderson, [rcd 15/12/1943], Anderson Papers* (Alabamans at the FAW); SMF to Frank Ryland, 21/4/1943, FP vol. 37. Flora Eldershaw (1897–1955) joined the Commonwealth Dept of Labour and National Service in Canberra in 1941and subsequently worked in the division of postwar reconstruction (*ADB* vol. 14). Frank Ryland (1904–87), soldier and journalist, served in Singapore and with the *British Commonwealth Occupation News*, Tokyo, post-1945. Hazel de Berg interview, NLA, no. 1173, 1980, other sources.

89   Douglas Stewart to SMF, 28/1/1943, FP vol. 37; SMF to Beatrice Davis, 30/12/1943, FP vol. 38.

90   'Joseph Furphy's Centenary', *ABC Weekly*, 4/12/1943, p. 6; 'Letters from Joseph Furphy to Miles Franklin', *Meanjin Papers*, Spring 1943, pp. 14–16; *Communist Review*, Sept. 1943, pp. 22–4, repr. *A Gregarious Culture*. The statement is printed in *My Congenials*, vol. 2, p. 98.

91   SMF to Margery Currey, 13/7/1948, FP vol. 22; SMF to Alice Henry, 8/7/[1942], FP vol. 11, and Alice Henry to SMF, 14/7/1942, FP vol. 115; SMF to WEA, 10/5/1944, FP vol. 38.

92   'Australia, the Incredible Feat', *Think Tank*, 29/7/1943, p. 4 (commissioned 22/3/1943, Mildred Seydell to SMF, FP vol. 37), repr. *A Gregarious Culture*; Miles first met Mildred Seydell, an American publisher and writer, when Seydell visited Australia in 1937 (SMF to Mary Fullerton, 27/10/1937, FP vol. 119); the *Think Tank* appeared 1940–8 (*World Who's Who of Women*). 'Birth Pangs of the Australian Novel', ML MSS 6035/10, *ABC Weekly*, 23/10/1943, p. 2; 'Need for Australian Literature', *Newcastle Morning Herald*, 1/5/1944, p. 2, and ML MSS 445/37/14; ML MSS 445/37/7 (Australian books); ML MSS 772, 27, p. 93, and *Tribune*, 5/10/1944, p. 4; PD, 2/11/1944; FP vol. 73/7, and *A Radical Life: The Autobiography of Russel Ward*, Macmillan, South Melbourne, 1988, p. 179. The broadcasts included an interview re 'Australian Writers Speak', 21/10/1944 (script at ABC Archives, NAA Talks, SP 300 series), for which she was paid three guineas; she may also have broadcast on 'Advice to Young Writers' (SMF to Mrs J. Moore, 4/9/1944, FP vol. 92, text at FP vol. 76/7). Mildred Seydell (1889–1988), *New Georgian Encyclopedia* (online). Donald McLean (1905–75) became one of Australia's foremost educationists (*OCAL*).

93   SMF to Frank Ryland, 27/4/1943, FP vol. 37.*

94   'Three Women and Love' by Punica Granatum, FP vol. 88 and ML MSS 6035/16. For 'Virgins and Martyrs', see ML MSS 445/11 and 25; the Glenties play is at ML MSS 6035/10 (later 'The Scandal-monger', ML MSS 445/26); 'Comedy at Runnymede' is at ML MSS 6035/3. Susan Pfisterer and Edel Mahony eds, *A Fringe of Paper: Offshore Perspectives on Australian Literature & History*, Sir Robert Menzies Centre for Australian Studies and the British Australian Studies Association, London, 1999, p. 76 (phases as playwright).

95   SMF to Mary Anderson, [rcd 15/12/1943], Anderson Papers; Catherine Duncan to SMF, 21/12/1943, FP vol. 38; SMF to Cusack, 13/10/1943, Cusack Papers;* PD, 27/3/1942. Camilla Wedgwood (1901–55), a member of the famous English Wedgwood pottery family, was principal of Women's College, Univ. of Sydney 1935–43 (*ADB* vol. 16). Joseph Daniel Unwin (1895–1936), *Who Was Who, 1929–1940*. Catherine Duncan (1915–2006) was an actor, playwright and film-maker; she died in Paris, *Herald Sun* (Melbourne), 17/8/2006.

96   Nettie Palmer to SMF, 9/5/1935, FP vol. 24.*

97   SMF to Godfrey Bentley, 5/1/1943, FP vol. 37; SMF to Henrietta Drake-Brockman, 2/9/1943, FP vol. 33

98   Muir Holburn (1920–60), president FAW 1948–50, and Marjorie Pizer (b. 1920), were poets (letters beginning 1944 when still in Melbourne are at FP vol. 39 and Holburn Papers, uncat. mss, 530/8). Neroli Whittle (1897–1967), director of the Australian Playwrights Theatre and the Greenwich Drama Group, later went to England (ADB files). Musette Morell [Moyna Martin] (1898–1950) wrote plays, books and radio programs for children (AustLit); Harry Hooton published three volumes of poetry 1941–61 (*OCAL* and *ADB* vol. 14); Harry Hooton to Marie E. J. Pitt, 5, 6, 12/10/1942, J. K. Moir Colln. Harry Hooton to SMF, 19/10/1943, and 1945, 'I'm a Rebel Too', ML MSS 3659/1; Glennie Millicent Fox (1906–76), née Mills, from 1955 Crouch, b. Queescliff, Vic, married Len Fox (1905–2004) in 1943 and they divorced early 1950s. SMF to KSP, [?]Jun. 1943, FP vol. 21, repr. Ferrier, *As Good as a Yarn with You*, and Glen Mills Fox to SMF, 2/9/1947, FP vol. 40.

99   Roe, '"Tremenjus Good"', re the relationship between literature and society.

100 Harold Ickes to SMF, 27/1/1944, FP vol. 12;* SMF to Elisabeth Christman, 3/4/1944, FP vol. 38; Kathleen Ussher to SMF, 20/11/[1944], ML MSS 3659/1; SMF to Mary Fullerton, 24/3/1944, FP vol. 18;* *Australian Women's Digest*, Sept. 1943, vol. 1, no. 2, inside cover (SMF's contributions are listed Bettison and Roe, *ALS*, listing, 2001); PD, 19–20/11/1943, *Tribune*, 13/7/1944, p. 7 (Ed. Bd); Vivienne Newson (1891–1973), *ADB* vol. 15.

101 SMF to Mary Fullerton, 4/7/1943, FP vol. 18 (Langley); Hilda Esson to SMF, 15/12/1943, FP vol. 38.* Hilda Esson (later Bull) (1885–1953) was a Melbourne medical practitioner and theatre director, (*ADB* vol. 8). *Point Counter Point* was published in 1928, Plato's *Dialogues* in 1871.

102 SMF to Mary Fullerton, 24/3/1944, FP vol. 18. Lindsay Franklin (1921–2007) recalled the visit for this book: 'She and Dad would go riding … then come in, talk, and play cards' (conversation with Margaret Francis, Tumut, 1/4/2006, notes in my possession).

103 SMF to Mary Fullerton, 24/3/1944, FP vol. 18; Fox, *Dream at a Graveside*, p. 106; Frank Ryland to SMF, 11/10/1944, FP vol. 37;* PD, 31/8/1945 (prize).

104 PD, 1/11/1944; SMF to Mary Fullerton, 3/11/1944, FP vol. 19; 'S', 'Partly Joseph Furphy', *Bulletin*, 13/12/1944, p. 2; SMF to Kate Baker, 14/11/1944 and 8/12/1944, both FP vol. 9A; *Bulletin*, 13/12/1944, 'Red Page', A. D. Hope, 'Review of Miles Franklin's Joseph Furphy', *Meanjin Papers*, 1945, vol. 4, no, 3, repr. *The Australian Nationalists*, ed. Chris Wallace-Crabbe, Oxford Univ. Press, Melbourne, 1971; *Fellowship* Feb. 1945, p. 2 (Patricia Thompson); *SMH*, 10/3/1945, p. 7; *Southerly*, 1945, vol. 6, no. 2, p. 56 (H. J. Oliver); *Argus Literary Supplement*, 27/1/1945, p. 1. Alec Derwent Hope (1907–2000) lectured in English at Sydney Teachers' College 1938–44 and was appointed professor of English at Canberra Univ. College in 1951.

105 Ian Mudie, *The Australian Dream*, Jindyworobak, Adelaide, 1944, p. 32. SMF to Ian Mudie, 31/8/1944, Mudie Papers ;* SMF to MDR, 19/2/1942, MDR Papers; SMF, 'Ian Mudie — Poet and Patriot', 1944, FP vol. 60/17. SMF's copy of *John Brown's Body* (Doubleday, New York, 1928) is at PBC 540(a).

106 KSP to SMF, 29/3/1944, FP vol. 21, repr, *As Good as a Yarn with You*. Leslie Loval Woolacott (1885–1961, NSW BMD index), half-brother of Esme Fenston (ed. *Australian Women's Weekly* 1950–72), wrote *The Garage Skeleton*, Currawong, Sydney, 1941, Miller & Macartney, *Australian Literature*, p. 498.

107 *SMH*, 21/4/1944, p. 3, and PD, 21–28/4/1944; Martyn Lyons, 'The Book Trade and the Australian Reader in 1945', *History of the Book in Australia*, vol. 2, eds Martyn Lyons and John Arnold, Univ. of Qld Press, St Lucia, Qld, p. 402. *Southerly*, 1945, vol. 6, no. 2, pp. 14–15, and *SMH*, 29/4/1944, p. 6; R. G. Howarth to SMF, 20/5/1944, and SMF to R. G. Howarth, 22/5/1944, FP vol. 33, both ;* 'Miss Gillespie's tragedy', FP vol. 4, pp. 141–8. George Clune (1889–1953) was also a restaurateur (NSW BMD index, Sydney *Telephone Directory*, 1946).

108 George Clune to SMF, 9/11/1944, and SMF to George Clune, 1/12/1944, ML MSS 3659/1, George Clune to SMF, 7/6/1946, FP vol. 81; Lesley Heath, 'Sydney Literary Societies of the Nineteen Twenties', PhD thesis, p. 59.

109 PD, 9/8/1944; *Diaries*, pp. 156–7.

110 Barnard, *Miles Franklin*, p. 3.

111 'Miles Franklin and Brent of Bin Bin', Barnard Papers, ML MSS 451/3.

112 FP vol. 3, 1944, repr. *Diaries*, pp. 155. *The Glasshouse* was published in 1936.

113 SMF to Mary Fullerton, 15/1/1944, FP vol. 120; SMF to Ian Mudie, 31/8/1944, Mudie Papers, re A. D. Hope, 'Confessions of a Zombie', *Meanjin Papers*, 1944, vol. 3, no. 1; R. G. Howarth to SMF, 20/5/1944, FP vol. 33,* and R. G. Howarth, 5/4/1949, *Bulletin*, 5/1/1949, 'Red Page'. No comment on the 'Ern Malley' hoax has been located to date.

114 Roderick, *Miles Franklin*, p. 166; Colin Roderick to SMF, 15/11/1944, FP vol. 38; SMF to Vance Palmer, 25/11/1944, and SMF to Colin Roderick, 22/11/1944, both Palmer Papers. Colin Roderick (1911–2000) was foundation professor of English at Townsville University College (later James Cook Univ.), 1965–76. *The Australian Novel* was published by William Brooks & Co, Sydney, 1945.

115 Colin Roderick to SMF, 2/12/1944, SMF to Colin Roderick 6/4/1945, both ML MSS 3659/1, SMF to Colin Roderick 17/6/1945, FP vol. 38; *SMH*, 14/4/1945, p. 10 (a positive review of the anthology).

116 Paul Frolich to SMF, 5/4/1944, FP vol. 38; SMF to Mary Fullerton, 1/9/1944, FP vol. 19; *Society of Artists Annual Exhibition Catalogues, 1940–51* (1944) lists the bust as 'a sketch', 'not for sale'; *SMH*, 22/1/1944, p. 8 (Dobell's entries). Paul Frolich (1918–89), public servant, was a music lover and *Bulletin* contributor.

117 People's Conference on Culture in the War and the Peace pamphlet, 1944 (ML), *DT*, 3/7/1944, p. 7, and *SMH*, 3/7/1944, p. 4; ['Australian war novels'], c.1944, FP vol. 3, repr. *Diaries*, p. 157.

118 SMF to E. H. Burgmann, 6/7/1944, FP vol. 27* ('human epizoa' probably refers to a population debate sponsored by the ABC mid-1944); SMF to Mary Fullerton, 10/8/1944, FP vol. 19.

119 SMF to Ian Mudie, 19/1/1945, FP vol. 36, and Mudie Papers; SMF to Kate Baker, 18/1/1945, Baker Papers; SMF to Colin Roderick, 17/6/1945, FP vol. 38. Roderick's *Twenty Australian Novelists* was published by Angus & Robertson in 1947; expatriates included G. B. Lancaster and Christina Stead. Charles Currey (1890–1970), *ADB* vol. 13.

120 SMF to Ian Mudie, 2/4/1945, and 4/2/1945, FP vol. 36.

121 SMF to Ian Mudie, 4/2/1945, FP vol. 36.

122 SMF to Catherine Duncan, 22/2/1945, FP vol. 38.*

123 North, *Yarn Spinners*, pp. 63–5, 70; Dymphna Cusack, 'My Friendship with Miles Franklin', *Ink* no. 2, 50th Anniversary edn, Hilarie Lindsay, Society of Women Writers, Sydney, 1977. Catherine Mackay Elliott, née Edmunds (1900–60), 'a true Aussie battler', had been a barmaid in Sydney in the 1930s, also an SP bookie (North, *Yarn Spinners*, pp. 71, 403). Florence James (1902–93) had been a social worker (AustLit); 'Pinegrove' is located in Valley Rd, Hazelbrook, (pers. comm., Marilla North). *Caddie* was published in 1953.

124 'Call Up Your Ghosts!', FP vol. 62 and ML MSS 445/25, repr. *Penguin Anthology of Women's Writing*, ed. Dale Spender, Penguin Books, Ringwood, Vic, 1988; research material for *Sydney Royal*, FP vol. 56, pp. 104–43.

125 Dymphna Cusack to SMF, 25/7/1945, FP vol. 30. 'Ghosts' played in Perth in 1948. (Sir) Mungo MacCallum (1854–1941) developed a tradition of Elizabethan scholarship at the Univ. of Sydney (*OCAL* and *ADB* vol. 10).

126 SMF to Frank Ryland, 28/9/1945, FP vol. 37;* SMF to F. T. Macartney, 22/1/1945, Macartney Papers. Frederick Macartney (1887–1980) was also prominent in literary circles (*OCAL*).

127 George Clune to SMF, 17/5/1945, FP vol. 81; SMF to Lucy Spence Morice, 18/4/1945, FP vol. 22;* Miles Franklin, 'Australian Classic No. 4: Clara Morrison', *Australian New Writing*, Current Book Distributors, Sydney, 1945, pp. 42–6.

128 SMF to Nettie Palmer, 28/3/1945, Palmer Papers; SMF to Ian Mudie, FP vol. 36, p. 287; *Bulletin*, 23/5/1945, p. 9, and *SMH*, 5/6/1945, p. 4; 'Australian Writers Need Courage', *SMH*, 21/7/1945, p. 6, repr. *A Gregarious Culture*; David Carter, 'The Mystery of the Missing Middlebrow, or the C(o)urse of Good Taste', *Imagining Australia: Literature and Culture in the New New World*, eds Judith Ryan and Chris Wallace-Crabbe, Australian Studies Committee, Harvard Univ. Press, Cambridge Mass., 2004, p. 192; Miles Franklin, 'You Can Share in this Job for Australian Literature', *Book News*, Aug. 1945, no. 1, p. 1 (copy, Ingamells Papers). Henry Seidel Canby (1878–1961) served as a liaison officer for the US Office of War Information while lecturing in Australia in 1945 (*ANB*).

129 SMF to KSP and others, 6/10/1945, p. 2, report on the progress of book selection, FP vol. 21. Sidney J. Baker (1912–76), *ADB* vol. 13.

130 Corres. between W. Blake and Dymocks Book Arcade 5/12/1944–16/1/1945, FP vol. 86; SMF to Ian Mudie, 4/4/1945, FP vol. 36.
131 SMF to Mary Fullerton, 5/6/1945, FP vol. 19; SMF to Catherine Duncan, 22/2/1945, FP 38.* 'Australian Drama — Its Dearth and the Remedy', *New Theatre Review* (Melbourne), Aug.–Sept. 1945, pp. 2, 8; Annette Bain, '"Brighter Days?": Challenges to Live Theatre in the Thirties', *Twentieth Century Sydney*, ed. Jill Roe, Hale & Iremonger, Sydney, 1980.
132 'People's Council': see n. 117 above, People's Conference on Culture in the War and the Peace pamphlet, 1944 (ML); PD, 22/4/1945, and FP vol. 3, repr. *Diaries*, pp. 158–60, 165; Pfisterer, *Playing with Ideas*, pp. 244–5; Mila Kronidov to Stephanie Liau, 1983; PD, 6/8/1945. Dulcie Deamer (1890–1972) was a writer and bohemian (*ADB* vol. 8).
133 'Sophistication': ML MSS 445/25 and ML MSS 6035/10; 'Tom Collins at Runnymede', prev. 'Comedy at Runnymede', ML MSS 6035/3 and ML MSS 445/27 (the reading version); 'The Thorny Rose', ML MSS 6035/13. Montague Grover (1870–1943) was a Sydney journalist and playwright (*OCAL*). Henry Kingsley (1830–76), *ADB* vol. 5.
134 The program and cast for 'Release', apparently a version of 'No Family', is at ML MSS 445/27.
135 *Companion to Theatre in Australia*, ed. Philip Parsons with Victoria Chance, Currency Press in association with Cambridge Univ. Press, Sydney, c.1995, pp. 437–8 (competitions), entry by Leslie Rees; Arrow, *Upstaged*, ch. 1; Pfisterer, *Playing with Ideas*, p. 243.
136 'Australian greetings', FP vol. 76. She was paid five guineas for the Lancaster broadcast, ML MSS 364/92; 'Her Scene Was Worldwide', *Australasian Book News and Library Journal*, Oct. 1946, pp. 127–8, and 'Profile of the Month: G. B. Lancaster', *Talk*, Apr. 1946; G. B. Lancaster to SMF, 7/5/1942, ML MSS 3659/1. SMF to Ian Mudie, 18/12/1945, Mudie Papers; 'Bishop Burgmann's Education', *Australian Women's Digest*, May 1945, repr. *A Gregarious Culture*; SMF to [Sir], 3/4/[1945], FP vol. 46; Barrymore, *Australasian*, 13/10/1945, pp. 18–19, and ML MSS 445/37. Jessie Street (1889–1970) was a leading NSW feminist (*ADB* vol. 12). Margaret Trist (1914–85) wrote *Now That We're Laughing* (1945) and *Morning in Queensland* (1958). *Fellowship* appeared 1944–c.1948 (ML).
137 SMF to J. B. Chifley, 14/10/1945, FP vol. 39;* Richard Nile and David Walker, *History of the Australian Book*, vol. 2, eds Martyn Lyons and John Arnold, Univ. of Qld Press, St Lucia, Qld, p. 17; SMF to Ian Mudie, 18/12/1945, Mudie Papers. Joseph Benedict Chifley (1885–1951), Labor Prime Minister of Australia 1945–9, Leader of the Opposition 1950–1 (*ADB* vol. 13). John Curtin (1885–1945), Labor Prime Minister of Australia 1941–5 (*ADB* vol. 13).
138 PD, 12/9/1945; SMF to Elisabeth Christman, 20/4/1945, and Elisabeth Christman to SMF, 20/7/1945, FP vol. 24, both;* SMF to RR, 20/4/1945, MDR Papers.
139 Arnold Dresden to SMF, 5/11/1945, FP vol. 35;* SMF to Rika Stoffel, 12/9/1945, and Rika Stoffel to SMF, 1/10/1945, FP vol. 15; SMF to Phil & May Meggitt, 17/12/1945, FP vol. 39.*
140 SMF to Mabel Singleton, 16/11/1945, FP vol. 25; SMF to Frank Ryland, 28/9/1945, FP vol. 37.

Chapter 13 — The Waratah Cup: 1946–1950

1 SMF to Frank Ryland, 11/1/1948, FP vol. 37.
2 SMF to Kathleen Monypenny, 5/2/1946, FP vol. 22, and SMF to P. R. Stephensen, 4/3/1946, FP vol. 28 (both*).
3 SMF to Mary Fullerton and Mabel Singleton, 5/2/1946, FP vol. 19.
4 SMF to Mabel Singleton, 27/2/1946, FP vol. 25;* SMF to Lydia Chester, 3/5/1946, FP vol. 35. In addition to the two volumes of verse published by Angus & Robertson, at least 29 single poems by Mary Fullerton appeared in anthologies 1942–6, thanks to SMF's efforts.
5 'Books Published in Australia', *Australasian Book News and Library Journal* (hereafter *Book News*), Oct. 1946, p. 162. Reviews of *The Wonder and the Apple*, e.g. *Bulletin*, 29/5/1946, p. 2, and *Southerly*, 1947, no. 2, pp. 115–16, suggest a polite acceptance, and few copies of the slim volume were sold, Angus & Robertson to SMF, 6/9/1948, Angus & Robertson Corres., ML MSS 3269, vol. 274, p. 515.
6 Sylvia Martin's *Passionate Friends*, offers an illuminating exposition of the Franklin–Fullerton corres.
7 SMF to Mary Fullerton, 13/1/1946, FP vol. 19; SMF to Mabel Singleton, 27/2/1946, FP vol. 25,* Mabel Singleton to SMF, 31/1/1946, FP vol. 25; Mary Fullerton to SMF, 3/2/1946, FP vol. 19.

8   SMF's corres. with Georgian House is at FP vol. 84; see also Edgar Harris, FP vol. 39. Beatrice Davis to SMF, 21/8/1946, FP vol. 38; Henrietta Drake-Brockman to SMF, 2/9/1946, and SMF to Henrietta Drake-Brockman, 9/9/1946, FP vol. 33 (and review, *Fellowship*, 1946, no. 3); Dymphna Cusack to SMF, 14/8/1946, FP vol. 30 (* all four letters); Rose Lindsay to SMF, 20/1/1949, ML MSS 3659/1; Aileen Goldstein to SMF, 23/2/1947, and SMF to Aileen Goldstein, [22/6/1947], FP vol. 10; SMF to RR, 4/9/1946, FP vol. 39. Reviews: 'Sybylla's Career', *Bulletin*, 21/8/1946, 'Red Page'; *Meanjin*, 1947, vol. 6, no. 2, p. 134–5; H. M. Green, *Southerly*, 1947, no. 4, p. 123. Rose Lindsay (1885–1978), artist's model, esp. of husband Norman, and writer (*ADB S*).

9   'What Can be Done…?', ABC Talks and Scripts, SP 300, series 1, Box 25, NAA; 'Reading Australian Books', 25/1/1946, for 2KY, FP vol. 76/9; PD, 22/2/1946, and FP vol. 105, p. 19 (*Swagger* extracts); 'Her Scene Was World-wide', *Book News*, 1946, vol. 1, no. 4, pp. 127–9; *Tribune*, 18/10/1946, p. 9, *Australian Women's Digest*, Oct. 1946, vol. 2, no. 10, pp. 14–15, and *Labor Digest*, Aug. 1946, pp. 89–93, repr. *A Gregarious Culture*; KSP celebration program, ML MSS 3659/1, encl. 387. The *Roaring Nineties* and *The Southern Cross and Other Plays* were both published in 1946.

10 Pixie O'Harris to SMF, 29/7/1946, FP vol. 35.*

11 SMF to KSP, 5/7/1946 and 29/7/1946, FP vol. 21, repr. Ferrier, *As Good as a Yarn with You*; SMF to Dymphna Cusack and Florence James, n.d. [early 1947], FP vol. 30, repr. North, *Yarn Spinners*, and *SMH*, 28/12/1946, p. 1 (prize); LN, FP vol. 3, [c.Aug.1946], repr. *Diaries*, pp. 172–3; Dymphna Cusack to SMF, 16/10/1949, FP vol. 30.*

12 SMF to Dear Girls, [n.d., Sept./Oct. 1946], FP vol. 30,* and Dymphna Cusack to SMF, Monday [Sept./Oct. 1946], FP vol. 30; North, *Yarn Spinners*, pp. 97, 385; Cusack, 'My Friendship', p. 113.

13 'The Pursuit of Glamour', 1946–7, FP vol. 84; Bridget Griffen-Foley, 'Revisiting the "Mystery of a Novel Contest": The *Daily Telegraph* and *Come in Spinner*', *ALS*, vol. 19, no. 4, 2000.

14 SMF to Nettie Palmer, 26/7/1946, FP vol. 24; 'No Family' (1937, ML MSS 3659/1, text repr. *Tremendous Worlds: Australian Women's Drama 1890–1960*, ed. Susan Pfisterer, Currency Press, Sydney, 1999, pp. 129–142); PD, 4/7/1946, and *Fellowship*, Nov. 1946; *SMH*, 6/6/1946, FP vol. 86; Kent, *A Certain Style*, p. 199; Bridget Griffen-Foley, *The House of Packer*, HarperCollins Australia, Pymble, NSW, 1999, p. 146.

15 ML MSS 6035/5, no. 2, p. 354 with insert.

16 PD, 17/12/1946. (Sir) William Dobell (1899–1970), *ADB* vol. 14. Alice Cooper Stewart (1902–97), wife of Sydney financier Bayliss Stewart, was a Paddington painter (*Bulletin*, 27/8/1955, p. 56). *Diaries*, p. 176.

17 These encounters are published *Diaries*, pp. 174–89.

18 J. Lane, 'Stella Maria Sarah Miles Franklin — A Personal Memoir', unpub. copy in my possession, courtesy author. Helena Lampe moved to Walker St, North Sydney, c.1947, was at Lyndhurst Rest Home in Stanley St, Hunters Hill, c.1951–8, moving to another guesthouse at Gordon in her final years (d. 1964). For Thelma Perryman and Phillis Moulden, see Appendix 2. Les (T. E.) Franklin died Queanbeyan, 25/11/1946 (*SMH*, 27/11/1946, p. 24).

19 The corres. with Emmy Lawson is FP vol. 39 (SMF to Emmy Lawson, 13/1/1947, details the contents of a food parcel.*) Henry R. Aldridge, *If You are Blitzed. How to Claim Compensation etc*, *Reynolds News*, London, 1944, p. 16.

20 SMF to Emmy Lawson, 13/1/1947, FP vol. 39.

21 Florence James to SMF, 7/10/1947, FP vol. 30.*

22 Florence James to SMF, 20/11/1946, FP vol. 30; Marjorie Pizer to SMF, Thurs. 17 [late 1946], FP vol. 39.*

23 Rex Ingamells to SMF, 18/3/1947, and reply 19/3/1947, FP vol. 40. Roland Robinson (1902–92) was a distinguished poet, regarded as the best of the 'Jindy' poets at the time (*OCAL*). Gina Ballantyne (1919–73), poet and painter, edited the 1945 Jindyworobak anthology. Flexmore Hudson (1913–88), was an Adelaide-based teacher and poet (*ADB* vol. 7).

24 ML MSS 445/26 and ML MSS 6035/10 (includes also 'Glenties' as a radio play by 'Jim Barrington').

25 *Newcastle Morning Herald*, 12/7/1947–28/8/1947, and Glen Mills Fox, 'A Not So "Thorny Year" for Serial Author', *Newcastle Morning Herald*, 12/7/1947, p. 4; ML MSS 6035/13–14 (radio play and edited pages). 'The Thorny Rose', ML MSS 445/13, with undated *Newcastle Morning Herald* cutting.

26   'The Thorny Rose', ML MSS 445/13, pp. 244, 245, 171, 205–9.
27   SMF to Florence James, 14/7/1947, FP vol. 30, repr. North, *Yarn Spinners*, p. 122; SMF to Florence James, 16/11/1947, FP vol, 30;* Oliver Holt to SMF, 23/8/1947, FP vol. 40. Lawson Glassop (1913–66), journalist, wrote *We Were the Rats* (1944, banned 1946) (*ADB* vol. 14).
28   SMF to Glen Mills Fox, 31/12/1947 (post office work), FP vol. 40; George Ferguson to SMF, 3/2/1947, ML MSS 3659/1. Angus & Robertson Royalty Statements, FP vol. 82. George Ferguson (1910–98), grandson of George Robertson, joined Angus & Robertson in 1931 and was director of publishing 1949–71 (*SMH*, 15/1/1998, obit.).
29   'Books published in Australia', *Book News*, Jun. 1947, p. 570; Pixie O'Harris to SMF, 18/2/c.1948, FP vol. 35; *Sydney Royal: Divertisement,* Shakespeare Head Press, London, Sydney, [1947], pb., back cover; Griffin-Foley, *House of Packer,* HarperCollins Australia, Pymble, NSW, 1999, p. 153; SMF to Dymphna Cusack and Florence James, 1/12/1946 and 11/2/1947, Cusack Papers, NLA, repr. North, *Yarn Spinners.* Nan Knowles was a freelance illustrator who had shared a studio with Florence James after she came back from London in 1938, and later returned to London (North, *Yarn Spinners,* pp. 101, 204).
30   Brian H. Fletcher, *The Grand Parade: A History of the Royal Agricultural Show Society of NSW,* Royal Agricultural Society of NSW, Paddington, NSW, 1988, p. 312.
31   J. K. Moir to SMF, 12/7/1947, FP vol. 34; Beatrice Davis to SMF, 3/5/1947, ML MSS 3659/1;* Alice Springs Kindergarten to SMF, 12/12/1947, FP vol. 40; Griffen-Foley, *House of Packer,* HarperCollins Australia, Pymble, NSW, 1999, p. 153; *Fellowship,* Jun. 1947, p. 3; SMF to Lorna Salter, 22/2/1951, FP vol. 43. Miles' view is cited in Sircar Sanjay, 'Transformative "Australianness" and Powerful Children. Miles Franklin's *Sydney Royal*', *Bookbird*, 1999, vol. 37, no. 1, p. 26; Glen Mills Fox, 'A Not So "Thorny Year"', *Book News*, Aug. 1947, p. 96.
32   *Sydney Royal: Divertisement,* Shakespeare Head Press, London, Sydney, [1947], p. 33. PD, 24/3/1948 (1898); the earlier date could be another instance of secretiveness about her age.
33   SMF to Glen Mills Fox, 3/12/1947, FP vol. 40. Leslie Haylen (1898–1977), b. near Queanbeyan, was a writer and politician (*ADB* vol. 14).
34   SMF to KSP, 20/11/1947, FP vol. 21; Jill Roe, 'The Historical Imagination and its Enemies: M. Barnard Eldershaw's *Tomorrow and Tomorrow and Tomorrow*', [1983 edn], *Meanjin*, 1984, vol. 43, no. 2; SMF to Henrietta Drake-Brockman, 3/4/1947, FP vol. 33.
35   SMF to Glen Mills Fox, 28/11/1947, FP vol. 40* (part); Fox, *Dream at a Graveside* provides a useful if episodic account of the FAW. Nicole Moore, 'Obscene and Over Here: National Sex and the *Love Me Sailor* Obscenity Case', *ALS*, 2002, vol. 23, no. 4, also 'An Indecent Obsession', *Memento*, Spring–Summer 2005, p. 15. Robert Close (1903–95) was sentenced to three months' jail in 1948, and although released after ten days, left Australia soon after and spent many years in France. Howard Fast (1914–2003), American author and political radical, was blacklisted by the Congress House of Un-American Activities Committee in the late 1940s and jailed in 1950 (*Current Biography* 2003).
36   SMF to KSP, 20/11/1947, FP vol. 21;* SMF to RR, 5/1/1946 [1947], FP vol. 39. William Charles Wentworth (1907–2003), MHR for Mackellar 1949–77, Minister for Aboriginal Affairs 1968–72, returned from the war in 1943 and became a businessman and anti-communist campaigner, writing several anti-socialist pamphlets 1947–8.
37   Although the Australian Security Intelligence Organisation (ASIO) was not established until 1949, data was gathered before then by several Commonwealth departments such as Defence and as in the case of Australia First, state authorities undertook political surveillance.
38   PD, 14/10/1947 (re John Franklin).
39   Dan Clyne to SMF, 15/5/1947, FP vol. 22. Clive Raleigh Evatt, MLA (1900–84), barrister, was state Labor member for Hurstville 1939–59 (*ADB* vol. 17); his brother Dr Herbert Vere Evatt, MHR (1894–1965), was federal Labor member for Barton, 1940–58, *ADB* vol. 14.
40   SMF to Emma Pischel, 6/5/1947, FP vol. 15, and Vida Goldstein to SMF, 22/12/1947, FP vol. 10.*
41   SMF to Anne Barnard, 1/8/1947, FP vol. 40;* Eileen Geddes Barnard-Kettle (d. 1986) was associated with Quaker peace groups.
42   Fox, *Dream at a Graveside,* p. 124; *SMH*, 1/3/1947, p. 24; 'Puritanism', ML MSS 445/35, pp. 137–57.
43   'The War Comes to Jones Street', ML MSS 6035/15, annotation.

44 Graeme Davison, 'The Exodists: Miles Franklin, Jill Roe and "the Drift to the Metropolis"', *HA*, 2004, vol. 2, no. 2; 'High Valley' by George and Charmian Johnston [sic] was awarded first prize in the *Herald* competition.

45 SMF to Kate Baker, 26/8/1947, Baker Papers; SMF to Mabel Singleton, 4/7/1947, FP vol. 25; SMF to Emma Pischel, 6/5/1947, FP vol. 15.

46 Nettie Palmer to SMF, 3/8/1947, and SMF to Nettie Palmer, 7/8/1947, FP vol. 24.

47 *Newcastle Morning Herald*, 2/9/1947, p. 2 (death of Bentley).

48 Harley Matthews to SMF, 7/10/1947, FP vol. 31; Lute Drummond to SMF, 28/9/1947, FP vol. 40.

49 *Official Year Book of the Commonwealth of Australia*, 1964, pp. 450–5; Roderick, *Miles Franklin*, p. 170.

50 FP vol. 104, p. 189.

51 SMF to Beatrice Davis, 11/11/1948, FP vol. 38;* [Mar. 1948], FP vol. 4/5, repr. *Diaries*, p. 197.

52 SMF to Florence James, 11/11/1948, FP vol. 30; PD, 11/11/1948.

53 The muddled layout of 'Twas Ever Thus' (*Jindyworobak Review 1938–1948*) is corrected in *A Gregarious Culture*; *Bulletin*, 29/9/1948, p. 2.

54 'Difficulties of Australian Writing', ML MSS 445/37, and 'Problems of Writing Today', *Book News*, Feb. 1948, p. 439, SMF one of five lecturers on Australian literature at Sydney Teachers College; SMF to Leonora Pease, 26/1/1948, FP vol. 13.

55 FP vol. 4/5, repr. *Diaries*, p. 198. Jean Devanny was expelled from the Party in 1940, rejoined 1944, and left for good in 1950 (*ADB* vol. 8 and Carole Ferrier, *Jean Devanny: Romantic Revolutionary*, Melbourne Univ. Press, Carlton, 1999, p. 254.)

56 *Diaries*, p. 203; SMF to KSP, 9/4/1948, FP vol. 21, repr. Ferrier, *As Good as a Yarn with You*. Morrisby (see ch. 11, n. 108) is not identified as a significant figure in Catholic Action in Sydney in Bruce Duncan, *Crusade or Conspiracy: Catholics and the Anti-communist Struggle in Australia*, Univ. of NSW Press, Sydney, 2001.

57 SMF to KSP, 9/4/1948, and KSP to SMF, 4/5/1948, FP vol. 21, both repr. Ferrier, *As Good as a Yarn with You*; Fox, *Dream at a Graveside*, Appendix.

58 Dymphna Cusack to Florence James, 24/10/1948, FP vol. 30, repr. North, *Yarn Spinners*; SMF to KSP, n.d., 1948, FP vol. 21, repr. Ferrier, *As Good as a Yarn with You*, p. 201; SMF to Australian Russian Society, 1/8/1948, FP vol. 41. UNESCO commenced in 1946.

59 SMF to Jean Hamilton, 11/1/1948, FP vol. 26, and SMF to St John Ervine, 12/5/1948, FP vol. 14;* Jalland, *Changing Ways of Death in Twentieth-century Australia*, ch. 2.

60 SMF to Leonora Pease, 26/1/1948, and 28/5/1948, FP vol. 13; SMF to Hildegarde Pischel, 19/2/1948, FP vol. 41; SMF to Florence James, 3/5/1948, FP vol. 30, repr. North, *Yarn Spinners*. Kay Keen (1910–48) died of tuberculosis, *ibid*., p. 409.

61 PD, 31/3/1948; SMF's will, probate no. 42952, repr. North, *Yarn Spinners*. 'Edwin' Graham was registered at birth as Edward John Mervyn Graham, NSW BMD indexes.

62 Ian Hamilton, *Keepers of the Flame: Literary Estates and the Rise of Biography*, Hutchinson, London, 1992, has case studies from John Donne to Sylvia Plath and Philip Larkin.

63 Jalland, *Changing Ways of Death in Twentieth-century Australia*, p. 128, ch. 6 (drinking by airmen to cope with stress); PD, 21/1/1948. 'War neurosis' is a term dating from World War I, devised to describe various psychological disorders suffered by soldiers. The Woomera rocket range, a joint UK–Australia missile testing facility, was under construction by 1948.

64 SMF to Leonora Pease, 20/2/1948, FP vol. 13; 'Sixteen Airmen Killed', *SMH*, 20/2/1948, p 1; Dymphna Cusack to Florence James, 8/3/1948, in North, *Yarn Spinners*, p. 172.

65 SMF to Frank Ryland, 2/2/1948, FP vol. 37.*

66 SMF to Emmy Lawson, 3/6/1948, FP vol. 39 (also refers to another appalling crash, killing the last of the squadron John flew with at Balikpapan in east Borneo); SMF to Mary E. Dreier, 3/6/1948, FP vol. 14;* SMF to B. Dobbyn and J. Adam, 13/1/1948, FP vol. 40.

67 SMF to KSP, 11/1/1948, FP vol. 21, repr. Ferrier, *As Good as a Yarn with You*; SMF to Ian Mudie, 18/5/1948, FP vol. 36; SMF to Frank Ryland, 1/11/1948, FP vol. 37 ('marooned').

68 PD, 2–3/11/1948. KSP to SMF, 13/8/1948, FP vol. 21, repr. Ferrier, *As Good as a Yarn with You*, pp. 183–8; Nettie Palmer to SMF, 21/10/1949, FP vol. 24; SMF to Margery Currey, 24/11/1948, FP vol. 24 (cesspits). George Langrigg Leathes Lawson (18??–1948) was a partner in the 'Goulburn Dispensary' in 1895, and medical officer to NSW Imperial Bushmen in the Boer War (NSW Government *Gazette*, 3/1/1903, p. 104, and Wyatt, *History of Goulburn*, p. 313).

69   O'Harris, *Was It Yesterday?*, p. 74.

70   ML MSS 445 and ML MSS 3065 (texts); FP vol. 88–9 (publishing papers); Pfisterer, *Playing with Ideas*, pp. 241–3 (re 'Johanna' plays, pp. 237–40); Jill Roe, 'Miles Franklin's pseudonyms', *SMH*, 28/2/2004 (*Supp.*), p. 4.

71   SMF to St John Ervine, 12/5/1948, FP vol. 14;* Lenore Layman & Julian Godard, *Organise! A Visual Record of the Labour Movement in Western Australia*, Trades and Labor Council of WA, E. Perth, WA, 1988, p. 243, and *West Australian*, 10/8/1948, p. 8; Annette Bain, '"Brighter Days?": Challenges to Live Theatre in the Thirties', *Twentieth Century Sydney*, ed. Jill Roe, Hale & Iremonger, Sydney, 1980, p. 45; SMF to Sumner Locke Elliott, 31/10/1948, FP vol. 41.* (Dame) Doris Fitton (1897–1985), *ADB* vol. 17. (Baron) Laurence Olivier (1907–89) and Vivien Leigh (Lady Olivier) (1913–67), *ODNB*; Sumner Locke Elliott (1915–91) left for New York before the first production (*OCAL*); his play was censored for swear words such as 'bloody'.

72   FP vol. 41 (SMF–Collinson corres.). Laurence Collinson (1925–86), who was English-born and returned to England in 1964, wrote numerous plays, mostly unpublished (*ADB* vol. 17, *OCAL*).

73   *Letty Fox: Her Luck*, and *Sexual Behaviour of the Human Male*, were both published in 1946. SMF to Margery Currey, 13/7/1948 and 24/11/1948, FP vol. 22; SMF to Beatrice Davis, 11/11/1948, FP vol. 38.*

74   SMF to Frank Ryland, 11/1/1948, FP vol. 37 (Japan); SMF to Leonora Pease, 28/5/1948, FP vol. 13; SMF to Emmy Lawson, 3/6/1948, FP vol. 39. *ABC Weekly*, 1/5/1948 ('Reflections on an atomic age', Oliphant), 2/6/1948 ('Social Security and Freedom', Beveridge), *SMH*, 6/5/1948, p. 1 ('Warning on World Food Crops', Orr). (Sir) John Boyd Orr (1880–1971) had just resigned as director-general of the Food and Agriculture Organization; (Sir) William Beveridge (1879–1963) visited Australasia in 1948; (Sir) Marcus Oliphant (1901–2000) later became governor of South Australia (all *ODNB*).

75   SMF to Emmy Lawson, 3/6/1948, FP vol. 39. The prelates were en route to the centenary of the Melbourne archdiocese, *SMH*, 29/4/1948, 1/5/1948, p. 5. *Bulletin*, 19/5/1948, p. 10 (re) Francis Joseph Spellman (1889–1967) was created a cardinal in 1946; Fulton John Sheen (1895–1979) became auxiliary bishop of New York in 1951 and was America's first successful television preacher (both *ANB*).

76   SMF to Leonora Pease, 28/5/1948, FP vol. 13; SMF to Mary E. Dreier, 3/6/1948, FP vol. 14.*

77   SMF to Mary E. Dreier, *ibid.*; KSP to SMF, 4/4/1948, FP vol. 21, repr. Ferrier, *As Good as a Yarn with You.*

78   Margery Currey to SMF, 21/10/1948, FP vol. 22.

79   [1948], FP vol. 4/5, repr. *Diaries*, pp. 211–12.

80   SMF to Margery Currey, 13 and 30/7/1948, FP vol. 22.

81   SMF to Beatrice Davis, 11/11/1948, FP vol. 38.*

82   SMF to Magdalen Dalloz, 31/7/1948, FP vol. 41; SMF to Margery Currey, 24/11/1948, FP vol. 22.

83   SMF to Dymphna Cusack, 31/5/[1949], FP vol. 30,* has the exchange. Sydney John Tomholt (1884–1974), *ADB* vol. 12.

84   SMF to J. K. Moir, 29/12/1948, J. K. Moir Colln.* *Spinner* was finally published by William Heinemann. Unfortunately the dedication is omitted from the 1990 edition, though Florence James does refer to it in her introduction.

85   SMF to J. K. Moir, 29/12/1948, J. K. Moir Colln.* See http:// www.austlit.edu.au for an up-to-date listing of editions of *Swagger.*

86   PD, 1948, *passim* (reading); *SMH*, 7/8/1948, p. 6; David Marr, *Patrick White: A Life*, Random House, Sydney, 1991, pp. 257–8; R. G. Howarth, *Southerly*, 1950, vol. 11, no. 4, pp. 209–10; Marjorie Barnard, 'The Four Novels of Patrick White', *Meanjin*, 1956, vol. 15, no. 65, pp. 156–70 was the first major appreciation.

87   'Gentleman Encounters Lady', by 'Johnny Palms', ML MSS 445/22, dated 17/2/1949, was written for a *SMH* literary competition; see also ML MSS 6035/3. White attended preparatory school at Moss Vale in the Southern Highlands in the early 1920s; Miles stayed with Edward and Maggie Bridle at nearby Tallong in the 1930s.

88   Adrian Mitchell, 'Fiction', *Oxford History of Australian Literature*, Oxford Univ. Press, Melbourne, ed. Leonie Kramer, p. 149.

89   John Franklin certificate of service and discharge, FP vol. 113X.

90 SMF to My dear little Enid [Norvill], 23/12/1949, FP vol. 46. See ch 10, n. 60 for data on John Franklin's relatives.

91 Corres. re Dymock's proposal 4/6/1943–16/4/1944 is at ML MSS 6329, and for 1944–16/1/1945, see FP vol. 86; Colin Roderick to SMF, 5/5/1945, and SMF to Colin Roderick, 15/6/1945, 2/7/1945, FP vol. 38.

92 Corres. between Charles Peters and J. H. Blackwood, 16/11/1945–8/2/1946 is at ML MSS 6329; William Blake to Charles Peters, 26/6/1947, FP vol. 86

93 Blackwood to William Blake, 30/12/1946, ML MSS 6329; W. G. Cousins to SMF, 6/1/1947, FP vol. 86; Brent of Bin Bin to Blackwood, 9/4/1947, and Marjorie Hetts to Blackwood, 22/2/1948, ML MSS 6329.

94 Brent of Bin Bin to Colin Roderick, [24/3/1947], and reply 5/4/1947, FP vol. 86; Angus & Robertson [Colin Roderick] to SMF, 20/6/1947, FP vol. 86.

95 SMF to Dymphna Cusack, 18/7/1949, FP vol. 30 (Roderick); Beatrice Davis to Brent of Bin Bin, 16/9/1948, Angus & Robertson Corres., ML MSS 3269, vol. 274, p. 229; FP vol. 86.

96 SMF to Beatrice Davis, 2/3/1949, Angus & Robertson Corres., ML MSS 3269, vol. 274; Ric Throssell to SMF and reply, 21–22/1/1949, FP vol. 41; Pfisterer, *Playing With Ideas*, p. 246. Mary Elizabeth ('Maie') Hoban (1887–1984), speech and drama teacher, established the Pilgrim Theatre in 1939 (*ADB* vol. 17).

97 *A Gregarious Culture*, pp. 218–20, has the full text (source, ABC Archives) .

98 'Writers from the universities', *Bulletin*, 5/1/1949, 'Red Page', and 'Syntax is not Sufficient', ML MSS 445/37; 'Gentleman Encounters Lady', 'The Robinson Story', 'The Hat' (pen-name 'Felt Hat'), ML MSS 445/22; SMF [two paras], Donald McLean, *Easy English for Young Australians*, Shakespeare Head Press, Sydney, 1951, p. 11.

99 SMF to Beatrice Davis, 2/3/1949, Angus & Robertson Corres., ML MSS 3269, vol. 274; Pearl Cotterill, d. May 1986 aged 82 (*Tumut & Adelong Times*, 27/5/1986, p. 2).

100 PD, 2 and 4/3/1949 (the new pine plantations).

101 SMF to Beatrice Davis, 2/3/1949, Angus & Robertson Corres., ML MSS 3269, vol. 274, p. 237; SMF to Ian Mudie, 8/7/1949, FP vol. 36.

102 SMF to J. K. Moir, 16/2/1949, J. K. Moir Colln; *DT*, 12/2/1949, p. 4, and 16/2/1949, p. 10; *SMH*, 10/3/1949, p. 3.

103 SMF to Beatrice Davis, 12/4/1949, Angus & Robertson Corres., ML MSS 3269, vol. 274; PD, 12 and 17/4/1949.

104 Beatrice Davis to SMF, 14/4/1949, Angus & Robertson Corres., ML MSS 3269, vol. 274.

105 Angus & Robertson to SMF, 19/5/1949, and page of Blackwood contract, Angus & Robertson Corres., ML MSS 3269, vol. 274, p. 477. Miles nominated as Brent's rep. in Jan. 1949: cited Beatrice Davis to SMF, 19/5/1949, FP vol. 86, but the letter does not seem to survive.

106 SMF to Beatrice Davis, 21/4/1949, Angus & Robertson Corres., ML MSS 3269, vol. 274; SMF to Ian Mudie, 8/7/1949, FP vol. 36.

107 Kent, *A Certain Style*, pp. 106, 112; Neil James and Elizabeth Webby, 'Canon around the Hub: Angus & Robertson and the Post-war Literary Canon', *Southerly*, 1997, vol. 57, no. 3. Beatrice Davis, 'An Enigmatic Woman', *Overland*, 1983, no. 91, p. 26 ('it says a lot for her personality and persuasiveness that any sensible publisher should have agreed to such madness'). See n. 85 above re editions of *Swagger*.

108 SMF to [Dr Young], Good Friday 1949, FP vol. 20; SMF to Dymphna Cusack, 31/5/[1949], FP vol. 30.*

109 PD, 27 and 31/7/1949.

110 SMF to W. G. Cousins, 10/5/1949, Angus & Robertson Corres.; J. Lane, 'Stella Maria Sarah Miles Franklin — A Personal Memoir', unpub. copy in my possession, courtesy author. Alan Paton (1903–88) South African writer and politician (*ODNB*). The three novels mentioned were all published in 1948.

111 Pixie O'Harris to SMF [rcd 7/2/1949], FP vol. 35.

112 SMF to Beatrice Davis, 19/8/1949, FP vol. 38;* SMF to Nettie Palmer, 10/7/1949, Palmer Papers; Smith (ed.), *Nettie Palmer*, p. 141 (stating that in 1935 Miles farewelled the Palmers en route to Europe with a pot of pineapple jam).

113 Beatrice Davis to SMF, 20/10/1949 and 26/10/1949, Angus & Robertson Corres., ML MSS 3269, vol. 274, pp. 271–3.

114 David Martin to SMF, 5/8/1949, and SMF to David Martin, 23/8/1949, FP vol. 41 (*both, edited text). David Martin (1915–97), b. into a Jewish family in Hungary, worked as journalist in England 1938–48, when he travelled to India, moving to Australia in 1949; he left the Communist Party in 1958 (obit., *SMH*, 12/7/1997).

115 SMF to Mollye Menken, 19/12/1949, FP vol. 20.

116 SMF to Elisabeth Christman, 28/11/1949, FP vol. 24.

117 SMF to Dymphna Cusack, 24/9/1949, FP vol. 30. John Wallace Metcalfe (1901–82) was principal librarian, Public (now State) Library of NSW, 1942–59 (*ADB*, vol. 18 forthcoming).

118 *Newcastle Morning Herald*, 22/9/1949, p. 2; *Union Recorder*, 24/11/1949, n. p. Denis Winston (1908–80), architect and town-planner, was regarded as the most influential planner in postwar Australia (*ADB* vol. 16).

119 Miles Franklin re-appeared in *Who's Who in Australia* in 1938 after a long absence; entries often omitted a birth date altogether, e.g. 1938, 1950; *Bulletin*, 5/12/1951, p. 30, and Geraldine O'Brien, 'Author's Light Falls on the Poets of Waverley', *SMH*, 17/1/1998, p. 15; SMF to Nell Malone, 18/12/1949, FP vol. 15.

120 Allan Edwards to SMF, 16/1/1950, FP vol. 89; Registrar, Univ. of Tasmania to SMF, 20/5/1947, 12/6/1947, and SMF's reply, 23/5/1947, FP vol. 92. William Allan Edwards (1909–95) was professor of English, Univ. of Western Australia, 1941–74/5 <www.museum.wa.gov.au/welcomewalls/albany>.

121 Tom Shapcott, *The Literature Board: A Brief History*, Univ. of Qld Press, St Lucia, Qld, 1988, pp. 262–4 (the scheme operated 1940–64); Allan Edwards,16/1/1950, FP vol. 89.

122 V-C Currie to SMF, 6/4/1950, and reply SMF to Currie, 11/4/1950, Univ. of WA Archives, FP vol. 89; Allan Edwards to SMF, 23/1/1950, and SMF to Allan Edwards, 18/1/1950, 4/2/1950, *ibid.* (Sir) George Alexander Currie (1896–1984) was vice-chancellor of Univ. of WA 1940–52 (*ADB* vol. 17).

123 Henrietta Drake-Brockman to SMF, 23/5/[1950] and SMF to Henrietta Drake-Brockman, 7/6/1950, FP vol. 33.*

124 SMF to KSP, 24/4/1950, FP vol. 21;* SMF to Allan Edwards, 5/6/1950, FP vol. 89, attachment.

125 'JvH', Handcard, FP vol. 91/1, citing St John Ervine, Henrietta Drake-Brockman; James Pratt to SMF, 26/1/1950, 3/2/1950, FP vol. 88; SMF to Kevin Brennan, 4/2–2/8/1950, FP vol. 88.

126 SMF to Mabel Singleton, 5/3/1950, FP vol. 25; Elisabeth Christman to SMF, 2/2/1940, WTUL Papers, m/film reel 12, folders 707–8; SMF to Margery Currey, 14/3/1950, FP vol. 22;* F. W. E. Burnham to SMF, 6/11/1948 and 20/3/1950, and SMF to F. W. E. Burnham, 12/6/1950, FP vol. 24, also SMF to 'Dear Canadian Friend', 6/3/1950, FP vol. 42; SMF to Emmy Lawson, 6/3/1950, FP vol. 39.

127 SMF to Margery Currey, 14/3/1950, FP vol. 22;* SMF to David & Richenda Martin, 3/1/1950, FP vol. 41; Myrtle Rose White to SMF, 3/3/1950, FP vol. 42.* Myrtle Rose White (1888–1961) wrote *No Roads Go By* (1932) and two sequels (*ADB* vol. 12).

128 SMF to Henrietta Drake-Brockman, 4/4/1950, FP vol. 33.

129 The following account is based on PD entries.

130 The story of John Franklin's committal accords with the analysis in Garton, *Medicine and Madness*, pp. 121–6, 130–1, regarding young men in the inner suburbs, who often directed their anger against mothers when a male authority figure was absent, the role of neighbours when the situation became public as in the street scene, and the effect of the law and the police in dealing with inebriates, to which must be added in this instance the effects of war; SMF to Dymphna Cusack, 16/5/1950, FP vol. 30, is one of several accounts in letters at this point. 'DTs': *delirium tremens* caused by excessive alcohol (*MD*).

131 Persia White: Miles once referred to her as Mrs Persia White and wished she was free to marry John. Further information has not been located to date.

132 Garton, *Medicine and Madness*, p. 169 (patients often died during the initial course of ECT, i.e. electro convulsive therapy). With the medicalisation of mental problems, 'schizophrenia' replaced 'mania' in clinical usage.

133 SMF to Mabel Singleton, 29/5/1949, FP vol. 25 (blames the air force); Garton, *Medicine and Madness*, p. 165. Apparently the legal maximum time for committal to an asylum on the grounds of inebriation was six months (SMF to Dymphna Cusack, 27/9/1950, FP vol. 30).

134 SMF to Renee & Ian Mudie, 5/6/1950, Mudie Papers; SMF to David Bradley, 25/11/1950, FP vol. 43;* SMF to KSP, 7/6/1950, FP vol. 21. David Bradley, b. 1925, then an English lecturer, later became professor emeritus of English, Monash Univ.

135 SMF to [Emmy Lawson], 6/3/1950, FP vol. 42; SMF to David Martin, 18/4/1950, FP vol. 41; SMF to Henrietta Drake-Brockman, 7/6/1950, FP vol. 33;* SMF to Clive Evatt, 22/6/1950, FP vol. 42;* SMF to KSP, 7/6/1950, FP vol. 21.

136 KSP to SMF, 5/3/1950, FP vol. 21; Rex Ingamells to SMF, 20/2/1950, FP vol. 40; SMF to KSP, 26/3/1950 and 24/4/1950, FP vol. 21 (all KSP/SMF letters repr. Ferrier, *As Good as a Yarn with You*), and SMF to Margery Currey, 14/3/1950, FP vol. 22;* Throssell, *Wild Weeds and Wind Flowers*, n. 95. The Nobel Prize for literature was won by Bertrand Russell in 1950 and the poet Pär Lagerkvist in 1951. John Keith Ewers (1904–78), *OCAL*.

137 PD, 16/6/1950, 21/6/1950.

138 'Jonesie' to SMF, 5/8/1937ff., FP vol. 10. 'Jonesie' returned from America in 1911 and married Harold Partridge McKenzie in 1917 in South Australia, where she died.

139 FP vol. 91, *Sydney Royal* distribution list.

140 SMF to Bob Saunders, 26/8/1950, FP vol. 42; *West Australian*, 3/7/1950, p. 12; *Australian Women's Weekly*, 8/7/1950, p. 28. Jean Bradley, née Tweedie (d. 1991), Parsons, *Companion to Theatre in Australia*, ed. Philip Parsons with Victoria Chance, Currency Press in association with Cambridge Univ. Press, Sydney, c.1995. Dorothy Lucie Sanders ('Shelley Dean') (1907–87), was a popular West Australian writer (AustLit).

141 PD, 2/7/1950. Dr Roberta Jull (1872–1961), *ADB* vol. 9.

142 Henrietta Drake-Brockman, 'Miles Franklin', *Walkabout*, 1/3/1951, pp. 8–9. Sylvia (Silvia) Pallot, née Furphy (1875–1967), Barnes, *The Order of Things*, WA BMD Indexes.

143 SMF to Allan Edwards, 5/6/1950, FP vol. 89 (page of notes attached); 'D.S.' [possibly Donald Stewart], 'A Gifted Australian Writer', *West Australian*, 5/8/1950; 'Interview with Miles Franklin', *Pelican*, 4/8/1950, p. 7. Geoffrey Bolton, AO, b. 1931 (*OCAH*).

144 SMF to Pallots, 8/8/1950, FP vol. 43;* *All That Swagger*, inscription, Irene Greenwood Book Collection, Murdoch Univ. Archives. Mary Louisa (Mollie) Skinner (1876–1955), *ADB* vol. 11. Irene Greenwood (1898–1992), *Australian Feminist Studies*, 1993, vol. 17, no. 104.

145 FP vols 90 and 92 (payments); 'The Australian Theatre', *West Australian*, 23/9/1950, p. 21, repr. *A Gregarious Culture*.

146 Allan Edwards, 'Report of Miss Miles Franklin's visit as Australian Commonwealth Fund Lecturer', 15/8/1950, Univ. of WA Archives, cited Roderick, Guard Book 10, Roderick Papers, pp. 21–3. (Dame) Alexandra Hasluck (1908–93) later published numerous distinguished works of history and biography (*OCAL*).

147 SMF to Henrietta Drake-Brockman, 8/8/1950, FP vol. 33.

148 KSP to SMF, 8/8/1950, FP vol. 21; 'Parade of Australian Fiction', *West Australian*, 15/7/1950, p. 19 (review of Roderick).

149 Angus & Robertson to SMF, 6/6/1950, FP vol. 90 (promotions in Perth); Beatrice Davis to SMF, 14/8/1950, and SMF to Beatrice Davis, Sunday night, FP vol. 38; Beatrice Davis to SMF, 25/8/1950, FP vol. 86, and Sydney *Sun*, 12/8/1950, p. 5, 'Remember the Controversy about the Authorship of the Brent of Bin Bin Books?'.

150 FP vol. 5/11 and draft entry, 'Notes on Australian Fiction', by 'Bunyip', Commonwealth Literary Jubilee Literary Competition brochure, FP vol. 89, p. 115.

151 *Laughter, Not for a Cage*, p. 230.

152 *ibid.*, p. 15.

153 *ibid.*, pp. 1, 3, 15; *ibid.*, chs 9, 10, 11. Mentioned above: Morris Miller (1881–1964), scholar and bibliographer (*ADB* vol. 10); for Eris O'Brien, see ch. 14, n. 79.

154 The full title of *Tomorrow and Tomorrow and Tomorrow* was restored by Virago, London, 1983; Elizabeth Webby, 'Miles Franklin as Literary Critic' (unpub. paper, copy in my possession, courtesy the author); *Laughter, Not for a Cage*, p. 206.

155 *ibid.*, pp. 211, 220.

156 *ibid.*, p. 217.

157 *ibid.*, pp. 226–7, 181, 228.

158 *ibid.*, pp. 118–19; for Stephens, 'Wizard of the South', see ch. 10, n. 75.

159 KSP to SMF, Christmas Eve, 1950, FP vol. 21;* Henrietta Drake-Brockman, 18/8/1950, FP vol. 33; 'D. E.' [John Edward Webb], *SMH*, 23/12/1950, p. 6; 'Miss Bronte', 'No Applause for Brent', *DT*, 25/11/1950, p. 19 ['Miss Bronte' was a pen-name of editor Brian Penton] and SMF to C. B. Christesen, 4/3/1951, MA ('spiteful'); *Sun*, 25/11/1950, p. 4; *Argus*, 7/4/1951, p. 16; SMF to David Martin, 22/11/1950, FP vol. 41. A review by H. M. Green ('misguided' according to Miles) appeared in *Southerly*, 1951, no. 4, pp. 182–9.

160 SMF to David Martin, 22/11/1950, FP vol. 41; David Martin, *Meanjin*, 1951, vol. 10, no. 2, pp. 187, 189.

161 Jean Hamilton to SMF, 29/12/1951, FP vol. 26.

162 SMF to United Associations of Women, 23/10/1950, FP vol 41.*

163 SMF to David Martin, 16/11/1950, FP vol. 41* (conscientious objectors); SMF to Ric Throssell, 20/12/1950, FP vol. 41.*

164 Beatrice Davis to SMF, 11/9/1950, FP vol. 38; J. Lane, 'Stella Maria Sarah Miles Franklin — A Personal Memoir', unpub. copy in my possession, courtesy author.

Chapter 14 — 'Shall I Pull Through?': 1951–1954

1 SMF to Tom Ronan, 13/2/1953, FP vol. 44.*

2 Electoral Roll, 1950; Sands' *Directory*, 1932–3.

3 *SMH*, 9/8/1940, p. 6 (re the widowed May Smales, née Fogden).

4 The older shops on High St were nearer, Ron Rathbone, pers. comm., 24/5/2006; see also his *History of Carlton,* R. W. Rathbone, Kogarah, 196—?, and Carlton Parade Rate Valuation book, 1950, information courtesy Rockdale City Library. (Carlton, previously part of Bexley, was absorbed into Rockdale c.1948.) On south Carlton today, see 'Up Your Street', *SMH*, 20/5/2004, Domain, p. 22.

5 NAA records C95422 and A6122/2 show that from 1949 the FAW was regarded by ASIO as 'a purely political organisation' dominated by leftists and communists.

6 SMF to Mrs Howarth, 26/5/1954, FP vol. 43.

7 Joe Salter (1917–2003) was a poet who worked as a locomotive fireman (AustLit and Ryerson Index). Allan John Dalziel (1908–69) was a social reformer and political secretary (*ADB* vol. 13). Arthur Cross (1904–1974) and Delys Cross (1910–1993) were originally from Western Australia.

8 Nancy Keesing, *Riding the Elephant*, Allen & Unwin Australia, 1972, pp. 71–3; Rex Ingamells to SMF, 16/8/1951, FP vol. 40,* and SMF to Rex Ingamells, 24/12/1951, Rex Ingamells Colln. Nancy Keesing, AM (1923–1993) was a Sydney writer active in literary affairs for many years (*OCAL*).

9 Sale notice, Franklin Estate, *SMH*, 22/11/1961, p. 7, lists furniture.

10 A Hoover electric washing machine cost as much as £43/10/– in 1951 (*Australian Women's Weekly*, 21/1/1951), i.e. approximately a third of SMF's annual income.

11 'Bagging the figs': to protect them from birds; mowing: by push mower so hard work.

12 SMF to Magdalen Dalloz, 28/12/1953, FP vol. 41; Ron Rathbone, pers. comm., 24/5/2006 (paper boy in 1942); Dymphna Cusack to SMF, 14/1/1951, FP vol. 30.

13 SMF to Theo Lampe, 21/1/1950, FP vol. 49; PD, 20/11/1951; SMF to Ethel Nielsen, 29/11/1951, FP vol. 21.

14 Dymphna Cusack to SMF, 8/10/1950, SMF to Dymphna Cusack, 2/11/1950, FP vol. 30, repr. North, *Yarn Spinners*. Corres. with William Farquhar Fraser (1898–1979) between 1951 and 1953 is at FP vol. 44 (NSW BMD, Medical Directories); Fraser's uncle Alex McFarlane, from the Clarence River region, was a fan of Miles Franklin.

15 SMF to Dymphna Cusack, 10/11/1951, FP vol. 30, repr. North, *Yarn Spinners*. John Franklin had four maternal cousins: *SMH* 3/11/1956, p. 56 (his death notice), lists Enid (Mrs Norvill), Rose (Mrs Thompson), Claire (Mrs O'Connor) and Brenda (Mrs Fitzpatrick).

16 Marie Isabell Edith (known as 'May') McNiven, née Beattie (1888–1962) several sources, including NSW BMD indexes. Herbert Kemble, b. 1920, was a painter who worked as an illustrator in the 1940s (Griffen-Foley files).

17 SMF to Arnold Dresden, 8/7/1951, FP vol. 35; SMF to Margery Currey, 6/6/1951, FP vol. 22. (The *Walkabout* article, 1/3/1951, pp. 8–9).

18 SMF to Bruce Graham, 12/2/1951, and Bruce Graham to SMF, 22/3/1951, FP vol. 43. For laments for the old Australia, see e.g.: SMF to Jean Hamilton, 4/5/1951, FP vol. 26; SMF to Ian Mudie, 5/7/1951, FP vol. 36* and SMF to P. & M. Meggitt, 10/12/1951, FP vol. 39. Bruce Graham, b. 1919, *Who's Who in Australia* (1985).

19 J. Staedter, *Sydney's Jewish Community: Materials for a Post-war (II) History*, Australian Jewish Communities series, Pennant Hills, NSW, 1955. William J. Hobbin (1905–93) was director, Methodist Social Service Department (*SMH*, 27/2/1951, pp. 1, 4). See also 'Keep Out the Nazis', FP vol. 445/39, 1 (*verso*), and Mark Aarons, *Sanctuary: Nazi Fugitives in Australia*, Heinemann Australia, Port Melbourne, 1989.

20 *SMH*, 2/6/1951, p. 9, and 4/6/1951, p. 2; SMF to Arnold Dresden, 8/7/1951, FP vol. 35; Raymond Fitzpatrick (1909–67), *ADB* vol. 14. Ronald Fogarty, *Catholic Education in Australia 1806–1950*, Melbourne Univ. Press, Carlton, Vic, 1959, vol. 2, p. 449. For Howard Mowll (1890–1958) and Daniel Mannix (1864–1963) see *ADB* vols 15, 10.

21 Anne V. Player, 'Bishop William Lanigan of Goulburn and the Making of a Catholic People, 1867–2004', PhD thesis, ANU, 2004, ch. 5; SMF to Jean Hamilton, 4/5/1951, vol. 26.

22 PD, 13/9/1951, 22/9/1951, 24/11/1951. In NSW, 53% voted 'No' at the referendum on wider Commonwealth powers to combat communism, the highest of any state (overall, 50.56%).

23 SMF to KSP, 25/5/1951, FP vol. 21, repr. Ferrier, *As Good as a Yarn with You*; P. & M. Meggitt, 10/12/1951, FP vol. 39; Dymphna Cusack to SMF, 14/2/1951, repr. North, *Yarn Spinners*, and SMF to Florence James, 27/2/1951, FP vol. 30 ('peace movement 'commo dominated''); Barbara Curthoys and Audrey McDonald, *More than a Hat and Coat Brigade: The Story of the Union of Australian Women*, Bookpress, Sydney, 1996, p. 70. Re communist dominance of the peace movement in Australia: John McLaren, 'Peace Wars: The 1959 ANZ Peace Congress', *Labour History*, 2002, no. 82, and Barbara Carter, 'The Peace Movement in the 1950s', in Ann Curthoys and John Merritt eds, *Better Dead than Red: Australia's First Cold War 1945–1959*, vol. 2, Allen & Unwin, Sydney, 1986, p. 65.

24 SMF to KSP, 25/5/1951, FP vol. 21.

25 Miles Franklin ASIO Files, NAA, CT 64/165 MF 4734:75; '[Sydney] Conference attack on Red Bill', *SMH*, 29/5/1950, p. 9; Fiona Capp, *Writers Defiled: Security Surveillance of Australian Authors*, McPhee Gribble, Ringwood, Vic, 1993, p. 45. Of Russian descent, railway worker Alexander Bookluck (?–1967) was a long-serving treasurer of the FAW from 1938. Frank Hardy (1917–94), Victorian-born writer who joined the Communist Party of Australia in 1939, wrote *Power Without Glory* (1950), a section of which was allegedly based on the life of Melbourne underworld figure John Wren (*OCAL*).

26 R. G. Howarth to H.S. Temby, 13/10/1950, NAA CLF files, A 463/34; SMF to H. S. Temby, 25/2/1951, and Temby's file note, *ibid.*, 1968/4178; SMF to Marjorie Pizer, 15/2/1951, FP vol. 39.

27 'Famous Women in Australian History: Rose Scott', to air 23/1/1951, *ABC Weekly*, 17/2/1951; 'The Dead Must Not Return', ML MSS 445/26, and FP vol. 88, also ML MSS 6035 (pseud. 'Field Hospital Orderly').

28 'The Dead Must Not Return', ML MSS 445/26, p. 57.

29 David Martin to SMF, 29/1/1952, FP vol. 41;* SMF to Margery Currey, 6/7/1951, FP vol. 22; SMF to Florence James, 23/6/1951, FP vol. 30. Thomas Arthur Guy Hungerford (b. 1915) shared second prize with Barbara Jefferis, '*Herald* Novel Awards' 1950–1, *SMH*, 5/5/1951, p. 1.

30 '*Herald* Novel Awards', *SMH*, 5/5/1951, p. 1; FP vol. 88, pp. 401, 425, 419 and 407 (entries); 'A Bun for the Playwrights', *Bulletin*, 14/11/1951, p. 6; Henrietta Drake-Brockman to SMF, 16/8/1951, FP vol. 33; James Crawford (1908–73), journalist and playwright (*ADB S*); SMF to Keith Macartney, 7/4/1951, FP vol. 42 (states the play was 'noncompetition'), and Henrietta Drake-Brockman to SMF, 7/1/1951, FP vol. 33; Fred Robinson to SMF, 28/12/1951, FP vol. 39. Keith Lamont Macartney (1903–71), *ADB* vol. 15. On Frederick Walter Robinson (1888–1971) and his scholarly aspirations for the emerging field Australian literature, see Leigh Dale, *The English Men: Professing Literature in Australian Universities*, Association for the Study of Australian Literature, Univ. of Southern Qld, 1997, pp. 148–9 and *ADB* vol. 11.

31 PD, 16/9/1951; John Barnes to SMF, 9/7/1951, SMF to John Barnes, 16/7/1951, FP vol. 44. Richard John Barnes, b. 1931, professor emeritus, La Trobe Univ. (AustLit).

32 Eleanor Witcombe to SMF, 18/3/1951, FP vol. 43,* and SMF to Eleanor Witcombe, 7/4/1951 and [15]/5/1951, FP vol. 43; SMF to Warwick Fairfax, 3/8/1951, FP vol. 44* and Warwick Fairfax to SMF, 7/8/1951, FP vol. 44; SMF to KSP, 30/3/1951, FP vol. 21, repr. Ferrier, *As Good as a Yarn with You*, and Ric Throssell to SMF, 23/5/1951, FP vol. 41; SMF to Sumner Locke Elliott, 3/10/1951,* and Sumner Locke Elliott to SMF, 26/11/—[?] FP vol. 41. Eleanor Witcombe (b. 1923) is a Sydney playwright and author with a particular interest in the life of Daisy Bates. (Sir) Warwick Fairfax, see *ADB* vol. 17.

33 SMF to Margery Currey, 6/6/1951, FP vol. 22.

34 SMF to Eleanor Witcombe, 7/4/1951, FP vol. 43. Jean Campbell (1901–84), *ADB* vol. 17, who mainly wrote light novels, dismissed 'The Dead Must Not Return' as a complete failure and hackneyed (Jean Campbell to SMF, 9/3/1952, FP vol. 44); PD, 13/10/1951 ('shocking'), and LN, FP vol. 3, pp. 523–4 (Thornford).

35 *Bulletin*, 16/5/1951, p. 18; SMF to Dymphna Cusack, 27/5/1951, FP vol. 30; PD, 9/5/1951, 21/9/1951.

36 'Bunyip': an imaginary creature of Aboriginal legend said to haunt swamps and billabongs: an impostor (*MD*); FP vol. 89, p. 115 (brochure). SMF to Dymphna Cusack, 9/5/1952, FP vol. 30 (the awards).

37 SMF to David Martin, 2/10/1951, FP vol. 41; entry materials, FP vol. 89, pp. 115–21; 'Two Share Prize for Serial', *SMH*, 27/11/1951, p. 3 and 'Prize of £200 to Author', *SMH*, 24/12/1951, p. 2 (Palmer wins). In fairness to Inglis Moore, his study was begun in the 1930s, and publication was delayed by teaching responsibilities at the ANU (Preface, *Social Patterns in Australian Literature*, Univ. of California Press, Berkeley and Los Angeles, 1971, p. viii). Perth-born Tom Ronan (1907–76), *ADB* vol. 16, lived at Katherine and wrote five outback novels 1952–61 and several volumes of non-fiction to 1977 (*OCAL*).

38 PD, 13/6/1951 (will power); SMF to Dorothy Sanders, 8/3/1951, FP vol. 43.

39 SMF to Dorothy Sanders, 8/3/1951, FP vol. 43.

40 SMF to Florence James, 21/11/1951, FP vol. 30. Katherine Mansfield (1888–1923) was a New Zealand-born writer (*ODNB*).

41 Em Fullerton had been in Sydney from c.May 1937 and with financial help from Miles in Aug. 1938 set up a residential at Kirribilli, FP vol. 104, p. 171; Nell Malone to SMF, 31/5/1951, FP vol. 15; SMF to Rex Ingamells, 10/11/1951, Ingamells Colln; SMF to Dymphna Cusack, 27/7/1949, FP vol. 30, part repr. North, *Yarn Spinners*. Nell Malone was last heard of in 1953 (Kathleen Ussher to SMF, 30/10/1953, FP vol. 15, postcard).

42 SMF to David Martin, 2/10/1951 and 23/11/1951, FP vol. 41. David Martin, main titles: *The Young Wife* (1962), *Armed Neutrality for Australia* (1984), and *My Strange Friend* (1991). Aldous Huxley (1894–1963), whose books include *Brave New World* (1932) (*ODNB*). 'Nevil Shute' (Nevil Shute Norway, 1899–1960), *ADB* vol. 15, an English-born novelist best known for *A Town Like Alice* (1950) and *On The Beach* (1957), interested her possibly because of themes close to her heart, the outback and strong women in the former work (Christina Twomey, unpub. Australian Hist Assoc. conference paper, Newcastle, 2004).

43 'Books', *Unity*, Mar.–Apr. 1951, p. 24.

44 *Unity* to SMF, 4/1/1951, FP vol. 90; *Meanjin*, 1951, vol. 10, no. 2, pp. 187–9; SMF to Vance Palmer, 9/8/1951, Palmer Papers;* *Bulletin* 17/1/1951, p. 2.

45 *Meanjin*, 1951, vol. 10, no. 1, pp. 81–2, repr. *A Gregarious Culture*; SMF to Dymphna Cusack, 27/2/1951, FP vol. 30, and SMF to Dymphna Cusack and Florence James, 10/4/1951, both repr. North, *Yarn Spinners*; also Dymphna Cusack to SMF, 21/4/1951, FP vol. 30. Re 'for the first time', she gave the proofs to Dymphna's friend and occasional go-between Nell Jordan (Fraser) (1906–82), and others failed to return her gift copy.

46 SMF to Dymphna Cusack, 27/7/1949 and 31/12/1951, and Dymphna Cusack to SMF, 26/3/1952, FP vol. 30; SMF to Emmy Lawson, 9/12/1951, FP vol. 39. Re Freehill, see n. 78 below.

47 SMF to Dymphna Cusack, 10/11/1951, FP vol. 30 (re *Swagger*); Brent royalty statements, Angus & Robertson, FP vol. 86.

48 PD, 2/6/1951; the dust jacket is reproduced in this volume. *Bulletin* 11/7/1951, p. 35, ad. ('a spirited Australian novel of adventure, humour and hardihood', price 6 shillings). Steele Rudd (Arthur Hooey Davis) (1868–1935), *ADB* vol. 8.

49 Beatrice Davis to SMF, 4/6/1951 and 29/6/1951, FP vol. 86.

50 Dymphna Cusack to SMF, 21/4/1951, FP vol. 30; 'Comparing the Critics', *Austrovert*, 1951, no. 1, p. 7; *Bulletin*, 18/7/1951, 'Red Page'; *Age*, 7/7/1951, p. 9.

51 Eng. Ass. Annual Dinner, *Union Recorder*, 29/11/1951, p. 237, p. 30; SMF to Dymphna Cusack, 1/5/1951, FP vol. 30; ML MSS 3659/1 (card). Bruce Sutherland (1904–70), AustLit.

52 J. K. Moir to SMF, 25/11/1951, FP vol. 34; SMF to Mabel Singleton, 1/4/1952, FP vol. 25 (* in part); on Moir, 'Knight Grand Cheese', *People*, 23/4/1952, and see ch. 12, n. 30.

53 SMF to Mabel Singleton, 1/4/1952, FP vol. 25.*

54 *Argus*, 27/2/1928, p. 8. Roland Robinson, Nancy Keesing and the Holburns were leading Lyre-Bird Writers. Freda Irving (1903–84), *ADB* vol. 17.

55 SMF to J. K. Moir, 4/2/1951, JK Moir Colln. Harold Blair (1924–76), *ADB* vol. 13. Bernard O'Dowd (1866–1953), poet, radical, and parliamentary draughtsman (*ADB* vol. 11).

56 Clem Christesen to SMF, 15/5/1952, MA (his invitation); SMF to Arthur Phillips, 28/1/1952, FP vol. 44; SMF to Dymphna Cusack, 15/3/1952, FP vol. 30;* Bruce Muirden, cited Mathew, *Miles Franklin*, p. 35. Arthur Phillips (1900–85), Bruce Muirden (1928–91), AustLit.

57 Everill Annie Venman (1907–c.80), who came to Melbourne c.1948 from Brisbane, resided at South Yarra and worked at Myer dispensary (Kristin Ashman, *A Tribute to Jack Venman: In Honour of a True Bushman*, Kristin Ashman, Qld, 1988, pp. 93–5).

58 SMF to J. K. Moir, 14/3/1952, J. K. Moir Colln.*

59 P. R. Stephensen to SMF, 1/3/1952, FP vol. 28, and SMF to J. K. Moir, 10/3/1952, FP vol. 34, also 14/3/1952, J. K. Moir Colln.*

60 SMF to J. K. Moir, 14/3/1952, J. K. Moir Colln;* SMF to P. R. Stephensen, 21/6/1951, FP vol. 28.

61 SMF to J. K. Moir, 14/3/1952, J. K. Moir Colln.*

62 'The Hansom Cab Mystery', *Bulletin*, 17/12/1952, p. 35, repr. *A Gregarious Culture*. Author Fergus Hume (1859–1932) left Australia permanently for England in 1888 (*ADB* vol. 4).

63 Pixie O'Harris, *Bulletin*, 5/10/1963, p. 53, and *Was It Yesterday?*, p. 72. A marked-up ts. of *Childhood at Brindabella* with the original photographs survives, Angus & Robertson Archive, ML MSS 314, Box 38, also a fair copy of 'I remember' made by Ruby Bridle (presently in my possession); but the original has not been sighted, nor the possible draft foreword, dated 14/8/1952 mentioned in the Publisher's Note, *Childhood at Brindabella*, 1987 edn.

64 SMF to Pixie O'Harris, letter cited in the Publisher's Note, *Childhood at Brindabella*, 1987 edn.

65 Joy Hooton, *Stories of Herself When Young: Autobiographies of Childhood by Australian Women*, Oxford Univ. Press, Melbourne, 1990, pp. 104–5; David McCooey, *Artful Histories: Modern Australian Autobiography*, Cambridge Univ. Press, Melbourne, 1996, pp. 54–7, discusses 'the Edenic myth'; *Childhood at Brindabella*, p. 121.

66 *Was It Yesterday?*, p. 74; Frank Eyre to Pixie O'Harris, 31/3/1953, FP vol. 89; Thelma Forshaw, *Nation*, 16/8/1962, p. 23. Manchester-born Frank Eyre (1910–88), arrived 1949 as editorial manager of Oxford Univ. Press, became general manager in 1951 (AustLit, *ADB* vol. 17).

67 The Cooper portrait has not so far been traced. One of the McNiven photos is reproduced in this book.

68 SMF to Bruce Sutherland, 6/3/1954, FP vol. 44; Roe, 'Changing Faces: Miles Franklin and Photography', *Australian Feminist Studies*, 2004.

69 SMF to J. K. Moir, 3/4/1952, 30/8/1952, J. K. Moir Colln; Brian Fitzpatrick, 'The Winter at Bay', *Overland*, 1954, no. 1, p. 3.

70 SMF to C. B. (Clem) Christesen, 17/5/1952, FP vol. 35. No first prize was awarded for fiction. The exchange is as follows: Clem Christesen to SMF, 12/5/1952, MA, SMF to Clem Christesen, 17/5/1952, FP vol. 35, Clem Christesen to SMF, 22/5/1952, MA, and SMF to Clem Christesen, 5/6/1952, MA. Dominic Mary Paul Maguire (1903–78), *ADB* vol. 15.

71 SMF to Ian Mudie, 5/7/1951, FP vol. 36.* Dr Anderson to SMF, 10/3/1951, FP vol. 43. Douglas Joseph Anderson, MD (1907–70), was a prominent Macquarie St physician, with expertise in tuberculosis (*ADB* file).

72 Jean Devanny to SMF, 28/4/1952, FP vol. 32; SMF to Les Woolacott, 28/4/52, FP vol. 44.

73 PD, 9/4/1952, 19/6/1952, *SMH*, 19/6/1952, p. 15; SMF to Dymphna Cusack, 21/6/1953, repr. North, *Yarn Spinners*; SMF to Rex Ingamells, 3/6/1952, Ingamells Colln. Edouard Borovansky (1902–59), *ADB* vol. 13.

74   Gertrude Kinred to SMF, 19/2/1952, FP vol. 49; SMF to Ethel Ruby Bridle, 10/2/1954, FP vol. 47.

75   SMF to J. K. Moir, 2/4/1952, J. K. Moir Colln; SMF to Henrietta Drake-Brockman, 15/4/1952, FP vol. 33;* SMF to J. K. Moir, 26/5/1952, FP vol. 34; SMF to Ian Mudie, 9/5/1952, FP vol. 36; SMF to J. K. Moir, 14/8/1952, J. K. Colln ('a new Australian').

76   J. K. Ewers to SMF, 7/8/1952, FP vol. 42; KSP to SMF, 25/8/1952, FP vol. 12;* SMF to Rex Ingamells, 14/6/1952, Ingamells Colln. The 'academic practitioners' she had in mind were probably Inglis Moore and Fred Robinson.

77   Barnard, *Miles Franklin*, p. 143 (but Barnard relied heavily on Miles' letters to Nettie Palmer, which petered out in the 1940s, and she always insisted on her own behalf that history is one of the creative arts, *ADB* vol. 17). *Swagger* was published in the UK, on 24/7/1952 (*English Catalogue of Books*).

78   SMF to Florence James, 3/6/1952, FP vol. 30;* SMF to Dymphna Cusack, 15/4/1954, FP vol. 30; PD, 4/10/1952. For Norman Randolph Freehill (1892–1984), journalist and communist, see North, *Yarn Spinners*, pp. 404–5 and p. 314, n. 70 ('a more complex situation'). Glen Mills' second husband was Arthur Crouch.

79   Lucy Cassidy, OBE (c.1880–1968), was a founder and first publicity officer of the FAW (*SMH*, 24/2/1968, death notice, and Fox, *Dream at a Graveside*); Nellie Stewart (1858–1931) sang at the opening of the Commonwealth Parliament (*ADB* vol. 12). Eris O'Brien (1895–1975) was appointed auxiliary archbishop of Sydney diocese in 1951, and archbishop of Canberra–Goulburn in 1953 (*ADB* vol. 15). James Meagher (1894–1975) was a Sydney solicitor and raconteur (*ADB* vol. 15).

80   Angus & Robertson Royalty Statements 1951–2, FP vol. 86; SMF to J. K. Moir, 19/10/1952, J. K. Moir Colln; SMF to Dymphna Cusack, 12/1/1952 and 26/10/1952 (the cheque filed there). The female basic wage (NSW) for 1952 was £403.

81   (Dame) Eadith Walker (1861–1937), *ADB* vol. 12.

82   SMF to J. K. Moir, 7/7/1952, J. K. Moir Colln.

83   Arnold Dresden to SMF, 23/2/1952, FP vol. 35.

84   'Sequel', ML MSS 445/22.

85   SMF to Mary Fullerton, 24/3/1944, FP vol. 18; SMF to Leonora Pease, 29/1/1948, FP vol. 13. The sympathetic clergyman may have been based on the Rev. Stanley Best of Lake Bathurst (Stanley Best to SMF, 30/12/[1901], FP vol. 10); see also the Rev. Mr David, *My Career Goes Bung*, p. 292, who speaks of Sybylla's 'glorious eyes', and 'the pretentious canon' (possibly an irritable version of the Rev. Charles Kingsmill (1833–1910), English-born canon of Goulburn diocese for many years.

86   SMF to unident., n.d., FP vol. 46, p. 125; Vida Goldstein to Edith How Martyn, 26/1/1944, VG Papers.

87   SMF to Mary Fullerton, 5/2/1946, FP vol. 19; David Myton, 'Miles Franklin and Religion', 2001, unpub. paper 2001, copy in my possession.

88   Charles Graham to SMF, 27/3/1928, and SMF to Ted Graham 9/7/1938, FP vol. 49. SF Notebook, FP vol. 107, pp. 40, 30. SMF to Farquhar Fraser, 5/8/1952, FP vol. 44, mentions a phone call from John, 'who had a week's leave, whatever that may mean' (though he did not call by as arranged).

89   Eris O'Brien to SMF, 'Dear Miss B of B Bin', 3/2/1952, FP vol. 44;* SMF to David Martin, 3/2/1952, FP vol. 41.*

90   Les Woolacott to SMF, 6/4/1952, SMF to Les Woolacott, 6/5/1952, FP vol. 44. Miles steered well clear of Woolacott's marriage troubles (Leila Woolacott to SMF, 7/5/1952, and reply 9/5/1952, FP vol. 39).

91   Dal Stivens, 'The Squatters', *John O'London's Weekly*, 17/10/1952, pp. 1–2; Florence James to SMF, 20/10/1952, FP vol. 30 (Stivens quote). Dal Stivens (1911–97) published over 130 books in a range of genres (*OCAL*).

92   Viera Jones, 'Australian Imprint', PhD thesis, *passim*; Beatrice Davis, 'An Enigmatic Woman', *Overland*, 1983, p. 26; Florence James to SMF, 20/10/1952, FP vol. 30; SMF to P. R. Stephensen, 21/6/1952, FP vol. 28.

93   SMF to KSP, 23/10/1952, FP vol. 21. Brian Elliott (1910–91), AustLit.

94 SMF to Rex Ingamells, 25/9/1952, Ingamells Colln.* SMF to Erle Wilson, 4 and 7/11/1953, FP vol. 43; SMF to Nettie Palmer, 22/3/1952, FP vol. 24; SMF to Joyce Ralph, 14/12/1953, FP vol. 43. *Blue Hills* by Gwen Meredith (1907–2006), ran 1949–76. For Jon Cleary (b. 1917) and Erle Wilson (1898–1970), *SMH*, 11/7/1970, p. 124 and AustLit.

95 *SMH*, 10/2/1952, p. 2 (also mis-spelling her first name); SMF to KSP, 11/9/1952, FP vol. 21.* KSP eventually withdrew from the case because it was affecting her blood pressure, the last phase being played out in Feb. 1956 when it was decided in favour of the *SMH*, with costs to KSP: the saga is outlined in Carolyn Skinner, 'Christian Jollie Smith: A Biography', PhD thesis, Macquarie Univ., 2008, pp. 321–3; see also Throssell, *Wild Weeds and Wind Flowers*, p. 181 and North, *Yarn Spinners*, p. 324, n. 76. Russel Ward (1914–95), AustLit.

96 SMF to Dear Girls, 24/11/1952, FP vol. 30.

97 *Bulletin*, 26/11/1952, p. 18; *Southerly*, 1953, no. 3, pp. 196–202. The flats are at 127 Brighton Bvde. Assoc. Prof. Mentor L. Williams, a folklorist from the Illinois Institute of Technology, was Fulbright Fellow in American Literature at the Univ. of Sydney, succeeding Bruce Sutherland in 1952 (*Fulbright Program in Australia: The First Eight Years and the Future*, The Foundation, 1958, n.p.); Mentor L. Williams, 'Boosting our own Books', *Sunday Herald*, 12/6/1952, p. 11, and *Bulletin*, 2/7/1952, p. 23.

98 Diary excerpts, 1952, cited Mathew, *Miles Franklin*, 1963, Appendix II.

99 Ray Mathew to SMF, 17/12/1952,* and SMF to Ray Mathew, 7/2/1953, FP vol. 44.

100 *OCAL*, p. 522; Myfanwy Horne, 'Literary Wit with the Brown Wavy Hair', *SMH*, 25/6/2002, p 27.

101 Mathew, *Miles Franklin*, p. 30.

102 *ibid.*, p. 23.

103 *MD*, Federation edn.

104 SMF to David Martin, 3/2/1952, FP vol. 41.

105 P. F. McDonald, *Marriage in Australia: Age at Marriage and Proportions Marrying 1860–1971*, ANU Press, Canberra, 1974, pp. 133–4, Table 40.

106 *ibid.*, pp. 95, 112, 121; 'marriageable age' for males here means men between ages 20 and 49 and women between ages 20 and 44. Kathryn M. Hunter, *Father's Right-Hand Man: Single Women on Australia's Family Farms in the Age of Federation 1880s–1920s*, Aust. Scholarly Publishing, Melbourne, 2004, examines the roles played by single women in rural life.

107 P. F. McDonald, *Marriage in Australia: Age at Marriage and Proportions Marrying 1860–1971*, ANU Press, Canberra, 1974, pp. 131, 134, Table 40.

108 *ibid.*, p. 112; Graeme Davison, 'The Exodists: Miles Franklin, Jill Roe and "the Drift to the Metropolis"', *HA*, 2005, vol. 2, no. 2; Helen Heney, review of Rebecca Patterson, *The Riddle of Emily Dickinson* (1953), *SMH*, 27/3/1954, p. 13, and SMF to Helen Heney, draft letter (c.Mar. 1954).*

109 Hera Cook, *The Long Sexual Revolution: English Women, Sex, and Contraception 1800–1975*, and '"Unseemly and Unwomanly Behaviour": Comparing Women's Control of their Fertility in Australia and England from 1890 to 1970', *J. Population Research*, 2000, vol. 17, no. 2.

110 'Divorces Demarest Lloyd', *NYT*, 20/1/1937, p. 19.

111 SMF to Jean Devanny, 13/1/1954, FP vol. 22, and Ferrier, *As Good as a Yarn with You*. The 'utterly revolting' behaviour was probably sex with children (though age of consent was variably defined in the US, J. Gathorne-Hardy, *Alfred C. Kinsey: Sex the Measure of all Things*, Chatto & Windus, London, 1998, p. 377).

112 SMF to Theo Lampe, 26/12/1953, FP vol. 49.

113 SMF to Margery Currey, 14/2/1953, FP vol. 22; SMF to Mabel Singleton, 29/10/1953, FP vol. 25. The coronation of Queen Elizabeth II occurred 2/6/1953.

114 SMF to Jean Campbell, 27/11/1953, FP vol. 44;* PD, 28–9/11/1953; David Martin, '1954: Meeting Miles for the Last Time', *Overland*, 1975, no. 62, p. 37.

115 P. R. Stephensen, 'Miles Franklin', in Bread and Cheese Club, *Miles Franklin, by Some of her Friends*, p. 39; SMF to Magdalen Dalloz, 28/12/1953, FP vol. 41; SMF to J. K. Moir, 17/10/1953, J. K. Moir Colln.

116 SMF to Frank Eyre, 20/4/1953 and 22/6/1953, FP vol. 89.

117 SMF to Frank Eyre, 22/6/1953, and Frank Eyre to SMF, 25/6/1953, SMF to Frank Eyre, 2/8/1953 and 21/10/1953, FP vol. 89.

118 SMF to Rex Ingamells, 1 and 10/7/1953, Ingamells Colln; SMF to Mr Hall, 12/9/1953, FP vol. 89, and related corres. with Hallcraft.

119 North, *Yarn Spinners*, has the sequence of letters between Franklin, James and Cusack, cited here and subsequently.

120 SMF to Mabel Singleton, 29/10/1953, FP vol. 25.*

121 Myrtle Rose White to SMF, 28/7/1953 and 14/3/1954, SMF to Myrtle Rose White, 24/8/1953, FP vol. 42.

122 PD, 31/3/1953, and SMF to Dymphna Cusack, 28/4/1953, FP vol. 30, repr. North, *Yarn Spinners*; PD, 8/7/1953. *Caddie: The Story of a Barmaid*, ed. Dymphna Cusack, Constable, London, 1953; see ch. 12, n. 123 for biodata. Jean Devanny's autobiography was published in 1986 (*Point of Departure*, ed. Carole Ferrier, Univ. of Qld Press, St Lucia, Qld).

123 SMF to Henrietta Drake-Brockman, 2/10/1953, FP vol. 33. 'Alex Sheppard, MC, 1913–1997', *SMH*, 14/6/1997, p. 24. (Viscount) William Slim (1891–1970), *ADB* vol. 16.

124 Delys Cross to SMF, n.d, 1953, FP vol. 43; *SMH*, 26/9/1953 (death notices); SMF to Henrietta Drake-Brockman, 2/10/1953, FP vol. 33.

125 SMF to Mabel Singleton, 29/10/1953, FP vol. 25.

126 Mabel Florence Neely Knox (1885–1973), widowed in 1924, was a hospital matron in Qld in the interwar years, pers. comm., Mrs M. C. Knox; Berta Donald to SMF, 7/12/1953, and SMF to Berta Donald, 29/12/1953, FP vol. 27.

127 SMF to Rene Laws, 3/10/1953, FP vol. 45. Louise Blanche de Guerry de Lauret (1871–1947), *Penny Post*, 30/9/1947, p. 2.

128 PD, 27/1/1953, 16/10/1953; Amy Somerville, b. Penrith 1905, m. Alec McCutchan in Vic in 1929, moved to Pymble, NSW, c.1950; for her mother, see ch. 11, n. 26. Charles Graham died at Dalveen in 1950 and was buried at nearby Stanthorpe, pers. comm., Mrs Shirley Graham.

129 PD, 16/10/1953 (Phoebe W.); SMF to Isabel Newsham, 31/10/1953, FP vol. 29; SMF to Mabel Singleton, 29/10/1953, FP vol. 25;* SMF to KSP, 31/8/1953, FP vol. 21.

130 SMF to J. K. Moir, 17/8/1953, J. K. Moir Colln. Henrietta Barnett (1851–1936), *ODNB*.

131 *SMH*, 2/6/1953, p. 6 (medal); PD, 18/3/1953.

132 SMF to Rex Ingamells, 9/9/1953, Ingamells Colln; Roe, 'Miles Franklin: Bush Intellectual' explores these concepts.

133 D. S., 'The New Brent of Bin Bin', *Bulletin*, 14/1/1953, 'Red Page'. 'E.', 'Study of Spacious Days', *SMH*, 1/11/1952, p. 10. The contract for *Cockatoos* was finalised Jan. 1954 and returned in Jun. (Angus & Robertson to SMF, 21/1/1954, FP vol. 86, and Angus & Robertson to SMF, 8/6/1954, Angus & Robertson Corres., ML MSS 3269, vol. 274, p. 39).

134 Angus & Robertson Royalty Statements, FP vol. 86, and Angus & Robertson Corres. files, ML.

135 SMF to John Casson, 3/4/1953 and 27/4/1953, FP vol. 44; SMF to Henrietta Drake-Brockman, 13/11/1953, FP vol. 33;* PD, 10/12/1953. John Casson (1909–99), son of Sir Lewis Casson and Dame Sybil Thorndike, was senior manager for J. C. Williamson Theatres in Australia after World War II (*ODNB*). The talk on religious drama was given at St Columba's, Woollahra, the radical Presbyterian Rev. Keith Dowding incumbent (1911–2008, *SMH*, 7/10/2008, p. 76). *Reedy River*, scripted by Dick Diamond, dealt with the aftermath of the 1890s shearers' strike (*OCAL*).

136 *SMH*, 18/7/1953, p. 2. Baker's article 'The Great Australian Novel' appeared in *SMH*, 11/7/1953, p. 8; Miles' response is repr. *A Gregarious Culture*. Suzanne Baker, 'Realising an Absent Presence: Women Writers as Keepers of the National Language Culture', BA (Hons) thesis, Univ. of Sydney, 2005, shows Baker paid close attention to the works of women writers of the 1930s, despite a patronising attitude.

137 PD, 19/11/1953; *Bulletin*, 2/12/1953, p. 18, and *Southerly*, 1954, no. 3, pp. 201–4. 'Off to South Africa', *Bulletin*, 29/12/1954, p. 6. Ruth Bedford (1882–1963), *ADB* vol. 13; J. M. D. Pringle (1912–99), AustLit; Charles McLelland (1904–88), *Aust. Law Journal*, 1985, no. 59, p. 580. Kenneth Slessor (1901–71), was a poet and journalist (*ADB* vol. 16).

138 SMF to Jean Devanny, 3/10/1953* and 22/12/1953, FP vol. 32; Jenn Lane, pers. comm., 26/9/1993.

139 PD, 8/12/1953, and 'Training Ended', *SMH*, 9/12/1953, p. 12 (but SMF not mentioned); PD, 15/5/1953, and *Bulletin*, 13/5/1953, p. 30.

140 SMF to Frank Eyre, 21/10/1953, FP vol. 89; SMF to Jean Devanny, 31/10/1953, FP vol. 32, repr. Ferrier, *As Good as a Yarn with You*; SMF to Florence James, 16/12/1953, FP vol. 30, repr. North, *Yarn Spinners*.

141 SMF to Theo Lampe, 26/12/1953, FP vol. 49; PD, 1/12/1953, 18/12/1953, 20/12/1953; SMF to John Franklin, 23/12/1953, FP vol. 50; SMF to Farquhar Fraser, [Jul. 1953?], FP vol. 44.

142 Florence James to Dymphna Cusack, 15/2/1954, James Papers; Florence James to SMF, 18/3/1954, FP vol. 30; telegram, Dymphna Cusack to SMF, 8/4/1954, FP vol. 30;* Dymphna Cusack to SMF, 12/4/1954, FP vol. 30; SMF to Dymphna Cusack, 1/5/1954, FP vol. 30* (all repr. North, *Yarn Spinners*).

143 SMF to Frank Eyre and replies, 1/2/1954–30/3/1954, FP vol. 89 (Moir's notes, pp. 159–85).

144 Dymphna Cusack to SMF, 12/4/1954, FP vol. 30; SMF to Dymphna Cusack, 1/5/1954, FP vol. 30* (both repr. North, *Yarn Spinners*).

145 O'Harris, *Was It Yesterday?*, p. 72; SMF to Beatrice Bridle, 5/3/1954, FP vol. 47.

146 SMF to Winifred Stephensen, 16/1/1954, FP vol. 39; SMF to Bruce Sutherland, 18/3/1954, FP vol. 44;* Jane Connors, 'The 1954 Royal Tour of Australia', *Australian Historical Studies*, 1993, vol. 25, no. 100; SMF to Dymphna Cusack, 23/3/1954, FP vol. 30; Ethel Ruby Bridle to SMF, 15/2/1954, FP vol. 47. The Statute of Westminster provided for the sovereignty of the parliaments of the self-governing dominions within the emergent British Commonwealth (but Australia did not ratify it until 1943).

147 The incident is detailed in the Moir–Franklin corres. Feb.–Mar. 1953 (and Georges [store, Melbourne] to Everill Venman, 16/2/1954, FP vol. 121).

148 On Everill's later years, see Kristin Ashman, *A Tribute to Jack Venman: In Honour of a True Bushman*, Kristin Ashman, Qld, 1988, pp. 94–5.

149 SMF to 'Dear Things' [the Crosses], Tuesday, Cross Papers; SMF to Jean Devanny, 17/2/1954, FP vol. 32, and SMF to KSP, 13/3/1954, FP vol. 21; SMF to Winifred Stephensen, 1/5/1954, FP vol. 39; SMF to J. K. Moir, 1/5/1954, J. K. Moir Colln.

150 SMF to Rex Ingamells, 29/3/1954, Rex Ingamells to SMF, 9/4/1954, SMF to Rex Ingamells, 20/5/1954, Ingamells Colln, and Rex Ingamells to SMF, 1/6/1954, FP vol. 40; SMF to Henrietta Drake-Brockman, 31/3/1954, and Henrietta Drake-Brockman to SMF, 18/5/[1954], FP vol. 33, and Allan Edwards to SMF, 22/4/1954, FP vol. 45.

151 SMF to E. Venman, 21/5/1954, FP vol. 43; SMF to David Martin, 16/5/1954, FP vol. 41; A. D. Hope, 'The Party Line on Poetry', *SMH*, 1/5/1954, p. 11; SMF to Jean Devanny, 31/5/1954, FP vol. 32.

152 SMF to Mary Alice Evatt, 24/4/1954, Evatt Colln;* SMF to J. K. Moir, [31/5/1951], FP vol. 34; SMF to Eris O'Brien, 15/5/1954, FP vol. 44.* Robert Manne, *The Petrov Affair: Politics and Espionage*, Pergamon Press, Sydney, 1987, p. 96. Vladimir (1907–91) and Evdokia (1914–2002) Petrov. Henry Parkes (1815–96) was the best known politician of nineteenth-century Australia, five times premier of NSW, and leading advocate of federation (*ADB* vol. 5).

153 SMF to L. & R. G. Howarth, 26/5/1954, FP vol. 43; SMF to Magdalen Dalloz, 2–4/6/1954,* Magdalen Dalloz to SMF, 28/12/1953, Magdalen Dalloz to SMF, 11/6/1954, FP vol. 41; SMF to Beatrice Davis, 24/8/1954, Angus & Robertson Corres., ML MSS 3269, vol. 274, p. 447 ('a grand dictionary').

154 Joan Lampe to SMF, 20/6/1954, FP vol. 49.

155 Helena Lampe to SMF, 23/6/1954, FP vol. 49; SMF to Vance Palmer, 23/7/1954, Palmer Papers* ('I was taken with a heart attack five weeks ago').

156 Delys Cross to KSP, 'Sunday', Cross Papers; SMF to Dymphna Cusack, 18/8/1954, James Papers, repr. North *Yarn Spinners*.

157 Delys Cross to KSP, 'Sunday', Cross Papers; Rex and Mabel [Florence] Knox, 28/6/1954, FP vol. 45.

158 SMF to Beatrice Davis, n.d. [28/6/1954], Angus & Robertson Corres., ML MSS 3269, vol. 274, p. 393; Delys Cross to Beatrice Davis, Monday, *ibid.*, pp. 415–17.

159 Beatrice Davis to SMF, 29/6/1954, Cross Papers, and SMF to Dear George, Angus & Robertson Corres., ML MSS 3269, vol. 274, p. 419. 'S. H.', 'That Bin Bin Bird' *Sun-Herald*, 25/7/1954, p. 48; 'More Brent of Bin Bin', *Bulletin*, 8/9/1954, p. 2. Stewart Howard (see ch. 11, n. 69) was said to be 'doing Menzies' flap-doodle', and allegedly was paid by Angus & Robertson to write reviews (SMF to Dymphna Cusack, 14/12/1950, FP vol. 30, and SMF to Dymphna Cusack, 18/8/1954, James Papers, both repr. North, *Yarn Spinners*).

160 Delys Cross to Beatrice Davis, 'Monday', Angus & Robertson Corres., ML MSS 3269, vol. 274, p. 417; Delys Cross to Henrietta Drake-Brockman, 22/8/1954, NLA MS 1634/3/5; Rex Ingamells, 'Miles Franklin', ts., 1954, Ingamells Colln.

161 Beatrice Davis to Rex Ingamells, 22/10/1954 (seven weeks), ML MSS 3269, Box 35; Delys Cross to Henrietta Drake-Brockman, 22/8/1954, Delys Cross to SMF, 20/7/[1954], SMF to Delys Cross, 23/7/1954, Cross Papers.

162 SMF to Vance Palmer, 23/7/1954, Palmer Papers.* There is no record of a reply, but he did receive the letter, see his eulogy for SMF, cited Afterlife, n. 2.

163 SMF to David Martin, 16/5/1954, FP vol. 41; Beatrice Davis to Charles Hall, 3/8/[1954], Angus & Robertson Corres., ML MSS 3269, vol. 274, p. 427; SMF to Delys Cross, 30/8/1954, Cross Papers.

164 SMF to Delys Cross, 30/8/1954, Cross Papers; David Martin, '1954: Meeting Miles for the Last Time', *Overland*, 1975, no. 62, pp. 36–7.

165 Beatrice Davis to Rex Ingamells, 22/10/1954, ML MSS 3269, Box 35; SMF to Beatrice Davis, 'Sun', and Dr Anderson to Beatrice Davis, 28/8/1954, Angus & Robertson Corres., FP vol. 274, pp. 451, 453; SMF to Dymphna Cusack, 18/8/1954, James Papers, repr. North, *Yarn Spinners*.

166 SMF to Beatrice Davis, 24/8/1954 and [27/8/1954], Angus & Robertson Corres., ML MSS 3269, vol. 274, pp. 447, 449, also 'Sun', Angus & Robertson Corres., ML MSS 3269, vol. 274, p. 451; SMF to Delys Cross, 30/8/1954, Cross Papers.

167 J. Lane, 'Stella Maria Sarah Miles Franklin — A Personal Memoir', unpub. copy in my possession, courtesy author; Robert Manne, *The Petrov Affair: Politics and Espionage*, Pergamon Press, Sydney, 1987, p. 152.

168 SMF to Beatrice Davis, 'Sun', Angus & Robertson Corres., ML MSS 3269, vol. 274, p. 451; SMF to Marjorie Pizer, Beecroft, Thursday, and SMF to Marjorie Pizer, Wednesday (p.m. 2/9/1954), Holburn Papers,* and SMF to Pixie O'Harris, 3/9/1954, ML Doc. 3233.* *Overland* magazine began publication in Melbourne in 1954 (motto 'Temper democratic, bias Australian'), and is one of Australia's major literary magazines.

169 SMF to Marjorie Pizer, Wednesday (p.m., 2/9/1954), and SMF to Pixie O'Harris, 3/9/1954, ML Doc 3233.*

170 Beatrice Davis to Rex Ingamells, 22/10/1954, ML MSS 3269, Box 35, no. 1.

171 KSP to Dymphna Cusack, 28/9/1954, repr. North, *Yarn Spinners*.

172 O'Harris, *Was It Yesterday?*, p. 79.

173 This account is from several sources, especially letters by Florence Knox, KSP, Delys Cross and Beatrice Davis.

174 *ADB* file; Florence Knox to Dymphna Cusack, 20/9/1954, James Papers, ML 5877, repr. North, *Yarn Spinners*.

175 Bridle family cuttings ML MSS 3732/2, vol. 2, and Leslie Bridle to J. K. Moir, 19/9/1954, J. K. Moir Colln, Box 32/4. Edmund Keith Cole, b. 1919 (*ADB* file).

176 Leslie Bridle to J. K. Moir, 19/9/1954, J. K. Moir Colln, Box 32/4.

177 *All That Swagger*, 1936 edn, pp. 598–9.

Afterlife

1 'Death of Miss Miles Franklin', *SMH*, 21/9/1954, p. 5 (where her age at death is given as 71); Marie Marshall, 'Australian Spirit in Writing', *SMH*, 22/9/1954, p. 2; Henrietta Drake-Brockman, 'We Have Lost a Fine Wit', *West Australian*, 25/9/1954, p. 22. The *Bulletin*, 22/9/1954, p. 18, gave Miles' age at death as 69.

2 Beatrice Davis, 'A True Australian', *Southerly*, 1955, vol. 16, no. 2, pp. 83–5; David Martin, 'Miles Franklin', and Jean Devanny [untitled], *Overland*, 1954–5, no. 2, pp. 17, 18; Florence James, *Times* (London), 19/11/1954, p. 10, repr. with additions, *Miles Franklin by Some of her Friends*, p. 30; O. C. R[oberts], 'Miles Franklin and our Literature', *Age Lit. Supp.*, 9/10/1954; R. J. B., 'Miles Franklin', *Voice*, Jan. 1955, p. 26; Vance Palmer, 'Miles Franklin', *ABC Weekly*, 11/12/1954, p. 11.

3 'Writer's Death Has Left Literary Mystery Unsolved', *SMH*, 21/9/1954, p. 2; Zelie McLeod, 'Miles Franklin: Our Literary Enigma', *DT*, 25/9/1954, p. 19; Nigel Muir, 'Miles Franklin Confesses', *SMH*, 16/7/1966, p. 15. The kindest review of *Gentlemen at Gyang Gyang* (1956)

was by Norman Strachan, 'fiercely Australian ... and very readable' (*DT*, 19/5/1956, p. 12), cf. Kenneth Slessor, 'artificial' (*Sun*, 23/5/1956, p. 37); 'D. S.' (*Bulletin*, 2/10/1957, p. 2) conceded 'some merit' to *Back to Bool Bool*, but for Sidney J. Baker it was 'repetitious twitterings' (*SMH*, 24/8/1957, p. 12).

4   Miles Franklin, deceased estate file, SRNSW, B 104683; Roderick, *Miles Franklin*, p. 179; 'Franklin Fund for Novelists', *SMH*, 19/1/1955, p. 4; *Official Year Book of the Commonwealth of Australia*, 1964, ch. xiii, s. 5. See ch. 13 for further details of the will; North, *Yarn Spinners*, Appendix, has a copy. Harry Heseltine, *The Most Glittering Prize: The Miles Franklin Literary Award 1957–1998*, Permanent and Australian Defence Force Academy, Canberra, 2001, is the authoritative account.

5   'Here We Go Again', *Australian Book Review*, May 2006, p. 1 (re ongoing failure to appreciate the terms of the award). The award has not been made for a play.

6   Sidney J. Baker, *SMH*, 24/8/1957, p. 12; Peter Ward, 'Miles on Miles', *Australian Book Review*, Aug. 1963, p. 167, and Thelma Forshaw, 'Stella and Miles', *Nation*, 10/8/1963, p. 22.

7   Judith Armstrong, *The Christesen Romance*, Melbourne Univ. Press, Carlton, Vic, 1996, p. 27; Marjorie Barnard to C. B. Christesen, 27/4/1955, and ensuing corres., MA; Marjorie Barnard, 'Miles Franklin', *Meanjin*, no. 63, vol. 14, no. 4, 1955, pp. 483, 487.

8   Barnard, *Miles Franklin: A Biography*, Twayne, New York, 1967 (and a new edn, *Miles Franklin: The Story of a Famous Australian*, St Lucia, Qld, 1988), reviewed by Kylie Tennant, *SMH*, 2/12/1967, p. 21; Marjorie Barnard to C. B. Christesen, 14/8/1955, 16/3/1963, 1/1/1964, MA; Roderick, *Miles Franklin*.

9   'The Mysterious Miles Franklin', *ABC Weekly*, 24/6/1959, p. 4; *SMH*, 21/11/1960, p. 26 (sale advertisement); *Miles Franklin's Manuscripts and Typescripts*, 150th Anniversary Catalogue, Berkelouw, Sydney, 1962.

10 Susan Sheridan, 'The Career of the *Career*', *ALS*, 2002; Veronica Brady, *South of My Days: A Biography of Judith Wright*, Sydney, 1998, p. 30, and *Half a Life Time*, ed. Patricia Clarke, Text Publishing, Melbourne, 1999, p. 53.

11 Publication data here and subsequently is drawn from the AustLit database. A few re-issued writings have appeared in edited form, e.g. ch. 2 of 'A Ministering Angel', repr. *A Gregarious Culture*.

12 The remaining stock of *Some Everyday Folk and Dawn* was pulped at the time of takeover, and the introduction to *The Net of Circumstance*, which I was invited to prepare, was not needed.

13 *Newcastle Herald*, 36 episodes, 14/12/1992–25/1/1993.

14 *My Brilliant Career: Miles Franklin*, ed. Bruce K. Martin, Broadview Edns, Toronto, Canada, 2007. HarperCollins Australia published a new combined edition of *My Brilliant Career* and *My Career Goes Bung* in 2004.

15 Alan Ramsey, 'Oh How He Loved to Reel Them In', *SMH*, 13–14/5/2006, p. 37.

16 See the Bibliographic Note for the works referred to.

17 'You Have Mail', *SMH*, 6–7/6/2006, p. 22; Nicole Moore and Brigid Rooney, 'Centenary Celebrations/Symposium of Miles Franklin's *My Brilliant Career*', *Australian Historical Association Bulletin* [now *HA*] 2001, no. 93, and 'Focus on Miles Franklin' *ALS*, 2002, vol. 20, no. 4 (selected seminar papers). See Appendix 1, Principal Published Writings, for the works referred to.

18 'A Century of Democracy', *SMH*, 10/5/2001, p. 6; Angela Bennie, 'The Books that Tell Us Who We Are and What Australia Is', *SMH*, 26/1/2001 (Holiday Metropolitan), p. 6; 'Unusual Suspects', *SMH*, 8–26/1/2001 (serial); Andrew Byrne and Elizabeth Drake, 'Miles and Furphy', Seduction Opera, North Melbourne Town Hall, 5/5/2001 <www.theatre.asn.au/node/20873>; Goulburn Regional Art Gallery, 14/10/2001 (leaflet in my possession).

19 Colin Roderick, Guardbook 10, p. 141, Roderick Papers; 'Bush Wedding Goes Horribly Wrong', *Goulburn Post*, 11/3/2002, p. 6; Francis *et al.*, eds, *The Buddong Flows On*; *The Norvill Art Prize: A Background to the Award*, c.1999, courtesy Peter Norvill.

20 *Miles Franklin by Some of her Friends*, p. 21; 'My Brilliant Blunder', *SMH*, 5/4/2004, p. 18; 'Moorhouse Gets the Last Laugh with Aussie Edith', *SMH*, 6/6/2001, p. 3.

21 Ruth Park, *Fishing in the Styx*, Penguin, Ringwood, Vic, 1993, p. 151 (a 'dark side').

22 David Martin, 'Miles Franklin', *Overland*, 1954–5, no. 2, p. 17.

23 Martin, *My Strange Friend*, p. 215.
24 Michele Le Doeuff, *The Sex of Knowing*, Routledge Kegan Paul, London, 2004, as reviewed by Elizabeth Fallaize, 'Ladies Intellectual', *TLS*, 21/5/2004, p. 6; Stephensen, *Miles Franklin by Some of her Friends*, p. 39; SMF to David Martin, 3/2/1951, FP vol. 41.*
25 Bruce Sutherland to SMF, 3/9/1954, ML MSS 1128.
26 Leslie Bridle to J. K. Moir, 19/9/1955, J. K. Moir Colln, Box 32/4.

Brief guide to main and frequently cited sources and titles of general significance

Reference works

AustLit database <www.austlit.edu.au>

Australian Dictionary of Biography, Melbourne University Press, Melbourne, 1966–2005, vols 1–17 and Supplement

Margaret Francis, Stella Vernon, Colin Wilkinson, Barbara Crichton (eds), *The Buddong Flows On*, vol. 1: *The Old Hands*, and vol. 2: *Genuine People*, Buddong Society, Wagga Wagga, NSW, 1993, 2003

E. Morris Miller and Fredrick T. Macartney, *Australian Literature: A Bibliography to 1938. Extended to 1950*, Angus & Robertson, Sydney, 1956

Notable American Women, Belknap Press of Harvard University Press, Cambridge, Mass., 4 vols, 1974–1980

Oxford Companion to Australian Literature, Oxford University Press, Melbourne, 2nd edn 1994

Oxford Companion to Australian History, Oxford University Press, Melbourne, 1998

Oxford Dictionary of National Biography, Oxford University Press, Oxford, UK

Guides

Guide to the Papers and Books of Miles Franklin in the Mitchell Library, State Library of New South Wales, Library Council of New South Wales, 1980, 158 pp.

Papers of the Women's Trade Union League and its Principal Leaders: Guide to the Microfilm Edition, published for the Schlesinger Library, Radcliffe College, by Research Publications, Inc., Woodbridge, Conn., 1981

Papers

Angus & Robertson Records, 1882–1932, Further Records (Part 2), 1880–1972, Mitchell Library, State Library of NSW

Australian Federation of Women's Societies Papers, National Library of Australia

Kate Baker Papers, National Library of Australia

Marjorie Barnard Papers, Mitchell Library, State Library of NSW

Commonwealth Literary Fund, Records, National Archives of Australia

Delys Cross Papers, Mitchell Library, State Library of NSW

Dymphna Cusack Papers, National Library of Australia

Dorothea Dreier Papers, Library of Congress

Fellowship of Australian Writers Collection, Mitchell Library, State Library of NSW

Miles Franklin Papers, Mitchell Library, State Library of NSW,
 including literary and other papers received from the Mary Fullerton Estate and papers from
  the Alice Henry Estate, 124 vols
 Further Papers, 1908–1950, undated
 William Blackwood & Sons, Publishing file for Miles Franklin's 'Brent of Bin Bin' novels,
  1927–1948
Mary Fullerton Papers, National Library of Australia
Vida Goldstein Papers, Women's Library, London
C. H. Grattan Papers, Harry Ransom Collection, University of Texas at Austin
Holburn Papers, Mitchell Library, State Library of NSW
Rex Ingamells Collection, Flinders University of South Australia Library
Florence James Papers, Mitchell Library, State Library of NSW
Victor Kennedy Papers, State Library of Victoria
Lothian Papers, Baillieu Library, University of Melbourne
Meanjin Archive, Baillieu Library, University of Melbourne
J. K. Moir Collection, State Library of Victoria
George Mackaness Papers, National Library of Australia
Ian Mudie Papers, State Library of South Australia
Mutch Papers, Mitchell Library, State Library of NSW
National Housing and Town Planning Council Records, London
National Women's Trade Union League of America, Records, Library of Congress
NSW Department of School Education, Archives, State Records NSW
Palmer Papers, National Library of Australia
Margaret Dreier Robins Papers, University of Florida, Gainsville
Raymond Robins Papers, Wisconsin Historical Society
Colin Roderick Papers, including Guard Books 1–10, National Library of Australia
Scottish Women's Hospitals Collection, Mitchell Library, Glasgow
Scottish Women's Hospitals Records, Women's Library, London
Rose Scott Correspondence, Mitchell Library, State Library of NSW
P. R. Stephensen Papers, Mitchell Library, State Library of NSW
Women's Freedom League Records, Women's Library, London
Women's Trade Union League Papers, Library of Congress, microfilm edition, including:
 WTUL Papers at the Schlesinger Library
 Mary Anderson Papers
 Agnes Nestor Papers
 Leonora O'Reilly Papers
 Rose Schneiderman Papers

Newspapers and Magazines

Age (Melbourne)
Chicago Daily Tribune
Daily Telegraph (Sydney)
Chicago Daily Tribune
Goulburn Evening Penny Post
Life and Labor
Meanjin Papers (from 1947, *Meanjin*)
Nepean Times
Southerly
Sydney Morning Herald

Books, Journals and Interviews

Allen, Judith A., *Rose Scott: Vision and Revision in Feminism*, Oxford University Press, Melbourne, 1994
Arrow, Michelle, *Upstaged: Australian Women Dramatists in the Limelight at Last*, Currency Press,
 Sydney, 2002

Ashworth, W., *The Genesis of Modern British Town Planning*, Routledge & Kegan Paul, London, 1954

Australian Literary Studies, vol. 20, no. 4, 2002, 'Focus on Miles Franklin', Special Section

Barker, A. W., *Dear Robertson: Letters to an Australian Publisher*, Angus & Robertson, Sydney, 1982

Barnard, Marjorie, *Miles Franklin*, Hill of Content, Melbourne, 1967

Barnes, John, *The Order of Things: A Life of Joseph Furphy*, Oxford University Press, Melbourne, 1990

Bettison, Margaret and Jill Roe, 'Miles Franklin's Topical Writings', *Australian Literary Studies*, vol. 20, no. 1, 2001

Bland, Lucy, *Banishing the Beast: English Feminism and Sexual Morality 1885–1914*, Penguin, London, 1995

Bomford, Janette *'That Dangerous and Persuasive Woman': Vida Goldstein*, Melbourne University Press, Melbourne, 1993

Boone, Gladys, *The Women's Trade Union Leagues of Great Britain and the United States of America*, Columbia University Press, New York, 1942

Bread & Cheese Club, *Miles Franklin by Some of Her Friends*, Melbourne, 1995

Buhle, Mari Jo, *Feminism and its Discontents: A Century of Struggle with Psychoanalysis*, Harvard University Press, Cambridge Mass., 1998

Clarke, Patricia, *Pen Portraits: Women Writers and Journalists in Nineteenth Century Australia*, Allen & Unwin, North Sydney, 1988

Coleman, Verna, *Miles Franklin in America: Her Unknown (Brilliant) Career*, Angus & Robertson, Sydney, 1981

Cook, Hera, *The Long Sexual Revolution: English Women, Sex, and Contraception 1800–1975*, Oxford University Press, Oxford, 2004

De Berg, Hazel, interview with Leslie and Ruby Bridle, 1977, NLA Oral History Collection, transcript 1001

De Garis, Mary C., *Clinical Notes and Deductions of a Peripatetic: Being Fads and Fancies of a General Practitioner*, Bailliere, Tindall & Cox, London, 1926

Dreier, Mary E., *Margaret Dreier Robins: Her Life, Letters and Work*, Island Press, New York, 1950

Elshtain, Jean Bethke, *Jane Addams and the Dream of American Democracy: A Life*, Basic Books, New York, 2002

Ferrier, Carole (ed.), *As Good as a Yarn with You: Letters between Miles Franklin, Katharine Susannah Prichard, Jean Devanny, Marjorie Barnard, Flora Eldershaw and Eleanor Dark*, Cambridge University Press, Cambridge, England, Oakleigh, Vic., 1992

Fox, Len (ed.), *Dream at a Graveside: The History of the Fellowship of Australian Writers 1928–1988*, Fellowship of Australian Writers, Sydney, 1988

Garner, Les, *Stepping Stones in Women's Liberty: Feminist Ideas in the Women's Suffrage Movement 1900–1918*, Heinemann, London, 1984

Garton, Stephen, *Medicine and Madness: A Social History of Insanity in New South Wales 1880–1940*, University of NSW Press, Kensington, NSW, 1988

Gibbs, A. M., *Bernard Shaw: A Life*, University of NSW Press, Kensington, NSW, 2005

Gilchrist, Hugh *Australians and Greeks 2: The Middle Years*, Halstead Press, Sydney, 1997

Goldstein, Vida, *To America & Back: 1902*, ed. Jill Roe, Australian History Museum, Macquarie University, 2002

Goulburn Regional Art Gallery Exhibition Research Project, *Reflections on Miles Franklin's 'My Brilliant (?) Career'*, including Jennifer Lamb, comp., 'Miles Franklin's "My Brilliant (?) Career": Goulburn and District References', and Marcelle Leicht, 'Miles Franklin's Life in the Goulburn District', Goulburn Regional Art Gallery, 2001

Heilbrun, Carolyn G., *Writing a Woman's Life*, Women's Press, London, 1989

Hergenhan, L. T., *No Casual Traveller: Hartley Grattan and Australia*, University of Queensland Press, St Lucia, Qld, 1995

—— (ed.), *Penguin New Literary History of Australia*, Penguin Books Australia, Ringwood, Vic, 1988

Heseltine, Harry, *The Most Glittering Prize: The Miles Franklin Literary Award 1957–1998*, Permanent and Australian Defence Force Academy, Canberra, 2001

Hutton, I. Emslie, *With a Woman's Unit in Serbia, Salonika and Sebastopol*, Williams and Norgate, London, 1928

Jacoby, Robin Miller, *The British and American Women's Trade Union Leagues: A Case Study of Feminism and Class*, Carlson Publications, Brooklyn, New York, 1994

Jalland, Patricia, *Changing Ways of Death in Twentieth Century Australia: War Medicine and the Funeral Business*, University of NSW Press, Kensington, NSW, 2006

Kent, Jacqueline, *A Certain Style: Beatrice Davis. A Literary Life*, Penguin Books, Ringwood, Vic, 2001

Kingston, Beverley, *My Wife, My Daughter and Poor Mary Ann: Women and Work in Australia*, Nelson, Melbourne, 1975

——, *A History of New South Wales*, Cambridge University Press, Melbourne, 2006

Kirkby, Diane, *Alice Henry: The Power of Pen and Voice. The Life of an Australian-American Labor Reformer*, Cambridge University Press, Cambridge, UK, and Oakleigh, Vic, 1991

Kirkpatrick, Peter, *The Sea Coast of Bohemia: Literary Life in Sydney's Roaring Twenties*, University of Queensland Press, St Lucia, Qld, 1992

Kirkpatrick, Rod, *Country Conscience: A History of the NSW Provincial Press, 1841–1995*, Infinite Harvesting Publishing, Canberra, 2000

Knight, D., *Charlotte Perkins Gilman: A Study of the Short Fiction*, Twayne, New York, 1997

Leneman, Leah, *In the Service of Life: The Story of Elsie Inglis and the Scottish Women's Hospitals*, Mercat Press, Edinburgh, 1994

Linklater, Andro, *An Unhusbanded Life: Charlotte Despard, Suffragette, Socialist and Sinn Feiner*. Hutchinson, London, 1980

Magarey, Susan, *Unbridling the Tongues of Women: A Biography of Catherine Helen Spence*, Hale & Iremonger, Sydney, 1985

——, *Passions of the First-Wave Feminists*, University of NSW Press, Kensington, NSW 2001

Martin, David, *My Strange Friend*, Pan Macmillan, Chippendale, NSW, 1991

Martin, Sylvia, *Passionate Friends: Mary Fullerton, Mabel Singleton & Miles Franklin*, Onlywomen Press, London, 2001

——, *Ida Leeson, A Life*, Allen & Unwin, Crows Nest, NSW, 2006

Mathew, Ray, *Miles Franklin*, Oxford University Press, London, 1963

Mazower, Mark, *Salonica, City of Ghosts: Christians, Muslims and Jews 1430–1950*, HarperCollins, London 2004

Melman, Billie, *Women and the Popular Imagination in the Twenties: Flappers and Nymphs*, Macmillan, London, 1988

Meyerowitz, Joanne J., *Women Adrift: Independent Wage Earners in Chicago 1880–1930*, University of Chicago Press, Chicago, 1988

Modjeska, Drusilla, *Exiles at Home: Australian Women Writers 1925–1945*, Angus & Robertson, Sydney, 1981

Munro, Craig, *Wild Man of Letters: The Story of P. R. Stephensen*, Melbourne University Press, Melbourne, 1984

Newsome, Stella, *Women's Freedom League 1907–1957* [WFL], London, [c.1960]

North, Marilla (ed.), *Yarn Spinners. A Story in Letters: Dymphna Cusack, Florence James, Miles Franklin*, University of Queensland Press, St Lucia, Qld, 2001

O'Harris, Pixie, *Was It Yesterday?*, Rigby, Adelaide, 1983

Palmer, A., *The Gardeners of Salonika*, Andre Deutsch, London, 1965

Pfisterer, Susan, *Playing with Ideas: Australian Women Playwrights from the Suffragettes to the Sixties*, Currency Press, Sydney, 1999

Roderick, Colin, *Miles Franklin: Her Brilliant Career*, Rigby, Adelaide, 1982

Roe, Jill, 'Chivalry and Social Policy in the Antipodes', [*Australian*] *Historical Studies*, vol. 22, no. 88, 1987

——, '"Testimonies from the Field": The Coming of Christian Science to Australia, c.1890–1910', *Journal of Religious History*, Vol. 22, no. 3, October 1998

——, 'Forcing the Issue: Miles Franklin and National Identity', *Hecate*, vol. 17, no. 1, 1991

——, 'Miles Franklin: Bush Intellectual', NSW Premier's History Awards Address, Ministry for the Arts, Sydney, 2004

Smith, Vivian (ed.), *Letters of Vance and Nettie Palmer 1915–1963*, National Library of Australia, Canberra, 1977

—— (ed.), *Nettie Palmer*, University of Queensland Press, St Lucia, Qld, 1988

Spearritt, Peter, *Sydney's Century: A History*, University of NSW Press, Kensington, NSW, 2000

Spinney, Robert G., *City of Big Shoulders: A History of Chicago*, Northern Illinois Press, De Kalb, Ill., 2000

Throssell, Ric, *Wild Weeds and Wind Flowers: The Life and Letters of Katharine Susannah Prichard*, Angus & Robertson, Sydney, 1975

Trewin, J. C., *The Theatre Since 1900*, A. C. Dakers, London, 1951

Wilde, W. H., *Courage a Grace: A Biography of Dame Mary Gilmore*, Melbourne University Press, Carlton, Vic, 1988

Woollacott, Angela, *To Try Her Fortune In London: Australian Women, Colonialism, and Modernity*, Oxford University Press, Oxford and New York, 2001

Unpublished theses

Heath, Lesley, 'Sydney Literary Societies of the Nineteen Twenties: Cultural Nationalism and the Promotion of Australian Literature', PhD thesis, University of NSW, 1996,

Hedley, Jocelyn, 'The Unpublished Plays of Miles Franklin', MA thesis, University of NSW, 2007

Jones, Caroline Viera, 'Australian Imprint: The Influence of George Robertson on a National Narrative (1890–1935)', PhD thesis, University of Sydney, 2004

ACKNOWLEDGEMENTS

The origins of this book lie in the feminist ferment of the 1970s and in the then publishing program of Angus & Robertson, now an imprint of HarperCollins Publishers Australia. In December 1982, publisher Richard Walsh, a Franklin enthusiast, commissioned a 'life and times of Miles Franklin'. It has been a long time coming, due to other commitments and responsibilities, and because of the extent of previously unexamined source material. The encouragement and steady support of many individuals and the practical assistance of several key institutions have been vital to its completion.

The following individuals deserve special thanks: Margaret Bettison, whose exceptional research skills brought many previously obscure aspects of Miles Franklin's life to light; Chris Cunneen, whose unrivalled biographical expertise helped run numerous hitherto unidentified and partly or erroneously identified persons to ground; and Beverley Kingston, whose wise counsel ensured the project stayed on track, despite difficulties and diversions.

Without the support of the State Library of New South Wales, this book could not have been written. An honorary research fellowship in 2002 made possible a start on unexamined areas of the Franklin Papers. I thank especially Dagmar Schmidmaier and her successor, Regina Sutton; Elizabeth Ellis; Paul Brunton; and, on a day-to-day basis, Arthur Easton. Rosemary Moon facilitated a centenary symposium on *My Brilliant Career* in 2001 and a presentation on Miles Franklin's Sydney in 2004. Staff on the special collections desk, Mitchell Reading Room, and elsewhere in the library, have provided ongoing assistance.

A sabbatical fellowship at the Australian National University in 2003, and concurrent membership of the Petherick Room at the National Library of Australia, enabled research to be done on the poorly documented period of 1918 to 1927 and the drafting of related chapters, also the presentation of a paper on Miles Franklin and photography. Special thanks are due to the then head of the Research School of Social Sciences (RSSS) history program, Desley Deacon, and to Margy Burn, assistant director-general of the NLA. As well, proximity to the office of the *Australian Dictionary of Biography* was most beneficial; appreciative acknowledgement is made of assistance received then and at other times, in particular from Anthea Bundock, Martha Campbell, Christine Fernon and Diane Langmore, also research associates Sally O'Neill in London and Roger Joslyn in New York.

Macquarie University has provided in-kind support throughout the project, such as office space and library facilities. Minor funding enabled early-stage work on Franklin materials by my then students Sandra McKirdy and Ros Parsons. A travel grant arranged by Christina Slade, dean of humanities at the time, enabled me to review sites and materials in Chicago, the UK, and Macedonia, in 2004. As well, the weekly research seminar sponsored by the modern history discipline at Macquarie University provided a regular reality check. For their expertise, insights and good humour, I thank in particular colleagues Michelle Arrow, Lee Benness, Lisa Featherstone, Bridget Griffen-Foley, Tom Hillard, Alison Holland, Marnie Hughes-Warrington, Joan Kirkby, Nicole Moore, Alanna Nobbs, George Parsons, Carroll Pursell, Michael Roberts, Boris Skvoric, Mary Spongberg, Hsu-ming Teo, Duncan Waterson and Angela Woollacott. My recent postgraduate students Robyn Arrowsmith, Brother Howard Le Couteur and Carolyn Skinner have kindly shared relevant findings. Particular acknowledgement is due to administrative officer Jackie Anker, who entered the data on the first drafts of the family trees, and the staff of the university library, especially document supply staff and Robin Walsh.

A modest publisher's advance covered some costs along the way, such as indexing of materials by Lynne Milne and Tessa Milne, and problem-related data searches by Stephanie Liau and Katharine Bradley in London, and Valerie Wright in Glasgow.

Grateful acknowledgement is made of assistance and references received from institutions and individuals located as follows:

Australia

Adelaide: State Library of South Australia; Flinders University Library; Helen Bartley; Susan Magarey; Sue Sheridan; David Hilliard; Barbara Wall.

Brisbane: AustLit database project and staff, University of Queensland, in particular Carol Hetherington; Leigh Dale; Jennifer Harrison; Laurie Hergenhan; Deborah Jordan; Helen Malone; Barbara Poniewierski.

Canberra: Australian War Memorial; National Archives of Australia; RSSS history program colleagues, in particular Barry Higman, Patricia Jalland and Barry Smith; the National Archives of Australia; Terry Hull; Rebecca Lamb; Chris Poll; Claudia Thame.

Hobart: University of Tasmania Archives.

Melbourne: Baillieu Library, University of Melbourne; State Library of Victoria; John Barnes; Graeme Davison; Maryanne Dever; Diane Kirkby; Stuart Macintyre; Poppy Malone; Anne Mitchell; Mark Peel; the late Sasha Soldatow; Lucy Sussex; Chris Wallace-Crabbe.

Perth: Battye Library, State Library of Western Australia; University of Western Australia Archives; Murdoch University Archives; Geoffrey Bolton; Brian de Garis; Lenore Layman; Bob Reece; Tom Stannage.

Sydney and regional NSW: Fisher Library, University of Sydney; Concord Historical Society; Goulburn Historical Society; Goulburn Regional Art Gallery; Hurstville City Council Library; Nightingale Museum Sydney Hospital; Penrith City Library; Randwick Public Library; Rockdale City Library; State Records of NSW; Railway Historical Society; Yass & District Historical Society; the late Don Adamson; Suzanne Baker; Tony Barker; Bill Blinco; the late Ken Cable; Jeanne Kellett Cox; Barbara Dale; Ian Frazer and Mrs Rose Frazer; Laurie Ferguson, MHR; Gwen Frolich; Laurence Gooley; Mrs Shirley Graham; Jocelyn Hedley; Mrs M. C. Knox; Jennifer Lamb; Robyn and Robert Lance; David McNight; Diane McQuillan; Bruce Mansfield; Barbara Mebberson; Drusilla Modjeska; Ray Mooney; David Myton; Marilla North; Marjorie Pizer; the late Ron Rathbone; Brigid Rooney; Lyndall Ryan; Alison Spencer; Lynn Stevens; Greta Stone; Sue Tracey; Ian Tyrrell; Christine Yeats; Robin Walker; Eizabeth Webby; James Weirick; Mr A. J. Willett; Elinor Wrobel.

America

Arthur and Elizabeth Schlesinger Library, Harvard University, Boston; Chicago Historical Society; Mary Baker Eddy Library, Boston, in particular Judith Heunneke; New York Public Library (Berg Collection); University of Illinois at Chicago Library (Special Collections); John Boaz; Sheila Fitzpatrick; Maria Whitney Lloyd (preliminary researches, Boston, 1999); Bruce K. Martin; Gilbert and Glenn Nelson.

United Kingdom
England: British Library, London; Bristol University Archives, in particular Hannah Lowery; City of Bradford Central Library; Royal Mail Archive, London; Society of Friends Library, London; Women's Library, London; Hera Cook; John Thane; Pat Thane.

Scotland: Mitchell Library, Glasgow; University of Edinburgh Archives.

Greece
Christos Gandos, Australian Consul, Salonika; Ambassador Stuart Hume, Richard Mathews, Australian Embassy, Athens; and information officers, Edessa; with special thanks to Leonard Janisweski and the late Deborah George who facilitated contacts.

Miles Franklin's family
The interest and quiet encouragement of members of Miles Franklin's family has been much appreciated. Bridle/Lampe family historians Margaret Francis, Stella Vernon and Colin Wilkinson, also Barbara Crighton, have been unfailingly helpful. The late Lindsay Franklin, Shirley Graham, Jenn Lane, Pamela Mathers, Peter Norvill and Claire O'Connor have provided valuable new data and insights, the latter two regarding Miles Franklin's nephew John Franklin.

Readers
For their great kindness and helpfulness in perusing some or all of the manuscript at various times, I thank Judith Allen, Eileen Chanin, Chris Cunneen, Desley Deacon, Lisa Featherstone, Stephen Garton, Laurie Hergenhan, Jacqueline Kent, Beverley Kingston, Diane Kirkby, Sylvia Martin, Nicole Moore, Marilla North, Michael Roberts and Elizabeth Webby, also the publisher's editors. Considering that Miles Franklin had a very low tolerance for error and obscurity, I have been grateful for all and every comment. However, none but my editors and I have seen the final version, and responsibility for any infelicities or error rests solely with me.

Every effort has been made to acknowledge assistance received. Nonetheless, due to the lengthy period of research and writing, oversights may have occurred. Any such oversight is deeply regretted and will, if made known to me, be remedied in future editions.

Graphics

The photographic portrait of Miles Franklin taken in Chicago in 1914 on the dustcover is reproduced from the Franklin Papers, pictorial material, by permission of the State Library of New South Wales; background text of the first page of the first draft of *All That Swagger* (1933) is reproduced by kind permission of Trust Company Limited, Sydney, custodian of Miles Franklin's literary estate. Permission to reproduce picture-section images has been granted by the institutions and individuals specified therewith. Where images are held in more than one collection, acknowledgement is made according to where the reproduction was originally obtained.

The publisher

Miles would surely have been pleased that her name is being kept before the public by HarperCollins Publishers Australia. The Fourth Estate imprint seems just right for her. The professionalism and generous production values of staff have been much appreciated. Special thanks go to publisher Linda Funnell, who went well beyond the call of duty in making it all happen.

A final acknowledgement is due to Miles herself. She has been good company and taught me much. May this be so for others.

Jill Roe
August 2008

INDEX